FROMMER'S
DOLLARWISE GUIDE
TO THE CARIBBEAN

By Darwin Porter
Assisted by Danforth Prince

1986-87 Edition

Published by Frommer/Pasmantier Publishers
A Division of Simon & Schuster, Inc.
1230 Avenue of the Americas
New York, NY 10020

ISBN 0-671-54720-8

Manufactured in the United States of America

CONTENTS

MAPS

To Stanley Haggart

Acknowledgment

I wish to thank Margaret Foresman, Key West, Florida, and Staten Island, New York, for her tireless editorial assistance.

What the Symbols Mean

Travelers to the Caribbean may at first be confused by classifications on rate sheets. I've used these same classifications in this guide. One of the most common rates is **MAP,** meaning "modified American plan." Simply put, that usually means room, breakfast, and dinner, unless the room rate has been quoted separately, and then it means only breakfast and dinner. **CP** means continental plan—that is, room and a light breakfast. **EP** is European plan, which means room only, and **AP** (American plan) is the most expensive rate of all, because it includes not only your room but three meals a day.

INFLATION ALERT: I don't have to tell you that inflation has hit the Caribbean as it has everywhere else. In researching this book I have made every effort to obtain up-to-the-minute prices, but even the most conscientious researcher cannot keep up with the current pace of inflation. As the guide goes to press, I believe I have obtained the most reliable data possible. Nonetheless, in the lifetime of this edition—particularly its second year (1987)—the wise traveler will add 15% to 20% to the prices quoted throughout these pages.

A Disclaimer

Although every effort was made to ensure the accuracy of the prices and travel information appearing in this book, it should be kept in mind that prices do fluctuate in the course of time, and that information does change under the impact of the varied and volatile factors that affect the travel industry.

Readers should also note that the establishments described under Readers' Selections or Suggestions have not in many cases been inspected by the author and that the opinions expressed there are those of the individual reader(s) only. They do not in any way represent the opinions of the publisher or author of this guide.

A DOLLARWISE GUIDE TO THE CARIBBEAN

The Reason Why

ONE OF THE WORLD'S greatest travel oases, the Caribbean spins its own sunny web of enchantment.

The dream is real enough, and all but the unimaginative can picture themselves part of the lazy life of these striking, dramatic islands, often called the "eighth continent of the world."

In just a few hours by plane from the North American continent, you're submerged in lands that have absorbed the cultures of other continents, including America, Europe, and Africa.

On a white sandy beach, shaded by a row of palm trees, you've just returned from a swim in gin-clear waters and are lying in the tanning sun, listening to the murmur of the surf, cooled by trade-wind-fed breezes, waiting for your tall rum punch drink as a sundowner before you dine on a West Indian buffet and dance to a steel band as you look out upon a shimmering sea under moonlight.

Although this fantasy comes true often enough for dreamers and lovers, I do not suggest that the complex, often perplexing Caribbean region is just a romantic mirage, without its problems. Few single travel destinations pose such confusion and require such advance, detailed information—data you need to know not just when you get off the plane, but material to review in advance when you ask the important question, "Which island should I choose?"

Leading you through this maze of emerging nations and colonial outposts is the purpose of this guide.

WHAT IS THE CARIBBEAN? This question may seem too obvious at first, but it is a legitimate one. The bewildering variety of islands in the sun sowed confusion in its first tourist, Christopher Columbus, back in 1492. To Isabella back home in Spain, he wrote in a rapturous letter, "I saw so many islands that I could hardly decide which to visit first." As far as decisions go, things haven't changed that much for today's southbound, sun-seeking tourist.

As diverse in mood as they are in number, the islands of the Caribbean are each gifted with a distinctive sparkle and style, even when part of the same nation. The short trip from St. Kitts to Nevis, when the plane goes up merely to set down again, has taken you not just to a sister state, but a nostalgic island, of decaying, once-flourishing plantations, remarkably unlike the place you left only ten minutes ago.

First, some basic orientation. The Caribbean Sea is ringed by the Greater Antilles in the north (Cuba, Jamaica, Hispaniola, and Puerto Rico), the Lesser Antilles on the east, the coasts of Venezuela, Colombia, and Panama on the south (once referred to as the Spanish Main), and the countries of Central America and the Mexican Yucatán peninsula on the west. Its total area is somewhat over one million square miles!

For the purposes of this book, I've concentrated primarily on the West Indies, which form the border between the chilly Atlantic and the warm, calm Caribbean Sea. The West Indies begin with Cuba, curving south to Trinidad, lying between the peninsula of Florida and the northern coast of South America. The Netherlands Antilles, often called the "ABC Islands," lie off the coast of the Spanish Main or what is today Venezuela.

The question of a specific destination depends largely on who you are and what your vacation goals are—to sunbathe in the buff on the nudist beaches of Guadeloupe; to snorkel and scuba-dive off Bonaire; to scale a volcanic crater in Saba; to sail as Lord Nelson did from English Harbour in Antigua more than 200 years ago; to take a donkey ride in Haiti to the Citadelle (one of the seven man-made wonders of the world); to explore Santo Domingo, the oldest city in the Americas; or to shop the winding alleys in the merchandise-loaded bazaars of St. Thomas and St. Croix in the U.S. Virgin Islands.

If deciding on the island or islands to visit seems complicated, selecting the place to live once you get there may be even more perplexing. Few travel destinations in the world offer such a wide range of accommodations: a tropical villa in St. Thomas, a millionaire's estate in Jamaica, a 17th-century great house in St. Kitts, a 200-year-old sugar warehouse in St. Vincent, or a beachfront apartel in Puerto Rico. You can even perch in a treehouse by the sea! In this guide, I've surveyed the widest range possible of accommodations, from deluxe citadels to simply furnished, low-cost cottages near the sea.

DOLLARWISE—WHAT IT MEANS: In brief, this is a guidebook giving specific, practical details (including prices) about the hotels, restaurants, sightseeing attractions, and nightlife of the Caribbean. Establishments in *all* price ranges have been documented and described, from the classily elegant Round Hill on a 98-acre peninsula in Montego Bay, Jamaica (where everybody from Coward to Porter to Rodgers used to play the resident piano), to a "Mom and Pop"-run, informal inn in Tortola in the British Virgin Islands.

In all cases, establishments have been judged by the strict yardstick of value. If they "measured up," they were included in this book—regardless of the price classification. The uniqueness of the book, I think, lies in the fact it could be used by everybody from Jacqueline Kennedy Onassis to a free-wheeling, adventure-seeking collegian who seeks a different type of vacation—not just the sand and sea, but wants to learn something about other people and their lands, the intoxicating power of the Haitian Créole or the mystery of the Rastafarians who consider themselves Africans, not Jamaicans, and worship the late Emperor Haile Selassie I of Ethiopia as the Messiah.

But the major focus of the book is not centered either on the impecunious whose sole resources jingle in their pockets, or the affluent whose gold rests in numbered accounts in the Cayman Islands. Rather, my chief concern is the average, middle-income-bracket voyager who'd like to patronize some of the less documented hotels of the Caribbean, those places travel agents are sometimes reluctant to tell you about because the commission is not high.

THE CARIBBEAN ISLANDS

The *Dollarwise Guide* attempts to lead the reader through the maze of attractions, such as Old San Juan, then introduce you to a number of more esoteric locales, such as the ghost town of Oranjestad on St. Eustatius. Most important, the hours of operation and the prices of admission of these attractions have been detailed.

All these specifics are presented against a backdrop of history and culture that has spanned centuries, ever since the Age of Discovery when flagships of every major European power cruised through these blue waters.

On the trail of Columbus followed such explorers as Ponce de Leon, Balboa, DeSoto, Nelson, Hawkins, and Drake. The influence of their colonies remains today. You see it everywhere. For example, in Barbados the harbor police wear the British sailor's uniform of Lord Nelson's era, and in Haiti the night air is filled with a drumbeat born in Africa long ago.

I think the guide has struck the proper balance among sightseeing atttractions, hotels, and restaurants, as well as fun-time resorts, good shopping buys, the sporting life (such as tennis, golf, scuba, and snorkel holidays), and night-time diversions.

A TRAVELER'S ADVISORY: This is one of the questions most often asked by the first-time visitor, and it's one of the most difficult to answer. Can a guidebook writer safely recommend traveling to New York or any major American city? Are you, in fact, free from harm in your own home?

The "attitude toward the visitor" takes on a wide range of meaning depending on whose attitude you are talking about. The Caribbean is composed of many nations, some of whom have broken, at least on paper, from colonial powers which dominated their cultures for years, others such as Montserrat preferring to retain their safe links with the past. Some islands, such as Guadeloupe and Martinique, are actually part of France, while other Caribbean nations prefer to seek help anywhere else but from their former colonial masters.

That attitude I mentioned might mean friendliness and hospitality, or it could encompass everything from indifferent service in a hotel dining room to theft and perhaps violence.

Many tourist boards are increasingly sensitive to the treatment of visitors, because their fragile economies depend on how many people their islands attract. Rudeness, room burglaries, anything that results in unfavorable publicity can cause damage. As a result, many islands, such as St. Lucia, are taking steps to make their own people more aware of the importance of tourism, and to treat and respect their guests as they themselves would want to be treated if traveling in a foreign land.

Of course, many of the problems in the past have come from the tourists themselves. A white person arriving in a predominantly black society may feel threatened—or worse, superior—and that can create difficulties. The people of the Caribbean must be given their respect and dignity. A smile usually wins a smile.

In addition, many of the islanders are deeply religious, and are offended by tourists who wear bikinis on shopping expeditions in town. One West Indian woman who runs a small hotel in Antigua had rented rooms to a film crew making a pirate adventure. When the men on that crew started running drunk and nude on the beach, a sight witnessed by the woman's two teenage daughters, she was deeply shocked. She handled the situation by posting a sign—"Pirates Must Wear Bathing Suits on the Beach."

Don't leave valuables such as cameras and cash-stuffed purses lying unattended on the beach while you go for a swim. Would you be so careless of your possessions in any town or city in Europe or America? Caribbean tourist officials often warn visitors, "If you've got it, don't flaunt it."

Problems do exist, and tomorrow's headlines may carry the story of a Caribbean disaster. Let me point out, however, that trouble in, say, Kingston, Jamaica, doesn't mean trouble in Barbados, no more than a bombing in London means you should cancel your trip to Munich.

Know that most of the people in the West Indies are proud, very proper, and most respectable, and if you treat them like such, they will likely treat you the same way. Others—certainly the minority but a visible minority—are downright antagonistic. Some, in fact, are skunks. But, then, any country on the globe has its share of that type.

Some islands are more hospitable to tourists than others. Your greeting in Montserrat is likely to be friendlier than it is in more jaded St. Thomas. But, then, Montserrat doesn't have five cruise ships a day docking at its harbor.

To show how difficult it is to assess the honesty and friendliness of a people, let me cite one example. By accident, I left a travel bag containing documents, cash, credit cards, and travelers checks in the back seat of a taxi. The driver pulled out before the bag could be retrieved. A bartender at the hotel tracked down the driver at carnival where he had the bag on his person. Under threat of calling the police, the bartender forced the driver to turn over the property. Both were citizens of the British Virgin Islands, but in honesty, integrity, and responsibility they were a world apart, just like the people in your hometown.

TRAVELING IN WINTER: The so-called season in the Caribbean runs roughly from the middle of December to the middle of April. Hotels in the Caribbean charge their highest prices during the peak winter period when visitors fleeing from the cold north winds crowd into the islands. Winter is the dry season in the islands, and most of the days are invariably sunny.

During the winter months, make reservations two to three months in advance, and if you rely on writing directly to the hotels, know that the mails are unreliable and take a long time. At certain hotels it is almost impossible to secure accommodations at Christmas and in February. One hotel in particular, Caneel Bay Plantation in St. John, books its rooms in February about a year in advance. Instead of writing to reserve your own room, it's better to book through one of the many Stateside representatives all major and many minor hotels use, or else to deal directly through a travel agent. If you don't want to do that, you should telephone the hotel of your choice in the Caribbean, agree on terms, and rush a deposit to hold the room.

Air-conditioned by trade winds, the temperature variations in the Caribbean are surprisingly slight, ranging between 75° and 85° Fahrenheit in both winter and summer. In other words, it's like a perpetual June.

20% TO 60% REDUCTIONS: The off-season in the Caribbean—roughly from mid-April to mid-December (although this varies from hotel to hotel)—virtually amounts to a summer sale. Except that summer in this context is eight months long, stretched out to include spring and autumn, often ideal times for travel.

In most cases, hotel rates are slashed a startling 20% to 60%, and these rate reductions are emphasized in this guide by being set in *italics*.

It's a bonanza for cost-conscious travelers, especially families who like to go on vacations together. Unbelievable, you say. You need proof.

In the chapters ahead, I'll spell out in specific dollars the amounts hotels charge during the off-season. In the meantime I'll cite percentages to back up my case. These percentages, incidentally, were tabulated by the Caribbean Tourism Association, and released to the press only after a careful screening for verification.

In the French island of Guadeloupe, which possesses some of the finest beaches in the Caribbean, and is covered with rain forests and topped by a sulfurous volcano, the PLM Arawak cuts its rates by 45% in the off-season. A skyscraper on the shore, it offers ten floors of "modern Créole rooms."

On the popular island of Barbados, the easternmost island in the West Indies, the Barbados Hilton cuts rates by about 33%. Built around a central court full of tropical gardens, right on the beach, it's a citadel of luxury living, Bajan style.

On the "spice island" of Grenada, southernmost island of the Windward Antilles, the Calabash, one of the finest hotels in the island country, slashes its rates by a whopping 57% on certain rooms.

On Nevis, once known for its sugarcane estates, the Nisbet Plantation Inn, a gracious estate house on a copra farm, the former home of Lord Nelson's bride, cuts tariffs by 43%.

In Tortola, the capital of the British Virgin Islands, Long Bay Hotel, a low-rise hotel complex set in a 50-acre estate with nearly a mile of white sand beach, cuts charges in summer by a big 55%.

Finally, the best for last. In the Dominican Republic, the Casa de Campo, the most fabulous resort in the West Indies, reduces its winter tariffs by 51% in the off-season, which makes it so reasonable that many middle-class Dominican families plan their holidays in this super-complete, luxurious resort dedicated to sports.

THE WEST INDIAN GUEST HOUSE: An entirely different type of accommodation is the guest house, where most of the Antilleans themselves stay when they travel in the Caribbean. Some of these are surprisingly comfortable, often with swimming pools and private baths with each room. You may or may not have air conditioning. The rooms are sometimes cooled by ceiling fans or trade winds blowing through open windows at night. Of course, don't expect the luxuries of a fabulous resort, but for value the guest house can't be topped. Staying in a guest house, you can journey over to a big beach resort, using its seaside facilities for only a small charge, perhaps no more than $3.

Although bereft of frills, the guest houses I've recommended are clean, decent, and safe for families or single women. Many of the cheapest ones are not places you'd like to live in all night and day too, because of their simple, modest furnishings.

However, many of today's new breed of travelers to the Caribbean don't want to spend more than eight hours in their rooms anyway. Otherwise, you'll find them on the beach, snorkeling or going scuba-diving, and at night patronizing the native taverns serving local food and just getting to know people. To this type of traveler a hotel is a mere convenience, to go to for sleep after an activity-filled day and a nightlife-packed evening.

Dressing up for dinner and otherwise practicing a routine familiar at American country clubs may not appeal to many of today's more adventurous travelers, who often arrive in the West Indies with a bikini, a T-shirt, and a pair of jeans.

In the Caribbean, the term "guest house" can mean anything. Sometimes so-called guest houses are really like simple motels built around swimming pools. Others are small individual cottages, with their own kitchenettes, constructed around a main building in which you'll often find a bar and a restaurant serving local food.

Giving fair warning, I'll point out that many of these guest houses are very basic. You must remember that nearly every piece of furniture must be imported, at often outrageous prices to the owner of the establishment. Salt spray on metal or fabric takes a serious toll, and chipped paint is commonplace. Bathrooms fall into the vintage category, and sometimes the water isn't heated. But when it's 85° to 92° Fahrenheit outside, you don't need hot water.

Guest houses are rarely built on the beach, but lie across the street or perhaps a five- or ten-minute stroll from the sands. That's why they can afford to charge such low prices.

Although not said to disappoint, these comments are made to anyone experiencing cultural shock or to a first-time visitor to the Caribbean who may never have encountered such a leisurely, beachcombing life as prevails in the West Indies.

Having said this, let me add another word about the friendliness, hospitality, and convivial atmosphere often created in these small, family-run places, which not only attract Antilleans, but are most often Antillean owned and run.

Staying in a guest house is for the serious tourist who'd like to meet some of the local people as well as fellow visitors with similar interests. Often, spontaneous barbecues are staged, and even in some of the smaller places a steel band is brought in on Saturday night for a "jump-up" session.

SELF-CATERING HOLIDAYS: Particularly if you're a family or friendly group, a housekeeping holiday can be one of the least expensive ways of vacationing in the Caribbean. These types of accommodations are now available on nearly all the islands previewed. Sometimes you can rent individual cottages; others are housed in one building. Some are private homes rented when the owners are away. All have small kitchens or kitchenettes where you can do your home cooking, shopping for groceries, and whenever possible, buying freshly caught fish and some Caribbean lobster.

Life this way is easy and pleasant. You can get up any time you choose, preparing your own breakfast with eggs just as you like them. You can even turn shopping into an adventure, particularly at a local marketplace where you may see fresh vegetables such as christophenes (a kind of squash) that you've never tried before. The fruits are luscious as well.

A housekeeping holiday, however, doesn't always mean you'll have to do maid's work. Most of the self-catering places have maid service included in the rental, and you're given fresh linen as well.

Cooking most of your meals yourself and dining out on occasion, such as when a neighboring big hotel has a beachside barbecue with entertainment, is the surest way of keeping holiday costs at a minimum.

IS THE SUMMER TOO HOT? For many travelers the islands of the Caribbean simply do not exist except when fearsome winds beat around corners and ice and slush pile up on the sidewalks up north. Regrettably, because everybody wants to visit the islands—"just anyplace warm"—at these times, "the season" developed. Knowing they had a hot item to sell—warm, sandy beaches when much of North America was hit by blizzards—hotel entrepreneurs charge the maximum for their accommodations in winter, "the maximum" meaning all that the traffic will bear.

When North America warms up, vacationers head for Cape Cod or the Jersey shore or the beaches of California, forgetting the islands in the sun, thinking perhaps that the Caribbean is a caldron. This is not the case. The fabled Caribbean weather is balmy all year, with temperatures varying little more than five degrees between winter and summer. The mid-80s prevail throughout most of the region, and trade winds make for comfortable days and nights, even in cheaper places that don't have air conditioning.

Truth is, you're better off in the West Indies most of the time than you are suffering through a roaring August heat wave in Chicago or New York.

Dollar for dollar, you'll save more money by renting a house or self-sufficient unit in the Caribbean than you would on Cape Cod, Fire Island, Laguna Beach, or the coast of Maine. Sailing and water sports are better too, because the West Indies is protected from the Atlantic on its western shores which border the calm Caribbean Sea.

In essence, because of the trade winds and the various ocean currents, the Caribbean is virtually "seasonless."

OTHER OFF-SEASON ADVANTAGES: In addition to price slashes at hotels, there are some other important reasons for visiting the Caribbean in spring, summer, and autumn.

- After the winter hordes have left, a less hurried way of life prevails. You'll have a better chance to appreciate the food, the culture, and the local customs.
- Swimming pools and beaches are less crowded—perhaps not crowded at all.
- Because summer business has grown, year-round resort facilities are offered, often at reduced rates. This is likely to include, among other activities, snorkeling, boating, and scuba-diving.
- To survive, resort boutiques often feature summer sales, hoping to clear the merchandise they didn't sell in February. They've ordered stock for the coming winter, and must clean their shelves and clear their racks. Duty-free items in free-port shopping are draws all year too.

You can often walk in unannounced at a top restaurant and get a seat for dinner, a seat that would have been denied you in winter unless you'd made reservations far in advance. When the waiters are less hurried, you'll get far better service too.

- The endless waiting game is over in the off-season. No waiting for a rented car (only to be told none is available). No long tee-up for golf. More immediate access to the tennis courts and water sports.
- The atmosphere is more cosmopolitan in the off-season than it is in winter, mainly because of the influx of Europeans. You'll no longer feel as if you're at a Canadian or American outpost. Also, the Antilleans themselves travel in the off-season, and our holiday becomes more of a people-to-people experience.
- Some package-tour fares are as much as 20% cheaper, and individual excursion fares are also reduced between 5% and 10%.
- All accommodations, including airline seats and hotel rooms, are much easier to obtain.
- Summer is the time for family travel, which is not possible during the winter season. Or else parents can travel while children are away at camp.
- Finally, the very best of wintertime attractions remain undiminished—that is, sea, sand, sun, and surf.

FOR SINGLE TRAVELERS: If you've ever read bargain-travel advertisements, you'll sometimes see an asterisk, indicating below (in fine print) that the tempting deal being presented is based on "double occupancy." If you're a lone wolf or without a traveling companion, you'll often get hit with a painful supplement called a "surcharge" in the industry. That surcharge can be at least 35% and perhaps a lot more. The hotelier in the Caribbean, of course, likes to shelter at least two in a room, and sometimes they crowd in three or four. It's the same room, and two to three persons spend a lot more on drinks, water sports, and food.

In addition to the cruises for singles that have gained mass popularity in the past few years, there is another way to keep costs bone-trimmed and take advantage of some of the package tours, cruises, and cut-rate hotel deals. But it means you may have to join a club.

One of the most successful such groups is **Gramercy's Singleworld,** 444 Madison Ave., New York, NY 10022 (tel. 212/758-2433), which for nearly 30 years has catered to single and unattached persons—the never-married, the separated, divorced, widowed, and those traveling alone. They have no age limits, although most of their club members are under 35. Certain cruise and tour departures are designated for people of all ages or under 35.

Anyone who is single or traveling alone is eligible for membership. The membership fee is $18 (nonrefundable). However, it is effective from the date of a departure for one full year. Singleworld emphasizes that they are *not* a lonely-hearts club, *not* a matrimonial bureau, and do *not* guarantee equal numbers of men and women in their groups.

Because Singleworld offers more than 500 departures a year, the prices offered for the cruise and tour departures are competitive. In addition, you can avoid the extra expense of a single-room accommodation by sharing a unit with another member.

TELEPHONING: While the area code for most of the Eastern Caribbean is 809, for many locations it is not possible to place a direct-dialed long-distance call from North America. (In fact, in some of the places I have listed, telephoning is not possible!) If you want to call ahead in the Caribbean, the Bell System has suggested that you call information for the area (dial 809/555-1212) and the operator will tell you the procedure for direct dialing.

However, to call station to station to one of the French-held islands, such as Guadeloupe, Martinique, St. Barts, or St. Martin, dial 011-596, then the local number.

The Dutch-held islands of Aruba, Bonaire, and Curaçao also have a different system. To call Aruba station to station, dial the international code 011, followed by the prefix 5998, then the local number. To reach Bonaire, dial 011/5997, followed by the local number; and to call Curaçao, dial 011/5999, then the local number. Dutch-held St. Maarten is reached by calling 011/596, followed by the local number. To reach little Saba, dial 011/5994 and the local number. Finally, for St. Eustatius, call 011/5993 and the local number.

Even within the 809 international access code, there are prefix numbers which must be dialed before the local number. Each island has its own. The procedure is to dial 809 first, then the island prefix number, then the local number.

The various prefix codes for the islands, *in each case following the 809 number, and coming before the local number,* are as follows:

Anguilla (497); Antigua (46); Barbados (42); the British Virgin Islands (49); the Cayman Islands (94); Dominica (445); Montserrat (491); St. Kitts (465); Nevis (also 465); St. Lucia (455); St. Vincent (45); Trinidad and Tobago (also 45).

You can dial Jamaica, Puerto Rico, the U.S. Virgins, and the Dominican Republic by dialing 809, then the local seven-digit number.

Haiti is a special case. Dial 1/509, followed by the local number in Haiti.

WHAT TO WEAR: In this day when dress is such a personal statement, I can no longer present checklists of what to pack. Many beachcombers arrive in the Caribbean with the jeans they're wearing, a toothbrush, and a bikini (perhaps!). Most travelers today are aware of clothing needed in subtropical or tropical climates. You'll want to dress casually to stay cool, and you'll want to select apparel that is easy to clean, of course.

If you're living at deluxe and first-class hotels, women should be prepared for at least an evening cocktail party. Some restaurants and hotels—and admittedly it's a hopeless battle—still require men to wear a jacket and tie in the evening.

Treading the balance between a personal statement in apparel and a concern for others, clothing in the Caribbean ultimately becomes a matter of taste. Some resorts which used to have dress codes—that is, men required to wear jackets after 6 p.m.—have, in despair, posted signs that dress should be "casual but chic." You are allowed to interpret that according to your wishes. I have attempted to give clues in individual writeups when hotels have set particular standards of dress.

Obviously, you should take coordinated clothing so that you can travel lightly.

AN INVITATION TO READERS: Like all its sister Dollarwise books, *Dollarwise Guide to the Caribbean* hopes to maintain a continuing dialogue between its author and its readers. All of us share a common aim—to travel as widely and as well as possible, at the best value for our money. And in achieving that goal, your comments and suggestions can be of tremendous help. Therefore, if you come across a particularly appealing hotel, restaurant, shop, even sightseeing attraction, please don't keep it to yourself. Your letters need not apply to new restaurants only, but to hotels or restaurants already recommended in this guide. The fact that a listing appears in this edition doesn't give it squatter's rights in future publications. If its services have deteriorated, its chef grown stale, its prices risen unfairly, whatever, these failings should be known. Even if you enjoyed every place and found every description accurate—that, too, can cheer many a gray day. Every letter will be read by me personally, although I find it well-nigh impossible to answer each and every one. Send your comments to Darwin Porter, c/o Frommer/Pasmantier Publishers, 1230 Avenue of the Americas, New York, NY 10020.

TIME OUT FOR A COMMERCIAL: Many visitors erroneously consider The Bahamas part of the Caribbean, and may wonder why this world tourist mecca is not covered in this guide. I do not mean to overlook The Bahamas. In fact, the publisher of this guide considers them important enough to create a companion volume, the 1986–1987 edition of *Frommer's Dollarwise Guide to Bermuda and The Bahamas,* which you may want to peruse in your search for an island hideaway.

1. Getting There

FLYING SOUTH: From North America, it's easy to wing your way south to the Caribbean. In just a matter of hours you can flee the Arctic winds and be lying on the beach, sipping your rum punch.

Travel agents who keep up-to-the-minute schedules can inform you about special stopover privileges, as "island hopping" is becoming an increasingly popular diversion for both a summer or winter holiday.

All the biggest islands have air links to the North American continent, with regularly scheduled service. The smaller islands are tied into this vast network through their own carriers, such as Prinair. For example to reach Montserrat, you fly, say from New York to Antigua, where a smaller craft will take you the rest of the short distance.

For a specific description of how to reach each island in this guide by plane, refer to the "Getting There" section at the beginning of the description to every destination.

TOURING BY PLANE: Chances are, you'll spend less than half a day flying from your point of embarkation in North America to your Caribbean island, and unless connecting links are impossible, that includes time lodged in waiting for inter-island flights. Obviously, the less time spent in getting there means more time on the beach. Direct flights from, say, New York, are possible to all major cities or islands of the Caribbean, including Antigua and Puerto Rico.

You face a choice of booking a seat on a regularly scheduled flight or else a charter plane, the latter being cheaper, of course. On a regular flight you can cancel your ticket without penalty. On a charter you do not have such leeway.

Charter Flights

Now open to the general public, charter flights allow visitors to the Caribbean to travel at rates cheaper than on regularly scheduled flights. Many of the major carriers offer charter flights to the Caribbean at rates that are sometimes 30% (or more) off the regular air fare.

There are some drawbacks to charter flights that you need to consider. Advance booking, for example, of up to 45 days or more may be required. You could lose most of the money you've advanced if an emergency should force you to cancel a flight. However, it is now possible to take out cancellation insurance against such an eventuality.

Unfortunately, on the charter flight you are forced to depart and return on a scheduled date. It will do no good to call the airline and tell them you're in Trinidad with yellow fever! If you're not on the plane, you can kiss your money good-bye.

Since charter flights are so complicated, it's best to go to a good travel agent and ask him or her to explain to you the problems, and advantages. Sometimes charters require ground arrangements, such as the prebooking of hotel rooms.

While there, ask about Apex Excursions, meaning advance purchase. These individual inclusive fares include land arrangements along with your excursion fare, and can represent a considerable savings to you.

TOURING BY CRUISE SHIP: If you'd like to sail the Caribbean, having a home with an ocean view, the cruise ship might be for you. It's slow and easy, and it's no longer to be enjoyed only by the idle rich who have months to spend away from home. Most cruises today appeal to the middle-income voyager who probably has no more than one or two weeks to spend cruising the Caribbean. Some 300 passenger ships sail the Caribbean all year, and in January and February that figure may go up another hundred or so. That's why it is impossible for me, given my space limitiations, to recommend particular cruises to readers.

Most cruise-ship operators suggest the concept of a "total vacation." Some promote activities "from sunup to sundown" while others suggest the possibility of "having absolutely nothing to do but lounge." Cruise ships are self-contained resorts, offering everything on board but actual sightseeing once you arrive in a port of call.

If you don't want to spend all your time at sea, some lines offer a fly-and-cruise vacation. Terms vary widely under this arrangement. You spend a week cruising the Caribbean, another week staying at an interesting hotel at reduced prices. These total packages cost less (or should) than if you'd purchased the cruise and air portions separately.

On yet another interpretation of "fly and cruise," you fly to meet the cruise and to leave it. Although multifarious in nature, most plans offer a package deal from the principal airport closest to your residence to the nearest major airport to the cruise departure point. Otherwise, you can purchase your air ticket on your own—say, from Kansas City to Fort Lauderdale—and book your cruise ticket separately as well, but you'll save money by combining the fares in a package deal.

Miami is the "cruise capital of the world," and vessels also leave from San Juan, New York, Port Everglades, Los Angeles, and other points of embarkation as well.

As in a hotel, if you're keeping costs at a minimum, ask for one of the smaller, inside cabins when booking space on a cruise ship. If you're the type who likes to be active all day and for most of the night, spending little time in your cabin except to sleep or whatever, you need not pay the extra money, which can be considerable, to rent luxurious suites aboard these seagoing vessels. Nearly all cabins rented today have a shower and a toilet, regardless of how cramped and confining it is. If you get a midship cabin, you are less likely to experience severe rolling and pitching. Most of the modern vessels have standardized accommodations, and the older vessels offer cabins of widely varying sizes, ranging from deluxe stateroom suites to "steerage."

Dress is more casual on cruise ships than it used to be in the "white tie and tails" days. Men still can use a dark suit occasionally, and women should have at least one cocktail dress. Most passengers on cruise ships don't dress up every evening, and some don't dress up at all. Men often wear sports coats and slacks with open shirts; women, pants suits or sports dresses.

Some evenings may be cool and you'll need a sweater. For women, a sun hat or scarf will do nicely. Plenty of casual, comfortable clothes are suggested for the day. For actual touring in the islands, or participating in the deck activities, men wear sport shirts, walking shorts, slacks, and a comfortable pair of walking shoes. Women will need sun dresses, skirts, blouses, shifts, culottes, and shorts. Walking shoes are preferred to city footwear.

Naturally, you'll need a bathing suit or a bikini. For women, even that kooky dress may be worn too, as Caribbean cruises lend themselves to masquerades.

Most of the cruise ships prefer to do their traveling at night, arriving the next morning at the day's port of call, as anybody who has ever had a hotel room overlooking the water in St. Thomas can testify. In port, passengers can go ashore for sightseeing and shopping (it's also possible to have lunch at a restaurant of your choice to sample some of the island specialties and break the monotony of taking every meal aboard ship).

Prices vary so widely that I cannot possibly document them here. Sometimes the same route, stopping at the identical ports of call, will carry different fares.

Unfortunately, the one ingredient needed for a successful cruise is the hardest to know in advance—and that's the list of your fellow passengers. The right crowd can be a lot of fun. A group incompatible with your interests can leave you sulking in your cabin.

TOURING BY CHARTERED BOAT: There is perhaps no more dream-making way of having a holiday in the Caribbean than from the deck of your own yacht. An impossible dream? Not really. No one said you had to own that yacht. You can charter it or go on a prearranged cruise.

Experienced sailors and navigators, with a sea-wise crew, can charter "bareboat," a term meaning a rental with a fully equipped boat but with no captain or crew. You're on your own, and you'll have to prove you can handle it before you're allowed to go on such a craft. Even if you're your own skipper, you may want to take along an experienced yachtsman familiar with local waters, which may be tricky in some places. (The company which insures the craft will definitely want to know that the vessel in question is in safe hands.)

Of course, if you can afford it, the ideal way is to charter a boat with a skilled skipper and a fully competent crew. Four to six people, maybe more, often charter yachts varying from 50 to more than 100 feet. Sometimes a dozen people will go out; at other times, a more romantic twosome.

Both the U.S. and British Virgin Islands are good cruising grounds, as are the Leeward and Windward Islands, which stretch from Antigua to Grenada, taking in such jewels of the French West Indies as Martinique and Guadeloupe. St. Vincent and the satellite Grenadines are also beautiful cruising grounds.

Most yachts are rented on a weekly basis, with a fully stocked bar, plus equipment for fishing and water sports. More and more bareboat charters are learning that they can save money and select menus more suited to their tastes by doing their own provisioning, rather than relying on the yacht company which rented them the vessel.

Unless money is no problem to you, the immediate question the average sailor asks is "How much will it cost?" Depending on the type of boat and the facilities offered, one person can count on spending from $90 to $150 a day. That doesn't mean you can't go out for less, and you certainly can sail for a lot more. Perhaps in summer, when business might be slow, you might get some yacht companies to charter you a boat for four or five days instead of a week or longer.

Some of the best known firms in the charter business include the following:

Stevens Yachts, 183 Madison Ave., Suite 1106, New York, NY 10016 (tel. 212/686-3822 within New York state and toll free 800/638-7044 elsewhere in the U.S.). This outfit specializes in yacht chartering from its bases in Tortola (the British Virgin Islands) and St. Lucia. Bareboat and crewed yachts between 39 and 56 feet are available from a well-maintained fleet of Sparkman and Stephens–designed sailing craft. Heidi Patty, the charter manager, suggests that four- to six-month bookings (which require a 50% deposit) are a good idea for locked-in dates. Clients whose schedules are more flexible need only about a month's reservations in advance. Insurance and full equipment are included in the rates.

Windjammer Barefoot Cruises, Ltd., P.O. Box 120, Miami Beach, FL 33119 (tel. 305/373-2090; toll free 800/327-2600; in Florida, 800/432-3364), offers trips on large sailing ships through The Bahamas and the Caribbean. Its *Flying Cloud* goes through the British Virgin Islands; its *Polynesia* sails the Leeward and Windward Islands; its *Yankee Clipper,* sails from Antigua; and *Fantome,* from The Bahamas. The newest ship, *Mandalay,* makes 12-day cruises out of Barbados and Antigua. Rates start at $450. Air-sea package deals are offered. S/V *Fantome,* S/V *Polynesia,* and S/V *Yankee Clipper* are registered in the British Virgin Islands, and the *Flying Cloud* is registered in The Bahamas. All ships comply with international safety standards except 1966 fire safety standards.

Nicholson Yacht Charters, 9 Chauncy St., Cambridge, MA 02138 (tel. 617/661-8174), or write P.O. Box 103, St. John's, Antigua, West Indies. This company, one of the best in the business, handles charter yachts for use throughout the

Caribbean basin, particularly the route between Dutch-held St. Maarten to Grenada, as well as the routes around the U.S. and British Virgin Islands. Specializing in boats of all sizes, they can arrange rentals of motor or sailing yachts of up to 164 feet long (in this case, a Hanse motor yacht), with a skipper and crew, or smaller boats accommodating anywhere from 2 to 12 people in private single or double cabins. Especially popular are arrangements where two or more yachts, each sleeping eight guests in four equal double cabins, race each other from island to island during the day, anchoring near each other in secluded coves or at berths in Caribbean capitals at night. Nicholson's offers a series of possibilities. An average package, according to the owners, costs approximately $4000 per week.

Windward/Leeward Sailing Tours, 680 Beach St., Suite 494, San Francisco, CA 94109 (tel. 415/441-1334), is another professional yacht charter agency, representing the major bareboat charter fleets, crewed yachts, and sailing ship opportunities throughout the world. It costs no more to utilize their services, and you'll benefit from their years of experience as charter agents.

It's also possible to cruise in the Caribbean on yachts which have set sailing dates. On this type of craft, depending on its size, of course, there might be anywhere from 6 to 50 passengers. You are in fact a cruise passenger.

PACKAGE TOURS: If you want everything done for you, plus want to save money as well, you might consider traveling the Caribbean on a package tour. General tours appealing to the average voyager are commonly offered, but many of the tours are very specific—tennis packages, golf packages, scuba and snorkeling packages, and, only for those who qualify, honeymooners' specials.

Economy and convenience are the chief advantage of a package tour in that the cost of transportation (usually an airplane fare), a hotel room, food (sometimes), and sightseeing (sometimes) are combined in one package, neatly tied up with a single price tag.

There are extras, of course. There are always extras, but in general you'll know roughly what the cost of your vacation will be in advance, and can budget accordingly.

If you booked your flight separately, likewise your hotel, you could not come out as cheaply as on a package tour—hence their immense and increasing appeal. There are disadvantages too. You may find yourself in a hotel you dislike immensely, yet you are virtually trapped there, as you've already paid for it.

Everybody from Idaho potato growers to birdwatchers of Alcatraz seemingly offers package tours to the Caribbean. Choosing the right one can be a bit of a problem. Your travel agent may offer one. Certainly all the major airline carriers will. It's best to go to a travel agent, tell him or her what island (or islands) you'd like to visit, and see what's currently offered.

These packages are available because tour operators can mass-book hotels and make volume purchases. Another disadvantage is that you generally have to pay the cost of the total package in advance. Transfers between your hotel and the airport are often included, and this is more of a financial break than it sounds at first, as some airports are situated a $40 or more taxi ride from a resort.

Many packages carry several options, including the possibility of low-cost car rentals.

The single traveler, regrettably, usually suffers, as nearly all tour packages are based on double occupancy.

Personally, I find one of the biggest drawbacks to taking a package tour to the Caribbean to be the hotel selected. I am especially fond of West Indian inns, small, family-run places, and I don't get these on package tours. Rather, tour operators who have to deal in block bookings can get discounts only at the large, more impersonal resorts.

Also, I find that many package deals to the Caribbean contain more hidden extras than they should. The list of "free" offerings sometimes sounds better than it is. Forget about that free rum punch at the manager's cocktail party, and peruse the fine print to see if your deal includes meals and other costly items.

2. The $25-a-Day Travel Club—How to Save Money on All Your Travels

In this book we'll be looking at how to get your money's worth in the Caribbean, but there is a "device" for saving money and determining value on *all* your trips. It's the popular, international $25-a-Day Travel Club, now in its 23rd successful year of operation. The Club was formed at the urging of numerous readers of the $$$-a-Day and Dollarwise Guides, who felt that such an organization could provide continuing travel information and a sense of community to value-minded travelers in all parts of the world. And so it does!

In keeping with the budget concept, the annual membership fee is low and is immediately exceeded by the value of your benefits. Upon receipt of $18 (U.S. residents), or $20 U.S. by check drawn on a U.S. bank or via international postal money order in U.S. funds (Canadian, Mexican, and other foreign residents) to cover one year's membership, we will send all new members the following items.

(1) *Any two* of the following books

Please designate in your letter which two you wish to receive:

Europe on $25 a Day
Australia on $25 a Day
England on $35 a Day
Greece including Istanbul and Turkey's Aegean Coast on $25 a Day
Hawaii on $35 a Day
Ireland on $25 a Day
India on $15 & $25 a Day
Israel on $30 & $35 a Day
Mexico on $20 a Day
New York on $35 a Day
New Zealand on $20 & $25 a Day
Scandinavia on $35 a Day
Scotland and Wales on $35 a Day
South America on $25 a Day
Spain and Morocco (plus the Canary Is.) on $35 a Day
Washington, D.C. on $40 a Day

Dollarwise Guide to Austria and Hungary
Dollarwise Guide to Bermuda and The Bahamas
Dollarwise Guide to Canada
Dollarwise Guide to the Caribbean
Dollarwise Guide to Egypt
Dollarwise Guide to England and Scotland
Dollarwise Guide to France
Dollarwise Guide to Germany
Dollarwise Guide to Italy

Dollarwise Guide to Japan and Hong Kong
Dollarwise Guide to Portugal (plus Madeira and the Azores)
Dollarwise Guide to Switzerland and Liechtenstein
Dollarwise Guide to California and Las Vegas
Dollarwise Guide to Florida
Dollarwise Guide to New England
Dollarwise Guide to the Northwest
Dollarwise Guide to the Southeast and New Orleans
Dollarwise Guide to the Southwest
(Dollarwise Guides discuss accommodations and facilities in all price ranges, with emphasis on the medium-priced.)

A Guide for the Disabled Traveler
(A guide to the best destinations for wheelchair travelers and other disabled vacationers in Europe, the United States, and Canada by an experienced wheelchair traveler. Includes detailed information about accommodations, restaurants, sights, transportation, and their accessibility.)

A Shopper's Guide to the Best Bargains in England, Scotland, and Wales
(Describes in detail hundreds of places to shop—department stores, factory outlets, street markets, and craft centers—for great quality British bargains.)

Bed & Breakfast—North America
(This guide contains a directory of over 150 organizations that offer bed & breakfast referrals and reservations throughout North America. The scenic attractions, businesses, and major schools and universities near the homes of each are also listed.)

Dollarwise Guide to Cruises
(This complete guide covers all the basics of cruising—ports of call, costs, fly-cruise package bargains, cabin selection booking, embarkation and debarkation and describes in detail over 60 or so ships cruising in Alaska, the Caribbean, Mexico, Hawaii, Panama, Canada, and the United States.)

Dollarwise Guide to Skiing USA—East
(Rates and describes the many resorts in Massachusetts, Vermont, New Hampshire, Connecticut, Maine, Quebec, New York, Pennsylvania, plus new areas in North Carolina, the Virginias, and Maryland. Includes detailed information about lodging, dining, and non-skier activities.)

Dollarwise Guide to Skiing USA—West
(All the diverse ski resorts of the West—in California, Colorado, Idaho, New Mexico, Montana, Oregon, and Wyoming—are fully described and rated. Lodging, dining, and non-skier activities are also included.)

Frommer's Travel Diary and Record Book
(A 72-page diary for personal travel notes plus a section for such vital data as passport and traveler's check numbers, itinerary, postcard list, special people and places to visit, and a reference section with temperature and conversion charts, and world maps with distance zones.)

How to Beat the High Cost of Travel
(This practical guide details how to save money on absolutely all travel items—accommodations, transportation, dining, sightseeing, shopping, taxes, and

more. Includes special budget information for seniors, students, singles, and families.)

Marilyn Wood's Wonderful Weekends
(This very selective guide covers the best mini-vacation destinations within a 175-mile radius of New York City. It describes special country inns and other accommodations, restaurants, picnic spots, sights, and activities—all the information needed for a two- or three-day stay.)

Museums in New York
(A complete guide to all the museums, historic houses, gardens, zoos, and more in the five boroughs. Illustrated with over 200 photographs.)

Swap and Go—Home Exchanging Made Easy
(Two veteran home exchangers explain in detail all the money-saving benefits of a home exchange, and then describe precisely how to do it. Also includes information on home rentals and many tips on low-cost travel.)

The Fast 'n' Easy Phrase Book
(The four most useful languages—French, German, Spanish, and Italian—all in one convenient, easy-to-use phrase guide.)

The New York Urban Athlete
(The ultimate guide to all the sports facilities in New York City for jocks and novices.)

Where to Stay USA
(By the Council on International Educational Exchange, this extraordinary guide is the first to list accommodations in all 50 states that cost anywhere from $3 to $25 per night.)

(2) A one-year subscription to *The Wonderful World of Budget Travel*
This quarterly eight-page tabloid newspaper keeps you up to date on fast-breaking developments in low-cost travel in all parts of the world bringing you the latest money-saving information—the kind of information you'd have to pay $25 a year to obtain elsewhere. This consumer-conscious publication also features columns of special interest to readers: **Hospitality Exchange** (members all over the world who are willing to provide hospitality to other members as they pass through their home cities); **Share-a-Trip** (offers and requests from members for travel companions who can share costs and help avoid the burdensome single supplement); and **Readers Ask . . . Readers Reply** (travel questions from members to which other members reply with authentic firsthand information).

(3) A copy of *Arthur Frommer's Guide to New York*
This is a pocket-size guide to hotels, restaurants, nightspots, and sightseeing attractions in all price ranges throughout the New York area.

(4) Your personal membership card
Membership entitles you to purchase through the Club all Arthur Frommer publications for a third to a half off their regular retail prices during the term of your membership.

So why not join this hardy band of international budgeteers and participate in its exchange of travel information and hospitality? Simply send your name and address, together with your annual membership fee of $18 (U.S. residents) or $20 U.S. (Canadian, Mexican, and other foreign residents), by check drawn on a U.S. bank or via international postal money order in U.S. funds to: $25-A-Day Travel Club, Inc., Frommer/Pasmantier Publishers, 1230 Avenue of the Americas, New York, NY 10020. And please remember to specify which *two* of the books in section (1) above you wish to receive in your initial package of members' benefits. Or, if you prefer, use the last page of this book, simply checking off the two books you select and enclosing $18 or $20 in U.S. currency.

Once you are a member, there is no obligation to buy additional books. No books will be mailed to you without your specific order.

THE CAYMAN ISLANDS

COLUMBUS FIRST SIGHTED the Cayman Islands in 1503, calling them "Las Tortugas," or the turtles. The first inhabitants consisted of a motley crew— buccaneers, beachcombers, bands of shipwrecked sailors. Rollicking Sir Henry Morgan once lived here, but in time the descendants of Scottish farmers arrived to forge a quiet, peaceful, God-fearing chain of islands that is an oasis of tranquility at the western edge of the Caribbean.

Don't go to the Cayman Islands for the fast-paced excitement of some of the Caribbean islands to the south. The world of the Cayman Islands centers around the sea. Snorkelers find it a paradise, as do beach buffs who are attracted to the powdery sands of West Bay Beach, renamed Seven Mile Beach with the opening of the Holiday Inn.

The Cayman Islands, 480 miles due south of Miami, consist of three islands —the pretentiously named Grand Cayman, Cayman Brac, and Little Cayman. Despite its name, Grand Cayman is only 22 miles long and 8 miles across at its widest point. The other islands are considerably smaller, of course, containing very limited tourist facilities. In contrast, Grand Cayman has become well developed just in the past decade or so.

This islands were once a dependency of Jamaica. But when that island opted for independence in 1962, the Cayman Islands preferred to remain a British Crown Colony, a land where there is no income tax.

Unlike the rest of the Caribbean, the population of the Cayman Islands is predominantly mixed. Essentially, the islanders are a self-reliant people who for years have enjoyed their unspoiled natural beauty in isolation, but at long last are inviting the world to come and share it with them.

Appointed by Queen Elizabeth II, a governor heads the local government, and English is the official language of the islands, although often spoken like an English slur mixed with the American southern drawl and finished off with a lilting Welsh accent.

George Town on Grand Cayman is the capital, the hub of government, banking, and shopping. Money rests here in more than 400 banks, free of the tax bite.

PRACTICAL FACTS: In **currency,** the legal tender is the Cayman Islands dollars, its value based on the U.S. dollar. At prevailing exchange rates, one Cayman dollar equals about $1.25 in U.S. currency. Or one U.S. dollar brings about C.I. 80¢. Canadian, U.S., and British currencies are readily acceptable throughout the Cayman Islands. Most hotels quote rates in U.S. dollars. However, many restaurants quote prices in Cayman Islands dollars, leading you to think that food is much cheaper than it is. Unless otherwise noted, quotations in this chapter are in U.S. dollars.

The best time to go is from mid-November to March, as violent rains often lash these islands in summer. Mosquitoes, once the scourge of the islands, are now kept under control through a government program.

No passports are required for U.S. or Canadian citizens. However, proof of citizenship is (voter registration card, birth certificate). Your return ticket is also required. A departure tax of $5 (U.S.) is collected when you leave the island.

Telephone: A modern automatic telephone system links the islands to the world via a submarine coaxial cable. Automatic-switching links in Jamaica enable the Cayman operators to dial numbers worldwide as a 24-hour service. International direct dialing was introduced in 1984.

Telegraph and Telex: The Cable and Wireless handling these is open from 8 a.m. to 5 p.m. weekdays, to 1 p.m. on Saturday, and to 11 a.m. on Sunday.

Time: Eastern Standard Time is in effect all year. Daylight Saving Time is not observed. Therefore, when Miami is on Daylight Saving Time and it's noon there, it's still 11 a.m. in the nearby Cayman Islands.

Banks: That most important part of Cayman Island life, the bank (or banks) is open from 9 a.m. to 2:30 p.m. Monday to Thursday and from 9 a.m. to 1 p.m. and 2:30 to 4:30 on Friday.

Drugs: The Cayman Islands have very severe laws on the use of marijuana and other drugs. Large fines and prison terms are given out to offenders.

Post Office: In Grand Cayman at George Town, the post office is open from 8:30 a.m. to 3:30 p.m. Monday to Friday and 8:30 to 11:30 a.m. on Saturday. It also has a Philatelic Bureau.

Electricity: It is 110 volts, 60 cycles—therefore American appliances will need no adapters.

Taxes: A government tourist tax of 6% is added to your hotel bill.

Tipping: Many restaurants add a 10% to 15% charge in lieu of tipping.

GETTING THERE: From Miami, the Cayman Islands are service by both **Cayman Airways** and **Republic Airways.** These airlines make the hour-long flight twice daily to Grand Cayman. Cayman Airways also flies direct from Houston daily, and Republic Airways offers a through flight from Detroit, stopping at Atlanta and Miami, to Grand Cayman. Once on Grand Cayman, Cayman Airways will fly you to Little Cayman or Cayman Brac.

To reach Miami, of course, visitors have a choice of several airlines, including TWA, Eastern, and Pan Am. However, it's cheaper to ask about a package service offered by **Cayman Express Ltd.** in conjunction with Cayman Airways. This is a seven-night package which includes *direct* round-trip air fare between New York and Grand Cayman, along with accommodations. This package, naturally, may not be available at the time of your visit, but check with a travel agent. If offered, the package is likely to be available only during the winter months.

GETTING AROUND: **Taxis** meet all arriving flights, and rates are fixed by the Cayman Islands Taxi Cab Association. A typical one-way fare from the airport to George Town is $5. However, to the Holiday Inn on Seven Mile Beach, the fare is $8.75. If you've booked a hotel at Rum Point on the North Shore, the fare is about $28. Taxis also transport visitors on around-the-island tours at $25 an hour. Five people can ride in the same cab.

Between George Town and West Bay, there is **bus** service approximately hourly. Many visitors use the much cheaper buses when shopping or dining in George Town, where you can catch buses at Panton Avenue, near the By-Rite Super Market.

Several car-rental firms operate on the island, including such familiar companies as **Avis** (tel. 9-2468); **Budget** (tel. 9-5605), and **Hertz** (tel. 9-2280). A reliable local company is **Coconut Car Rentals** (tel. 9-4037). Upon presentation of your own valid licencse, the car-rental agency is authorized to give you a driving permit at a cost of $3. *Remember, however, to drive on the left.* The cheapest car rentals start at about $28 per day. Many companies do not grant unlimited mileage unless you stay more than three days. In summer, prices are cut by about one-quarter. You should reserve a car several weeks in advance, particularly during the height of the winter season. You can return your car to the airport upon your departure, but it can't be picked up upon arrival. Rather, take a taxi to your hotel. After a phone call, your car will be delivered.

Another increasingly popular means of transport is a Honda, rented from **Caribbean Motors,** opposite Burger King (tel. 9-4051) and opposite the Holiday Inn (tel. 7-4466), for from $12 to $20 per day. These motorcycles can carry two persons. The same outfit also rents Mopeds from C.I. $9.60 ($12) a day.

1. Where to Stay

The true dollarwise hotel shopper will rent an apartment or villa (most often shared with friends or families), as in my opinion these units offer the best value. As they're furnished with kitchenettes, you can cut costs considerably by cooking your own breakfast, perhaps preparing a light lunch, then dining out for

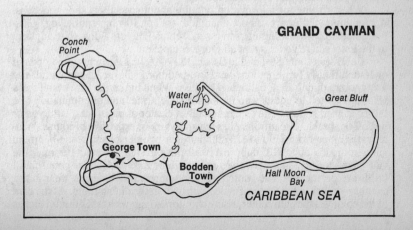

only one main meal of the day. Divers are often attracted to hotels or small resorts which include a half day's dive in their tariffs. I'll lead off with the most pleasing choices along Seven Mile Beach, beginning with a complete resort hotel:

ALONG SEVEN MILE BEACH: Holiday Inn Grand Cayman, Seven Mile Beach (tel. 7-4444), is an all-purpose, all-inclusive resort just a ten-minute taxi ride from the airport. Bedrooms have a bright, tropical flair, with floral island prints (most of them have sitting areas)—all have a bath with a dressing room and air conditioning. This is a very modern, 215-room beachfront hotel. There is a theatrically designed swimming pool—lagoon-like, with arched bridges and surrounding areas for sunbathing and entertainment. You can order tall rum punches beside the pool. Bars include the Corsair's Wharf, poolside, plus the Wreck of the Ten Sails for evening entertainment with a live band. Dining is varied. At Chez Jaques, with attentive service, you might order a conch salad or steamed shrimp, a sizzling turtle steak, the feature of the island, or roast prime ribs.

Ocean-view and oceanfront rooms are more expensive, of course, than island-view units. Depending on the accommodation, one person in winter pays from $137 to $220 per day; two persons, from $142 to $225 per day. There is no extra charge for a third or fourth person. *In summer, these tariffs are reduced to $98 to $135 per day for one person, from $103 to $139 per day for two persons.* For oceanfront rooms with private balcony or patio, add $20 per day, plus an energy surcharge of $3 per day per room. There is a fully equipped dive shop on the premises, and sailboats, waterskiing, and deep-sea fishing boats are available. Tennis is played on the inn's four courts (lit at night).

Beach Club Colony Resort, Seven Mile Beach (tel. 9-2023), is a 41-room resort two miles from George Town and five miles from Owen Roberts Airport. Each bedroom is air-conditioned, and most have balconies offering either an ocean or a garden view. You dine evenings in the Marlin Room. Informal luncheons and breakfasts are served on the Sea Grape Terrace. Guests congregate at the Escape Hatch Bar for tropical drinks.

Accommodations face the beach, ocean, or garden, and cottage units nestle in the garden as well. In winter, singles pay from $109 to $180 daily; two persons, from $127 to $188 daily. *In summer, these tariffs are lowered to $60 to $96 per day in a single, and from $72 to $108 per day in a double.* Add another $40 per person daily for breakfast and dinner.

When writing for information, inquire about special package vacations. Recreation facilities are almost unlimited—sailing, diving, snorkeling, glass-bottomed boat rides, cruising picnics, and tennis. There is a dive shop adjacent to the hotel where you can rent all sports equipment.

Caribbean Club, Seven Mile Beach (tel. 7-4099), is an exclusive compound of 18 luxuriously furnished one- and two-bedroom villas, each with a full-size living room, dining area, patio, and kitchen. When the owners are away, these villas are rented to guests who prefer the style, taste, and discrimination of a self-contained retreat. The club is actually a cluster of pink villas, either on or just off the beach. Oceanfront villas are always more expensive of course. Winter rates range from $190 to $237.50 daily for two persons in a one-bedroom villa, from $157.50 to $185 daily in a two-bedroom villa. An extra person in the villa pays another $24. *In summer, reductions of 25% to 40% are granted.* All tariffs are on the EP. The winter season requires casual elegant wear in the evening—either in the Green Turtle Lounge or in the dining room. At the core of the colony is the club center, rising two stories high with tall, graceful arches and picture windows. On the grounds is an abundance of foliage—many palm trees and flowering shrubbery—and there's a profesional tennis court as well.

Tarquynn Manor, P.O. Box 1362, West Bay Beach (tel. 7-4038), is a condominium of 20 apartments on the upper stretch of Seven Mile Beach. As an innovative concept for the Cayman Islands, two L-shaped apartment blocks face the sea, each block rising two stories high and containing four first-class apartments furnished in a nautical theme with individually controlled air conditioning. Standard apartments contain two bedrooms with two baths, costing $186 per day for up to four persons from December 15 to April 15. For families this can be a bargain, as a maximum of four persons can rent just one non-oceanfront apartment. Taxes and a service charge are extra (a maid cleans the units daily). For the more luxurious oceanfront and penthouse apartments, six persons are charged from $279 to $352 daily. *However, in the off-season, tariffs are lowered to $138 daily in the non-oceanfront apartments, each additional person paying $11 per day. The oceanfront and penthouse apartments in summer rent for anywhere from $207 to $259 for six persons.* Kitchens are all-electric, and the furniture is rattan. Either square-shaped porches or V-shaped balconies look out onto the freshwater swimming pool and beach areas.

West Indian Club, P.O. Box 703, West Bay Beach (tel. 9-2494), true to its name, is like a small private club, right on the white sands. It offers the poshest comfort on the entire island, with nine individually decorated one- and two-bedroom housekeeping apartments. Each apartment, furnished in a tropical idiom, has a large living room with patio or balcony overlooking the beach. Best of all, a full-time maid comes with each apartment. She will not only cook, clean, and do your laundry, but she can prepare native foods and is also trained in the standard American repertoire. Her hours are from 8:30 a.m. to 3:30 p.m. (never on Sunday). This imitation Tara, painted in salmon pink, is reached by going up a row of stately royal palms. Rates are expensive in winter—$222 per day for two persons in a one-bedroom unit. $288 daily for four in a two-bedroom accommodation. *In summer, these same tariffs drop to $135 to $170 per day.* One efficiency for two is available, *costing $114 in summer,* $132 in winter. Each unit has a private phone for local calls. There is an $11 surcharge for air conditioning, and guests must book for at least a week. Boats can be arranged for deep-sea fishing for wahoo, marlin, and sailfish.

Victoria House, West Bay Beach (tel. 7-4233), is an apartment complex standing at the north end of the beach. The management is among the friendliest and most helpful on the island. Twenty-five studio, and one- and two-bedroom apartments are rented, each with an open, airy feeling, furnished tastefully, generally in white bamboo with colorful fabrics. Kitchens are not only equipped with dishes and cutlery, but have a stylish appearance, and the dining area is in the living room. In high season, December 1 to April 30, two persons pay from $102 to $126 daily in either a studio or one-bedroom apartment; and four persons are charged from $162 in a two-bedroom unit up to $178 in a penthouse. *Off-season, for these same units, two persons are charged from $72 to $90; four persons, from $110 to $119.* Daily hotel-type maid service is included, but not tax and service. Between swims, string hammocks are strung up between the trees for naps, and a professional tennis court is nearby.

Coral Caymanian, P.O. Box 1093, Seven Mile Beach (tel. 9-4054), has an informal atmosphere. Right on the beach, it provides a wide range of accommodations—from oceanfront rooms to standard, from beach cottages to studios with kitchenettes—all air-conditioned. Units are sheltered from the hot sun by tall tropical trees, and near the shoreline is a thatched gazebo for even more shade. In a pleasantly decorated coffeeshop, guests enjoy a breakfast with fresh tropical fruits or a light lunch. From December 1 to April 30, superior and oceanfront rooms rent for $144 and up in a double. If you're traveling with a child who shares your room, the cost is another $14 per person. *In summer, these same superior and oceanfront rooms go from $96 daily.*

The **Royal Palms,** West Bay Road on Seven Mile Beach (tel. 9-2636), adjoins the Coral Caymanian, whose facilities are shared as they are under the same ownership. Established two decades ago as La Fontaine Hotel, the Royal Palms is an 83-room resort, owned by Capt. Charles Kirkconnell. They also have 40 condominium units. A major renovation program has taken place here, and new fixtures and furniture have been installed. The best accommodations are those with private patios or balconies overlooking the beach. Standard rooms, also refurbished, are in the main building.

Winter rates are $92 daily in a standard single, going up to $104 in a double and $116 in a triple. In the pool-view units, singles cost $114; doubles, $125. Condominium apartment rates are $132 for two guests in a one-bedroom, rising to $162 to $175 daily in a two-bedroom, one-bath apartment, the latter suitable for three to four guests.

In summer, standard singles on the EP range from $55 to $100 daily, going up to $68 to $105 in a double. A one-bedroom apartment costs two persons $102. For MAP, add $32 per person daily. Honeymoon, scuba-diving, and vacation packages are also available.

The beachfront bar is a popular rendezvous for residents and visitors at the happy hour from 5 to 6 p.m. Monday to Friday. The Royal Palms also has a beauty salon.

Don Foster's Dive Grand Cayman provides all scuba-diving and water sports (a dive shop and retail store is in the lobby of the resort). They offer daily two-tank morning dives and afternoon one-tank dives aboard the 26-foot Bristol Blue Water flattop *Adventure Diver* and the 36-foot custom flattop *Undersea Diver,* plus two others. PADI scuba resort courses are also available from Don Foster.

London House, P.O. Box 1356, West Bay Beach (tel. 7-4060), is a residential community of 20 deluxe apartments, directly on the beachfront. Each three-story apartment complex overlooks a kidney-shaped freshwater swimming pool with sun lounges. It is ten minutes from the airport and five minutes from town. The apartments are air-conditioned, well furnished, with fully equipped kitchens, and hotel maid service is included. Furnishings are in white bamboo with bright floral prints. The two-bedroom apartments have two full bathrooms. The two-bedroom apartments at ground level are one-story; the upper-floor two-bedroom apartments are two-story. The manager is Miriam M. Bodden. Rates are $186 daily in winter for a one-bedroom apartment, rising to $234 for a two-bedroom unit. Each additional person pays about $18 daily. *In summer, a one-bedroom apartment goes for $126 daily, increasing to $120 daily in a two-bedroom unit.*

Christopher Columbus, West Bay Beach (tel. 7-4354), is a new resort, actually a condominium where transient visitors can rent accommodations when the resident owners are away. Altona and Olney Ebanks always seem to be around, however, welcoming and directing guests to one of 30 luxurious two- and three-bedroom apartment homes opening onto Seven Mile Beach. Well equipped, each suite contains two baths, a well-supplied kitchen, tropical-style furnishings, and central air conditioning. In winter, four persons can take a two-bedroom apartment for $180 to $236, depending on the type of accommodation, or $266 for a penthouse. *Rates are slashed off-season, ranging from $110 to $156 for four persons in a two-bedroom apartment to $174 in a pent-*

house. On the grounds are two tournament-size tennis courts, plus a 50-foot freshwater pool.

Lime Tree Bay, Seven Mile Beach (tel. 7-4045), is a luxurious and handsome condominium community of 72 residential apartments surrounded by five acres of parkland, with direct access to the beach. Guests live in their own private worlds but occasionally meet and mix at impromptu sundown gatherings. Lime Tree Bay boasts a recreational area with two tennis courts (lit in the evening), plus an air-conditioned lodge with a swimming pool and shuffleboard. There's also a landing dock for sailing boats and yachts. All places are harmoniously decorated, with a combination of tropical and traditional. Units serve a wide range of needs. In high season, two persons can opt for anything from a studio at $118 daily to a deluxe one-bedroom apartment at $166, and four persons can be housed in facilities ranging from a two-bedroom apartment at $215. *Off-season, May 1 to November 1, reductions are dramatic: two persons pay anywhere from $79 to $106; four persons, from $144.*

Silver Sands, P.O. Box 205, West Bay Beach (tel. 9-3343), is a modern, eight-building complex arranged horseshoe fashion directly on the beach, taking up to 550 feet of frontage. After breakfast on your private sea-view balcony, guests hit the sands for a morning constitutional and a swim. The air-conditioned apartments are grouped around a freshwater pool. The eight apartment blocks contain either two-bedroom, two-bath, or three-bedroom, three-bath units. Kitchens are fully equipped, and hotel-type maid service is offered. The resident manager will point out the twin tennis courts and two utility rooms with washer-dryers. In the winter season, two persons rent a two-bedroom apartment for $180 daily, the cost going up to $216 for three to four persons. Six persons are given a three-bedroom unit at a cost of $264 daily. *Rates are greatly lowered off-season—from $120 daily for two in a two-bedroom to $144 daily for three to four persons in the same apartment. The three-bedroom units cost from $180 daily, and six guests are sheltered for that tariff.*

Harbour Heights, P.O. Box 688, West Bay Beach (tel. 7-4295), is a beachfront condominium, where you can stay in style and comfort by the day, week, or month. You're "on your own" for meals, but there's a good-size recreation area and a large free-form swimming pool with a surrounding tiled terrace (filled with white lounge furniture). The gardens are planted with palms and subtropical shrubbery. Apartments are of generous size, each having a living room and dinette, an attractive and complete kitchen, two bedrooms, two baths, and ample closet space. Each apartment has its own balcony or patio; furnishings are all in white tropical designs with decorative fabrics and accent rugs. Daily maid service is included. It's a short distance into George Town for shopping or restaurants. In the high season, a two-bedroom, two-bath apartment rents for $174 for two persons, with each additional person charged another $18 daily. A minimum stay of five days is required year round. *In the off-season, April 22 to December 12, that same apartment costs two persons $126, with each additional guest charged another $18.*

George Town Villas, P.O. Box 1169 (tel. 9-5172). A condominium complex, occupies a secluded position on Seven Mile Beach, within one mile of George Town. Around a central swimming pool rises a cluster of three-story, red-roofed buildings. Each of the 54 units contains two bedrooms, two baths, a kitchen and dishwasher, along with central air conditioning, a wet bar with icemaker, and a patio or balcony. Restaurants and grocery stores are within a short walk of the property. A tennis court is on the premises. In winter, between one and four persons can share a condo for $215 a day. *In summer, one to four guests pay $160 per day,* plus tax and service charged year round.

Pan-Cayman House, P.O. Box 440 (tel /-4002). The Georgian-style beachfront facade of this longtime favorite was attractively altered to suit its Caribbean setting. Only ten apartments are contained within this long, two-story building. Each has its own fully equipped kitchen, air conditioning, a private balcony or patio with an unrestricted view of the sea, and comfortable summer-type furniture. Hotel-type maid service is provided as part of the rentals of these two- and three-bedroom apartments. Rates vary with the season and according to the number of persons staying in an accommodation. In high season, two-bedroom apartments rent between $190 and $225 daily, while a three-bedroom unit, holding up to six persons, costs $290. *In summer, two-bedroom apartments rent for $95 to $150 daily, while three-bedroom accommodations go for $170 and $210.* A service charge of 5% is added. This place tends to be so popular that it's sometimes fully booked long in advance of the winter season.

The Beachcomber, P.O. Box 1799 (tel. 7-4470), a beachfront complex only five minutes from George Town, contains 24 luxury condominiums. These are contained in two- and three-story buildings whose angular facades include private verandas and sunrooms. Furnishings tend to modern pieces of bentwood well suited to hot climates. The big windows keep the interiors cool, when occupants aren't enjoying the central swimming pool or the wide sandy section of Seven Mile Beach reserved for the hotel. Each accommodation is air-conditioned, contains a fully equipped, all-electric kitchen and a private screened-in patio or balcony, and offers six-day-a-week maid service.

Winter rates for one or two persons in a two-bedroom apartment range from $155 to $200 per day. For between one and four persons in an oceanfront apartment, the high-season rate is $300 daily. *In summer, one or two persons can stay in a two-bedroom apartment for between $120 and $145, while between one and four persons can occupy an oceanfront unit for $235.* Each extra person, up to a total of four to six, depending on the rental, pays additional fees ranging from $12 to $18, depending on the season. Service and tax are extra.

The Islands Club, P.O. Box 1764 (tel. 9-5411). Many residents check in here simply for the uninterrupted view of the sea from the windows of each of the 27 condominiums. It has its private section of a very long beach, tennis courts (lit at night), and a clubhouse. Bud and Melissa Bodden, the resident managers, make sure that the amenities of each unit (which include a dishwasher, central air conditioning, microwave oven, washer and dryer, and a patio or balcony) are in working order. In winter, two-bedroom apartments for one to four persons rent for $290 per day. A three-bedroom unit for one to six persons costs $400 per day. *In summer, two-bedroom apartments go for $210 daily, while three-bedroom units cost $275, plus service.*

ON THE NORTH SHORE: Cayman Kai, P.O. Box 1112, Rum Point (tel. 7-9556), is an attractive collection of beach villas and lodges that have interesting architectural features: many are circular, some are square-shaped, others rectangular; all have unusual white tent-like roofs. There are 26 one- and two-bedroom sea lodges, and 16 luxurious beach villas, complete with dining area, kitchen, and patio, overlooking miles of reefs. Set among coconut trees on 200 acres of the village community of Cayman Kai on the north shore, the beach is ideal for snorkeling. Top of the Kai Lounge offers native entertainment several nights a week. The Kai offers two dive boats and has complete diving equipment available for guests. Caymanian and international cuisine—everything from beef Wellington to whelks—is served.

For a sea lodge, one or two guests pay from $67 per day in summer, and four guests in a two-bedroom, two-bath lodge are housed for $127. In winter, both these rates rise, to $118 to $222 per day respectively. *In the off-season, beach villas, depending on their size (one bedroom, two bedroom, or four bedroom), range in price from $89 daily for two, going up to $154 for up to six guests.* In winter, these same rates are $140 daily to $253 respectively.

For the full-board plan, add $34 per person daily to the rates quoted. When writing for reservations, ask about attractive package deals, such as scuba holidays.

Spanish Cove, P.O. Box 1014, Spanish Bay (tel. 9-3765), is a luxury resort for divers located on a remote, rugged beach on the northern tip of the island, which offers good scuba-diving. A handsomely designed dining room and bar is constructed out of coral rock and natural wood. There are 46 rooms, pleasantly designed with ceramic tile floors and rough wood trim. The restaurant is outstanding on the island. The food is well prepared, with luncheon served buffet style. The dining room is at beach level with a large outdoor patio and barbecue. The bar and lounge are on the second floor overlooking the water. There is a pool on the premises. All rooms have two queen-size beds, air conditioning, and ceiling fans. Four rooms are suitable for families or small groups.

The double rate is $114 year round, EP, with an additional person paying $12 daily.

Spanish Cove is a full-service dive resort and that means a NAUI/PADI training facility. Facilities include a sheltered three-boat slipway, four outstanding dive boats, and the latest in rental equipment.

IN AND AROUND GEORGE TOWN: Sunset House, P.O. Box 479, South Church Street (tel. 9-5966), attracts serious divers and is one of the few resorts in the capital. In fact, it's known for its program of night dives, including a descent down "The Wall," a sheer dropoff into a submarine world of caves and coral, sponges, sea fans, and brilliantly colored fish. A special feature of Sunset House is its "Diver's Package" (based on double occupancy), including an air-conditioned room with bath, breakfast, dinner, airport transfers, surprise package, a cocktail, service, taxes, and boat trips with two tanks and weight belts.

Hotel rooms cost $78 in a single, $126 for two in winter. In addition, efficiencies and apartments, sleeping from four to six persons in the modern block, are rented on the EP. In winter, the double rate in an apartment ranges from $126,with an extra person paying $11 for the cost of the room. *In summer, one person can stay here on a half-board arrangement, paying from $54 to $66 daily; two persons are charged from $66 to $78 daily, also halfboard. A one-bedroom apartment (no meals) rents for $102 per day, with each additional person sharing assessed another $11.* At the end of the day, divers meet at the waterfront Thatch Bar to enjoy a sundowner with fellow divers and local residents. Meals, featuring a range of native and international dishes, are served family style.

South Cove Diving Resort, P.O. Box 637, near George Town (tel. 9-2514), is a small, friendly hotel primarily for dive buffs. The resort—some would call it a guest house—opens onto the sea. Guests can swim to the offshore wall, visit Waldo, a friendly moray eel, or go on night dives. Short boat trips are offered on a 36-foot platform dive boat or a 42-foot Bruno Stillmann with rear platform entry *(Gypsy* and *Gypsy Diver)*. Nondivers can enjoy a quiet stay here as well, relaxing and meeting people. There is a bar, and good local food is served in the restaurant. All rooms are air-conditioned, and there are six two-bedroom apartments directly across the road offering more luxurious accommodation and catering to families. Cooking facilities are available. On the AP, singles pay $92 daily; doubles, $137 daily. Ask about special seven-night, eight-day dive packages, with three meals included.

ELSEWHERE ON GRAND CAYMAN: Tortuga Club, P.O. Box 496, East End (tel. 7-7551), is a group of long, low buildings set in a grove of coconut trees. The windows open to the sea breezes. The club is small, only 14 rooms with air conditioning and ceiling fans. *Town & Country* magazine rated the club as one of the leading 125 world resorts. The dining room is built of rugged stone, with Spanish elm beams, flagstone floors, and a water view. The shell bar has tables made from hatch covers and local mahogany. The spacious bedrooms have indoor/outdoor life with wall-wide glass doors opening onto a terrace with white furniture. Everything is homemade—conch pie, turtle steak, lobster, whatever. One morning one guest ordered beer pancakes—and got them! In winter, a single person can stay here on the MAP for $138 daily, the cost going up to $190 for two, $234 for three. A fourth person sharing a room is charged $60 daily for half board, and children under 12 in their parents room need pay only $22 per day. *From April 15 to mid-December a MAP single rents for $96 daily, $138 for two.* Scuba packages are also offered. Snorkeling and deep-sea fishing are available.

    Cayman Diving Lodge (tel. 7-7555 or toll free 800/327-8223), is primarily for divers. It was taken over in late 1984 by Ron Kipp, owner of Bob Soto's Diving, Ltd., the biggest dive operator on the island. The lodge is a two-story building set against a backdrop of tropical trees on a private beachfront. Oceanview rooms are modern, pleasant, simple, and air-conditioned. In the southeast corner of the island, the lodge is on a coral sand beach with a live coral barrier reef just offshore. Meals are prepared by native Caymanian chefs who serve abundant portions. The accent is on fish.

    Package bookings—the acceptable method of checking in here—are usually for seven nights. The Cayman dive package includes not only the room but all meals, as well as two tank dives daily, unlimited tanks, backpacks, weight belts, and weights. One person on this seven-day plan pays $750, double occupancy. Nondivers are given reductions, of course. Also offered is professional underwater cinematography equipment. Heindl, well-known veteran underwater cameraman, and master photographer Gerry Hytha conduct underwater photography classes.

    Windsor House Apartment, P.O. Box 487 (tel. 9-2604), is one of the least expensive accommodations on the island. The owner, Mrs. Bernard St. Aubyn, rents out a self-contained apartment, separated from her own private residence by a breezeway, ensuring complete privacy. In the best residential area, with a fine view of the harbor, the house stands in a well-kept garden with plenty of flowering shrubs, trees, and birds. The Windsor is about ten minutes by car from Seven Mile Beach and a mile from a small sandy cove in the opposite direction. Each bedroom (there are two) contains twin beds, making the apartment suitable for four persons. The kitchen is fully equipped, and a large living room opens onto an enclosed veranda. Mrs. St. Aubyn says, "Don't be put off by our low rates. We want repeat business." *In summer, the tariffs are $36 per day for two persons, plus $6 for each additional person,* increasing to around $48 in winter. The apartment is not air-conditioned, but there is a large standing fan and an attic fan. Guests are on their own as far as maid service is concerned.

2. Eating Out

    American and continental dishes predominate, although there is also a cuisine known as Caymanian, featuring specialties made from turtle, even turtleburgers, certainly turtle soups and steaks. Fresh fish is the star, and conch is used in imaginative ways. Native lobster is in season from late summer through January. While most visitors dine at their hotels, many of my recommendations are apartments or villas, which do not always serve meals, allowing you to sample some of the island's many restaurants. Since most dining places have to rely on imported ingredients, prices tend to be high.

The Grand Old House, Petra Plantation, South Church Street (tel. 9-2020), is my favored dining spot in Grand Cayman. This beautiful old mansion, a former Caymanian residence built at the turn of the century by a Bostonian, lies less than five minutes south of George Town. Built on bedrock, it stands on 129 ironwood posts.

Stop off in the Batik Bar for a predinner drink. There the fine wood floors have been burnished, and flickering candles set off the batiks. Tables are placed on a broad Victorian veranda, with a view of the Caribbean. Your hosts, Timothy and Phyllis Kelly, have hired a lovely group of Caymanians to serve you.

The menu is wide ranging, from U.S. dishes to West Indies specialties to continental selections. You might begin with marinated Cayman conch or shrimp Old House, a specialty. The soups are very good, including clear turtle consommé with sherry. The maître d' will guide you through the main-dish specialties, which include every item from an Indonesian rijsttafel to snapper caprice (Cayman snapper served with banana and mango chutney sauce). Your final tab is likely to be from $35 to $40 per person.

There is a fine wine list. Only dinner is served, from 6 to 10:30 p.m.; and reservations are advised. No credit cards are honored.

Caribbean Club, Seven Mile Beach (tel. 7-4099), is one of the best places for dining in Grand Cayman (already recommended for its accommodations). A popular luncheon stopover, it offers such hot dishes as Cayman turtle Stroganoff, served with rice and cole slaw. For an appetizer, I suggest the marinated conch. A selection of sandwiches is also available. Each day a special is featured. Lunch begins at $15. In the Governor's Dining Room, the setting is elegant, and there's a view of the sea. A German chef prepares excellent international dishes. The appetizers are tempting, ranging from something continental like escargots bourguignonnes, to something local, like conch fritters. The specialty of the house is tournedos (two small filets, wrapped in bacon and topped with mushrooms and a light madeira sauce). The deep-fried crab claws are also superb. A dinner here can easily run around $35 or more. Reservations are required in the evening.

Lobster Pot, North Church Street (tel. 9-2736), is one of the island's best known restaurants, overlooking the water from its simple, second-floor perch right outside George Town. True to its name, it offers an assortment of seafood dishes, including the classic seafood platter—lobster, turtle, and the catch of the day. The increasingly rare turtle steak is offered here just by itself. The spicy seafood curry is also excellent. An unusual opener might be "Cayman delight," that is, wahoo (a game fish) marinated in coconut milk. The turtle soup is laced with sherry, and the cherries jubilee flamed at your table makes a spectacular finish. Count on spending from $30. In the bar, styled like an English pub, the dart board is kept busy and the drinks are good. From the dining room, the views at sunset are magnificent. You're asked to make a reservation.

The Cayman Arms, Harbour Drive (tel. 9-2661), overlooks the waterfront and is a popular gathering point for an expatriate colony—that is, a number of business people and bankers who find the Cayman Islands an ideal place in which to carry on international transactions. Therefore, it gets very crowded at lunchtime. The food is good, as is the service. At lunch you can order such appetizers as marinated Cayman conch or escargots in garlic butter, followed by such main-dish selections as "mushrooms Cayman Arms," a casserole and onion dish with a loyal following. At dinner, appetizers include the mushrooms ordered in a smaller portion before your main course. Among the recommended main dishes are turtle in garlic butter, English fish and chips, and oysters Cayman Arms. Desserts include homemade pies and cakes. Count on spending around $15 for lunch, $25 to $30 for dinner. The restaurant is closed for Sunday at lunch.

Ports of Call, North Church Street (tel. 9-2231), gives you excellent dining in an elegantly appointed setting for both lunch and dinner. Saturday night the restaurant features an island-style buffet with five native dishes to choose from. Sunday, guests spend the afternoon on the Edgewater Patio where barbecued chicken, ribs, and hamburgers are served in the casual and relaxed atmosphere. Happy hour is every weeknight from 5 to 7 p.m. Lunch features are daily specials as well as such delights as smoked salmon on toast, french onion soup, open steak sandwich, and Cayman-style turtle steak or conch fritters. The dinner menu offers a Cayman seafood platter among its delicacies. Special coffees are popular after your meal, which is likely to cost $30 or more. Reservations are needed only for dinner.

Almond Tree, North Church Street (tel. 9-2893), is an informal restaurant run by Jim and Kelly Wall. The place has a tropical atmosphere and attracts a casually dressed diner. The Almond Tree is famous for its tropical drinks, and the cooks produce some of the finest turtle and fish dinners in the islands, including baked turtle steak, Cayman style, and the fresh catch of the day. Caribbean lobster is also featured on the menu, as well as a variety of homemade desserts. Meals csost from $25. Open in the afternoon is the patio, where you can enjoy a piña colada and a light snack, including such island favorites as marinated conch and turtle soup, in the shade of towering almond and breadfruit trees. Reservations are a must.

Coconut Place Liquor & Deli, West Bay Road (tel. 7-4442), stands just south of the Holiday Inn. It's *the* place for delectable sub sandwiches, costing from $3.50, with a quick take-out service. It's recommended for après-dive appetites. There's also a large selection of munchies, along with fresh fruit and liquor, plus cold soft drinks. The place is convenient to Seven Mile Beach, and you shouldn't miss its "black coral" brownies. Closed Sunday.

The Cracked Conch, Red Bay Plaza (tel. 9-5717), invites you to eat as "Caymanians eat." After that, the menu lists what they mean: conch in every known way, ranging from conch burgers to conch fritters, from cream-style conch chowder to Manhattan conch chowder, not to mention marinated conch and cracked conch, as well as conch stewed in coconut milk. If you don't like conch, a turtle sticks its head out and becomes turtle burger, turtle Cordon Bleu, turtle steak, and turtle schnitzel. If any of that is too exotic for you, order vichyssoise, followed by lobster tails or the fish of the day. Stuffed shrimp, filets, and chicken Cordon Bleu round out the selections. Lunch and dinner are served daily from 11 a.m. to 5:30 p.m. and dinner from 6:30 to 10 p.m. You'll spend from $10 to $25 for a meal. Closed Sunday. The location is about a five-minute drive from George Town. The restaurant, staffed by Caymanians, is a family operation.

Welly's Cool Spot, North Sound Road, George Town (tel. 9-2541). Go here for native dishes, and by that I mean the emphasis is on our old reliable friends, the conch and turtle. But they also do lobster superbly, and in fact offer different dinner specials every night. Lunch is from noon to 3 p.m. and dinner from 6:30 to 10 p.m., costing around $25 to $30 maybe less. In the evening you should call ahead for a reservation. If you give him advance notice, Welly will do something special, maybe curried goat.

Tortuga Club, East End (tel. 7-7551). You can head out to Tortuga Club for a great "day-away" from Seven Mile Beach. There you can go snorkeling and diving, then enjoy some of the island's best rum punch while relaxing in one of the shady beachside hammocks. Don't fail to make a reservation for dinner, costing from $25. Miss Cleo, a Caymanian woman of great culinary talent, is the club's cook, and has been for more than 20 years. Her banana cream and coconut cream pies are unsurpassed. Save space for them after ordering a fresh lobster. Later, you can waddle out to the bar where a friendly "East Ender" like manager Frank Conolly will teach you the fundamentals of "warry," a Caymanian board game.

3. The Sporting Life

What they lack in nightlife, the Caymans make up in water sports—fishing, swimming, waterskiing, and of course, diving are among the finest in the Caribbean.

DIVING: *Skin Diver* magazine wrote, "Grand Cayman has become the largest single island in the Caribbean for dive tourism." There is lots of marine life, a large variety, and many coral formations. There are plenty of boats and scuba facilities. Coral reefs encircle the islands, and these reefs are filled with marine life. However, the government bans scuba-divers from taking any form of marine life. It's easy to dive close to shore—therefore, boats aren't necessary.

But for certain excursions I recomment a trip with a qualified dive master. For rentals, the island maintains many "dive shops." Hotels also rent in-house facilities as well; however, a dive shop will not rent scuba gear or supply air to a diver unless he or she has a card from one of the national diving schools, such as NAUI or PADI. In most places in Grand Cayman, air refills cost from $3.50 upward. Hotels arrange snorkeling and scuba-diving trips. A morning, two-tank diving trip is likely to cost about $35. Night dives to for about $30 for two hours. A half-day snorkel trip costs around $25.

The largest dive operator in the Cayman Islands is **Bob Soto's Diving, Ltd.,** P.O. Box 1801, Grand Cayman (tel. 9-2022). Established in 1957, the headquarters are below the previously recommended Lobster Pot restaurant. Dive shops are also found at the Holiday Inn, Scuba Centre, and the Cayman Islander. Bob Soto's offers two-tank scuba dives in the morning at $35, one-tank scuba dives in the afternoon at $25, and night scuba dives at $30. Scuba instruction is also available, and snorkel and boat trips operate daily. In addition, you can rent sailboats, jet skis, windsurfers, and Hobie Cats. For example, a Sunfish rental costs only $15. Equipment such as snorkeling vests, masks, and fins can also be rented. A full range of water sports awaits the visitor, and Bob Soto's people, as they're called, are the friendliest and most helpful I've ever encountered in the islands.

Surfside Watersports, Ltd., P.O. Box 891 (tel. 7-4224), which Joseph P. Donahue operates out of the "new" Le Club Cayman on Seven Mile Beach, has undergone extensive renovation and is the island's most complete water-sports center, offering much more than just diving. A morning, two-tank dive costs $35 and an afternoon one-tank trip goes for $25. Various diving courses are offered, and gear can be rented. Besides snorkel trips ($12.50) and beach lunch trips ($25), the following are for rent: Hobie Cats, day sailors, jet skis, windsurfers, aquabikes, and kayaks. Daytime glass-bottomed boat trips cost $12.50 and a nighttime trip is $15. Additionally, Surfside is the only operation at Grand Cayman offering parasailing.

At **Tortuga Club,** East End (tel. 7-7551), is the dive master/instructor in charge of the dive operation. He offers daily two-tank dives on some of the island's most dramatic east-coast dive sites. Full certification and resort courses are available for $375 and $50, respectively.

The **Spanish Cove Diving Resort** (tel. 9-3765), previewed earlier as a hotel, offers a one-tank boat dive for $25 and a two-tank boat dive for $37.50. They also do one-tank night dives for $30.

South Cove Diving Resort, near George Town (tel. 9-2514), was already previewed as a resort. It offers daily trips to nearby reefs and wrecks, including two full tanks, backpack, weights, and belt at a cost of $30 per half day. Dive boats, both 42 feet and 36 feet, also go out on one-tank night dives at a cost of $25 per person.

FISHING: Grouper and snapper are most plentiful for those who bottom fish along the reef. Deeper waters turn up barracuda and bonito. The flats on Little Cayman are said to offer the best bonefishing in the world. Sports people from all over the world come to the Caymans for the big ones—tuna, wahoo, marlin. Most hotels can make arrangements for charter boats. For a typical rate, a maximum of six fishermen pay about $255 per day and up on an open-boat trip. Experienced guides are also available.

At **Tortuga Club,** East End (tel. 7-7551), an experienced local guide will escort anglers seeking blue-water action from marlin, wahoo, dolphin, and a variety of tuna, for $150 per half day (up to four passengers), bait and tackle included.

SAILING: Nearly all the hotels I've recommended offer sailboats, jet skis, Hobie Cats, windsurfers, and guided sailboat cruises for their clients. Calm waters please skiers. The previously cited **Bob Soto's Diving Ltd.** can arrange for small-boat rentals at prices ranging from aboukt $25 to $100 a day.

SWIMMING: About the finest in the Caribbean. Grand Cayman's Seven Mile Beach has sparkling white sands with Australian pines in the background. In addition, beaches on the east coast and north coast are also fine, as they are protected by an offshore barrier reef. In winter the average water temperature is 80°, rising to 85° in summer.

4. Exploring the Island

The capital, **George Town,** can easily be explored in an afternoon. It is principally a place to visit for its restaurants and shops (or banks!)—not sightseeing. It does offer a clock monument to King George V and the oldest government building use today, the post office on Edward Street, where stamps sold there are an avid prize to collectors.

Elsewhere on the island, you might go to **Hell!** That's at the north end of West Bay Beach, a jagged piece of rock named Hell by a former commissioner. There the postmistress, Mrs. Mary Ebanks, will stamp Hell, Grand Cayman, on your postcard to send back to the States.

Cayman Turtle Farm, at Northwest Point, houses giant turtles and is in fact the world's only sea turtle farm, with thousands of turtles on view ranging in weight from six ounces to 600 pounds. Admission is $5 for adults and $2.50 for children. There is also a large gift shop.

At **Botabano,** on the North Sound, fishermen tie up with their catch, much to the delight of photographers. If you've got your own kitchenette, you can buy lobster (in season), fresh fish, even conch and turtle meat, from these fishermen. A large barrier reef protects the sound which is surrounded on three sides by the island, a mecca for divers and sports fishermen.

If you're driving, you might want to go along **South Sound Road,** lined with pines and, in places, old wooden Cayman Island houses. After leaving the houses, including many modern ones, behind, you'll find good spots for a picnic.

Pedro's Castle is reached by going along Old Prospect Road to Bodden

Town. A few miles from there, you turn right at the crossroads at Savannah. Originally called St. James Castle, Pedro's is the oldest standing building in the Caymans. Erected by slave labor, today it houses a restaurant.

Also, just outside Savannah, on Spots Bay, is the island's best known cave, **Bat Cave.** Frankly, I recommend this attraction to cave buffs only. Backtracking from Pedro's Castle, you go just beyond the speed restriction sign, as if heading back to George Town. On your left (the sea side of the road), you'll see a dirt road. Follow it to the end. Once you reach the sea, turn left. Walking along the cliff edge for some 30 yards, you'll reach a sandy beach. After climbing down ten feet, you'll spot the cave's low mouth. The cave is explored on your hands and knees (thankfully, the floor is sandy). The bats will squeak loudly at your entrance but they're harmless.

On the road again, you reach **Bodden Town,** which was once the largest settlement on the island. At Gun Square, two cannons commanded the channel through the reef. They are now stuck muzzle-first into the ground.

On the way to the **East End,** just before Old Isaac Village, you'll see the onshore sprays of water shooting up like geysers, their sound like the roar of a lion. These are called "blowholes."

Later, you'll spot the fluke of an anchor sticking up from the ocean floor. As the story goes, this is a relic of the famous "Wreck of the Ten Sails" in 1788. A modern wreck can also be seen—the *Ridgefield,* a 7500-ton Liberty ship from New England which struck the reef in 1943.

Finally, **Old Man Bay** is reached by a new road that opened in 1983. Head back to town along the cross-island road through savannah country, where royal palms sway in the breeze and the appearance is veldt-like. You might even spot the green Cayman parrot. At Old Man Bay, you can travel along the north shore of the island to **Rum Point,** with its lovely beach, which is as good a place as any to end the tour.

5. Free-Port Shopping

This is not the most compelling reason to take a vacation in Grand Cayman. However, having said that, it should be noted that there is free-port shopping, with merchandise from all over the world available in the stores of George Town. Often you'll find bargains in silver, china, crystal, Irish linen, French perfumes, British woolen goods, and such native crafts as black coral jewelry and thatch-woven baskets. However, you should know the prices prevailing in U.S. stores. I have found them to be the same on many items.

Don't purchase turtle products. They cannot be brought into the U.S.

In George Town, my recommendations follow:

Caribe Island Jewelry, North West Point, West Bay (tel. 9-3448), offers locally made jewelry from black coral, caymanite, whelk, and conch. The jewelry is produced in many forms, including necklaces, bracelets, and earrings. The store is on the way to the turtle farm.

Viking Gallery, Harbour Drive on the waterfront (tel. 9-4090), offers two floors of handicrafts, as well as hand-painted skirts and tops, a calypso boutique, native bolt material, and local and Caribbean paintings. They also sell pewter, crystal, black coral items, fine jewelry, porcelain, and bank tax-haven books.

Bridget's Fashions and Fragrances, Harbour Drive, Freeport Plaza (tel. 9-2699), opposite the cruise-ship passenger landing, offers a selection of fashions from around the world. These include Gottex swimwear from Israel, handcrafted batik from Bangkok, Irish linen, Cayman map wall hangings, special design (woven) turtle ties for men, and Cayman coat-of-arms ties, along with sportswear for men.

Far Away Places, at the end of the Olde Fort Building, sells sterling silver, gold jewelry, gifts from nearly every part of the globe, including a tasteful, unusual selection of jade, silk fans, American petit-point.

McArthur's Black Coral Jewelry, Jack & Jill Building, Fort St. George, has black coral jewelry designed by McArthur in gold and silver settings. Items are handmade at the shop's own factory.

Caymandicraft, South Church Street (tel. 9-2405), a short distance from the center of George Town, imports Braemar all-wool sweaters, cashmere scarves, kilts, mohair stoles, and blankets from Scotland, Irish linen, and a wide range of Liberty of London fabrics.

English Shoppe, on the seafront (tel. 9-2457), stocks duty-free perfumes, along with a fine collection of watches and other fine jewelry. They also carry Irish Belleek china, Irish crystal, and collectors' items. Travelers checks and major credit cards are accepted, and all prices are quoted in U.S. dollars.

The Jewellery Factory, Fort Street (tel. 9-2719), is one of the most popular jewelry shops on Grand Cayman. Gold jewelry is sold by weight, according to the London bullion price the day you make your purchase. You can also purchase black coral items and gold-framed doubloons.

6. The Sister Islands

The lesser Caymans are usually explored by people who have gotten waterlogged after too many days on the beach or those seeking a more remote oasis than Grand Cayman itself.

Both Cayman Brac and Little Cayman were resettled as recently as 1833 when a few Cayman families moved there, living in almost complete isolation until 1850. The first settlers before them had been prey to Spanish pirates and had abandoned the colony.

Cayman Brac is high and wild, with windy cliffs and bluffs *(brac* is Gaelic for bluff). A bluff runs the entire length of the island. At one point it's at sea level, but at the opposite end it rises to a sheer cliff of 140 feet. This limestone bluff is honeycombed with caverns that are reputed to contain treasure left by long-ago pirates, including Blackbeard.

The island is about 89 miles east-northeast of Grand Cayman, and it's about 12 miles long and a little more than a mile wide.

The dedicated fisherman in pursuit of bonefish and wahoo heads for Little Cayman, which is only 10 miles long, 2 at its widest point. The population there numbers only a few dozen. Iguanas and wild birds can be seen on the tiny island, which is dotted with beaches and reefs.

Cayman Airways flies nonstop to Cayman Brac from Miami twice weekly. There is also inter-island service from Grand Cayman to Cayman Brac and Little Cayman several times a week.

CAYMAN BRAC: Brac Reef Beach Resort, Cayman Brac (tel. 305/987-8880 in Florida; 800/327-3835, toll free, elsewhere in the United States), is on a palmshaded white sand beach inside the barrier reef. The resort, owned by the Divi Divi Caribbean hotel chain, is on a narrow strip of land stretched between two bodies of water; there is no bedroom that doesn't have a water view. Most rooms in the Caribbean-modern-style building have surrounding lower and upper verandas. The modern rooms have attractive furnishings, with bright floral prints contrasting with the simplicity of the walls. All rooms are air-conditioned; many of them overlook a large swimming pool. There are two double beds in each unit and wall-to-wall carpeting. An oceanfront restaurant presents appetizing native and American-style meals, but most guests are more enthusiastic about the island cookouts at the poolside patio. Drink in Duppy's Roost lounge where there's usually a scattering of guests from all over the world

—anybody is likely to show up at this remote, offbeat oasis. *In summer, singles rent from $70 per day; doubles, from $75 per day. Some rooms are suitable for three to four persons, costing from $70 to $80 daily.* Rates quoted are on the EP. In winter, singles rent from $90 daily; doubles, from $96 per day. There is a tennis court available for guests' use, as well as bicycles, video movies, and a full dive operation.

Buccaneer's Inn (tel. 5-9968) has been the Brac's long-established hotel before the opening of Brac Reef. At the north shore, near West End, it's a quiet place to go for a relaxing fishing holiday, if you can snare one of its 34 moderately furnished bedrooms. It's been an inn since the mid-1950s, having grown into its present complex from very modest beginnings. The simpler singles rent for $80 daily, full board, and doubles cost from $85. More expensive accommodations are also offered. The hotel is the social center of Brac, and residents mingle freely with guests, particularly at the poolside bar. Friday and Saturday is hoedown night, with a good local band. The fare is plentiful and good tasting. If you'd like to explore on your own, the hotel will rent you a car or perhaps a bicycle.

Tiara Beach Hotel (tel. 8-7313) is a 33-room hotel with a white sandy beach, good diving and fishing, and a swimming pool and tennis court. Divers and honeymooners are offered special package rates. Otherwise, the charges are $80 to $90 for a double in winter, *$55 to $65 for the same accommodations in summer.*

LITTLE CAYMAN: Little Le Club (tel. 8-8324), formerly Kingston Bight Lodge, was recently purchased and refurbished by the owners of Grand Cayman's Le Club Cayman. It is a modern inn overlooking South Hole Sound lagoon and Owen Island, a tiny unpopulated cay. The lodge caters almost exclusively to serious sportsfishermen, who often share one of the extremely simple bedrooms, much like an average-priced motel on the mainland. All units have private baths and are cooled by overhead fans and island breezes. Rates were undecided at press time.

Pirates Point (tel. 8-4210) has beefed up the island's accommodations, but not by much. Run by Dana and Sara Vied, Pirates Point has only eight comfortably furnished bedrooms. They're filled up with guests who like the quiet, quiet life. A single or double rents for $80 in winter with dive packages being offered for $110. *In summer, the charge is $60 in a single or double, with a dive package going for $88.* These tariffs include meals. After seeking out the bird rookery, the tarpon pond, and the pink sands of the beach, you'll be ready for some of the filling fare served here, which naturally places its emphasis on seafood.

Southern Cross Club (tel. 8-3255) is a ten-unit resort recently completely redone. Hosts are Mike and Donna Emmanual. Scuba-diving and fly-fishing are among the attractions. Guides are available. A double room with three meals a day rents for $98. It overlooks Owens Island.

PUERTO RICO

IT WAS ON COLUMBUS's second voyage to the New World in 1493 that he discovered the island of San Juan (St. John the Baptist), later renamed Puerto Rico. The island's government has undergone many changes since the days of its first governor, Ponce de Leon, to its present status as an American Commonwealth.

However, the beauty and charm have remained since the first navigators set foot on Puerto Rican soil. They called it "the island of enchantment."

Even though the island is in the "torrid zone," found between the Tropics of Capricorn and Cancer, it enjoys a lower temperature than that typical of the region. Trade winds blow in from the northeast toward the southwest of the island, acting as a gigantic fan, cooling and protecting the island from excessive heat. The sea, land, and mountain breezes further contribute to maintaining the temperature at a comfortable level.

Puerto Rico's climate, one of the best in the Caribbean, is fairly stable all year, with an average temperature of 76° Fahrenheit. The only variants are found in the mountain regions, where the average temperature fluctuates between 66° and 76° Fahrenheit, and on the north coast, where the temperature goes from 70° to 80°.

It may date from the discovery of the New World, but Puerto Rico, at least in San Juan, its capital, is as modern as tomorrow. The "bootstrap" island is remaking itself and holding out much promise for a bright future. It is no longer called "the poorhouse of the Caribbean."

Lush, verdant Puerto Rico is only half the size of New Jersey, roughly speaking. Its location is some 1000 miles southeast of the tip of Florida. As such, it is at the hub of the Caribbean chain of islands, and you'll probably fly in and out of San Juan at least once or twice if you're doing much touring in the area, as its international airport is the center for many connecting flights.

After a slump in the mid-'70s and early '80s, tourism has improved. Now you'll find some of the best golf and tennis in the Caribbean at such posh resorts as Dorado Beach and Palmas del Mar. Accommodations have also greatly improved at out-on-the-island cities such as Mayaguez with its Hilton and Ponce with its Melia. Paradores—government-sponsored inns—are now sprinkled across the country for visitors who want a deeper look at the island than that provided by the posh hotels and gambling casinos of San Juan, with their Las Vegas–type shows.

To get into Puerto Rico, American citizens do not have to have a passport or visa. Canadians, however, should carry some form of identification, such as a birth certificate. The Yankee dollar, of course, is the coin of the realm.

All the major U.S. banks, such as Chase Manhattan, are located in San Juan, and hours are from 9 a.m. to 2:30 p.m. Monday to Friday. Canadian currency will be accepted in some big hotels in San Juan, although reluctantly. English is understood at the big resorts and in most of San Juan, but out on the island the language of Ponce de Leon is still *numero uno*.

The electric current is 110 volts, 60 cycles, as it is in the continental U.S. and Canada. Puerto Rico operates on Atlantic Standard Time, which is one hour before Eastern Standard Time. However, when the eastern part of the U.S. goes on Daylight Savings Time, Puerto Rico and the mainland keep the same clocks.

GETTING THERE: Any travel agent can tell you that one of the cheapest ways to reach Puerto Rico from several parts of North America is on an airline that many travelers have never before heard of. The airline is **Arrow Air,** which carries passengers on a flight network (both scheduled and chartered) that, at the time of this writing, spanned 245 cities in 72 countries. When the airline was founded in California in 1947, it was used by professional sports teams, movie crews, and doctors for ferrying athletes, technical equipment, and ambulance services around America. Reorganized in 1981, Arrow Air is today a Miami-based carrier one of whose principal functions is to make frequent runs into San Juan and Aguadilla.

Today, in any season, Arrow's DC-10s and DC-8s—some of which used to belong to Freddy Laker's Skytrain service—are likely to be jammed with holiday and business travelers, so ironclad advance reservations are important. If you choose Arrow, don't expect luxury. Flights are somewhat spartan, and every seat is usually filled. Still, Arrow's fares were cheaper than any of the major airlines at the time of this writing.

Call your travel agent or Arrow Air toll free at 800/872-8000 for information or reservations. Arrow makes a daily run from New York's JFK airport to both Aguadilla's Borinquen airport and to San Juan, as well as several round-trip flights every week between San Juan and Miami, Philadelphia, Toronto, and Montréal.

Other airlines that make the run from North America to Puerto Rico include some of the big carriers, which often make nonstop flights from cities not serviced by Arrow. **Eastern** flies nonstop from New York (Newark), Philadelphia, Miami, and Atlanta, and flies direct (with one stop along the way) from many more cities, including Orlando and Boston. **Delta** services more than 100 North American cities, most of which can be connected through the airline's headquarters in Atlanta. From Atlanta, Delta flies twice daily round trip to San Juan. **American Airlines** has nonstop daily flights to San Juan from New York's JFK, Newark airport, and Dallas/Fort Worth. American also offers direct serv-

ice from Chicago and Los Angeles, both of which make one stop before continuing on to San Juan.

SAN JUAN

The capital of Puerto Rico is today an urban sprawl, one muncipality flowing into another to form a great metropolitan area. San Juan introduces you to Puerto Rico, and the look of this old city ranges from decaying ruins that recall the heyday of the Spanish empire to modern, plush, beachfront hotels that evoke Miami Beach.

The city roughly breaks down into general divisions, including the old walled city on San Juan Island (see "What to See in San Juan"); the city center on San Juan Island containing the Capitol building; Santurce, on a larger peninsula, which is reached by causeway bridges from San Juan Island (the lagoonfront section here is called Miramar); and Condado, that narrow peninsula which stretches from San Juan Island to Santurce.

The Condado strip of beachfront hotels, restaurants, casinos, and nightclubs is separated from Miramar by a lagoon. Isla Verde is in the vicinity of the airport, which is detached from the rest of San Juan by an isthmus.

1. Where to Stay in San Juan

From a guest house directly on the beach to a restored convent in Old San Juan, the choice of accommodations in the Puerto Rican capital is wide ranging, as are the tariff sheets. It's easy to spend $200 a day here, or else get by for $35. There are package deals galore, and you may want to check with a travel agent to see if one fills your needs.

Most of the hotels lie in Condado and Isla Verde, out by the airport. Both these sections border the beach. However, I'll also have other choices for those who prefer to live in sectors such as Ocean Park. I'll start where San Juan started, even though you'll find fewer accommodations in the Old Town than anywhere else.

Note: All hotel rooms in Puerto Rico are subject to a 6% tax.

LIVING IN OLD SAN JUAN: El Convento, 100 Cristo St. (tel. 723-9020), is considered by many as the "Grand Hotel of Puerto Rico." It is an authentically restored, 300-year-old Carmelite convent boasting of a solid Spanish brick and limestone structure. It stands directly across the street from a building which was the original city hall in 1521 (during the Spanish colonial period) and a few steps from the cathedral where the remains of Juan Ponce de Leon are buried. Most of the historical landmarks of the colonial walled city are within walking distance.

Some of the rooms, furnished in a Spanish style of heavy wood, have a view of either the old town square (Little Plaza of the Nuns) or of San Juan Bay, where one can spot modern ships and island schooners go past the ancient fortress of El Morro.

Because of its location there are no beach facilities, but the pool in the downstairs patio will serve you daily buffets.

In summer, singles range in price from $75 to $100 daily, while doubles go for $80 to $120. In high season, a single costs from $85 to $135 daily; doubles begin at $95, climbing to $160.

PUERTA DE TIERRA: Caribe Hilton, P.O. Box 1872 (tel. 721-0303), stands near the old Fort San Jeronimo, which has been incorporated into its complex. With Old San Juan at its doorstep and San Juan Bay as its backyard, the Caribe Hilton can be called the gateway to the walled city of San Juan. Near what was once the ultra-exclusive Escambrón Beach Club, it is today the only major luxury hotel in the Old San Juan sector. There was a time when tourists to the island would arrive at the airport, go directly to the Caribe Hilton, and stay within the hotel confines and in Old San Juan for the duration of their vacation. The main reason for this was (and still is) that the hotel had so much to offer that, according to the less adventurous visitor, there was no need to venture farther inland or anywhere else.

Built in 1949, the Caribe Hilton was a new breed of resort, offering total entertainment and luxury. It still offers all that and more. Set in a 17-acre tropical park, it has a private palm-shaded beach and swimming cove. One can walk to the 16th-century fort or spend the day on a tour of Old San Juan, then come back to either of two freshwater swimming pools, work out at the health club, play a tennis match (day or night), swim at the beach, or simply lie on the white sand under a palm tree.

If you have a meal, the variety of food and ambience is so extensive that you may have to pull straws or toss a coin to help you decide. For breakfast you can try the Terrace Café (coffeeshop), open from 6 to 11 a.m. If you decide to go for a morning swim, you can order your breakfast at poolside at the Pool Terrace Restaurant, open from 8 to 11 a.m. Dinner at the Terrace Grill is served from 6 p.m. to midnight, featuring a full-course menu of international, American, and Puerto Rican cuisine. Monday night is "Jibaro Night" (Puerto Rican folklore evening) from 6:30 to 11 p.m. Informal attire is suggested. This event is very popular, so make sure you have reservations. On Friday, between 6:30 and 11 p.m. the terrace becomes the "Fish Market." Stands and carts filled with crabmeat, oysters, shrimp, and clams are set up, and you can also order swordfish and lobster, as well as cioppino, paella, and poached sea trout. Reservations are important.

Other eating facilities at the Caribe Hilton are La Rôtisserie (see the dining recommendations) and the Club Caribe, which also features headline entertainment (see "After Dark in San Juan"). One of San Juan's leading discos, Juliana's, is also on the premises.

The newer rooms, and I prefer these, are in the 20-story tower which was added in 1972. The Garden Wing rooms are decorated in tropical fashion. On the family plan, there is no charge for children, regardless of age, if they share the same room as their parents. *In summer, guests on the EP pay from $117 to*

$163 daily, with doubles going for $123 to $170. The MAP supplement is $45 per person. In winter, EP rates go up to $160 to $220 daily in a single, from $170 to $225 in a double or twin. Two persons can stay here on the MAP in season, paying from $253 to $313 daily.

CONDADO: Condado used to be an exclusive residential section near the beach, but it isn't anymore. Over the years private villas have been torn down to make way for high-rise hotel blocks, restaurants, and nightclubs, many with a kinky bent. Old San Juan has a lot of action at night, and Condado does too, regardless of your sexual persuasion. There are good bus connections into the old town, or you can take the taxis which are usually available. Attempts are made periodically to clean up the beach area, but many readers have written complaining about "the broken glass and dog-walkers." Watch your step!

If you like a Caribbean Coney Island by the sea, then the Condado area might be for you, especially if you're gay. Condado has now become the homosexual stamping ground of the Caribbean. There's plenty of straight action too, much of it for sale.

The Leading Hotels

Condado Plaza Holiday Inn Resort and Sands Casino, 999 Ashford Ave. (tel. 721-1000), is a two-in-one hotel complex, an original beachfront structure linked by an elevated passageway across Ashford to its Laguna section. It now ranks as the city's second-largest hotel, containing 580 units. Just as the Caribe Hilton is the gateway to Old San Juan, so is the Holiday Inn the gateway to San Juan's Condado area.

Every room is air-conditioned (sometimes a bit too much) and has a private terrace. Units have king-size and double beds. The management claims to have the largest casino on the island, and when your gambling fever won't come down, there are slot machines as well. If the San Juan temperature becomes unbearable, take a dip in any of the four swimming pools or the beach at the back entrance of the hotel. In the cool of the evening, stroll over to the Copa Room which features a Vegas-style revue. Or else patronize Isadora, a disco (see my nightlife suggestions).

The hotel has some of the finest dining choices—in several price ranges—of any hotel in Puerto Rico. Besides the Lotus Flower, the finest Chinese restaurant on the island, right next door there's the Au Cheval Blanc, an elegant French dining room. The Capriccio has pizzas and homemade pastas, and also a collection of classic Italian dishes. La Cantina is an attractive bar—cozy, dark, intimate—and La Posada with its Spanish-style decor is known for its prime western beef. Sunday is usually Criollo Night at the Holiday Inn. Puerto Rican food is served poolside with dancing. While dining on octopus salad and rabbit fricassée, guests are entertained by a live folkloric show. The ground-floor La Fiesta also has live entertainment and Latin rhythms.

The deluxe part of the hotel is the Plaza Club, which covers two floors, a total of 72 units with three suites. A stairway connects the two floors, and a VIP lounge is reserved for guests. Accommodations have cable TV, and there is a special keyed elevator so that members can avoid the crowds in the other sections of the hotel.

The least expensive rooms are labeled Ashford, and the higher priced units are either laguna view or oceanfront. From December 1 to the end of April, singles range from $205 to $230 daily; two persons pay $215 to $240. *Summer tariffs (room only) range from $155 to $190 daily in a single, from $162 to $200 in a double,* plus another $20 charged for an extra person sharing a unit. While at the beach and at poolside, the chaise longues and towels are provided free.

There are two tennis courts (lit at night) and water sports are featured in the lagoon (at no cost) right behind the hotel. Make arrangements at the front desk for the use of any sport facility and equipment.

Condado Beach–La Concha Hotel, Ashford Avenue (tel. 721-6090), is a two-hotel complex on beachfront property that is operated by HUSA Hotels International, which is also in the hotel business in Spain. These hotels are linked by the cavernous Convention Center to form the three-part "El Centro." When it opened its doors to the tourist trade in March 1919, the Condado Beach was then known as the Condado-Vanderbilt. La Concha is of much more recent vintage, opening in 1956, and named for its seashell-shaped roof. The land where both hotels stand is approximately where the British attempted an unsuccessful attack on San Juan (the walled city) in 1797. The union of the hotels provides the romance of Old San Juan at the Condado Beach and the excitement of today at La Concha.

The Condado Beach offers a choice of rooms with either a view of the ocean or of the lagoon. All the rooms at La Concha face the ocean beach. Whichever of the two hotels you choose, you will have two swimming pools, tennis courts, and a stretch of beach to enjoy, plus the Condado Beach Hotel Casino.

The complex also includes dining facilities at the Condado Beach restaurants. El Gobernador is open from 11 a.m. to 11 p.m., El Patio Terrace Restaurant from 7 a.m. to 10 p.m., and La Concha Seafood Restaurant from 6 to 11 p.m. The complex is not without nightlife.

The most exclusive way to stay at the Condado Beach Hotel is by asking for an accommodation in the Vanderbilt Club, which is entered by a private elevator. Winter rates at the Condado Beach range from $130 to $190 in a single, from $140 to $200 daily in a double. Accommodations in the Vanderbilt Club cost from $220 daily. *In summer, tariffs fall to $90 to $135 daily in a single, from $100 to $145 in a double.*

La Concha is slightly cheaper, renting in winter for $115 to $160 daily in a single, from $130 to $170 in a double. *In summer, EP tariffs fall to $85 to $110 daily in a single, from $95 to $120 in a double.* For MAP, expect to pay another $35 per person daily at either hotel.

Dupont Plaza San Juan, 1309 Ashford Ave. (tel. 724-6161). Take 450 air-conditioned rooms, each with a private balcony, add 2000 feet of ocean beach, a gambling casino, an Olympic-size swimming pool, water sports, and everything you expect from a vacation resort—and you have this hotel, once known as the Puerto Rican Sheraton.

A vacation is something people indulge in when they want to get away from the everyday routine and sometimes even from the children. However, there are times when the children are an integral part of that get-away safari. When you take the children to Dupont Plaza, you will still feel you are on vacation. The children's play area is fully equipped to set any child's imagination afire. There is also a separate wading pool. Both the play area and the pool are safe and loaded with fun.

You also deserve some fun, and you can have a lunch outdoors at the ocean terrace. There is no music playing in the background, just the sound of the Caribbean nearby. If you're a romantic, then dinner at the Penthouse Restaurant offers a 360° view. Attached to the hotel is the Fontana di Roma, a restaurant specializing in northern Italian cuisine.

The hotel also has a supper club with performers from both the States and the Caribbean. Whatever the program is, you can count on this hotel for action, a frenzy which reaches its peak in the hotel's gambling casino.

In winter, singles range from $125 to $170 daily; twins or doubles, from

$135 to $180. *In summer, tariffs are lowered to $90 to $135 in a single, from $100 to $145 in a double.* Even more expensive suites are available. An additional adult sharing a room pays $22 per day, and breakfast and dinner are available at an extra $35 per person daily.

First-Class Hotels at Condado

Dutch Inn & Tower, corner of Condado and Ashford (tel. 721-0810). In spite of its name, this is a very Latin hotel, drawing not only foreigners but many islanders visiting San Juan as well. It consists of twin buildings, one on the Condado, with a reception area on a side street. Each unit has a light-blue balcony. One building contains a series of suites; the other, standard hotel units.

The hotel has no beach facilities, but the Condado beach is only a minute away. There is a sun roof available for sunbathing, and the freshwater swimming pool is invigorating.

Every room has a TV set with cable TV and a radio. The air conditioning is individually controlled (this is a convenience since most of the hotels featuring air conditioning control it from a central unit which may not provide sufficient cooling, or may freeze you out of your room).

For breakfast, or dinner, you can try New England Seafood, a restaurant and lounge which provides live entertainment. For lunch or dinner, you can also choose the Green House sidewalk café opening onto the sea. The Green House has a piano bar where the entertainment is intimate yet lively until 5 a.m.

In summer, singles range in price from $60 to $65 daily; doubles, from $65 to $70. Winter rates are $85 to $105 for singles, from $90 to $110 for doubles. For MAP, add $35 per person daily to the room rates. An extra adult in a room costs $30 more. The rates are subject to 6% government room tax.

Howard Johnson's Nabori Lodge, 1369 Ashford Ave. (tel. 721-7300), offers a total of 150 guest rooms decorated in a contemporary mood (each with balcony, radio, and cable color TV). Combined with a nearby beach and lots of American food, the inn offers a lot more than just 28 flavors of ice cream. Space is at a premium in the Condado area, and the free parking offered lodge guests is another convenience.

In the heart of Condado, the lodge offers all the basics of a Stateside family-style hotel. Beds are large, and private balconies open onto views and trade-wind breezes. *In summer, singles are charged $100 daily; doubles going for $110.* In winter, the single rate jumps to $136 and doubles pay $150 an additional person is charged another $18 daily. Children under 18 are housed free under the family plan.

There's a good view from the rooftop sundeck and swimming pool. The hotel has no beach facilities, but you can swim about a block from the lodge.

Ramada San Juan Hotel and Casino, 1045 Ashford Ave. (tel. 724-5657), is the first major hotel to be built in ten years in the Condado section, and it's the only hotel in San Juan with concierge service for every one of its rooms and suites, all of which contain views of either the ocean or lagoon. Rooms are classified standard, superior, and deluxe. In winter, singles pay from $140 to $170 daily; doubles, $150 to $180. *In summer, singles range from $100 to $140 daily; doubles, $110 to $150.*

The hotel has a friendly management, and its location is directly on 300 feet of private Condado Beach real estate. A favorite with the business traveler, the 11-story complex contains guest rooms that are spacious and well appointed. The Polo Room and lounge serve good food, dished up along with live entertainment, and an open-air patio overlooks the beach and swimming pool. Its casino, incidentally, is open from 1 p.m. to 4 a.m. with roulette, blackjack, and craps in an oceanview room above the restaurant and lounge.

The **Regency Hotel,** 1005 Ashford Ave. (tel. 721-0505), next to the Condado Plaza Holiday Inn, is a simple, attractive place where accommodations cost slightly less than those at its better known neighbors. After registering in the stucco-walled lobby, of of which the Royale Palm Restaurant usually does a thriving lunchtime business, you'll proceed to your balconied room, which will have a view of either the sea or the lagoon. In back, built on a terrace over the rocky shoreline, the pool is set into the checkerboard terrace.

In winter, singles range from $90 to $210, while doubles cost between $100 and $210. *In summer, singles range from $60 to $180, while doubles cost between $96 and $180.* An additional person lodged in a double room costs an extra $18 per day.

A Budget Hotel at Condado

Condado Lagoon Hotel, P.O. Box 13145, Santurce, on Clemenceau at the corner of Joffre (tel. 721-0170), boasts of its smallness and the fact that because it is not a gigantic, cavernous hotel, one can get friendly, personal service. If you are booking from the States, allow plenty of time (two to three weeks will do) since the lodge has only 49 rooms, which go very fast both in and off-season. The suitably furnished rooms all have TVs and refrigerators. The Tabarin cocktail lounge offers no entertainment other than a piano-bar atmosphere in the evening. There are no beach facilities—one has to walk to the sands (nearby)—but there is a swimming pool. The hotel is one block from the main drag of Condado where entertainment, casinos, and restaurants are all a short walk away. There is parking available at no extra charge.

Year round, singles rent for $65 daily, going up to $75 in a double. An extra person is charged $15. Tariffs include use not only of the swimming pool but also the gym. There is a mini-market on the premises.

Condado Guest Houses

El Canario Inn, 1317 Ashford Ave. (tel. 724-2793), a bisque-colored villa next to the Dupont Plaza Hotel offers one of the best bed-and-breakfast values in San Juan. You'll recognize the building by its arched veranda and the porte-cochère which covers a side yard filled with plants. Keith and Judy Olson are the accommodating owners. The hotel consists of a main house and two nearby sets of servants' quarters, all linked by a terrace. There's a small, exquisite pool designed like a jungle pond, where water splashes down a stone wall into the bathing area.

On the premises is an outdoor bar and lots of quiet corners for conversation. The simple bedrooms are air-conditioned and filled with unpretentious furnishings. There's a communal kitchen if guests feel like cooking. *In low season, the 25 bedrooms cost $36 for a single, between $48 and $60 in a double. An efficiency unit with its own private kitchen rents for $72.* High-season rates range from $54 in a single to between $66 and $72 for a double. Efficiency units in high season cost around $90. An additional person in any double is an extra $12 per night.

Arcos Blancos, 10 Carrion Court (tel. 728-6725). Three former private mansions in the Condado area now make up Arcos Blancos (White Arches), a guest house which derives its name from the arches in the library. Peter Bessi, owner and host of the guest house, seems never to be away or sleeping, always ready to cater to your needs as a guest. His guests, incidentally, consist of a lot of repeat customers, drawn in part from the colony of Greenwich Village's gay men.

Right in the heart of Condado, you step out the front door into the hub of dining and entertainment. However, the peaceful atmosphere of the guest house provides a relaxing contrast to the world outside. A dip in the pool may lead you to expect Dorothy Lamour to emerge from the tropical greenery surrounding the inner courtyard. There is also a Jacuzzi. You may also choose to have your breakfast served al fresco in the patio. The beach is within walking distance.

You may be in for a pleasant surprise when you arrive to find your host waiting for you with a tall piña colada or a cool planters' punch at the Oasis Bar. The Arcos Blancos has fantastic package deals which include "free" guided tours of Old San Juan and guided tours of El Yunque and Luquillo Beach.

Rooms, 37 in all, contain private baths and are air-conditioned. *Singles range in price from $45 to $55 daily in the summer* to $58 to $70 in the winter, and *doubles off-season are charged $55 to $65,* going up to $68 to $80 in season.

A BUDGET HOTEL IN MIRAMAR: Miramar, a quiet, residential sector, is very much a part of metropolitan San Juan, and a long brisk walk will take you where the action is. The beach, regrettably, is at least half a mile away.

Olimpo Court, 603 Miramar (tel. 724-0600), looks much like an apartment house (100 rooms, some with balconies). It's considered a commercial hotel as opposed to a tourist hotel. The reason for this is that the Olimpo is landlocked on the other side of the Condado Lagoon. Thus it has no beach, nor a swimming pool to compensate. It does have a roof deck with a view of metropolitan San Juan and some of the nearby mountains.

The entrance lobby has echoes of Somerset Maugham's *Rain* with its rattan and bamboo furnishings. There is a restaurant on the premises, La Fabrada, where continental food is available.

In winter, singles rent for $44 daily, doubles for $50; *although these tariffs are lowered off-season to $42 in a single, $45 in a double.*

GUEST HOUSES AT OCEAN PARK: Arcade Guest House, 8 Taft St. (tel. 728-7524), on a private residential street, is a former private residence itself. For some 15 years, it's been owned by Aurelio Cinque and his charming wife, Renée, who offer privacy, plus the convenience of being within walking distance of Condado. True to his name Mr. Cinque ("Mr. Five") speaks five languages— English, Spanish, Italian, French, and Portuguese.

The rooms are comfortable and spotlessly clean. Sea breezes keep them pleasantly cool—you will seldom need to use your air conditioner. The Condado Beach is just a few short yards away. Your host, Aurelio, is a master chef at heart, and can fix you a fast breakfast, lunch, or snack. The Arcade is very popular, so I advise booking well in advance. Parking is available on street.

In winter, singles are accepted for $30 to $36 nightly, doubles for $36 to $44, and triples for $53. *In summer, single rates go down to just $20 to $30 daily; doubles, $30 to $38; and triples, $40.*

La Condesa Inn, 2071 Calle Cacique (tel. 727-3698), was formerly the private residence of the Spanish consul. It still is all you would want your own home to be. You're a long way from most of the casinos, restaurants, and entertainment centers. The Dupont Plaza Hotel on the Condado strip is about the closest, but it's a $2 cab fare away. Because La Condesa is limited to just 20 accommodations, I recommend that you book and plan accordingly. It is in the residential Ocean Park–Condado area, just 60 yards from San Juan's most spacious beach. All but the upstairs suites have their own private entrances. Some rooms contain complete individual kitchens and dining bars. There is also a pool restaurant.

In off-season, a single rents for $30 and a double goes for $33. In winter, regular singles cost $50 and doubles are $57. A third person in a room pays $10 extra. A 15% service charge is levied, plus a $3-a-day energy surcharge.

A GUEST HOUSE AT PUNTA LAS MARIAS: Tres Palmas Guest House, 2212 Park Blvd. (tel. 727-4617), received so many favorable reports from readers that I went to investigate myself. Its manager, Paul Thomas, along with co-owner Bud Parker, could not be more accommodating. The outside of the half-century-old Puerto Rican house is neat and freshly painted, and the furniture, as of this writing, is new and pretty. Towels, sheets, whatever, are sparkling clean, and Mr. Thomas will even see that your laundry is done (but don't count on that!).

The location is ten minutes from the airport, midway between Isla Verde and Condado. You can walk to Condado Beach if you wish, even though it's a mile away. Tres Palmas lies on the ocean, between Parque Barbosa and Punta Las Marias. The living area of the main house becomes like a private "at home" den, where guests relax on the sofas, talking or reading. Original paintings and mirrors decorate the walls, and on holidays the big dining table becomes a social center, as guests join the friends of management to celebrate.

Bedrooms are comfortable, and most of them contain a private bath. Each room is air-conditioned, decorated with tropical print wallpaper. The most expensive ones contain HBO cable TV sets. In all, there are only eight units, renting in winter for $45 to $60 daily in a single, $55 to $70 in a double. *Off-season, tariffs are reduced: a single costs $35 to $50 daily and a double goes for $40 to $55.*

The food is good, including American, Puerto Rican, and Italian specialties. Up 17 steps leads to a rooftop deck, fronting the ocean, and it's not only a place to get a suntan, but to watch the sunset.

In my opinion, this is one of the best bargains on the island. Not only that, but they know how to make a great piña colada here!

ISLA VERDE: Beach-bordering Isla Verde is closer to the airport than the other sections of San Juan. Hotels here lie farther from the old town than do those considered in Miramar, Condado, and Ocean Park. If you don't mind the isolation and want access to the fairly good beaches, then you might consider one of the following hotels. However, that proximity to the airport presents distinct disadvantages. I agree with reader John F. Brown of Barton, Vt., who wrote: "Each commercial jet aircraft that takes off rattles the windows in your room and leaves a lingering smell of jet fuel exhaust." I'll begin with the most expensive and work down the list:

The Palace Hotel and ESJ Towers

The **Palace,** P.O. Box 6676, Loiza Station (tel. 791-2020). Just a skip to the beach, this hotel has 450 fully air-conditioned rooms. The Palace has an imposing collection of balconies on its high-rise facade constructed near a busy road. The first thing you'll see as you enter is a rattan bar in the terrazzo-floored lobby with a verdant screen of greenery behind it. It has so many restaurants, bars, and nighttime diversions that you need never leave the hotel. Swimming can be enjoyed either at the beach or in the Olympic-size pool. If the children come along, there is an area for them which includes numerous games and amusements, plus some electronic ones.

For dining and entertainment the Palace offers the Club Tropicoro, featuring revues by international headliners (after the show, there's dancing). If you don't want to dance, walk over to the Carioca, a cocktail lounge, and listen to fast and sometimes fanciful music in an intimate atmosphere. If you want the intimacy but not the music, the Quicksilver Lounge is for you. You may spoil your appetite if you go to the Quicksilver Lounge before dinner, as the lounge is very generous with the cheese snacks and other goodies. The salad bar is an attraction at Prime Time, a steakhouse featuring prime-quality meats from the rôtisserie or the grill. Seafood is also served. A more informal setting is offered by the Sand Castle (indoor restaurant and open-air café bar). The Sand Castle is open at 6 a.m. for breakfast, then lunch, dinner, and late-night snacks. At poolside you can have snacks and drinks. Other restaurants include La Trattoria, serving Italian specialties (naturally), and the House of Hunan, offering zesty, spicy fare. You can take Lady Luck to the casino, where blackjack tables, dice, roulette, baccarat, and slot machines are active from 1 p.m. to 4 a.m.

Rooms are well furnished. Package-tour groups are often booked into this high-rise block. If you're not in here on some cut-rate deal, you are likely to pay $125 to $175 daily in a single in winter, $130 to $180 in a double. A third person sharing is charged another $30 daily, and breakfast and dinner on the MAP cost $42 per person additional. *Spring, summer, and fall tariffs are lower, costing $80 to $110 daily in a single, $85 to $115 in a double.*

El San Juan Towers, P.O. Box S3445, Isla Verde (tel. 791-5151, or toll free 800/468-2026), offers the closest thing a vacationer can get to apartment living. About a third of the 451 units are privately owned and occupied year round, while the rest are rented for at least part of the year as hotel accommodations.

Each accommodation is completely air-conditioned, with a fully equipped kitchen, cable color TV, and a private balcony. *Off-season rates range from $125 daily in a minimum studio or efficiency for two, rising to $150 in a deluxe. A one-bedroom unit costs from $190 minimum to $260 daily, and two- and three-bedroom accommodations are also available.* In winter, studios and efficiencies for two range from $150 to $250 daily, while one-bedroom units cost anywhere from $260 to $325 daily.

While at the hotel, you have access to the well-equipped private health club, with separate facilities for men and women. An outdoor playground and an indoor nursery for children are both supervised. The ground-floor restaurant, the Happy Apple, is open for breakfast and lunch, closing just before dinnertime. In a bar and lounge, the Mano-a-Mano, you can dance to low-key disco music after doing your daily shopping at the lobbyside mini-market. A car wash and a laundry are on the premise.

A First-Class Choice

Carib-Inn of San Juan, Route 187 (tel. 791-3535), is a complete tropical resort and casino just eight minutes from the airport. The 225 high-ceilinged bedrooms and the cabanas, many with balconies, have outside views. Most overlook a giant racquet-shaped swimming pool, with a generous sunning and refreshment terrace, plus a Bohio Bar. The rooms are traditionally furnished, most having two double beds. Rooms are graded moderate, superior, and deluxe. *Summer tariffs are: singles $48 to $68; doubles, $76 to $120.* In winter, prices are: singles, $85 to $95; doubles, $95 to $110. Meal plans are available for a seven-day stay.

Action is lively at night, particularly in the intimate casino. La Tinaja Restaurant serves local and international cuisine, and Cousin Ho's, a Chinese eatery, is one of the best restaurants in town. La Tinaja lobby bar often provides live entertainment and dancing until the early hours.

Tennis is taken seriously here, with eight professional Laykold-surfaced courts, of which four are lit for night games. The largest tennis facility in the San

Juan area, the Carib-Inn features a group of tennis professionals at your command to sharpen your game. A ball-throwing machine and a large tennis club membership always ensure an opportunity to play. There's a health center for men and women, including a gym, steam room, and sauna.

On a Budget in Isla Verde

La Playa, 6 Amapola St. (tel. 791-1115), is a true bargain. Its situation and atmosphere make it a persuasive choice. It's a two-story, L-shaped hotel, directly on the water, with rooms overlooking a courtyard crowded with lush, semitropical trees and shrubbery. The second-floor bedrooms, with long balconies, are preferred. Across from the front entrance lies the beginning of a two-mile-long beach. Each of the 14 well-furnished bedrooms has a private bath and a bright, colorful ambience. Bold-patterned draperies match the bedspreads. *In summer, doubles cost from $40, singles from $35.* Tariffs go up to $55 in a double in winter, $47 in a single. All units have private bath and air conditioning. The hotel's waterfront bar is one of the most popular on the island (see my nighttime suggestions).

The **Duffy's,** 9 Isla Verde Rd. (tel. 726-1415), has a certain charm. Dating from 1946, it resembles a secluded California bungalow-court compound hidden by flowering trees, with a set-back front fence where you can park your car. Everything is a bit time worn, but this is what makes the place so mellow, that and the congenial company. Informality reigns, and guests gather in the courtyard for dinner at Duffy's Restaurant. You reach your bungalow via sidewalks wending through lush flowering shrubbery and trees. Each bedroom, 14 in all, has a private bath and a personality. In winter, singles pay $50 daily, the tariff going up to $60 in a double. *In summer, singles cost $40; doubles, $50.*

Mario's Hotel & Restaurant, 2 Rosa St., P.O. Box 12366 (tel. 791-3748), has been a longtime favorite of airline and government employees who want to save dollars during their San Juan stopover. You'll find singles, doubles, and one-bedroom suites, all air-conditioned, with phones, radios, and private baths. *Singles or doubles cost $27 daily, off-season, and suites go for $65.* In winter, rates go up to $50 in a single or double, $85 in a suite. Of course, those employees get discounts. The location is in front of the Isla Verde cockfight coliseum, one block from the beach, and a half block from the Palace Hotel. A seafood restaurant is attractively decorated. At the cozy piano bar, you may meet the pilot or the flight attendant of your dreams.

Don Pedro Hotel, 4 Rosa St. (tel. 791-2838), was created in the old Spanish style, with its L-shaped room block overlooking a courtyard, a swimming pool,

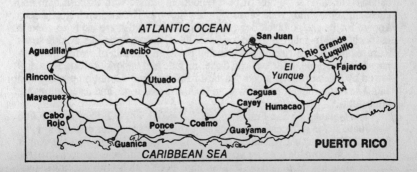

and an adjoining garden restaurant. It's quite informal, the tone set by the youthful staff. Each of the bedrooms has tiled floors, basic furnishings, with good-size closets and a tiled bath. The furnishings are hit and miss, with older chests, maybe a vintage rocker, simple beds—in all, good for sleeping, and most important, clean. Each room is air-conditioned, and some have tiny kitchenettes opening onto a bed-sitting room. In winter, a single costs $38 daily, and a double goes for $42. Efficiencies with kitchenettes are tabbed at $52. *In summer, singles cost only $28, with doubles going for $32 and efficiencies for $38 daily.*

2. Dining Out in Puerto Rico

In recent years San Juan restaurants have returned to a greater appreciation of Puerto Rican cooking. Now many of the leading restaurants, although they still offer Stateside dishes, also feature a selection of local specialties as well. Even big hotels such as the Caribe Hilton are getting in on the act. While Puerto Rican cookery has similarities to both Spanish and Mexican cuisine, it is quite different.

Among local dishes you'll want to sample are black bean soup, invariably good and eaten with chopped raw onions; pasteles (little meat patties which have been wrapped in a dough made of plantain flour, often served as hors d'oeuvres); tiny codfish fritters known as bacalitos; asopao (a soupy rice dish made with chicken, seafood, or whatever inspires the chef that day—perhaps squid); roast suckling pig (sometimes sold along the road on your way to the beach) and known here as lechon asado; arroz con pollo (chicken and rice, a national dish); tostones (plantains fried in deep fat); and jueyes (land crabs).

Of course, out on the island ask for any fresh fish dish and chances are you'll be pleased. Finish your meal with Puerto Rican coffee, which is strong, black, aromatic. Perhaps you'll have only a small cup. Rum is the national drink, and you can buy it in almost any shade. In Puerto Rico, it's quite proper to order a cold beer before one even looks at the menu. Popular among the locals is India, brewed in Mayaguez, famous for its pure water.

MEALS IN OLD SAN JUAN: La Zaragozana, 356 San Francisco (tel. 723-5103), recaptures Old Spain, with its white adobe walls, rough-hewn beams, slate and terracotta floors, as well as antiques, murals, brass lamps, and wine racks. In the beamed bodega, you can enjoy a before-dinner drink.

The restaurant, which specializes in Spanish, Cuban and Puerto Rican cuisine, is run by the much-awarded Nick Leon. On my most recent rounds I was served my finest meal in Old San Juan in this restaurant. The top specialty is called "The Chef's," a filet of beef tenderloin stuffed with Spanish ham and cheese in a burgundy wine sauce with mushrooms. The kitchen has long been known for its classic black bean soup, but other kettles are likely to contain gazpacho, caldo gallego, garlic, or fish soup. Other temptations include snails Zaragozana, beef Stroganoff, Valencian paella, a zarzuela of seafood, or perhaps lobster creole. Puerto Rican dishes include filet of pork Old San Juan, followed by a dessert nicknamed "custard from heaven." Count on parting with $30. The restaurant is open daily from 11:30 a.m. to 1 a.m., and reservations are important.

Los Galanes, 65 San Francisco (tel. 722-4008), links Old Seville with Old San Juan. It's a 16th-century setting on a one-way street, an easy walk down from El Convento. As you enter, on your right is a small bar for a before-dinner drink (it's fashionable to order a dry sherry). The restaurant is the domain of the dancer Manolo Galan, and portraits of him, along with his two dancing sisters, grace the walls. The maître d' and his staff are courtesy oriented, and you know you can dine comfortably in good hands.

The familiar selection of international appetizers is presented on the elaborate scroll of the parchment menu, including gazpacho, homemade pâté, and escargots bouguignonnes. However, for something different, try coquilles Manolo, named after the proprietor. This appetizer consists of shrimps cooked in a shell with tomatoes and laced with béchamel sauce and cheese, and then baked. The main courses are usually good and sometimes excellent—filet of sole meunière, shrimps in garlic sauce, veal Marsala, filet mignon, and chicken Cordon Bleu. Another specialty is paella, prepared for two or more. For dessert, most diners seem to prefer the chocolate cheesecake. For a complete dinner here, expect to spend $25. The restaurant is open from 7 to 11 p.m. for dinner only, and reservations are imperative. It is closed Sunday and Monday.

Café del Puerto, 3 Frente al Muelle (tel. 725-1500). You may be tempted to browse in the crafts shops on the ground floor of the building that contains this restaurant, but the lure of the good food will eventually pull you up to the third floor. The café is in a harborfront building opposite the wharfs of the old city, but the decor is unabashedly modern. The windows look out to the port, and added illumination comes from the skylights, which are set off by curved pipes painted in a wide array of trendy colors.

This is one of the newest and most cosmopolitan clubs in town. It is technically a members-only place, but out-of-town visitors are always welcome for lunch and are usually admitted in the evening as well. There's a bar near the entrance reserved just for backgammon tables. A second bar a few yards away is tastefully decorated with nautical signal flags, ceiling fans, and varnished planking.

Dinners cost from $30; lunches from $12. Specialties at lunchtime include black bean soup, club sandwiches, fresh fish of the day, marinated octopus salad, pineapple boat filled with seasonal fruits, New York sirloin, and coconut custard. Dinner is more elaborate, although since the policy about evening admission for nonmembers tends to vary, it's a good idea to telephone in advance.

El Patio de Sam, 102 San Sebastian (tel. 724-9254), stands across from the San José Church, the oldest building on the island, and faces the statue of Ponce de Leon, the island's first governor. This popular place is a gathering spot for American expatriates, newspeople, and shopkeepers in the old town. It's known for having the best hamburgers in San Juan, and they're served from noon to 1 a.m.

Even though the dining room is not on the outside, it has been cleverly transformed into a patio. The illusion is so credible you'll swear you're dining al fresco. Every table is strategically placed near a cluster of potted, outdoor plants, and the canvas panels and awnings covering the skylight give the dining area the feeling of being outside (rain or shine).

For a cooling and satisfying lunch, ideal after you've strolled through the streets of the old town, try the black bean soup, followed by the cold meat platter, and topped with a key lime tart. Other main dishes include various steaks, barbecued ribs, filet of sole stuffed with crab, and fish and chips. At lunch, expect to pay around $15, the tab rising to $20 and up for dinner. It is open daily from 10 a.m. to 2 a.m.

Restaurant El Callejon de la Capilla, 317 Fortaleza (tel. 725-8529). Charming Yolanda Muñoz is the owner of this old-fashioned restaurant, which does everything it can to recapture the aura of colonial San Juan.

Dinner guests pass an antique carriage in the vestibule before entering the high-ceilinged, heavily beamed room where the work of dozens of local artists is displayed. There's a live pianist, and a house brand of sangría will liven up your party. Menu items are based on Puerto Rican specialties such as ripe plantains stuffed with ground beef, rabbit fricassée, fried rabbit in garlic sauce, asopao of chicken, lobster, or shrimp, and roast pork. Meals, which are served daily except Sunday from 11:30 a.m. to 10:30 p.m., cost from $28.

La Mallorquina, 207 San Justo (tel. 722-3261), is San Juan's oldest restaurant, founded in 1848. A bit of Old Spain transplanted to the New World, the restaurant is in a three-story, glassed-in courtyard with arches and antique wall clocks. Even if you've already eaten and are shopping in the old town, you might want to visit just to perch at the old-fashioned wooden bar which runs the length of the left wall as you enter. The waiters appear as if they've been hired by central casting, and they slip in the back to eat the food too. The chef specializes in the most typical Puerto Rican rice dish—asopao. You can have it with either chicken, shrimp, or lobster and shrimp (if you're feeling extravagant). Arroz con pollo is almost as popular. I suggest you get your dinner rolling by ordering garlic soup. If that frightens you, gazpacho is served also. Among other recommended main dishes are grilled pork chop with fried plantain, and beef tenderloin, Puerto Rican style. Imaginatively prepared, the assorted seafood stewed in wine is good. Lunch is busy, and dinners are sometimes quiet. A full dinner should cost somewhere between $15 and $25. It is closed Sunday.

El Meson Vasco, 47 Cristo St., corner of San Sebstian (tel. 725-7819), serves savory Basque specialties right in the old town, near the more popular El Patio de Sam. A corner building, the restaurant opens directly onto the Plaza de San José. Even if you prowl the streets of Seville, you couldn't find a more Spanish restaurant. High arched windows and a beamed ceiling add the right architectural details, and as you sit on raffia-covered chairs you can check out the paintings, woodcarvings, and bullfight posters placed against the white stucco walls. The very leisurely service is from 11:30 a.m. to midnight. I've seen visitors stroll in here and order a hamburger, but it's better to stick to the chef's specialties—garlic chicken, codfish Bilbaina, Spanish hake in green sauce, trout molinera, eggs Bilbaina. Every time I'm in San Juan I journey here for an order of the small white beans, Basque style (with sausages), a meal in themselves. Soups are good, especially the porrusalda (potato and leek). If you eat here, expect a tab ranging from $18.

La Chaumière, 367 Tétuan (tel. 722-3330), is decorated like an inn in provincial France, with heavy ceiling beams, black and white checkerboard floors, large rows of wine racks, and half-timbered walls. Menu items include beef Wellington, a surprise in a French restaurant, rack of lamb for two, chateaubriand for two, pheasant flambéed with Calvados, onion soup, vichyssoise, pâté maison made with pork, chicken, and duck liver, and daily specials, such as fish soup. Full meals range upward from $40. There's a crêperie on the upper floor if you prefer a lighter meal.

The **Butterfly People,** 152 Fortaleza (tel. 725-0756), has gossamer wings. This butterfly venture (see my shopping recommendations) is the special world of Drakir Purington and his wife, Attendaire. He was a Harvard graduate and she a Jordanian translator at the United Nations before opening this second-floor café in a restored mansion in Old San Juan. Next to the world's largest gallery devoted to butterflies, you can dine in the Palm Court Café, opening to a patio. It is mainly a bar, with 15 tables serving drinks and lunch from 11 a.m. to 6 p.m. Monday to Saturday, on Sunday to 5 p.m.

The cook specializes in crêpes. You might begin with gazpacho and then follow with a quiche with a salad. The omelets are also good. For dessert, try a piece of homemade cheesecake, before settling a tab which is likely to cost from $12 to $15 per person.

Wherever you look, framed butterflies will delight you. At times, especially the afternoons when cruise-ship passengers aren't visiting, the place has a private-club atmosphere, where the customers play chess and backgammon. Drakir himself is quite an attraction as he goes about the premises. With his long gray hair, he is almost mystical in demeanor. The clothes he wears are as striking as he is, but then one must work hard to compete in a room full of butterflies.

La Danza, corner of Cristo Street and Fortaleza (tel. 723-1642), is known to San Juaneros as one of the best budget restaurants in the old city. A corner eating place opposite the Museum of Modern Art, it is somewhat of a shrine to the famous composer Don Juan Morell Compos, father of the Puerto Rican *danza*. The composer's sheet music is all over the walls, but guests don't come here just for the music.

The food is cooked native style, and it's good and plentiful. Nearly every kind of fresh shellfish is offered, with Puerto Rican hot sauce (mojito isleño). Guests may try the special, paella for two persons, for $15. This is paella, salad, green plantain, one 12-ounce bottle of wine, dessert, and coffee. Rice stews served with green plantain are the chef's pride, made with everything from squid to crab. You might also order pateles (two are served with a salad). These are stuffed green plantains and other vegetables which have been boiled and mashed, wrapped in a banana leaf. All meats are cooked Puerto Rican style. The classic dessert is guava with cream cheese, followed by Puerto Rican coffee. The restaurant stays open daily until 8 p.m.

Maria's, 204 Calle Cristo (tel. 724-9850). Every time I get off the plane in San Juan, I head for this narrow little bar with back tables in the old part of town. There, perched on a stool, you'll be served some of the coolest and most refreshingly original drinks in the capital—a banana frost, a pineapple frost, an orange freeze, a papaya freeze, a chocolate frost, a lime freeze, a mixed fruit frappe. Two drinks generally cost $6. The students, TV personalities, writers, and models who gather here also enjoy Mexican dishes such as chili with cheese, a taco, or an enchilada. If that sounds too heavy on a hot day, then I suggest the fruit salad. Count on spending from $6 up for a drink and a snack. The blender continues to whir from 11 a.m. until 3 a.m.

PUERTA DE TIERRA: La Rôtisserie, Caribe Hilton (tel. 721-0303), is one of the most elegant—and best—restaurants in Puerto Rico. The chef, August Schreiner, has won many awards for his outstanding international cuisine. The restaurant is tastefully appointed, located on the second floor of the deluxe hotel next to the Casino. Fashion shows are presented at lunchtime on Tuesday and Thursday. Reservations are necessary, and in the evening men are requested to wear a jacket and tie.

Meals usually average around $35. For that, you are likely to be tempted with roast prime rib of beef, two succulent double lamb chops, perhaps duckling with wild rice. There is always fresh fish, such as red snapper, as well as the ever-popular steak Diane. The chef shows his imagination in such dishes as medallions of veal and lobster flavored with tarragon. For an unusual opener, if featured, try the pumpkin bisque with lobster flavored with coriander. The Caesar salad is always spectacular, and you might want to conclude your repast with a hot chocolate soufflé.

CONDADO: The Charthouse, Ashford Avenue (tel. 728-0110), is one of the best restaurants on the island and also one of the most popular bars in the Caribbean. The lattice-trimmed villa, built in 1910, stands across from the Dupont Plaza Hotel, attracting on any night literally hundreds of sociable local residents, aged 18 to 40, to its long bar in what used to be a spacious salon.

Today the heavy ceiling beams have been exposed, track lighting installed, and glamorous paintings added to create a warm ambience. The large ground-floor salon contains an almost endless Victorian-style series of shelves, complete with Corinthian columns and beveled mirrors.

If you show up here just for a drink, you'll have some of the most attractive (and eligible) company in town at your elbows. If dining is your aim, you should reserve early and skip lunch, since the portions here are more than enough for even the most dedicated gourmand. You can request a table on one of the three wrap-around verandas unless you prefer the constantly changing cast which promenades through the large interior.

The food here is beautifully prepared. The prime rib dishes may be the best in the entire Caribbean. You can enjoy New England clam chowder, the copious salad which comes with all main courses, blue marlin, scrumptiously steamy twice-baked potatoes, fresh broccoli, top sirloin, shrimp teriyaki, one-tail Australian lobster, Hawaiian chicken, and a dessert affectionately known by the staff (most of whom are Californians) as "mud pie."

Full meals here are often less expensive than those at less desirable restaurants in San Juan. They begin at around $30, although if you drink a lot (and that's part of the fun here) you can spend a lot more. The Charthouse is part of a chain of ambience-filled restaurants scattered across the American West, based in California. It's open every evening for dinner with bar service from 5 p.m. Reservations are imperative.

Lotus Flower, 999 Ashford Ave., Laguna Wing of the Condado Plaza Hotel and Casino (tel. 722-0940, ext. 1950), in the Holiday Inn on Condado Beach, is one of the finest Chinese restaurants in the Caribbean. Overlooking the Condado Lagoon, the restaurant serves dishes that are a wonderful medley of flavors. It is open Monday to Friday from noon to 3 p.m. and 6 to 11:30 p.m. On Saturday it is open only from 6 to 11:30 p.m., and on Sunday from 1 to 11:30 p.m. The decor consists of warm colors, a beamed ceiling, hanging plants, and a miniature Buddha on each table.

The chef is equally at home in turning out Hunan, Szechuan, or Cantonese cookery. He'll even do a Peking duck if you order it far enough in advance. Specialties include lemon chicken, beef with scallops and shrimp in a hot sauce, and Szechuan Phoenix, made with prime beef and chicken in a hot sauce. Open your meal with the noodles in sesame sauce, a delectable dish. Count on spending around $30, but you can do it for less.

Au Cheval Blanc, Condado Plaza Holiday Inn, 999 Ashford Ave. (tel. 721-1000), is one of the chicest French restaurants of Puerto Rico. Attracting both well-heeled locals along with the "smart set" foreign crowd, it is a reservations-only dinner restaurant. From one of its best tables, you can look out upon a panoramic view of the lagoon. The restaurant is elegantly appointed, vaguely Louis XIV in style. It is adorned in shades of blue and gray, with a bar at the entrance. Meals, costing from $30, are likely to include duckling in orange sauce, veal kidneys in a Dijon mustard sauce or veal Cordon Bleu, along with lobster thermidor. Among the chef's best fish dishes is sole stuffed with crabmeat.

El Cid, Joffre and Marseille (tel. 723-5894), stands removed from the garish, sign-studded Ashford Avenue on Condado. Offering high-quality Spanish and international specialties, and opening onto a lagoon, it occupies the lower level of an apartment house. A wine rack divides the two dining areas of different levels. In a subdued, refined atmosphere, you get good service and food, both at lunch and dinner. The owner is José Fernández, whose family came from northern Spain. Bluepoint oysters on the half shell are a good opening, followed by caldo gallego, the Spanish white bean soup.

The classic dish to order here is paella El Cid, although among the fish and seafood entrees I prefer the filet of red snapper Madrilena or the Puerto Rican freshwater shrimp in garlic sauce. Under a large listing of the house specialties, I am fond of four in particular—veal piccata, boneless chicken Andaluza, calf brains in black butter and capers, and medallions of beef tenderloin with wine, Spanish ham, and mushrooms. For dessert, you might try "tocino del cielo," which means custard from heaven. A three-course meal will average between $25 and $35. The restaurant is open Monday to Saturday from 11:30 a.m. to 11:30 p.m.

Oasis, 1043 Ashford Ave. (tel. 724-2005), between the Regency Hotel and the Ramada Inn, has a lot of friends, attracted by its seafood and Cuban and Creole specialties. The classic Puerto Rican rice dish, shrimp asopao, is offered here, and I'm always partial to the mixed seafood casserole. The menu is large, and you may have trouble making up your mind. Certainly the filet of red snapper is appealing, as is the Andalusian-style chicken. Among the Cuban and Creole repertoire, I'd recommend the fried beef, Cuban style, or the Creole hash. The most expensive item on the agenda is the grilled lobster. If you're going local all the way, why not garlic soup? Depending on your selections, your tab might be as little as $18. Oasis is open daily from 11:30 a.m. to 2 a.m.

Scotch 'n Sirloin, La Rada Building, 1020 Ashford Ave. (tel. 722-3640), is a lagoon-side setting, has long been considered the quality steak and lobster house of Puerto Rico. In the old days it used to attract a lot of celebrities such as Jackie Gleason. You dine inside in a snug, wood-paneled interior or at one of the dockside tables. Most diners ask for the top sirloin or the prime rib of beef. King crab and scallops is a favorite combination, as is the lobster and sirloin. Alaskan king crab is another specialty. If you order any of the above dishes, you can enjoy a limitless selection from the crisp salad bar. Homemade bread, soup, and coffee are included in the price of the entree. Meals cost from $30. Service is from 6 p.m. to midnight. Many famous artists, such as Jimmy Durante, have appeared here. The tradition of cabaret continues, at least on Thursday, Friday, and Saturday from 5 p.m. to 4 a.m.

L'Escargot, 1106 Magdalena Ave. (tel. 722-2436), is one of the best and most reasonably priced French restaurants in San Juan. Open Monday through Saturday, it is housed in a building that evokes a private hacienda, with red awnings and a tile roof. When guests at one of the hotels flanking the Convention Center hear about this place, they often head here and are rarely disappointed. The price is right too: about $25 for dinner. My most recent meal began with a potage du jour and was followed by a delectable roast veal. My dining companion ordered filet of red snapper in escargot butter. Each night a different dessert maison is offered. The wine list is limited but well chosen.

SANTURCE: Swiss Chalet, Hotel Pierre, De Diego (tel. 721-2233), has operated for some 30 years. The menu is large, with a host of cheese dishes and other Swiss specialties, including everything from sauerbraten to minced veal in white wine sauce with mushrooms, a favorite in Zurich. Hors d'oeuvres offered are a dozen escargots du Jura maison and soups such as French onion, green pea, and vichyssoise. The main dishes are well prepared, and you can enjoy a Swiss-style bratwurst with onion suuce or roast rack of lamb Provençale. Fish and seafood are good too. Try the Mexican Gulf shrimp sauteed in garlic and herb butter. Among the desserts, I like Bavarois au kirsch with raspberry sauce. Meals average around $25. The management suggests that you dress "elegantly casual." Hours are until 1 a.m.

MIRAMAR: La Fragua, in the Capitol Hotel, 800 Ponce de Léon Ave. (tel. 722-4699), is one of my favorite restaurants in and around San Juan. Go here for their fresh-tasting and well-prepared fish dishes, along with impeccable service. Sea bass is a specialty (it appears on the menu as mero). Don't go here for the decor. The restaurant is vaguely Spanish, and the average meal is priced at $25. The waiters are helpful in explaining what's available on a particular day. Many professionals, such as lawyers, in the San Juan community patronize this establishment, considering it their "secret" address. It is open Monday to Friday from noon to 3:30 p.m. and 6:30 to 11 p.m., on Saturday from 6:30 to 11 p.m. only.

ISLA VERDE: Cousin Ho's, Carib-Inn, Route 187 (tel. 791-4089), provides a powerful kitchen in its palate-perking Szechuan and Hunan dishes, but also soothes those diners seeking milder Cantonese specialties. On the second floor of this modern Isla Verde hostelry, the chefs prepare Chinese dishes from 6 to 11:30 p.m., and will begrudgingly serve you American dishes if you insist. Try, for example, their Szechuan Phoenix—shredded beef and chicken sauteed with scallions and blended in a spicy hot sauce. Before launching into that, you might be game for their special soup, served to two persons. I'd also suggest their seafood combination with sizzling rice, and their subgum wonton. I've also sampled and approved of their "softy" fried chicken, and their large marinated shrimp, served with Chinese vegetables. Depending on your selection, your final bill will range in price from $15 to $22.

Restaurant Metropole, Carretera Boca de Cangrejos, Anexo Club Gallistico, Isla Verde (tel. 791-4046), is a pleasant restaurant off a busy road in a low-lying white building whose entrance parapet is partially concealed by burgeoning plants. You'll find lots of parking, a kindly staff, and one of the most attractive bars in the neighborhood in a large, square room off the main restaurant. The modern dining room draws many of the local residents for succulent examples of both Cuban and Puerto Rican specialties. These include platter specials such as pork chops with congri and plantains, shrimp Creole, six kids of omelets, and asopao of chicken, shrimp, or lobster. There's also Galician soup, shrimp or lobster salad, a skewer of grilled filet steak, Creole-style beef, and fried sliced kingfish. Full meals here will cost from around $13 and are served seven days a week from 11:30 a.m. to 10:30 p.m.

FOOD ON THE ISLAND: In your tour out on the island, you'll find few well-known restaurants, except those in the major hotels. However, there are plenty of roadside places and simple taverns. The following recommendations, however, deserve special mention and you may want to plan meals there during your island tour. The most popular restaurant outside of San Juan follows:

El Yunque Restaurant, at El Yunque (tel. 790-4237), right in the heart of the island's exotic rain forest. You can dine on some of the most authentic Puerto Rican specialties offered on the island. On the narrow ledge of a mountain road, this chalet restaurant is made of wood, with a stone fireplace at each end. The side of the dining room with the best view has an all-glass wall. The atmosphere is rustic, and at some time during your meal it will definitely rain—I can guarantee that! You park your car on the road above, walking down a covered staircase to this seemingly remote spot.

The soups, served in pewter bowls, are excellent and homemade, ranging from a peasant garlic version to the classic caldo gallego. The specialty is asopao, that soupy Puerto Rican rice dish, prepared here with everything from land crab to squid. The best, I think, is the asopao paella, a really big meal.

Also good are white turtle-meat steak, land crab prepared native style, and a casserole of shrimp and lobster in wine sauce. First-timers might be attracted to the yuquiyu. This is half a pineapple shell filled with turtle meat and Spanish sausage, pigeon peas, and crushed fresh pineapple. If you don't want such heavy food for lunch, try a native fruit salad, followed by custard. A full repast will cost from $22 per person. Hours are daily from 9 a.m. to 6 p.m.

Jajome Terrace, at Cayey (tel. 738-4016), is reached by taking Highway 52 (limited access) up to exit 40 in Cayey to Route 15, km. 18.6. Zaida Clemons likes to share with diners her taste of New Orleans cuisine, creating dishes enjoying equal billing with well-prepared local specialties. The staff is there to tell you about the "all you can eat" special for $12. Drinks and desserts are extra, and children under 12 pay half price. The restaurant is not easy to reach, but it's fun and well worth the search. Hours are Wednesday to Saturday from noon to 10 p.m. and Sunday and holidays from noon to 7 p.m. Reservations are necessary to dine after 6 p.m. any day.

Heading west from San Juan along the northern coast, you reach Vega Baja. There I suggest dining at **Dino's Steak House,** Route 2, no. 12, in the Jardines de Vega Baja (tel. 858-1100). It's an Italian steakhouse and seafood oasis right off Route 2 in Vega Baja. If you're headed toward the west coast, a stopover here for a meal would be in order. Hours are 11 a.m. to 10 p.m. seven days a week.

The ambience is friendly and relaxed, and musical entertainment is offered at dinner on weekends when the mood is informal. The most expensive steak is a 14-ounce prime, and the menu includes a variety of local seafood dishes, depending on what's available. Try the lobster salad supreme.

Most dishes include side orders of spaghetti, with a savory Italian sauce to which only Dino has the recipe, and he's not talking! Meals cost from $25.

On the road between Ponce and Mayaguez, you'll find several worthy stopovers, some of them offbeat.

Restaurante La Guardarraya, Route 128, is in Yauco, the coffee-growing area. The town is on the main road just past Ponce. This is a roadside place in a painted green building, very rustic but clean. There's even a little sink right in the dining area in addition to rest rooms. It might put some people off, but many locals rave about it, including some of the island's politicians.

The specialty of the house is called Can Can pork chops. It's what everybody has, and many diners come from as far as San Juan to sample it. The pork chops are easily two inches thick and a foot long, two to a portion (can be shared). They are deep-fried three times according to a special recipe—crisp outside, but moist inside. The meat is butchered on the premises. The rice dishes are also superb. The arroz Guisado is stewed with pigeon peas, the plain rice served with the pink beans to be poured over, and the manpostiao is done with kidney beans and sausage. Desserts consist of homemade flan and an assortment of preserved fruits in syrup with native white cheese. A full meal will cost from $15 and up.

The whole area of **Cabo Rojo** on the west coast is well known for its small rustic seafood restaurants that line the water on both sides of the road, principally Route 102 in the town of Joyuda. I have eaten at several over the years, and all of them serve the same assortment of seafood, prepared in a similar way.

3. What to See in San Juan

The streets are narrow and teeming with traffic, but a walk through Old San Juan—in Spanish, El Viejo San Juan—is like a stroll through five centuries of history. You can do it in less than a day. In a historic landmark seven-square-block area in the westernmost part of the city, you can see on foot many of Puerto Rico's chief historical sightseeing attractions, and when you tire of monuments, you can combine your tour with some shopping along the way. Many of the museums in Old San Juan close at 11:45 a.m. for lunch and don't reopen until 2 p.m.

The Spanish moved to Old San Juan in 1521, and the city founded there was to play an important role as Spain's bastion of defense in the Caribbean. Once the city was called Puerto Rico (Rich Port), as the name San Juan was given to the whole island.

I'll begin our tour at the northeast corner of Old San Juan. On Calle Norzagaray stands the 1783 **Fort San Cristobal,** which was built to defend San Juan against attacks by land, as well as to form backup support for El Morro if that fort were attacked from the sea. Composed of six independent units, the fort is connected to a central structure by means of tunnels and dry moats. You'll get the idea if you look at a scale model on display. On a site of 27 acres, the fort is overseen by the National Park Service. Be sure to see the Garita del Diablo, or the Devil's Sentry Box. The devil himself, it is said, would snatch away soldiers on guard duty at the box. Free guided tours are offered daily at 9:30 and 11 a.m. and at 2 and 3:30 p.m.

The **Tapia Theater,** Avenida Ponce de Léon, was paid for by taxes on bread and imported liquor. Standing across from the Plaza de Colón, it is one of the oldest theaters in the western hemisphere, built about 1832. In 1976 a restoration returned the theater to its original look. Much of Puerto Rican theater history is connected with Tapia. It's named after the island's first prominent playwright, Alejandro Tapia y Rivera (1826–1882), and Adelina Patti (1843–1919), the most popular and highly paid singer of her day, made her operatic debut here when she was barely 14.

Before you leave, pause to look at the **Plaza de Colón.** Once named the Plaza de Santiago, it had its name changed to honor Columbus on November 19, 1893, the 400th anniversary of the island's discovery. In the center of the square is a statue of Columbus, and at its base are plaques tracing incidents in his globe-trotting life.

La Casa del Callejon, Calle San Francisco (tel. 725-5250), run by the Institute of Culture, houses two museums. On the first floor of this 18th-century house, the Museum of Colonial Architecture has scale models of El Morro and La Fortaleza which may give you some perspective before you see the real thing. Exhibits of iron and woodwork, along with ceramic tiles, can also be seen. I find the second-floor Museum of the Puerto Rican Family much more interesting, as it gives you a glimpse into the life of how these island people lived in the 19th century. The rooms are small, and the life, as depicted here, was definitely middle class. Hours are 9 a.m. to noon and 1 to 4:30 p.m., costing adults 50¢ (children are admitted free). Guided tours are conducted Tuesday through Saturday at 9 a.m. and again at 4:30 p.m.

El Arsenal, La Puntilla (tel. 725-5584). The Spaniards used a shallow craft to patrol lagoons and mangroves in and around San Juan. Needing a base for these vessels, they constructed El Arsenal at the turn of the century, and it was at this same base that they, so to speak, staged their last stand, flying the Spanish colors until the final Spaniard was removed in 1898, at the end of the Spanish-American war.

La Princesa Jail, Paseo de la Princesa, was until very recently a prison, dating from 1837. As you face the jail from the wall on Cristo Street, you can better appreciate the height of the city's wall from which the structure can best be seen. After a restoration (hopefully), the former home to prisoners and exiles may be turned into a museum.

Cristo Chapel, on Calle Cristo, was built to commemorate what legend says was a miracle. Horse racing down Cristo Street was the highlight of the fiestas on St. John's Day, the patron saint of the city. In 1753 a young rider lost control of his horse and plunged over the precipice. Moved by the accident, a spectator, the secretary of the city, Don Mateo Pratts, invoked Christ to save the youth. He had the chapel built that same year. Today it is a landmark in the old city and one of its best known historical monuments. The Campèche paintings and gold and silver altar can be seen through its glass doors.

La Casa de Libro, 255 Calle Cristo (tel. 723-0354), is a restored 18th-century house sheltering a library devoted to the arts of printing and bookmaking, with examples of fine printing from the 15th century to the present, as well as some medieval illuminated manuscripts. Special exhibits are usually shown on the first floor, open from 11 a.m. to 4:30 p.m. except weekends and holidays.

La Fortaleza, at the west end of Calle Fortaleza overlooking the San Juan harbor (tel. 721-7000, ext. 2370), is the office and residence of the governor of Puerto Rico. The oldest executive mansion in continuous use in the western hemisphere, it has served as the island's seat of government for more than three centuries. Yet its history goes back even further, to 1533, when construction began for a fortress *(fortaleza)* to protect San Juan's settlers during raids by cannibalistic Caribs. The original medieval towers remain, but as the edifice was subsequently enlarged into a palace, other modes of architecture and ornamentation were also incorporated, including baroque, Gothic, neoclassical, and Arabian. La Fortaleza has been designated a National Historic Site of the U.S. government. Tours, in English and Spanish, are conducted every half hour on weekdays at 9, 10, and 11:30 a.m., and at 2 and 3:30 p.m.—but don't show up in your bikini.

San Juan Gate, Calle San Francisco and Calle Recinto Oeste, built around 1635, just north of La Fortaleza, was the main gate and entry point into San Juan—that is, if you came by ship in the 18th century. The gate is the only one remaining of the several entries to the old walled city. It stands today as a sign of welcome.

The **City Hall,** Calle San Francisco, was ordered built in 1604, but work suffered many delays because of lack of money. Rebuilt twice in the 18th century, in was finally ready to be occupied in 1789. The clock in the tower was installed in 1889. Flanked by two towers, the building has a double arcade. Guided tours are given Monday through Friday, except holidays, from 8 a.m. to 4:15 p.m.

San Juan Cathedral, Calle Cristo and Caleta San Juan, was begun in 1540. Since that time it's had a rough life. Restoration today has been extensive, so it hardly resembles the thatched-roof structure that had stood there until 1529 when it was wiped out by a hurricane. Hampered by lack of funds, the cathedral slowly added a circular staircase and two adjoining vaulted Gothic chambers. But along came the Earl of Cumberland in 1598 to loot it, and a hurricane in 1615 to blow off its roof. In 1908 the body of Ponce de Leon was brought here. After he'd died from an arrow wound in Florida, his body had originally been taken to San José Church. The cathedral faces the Plaza de las Monjas (or the Nuns' Square), a tree-shaded old town spot where you can rest and cool off, taking a break in the tour.

Plazuela de la Rogativa, Caleta de las Monjas, basks in legend. In 1797 the British across San Juan Bay at Santurce held the old town under siege. However, that same year they mysteriously sailed away. Later, the commander claimed he feared the enemy was well prepared behind those walls, apparently seeing many lights and thinking them to be reinforcements. Some people believe those lights were torches carried by women in a rogativa, or religous procession, as they followed their bishop. A handsome statue of a bishop, trailed by a trio of torch-bearing women, was donated to the city on its 450th anniversary.

Casa Blanca, 1 Calle San Sebastian (tel. 724-4102). Ponce de Leon never lived here, although construction of the house (built in 1523) sometimes is attributed to him. The house was erected two years after the explorer's death, and work was ordered by his grandchild, Juan Garcia Troche, who later adopted his grandfather's name. The parcel of land was given to Ponce de Leon as a reward for services rendered to the Crown. Descendants of the explorer lived in the house for about 2½ centuries until the Spanish government took it over in 1779 for use as a resident for military commanders. The U.S. government as well used it as a home for army commanders. Today it's a museum, showing how Puerto Ricans lived in the 16th and 17th centuries. Guided tours are Tuesday through Saturday at 9 a.m. and 4:30 p.m. On Sunday it can be visited from 9 a.m. to noon and 1 to 4:30 p.m.

Back on Calle Cristo, **San José Church** is centered in San José Plaza, right next to the Dominican monastery. Initial plans were drawn in 1523 and work, supervised by Dominican friars, began in 1532. Before going into the church, look for the statue of Ponce de Leon on the adjoining plaza. It was made from British cannons captured during Sir Ralph Abercromby's unsuccessful attack on San Juan in 1797.

Both the church and its monastery were closed by decree in 1838, the property confiscated by the royal treasury. Later, the Crown turned the convent into a military barracks. The Jesuits restored the badly damaged church. The church was the place of worship for Ponce de Leon's descendants, who are buried there under the family's coat-of-arms. The conquistador was interred there until his removal to the cathedral in 1908.

Although badly looted, the church still has some treasures, including *Christ of the Ponces,* a carved crucifix presented to Ponce de Leon. Packed in a crate, the image survived a terrible shipwreck outside San Juan harbor. The church has four oils by José Campèche and two large works by Francisco Oller. Many miracles have been attributed to a painting in the Chapel of Belem. It's a 15th-century Flemish work called *Virgin of Bethlehem.*

Adjacent to the church, at the corner of the square, the **Pablo Casals Museum** (tel. 723-9185) is devoted to the memorabilia left by the artist to the people of Puerto Rico. Born in 1876, Casals of course achieved fame as a cellist, and also won renown as a conductor and composer of symphonies and symphonic poems. Later in Puerto Rico, his "Casals Festivals" drew worldwide interest, attracting some of the greatest performing artists. The maestro's cello is here, along with a library of videotapes, played on request, of some of the festival concerts. This small, 18th-century house also contains manuscripts and photographs of Casals. It is open daily: from 9 a.m. to 5 p.m. Monday through Saturday, and from 1 to 5 p.m. on Sunday.

The **Casa de los Contrafuertes** ("House of the Buttresses") stands adjacent to the Pablo Casals Museum at Calle San Sebastian. The building with its thick buttresses is believed to be the oldest residence remaining in El Viejo San Juan, and it's open from 9 a.m. to noon and 1 to 4:30 p.m. Wednesday through Sunday. It is a three-in-one museum, containing a Pharmacy Museum, which existed in the 19th century in the town of Cayey. Even more interesting is its Museo de Santos (saints carved in native woods). Both of these museums are on the ground floor. If you go upstairs, you'll find a Graphic Arts Museum, displaying an exhibition of watercolors, prints, and paintings by local artists.

Dominican Convent, Calle Norzagaray, was started by Dominican friars in 1523, shortly after the city itself was founded. It was the first convent in Puerto Rico, and women and children often hid out here during Carib Indian attacks. The friars lived here until 1838 when the Crown closed down the monasteries, turning the building into an army barracks. The American army used it as its headquarters until 1966. Today it is the center of the Institute of Puerto Rican Culture. The institute promotes cultural events all over the island. On the ground floor is a permanent display of treasures, featuring a medieval altarpiece. Gregorian chants help re-create the long-ago atmosphere. For more information, call 725-5584. It is open daily from 8 a.m. to 4:30 p.m.

The **City Walls,** Calle Norzagaray, around San Juan were built in 1630 to protect the town against both European invaders and Caribbean pirates. The width of the walls averages from 20 feet at the base to 12 feet at the top, with an average height of 40 feet. Between San Cristobal and El Morro, bastions were erected at frequent intervals. You can start seeing the walls from your approach from San Cristobal on your way to El Morro.

The **San Juan Cemetery,** Calle Norzagaray, officially opened in 1814 and has since been the final resting place for many prominent Puerto Rican families. The circular chapel is dedicated to Saint Magdalene of Pazzis and was built in the 1860s. Necrophiles can wander through marble monuments, mausoleums, and statues, marvelous examples of Victorian funereal statuary. However, there are no trees or any form of shade in the cemetery, so don't go wandering in the noonday sun.

Museo del Niño is a museum devoted to children and sheltered in an 18th-century powder house, within the grounds of El Morro. It deals with arts and sciences, concentrating on exhibits that can be touched. Displays are devoted to sun, earth, and family. Hours are daily, except Monday and Thursday, from 9 a.m. to noon and 1 to 4:30 p.m.

El Morro, Calle Norzagaray (tel. 724-1978), stands on a rocky promontory, dominating San Juan Bay. Called the Castillo San Felipe del Morro, it was ordered built in 1539 and construction started the following year. The original fort was a round tower which can still be seen inside the main bastion of the castle. More walls were added, a line of batteries installed. By 1787 the structure reached its present stage. Sir Francis Drake was turned away in 1595. The fort is run and administered by the U.S. National Park Service. As one of the loftiest points in the old town, it is a labyrinth of dungeons, barracks, outposts, and ramps. Free guided tours are offered daily at 9:30 and 11 a.m., and at 2 and 3:30 p.m.

Unless you've grown weary of forts, there's one more. **Fort San Jeronimo,** or what's left of it, stands east of the Caribe Hilton at the entrance to Condado Bay. Completed in 1788, it was badly damaged in the English assault of 1797. Reconstructed in the closing year of the 18th century, it has now been taken over by the Institute of Puerto Rican Culture. A museum has been lodged there, with life-size mannikins wearing military uniforms. Ship's models and charts are also displayed. Charging adults 50¢ admission, the museum is open from 8 a.m. to 5 p.m. (on Saturday it's free).

READER'S SIGHTSEEING TIP: "I enjoyed the museum on the campus of the **University of Puerto Rico** in Río Piedras very much. They had a good collection of paintings by the promiment Puerto Rican artist, Francisco Oller, and a very large collection of pre-Columbian Puerto Rican Indian artifacts from the Ingeri, sub-Taino, and Taino civilizations. This museum is free and open from 9 a.m. to 5 p.m. every day except Sunday" (Barry Isaac, Miami Beach, Fla.).

4. A Shopping Tour

Puerto Rico has the same tariff barriers as the U.S. mainland. That's why you don't pay duty on items brought back to the United States. That means you don't walk away with great bargains, either. Nevertheless, there are a number of boutiques and specialized stores—especially in the old town—that may tempt you into a purchase.

Native handicrafts can be good buys. Look for "santos," hand-carved wooden religious figures, needlework (women no longer get 3¢ an hour for it!), straw work, ceramics, hammocks, guayabera shirts for men, papier-mâché fruit and vegetables, and paintings and sculptures by Puerto Rican artists.

IN OLD SAN JUAN: You might begin your shopping tour as you emerge from El Convento onto Cristo Street.

Galería Botello, 208 Cristo St. (tel. 723-2879), is almost a museum or art gallery. It's a living tribute to the fiery success story of Angel Botello, now considered one of the most outstanding artists working in Puerto Rico. He was born in a small village in Galicia, Spain, although he fled after the Spanish Civil War to the Dominican Republic. Then there was a 12-year period in the dynamic, art-conscious country of Haiti. His paintings and metal sculpture, while to the knowing eye evocative of his colorful background, have a style very much his own. This galería is his former home, and he did the restoration on the colonial mansion himself. Today it's an appropriate seting to display his paintings and sculpture. Most of the salons open onto couryards. The gallery offers a large collection of Puerto Rican antique santos, which are small, carved wooden figures of saints, and it carries the work of some of Puerto Rico's leading artists. You'll also find colorful posters.

José E. Alegría & Associates, 152–154 Cristo St., opposite El Convento, is housed in an impressive old Spanish-style building dating from 1523 with rooms opening onto patios and courtyards. It displays antique furniture and paintings, its collection considered the finest in San Juan. Intermingled are the paintings of contemporary artists who live in Puerto Rico. Prices are not low, but the quality is very high. There is a wine boutique in the old cellars.

The Gentle Swing, 156 Cristo St. (tel. 724-6625). Owner-manager Étienne Dusart has brought together an exciting collection of hammocks of every description, not only from Puerto Rico but from the Caribbean and Latin American countries as well. You'll find at least 15 highly original designs, suitable for beach or home. Many varieties of string, cord, and decorative tassels are used. You can pick one that is suitable for packing in your suitcase for as little as $18, although the price tag could climb to $1000, depending on how elegant you wish to be.

The Gentle Swing is also home of the original HAMOK chair, which is natural cream or multicolored woven string held apart by a wooden bar and suspended from the ceiling. The HAMOK chair, from $65, is made by hand with the same weaving technique that was known to the Taino Indians of Puerto Rico in pre-Columbian times, but the design is contemporary, the work of owner-architect Étienne Dusart. It is protected by a U.S. patent and received the Designer's Choice 1980 Award by *Industrial Design* magazine. The arms and loop ends have been crafted and individually macraméed for resistance to stress. Besides hammocks, the Gentle Swing also offers local quality crafts such as santos and woodcarvings (some by famous sculptor Emilio Rosado) and the traditional carnival masks in papier-mâché original to Puerto Rico. There is also an entire section of batik garments and wall hangings featuring Caribbean designs in bright colors.

Casa Cavanagh, 202 Cristo St. (mailing address: P.O. Box 3282; tel. 725-3520), about half a block from El Convento, is famous. For more than 28 years the owners have traveled around the globe on purchasing trips to buy the exotic and different. Fine gifts of china and crystal imported from England, France, and Italy are featured, as well as an array of items made by Puerto Rican artisans. Accessories for decorating your home or office include bronzes, porcelain, lacquerware, and more from the markets of India, Singapore, Thailand, Latin

America, and Sri Lanka. Casa Cavanagh also has stores in Plaza las Americas, Puerta de Tierra, and several major hotels.

Don Roberto, 205 Cristo St. (tel. 724-0194), is one of the oldest and most established shops in Old San Juan. It's owned by Tom Catlett, who seems to know everything there is to know about unusual sources for gifts. His taste is excellent, his prices realistic. The collection is eclectic. He offers a superb collection of soft leather items imported from Bogota, Colombia, at prices sometimes half those of the U.S. Another hard-to-find item is antique santos (saints), and he has a fine collectiton of ceramics, molas, tapestries, hammocks, and swings. You'll find an intriguing collection of "gold" jewelry (actually pewter, gold plated, and replicas of jewelry) from Bogota. You may be tempted by the replicas of coquí, the tree frog that sounds like a bird.

Reinhold, 201 Cristo St. (tel. 725-6878), is perhaps the most distiguished jewelry store in Old San Juan. It's family owned, and has its own diamond mines to make a stunning collection of jewelry. Look at the display case on your right as you enter. The collection of glittering semiprecious and precious rings will fascinate you. Reinhold's occupies the entire two-story colonial building, a minute's walk from El Convento.

The **Butterfly People,** 152 Fortaleza (tel. 723-2432). Once Drakir Purington used to sell his butterflies in the snow outside the Seagram Building in New York. And again, on the beach in St. Thomas. But now he has a café and museum of his own in a handsomely restored building in Old San Juan. There he and his wife, Attendaire, along with their assistants, have artfully arranged butterflies in lucite boxes. The cost could range from $20 for a single butterfly to as much as $70,000 for a swarm. What began as a decorating scheme for the room of their coming child has turned into a successful business. Their butterflies come from farms in New Guinea and South America, among other places. The butterfly bodies are preserved by a secret formula, and the color is forever. The signed and dated lucite boxes of butterflies are guaranteed for a lifetime.

Puerto Rican Art and Crafts, 204 Fortaleza (tel. 725-5596), is a large, high-ceilinged brick room loaded with handmade products from around the country. Owned and operated by the Amador family, the shop offers vividly painted papier-mâché carnival masks which leer down at visitors with macabre grins. Other items include pottery, textiles, serigraphs and original artworks, batiks, woodcarvings, hand-knotted hammocks, ceramic jewelry, and a colorful series of posters. The shop is open daily except Sunday from 9 a.m. to 6 p.m.

Olé, 105 Fortaleza (tel. 724-2445), is the kind of store where even if you don't buy anything, you can still learn a lot about the crafts displayed. Practically everything here that wasn't made in Puerto Rico came from a different part of South America, all artistically displayed in a high-ceilinged room decorated clear to the top. If you want a straw hat from Ecuador, hand-beaten Chilean silver, Peruvian woodcarvings, or Puerto Rican santos, this is the place to buy them. Olé is open daily except Sunday.

Hathaway Factory Outlet, 204 Cristo St. The selection of shirts, known for their "Red H," may vary widely in this factory outlet, but if you happen to be there shortly after stock is replenished, you can stock up at bargain prices on shirts that could easily cost twice as much back home. Most items are top-quality dress and knit shirts from the Hathaway factories in Waterville, Maine, and while you shop, a video will play over and over again a story about how the shirts are sewn. Most items, including articles by Chaps, Ralph Lauren, or Christian Dior, are reduced by 50%. Service is efficient and friendly, and if you need shirts, you might conceivably walk out with a full year's supply.

Carmen's Watch and Gem Center, 204 San José (tel. 725-2284), carries a full selection of jewelry, watches, and chains, each of which will be shown by an attractive saleswoman whose smile seems genuinely friendly.

200 Fortaleza, Fortaleza and Cruz (mailing address: P.O. Box 607; tel. 723-1989), is known as a leading place to buy fine jewelry in Old San Juan. It has famous-name watches, and you can purchase 14- and 18-karat gold chains, which are measured, fitted, and sold by the weight, priced accordingly to the gold market. And they're duty free! I looked at 14-karat gold diamond studs priced from $38 to $125, a 14-karat gold heart-shaped ring with diamond for $95, and a matching gold pendant with diamond-studded heart for $110. You can even find 14-karat gold rings with a single diamond for $28!

La Plazoleta del Puerto, Marina Street in front of Pier 3 (tel. 722-3053), is one of the most important achievements of San Juan's municipal government: the first Puerto Rican crafts market. Once a depressed waterfront building, the structure has been restored by city hall to simulate a typical street of Old San Juan. It attracts local visitors as well as tourists. The artisans' shops are open between 9 a.m. and 6 p.m. daily. Folk art is displayed in various forms, including the work of ceramists, doll-makers, needle-workers, and other craftspeople.

ON THE CONDADO: **Ambiance,** Condado Beach Arcade, Ashford Avenue (tel. 724-6426), is a well-stocked gift shop near the Ramada Inn, selling a wide selection of porcelain, crystal, jewelry, and china. It's considered by many to be the finest store in the Caribbean, and a quick look at its stock will tell you why. If you want products from Lladro to Lalique, from Aynsley to Wedgwood, Ambiance will probably have them in dozens of patterns. They also sell watches. Don't ignore the second floor if you're interested in china, since there is a considerable display upstairs as well. The store is open from 9 a.m. to 6 p.m. daily except Sunday, when it is open from noon to 5 p.m.

Artisans Market. From about 10 a.m. to 5 p.m. on weekends, handicraft stalls are set up at El Centro, the Convention Center linking the Condado Beach and La Concha Hotels. Here you'll find all the items typical of Puerto Rico, including the small carved religious figures called santos. Devil's masks are imaginatively shaped from coconut husks, and much embroidered clothing is offered, as well as woven straw items, including hats. Papier-mâché fruits and vegetables are sold along with local ceramics and pottery.

PLAZA LAS AMERICAS: The biggest and the most up-to-date shopping plaza in the Caribbean Basin is Plaza Las Americas, which lies in the financial district of Hato Rey, right off the Las Americas Expressway. The complex, with its fountains and advanced architecture, has a total of 200 shops, most of them upmarket.

Bon Voyage Luggage & Gifts (tel. 751-2933) has the most complete selection of travel-related items, including suitcases and travel clocks. There is also a section devoted to Gucci accessories.

Almacenes Linda (tel. 753-0115). Many of the big designer names, such as Oscar de la Renta, are displayed in this sportswear shop. Look for those bathing suits by Dior.

Casa Cavanagh (tel. 753-0133), already previewed in the preceding section, also has a branch here. Although known for their items from the exotic corners of the world, they also sell work by island artisans as well.

Clubman (tel. 753-1965) is the best of the men's specialty stores, with both casual and formal wear.

Galería (tel. 753-1108) is an interesting concept. On the second floor of the shopping arcade, it offers a total of seven footwear boutiques, including many imports from Italy.

Suit City (tel. 753-7134) is aptly named. It'll give men that continental look, with a Spanish or an Italian suit. It also sells much sportswear for men, including jackets and bathing suits.

La Fragrance (tel. 753-0506), as its name suggests, is devoted to cosmetics. It has one of the most comprehensive—and the finest—perfume collections in Puerto Rico.

5. After Dark Around the Island

CASINOS: These are one of the island's biggest draws. Many visitors come here on package deals, staying at one of Condado's plush hotels, with just one intent —to gamble at games ranging from blackjack to baccarat.

The biggest, splashiest game room is at **El Centro,** the Hilton-operated, government-owned complex that connects the Condado Beach and La Concha Hotels, reviewed earlier.

All the other game rooms are in hotels, the plush ones certainly. Therefore you can try your luck at the **Caribe Hilton** (one of the better ones), the **Carib-Inn,** way out in Isla Verde, the **Dupont Plaza,** the **Palace,** and the **Condado Holiday Inn** (largest on the island). There are no passports to flash, admissions to pay, or whatever, as there often is in European gambling casinos.

The best casinos "out in the island" are those at the **Dorado Beach Hotel** and its sister, the **Cerromar Beach.** In fact, you can easily drive to either of these hotels from San Juan to enjoy their nighttime diversions. There is also a new casino at Palmas del Mar.

Drinking, incidentally, is not permitted at the tables. Most casinos open between 1 and 4 p.m., and again from around 8 p.m. to 4 a.m. Jackets and ties for men are often requested, as the Commonwealth is trying to keep a "dignified, refined atmosphere."

SHOWS AT HOTELS: For after-dark amusements, the resort hotels have the most beautiful, swank (and expensive) meccas, ranging from Las Vegas–type shows (everybody from Liza Minnelli to Sammy Davis, Jr.) to discos.

The Caribe Hilton at Puerta de Tierra (tel. 721-0303) contains one of the most complete entertainment complexes on the island, drawing thousands of visitors into its nightlife facilities every season. The most prominent is the **Club Caribe** where the live music from some of the western hemisphere's biggest entertainers—as well as a promising crop of newcomers—sometimes wafts down to the customers at the surrounding bars and restaurants. Some of the big names who have appeared at the Club Caribe include Chita Rivera, Robert Goulet, and Diahann Carroll.

You need not eat dinner to enjoy the show, but if you do, à la carte evening meals cost between $18 and $40. The music begins between 10 and 10:30 p.m., and if you just want to enjoy the show, you'll be charged around $17 to enter Sunday to Thursday, around $22 on Friday and Saturday. A two-drink minimum, costing around $10 per person, is required. Men must wear jackets and ties. Service and taxes are not included in these prices.

One of the popular weekend pastimes in San Juan is to attend the Club Caribe's international buffet, held from 6:30 to 9:30 p.m. every Sunday. The price is around $28 per person and includes all you can eat from the well-stocked tables.

If you're looking for a less high-powered ambience, you can enjoy a drink at the adjoining **Caribe Lounge** (not to be confused with the club), which is also on the second floor near the entrance to the casino. Live music is presented here on Friday and Saturday, at which time a $6 cover charge is added to each listener's bar tab. Piña coladas here are delicious, and many habitués welcome the chance for a quiet drink after a visit to the casino.

The casino, of course, offers all the glitter and excitement of money changing hands, with row on row of flashing lights and excited clusters of players gathered around tables devoted to craps, 21, or roulette. Jackets and ties are required for men. Cold nonalcoholic drinks or coffee will be served to your gaming table free.

The **Tropicoro Club** at the Palace Hotel (tel. 791-2020), out at Isla Verde, near the airport, bounces into the supper club competition with a Las Vegas–style revue. The most recent one I saw there was called *Scandalous*. For $25 you can see the show and get two drinks as part of your minimum. It's also possible to dine at the club, with dinners costing from $35. You can also enjoy a drink at the Palace in either the Carioca cocktail lounge or the lobby bar, listening to live music. The Latin Lounge also has live music, and later you can check out the casino action.

There's always something happening at the **Condado Plaza Hotel and Sands Casino,** 999 Ashford Ave. (tel. 721-1000). It bills itself quite rightly as "San Juan's entertainment center." There is continuous live music nightly in the La Fiesta lobby bar. But for the best of international revues, head for the Copa Room, where your cover charge and two-drink minimum is settled for $25. A dinner and show, Thursday through Saturday only, is from $40. The club is open Monday through Saturday from 7 p.m. to midnight. Shows are Thursday through Monday (excluding Sunday) at 10 p.m. On Tuesday and Wednesday shows are at 9:15 and 10:15 p.m.

One of the best flamenco shows in town is presented at **El Convento,** 100 Cristo (tel. 723-9020), in the heart of the old town. The cost is only $5 per person if guests are registered at the hotel and if they plan to dine there. Otherwise, nondining outsiders pay around $10. Shows are most often presented around 9 p.m. on Thursday, Friday, and Saturday.

Polo Lounge, Ramada San Juan Hotel and Casino, 1045 Ashford Ave. (tel. 724-5657). Partly because of its location inside one of the Condado's smaller hotels, this nightspot with live entertainment perhaps conveys more than its share of intimate camaraderie. The color scheme around the big windows facing the ocean reminds the convivial drinkers from the north of the full spectrum of autumn, especially as the chairs and carpets are in shaded tones of russet with strong reminders of colonial accents. There's a piano to liven up the early-evening hours. Downstairs from the casino and near the reception area, the bar is open daily from noon to 4 a.m. There's no cover charge, and drinks cost around $2.50.

DISCO FEVER: Juliana's, Caribe Hilton (tel. 725-0303), in the Puerta de Tierra section, is affiliated with Juliana's of London. It's a private disco club at this deluxe hotel, drawing some of the most sophisticated of San Juaneros along with visitors every night from 9 p.m. till 4 a.m. It's considered "the right sound and the right place." You may prance to every beat from merengue to salsa to a waltz. It's even considered possible to converse because of discreet sound engineering. It is built arena style, with bamboo and rattan seating and graceful art nouveau lighting. Singles drink at a bar on the upper ledge. There are two kinds of prices (guests of the hotel get a reduction). Nonguests on Friday and Saturday pay a $20 cover with a two-drink minimum (at $4 per drink). On weekdays and Sunday the cover charge is lowered to $14. It opens earlier, but the action doesn't get under way until 10:30 p.m. or later.

Jeen's Discotheque, Dupont Plaza San Juan, 1309 Ashford Ave. (tel. 724-

6161), has opened its door to become a formidable rival to Juliana's at the Caribe Hilton. The place is elegant and very packed, especially on weekends. The decor may be more fitting to an older crowd, but the patronage is from 18 to 40 years of age. The dress code is casually elegant. Cover charges range from $8 to $15.

Isadora's, Condado Plaza Holiday Inn, 999 Ashford Ave. (tel. 721-1000), is one of the most elegant discos and after-dark rendezvous points in Puerto Rico. This strobe-lit jungle garden is named after the legendary dancer. Sometimes you get music from the '50s—or what John Lennon's son, Sean, called "the old stuff from the '70s." The interior is in shades of russet and peach, with etched glass, mirrors, and padded corners. The $15 minimum includes the first two drinks, and the club opens at 9:30 p.m.

Actually, Puerto Rico's liveliest club is out of San Juan. It's **El Coquí,** at the Cerromar Beach Hotel, at Dorado (tel. 796-1010). Because of the effective sound system here, you can actually talk if you don't want to dance. Favored perches are the basket couches. Glass-etched coquís, those singing tree frogs, are lit in the corners. There's action from 9:30 p.m. to 4 a.m., and don't count on spending less than $15.

FLAMENCO: Copacabana, 1020 Ashford Ave., in the La Rada building in Condado (tel. 723-0691), features flamenco entertainment nightly, with typical Spanish food in the true Spanish fashion and tradition. Entrees incude paella Valenciana as well as lobster and beefsteak. You can also order highly seasoned red snapper filet. Dinner and show usually run as little as $18 per person. Check at the lobby at La Rada for announcements of who is currently appearing in the show.

BAR HOPPING: 1919, Hotel Condado Beach, Ashford Avenue (tel. 721-6090). The room which this club occupies is in the very heart of the hotel in a windowless area near a collection of boutiques. Its unpretentious setting, however, doesn't prevent it from being almost overfull on busy nights. Jazz lovers from around the Condado reserve one of the art deco tables hours or days in advance. On weeknights it's just another pleasant bar, with rose-colored walls, soft lighting, black lacquer tables, and a pianist/singer. On Thursday, Friday, and Saturday, however, two nightly shows are offered, presenting the island's best jazz. at those times a cover charge of around $12 is imposed, after which drinks cost $3. There's a happy hour weekdays from 5 to 7:30 p.m. The place closes on Sunday.

Café 1897, 105 Cristo in Old San Juan (tel. 725-7761). The original well inside this former private home, still filled with water, has been transformed into a wishing well into which poets, politicians, and trysting lovers toss coins. As any Puerto Rican knows, 1897 was the last year of the Spanish occupation of the island, but the Spanish provincial flavor has been re-created at this café/bar.

You enter through a long hallway, past a formal green and white facade, to reach the accommodating and friendly bar. Table-sitters may prefer a place in the inner room, below a skylit ceiling. Some guests are likely to be registered at the Hotel El Convento just across the street. Many will savor the house drink, "Sweet Love," containing "43" liquor, vanilla liqueur, coconut cream, orange juice, and grenadine. This libation costs about $4. Beer is $2.50, and there's a cover charge of $2.50 whenever there's live music. This is usually Wednesday through Saturday. The bar opens daily at 5 p.m. and stays open as late as 4 a.m. on weekends.

Tiffany's, 213 Cristo in Old San Juan (tel. 725-0380). Many guests have wandered in here expecting a quick piña colada or daiquiri, only to stay all evening. The drawing card is the video rock concerts and occasional full-length movies which the bartender shows on a big screen behind the hanging Tiffany-style lamps and the dark-wood bar. If you order beer, it will probably be served in the can. Tropical drinks and frappes (chocolate-peanut is a favorite) are also popular. To add to the electronic ambience, you'll find a collection of video games off to the side of the movie screen. The establishment, lying behind a wooden facade and a big window on one of the main streets of Old San Juan, is open from 11:30 a.m. to 2 a.m. On Friday and Saturday, it closes at 3 a.m. The bar is closed on Sunday.

SUNSET WATCHING: Hotel La Playa, 6 Amapola St., Isla Verde (tel. 791-1115), is a busy nightspot built out over the water in back. It's a disco bar, and although no one might actually be dancing, it's still one of the hottest places in town every night during and after happy hour, weeknights from 4 to 7 p.m. The boat-shaped bar is open to the breezes from the ocean, and colored lights hang from the beamed ceiling, illuminating everyone from athletes to artists to bona fide tourists. There's live music on Wednesday and Thursday from 7 to 11 p.m. Free drinks are given to women for a one-hour period on Wednesday and to men for a similar period on Thursday.

An adjoining restaurant, in addition to the bar, serves hamburgers, chili, and roast chicken. Drinks costs from $2.50. The restaurant is open from 8 a.m. to 11 p.m., with the bar being in operation from 11 p.m. till 2 a.m. seven days a week.

CULTURAL EVENTS: The Performing Arts Center (tel. 724-4747) was built in 1981 in the heart of Santurce, a six-minute taxi jaunt from most of the hotels on Condado Beach. Built at a cost of $18 million (relatively modest for such a complex), the center contains 1883 seats in the Festival Hall, 760 in the Drama Hall, and 210 in the Experimental Theater. Some of the events here are of interest only to Spanish-speaking readers, while others attract an international audience. When the Puerto Rico Symphonic Orchestra performs, seats generally sell for $12 to $20.

LE LO LAI FESTIVAL: This is a year-round vacation package that has many savings for the visitor who plans to stay in Puerto Rico at least a few days. Le Lo Lai is a name created by the island people to express their love of song and dance and a cultural heritage that comes from Spanish, Indian, and African traditions. The government-sponsored Le Lo Lai Festival welcomes visitors to a complimentary week-long celebration, with the pre-purchase, at several participating San Juan hotels, of a seven-night stay from December 15 to April 14 and a five-night stay from April 15 to December 14.

A 26-page discount booklet offers additional sightseeing suggestions and cents-off coupons to many of the island's boutiques and shops. There are coupons for a free T-shirt, Pava hat, and poster, as well as discounts on water sports at hotels such as the Condado Holiday Inn, the Palace, and La Concha. Avis and Budget Rent-a-Car discount coupons for a two-day (or more) auto rental are also part of the package.

For further information, write to the Le Lo Lai Festival, P.O. Box 4195, San Juan, PR 00905, or call 723-3135. If in Puerto Rico, you can drop in at the Le Lo Lai Festival office at the street level of the Convention Center in the Condado area.

6. Getting Around

After you land at Isla Verde International Airport in San Juan, your first problem is to get to your hotel. Less expensive than taxis, limousines run to various parts of the city for low rates: $1.25 to Isla Verde Hotels, $1.50 to Condado, and $1.75 for the San Juan metropolitan area, including the old town. Stops are made en route, and you share the ride, of course. On the way back to the airport, however, you'll have to take a taxi, as limousines aren't allowed hotel pickups.

Taxis are metered in San Juan, and the meter handle should be up when you get in, down as the taxi pulls out. Rates begin at 80¢, going up 10¢ for each additional mile. Each suitcase carries a supplement of 50¢. From the airport to a Condado hotel costs about $5 to $8, and tipping is very much allowed. Waiting time costs $8 per hour.

Publicos are cars or mini-buses which provide low-cost transportation and are designated with the letters "P" or "PD" following the numbers on their license plates. They run to all the main towns of Puerto Rico. Passengers are either let off or picked up along the way. Rates are set by the Public Service Commission. Publicos usually operate during daylight hours, departing from the main plaza (central square) of a town.

Buses run both day and night and operate on a fixed-fare system. Some are air-conditioned. City terminals are on the Plaza Colón and at Pier One. The **Puerto Rico Motor Coach,** 327 Recinto Sur in Old San Juan (tel. 725-2460), runs daily service between San Juan and Mayaguez and San Juan and Ponce, a one-way fare costing $6.

Car rentals are readily available, and some local agencies may tempt you with special slashed prices. But if you're planning to tour out on the island, you won't find any local branches should you run into car trouble. Also, some of the agencies widely advertising low-cost deals don't take credit cards and want cash paid in advance. If you plan to do much touring, it's better to stick with one of the international reliables, including **Avis** (tel. 721-8605), or **Hertz** (tel. 791-0840), both recommended in previous editions of this guide.

For my latest trek across Puerto Rico, I tried out the services of **Budget Rent-a-Car** (tel. 791-3685), which maintains two offices in San Juan. As soon as visitors pick up their luggage, they can call Budget for a van which will transport them to the main office at 187 km., 12 Isla Verde Rd., across from the Palace Hotel. Hours are from 6 a.m. to 11 p.m. No advance reservation is required, but to protect yourself you should have a vehicle set aside by calling toll-free 800/527-0700.

Added security comes from antitheft double-locking mechanisms which have been installed on most of the agency's cars. The inventory consists mainly of Japanese-made Datsuns which perform well on the narrow roads of the island. There is also a fleet of American-made cars, such as four-door Chevrolet Cavaliers.

As an indication of prices, the Cavalier with unlimited mileage included costs $48 for a one-day rental, or $288 for the week. Most visitors, however, will settle for a less expensive model, a peppy Datsun Sentra with manual transmission. A daily rental costs from $33; a weekly contract, from $195. Unlimited mileage is included. There are many other cars which don't fit into either category.

Reader Sylvia Dick, of Roxbury, Mass., points out (accurately, I feel) that driving conditions in Puerto Rico are less than desirable. She writes: "Many of the roads you mention are barely one lane in either direction and take tortuous paths through the mountains. Roads are sometimes poorly or incorrectly labeled. People drive *fast* and rarely rely on their horns. The quality of roads varies greatly and looking at a map is not reliable."

Renting a car in Puerto Rico is easy. Motorists should remember that distances are often posted in kilometers rather than miles, but speed limits are in miles! Drivers on the island must be at least 21 years old. Those who don't purchase collision damage waivers (around $6 per day) are responsible for the first $1500 worth of damage to their vehicles in case of an accident.

Sightseeing bus tours are convenient for people who don't want to drive. The **Gray Line Sightseeing Tours** of Puerto Rico, P.O. Box 7342 (tel. 727-8080), operates some of the best tours. Reservations are required on all tours, and pickup at your hotel can be arranged. Usually someone at your hotel desk will book you on a tour.

One of the most popular full-day tours, leaving at 9 a.m. and costing around $20, takes in the rain forest, El Yunque, and Luquillo Beach.

There is also a tour of the city of San Juan, leaving year round at 9 a.m. and 1:30 p.m., costing $12 and taking about 2½ hours. Other tours are also available.

For a sea excursion, **Capt. Jack Becker** invites you to go out aboard his 40-foot catamaran, *Spread Eagle,* at a cost of $30 per person, including a buffet lunch and snorkel gear. It ties up at the Villa Marina Yacht Harbour in Fajardo, about an hour's drive east from San Juan. Departures for Icacos Island are at 10 a.m. Once there, you can swim, beachcomb, snorkel, or whatever. The *Spread Eagle* sails back at 2:30 p.m., the trip taking about an hour. To make reservations, telephone Captain Jack after 6:30 p.m. Dial 129 for long distance and ask for 863-1905. Transportation is available from metro San Juan for $10 round trip. Sixty percent of the passengers on the *Spread Eagle* are repeats or referrals. For information, write P.O. Box 445, Puerto Real, PR 00740.

ISLAND AIR SERVICES: Prinair (tel. 724-4220) is the Commonwealth's national carrier. It flies twice a day round trip from San Juan to Ponce, costing $60 round trip per person. By far the most popular inter-island route is between San Juan and Mayaguez, which the airline flies 10 times a day on weekdays and 23 times a day on weekends. The round-trip fare is $68 per person.

If you want to reach one of Puerto Rico's offshore islands—Vieques or Culebra—call **Vieques Air-Link** (tel. 722-3736). One-way fare to Vieques from San Juan is $23; to Culebra, $30. **Dorado Wings** (tel. 725-2927) will fly you from San Juan to Dorado for $26 one way, while **CrownAir** (tel. 728-2828) flies four times a day between San Juan and Palmas del Mar, charging a round-trip fare of $58 per person.

OUT IN THE ISLAND

The Puerto Rico Company of Tourism (a government agency) has been quite successful in its efforts to have Puerto Rico known as "The Complete Island." Tourism promoters in the island agree with this concept and add that since it is the complete island, why then stay in only one place and say that one has seen Puerto Rico?

After seeing and enjoying San Juan, there is a lot more yet to see, do, and enjoy in the rest of the island. It's amazing how many visitors return home unaware of the many attractions and places they could have visited beyond the San Juan area. There are 79 towns and cities, each having its unique charm and flavor. Puerto Rico has a rich countryside with many panoramas, centuries-old coffee plantations, sugar estates still in use, foreboding caves and enormous boulders with mysterious petroglyphs carved by the Taino Indians (original settlers of the island), colorful but often narrow and steep roads, and meandering mountain trails leading out to tropical settings.

7. Hotels Out in the Island

Until recently, this other Puerto Rico was thought of as "too far out" for the fast-moving visitor. Because of the efforts of Paradores Puertorriqueños, a chain of privately owned and operated inns under the auspices and supervision of the Commonwealth Development Company, today everyone can enjoy the Puerto Rican countryside.

THE PARADORES: These hostelries are easily identified by a Taino grass hut in the signs and the logo of each inn. There are three categories of paradores scattered throughout the island:

Hotel—where you have full-service facilities very much like the tourist hotels of the big cities, but set in a coastal or countryside setting.

Guest house—having all the basic large hotel facilities except dining facilities. Breakfast menus are available at most.

Villa or lodge—here you find the minimum tourist facilities in a rural setting. These paradores are composed of individual cottages or units centered around a main building where all the basic services, dining facilities, and entertainment take place. In this type of parador you are expected to do your basic housekeeping and cooking.

My survey of the paradores of Puerto Rico follows. For yet another parador, refer to the section on San German.

Parador Baños de Coamo, P.O. Box 540, Coamo (tel. 825-2186). Legend has it that the hot springs of Baños de Coamo were the fountain of youth sought by Ponce de Leon. It is believed the Taino Indians, during pre-Columbian times, held rituals and pilgrimages here as they sought health and well-being. For more than 100 years (1847 to 1958) the site was a center for rest and relaxation where many Puerto Ricans as well as others had enjoyable stays, some on their honeymoon, others in search of the curative powers of the thermal springs, which lie about a five-minute walk from the hotel.

The spa is now a parador offering hospitality in the Puerto Rican tradition. Even so, the place has a somewhat Mexican atmosphere. Buildings range from a lattice-adorned, two-story motel-style unit with wooden verandas, to a Spanish colonial pink stucco building housing the restaurant. All 48 units are air-conditioned and roomy. The decor has been restored to its original 19th-century style. Coamo is inland on the south coast, about two hours from San Juan, and swimming is limited to an angular pool, but one can always drive to a nearby public beach. Horseback riding is unique at Baños de Coamo—here you can ride Paso Fino horses. This beautiful breed of Arabians is the pride of Puerto Rico's equestrian breeders. The cuisine is both creole and international, and the coffee Baños style is a special treat. The Baños lists many notables among its past visitors, including F. D. Roosevelt in 1933, as well as Frank Lloyd Wright. Alexander Graham Bell and Thomas Edison were also visitors.

All year the parador charges the same rates—$40 daily in a room with twin beds, $35 in a single.

Parador Hacienda Gripiñas, P.O. Box 387, Route 527, km. 2.5 (tel. 721-2884), at Jayuya, is a former coffee plantation in the very heart of the Central Mountain Range, reached by a long, narrow, and curvy road. This home-turned-inn is a delightful blend of hacienda of days gone by and the modern conveniences of today. The plantation's ambience is found everywhere—ceiling fans, splendid gardens, hammocks on a porch gallery, and more than 20 acres of coffee-bearing bushes. You'll taste the home-grown product when you order the inn's aromatic brew.

You can swim in the pool (away from the main building), soak up the sun, or go and enjoy the nearby sights such as the Indian Ceremonial Park at Utuado or the Pool of the Petroglyphs. Boating and plenty of fishing are just 30 minutes away at Lake Caonillas.

The restaurant of the parador, reached from San Juan in about 2½ hours, features a Puerto Rican and international cuisine. Complete meals can range from as little as $5 to a high of $25, depending on your selection. Rooms in the two-story frame building with green trim are supervised by Edgardo and Milagra Dedos, perhaps the friendliest and most helpful innkeepers you are likely to encounter out on the island of Puerto Rico. Each of their 19 rooms has a private bath, and most come with ceiling fans. Rates are modestly priced at $35 in a double and $30 in a single. These are in effect year round. If you can spend only one night in a Puerto Rican parador, make it Hacienda Gripiñas.

Parador Martorell, 6A Ocean Dr., Luquillo (tel. 889-2710). Back in 1800 the Martorell family came to Puerto Rico from Spain and fell in love with the island. Today their descendants own and manage the Parador Martorell in Luquillo, in the vicinity of the most impressive beach in all of Puerto Rico. The Martorells think of themselves as pioneers, and keep this feeling alive by blending modern household furnishings with the simplicity of Spanish decor. When you arrive at the parador, you will enter an open courtyard by a tropical garden. Later, when you have time to explore, among the foliage you will find Spanish tiles imprinted with proverbs. Some are humorous, and most of them will encourage you to relax—as in the one that states: "el trabajo es sagrado, no lo toques" ("work is sacred—don't touch it!"). The main reason for staying at the Martorell is Luquillo Beach, with its shady palm groves, crescent beaches, coral reefs for snorkeling and scuba-diving, and the surfing area.

Lunch in the patio of the guest house comes with fragrant flowers, the elusive hummingbirds, and the occasional music of the coquí, the tiny Puerto Rican tree frog that very few people are privileged to see. Breakfast at the Martorell is a surprise. The buffet-style breakfast always features plenty of freshly picked fruit and baskets full of homemade breads and compotes. The Martorells have also opened the Coquí Garden Bar and Restaurant, which operates only during the winter season on a reservations-only policy. Specialties include Spanish paella and crêpes.

While at the parador, you must include the rain forest in your itinerary. At day's end you can come back to the parador, where guests often gather on the patio to swap anecdotes and taste the homemade "Ponche María" as an apéritif.

Low-season rates are $30 daily in a single and from $39 to $42 in a double, while high-season rates are from $40 in a single and $55 in a double.

Parador Hacienda Juanita, Apartado 838, Carr. 105, km. 23.5, Maricao (tel. 838-2550). Right at the foot of the state forest in the mountain region where the Taino Indians offered their final resistance to the Spanish conquistadores, the Hacienda Juanita has preserved intact the flavor of an old coffee plantation. Every room has a private bath. There is a bar featuring a balcony from which you get a magnificent view of the country greenery surrounding the parador. For relaxation, the swimming pool is always available. There is always a volleyball or basketball game in progress.

Near the former plantation house, the new rooms are pleasantly furnished, containing private baths. In all, 21 units are rented out. Despite their modernity, the accommodations still have a traditional feeling. The same rates are charged all year—$30 daily in a single, $35 in a double. Children under 12 are sheltered free, and a third adult in the room pays $16. For MAP (breakfast and dinner), add another $25 per person daily. The hearty cuisine includes many regional dishes, and every single plate served you is enough for two.

From the parador, you can visit the only fish hatchery that supplies the lakes and rivers of Puerto Rico with native fish, tour the town's grotto dedicated to its patron saint, John the Baptist, visit a colonial cemetery, trek through the state forest, and explore the town of Maricao, one of the smallest in the island (population 3000), which still retains many of its colonial traditions. Mayaguez is only 12 miles away.

Parador El Guajataca, P.O. Box "H," Route 2, km. 103.8, Quebradillas (tel. 895-3070), lies along the north coast 60 miles west of San Juan. Service, hospitality, and the natural beauty surrounding El Guajataca—all this, plus modern conveniences and a family atmosphere, add up to a good visit. Your host is German Chavez.

The parador is set on a rolling hillside which reaches down to the surf-beaten beach. Each of the 38 air-conditioned rooms is like a private villa with its own entrance and private balcony opening onto the turbulent Atlantic. Breakfast is an experience, with eggs and fresh fruit tasting as if they were brought directly from the farm to your table. Room service is available, but meals are more enjoyable in the glassed-in dining room where all the windows face the sea.

Dinner is a unique experience, with a cuisine that is a mixture of creole and international specialties. A local musical group plays for dining and dancing on weekend evenings. On Sunday there is a traditional buffet dinner from noon to 3 p.m. The native bar is open daily from 11 a.m. to 10 p.m. (until 1 a.m. on weekends). Friday is creole night, when the chef pulls out all the stops with an array of Puerto Rican dishes, buffet style.

For the shell and fossil collectors, early-morning jaunts along the beach and along the cliffs where the ocean and mountains meet may turn up some interesting finds.

All year, prices are the same—$57 to $65 daily in a single, $60 to $65 in a double; a third person sharing a room pays $10. On the grounds are two swimming pools, one for adults, another for children, and there are two tennis courts free to guests, plus a playground for children.

Parador Montemar, Route 2, km. 125.4 (tel. 891-4383), at Aguadilla, is a good choice for those motorists exploring the west coast of Puerto Rico. It offers a total of 40 pleasantly furnished accommodations, most of which open onto views of the Atlantic. Rates, in effect all year round, are $50 in a single, rising to $60 in a double. Each unit is air-conditioned.

Near the Punta Borinquen golf course, the hotel was built on a land site above the Mona Passage. It is also near one of the finest surfing beaches in Puerto Rico at Rincon, but you'll have to drive to it. On weekends live groups are brought in to entertain the guests, many of whom are native islanders.

Even if you're not staying at Montemar, you might want to visit for lunch, enjoying a meal in one of two restaurants. Open to the trade winds, one of these restaurants is an open-air Bohio with 180° views of the sea. Local dishes, including dark Puerto Rican coffee, are served. During the day you can drive to the mountains and the Taino Indian Ball Park.

Parador Villa Parguera, off Route 304 (tel. 721-2884 in San Juan and 899-3975 in La Parguera). Although the water in the bay alongside this hotel is too polluted for swimming, guests still benefit from a view of the water, a swimming pool, and a pleasantly isolated kind of peacefulness. This parador is known for its seafood dinners, the air-conditioned comfort of most of the rooms, and its location beside the glistening phosphorescent waters of one of the coast's best known bays. The establishment is set behind a white wall on a quiet street. The reception area is in an alcove off the screened-in dining room, where ceiling fans supplement the sea breezes.

Each of the 45 rooms contains a private or semiprivate bath. Prices year round are $52 in either a single or double room with air conditioning. Units without that amenity cost $42. The dining room offers daily specials priced at around

$4.50 each, plus chef's specials of filet of fish stuffed with lobster and shrimp as well as several other dishes.

Parador Vistamar, Box T-38, Quebradillas (tel. 895-2065). High atop a mountain, overlooking greenery and a seascape in the Guajataca area, this parador sits like a sentinel surveying the scene. There are gardens and intricate paths carved into the side of the mountain where you can stroll while you take in the fragrance of the tropical flowers that grow in the area. Or you may choose to search for the calcified fossils which abound on the carved mountainside.

For a unique experience, visitors can try their hand at freshwater fishing in the only river in Puerto Rico with green waters, just down the hill from the hotel. Flocks of rare tropical birds are frequently seen in the nearby mangroves. Whether you are a seasoned professional photographer or just like to tote an Instamatic about with you, you are sure to get some of the best pictures you've ever taken.

A short drive from the hotel will bring you to the popular Punta Borinquen Golf Course. Tennis courts are just down the hill from the inn itself. Sightseeing trips to the nearby Ionospheric Observatory in Arecibo, with the largest radiotelescope in the world, and to Monte Calvario (a replica of Mount Calvary), are side trips available. Another popular visit is to the plaza in the town of Quebradillas, where you can tour the town in a horse-driven coach. Back at the hotel, prepare yourself for a typical Puerto Rican dinner, or choose from the international menu, in the dining room with its view of the ocean.

Rates are in effect all year—$35 daily in a single, $45 in a double. Each additional person sharing a room pays another $12, and children under 12 in the same room stay here free (a maximum of two).

BUDGET ISLAND HOTELS: If you're seeking a holiday "out in the island," but want something far removed from the big, expensive resort hotels, I have a few suggestions. (For some other recommendations, read the list of island guest houses immediately following.)

Borinquen Resorts, Box "G," Ramey Station, at Aguadilla (tel. 890-4560), stands at the northwest "corner" of Puerto Rico, where the Atlantic meets the Caribbean at Ramey on the grounds of a former U.S. Air Force base, next to Borinquen International Airport. The simply furnished hotel features 40 rooms —singles, doubles, and suites. All units are fully carpeted, with air conditioning. At this tourist complex, you can also rent two-bedroom apartments, fully equipped with many conveniences. Among the facilities are a pool for swimming enthusiasts, the largest golf course on the island, tennis courts, a bowling alley, and of course, dining areas.

From September to December, singles pay $33, doubles cost $39.10, and suites run $55. From December to spring, the rates are $44.40 single, $55 double, and $65.50 for suites, which have kitchenettes.

Delicias, Playa de Fajardo (tel. 863-1818), lies right on the waterfront in Fajardo, but not on the beach. Still, it's only ten minutes from the island's finest beach, Luquillo, and not far from El Yunque (rain forest). The bedrooms are very modestly but still comfortably furnished, and all the units are decorated with engravings and paintings by well-known Puerto Rican artists. Year round, singles cost $30 and doubles run $35 to $55. There is a cocktail lounge in the hotel, and good food is served in the restaurant (the owner-manager operates the famous Delicias restaurant). The cuisine is American and international. There is also a courtyard filled with plants. Once this was about the only place to stay in this part of eastern Puerto Rico, but that's all changed now.

Boquemar, P.O. Box 133, Boquerón, Cabo Rojo (tel. 851-2158), lies on Route 101, near Boquerón Beach in the southwest corner of Puerto Rico, between Mayaguez and Ponce. The beach at Boquerón is considered one of the best bathing beaches on the island. The hotel is not right on the beach, but it's just a short walk away. There is also a swimming pool—popular with Puerto Rican families—in back of the hotel. The Boquemar rents out 41 rooms, all air-conditioned. Refrigerators are small but serve the purpose. There is a communal TV set in the lobby, and for dining, several seafood restaurants are in the vicinity. Year-round rates are $35 in a single, rising to $48 in a double.

Copamarina, P.O. Box 589, Route 333, Guanica (tel. 842-8300), in southwest Puerto Rico, also lies between Ponce and Mayaguez. At the Copamarina, you can step out of your room into the warm sand of the private beach. Some say the footprints of the pirate Cofresi can still be seen in the sand. Next to this private beach is Cana Gorda, the best known beach on the south shore, where you can mingle with local people from all over the island who travel here to swim and enjoy the sand. At Cana Gorda, mountains skirt the sea, and you can hike for hours as you collect coral, shells, dried sea urchins, and plenty of volcanic rocks with fossils. The parking lot is a coconut grove offering plenty of shade.

The food at Copamarina is excellent, a combination of international and Puerto Rican cuisine. The personnel know the meaning of courteous and efficient service. The rooms, since they all face the beach, are airy, sunlit, and air-conditioned. The garden surroundings are ideal for strolling in the moonlight, and the long stretch of sand is suitable for beachcombing. All year, rates are the same—$54 daily in a single, $62 in a double.

Monte Río, 17 César Luís González (tel. 829-3705), lies up in the cool mountains of Adjuntas, northwest of Ponce. This is strictly a hotel for the budget-minded who want to get away from the noise and hectic pace of cities. The town is very conservative and closes early. The only diversion other than television and the plaza is the local movie house or cine. Adjuntas is known as the "Town of the Sleeping Giant," named after a mountain that resembles a giant's body lying on his side. The relaxed ambience of Monte Río is welcomed after driving south on the twisting, almost perpendicular mountain roads. The rooms, 23 in all, are simplicity itself, renting year round for $18 daily in a single, $31 in a double. There is a restaurant and bar.

PONCE: A description of the sightseeing possibilities of Ponce is carried in the following section ("Touring the Island"). However, those not going back to San Juan will find some good accommodations in Puerto Rico's second city:

Meliá, 2 Cristina St. (tel. 842-0260), offers southern hospitality. A city hotel, often attracting business people, it has no connection with other hotels in the world bearing the same name. The location is a few steps away from Our Lady of Guadaloupe Cathedral and from the famous Parque de Bombas (the red and black firehouse). The lobby floor and all stairs are covered with Spanish tiles of Moorish design. The desk clerks, oftentimes family members, are well versed in English, and in their charming and courteous way will attend you.

Once you have checked in and parked your car in the lot nearby, a very pleasant surprise awaits you when you open your room door. The central air conditioning is turned on just right for comfort, every room has a television set, and most have a balcony facing either busy Cristina Street or the old plaza.

The rooms are comfortably furnished, pleasant enough. Year-round rates are $40 daily in a single, $55 in a double. Breakfast is served on a rooftop terrace with a good view of Ponce, and the hotel's dining room serves some of the best cuisine in town.

El Coche Hotel, La Rambla (tel. 842-9607), stands on Highway 14 in the northern section of Ponce known as "La Rambla." It's a commercial hotel—not too fancy, not too big. But each room has air conditioning and a private bath.

The units have been recently redecorated. Prices are $22 in a single, from $28 to $35 in a double or twin, tax included. El Coche (The Coach) restaurant next door is run by the same management, offering German, international, and Puerto Rican dishes.

If you're touring in Ponce, the best luncheon stopover is **Lydia's,** 52 Ramal (tel. 844-3933), in the Los Caobos Shopping Center. Open daily from 11:30 a.m. to 10 p.m., Lydia serves some of the best seafood not only in Ponce but on the island. Her reputation has grown steadily over the years. Even though her prices are higher than many local establishments, the food is well worth the cost: about $20 and up for a complete meal.

The location is about five minutes from the center of Ponce in a nondescript shopping center. The area is called Los Caobos. The place is very crowded with local business people at lunch, but dinner is much quieter. It is plain, plain, in decor. To reach her place, one must ask directions or else take a cab.

Some of the best dishes aren't on the menu. These are likely to include empanadillas filled with lobster and a side dish known as manpostiao (a rice dish with red beans and sausage). Tostones (fried plantains) are served almost automatically. Lydia's lobster deserves its fine reputation, and you can also have it prepared in a number of other ways, including in garlic sauce. Her octopus creole is excellent, as are her shrimps in butter sauce. Perhaps you'll try her "chili conch." Her flan is superb, and it comes in four different flavors: pineapple, coconut, cheese, and vanilla.

If you're heading east from Ponce, I suggest a stopover in Salinas, which is known for its seafood restaurants. One of the best of these is **Ladi's Place,** Route 701, km. 1 (tel. 824-2035). Here the specialty is whole fried snapper (chillo) and fried sliced grouper, both done *al mojo,* which is in a tasty onion sauce. They also serve the usual variety of seafood and asopaos (seafood stews). But their fresh fish is the best. Also better than I've had elsewhere out on the island are their surrillitos (corn sticks), a staple in Puerto Rican restaurants. They are normally quite dry and need to be dipped in a sauce to be appreciated. At Ladi's, they are plump and moist, slightly sweet, and difficult to stop eating.

The setting at Ladi's is another plus, since it lies right on the water. You can dine on a terrace overlooking the sea. The whole experience of eating there is always a pleasure. It is recommended more for lunch or at sunset when the view can be appreciated. The menu is printed on a giant wooden board in the shape of a fish. Prices are cheap, a complete meal rarely costing more than $18. It is open Monday to Thursday from 8 a.m. to 8 p.m., on Friday and Sunday to 9 p.m., and on Saturday to 10 p.m.

MAYAGUEZ: Overnighting in Puerto Rico's "third city" has some interesting possibilities, as reflected below:

Hilton International Mayaguez (tel. 834-7575) is a country club–style hotel set on 20 acres of lushly planted tropical gardens. Reasonable in price, it is nevertheless the finest hotel to be found in western Puerto Rico. Its grounds have been designated as an adjunct to the nearby Mayaguez Institute of Tropical Agriculture by the U.S. Department of Agriculture. There are no fewer than five species of palm trees, including the royal palm (native to Puerto Rico), eight kinds of bougainvillea, and numerous species of rare flora. If you want to get deep into botany, the nearby Mayaguez Institute of Tropical Agriculture has the largest collection of tropical plants in the western hemisphere.

The hotel stands at the edge of the city, and can be reached from San Juan after a scenic 2½-hour drive. Or else it's a half-hour flight aboard either CrownAir or Prinair. It's also possible to take a Capitol Airlines flight from San Juan to Borinquen Field (the Hilton is a 30-minute limousine drive away).

Built in 1964, the hotel has been completely refurbished, and in fact is better than ever. Some 150 well-appointed rooms open onto an Olympic swimming pool. Many units contain private balconies. Year-round rates in effect depend on whether you take a standard, superior, or a deluxe accommodation. Singles cost from $116 to $136; doubles, $135 to $160. MAP is another $40 per person daily.

The hotel is very sports oriented. Not only does it offer excellent courts, but there are also physical fitness trails. Near the hotel is a small, well-stocked lake filled with Congo perch. It's possible, if enough time is allowed, that the chef might prepare your catch for the evening. Deep-sea fishing can also be arranged, as can skindiving, surfing, and scuba-diving. An 18-hole golf course lies at Borinquen Field, a former SAC airbase, about 30 minutes from the Hilton. Of course, some of the most beautiful beaches on the island can be reached in an easy drive. Boqueron, for example, is a four-mile stretch adorned with coconut palms.

The elegant Rôtisserie Dining Room turns out the best food on the west coast of Puerto Rico. The food is a blend of Puerto Rican and international specialties. There is even a section called flambé fireworks which features "El Pescador," fresh lobster and jumbo shrimp sauteed with local herbs. Freshly caught fish of the day is also a specialty. The chef also prepares international beef recipes featured in sister Hilton hotels around the world.

The Hilton is also the entertainment center of the city. On Saturday, a "Wild West" barbecue is staged, including grilled spareribs and corn on the cob, along with cold beer. The cost is only $15 per person ($8 for children). Otherwise, there is always something happening in the Cacique Lounge, including such events as a merengue contest. One night a week is ladies' night, when female guests don't pay.

La Primavera Beach Hotel, Barrero-Rincon, P.O. Box 99, lies to the northwest of Mayaguez. It features studio as well as deluxe apartments and two big beach houses of three bedrooms and three baths, large, well-equipped kitchens, dining and living rooms, and patios or balconies over the water. Each unit has a balcony facing the beach, a living room, kitchen, bedroom, and bath. The studio can accommodate two adults comfortably; the deluxe, two adults and two children. The beach houses are suitable for families or groups of friends, usually attracting professional people. The price of each accommodation includes bed linen, towels, kitchen equipment, cooking utensils, glasses, and flatware.

The ambience of the hotel is a mixture of European warmth, Puerto Rican flavor, and American budget consciousness. In winter, the charge is $245 per week or $42 daily for one of the deluxe apartments, $195 weekly ($35 daily) for a studio apartment. An extra bed can be placed in each unit for $10. The charge for a beach house is $420 per week, $65 daily. *In summer, rates are 20% cheaper.*

The building appears to be encrusted in the mountain and faces the Caribbean Sea. The structure is of Mediterranean architecture and is surrounded by bougainvillea and a myriad of other tropical flowers and greenery. There is also a four-acre landscaped garden yielding a selection of exotic fruit, which is available in season to the hotel guests. The beach has reefs for snorkeling, smooth sand for sunning, and Sailfish boats available for rent for a modest fee.

GUEST HOUSES: That hidden little guest house "out in the island" may appeal to a certain type of traveler interested in a more offbeat experience. If so, I have a few recommendations:

Caribe Playa Resort, at Guardarraya, Patillas, Route 3, km. 112, in the southern edge of Puerto Rico, appeals to nature lovers and environmentalists. The 26-unit resort is sheltered in tropical greenery (45 acres) with a coconut farm, just 75 feet from a crescent-shaped Caribbean beach. The reefs at this beach make it a good spot for snorkeling, scuba-diving, surf fishing, or just swimming. Walking along the shore in a spot nicknamed "Scrounge Point," you can collect numerous shapes of seashells and odd-shaped colored glass and stone formations washed ashore.

To get to the Caribe Playa Resort, you must either rent a car (a 1½-hour drive from San Juan), use a publico, or make arrangements with the management. However you choose to get there, your visit, with some of the most beautiful and interesting scenery on the island, will be well worth the trip.

Accommodations are in three modern two-level breezeway-style concrete buildings. The interior-room units are large and well appointed, with private toilets and showers. Up to four persons can be accommodated in each of these units. Outdoor patios and balconies come with each rental. Seabeach rooms cost $42 nightly, whether occupied by one or two persons. For seabeach efficiencies, however, the charge is $55 for one or two persons, $68 for three guests, and $80 for quartets. Children under 6 sharing a room stay free. Rates apply year round. These rates do not include government tax and service. Call 212/988-1801 in New York for Stateside information.

Posada Porlamar, Route 304, La Parguera, Lajas (tel. 899-4015), offers life in a simple, informal fishing village where you can enjoy the restful tempo of the Caribbean. That and all the modern conveniences you want in a vacation are what you find at the Posada Porlamar (Guest House by the Sea).

In the Parguera section of Lajas in the southwestern part of the island, the area is famous for its Phosphorescent Bay and good fishing, especially snapper. The guest house is near several fishing villages and other points of interest.

If you like to collect seashells, you can beachcomb. Other collectors' items found here are fossilized crustacea and marine plants. If you prefer fishing, you can rent boats at the nearby villages, and even bring your catch back to the guest house, where you can prepare it in your own kitchenette.

The drive to Lajas is several hours from San Juan, but if you prefer, you can fly from San Juan to Mayaguez and then take the much shorter drive to Lajas. Porlamar has only 13 rooms, so early reservations are necessary to ensure a booking. All the rooms are air-conditioned and include kitchen facilities. All year, rates are the same: $32 daily in a single, $40 in a double.

Villa Antonio, P.O. Box 68, Route 115, km. 12.3, at Rincon (tel. 823-2645), offers air-conditioned cottages and apartments by the sea with sand at your doorstep, privacy, and tropical beauty around you. On the westernmost point of the island, Rincon has one of the most exotic beaches on the island, drawing surfers from around the world. The most sensible way to get there is by way of Mayaguez airport, just 15 minutes by car from Villa Antonio. Facilities at this guest complex incude a children's playground, two tennis courts, and a swimming pool. Surfing and fishing can be done just outside your front door. And you can bring your catch right into your cottage and prepare a fresh seafood dinner in your own kitchenette.

All year, the rates charged by the hosts, Ilia and Hector Ruiz, are the same, with two-bedroom units renting for $52 to $70 daily (the latter for the beachfront properties) for up to four persons. A one-bedroom apartment with kitchenette rents for $36 daily for two persons, $40 for three. A single with kitchenette costs $28 daily. Tax and an energy surcharge are extra.

8. Dorado

The name itself evokes a kind of magic. Along the north shore of Puerto Rico, about a 40-minute drive west of the capital, a world of luxury resorts and villa complexes unfolds. The big properties of the Dorado Beach Hotel and

Cerromar Beach Hotel, occupy choice real estate in this section of Puerto Rico, enjoying white sandy beaches.

Many clients book into either of these hotels directly, stopping off in San Juan only to arrive and leave by plane. Others, particularly first-timers, may want to spend a day or so sightseeing and shopping in San Juan before heading for one of these complete resort properties, since, chances are, once there they'll never leave the grounds. The hotels are self-contained, with beach, swimming, golf, tennis, dining, and nightlife possibilities.

Dorado Beach Hotel (tel. 796-1600) sprawls across a 1000-acre coconut and citrus plantation, filled with palms, pine trees, and purple bougainvillea, and a two-mile stretch of sandy ocean beach. It's 20 miles west of San Juan. Two side-by-side 18-hole championship golf courses, designed by Robert Trent Jones, are its big draw (see "The Sporting Life," below). Tennis buffs find seven all-weather courts, and there are the expected swimming pools, as well as a private airfield and a casino. The place is so large, in fact, that during the day guests can bicycle all over the grounds.

The present hotel opened in 1958, and many repeat guests have been going back ever since that time. After several owners, Hyatt Hotels Corporation is in charge. When this book was written, the papers for the transfer from the previous owner had just been signed, but plans were being drawn for a renovation costing between $20 and $30 million, to be distributed between this property and the neighboring Cerromar Beach Hotel. Although nothing is ever definite about the scheduled opening of Caribbean resort properties, at press time Hyatt planned for the major work to be completed in time for the winter season of 1985–1986. Before you go, check with your travel agent or call Hyatt's reservation system toll free at 800/228-9000. In any event, Hyatt plans to keep basically the same format that made the property famous.

Rooms are available on the beach or in villas tucked in and around the lushly planted grounds. The villas bordering the golf course fairways are concealed by verdant foliage. You pay for what you get here, but there are a lot of extras. In winter, standard singles rent for $250 daily, going up to $320 deluxe. Doubles range from $280 to $310, with triples going for $65 additional per person, all tariffs on the MAP. Casitas, private beach houses, cost $380 daily in a single, $400 in a double, also on the MAP. *In summer, singles on the MAP can stay here for $160 to $190; doubles go for $190 to $230, and triples to a peak $275. Casitas cost $225 in a single, $250 in a double, all MAP.*

Breakfast can be taken on your private balcony and lunch on an outdoor ocean terrace. Dinner is served in a three-tiered main dining room where you can watch the surf. Frankly, I prefer Su Casa, although MAP guests have to pay extra for this. It's the original plantation house, a Spanish hacienda with tile courtyards. Diners enjoy the candlelit tables and the serenade of strolling guitarists. The restaurant may be closed in summer, however. Dorado chefs have won many awards and are considered among the finest in the Caribbean.

Cerromar Beach Hotel (tel. 796-1010) stands near its elegant sister, the Dorado Beach Hotel, although occupying its own sandy crescent beach. Cerromar is a combination of two words—*cerro* (mountain) and *mar* (sea)—and true to its name, you're surrounded by mountains and ocean. Approximately 22 miles west of San Juan, Cerromar shares a 1000-acre estate with the Dorado, enjoying the two 18-hole Robert Trent Jones golf courses. Guests of Cerromar have the use of the facilities at the next-door hotel. A shuttle bus runs back and forth between the two resorts every half hour.

Every room or suite has a sweeping ocean view. The rooms have luxury appointments and are well maintained. Naturally, they are air-conditioned and contain private baths. *In summer, attractive package deals are offered (ask your* *travel agent). Otherwise, you pay $95 daily in a standard single or double, June 1 to October 1. Shoulder-season tariffs are quoted too—that is, from April 1 to June 1 and October 1 to December 20: $130 daily in a single or double, with extra persons paying $35 in each triple or quad. MAP is an additional $35 per person daily.* In winter, guests on the MAP pay $200 in a single, $230 in a double, $285 in a triple, and $340 in a quad.

Like its sister resort, this property was acquired by the Hyatt Hotels Corporation in 1985. Although Hyatt's plans weren't known at press time, company sources, as already mentioned, stressed their willingness to invest between $20 and $30 million in the total renovations of this and the Dorado Beach Hotel. The old format, which Hyatt claims was the key to the resort's appeal, will be maintained as strictly as possible. One thing is true: whoever maintains the property, the lush vegetation surrounding the two hotels is likely to be even better by the time of your visit.

Nightly live entertainment lights up El Yunque Lounge and El Bucanero Terrace. El Coquí (see my nightlife recommendations) is even livelier as a disco. For a full-course evening, elegant meals and dancing add to the excitement of the first-rate shows at Club Cerromar, the supper club next door to the casino. Alternatively, you can make a reservation and go over to the already-described Su Casa at Dorado Beach. The big dining room, the Surf Club, is at beach level.

In addition to 14 tennis courts, there is a children's day camp, drawing kids aged 5 through 13. The camp is open from mid-June to Labor Day, at Christmas, and at Easter. While the children are at play, you can enjoy the beach, the swimming pools, bicycle riding, or just plain sunning. Snorkeling and scuba equipment are available for a reasonable fee.

9. Palmas del Mar

It's called a "new American Riviera" in the making. The resort residential community of Palmas del Mar lies on the island's southeastern shore, 45 miles from San Juan, outside the town of Humacao, about an hour's drive from the San Juan airport. It's also possible to fly in from San Juan; a CrownAir craft lands at the resort's small airstrip.

Once there, you'll find the place so vast you'll need a rental car to reach your friends staying somewhere else on the grounds. Hiking on the resort's grounds is another favorite activity. There is a forest preserve with giant ferns, orchids, and hanging vines.

The resort also has one of the most action-packed sports programs in the Caribbean (refer to "The Sporting Life" section, coming up, for more details).

ACCOMMODATIONS: Palmas del Mar, P.O. Box 2020 (tel. 852-6000), lies on 2700 acres, a former sugar plantation including a stretch of the Caribbean coastline. Guests are housed in villas built around a marina, a tennis complex, and a championship golf course. You have a choice of either rooms or villas, depending on your space needs. Within the same complex are some privately owned condominium homes which the landlords make available to guests when they're not living in them.

In addition to the villas, guests can stay at the luxurious Palmas Inn or the newer Candelero Hotel, which opened in the '80s.

The **Palmas Inn** is a gem, containing only 23 deluxe junior suites, each with a panoramic vista of sea and mountains. The inn also shelters El Jumacao restaurant and La Galería lounge, previewed below. Accommodations are decorated in a Spanish antique style, and baths are designed so that you can sit in the tub while drinking in a view of the Caribbean. Your continental breakfast is left on a service counter in the entrance hall. The inn's decor evokes that of a Mediterranean villa, with a spacious, airy feeling. Most rooms are rented as a double, costing from $220, EP, in winter, *dropping to around $150 daily in summer.* Singles, however, are accepted at $190 daily in winter, *falling to $130 in summer.* For breakfast and dinner, add $35 per person.

At the **Candelero Hotel,** rooms come in a variety of sizes, some with king-size beds. High cathedral ceilings accentuate the roominess which is further extended by patios on the ground floor and balconies on the top floor. Room colors are light—pastels offset by strong colors on bedspreads—with original watercolors decorating the walls. The Candelero lobby, in common with that of the Palmas Inn, has a very open feeling. All around, the rattan furniture is of Puerto Rican make, the same style and quality that has marked the Palmas Inn since it opened in 1974. In all, there are 102 rooms and mini-suites. Its main dining spot is Las Garzas restaurant, previewed below. Many of the units have private balconies, with views of the sea. The beach and golf course are near at hand. The hotel doesn't have the charm of the Palmas Inn, but many of its units are cheaper. In winter, a single rents for $140 to $180 daily, while a double goes for $150 to $190. MAP is another $35 per person. *Summer tariffs are lowered to $130 to $175 daily in a single, from $140 to $185 in a double.*

Candelero Villas, adjacent to the hotel, might be more suitable if you're a group. The management rents out one-, two-, and three-bedroom villas, each handsomely furnished and well equipped. Accommodations are in attached houses, and these villas are privately owned. However, when the owners are away, villas are rented out to transient guests. Villas overlook the beach, the golf course, or else are built on a hillside overlooking the tennis courts. Those called "Harborside," naturally, overlook the waterfront.

In winter a one-bedroom villa for up to two persons costs $230 daily; two bedrooms, $320; and three bedrooms, $420, the latter suitable for up to six persons. *In summer, rates go down: a one-bedroom costs $200; two bedrooms, $310; and three bedrooms, $410.*

Rates quoted are individual tariffs. However, most guests at Palmas del Mar book in here on a package plan, perhaps taking one of the sports options such as golf. Most packages are for seven days and six nights. Reservations can be made by calling Palmas del Mar's New York reservation office toll free (800/221-4874). In New York state, call 212/889-0628.

WHERE TO DINE: Moods for dining come in a wide variety, depending on which "village" you're staying in. Paolo's Ristorante Italiano is arguably the best, serving northern Italian food, but the choice is vast. If management continues its policy of a dine-around plan, MAP guests need not be bored. On my most recent visit, MAP guests could select from a choice of six specialty restaurants on the grounds, as well as five restaurants off the property. They could also enjoy five theme nights, including a Western night and a Mexican night.

Paolo's Ristorante Italiano, at the Palmas del Mar complex at Humacao (tel. 850-3450), is an open-air selection in the resort's "Sun Fun Hut," serving a strictly northern Italian cuisine. It is a venture for tennis entrepreneur and former Italian Davis Cup star Paolo Bodo. Bodo claims that his is the only Puerto Rico restaurant serving *real* northern Italian food. "The Italian restaurants in San Juan are all southern Italian, overlaid with U.S.–Puerto Rican flavors." The bar opens onto a deck for drinks or barbecues, extending almost to the beach. For most of the day, a snackbar attached to the rear of the kitchen serves pizza and heroes to guests in the pool area, abutting the restaurant. Snacks are served between 11 a.m. and 4 p.m. The restaurant opens at 7 p.m. and stays open until the last guests leave. A complete meal will easily cost from $28, plus your wine. In the bar after 11 p.m., snacks are also served, a sort of after-theater supper. They also offer special ice creams—some that look like pizza or spaghetti.

Adjoining the restaurant, actually a part of it, is **Avo's Piano Bar,** where Avo Uvezian entertains nightly from 8. You can also enjoy lunch here, including pizzas, hot heroes, and a good salad bar, costing from $12.

The premier restaurant of the resort is **El Jumacao,** the four-star dining room in the Palmas Inn. It sits atop a 100-foot promontory overlooking the sea, and in the distance you can see the offshore island of Vieques. Portuguese blue and white tiles, specially made in Lisbon, enhance the decor. The restaurant comes complete with painted ceiling fans and a wide veranda. On Friday there is a seafood buffet, and on Saturday the staff decorates the restaurant with palm fronds for a Caribbean buffet with creole specialties. Buffets cost about $32 per person; otherwise you can count on spending from $40 if you drop in for an à la carte dinner.

Las Garzas is the outstanding restaurant in the Candelero Hotel. Cooled by trade winds, it overlooks a courtyard and swimming pool, and is an ideal choice for either breakfast, lunch, or dinner. Lunches cost from $12 and up, and are likely to include sandwiches and fish and chips. If you want heartier fare, you can ask for the Puerto Rican specialty of the day, perhaps red snapper in garlic butter, preceded by black bean soup.

Dinner is more elaborate, costing from $25. Perhaps you'll begin with oysters over rock salt, following with stuffed eye round or perhaps prime rib of beef au jus. The chef always prepares the catch of the day, and you can invariably count on a good filet mignon.

Independently operated, **La Marina** is a good French restaurant standing at the marina. It serves until 11 p.m., having opened at 9 a.m. for breakfast. Martine and Robert Gaffori operate this restaurant in a boat dock–style room with a plank floor and lattice ceiling. Lobster is prepared five ways here, and you can expect a classic repertoire of French dishes, including coq au vin, entrecôte Bordelaise, escargots, and lobster bisque. Count on spending from $30 per person. Lunch will cost less: around $15. You can order their French onion soup or a savory fish soup that evokes those you are likely to find on the Mediterranean. They also serve salads and burgers at noontime.

La Cantina at Monte Sol is popular with a younger crowd. Under heavy wooden beams (or at an outside table) diners enjoy chili and other Mexican dishes Wednesday to Monday from 6:30 to 10:30 p.m. Live music is often played. Sometimes Monday is devoted to a special Mexican fiesta. The cost is about $15 and up for dinner.

The **Café de la Pace** is also to be considered Evoking Old Spain, it occupies a village square setting in the evening to serve its buffets. Here, families bring their children to enjoy hamburgers, crêpes, and spaghetti, dinners costing from $15. Each night a different Puerto Rican specialty is featured.

These are only a preview of the dining possibilities. You will discover several more on your own. All the restaurants are open during the winter season; however, in summer, only three or four may be fully functioning.

AFTER DARK: The most romantic spot in Palmas del Mar is **La Galería,** a lounge bar where guests can drink and dance to live music five nights a week, Wednesday through Sunday, from 8 p.m. to 2 a.m. Live music is performed by the house band, "Coffee." The $8 minimum includes your first drink. The location is adjoining El Jumacao restaurant in the Palmas Inn.

The **Palmas Casino,** next door, is one of the newest in Puerto Rico. It is open from 6 p.m. to 2 a.m., offering blackjack, roulette, and dice. Cash is available on credit cards.

10. Touring the Island

Even though Puerto Rico is an island barely 100 miles long by 35 miles wide, it offers a variety of scenery, from the rain forests and lush mountains of El Yunque to the lime deposits of the north and the arid areas of the south shore, where irrigation is a necessity and the cactus grows wild. In Puerto Rico you will find some of the most complicated geological formations in the world.

While driving on the mountain roads of Puerto Rico, blow your horn before every turn, contrary to urban zone regulations. Commercial road signs are forbidden, so make sure you take along a map and this guide to inform you of restaurants, hotels, and possible points of interest. The kilometer information refers to the roadside markers painted on a white background with black letters telling you the kilometer and hectometer.

Puerto Rico is a subtropical country, yet you can see seasonal changes. In November the sugarcane fields are in bloom, and in January and February the flowering trees along the roads are covered with red and orange blossoms.

When spring comes, the Puerto Rican oak is covered with delicate pink flowers and the African tulip tree is ablaze with its deep-red blossoms. Summer is the glorious flamboyant time when the roadsides seem as if on fire.

A HALF-DAY TRIP AROUND SAN JUAN: I'll suggest a number of itineraries, beginning with a half-day trip around the metropolitan San Juan area up to a rum distillery, Isla de Cobras, Loiza Aldea, and Boca de Cangrejos.

From San Juan, take Route 2 up to km. 6.4. To the right you will see a small park containing the ruins of the house erected in 1509 by Juan Ponce de Leon in Caparra, the first Spanish settlement in Puerto Rico.

Continue on Route 2 until you reach Bayamon. Facing the town plaza you have the old church, built in 1877, an excellent example of period architecture.

Afterward, you can then continue on Route 167 toward Cantano, turning left at km. 5.2. Within a short distance you will find yourself in the **Barrilito Rum Distillery.** To the left you will see a 200-year-old mansion with grand outdoor staircases leading to the second-floor galleries. This is the original mansion of the Santa Ana plantation (which once covered 2400 acres) and is still occupied by members of the family, owners of the distillery. There's an office on the right, near a tower which was originally a windmill from which the entire valley and bay could be seen. It was from this vantage point that a former head of the family, as a boy, observed the bombing of San Juan by Admiral Sampson's fleet, and the cannon blasts from El Morro in 1898.

Back on Route 167, drive until you reach Catano, then take Route 165 going west and turning left (hugging the shoreline) until you reach **Isla de Cabras.** From this point, you can see the entire bay of San Juan. At the end of the road in Isla de Cabras you will come upon Fort Canuelo, erected in 1610 and reconstructed in 1625 after the Dutch attack on Puerto Rico. Originally built on what was then a tiny islet, the fort seemed to be emerging from the water. Today, however, because of modern landfill techniques it is connected to Isla de Cabras. Picnic facilities are available. Here, the breezes are cool and you have a good view of San Juan Bay and El Morro, built in 1539.

On the way back, drive toward Catano where you can take a short ferry ride to Old San Juan. Boats leave every 15 minutes,, taking the same time to cross each way. The fare is 20¢ per person, round trip. A more extensive tour of the bay is offered by the Port Authority, leaving from the San Juan Terminal only on Sunday and holidays at 2:30 and 4:30 p.m. The tour takes you near the Coast Guard base, and you have a view of the governor's palace, the San Juan door (Puerta de San Juan), and El Morro. The trip lasts 1½ hours and the price is $1.50 for adults and $1 for children.

From Catano, continue on Route 24 until the Caparra intersection on Route 20; then take Route 20 to Guaynabo until you reach Route 21. After going past the psychiatric hospital, the medical center, and the state penitentiary, continue until the Río Piedras intersection, turning left toward Carolina by way of Avenida 65 de Infantería (Route 3), from which you can see El Yunque. When you reach km. 18.3, turn onto the bridge and stay to the left to reach **Loiza Aldea.** If you are in Puerto Rico between July 19 and 29, the trip to Loiza Aldea will be quite an experience. This is when the whole town comes out to celebrate the feast day of its patron saint (Santiago Apostol). The festivities are very unusual and bizarre, a mixture of pagan Afro-Caribbean and Christian elements forming part of the celebration and carnival.

The Church of San Patricio (St. Patrick), dating from 1645, in Loiza Aldea is in front of the road that leads you to the barge for crossing the Río Grande de Loiza. It is a bit of a thrill to cross this river (with your car) on a barge propelled by a man with ropes. Continue for half an hour on a sandy (but hard) road lined with coconut palms and shady trees until you reach the Nautical Club, then on to Santurce and San Juan.

RAIN FORESTS AND BEACHES: From San Juan, if you have two days to explore, you can take the following itineraries, going on the first day to Trujillo Alto, Gurabo, El Yunque (rain forest), Luquillo Beach, and Fajardo. Perhaps you'll find the makings of a picnic lunch at one of the thatched stands along the road, eating it at El Yunque (there is also a restaurant in the rain forest—see "Dining Out in Puerto Rico"). On the second day you can explore Fajardo, Naguabo, Humacao, Yabucoa, Patillas, and Caguas, returning to San Juan in the late afternoon.

Water is considered one of Puerto Rico's most important resources; the other is its fertile soil. During the period of a year, 400 billion cubic feet of rain fall on the island. The Spaniards nicknamed the island "The Land of Rivers." To harness this water for public consumption, many dams were built, creating lakes which can be visited.

From San Juan, go to Río Piedras and take Route 3 (Avenida 65 de Infantería, named after the Puerto Rican regiment which battled in World War II and in Korea). Turn, heading south on Route 181 toward Trujillo Alto, then take Route 851 up to Route 941. At the end of the valley you can spot the **Lake of Loiza.** Houses can be seen nestled on the surrounding hills. You can even see local farmers (jibaros) riding their horse laden with produce, on the way to and from the marketplace. The lake is surrounded by mountains.

Your next stop is the town of **Gurabo.** This is tobacco country and you'll know you are nearing the town from the sweet aroma enveloping it (tobacco smells sweet before it's harvested). Part of the town of Gurabo is set on the side of a mountain, and the streets are made up of steps. One street has as many as 128 steps.

You will leave the town by way of Route 30. Then get on Route 185 north, then Route 186 south. This road has views of the ocean beyond the valleys. You will at this stage be driving on the lower section of the Caribe Experimental Forest; the vegetation is dense and you'll be surrounded by giant ferns. The brooks descending from El Yunque become small waterfalls on both sides of the road. If you have plans to have lunch at El Yunque, turn to go up on Route 191.

At about 25 miles east of San Juan, **El Yunque** consists of about 28,000 acres and is the only tropical forest among those in the U.S. National Forest system. It is said to contain some 240 different tree species native to the area (only half a dozen of these are actually found on the mainland). In this world of cedars and satinwood (draped in tangles of vines), you'll hear chirping birds, see wild orchids, and perhaps hear the song of the tree frog, the coquí. The entire forest is a bird sanctuary, and may be the last retreat of the rare Puerto Rican parrot.

El Yunque is 3493 feet high, and the peak of El Toro rises 3526 feet. You know you'll be showered upon, as more than 100 billion gallons of rain fall on the forest annually. However, the showers are brief, and there are many shelters.

You might go first to the Visitor Center, at km. 11.6. It is open daily from 9 a.m. to 5:30 p.m., and guides here will give lectures and show slides. Groups, if arranged in advance, can go on guided hikes.

To make your way back, head north along Route 191, connecting with Route 3. If you drive east for five miles, you will reach **Luquillo Beach,** lying about 30 miles east of San Juan.

Edged by a vast coconut grove, this crescent-shaped beach is not only the best in Puerto Rico, it's one of the finest in the Caribbean. You pay to enter with your car, and you're allowed to rent a locker, take a shower, and have a place to change into your bathing suit or bikini. Luquillo gets very crowded on weekends, and if possible I suggest a weekday visit when you'll have more sand to yourself. Picnic tables are available as well.

The beach is open from 9 a.m. to 6 p.m. daily. It is closed on Monday, however. If Monday is a holiday, then the beach will shut down on Tuesday that week. Before entering the beach, you may want to stop at one of the roadside thatched huts, selling Puerto Rican snacks, the makings for your picnic. (I had a similar suggestion for eating at El Yunque, of course.)

Continuing east, Route 3 leads to **Fajardo,** a fishing port hotly contested in the Spanish-American War. Fishermen and sailors are attracted to its shores and to nearby **Las Croabas,** which has a lot of native fish restaurants. Puerto Ricans are fond of giving nicknames to people and places. For many years, the residents of Fajardo have been called "cariduros" ("the hard-faced ones"). However, don't be misled by that. The people here are very friendly.

At Fajardo you can also rent boats or take the ferry ride to the islands of Vieques and Culebra (see "The Offshore Islands").

On the second day, you can continue south on Route 3, following the Caribbean coastline. At **Cayo Lobos,** not far from the Fajardo port, the Atlantic meets the Caribbean. Here, the vivid colors of the Caribbean seem subdued compared to those of the ocean.

Go across the town of Ceiba, near the Roosevelt Navy Base, to reach **Naguabo Beach,** where you can have coffee and "pastelillos de chapin," pastry turnovers used as tax payments in Spanish colonial days. At km. 70.9, briefly detour to Naguabo and enjoy the scented shady laurel trees from India in the town's plaza.

Continue on Route 3, going through **Humacao** and its sugarcane fields. When the cane blooms around November and December, the tops of the fields change colors according to the time of day. Humacao is of little interest, but it has a balneario-equipped beach. From here you can detour to the 2800-acre resort, Palmas del Mar, already described.

After the stopover, you can continue until the town of Yabucoa, nestled among hills. The road suddenly opens up through **Cerro** (mountain) **La Pandura,** giving you some of the most spectacular sights in Puerto Rico. Take note of the giant boulders, beyond which you will see the Caribbean.

After passing the town of Maunabo along Route 181 (a tree-lined road which runs next to Lake Patillas), stay on the highway until you reach San Lorenzo, across the mountains. You then take Route 183 to reach Caguas, then Route 1 back into San Juan.

PINEAPPLES AND COFFEE PLANTATIONS: To take the trip outlined below takes two days, as you cross an extraordinary limestone region. However, the itinerary can be cut down to one day if you eliminate a stay at the coffee plantation.

The trip takes you across the famous "Karst" district in Puerto Rico, one of the most developed regions of this type in the world. This area was formed by the wearing down of limestone by acids in the water, leaving a maze of deep fissures and mounds. Some of the depressions in the area are 400 feet across and as deep as 160 feet. The radiotelescope in nearby Arecibo is built inside one of these craters, more than 300 feet deep and 1300 feet wide. Underground rivers are sometimes formed in this type of geological environment. An example of this is the Tanama River, which emerges and disappears at five different places.

From San Juan, take Route 2 heading west toward Manati, after which you will pass the pineapple region. At km. 57.9, turn onto Route 140 south to Florida. At km. 25.5 you will find a coffee cooperative where during harvest time the beans are processed, ground, and packed. At km. 30.7, turn right toward Hacienda Rosas. A coffee plantation is interesting at all times, but especially around harvest time (from September to December, sometimes as late as January) when the pickers, gathered in groups, walk under the bushes and pick the crimson beans while other workers process the already-picked yield.

Continuing, take Route 141 to Jayuya, where you can stay at the Parador Gripiñas (refer to "Hotels Out in the Island").

After a restful day there, take Route 141 north until you are back on route 140. Head west on Route 140 until you pass Caonillas Lake. There, turn onto Route 111 west, go across the town of Utuado, and continue to km. 12.5. Here you will find the **Taino Indian Ceremonial Ball Park.** Archeological clues date this site to approximately two centuries before the discovery of the New World. It is believed that Indian Chief Guarionex gathered his subjects on this site to celebrate rituals and practice sports. Set on a 13-acre field surrounded by trees are some 14 vertical monoliths with colorful petroglyphs, all arranged around a central sacrificial stone monument. The ball complex also includes a museum. It is open from 9 a.m. to 5 p.m., charging no admission. There is also a gallery, Herencia Indígena, where visitors can purchase Indian relics at very reasonable prices, incuding the sought-after Cemi (Taino Indian idols) and the famous little frog, the coquí.

Continue next on Route 111 up to Route 129 north and head toward Arecibo (going across the Karst region) until you reach km. 13.6. Take route 489 south to La Cueva de la Luz (Cave of Light).

Next, follow Route 489 until the Barrio Aibonito, Pagan sector. If you have any doubts, ask anyone for **"La Cueva de Pagan Pagan"** (Pagan Pagan's cave). A narrow road will lead you, only to end at a general store where anyone will find Pagan for you. Only the agile and those who like to explore should venture inside the cave. The cave is lit by daylight, but the floor is rough and irregular. Women should wear slacks and possibly sneakers or rubbersoles. There are no bats in the cave. Inside, a stone vessel contains fresh water which some believe has rejuvenating qualities. Other caves in this area have not been explored fully, but Indian relics have been found. Return by way of Route 489 to Route 129 north, to Arecibo.

The **Arecibo Observatory,** referred to earlier, is a 35-minute drive south from the commercial city of Arecibo. Take Routes 129, 635, and 625. Operated by Cornell University, this is the largest radar-radiotelescope on earth. The grounds are open to the public on Sunday only from 2 to 4:30 p.m. On a site of 20 acres, the reflector is a curving expanse of some 40,000 aluminum panels which have been installed over a sinkhole 300 feet deep and 1300 feet wide. The observatory is operated by Cornell University for the National Science Foundation and carries out research in the fields of astronomy and atmospheric science. For more information, write to Cornell University, P.O. Box 995, Arecibo, PR 00613.

After you return to Arecibo, you can take Route 2 east back to San Juan.

A FOUR-DAY TRIP: More ambitious than the itineraries considered so far, this next trip takes you to the west coast and south on the island:

On the first day, follow Route 2 from San Juan west up to **Guajataca.** Just before you reach km. 103.4, you will spot a sign for the Guajataca recreation area. Make a right turn and staay on the road to the parking area.

Go back to Route 2 and to the Guajataca Beach. It is so fine a beach you may want to stay there for at least one more day. (The Parador Guajataca is just above the hill from the beach.)

When you decide to continue, take Route 2 up to km. 91 and turn toward the south, across the Karst region (see the previous tour) until you reach manmade Guajataca Lake. Follow the lake's shoreline for about four kilometers and turn left at km. 19 to Route 455 until you reach a bridge spanning the Guajataca River, which runs through the lush mountainside.

Return by way of Route 119 and continue toward San Sebastian and to Route 109 across coffee plantations to Anasco. Turn onto Route 2 and head for Mayaguez.

Mayaguez

On your second day you can explore what Puerto Ricans have nicknamed "The Sultan of the West." This busy port city, not architecturally remarkable, is the third largest on the island. Once considered the needlework capital of the island, it still has women who do fine embroidery and drawn-thread work. Some of the older downtown shops sell it, and the clever shopper will seek out some good buys.

Mayaguez dates from the mid-18th century. It was built to control the location of the Mona Passage, a vital trade route for the Spanish empire. Queen Isabel II of Spain recognized its status as a town in 1836. Her son, Alfonso XII, granted it a city charter in 1877.

Mayaguez is the honeymoon capital of Puerto Rico. The tradition dates from the 16th century, when, it is said, local fathers kidnapped young Spanish sailors who stopped for provisions there enroute to South America. Because of the scarcity of eligible young men, they needed husbands for their daughters.

The major industry is tuna packing, representing about 60% of all U.S. tuna consumption.

The chief sight is the **Tropical Agriculture Research Station.** At the administration office, ask for a free map of the tropical gardens, which contain one of the largest collections of tropical species useful to people, including cacao, fruit trees, spices, timbers, and ornamentals.

The location is on Route 65, between Post Street and Route 108, adjacent to the University of Puerto Rico at Mayaguez campus and across the street from the **Parque de los Próceres** or patriots' park. The grounds are open Monday through Friday from 7:30 a.m. to noon and 1 to 4:30 p.m., charging no admission. For more information, call 834-2435.

The **Puerto Rico Zoological Garden,** Route 108 (tel. 832-8110), at Mayaguez, exhibits birds, reptiles, and mammals, plus a new South American exhibit, all contained in a luxurious tropical environment. Hours are 9 a.m. to 4 p.m. Tuesday through Sunday, and admission is $1 for adults, 50¢ for children.

Mayaguez might also be the jumping-off point for a visit to **Mona Island,** which enjoys many legends of pirate treasure and is known for its white sand beaches and marine life. Accessible only by private boat or plane, the island is virtually uninhabited, except for two policemen and a director of the institute of natural resources. A private plane, seating about five persons, can be rented for $150 for the day.

The island attracts hunters seeking pigs, iguanas, and wild goats, along with big-game fishermen. But mostly it is intriguing to anyone who wants to escape civilization.

Playa Sardinera on Mona Island was a nesting ground of pirates waylaying the unsuspecting Armada. On one side of the island, Playa de Pajaros, there are caves where the Taino Indians left their mysterious hieroglyphs.

After touring Mayaguez, you can pick up the tour by taking Route 105 up to Route 120 as far as **Maricao.** The town is colorful and rather small. On the outskirts look for a sign that reads "Los Viveros" **(The Hatcheries);** then take Route 410. Here, the Commonwealth Department of Agriculture hatches as many as 25,000 fish for stocking the Puerto Rican freshwater lakes and streams.

Go back to Maricao to Route 120 south up to km. 13.8 until you reach the **Maricao State Forest** picnic area at a height of 2900 feet above sea level. The observation tower provides a splendid view across the green mountain range up to the coastal plains. Continue on Route 120 across the forest to the town of Sabana Grande (Great Plain). Route 2 will then take you to San German.

San German

This town is a little museum piece of a city. It was founded in 1512, although destroyed by the French in 1528. Rebuilt in 1570, it was named after Dona Germana de Foix, King Ferdinand of Spain's second wife. Once it rivaled San Juan in importance, although it has now settled into slumber, a living example of Spanish colonization.

Gracious old-world buildings line the streets, and flowers brighten the patios as they do in Seville, Spain. Also as in a small Spanish town, the population turns out to stroll in the plaza in the early evening.

On a knoll at one end of the town stands the chapel of **Porta Coeli** (Gate of Heaven), dating from the 17th century, oldest in the New World. Restored by the Institute of Puerto Rican Culture, it contains a museum of religious art which is open (admission free) from Tuesday to Sunday from 9 a.m. to noon and 2 to 4:30 p.m. The museum has a collection of ancient santos, carved holy figures and saints. Guided tours are offered Wednesday through Sunday. For more information, call 892-5845.

It's now possible to spend the night in comfort in the town at the **Parador Oasis,** 72 Luna St. (tel. 892-1175), housed within a 200-year-old building. Originally this parador was a fashionable private home and later a winery. It was also a small family-run hotel. Today it offers the same ornate verandas and decorative latticeworks—called *soles truncos*—that it used to, except everything has been considerably restored. Here visitors will see examples of *mediopunto,* a decorative room divider usually made of fine wooded lacework, highly characteristic of architecture in Puerto Rico between 1890 and 1940. Below are underground tunnels once believed used for contraband. All the pleasantly furnished rooms are air-conditioned. EP singles rent for $40 daily, going up to $45 in a double, $55 in a triple. Units contain private baths, and some face the inner patio, which is a gathering place for both guests and local patrons. Good regional food is served in the 18th-century dining room, known for its frescos.

From San German, take Route 320 to Route 101, then on to Lajas where Route 116 will lead to Route 304 which will take you to La Parguera where you can visit the **Phosphorescent Bay** (best on a moonless night). A boat leaves Villa Parguera pier nightly at 7:30 p.m. ($3 per person). The experience of seeing fish jump out of the water and emit a luminous streak on the surface and watching the water ripples created by the boat glimmer in the dark is extremely rare. Phosphorescent Bay is near the fishing village of Paraguera. The phenomenon, incidentally, is caused by a big colony of dinoflagellates, a small form of marine life. They produce these sparks of chemical light when their nesting is disturbed.

On the third day, take Route 104 up to Route 116 to Enseñada. From there you can continue on Route 116 to Guanica Bay. Or you could turn off on Route 333 to Cana Gorda Beach, to have a swim or lunch at the already-previewed Copamarina Hotel. While there, look for the species of cacti typical of the region. Continue on Route 2 to Yauco, then take Route 132 and head for—

Ponce

Puerto Rico's second-largest city, Ponce—called "The Pearl of the South" —was named after Ponce de Leon. Founded in 1692, it is today Puerto Rico's principal shipping port on the Caribbean. The city is well kept and attractive, as reflected by its many plazas, parks, and public buildings. There is something in its lingering air that suggests a provincial Mediterranean town. Look for the rejas, or framed balconies of the handsome colonial mansions.

Any of the Ponceños will direct you to their **Museum of Art,** at Las Americas Avenue (tel. 842-6215). This excellent museum was donated to the city by Luís A. Ferré, a former governor. The building in which the museum is housed was designed by Edward Durell Stone (who was the designer of New York's Museum of Modern Art), and it's been called "The Parthenon of the Caribbean." In spite of such a fanciful label, its collection represents principal schools of American and European art of the past five centuries. Hours are 10 a.m. to noon and 1 to 4 p.m., Monday through Friday; 10 a.m. to 4 p.m. on Saturday, to 5 p.m. on Sunday and holidays. The museum is closed on Tuesday. Adults pay $1.50; children under 12, 75¢.

All visitors as well head for the **Parque de Bombas,** on the main plaza of Ponce. This old firehouse is fantastic—painted black, red, green, and yellow. It was built for a fair in 1883, and is today the headquarters for the government tourism agency's Ponce Information Office.

Around from the firehouse, the trail will lead to the **Cathedral of Our Lady of Guadalupe.** The church rises between two plazas.

The marketplace at Atocha and Castillo Streets is colorful, the Perla Theater historic, and the Serralles rum distillery worth a visit. Or perhaps you'll want to just sit at the plaza, watching the Ponceños at their favorite pastime, strolling in the plaza.

The oldest cemetery in the Antilles, excavated in 1975, is located on Route 503, km. 2.7. The **Tibes Indian Ceremonial Center** contains some 186 skeletons, dating from A.D. 300, as well as pre-Taino plazas from A.D. 700. Bordered by the Portugués River, the museum is open daily from 9 a.m. to 4:30 p.m. Admission is $1.50 for adults and 50¢ for children. Guided tours are conducted through the grounds (for more information, call 844-5575). Shaded by such trees as the calabash, seven rectangular ballcourts and two dance grounds can be viewed. The arrangement of stone points on the dance grounds, in line with the solstices and equinoxes, suggest a pre-Columbian Stonehenge. A re-created Taino village includes not only the museum, but an exhibition hall which shows a documentary about Tibes and, later, has a cafeteria where you can find refreshments.

On the fourth and final day, leave Ponce by Route 1. As vast sugarcane fields fade from view, take Route 3 to **Guayama,** one of the handsomest towns in Puerto Rico. There, find Route 15, going north. If you travel this road in either spring or summer, you'll be surrounded by the brilliant colors of flowering trees.

At km. 17.1, in Jajome, you can see the governor's summer palace, an ancient, now restored and enlarged roadside inn. Continue on Route 15; then get on Route 1 which leads directly back to San Juan.

BEACHES ALONG THE ATLANTIC: An interesting scenic trip to the beaches between San Juan and Arecibo follows. Allow at least 5½ hours, not counting beach time.

The ever-changing colors of the Atlantic make this trip a memorable experience. Start at Route 2 to the Caparra intersection, where you turn onto Route 24 to Catano; then continue west on Route 165. El Morro and Old San Juan can be seen across the bay.

After passing a dense coconut grove, you will reach Livittown City (a housing development). The sea turns a blue-green shade at this spot. Continue up to the river and the town of **Dorado** by way of Route 690 north. Within a short distance, you will reach **Cerro Gordo Beach.** Watch your time, for you might be mesmerized by the natural beauty of this beach and stay longer than planned.

If you can break away from Cerro Gordo, take Route 688 back to Route 2 headed toward **Vega Baja** (founded in 1776). The residents of Vega Baja are nicknamed "melao-melao" ("molasses-molasses") because of the large amount of molasses produced in the town.

Route 676 north takes you to a spectacular beach in the west, where the water turns jade green with touches of purple and lots of white foam. Over to the east of this beach the water is less turbulent, held back by a giant rocky barrier where the waves crash thunderously. This beach is dotted with cabins and cabanas belonging to the local residents. Continue on Route 686 until you reach Route 648, which will take you to **Mar Chiquita,** where the high rocks enclose an oval lagoon perfect for swimming.

Return by way of Route 648 to Route 685, which will lead you to Route 2. Head north on Route 2 to Route 140 until you get to Barceloneta; then take Route 681 up to the Plazuela sugar mill and go through sugarcane fields bordered with almond trees.

Continue toward the beach and look for a sign which reads **"La Cueva del Indio"** (The Indian Cave). Many Indian symbols can be seen on the cave walls.

Leave the area by way of Route 681 up to where it meets Route 2 in Arecibo. Route 2 east will take you back to San Juan through cane fields and perfumed pineapple plantations.

11. The Sporting Life

Dorado Beach, Cerromar Beach, Palmas del Mar, and Río Mar are the chief centers for those seeking the golf, tennis, and beach life. However, hotels along the Condado/Isla Verde coastline also have, for the most part, complete water sports.

BEACHES: Beaches in Puerto Rico are open to the public, although you will be charged for parking and for use of balneario facilities, such as lockers and showers. The public beaches on the north shore of San Juan at Ocean Park and Park Barbosa are good, and can be reached by bus. Luquillo, on the north coast, some 30 miles east of San Juan, is discussed separately in the touring section. Also refer to the touring section for more tips on beaches west from San Juan. Public beaches shut down on Monday. If Monday is a holiday, the beaches are open then but close the next day, Tuesday. In winter, beach hours are 9 a.m. to 5 p.m., to 6 p.m. in summer.

Along the coastal roads of Route 2, to the north of Mayaguez, lie what are reputed to be the best surfing beaches in the Caribbean. Surfers from as far away as New Zealand are attracted to these beaches. The most outstanding of all, comparable to the finest surfing spots in the world, according to competitors in the 1968 World Surfing Championship held there, is at Punta Higuero, on Route 413 near the town of Rincon. In the winter months especially, uninterrupted Atlantic swells with perfectly formed waves averaging five to six feet in height roll shoreward and rideable swells sometimes reach 15 to 25 feet.

SNORKELING AND SCUBA: The coral reefs and cays around Puerto Rico make it ideal snorkeling country. Most major hotel water-sports offices also offer scuba-diving instructions. All the major hotels have water sports, but one of the most professional outfits is **Caribe Aquatic Adventures,** P.O. Box 1872 (tel. 721-0303, ext. 447), at the Caribe Hilton on Puerta de Tierra in San Juan. Karen Vega, the president of the resort division, is a NAUI-PADI certified instructor. She's helped by her husband, Tony, a NAUI divemaster. Their shop is a NAUI Pro facility. The best dive sites in San Juan are off the Hilton's beach. The Inside Reef has a large array of marine life including hand-feedable tropical fish. The Outside Reef has underwater caves with a 30-foot drop. Mask, fins, and snorkel are rented for $5 an hour, and the Inside Reef dives cost $25. Experienced divers can take the cave or night dives at $30. Deserted island sailing trips are also available, costing $55 for nondivers, $75 for divers. All prices include full equipment.

A nearby competitor of the Hilton, the **Condado Plaza Holiday Inn,** 999 Ashford Ave. (tel. 721-1000), operates a full dive shop on its premises also. Capt. Greg Korwek, a certified NAUI instructor, directs scuba facilities. Programs are available for everyone from novices to advanced divers. A half-day program, which includes classroom, pool, and underwater work, costs around $60 for a complete introduction to scuba. Once a beginner has completed this, he or she can qualify for one of the most comprehensive expeditions on the Condado, the Island Safari Tour.

Depending on the weather at any one of several dive spots along Puerto Rico's east coast, Captain Korwek or a member of his staff will lead selected groups for a full day of picnicking, sightseeing, skindiving, and exploring. An hour's minibus ride takes participants through the rain forest to a boat called the *Innovation.* Lunch is included in the special cash price of $60 for snorkelers and $85 for scuba-divers. All equipment is included, as well as the services of a guide.

You can also sail and snorkel at **Palmas del Mar** at Humacao (tel. 726-6132). A full day, including lunch, costs $65 per person. A popular sunset cruise, offered between 5 and 6 p.m., including wine, costs $17 per person. You get complimentary use of the snorkeling equipment.

DEEP-SEA FISHING: It's top-notch. Allison tuna, white marlin, sailfish, wahoo, dolphin, mackerel, and tarpon are some of the fish that can be caught in Puerto Rican waters where 30 world records have been broken.

It is said in Puerto Rico that **Capt. Mike Benitez** sets the standards by which to judge other captains. He is especially praised by marlin fishermen. You can write him directly at P.O. Box 5141, Puerta de Tierra, San Juan, PR 00906 (call 723-2292 daily to 9 p.m.), or else get in touch with him at Caribe Aquatic Adventures in the Hilton Dive Shop (tel. 721-0303, ext. 447). The captain has chartered out of San Juan for nearly 35 years. He takes his clients out on his 53-foot, custom-built sportfisherman, *Sea Born.* Fishing tours cost $285 for a half day, $490 for a full day, and take up to six sportsmen.

You can also go out with **Capt. Jorge L. Torruella,** the owner of the *Gin Pole,* a 41-foot Hatteras sportfisherman which is fully equipped and diesel powered. A half-day tour costs $240, a full day going for $450. It's cheaper to go on a split charter, which costs only $80 per angler. A maximum of six passengers is taken out. For more information, write Captain Torruella, Apt. 204, Condado Gardens, 1436 Estrella St., Santurce, PR 00907 (tel. 725-1408).

Some of the best year-round fishing in the Caribbean is found in the waters just off Palmas del Mar, the resort complex on the southeast coast of Puerto Rico (tel. 850-7442 after 6 p.m.). There **Capt. Bill Burleson** operates charters out of Palmas's harbor. His 44-foot customized sportsfishing boat *Karolette* is the second-largest charter fishing vessel operating out of Puerto Rico. He has fished the Caribbean for more than 20 years. Burleson prefers to take visiting fishermen to Grappler Banks, 18 nautical miles away. The banks are two sea mounts, rising to about 240 feet below the surface and surrounded by deeps of 6000 to 8000 feet. They lie in the migratory paths of wahoo, tuna, and marlin. Reservations can be made at Palmas del Mar's Candelero Hotel, at the guest services desk. The cost is $395 for a half day, $575 for a full day.

SAILING: In Humacao, **Palmas del Mar's Sailing Center** offers waterskiing, windsurfing, Sunfish sailing, and deep-sea fishing. A windsurfer rental costs $15 per hour, a Sunfish rental going for the same price. Pedal-boats can be rented for $20 per hour. In addition, bareboat and/or captained 27- to 46-foot sailboats are available for rent. Telephone 852-3450, ext. 2424, for reservations.

The **Condado Plaza Holiday Inn,** 999 Ashford Ave. (tel. 721-1000), offers a wide selection of boats for rent to visitors who want to sail in the sheltered lagoon near the heart of town. A 35-foot Pierson, holding a maximum of six passengers, can be chartered for a half-day excursion, costing around $350. On a less grand scale, Sunfish can be rented for $23 an hour. If you need a lesson, someone from the hotel will sail with you for the first hour, charging around $25. Hobie Cats are available for qualified sailors and cost $30 an hour, with lessons costing around $30. Paddleboats operated with a different kind of wind—your own—cost $18 per hour and carry two passengers.

GOLF: A golfer's dream, Puerto Rico has some splendid courses, too many for me to document here. The Dorado Beach and the Cerromar Hotel, its sister, with 72 holes of golf, constitute the greatest concentration of the sport in the Caribbean. The course at Dorado Beach is rated as one of the finest anywhere. These side-by-side 18-hole courses were designed by Robert Trent Jones. You pay a $12 greens fee for 9 holes. Each golf course is so gigantic that the only way to enjoy the game is to do so by means of a motorized golf cart. Rental of these four-wheeled bugs runs to $15.

The **Club de Golf,** at Palmas del Mar in Humacao (tel. 852-3450, ext. 2526), is one of the leading courses for golf in Puerto Rico. On Puerto Rico's southeast coast, it has a par-72, 6690-yard layout designed by Gary Player. It's under the direction of club professional Seth Bull. Greens fees are $19 for 18 holes, $12 for 9 holes if you're a guest of the hotel; otherwise, $25 to the general public. Carts, use of which is mandatory, cost $20 for 18 holes, $14 for 9 holes. Clubs can be rented for $10 for 18 holes, $7.50 for 9 holes. Seth Bull and his assistant pro,

Pepe Rosa, charge guests $20 for a private half-hour lesson ($15 for club members).

Other leading resorts with golf courses include Río Mar, in Río Grande. The Mayaguez Hilton makes arrangements for guests to play at a nine-hole course at a nearby country club. Punta Borinquen, at Aguadilla, the former Ramey Air Force Base, has an 18-hole public golf course which is open daily, charging greens fees of $5 on weekdays, $7 on Saturday, Sunday, and holidays.

TENNIS: Again, the sister resorts of Dorado and Cerromar have the monopoly on this game, a total of 21 courts between them. These all-weather courts charge $5 an hour for night lights. Take your racquet and tennis outfit along (attire and equipmment are often available in shops, but prices are outrageous, the selection minimal). If your backhand is a bit rusty or your game needs a few pointers, take advantage of the professional tennis clinic.

In San Juan, the Caribe Hilton, the Condado Holiday Inn, the Dupont Plaza San Juan, Carib Inn, and the combined Hilton-operated Condado Beach and La Concha have tennis courts. Also in the San Juan area there's a public court at the old navy base, Isla Grande, Miramar. The entrance is from Fernandez Juncos Avenue at Stop 11.

The Tennis Center at Palmas del Mar in Humacao, run by All American Sports, features 20 courts (5 Hartru, 15 Tenneflex). Court fees are $16 per hour for doubles in prime time. Call 852-3450, ext. 2527, to reserve court time.

HORSE RACING: Great thoroughbreds and outstanding jockeys compete all year at **El Comandante,** Route 3, km. 15.3 at Canóvanas (tel. 724-6060), in this ultramodern track. Races are held Wednesday, Friday, Sunday, and holidays at 2:30 p.m. Admission to the clubhouse is $3, and you pay only $1 for the grandstand. An air-conditioned terrace dining room opens at 12:30 p.m. on each race day. Telephone 724-6060 for luncheon reservations. Most credit cards are accepted.

COCKFIGHTING: Puerto Ricans are tremendously fond of this sport, as is most of Latin America. The **Club Gallistico,** Route 187, km. 1.5, Isla Verde (tel. 791-1557), is air-conditioned, complete with restaurant and cocktail lounge. General admission is $8; ringside admission, $15. It is open Saturday from 1 to 7 p.m.

CAMPING: Although not highly publicized, Puerto Rico is considered one of the best islands in the Caribbean for camping, with a total of seven locations. These range from beachfront properties to the cool hills. Many are bare sites, yet others have cottages or tents available. For information, write to the **Department of National Resources,** Forest Service Area, P.O. Box 5887, Puerta de Tierra Station, San Juan, PR 00906, or else phone 721-8774.

RIDING: In Humacao, at the **Palmas del Mar Equestrian Center,** guided trail rides follow the beach through the tropical forest on horses suitable for all ages and abilities. No experience is necessary. They also feature equestrian classes through various levels. Trails are crossed Tuesday to Saturday from 9:30 a.m. to 5:30 p.m. and on Sunday to 3 p.m. Classes are by appointment only. Reservations can be made by calling the hotel at 852-3450 or by dialing the stables direct at 852-4785. The hourly cost is $17.

12. The Offshore Islands

From Fajardo, the islands of Culebra and Vieques are reached by a dramatic ferry ride. It's not recommended to landlubbers, however, because the water can be quite rough off the island's eastern coast. The launch leaves Fajardo for Vieques daily at 9:15 a.m., costing $2 for the one-way ride, which lasts about an hour and a half. Another launch departs at 4:30 p.m.

The morning launch goes on to Culebra, for a total one-way cost of $2.25. The trip to Culebra takes about two hours.

From Culebra to Fajardo, a passenger ferry departs Tuesday through Saturday at 7 a.m. (on weekends and holidays at 3 p.m.). On Monday there is a departure via Vieques at 1:30 p.m.

From Vieques to Fajardo, a passenger ferry departs daily at 7:30 a.m. and again at 3 p.m.

You can also get to Culebra on a plane from the International or Isla Grande airport at San Juan, the flight costing about $25 each way.

CULEBRA: At this volcanic island off the east coast of Puerto Rico, the beaches are sometimes almost completely deserted. The chief activities are, of course, swimming, fishing, and dining on the local seafood. There are no forms of nightlife on the island, so be prepared to relax and retire early.

The roads aren't seriously paved, making it a perfect setting for hiking and birdwatching. The latter pastime is rewarding here, since part of the island has been set aside as a bird sanctuary. Snorkeling and sailing are popular as well, as this portion of the island has several coral reefs.

Where to Stay

Seafarer's Inn, 6 Pedro Márquez, P.O. Box 216 (tel. 742-3171), is not a place you come to for a single night's stay, considering how hard it is to get here. Run by Druso and Jane Daubon, this inn rents out plain but clean units, costing only $20 a day in a double all year round. At the inn the art of enjoying local seafood is well developed. The menu varies with the day's catch. There are always plenty of fresh fruits and vegetables, many grown in the inn's own backyard. The dining room is cozy and intimate, seating only 20 persons. Depending on what kind of person you are, you may like it a lot.

Villa Boheme, Enseñada Honda, P.O. Box 218 (tel. 742-3508). Trade winds blow through the five bedrooms and one apartment offered for by-the-week rental by Jane and Huss Malik. Formerly a resident of Oregon, Huss met his charming wife while teaching graduate courses in counseling and education at the University of Maine. He packed his Yankee bride off to a palm-studded harborside location where guests appreciate the calm and the rentals by the sea. The Maliks maintain what's become almost a mini-marina, where access to the many craft bobbing in the harbor is made easier by the on-site wharf extending into the bay from the backyard of the guest house.

The units are arranged in a split-level format, each with its own private entrance, a view of the harbor, a king-size bed, a table or ceiling fan, windows protected by metal louvers, and a private bath. No meals are served, but the Maliks maintain two communal kitchens where guests can prepare their own meals. Also, several restaurants are within walking distance. The apartment includes a full kitchen and rents for $475 per week year round, although it is usually left vacant in summer. The five rooms cost $350 a week in winter and *$310 in summer,* single or double occupancy.

Where to Eat

El Batey (no phone) across from the harbor, is a large, clean place which maintains a full bar as well as an array of deli-style sandwiches, costing around $4. Beer is a popular drink, and the pool tables make the place lively, especially on weekends when many locals throng in. Weekdays, it's much calmer. The owners are friendly and have many fans on the island. Breezes from the harbor cool the place.

Happy Landing (no phone) is appropriately named for its location near the airport. It doesn't win any awards in the decor department, but it's the kind of local haunt where guests come for the ambience and the simple foods, which include Spanish-style chicken, fish, and pork. Full dinners cost around $8. This is a good place to go for a full breakfast. You can also lunch here.

VIEQUES: Seven miles off the eastern tip of Puerto Rico is Vieques (pronounced Bee-*ay*-kase), the second of Puerto Rico's trio of island possessions (in addition to already-reviewed Culebra and Mona, a barren plateau). Vieques, about twice the size of Manhattan, offers scores of palm-lined white sand beaches. Nearly all of the 21-mile-long island is a U.S. military base, a fact which has led to hostilities in the past. Occasional military maneuvers might limit certain parts to visitors.

The main town is Isabela Segunda, on the northern shore, where most of the island's population does its business. Fishing and farming are the main occupations of the 8000 residents.

From Isla Grande Airport in San Juan, air service is available to Vieques for about $25. Your small plane lands at the airstrip about 15 minutes away from the small fishing village of Esperanza, which is at the center of some of the island's loveliest beaches, including Sun Bay. It is said that Vieques possesses some 50 beaches, many quite small, of course.

La Casa del Francés, Barrio Esperanza, P.O. Box 458 (tel. 741-3751), is just outside of the village on the south shore of the island. Recently designated a historical landmark, this turn-of-the-century plantation home has been converted to a charming and very informal guest house with Haitian paintings and wicker furniture. The casual atmosphere is not luxurious but offers peaceful quiet in a tropical setting for self-sufficient types. The 12 rooms range *from $55 to $60 for a double off-season* and $60 to $65 for the same double from December 1 to April 30. All rooms have private baths. Cooling is by trade winds and ceiling fans, and a two-story atrium is in the central courtyard. An outside bar and terrace are the preface to excellent dining on the veranda, which is informal.

There is a pool on the premises, and the inn is within walking distance of at least one fine beach. Scuba-diving, snorkeling, sportsfishing, sunset watching, and relaxing are the available activities.

Bananas, Barrio Esperanza (tel. 741-8700), is a pleasant guest house better known for its popular bar and restaurant than for its rooms. However, Boston-bred Tom Lugrin rents nine accommodations to persons seeking a laid-back ambience. The cost in the most expensive doubles, which have ceiling fans, is $38; the less expensive, very basic, units cost $32.

The front of the guest house is devoted to the bar and veranda restaurant, which are cooled by the ocean breezes. Meals at the restaurant begin at $12 and include everything from local fish to lobster. A burger and fries is a popular luncheon choice. The restaurant is open all year, daily in winter and on weekends only from May to September.

The sandy beach just across the street is especially appealing because of the calm waters created by the presence of a small, unnamed rocky islet a little distance away. It was used some 20 years ago by the makers of the film *Lord of the Flies.*

Chapter III

THE U.S. VIRGIN ISLANDS

1. St. Thomas
2. St. John
3. St. Croix

SEPARATING THE ATLANTIC from the Caribbean, the U.S. Virgin Islands—St. Thomas, St. John, and St. Croix—enjoy one of the most perfect year-round climates in the world. They lie directly in the belt of the subtropical, easterly trade winds. At the eastern end of the Greater Antilles and the northern tip of the Lesser Antilles, the U.S. Virgins are some 40 miles east of Puerto Rico, 1400 miles southeast of New York City, and 1000 miles east-southeast of Miami. Some of their sugar-white beaches, experts cite, are among the most beautiful on the globe.

Christopher Columbus (there's that name again) discovered the Virgin Islands on his second voyage to the New World, in 1493. He anchored at Salt River on St. Croix, naming the islands for St. Ursula and her 10,999 virgins martyred by the Huns at Cologne in the Middle Ages.

In 1666, the Danes took formal possession of St Thomas, changing the name of its capital to Charlotte Amalie in 1691. St. Thomas was divided into plantations, and an attempt was also made to colonize the island with convicts and prostitutes.

To help guard the Panama Canal, the United States purchased the islands in 1917 at a cost of $25 million, a price considered scandalously high at the time. Of course, the Americans feared German U-boat flotillas. These American outposts in the Caribbean today have territorial status, governed by an elected 15-member legislature and a governor.

PRACTICAL FACTS: Since the Stars and Stripes fly over these islands, with their old-world Danish towns, you don't have a language barrier, and you don't have to exchange the Yankee dollar for some other currency.

Of course, the big attraction of St. Croix and St. Thomas, in addition to serving as a winter playpen and an increasing summer destination, is that every U.S. resident can bring home $800 worth of duty-free purchases, including a gallon of alcoholic beverages per adult. In addition, one can mail home an unlimited amount in gifts valued at up to $100 each. (At other spots in the Caribbean, U.S. citizens are limited to $400 worth of merchandise and a single bottle.)

Whatever appliances you use on the mainland (hair dryer, etc.), should work for you in St. Thomas. The **electrical current** in the Virgin Islands is the same as on the mainland: 120 volts, 60 cycles, A.C. No adapter or converter is necessary.

As for **time,** when it's 6 a.m. in Charlotte Amalie, it's still 5 p.m. in Miami. The U.S. Virgins are on Atlantic Time, which places the islands an hour ahead of EST. When the east coast goes on Daylight Saving Time, Virgin Island clocks and those on the mainland record the same time.

Several major banks are represented in St. Thomas, and they are usually open from 9 a.m. to 2:30 p.m. Monday to Thursday. Friday hours are different: 9 a.m. to 2 p.m. and 3:30 to 5 p.m.

Since the Virgin Islands are part of the U.S. Postal System, postage rates are the same as on the mainland.

Remember to drive on the left, a carryover from Danish rule, and obey speed laws, which are 20 m.p.h. in town, 35 m.p.h. outside.

Virgin Islanders celebrate a total of 24 legal **holidays!** In addition to the standard ones, they observe the following: January 6 (Three Kings' Day); January 15 (Martin Luther King's birthday); March 31 (Transfer Day—tranfer of the Danish Virgin Islands to the Americans); April 29 (Children's Carnival Parade); April 30 (Grand Carnival Parade); June 20 (Organic Act Day; in lieu of a constitution, they have an "Organic Act"); July 3 (Emancipation Day, commemorating the freeing of the slaves by the Danes in 1848); July 25 (hurricane supplication day); October 17 (hurricane thanksgiving day); November 1 (Liberty Day); and December 26 (Boxing Day).

For a local call at a **telephone** booth, place 25¢ into the meter. From many points on the mainland, you can dial direct to the Virgin Islands (or vice versa). Cable service is available as well.

Daily newspaper from the mainland are flown in to St. Thomas and St. Croix every day, and local papers such as the *Virgin Island Daily News* on both islands also carry the latest news.

St. Thomas receives both cable and commercial TV stations. Radio weather reports can be heard at 7:30 p.m. and 8:30 a.m. on 99.5 FM.

In **hospitals,** St. Thomas has the 200-bed Knud Hansen Memorial (tel. 774-9000), with an emergency room open 24 hours a day. There is also the St. Thomas Hospital and Community Center (tel. 776-8311).

In St. John there is the DeCastro Clinic (tel. 776-6461) in Cruz Bay and the more recent St. John Hospital and Community Center at Centerline (tel. 776-6400).

St. Croix is well equipped with hospitals, including the Charles Harwood Memorial (tel. 773-2099) and the St. Croix Hospital (tel. 773-8311) both at Christiansted, and Ingerborg Nesbitt Clinic at Frederiksted (tel. 772-0260).

As a general tipping rule, it is customary to tip 15%. Some hotels add a 10% to 15% surcharge to cover service. When in doubt, ask.

There is ample water for showers and bathing in the Virgin Islands, but you are asked to conserve. Hotels will supply you with all your water for drinking.

GETTING THERE: Travelers living in the northeast quadrant of the United States will probably find that **American Airlines** offers the easiest connections to and from St. Thomas. Two DC-10s leave within 75 minutes of one another from New York's JFK airport every morning. The first flies nonstop to St. Thomas, and the second lands first in St. Croix, with continuing service on another aircraft to St. Thomas.

Travelers opting for the second morning flight can arrange to have their luggage routed directly through to their final destination. In the afternoon, both flights return to New York, the first flying nonstop from St. Thomas to JFK and the second making a 40-minute stopover in St. Croix before continuing on to

New York. This flight is convenient for Boston-based passengers, since American offers excellent connections to and from that city for passengers embarking or disembarking from its Virgin Islands flights.

American's fare structure is considerably simpler for its Virgin Islands routes than for other islands it services in the Caribbean. Except for passengers traveling at Thanksgiving, Christmas, or New Year's (when fares go up about $60 each way), the year-round one-way fare between New York and either St. Thomas or St. Croix is $193 for midweek travel and $206 for weekend travel. Weekend travel is defined as Friday, Saturday, and Sunday for southbound traffic, and Saturday, Sunday, and Monday for northbound traffic.

American uses wide-body DC-10s for the longest stretches of the New York–USVI route, which usually lasts around 3½ hours, and 727s for the inter-island shuttles, which require about 20 minutes of flight time.

Bargain-seeking passengers can always call American and ask to be connected with the tour desk. There, someone can arrange discounted air passage if a hotel reservation is made through American at the same time. A wide array of accommodations and flight dates are available, although the options are so varied and complicated that only an airline staff member (or a travel agent) can describe them in detail.

If you're coming from Miami, you'll find that **Eastern Airlines** has nonstop jet service from Miami to St. Thomas / St. Croix. From flights connecting in Miami, Eastern also provides connections to the U.S. Virgins from such cities as Atlanta, Baltimore, Boston, Chicago, Cleveland, Detroit, Hartford, and St. Louis.

If you're in San Juan, you can take a 30-minute flight from Puerto Rico to St. Thomas aboard **Prinair**, or one of several smaller airlines.

For Pan Am's more recent service to the U.S. Virgin Islands, refer to the "Getting There" section of St. Croix.

1. St. Thomas

The busiest cruise-ship harbor in the West Indies, St. Thomas is the second largest of the U.S. Virgins, lying about 40 miles north of St. Croix, which is larger. St. Thomas, with its capital at Charlotte Amalie, is about 12 miles long and 3 miles wide. The capital is also the shopping center of the Caribbean (refer to the section on what to buy).

Hotels on the north side of St. Thomas look out onto the Atlantic, and those on the south side front the calmer Caribbean. It's possible for the sun to shine in the south as the north experiences showers.

January and February are the coolest period, recording lows around 60° Fahrenheit, but highs in the 80s. August is the hottest time, with daily peaks in the high 80s. The temperature drops to the 70s at night.

Holiday makers discovered St. Thomas right after World War II, and they've been flocking back ever since in increasing numbers. Shopping, sights, and sun prove a potent lure. Tourism has raised the standard of living here until it is one of the highest in the Caribbean. Condominium apartments have grown up over the debris of bulldozed shacks.

In all honesty, I must point out that St. Thomas is not paradise for all our visitors. Many readers have written in to make the same point: "It's strictly for cruise ship passengers in town to shop." There have been many complaints about hostility to visitors, and the area around the waterfront and the little alleyways shooting off from Back Street are not considered safe at night. Be duly warned.

If you're visiting in August, make sure you carry along mosquito repellent.

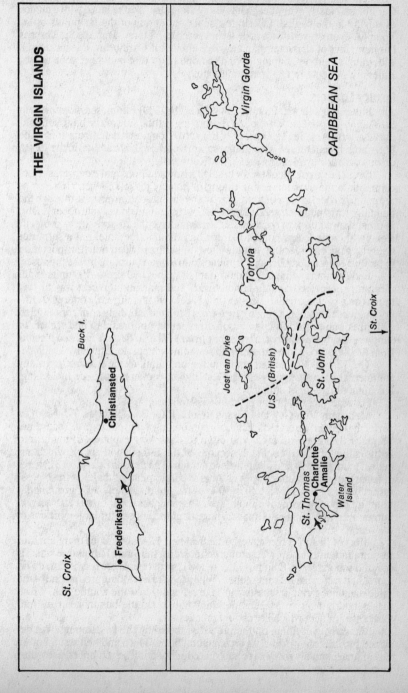

THE VIRGIN ISLANDS

CARIBBEAN SEA

Virgin Gorda

Tortola

Jost van Dyke

U.S. (British)

St. John

St. Croix →

St. Thomas
Charlotte
Amalie
Water
Island

Buck I.

Christiansted

Frederiksted

St. Croix

HOTELS: There are more hotels in the Virgin Islands than anywhere else in the Caribbean. Nearly every beach has its own hostelry. You're faced with a choice of staying in the capital, Charlotte Amalie, or at any of the far points of St. Thomas, even on your own little island reached by ferry. Perhaps St. Thomas has more inns of character than anyplace else in the Caribbean. I've included a wide-ranging survey, hoping to find the one place that will meet your needs. Rates are subject to a 5% government tax.

Luxury Leaders

Bluebeard's Castle, P.O. Box 7480 (tel. 744-1600), is almost a monument in St. Thomas, a popular, all-around resort lying on one side of the bay overlooking Charlotte Amalie. The history of this spot is long, as it dates from 1665. The U.S. government turned what had been a private home into a hotel in the 1930s, on one occasion attracting Franklin D. Roosevelt.

Over the years, Bluebeard's has had many additions and extensions to accommodate the ever-increasing throng of holiday makers. When cruise ships are in the harbor, groups of tourists arrive by the busload, swarming through the buildings with their well-tended gardens, old trees, and flowery shrubbery. But, in time, they go back to their vessels, and you have the 20-acre site to yourself, along with your fellow guests. Not for beach buffs, the hotel has a saltwater swimming pool and Jacuzzi, but the guests are also provided free transportation to famous Magens Bay Beach. Championship tennis courts are on the premises.

Bedchambers come in a wide variety of shapes and sizes—100 units in all, pleasantly decorated and air-conditioned. You may find the best way to stay here is on a package deal (ask your travel agent what is currently offered). Otherwise, winter rates in a single range from $172 to $202 daily and from $175 to $205 in a double. Add $42 per person extra per day for breakfast and dinner. *In summer, tariffs are lowered. Singles pay from $132 to $162 daily and two persons from $135 to $165.* More expensive suites, some with parlors, are also available.

The Terrace Restaurant commands a breathtaking view and offers many continental specialties as well as West Indian cookery, open-air brunching, lunching, or late-night dining.

For reservations, phone 800/524-6599 toll free.

Mahogany Run Golf and Tennis Resort, P.O. Box 7517 (tel. 775-5000), is perfectly situated on a verdant hilltop overlooking a jagged, forested coastline. To reach the reception area, you drive through long expanses of manicured lawns, some of which double as sections of the 18-hole golf course which has helped to make this sophisticated place famous. The fact that it's set on 315 acres of rolling grasslands dotted with clusters of condominiums makes it the biggest resort in St. Thomas. More than 90% of the approximately 300 accommodations are privately owned, although the absentee landlords turn their vacation homes over to Mahogany Run's management to rent out for large portions of the year.

Most of the units contain cooking facilities. However, since there are four restaurants scattered over the property (including the Stone Farmhouse which is covered separately in "Dining Out," below), most people are tempted to do no more than just make morning coffee. When they're not lolling around one of the three swimming pools, guests can take advantage of the shuttle bus, which makes hourly runs to Magens Beach. Another shuttle bus makes runs into Charlotte Amalie, which lies about ten miles away.

Virtually everything on the property, including the landscaping, was designed by different world-class architectural firms. The combined result is a series of imaginatively modern terraced accommodations, each priced according to its location and scenery.

If you're a sports enthusiast, you can arrange for a full slate of water activities, including sailing, scuba, snorkeling, and much more. Tennis is important here, with ample opportunity for day or night playing.

Rates are extremely complicated, based on such items as views and number of bedrooms. In winter, the basic rates for two persons, EP, range from a low of $160 to a high of $280 per day, the latter the price of a one-bedroom villa. Naturally, suites and two- and three-bedroom villas are more expensive. For single occupancy, deduct $25. No MAP tariffs are quoted. *In the off-season, two persons can stay here at prices beginning at $100 daily for the simplest accommodations. A third person sharing pays another $25.*

Frenchman's Reef, P.O. Box 7100 (tel. 774-8500), has a winning southern position on a projection of land overlooking both the harbor at Charlotte Amalie and the Caribbean. The hotel is a Holiday Inn and stands in such a conspicuous position that the traveler with the worst possible sense of direction can't help but find it.

Everywhere you look are facilities devoted to the good life—two giant swimming pools, suntanning areas, a poolside bar, tennis courts, every kind of water sports (snorkeling, scuba-diving, sailing, deep-sea fishing). Whatever your holiday needs, chances are you'll find them met at "The Reef." To reach the private beach, you merely take a glass-enclosed elevator.

The bedrooms vary greatly, but in general are furnished in a traditional manner, with various color groups and quite good taste. In winter, except during the Christmas season when prices are increased about $10, singles range from $186 to $226 daily, two persons paying from $188 to $228. For breakfast and dinner, add about $42 per person to the room tariffs. *In summer, singles cost from $136 to $176 daily; doubles, from $138 to $178.*

Good food is served in the Gazebo Room, which has a view of the harbor, and you can also get simple meals at the Lighthouse Bar, once an actual lighthouse. In the evening, the Top of the Reef, a supper club, offers entertainment, or you can go to La Terraza lounge. The Lighthouse Bar is another possibility.

First Class

Yacht Haven Hotel, P.O. Box 7970, Long Bay Road (tel. 774-9700), is a fashionably styled resort directly on Long Bay, adjacent to the port where cruise ships dock. The life here is marina oriented, yet the site is close to the best shops of Charlotte Amalie. Large blocks of tall arches overlook a garden of palm trees and the waterfront. Guests have a choice of two swimming pools, plus one for children. There are also two tennis courts.

In the summer of 1982 the hotel and marina underwent a $2.5-million renovation. It now has 220 spacious and attractively furnished bedrooms, plus nine well-appointed suites. Units open either onto harbor views or else overlook the gardens. The rate is the same, whether occupancy is by one or two persons. In winter, tariffs range from $140 to $180 daily, *and in summer from $90 to $110 daily.*

The Harbour Room restaurant offers seafood dining and evening entertainment. You can also take breakfast or lunch in the Greenhouse, followed by an evening meal at the Bilge Restaurant, enjoying the surrounding yachts at the marina.

For all types of water activities, the 180-slip marina offers many possibilities, ranging from windsurfing to day sailing to chartering yachts.

Virgin Isle Hotel, P.O. Box 3188 (tel. 744-1500), is a beach and racquet resort with 225 tastefully appointed, air-conditioned rooms and suites, most with private terraces overlooking the harbor of Charlotte Amalie. Rates based on double occupancy, EP, are $135 to $175 daily in winter, *$100 to $135 in* *spring, summer, and fall.* An extra person is charged $30 daily, and children 17 and under sharing a room with two adults stay free. Add another $35 per person for breakfast and dinner. For single occupancy, deduct $5 from the tariffs quoted. Lunch is served by the sea in a French country-style restaurant.

At the hotel's beach club, a complete water-sports center offers snorkeling, scuba-diving, windsurfing, and other sports. There are two tennis courts, lit for night play, and an Olympic-size freshwater pool with a deck overlooking the harbor.

The hotel is one of the liveliest in St. Thomas. On Tuesday night a "Wild West" barbecue is the attraction, and a steel band performs all evening. On Friday night there's a West Indian luau complete with roast pig and a help-yourself salad buffet, a local favorite. Milo and the Kings add island flavor for dancing under the stars. More dancing and live entertainment are held at the Virgin Bar nightly, and later you can dance at Studio 54, one of the major nightspots of St. Thomas.

To make toll-free reservations, call 800/524-2004.

Pavilions & Pools, Route 6 (tel. 775-1110), is ideal for either a honeymoon or an off-the-record weekend. It seems the ultimate in small-scale luxury—your own air-conditioned villa, with floor-to-ceiling glass doors opening directly onto your own private swimming pool. The resort is a string of condominium units, built and furnished with good taste. After checking in and following a wooden pathway to your attached villa, you don't have to see another soul until you check out, if that is your desire.

The fence and gate are high, and your space opens into tropical greenery. Around your own swimming pool is an encircling deck. Inside, a high room divider screens a full, well-equipped kitchen. Each bedroom has its own style, with plenty of closets behind louvered doors. The bath may intrigue you, as it has a garden shower where you can bathe surrounded by greenery, yet are protected from Peeping Toms. Inquire about honeymoon packages if that's what you're on. Otherwise, expect to pay, in winter, from $177 to $187 daily in a double. *Two persons in summer pay from $130 to $140 daily.*

A small bar and barbecue area is set against a wall on the reception terrace, and here rum parties and cookouts are staged. There's also an informal dining room. Occasionally a musician or singer will entertain. There's free use of snorkeling gear, and you also can play on adjacent tennis courts. The resort adjoins Sapphire Bay with its good beach.

Limetree Beach Hotel, P.O. Box 7307 (tel. 776-4770), nestled on Frenchman's Cove, is a very private, very pleasant collection of well-built three-story bungalows set on a hillside above the sea. After registering in the comfortably airy public rooms, guests move into their simple but attractive units, each of which is air-conditioned, contains a phone and a private bath, and lies only a few steps from the white sands of the palm-fringed beach.

On the premises are two floodlit tennis courts and an amply proportioned swimming pool shaped like a modified boomerang. The cheerful staff presents live entertainment every night, which is likely to include a King Voodoo show. Snorkeling, scuba, and sailing can be arranged upon request. Charlotte Amalie is only a ten-minute drive away, but because of the resort's southern shore seclusion, you'd think it was far more distant.

In winter, singles range from $140 to $160, while doubles cost from $170 to $180. Each additional person pays an extra $30. *In summer, singles range from $110 to $120 and doubles go for $120 to $145. Triples cost from $140 to $170, while quads are from $170 to $190.* Refrigerators can be rented for an additional $6 a day. For reservations, call 800/524-2007, toll free.

Inns of Character

Hotel 1829, P.O. Box 1567, Kongens Gade (Danish for Kings Street; tel. 774-1829), is my favorite nest in St. Thomas. After a major renaissance, this once-decaying historical site has become one of the leading small hotels of character in the Caribbean. Right in the heart of town, it stands about three minutes from Government House, built on a hillside with many levels and many steps (no elevator). It is reached by a climb. The hotel is the prize possession of Vernon and Eva Ball. He's from Ohio—and known as the "Bobby Fishers of backgammon"—and she's from the enchanting little German village of Dinkelsbuhl. The Baron and Baroness Ball (he purchased the title from an Italian nobleman) have wisely selected a considerate, thoughtful staff, many of them virtually in the "family retainer" category. The 1829 has actually been a hotel since the 19th century, entertaining such celebrated guests as King Carol of Rumania (and his mistress, Madame Lupescu), Suzy Parker, Edna St. Vincent Millay, and Mikhail Baryshnikov.

Amid a cascade of flowering bougainvillea, you can reach the upper rooms which overlook a central courtyard with a miniature swimming pool. The units, some of which are small, are beautifully designed, comfortable, and attractive, but don't expect phones, TVs, or room service. In the restoration, the old was preserved whenever possible. In high season, the cheapest and smallest double rents for $90 daily, a single for $80. All have baths and air conditioning. However, superior and deluxe doubles range in price from $120 to $165 daily, with singles in that category costing from $105 to $155. A few special suites cost from $210 for two persons ($200 if rented as a single). There are only a dozen rooms in all, most of which face the sea. A few have antiques such as four-poster beds. *In summer, double rates drop 25% to 30%.* The hotel cannot take children under 12.

The Inn at Mandahl, P.O. Box 2483 (tel. 775-2100), is a time-sharing hotel, tiny and informal, lying about 250 feet overlooking Mandahl Bay on the north coast, reached by a winding, circuitous road. It is next door to the golf and tennis resort of Mahogany Run, and a Magens Beach lies about two miles to the west.

The managers welcome you to one of their eight good-size units, each with terrace and what they call a "down-island" view. *In summer, singles rent for $80 daily; doubles pay $90, and another person sharing a room $12.* In winter, tariffs go up to $120 daily in a single, $130 in a double, plus another $18 for an additional person.

The inn has a cliff-hung pool, and offers beach towels free, as it does snorkeling equipment. A continental breakfast is also served free in your room. Everybody seemingly drives up here for the Banana Pancake Brunch, an island tradition, served on Sunday between 9 a.m. and 2 p.m. You can also enjoy a remote beach, next to a jetty. Dinner is casual (but not that casual!), featuring such local specialties as black-bean soup and grilled local fish. Of course you get the usual assortment of steaks and chops as well. You can take your meals here or else, for variety, dine at the Mahogany Run Golf Course Club House.

Harbor View, Frenchman's Hill, P.O. Box 1975 (tel. 774-2651), was a once-scandalous *maison de tolerance,* built in the 1700s by French Huguenot political refugees at the western edge of Charlotte Amalie. After a remarkable transformation by two cosmopolitan American women, Arlene Lockwood and Lenore Wolfe, it became not only one of the finest restaurants in St. Thomas (see my dining recommendations) but an inn, often touted as "the most sophisticated small hotel in the West Indies." The women visited the hotel when it was a wreck. When word reached them in New York that it was for sale, they flew here and bought it, creating a small wonder and opening it in the early 1960s.

They brought individuality and chic to the ten air-conditioned bedrooms, which contain many four-poster beds, old chests, dressing tables, mellow paintings, flower prints, and, of course, coordinated fabrics at the windows and on the beds. Guests have access to the garden living room and a swimming pool combined. It's like a classic terraced garden in Portofino *Harper's Bazaar* called it "very Tennessee Williams."

Winter rates, in effect from November 1 to May 1, are $110 in a double, $90 in a single, and $122 daily in a triple. *In the off-season, lasting from May 1 to Labor Day, prices go down: $80 daily in a double, $60 in a single, and $88 in a triple.* Rates include a continental breakfast, and a full breakfast is available at an extra charge. Lunch is available to house guests, except on Tuesday.

Galleon House, P.O. Box 6577 (tel. 774-6952). You walk up a long flight of stairs past a neighboring restaurant's veranda to reach the concrete terrace which doubles as this hotel's reception area. The ten rooms are scattered in several hillside buildings, and each contains a ceiling fan or air conditioning. There's even a small pool on the grounds. The main attraction of this place is its location, set as it is next to the Hotel 1829 on Government Hill about one block from the main shopping section of St. Thomas.

Cordell and Elise Tittle are the directors of this bed-and-breakfast house, having rebuilt it after a disastrous fire which closed an older establishment on the same premises. Winter rates for singles range from $41 to $85, while doubles cost between $48 and $110. *Summer prices go down to between $36 and $48 in a single, between $40 and $75 in a double.* A third person in any double costs an additional $12 per day. A continental breakfast is included in the tariffs. For reservations, call 800/524-2052 toll free.

Small, Special Resorts

Secret Harbour Beach Hotel, P.O. Box 7576 (tel. 775-1010), overlooks Nazareth Bay in the east, built in a contemporary style on the south coast, about a 15-minute ride from Charlotte Amalie. At first you'll think you've arrived at a South Seas island beach resort, set apart from civilization. Spread out in a setting of tall palm trees is a row of air-conditioned accommodations. Dating from 1969, it was the first condominium apartment complex to open in St. Thomas.

Each suite or bedroom has its own private veranda, and the rooms have a distinct charm, as they are decorated to the taste of each individual owner. There are three kinds of accommodations: studio apartments with a bed-sitting room, patio, and bath, as well as a dressing room; one-bedroom suites with a living/dining area, a separate bedroom and bath, plus a sun gallery; and the most luxurious—a two-bedroom suite with two baths. Accommodations have fully equipped kitchens.

In summer, a studio apartment for two persons costs $105 daily, going up to $120 for a one-bedroom apartment and peaking at $185 for a two-bedroom unit suitable for four guests. In winter, a two-person studio apartment costs $160 daily, rising to $200 for a one-bedroom apartment, and peaking at around $300 for a two-bedroom apartment suitable for four guests. Certain shoulder-season reductions are granted, usually from mid-November to right before Christmas and for most of the month of April.

The Bird of Paradise restaurant, previewed later, offers lunch on an outdoor terrace in a setting on the beach. Or else you can dine inside. Before that, you may want to go to the Beach Bar or Gazebo for drinks. There's a full water sports center on the beach, as well as a freshwater pool and three tennis courts. For reservations, you can telephone toll free by dialing 800/524-2250.

Secret Harbour House III, Route 6 (tel. 775-3304), is a hill-hugging cluster of white buildings which, as a business entity, is distinctly different from Secret

Harbour Beach Hotel a short distance away. It's only a short walk to the beach here, although guests can always stay in their eyrie and use the on-the-premises pool if they prefer freshwater to saltwater bathing. There are also a Jacuzzi and three tennis courts, while a number of water sports—snorkeling, scuba, and sailboat rentals—can be arranged nearby.

Each accommodation includes air conditioning, a telephone, a fully equipped kitchen, a living/dining area, and a wood-rail balcony, some with a view of the sea. In winter, single or double studio or one-bedroom apartments cost between $160 and $200 a day. Two-bedroom units, suitable for two to four persons, cost around $270 per day. *In summer, studios or one-bedroom accommodations rent for $100 to $110, while two-bedroom apartments go for $140 a day.* For reservations, call 800/221-4588 toll free.

Bolongo Bay Beach & Tennis Club, P.O. Box 7337 (tel. 775-1800), is really like your own private beach club, where informality prevails. The owner-managers, Dick and Joyce Doumeng, are among the friendliest and most hospitable people on the island, and they give you a lot for your money. Likewise, they've picked a good and talented staff who seem to appreciate your staying with them. What makes the resort so appealing is that it gives you an inclusive sports package in the rates. Beach attendants supply you with snorkeling equipment, the Sunfish sailboats are yours for the asking, and the club has its own boats for scuba, with three compressors and tanks and a diving instructor. Tennis fans find four courts which they can use free—even for night play.

In all, 36 modestly furnished rooms are rented out. Single units go for $160 daily in winter, going up to $170 in a double, with each additional person charged $18. *In summer, the single tariff is $110 daily; the double, $115.* When booking, ask about special package deals too. Units have efficiency kitchens, and small areas have been set outside for do-it-yourself cookouts.

Meals are also served at a waterside restaurant, with a canopy. Around the palm-fringed swimming pool is a covered terrace with yellow garden furniture. On some evenings a steel band and calypso singers entertain you. You may even be asked to join in on the calypso singing. The location is ten minutes from downtown.

Island Beachcomber Hotel, Lindbergh Bay, P.O. Box 1618 (tel. 774-5250), is the beach hotel closest to town, and one of the most casual and informal on the island. Guests wear swimsuits most of the time—never shoes, except to go into town. At their place near the airport, Michael and Lorette Resch have shown thoughtful concern in running this establishment, drawing a large repeat clientele, many of whom are writers. Once part of a military chapel and a navy golf range, the resort has some motel-type units and a camaraderie among fellow guests is ingratiating. One night there might be a beach cookout or a rum party.

However, don't think it's primitive—it isn't. A row of smart Spanish-style units has overhanging balconies and arches on the lower apartment courtyard between units. The interior design features wood paneling and modified tropical furniture, much of it dark bamboo with electrified lantern wall lights and small refrigerators for your own cocktail parties. Both standard and beachfront rooms are rented. In winter, singles pay from $100 to $110 daily; doubles, from $105 to $115. *Off-season, singles range from $85 to $95; doubles $90 to $100.*

Water sports are strong here. You get complimentary snorkeling equipment, water rafts, and lounges. Caribbean dishes are served in the garden restaurant—right at beachside under a moonlit sky. Fishing and sailing are also possible off that beach.

For reservations, call 800/982-9898 toll free.

Magens Point Hotel, Magens Bay Road (tel. 775-5500), has a personality and charm of its own. On the northern shoreline, an eight-minute ride from downtown, it lies on a hillcrest overlooking Magens Bay with its beach which the *National Geographic* called "one of the ten best in the world." Naturally, there's regularly scheduled transportation to and from the beach and the adjacent Mahogany Run Golf Course as well as to the downtown free-port shopping. The hotel is small enough to retain its individuality, yet large enough to provide excellent holiday facilities. The main building is constructed with taste in native stone, with two rows of view balconies and a shingled town-house style of roofing. There's a wide, tree-shaded terrace with in- and outdoor dining. Buffets are often set out on long tables decorated with hibiscus bushes.

On a cliff, the swimming pool is set in the midst of rough stones, giving it a rain forest look, with a sunbathing ledge on one side. Bedrooms are air-conditioned, each with color TV and telephone, framed watercolors, and Caribbean-style furnishings. From every unit there's a generously proportioned veranda where you can order breakfast if you wish. A single in winter, on the EP, rents for $105 to $140 daily, going up to $105 to $150 in a double, with a third person sharing paying $35. *In summer, singles on the EP rent for $95 to $105 daily; doubles, $110 to $115.* Inquire about special honeymoon packages.

For your use are several tennis courts, lit at night, and you can also make arrangements for golf, scuba-diving, deep-sea diving, and sailing. Overlooking the sea is the popular restaurant, the Green Parrot. Unfortunately, a condominium blocks the view of the bay at sunset. Sometimes entertainment is provided. If you don't stay here, call before striking out from Charlotte Amalie or wherever.

Call 800/524-2031 toll free for reservations.

Point Pleasant Estate, Smith Bay, No. 4 (tel. 775-7200 or toll free 800/645-5306), is a very private, unique resort on Water Bay, on the far southeastern tip of St. Thomas, remote enough to connect you with the sea and islands. From your living room gallery, you look out on a Virgin collection—Tortola, St. John, and Jost Van Dyke. The hotel complex is set on a bluff with flowering shrubbery, century plants, frangipani trees, secluded trails, old rock formations, and lookout points. Hummingbirds share your breakfast. An open-air restaurant offers elegant dining.

Living arrangements are varied, and all units (except the bedrooms) feature fully equipped kitchens and private galleries facing that view. Guests are always close to the three freshwater swimming pools. You'll have a choice of living in a two-bedroom suite with two or three baths, a one-bedroom villa with two baths, a studio, an efficiency, or a bedroom. The studio is approximately 800 square feet with a bedroom closed off by louvered doors. The efficiency of about 500 square feet has a sleep-living room. The regular bedrooms have a full bath and are hotel size, with a balcony or sunken garden. The furnishings are light and airy, mostly rattan with floral fabrics.

On the EP, one person in summer pays from $660 to $875, and two persons pay from $690 to $1200 weekly, the latter for a villa. Four persons can occupy a studio in summer for $1200 weekly, a villa for $1500 a week. In winter, the rates go up. Then a single on the EP ranges from $900 weekly in a bedroom to $1350 for a villa. Two persons pay $950 for a bedroom, $1800 for a villa. Up to seven persons can stay in a suite for $3500 per week.

Many free offerings tip the scale. There is use of tennis courts, snorkeling equipment, and Sunfish sailboats. Free use of a car for four hours daily is allowed on a sign-out basis. You're also given free introductory scuba or windsurfing lessons.

Sapphire Beach Resort, P.O. Box 8088 (tel. 775-6100), opens onto one of the best beaches in St. Thomas. It is a beachfront resort with a lot of activities, including such water sports as scuba diving, snorkeling, windsurfing, and sailing. If you're not competent in any of these sports, instruction is available. Guests of the beachfront resort are allowed to use the four tennis courts as well. Rooms are pleasantly but simply furnished in a tropical motif, and you face a choice of living in one of the beachfront units or in one of the hillside studio condominiums, which tend to be cheaper.

It's best to book in here on one of their hotel package deals (see your travel agent), although these aren't applicable to condominium units. If not, expect to pay from $140 to $155 daily in a beachfront single, from $155 to $170 daily in a double, all winter tariffs, EP. Two persons in a hillside condo pay $130 daily, the cost going up to $150 in a one-bedroom hillside condo which can sleep as many as four persons. *In summer, beachfront singles range in price from $90 to $100 daily, with doubles priced from $100 to $110; hillside condos begin at $105 for two persons, going up to $120 for a maximum of four, plus tax.*

A Diving Resort

St. Thomas Diving Club, at Villa Olga, P.O. Box 4976 (tel. 774-1376), provides the illusion that it is on some remote island. It stands on a small projection of tree-covered land, with a sheltered waterfront swimming pool. At its core is Villa Olga, a handsomely rebuilt Danish West Indian–style gingerbread house which earned its name when it was the seat of the Russian consulate in the 1800s. When it was no longer the consulate, it was a brothel. It is now the Chart House Restaurant.

Today the club is the only total diving resort in the Virgin Islands. It's reached by going through Frenchtown. Experienced divers make their headquarters here. The inn rents out both hillside cottages and beachfront units.

Dick Doumeng, president of the club, offers a year-round dive package. For eight days and seven nights, based on double occupancy, one person pays about $700, which includes unlimited diving (reef, wreck, and nighttime), plus tanks, airfills, weights, and backpacks. If you'd like to go with a nondiver, he or she is welcomed for $375 weekly on the same package. These rates are in effect from December 20 to mid-April. After that, the dive package as described is reduced to $550 per person, the nondiver package going for $275, each one based on double occupancy. Activities are also planned for nondivers. Mr. Doumeng says, "We don't want any diving widows around here, and we see to it that that doesn't happen."

Every room has its own bath and a view of the harbor or sea. At water's edge, the club has a protected swimming pool surrounded by a bulkheaded sandy beach and palm trees.

Budget Inns and Guest Houses

Miller Manor, P.O. Box 1570, Princess Gade (tel. 774-1535), has been around for a long time, but it wasn't always a guest house. This is a 150-year-old Danish town house/villa, built on a bluff up in the residential section on Frenchman's Hill, about five minutes from downtown Charlotte Amalie. The owner-manager, Aida Miller, has lived here since she was seven years old. The house has a heavy collection of antiques, mixed with modern pieces. You enter through wrought-iron gates into a small courtyard with flowering bushes. The two lounges have crystal chandeliers, island antiques, and adjoining is a covered dining terrace with a view of the bay. The bedrooms are on four levels, each with its own style and furnishings. Many have tropical bamboo, ornate headboards, brass chandeliers, and a few have exposed-brick walls. There are 22 rooms in all, each with private bath and some with ceiling fans, others with air conditioning. *In summer, a single with bath costs $32; a double, also with bath, goes for*

$36 and $39. In winter, singles range in price from $38 to $42 and doubles pay from $46 to $49.

Villa Santana, Denmark Hill (tel. 774-1311), is a small estate house, high on a hill, with a surrounding garden. This very old villa, with its winding driveway and surrounding view terrace, was built by General Santa Anna during his third exile from Mexico. The building is so well known that many tour bus drivers point it out as part of island orientation. Even though now converted into a guest house, it still retains the flavor of those old days. The Danish architecture is untouched, and there are many antiques sprinkled throughout the main house. With its wooden coved ceiling, the living room opens toward a view of the harbor and is furnished in red bamboo.

While there are only six rooms in the main house, adjoining buildings have been converted into efficiency units all but two of which have kitchenettes. Room 2 is my favorite, furnished with period pieces, including a four-poster bed, an old chest, and a bentwood rocker. This is a friendly place to stay—they are beguiling hosts. In winter, accommodations cost from $42 to $55 per day for two in a double room, with each additional person paying an extra $12 per day. *In summer, two persons pay from $42 to $55 per day.* No meals are served, but many guests think the sweeping view more than makes up for that lack.

Mafolie, Mafolie Hill, P.O. Box 1528 (tel. 774-1506), stands high on a side of a hill, 800 feet above the harbor, with remarkable views of the bay and islands. To the south you can see St. Croix; to the west, Puerto Rico. The inn was built in the style of a Mediterranean villa. Everything is terraced. Although it can get lively when the crowd flocks in to enjoy steak at its restaurant, serenity prevails when they go back down the mountain. Sometimes calypso singers and a small steel band entertain. Therefore, if you like to go to bed early, this is not the place for you.

Rooms are modestly furnished in a homey fashion, and most of the units are air-conditioned. In winter, doubles range from $72 to $76 daily; singles, from $58 to $64. *In summer, tariffs are lowered to from $52 to $55 daily in a double, from $42 to $46 in a single.*

The hotel looks down upon a cliff-ledge swimming pool, and breakfast is served on the terrace. (For a description of the food served here, see the dining recommendations.) A free trip is scheduled daily to Magens Bay Beach, and fishing trips can be arranged. Unless you have a rented car, you may not want to stay here. The hotel is only a mile from town, but it's reached by steep, switchback roads, with loco drivers. If you don't have a car, it will cost from $5 or more each time you want to go downtown and return to the hotel.

Island View, P.O. Box 1903 (tel. 774-4270), is a nine-room guest house 545 feet up Crown Mountain overlooking St. Thomas harbor and the town of Charlotte Amalie. You enter onto a large gallery with this breathtaking view. The Island View is moderately priced for the budget-minded guest. Poolside rooms and one suite have private baths. Main-floor rooms, of which there are four, share hall baths. All bedrooms are cooled by natural breezes. The fresh-water pool provides a view of the town and harbor. Tropical fruits and flowers abound.

In winter, on the main floor singles pay $40 daily, the rate going up to $50 at poolside with a private bath. Doubles pay $50 on the main floor, $72 for a poolside room. *In summer, these rates are lowered to $30 in a single, $40 in a double.* All rates include a continental breakfast, with a full breakfast available. The self-service, open-air bar on the gallery is run on the honor system.

Bunkers' Hill View Guest House, Bunkers' Hill, 9 Commandant Gade (tel. 774-8056), is a clean and centrally situated guest lodge that would be suitable for students and others on an economy budget who don't want to sacrifice comfort and safety. Hubert V. Rawlins, the owner and manager, operates this establishment, renting pleasant rooms, most of which contain air conditioning and TV. Bunkers' Hill View lies right in the heart of town, just a short walk from the Main Street and all the major restaurants of Charlotte Amalie. Daily rates in winter are from $40 in a single, going up to $50 or more in a double. *Summer tariffs are $35 daily in a single, $45 in a double.* Rates include breakfast and limousine service to the airport. A kitchenette is provided if you want to prepare your own meals, and a laundromat stands about 25 yards from the guest house.

DINING OUT: The restaurants in St. Thomas have a cuisine that puts them among the top in quality in the entire West Indies. Prices, unfortunately, are high, and many of the best spots can only be reached by taxi. With a few exceptions, the finest and most charming restaurants aren't in Charlotte Amalie but out on the island.

Dining in Charlotte Amalie

Hotel 1829, Government Hill (tel. 774-1829), has some of the finest food in St. Thomas. The building is graceful and historic, too (see the previous hotel accommodations). For carefully prepared food and drink, with a distinctive European flavor, guests walk up the hill and climb the stairs of this old structure, heading for the attractive bar for a predinner drink. Dining is on a terrace or in the main room whose walls are made from ships' ballast and whose cooling is by ceiling fans. The floor is made of Moroccan tiles, two centuries old. Baron and Baroness Ball are your hosts.

The bartender specializes in frozen daiquiris, including coconut and strawberry. For an appetizer, you might select the escargots maître d'hôtel or perhaps one of the velvety-smooth soups such as cold cucumber. Try also the lobster bisque, which is made here fresh daily.

Fish and meat dishes are usually excellent. Among favorite dishes are the red snapper à la meunière and the grouper Dijon (served in a light mustard sauce). A thick cut of expertly prepared prime ribs is also featured. Try also a goose liver pâté or veal kidneys and scallops Domingo in a Pernod sauce. The homemade chocolate mousse is so good *Gourmet* magazine wrote the chef for his recipe. If you plan to dine here, expect to spend from $35 per person. Dinner is from 5 to 11 p.m., and reservations are requested. Closed Sunday.

L'Escargot, 3 Creques Alley (tel. 774-8880), has the same good food as its sister "Snail" (see below), but its menu is nowhere near as extensive. For the downtown shopper seeking some Gallic specialties, it offers good food, reasonable prices, and fine service. The location is in the Royal Dane Mall in a restored Danish building which is air-conditioned. Lunch is served from 11:30 a.m. to 3 p.m. and dinner from 6 to 10 p.m., except Sunday. Lunch has a range of well-chosen appetizers, including the namesake escargots. Soups are especially good, especially lobster bisque and onion soup au gratin. You help yourself to the salad bar. Otherwise, prime rib is a specialty, and roast duck with orange sauce is another winner. Count on spending about $15 per person for lunch or dinner. Children under 5 years of age are given a hamburger, french fries, and Coke free if accompanied by their parents (few 5-year-olds dine out unaccompanied). The offer is good until 7:30 p.m.

Sinbad, Bakery Square, off Back Street (tel. 774-2434), is a Middle Eastern bakery and restaurant, the finest of its kind in the Virgin Islands. Tiring of feeding sheiks in Miami, a Lebanese-American, Magdi Kassab, decided to open this charming corner of an old bakery site in Charlotte Amalie. It's an open-air complex on several levels, with natural wood, open beams, and hanging basket lamps as well as plants in handmade macramé holders. Haitian tables and chairs are used, and the courtyard atmosphere makes this a good choice for a luncheon of Middle Eastern sandwiches served in freshly baked pita bread, afternoon Turkish coffee, or a fabulous dinner. The bakery also serves breakfast, but no dinner.

Sinbad's serves a good breakfast such as omelet suprême with homemade yogurt and strawberries. For lunch, it offers sandwiches such as "sinburgers," shrimpburgers, and lobsterburgers. Sinbad's bakery specializes in delightful pastries, among them baklava, birdnest with strawberries or blueberries, apples and walnuts, and many more. Besides the sandwiches, the luncheon menu also offers stuffed mushrooms, hummos tahina, stuffed shrimp, and a seafood platter. Meals cost from $15 up. All these recipes are created after years of experience in the restaurant business. Closed Sunday.

Yesterdays, 1 Commandant Gade (tel. 774-3088), begins where Back Street ends. Cooled by ceiling fans, it's a casual place, a favorite with the locals who gravitate to the relaxed atmosphere. You can select a table outside on the veranda fronting the street, or else one covered with a gingham cloth resting under ceiling fans. Wood floors, a good-size bar (with the coldest beer in town), a dart game, paintings on driftwood for sale—you get the picture. All patrons seem to know each other. Table hopping is commonplace. Sandwiches, a lunch in themselves, are served on pita or french bread. The chef's special is a hamburger seasoned with sweet vermouth. But that is only one of many hamburgers from around the world which are served, ranging from Texas to Japan. You can also order the baby back ribs in the evening, the chef's specialty. You might begin with a banana daiquiri, arguably the best on the island. The typical meal will cost from $10. One of the oldest bars on the island, Yesterdays is behind the Chase Manhattan Bank. For amusement, you can watch rock concerts on the video screen.

On Frenchman's Hill

Harbor View, Frenchman's Hill (tel. 774-2651). Two very sophisticated American women, Arlene Lockwood and Lenore Wolfe, have welcomed guests to their gracious 19th-century Danish manor house for more than two decades. When magazines such as *Mademoiselle, Cosmopolitan,* and *Harper's Bazaar* started publishing reports of their imaginative cuisine—true creative cookery—the world came to their doorstep. Countless diners return again and again, and have become friends of the management.

The setting alone is dramatic (described in part in the hotel recommendations). You enter to the sounds of a tinkling concert grand piano. One of the staff shows you to a terrace with a spectacular view of Charlotte Amalie and the harbor. While you quietly sip your apéritif, menu selections are made.

Later you are shown through a montage of sweeping brick arches to your shimmering candlelit table, a polished mahogany which has been set with a pewter service. One of the three dining rooms is in the original kitchen. Forget the expense for one night, and sit back to enjoy fine food, a Mediterranean cuisine, and impeccable service.

Recommended appetizers include West Indian meat "pattes" (beef) and a cassolette of fresh mushrooms prepared with sour cream and herbs. The chef is noted for his classic gazpacho, but one should also inquire about the soup du jour (I recently enjoyed the best carrot soup I've ever had).

Main dishes are served with salad greens and a choice of potato soufflé or a side order of pasta. My favorite orders include a delightfully delicate dish of sauteed shrimp and cream sauce embellished with grated cheese and dry sherry, scaloppina maison (thin slices of veal stuffed with cheese and served with a fresh mushroom sauce), steak pizzaiola (filet mignon cooked to order and prepared with a herbed tomato sauce), and spanaki tou fournou (Greek-style spinach casserole baked with a creamy blend of cheeses).

Each day the cooks bake good-tasting pies from their collection of house recipes. Dinner is served nightly, except Tuesday, and reservations are imperative. Count on spending $35 or more for a complete dinner. On certain nights in season it seems that half the denizens of St. Thomas drive up the narrow, wiggly road from the marketplace to this hillside-hugging gastronomic retreat. I suggest you join them. The restaurant is open year round except for a vacation period just after the Labor Day weekend.

At Compass Point

Raffles, Compass Point (tel. 775-2850), named after the legendary hotel in Singapore, is an establishment filled with tropical accents more evocative of the South Pacific than of the Caribbean. Because of that, no one will mind if women wear flowers in their hair or if men dress in sports clothes for dinner on the outdoor terrace. The furnishings include peacock chairs, lots of wicker, ceiling fans, and the kind of bar where you may want to toss off a few rounds before dinner, perhaps sampling the daiquiris which are known throughout the island. Dinner is served daily except Sunday from 6:30 to 10:30 p.m. A pianist plays during the dinner hours from Tuesday through Saturday.

You can choose from dishes which are organized on the menu into categories, including beef, veal, lamb, chicken, and shrimp. The fish of the day is freshly caught and well prepared, with various tasty sauces. You may also enjoy coconut shrimp, "two-day duck," steak Raffles prepared at your table, veal tsaritsa, a mixed English grill, or chicken Rangoon. Full meals range from $25 upward. You'll find this place outside the lagoon at Compass Point, a few miles east of Charlotte Amalie.

The **Windjammer Restaurant,** Compass Point Seaport (tel. 775-2275). Much of the paneling and the smoothly finished bar of this pleasant place are crafted from thick slabs of island mahogany, which is illuminated by light streaming in from the open windows looking out onto the nearby marina.

Uwe Dedekind, the Germany-born owner, lived in Bremen and later in Costa Rica before opening this nautical-style hideaway. Dinner is served seven days a week from 6:30 to 10 p.m. Of course, no one will mind if you want to join the drinkers at the commodious bar for a round or two before tucking into a few of the house specialties. The selection of house drinks ranges from a "Shiver Me Timbers" to the "Half Hitch" to the "Drunken Sailor."

On the menu is a wide selection of seafood, such as queen triggerfish, a Caribbean delicacy locally referred to as "whole ole wife," five different shrimp dishes, a Teutonic rahmschnitzel (veal cutlets with spices in a heady cream sauce), snapper and dolphin prepared in many different ways, some of them stuffed with lobster, a well-prepared wienerschnitzel, and a fisherman's platter. Full meals range from $25, although your bar tab could make it go much higher.

At Frenchtown

The **Café Normandie,** rue de St. Barthélemy, at Frenchtown (tel. 774-1622) is my favorite dining nook in this colorful section of St. Thomas. It also offers one of the best dining values on the island. From 6:30 to 10 p.m. daily you can order a table d'hôte menu for just $20, which might begin with hors d'oeuvres, perhaps made with seafood, plus soup, perhaps French onion. You're served not only a salad and sherbet (to clear your palate), but are allowed to choose from a selection of main-dish specialties ranging from langouste to beef Wellington (an odd name for a French restaurant), or hasenpfeffer (pieces of hare, bacon, and steak in a rich, savory sauce). The dessert special (not featured on the set meal) is their original chocolate fudge pie. All the food writers from such magazines as *Food and Wine* and *Gourmet* have so far been unsuccessful in getting the chef to part with the secret recipe. The restaurant is air-conditioned, and the glow of candlelight makes it quite elegant. It's beautifully run, and the service is excellent. There is a relaxed informality about the dress code, but you shouldn't show up in a bikini. Reservations are absolutely mandatory, and if you're dining there from mid-December to May 1, you may need to call several days in advance.

Bartolino's (tel. 774-8554) is one of the best of the cluster of restaurants in this little sea-bordering hamlet. The chef specializes in northern Italina fare, which, unlike the cookery of southern Italy, is a butter-based cuisine. Sit on his porch with its harbor view, enjoying a sundowner, served between 4:30 and 6:30 p.m. The lighting is subdued in the main dining room which has a tropical look. Early birds begin their dinner at 6:30 p.m., and service is until 10:30 p.m. Pasta dishes are well made here, and you get good fresh fish. If you're into meat for a main course, try one of the veal dishes. Desserts are smooth. Count on dropping about $25 or more for a fine meal with good service. The doors shut on Monday.

Alexander's, Frenchtown (tel. 774-4340), will warmly accommodate you. Its walls are painted a pale shade of gray, while the thick mahogany bar is lined with a moveable collection of stools, which, of course, change positions as different crowds of drinkers come and go. This is especially true during the happy hour, 4 to 6 p.m., when your second drink costs only $1.

In addition to serving drinks—a brandy Café Alexander is a favorite—the place is a well-run restaurant as well. There are only ten tables, but on them, Austrian specialties are served with flair. A few seafood dishes are offered, among them a conch schnitzel, but most of the others are strictly Middle European. They include a mouthwatering wienerschnitzel, Nürnburger röstbraten, goulash, breaded mushrooms, schweinbraten with dumplings and sauerkraut, and homemade pâté. For dessert, you might try the homemade strudel, either apple or cheese, or else the richly caloric Schwartzwald torte. A full dinner, served from 6:30 to 10 p.m. seven days a week, costs from $25. Lunches are considerably cheaper, around $10. Midday meals consist of a variety of crêpes, quiches, and a daily chef's special. You'll find this place on the waterfront overlooking the harbor.

Barbary Coast, Frenchtown (tel. 774-8354). Chianti bottles hang from the walls of this dimly lit restaurant which serves the best Italian food on the island. The ambience is informal and can be a lot of fun, especially around the large bar in the outer room which many patrons abandon only reluctantly to head inside to dinner. This lighthearted establishment is owned by three young partners, Al, Steve, and Dan, who work hard to keep it going seven days a week.

If you want a touch of the Caribbean, you might try the conch parmigiana. Otherwise, you'll have to stick to savory dishes such as veal served either piccata, marsala, or parmigiana, eggplant parmigiana, many versions of pasta, homemade minestrone, and a fresh fish dish of the day, which might be grouper served four different ways. Other choices are prime rib, filet mignon, New York strip steak, fresh garlic bread, and shrimp cocktail. Wine is sold by the bottle or by the glass. The restaurant is closed for lunch. The bar opens daily at 5 p.m., staying open till around 4 a.m. Full meals cost from $20.

Red Hook

New York, New York, at Red Hook (tel. 775-2979). Except for the New York City memorabilia dotting the plank walls and the Big Apple–style deli food featured on the menu, the aura of this place is inspired more by California than by New York. From the outside, it looks a lot like one of the warehouses dotting the outskirts of Red Hook, but what you're likely to see is a lively and sometimes hard-drinking crowd of Stateside refugees who seem to have made this their favorite island hangout.

Every Saturday, a guitarist plays and sings to a full house, beginning at 9 p.m. Weekends, a special brunch is offered from 11 a.m. to 4 p.m., costing a bargain $9 per person with unlimited Bloody Marys, mimosas, or champagne. The rest of the week, food is served from 10 a.m. to 4 p.m. daily, with a menu featuring Reuben sandwiches, tuna melts, nine-ounce "monster burgers," french-fried zucchini, breaded mushrooms and mozzarella fingers. Full meals, served on red-checked tablecloths, cost from $11.

The Sub Base

L'Escargot (tel. 774-6565) has a loyal group, including one American expatriate who told me she wouldn't dine anywhere else except perhaps at the downtown L'Escargot. I'm not *that* devoted to "The Snail," but I admire its Gallic tradition of fine food and expert service. The pseudo-Spanish exterior as well as the interior are less enviable, but no diner comes here for the decor. Backed up by a good wine cellar, the menu is extensive, including the classic French specialties. About the largest selection of hors d'oeuvres, in town—both hot and cold—are offered, including such unusual ones as mousse of red snapper and/or the better known pâté de foie gras. The Boston clam chowder is creamy delicious, and you might also order a spinach salad. Frog legs with butter and garlic will rest on your china plate, unless you prefer one of the many specialties such as wienerschnitzel or orange duckling. The beef Wellington is another chef's specialty. The chocolate soufflé for two is considered the best in town. You'll spend from $30 to $35 here for dinner. Lunch is served Monday to Friday from noon to 2 p.m. and dinner nightly except Sunday from 6:30 to 10:30 p.m. The restaurant overlooks the Gregorie Channel.

Scattered Choices

Au Bon Vivant (tel. 774-2158) sits atop Government Hill, and is known for its superb view of Charlotte Amalie and the lights in the harbor. It is also known for its classic French cookery, carefully supervised by José Chevrotée, the owner and chef. You may order French champagne by the glass while choosing from an extensive selection of fine dishes. Hot hors d'oeuvres are likely to include an onion tart or else escargots de Bourgogne. Soups are imaginative and include cream of watercress and fresh fish flavors. The chef also takes care with his salads, avoiding the iceberg lettuce monotony by using endive, fresh mushrooms, and romaine lettuce, each served with a different dressing. Main-dish specialties include a rack of lamb aux herbes and fish Normande. You might also select the filet mignon with Madagascar pepper, Dover sole stuffed with fish mousse, or baby veal sauteed and steamed with plums and flamed with champagne. The chef also prepares chicken breast with lime and coconut. Dinner, costing from $30, is served Monday to Saturday from 6:30 to 10 p.m. Reservations are necessary.

The Stone Farmhouse, Mahogany Run Golf and Tennis Resort (tel. 775-5000). Decorated with antiques and 19th-century farm implements, this restored farmhouse is one of the most charming culinary hideaways in all of St. Thomas. Built some 150 years ago, the stone-walled house used to shelter the plantation's dairy workers, but today, the occupants are vacationing gourmets enjoying the view of the golf course, the well-prepared specialties, and the upbeat rhythms from the evening dance bands.

Set beneath the interior stone arches are enough high-backed chairs to seat

100 diners, who savor the kinds of specialties which won the establishment the Golden Pelican Award for the finest food on St. Thomas. Open only for dinner every night except Tuesday, the place serves such appetizing dishes as a terrine of chicken and crabmeat, scallop and salmon mousse with tarragon sauce, Strasbourg foie gras, fettuccine with salmon, fresh broccoli with cream sauce, stuffed quail with grape sauce, shrimp with frog legs creole style, veal with lobster in béarnaise sauce, Caribbean-style bouillabaisse, shrimp stuffed with ripe bananas in coconut batter served with a curry sauce, tournedos Rossini, and many others. For dessert, you choose from a collection of mousses, homemade ice creams, and pastries, with the final note set by a selection from eight exotic coffees. Full meals range from around $50.

The resident musician is Nat Blake, who has become so popular since the restaurant and the resort were established in 1980 that some guests claim they return year after year just to hear him.

Fiddle Leaf, Watergate Villas (tel. 775-2810). Occasionally a chef comes along who is imaginative and creative, enough so that his or her place becomes *the* restaurant to dine in a city or on an island. In St. Thomas, that honor goes to Patricia LaCorte, who, in spite of her Cordon Bleu training, has broken through with innovative recipes all her own, a kind of French and Stateside nouvelle cuisine. Her restaurant, opening onto Bolongo Bay, has awakened the sleepy tastebuds of St. Thomas.

First, the location is romantic: an open-air garden atmosphere in a pavilion setting. Flickering candlelight enhances the atmosphere, and only dinner is served nightly except Monday from 6:30 to 10 p.m. Most dinners cost from $35 and up, and reservations are essential.

Backed up by an expert culinary team, Ms. LaCorte is likely to tempt you with one of her soups. Ever had carrot and orange? Perhaps cannelloni and escarole soup will be served on the night of your visit.

The main dishes are skillfully prepared, including the well-known pecan chicken. The catch of the day is also reliable. Each dish, such as filet mignon filled with brie, is prepared to order—so don't come here in a rush. For dessert, perhaps you'll sample, if featured, the delectable tart made with four fresh island fruits. If you're staying in or around Charlotte Amalie, count on a 25-minute ride.

Entre Nous (Between Us), Bluebeard's Castle Hotel (tel. 774-1600), is one of the finest dinner restaurants serving a French cuisine in St. Thomas. An open-air restaurant with a view, it occupies space at this world-famed hotel. All food is cooked to order, so allow plenty of time. Count on spending around $30 for a superb dinner which is likely to include the chef's specialty, filet Entre Nous with shrimp and scallops. On my most recent rounds, I ordered a well-prepared Caesar salad to accompany the dish. I could also have selected medallions of veal Oscar, roast Long Island duckling flambéed with Calvados, or else a casserole of fruits de mer. To begin your fine repast, you might select escargots en croûte, finishing off your meal with a Café Sambucca. If you are a vegetarian, the chef will prepare special plates, perhaps linguine primavera. Always call for a reservation.

At the **Bird of Paradise,** Secret Harbour Beach Hotel (tel. 775-5686), you can touch the mast of a beached catamaran from the veranda. This outdoor restaurant, set up beside an amply stocked bar by the water, is the domain of Liverpudlian Frank Godin and his New York City sweetheart, Sherie Berk. In many ways, the restaurant is as exotic as the bird for which it is named. Large wicker chairs and ceiling fans add a touch of Somerset Maugham, although the menu quickly brings diners back to a late 20th-century appreciation of some of the most sophisticated cuisine on St. Thomas.

Specialties change frequently, but at the time of your visit, they might include three-spice West Indian chicken, duck à l'orange flambéed near your table, sirloin with cabernet-flavored butter, or boneless rack of lamb en croûte. This is stuffed with fresh spinach, Montrachet goat cheese, and pignoli, then rolled in puff pastry, sliced into medallions, and served with a cabernet sauce. Other special dishes are a fresh fish of the day, often stuffed with spinach and brie and served in a cream sauce, veal chop almondine with vinaigrette honey glaze, chicken mimosa with orange, ginger, and champagne, filet mignon with three spices, and fresh lobster stuffed with crabmeat and scallop mousse. Mushroom strudel is a favorite appetizer, fairly bursting with mushrooms and cream sauce, while for dessert, you might like a white chocolate mousse or a native Linzertorte with tropical fruits. Finally, for an after-dinner drink which is as theatrical as it is delicious, try the café diablo, whose hissing elaborate tableside preparation enhance the orange-and-clove-laden perfume of the alcoholic coffee. Full meals range from $40 per person. Reservations are suggested.

Chart House Restaurant, at the St. Thomas Diving Club (tel. 774-4262), was the site of the Russian consulate in the 19th century. The club itself was recommended separately for its diving resort (see hotels), which is on the same property but run separately from the restaurant. However, even if you aren't one of the experienced divers staying here, you may want to journey out past Frenchtown Village for lunch or dinner in this tranquil spot. The restaurant is in the rebuilt Villa Olga, which is Victorian in style. In the bar area you can listen to divers' "bull sessions." The dining gallery is a large open terrace fronting the sea.

Dinner at the Chart House is served Monday through Thursday from 5:30 to 10 p.m. and Friday through Sunday at 5:30 to 11 p.m. Cocktail service starts at 5 p.m. seven days a week, and the bartender will make you his special drink called a Bailey's colada. The restaurant features the best salad bar on the island, with a choice of 30 to 40 items nightly. Dinners begin at $20, going up to $35, and menu choices range from chicken to Alaskan king crab. Of course, this chain is known for serving the finest cut of prime rib anywhere, and here it comes loading down a plate at 22 ounces. Dinners are complemented with fresh bread.

If you arrive before sunset, you'll get to watch the seaplanes land directly in front of the restaurant. For dessert, you can order the famous Chart House "mud pie," which, in spite of its name, is a shockingly calorie-loaded ice-cream concoction. You don't make a reservation—just arrive and hope you'll get a table.

Royal Rum Barrel, Government Hill (tel. 776-1854), occupies a charming, secluded nook in an 1854 house. Tables for food and drink are set up in one of the most tucked-away little courtyards in St. Thomas, with a fountain and enclosing stone walls. If you find your way here to this Government Hill spot, you'll be served sandwiches and salad plates at lunch, and such tempting dinner fare as conch native style and steak in a Dijon mustard sauce, along with "regal coffees" and a new dessert every evening. Full meals cost from $20 and up, but you can always drop in for a drink on a hot afternoon. Ever had baked potato soup? You might try it here, along with local fish prepared in the West Indian manner.

Driftwood Inn, 46 Aguas Fancy (tel. 774-2390), serves very good Italian food, and even if it didn't, you might want to come here just for the view—which is spectacular, overlooking the town and harbor. Arrive in time to enjoy a sundowner after you drive into the mountains. As you go down the steps, the wafting aroma of a rich tomato sauce usually greets you. The owner has hired a friendly and most hospitable staff who will show you to an al fresco terrace table. Bolla wine bottles are wrapped around the posts holding up the ceiling.

I suggest you begin with the antipasto for two or perhaps the minestrone. Dinner is prepared from basic ingredients right in the kitchen, and it is cooked only after you order it. So sit back, relax, and spend a while. The inn offers the usual selection of steak, chops, and seafood, but most guests come here for the Italian specialties, including saltimbocca, eggplant parmigiana, veal piccata, and linguine with red clam sauce. Desserts usually include an Italian cake, followed by espresso. The price for dinner ranges from a low of $20, going up to $30. Meals are served from 6 to 11 p.m. seven days a week. You're asked to reserve a table.

Parkside Swiss French Restaurant (tel. 774-1695), lies at the foot of Government Hill, about a couple of blocks east of Post Office Square and fronting Roosevelt Park. In a historic 1822 house, its chef-owner, René Tornier, a Swiss citizen, has opened this relaxed continental restaurant which, in spite of its food, has a West Indian ambience. Ask for a table in the garden if the weather is right (which it almost always is), or else you can select a spot on the veranda or perhaps in the attractive living room of this town house.

Reservations are necessary, and you can count on spending from $30 and up for a superb meal which might include fondue Bacchus, frog legs, filet mignon with a superb sauce, le veau française, sweetbreads, duck, even dolphin caviar. There is a selection of flambé desserts, but most guests seem to prefer what is considered the best chocolate pie in St. Thomas. The restaurant serves dinner only daily except Sunday. Be prepared to make an evening of it since each course is prepared to order.

The Frigate, Mafolie Hotel, Mafolie Hill (tel. 774-2790), occupies one of the most spectacular dining terraces in St. Thomas. This hotel, previously described, is certainly the inn with the view. The moon lights this tropical place, which you reach after a taxi ride from the harbor, along Magens Bay Road. The menu is presented to you on a little brown jug, and it's wisely kept simple, as this is primarily a steak and lobster place. The food that is charcoal broiled is done so to perfection at the outdoor grill. I suggest the beef kebab or the New York strip. For that price you can not only help yourself at a most presentable salad bar, but get a baked potato, even a soup (such as vichyssoise). The lobster tail is also a big, popular specialty. For dessert, you'll happily settle for cheesecake, if you're like most diners. The inn opens for drinks at 5:30 p.m., serving dinner (no lunches) every night from 6:30 to 10:30 p.m. Your total bill will probably run about $25 per person. Reservations are recommended.

Sparky Cloud Room, Smith Bay Road (tel. 775-1055), is one of the best places on the island for good native cookery. Ever had an oldwife? That's trigger fish, and the taste is far better than the name. Other local fish such as grunt and hind are also served West Indian style, which often means in a zesty creole sauce. Try the stewed conch Anegada (from the British Virgin Islands) along with okra fungi which has been batter fried in cornmeal. Curried chicken and steaks form a tasty array of good cooking, along with a superb seafood casserole in a creamy sauce with chunks of lobster. Callaloo soup is regularly featured. Count on spending around $20 to $25 for a meal.

On some nights calypso shows are staged here. Sparky is to the east of Charlotte Amalie. It's customary to begin your meal with a Vicious Virgin. That's the house drink, and it lives up to its name! The Cloud Room serves seven nights a week, from 6:30 to 10:30 p.m.

Eunice's Terrace, 67 Smith Bay (tel. 775-3975). This unpretentious plank-covered building welcomes a hard-fisted collection of Stateside construction workers, West Indian locals, and an occasional tourist into its confines for savory platters of island food served in generous portions. The number of tables (about seven) is so limited that many diners wait at the bar with a drink before eventually seating themselves. A popular concoction called a Queen Mary (a combination of tropical fruits laced with dark rum) is a favorite.

Eunice Best, formerly of Charleston, South Carolina, set up this restaurant years ago after marrying a resident of St. Thomas. She spends her days as a guidance counselor in a public school, sometimes leaving the lunch crowd in the capable hands of Mrs. Thelma Small, although in the evening, Mrs. Best is likely to be on hand. The establishment is open from 9 a.m. to midnight seven days a week. You'll find it just east of the Coral World turnoff.

Dinner specialties include conch fritters, boiled or fried fish, especially dolphin, sweet potato pie, and a number of chalkboard specials which are usually served with fungi, rice, or plantain. Full dinners cost from $18 and lunches $10. On the lunch menu are fishburgers, sandwiches, and such daily specials as Virgin Islands–style pork or meat loaf. Key lime pie is a favorite dessert. Reservations are a good idea at dinnertime.

El Papagayo, at the Tillett compound, 125 Estate Anna's Retreat (see "Shopping"; tel. 775-1550), is an unusual choice for dining. Out near Red Hook, "The Parrot" serves a tasty array of California-style Mexican dishes, along with some Stateside favorites. You'll find the usual assortment of chiles rellenos, enchiladas, tacos, burritos, and stuffed quesadilla. Contrary to some people's belief, the Tilletts aren't back there slaving in the kitchen. Rather, it's Fred and Vivian Wilkins, a friendly couple who make this a pleasant luncheon stopover or an eatery worth the trek out there at night.

In the garden bar, order a strawberry margarita, and I bet you can't stop with just one. Main dishes include rice-and-bean combination plates, and a full meal can be had for around $12. They serve all day until 10 p.m., but in the evening you should reserve.

GETTING AROUND: The chief means of transport is the taxi, which is unmetered. Therefore it is important to agree with the driver *before* you get into the car. Actually, taxi fares are controlled and are widely posted, perhaps at your hotel desk. In St. Thomas cabs are plentiful. Most trips cost only $3.50 to $7. For example, a transfer from the airport to Bluebeard's Hotel is about $9 for the first passenger. Surcharges, ranging from $1 to $1.50, are added on after midnight. If you rent a taxi and a driver (who just may serve as a guide) for the day, the cost is about $25 for two persons for two hours of sightseeing. Each additional passenger pays another $12.

St. Thomas has what they call an open-air "taxi bus." Departures are from Red Hook dock on the hour from 7:15 a.m. to 6:15 p.m. They also depart from the Market Place for Red Hook on the hour from 8:15 a.m. to 5:15 p.m., costing $2 for a one-way ticket.

Manassah Country Bus goes between Charlotte Amalie and Red Hook nearly every hour. Service starts at 6 a.m. from Charlotte Amalie, ending at the last run at 8 p.m. from Red Hook, all for a one-way ticket cost of 75¢. Throughout the day, other buses depart from the Market Place in Charlotte Amalie, heading across St. Thomas as far west as Bordeaux, a one-way passage going for 75¢. For information about exact schedules, telephone 774-5678.

A **Safari Bus,** which goes from Market Square to Red Hook, departs hourly on the quarter hour at a one-way cost of $2 per passenger.

Car Rentals

St. Thomas has a lot of cars to rent and a lot of agencies, and rates, I feel, are pretty steep. Naturally, the big names, such as **Hertz** (tel. 774-0841) and **Avis** (tel. 774-1468), are here, as is **National** (tel. 774-6220). You'll find these companies operating out of expensive kiosks at the airport.

Adhering to my policy of trying different car-rental companies on various research trips, I used **Budget Rent-a-Car** and found that their high-season rates in all categories, including insurance, were less than that charged at Hertz. In addition, except for a promotional fare (subject to change) on week-long rentals of a limited number of Isuzus as Avis, Budget's rates were almost always cheaper across the board than those at Avis as well.

Circumstances could change by the time of your visit. If so, you can call Avis toll free at 800/331-1212 or Hertz toll free at 800/654-3131.

Budget maintains offices at the St. Thomas airport (tel. 774-5774) and at the St. Thomas Sub Base (tel. 776-5774). Most travelers will use the airport branch, which is in the arrivals hall.

All vehicles rented by Budget in St. Thomas come with automatic transmission as a standard feature. The least expensive car in high season is a Mazda station wagon, which seats four to five persons in comfort, with space for luggage. Weekly rentals without air conditioning, but with unlimited mileage included, cost $240 per week or $39 a day. With air conditioning, the cost goes up another $20 per week or $3 per day.

These rates are high-season tariffs, and they are lowered in the summer. Budget also offers a line of mini-vans that seat 8 to 15 persons, plus a line of well-appointed sedans.

To qualify for these rates, you must reserve a vehicle at least two business days in advance by calling Budget's toll-free reservations service (tel. 800/527-0700).

All of St. Thomas's major rental companies require that in the event of an accident, the driver must pay for the first several hundred dollars of the repair costs unless additional insurance is arranged. If the driver does not purchase the added insurance, he or she is obligated to pay up to the first $600 worth of damage should a mishap occur with a Budget car. At both Hertz and Avis, uninsured drivers are responsible for up to $1500 worth of collision damage. All three agencies charge about $7 per day for this extra insurance. Additional personal accident insurance is available at all agencies for $2.50 a day.

Cycle Rentals

Honda and Yamaha Rental, 80 Veterans Dr. (tel. 774-2018), handles this type of rental right downtown in Charlotte Amalie on the waterfront. The cost is from $40 a day. Bring along your driver's license.

Sightseeing by Surrey Bus

Booked mainly by cruise-ship passengers, this 2½-hour tour by fringe-topped surrey bus costs $12 per person (minimum of eight persons), and covers all the major sights such as Bluebeard's Castle, Drake's Seat, and Frenchman's Reef. Reservations must be made in advance. Across from the post office in Charlotte Amalie, try **Travel Services Inc.** (tel. 776-0935).

Local Air Services

If you'd like to hop over to St. Croix or perhaps Tortola (the capital of the British Virgin Islands), call on **Virgin Islands Seaplane Shuttle.** For reservations, telephone 773-1776, the last four digits of whose numbers any American can remember. The seaplane also flies to St. John in case you don't want to take the ferry boat.

SHOPPING: The $800 duty-free allowance makes every purchase a double bargain. Often well-known brand names are presented at savings of up to 60% off

Stateside prices. However, that is likely to be an exceptional purchase. I don't want to paint too optimistic a picture. To find true value, you often have to plow through a lot of junk. Many items offered for sale—binoculars, stereos, watches, cameras—can be matched in price at your hometown discount store. Therefore, you need to know the price of the item involved back home to determine if you are in fact making a savings. Having sounded that warning, I'll survey some St. Thomas shops where I personally have found good buys. Know that there are lots more you can discover on your own.

Most of the shops, some of which occupy former pirate warehouses, are open from 9 a.m. to 5 p.m., regular business hours, and some stay open later. Nearly all stores close on Sunday and major holidays—that is, unless a cruise ship is in port. Few shopkeepers can stand the prospect of dozens of potential customers, their purses full, wandering by their padlocked doors. Therefore, those gates are likely to swing open, at least for half a day on Sunday. Friday is the biggest cruise-ship visiting day at Charlotte Amalie (one day I counted eight at one time)—so try to avoid shopping then.

Cardow Jewelers, 39 Dronningens Gade (tel. 774-1140), often called the Tiffany's of the Caribbean, is the first store on Main Street. It boasts the largest selection of fine jewelry shown in the world. This fabulous shop, where there are more than 6000 rings displayed, offers its customers enormous savings because of its worldwide direct buying, large turnover, and duty-free prices. Unusual and traditional designs are offered in diamonds, emeralds, rubies, sapphires, and Brazilian stones, as well as pearls and coral. Cardow has a whole wall of Indian gold chains at savings of 40% and 50%. Also featured are antique coin jewelry and Piaget watches. The Treasure Cove has case after case of gold jewelry.

A. H. Riise Gift Shops, 37 Main St. at Riise's Alley (tel. 774-2303), offers the customer a memorable shopping experience. Displayed in a restored 18th-century Danish warehouse that extends from Main Street to the waterfront is an unusually wide and fine selection of quality imported merchandise. Special attention is given to the collection of fine jewelry and watches from Europe's leading craftspeople, including Patek Philippe, the most prestigious watch in the world, Ebel, Concord, and many others. Waterford, Lalique, Daum, Baccarat, Wedgwood, Royal Crown Derby, Royal Copenhagen, and Lladro are but a few of the internationally known names found in the crystal and china departments. The perfume and cosmetics are found in one of the largest parfumeries in the Caribbean. Specialties also include Crabtree & Evelyn and Liberty of London shops, as well as a complete duty-free art gallery featuring original Caribbean art.

Tropicana Perfumes Shoppes, 2 Dronningens Gade (tel. 774-0010), stand at the beginning of Main Street near the Central Post Office. They are the exclusive agents of Yendi by Capucci. The first of these two shops is billed as the largest perfumerie in the world. Behind its rose and white facade, it offers all the famous names in perfumes, colognes, as well as cosmetics and toilet water, including Anaïs Anaïs, named after the famed diarist, Anaïs Nin. Men will find Europe's best colognes and aftershave lotions.

Little Switzerland, 5 Dronningens Gade (tel. 776-2010), with three stores in downtown Charlotte Amalie and one on the dock at Havensight Mall, sells only the finest watches, as well as a wide selection of jewelry and the best in crystal and china. The watches are priced as they are in Switzerland, which is a good saving on such name brands as Rolex, Ebel, Girard-Perregaux, Vacheron & Constanin, Concord, and many more. Incidentally, the owners employ Swiss watchmakers to ensure that every watch is perfectly adjusted. Names in chinaware and crystal such as Baccarat, Lalique, Rosenthal, Aynsley, Royal Doulton, Wedgwood, and many more are here. This is also the official Hummel and Lladro shop, as well as being the largest Waterford crystal importer in the West Indies.

Cavanagh's, Havensight Mall (tel. 776-0737), at the West Indian Company Docks, is a name that suggests casual island living to both visitors and residents. From furniture to fashions, the selection is varied, and is likely to come from anywhere around the globe. Seek out, in particular, the items in Thai silk and cotton. The shop has had more than a quarter of a century's experience in the Virgin Islands, selling fashions, gifts, and labels from more than 50 countries, along with accessories and wearing apparel for the whole family. Liberty of London and Pringle and Barrie Knitwear of Scotland are just some of the names carried.

H. Stern, Main Street (tel. 774-1939), is an outlet of one of the world's leading jewelers. This chain store designs as well as manufactures most of the jewelry it sells. Rubies, emeralds, sapphires, diamonds—you name the size and shape, and Stern has it in its showcases. Many of the designs are one-of-a-kind pieces. Stern, of course, is South America's leading jeweler, and the firm is known for its Brazilian gemstones. Other locations in St. Thomas include Bluebeard's Castle Hotel, Havensight Shopping Mall, and Frenchman's Reef Holiday Inn.

If you want to combine a little history with shopping, you might go into the courtyard of the old **Pissarro Building,** entered through an archway off Main Street. The celebrated impressionist painter lived in this same building as a child. The old apartments have been turned into a warren of interesting, merchandise-loaded shops.

The Leather Shop, 1 Dronningens Gade (tel. 776-3995), across from Little Switzerland, Main Street, has a good selection of leather from Italian designers. Some of the handbags are carried by the chic Italian boutiques, Fendi and Bottega Veneta. For example, you'll find belts handmade in oiled calfskin by Pugi of Florence. There are more than two dozen different styles of buckles from which to choose. The store claims to hold the largest selection of handmade leather goods in the Caribbean. You can walk through to enjoy an attractive Italian garden, built in 1820 and faithfully restored.

The Guitar Lady, on Raadets Gade (tel. 774-5121), near the waterfront opposite Shane Co. and the Blue Parrot, sells guitars made in Brazil. The cost can run as low as $75, but it can also jump to $250 and beyond. Tambourines and drums are sold as well, as are small steel drums. The "guitar lady," Joyce La Motta, will also show you her congas, bongos, ukeleles, mandolins, and Hohner harmonicas, as well as her good selection of West Indian records and tapes.

Sweet Passion (tel. 774-2990), close by the fountain, across from L'Escargot Restaurant in the Royal Dane Mall, facing the square, sells antique jewelry, with many items from the Georgian and early Victorian periods. On these items —that is, anything more than a century old—there is no duty. The shopkeepers will also show you jewelry of a later design, including art nouveau and 1920s deco. The shop also carries a line of luxury gifts in sterling and crystal as well as a fun line of early plastic and paste "fashion" jewelry.

The Straw Factory, 24 Garden St. (tel. 774-4849), a stroll up from Post Office Square, has the island's largest selection of straw hats, from classic Panamas to beachcomber bargains, as well as handcrafted wares. Be sure to check out the modestly priced Haitian terracotta figurines and the wide selection of all-cotton sportswear. There are shopping bags with embroidered flowers, but most of the shop is filled with one-of-a-kind items, both decorative and useful. Stop at the counter outside for an ice-cream cone and eat it seated in the shade of the Straw Factory patio.

The wafting aroma of spices will lead you to **Down Island Traders,** 9 C Contant (tel. 774-3419). It has an attractive array of spices, teas, seasonings, jams, and condiments, most of which are packaged from natural Caribbean products. Look also for its nuts, candies, and jellies—it's an original native market. The owner also carries a line of local cookbooks, as well as silkscreened island designs on T-shirts, scarfs, and bags.

Blue Carib Gems and Rocks (tel. 774-8525), the Bakery Shopping Square, is perched behind Little Switzerland on Back Street. For a decade the owners prospected for gemstones in the Caribbean, and these stones have been brought direct from the mine to you. The raw stones are cut and polished and then fashioned into jewelry by the lost-wax process. On one side of the premises you can see the craftspeople at work, and on the other side view their finished products, including such handsomely set stones as larimar, the light blue turquoise from the Dominican Republic. Since the items are locally made, they are duty free and not included in the $800 exemption.

Java Wraps (tel. 774-3700), in Palm Passage on the waterfront in Charlotte Amalie, is all white tiles with traditional Javanese matting decorated with exotic Balinese wood carvings on the walls. Locals and tourists alike buy the hand-batiked resort wear line specializing in shorts, shirts, sundresses, and children's clothing. Java Wraps is known for its sarong pieces and demonstrates the tying of them in at least 15 different ways.

Irmela's Jewel Studio has made a name for itself in the highly competitive jewelry business in St. Thomas. It has two locations: in the old Grant Hotel (tel. 774-5875) and in Drake's Passage (tel. 774-8244). Both branches have a big selection of unset gemstones which come cut and polished. Each displays a wide selection of gems, Biwa pearls, Japanese cultured pearls, as well as many clasps and pearl shorteners.

The **Royal Caribbean,** 33 Main St. (tel. 776-4110), is considered to be one of the largest camera stores in the Caribbean. Since 1978, it has offered good value in camera equipment, including all accessories. You get a wide assortment of all the big names, including Nikon. The store also has good buys in linens.

The **Linen House** is considered one of the best stores for linens in the West Indies. It has two locations, one at 7A Royal Dane Mall (tel. 774-8117), and another at Palm Passage (tel. 774-8405). You'll find a wide selection of placemats, decorative tablecloths, and many hand-embroidered goods. There are many high-fashion styles.

The **Octopus' Garden** (tel. 774-7010), in Trompeter Gade near the waterfront end, is a gallery-boutique ablaze with tropical color. Hand-batiked fashion from four continents is a special feature: sarong wraps, day dresses, pantsuits, harem pants, men's shirts, bikinis, scarves, and belts. The gift gallery has jewelry from award-winning designer Roberta L. Newman.

The **Cloth Horse,** Bakery Square (tel. 774-4761), sells the celebrated Marimekko of Finland fabric as well as the French Oulivado fabric from Provence, both at a 40% saving over Stateside prices. You can also buy ready-made items such as scarves, handbags, and pillow covers. The Caribbean products carried here are natural cotton bedspreads, wall tapestries, placemats, baskets, and mahogany plates from Haiti.

At **Al Cohen's** big warehouse at Havensight, 18A Estate Thomas (tel. 774-3690), across from the West Indian Company dock, where cruise-ship passengers come in, you can purchase discount liquor. Your purchases are delivered free to the airport or your ship.

A visit to the boutique, art gallery, and craft studios of **Jim Tillett** (tel. 775-1405) is like a combined shopping and sightseeing expedition. The Tillett compound—converted from a Danish farm—stands in a section of the island called "Tutu." The Tillett name conjures up high-fashion silkscreen printing by the famous Tillett brothers, who for years have had their exquisite fabrics used by top designers and featured in such magazines as *Vogue* and *Harper's Bazaar.* Jim Tillett long ago settled in St. Thomas, after creating a big splash in Mexico, where his work was featured in *Life* magazine.

At his compound you can casually visit the adjoining workshops, where you can see silkscreening in progress. Mr. Tillett and his staff produce about 40,000 yards a year. He's daring in his color consciousness, and as you enter the shop, operated by his wife, Rhoda, you're struck by the power of the colors used.

The boutique is stocked with fabric sold by the yard, costing from $10 (silk starts at $20). Out of this fabric, resort wear has been fashioned, including dresses and caftans from $45, scarfs from $5. If you don't see what you want, just ask—it'll be made up for you. Bargain hunters might also want to ask Mrs. Tillett or one of the staff "about some special sale stuff" which is usually available.

Adjoining the boutique is an art gallery which has an abundance of maps, paintings, and graphics made by Mr. Tillett himself. He's created a series of maps on fine cotton canvas which have been bestselling items. Silkscreened maps of St. Thomas on canvas start at $18.

Shopping tip: Buy a square of florid Tillett fabric and frame it when you return home. It can make a vivid wall hanging.

WHAT TO SEE: The color and charm of a real Caribbean waterfront town vividly come to life in the capital of St. Thomas, Charlotte Amalie, where most visitors begin their sightseeing exploration of the small island. In days of yore seafarers and adventure seekers from all over the world, including the prostitutes who kept them amused, flocked to this old-world Danish town, as have pirates, slaves, and members of the Confederacy using the port during the American Civil War. St. Thomas was the biggest slave market in the world.

The old warehouses, once used for storing pirate goods, still stand, for the most part housing the merchandise. I've already previewed in the shopping expedition. Cruise-ship passengers have taken the place of Captain Kidd and Blackbeard the pirate, walking the same old streets, called "gade" here in honor of their Danish heritage.

The main streets of town are now a virtual shopping mall, and are usually packed. Sandwiched among these shops are a few historic buildings, most of which can be covered on foot in about two hours.

Before starting your tour, you might stop off in the so-called **Grand Hotel.** Mercifully, it's no longer a hotel, for which its last tenants can be grateful. Along with shops, it also contains a Visitors' Bureau, near tiny **Emancipation Park** where a proclamation freeing the slaves was read on July 3, 1848. The architectural relic was built in 1841.

West of the park, and across the street, the **Central Post Office** displays WPA-type murals by Stephen Dohanos, who later became famous as a *Saturday Evening Post* cover artist.

Next, you can climb a steep street, Kongens (Danish for king) Gade , passing the entrance to the historic **Hotel 1829,** which has already been previewed in both the hotel and restaurant sections.

Continue past the hotel until you reach **Government House,** the administrative headquarters for all the Virgin Islands. It's been the center of official life in the islands since it was built around the time of the American Civil War. Visitors are allowed on the first two floors, weekdays from 8 a.m. to noon and from 1 to 5 p.m. Some paintings by former resident Camille Pissarro are on display, plus works by other St. Thomian artists.

Nearby is one of the few remaining streets of the old Danish town. Called the **99 Steps,** it was erected in the early 1700s.

After climbing the stairs, you can see the facade of **Crown House,** built in the mid-18th century, a stately home which was the residence of two of the past governors of the Virgin Islands. Here the rich and privileged lived in the 18th century, surrounded as they were by Chinese wall hangings, a crystal chandelier from Versailles, and carved West Indian furniture. It was once the home of von Scholten, the Danish ruler who freed the slaves in the 1848 proclamation.

Southeast of Emancipation Park stands **Fort Christian,** dating from 1672. Named after the Danish king Christian V, the structure has been everything from a governor's official residence to a jail. Many pirates, it is said, were hanged in the courtyard. In some cells the Virgin Islands Museum has been installed, displaying some minor Indian artifacts. Admission free, it is open Monday to Friday from 8 a.m. to 5 p.m. and on Saturday from 1 to 5 p.m.

The oldest **synagogue** building in continuous use under the American flag still maintains the tradition of sand on the floor, commemorating the exodus from Egypt. It stands on Crystal Gade, and is reached by a steep walk up from Main Street. Not as old as the synagogue in Curaçao, this one was erected in 1833 by Sephardic Jews. It marked its 150th anniversary in 1983. The synagogue was built of native stone, along with brick from Denmark and mortar made of molasses and sand. It is open from 9 a.m. to 4 p.m. Monday to Friday for visitors, and conducts its religious school for children on Saturday morning from September through May.

At the point where Main Street intersects Strand Gade, **Market Square** or "de market" as it is known locally, was the center of a large slave-trading market before the emancipation was proclaimed. Roofed over, it is an open-air fruit and vegetable market today, selling, among other items, genips (you break open the skin and suck the pulp off a pit). The wrought-iron roof came from Europe, and at the turn of the century covered a railway station.

It's open every day but Sunday, reaching the peak of its activity on Saturday.

If the genip didn't satisfy you, you can take Strand Gade down to the waterfront. There you can purchase a fresh coconut, getting the vendor to whack off the top with his machete. Then you can drink the sweet milk from its hull.

After finishing your tour in Charlotte Amalie, head west on Main Street until you connect with Hardwood Highway. Turn off at the Villa Olga sign to visit "Cha-Cha Town," or **Frenchtown** as it's called. The French people who settled here—named for the "cha-chas" or straw hats made and worn here—are descendants of immigrants from the French islands, speaking an unusual patois. The colorful little town, most of whose residents seem to be engaged in fishing, contains some interesting restaurants and taverns.

Later, you can strike out for **Mountain Top,** the traditional stopping-off point for a banana daiquiri.

To cap your tour, locate **Drake's Seat** on a good map and head there for the most spectacular view in St. Thomas. According to legend (and not really to be believed), Sir Francis Drake sat there charting the channels and passages of the Virgin Islands. Nevertheless, you have spread at your feet the entire sweep of almost 100 Virgin Islands, both U.S. and British.

St. Thomas's most popular attraction is **Coral World,** Route 6 (tel. 775-1555), a marine complex that includes a three-story underwater observation tower 100 feet offshore. Through windows large and clear you get to see sponges, deep-sea flowers, fish, and coral—underwater life in its natural state. In the Marine Gardens Aquarium, 21 saltwater tanks display everything from seahorses to urchins. The entire complex is at Coki Beach on the northeastern shore, 15 minutes from downtown, and is open seven days a week from 9 a.m. to 6 p.m. Adults pay $7; children, $3.50. Shark and fish feeding is at 11 a.m. Shuttle service is available from downtown and major hotels. The shuttle departure is from the Gray Line Tour office at the Grand Hotel in Charlotte Amalie. Departures are daily excepting Sunday at 9:30 a.m. and again at 12:30 p.m. A one-way ticket costs $3.50 for each passenger.

West of the center of Charlotte Amalie, on the campus of the College of the Virgin Islands, the **Reichhold Center** (tel. 774-8475) is one of the major cultural centers in the Caribbean. Frequent art exhibits of local artists are staged here at this Japanese-inspired amphitheater set in a natural valley. About 1200 spectators are accommodated here, and big-time cultural entertainment has arrived in St. Thomas. Ask about possible events during your visit. You might see, perhaps, the Joffrey Ballet. The smell of gardenias will only add to the evening's pleasure. If no event is being sponsored, you can still take a guided tour of the center Monday through Friday by calling the number given above. Lawrence O. Benjamin is the director.

A SIDE TRIP TO WATER ISLAND: The fourth largest of the U.S. Virgins, Water Island is only half a mile long and about a half to one mile wide. At its nearest point, it comes about three-eights of a mile from St. Thomas. Visitors go there to spend the day on Honeymoon Beach where they swim, snorkel, sail, water-ski, or just sunbathe while they relax under the palm-shaded beach, ordering lunch or a drink from the beach bar. The highest elevation is only 300 feet above sea level, and the Arawak Indians were the first to inhabit it. Originally the island had freshwater ponds to which sailing vessels came to replenish their casks. The army used Fort Segarra as a base in World War I.

It's possible to go on your own. A ferry runs between Water Island Dock and the Sub Base at St. Thomas, a seven-minute ride costing $5 for a round-trip ticket. The first ferry leaves Water Island at 7:30 a.m., St. Thomas at 7:45 a.m. On Sunday, the first ferry leaves Water Island at 9:30 a.m., St. Thomas at 9:45 a.m. During the day there is an intermittent schedule. Don't get caught on Water Island. The last ferry leaves there at 6:30 p.m. However, on Saturday the last ferry departs Water Island at 9:45 p.m., on Sunday at 4:30 p.m.

THE SPORTING LIFE: Chances are, your hotel will be right on the beach, or very close to one, and this is where you'll anchor for most of your stay, perhaps occasionally going out in a Sailfish or Hobie Cat. All the beaches in the Virgin Islands are public, incidentally.

Most of the beaches lie anywhere from two to five miles from Charlotte Amalie. I've already extolled the glory of **Magens Bay,** three miles from the capital, which charges 50¢ for adults and 25¢ for children. Dressing rooms are provided, and snorkeling equipment and small sailboats can be rented. There is also a restaurant.

Others include **Morning Star Beach,** about two miles outside Charlotte Amalie, which also has dressing rooms and a restaurant, charging adults an admission of $2 (children under 12 are admitted free). **Lindberg Beach,** adjacent to the airport, is another favorite, as is **Coki Point** at Coral World (at the latter you can rent snorkeling gear).

Boating

The biggest charter business in the Caribbean is done by Virgin Islanders. In St. Thomas most of the business centers around the Red Hook and Yacht Haven marinas.

Perhaps the easiest way to go out to sea is to charter "your yacht for a day," from **Spur-of-the-Moment Charters,** Red Hook, P.O. Box 71 (tel. 775-1110), for only $50 per person. No more than six passengers are taken out at one time. You're granted a full-day sail with a champagne tropical lunch and open bar, aboard the 50-foot yawl *Nightwind.* You're also given free snorkeling equipment and instruction. For reservations, call between 8 a.m. and 9 p.m. daily.

My Way is a 35-foot Pearson sloop which sails to the uninhabited island of Hans Lollick for $35 per person (call 776-9547 for reservations). Snorkeling equipment and instruction are provided, and there's an all-day bar. You take lunch on a deserted beach. Everything is included. Sailings leave from the north side of St. Thomas. The cost is $40 per person per day.

True Love is a sleek Malabar schooner, used during the filming of *High Society* starring Bing Crosby and Grace Kelly. It gave its name to the Cole Porter duet they sang. At 54 feet in length, it sails at 9:15 a.m. from Red Hook into Pillsbury Sound. Bill and Sue Beer have sailed it since 1965. You can join one of Bill's snorkeling classes and later enjoy one of Sue's gourmet lunches with champagne. Call 775-6547 for reservations. The cost is $50 per person.

The day sail to St. John on the catamaran *Ho-Tei* is a bargain at $25. You'll have time to explore the sandy beaches too. Ask your hotel travel desk to book it for you, or else telephone 774-2435 for reservations.

Of course, if you want something more elaborate, you can go bareboating —that doesn't suggest nudity, but means renting a craft where you're the captain. However, you must prove you're able to handle the craft before you're allowed to go out in it alone. If you'd like everything done for you—that is, go out in a manned boat, with the captain and crew at your service—you can join one of the one-week charter plans.

This type of charter rental is available through **Avery's Boathouse,** P.O. Box 3693 (tel. 774-0111); **Caribbean Yacht Charters,** Compass Point, Frydenhoj (tel. 775-3604); and **Watersports Center,** P.O. Box 2432, Sapphire Bay (tel. 775-0755).

Captain Cook's glass-bottomed boat will take you for a look at the island's Marine Gardens and the harbor of Charlotte Amalie, which occupies an extinct volcano crater. Departures are Monday through Saturday at 10 a.m., 11 a.m., 1 p.m., 2 p.m., 3 p.m., and 4 p.m. from the waterfront in Charlotte Amalie. The cost is $12 per person; children under 12 need pay only $6.

Deep-Sea Fishing

It's very good in the U.S. Virgins. Nineteen world records have been set in recent years (eight for blue marlin). Sports fishing is offered on the *Fish Hawk.* Al Petrosky of New Jersey sails from Fish Hawk Marina Lagoon at the East End on his 43-foot diesel-powered craft, which is fully equipped with rods and reels.

Golf

Mahogany Run, P.O. Box 7517 (tel. 775-5678), is a golf and tennis community, along with a luxurious condo complex. On a 315-acre site, the first championship 18-hole golf course ever built in St. Thomas opened in 1979. The 13th, 14th and 15th holes make up the "Devil's Triangle," with the 14th acclaimed as "one of the great golf holes in the world." It juts out of a cliff overlooking the Atlantic. Greens fees are $20 for 18 holes, and a golf cart is required, costing $20 for two players for 18 holes.

Tennis

Many courts are lit for night play, and St. Thomas has a lot of them. Outstanding ones are at the **Bolongo Bay Beach and Tennis Club** (tel. 775-2489), which has four courts, two of which are lit until 11 p.m. It caters to members and hotel guests only except for lessons which cost $65 for a three-hour series.

At **Frenchman's Reef Tennis Courts** (tel. 774-8500, ext. 350), four courts are available and those not hotel guests are charged $5 a half hour per court. Lights stay on until 10 p.m.

There are two courts at **Mahogany Run Tennis Club** (tel. 775-5678), and more may be added. Hotel guests pay $6 an hour during the day, $10 an hour at night. If you're not a guest, $8 an hour is charged during the day, $12 at night.

There are also two courts at the **Virgin Isle Hotel** (tel. 774-1500), which charges $4 per hour during the day, $6 per hour at night.

Scuba and Snorkeling

With 30 spectacular reefs just off St. Thomas, the U.S. Virgins are rated as one of the "most beautiful areas in the world" by *Skin Diver* magazine. Since 1960 your best place for dive operations is **Joe Vogel Diving Co.,** 12B Mandal Rd., Route 42, a one-minute drive east of the Mahogany Run Golf Course (tel. 775-7610 between 9 a.m. and 9 p.m.). It's run by an ex-U.S. Navy frogman, Joe Vogel, aided by Debby Powers-Vogel, its manager and an underwater photographer herself. Joe pioneered night diving in the Virgin Islands and still goes out. On his dives, which he conducts himself, he limits his crew to six or fewer for the divers' safety and better enjoyment.

A beginner scuba class is given for $45, a snorkel tour for $22. Daytime reef dives range from $26 to $30, according to the gear a diver brings, and night and offshore wreck dives cost from $31 to $35. Scuba portraits by Debby cost $40 for professional-quality color shots of your dive. For more information, write them at P.O. Box 7322, St. Thomas, USVI 00801.

Watersports Center (tel. 775-0755) stands at the Sapphire Bay Marina, and can outfit 60 divers a day. At the eastern tip of St. Thomas, it has a staff of certified PADI and NAUI guides and instructors. Usually, however, only four to five divers go out at a time. They have a regular dive program, but also offer double tank dives, night dives, and all-day trips to the wreck of the *Rhone,* which you may remember if you saw the film, *The Deep.* Scuba tours (a single tank) cost $40, rising to $65 for a double tank. Most night dives cost $50, and the *Rhone* dive is $80.

AFTER DARK: There are no casinos, no supper Las Vegas–type shows. However, there's some action. You just have to look for it:

Frenchman's Reef (tel. 774-8500) has the most nightlife, and enjoys a deserved reputation as "the entertainment center of St. Thomas." Occasionally top acts are imported to perform at the stage show at its **Top of the Reef Supper Club,** Monday through Saturday, with dancing offered not only before the show but until the early hours of the morning. Most people go for dinner, at which time they can order the chef's specialties, meals costing from $30. If you go just for the show, you pay no cover charge or minimum, with all drinks priced at $3.50.

In addition, the hotel also offers **La Terrazza,** where a steel band plays and a limbo show is staged for the entertainment. Check at the desk for what's on. No minimum is charged, and drinks cost $3.50.

Bluebeard's Castle Hotel (tel. 774-1600) is another entertainment center. Call and see what's playing. Overlooking the pool and yacht harbor, the Dungeon Bar offers piano bar-type entertainment nightly except Thursday. You can dance, too. On Thursday and Friday nights, there's a lively steel band. On Saturday night, you can dance the night away to the music of one of the island's great combos. There is continuous entertainment until 1 a.m. All drink specialties are named after Bluebeard himself—Bluebeard's wench, cooler, and ghost. Most drinks cost from $2.50, although some specialty drinks are priced from $3. The Dungeon Bar is a popular gathering spot for both residents and visitors.

The **Carib Beach Hotel** (tel. 774-2525) is another lively spot. Perhaps you'll journey out here on Friday night for their West Indian buffet with a steel band and limbo show. You'll see a little fire-eating, walking on broken glass, stuff like that. Count on spending from $25 per person. Always call to make sure that Friday night is *the* night. St. Thomas hotels are known for switching the dates of their entertainment activities.

In town, I like the **Greenhouse,** Waterfront Drive (tel. 774-7998), which enjoys a harbor view and often features rock-'n-roll entertainment. At this restaurant-lounge, the chef offers a full breakfast from 7 to 11 a.m. and a lunch menu with a native special. There are also eight kinds of hamburgers. Light dinner is served every night, costing from $15. The lounge features live entertainment seven nights a week, usually from 9:30 p.m. to 2 a.m. A friendly, breezy waterfront oasis, the Greenhouse will answer your questions about specials and entertainment if you give them a ring.

The **Ritz Cabaret,** on Dronningens Gade, popularly known as Back Street (tel. 774-6597), is clustered among a colony of nightlife places, outside of which it's sometimes dangerous to walk alone. Once you get inside the whimsically decorated, high-ceilinged interior of what used to be a warehouse, you'll forget any problems about the neighborhood and concentrate on one of the most glamorous urban-inspired milieus in Charlotte Amalie. Geraldine Ferraro dropped in here for a strawberry daiquiri after the 1984 presidential election, although few of the staff (including bartender Cathy Zent, once referred to by *Vogue* magazine as a Betty Hutton type) recognized her at the time.

A New York City artist painted a huge mural of jazz musicians on one of the walls. Ceiling fans whir, mirrors glisten, and, during lunchtime, daily from 10 a.m. to 4 p.m., a cabaret-style pianist tickles the ivories as diners enjoy generous salads, sandwiches, or summer avocados or pineapples stuffed with various fillings.

Later in the day, the establishment's bar does a thriving business. Movies are sometimes shown between 7 and 9 p.m., after which the place becomes a disco. Guests, many of whom don't leave until around 4 a.m., pay $3.50 for a mixed drink and $3 for a beer. On Sunday, the place is open only as a disco, from 9:30 p.m. to 4 a.m.

Walter's Living Room (tel. 774-5025), at the foot of Government Hill, corner of Roosevelt Park, draws a lively crowd, often native Virgin Islanders. Sometimes live jazz groups appear at this old Danish cottage, and when they do there's a $3 minimum. The host who invites you into his "living room" is Walter Springette, a veteran of some 25 years in the nightclub business. The Living Room has a tropical atmosphere.

There is now **Walter's II,** lying at upper Raadets Gade, across from Gracie's Sandwich Shop. It is also open from noon to 4 a.m. The second version of Walter's, just off Back Street, is housed in a restored early 20th-century wooden town house. It too has a lively ambience. You're never sure at which club Walter will turn up.

Safari Lounge Bar, 7 Wimmels Kafts (tel. 774-7338), is a well-liked and well-patronized disco, with flashing lights and the latest sounds. Go there late. The location is just off Back Street, and the crowd is young, both Virgin Islanders and college-age tourists. When live groups perform, you're likely to be assessed a cover up to $6. Otherwise, drinks are inte $3 range.

In Charlotte Amalie, a popular nighttime diversion is to patronize one of the local pubs along "Back Street," which is literally in back of the shopping malls fronting the waterfront. However, this street can be extremely dangerous at night—so don't go alone.

Along this row, I prefer **Chaps Western Saloon,** 11 Dronningens Gade (tel. 774-6597), which is a westernized pub with wide plank floors and food inspired by Texas and Mexico, rib-sticking fare like chili con carne, big beefburgers, and tacos. Drinks are generous, and the cost is low, around $15 for an evening with plenty of beer. Electronic games are the current rage.

Rosie O'Grady's, on Dronningens Gade (no phone). The original owners of this very old brick-walled bar were Irish, as you might guess from the name. Before retiring, they decorated the walls with memorabilia from the Emerald Isle and encouraged guests to sing whenever the spirit moved them. Today, the spontaneous singing has been replaced with recorded music, although there's still a Gaelic kind of charm in the attitude of the friendly barmaids (yes, they're still called that here) and an occasional rowdiness worthy even of a pub in Killarney. No food is served here, so no one minds if you bring it in from the pizzeria across the street. Beer costs between $2.50 and $3. Every day except Sunday, the establishment opens for business at 10:30 a.m. On Sunday it opens at 6 p.m. Closing is between 1 and 2 a.m.

2. St. John

About two miles east of St. Thomas, little St. John lies just across Pillsbury Sound. It is about seven miles long and three miles wide, with a total land area of some 19 square miles.

The smallest and least populated of the three main U.S. Virgins, St. John has more than one half of its land mass, as well as its shoreline waters, set aside as the Virgin Islands National Park, dedicated in 1956.

Once it was slated for big development when it was under Danish control, but a slave rebellion and a decline of the sugarcane plantations signaled the end of many a man's dream. For that reason St. John has remained truly virginal, unlike some other U.S. Virgins.

GETTING THERE AND AROUND: Among the many methods of reaching the island, the easiest and most frequented is by ferry boat, leaving from Red Hook landing on St. Thomas, the trip taking about 20 minutes. Beginning at 6:30 a.m., except weekends and holidays, boats depart every hour on the hour. The last ferry back heads out of the harbor at St. John at 10 p.m.

Because of such frequent departures, even cruise-ship passengers, anchored in Charlotte Amalie for only a short time, can visit St. John for a quickie island tour, perhaps a picnic and a swim at one of its fine sandy beaches, returning in time for dinner. The one-way fare is $2 per adult, $1 for children.

Should you ever get stranded, water taxi service is available 24 hours a day for about $35 for two persons.

To reach the ferry, you can take an open-air shuttle which departs from the Market Square in Charlotte Amalie. It will take you on weekdays (not on Sunday) to the ferry dock at Red Hook. The fare is $2 per person each way. It is also possible to board a boat directly at the Charlotte Amalie waterfront for a cost of $4 one way, the ride taking 45 minutes. Boats depart St. Thomas at 9 a.m., 11 a.m., and again at 5:30 p.m. They leave Cruz Bay on St. John at 7:15 a.m., 9:15 a.m., and finally at 3:45 p.m. (the latter departure from the National Park Dock).

Also, a launch service leaves from the dock at Caneel Bay at St. John heading for the National Park Dock at Red Hook on St. Thomas. This one-way fare, however, costs $9 per person.

In addition, **Virgin Islands Seaplane Shuttle** will take you from either St. Thomas or St. Croix for $30 round trip on either Tuesday or Thursday. For reservations, telephone 773-1776.

Once on St. John, there are several methods of getting around, the most popular of which is by surrey-style taxi. If you just want to go from the ferry landing dock to Trunk Bay, for example, the cost is about $6 for two passengers. Between midnight and 6 a.m., fares are increased by 40%.

The **St. John Taxi Association** (tel. 776-6060) also conducts a historical tour of St. John, including swimming at Trunk Bay and a visit to the Caneel Bay resort, at a cost of $12 per person. Tours depart Cruz Bay seven day a week at 9:45 a.m., 10:45 a.m., and 11:45 a.m.

It's also possible to use the bus service running from Cruz Bay to Maho Bay, stopping at Caneel and Cinnamon Bays. The one-way bus fare costs $3.50 for adults.

Incidentally, there's only one gasoline station on St. John, so better fill your tank up at that pump before striking out on an exploring adventure.

Varlack Ventures, P.O. Box 36 (tel. 776-6412). Many visitors feel that the real beauty of St. John lies away from Cruz Bay, along some of the relatively inaccessible coastline. Should you wish to reach such places, a Jeep might be the best means of getting there. Rentals of these four-wheel drives cost $40 per day, with $5 per day for insurance. Renters are required to post a $35 deposit and must be between the ages of 25 and 65. Gas is not provided, although there's usually just enough in the Jeep to get you to one of the two gas stations on the island. It's never a good idea to drive around St. John with an almost-empty tank. Varlack, which is about a block from the ferryboat pier, also rents a limited number of air-conditioned cars, priced at the same rates as the Jeep.

WHERE TO STAY: From a tropical retreat, one of the most spectacular in the Caribbean, to a campsite, the choice of accommodations in St. John is severely limited, and that's how most people would like to keep it.

Caneel Bay, Inc., National Park, P.O. Box 720 (tel. 776-6111), is the fulfillment of an idealistic man, Laurance S. Rockefeller, and it's a remarkable achievement. It's a super-luxurious resort placed on a 170-acre portion of St. John, built on the site of a mid-1700s sugar plantation directly on the bay, with a choice of seven beaches. Resort owners throughout the Caribbean speak of Caneel Bay with supreme respect. It's operated by Rockresorts.

The retreat of many an industrialist and government leader, the hotel caters to people with full purses who know their needs can be met with style. The main buildings are strung along the bays, with a Caribbean-style lounge and dining room at its core. Other, separate units—really bedroom villas—stand along the beaches, so all you have to do is step from your private veranda onto the sands.

Not all of the 170 rooms, however, are on the beaches. Some are set back on low cliffs or headlands. AP rates in winter range from $285 to $420 daily in a single, from $320 to $460 daily in a double. *In summer, daily AP rates in a single go from $170 to $275, from $210 to $310 in a double.* But if you're coming down for the summer, you should ask about one of the special packages likely to be offered, everything from honeymoon to boating to one that combines a visit at Caneel Bay with a stay at Little Dix Bay in the British Virgins.

The most loyal devotees of Caneel Bay book their favorite room in winter a year in advance, and February is almost always sold out.

The buildings have a quiet understatement in decor, and I suspect the habitués of the place would rebel if the management tried to change the dark bamboo. The choice spot at Caneel Bay is the Turtle Bay Estate House, part of the 18th-century Dutch sugar plantation, serving now as one of a trio of dining locations (for the most part, only guests dine here; the other dining facilities are described in the "Where to Eat" section, which follows the hotel recommendations).

Surrounding all buildings is a skillfully planted garden, filled with sea grape, brilliant-red flamboyant, the geranium tree, the golden shower tree, poinsettias, hibiscus, oleander, the red ixora, and of course plenty of bougainvillea that washes everything with color. When man has intruded architecturally, it is generally with natural elements such as wood and native stone.

There are many, many scheduled activities per week, ranging from a fishing trip to a walk through the ruin of the old sugar mill. Of course, in addition to its beaches, the plantation also opens onto an undersea world, as there are endless inlets and secret reefs to explore. Snorkeling lessons are given free each day, and divers can go on trips to the many historic shipwrecks. A fleet of boats awaits your command, and there is complimentary use of the resort's sailboards for windsurfers. Perhaps the pursuit of the elusive wahoo will send you on a deep-sea fishing trip. In the evening you can listen to calypso music, dance, perhaps enjoy a steel band.

Maho Bay, P.O. Box 310, Cruz Bay, St. John (tel. 776-6240). What I like most about this place is that there is a help-yourself center where groceries, books, and magazines are left by departing campers for new arrivals to take. That sets the tone for this interesting concept in ecology vacationing, where you get about as close to nature as you can, but with considerable comfort. Maho Bay is a deluxe campground set in the heart of the National Park Reserve, seemingly inspired by Fire Island (New York) where the technique of running wooden walkways through vegetation was advanced. Utility lines and pipes are hidden underneath.

You stay in a tent-like cottage made of canvas. Each unit has a choice of a double bed or two built-in single beds, a couch that converts into a double bed, electric lamps and outlets, a round dining table, chairs, a propane stove, and an ice chest (cooler). That's not all—you're furnished linen, towels, dinner service, and utensils. You do your own housekeeping and cooking, although you can eat at the camp's outdoor restaurant. Guests share a community bathhouse. Each unit is cantilevered over a thickly wooded area, providing a view of the sea, sky, and beach.

From mid-April to mid-December, no minimum stay is required, with cottages (limited to two adults) renting for $45 per day. Children under age 7 pay $7 per night per person; over 7, $10 each. In season, the minimum stay is seven nights, and the cost is $60 per cottage, occupancy by two persons. Others sharing a cottage pay from $10 per person nightly.

There's a store where you can buy expensive supplies, and in season you can help yourself from a garden with fruit, vegetables, and herbs. The camp attracts an interesting array of guests, everybody from honeymoon couples to botanists to college students. Don't expect a bar or entertainment. It's a camp for people who love the sounds, smells, textures, and visual splendor of a beautiful preserve. The location is an eight-mile drive from Cruz Bay, and there's regularly scheduled bus service. The camp also has the best program of water sports on the island (see below).

Maho Bay has a community center, housing a restaurant which serves breakfast every morning for up to $3. This includes juice, eggs or french toast, and coffee. There is no charge for extra juice or coffee. For dinner, they have asked some of the best cooks on St. John to cater. Menus are posted and people who are interested sign up in advance. Typical meals are fresh fish or chicken, goat stew, whelk stew, conch stew, quiche, and lasagne. Prices range from $7 to

$10 for a full dinner. This allows guests to meet the local people who function as entrepreneurs rather than staff, and also to taste local cooking. The islanders, by making the food preparation a family endeavor, can offer a good meal much cheaper than the camp could.

Meals are served on a covered patio which overlooks the water. This same patio functions as an amphitheater where they have nature lectures, concerts of folk music, scuba and sailing movies, and lectures by park rangers. The bathhouse which services the community center is testing the Clivus Multrum composting toilets which use no water at all. So far, the word is that they are a miracle.

Cinnamon Bay, P.O. Box 720, Cruz Bay (tel. 776-6330), established by the National Park Service in 1964, is the most complete campground in the Caribbean. The site is directly on the beach, and thousands of acres of tropical vegetation surround you, an opportunity to get insect-repellent close to nature. Life is simple here, and you have a choice of three different ways of sleeping—tents, cottages, and bare sites.

In winter, a cottage rents for $50 a day for two persons, a tent for $40, and a bare site for $9. *In the off-season, cottages cost from $32 to $43 per day for two persons, tents from $25 to $35, and bare sites from $9.*

At the bare campsites, nothing is provided except general facilities. Canvas tents are 10 by 14 feet with floor, and a number of facilities are offered, including all cooking equipment. Even your linen is changed weekly. Cottages are 15 by 15 feet, a screened room with two concrete walls and two screen walls. They consist of four twin beds, and two cots can be added. Cooking facilities are also supplied. Lavatories and showers are in separate buildings nearby. Camping is limited to a two-week period in any given year. Near the road is a camp center office, with a grocer, a cafeteria (serving $5 dinners), and an arbor-covered picnic area. Budget travelers, wanting to keep costs bone-trimmed, can purchase supplies in Charlotte Amalie and transport them over on the ferry from Red Hook.

Management is handled by Rockresorts, and reservations can be made at 30 Rockefeller Plaza, Room 5400, New York, NY 10112 (tel. toll free 800/223-7637; in New York City, call 212/586-4459, or in New York state, toll free 800/442-8198).

Housekeeping Holidays

Gallows Point, P.O. Box 58, Cruz Bay (tel. 776-6434). Visitors sailing into Cruz Bay will notice an appealingly contemporary cluster of cottages whose design was patterned after 18th-century colonial models. The clapboards, the latticework, the fan-shaped windows, and the louvered French doors of this attractive resort were stained a dignified shade of gray.

Each cottage contains four one-bedroom apartments, some of which have duplex-style arrangements where the loft-style bedrooms look down on well-furnished living rooms whose illumination is increased by skylights. Garden-level suites have wooden decks facing the water, sunken living rooms, and bathrooms filled with plants. Each accommodation contains a fully equipped kitchenette, and several ceiling fans.

In winter, a garden suite costs $170 daily, while a loft suite rents for $190. *In summer, garden suites are $120 daily, with loft suites costing $135.* These rates apply to either one or two persons. Additional guests must pay another $18 per person.

The **Holiday Homes of St. John,** P.O. Box 40 (tel. 776-6776), is for those who seek serenity in tasteful surroundings, free of hotel life. Holiday Homes is a generic name given to ten privately owned homes on the island. When not lived in by their owners, these homes are rented out by a local realty office. You get not only privacy, but in most cases (at least those I inspected) individualized charm. They are well furnished, according to the tastes of each owner. All of them, however, are fully equipped. When making inquiries, state the number of your guests and the style of home you prefer. That doesn't mean you'll get it, but you can try.

A two-week minimum is preferred, but in summer this stipulation may be a bit more flexible. I haven't the space to describe each home. However, I'm fond of one called "Eagle's Nest," a handsome redwood and stone house on a cliff overlooking the bay, with spacious living quarters; and "Haiku," contemporary living in a Japanese-inspired home with a covered pavilion opening onto terraces and tropical gardens.

In winter, two guests pay from $120 daily, plus $45 for each additional person. *In summer, tariffs are lowered to $90 daily for two guests, plus $30 daily for each additional person.*

Serendip Apartments, P.O. Box 273, Cruz Bay (tel. 776-6646), is a condominium apartment building set in the midst of private homes, surrounded by brilliant flamboyant trees. The apartments are built for full living, each with a veranda, a living room with two convertible couches, a fully equipped kitchen, a bath, plus a twin-bedded room. The furnishing style is informal and casual, not style conscious, pleasantly basic. Maid service is by arrangement—and at your expense—but it doesn't cost much. In winter, daily rates, either single or double occupancy, are from $75 to $90, *and these tariffs are lowered off-season to $60 to $75 for one or two persons.*

Villa Bougainvillea, P.O. Box 349, Cruz Bay (tel. 776-6856), might be a perfect accommodation for travelers looking for an apartment rental without the surroundings of a large resort complex. Donald and Deborah Schnell are the owners of this two-unit building whose fieldstone walls open onto a view of the sea. There's a covered porch looking seaward and a flower garden surrounded with a wall.

Each unit contains a fully equipped kitchen, two bedrooms, comfortable chairs, good-quality furniture (some of it crafted from teak), and big windows open to the breezes on three sides. In winter, two persons can rent the less expensive apartment for $100 per day. The more expensive one upstairs, with the wider view, costs $120 per day. *In summer, the less costly quarters go for $80 per day, while the more expensive apartment costs $100 daily.* In any season, each additional adult pays an $18 a day supplement, while each child costs an extra $9. Children under two stay free.

Selene's, Cruz Bay (tel. 776-7850), sits on a hillside a short distance above the port. It's a clean, pleasant apartment-hotel, each unit of which contains a kitchen, ceiling fan, separate bedroom, living room with convertible couch, and a modern tile bath. There are a total of six accommodations, several with wood-railed balconies facing the harbor. Each unit can sleep four persons more or less comfortably. In winter, they rent for $510 to $600 weekly and *in summer for $360 to $480.*

D and E Apartments, Cruz Bay (tel. 776-6637). The owners of this place manage a handful of two-bedroom apartments a short walk from the center of town. The slightly spartan interiors are nonetheless sunny and breezy, some having verandas. In winter, two persons rent an apartment for $120 per day. *In summer, the price for two persons drops to $90 per day.* Guests who rent a unit for six days get an extra day free. Each additional person pays a $30 supplement per day.

WHERE TO EAT: Visitors over just for the day generally like to have lunch at the

Sugar Mill Kitchen on the grounds of Caneel Bay (tel. 776-6111). From 11:30 a.m. to 3 p.m., it offers grilled items, salads, and sandwiches. Up until 3 p.m. you can order good-tasting tropical drinks, such as a plantation punch or a peach daiquiri. From the restaurant there is a panoramic view overlooking St. Thomas and its surrounding cays. Diners are seated on a "horse-mill" platform (when the wind was insufficient to turn the mills in the old days, beasts of burden such as one-eyed donkeys were used. Lunch specialties include lobster salad, ginger barbecued chicken, and broiled chopped sirloin. There is always a cake of the day. Guests come here for sundowners at 6:30. For about $40, you can enjoy a buffet dinner served nightly except Sunday on a reservation-only basis. Featured are a choice of grilled entrees, a salad bar, and a dessert table. Dining is only from 7 to 8:30 p.m.

Before someone has settled into St. John, he or she has been told about the buffets served overlooking the water at the **Caneel Bay Beach Terrace Dining Room** (tel. 776-6111), on the grounds of the Caneel Bay Hotel, right below the Sugar Mill. The $20 buffet luncheon is one of the best in the Virgin Islands. It is always necessary to make a reservation. After you're assigned an open-air table overlooking the beach and the water, and you've given your drink order, you proceed to the buffet counter. I suggest a visit first to a side counter where freshly cut tropical fruit such as pineapple is spread around a bowl of cold soup (my recent bisque of almond sent me rushing back to the chef for the recipe). After soup and fruit, you can proceed to the tempting array of salads (usually one made of avocado) and cold meats. As an elegant touch, fresh mushrooms are sliced, awaiting your favorite dressing. Corn chutney, smoked oysters, and many other plates await your selection. If, after all that, you still have room for hot dishes, you'll find those followed by a big table of desserts, including such delectable pies as blueberry cheese. Drinks are extra.

In the evening, if you return for dinner from 7 to 8:30, you should make a reservation. At that time you can have a complete dinner for $40 per person. Appetizers might include papaya with prosciutto, or perhaps artichoke bottoms Carla, followed by excellently prepared soups (perhaps potato leek, maybe cold strawberry tapioca). Salads are invariably good, including the marinated green bean or the tossed garden greens mimosa. Entrees are likely to include baked filet of red snapper (with onions, tomatoes, and green peppers), beef tenderloin à la Stroganoff, or roast prime rib of blue-ribbon beef carved to order with natural juices. There are always some calorie-loaded desserts such as strawberry cheesecake or Boston cream pie. Menus are changed nightly. On Sunday the chef offers a sumptuous buffet of West Indian, continental, and American dishes between 7 and 9 p.m.

The **Upper Deck,** Cruz Bay (tel. 776-6318), has the best view and the most atmospheric location of any restaurant on St. John, outside of Caneel Bay. Reached by a bumpy Jeep ride, it's a honey. The bar opens at 5 and I recommend that you go then for your sundowner, enjoying that view while it's still daylight. You don't need a reservation—just arrive, but only Wednesday through Sunday. No luncheons are served, only dinner, anytime between 6:30 and 9 p.m. The decor is casual and rustic, like an overscale mountain cabin. Tables, lit by candlelight, are placed on an open deck. The location is about five minutes from Cruz Bay dock.

Your hosts are Clarence and Sis Thoman, both Americans. He worked for an advertising agency in New York, producing TV shows, before finding his little oasis on St. John. Sis never went to cooking school, and she has no pretensions in that direction: "At 16 I learned to cook for hungry farmers in Pennsylvania." She offers plain, ordinary cookery, and it's good.

Each day she makes a pot of soup such as New England–style clam chowder. Many of her dishes come from the charcoal grill, including lamb chops, sirloin steak, and pork chops. These dishes are served with a choice of tossed salad or cole slaw. Each night she offers a special, perhaps spare ribs or chicken à la king. From the sea, a nightly fish special with accompaniments is served. Try also her fried scallops followed by one of her homemade desserts. An average repast here is likely to cost from $15 per person.

Ric's Hilltop Restaurant (tel. 776-6383), one block from the Julius Sprauve School in Cruz Bay, serves some of the best West Indian food on the island. You don't need a reservation, and any taxi driver knows how to deposit you there. Once on the premises, you're in the capable hands of Robert O'Connor, Jr.

Go only for lunch, which is served Monday to Friday from 11:30 a.m. to 3 p.m. Two daily hot specials, perhaps freshly caught yellowtail, are featured. Desserts are homemade too, and an array of buffet-style native dishes are often presented. Meals cost $15 and up.

Mongoose Restaurant, Café, and Bar, Mongoose Junction (tel. 776-7586), is like a Japanese/Caribbean birdcage, set among trees and built above a stream. It is like something you'd come across in Marin County of northern California. Of avant-garde design, this delicatessen-restaurant utilizes bamboo and natural wood. The place is a popular social center during the day, especially among a young crafts-oriented crowd of local people who live on St. John. Some of these people drop in and buy deli food or their favorite cheese, perhaps Monterey Jack.

The place is open for breakfast, lunch, and dinner daily, as well as for Sunday brunch. Dinner is served between 6 and 10 p.m. and costs from $24. Typical dishes include shrimp Newburgh, Caribbean chicken with orange and coconut curry sauce, a fish of the day served several different ways, beef Stroganoff with fresh mushrooms, steaks, and homemade cheesecake. The lunches are less elaborate, consisting of sandwiches and hot dish specials. Full noon meals cost from $12. Breakfast is served daily between 9 and 11 a.m. Of course, you can drop in for a drink at the sunken bar any time of day, enjoying one of the 20 tropical drinks which the residents like.

Il Bucanière Restaurant and Cruz Quarter Bar (tel. 776-6908), is set in the main square of town near the ferryboat landing. If you're not sure of whether you'll lunch or dine here, you can always decide over a drink at the long mahogany bar or while seated at one of the outdoor iron tables looking over the trees and passersby.

Lunch might include a selection of omelets, salads, hot and cold sandwiches, and homemade desserts for about $12 per meal. The candlelit dinners are more elaborate, with a fish of the day, Caribbean lobster when available, coconut chicken tempura, vegetables in beer batter, Kansas-bred steaks, and an assortment of stir-fried dishes which include everything from strictly vegetarian recipes to ones laden with beef. Full meals cost from $30. The restaurant is open seven days a week from 11 a.m. to 9:30 p.m.

The **Bird's Nest** (no phone) is a sunny restaurant on the upper level of an unimposing concrete building not far from the ferryboat landing. To get here, you climb a flight of exterior concrete steps which lead to a room filled with silkscreen prints, caged birds, thick plank tables, rock music, high peaked ceilings, hanging plants, and big open windows.

If anyone in St. John is traveling on a budget or just living cheaply in the sun, you're likely to find him or her at a table adjacent to you. Meals are served from 7 a.m. to 10 p.m. daily except Sunday, when hours are from 7 a.m. to noon. Dinners range from around $12 and might include snapper as the fish of the day, conch, chicken, sirloin steak, West Indian stewed goat, vegetable combination platters, and Trinidadian sauté of beef with pineapple. Main dishes are served with salad, Spanish rice, and beans. Sandwich meals and breakfasts cost from $4.

The **Lobster Hut** (tel. 776-6533) is near Mongoose Junction. After climbing up the steps to this open-air shack, ask for Mr. Nose. Tell him you're hungry and ask him what fresh fish he's got that day. In honor of his restaurant's namesake, he often has lobster, but he prefers you to let him know if you'll be wanting that for dinner. You might settle instead for a lobster roll. You can always order two pieces of fresh fish, and you'll be served the best conch fritters on the island. Lunch is served, but the place comes alive at night, when you're placed at a candlelit table, probably near a hanging plant. Meals cost from $15. The hut opens toward the water, a short walk from the ferry and operates seven days a week.

WHAT TO SEE: I personally like to spend lots of time at Cruz Bay, where the ferry docks. In this West Indian village, the capital, there are interesting bars, restaurants, boutiques, and pastel-painted houses. It's pretty sleepy, but amusing to some after the fast pace of St. Thomas. The museum at Cruz Bay isn't big, but it does contain some local artifacts and will teach you something about the history of the island. It's at the Battery, and can be visited from 10 a.m. to 2 p.m., Monday through Friday.

Most cruise-ship passengers seem to dart through Cruz Bay, heading for the island's biggest attraction, the **Virgin Islands National Park.**

Before going to the park, you may want to stop at the Visitor's Center at Cruz Bay, which is open daily from 8 a.m. to 5 p.m. There you'll see some exhibits and learn more about what you'll be viewing. Regular briefings and slide talks are given. The park rangers also lead nature walks, and you can find out if you can join up.

By 1981 the size of the park totaled 12,624 acres, including submerged lands and waters adjacent to St. John, and since 1956 a trail system aggregating 20 miles has been developed. This is the only national park in the Caribbean area.

In 1952 Laurance S. Rockefeller purchased a small resort here and developed it, eventually donating it to the nonprofit Jackson Hole Preserve, an organization founded and supported by the Rockefeller family. Jackson Hole, in turn, after purchasing more than 5000 acres of St. John, about half the island, donated the lands to the U.S. government.

If time is very limited, try a visit to the vast estate of the **Annaberg Ruins,** where the Danes launched sugar-mill plantation life in 1718. On Tuesday, Wednesday, and Friday from 10 a.m. to 1 p.m., St. John islanders show you their own style of native cookery and explain basketweaving.

Trunk Bay is considered by those who know such things as "one of the world's most beautiful beaches." The beach is also the site of one of the world's first marked underwater trails.

Park rangers conduct **national park tours** of St. John. You can explore a three-mile trail which goes by the petroglyphs, figures (still undeciphered) carved on boulders by mysterious people of the past. You'll also pass by the ruins of sugar mills and a great house. You must make a reservation for all tours by calling 776-6201. A bus tour leaves on Monday. To catch up with it, you must be on the 8 a.m. ferry from Red Hook. Once on St. John, you board a special bus for $10 per passenger, leaving from the National Park Visitor's Center at 9 a.m. The tour lasts three hours.

Every Friday the rangers conduct a Reef Bay hike at 9 a.m. This time, it is necessary to take the 9 a.m. ferry from Red Hook in St. Thomas. The bus ride, costing $2, leaves from the National Park Visitor's Center at 9:45 a.m. A special boat, costing $5 per passenger, takes you back to Cruz Bay at 3:30 p.m. when you can catch another ferry to take you to St. Thomas. You're to bring your own food and beverage.

Fort Berg (called Fortsberg) at Coral Bay dates from 1717 and played a disastrous role in history in the 1733 slave revolt that devastated the economy of St. John. The fort may be restored as a historic monument.

THE SPORTING LIFE: Don't visit here expecting to play golf. Rather, anticipate some of the best snorkeling, scuba-diving, swimming, fishing, hiking, sailing, and underwater photography in the Caribbean. The island is known for its coral-sand beaches, winding mountain roads, trails, past decaying, bushcovered sugarcane plantations, and hidden coves.

Swimming

Trunk Bay is the word. It's the biggest attraction on St. John and a beach collector's find. To miss its great white sweep would be like going to Europe and skipping Paris. As mentioned, **Caneel Bay** fronts seven beautiful beaches, and the camps at **Cinnamon** and **Maho Bay** have their own beaches where forest rangers constantly have to remind visitors to put their swimming suits back on, if they have any.

Hiking

The big thing here, and a network of trails covers the national park. However, I suggest a tour by Jeep first, just to get your bearings. At the Visitor's Center at Cruz Bay, ask for a free trail map of the park. It's best to set out with someone experienced in the mysteries of the island. Both Maho and Cinnamon Bays conduct nature walks.

Tennis

Caneel Bay Plantation monopolizes the game, with seven courts and a pro shop. However, these courts aren't lit at night, and are likely to be used almost exclusively by guests. There are two public courts at Cruz Bay, however.

Snorkeling, Scuba, and Sailing

The action is at Trunk Bay's signposted underwater trail. Your best bet is to check with **Watersports Centers** at Sapphire and Cruz Bay (tel. 775-0755). After 6:30 p.m., call 774-5649. This center arranges a half-day sail to St. John with snorkeling gear, at a cost of $25 per person. Sailboat rentals can also be arranged. The center also offers scuba lessons and scuba tours for both intermediate and experienced divers. Lessons and a boat dive cost from $40, and include dives to wrecks and night dives.

Horseback Riding

Pony Express Riding Stable (tel. 776-6902 or 776-6922 for reservations) invites you to "view a tropical paradise on horseback." If you call from St. Thomas, one of the staff members will meet the Red Hook Ferry (but not on horseback). You'll be driven to their stables on Bordeaux Mountain, where you can go on nature trail rides. Then you'll be delivered back to Cruz Bay for your return to St. Thomas by ferry. The cost of the ride is $20 an hour with a 1½-hour ride minimum for two people. Special arrangements for beach rides can be made by request.

SHOPPING: Compared to St. Thomas, it isn't much, but what there is is interesting. The **Caneel Bay Plantation Boutique** is the place to go for island resort wear

—no contest. The style here is casual but sophisticated, and naturally the prices are high.

The boutiques and shops of Cruz Bay are highly individualized, and quite special. Most of the shops are clustered at **Mongoose Junction,** in a woodsy area beside the roadway, about a fast five-minute walk from where the ferry docks. I've already endorsed dining in this avant-garde complex, and it also contains shops of merit.

Donald Schnell Studio (tel. 776-6420) is a working studio and gallery at Mongoose Junction on St. John. Michigan-born Mr. Schnell and his assistants feature one of the finest collections of handmade pottery, sculpture, and blown glass in the Caribbean. They can be seen producing daily and are especially noted for their rough-textured coral work. Water fountains are a specialty item, as are house signs. The complete six-piece coral pottery dinnerware is unique and popular. The studio will mail works all over the world.

The **Canvas Factory** (tel. 776-9196) produces its own handmade, rugged, and colorful canvas bags in the "factory" in Mongoose Junction. They also specialize in well-made, practical, 100% canvas clothing.

The **Clothing Studio** (tel. 776-3585) features one-of-a-kind original hand-painted designs on fine tropical fashions by well-known artists such as Linda Smith, Palmer, and others. The shop studio will create custom designs just for you.

You'll find some exciting fabrics at **Fabric Mill** (tel. 776-6194), another Mongoose Junction shopping attraction. Specializing in silkscreened and batik prints from around the world, Fabric Mill also carries locally silkscreened fabric displaying island motifs. You'll also find interesting accessories, soft sculptures, and unique gift items made in this studio shop.

R and I Patton Goldsmithing (tel. 776-6548), by the entrance to Mongoose Junction, has a large selection of Rudy and Irene Pattons' island-designed jewelry in sterling, karat gold, and precious stones.

3. St. Croix

The largest of the U.S. Virgin Islands, 84 square miles of real estate, St. Croix was discovered by Columbus on November 14, 1493, but the reception committee of Carib Indians was far from friendly. He anchored his ship off Salt River Point, on the north shore of St. Croix, before the Indians drove him away. However, before leaving he named the island Santa Cruz (Spanish for Holy Cross). Those cannibalistic Indians made later colonizing parties less than eager to settle in St. Croix.

However, the Dutch arrived, as did the English, and for a short time St. Croix was owned by the Knights of Malta, no great pioneers. The Spanish drove the British out, only to be driven out themselves by the French, and so the familiar story of Caribbean colonization went. It wasn't until 1650 that the French laid claim to the island, later abandoning their attempts at colonization.

The Danes purchased St. Croix in 1773, attracted to the island because of its slave labor and sugarcane fields. This marked the golden era of St. Croix, as both planters and pirates grew wealthy. However, the sugar boom ended, with eventual slave uprisings, the introduction of the sugar beet in Europe, and the emancipation of 1848. Even though seven different flags have flown over St. Croix, it is the nearly 2½ centuries of Danish influence that still permeates the island and its architecture.

St. Croix has some of the best beaches in the Virgin Islands, and ideal weather. It doesn't have the sophisticated nightlife of St. Thomas, nor would its permanent residents want that.

African tulips are just some of the flowers that add a splash of color to the landscape, and stately towers that once supported grinding mills are but lonely ghosts on moonlit nights.

At the east end of St. Croix, which, incidentally, is the easternmost point of the United States, the terrain is rocky, arid, with cacti growing, evoking in some memories of parts of Arizona. However, the west end is lusher, with a rain forest of mango and mahogany, tree ferns, and dangling lianas. Rolling hills and upland pastures characterize the area lying between the two extremes.

GETTING THERE: For a description of the air transportation offered by both **American** and **Eastern,** refer to the "Getting There" section of St. Thomas at the beginning of this chapter.

Pan American initiated service from New York to St. Thomas and St. Croix late in 1984. With its feeder flight hookups to dozens of midwestern American cities, it often offers the most convenient connections from such places as Detroit, Chicago, Minneapolis, Pittsburgh, and dozens of others to the U.S. Virgins.

Such flights are scheduled to arrive from the departures of Pan Am's two daily nonstop flights to St. Thomas. The 10:15 a.m. flight lands at St. Thomas at 2:55 p.m., then continues on the same plane to St. Croix, landing there at 4:05 p.m. A 12:30 p.m. flight goes to St. Thomas, then on to St. Croix.

Returning flights leave St. Thomas at 10:10 a.m., stopping 30 minutes at St. Croix, and arriving at New York's JFK Airport at 1:50 p.m. with enough time remaining to catch feeder planes to the Middle West. A 3:45 p.m. flight leaves St. Thomas, with a stopover in St. Croix, before reaching its final destination, New York's JFK at 7:35 p.m.

Pan Am also routes Middle Atlantic passengers through Miami. There's a daily nonstop flight at 1:55 p.m. to St. Thomas. A hookup to St. Croix is then possible via Sun Aire. The return from St. Thomas leaves for New York City daily at 9:55 a.m.

Pan Am also has direct daily stops to St. Thomas and St. Croix from Washington's National Airport. These daily flights originate in St. Kitts, routing themselves through St. Croix, St. Thomas, Miami, and Washington.

Through Pan Am's cooperative agreement with Empire Air, most of the New York state traffic to the U.S. Virgins is conveniently routed through New York's JFK Airport.

WHERE TO STAY: You can stay at one of the many charming waterfront inns at Christiansted, or at one of the resorts, plantations, or condominium units scattered throughout the island, many at beachside perches. Tariffs for the most part are steep, and all rooms are subject to a 5% hotel room tax.

The Luxury Leader

The **Buccaneer,** P.O. Box 218 (tel. 773-2100), is the big fancy hotel of St. Croix, the only really serious resort. Among other offerings, it opens onto a trip of the island's best beaches. With its hilltop perch and its beachside sites, it is almost two resorts rolled into one. The location is about a four-mile drive from the lure of Christiansted, on a sweeping, rolling landscape.

Pink and patrician, the hotel offers you a choice of rooms in its main building or in one of its beachside properties. The baronially arched main building has a lobby opening toward drinking or viewing terraces, with a sea vista on two sides. Once the Buccaneer was a sugar plantation, and its first estate house, dating from the mid-17th century, stands near the freshwater swimming pool. The Buccaneer's present history as a resort hotel dates from the postwar era when it was opened by the Armstrong family. The Armstrongs are still going strong at the Buccaneer. Robert D. Armstrong is the owner and general manager.

The architecture is inspired by the Danish custom of free use of arched colonnades. Throughout the estate are units of varying sizes with this architectural theme. The interiors of the suites and rooms effectively use slanted wood ceilings, chalk-white walls, and all-white furniture to create a fresh, uncluttered look. Rooms are categorized as deluxe, sea-view, and standard. *In the off-season, single EP rates range from $80 to $115 daily, with doubles going for $90 to $125.* For breakfast and dinner, add another $35 per person. However, in winter double occupancy costs from $160 to $240 daily.

Prices quoted are on the EP, but there are many choices for meals. Most guests lunch lightly in the sun at the Grotto, tanning as they enjoy lobster salad. The Little Mermaid serves food at the beach. You can dance and drink at the al fresco bar. One of the most elegant places to dine is the resort's Brass Parrot Restaurant (see the recommendations to follow).

The resort has the best sports program in St. Croix—eight championship tennis courts and an 18-hole golf course, as well as sports fishing, scuba-diving, and snorkeling available from its own dock. Excursions are arranged to Buck Island's reef.

For reservations, get in touch with Ralph Locke, 315 E. 72nd St., New York, NY 10021 (tel. 212/586-3070, or 800/223-1108 toll free).

First-Class Hotels

Grapetree Beach Hotels, P.O. Box Z, Christiansted (tel. 773-4161), are two shoreline properties at Grapetree Bay—the former Beach Hotel and Grapetree Bay—now merged into one resort. About nine miles from Christiansted, they occupy a vast acreage at the easternmost point of the United States. To go from one property to the other means either a long walk or a short bike ride.

The visitor is faced with a choice of accommodations—family suites, regular hotel rooms, ocean-view cabanas, and beach lanais. Of course, all are air-conditioned and have patios and terraces which open onto beach or bay. Each unit also has a refrigerator-bar. *In summer, singles go for $95 daily; doubles $125.* In winter, tariffs go up—$135 daily in a single, $145 in a double. For breakfast and dinner, add $35 per person daily to the room charge. You might find yourself in the hills, housed in a wide, ultramodern block of rooms facing an angular swimming pool, or else near the beach in another block of units. Furnishings are colorful and contemporary.

There are two places at which to dine—informally near the pool where you need wear only your bathing suit, or else at the waterfront restaurant which offers a Stateside, West Indian, and continental cuisine. When the house count merits it, the management brings in a steel band and calypso singers. Weekly barbecues, cocktail parties, and buffets manage to keep the place lively when it's full. A fleet of the hotel's trimarans will take you on Buck Island sailing excursions, and boats can also be rented for deep-sea fishing. Tennis courts are lit for night games. A highlight is the Sunday brunch, with many platters of both continental and West Indian foods. You get not only free champagne, but can hear steel band music.

The **Hotel on the Cay,** on Protestant Cay in Christiansted Harbor, P.O. Box 4020 (tel. 773-2035), is an isolated resort, just a one-minute ferry ride from Christiansted to its dockside. The hotel offers ferry service to its guests and visitors from 6 a.m. to 1:45 a.m. daily. The establishment has the only beach in Christiansted, as well as clean freshwater pool. For guests who wish to adventure more extensively in the world of water sports, a complete program is offered, with on-property experts to teach, guide, and recommend activities for everyone from the novice to the more experienced. For the tennis lover, the Cay has four fine, well-kept courts. Play is complimentary to guests.

Continental and West Indian fare are offered in the hotel's main dining room and tropical terrace, with a less formal beach barbecue on Tuesday night and a steak-and-lobster beach party on Saturday. Island entertainment accompanies dinner on most evenings, followed by dancing.

The 55 clean, air-conditioned rooms are decorated in good taste, with cypress and fine ceramic tile. All units have either a sea view or overlook the gardens and waterfalls. *Accommodations are available in summer at $78 to $85 single occupancy, $85 to $95 double occupancy.* In winter, singles range from $123 to $130; doubles, $149 to $159. Breakfast and dinner may be included for an additional $32 per person daily.

Queen's Quarter Hotel, P.O. Box 770 (tel. 778-3784), is a lushly verdant resort in the center of the island, established when a group of doctors in Chicago banded together to finance a hotel which would welcome children as well as adults. Today, the well-built villas scattered over the rolling hillsides of this property are likely to host educational conferences, perhaps from Cornell or the University of Kentucky, in addition to the regular clientele of sunworshippers from colder climates.

The space of the public rooms flows gracefully onto an open veranda exposed to the swimming pool. There, dining tables allow the serving of succulent meals to hotel guests and people from outside (see "Where to Dine," below).

In 1979 most of this place was rebuilt, so that accommodations today are pleasantly shaded refuges, complete with exposed stone, ceiling fans, sweeping views over a forest, or a series of landscaped gardens, and lots of extra comforts. The managing partner is the sophisticated Kentucky-born hotelier, James B. Morgan, whom his friends call J.B. He, with his staff, arranges four-times-daily transportation to and from the island's beaches.

Many of the accommodations have private kitchens, patios, and views onto masses of bougainvillea, trumpet-blossomed allamandas, and mahogany trees. In winter, studios and one-bedroom suites range from $120 to $140 daily, while one-, two-, and three-bedroom villas cost between $160 and $400 per night. *In summer, studios and one-bedroom suites go for $72 to $85 per night, while villas containing one, two, or three bedrooms cost $140 to $200.* In the villas, the bedrooms have extra-long double beds.

The Special Inns of Christiansted

Club Comanche, 1 Strand (tel. 773-0210), lives up to my idea of what a West Indian inn should really be like. Right on the Christiansted waterfront, it is the domain of its friendly innkeepers, Dick Boehm and Ted Dale. The main house is old, but it's been completely adapted to modern tastes in its remodeling. At every turning, you come upon a charming setting. Take the open iron-cage elevator, where you expect Katharine Hepburn to descend in *Suddenly Last Summer.* Some of the bedrooms have slanted ceilings with handsomely carved four-poster beds, old chests, and mahogany mirrors.

Reached by a glassed-in covered bridge, the newer addition passes over the colorful shopping street to the waterside. Other rooms, more recently constructed, are the poolside and harborfront buildings. One row of bedroom units is stretched along the swimming pool area, edged by a stone balustrade and flowering shrubbery. At one side is a waterfront refreshment bar where you can order drinks and watch yachts come into dock. On the EP, four different sets of rates are offered. The highest prices are charged from December 15 to mid-April: doubles for $65 to $125 daily; singles, $45 to $65. *From mid-April to December 14, doubles go for $45 to $75; singles, $35 to $48.*

The club is also one of the leading choices for dining in town (refer to my recommendations).

Anchor Inn, 58A King St. (tel. 773-4000), is one of the few hotels lodged directly on the waterfront, close to such historic buildings as Government House and the Old Danish Customs House. Of course, it's right in the heart of the shopping belt as well.

The space is so compact and intimate you might not believe it holds 30 units, each with twin beds, small refrigerator, radio, telephone, cable color TV, bath, and a tiny balcony. Air conditioning is individually controlled. A few suites have double beds, no balconies. *In the off-season, EP singles rent for $54 to $60 daily; doubles, $65 to $72; and triples, $75 to $81.* In winter, tariffs go up: $75 to $84 daily in a single, $86 to $95 in a double, and $105 to $115 in a triple, all EP. Furnishings for the rooms are warmly conventional, with good color combinations used.

Lon Southerland "anchored" here more than a decade ago, and he's hired Jean Perigord, his manager, to ease your adjustment into Christiansted. (The Anchor Inn restaurant, under separate management, is recommended in the "Where to Dine" section, following.)

Directly on the waterfront is a sundeck and small swimming pool, as well as the Anchor Inn's own boardwalk, where catamarans and glass-bottomed boats operate daily to Buck Island. There are also deep-sea fishing boats.

Pink Fancy, 27 Prince St. (tel. 773-8460), is my favorite hotel on the island. Sam Dillon, your host, has restored this small, unique private hotel in downtown Christiansted, offering 13 efficiency rooms in four buildings. Units are furnished in a Caribbean motif, with ceiling fans, air conditioning, and color TV. *In summer, the rate is only $85 daily, either single or double occupancy,* rising to $160 daily in winter. The location is one block from the Annapolis Sailing School and the V.I. Seaplane Shuttle.

The oldest part of the four-building complex is a 1780 Danish town house, now one of the historic places of St. Croix. Years ago the building was a private club for wealthy planters on the island. Fame came when Jane Gottlieb, the Ziegfeld follies star, opened it as a hotel in 1948. In the '50s the hotel became known as a mecca for writers and artists, attracting among others, Noel Coward.

To date, its present owner, Mr. Dillon, has spent some $1 million in restoration. Before Pink Fancy, he was an orchard owner, a navy vet, a legislator from Maryland, and a former newspaper owner. He also served for a time in the State Department.

Built on different levels, the units are clustered around the swimming pool and a monkey puzzle tree. At the free bar there, guests easily get acquainted. A complimentary continental breakfast is served every morning; otherwise, you're on your own for meals. Units are known by estate names such as "Sweet Bottom." If that's too suggestive a selection for you, ask instead for say, "Upper Love."

King Christian Hotel, P.O. Box 3619, King's Wharf (tel. 773-2285), is Betty Sperber's own special place, and she's one of the finest innkeepers on the island. The location is right in the heart of everything, directly on the waterfront, within walking distance of the duty-free shops, major restaurants, and water-sports activities. All its front rooms have two double beds and private balconies overlooking the harbor. However, the "no frills" economy wing has rooms with two single beds or one double bed, but no view or balconies.

All units are air-conditioned and contain private baths. Winter EP tariffs range from $60 daily in a single for the "no frills" room up to $90, with doubles costing from $70 to $100. *In summer, it's a real bargain; no-frills singles cost only*

$45, going up to $55 in a double. The superior units rent for $65 in a single; $75 in a double.

The staff will also make arrangements for golf, tennis, horseback riding, and sightseeing tours. You can relax on the sun deck, shaded patio, or freshwater pool. There's a beach just a few hundred yards across the harbor, reached by ferry. On the premises is the Chart House, one of the best restaurants in St. Croix (it's noted for its Sunday brunch).

King's Alley Hotel, 55 King St. (tel. 773-0103), stands at water's edge, surveying Christiansted Harbor's yacht basin. The hotel, a series of air-conditioned bedrooms, is furnished with a distinct Mediterranean flair. Many of its units overlook a swimming pool terrace, with its oval pool surrounded by tropical plants. The galleries opening off the bedrooms are almost spacious enough for entertaining. *The meticulously cared for rooms rent for $55 to $75 per day double occupancy, in summer; $50 to $70 per day for single occupancy.* All the rooms, incidentally, are twin-bedded or king-size. In winter, either single or double occupancy costs from $70 to $100 daily. The Marina Bar features nightly entertainment by the pool. Right outside your door you'll find boutiques and restaurants, including the King's Alley Café, an open-air bar and restaurant next door which is a popular bar for sundowners. A table here is always set aside for boat captains, who can be seen cleaning their catch of the day on the pier opposite the patio.

Hotel Caravelle, Queen Cross Street (tel. 773-0687). The facade of this sprawling hostelry is painted a dark Mediterranean pink and pierced with the high, arched windows which illuminate the pleasant accommodations. This establishment, biggest of the downtown hotels, usually caters to a clientele of international business people who prefer to be near the center of town.

There's an Andalusian-style tile fountain splashing near the rectangular bar in the middle of the ground-floor reception area. One of the most dramatically located restaurants in town, the Binnacle (see "Where to Dine," below), is a few steps away. Many resort activities, such as sailing, deep-sea fishing, snorkeling, scuba, golf, and tennis, can be arranged from the reception desk. A swimming pool and sun deck face the water, a health club is on the premises, and all the shopping and activities of the town are close at hand.

Accommodations, each with color TV, air conditioning, a phone, and a private bath, are priced according to their views. In winter, singles go from $75 to $100 daily, while doubles cost $90 to $110. *In summer, singles are priced at $62 to $85 daily, while doubles range from $72 to $93.* An additional person staying in any double is charged an extra $14 a day. For reservations and information, call 800/524-0410 toll free.

Holger Danske Hotel, 1 King Cross St. (tel. 773-3600), named after World War II's Danish resistance movement, is a pleasant garden-style hotel stretching along a concrete walkway leading from the outlying reception area. The feeling here is a lot like that in a suburban apartment complex in the Sunbelt. A restaurant and a pool are on the premises.

The decor of each of the 44 accommodations is unfussy, spacious, and comfortable, and most have a simple kitchen, a patio or veranda, air conditioning, TV, a phone, and a radio. Best Western, the management company, charges winter rates of $70 to $80 daily in a single, $80 to $93 in a double, and $18 for each additional person lodged in a double room. *In summer, singles rates range from $50 to $65 daily, doubles from $65 to $75, and additional occupants in double rooms pay $12 per day.*

Cathy's Fancy, P.O. Box 1668, Pelican Cove (tel. 773-5595), is one of the better bargains on the island. Cathy and Bill Gilmour, the owners, rent out 21 fully furnished self-contained units, ranging from compact and efficiency apartments suitable for two guests through one- and two-bedroom suites and cottages with enough room for three to five guests, all the way to a large three-bedroom, seven-person villa right at the water's edge. That water's edge, incidentally, is on one of the prettiest beaches on the island, Pelican Cove, protected by two reefs which almost completely close the cove. Waves break against the reefs outside the cove before rolling in gently, making the water good for swimming and snorkeling. The location is two miles outside Christiansted.

EP rates in summer are $55 daily for two persons in a studio, $60 for two in a one-bedroom unit, and $95 for up to six persons in a three-bedroom accommodation. In season, expect prices to average about 60% more than in summer. The seventh night is always free. The open-air Beach Bar is pure fun. Drinks are reasonably priced, and every Sunday guests and many locals come to enjoy their beach barbecue for around $10, including live entertainment, such as an island steel drum band or a lively reggae combo.

As for a dress code, the management has a rule: you must wear something!

The **Lodge**, 43A Queen Cross St. (tel. 773-1535), is a modest, attractive little hotel in the heart of 18th-century St. Croix. The prices are kept low, and most of the rooms overlook a vine- and tree-filled courtyard. You pass through iron gates, going under thick stone arches. The place is managed by Swiss-born Romi Truninger, usually found at a crowded little check-in office near the entrance. She'll tell you that the Lodge offers a continental breakfast free, plus extra towels for beach and pool privileges. Rebuilt units, 17 in all, open onto the brick-paved courtyard. The rooms are nicely furnished, containing private baths, air conditioning, and small TVs. *Double rates off-season are $60 daily, $50 in a single.* In winter, double charges range from $70 to $75 daily; singles, $60 to $66, with an extra person paying $15 year round. The hotel has a good breezy bar, tropical foliage, and umbrella tables on the patio set against a backdrop of banana trees.

Charte House Hotel, 2 Company St. (tel. 773-1377), is built around an old Danish courtyard and a freshwater pool right in the heart of Christiansted. It's a compound that combines the very old and the very new. The hotel was erected on the site of a Danish West Indies Company's counting house. An L-shaped three-story addition stands in the rear, with spacious, air-conditioned rooms with encircling balconies and private baths. All units overlook an intimate courtyard, dominated by an ancient mahogany tree. The entrance to the courtyard is through old arches. *The owner charges from $35 daily in a single in summer, $40 daily in a double.* Tariffs rise in winter to $40 daily in a single, $50 in a double. These charges include morning coffee. There is occasional entertainment in the bar, Two's Company, a tropical lounge.

The Special Inns of Frederiksted

The **King Frederik on the Beach,** P.O. Box 1908 (tel. 772-1205), has many recommendable assets. For those who'd like to stay near Frederiksted, it's within walking distance of the town, with its own beach and private swimming pool. Hidden behind a high stone facade wall is a cluster of apartments opening onto gardens. You enter through a reception patio, with its Italian-tile floor apartments and efficiencies. At the end of the pathway is the small pool area with its rustic beverage bar. Next comes the sea, with a gentle surf.

Each of the apartments has a good view, as they are built in a staggered fashion so that one unit doesn't block the other's vista. The complex is owned by a California educator, William Owens, who is very helpful to new arrivals. His (also helpful) assistant manager is Reba McCain Finley, a former school secretary from Los Angeles. The apartments have a veranda and covered gallery where you can dine. The living rooms have a clean-cut decor, furnished in part with reed and bamboo. The bedrooms contain twin beds, and the baths are quipped with closets. It's possible to prepare a full meal in the walk-in kitchen. The efficiences have the same concept, but there are no bedrooms. Maid service is provided.

All units, even the lowest priced, have air conditioning and kitchens (except for the beachfront homes). *In the off-season, singles rent for $34 to $62 daily, with doubles going for $38 to $70.* In season, singles cost from $55 to $84 daily; doubles, $59 to $94. Mr. Owens has two large beachfront homes, on both sides of his hotel. Each home has two bedrooms, two baths, a large kitchen and living area, and a private dining patio with a sea view. It's ideal for couples or families traveling together. *The off-season rate for four persons is $90 daily,* going up to $140 in season. He's also added six efficiency units directly across the street from the main building. *Rates off-season are $42 in a single, $48 in a double.* In season, tariffs go up to $64 daily in a single, $64 in a double. Rates include coffee, juice, and rolls every morning and all the Bloody Marys you can drink on Sunday.

The hotel provides five hibachi grills on the beach patio where you can grill your dinner while watching the sunset. It's both inexpensive and romantic. A daily morning shuttle service is provided to the large Sunshine Supermarket for shopping. Also, several restaurants in Frederiksted provide free round-trip transportation if you wish to eat out.

The Frederiksted Hotel, 20 Strand (tel. 772-0500). If you don't demand a location right on the beach, this interesting little hotel might be an offbeat choice. It's on the waterfront in Frederiksted, and it was certainly good enough for her royal highness, Queen Margrethe II, who stayed here with her Prince of Denmark. Room are well designed, each furnished with two double beds. There's a fresh, airy feeling throughout. In winter, two persons can stay here on the EP at rates ranging from $69 to $78 daily, with doubles going for $86 to $90, an extra person sharing paying another $20. *In summer, tariffs are lowered to between $46 and $50 daily in a single, between $55 and $60 in a double.* For breakfast and dinner, add another $22 per person daily.

The location is about a ten-minute taxi ride from the airport. The Frederiksted has a pool, or else you can drive or walk to a good beach club. The hotel itself provides regular transportation to and from the beach spot. In addition, the reception desk can make arrangements for many sporting activities, including fishing, snorkeling, horseback riding, tennis, and golf at the Fountain Valley Golf Course. The best shops of Frederiksted are also near at hand. For toll-free reservations in the United States, call 800/223-1900. (In New York state, call collect at 212/867-8663).

The **Royal Dane Hotel,** 13 Strand St. (tel. 772-2780). Visitors to the harbor at Frederiksted have always noticed the 200-year-old house with the sweeping stone staircase angled against the building's side, deploring its apparent abandonment for a number of years. However, late in 1984, it was reopened as a sophisticated and charming 15-room hotel operated by partners Warren Singer and Michael Zullo. Built of local bricks, thick stone blocks, and clapboards, the structure is capped with an upper story done with lattice work and open verandas. It's about half a mile from some of the best beaches on the island, expeditions to which are made convenient through the frequent free transportation which the hotel arranges for guests, who also have free access to transport to a nearby tennis club.

Each of the air-conditioned accommodations is an imaginatively decorated refuge with unusual prints, framed posters, and comfortable furnishings. No children under 14 are admitted to the hotel. In winter, singles range from $36 to $60 per day, while doubles cost about $5 more per night per room. *In summer,* *singles cost $30 to $60 daily, with doubles ranging from $36 to $65, depending on the week and the accommodation.* These prices include a continental breakfast, daily maid service, and a welcoming drink. A 10% energy surcharge is added to the rates. An extra person can be housed in any double for $10 to $15 per night, depending on the season.

The restaurant serves West Indian and continental dinners, which cost from $20. Lunches are less expensive, costing from $12.

Plantation Life

The **Sprat Hall Plantation,** P.O. Box 695, one mile north of Frederiksted (tel. 772-0305), can never be duplicated. It's the oldest plantation great house in St. Croix, dating back to the French occupation of 1650–1690, and set on 20 acres of grounds, with private white sandy beaches. The chatelaine of Sprat Hall, Joyce Hurd, was born here, and she'll show you the four-poster bed where that happy event took place, as she guides you through her home. For generations and generations this has been the family home. She married Jim Hurd. Joyce, a rosy-faced, cherubic, but dynamic-looking woman of natural charm, still operates the plantation, growing most of the food she serves guests or people who drop in (see the dining recommendations).

She seems to take delight in every visitor who finds himself or herself at her doorstep, right near the ruins of the original sugar mill and rum factory. Of course, only arrive on the threshold of this ancestral manor if you want to experience the casual life of yesterday. It's totally wrong for you if you want to be pampered. On my most recent visit, she rushed to bring me a cool glass of pure well water and huge slice of papaya she'd grown herself. If you wash up in the hall bath, under an open winding staircase, you'll find the soap resting on fresh green leaves. That's a telltale clue as to how natural this place is.

Guests keep returning and sending their friends. I hope you'll stay in the main house, furnished with a helter-skelter collection of antiques, with many old mahogany pieces dating from the various eras of occupation. Some units are converted slave quarters on the grounds, and for those who want to get away from everything, Joyce will rent you one of her Arawak cottages, air-conditioned and equipped only in a basic way, for families who like to rough it.

In summer, rooms at the house rent for $55 daily in a single, $70 in a double, and $90 in a triple. In winter, the single rate is $75 daily; double, $90 to $105; and triple, $115—all EP. *The cottages in summer range in price from $80 for one to $130 daily for a two-bedroom unit suitable for four persons.* In winter, the single or double tariff is $110, and the four-person charge, $190.

On the grounds is the best equestrian stable in the Caribbean. At the beach the Hurds offer skin- and scuba-diving, Sunfish sailing, waterskiing, and deep-sea fishing.

Self-Sufficient Units

If St. Croix's high hotel tariffs deflate your budget too severely, there is an alternative. In general, condominiums are rented at half or a third the going hotel rates. Particularly in the Frederiksted area, you'll find some excellent bargains. And if you wait until after April 15, prices are often half what they are in high season. My recommendations follow.

Tamarind Reef Beach Club, P.O. Box 1112 (tel. 773-0463), named after the tamarind trees growing on the property, was built on a flat, sandy area between a beach and one of the fastest-growing marinas in the Caribbean. Accommodations are clustered in semi-private cabanas and low-lying bungalows which are partially sheltered by shrubs and flowering trees. Each of the 16 units contains its own kitchenette, computerized safe, ceiling fans, and pleasantly simple furniture. Between December 20 and April 15, prices, depending on the week and the size of the accommodation, range from $110 to $185, either single or double occupancy. *Between April and December, they cost anywhere from $72 to $120, either single or double.*

There's a swimming pool on the premises, and a nearby tropical bar, The Deep End, is often peopled with escapees from Christiansted who enjoy the all-day happy hour (two drinks for the price of one) stretching from 11 a.m. to 9 p.m. Children are welcome here and can enjoy spending most of their day on the half-moon-shape beach which has a view of an uninhabited cay just across the water. There's no restaurant on the property, but light meals and snacks are served beside the pool. Clients can use the club's Sunfish, snorkeling gear, paddleboat, and rowing dinghy free.

Sugar Beach Condominiums, Golden Rock Estate (tel. 773-5345), is a row of modernized, stylized one-, two-, and three-bedroom apartments strung along the famous white Sugar Beach. When you tire of its white sands, you can swim in the curvy freshwater swimming pool nestled beside a sugar mill where Virgin Islands rum was made three centuries ago. Under red tile roofs, the apartments are staggered with patios set back to provide privacy. The units, opening toward the sea, are complete with kitchens and are tastefully furnished. In winter, a studio costs $105 daily, ranging upward to $165 for a two-bedroom unit. *In summer, studios go for $60 daily, two-bedroom villas for $95.* Maid service costs extra, but the charge is nominal. The property has two lit tennis courts with Laykold playing surfaces. The Fountain Valley Golf Course is only a short drive away.

Mill Harbour, Estate Golden Rock (tel. 773-3800), is a condominium complex made up of two- and three-bedroom, fully furnished and equipped apartments, ideal for those who like both the privacy of home living as well as the facilities of a resort hotel on the grounds. Just five minutes by car from Christiansted, and two minutes from the local supermarket, Mill Harbour has shuttle bus service running back and forth from resort to town. Manager Hank Walters runs a very good operation, and his buildings are attractive architecturally. Bamboo-furnished living rooms overflow onto the terrace where you can dine on a meal you cook yourself.

In winter, a two-bedroom apartment for four persons rents for $185 per day, going up to $225 in a three-bedroom unit for six persons. *These same rates in summer are reduced to $95 per day in the two-bedroom units, $125 per day in the three-bedroom apartments.* Rooms are air-conditioned; and on the grounds is a freshwater pool. The complex is built on a white sandy beach. Tennis can be played on the resort's own professional courts, and golf at Fountain Valley is a 20-minute drive away.

The nicest Saturday evening dining is at the Serendipity Inn at Mill Harbour, where you can enjoy prime ribs (thick cut) or dolphin (the fish, not the mammal) and a steel band. Listening and dancing makes for a mellow island fantasy feeling under the stars. The Friday night buffet featuring chicken and barbecued ribs is the best value for eating out at a sit-down restaurant.

Colony Cove, Golden Rock (tel. 773-1965), is a luxury beachfront resort whose clusters of three-story accommodations are angled rhythmically between the surf and the palm-dotted lawn into which the builders sank a free-form swimming pool. An on-the-premises water-sports instructor gives lessons in windsurfing or snorkeling, while a handful of new tennis courts is illuminated for night play.

Each unit here is more like a private home than a hotel accommodation, containing two bedrooms, a well-equipped kitchen, two baths, a washing machine and clothes dryer, a semi-private veranda, and tasteful contemporary furnishings. In any season, the price varies with the number of occupants. During the winter, rates for two persons are $125 daily; for three persons, $155; and for four, $180. *In summer, the charges are $80 daily for two guests, $95 for three, and $115 for four.*

Cane Bay Reef Club, P.O. Box 1407, Kingshill (tel. 778-2966). Nine suites overlook the surf, each with a fully equipped kitchen, bedroom, living room, bath, and balcony where you can dine out. The suites have been painted white, carpeted, and redecorated. The living room couches make into two single beds, so one suite can become a family accommodation, suitable for five guests. From your own private balcony, you'll have a view of the surf of the Caribbean. *In summer, one person pays from $40 daily or $260 weekly; two persons, $50 daily or $320 weekly.* In winter, only weekly rentals are accepted, costing $440 for two persons, each additional person paying $15 daily.

When you want to leave your own private retreat, you'll surely meet the hosts, Dulcy and Carl Seiffer, who always seem to be about, keeping a smooth control. When you tire of nearby beaches or their own 40-foot swimming pool, they'll direct you to the island's restaurants and nightspots. Or perhaps you'll stick around, joining other guests in an outdoor barbecue. The hotel lies within walking distance of Cane Bay Plantation, where you can dine if you make a reservation. According to *Skin Diver* magazine, the club is one of the ten best dive spots in the Caribbean. It's also the closest resort to the famed Fountain Valley championship golf course.

The **Waves at Cane Bay,** P.O. Box 1749, Kingshill (tel. 778-1805), is a pleasantly decorated nine-unit country inn with sweeping views over the seaside, directly on the island's north shore. The hotel was bought and refurbished by former Chicagoans John and Betty Silander. Before moving to St. Croix, he was a hotel supplier and she was a realtor. Wanting to put their expertise into practice on the island, they took over the ten units here and quickly made their focal point the wide stone terrace which looks over the rocky surf of the Caribbean.

The comfortable bedrooms are only a short walk to a nearby beach. Each unit includes cooking facilities as well as a ceiling fan, maid service on weekdays, and screened-in galleries facing the sea. In winter, singles range from $60 to $70, from $385 to $485 for a full week. Doubles go from $75 to $90 per day, with a full week costing $460 to $560. Additional adults in a double room pay an extra $18 per day. *In summer, singles range from $35 to $40, while doubles go for $45 to $50 per day, with a full week costing $215 to $240 in a single, $250 to $270 per week in a double.* Additional adults in a double pay an extra $12 per day. Some adjoining units connect through an inner door and can be rented as a combined accommodation if they're available.

WHERE TO DINE: Don't limit yourself to the mainly continental places in Christiansted, but head also for Frederiksted, not just for food but for what might be called "dining adventures" in establishments reeking with character.

In Christiansted

Top Hat Restaurant, opposite Market Square on Company Street (tel. 773-2346), represents the culinary adventure of two Scandinavians, Bent and Hanne Rasmussen, who sought the sun and wanted to make an income-producing, creative statement while in that pursuit. Mr. Rassmussen was a photographer in Copenhagen where he married his blonde and beautiful wife. They took this second-floor space over an arcade, creating the aura of a Danish kro (inn). Mrs.

Rasmussen has suspended a series of cloudlike large white paper balloon lights from the old beamed ceiling. Only dinner is served, offered Monday through Saturday from 6 to 10 p.m. from November 1 to May 1. I find theirs the best place among St. Croix eateries.

Appetizers range from smoked eel to cheese croquettes, as well as small Ping-Pong meatballs so popular in Denmark. My favorite soup is the home-made split pea. From the sea you might try filet of plaice Hanne (served with a white wine sauce). I'd also suggest the crêpes stuffed with shrimp from Green-land and topped with a white wine sauce. The inevitable frikadeller (Danish meatballs with red cabbage) is here, and the Copenhagen steak (tenderloin topped with onions). You can also order a herring platter, steak tartare, roast duck, wienerschnitzel, and tournedos béarnaise. A good selection of desserts is offered, or else you might finish with their Viking coffee. Dinners begin at $30 per person.

Perhaps the finest and most authentic smörgåsbord in the Caribbean is served on Sunday, costing about $25 per person and drawing such longtime smörgåsbord devotees as local resident, Victor Borge. You are presented with an array of at least 20 delectable dishes, including homemade herring in wine sauce, fried filets of plaice, boiled beef tongue slices, and curried codfish balls, along with a salad of those small Greenland shrimp. Naturally, the drink to order is Danish aquavit, followed by a frosty Carlsberg beer.

Comanche, 1 Strand St. (tel. 773-2664), is one of the best liked restaurants on the island. You can dine in the older part of this inn, or at a newer covered deck added on the water side of the premises. The size, openness, hanging plants, and rattan chairs create a real West Indian aura, and the welcome by Dick and Mary Boehm (or Vernon) is really superb. Even though relaxed, it is quietly elegant in its own way. It's a very busy place, and you'll really need a reservation. Lunch is served from 11:30 a.m. to 3 p.m. and dinner from 6 to 10 p.m.

The menu of West Indian and continental specialties is eclectic—an assort-ment of mouthwatering delicacies likely to include everything from fish and conch chowder to Cantonese shrimp balls. In the evening, most people seek the roast prime ribs of beef, sweetbreads, barbecued baby back ribs, duckling in orange sauce, the lime-broiled chicken, or the fresh island fish, steamed and broiled, or served with a creole sauce. Each night a different special is featured (mine was roast chicken with an oyster stuffing). Desserts include a bread pud-ding with rum sauce. Dinner tabs average around $30 per head.

Donn's Anchor Inn Restaurant, 58A King St. (tel. 773-0263), is downtown in Christiansted, right on King's Wharf, but it reminds some diners of a Sau-salito bistro. Guests who live elsewhere keep drifting in for an occasional meal. It's on the second floor, so from your dining perch you can see the boats in the harbor. Run by Glenn L. Hesselgrave, Jr. of California, the restaurant occupies a simple covered terrace, with comfortable captain's chairs. It's the perfect place to meet your friends for a late breakfast, enjoying their custardy french toast with sliced ripe bananas covered in real whipped cream. The cost is $6. You might also try their beer buttermilk pancakes.

At lunch the menu is predictable—burgers, chef's salad, 14 in all, and shrimp Louis served San Francisco style. "Creative" omelets here are quite good too. At dinner the menu improves considerably. You might order conch fritters as an appetizer or one of the soups of the day. I'd suggest a variety of fresh island fish, such as lobster and conch, which are brought in almost daily from the local charter boats and fishermen. The catch of the day is usually pre-pared West Indian style (sauteed in butter, then stewed with fresh onions, green peppers, tomatoes, and spices). Donn always manages to have a continuing supply of fresh local lobster. Count on spending from $18 to $25 for dinner. It's open seven days a week.

Golden China, 28 King Cross St. (tel. 773-8181), serves food as fine as that enjoyed in the Chinatowns of New York or San Francisco. The best experience is to get a group of six couples and arrange for the special Chinese banquet. You'll hardly believe it. If you don't know that many people, you can still enjoy many specialties, including those from the Hunan and Szechuan kitchens. Each dish is prepared to order, and only the finest quality ingredients are used. Of course, from time to time certain ingredients may not be available because of the vagaries of supply in St. Croix. Dinner is likely to run around $22 per person. However, lunches, served Monday to Saturday from 11:30 a.m. to 2:30 p.m., go for only about $8.

Eccentric Egret, 52 King St. (tel. 773-7644), run by Tony Romney, is an across-the-board mixture of dishes from the continent, the States, and the West Indies. He found this second-floor restaurant, which isn't large, but has a warm ambience, its walls covered with mementos, usually theatrical, he is fond of. It's reached after a climb up brick stairs. It's almost like a glorified tearoom, with a dash of bistro thrown in. The owner can be seen in the kitchen, adding finishing touches to the dishes served. He's assisted by a very friendly, able young staff.

Meals, costing from $22, are likely to include baked dolphin, shrimp with curry, sauteed conch, grilled beef with cognac sauce, marinated scallops, and the house specialty, asopao (a stew made with shrimp, conch, or lobster).

Tivoli Gardens, upstairs over the Pan Am Pavilion (tel. 773-6782), is a favorite local rendezvous, run by Gary Thomson. From this large second-floor porch festooned in lights, you get the same view of Christiansted Harbor that a sea captain might. White beams hold up the porch, and trellises and hanging plants help to evoke its namesake, the pleasure gardens of Copenhagen. The owner was a Wall Street executive before heading for St. Croix, and he often plays the guitar and entertains his guests with time-tested favorite songs.

The menu is international, everything from an Andalusian-style gazpacho to a country terrine, to a quiche made with snails, to a goulash inspired by a recipe concocted in the day of the Austro-Hungarian Empire. When available, lobster is featured, along with fresh fish and kebabs. Chicken, shrimp, and steak are given imaginative touches, and for dessert, those in the know order a wicked, calorie-heavy chocolate velvet cake. Save room for it, and count on spending from $25 to dine here.

Often there is live dancing from 7 p.m. when reservations are advised. The Sunday brunch served between 10:30 a.m. and 2:30 p.m. is one of the most popular in town.

Queen's Quarter Hotel Chandelier Room and Gallery Restaurant (tel. 778-3784) is in a hotel already covered in the accommodation section above. This restaurant in the center of the island is by many accounts one of the best and most romantic places to dine in all of St. Croix. Diners pass through the gracefully contemporary entrance portico, pass by the hotel reception desk, and eventually find themselves on a sweeping veranda looking over a curved pool surrounded by tropical plants.

Menu selections include crabmeat cocktail, lobster bisque, chicken Kiev, filet mignon, beef Stroganoff, fish of the day, and an array of stir-fried specialties. Full dinners cost from $30. In addition to its à la carte offerings the restaurant arranges a series of weekly events: Wednesday is a West Indian buffet, Sunday a well-attended brunch, and Friday surf-and turf. There's also live music during the dinner hour most nights between 7 and 10.

The **Binnacle,** Hotel Caravelle, Queen Cross Street (tel. 773-0687), is an outdoor restaurant set directly on the water. The waves of the harbor lap at a rocky foundation only a few feet from the bases of the dining tables. This provides patrons with an almost fish-eye view of the yachts and freighters passing into and out of one of the busiest harbors of the Virgin Islands. To reach the restaurant, you go by the Andalusian-style fountain of the Hotel Caravelle's public rooms.

Full dinners cost $25 and up and might include dishes such as veal Oscar with crabmeat, conch chowder, pepper steak, and a fresh fish of the day, possibly tuna, wahoo, dolphin, grouper, or snapper. Lunch is less expensive, from $12, and less formal. The luncheon menu includes a conch fritter plate and many types of burgers—one an Old Chinatown pork burger. A teriyaki steak sandwich is a specialty.

The Chart House, 59 King's Wharf (tel. 773-7718). This nautically decorated waterfront restaurant opens onto the waterfront in Christiansted. Normally, I don't like chain restaurants. However, when I'm on an island such as St. Thomas or Puerto Rico, I always head for a Chart House, knowing that I am likely to get one of my finest meals. The Chart House in St. Croix lives up to the well-deserved reputation of this U.S.-based chain.

To begin with, it has the best salad bar on the island, and many come here just for that. However, I always order their celebrated prime rib, which is a huge slab of meat. You might prefer instead their lobster, shrimp teriyaki, dolphin, swordfish, or barbecued beef ribs. Regardless, try their baked potato: it's a palate-pleaser. The kitchen always takes care to turn out fresh steamed vegetables, and, for dessert, the mud pie is just renowned, as it is in other Chart Houses. Telephone for a reservation and visit only for dinner, seven nights a week from 6 to 10 p.m. Meals cost from $25.

Frank's, Queen Cross Street (tel. 773-0090), is one of the most attractively amusing places in town, serving well-prepared Italian meals with lots of atmosphere. When you enter the 300-year-old house, you'll be faced with a stone-walled bar where every painting or photograph on it depicts a different version of cigar-chomping Frank Gullace, the owner. Whether shown as Bismarck, the subject of a portrait by Velásquez, Harpo Marx, or a flame-bearing Statue of Liberty, he is the most omnipresent figure among the assembled extroverts who make up the clientele of this sprawling restaurant.

There's an inner room, formerly part of a Danish colonial house, filled with elegant tables and a graveled courtyard such as you might find in southern France, except for the dozens of director's chairs, each emblazoned with the word "Frank." Try for a garden table if you can.

In many ways, this is one of the most "dollarwise" restaurants in Christiansted. You get good value for your money, and the food is well prepared and served in plentiful portions. Among the dishes from the Italian kitchen, the veal is handled particularly nicely. Many boating types drop in here for the relatively inexpensive pasta dishes, not only spaghetti, but fettuccine, lasagne, and other combinations.

The chef knows how to make a rib-sticking minestrone, and you can also order good seafood, including fresh dolphin (the fish, not the mammal). When available, lobster is broiled and served with drawn butter, and the steaks are big and juicy, prepared as you like them. Either way, you'll end up paying around $25 for a complete meal, unless you ordered only a pasta, salad, and glass of wine. Only dinner is served, and since the place is a beehive of activity, it's best to reserve a table.

Around the Island

The **Brass Parrot** is at the Buccaneer Hotel (tel. 773-2100), which was already previewed as the leading resort on the island. It also comes up with one of the fanciest—and best—dining choices. Most of the diners are guests at this star resort on 240 hilly acres, but if you call to make a reservation, the air-conditioned Brass Parrot is open to nonresidents as well. Men should wear a jacket, and women should appear in their chicest resort wear.

The restaurant has been completely redone and installed in the "Great House" of the Buccaneer, a pink stucco building. Views of the hills are framed by large windows. Piano music plays softly in the background—in all, a romantic, candlelit evening. Bamboo furniture and thick pile carpeting add to the atmosphere of elegance.

Decor aside, the reason people come here is for the food. Flambé main courses are the chef's specialty. The kitchen is known for such delicacies as rack of lamb, chateaubriand for two, Caribbean lobster, and veal langoustina. All this glamour comes with a price: expect to spend from $35 per person.

Dining at Frederiksted

Barbara McConnell's, 45 Queen St. (tel. 772-3309), is practically a legend on the island, run by an unpredictable hostess who's a great cook, conversationlist, and grand character. Her restaurant and guest house is in the original building that comprised a 1760 Anglican vicarage and "a Jericho dining room" forming the core of the house, with arches, breeze, and space.

Most people drop in for lunch, if they've called first. She offers what she calls a party plate—roast beef with sherry onion sauce, devilled crab patty or salmon mousse, Hawaiian chicken, salads, aspics, garlic toast. As for fresh fish, she candidly confesses that depends on her fortitude at the moment in battling through a mob of "bahn heahs." If she emerges triumphant, it's usually because she buys the big ones, such as red snapper and grouper.

She admits that her salmon mousse isn't a real "mouse," but a chilled affair with horseradish and caper sauce. I prefer her baked ham with drunken beans, or else her devilled crab patties. Of course, if you're dining light, there are also sandwiches, including a crabburger and a hamburger, but it seems ridiculous to come all the way here to order only that! Her desserts are always good, including her "weird cheesecake." A complete dinner will cost from $30.

When the pace gets too slow, Mrs. McConnell will sit down at the piano and sing "Danny Boy," accompanying herself. Her voice is compelling. Her father, Rea Irvin, did those memorable Eustace Tilly covers for the *New Yorker*.

If you ring her up and give her plenty of advance notice, she'll prepare a dinner for your party. When I recently told her I'd like to drop in on Sunday night with friends, she looked askance: "You mean the Sabbath?" However, when I arrived, she had a lovely dinner set out. We had a choice of dishes from which we helped ourselves from her buffet table. There was, as well, a table of desserts. It turned out to be our most memorable evening in the Virgin Islands.

Mrs. McConnell also has some rooms to rent "If I know you." If you fall in love with the place and seem to fit in with the vaguely Victorian trappings, you might want to see if she could put you up (price to be negotiated).

Outside of Frederiksted, one mile to the north, stands **Sprat Hall Plantation** (tel. 772-0305), which I have endorsed with enthusiasm as a place to stay. However, if that isn't possible, you might want to call the chatelaine of Sprat Hall, Joyce Hurd, and tell her you'd like to come by for dinner. That won't fluster her a bit. She and her West Indian cooks have been feeding guests for years, and they've won their own kind of fame on the island for dining in what is the oldest plantation great house in St. Croix.

She runs everything in the kitchen, dashing out to see if everybody's pleased. I even dropped in once for a good country breakfast, costing $6. The dinners here, going for around $18, are recommended by *Gourmet* magazine.

Chances are, the vegetables you'll be served came right from the plantation gardens. Each night you face a choice of main dishes. It might be lobster, conch, duck, turkey, or lamb. The roast beef is a winner.

And you get "as much as you want to eat." Joyce will have made some soursop ice cream ("I think I invented it"). Dinners are served every night. "We never close," Joyce said. "People have to eat, don't they?"

Yes, they do, and they eat very well at Joyce's table.

Swashbuckler, Prince Philip's Passage (tel. 772-1773), is in a modern hip-roof structure finished with cedar shingles. It's one of the most tastefully designed modern buildings along the harbor, and the bar within serves arguably the best piña coladas in town. Guests enter through a wooden arch set near the road and climb to the second floor. The view is of an uninterrupted 180-degree horizon visible from your perch on a bar stool. The Neville family makes a point of giving the best tables to dinner guests rather than to bar clients.

If you choose to dine here, the menu includes a conch and seafood jambalaya, New York sirloin, roast rack of lamb, fish baked Cruzan style, sauteed calf liver with onions, several chicken dishes, sweetbreads, prime ribs, coq au vin with mushrooms, seafood chowder, and barbecued Canadian ribs. Full dinners cost from $18, although less elaborate lunches go for only $10. Lunch is served from 11:30 a.m. to 3 p.m., and dinner from 6:30 to 10 p.m.

GETTING AROUND: At the airport you'll find official taxi rates posted. Expect to pay about $5 from the airport to Christiansted, and about $4 from the airport to Frederiksted. As the cabs are unmetered, you'll want to agree on the rate before getting in.

Buses

Fares are cheap, the rates depending on the distance you go. The main route is between the towns of Christiansted and Frederiksted.

Car Rentals

This is a suitable means of exploring for some, but know that if you're going into "bush country," the roads are often disastrous. Sometimes the government smooths them out before the big season begins.

Three of North America's major car-rental companies maintain popular branches at the St. Croix airport. After reviewing the prices of all the "Big Three," I concluded that **Budget Rent-a-Car** (tel. 778-9636 locally in St. Croix) maintains the most consistently inexpensive rentals. Any of its fleet can be reserved by calling toll free 800/527-0700 at least two business days in advance.

As any dollarwise shopper should do, you might also compare up-to-the-minute prices at **Hertz** (tel. toll free 800/654-3131) or at **Avis** (tel. toll free 800/331-1212).

High-season prices at Avis and Budget cost about the same. However, more of Budget's cars offer air conditioning than similarly priced vehicles at Avis. On the other hand, tariffs for most of the cars at Hertz were almost always more expensive than either of its two major competitors. Keep in mind, of course, that Hertz at any time could initiate a series of promotional fares.

On my most recent visit, insurance premiums tended to buy more coverage at Budget than at either Hertz or Avis, and the number of days of advance booking at Budget is usually less than that required for rentals at Hertz and Avis. All the major car-rental companies usually announce off-season reductions after April 15.

All of Budget's rental vehicles come with automatic transmission as a standard feature. Its least expensive rental is a peppy four-door Mitsubishi capable of holding four passengers in air-conditioned comfort. A similarly priced Isuzu at Avis did not offer air conditioning. Budget's Mitsubishi rents for $216 a week, with unlimited mileage included. Day-long rentals of this car cost $36 with unlimited mileage included.

Budget also offers a wide range of other well-built Japanese cars in ascending price orders. If you're looking for a more substantial vehicle, Budget offers a solid Ford Fairmont with automatic transmission and air conditioning for $300 a week or $43 a day, including unlimited mileage.

Drivers at Budget's St. Croix subsidiary must be between the ages of 25 and 70. For more information about insurance costs, please refer to the section under "Car Rentals" in St. Thomas, since basically the same insurance situation applies to Hertz, Avis, and Budget on both islands.

Taxi Tours

Many prefer to see St. Croix this way, resting at their hotel or shopping for the rest of their stay after a strenuous day's outing which, for a party of four, will cost from $35 for three hours, plus $8 for each additional passenger. This fare is to be negotiated and definitely agreed upon in advance.

Local Air Services

The **Virgin Islands Seaplane Shuttle, Inc.,** Seaplane Ramp (tel. 773-1776 or toll free 800/524-2050), offers scheduled downtown-to-downtown flights to St. Thomas, St. Croix, and St. John in the U.S. Virgin Islands, Tortola in the British Virgin Islands, and San Juan, Puerto Rico.

WHAT TO SEE: The picture-book harbor town of the Caribbean, **Christiansted** is an old Danish port, handsomely restored (or at least in the process of being restored). On the northeastern shore of the island, on a coral-bound bay, it is filled with Danish buildings, usually erected by prosperous merchants in the booming 18th century. These red-roofed structures are often washed in pink, ochre, or yellow. A blaze of bougainvillea will add yet another color splash. Built of solid stone, these 18th-century buildings have such thick walls they form their own kind of air conditioning. Arcades over the sidewalks make ideal shaded colonnades for shoppers.

To maintain what Christiansted had, Government House—in fact, the whole area around the harborfront—has been designated as a historical site, and is looked after by the National Park Service.

You might begin your tour at the russet-red **Fort Christiansvaern,** the best preserved of the five remaining Danish forts in the U.S. Virgins. Displayed are cannons, dungeons, an officer's kitchen, and bastions from its old defensive days. The fort saw many additions in the 19th century, as the Danish army garrisoned here until 1878. For the most part, the fort was built of tough yellow bricks brought from Denmark as ballast.

As you leave the fort, walk through a park to Company Street, stopping at **Steeple Building,** which was once the Lutheran Church of the Lord of Sabaoth. This was the first church built by the Danes after they colonized the island in 1734. The steeple, for which it was named, was added around 1794.

Today it is the U.S. Post Office and Customs House, but the **Danish West India and Guinea Company,** also on Company Street, dates from 1749. Once it was a military depot.

In the old days, the customs house was **Scalehouse,** near the bandstand at the Wharf. Built in 1835, it was the office of the Danish weighmaster. Troops were also housed here, and today the premises are occupied by a Visitors' Bureau.

In the Steeple House and the Scalehouse, newly installed exhibits develop important facets of West Indian history. Choice examples of pre-Columbian Indian artifacts depict the life of these early inhabitants of the West Indies. European discovery and colonization, with special emphasis on the rise and decline of the plantation sugar economy, is graphically re-created. A special exhibit on the particular Danish colonial architecture developed on this island also displays restoration techniques. A focus on black history acknowledges the important contributions these citizens have played in the life of the island. Hours are from 9 a.m. to 4 p.m. Monday through Friday.

Government House, on King Street, was finished in 1747, and this cream-colored and white residence housed the Danish governor-general before America purchased St. Croix. You can still see the tiny red guardhouse at the foot of the staircase going up from the patio to the big ballrooms with crystal chandeliers. These chandeliers and mirrors were a gift of the Danish government in 1966, replacing the originals. This house was joined with another house built in 1794 for a wealthy planter merchant named Adam Sobotker.

The original **Alexander Hamilton House** was built at the end of 1750, and it is said that Hamilton worked here when he was a clerk. The present house is a reconstruction, the original having burned in the 1960s.

Finally, try to visit the **marketplace,** where fruit and vegetables are sold. It's open every day, reaching its peak activity on Saturday morning.

The next day, or that afternoon, you might go on a walking tour of **Frederiksted.** Set by recently freed slaves, a fire in 1879 swept over this harbor town. The denizens later rebuilt, using wood construction on top of the old Danish stone and yellow-brick foundations. In the reconstruction, Victorian gingerbread embellished the stone arches that remained, forming an elaborate jigsaw pattern.

The old Danish town lies at the western end of the island, about 17 miles from Christiansted. This is a sleepy port town, very old-world looking, which comes to life only when a cruise ship docks at its shoreline.

Most visitors begin their tour at **Fort Frederik,** considered the first fort to sound a foreign salute to the U.S. flag, in 1776. (St. Eustatius in the Dutch Windwards makes a convincing rival claim.) It was here on July 3, 1848, that Governor-General Peter von Scholten emancipated the slaves in the Danish West Indies. The fort has been restored to its 1840 look, and you can explore the courtyard and stables. The location is at the northern end of Frederiksted. An exhibit area has been installed in what was once the Garrison Room.

Just south of the fort, the **Customs House** is an 18th-century building which has a two-story gallery built in the 19th century. Here you can go into the Visitors' Bureau and pick up a free map of the town.

Nearby, privately owned **Victoria House** is a gingerbread structure built after the fire that swept over the town. In the rebuilding, some of the original 1803 structure was preserved.

Along the waterfront Strand Street, you reach the **Bellhouse,** the old Frederiksted Public Library. One of its owners, G. A. Bell, ornamented the steps with bells. The house today is an arts and crafts center and a nursery. Sometimes a local theater group presents dramas here.

Other buildings of interest include the **Danish School,** giving way in the 1830s to a building designed by Hingelberg, a well-known Danish architect. Today it's the police station and Welfare Department.

Two churches are of interest. One is **St. Paul's Episcopal Church,** founded outside the port in the late 18th century. However, the present building dates from 1812. **St. Patrick's Catholic Church,** on Prince Street, began in the 1840s.

Finally, the **marketplace,** on Market Street, is also from the early days, the mid-18th century, and is lively on both weekdays and Sunday.

North of Frederiksted you can drop in at **Sprat Hall,** the island's oldest plantation (see the hotel and dining recommendations), or else continue along to the **rain forest,** covering about 15 acres, including the **Creque Dam.** Mahogany trees and yellow cedar grow in profusion, as do wild lilies. The dam is 150 feet high. As you travel through the terrain, which is private property incidentally, you'll hear the call of the mountain dove. The owner graciously lets visitors go inside to explore.

Most people want to see **Salt River,** but there isn't much to see. That's where Columbus landed for a brief moment, sending a boat out to a village filled with naked natives. These inhabitants turned out to be Arawaks, peaceful Indians captured by the militant Caribs. On their return, one of the Spanish leaders captured a "very beautiful Carib girl" from a native canoe, later writing that she "seemed to have been raised in a school of harlots." Columbus himself didn't actually set foot on ground.

The **St. George Village Botanical Garden,** just north of Centerline Road, four miles east of Frederiksted, at Estate St. George, is a veritable Eden of tropical trees, shrubs, vines, and flowers. Built around the ruins of a 19th-century sugarcane workers' village, the garden is a feast for the eye and the camera, from the entrance drive bordered by royal palms and bougainvillea to the towering kapok and tamarind trees, the multicolored hibiscus and fragipani, and the vast poinsettia bed—almost a quarter acre of red and white blooms from December to March. Restoration of the ruins is a continuing project. Two workers' cottages are already completed, providing space for a gift shop, rest rooms, a kitchen, and offices. These have been joined together with a Great Hall which is used by the St. Croix community for various functions. Other completed projects include the superintendent's house, the blacksmith's shop, and various smaller buildings used for a library, a plant nursery, workshops, and storehouses. Visitors are welcome from early morning until late afternoon; however, maps are available at the Great Hall only from 9 a.m. to 3 p.m. Admission is free, but donations toward the continued development of the garden are welcome.

Out on West Airport Road, the **Cruzan Rum Factory** makes the famous Virgin Islands rum. Guided tours depart daily from the new visitors' pavilion Monday through Friday from 8:30 to 11:15 a.m. and from 1 to 4:15 p.m. For reservations and information, telephone 772-0799.

The best for last, **Whim Great House,** a restoration of the St. Croix Landmarks Society, is one of the most intriguing of the West Indian plantation houses. The house was built soon after its Danish owner, a life-long bachelor of great wealth, took over in 1794. It's actually small, with only a trio of rooms in the main section. The location is on Centerline Road, about two miles east of Frederiksted, and hours are from 10 a.m. to 5 p.m. daily. Admission is $3 for adults and $1 for children. Some of the antiques in the main house are from old Cruzan homes. Around the perimeter is a moat. The house has semicircular ends, and walls three feet thick held together in part with molasses. On the grounds is a series of outbuildings, one housing machinery once used in the sugar-making process.

SHOPPING IN CHRISTIANSTED: In Christiansted, where the core of my shopping recommendations are found, the emphasis is on hole-in-the-wall boutiques, selling one-of-a-kind merchandise. Handmade items are strong. Of course the same duty-free stipulations, as outlined earlier, apply to your shopping selections in St. Croix.

Knowing it can't compete with Charlotte Amalie, Christiansted has forged its own creative statement in its shops, and by reputation it has now become the "chic spot for merchandise" in the Caribbean. All the shops are easily compressed into half a mile or so, so on a day's tour (or half day) you'll be able to inspect all the merchandise before making your purchases.

Little Switzerland, King Street (tel. 773-1976), is the unquestioned elite shop on the island for prestige watches, jewelry, china, and crystal. Only the finest watches are sold here, only the best crystal. The watches are priced exactly as they are in Switzerland—which is quite a saving on such name brands as Rolex, Concord, Ebel, Girard-Perregaux, Rado, Vacheron & Constantin, and many others. Incidentally, the owners employ Swiss watchmakers to see that every watch is in perfect adjustment. It's validated for you. Names in chinaware —Rosenthal, Aynsley, Royal Doulton, and Wedgwood—are here. This is also the official Hummel and Lladro shop. In addition, the shop is the largest Waterford importer in the West Indies.

Nini of Scandinavia, 16AB Church St. (tel. 773-2269), is home base for Nini Cohn, who has at least two dozen of the outstanding clothing and accessory sources of Scandinavia lined up. She has rolls of fabrics brought in from Finland's famed designer Marimekko. Smart shoppers buy a square length of one of these designs (exploded and color wild) to frame at home. Just stretched over a simple frame and hung, it can bring renewed life to any room. Fabric from Sweden is also sold. Nini imports lots of ready-to-wear apparel, offering at least 2000 dresses at all times. In stock is a large swimwear and sportswear selection, plus avant-garde jewelry from Denmark. As Nini rightly says, "It's mainly the people who have traveled the world who know the bargains here."

Java Wraps, Pan Am Pavilion (tel. 773-7529), on the corner of Strand Street, sells what is perhaps the most avant-garde fashion in the Caribbean. The dedicated owner is Twila Wilson, originally from Colorado, who spends six months of the year in Java and Bali overseeing the production of her resort designs made of hand-batiked prints. It's made in the classical traditional manner. Twila, who naturally wears a slinky sarong herself, says her "designs and fabrics emphasize cool, easy-to-wear, clean good-looking things." Her shop on Strand Street is a perfect setting, with Haitian floor matting, straw fan-back chairs, and potted palms. You'll find kimonos, rompers, bikinis, quilted jackets, sun dresses, and shirts for men and boys. But the bestseller is the one-size sarong. If you purchase it, you're given a sheet of instructions on how to wear it. Her antique Dorothy Lamour sarongs sell for $250 and up, and new sarongs are as low as $30. She also has a collection of children's wear.

The Compass Rose, 5 Company St. (tel. 773-0444), has been firmly entrenched on the island since 1957. It is an authorized Seiko dealer, but, in addition, offers an array of well-selected items from the Orient, including pearls, jade, and coral. They also sell tablecloths from China.

Violette Boutique, 38 Strand St., at the corner of Queen Cross Street, is a blue and gold multishopping place, where on its three floors is a vast array of perfumes, Seiko watches, gold jewelry, and fine gold and silver costume jewelry. The mezzanine offers a good selection of leather goods and handbags. On the second floor is an extensive array of women's and men's imported sportswear. Owner Violette Hilty keeps abreast of European fashion, and hopes to get merchandise here before it reaches the New York stores.

The Spanish Main, Pan Am Pavilion (tel. 773-0711), off the Strand, is for those who favor handcrafted fabrics, especially when they have style and integrity. The owner of this shop puts it most accurately when she says she offers "memories by the yard." You'll find bolts of hand-screened island prints on fabric that is 65% polyester, 35% cotton. The subjects are happy ones—a garden of native flowers, sails against the water, or flying birds against the sky. You can make your own apparel. Ready-to-wear dresses and evening wear are intriguing buys.

Pegasus, 58 Company St. (tel. 773-6926), is both the retail outlet and workshop of three jewelers, including Laura T. Leblow, a certified gemologist. They specialize in diamonds, gold, and gemstones, and can be trusted. In their undulating showcase they offer earrings, pendants, bracelets, and many one-of-a-kind pieces. Tariffs are based on the fluctuating price of gold. They also have a varied selection of hand-crafted black coral, pink coral, and pearl jewelry.

Many Hands, Pan Am Pavilion (tel. 773-1990), is devoted exclusively to Virgin Islands handicrafts. There is also a collection of local paintings. You're invited to see their year-round "Christmas tree." They sell a gold and silver mill pendant designed on the spot and handcrafted by Rudy Patton, which is a popular item. Children get a lot of attention here, as there's an assortment of custom-made dresses and suits, along with stuffed toys. West Indian spices and teas are also sold, as are shellwork, stained glass, hand-painted china, and ceramic switch plates, as well as other ceramic objects and handmade jewelry.

Happiness Is, Pan Am Pavilion (tel. 773-3123). I was drawn to this shop by its catchy name. Inside, you'll find a collection of island-made handicrafts, along with a selection of jewelry, including some made out of black coral. There is also a collection of resort-style clothing. Ask for Jean.

Pan Am Liquors, 12 Pan Am Pavilion (tel. 773-5641), advertises itself as "the most charming liquor store in the West Indies." By the volume of alcoholic beverages the place sells, it's easy to believe the claim. The staff will deliver any purchase free in easy-to-carry cardboard boxes to your hotel, so you can drop in on your way to the beach and not have to bother with lugging your parcel around. There's a free tasting bar stocked with tiny paper cups for sampling the varieties available. These range from well-known, straightforward brands to exotica such as perfumed rums and rare European blends.

SHOPPING AROUND THE ISLAND: In your visit to the Whim Greathouse, east of Frederiksted on Centerline Road, you might also want to browse through the **Whim Gift Shop.** Offering a good selection of gifts, appealing to a wide age spectrum, it has many imported items, but also many that are Cruzan made. Some were personally made for the Whim Shop. And as any member of the staff will point out, if you buy something, it all goes to a worthy cause: the upkeep of the greathouse and the grounds.

On your tour of the island, especially if you're in western St. Croix in the vicinity of Frederiksted, you might want to stop off at the following offbeat shopping recommendations:

St. Croix Leap, Mahogany Road, Route 76 (tel. 772-0421), is a fascinating adventure. You can visit the factory in the open, where you can see stacks of rare and beautifully grained wood being fashioned into tasteful objects. It is a St. Croix Life and Environmental Arts Project, dedicated to the natural environment through manual work and self-development. The end result is a fine collection of mahogany boards for cutting hors d'oeuvres, table tops, wall hangings, bowls, and sections of unusual pieces of wood with special graining. They become a form of naturalistic art.

St. Croix Leap is two miles up Mahogany Road from the beach north of Frederiksted. Large mahogany signs flank the driveway. Visitors should bear to the right to reach the woodworking area and workshop. It is asked that you telephone for an appointment. For inquiries, write to Box 245, Frederiksted.

The **Tradewinds Shop,** 320 King St. (tel. 772-0939), at the corner of Market Street, is the best-stocked store in Frederiksted. Housed in a series of high-ceilinged, spacious rooms, variously devoted to jewelry and watches, liquor, cigarettes, and clothing, the place is hard to miss during a shopping expedition. Purchases will be delivered to the airport, although if you buy a watch or perfume, you may want to carry it with you. The store is open from 8:30 a.m. to 5:30 p.m. daily except Sunday.

THE SPORTING LIFE: Beaches are the big attraction. The drawback is that getting to them from Christiansted, center of most of the hotels, isn't always easy. It can also be expensive, especially if you want to go back and forth during every day of your stay. Of course, you can always rent one of those housekeeping condominiums right on the water.

In Christiansted, if you want to beach it, head for the **Hotel on the Cay** (see the previous recommendation). You'll have to take a ferry to this palm-shaded island.

Cramer Park, at the northeast end of the island, is a special public park operated by the Department of Agriculture. Lined wth sea grape trees, the beach also has a picnic area, a restaurant, and a bar.

I highly recommended **Davis Bay** and **Cane Bay** as the type of beaches you'd expect to find on a Caribbean island—that is, palms, white sand, good swimming, and great snorkeling.

If you'd like to enjoy nude bathing, then head for **Isaac's Bay.**

Snorkeling and Scuba

Spectacular sponge life, black-coral trees (considered the finest in the West Indies), and steep dropoffs into water near the shoreline have made St. Croix a diver's goal.

Buck Island, with a visibility of more than 100 feet, is the site of the nature trail of the Underwater National Park, and it's the major diving target. All the minor and major agencies offer scuba and snorkeling tours to Buck Island. Divers also like to go to **Pillar Coral,** with its columns of coral spiraling up to 25 feet; **North Cut,** one of the tallest, largest coral pinnacles in the West Indies; and **Salt River Dropoff,** plunging to well over 1000 feet deep, as well as **Davis Bay Dropoff,** with its unique coral and rock mound structures in grotesque shapes.

Your best bet in Christiansted is **Caribbean Sea Adventures,** Kings Wharf (tel. 773-5922). Write to them at P.O. Box 3015, Christiansted. They have guided snorkeling tours on catamarans, motorboats, and trimarans, heading for Buck Island. They also offer dive courses.

St. Croix's most complex diving and training facility is **Dive Experience** (tel. 773-3307), at Club Comanche Hotel in Christiansted. A one-tank boat dive costs $40, a two-tank boat dive, $55. They also conduct night dives for $35.

Windsurfing

The **Virgin Surf Windsurfing Schools** has three locations. Telephone 773-0000 for more information.

Tennis

It's best at the **Buccaneer Hotel,** previewed earlier, which has eight courts, two lit at night, as well as a pro shop, even a resident pro (Don DeWilde). The court fee is $4 per person hourly, $5 hourly for night games. Other setups are the 12 courts (7 lit) at the **Caribbean Tennis Club** (tel. 773-7285), with its fully stocked pro shop. The charge here is $6 per person. **Canegata Ball Park** has two courts, lit at night, and no fee is charged. In addition, **Hotel on the Cay** offers four Laykold courts, charging $4 per hour (there's a pro shop).

Golf

St. Croix has the best in the U.S. Virgins. In fact, guests at Caneel Bay Plantation on St. John, or other visitors from St. Thomas, often fly over for a day's round.

On the island are two 18-hole golf courses, the **Fountain Valley Course** (tel. 722-0738), designed by Robert Trent Jones on the northwest side of St. Croix, and another one at the **Buccaneer Hotel** (tel. 773-2100). Site of "Shell's Wonderful World of Golf," Fountain Valley is where "Chi-Chi" Rodriguez set the course record of 69. In winter it charges $22 for 18 holes, and *this is lowered to $16 off-season.* A cart costs $20 for two persons. The Buccaneer charges $14 for 18 holes, plus $18 for a rental cart. Golf pro Tim Johnson is on hand, and there's a completely stocked pro shop and bar.

Horseback Riding

Jill's Equestrian Stable is found on the sprawling grounds of Sprat Hall Plantation (tel. 772-0305), where you can also find lodgings and good food. Jill Fleming, the daughter of the dynamic Joyce Hurd, offers the only riding on the island, with both English and western saddles. Of course, you've got to weigh in under 180 pounds for men, 155 pounds for women. A ride through the rain forest costs $30 per person. Her special is a moonlight ride for $45 per person, which includes a jug of wine and a block of cheese. Riding lessons are also given.

Fishing

The fishing grounds at **Lang Bank** are within easy reach. Here you'll find kingfish, wahoo, and dolphin. On light-tackle boats gliding along the reef, the catch is likely to turn up jack or bone fish. At Clover Crest, in Frederiksted, Cruzan anglers fish right from the rocks. Sprat Hall's **Jim Hurd,** P.O. Box 695, Frederiksted (tel. 772-0305), at the old plantation north of Frederiksted, will also arrange deep-sea fishing for two persons at a cost of $150. Ring him up if you're interested.

Bottom fishing on the 47-foot **Providencia** (tel. 773-0754) costs only $25 per person, and tackle and bait are provided. Trips are arranged from 10 a.m. to 2 p.m. Their motto is "What you catch . . . you keep."

Boating

Most boats move out to Buck Island. St. Croix has many boats for hire at widely varying rates, depending on the craft. **Llewellyn's Charter Inc.** (tel. 773-5037) rents a 36-foot trimaran, and **Watersports Inc.** (tel. 773-0754) rents craft for sailing, fishing, and diving.

Windsurfing

This ever-popular sport can be arranged at **Chenay Bay Colony,** four miles from Christiansted (tel. 773-2918). Both instruction and rental equipment are available in this efficiency cottage cluster opening onto three beaches.

AFTER DARK: To find the action, you might have to hotel or bar-hop: nightlife in St. Croix is like a floating game of craps.

If he's playing, the one man to seek out is Jimmy Hamilton, Duke Ellington's "Mr. Sax." He and his quartet are a regular feature of St. Croix nightlife.

On my latest rounds I caught him at the Binnacle in the Caravelle Arcade (tel. 773-4755) in Christiansted, where he usually appears on Saturday night. The Binnacle is in the Caravelle Hotel.

Bombay Club, 5A King St. (tel. 773-1838). Owner Jeff Serugi has managed to squeeze much miscellany into what is one of the most popular jazz clubs on the island. A large photograph of John Lennon greets visitors near the entrance. Other ornaments include original paintings, posters, and an array of tropical plants. You enter through a low stone tunnel and eventually find yourself near a collection of bars and a courtyard garden with tables and chairs.

Live jazz is presented seven nights a week, and uncomplicated food is served daily for lunch and dinner. Menu choices include omelets, salads, five kinds of nachos, burritos, enchiladas, burgers, and sandwiches. Full meals cost from $10, but if you just want a sandwich to soak up your beer, it will be less.

Grandstand Play, 56 King St. (tel. 773-7625). Above the shop, Little Switzerland, this establishment offers a huge bar area, a dance floor, and an upper veranda where you can cool off with a tropical drink. It presents a wide range of Stateside dance bands, as well as nationally known recording artists who give concerts. Everyone from Leo Kodke to Phoebe Snow to Dave Mason to Livingston Taylor to the Belmonts plays their stuff to enthusiastic crowds. When no one is performing, customers enjoy a ten-foot video screen on which are presented concerts and sporting events. There's usually a $7 cover charge, after which a beer costs from $1.50.

I've also spent many a pleasant evening at the **Moonraker Lounge,** which often has some very good guitar music. The location is on the balcony upstairs at the Lodge Hotel on Queen Cross Street (tel. 773-1535). Drinks cost from $3.

Rumors, 54B Company St. (tel. 773-6602). When I visited this place, I found a popular and stylish rendezvous point for hamburger gourmets and drink lovers. On a good night, it can be a lot of fun, since there's live entertainment five nights a week by a local band singing in a wide variety of musical styles. In the outermost room, a red neon sign above the bar spells out the name of the place. There's a lot for everyone here. Surrounded by bentwood chairs, hanging fans, potted plants, and beamed ceilings, you can see locals watching wrestling on TV near the bar or observe a romance blossoming in a corner.

Sunday brunch here is a bargain, and costs $8 per person. If you drop in for dinner, served between 5 p.m. and 2 a.m., you'll pay that same price for a full meal. Bryan Gregory, the New Jersey-born entrepreneur who is the owner, offers a rear terrace where many of the evening concerts are held. Food items, a supplement to the hamburgers and chili which originally made the place well known, are chicken primavera, shrimp primavera, "black" steak teriyaki, linguine with conch, and fresh dolphin. Full dinners cost from $23, although if you just want a hamburger it will be less.

The big treat of St. Croix is the **Quadrille Dancers.** Try to catch a performance if you can. You have to check at your hotel as to where you are likely to see one of their dances, little changed since plantation days. The women wear long dresses, white gloves, and turbans; and the men are attired in flamboyant shirts, sashes, and tight black trousers. When you've learned their steps, you're invited to join the dancers on the floor.

BUCK ISLAND: The crystal-clear water and the white coral sand of Buck Island, a satellite of St. Croix, are legendary. Now the National Park Service has marked an underwater snorkeling trail. The park covers about 850 acres, including the land area, which has a sandy beach with picnic tables set out and pits for having your own barbecues. There are two major underwater trails for snorkeling on the reef, plus many other labyrinths and grottos for more serious divers.

Slithering through its undergrowth of days of yore, you were likely to run into Morgan, LaFitte, Blackbeard, the privateer Deidrich, or even Captain Kidd.

A barrier reef of elkhorn coral, the calm waters of Buck Island shelter many reef fish, including the queen angelfish and the smooth trunkfish. Buck

Island lies only 1½ miles off the northeast coast of St. Croix. Uninhabited, it is only a third of a mile wide and a mile long.

Now a parkland, the island was inhabited for a long time, since the 1750s in fact. It's been a place of residence and a garden for growing crops. It's also been used for pasturage, and its timbers have been cut to build houses on St. Croix. It became a park in 1948, and the goats were eliminated in the 1950s. The attempt was to return Buck Island to nature, and it's been successful. Even the endangered brown pelicans is producing young here.

Many skippers of small boats run between St. Croix and Buck Island, charging from $20 to $25, and snorkeling equipment is furnished. You head out in the morning, and nearly all charters allow an hour and a half of snorkeling and swimming.

Captain Llewellyn (tel. 773-5037) has been sailing to Buck Island for more than 20 years, and he'll take you there on *Charis,* a 36-foot trimaran, which is the only charter boat sailing from the east end. Both half-day and full-day sails are arranged, as are sunset sails.

Captain Heinz (tel. 773-3161 or 773-4041) is another skipper with some 20 years of sailing experience. His trimaran, *Teroro,* leaves King's Wharf at 9 a.m. and 2:30 p.m., usually filled with small groups, never more than 11 passengers. All gear and safety equipment are provided. The captain sailed the *Teroro* across the Atlantic, and he's not only a skilled sailor, but a very considerate and concerned host while you're aboard. He will even take you around the *outer* reef, which the other guides do not, for an unforgettable underwater experience.

The easiest, smoothest, and most popular way to get to Buck Island is aboard the glass-bottomed boat *Reef Queen,* which sails daily at 9:45 a.m. and again at 1:45 p.m. It's the only boat that stops at "Scotch Bank." There's a changing room as well as a complete sit-down bar. For reservations, call 773-0754.

On the island itself, you can take a hiking trail through the tropical vegetation that covers the island. There are restrooms, plus a small changing room for visitors.

Chapter IV

THE BRITISH VIRGIN ISLANDS

1. Anegada
2. Jost Van Dyke
3. Marina Cay
4. Peter Island
5. Tortola
6. Virgin Gorda
7. Mosquito Island
8. Guana Island

WITH ITS SMALL BAYS and hidden coves, once havens for pirates, the British Virgin Islands are considered among the world's loveliest crusing grounds by the yachting set who know of such things.

Strung over the northeast corner of the Caribbean are some 40 islands, although skeptics might consider many of these rocks, perhaps cays, and in some cases, "spits of land." Only a trio of the British Virgins are of any significant size, including Virgin Gorda (the "fat virgin") and Tortola ("dove of peace"), as well as Jost Van Dyke.

The islands have such names as Fallen Jerusalem and Ginger. Norman Island is said to have been the prototype for Robert Louis Stevenson's *Treasure Island.* On Deadman Bay, a rocky cay, Blackbeard marooned 15 pirates and a bottle of rum, which gave rise to the ditty.

Columbus came this way in 1493, gazing upon beautiful harbors and green hills, but the British Virgins apparently made little impression on him. Sir Francis Drake sailed into the channel in 1595, seeking Spanish treasure ships. Drake's arrival here was commemorated by having the channel named after him. Less than a generation later the British claimed the island, and the Spanish and Dutch contested it. Tortola was officially annexed by the English in 1672.

The British Virgin chain lies some 60 miles east of Puerto Rico. These islands, craggy and volcanic in origin, are just 15 "air minutes" from St. Thomas. There is regularly scheduled ferry service between St. Thomas and Tortola as well.

The vegetation is varied. In some parts of the British Virgins palms and mangoes grow in profusion, while other places are arid and studded with cactus. Everything depends on the rainfall.

The islands are a British colony, with their own elected government and a population of about 11,000, mainly black. English is the tongue of the realm, and the Yankee dollar is the coin, much to the surprise of arriving Britishers who find no one willing to accept their pounds ("but this is a British colony," they protest to no avail). The islands, covering about 59 square miles, have a perfect year-round climate, with temperatures averaging between 77 and 85 Fahrenheit.

Note: All prices in this chapter are given in U.S. dollars.

Even though there are predictions that mass tourism is on the way, the British Virgins are still a paradise for escapists. The British Home Office, according to a report I once read, listed them as "the least important place in the British Empire."

PRACTICAL FACTS: U.S. and Canadian citizens need produce only an authenticated birth certificate or a voter registration card to enter the British Virgin Islands. On that evidence, they are welcome for a stay of up to six months, but must possess return or ongoing tickets and show evidence of adequate means of support and prearranged accommodations during their stay. Upon leaving, the BVI levies a $5 departure tax for those leaving by air or $3 for those leaving by sea.

Another government tax—this one to the tune of 5%—is imposed on all hotel rooms. However, there is no sales tax.

Watch your clock. The island operates on Atlantic Standard Time. In the peak winter season, when it's 6 a.m. in the British Virgins, it's only 5 a.m. in Miami. However, when Miami and the rest of the east coast goes on Daylight Saving Time, the clocks are the same in both places.

Ten doctors practice in Tortola, and there is a hospital with X-ray and laboratory facilities. One doctor practices on Virgin Gorda. Your hotel will put you in touch with the BVI's medical staff.

Unlike some parts of the Caribbean, nudity is an offense punishable by law in the BVI. Drugs, their use or sale, are also strictly prohibited.

Your U.S.-made appliances can be used here, as the electrical current is 110 volts, 60 cycles.

GETTING THERE: There are no direct flights from New York to Tortola, but you can make good connections through San Juan, St. Thomas, or St. Croix, each of which is serviced by such major carriers as **American** and **Eastern.**

Air BVI is your best bet from San Juan. It has flights not only from there to Tortola, but on to Virgin Gorda as well. The little carrier also has service from St. Thomas to Tortola, as well as from St. Maarten, St. Kitts, and Antigua.

CrownAir also flies from San Juan to Tortola and from St. Thomas to Tortola. It has flights as well from San Juan to Virgin Gorda and from St. Thomas to Virgin Gorda.

From Canada it's best to fly to a U.S. city, such as Miami, and make a connecting flight to San Juan.

Passengers arriving from Europe can best make connections through Antigua. Antigua is serviced directly from London on **British Airways.** In Antigua, as mentioned, BVI takes over from there.

You can also go from Charlotte Amalie (St. Thomas) by **public ferry** to the West End of Tortola. Both the *Native Sun* and the *Bomba Charger* depart three times a day. Check with the tourist board about exact departure times (subject to change). On Sunday, one ferry goes over in the early morning, another in the late afternoon.

1. Anegada

The most northernly and isolated of the British Virgins, 30 miles east of Tortola, Anegada has more than 500 wrecks lying off its notorious Horseshoe Reef. It's different from the other British Virgins in that it's a coral and limestone atoll, flat with a 2500-foot airstrip.

At its highest point, its land mass reaches a height of 28 feet, and hardly appears on the horizon if you're sailing to it. At the northern and western ends of the island are some good beaches, which might be your only reason for coming here, as there are no accommodations, as of this writing, that I care to recommend.

The population numbers about 250, many of whom have looked for (but not found) the legendary hidden treasure on such sunken ships as the *Paramatta,* which has been at rest for a century.

While on the island, you may want to visit **Neptune's Treasure,** a seaside restaurant run by the Soares family, who serve fresh fish and fresh lobster which they catch themselves. One reader writes, "I had my first dogfish shark at this restaurant, and it was great!" Meals cost from $12 per person, and the people are friendly and helpful in explaining to you how to explore their island. To get in touch with them, their radio contact in the BVI is on Tortola Radio (tel. 494-3425).

The family also rents tents with single or double air mattresses if you'd like to stay on the island—and don't mind roughing it a bit. You can take a taxi to one of their sandy beaches and go snorkeling along their reefs.

If you decide to come here, know that you're at a remote little corner of the Caribbean: don't expect one frill and be prepared to put up with some hardships (such as mosquitoes).

2. Jost Van Dyke

This rugged island, on the seaward side of Tortola, was probably named for some Dutch pirate. About 130 people live in four square miles. On the south shore of this mountainous island are some good beaches at White Bay and Great Harbour.

In the 1700s a Quaker colony settled here to develop sugarcane plantations. One of the colonists, William Thornton, won a worldwide competition to design the Capitol in Washington, D.C.

Smaller islands surround the place, including Little Jost Van Dyke, the birthplace of Dr. John Lettsome, founder of the London Medical Society.

The island has only a handful of places to stay but several dining choices, as it's a popular stopping-over point for the yachting set.

WHERE TO STAY: White Bay Sandcastle (tel. 494-2462) is a four-villa colony that makes a perfect retreat for escapists. Cottages are built in an octagonal style and are surrounded by flowering shrubbery and bougainvillea. Nestled among the palms, these individual cottages take advantage of the tropical breezes and gain every inch of the view. This is a small, personalized place, catering to only a handful of guests. You're allowed to mix your own drinks at the beachside bar, the Soggy Dollar, but you'll also have to keep your own tab. Visiting yachtspeople often drop in here for a while, enjoying the beachside informality and ordering a drink called a "Painkiller." In the guest book you'll find this quotation: "I thought places like this only existed in the movies."

Daphne Henderson is your hostess, and she's come a long way south from the Vermont country inn she used to run. In winter, two persons can stay here on the full-board plan at a cost of $200 per day. A single person pays $150. *Also* *on the full-board plan, a couple in summer need pay only $165 per day and a single $120,* plus tax and service. The owner will pick up guests at West End in Tortola. Fly to Beef Island and take a taxi from there. Or else you can take the ferry from St. Thomas, which goes to the West End three times a day. There's a $75 transportation charge for stays of less than six nights. For information, write to Daphne Henderson, P.O. Box 11840, St. Thomas, USVI 00801.

Sandy Ground, Box 594, West End, Tortola (tel. 494-3391), offers eight villas with self-sufficient housekeeping units of the type you might see along Spain's Costa del Sol. The estates, as it is called, is built on a 17-acre hill site on the eastern part of Jost Van Dyke.

The colony rents out two- and three-bedroom villas. One of my favorites was constructed on a cliff that seems to hang about 60 or so feet over a good beach. If you've come all this way to reach this tiny outpost you might as well stay a week, which are the rates quoted. In winter, two persons are charged $800 weekly, each additional person paying another $100. *However, in summer, the charge is lowered to $600 for two persons weekly, with each additional person paying only $85.*

Sandy Ground was created by John Eastman, who once headed an art school in Maine. The airy villas are each privately owned, and each unit is fully equipped with such necessities as refrigerators and stoves. They have their own electric generator. Bob and Billie Grunzinger, formerly of New York state, do a good job of running the property for the absentee owners. They'll help guests with boat rentals and water sports.

WHERE TO EAT: Explorers on Jost Van Dyke don't have to bring a packed lunch before heading out. The previously recommended **White Bay Sandcastle** (tel. 494-2462) has good food, but it does require a reservation, as supplies in the kitchen are limited. You dine right on the beach, taking breakfast, lunch, or dinner. Naturally, attire is casual. Lunch costs from $8, and dinner, featuring fresh fish when available, is from $20. The owner, Daphne Henderson, is a Cordon Bleu chef, and a good one at that.

Yachtsmen like to drop in at **Ira's-by-the-Sea.** Perhaps that's because a free welcoming drink awaits the captain. If you're a passenger or one of the crew, you have to pay. The food is simply prepared and inexpensive. Conch is always available, prepared in several ways. A fish dinner of whelks is more expensive. A catch of the day is always featured, and it might even be lobster. Then, the price "depends." Otherwise count on spending around $20 with drinks.

Abe's by the Sea is a native bar and restaurant on Little Harbour where the cook knows how to please the sailors with a menu of fish, lobster, conch, and chicken. Prices are low too. Most diners escape for around $20, money well spent, especially when a fungi band entertains you with its music and plays for dancing. For the price of the main course, you get peas and rice, along with cole-slaw and beans, plus dessert. Sometimes Abe's has a pig roast, and these turn out to be festive nights. When approaching the harbor, you'll see Abe's restaurant on your right hand side. For reservations, call Abe's on Channel 16 Marine Radio.

3. Marina Cay

Near Beef Island, Marina Cay is a tiny islet of only six acres. Its only claim to fame was as the setting of the Robb White book *Our Virgin Island,* which was filmed with Sidney Poitier and John Cassavetes. The island lies only five minutes away by launch from the Beef Island dock.

The only reason I'm mentioning such a tiny cay is because it is the site of a cottage hotel, previewed below:

Marine Cay Hotel (write to P.O. Box 76, Road Town, Tortola; tel. 494-2174). This cottage colony run by Chris and Maria Tilling is spread over the whole island, offering 16 pleasant A-frame cottages, consisting of two units each. Built along the water, they were among the earliest resort structures to open in the British Virgins. Subsequently, newer ones were added. Depending on the accommodation, one person can stay here in winter for $190 to $275 daily, MAP; two persons, from $230 to $315. *In summer, single MAP rates range from $125 to $185 daily, with doubles going for $165 to $225.* The hotel shuts down in September and October.

You of course have the use of a private beach, guaranteed not to be crowded. Sailing, fishing, and scuba-diving can be arranged, and use of Sunfish as well as snorkeling gear is included in the rates. A feature here is the hotel's "castaway picnic." Their J-24 *Jolie Brise* is available for day sails. At the beach bar and restaurant, both lunch and dinner are offered, with menus changed daily. As you'd expect, fresh fish such as grouper and snapper is the best item to order. A lobster farm is built into their dock. That doesn't mean you can't also enjoy Virginia ham and roast beef. You can show up here in sports attire, providing you've let them know you're coming over to eat. On Wednesday night in winter local entertainment is presented. The decor of the pavilion keeps everything nautical with driftwood, turtleshell lamps, and conch shells.

4. Peter Island

Half of the 1050-acre island, with its good marina and docking facilities, is devoted to the yacht club described below. A ferry makes the run across Sir Francis Drake Channel to Peter Island. Leaving from the CSY Dock, the craft takes from 20 minutes to half an hour. The CSY Dock is approached before you reach Road Town on the road from Beef Island Airport. Beach facilities are found on palm-fringed Deadman Bay, which faces the Atlantic but is protected by a reef.

The island is so private that except for an occasional mason at work and the endless vegetation, about the only creature a guest will encounter is an iguana or a wild cat whose ancestors were abandoned generations ago by shippers (they are said to have virtually eliminated the rodent population).

Peter Island Hotel and Yacht Harbour (tel. 494-2561) is a maritime village resort on a 675-acre site created by Peter Smedvig, the Norwegian shipowner and now owned by Amway of Michigan. In eight "harbour houses," 32 air-conditioned rooms are rented. The upper-floor units have front and rear balconies, and the lower-floor rooms have private patios, each with a view. To judge by the deft design of the intimate cottage colony set in a charming cove, it has been a great success.

Special touches include built-in refrigerators, his-and-hers washbasins, and pull-out magnifying mirrors. To add to the room count, 20 new units have been constructed overlooking Deadman Bay. In all, there are five beachfront villas, each with four rooms. All of these open onto beautiful views, and the interiors are in a tropical motif. Broad louvered wooden doors across the front of each unit open to balconies on the second floor and patios at beach level. The villas were built from locally quarried stones in blues, sand-bleached grays, taupes, and browns.

The beach-house units, on the MAP, cost from $425 for two persons. It's cheaper for two guests to stay at one of the harbour houses. There MAP rates are $350 daily. *In summer, MAP tariffs are reduced: two persons pay from $245 to $285 daily.* Special package plans are also offered. The Crow's Nest, overlooking Deadman Bay, crowns the peak above the hotel. This four-bedroom villa, with its own saltwater swimming pool, is rented for $1500 for up to eight persons per day. In addition, Peter Island offers Sprat Bay villa, on the water's edge. It has three bedrooms, two baths a kitchen, terrace, and living room, plus a rustic wooden interior. The daily EP rate for Spray Bay is $400 for up to six persons. For two meals a day, cottage occupants can add another $45 per person.

Naturally, there is a main swimming pool, and the club's marina facilities are considered among the best equipped in the Virgin Islands. Horseback riding, tennis, and sailing are easily arranged, as are such water sports as scuba-diving, snorkeling, and skiing.

England-born David E. Benson, the general manager, is the kind of experienced hotelier who anticipates in advance the problems and needs of his international clientele, which has included actors Nick Nolte, Robert Shaw, and Jacqueline Bisset, who stayed there during the filming of *The Deep*.

To call toll free for reservations, dial 800/346-4451. For written requests, write Peter Island, 220 Lyon St., Grand Rapids, MI 49503.

For dining, the **Peter Island Hotel and Yacht Harbour** (tel. 494-2561) serves food that is considered among the best in the British Virgins. Even if you aren't staying in one of the previously recommended accommodations, you can go over just for the cuisine. Boats depart from CSY Baughers Bay at 10 a.m. and noon for lunch and at 6:30 p.m. for dinner (reservations are required). Barbecue lunches and dinners are featured on the beach, or you can eat in the main dining room decorated in a nautical motif.

The prix-fixe dinner, served nightly except Saturday, costs $30, plus service. Both European and local chefs prepare specialties.

On Saturday evening, a big smörgåsbord is prepared, the accent on local seafood. Meat or grilled fish is served from the rôtisserie. A prime rib is carved right at your table, and you can enjoy one of the best and most varied wine lists in the Virgin Islands, with some rare clarets. In season a jacket is required in the main dining room.

5. Tortola

On the southern shore of this 42-square-mile island, **Road Town** is more like a village. Still, it's the capital of the British Virgin Islands, the seat of Government House and other administrative buildings. The landfill at Wickhams Cay, a 70-acre town center development and marina in the harbor, has brought in a massive yacht-chartering business and has transformed the sleepy capital into more of a bustling, sophisticated center.

On the same southern coast as Road Town, Tortola is characterized by rugged mountain peaks which contain yellow cedar and frangipani, among other foliage. On the northern coast, however, are white sandy beaches, banana trees, mangoes, and clusters of palms.

No visit to Tortola is complete without a trip to **Mount Sage,** a national park rising 1780 feet. Here on its slopes you'll not only find traces of a primeval rain forest, but you can enjoy a picnic, overlooking neighboring islets and cays. The mountain is reached by heading west from Road Town.

Also west from Road Town for about 4½ miles, you come to **"The Dungeon,"** the island's oldest fort, erected by the Dutch in 1640. Botanists should look for the rare wild West Indian cherry tree growing on the unkempt grounds.

Nearby you can view the ruins (and I mean ruins) of **Thornton Great House.** Here lived Dr. William Thornton, the Quaker I've mentioned previously who won the competition to design the Capitol in Washington, D.C.

Close to Tortola's eastern end, **Beef Island** is the site of the main airport for passengers arriving in the British Virgins. The airstrip is 3600 feet long and can accommodate the Avro 748 turbo-jet 48-seaters.

The tiny island is connected to Tortola by the Queen Elizabeth Bridge, which the queen herself dedicated in 1966. The one-lane bridge spans the 300-foot channel which divides the little island from its bigger sister, Tortola. On the north shore of Beef Island is a good beach, Long Bay.

GETTING AROUND: In this remote part of the Caribbean, getting around can be a bit of a problem. However, there are **taxis,** which meet every arriving flight. Your hotel can also call up a taxi, and one will soon arrive at your doorstep. Only problem is, forget about the "official" taxi rates—they are generally ignored, as they're completely out of date. You negotiate your own fare. For example, it costs about $12 as of this writing to go from the airport into Road Town.

Car Rentals

Driving in the BVI is only for those who like hairpin turns on a Coney Island Cyclone terrain.

Budget Rent-a-Car (tel. 494-2639) now operates out of Tortola, renting Datsuns and Nissan Jeeps at rates ranging from $159 to $209 weekly. Better nail down a reservation before you get there by calling toll free 800/527-0700 (in Alaska and Hawaii, 800/527-0747). In Canada, call 800/268-8900. You'll need a Canadian or American driver's license, and in addition, you must pay $5 at police headquarters for a temporary British Virgins driving permit, good for about a month.

Driving is on the left, as I'd like to remind the policeman who nearly killed me recently as he came speeding down the pike on the right!

Local Air Services

CrownAir, formerly Dorado Wings, will fly you to Virgin Gorda and on to San Juan or St. Thomas. For reservations, telephone 495-2548 in Tortola (actually Beef Island) or 495-5555 in Virgin Gorda.

Air BVI also flies from Beef Island (Tortola) to Virgin Gorda several times a day. For flight information and reservations, telephone 494-2777 in Tortola.

Sightseeing Tours

This is probably your best bet for taking a look at Tortola. **Travel Plan Tours** (tel. 494-2348) will pick you up at your hotel (a minimum of two persons required) and take you on a 4½-hour tour of the island, for $25 per person. At night you can call 494-2154 and arrange for a morning tour.

WHERE TO STAY: Most of the places are small—"mom and pop" operations—and informality is the keynote at these inns. My favorites follow:

Long Bay Hotel, P.O. Box 433 (tel. 495-4252), on the north shore, about ten minutes from the West End, is a low-rise hotel complex set in a 50-acre estate with nearly a mile of white sand beach. It is the first port of entry to Tortola. Escapists who want a far-away corner of a half-forgotten island come here. Units are available in a wide range of styles, shapes, and sizes. Suites, including regular and superior, as well as cottages are scattered up the side of a hill planted with such flowery shrubbery as hibiscus. Cottages come with two bedrooms, a bath and shower, a kitchen, and a living room overlooking the ocean. Some elevated beachfront rooms set at the edge of the white sands, with twin beds, a bathroom, and a kitchenette, as well as a deck overlooking the ocean with a patio at beach level.

In winter on the EP, these rent for $130 double, $110 single. *In summer, rates go down quite a bit, to $70 double, $60 single.* Service and tax are added to all rates. In winter, suites range in price from $90 to $120 for double occupancy, EP. Cottages housing four persons peak at $160 daily, *this rate being lowered to $80 in summer. Doubles can book a suite here in summer at tariffs ranging from $50 to $70; singles, $40 to $60.* Suites, called hillside studios, are air-conditioned and have a dressing area with vanity.

The beach restaurant serves breakfast and luncheon and, in the winter, informal à la carte suppers. The Garden Restaurant serves dinner by reservation only, and the food is of excellent quality, including that rarity in the British Virgins, fresh vegetables. Boats can also be rented for sailing, diving, and exploring the out islands. If the surf is too rough for you, an oceanside saltwater swimming pool adjoins the beach house (which was once a distillery, incidentally). If you write the director, Terence M. Ford will be helpful in responding to your inquiries.

Sugar Mill Estate, P.O. Box 425, Apple Bay (tel. 495-4440), is one of my favorite inns in the entire Caribbean! The setting is in lush foliage, on the north side of Tortola, a long $20 haul from the airport. Built on the site of a 300-year-old sugar mill, the cottage colony sweeps down the hillside to its own little beach.

The estate is owned by Jeff and Jinx Morgan, formerly of San Francisco, who are travel, food, and wine writers. They provide a warm greeting and atmosphere, and make one feel immediately welcome. They also conduct classes called "Cooking in Paradise with Jinx and Jeff Morgan." Write them for details if you'd like to know how to manage with wild mountain thyme, star apples and mangoes, and a host of other dishes such as an almond roulade with pineapple ginger cream.

Comfortable, stylish apartments climb up the hillside. At the center is a circular swimming pool for those who don't want to go down to the beach. Accommodations are contemporary and beautifully thought out, ranging from suites and cottages to studio apartments, all self-contained with kitchenettes and private terraces with views. In winter, two persons (EP) pay from $95 to $120 daily, and *tariffs are lowered off-season to anywhere from $55 to $75 for two,* plus $30 per person extra for breakfast and dinner. The four suites rented are each suitable for four family members. Ceilings are sloped, made of native lumber, and to keep the sea breezes moving, you can turn on a ceiling fan.

The landscaping of the grounds is a delight to botanists and to anybody else who enjoys foliage. You'll find jasmine, oleander, hibiscus, avocados, plantains, citrus trees, gardenias, bougainvillea, mangoes, bananas, and pineapples, as well as sugar apples. Lunch is served down by the beach, and dinner in the old Sugar Mill Room, its stone walls decorated with Haitian paintings (see the dining recommendatins). Breakfast is on the terrace. The bars are on the honor system, and snorkeling equipment is loaned free. The estate is usually closed in August and September.

Treasure Isle Hotel, P.O. Box 68, Road Bay (tel. 495-2501), is the most complete and central resort on Tortola, built at the edge of the capital, on 15 acres of hillside overlooking a marina. The late Herbert Showering of Harvey's sherry spent time, money, and energy transforming the hotel. The general manager, Peter W. S. Wimbush, keeps the British traditions alive today and runs a fine "isle."

The core of the hotel is a rather splashy and colorful lounge and swimming pool area. Adjoining it is an open-air dining room (covered), also overlooking the harbor. The cuisine is respected here, with such delights from the barbecue as fresh grouper or snapper when available or a plump, tasty chicken with hot sauce. Every Friday and Sunday evening there's a barbecue. At the hotel's Caribbean evening on Wednesday, you get tasty native dishes, including local conch in a spicy liquor, callaloo soup, curried local beef, and a mango fool or pumpkin pie for dessert.

Along hillside terraces are more than two dozen hotel rooms on one level, more than a dozen efficiencies on another, and higher still, ten condominiums. Winter rates are $105 daily in a double, $100 in a single. For MAP, add $30 per person extra per day. *In summer, a number of low-cost package tours are offered. Otherwise, singles cost $70 daily; doubles, $78.* The atmosphere in each room is striking, with high bamboo beds, tiled floors, and white walls forming a fine background for the large framed Jim Tillett silkscreen prints.

While most guests stay here for the water-sports activities, there are two tennis courts and another for squash. The hotel's own marina has facilities for visiting yachting people. The big treat here is to go on a day trip to the hotel's own beach club at nearby Cooper Island. The hotel's power boat runs three times a week to Cooper Island for lunch, swimming, and snorkeling. This tour must be booked through Treasure Isle. The hotel also has a fully equipped dive facility, handling beginning instruction and ranging upward to full certification courses. The hotel's also the "home" in the Caribbean for an offshore sailing school.

Prospect Reef Resort, P.O. Box 104, Road Town (tel. 494-3311), is British-owned, managed by James St. John III, the largest and most up-to-date resort in the British Virgins. From this village built on a coral reef, panoramic views of Sir Francis Drake Channel unfold. Attractively modern buildings have been set tastefully on landscaped grounds of 38 acres, opening onto a bustling little private harbor. Built as condominiums, rental units consist of suites, town houses, villas, and apartments. Appointments are modern and colorful, in a Caribbean motif.

In winter, guests on the EP are charged from $108 to $178 in a single or double. A two-bedroom villa costs $425 daily for four persons. Breakfast and dinner carry a supplement of $39 per person daily. *In the off-season, EP singles or doubles cost $115. Two-bedroom villas suitable for four persons go for $325 daily.* Accommodations include private balconies or patios, private baths or shower, good-size living and dining areas, plus separate bedrooms or sleeping lofts.

There's a pool to swim in, another to dive in, plus sea pools for snorkeling or just fish watching. Six tennis courts with lights are available to buffs. There's also a pitch-and-putt course. Food at the Prospect Restaurant, a combination of continental specialties and island favorites, was praised by *Gourmet* magazine. Diners usually begin their meals with an apéritif at the Drop Inn Bar by Prospect Harbour. The chef's specialties include duckling in orange sauce, steak au poivre, and lobster in champagne. Count on spending about $25 at dinner, if you don't order lobster. Barbecue nights at the Pavilion Restaurant, enhanced by the rhythms of a steel band, offer the choice of chicken, steak, or spare ribs with an array of salads, vegetables, and desserts. Lunch can be taken at the Pavilion.

The water-sports desk can fill you in on what's available in day sailing, dinghy rental, snorkeling, scuba-diving, or sports fishing. A complete spa and conference center has been added.

Fort Burt Hotel, P.O. Box 187, Road Town (tel. 494-2587), offers one of the most pleasant British ambiences in Tortola. The recently refurbished stone and tile rooms give few hints of the Dutch fort that was constructed on the site in 1666, but in the interior stairway leading up from the steep driveway, you can see some of the massive foundations. Richard Hodgkins and Steve Robinson, the England-born owners, keep the antique cannon and the former magazine of the fort in good condition as a focal point in the garden.

Today, cascades of jasmine and a flowering plant called the Pride of Barbados conceal some of the angles of the pleasantly isolated accommodations (seven in all), which rent in winter at $100 for a single, $110 for a double. Weekly rates are $570 for a single and $650 for a double. *Summer prices are $55 daily in a single, $65 in a double. Summer weekly rates are $475 in a single and $460 in a double.* Each unit has a flowered sun terrace, a private bath, and lots of ocean breezes.

The real heart and soul of this pleasant retreat is the wrap-around sun terraces, which takes in a view of the low-lying cays, and the oval-shaped room sharing part of the terrace's inner wall. Inside the room, man-size drinks cost from $2 to $2.50. Late on Saturday night, the terrace and oval room turn into a disco.

The adjoining restaurant is well worth patronizing, whether you prefer to eat in candlelit intimacy inside or under flowering vines and an open-air canopy. Your choice from the witty menu might be fresh snapper Sir Thomas More (served with walnuts in a lime and garlic sauce). Meat dishes in this colonial milieu include steak-and-oyster pie Henry VIII.

Full meals begin at around $30 and are served at dinner seven days a week. Reservations are suggested. At lunch, less expensive meals are served, for around $7 per person with drinks included. Even if you request it "Virgin style," the fruit punch is refreshing. The hotel lies about half a mile from Road Town's center.

The Moorings/Mariner Inn, P.O. Box 139, Road Harbour (tel. 494-2332), is the Caribbean's only complete yachting resort, outfitted with 100 sailing yachts, some worth around $500,000. On an eight-acre resort, the inn was obviously designed with the yachting crowd in mind. Charlie and Ginny Cary, a couple from New Orleans who started the British Virgins' first charter service, manage it. They originally came to the Virgins in 1969 to "get away from the cold weather." Not only do yachting people find support facilities and service, but shoreside accommodations as well: lanai hotel rooms, a dockside restaurant, Mariner Bar, a swimming pool, a tennis court, a beach club, a gift shop, and a dive shop. Some 38 units are rented on the EP in winter at a rate of $110 daily in a double, $90 in a single. *Off-season, doubles are lowered to $68 daily, singles going for $55.* Suites are priced at $120 in winter, $75 *in summer.* Rooms are spacious, decorated in a light Caribbean motif. All have kitchenettes.

Village Cay Marina, P.O. Box 145, Road Town (tel. 494-2771), offers well-furnished air-conditioned rooms, and the manager will quote you not only room rates but a dockage rate schedule as well. Units come with private balconies and private baths. Two persons in winter pay $65 per night, a single going for $55. A few economy bunkrooms are rented for $34 double occupancy, $29 single occupancy. *In summer, the tariffs are $50 nightly in a double, $46 in a single. Double occupancy in one of the economy bunkrooms is $30 nightly, and a single person pays $28.* The waterfront restaurant looks out to the boat slips, and a bar is in the British-pub style.

Cane Garden Bay Beach Hotel, P.O. Box 570, Cane Garden Bay (tel. 495-4639), on the north shore of Tortola on a palm-fringed white sand beach, offers a handful of comfortable but simple rooms, each furnished with a private balcony and views of the sea, a kitchenette, ceiling fan, telephone, and maid service. Accommodations are priced at $60 for a double and $55 for a single in winter, *$40 in a double and $35 in a single in summer.* A third person in a double costs an extra $12 in any season.

The driving force behind this pink-walled hideaway is the energetic and jovial James Rhymer. He personally directs the kitchens of the adjacent restaurant, Rhymer's, which has built up an enthusiastic clientele since it opened. It's recommended separately (see below).

Water sports abound here, with Sunfish and windsurfers available for use by the guests.

Brewers Bay Campground, P.O. Box 185, Road Town (tel. 494-3463), offers 20 prepared campsites on the north shore of Tortola. Tent sites are rented to two persons at a cost of $16 per day, plus $3 for each additional person. The managers also rent out ten bare sites at a cost of $6 per day for two persons, with each additional person paying $1. Picnic tables, gas lamps, a propane gas stove, and a charcoal grill are offered campers.

WHERE TO EAT: Most guests dine at their hotels, but if you want to break the monotony of that, I have a few suggestions.

Sugar Mill Room, P.O. Box 425, Apple Bay (tel. 495-4440). You dine in an informal room which was transformed from a three-centuries-old sugar mill (see the hotel recommendations). Your hosts are Jeff and Jinx Morgan, formerly of San Francisco. They know much about food and wine. Together they write a monthly column, *"Cooking for Two,"* in *Bon Appétit,* and she is contributing editor for food and dining for *American Way,* the American Airlines in-flight magazine. Their most recent book is called *Two Cooks in One Kitchen.* Works by Haitian painters have been hung on the old stone walls of the dining room, forming a museum of primitive art. Big copper basins, once used as mortar cisterns, have been planted with tropical flowers.

Before going to the dining room, once part of the old boiling house, I suggest a visit to the charming little bar, everything open air in the true West Indian fashion.

Jinx Morgan supervises the dining room and is an imaginative cook herself. One of their most popular creations, published in *Bon Appétit,* is a curried banana soup. They are likely to prepare delectable chicken breasts in a number of ways, seafood soufflé, black bean soup, herb pasta with hearts of palm sauce, lobster creole, and a cold rum soufflé. That's just an opening repertoire. The next time around, you might try their breadfruit vichyssoise, conch ceviche with coconut cream, and homemade rum and raisin ice cream. Everything here is homemade, including many island specialties. You're asked to help yourself from a crisp salad bar, like those good ones found in New York. At dinner, the cost is around $22 and you must call for a reservation.

The **Cloud Room** (tel. 494-2821) provides a unique dining experience in Tortola. This restaurant and bar sits at the top of Butu Mountain, overlooking Road Town. When weather permits, which is practically every day of the year, the roof slides back, allowing you to dine under the stars. The catch is that the road there is bad (and there's no place to park), so the owner, Paul Wattley, prefers to arrange to pick you up when you make your reservation for dinner, served nightly from 7:30 to 10. For anywhere from $20 to $30, including wine, you'll get a selection of juicy sirloin steaks, filet mignon, lobster (if available), king crab, fresh fish in season, shish kebab (the house specialty), and shrimp in creole sauce. At the West Indian buffet every Tuesday night, you'll find such native dishes as curried shrimp, pineapple spare ribs, stewed mutton, or curried veal.

Brandywine Bay Restaurant, P.O. Box 151, Road Town (tel. 495-2301). Marti and Ben Brown over the years have developed quite a few fans in the Virgin Islands. You'll find them now at their latest perch, in a garden-like atmosphere on the south shore of Tortola, overlooking Drake's Channel, about ten minutes by taxi from Road Town.

This is an elite hideaway, attracting the yachting crowd whenever they want to get their feet on solid ground. The setting may be romantic, but it is mainly the food that attracts the patrons. Very fresh ingredients are used, and the menu is both West Indian and continental. That is, you might prefer cracked conch Bahamian style, but you can also get a perfect wienerschnitzel or a veal piccata. Their Sunday brunch from 11 a.m. to 2:30 p.m. is quicky becoming a legend on the island.

If the caviar crêpes don't tempt you, perhaps the chicken Kiev will. For dessert, you might try key lime pie or the coco-banana crêpe. Meals cost from $25, and are served nightly except Monday from 6:30 to 9:30. You should always make a reservation.

If you're staying in one of the efficiency apartments on Tortola and don't want to cook, I suggest you go over to **Carib Casseroles,** on Main Street, near the post office in Road Town (tel. 494-3271). Even the *New York Times* praised its "excellent frozen meals," which are called "Meals on Keels." Persons aboard yachts who don't want to be gallery slaves drop in here, selecting from a choice of 30 international dishes, including such West Indian specialties as beef and green banana curry, red snapper in fresh lime butter, shrimp with garlic, and Cuban picadillo. Meals begin at $15.

Very popular are the rotis (the celebrated Trinidadian taco stuffed with spicy curried meat or shellfish). These wonderful dishes are the creation of Canada-born Roslyn Griffiths, whose recipes were featured in *Cuisine* magazine. You can purchase these fast-food pouches which you cook by dropping in hot water.

If you're in town for lunch or dinner, you can go over to her little garden restaurant and "splice the mainbrace" with her ROZmatazz rum punch. In addition to the specialties named, you can enjoy her memorable soups, including creole fisherman's stew, tomato and eggplant, peanut creole, and pumpkin. For dessert, try the sugar Bum Bum pie (with custard and cream). The garden restaurnt is likely to be closed for two months beginning in August. Otherwise, hours are 11 a.m. to 3 p.m. and 7 to 10 p.m. daily except Sunday.

The Pub (tel. 494-2608) stands at water's edge, and locals on Tortola like to go here for a sundowner. It's a British-style pub in the Fort Burt Marina complex, with a good view of the sailing scene. Boat owners like to visit at opening time, 10:30 a.m., for drinks, and a few might make it to the 1 a.m. curfew, depending on how thirsty they are or how long at sea. Lunches are simply prepared and inexpensive, featuring dishes such as chicken and chips, fish and chips, hamburgers, sandwiches, and a special of the day. At dinner there is more of a choice, with shrimp, chicken, chicken Kiev, and prime ribs flown in from Puerto Rico on Thursday. Meals cost from $15. The atmosphere of the Pub is friendly and relaxed, dress is casual, and reservations are not required. On Friday and Saturday nights entertainment is provided all year, and there is a dartboard for daily use.

AN EXCURSION FOR THE DAY: If you've decided to risk everything and navigate the roller-coaster hills of the BVI, then you need a destination. **Cane Garden Bay** is one of the choicest pieces of real estate on the island, long discovered by the sailing crowd. Its white sandy beach is a cliché of Caribbean charm, with sheltering palms. It is nearly always semideserted. No one crowds you here.

Rhymer's (tel. 495-4639) is the place to go for food and entertainment at Cane Garden Bay. The success of the place depends very much on James Rhymer himself, who, to judge from the size of him, likes his own food alot. Skippers of any kind of craft are likely to stock up on supplies here; but you can also order cold beer and refreshing rum drinks. Turtle, conch, and whelk show up regularly on the bill of fare, and, when available, Caribbean langouste. If you're tired of fish, maybe James will make you some of his barbecued spare ribs. You might also try the mutton stew with peppers and herbs or the honey-dipped chicken. The beach bar and restaurant is open seven days a week from 8 a.m., serving not only breakfast, but lunch and dinner, which costs from $15 up. On some nights a steel drum band will entertain the mariners, and maybe the host himself will show you what a limbo dance is all about! Ice and freshwater showers are available (there are towels to rent as well), and you can ask about renting Sunfish and windsurfers.

THE SPORTING LIFE: Tortola boasts the largest fleet of bareboat sailing charter boats in the world, and is also one of the finest diving areas anywhere.

Snorkeling and Scuba

Marina Cay is known for its good snorkeling beach, and the one at Cooper Island (see the Treasure Isle Hotel recommendation) is another honey. Divers are attracted to Anegada Reef, which is the site of many shipwrecks, including the *Paramatta* and the *Astrea*. However, the one dive site in the British Virgins that lures them over from St. Thomas is the wreckage of the R.M.S. *Rhone,* near the western point of Salt Island. *Skin Diver* magazine called this "the world's most fantastic ship wreck dive." It teems with beautiful marine life and coral formations, and was featured in the motion picture *The Deep.*

Aquatic Centres, Road Town (tel. 494-2858). For a good swimmer interested in taking his or her first dive under careful supervision, this well-equipped outfit would probably be one of the best choices anywhere. George Marler, a devoted conservationist described by many of his friends as "the old man of the sea," is ably assisted in this venture by Bob Turrentine, a former lawyer from Minnesota. A resort course for amateurs includes lessons in a pool and a two-tank reef dive lasting a full morning or afternoon. The cost is $55 per person. One-tank dives for experienced divers cost around $30 each, while full-week certification courses go for $350. For already-certified divers, an unlimited diver's card, a bargain at about $300, gives the option of taking as many as three dives a day for as long as you stay in the area. All equipment plus the services of the guide are included in the package.

George Marler provides expeditions to many dive sites, including the R.M.S. *Rhone* which sank in 1867, as well as giving courses in underwater photography. For more information about this remarkable company, you can call toll free within the U.S., 800/345-6296. In Pennsylvania, call 800/362-5255.

Boating

The best for this is Charlie and Ginny Cary's **The Moorings,** P.O. Box 139, Road Town (tel. 494-2332), whose eight-acre waterside resort I've already previewed as a dockside hotel recommendation. This place, along with others, makes the British Virgins the cruising capital of the world. The Carys started the first chapter service in the British Virgins.

From their beautiful fleet of sailing craft, you can choose your own design, including a Moorings 50 and a Morgan 46, considered the queens of the Caribbean charter fleet. They can accommodate three couples in comfort and style. Arrangements can be made for bareboating or going out with a skipper.

They have a staff of some 60 mechanics, electricians, riggers, and cleaners. In addition, if you're going out on your own, you'll get a thorough briefing session about Virgin Island waters and achorages. Based on four passengers going out, *summer rates range from $389 to $560 weekly,* winter rates costing from $604 to $823. These rates are given only for general guidance, and are subject to change. To make reservations in the U.S., call 800/535-7289, toll free.

The **Shadowfax,** Treasure Isle Hotel Jetty, Tortola (tel. 494-2175), is a catamaran whose double-hulled construction permits smooth sailing even in rough seas, with an experienced crew taking the boat out for a day of snorkeling off reefs rich in marine life. Snorkel equipment, a buffet lunch, and an open bar are covered by the fee of $55 per person. The highlight of the outing is a tour through weirdly angled granite formations of Virgin Gorda "Baths." These shelter tidal pools, massive tree roots, exotic fish, and hidden catches of soft white sand. Considered haunted by the native Indians, these massive boulders offer one of the most bizarre and colorful expeditions in the islands.

AFTER DARK: There isn't much nightlife. Your best bet is to ask around and find out which hotel might have entertainment on any given evening. Fungi and scratch bands appear regularly. Nonresidents are usually welcome, but call first.

WHERE TO SHOP: Most of the shops are on Main Street, Road Town, in Tortola, but know that the British Virgins have no duty-free port shopping. British goods are imported without duty, and the wise shopper will be able to find some good buys among these imported items, especially in English china.

The **Cockle Shop** carries jewelry handmade in the British Virgins, including many gifts and souvenir items, even pieces of Wedgwood.

Go to **Past and Presents** to see china and pewter, as well as a collection of antique silver. They sell books too.

The **Shipwreck Shop,** depending on what "washed up" on its premises, usually has a collection of West Indian handicrafts, including placemats, sandals, grass rugs, straw bags, shell jewelry, and wooden bowls, all for sale in one of the more traditional structures in Road Town.

Pusser's Company Store (tel. 494-2467) is equally divided between a long, mahogany-trimmed bar accented with nautical artifacts and a souvenir store selling T-shirts, postcards, and gift items. Pusser's Rum is one of the bestselling items here, or perhaps you'd prefer polished brass mementoes of your visit. The place is open from 9:30 a.m. to 5 p.m. daily except Sunday.

6. Virgin Gorda

The second-largest island in the cluster of British Virgins, Virgin Gorda (Fat Virgin) remains truly virginal. However, seen from the sea, it doesn't look virginal at all—rather, like a pregnant woman lying on her back.

Virgin Gorda is ten miles long and two miles wide, with a population of some 1100. It lies 12 miles east of Road Town, and is reached by frequent flights from Beef Island off the shores of Tortola. Virgin Gorda is also frequently visited from St. Thomas, which lies only 26 miles away. **Speedy's Fantasy** (tel. 495-5240) operates a ferry service between Road Town and Virgin Gorda, the trip taking only half an hour and costing about $8. The ferry makes several trips daily, but does not operate on Sunday.

The northern side of Virgin Gorda is mountainous, a peak reaching 1370 feet. However, the southern half is flat, with large boulders appearing at every turn. The best beaches are at Spring Bay, Trunk Bay, and Devil's Bay.

Among the places of interest, **Coppermine Point** is the site of an abandoned copper mine and smelter. Because of loose rock formations, it can be dangerous to explore and caution should be used if you're going there. Legend has it that the Spanish worked these mines in the 1600s. However, the only authenticated document reveals that the English sank the shafts in 1838 to mine copper.

The Baths are on every visitor's list to Virgin Gorda. These are a phenomenon of tranquil pools and caves formed by gigantic house-size boulders. As these boulders toppled over one another, they formed saltwater grottos, suitable for exploring.

The best way to see the island if you're over for a day trip is to call Andy

Flax at Fischers Cove Beach Hotel (tel. 495-5252). He runs **Virgin Gorda Tours Assoc.,** which will give you a tour of the island for about $25 per person. The tour is operated twice daily from the hotel's parking lot.

Kilbride's Underwater Tours, Saba Rock (tel. 494-2746), is run by the Kilbride clan. Between them they have been diving for 75 years. The Kilbride family members have done everything from spending two weeks under the sea as "aquanauts" to underwater demolition work. They'll take you on underwater tours of the dive sites in the area, ranging from coral forests and wall-to-wall fish to wrecks (the *Rhone* among others). A one-tank dive costs $50; two-tank dive, $60. A half day's snorkeling costs $30 per person. Saba Rock is an island on the eastern end of Gorda Sound.

THE RESORT HOTELS: Little Dix Bay, P.O. Box 70 (tel. 495-5555). Millions of dollars after the discovery of the site by Laurance Rockefeller, this resort—the embodiment of understatement in luxury—opened in 1964 on the northwest corner of the "Fat Virgin," in the Sir Francis Drake Channel, where pirates once prowled. It has the same quiet elegance as its fellow Rockresort, Caneel Bay Plantation in St. John in the U.S. Virgins. On a 500-acre preserve, the 84-room resort is discreetly scattered along a crescent-shaped private bay.

All rooms, built in woods of purpleheart, mahogany, locust, and ash, have private terraces, with a view of the sea or of gardens. Some units are two-story rondavels raised on stilts to form their own relaxing breezeways. On the outside they may appear like South Seas huts, but on the inside intelligent decorating has brought a sophisticated contemporary styling with all the conveniences. They are often characterized by rough stone walls, open beamed ceilings, hanging red lamps, white chests, and Toledo-red fabrics.

From mid-April until mid-May and from November 1 through December 19, singles rent for $285; doubles, $320—including three meals daily. From mid-May until the end of October, the single rate is $245 daily, $285 in a double. Special plans, such as tennis specials, honeymoon packages, whatever, are also offered in summer. In winter, full AP rates are $420 daily for two persons, $365 in a single, $570 in a triple. Trade winds come through louvers and walls of screens, the air mixture further cooled by ceiling fans. In the rondavels, hammocks swing from the stilts.

At the Pavilion, with its peaked roofs, you can dine in the open, or else enjoy meals in the Sugar Mill Restaurant with its adjoining bar. If you're coming over for lunch at Sugar Mill, you can order such light fare as an Antilles fresh fruit salad with coconut sherbet or sandwiches. Figure on spending from $18 to about $33 for dinner.

Little Dix offers many extras. Guests have the use of Sunfish, floats, and snorkeling gear. They also have Boston whalers that take you to the beach of your choice with a picnic lunch, and horseback riding is also available (extra). On Thursday all the guests at Little Dix are transported by car or Boston whaler to Spring Bay for a barbecue luncheon with a steel band.

For reservations, call toll free 800/223-7637 (800/442-8198 in New York state and 586-4459 in New York City).

Biras Creek, P.O. Box 54 (tel. 495-5455), is a magnificent resort lying at the northern end of Virgin Gorda. It stands like a hilltop-crowning fortress, not to keep away pirates, but to welcome the sun and stunning views. On a 150-acre estate with its own marina, it occupies a narrow neck of land, flanking the sea on three sides. To create their Caribbean hideaway, Norwegian shipping interests carved out this resort in a wilderness, but wisely protected the natural terrain.

The estate is well planted with flowering trees and bushes, and there is a greenhouse on the grounds to keep the estate supplied in foliage and flowers.

Along the walks laid out, you can inspect diddle doe cactus, golden-barked turpentine trees, tamarind, frangipani, white cedar, and wild nutmeg. Looking like a prehistoric monster, a timid iguana may run across your path. Along the way, you might also see iridescent hummingbirds and the friendly little bananaquit.

Scattered along the shore, 16 cottages and 32 suites shelter guests. Cooled by ceiling fans, suites have well-furnished bedrooms and divan beds with a sitting room and private patio, plus a refrigerator. You can open your windows to enjoy the sea breezes. There are four sets of rates. *The cheapest is during the summer period from June 4 lasting until November 3. At that time, single AP rates are $230 a day, going up to $260 in a double.* Shoulder-season rates for the spring and part of the fall are slightly higher. Highest tariffs are charged from mid-December until the first of April: from $320 daily in a single, from $360 in a double, both AP. Tax and service are added to all bills. These tariffs include three meals a day, plus use of facilities and equipment, such as a pool, snorkeling gear, Sunfishes, paddleboards, and tennis courts. Also provided are free trips to nearby islands and beach barbecues twice a week. Special honeymoon packages are also offered.

The food has won high praise. You never know what you're going to be served. Take the soups—it might be gazpacho, perhaps clam chowder, maybe cucumber, or even curried apple or grapefruit soup. Hopefully, it'll be an iced, creamed, and curried pea soup. Grouper baked in a shell, chicken Kiev prepared just right, filet of pork with apricot sauce, moussaka with banana bread, and pheasant flown in from the British Isles are just some of the dishes you are likely to be served during your stay. The wine cellar is also superb.

At the peaked-roof hilltop main house, the dining room and its connecting drinking lounge are quietly elegant, with heavy hewn beams and a ceramic tile mural. There's always a table with a view. A barbecued lunch is served on the beach on Monday and Friday. A buffet lunch from 1 to 2 p.m. is served Tuesday, Thursday, and Sunday, and a curry dish—a Malayan rice specialty—is offered on Wednesday. Dinner, from 7:30 to 8:30 p.m., is priced from $30.

Guests arriving in Virgin Gorda can be met by a taxi and taken to the hotel's motor launch for a speedy trip to Biras Creek.

Bitter End Yacht Club, P.O. Box 46, John O'Point, North Sound (tel. 494-2746), is a rendezvous point for the yachting set cruising through the British Virgins. Bitter End offers an informal life, guests taking one of the well-appointed hillside villas overlooking the sound and yachts at anchor. If you're not a sailor, the helpful staff gives free on-the-beach instruction to get you started. Formal lessons are also available. A sailboat practically comes with your room, as rates include unlimited use of the club's fleet of Lasers, Sunfish, Rhodes 19s, and J-24s, as well as windsurfers and outboard skiffs. Or you can charter a CAL 2-27 for an overnight trip. There are great sheltered-water sailing, reef snorkeling as you hunt for that doomed Spanish galleon, expeditions to neighboring cays, shelling, endless beachcombing possibilities, marine science participation, whatever.

For something novel, you can stay aboard one of the 27-foot yachts, yours to sail, with dockage including daily maid service, meals in the Yacht Club dining room, and overnight provisions. On the AP *in summer, yacht liveaboards pay $140 daily in a single, $180 for two persons. Villa rooms are $160 to $220 in a single, $190 to $250 for two persons daily. For two adults with two, three, or four children under 16, a family plan includes a second room free on the eight-day seven-night Admiral's package. The summer package also provides for deep-sea fishing, lobster/champagne beach party, night snorkeling with lights, children's sailing classes, and a dinner sail on the world's largest catamaran. A ten-day, nine-night private yacht/villa package in summer is $720 per person. In the fall,* *daily yacht live-aboards pay $180 single, $220 for two persons, and villa rooms cost $215 to $265 single, $235 to $285 for two persons.* In winter, AP yacht live-aboards pay $230 single, daily, $260 for two persons. Villa rooms are $260 to $310 daily in a single, $290 to $340 for two persons. *In spring, AP yacht live-aboards pay $190 daily for a single, $220 for two persons, while villa rooms go for $215 to $275 daily in a single, $245 to $300 for two persons.* New marina rooms are the same rates as live-aboard yachts, a good saving. Furnishings are a Caribbean motif—a grass rug from Dominica, a hand-printed bedcover from the French West Indies.

The social hub of the place is the bar where you're likely to find everybody from the publisher of *Yachting* magazine to the sunstreaked Flying Dutchman and the Barefoot Contessa. At dinner you'll find fresh native fish, lobster, and steak, and every manner of burgee hanging gaily along the walls. Yachting people arrive for the buffet breakfast, costing $9, or the lunch, $15. Dinner, from 6 p.m., is by reservation only, and the cost ranges from $28. All meals are included for club guests. There are boat races, plus a special lunch on Sunday.

For reservations, call 312/944-5855 (collect), or write to Bitter End Yacht Club, 875 N. Michigan Ave., Chicago, IL 60611.

Olde Yard Inn, P.O. Box 26, The Valley (tel. 495-5544), is a charmer. It's got a lot going for it, namely its owners, Joseph and Ellen Devine, who confess that they know "nothing about the hotel business." Nevertheless, somebody does, because this little 11-room Caribbean inn is beautifully run, with good food, good beds, and hospitality that ranks among the best in the British Virgins.

Ellen is a Canadian diplomat's daughter, which has given her a checkerboard background of living everyplace from Charleston, S.C., to The Hague. Toronto-born Joseph Devine was a "sometime international lawyer," until he finally admitted he was allergic to the legal profession.

At the beginning, they built a structure for their well-stocked library. Here you can only read a good book, but enjoy a cool drink or after-dinner coffee in a comfortable armchair. Once in a while a guest will play a favorite piece on an aged Berlin upright piano. Otherwise, everything is tranquil.

Near the main house are two long bungalows with small but adequate bedrooms, each with its own bath and Haitian bedspreads. Scattered about are a few antiques and special accessories. On the MAP in winter, guests pay $185 daily in a double, $105 in a single. *From mid-April to mid-May, and again from mid-November to mid-December, MAP bookings are accepted at $125 daily in a double, $85 in a single. The EP charge is $45 per person. However, from mid-May until mid-November, you can stay here for $45 daily in a single, $65 in a double, and $85 in a triple, including a buffet-style breakfast.*

When you arrive you'll be asked about your interests. Perhaps you'll find a saddled horse waiting for a prebreakfast or a moonlight ride. Or you'll go for a sail on a yacht or a snorkeling adventure at one of 16 beaches, with a picnic lunch provided (perhaps lobster, pâté, champagne, or peanut butter sandwiches).

Under a banana-leaf thatched roof, the meals served here are one of the reasons for coming over. You might begin with snails or coquilles, follow with local fish or lobster. Steaks cut at the inn are from the finest fresh sirloin. Meals have a decided French accent. If you're just visiting for the day, you can enjoy a lunch from noon to 2 p.m., costing from $10. Dinners, from 7 to 9 p.m., begin at $15 but could run up to $30 if you want lobster.

On the premises is a small boutique full of bright, intriguing items such as local silkscreened clothes, arts and crafts, painting and sculpture, as well as other fun items such as Chinese and American kites in silk, nylon, cotton, and paper.

Fischers Cove Beach Hotel, P.O. Box 60 (tel. 495-5252), is a group of cottages nestled near the beach of St. Thomas Bay, with swimming at your doorstep. Erected of native stone, each house is self-contained, with one- or two-bedroom units having a combination living and dining room with a kitchenette. The design is attractive, with open pitched ceilings accented by dark wood beams. At a food store near the grounds, you can stock up on your provisions if you're doing your own cooking. A two-story unit (12 rooms) has been added to the resort. These are pleasant but simple rooms, offering a view of Drake Channel. Each has its own private bath (hot and cold showers) and private balcony.

The place was started in 1962 as a small bar by Andy Flax, who always wears his baseball hat and bears a faint resemblance to Reggie Jackson. His grandfather gave him the land. In winter, he rents one-bedroom cottages for $140 daily, and a two-bedroom cottage goes for $220. *In summer, one- and two-bedroom cottages are in the $100 to $135 daily range.* The hotel rooms are rented for $190 daily in a double and $140 in a single, both MAP tariffs. *In summer, the MAP tariffs are $105 in a double and $80 in a single in the hotel units.* The cottages are rented on the EP and the rooms on the MAP.

Andy's wife, Norma, is from Antigua, and she's known as one of the best cooks on the island. Lunch from noon to 2 p.m. costs around $10 and up, and dinner from 7 to 10:30 p.m. ranges from $22. A resident steel band provides entertainment most nights, and periodically a local scratch band plays. In whatever form, something nice is always happening here.

Guavaberry Spring Bay Vacation Homes (tel. 495-5227) are clusters of hexagonal redwood, white-roofed houses built on stilts and available for daily or weekly rentals. It's like living in a treehouse, with screened and louvered walls open to let in sea breezes. Each home has one or two bedrooms, and all have private baths, with a small kitchenette and dining area. The friendly hosts are Wing Commander Charles Roy, R.A.F. (Ret.), and his wife, Betty, who are assisted by Tina and Ludwig Goschler, their daughter and son-in-law. They'll show you to one of their unique vacation homes, each with its own elevated sundeck overlooking Sir Francis Drake Passage.

Two persons in winter pay $95 daily for a one-bedroom house, the rate rising to $140 per day for four persons in a two-bedroom house. An extra person pays $18 per day. *In summer, a one-bedroom house costs $65 per day; the two bedroom house, $90 per day, plus service.*

Within a few minutes of the cottage colony is the beach at Spring Bay. It's also possible to explore the "Baths" nearby. The owners provide a complete commissary for guests, and such tropical fruits as tamarind and soursop can be picked in season or else bought at local shops. The Roys will make arrangements for day charters for scuba-diving or fishing, and will also arrange for island Jeep tours and saddle horses.

7. Mosquito Island

The sandy, 125-acre Mosquito Island just north of Virgin Gorda wasn't named for those pesky insects we all know and few if any love. It took its name from the Mosquito (or Moskito) Indians, who were the only known inhabitants of the small land mass before the arrival of the Spanish conquistadors in the 15th century. Archeological relics of these peaceful Indians and their agricultural pursuits have been found here.

Today the privately owned island is uninhabited except for **Drake's Anchorage**, North Sound, Virgin Gorda (tel. 494-2254), which many repeat patrons consider their favorite retreat in the British Virgins. The hotel offers only ten comfortable rooms and two villas. All the accommodations are decorated with Haitian art, and each contains a private bath and sea-view veranda. The villas have private kitchens. Units at this idyllic oasis are managed by Brian Kohlweck. In winter, he charges $240 daily for a double room, $180 for a single, and $90 for a third person lodged in a double, all AP. *Summer rates are $180 in a double, $140 in a single, with a third person in a double paying an extra $75 daily, AP.*

The resort provides free use of windsurfers, Sunfish, and snorkeling equipment. For additional fees, you can go scuba-diving, take boat trips to a nearby deserted island or to the "Baths" at Virgin Gorda, go deep-sea fishing, make day sails, go horseback riding, or try your skill at waterskiing. The snorkeling and scuba here are considered so good that members of the Cousteau Society spend one week each year exploring local waters. There are four beaches on Mosquito Island, each with different wave and water conditions, so guests can choose what suits them.

The resort's restaurant is attractively tropical in design and conscious of both French and Caribbean culinary styles. It faces the water and offers a superb cuisine which features local and continental dishes, a fresh fish of the day, and a weekly pig roast, with a live band for entertainment.

Getting here requires taking a plane to the Virgin Gorda airport and a taxi ride from there to the Gun Creek Dock. The charge per taxi load is around $18. From there, if you call ahead, a boat will be sent from Drake's Anchorage to take you on the five-minute ride from the dock to the resort.

8. Guana Island

This 850-acre private island, part of which is a bird sanctuary, is one of the most isolated hideaways in the Caribbean. Don't go here seeking resort action, but if you want to retreat from the world, to envelop yourself in a natural setting where intrusion by people has been wisely controlled, then Guana Island might be for you.

It lies right off the coast of Tortola. To reach it, the **Guana Island Club,** P.O. Box 32, Road Town, Tortola (tel. 4-2354), will send a boatman to meet arriving guests at Beef Island airport from 9 a.m. to 5 p.m. Of course, you must give the club fair warning of your arrival. You should advise their office in New York of your arrival. Write or call Guana Island Club, Timber Trail, Rye, NY 10580 (tel. 914/967-6050). If you're late, you'll have to phone the club directly.

After your arrival on Guana Island, a Landrover will transport you up one of the steepest rocky inclines in the region. You arrive at a cluster of whitewalled cottages that were built as a private club in the 1930s on the foundations of a Quaker homestead.

The stone-trimmed bungalows never hold more than a total of 30 guests. Since the dwellings are staggered along a flower-dotted hillside, the sense of privacy is almost absolute. The panoramic sweep from the terraces is spectacular, particularly at sunset.

When guests hunger for company, they'll find a friendly atmosphere at the rattan-furnished clubhouse. Dinners by candlelight are served family style on the veranda, with menus which include home-grown vegetables and continental and Stateside specialties. Dinner is a casually elegant sit-down affair, whereas lunch is served buffet style every day. Children under 13 are not allowed in the living room during cocktail hour, and are supervised at a special dinner service at 6:45 every evening. The bars are self-service, and the hotel bills clients according to the honor system.

Each guest cottage, complete with shower (but don't use too much water), has an individual charm. The interiors are fairly rustic, with wood beams. Cottages are named after such islands as Grenada.

In high season, two persons pay $325 daily and a single is charged $250. *In* *the off-season, tariffs in a double range from $200 to $235 daily, with singles paying from $130 to $190.* Tariffs include all meals, but service and tax are extra, as is the $15-per-person round-trip boat transfer. If you'd like to round up 30 of your friends, you can rent the whole island!

Mary Randall is the thoughtful hostess here, directing a pleasant staff. Sports lovers and/or beachcombers will find six almost-deserted beaches, two of which require a boat to reach. There's also a clay tennis court, a five-hole putting green, a fleet of sailing craft, and a network of nature trails.

Chapter V

HAITI

SIGHTS, SOUNDS, TASTES, and smells come together uniquely in the oldest black republic in the western hemisphere. In the heart of the Caribbean, the republic is the size of the state of Maryland and shaped like the claw of a large Maine lobster. Bizarrely exotic, inescapably moving, it is the most flamboyant island in the Caribbean, a French-speaking land with a pure African cast.

These warm people, who extend a *bienvenue* to visitors, speak their special Créole tongue and maintain the songs and dances of their African past. They still very much practice voodoo with its richly symbolic ceremonies.

Haiti occupies the western port of the island of Hispaniola, lying some 643 air miles southeast of Miami, and even though it's on the same island, it bears almost no resemblance to the Spanish-speaking Dominican Republic.

A primitive rhythm seems to pulsate through Haiti, this teeming, turbulent land of stark contrasts and subtle blending. Its poverty is often masked in the blossoms of the flamboyant tree and the bougainvillea vine.

Just how poor is Haiti? To illustrate, one family lives in a tin-roofed hovel, only seven feet square, some of its rotting wooden boards missing. The family members, seven in all, sleep huddled together on a bed made of banana leaves. Yet they are considered rich enough to employ a servant.

The landscape is dominated by a trio of mountain ranges, the major ones of which are the Cibao Mountains and the Cordillera Central, their peaks climbing to 8000 to 9000 feet above sea level.

Some five million people live in Haiti, about 90% of whom are black. In addition to a scattering of whites, many of the remaining 10% are mulattoes, Haitian Créoles, descendants of the early French colonists who mixed with Africans. These Créole women are known for their café-au-lait beauty.

GETTING THERE: Haiti's international airport at Port-au-Prince is served by several major airlines, all offering good-quality service and usually prompt arrivals. For most passengers living in the northeastern part of the United States (especially in the New York area), the most attractive routing is on one of the **American Airlines** streamlined 747s from JFK airport to Port-au-Prince. American Airlines, in fact, is the only carrier to fly nonstop from New York to Haiti, departing every day for the approximately 3½-hour flight to the Haitian capital. Other airlines such as **Eastern** have nonstop flights to Haiti leaving daily from Miami.

A wide variety of ticket options is available on American, the prices varying with the time of year, the day of the week, and whether or not a passenger opts for a complete travel and hotel package. These sometimes represent impressive bargains when purchased simultaneously from a representative of American's tour department.

The cheapest ticket that is *not* a part of a package is an advance purchase excursion (APEX) ticket (not available during parts of the midwinter high season). The **APEX ticket** usually requires a seven-day advance purchase and a delay of between 3 and 21 days before using the return half. Both the departure and the return dates must be specified in advance, with a penalty (a procedure shared by practically all the airlines) imposed for alteration of the itinerary once the ticket is issued. Passengers wanting more leeway in planning a trip can opt for an **excursion ticket,** which requires no advance purchase.

More information about schedules, exact prices, tour options, and connections from the dozens of cities which the airline serves can be obtained by calling American Airlines on one of their local or toll-free numbers, available from your local telephone company's directory and directory assistance.

If you're in Miami or San Juan, you can take an **Air France** jet to Port-au-Prince. Connections from San Juan to the Haitian capital are also possible on **Prinair.** For Canadians, a popular routing is an **Air Canada** flight from Montréal. If you're resort-hopping, you'll find that **Air Jamaica** wings into Port-au-Prince from both Kingston and Montego Bay. It's also possible to take a **Bahamasair** flight from Nassau. Within the country, **Air Inter Haiti** will fly you on its most frequented run to Cap-Haitien.

PRACTICAL FACTS: The official **currency** of the country is the Haitian gourde. One U.S. dollar presently is exchanged for 5 Haitian gourdes. There is usually no problem in paying with U.S. dollars, except perhaps in some remote places. However, Canadian dollars are not freely exchanged and therefore should be converted into Haitian gourdes. In general, banks are open from 9 a.m. to 1 p.m. except Saturday and Sunday. *Unless otherwise stated, prices quoted in this chapter are in U.S. dollars.*

English is commonly spoken in all tourist centers (not in the country), but French is the **official language.** Créole is the unofficial second language, and it's filled with wonderful proverbs, such as "When a cockroach is giving a dance, he never invites a chicken."

Entering Haiti is rarely a problem if you're a U.S. or Canadian citizen. A **passport,** either current or expired, is accepted, or else a voter registration card or birth certificate. You'll also need to produce an ongoing or return ticket, a requirement common in the Caribbean. The tourist card issued is valid for a month (it can be extended upon application), and upon departing Haiti, you'll be charged a $10 departure tax.

In **electric current,** Haiti uses 110 volts, 60 cycles, so therefore most U.S. appliances do not need a converter.

Haiti operates on Eastern Standard Time. The mainland and Haiti keep the same time for most of the year, except when the conversion in the U.S. comes to Daylight Savings Time. Then the clocks of Haiti are one hour behind those of, say, New York or Miami.

All hotels in Haiti have a doctor on call, and more often than not he speaks English. Port-au-Prince has four hospitals, none particularly distingushed.

Someone once said that a shop in Haiti will open any time you want to buy something. This is an exaggeration, of course, but might be true for certain art galleries. In general, store hours are from 8 a.m. to 5 p.m. weekdays. Many owners take a long lunch break, from noon to 2 p.m., and often close on Saturday at 1 p.m. Nearly all shops close on Sunday.

Haiti observes the usual holidays, but has some unique ones as well; January 2 (The Day of the Forefathers); April 14 (Pan Am Day); May 1 (Workers Day); May 18 (Flag and University); May 22 (in honor of sovereignty); June 22 (honors the present and former dictator, the Father-son Duvalier team); August 15 (Assumption); October 17 (honors anniversary of death of liberator Dessaline); October 24 (honors the U.N.); November 1 (All Saints); December 5 (day Columbus discovered Haiti); along with Carnival or Mardi Gras, previewed in a separate section.

Driving is on the right, and to rent a car (see below) you'll need an international driver's license or else a valid U.S. or Canadian one.

Ten percent for service is added to most hotels and restaurant tabs; otherwise, tip from 10% to 15%. Curiously, taxi drivers (tap-tap operators, etc.) are not tipped!

Hotels add a 5% government occupancy tax.

A VIOLENT PAST: The first tourist, the Haitians say, was Columbus, who discovered the island of Hispaniola on his maiden voyage to the New World on

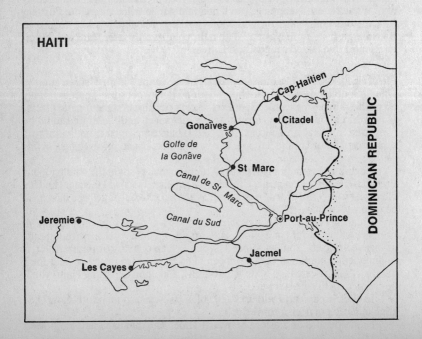

December 5, 1492. In time, Spain was to conquer the island, killing nearly one million peaceful Arawak Indians who made up the native population.

Under Spanish rule, a decree called for the importation of African blacks as slaves. When Spain failed to colonize the entire island, French buccaneers, from their base in Tortuga off the northwest coast, moved into what is now Haiti. Eventually they took control in the western part of Hispaniola, a move legalized by treaty in 1697. Spain officially ceded the territory to France.

In May 1801, a former slave and coachman, Toussaint L'Ouverture, was elected governor. Considering this secession, Napoleon ordered the rebellion quelled. Defeating the Haitians, the French took L'Ouverture prisoner.

However, revolutionists led by Jean-Jacques Dessalines and Alexandre Pétion, two Haitian generals, eventually defeated the French army, whose troops returned to Paris in 1803. Dessalines proclaimed Haitian independence on January 1, 1804. He also proclaimed himself emperor, a title he held until his death in 1806.

Henri Christophe, the prototype of Eugene O'Neill's *Emperor Jones,* was named as first president of the republic. But he proclaimed himself king. Pétion was to succeed him. However, Christophe's action divided the nation, and the north and west were ruled as an empire until the self-proclaimed king shot himself in 1820.

At the overthrow of Haitian president Guillaume Sam in 1915, the Americans, fearing a German invasion, occupied the country and didn't leave until 1934. After much turmoil and many leaders, Dr. François Duvalier ("Papa Doc") was elected president in 1957, launching an iron-fisted dictatorship until his death in 1971. He has been succeeded by his less militant son, Jean-Claude ("Baby Doc") Duvalier, as "president-for-life."

NOTES ON CARNAVAL: If you can arrange your trip to Haiti during the time between Epiphany, January 6, and Mardi Gras on Shrove Tuesday, you will be treated each Sunday to a true Haitian folk spectacle, **carnaval.**

In Port-au-Prince and all other towns of any size, groups parade through the streets, costumed in burlap bags or other outré garb, singing and making noise with any implement they can find. One popular "instrument" is the leaves from old automobiles springs, which are cut to varying lengths to give off different sounds when beaten together or pounded with a metal knife. They also use bongo drums, tambourines, washboards, saws, and cowbells. Some of the costumed people powder or paint their faces a ghostly white, while others wear masks that look like bulls' heads, with horns.

In the capital, groups of five or six start out in various parts of the city and are rapidly joined by happy Haitians (and sometimes by tourists) as they proceed. They serenade guests at the hotels close in. This all may begin sometime in the late morning, but the marching and chanting go on all day. Toward evening, all celebrants converge on the heart of the city and throng the streets, writhing in abandon in their serpentine march until late at night.

In other large towns, the celebration may start a little later in the day, but by nightfall the main streets are alive with a singing, whistling, shouting mass of humanity. In Cap-Haitien, a real steam calliope is mounted on a high, flatbed truck, with dancers capering around it on the truck as it inches its way through the main part of town. If a highway passes through a town, you might as well stop and watch the fun if you are there during carnaval, because the highway is where it all goes on, so that your passage is blocked by hundreds of moving bodies. However, the festivities conclude earlier in the outlying towns than in the capital, so you won't be stuck all night and be a prey to zombies.

With all this lead-up, you can be sure that Mardi Gras itself is a hysterically festive occasion, not highly organized with floats and masked balls and all that, like New Orleans, but nevertheless an unforgettable occurrence.

Fortified with some background, you can now plunge into the bustling capital. But don't come here for a quiet vacation. Go instead for an experience.

PORT-AU-PRINCE

Framed by mountains, the capital of Haiti, founded in 1704, is a jumble of bonbon-colored gingerbread houses, art galleries full of vivid, primitive paintings, and streets filled with vendors. If you're wearing a pair of shoes, you're prosperous looking enough to be approached by somebody selling something—perhaps a chandelier made of Pet Milk cans. In Haiti, everthing is used. Even old tires are made into sandals.

A bastion of American and French culture, uniquely mixed, Port-au-Prince is a kaleidoscope of brilliant, flashing colors, such as frangipani blossoms. The very heart of this magic country, the capital happily blends the Christian with the pagan. Modernity coexists with the past, a voodoo shop standing next door to a unisex beauty salon. European-style hotels—lush, sensual—often lie in some of the worst poverty belts in the western hemisphere.

Rich in sights by day, vivid in color and texture, Port-au-Prince comes alive at night, in mesmerizing enticement, with the blood-pounding beat of the merengue. And in the distant hills, you hear the beating of drums.

Home to some 700,000 residents, Port-au-Prince rises from the Gulf of Gonâve to the cool slopes of the resort of Pétionville. Many people may want to head for the hotel in Pétionville, leaving the city with its teeming markets and the scents of fresh spices. The route up is shaded by a canopy of poinciana trees. From Pétionville, Port-au-Prince 1500 feet below doesn't look as intimidating.

1. Hotels of Port-au-Prince

Perhaps the nicest thing about the hotels of Haiti is that the maids will still iron a shirt or sew on a button. The hotels of Haiti are among the most charming in the Caribbean, special inns, many converted from once-palatial mansions.

You have a choice of a mountain-cooled villa high in the hills or a gingerbread house right in the bustling heart of Port-au-Prince. Most of these hostelries are scattered on the eastern outskirts of the capital or in the suburban foothills of Pétionville.

THE UPPER BRACKET: El Rancho, P.O. Box 71 (tel. 7-2080), at Pétionville, is a leading Haitian resort hotel which grew as part of the fantasy of its Haitian/Lebanese owner, Albert Silvera. Using as a core the existing structure of his family home (now hardly visible owing to the sweeping changes he's made), he set out to build a lavishly designed extravaganza of curved surfaces, dramatic passageways, and hacienda-style decor, as well as a series of interconnected entertainment facilities. Built in the 1950s, El Rancho contains wings of rooms filled with mahogany furniture, some hand-carved, native sculpture, dramatically contrasting Italian marble floors, and primitive island paintings. There's even a Rolls-Royce Silver Shadow in constant attendance to pick up VIPs from their arrival points.

The swimming pool is two separate bodies of water, both gracefully curved into their settings, divided and traversed by an arched walkway vaguely reminiscent of something you'd find in a Japanese garden. At the top of a flight of stairs, there's a bar area sheltered from the sun, with a view over all the comings and goings of the hotel.

The first thing visitors see is a zigzag zebra-stripe tile walk capped with a curved cement awning and two splashing fountains. In the center of the patio garden is a key-shaped Jacuzzi, and near the sundeck is a whirlpool. On the grounds are tennis courts, plus a gymnasium and a sauna. As you sit on the terrace, strolling guitarists may serenade you. Later, you can enjoy music and dancing in the nightclub, L'Epicure. There's also one of the city's two casinos in a cabana-shaped building near the swimming pool. On some nights, barbecues are held, accompanied by a native Haitian revue and folklore show, one of the best known attractions in the Port-au-Prince nightlife scene.

In summer, singles range in price from $72 to $100 daily, white doubles cost from $85 to $132. In winter, singles range from $85 to $115, and doubles go for $100 to $140. A third person in a unit is assessed an additional $35 a day, while MAP costs a $20 supplement per person per day. Service and taxes are extra. You'll find TV, a radio, and a phone in each accommodation.

Splendid, P.O. Box 1214 (tel. 5-0116), is one of Haiti's oldest hotels. Built at the turn of the century as a family mansion, it was transformed beautifully into a hotel many years ago, entertaining as a grande dame in the country's early days of tourism. The Splendid is one mile from Port-au-Prince, four miles from the airport. It's within walking distance of both of Haiti's cultural centers, the Centre d'Art and the Musée d'Art Haitien du College St-Pierre.

Formal entry steps lead up to a long, open loggia with classic columns and potted palms. Set out for your pleasure is a row of handmade Haitian rockers. The hallway leads to a drawing room with antique furnishings, cretonne armchairs, and gilt mirrors, making for a restrained gentility. A central staircase goes up to a few of the handsomely furnished bedrooms.

In spite of its age, the house has been constantly improved and kept in top condition. You'll find all-white walls forming a good backdrop for the flamboyant Haitian bedspreads and matching draperies. French doors open onto balustraded balconies.

The director is Wolfgang Wagner, who offers all air-conditioned guest rooms, including seven in the original antique mansion, but most are in newer sections, built around the swimming pool with a courtyard feeling.

All year, he charges the same tariffs—from $60 to $75 daily in a single, from $70 to $85 in a twin, and from $80 to $95 in a triple, plus tax and service. The hotel has a very good restaurant, Gala, which is recommended separately in the "Dining Out in the Capital" section following.

Grand Hotel Oloffson, P.O. Box W120 (tel. 2-0139), is a 19th-century seedy-gingerbread palace. At great cost, all the lacy trim, the fretwork and dado, the tower with its intricate scrollwork, the zigzag entrance staircase, the ornate balconies with the absurd cupolas, and the sagging balustrades could be copied. But the character of the hotel could not be reproduced in the Walt Disney factories. It's a one-of-a-kind hotel, a gloriously bizarre birthday cake which has attracted some very talented and celebrated guests. Of course, it's been called a doodle by Steinberg. Charles Addams, a spiritual father of the place, has been a guest.

When it was built in the late 19th century, the Oloffson was the mansion of "President Sam of Haiti," and later it was a military hospital for the invading U.S. Marines in 1915. It's named, however, for the Norwegian sea captain who purchased it in 1935, installing crocodiles in the swimming pool. Eventually, it has become one of Haiti's first hotels.

When Roger Coster, a French photographer, and his wife, Laura, ran the hotel in the 1950s, it became known as "Greenwich Village of the Tropics," attracting writers, actors, and artists. Coster named accommodations after favorite guests such as James Jones, who was married in the converted surgical building of the U.S. Marines. Connecticut expatriate Al Seitz purchased the hotel in 1960 and became a firmly entrenched member, and legend, on the Haitian landscape. Graham Greene (who is forbidden to enter Haiti) used the Oloffson as his model of a "fragile absurd anachronism" in the novel (and subsequent movie) *The Comedians*. Mr. Seitz, now deceased, was like a movie character himself, with a cigar in his mouth day and night.

Under his guidance, he turned the Oloffson into a "refuge for friends." Sitting on the rickety veranda in a wicker peacock chair, you were likely to encounter Anne Bancroft, Sen. Barry Goldwater (although no one knows how he got in here), Peter Glenville, Rex Reed, Lillian Hellman, David Brinkley, or one of the Rockefellers. Mr. Seitz in turn was joined by his bride, the charming Suzanne Laury from Bucks County, Pennsylvania. Today Sue Seitz carries on the management of the hotel with her three sons in much the same tradition. Of course, the place is a bit more "spiffed up," with new plumbing and more wicker. However, Al's presence still seems to dominate the scene, and in a way, nothing has changed, not now at least.

Arched french doors lead to the slapdash lounge, with some original paintings, ceiling fans, wall hangings, tin lamps, peacock chairs, wicker sofas, a melange of clutter that is timid compared to the cast usually seen here. It's a coterie of characters unlike any gathered together since W. Somerset Maugham and his friend set sail for the South Seas in search of story material.

The rooms merge together into one glorious jumble. So the faucet doesn't work. Maybe there's an insect or two. It's considered provincial to dwell on such minor faults when you're absorbing so much character. There's every kind of wicker and bamboo resting under whirling ceiling fans, and each unit is different, furnished with "hit or miss" pieces. Some of the units and cottages are set in the shady, woodsy garden, at the foot of which is a swimming pool.

In the high season, singles range in price from $65 to $100, with doubles costing from $85 to $110. A two-bedroom suite with gallery is likely to range from $125 to $150 daily. I've stayed in the John Gielgud suite, a gazebo-like turret, which I consider the best accommodation in the house, although you may prefer the more secluded Marlon Brando cottage. *In summer, singles range in price from $54 to $82, with doubles costing from $70 to $82. Suites go for $100 to $120.* You can ask Mrs. Seitz about her honeymoon special, Oloffson Montrouis, a private house with a private beach about 45 minutes from Port-au-Prince.

Breakfast (the cook is known for his french toast) is served on an open veranda. At dinner, the food will consist of French, créole, and international specialties.

THE MIDDLE BRACKET: Ibo Lele, P.O. Box 1237 (tel. 7-0845), Pétionville, is one of Haiti's leading all-around resorts, perched high up in the hills. Named for a voodoo god, it has its own private beach on Cacique Island which you reach after a 20-mile, 30-minute ride from Pétionville to the site of a motor launch which in five minutes takes you to the island.

At Pétionville, modern buildings are spread over acres of terraced gardens, centered around an old mansion with its pool plaza, the social center of the hotel. Jacques and Conchita Baussan welcome you to their dramatic perch, 1575 feet above sea level. Much of the architectural harmony of Ibo Lele was achieved by its late president, Robert Baussan, a well-known local architect.

Accommodations are in 50 well-furnished rooms or 18 suites, all with private bath, color TV, and a terrace where you can take in that view. In winter, singles range in price from $65 to $90 daily; doubles, from $80 to $125; and triples, from $110 to $135—including breakfast. *In summer, also with breakfast,* *the single tariff ranges from $60 to $85 daily; the double, from $70 to $115; and the triple, from $90 to $135.*

French, Haitian, and seafood specialties are served in the hotel's restaurant, and guests can later enjoy the exotic Shango nightclub, which has voodoo shows. Friday is the big night. In the lounge is a good collection of Haitian art.

Villa Créole, P.O. Box 126 (tel. 7-1570), Pétionville, is a restored hilltop Spanish-style mansion that has seen graceful additions over the years. Now there are 80 bedrooms, all with private bath, phone, and air conditioning, plus a deluxe wing which opened in 1977. Private balconies open off each room, except on the lower level where the units face a private garden. The transformation is a result of the labor of one of the country's most distinguished personalities, Dr. Reindall A. Assad, and his daughter, Ms. Alicia Assad.

Both father (who is semi-retired) and daughter keep an atmosphere of pure Haitiana alive here. The walls have a vibrant collection of Rousseau-like primitive paintings, including murals by Dorcelly, who studied with Picasso. Each of the 70 bedrooms is in a restrained contemporary style with louvered doors, a painting by a local artist, color TV, and private bath. In winter, singles range from $65 to $100 daily, while doubles cost from $85 to $120. A third person in a room is an additional $30. *In summer, singles range from $60 to $90, while doubles go for $72 to $100, depending on the accommodations.* American breakfasts are included in the prices, although service and taxes are not. Guests desiring full MAP are charged an extra $17 per day per person.

The long terrace adjoining the big house has tables set under a pillared arbor. Dining in Villa Belle is by candlelight with a view of the free-form pool, which reaches the hillside terrace where there is an almond tree with widespread branches. Breakfast starts with freshly picked fruit, accompanied by the aromatic Haitian coffee.

The cuisine is French créole, the chef specializing in such dishes as Haitian rice with black mushrooms and lambi (conch) créole. Monday night is barbecue night with fresh lobster on charcoal. Thursday night is a créole buffet time, and on Monday and Thursday evening the bar by the pool features a one-man show with an organist. There are two Plexipave all-weather tennis courts, lit for night play.

Hotel Castelhaiti (tel. 2-0624) sits imposingly near the top of a forested hill high above the city. Built in a pleasantly airy 1950s style of geometrically angled balconies, curved walls, and large expanses of glass, it was designed to captivate as much of the view as possible.

To reach the hotel, your car or taxi will have to shift into low gear while negotiating one of the steepest cobblestone roads in town.

Visitors sitting in the dining room's breezeway enjoy the aroma from the flowering vines entwined around the balcony as well as a view of the boomerang-shaped pool, the sprawling city, and the ocean sparkling in the distance. The lobby is an open-air arrangement washed with breezes and filled with rich colors, vivid Haitian murals, and verdant plants. The staff is pleasant at this monumental hotel which is capable of accepting large conventions as well as individual guests.

Winter rates range from $52 to $84 daily in a single, from $59 to $90 in a double, and from $65 to $96 in a triple. *Summer rates go from $36 to $60 in a single, from $42 to $66 in a double, and from $48 to $72 in a triple.* Service and taxes are added to the tab. The manager here will probably get acquainted with you if you choose to accept the breakfast at $6 and the dinner at $14 per person. For reservations in the United States, call toll free 800/223-6510. In New York City, call 212/832-2277.

Haiti Holiday Inn, P.O. Box 1429 (tel. 2-3722), faces the city park. From the public square just outside the somewhat unimposing entrance to the hotel, you may think the building is rather run down. When you enter, however, you'll see a verdant and well-cultivated courtyard centered around an open-air pool, surrounded by the open balconies of this business people's hotel in the center of town. The bedrooms are simple, comfortable, and air-conditioned, all outfitted in typical bland Holiday Inn style, but appealing nevertheless.

On the premises are a bar and a restaurant, both filled most of the time with vacationing families and commercial travelers relaxing after a day of business. *In summer, single rooms, depending on the accommodation, range from $50 to $70, while doubles rent for $60 to $75.* Singles cost from $65 to $80 in winter, with doubles or twins going for $75 to $90 and suites costing more. All rooms include a full American breakfast for each occupant. A third person staying in any room must pay an additional $10 per night. Teens and younger children stay at no charge when occupying the same room as their parents. Service and taxes are extra, and the hotel imposes a 25% surcharge for visits during carnival week.

Royal Haitian Hotel and Casino, P.O. Box 1429 (tel. 4-0258), is one of the best landscaped and most extravagantly spacious hotels in the country as well as containing one of the biggest casinos in Haiti. Standing just outside the heart of the city, surrounded by a well and ringed with palms, the Royal Haitian, built in 1975, boasts many of the facilities of a resort, with the exception of a beach. If that isn't a top priority for you, or if you don't mind traveling outside Port-au-Prince to the beach resorts, you'll appreciate the splashing fountain connecting two swimming pools, the cultivated planting, and the restaurant set to the side, all in 16 acres of land which include the casino.

The reception area is reached by crossing a roofed terrace open on three sides and bedecked with singing birds in ornate cages and life-size Haitian sculptures of figures blowing conch shells or mending nets. The simple, sunny rooms are air-conditioned, and each has a private tiled bath. The 90-room units are clustered in compact groupings around the grounds, providing a feeling of lots of space around the living quarters. There are two tennis courts, as well. Rent in winter is $72 to $85 daily in a single, between $85 and $110 for a double. *In summer, the cost of singles is between $54 and $66, while doubles go for $66 to $78 per couple.* These prices include breakfast, but taxes and service are extra.

Le Résidence Katherine Dunham, P.O. Box 1283 (tel. 2-0562), is unique in the Caribbean and perhaps in the world. This Mediterranean-style house was built across from the now-closed Habitation Leclerc, which was constructed on land that Katherine Dunham, that world-famous figure in the annals of modern dance, sold to the hotel developers some years ago. Le Résidence is a personal statement of Ms. Dunham, still a dedicated choreographer, who lives here during those parts of the year that she doesn't spend near her foundation in St. Louis.

It would be inaccurate to call this a hotel, since only a select number of hand-picked guests are received in the siena-colored villa with arched arcade, tropical oak shutters, and some good Haitian sculpture. The five-acre plot on which the house stands is one of the most charming gardens in Haiti. In brief, Le Résidence is best described as a private home set into handsomely terraced landscaping, where paying guests are accepted only if it's convenient for the high priestess of American modern dance. Double rooms cost around $145 while singles rent for $110. Lunch, breakfast, and dinner are served only on special request.

A student of voodoo for half a century, Ms. Dunham made her courtyard, hemmed by a peristyle, suitable for the staging of voodoo rituals, which are arranged on special request if interested parties telephone far enough in advance.

Le Résidence is home in Haiti to Ms. Dunham and her husband, John Pratt, a set designer, and it is managed, more or less, by the dancer's close friend, Egyptian-born Rose Rubenstein. The establishment usually closes down in May and October.

BEST FOR THE BUDGET: Prince Hotel, P.O. Box 2151 (tel. 5-2765), was once an elaborate private mansion with a French colonial facade, standing in a residential area only minutes from the commercial heart of Port-au-Prince and next to the Gallery Issa. Its owner, Raymond Chancy, who is assisted by his daughter, Maryse, has adapted it skillfully to its present function, filling its high-ceilinged public room with Haitian paintings and sculpture and adding a modern wing which is reached through a labyrinthine series of internal and exterior staircases.

The long, narrow dining room has high-backed wooden chairs, a wall sculpture, and a large window opening onto a screen of greenery. Several tables are set up in the courtyard if you find the interior claustrophobic (some people do), where you find a West Indian cuisine with continental overtones is served, sometimes to the accompaniment of live music. On the way to the backyard pool, you'll pass a grotto bar whose serpentine banquettes offer an intimate hideaway from both direct sunlight and other guests.

This attractive, Haitian-owned hotel offers only 33 rooms, all different, ranging from the high-ceilinged and old-fashioned (number 12 is a favorite in this category) to a comfortably contemporary format which at its best matches much more expensive accommodations in Port-au-Prince hotels. Each of the units is air-conditioned, and they vary in size and treatment from standard to deluxe. All have bath and phone, and several have old-style furniture ranging from art deco to hand-carved Haitian.

In winter, the rates range from $36 to $55 in a single, from $46 to $68 in a double. *Summer rates range from $31 to $50 daily in a single and from $45 to $63 in a double.*

Montana, between Port-au-Prince and Pétionville, P.O. Box 523 (tel. 7-1920), is estate-like, surrounded by a hillside garden with well-tended flowers growing in a setting of palm trees and bougainvillea. Even the dining room, La Palmeraie, has a tropical look with palm trees and latticework. Those seeking a good buy like it here, enjoying the pool which avoids that sterile resort look, being surrounded by flowers and a sundeck area.

The rooms, 70 in all, are decorated with native mahogany contrasted with bold, strong colors used in draperies and bedspreads. Each room has a private bath and air conditioning, as well as color TV and a balcony. The charge in winter is from $56 to $75 for a double with breakfast, a single costs $42 to $56, and another $18 is charged for a third person in a double room. *In summer, CP rates range from $38 to $52 daily in a single and from $52 to $66 in a double.*

The cuisine, a mixture of French and Haitian, is good, and on Sunday a créole buffet is featured. There is a managment cocktail party and barbecue on Tuesday. The hotel provides a beach bus for a minimum fare three times a week.

Marabou Hotel, rue Archer, Parc de Pétionville, P.O. Box 991 (tel. 7-1934), is simple but a fine place at which to stay. It is run by owner-manager Odette Gerard Wiener, a Haitian choreographer. She is a person of unstudied charm and grace, who has converted her home into a smooth-running little hotel of 14 clean, comfortable rooms, each unit with a private bath and garden view.

In small, individualized rooms, you pay the same tariff year round—$32 daily in a single, $50 in a double, and $60 in a triple. The resident manager can arrange for you to be served dinner.

In the rear of the inn, overlooking a swimming pool, a few guests gather in the dining room. Around the walls of the lounge is a permanent art exhibit. The food is pure créole. The location is convenient to the well-known restaurant, Chez Gerard.

THE BEACH LIFE: The beaches are a long haul from the capital, involving expensive taxi commutes. Those tourists who come to Haiti "just for the beach" will do better by seeking out other islands in the Caribbean, such as the Cayman Islands or Antigua. However, those who'd like a holiday in Haiti with some beach life "thrown in" will do all right here if they don't mind coping with some transportation problems.

Ibo Beach on reef-rimmed Cacique Island is about a 35-minute taxi ride from the capital, and a five-minute motor launch from there. There, tiny huts and lockers can be rented for the day.

Club Med, Point of Montrouis (tel. 2-3118), is one of the most deluxe showcase resorts of this increasingly popular "holidays-in-the-sun" club, occupying 120 acres. This one lies 46 miles north of Port-au-Prince, about a 75-minute ride from the capital (or longer if too many pedestrians and roosters get in the pathway). At its peak, some 700 members, who must pay a $30 fee, can check in here, in one of the double-occupancy bungalows, furnished with rattan pieces and overlooking the sea. Perhaps to honor the color of Haiti itself, the bungalow are flamboyantly painted, and all are air-conditioned with a private bathroom (shower, no tub). The clusters of one-, two-, and three-story casitas with peaked roofs are built along the lush garden and good beach.

As of this writing, Club Med features a "fly free" program from New York to Miami (listed as their "Magic Isle" package). I cannot predict what the actual land/air package will be at the time of your arrival or journey there. *However, summer visitors are likely to be offered an all-inclusive land/air package for $650 a week and up,* the cost rising to about $900 and up per person per week in winter. Warning: Holiday weeks such as Christmas are higher.

In the typical Club Med fashion, activities revolve around a combined bar/dance floor, and theater complex facing a large pool and the beach in the distance. You have a choice of three dining possibilities, plus an open-air disco and an arts and crafts workshop, for which you must pay a small charge for materials.

The restaurants offer many Haitian-style specialities, along with fresh grilled fish and clubhouse buffets. It wouldn't be a Club Med without a lot of sports, and these include windsurfing, sailing, waterskiing, snorkeling to sponge beds, swimming, archery, yoga, basketball, and tennis (played on 14 courts, 6 of which are lit for night games).

For reservations in New York call 212/750-1670, or toll free nationwide at 800/528-3100.

Ibo Beach Hotel, P.O. Box 1237 (tel. 7-1200), is one of the most complete beach hotels in Haiti. It's owned and run by the same Baussan family who manage the Ibo Lele in Pétionville, which has exchange privileges with their spot on Cacique Island. The club occupies several acres dominated on one side by the sea and on the other by the surrounding mountains. This is the closest beach resort on the north side of Port-au-Prince.

On its grounds, visitors discover one of the most complete marinas in Haiti, highly popular with yachtsmen. President Duvalier and his wife, Michelle, often sail over from the capital for a weekend. If you don't have a yacht, park your car near a small shed beside a pier about three-tenths of a mile from the resort. Someone will telephone to have a boat come for you through islet-strewn shallow water.

The social center of the resort—the various parts of which are interconnected with cement jogging paths, covered breezeways, and scattered voodoo designs set mosaic-style into the pathways—is the bar/restaurant. This, filled with Haitian metal sculptures, woodcarvings, and sea breezes, leads up to a pair of swimming pools. Surrounded by cultivated foliage, the complex contains a private sandy beach. There are also tennis courts and a separate series of restaurant facilities serving the marina.

Throughout the flat spaces and palms of this scrub-covered coral island stand some 70 A-frame bungalows, with voodoo or Indian designs, private baths, and porches. Some are large enough to accommodate up to six persons. Natural wood has been used extensively, and units are decorated with pierced tin lanterns and ceiling fans.

In winter, singles cost $84, while doubles rent for $90, triples for $102, and quads for $120. *In summer, prices are $72 in a single, $84 in a double, $96 in a triple, and $110 in a quad.* These prices include breakfast. If you choose to stay here on the MAP, figure on spending $14 additional per day per person.

At the hotel, a full program of water sports is offered.

Kyona Beach Club, P.O. Box 1647 (tel. 2-6788), lies about an hour's drive north of the Port-au-Prince airport. A pleasant resort, this can be the focus of either a day's outing in the sun or a hospitable place to spend an entire low-key vacation. The white-sand is well raked and has unusual trees, thatched bungalows, and chairs clustered beneath coconut palms. The accommodations, scattered over a flat, grassy expanse, are constructed with cement and stucco walls, big glass windows, and thatched roofs, and have an unpretentious decor of summertime furniture, ceiling fans, iron headboards, and carved Haitian art.

This is a place for the simple beach life. The social center of the resort is a circular bar area with a thatched roof.

The international menu features beautifully prepared local fish, shrimp, and lobster dishes, efficiently supervised by the friendly manager, Jean Hervé. The hotel is owned by the former American fashion designer, Muriel Martin, from New York.

The 20 rooms rent for $55 daily in a single and $66 for a double in summer. Winter rates are around $66 single and $80 double, and an additional person in any unit pays an extra $30 in all seasons. Breakfast is included in the prices, but service and taxes are not. Clients wishing to stay here on the MAP pay an additional $15 per person per day. Children under 12 stay free with their parents but pay extra for meals.

Hotel Taino (tel. 2-6157). You almost need a Landrover to negotiate the bumpy road leading several miles from the main highway to this beachside collection of chalets. The resort was built in 1975 on a narrow strip of palm-studded beach near the Grand Goâve. Each of the accommodations is contained within part of a thatch-covered bungalow whose steep-roof design looks like a tropical version of a chalet in Switzerland.

The focal point of the resort is an open-air dining room with an adjacent bar where the palm fronds of the ceiling are held up by ceramic rams' heads supported by vertical wooden posts. The Taino has a raised dance floor near the dining area, a horseshoe-shaped swimming pool, a tennis court, and a scattering of Haitian art.

It would be difficult to find a more isolated resort, and in low season you could be one of very few guests using the facilities. Mrs. Camello Roland, the Haitian proprietor, charges around $95 MAP for a double room all year. The cedar-walled bungalows may be fairly hot during the day, since there are no ceiling fans and no air conditioning. Still, if what you're looking for is solitude, this might be the place for you.

A wide variety of water sports is available for an additional charge.

2. Dining Out in the Capital

Hotels and restaurants throughout Haiti offer a French créole cuisine among the finest and most imaginative served in the entire Caribbean. Local snails from the mountains end up on your plate swimming in garlic butter; chicken is offered flavored with cashew nuts; a velvety-smooth ice cream is made with coconut; whatever—the cuisine delights with surprises, happy ones. You can dine in expensive French restaurants in Pétionville or on simple native food. Everybody in Haiti seemingly knows how to cook.

Créole cookery is spicy, but not overly so. Tassot, an old Indian recipe, is a specialty. In its classic method of preparation, pork, beef, or fowl (often turkey) is dried on a hot tin roof all day, facing the burning sun before it's marinated in a highly seasoned lime juice, then grilled. Conch is called "lambi" here, and it's prepared in an infinite number of ways. Cabrit (goat) is barbecued in the ground (that is, under leaves) and marinated à la créole. A spicy, homemade peanut butter is known as "mamba," and it appears with a number of dishes.

Street food, incidentally, although readily available and plentiful, is only for the courageous or those with cast-iron stomachs, definitely not for delicate digestive systems. If you've survived Mexico, then you might be ready for a streetside snack called "griot," charcoal-roasted pork with a hot sauce.

La Cascade, corner of rue Oge and rue Clerveau in Pétionville (tel. 7-6704), the best place for French food, is a family-owned establishment named for a small artificial waterfall (cascade) which splashes across a rock wall just inside the entrance to what used to be a private home. The owners, Guy Augier and his English-speaking wife, Sylvie, originally from Grasse in the south of France, had owned or managed five restaurants before setting up this one, an airy place with especially constructed stone walls.

Patrons can enjoy a drink seated on one of the low-slung canvas-covered couches in the tropical bar, whose raised platform is open to the hillside breezes. Next, they'll be seated on one of the Empire cane-bottom chairs in the dining room, where, accompanied by the scent of flowers and the occasional sound of live music, they can enjoy full meals costing from around $30.

Specialties include conch with Noilly Prat and saffron, lobster flan, fresh filet of fish with scallions or sorrel, several kinds of lobster, roquefort filet, tagliatelle with cognac (homemade pasta with tomatoes, crème fraiche, garlic, Provençale herbs, and cognac), smoked trout, and filet of sole à la persillade. The dessert everyone seems to order is lightly caramelized cherries gratinée au chantilly. The restaurant is closed Sunday. The rest of the week it's open for dinner only, from 6 to around 11:30 p.m.

La Lanterne, 41 rue Borno (tel. 7-0479), in Pétionville, is generally conceded to be the finest deluxe restaurant in Haiti. It's owned by Budapest-born Georges Kenn de Balinthazy and his wife, Edwige, who is a seventh-generation Haitian. Guests, everybody from Mike Wallace to Walter Cronkite, dine (or have) around a swimming pool. Along with antiques and objects of art from his native Hungary, the owner displays an outstanding collection of Haitian paintings and sculptures. Georges is also a scuba instructor and has certified many of the steady customers in private lessons.

Guests enjoy an apéritif in the cocktail bar and are allowed to inspect the aquarium. Delectable dishes, served with fine wines, are offered every day except Monday for dinner from 6 p.m. to midnight. Call for a reservation. I suggest that you ask the chef to prepare you a cold avocado soup. The menu is international, as reflected by the spaghetti with snails and garlic, the beef Stroganoff, the fried frog legs, the filet of pike à la Lanterne, and the shrimp curry. I'm also fond of the fondue bourguignonne, the spring chicken à la Bruno (marinated in coconut juice and spices, sauteed and served with mustard butter), and the sliced pork marengo with steamed shrimp. A luscious dessert is the iced Grand Marnier Soufflé, and you can finish off your meal with a "zombie coffee." A complete meal will cost from $30 per person.

Chez Gerard, 17 rue Pinchinal (tel. 7-1949), is a stone structure, in a delightful garden setting, providing a panoramic view of Port-au-Prince at night. Before dinner, have an apéritif in the little bar to your left as you enter. Tables are placed on an open-air veranda or in an inside dining room with a timbered ceiling, formal chairs, and dozens of botanical prints elegantly framed in gold. The taste of the decor is high, as is the skill behind the essentially French cookery. In a quiet, relaxed ambience, you feel much as you would dining in a private home—that is, until you get the bill. The restaurant was created by its owner-chef, Gerard, an adventure-seeking Frenchman and a seafarer of great skill. Before his stunning Créole wife, Louison, drew him here, he'd founded the well-known Chez Gerard in Martinique.

If it flies, crawls, swims, creeps, or hops, the chef is likely to have it on the menu at some point during the year. The appetizers always intrigue me, especially the snails done in the Burgundy style or the clams with garlic.

Four kinds of terrine are usually offered. Among the most recommendable main courses, I suggest frog legs, poached red snapper in a wine sauce, wild duck with peaches, and guinea hen with black mushrooms. If none of the above tempts you, surely the chicken chasseur will. Desserts are spectacular—flambéed bananas or baked Alaska. Dinner is likely to cost around $60 for two persons, maybe more. Add 10% for service. Hours are noon to 3 p.m. and from 7 to 10:30 p.m. It is closed Sunday.

La Tour d'Argent, 19 rue Lamarre (tel. 7-6507), Pétionville, set around a reflecting pool, opened in 1984. In many ways it is a small outpost of eastern France transported directly to Haiti by Jean-Claude and Mireille Haupert, experienced restaurateurs formerly of Metz, France. They meticulously supervise the preparation and service of food within the stone walls of their open-air restaurant on the road leading from Port-au-Prince to the Pétionville suburb.

The kitchen was designed to be visible from some of the tables, so while you're waiting you may be able to watch Jean-Claude concoct one of his house specialties, the best of which are derived from ultra-fresh and strictly local fish and vegetables. Each of the main courses requires about 30 minutes to prepare.

Specialties of the house are lobster thermidor served on a half shell with cognac and cream, duck à l'orange with Grand Marnier, filet of red snapper, chateaubriand with choron sauce and essence of tomatoes, a ragoût of langoustes, and soupe de poissons aux ricard à la Marseillaise. Desserts may include a tempting selection of such specialties as lemon sorbet with vodka, an "omelette norvegienne" (cake filled with ice cream, garnished with meringue and flambéed with cognac), or a blanc manger (crushed coconut with cream sauce). Full evening meals cost from $30, although at lunchtime, when you may see children splashing in the reflecting pool, a fixed-price meal is served for around $15 per person.

The restaurant is open daily for lunch and dinner, except at noon Sunday.

Le Belvedere (tel. 7-1115) opens onto one of the most spectacular vistas of any Haitian restaurant, set on a mountainside overlooking Port-au-Prince. In such a lofty setting, you get a French cuisine of a very high standard. The owner, Patrice Amant, always gets requests for seats on the veranda, and it's small and can't accommodate everybody. But if you're seated inside near the windows, you'll also have a good view. From Pétionville, the restaurant is reached by heading toward Kenscoff and Fort Jacques, turning right at the clearly marked sign. Drive on until you reach its eagle's-nest position.

The architectural outlook is in explosive modern, with no attempt to re-create Old Haiti here. For your apéritif and slow perusal of the padded menu, you can go into the grotto bar, where some of the rocks and ferns of the mountainside are exposed. In contrast to the severe contemporary architecture, the decorations and accessories evoke 19th-century France. You dine on high-backed château-style chairs, your table set with fine stemware and china. The walls contain a collection of 18th-century gilt-framed oil paintings and 12th-century church music.

But it's not for the view or decor that people drive all the way up here—rather, the food. Begin with the snail soup, the "escargots" gathered from nearby Kenscoff. Or perhaps the lobster and shrimp bisque will be a worthy alternative. Great care and good ingredients go into the preparation of the main dishes—smoked salmon and green been salad, grapefruit stuffed with seafood, chicken liver mousse with almonds, filet of red snapper in a garlic sauce, filet of beef with a cream and green peppercorn sauce, and lamb in a raisin sauce. For your finish you can order the coupe Belvedere. No lunch is served on Sunday, and dinner will cost around $50 per person.

La Belle Époque, 23 rue Grégoire (tel. 7-0984), has a pleasant dining room, reached by an ornate flight of stairs on the exterior of the building. There's a popular bar on the ground floor, with a terrace extending under one of the upper parapets. You dine in a simple, high-ceilinged room where the vertical dado molding is white. Shadows of the gingerbread of the Victorian house structure housing the bar and restaurant sometimes play across the immaculate white tablecloths.

Beneath the swirling ceiling fans, you can enjoy such specialties as baby back spare ribs, sole Belle Époque, pot roast, Italian dishes such as lasagne, baked fish in cheese sauce, pepper steak, chicken in black mushrooms, duck in orange sauce, Kenscoff snails in garlic butter, and conch chowder. Your meal might be followed by a heady concoction called zombie coffee, bringing the grand total per person to around $30. A Haitian buffet is usually featured every Saturday night. The restaurant is open only at dinnertime daily, although lunches are sometimes served to large groups on request.

Le Picardie, Montagne Noire (tel. 7-1822), a hillside mansion in Pétionville, puts a Haitian accent on its tangy French créole cuisine. Just 15 minutes from Port-au-Prince proper, this restaurant, nestled on the hill, pleases the eye as well as the palate. It is family owned. Reached by a steep access road, the dining room is adjoined by a white dove aviary.

After tasting one of the chef's good, homemade soups, you'll know you've arrived at a place that has a healthy respect for cookery. The shrimp soup is made from fresh crustaceans. The fresh fish soup compares with some of France's finest, as does the onion soup gratinée. Specialties include grilled fresh lobster, shrimps in créole sauce, and frog legs Provençale. The natives prefer grilled conch, and perhaps you will too.

Out of the fish realm, I'd suggest chicken cooked with Haitian black mushrooms, calf brains in black butter, and duck with oranges. Grilled kidneys are served in flaming rum. Everything is prepared fresh here, so allow 20 to 30 minutes after placing your order. Meals can begin at $20 per head, but you can also spend from $30, particularly if you're a shellfish aficionado. The restaurant is closed on Sunday.

Le Recif, 430 rue de Delmas (tel. 6-2605), is the first seafood restaurant of any size in Haiti. Whatever is found in the deep waters of the Caribbean is likely to turn up here on your plate—lobster, octopus, conch, blue crab, red snapper, scallops, "monster" shrimps, sea turtle, hawksbill turtle, and sea urchins. A two-level, rustic restaurant, it has a pitched beamed ceiling, with rugged stone walls. There's also an outdoor terrace with bougainvillea.

One of the most native seafood dishes is a pimentade de lambi (conch). At luncheon the lobster salad is preferred. If you'd like a little bit of everything, order the assiette de fruits de mer. I'm partial to rice Le Recif (with lobster, conch, oysters, and other denizens of the deep). Try also spaghetti Le Recif, with about the same mixture of sea creatures.

There's a large barbeque pit for "buccaneer style" specialties. These are brochettes, and they come in a wide range. The house specialty, with a mixture of seafood, is brochette Le Recif, or you may prefer to stick to one taste sensation, perhaps ordering the turtle-steak brochette. Pan-fried turtle steak is also good. The menu features photographs of the dishes so you'll have some idea of what you're ordering. Incidentally, I find the king crab here tastier than Florida's stone crab. If you don't want fish, you can order "Rocky Mountain oysters," which the French call Jean Jolle. The restaurant is open from noon to midnight, offering meals for about $25 per person. It does not serve lunch on Sunday, when it is open only from 7 p.m. to midnight.

Restaurant Le Rond Point, Avenue Marie-Jeanne (tel. 2-0621). You might hesitate to enter this restaurant after you study the somewhat dismal facade, but once you come into the bar area near the entrance, you discover a pleasantly furnished and spacious interior. Owner Max Buteau directs a large staff of uniformed waiters, who serve inexpensive and well-prepared island specialties between the large windows and paneling of the interior. Full meals, costing from around $18, might include lobster créole, conch in sauce, brochette of seafood, guinea hen with black mushrooms, grilled steak with anchovy butter, and many versions of shrimp and chicken. The establishment, at a traffic circle not far from the Iron Market, is open from 8 a.m. to midnight every night of the week.

Restaurant Gala, Hotel Splendid (tel. 5-0116), one mile from Port-au-Prince, is in an antique Haitian mansion already recommended for its accommodations. Nonguests of the hotel who make a reservation for dinner can wander through its tropical gardens, and later enjoy the fragrance at their al fresco table. Arrive early for a sundowner, accompanied by a Haitian sunset. After relaxing over a tall drink, you are shown to your table where you are likely to be served native créole dishes if you've tired of "international fare." Not only will you get uniformly good food at pleasingly moderate prices, but you can enjoy a pianist as well. Hors d'oeurves are delectable, including the pâté maison or the lobster salad. Some good beef dishes are offered, along with white duck, oven roasted and spiced with green olives. Lobster thermidor is a specialty. Dishes are usually accompanied by Haitian white rice with fresh vegetables from Kenscoff. Fresh fruits in season are the traditional dessert offering. Expect to pay from $30 for a really good meal.

Le Tiffany, 13 Avenue Harry Truman (tel. 2-3506), serves Haitian-style and French food from its waterfront location in the downtown section. It was established in 1974 by an experienced New York restaurateur. Behind its stone facade it's like a disco, with dining tables set in free-form niches with cut-out circles. The chef prepares a wide range of dishes, none more typical than lambi (conch) créole. The snails for the "escargots à la Provençale" come down the mountain from Kenscoff. Soups get a hearty recommendation, especially the fish soup and the onion soup. If the owners were able to get fresh lobster that day, you can order langouste créole. Both the Tiffany steak and the steak au poivre are usually excellent. Try also the coq au vin. For dessert, a salad of tropical fruits is a tempting offer, and might even put you in a good mood for the bill, averaging from $12 to $20. It is open daily from 11 a.m. to 10:30 p.m. (on Sunday from 5 to 10:30 p.m.).

Vegedieta, 32 Avenue Christophe (no phone). The architecture of this vegetarian restaurant gives a hint as to what a private, upper-class Haitian home used to look like. At the corner of the rue Saint-Cyr, the restaurant extends from a high-ceilinged, very simple interior onto the sprawling verandas that are visible from the far end of the walled courtyard which separates the building from the dusty courtyard which separates the building from the dusty street outside. Paule Duncan, the Haitian director, may suggest an initial island tonic called Maby, whose essence comes from several kinds of local tree barks. This might be followed by home-style vegetable pâté, rice with black mushrooms, breadfruit and tomato cake, potato omelet, salad of avocado and green peppers, orange and beet salad, a selection of fruit juices (including soursop), and colonial pudding made with cassava and native fruits. The establishment, open for lunch and dinner daily except Sunday, serves a complete meal for around $12.

3. Getting Around

After you've gone through a thorough Customs inspection, you emerge from the crowded bustle of the airport into the bright sunshine where, waiting for you, will be some—

TAXIS: Drivers hang out in front of airports, major nightspots, and restaurants. But don't be surprised if after they've gotten you in the back seat, the vehicle breaks down on your way to your hotel. The cars, often in bad condition, aren't metered, so rates will have to be negotiated.

I will quote typical rates, but they are likely to be out of date by the time of your arrival in Port-au-Prince (high oil prices have dealt a serious blow to Haiti's economy). For example, from Port-au-Prince to Pétionville, the most frequented route, costs $5 per person, while from the airport to the Holiday Inn downtown costs about $12. It will cost $30 to $45 or more to go from the airport to a hotel on the beach! At that rate, you won't want to make a lot of trips between the beaches and Port-au-Prince. Rates for all vehicles are government controlled.

TAXI TOURS: The best way to go on a shopping or sightseeing expedition is by taxi. Navigating through the teeming streets of Port-au-Prince, where denizens casually run in front of cars, is for the adventuresome only. Of course, taxi drivers will try to take you to shops where owners have promised them commissions on every purchase. They'll tell you that the shop or gallery you wanted to visit "just burned down" or is a "tourist trap." Both are a possibility but don't necessarily believe what you're told, and be firm in what you want to see.

In hiring a car or a driver, it's best to have your hotel make the arrangements rather than trying to do it yourself. The people at your hotel desk are likely to know the most reliable people and will possibly make the best deal for you.

You can rent a taxi for four hours for $35, eight hours for $60.

PUBLIQUES: These public cars or jitneys are such an offbeat mode of transportation that I hesitate to suggest them to first-time or fastidious visitors. The fare is only one Haitian gourde or 20¢ and there is no cheaper method other than walking if you want to get around Port-au-Prince inexpensively. However, if the driver enters the grounds of your hotel, he is legally entitled to charge you more. You'll recognize the publique by the red kerchief or ribbon dangling from the rear-view mirror. Drivers rarely speak English and they stop wherever they choose, picking up whomever or however many passengers they want to.

CAMIONETTES: These are bus-like vehicles, usually Peugeot station wagons, charging one Haitian gourde or 20¢ on most runs. If you stop off the scheduled route, however, you'll have to negotiate the fare. Literally "little trucks," camionettes run between Port-au-Prince and Pétionville Square. Camionettes that take you to other places besides Pétionville are trucks with wooden benches in the back. They are canopied and painted like circus wagons, each with a name such as "La Petit Fleur" (The Little Flower).

TAP-TAPS: These gaily decorated station wagons, charging a gourde or 20¢ a ride, are like a circus carousel on wheels. The subject of countless paintings, the tap-tap has no springs, and your bad back will be in rotten shape after bouncing along the rough streets of Port-au-Prince. The government says "tap-taps are more often photographed by tourists than used by them for transportation." That's good advice, unless you like crowding in with a few chickens or maybe a live pig on the way to market!

CAR RENTALS: Roads are unmarked, and out in the country most often rutted. In many cases in exploring the hinterlands I've had to ford a stream when the road just gave out.

In overpopulated Haiti, people don't seem car conscious. In Port-au-Prince, in particular, you're often trapped in a mass of people and cars, a cacophony of shouts and horns. Women with half-naked children march in front of your moving car with seemingly reckless abandon for their own safety, much less their child's. As they're often colorfully clad in flaming reds, lime greens, and sunflower yellows, they're at least easy to spot.

But if you're willing to run the risk, and want to save the expense of a driver, you'd better stick to one of the bigger international car-rental firms. Over the years, I've encountered major problems with some strictly local companies.

Hertz (tel. 6-1132) is well represented in Haiti, although their selection of cars, at the time of this writing, consists mainly of several kinds of Eastern European Ladas. Confirmation of availability of any vehicle at Hertz requires a 36-hour advance notice. For toll-free information, call 800/654-3131.

I have also used **Avis** (tel. 6-2333) satisfactorily in the past. They rent rear-engine Volkswagen Beetles as their low-priced entry and higher-priced Datsuns for those who want more luxury and comfort.

For the purposes of updating this guide, I used the services of **Budget Rent-a-Car** (tel. 6-2324). My comments about certain of their policies, such as insurance, will pertain to all car-rentals in Haiti in general.

Budget has an exceptional and friendly staff in Haiti, and they seem eager to help with problems, which are likely to occur. The inventory at Budget emphasizes peppy Nipponese cars well-suited to the winding roads and steep inclines of Haiti.

You must have a valid driver's license, a major credit card (or else a cash deposit), and be between the ages of 25 and 65. Budget charges $4 per day for a collision damage waiver which, nonetheless, will mean that a driver must be responsible for the first $250 in damage costs in the event of an accident. Without the waiver, a driver is responsible for the *full* price of repairs to the vehicle. A local driver, if hired, must also be registered on the policy.

For rentals of three days or less, Budget charges for each kilometer driven. For rentals of four days or more, mileage is automatically included in daily or weekly rates.

Budget's cheapest car is a Pony or a Daihatsu Charade with manual transmission and a seating capacity of four persons. Rentals of three days or less cost $18 a day, with 12¢ charged for each kilometer. Rentals in this category for a full week, with unlimited mileage included, is $180. If a traveler keeps the car for between four and six days, the charge is $30 a day, with unlimited mileage included. Automatic transmission vehicles cost $32 per day with unlimited mileage or $192 per week with unlimited mileage. If the rental is for three days or less, the charge if $20 per day, plus 12¢ per kilometer.

From the top category listing of vehicles, there is a manual transmission Honda Civic or a Daihatsu Charmont with air conditioning. Per-day rentals with unlimited mileage cost $35, or $210 per week. Rentals for three days or less cost $20 per day, plus 16¢ per kilometer.

These rates require an advance reservation of 1½ business days through Budget's reservation center in Dallas. The toll-free number there is 800/527-0700.

BUS TOURS: All the companies in Port-au-Prince offer the same tours at similar prices. **Chatelain Tours and Travel Service,** rue Geffrard (tel. 2-4469), is the representative for Gray Line tours in Port-au-Prince. In minibuses or limousines they operate both large- and small-group excursions, not only to the sights within the periphery of Port-au-Prince, but to Cap-Haitien as well. Rates are very steep if only one person goes on the tour. However, they are considerably reduced if two or more persons go along. The most popular tour is the one previewing the highlights of Port-au-Prince, including the Iron Market. The three-hour Kenscoff Mountain Drive visits the Jane Barbancourt Rum Castle.

AIR TRIPS: Haiti Air Charter will fly you to Cap-Haitien where you can see the Citadel and Sans Souci Palace. Flights leave Port-au-Prince daily except Sunday. Call 6-2235. The round-trip fare to Cap-Haitien is about $60 per person. But once you land, you're on your own.

Most visitors prefer a conducted tour, which costs from $75 per person, plus the air fare, based on two or more going along. This escorted tour includes round-trip transfer between your hotel and the airport, and round-trip transfer by Jeep between Milot and the parking lot of the Citadelle, along with horses, guides, and a hot lunch. Departures are at 6:15 a.m. and reservations are required. Call **Chatelain Tours and Travel Service,** rue Geffrard (tel. 2-4469).

4. Sights, Galleries, and Markets

Haiti itself is a sightseeing adventure. A walk down any street in Port-au-Prince is a look at life and excitement, but you may want to give more definition to your tour through the capital. If so, seek out the following specific targets:

SIGHTS: The **Cathédrale de la Sainte Trinité,** at the intersection of rue Pavée and rue Msgr-Guilloux, about two blocks north of the Champ de Mars, has its walls covered with naïve biblical mural paintings, and is considered Haiti's finest showcase of regional art. Started in 1951, the murals represent the turning point in the country's art. Started in some unpromising beginnings it reached a full blossom. The apse and transepts of this Episcopal church are done in tempera by some of the country's best known artists, and as such it forms a fine and proper introduction to Haitian art before your visit to specific galleries.

In the wake of charges of "paganism," Bishop Voegeli agreed to have the murals painted, admitting that it "pays to be somewhat crazy at times." Called away, he returned only when the charcoal sketches had been completed. His comment? "Priase the Lord! They painted Haitians!"

Look for the *Marriage Feast at Cana,* on the south transept wall. It was painted by Wilson Bigaud, then only 25 years old. In 1947 at the age of 14 he'd been discovered by Hector Hyppolite, a voodoo priest and artist. The critic Selden Rodman considers Bigaud the Haitian Brueghel, "the most brilliant and technically advanced of the self-taught artists" of Haiti.

Other Haitian masters who painted murals include Rigaud Benoit (a former taxi driver), Castera Bazile (a former busboy), and Cap-Haitien-born Philomé Obin. Obin painted Christ without the traditional beard. Bazile painted his characters so that their fingers and toes were exposed flat. Gabriel Leveque did the murals overhead, placing his angels upside down. Incidentally, in *The Last Supper,* a black Christ is betrayed by a Judas in white face!

Le Musée d'Art Haitien du College St-Pierre, Place des Héros (also called Champ de Mars; tel. 2-2510), is often known as the "modern museum." It is a major museum of painting and sculpture, from its beginning postwar years to its present renaissance. Many of the paintings are from the DeWitt Peters collection, the founder of the Centre d'Art who discovered and popularized the creativity of Haitian artists in the late 1940s. Others are pieces of art sponsored by Bishop Voegeli of Sainte Trinité Episcopal cathedral.

The collection at the museum of art is an ever-changing one, as many paintings are in storage and others have been lent to museums throughout the world. As you enter, look straight ahead at the large canvas by Antonio Joseph, a protégé of the late Mr. Peters. While not primitive in subject, it portrays gentle yet powerful forces in a contemporary style. Other paintings often on display include works by Hector Hyppolite, as well as Wilson Bigaud and Philomé Obin, who did some of the murals at the cathedral. Displayed also are paintings and sculpture by such well-known aritsts as Jasmin Joseph and Georges Liautaud, and black iron pieces which usually depict voodoo symbols. At the rear of the museum is a boutique of handicrafts (see my shopping recommendations).

Hours, likely to vary, are Monday through Friday from 9 a.m. to 1 p.m.; Monday, Wednesday, and Friday from 4 to 6 p.m.; and Saturday and Sunday from 9 a.m. to noon. This museum is really underfinanced, and it thrives only on public help (you'll see the little box at the entrance).

La Maison Defly stands next door to the Musée d'Art Haitien du College St-Pierre, right off the Place des Héros. Here in this Haitian museum you have a chance to see what the inside of a Haitian army house looked like in 1898. General Defly was the commander of the Haitian army, and he lived here. The house is rich in gingerbread details. A tall four-sided wooden tower with a peaked roof dominates the facade. Surrounding half of the front portion is a wide veranda. A hostess will guide you through the house, telling you about the uses of the various rooms and pointing out authentic furnishings. The museum is open daily except Sunday from 10 a.m. to 1 p.m., charging $1 per visitor.

The **Musée du Panthéon National Haitien** (tel. 2-4560), the national shrine honoring the heroes of Haitian independence, is now in the center of Port-au-Prince on the Champ de Mars in a handsome building designed by French architect Alexander Guichard. Constructed to blend perfectly with the surrounding gardens, the museum is seen from outside as seven blue mosaic cones, arranged in a circle around a larger central cone of white marble. Inside, there are three circular sections. In the first and central part is the marble sarcophagus in which are kept the remains of the forefathers of Haiti—Toussaint L'Ouverture, Jean-Jacques Dessalines, Henri Christophe, and Alexandre Pétion.

The museum also has mementos of these men. For example, there is the gold pocketwatch said to have been the property of Toussaint L'Ouverture, who fought against the troops of General Leclerc, brother-in-law of Napoleon Bonaparte. L'Ouverture was arrested, deported, and imprisoned in a French prison, Fort de Joux, where he died in 1803. In the showroom is the silver pistol used by Henri Christophe to kill himself. The self-proclaimed king's jawbone is also on display, as is some silverware that belonged to one of his secretaries, Baron Alexis Dupuy.

A permanent historical display in the second arc-like section shows life of the Haitian people from pre-Columbian times to the present. In this section can be seen, among other historical relics, the towering anchor from Columbus's flagship, the *Santa Maria,* wrecked during his first voyage along the northern coast of Hispaniola in 1492. Also displayed is the splendid gold crown of Faustin I, which focuses attention on the 19th-century imperial state of Faustin Soulouque. A third section of the museum is used to present both visiting and Haitian art shows.

The museum is open Monday to Saturday from 10 a.m. to 5 p.m

Le Centre d'Art, 58 rue 22 Septembre 1957 (tel. 2-2018), is housed in a splendid old mansion with a garden. This art center is listed in the shopping section, but it is also an important sightseeing attraction. The gallery grew out of the inspiration of an American, DeWitt Peters, a painter of the Hudson River School, who founded it back in 1944.

Even before that, Mr. Peters had discovered the excitement of Haitian art when he came to Port-au-Prince in the early 1940s to teach English. A young man named Philomé Obin came to him with a painting, and immediately Mr. Peters sensed the vitality of the country's art. Obin, of course, is now collected by art patrons around the world. Mr. Peters met a voodoo priest, Hector Hyppolite, discovering his explosive talent, and there were others—enough so that he decided to devote his life to developing and encouraging the artists of Haiti.

He didn't show them how to paint, or even what to paint. Rather, he taught them how to apply their ideas to canvas, wood, beaverboard, or whatever backdrop they could find. Eventually he set up a government showcase for their works. He persuaded Bishop Voegeli and a wealthy patrician octogenarian, Mrs. Ann Kennedy, to assist the artists morally and financially. Mr. Peters was later assisted by Selden Rodman, the poet, author, and art critic who now runs a superb museum in Jacmel.

The Centre d'Art has some of the best collections of important artists in Haiti, and should be considered as a museum in itself. The lovely director, Francine Murat, will assist you, pointing out paintings of exceptional interest. They display works by Haiti's three great sculptors, George Liautaud, Murat Brierre, and Jasmin Joseph. Of course, the works of Benoit are found here.

Hours are Monday to Friday from 10 a.m. to noon and 2 to 4 p.m. It's closed on Saturday and Sunday.

The president, Jean-Claude ("Baby Doc") Duvalier, son of the dictator Dr. François Duvalier, lives in the **National Palace,** all glistening, gleaming in white, the official residence of the black republic, standing next to the barracks of the army.

It opens onto the **Place des Héros de l'Independence** which is more popularly known as Champ de Mars. This "Square of the Heroes of Independence" contains statues of Jean-Jacques Dessalines, who is considered the father of his country (Haiti's first emperor in 1804), as well as the ill-fated Henri Christophe, whose silver bullet ended his life, and Alexandre Pétion, for whom Pétionville was named. Large letters spell out "Duvalier—Président pour la Vie" in the center of the gardens. Look for the well-known bronze statue of the Unknown Marron blowing a call to liberty on a conch shell.

Adjoining the square is the Place Toussaint L'Ouverture, named after the popular hero. The Haitian sculptor, Normil Ulysee Charles, created the statue that stands there of his ill-fated hero.

THE BEST OF THE GALLERIES: Art is Haiti's fourth-biggest export. The country has seen such self-taught contemporary grand masters as Hector Hyppolite, Philomé Obin, Wilson Bigaud, and Rigaud Benoit—names known throughout the art world. It also, quite frankly, hawks and exports some of the worst primitive art of any nation on earth.

Ever since the 1940s when Haitian art began to bloom, there has been such an increase in painting that even the average Haitian, talented or not, has gotten on the bandwagon. As long as tourists will buy, Haitians will sell. You'll see some of the pathetic results on the walls of François Duvalier Airport as soon as you get off your flight. Every hotel lobby, every shop, every boutique, practically every street corner will be hustling primitive art.

Unfortunately, even some of the galleries I'm recommending display bad art. That's not why I'm recommending them, however. The galleries set forth below display the works of many good artists. You must know, however, what you're looking for.

The market, frankly, is filled with fraud. Obin never saw many of the paintings on which his name was shamelessly signed by others. So unless you're an expert, don't expect to find a winner among the unknowns. Of course, if you have a genuine Obin, a Georges Liautaud, a Rigaud Benoit, or a Gerard Valcin, you can't go wrong (as an investment), but you'll pay a high price for these. Therefore, a Haitian painting should be purchased if it fulfills your emotional needs. Don't count on buying cheap and reselling at a high price.

Le Centre d'Art, 58 rue 22 Septembre 1957 (tel. 2-2018), is housed in a former mansion with gardens. Established originally in another location, the Centre d'Art was the birthplace of Haitian art (see the previous sightseeing attractions), the inspiration of an American, DeWitt Peters, in 1944. It still remains the most trustworthy place to buy Haitian art, but only if you're interested in top-quality paintings or sculpture in iron. For example, some of the prestigious paintings sell for $10,000. However, you might pick up a Bigaud beginning at $800. Antonio Joseph, another well-known artist, has smaller paintings that sell here from $1000 (you might also consider some of his serigraphs for $50 to $60). Some of the iron sculptures are by Haiti's leading artist in the medium, Georges Liautaud, and thse go from $200 to $1000. Some pieces by lesser known artists are in the $250 to $500 range. I'm also enthusiastic about a number of handcrafted articles, all with a strong Haitian accent. A stool-size cedar-lined storage box, brightly decorated, will be yours for around $20, although some cost as much as $250. The art center is open Monday to Friday from 9 a.m. to 5 p.m., on Saturday to 1 p.m.

Galerie Issa, 9 rue Bonne-Foi (tel. 2-8522), gets a recommendation for fair play, fine art, and handicraft work. A Haitian dealer, Issa El Saieh, runs this air-conditioned gallery. He's an oldtimer in Haiti and once owned the first department store in the country, along with his older brother. He gave it up in 1957 to open Galerie Issa. He seems to know everyone, certainly all the established, good, or even promising painters.

His gallery is more a way of life than a place to buy. Artists often frequent the place, making it their second home. It's the kind of gallery where no deals are made with taxi drivers, and unlike the rest of Haiti, no one bargains. The price asked is the price Issa expects you to pay. The reason for this is that he keeps his tariffs low, and therefore his profits are only marginal.

Even though a merchant of art, he's hooked on believing in artists, which means he often has to come to their financial aid. A soft-spoken, low-key individual, he will share his knowledge of Haitian art willingly with customers. If you insist, he'll show you a few small paintings, although he won't pretend they represent great art. They are merely decorative, to be enjoyed if you like a whimsy.

Issa has backed many talented artists who went on to win fame. André Pierre is one such painter, as is Gerard Valcin. André Normil paints in the finest tradition of Haitian art. Pierre is a voodoo priest, and you'll find his religious symbols used significantly in his works. You might also ask Issa to see some of his new favorites.

The **Gallery of Aubelin Jolicoeur** (also called Claire's), 9 rue 3 (tel. 2-4752), near the Oloffson Hotel, is a very special place owned by one of the most colorful characters in the West Indies. He's Haiti's best known journalist and reputedly was the model for Petit Pierre in Graham Greene's *The Comedians*. A natty dresser, he is often called "The Butterfly" by Haitians, because he is known to flit from table to table at his hangout, the Oloffson, collecting material for his column. He knows everyone in town worth knowing, and the others he doesn't need to waste his time with. He is also known, quite simply, as "Mr. Haiti."

A most unforgettable person, he is a man of wit and wisdom, as he prances around with his cane. When he meets a woman, he bows and kisses her hand.

He has assembled a remarkable collection of paintings, some of which could begin at $10,000 and go up. He also handles talented but lesser known artists, some of whose works begin at $400. His gallery is also his home, and every room, even the garage, is filled with his paintings. André Malraux called the house "a museum of art."

Nader's Art Gallery, 92 rue du Magasin de l'État (tel. 2-0033), is operated by an enterprising merchant who is set to take over the mass art business in Haiti. Nader's is the largest and most varied center for paintings, sculpture, and art books in Port-au-Prince. In addition to his main showroom in the downtown area, Georges Nader has another outlet, Nader's Jewelries, opposite the First National Bank of Boston, rue des Miracles, one block from the art gallery, where you can purchase souvenirs.

Nader's energy is amazing, and it has made his store the best all-around place for purchases. He even has a collection at his private home at 4 Croix des Prez (tel. 5-4524), where he keeps his finest paintings. He handles the works of such prestigious artists as Gerard Valcin, Philomé Obin, Prefete DuFaut, André Pierre, Joseph Jean-Gilles, Lyonel Laurenceau, and others. At the other end of the canvas are tourist "cheapies," selling for as little as $20. In the middle-price bracket, however, are many fine works in the $200 to $500 range.

Of course, Nader has collected some excellent metal sculptures and mahogany carvings as well. This is the best place in Haiti to purchase books on the country's art, including a superb one by the Brooklyn Museum as well as others.

MARKETS, HANDICRAFTS, AND OTHER ITEMS: Shopping in Haiti is different from any other island in the Caribbean. On the big "shopping islands," visitors head for free-port areas, where merchandise is imported from other countries, usually Europe, and sold at prices often comparable to the land of its origin.

In Haiti you buy items actually made in the country. No islanders turn out as many handicrafts as do the Haitians—and not just paintings or mahogany carvings, although these items predominate. Seek out handmade furniture, baskets, sandals; hand-loomed fabrics for upholstery and draperies; and jewelry, articles of mahogany, sisal products, even stuffed voodoo dolls. Officials at the airport are now blasé about seeing visitors checking in with bulky packages.

The **Iron Market** is considered one of the leading attractions of Port-au-Prince, and true to its name, it's built of lacy ironwork, a block square open on all sides, right in the center of the city. It has a definite Haitian style and flavor.

Vendors have one or more stalls, and near the entrances everybody from gourde-less women to nagging children will accost you, urging you to buy. Frankly, many readers are intimidated by this outdoor emporium, which is probably the most competitive market in the western hemisphere.

It's not unlike a Tower of Babel, with churning noises and a nerve-wracking pace. To shop here can be exciting and stimulating; it can also be exasperating. Hardened shoppers will learn to ignore the hands, the faces, the voices that besiege you at every turn. Yet you have to keep your eyes open to find the purchase you might want. Some visitors engage a local youth as their guide, and I'd endorse that. To earn his gourdes, he'll ward off intruders or overly enthusiastic vendors.

Stalls crowded one upon the other, with merchandise sometimes wired in suspension, are bewildering. Try a systematic tour, going up one aisle, down the other. Almost no booth has a monopoly on one kind of merchandise.

Passing a stall with straw hats, a vendor asks $4. Your guide says, "Pay no more than $1.50." Bargaining is essential here. Everybody expects it. Ask the price, then offer half the amount quoted. Chances are, you'll get away with it.

The inevitable $10 bad primitives show up here, and you'll find cedar-lined coral boxes and every style of basket to be imagined. There are placemats, sandals, mahogany statues, some good mahogany plates, bowls, and masks. However, I suggest you consider fumigating these products to remove wood-craving beasties which might infest your house when you get back home.

Articles made of tin interest many shoppers, including the pierced lanterns which often sell for only $2. The iron plaques with voodoo motifs are, in my opinion, the best buys, ranging from $3 for a small one of the sun to $15 (an up) for more intricate designs.

The **Boutique of the Musée d'Art Haitien du College St-Pierre,** at the Place des Héros, Champ de Mars (tel. 2-2510), was already previewed as a museum. In the back of a boutique, displaying one of the best collections of handcrafted objects in Haiti. The work of only the finest artisans is sold here. After all, this is a museum, and must be concerned with its reputation.

New and unusual wood plaques depicting Haitian scenes are carved in hard, unvarnished wood. These are in such contrast to the highly varnished mahogany figure hawked on every street corner. The ones at the boutique sell from $20 to $50. Seek out also the unusual voodoo flags, about three feet square with designs made of sequins in various colors, in the $60 to $125 price bracket.

There's also a fine selection of iron plaques, some utilizing voodoo and folkloric symbols. The subjects are different—Adam and Eve, crabs, a bull. Eye-catching and outrageous papier-mâché figures are sold, as are carnaval masks, in the $20 to $75 range. Another enchanting collection is of Haitian gingerbread and lacy houses, made of paper and selling for as little as $30. However, you'll have to carry these back in the airplane on your lap, I fear. These houses appear only at Christmas but are available for several months afterward. The boutique also sells boxes of all shapes and sizes, painted with Haitian jungle scenes. The curator, or one of the staff, will be there to aid and assist.

Bagaille Boutique, 23 rue Panaméricaine in Pétionville (tel. 7-1694). Bagaille, in Créole, means "things," and that describes boutique's extensive offerings. Featured are fashions for women and men, including hand-dyed, embroidered fabrics, bikinis, gift items, jewelry, cushions, and some imports from Europe.

Caribbean Hand Craft Mahogany, 19 Lamartinnière, Bois Verna (tel. 5-5820), is a building selling every object made of mahogany. The place is an old, Haitian frame shop, and it's stuffed with wooden merchandise. Nearby, under the big trees, workmen chisel, saw, file, sand, and polish the items sold in the front building. The list of merchandise is extensive, including salad plates, bowls, stemware. The craftsmen will also make furniture to order. The owner and manager of Caribbean Hand Craft Mahogany is Philip R. Khawly. Hours are daily except Sunday from 7:30 a.m. to 4 p.m.

Ambiance, 15 Ave. M (tel. 5-2494), featured in *Town and Country,* was started by Nancy Chenet, the sister-in-law of Mrs. Mike Wallace, who, along with her husband, has a place in Jacmel. One of the most fashionable boutiques of Port-au-Prince, this shop in a gingerbread house is pure Haitian, offering camisoles, resort wear, sarongs, and other high-fashion outfits, ideally adapted for the Caribbean climate (or Hawaii for that matter). Many decorative accessories are sold other than clothes.

Anson Music Center, 62 rue Pavée (tel. 2-0123). Customers go here to buy recorded Haitian music. Ask for one of the records of Ti Ro-Ro, Haiti's foremost concert drummer. His hands are not only masterful, but one has a calloused heel from beating the Petro drum.

The **Haiti Perfume Factory,** 21 rue Panaméricaine (tel. 7-1304), in Pétionville, offers visitors the chance to watch as perfumes are frozen, filtered, blended, and bottled from a glassed-in area at the back of the store. There are many unusual kinds bottled here, including a blend called "Pauline" (created originally for guests of the now-closed Habitation Leclerc), as well as many jungle varieties such as jasmine, frangipani, white ginger, and belbagaille. The perfume factory is eager to do business daily except Sunday and holidays. Jean-Marie Louis-Charles is the charming bilingual manager.

When shopping has tired you, it's time to head for one of the following—

SIDE TRIPS: These major possibilities beckon to you.

To Sand Cay

Every morning except Sunday at 10 a.m., a catamaran leaves from the pier by the Casino International, returning at 1 p.m. It takes you to a natural coral reef with rainbow-colored fish so tame they eat from your hand.

The famed explorer and naturalist William Beebe once wrote, "A new world, an unsuspecting realm of gorgeous life and color. Huge pink and orange growths rise on all sides; an ostrich feather of a sea plume as tall as yourself sweeps against you; it is a royal purple and might well be some weird fern from Mars . . . unearthly, resplendent petals in hues of gold and malachite." The cost of tickets is $15 per person. A minimum of four persons is required. Phone 5-5583 for information.

Excursions to Grand Banc

Captain Alain Moureau will take you out on his catamaran, the *Yellowbird* (tel. 2-3906, or 7-7758 after 7 p.m.), leaving from the Beau Rivage Marina near the downtown casino. The boat goes to Grand Banc offshore, where you swim, snorkel, and explore the coral formations of the sandy bottom. The price of the cruise is $12 per person, and beverages and sandwiches are available on board.

Masks and snorkels are provided free. If enough passengers show up, the *Yellowbird* sails daily, except Monday, from 10 a.m. to 2 p.m. in season. From June through November, it sails from 10 a.m. to 2 p.m only on Friday, Saturday, and Sunday.

Water Sports

Port-au-Prince is not blessed with superior beaches, so on weekends many of the sunworshipers who can afford it head north to Cacique Island and the **Ibo Beach Club** (see my previous hotel recommendation). There, in addition to a 100-ship marina, are restaurants, bars, sandy beaches, and a wide range of water-sports facilities. You can rent scuba gear, if you're a certified diver, for $35 per dive ($25 for the second dive of the day). Equipment for snorkeling can be rented for $5 per day and for windsurfing for $8 per hour or $30 per day. Waterskiing costs $12 for ten minutes. Deep-sea fishing is also available, or you can charter a boat. There's even a boat excursion offered, costing around $55 per person, going to Gonâve Island. Requiring about three hours each way, the trip comprises a full day in the sun, with feasting on lobster, steak, fish, rum punches, beer, and wine. Snorkeling expeditions to the Arcadins, lasting half a day and including snacks, soft drinks, and snorkeling gear, cost around $30 per person.

Hotel Taino (tel. 2-6157). If you're looking for a day at the beach and want to take an excursion from Port-au-Prince to Grand Goâve (midway between the capital and Petit Goâve), you'll find, for a price, a wide range of rental equipment at the Hotel Taino. From a hut on a narrow strip of palm-studded sand (see my hotel recommendations) you'll find waterskiing (around $14 for 10 minutes and $36 for 30 minutes), parasailing ($25 for a 10-minute flight), Sunfish, scuba, and snorkeling facilities (mask, fins, and snorkel rent for $7 per hour).

5. Voodoo and Nightlife

Voodo is not the dark, secret society it is often depicted to be. It certainly isn't "black magic" or "snake worship," as some have labeled it; and it isn't just fun and folklore games staged for tourists either. However, know that many Haitians are willing to put on a voodoo show for you if you'll pay them.

First of all, voodoo is a vitally alive religion, with a dominant African heritage. It is frowned upon but tolerated by the Catholic hierarchy in Haiti, who apparently have recognized that it is here to stay. Millions of Haitians who call themselves Catholics also practice voodoo. Incidentally, there are many spellings of the word. In Haiti, you'll often see it written as "vaudou."

Instead of attempting a complicated explanation of voodoo, I'll make the following suggestions.

With only one night to spend in Haiti, ask your taxi driver to deposit you at **Le Peristyle de Mariani** (tel. 4-2818), which lies about a 30-minute trek outside the capital on the principal highway to Jacmel and the south of Haiti, beyond Carrefour. Once there, you'll be enthralled at Max Beauvoir, the houganproprietor and his "vaudou" ceremony. This may not be authentic voodoo, but you'll leave with a greater understanding of the often-baffling ritual.

Before the entertainment, Mr. Beauvoir gives a thorough introduction in English. The actual vaudou ceremony takes you through invocation, vevers, followed by dancing and drumming. You'll see a vaudou possession—that is, when the possessed one speaks in strange tongues, assuming the character of the divinity invoked. One is possessed, so to speak, when "mounted" by the loa, achieving communication with the gods.

To achieve this possession, hounsis are chosen who are considered most susceptible to trance. On many a night this ceremony, staged for tourists, has been known to produce an inadvertent trance in a member of the audience. On some evenings the vaudou ceremony is staged across the highway in a jungle-like setting where a Grecian-style amphitheater has been erected. Show time is nightly, except Sunday, at 9:30, and admission is $12 per person, with drinks beginning at $3.

Several of the leading hotels, such as the Oloffson and El Rancho, have an arrangement whereby each has live entertainment one night a week during the winter season. Guests are advised of the schedule. Shows start after dinner, and some of the best talent of Haiti and other islands is presented, usually consisting of folkloric groups, colorfully costumed in the garb of their native areas. Your hotel desk will know where the action is on any given night.

CASINO ACTION: There are only two major casinos in Port-au-Prince. When business is flourishing in the country, they are both often filled with excited gamblers, onlookers, and people-watchers, but otherwise they can be quite dull. The newest casino, constructed in 1975, is the one at the **Royal Haitian Hotel** (tel. 4-0258) in Port-au-Prince which, in addition to offering bedrooms in an estate-like setting (see my hotel recommendations) features a paneled decor with shades of scarlet within the walls of the casino. Players will find the ubiquitous rows of slot machines, as well as roulette, baccarat, and 21 tables. Drinks are free, even to small-stakes gamblers.

The casino is open nightly from 9 until the early hours of the morning, depending on business.

Haiti's other major casino is at **El Rancho Hotel** in Pétionville, where the roulette wheels begin to spin every night at 8:30. The casino is like a cabana, reached via a gently arched bridge leading over a section of the swimming pool. Visitors might also appreciate the hotel's nightclub, the Epicure, which occasionally offers live music and the chance to leave the gaming tables for a dancing break.

OUTSIDE THE CAPITAL

If you haven't time to go north to Cap-Haitien or south to Jacmel, you'll find some intriguing sights right on the doorstep of Port-au-Prince, except you'll have to head up in the hills to see them. On a hot day, that isn't a bad idea, as it's much cooler in the hills.

6. Day Trips from the Capital

KENSCOFF: When you go from the heart of Port-au-Prince at barely above sea level to Pétionville at 1500 feet, the change of climate is noticeable, as I've mentioned. Then, if you continue on the road for ten miles to Kenscoff at 6000 feet, you'll again be astonished that in such a short time you can pass through various climatic strata. Going to Kenscoff is an adventure, whether in a self-drive rental car or with a Haitian driver and car which you can engage by the hour or the day.

The drive to Kenscoff and back is breathtaking, both because of the frequent splendid panoramic views of the Cul-de-Sac, of Port-au-Prince, of the wide bay, deep valleys, and barren mountainsides; and because of the Haitian drivers' taking horseshoe curves and blind corners with a blithe insouciance.

Taking it from the top, Kenscoff is a select spot so far as climate goes, and a number of well-to-do Haitians have built summer homes in the area. Reputedly named for a French count who owned a beautiful estate there when France governed the country, the tiny town is mainly noted today because of the market held on Tuesday and Friday, when the street and the rocky hillside are alive with people, animals, and fowl, walking, standing, sitting, squatting—most of them hawking wares which range from fruit, vegetables, flowers, chunks of meat to items of clothing, goatskins, and baskets. The air is heavy with the aroma from tiny charcoal braziers and less pleasing odors exuded by unrefrigerated meat and decaying food scraps, as the day wears on.

Despite the sad squalor of much of the scene and a few beggars who may dog your footsteps but will be easily appeased by the gift of a dime or a quarter, any visitor must be impressed with the sheer lushness of vegetables and fruits in season—evidence that there is a great potential for productivity in this place. There are raspberries, strawberries, all types of root vegetables, mangoes, corn, beans, many kinds of squash, artichokes, avocadoes, and bananas to name a few, most of which can be had at any time of year because of the variation of belts of climate. Beautiful flowers are offered for sale here and along the roadside, ranging from tropical blossoms to daisies. Much of the year, all along the road from Pétionville to Kenscoff, you see vibrant flamboyant trees (poincianas) and tall poinsettia plants like small trees, bearing masses of bright blooms.

Also on the road you will see many Haitian women and girls strutting along (only a fortunate few travel by donkey), making their way from the high country around Kenscoff and other more remote areas, their heads laden with baskets, produce, eggs, chickens, or whatever, going all the way to the Port-au-Prince Iron Market and then walking all the way home again. Frequent Haiti visitor Frederic E. Cole of Key West, Florida, reports seeing one woman making this trek with 16 large baskets tied together and somehow balanced on her head.

Many Haitians have been kept alive, well, and educated through continuing missionary efforts by various churches. On the road between Pétionville and Kenscoff, on the right going up the mountain, is the **Baptist Mission's Mountain Maid Self-Help Project,** P.O. Box 1386, with a school and a shop where you can purchase at low prices items, such as a woman's string macramé bag, made by the Haitian students and their families. Men's shirts, patchwork skirts, wooden plates and bowls, and many other gift items are sold inexpensively. The mission also sells farm produce at a stand.

At the Baptist Mission, you'll be served what one enthusiastic newspaper reporter calls "one of the biggest, thickest, and juiciest grilled ham and cheese sandwiches anywhere." The cost is only $2.50. A cup of hot tea is complimentary.

If you're truly adventurous, you can turn off the road between the Baptist Mission and Kenscoff, to the left as you ascend, onto a rocky, unpaved road which leads to the ruins of **Ford Jacque** and **Fort Alexander.** You're sure to be offered small cannon balls which the Haitians find in the ruins and sell as souvenirs for a small price.

RHUM-LIQUEUR BY THE BARBANCOURT FAMILY:
Another trip upward from Pétionville will take you to the **Jane Barbancourt "castle"** at Laboule (tel. 7-0589), about five miles from Kenscoff, where you can sample free the rums (rhums) bottled by the Barbancourt family to your heart's content, although if you work your way through all 23 flavors your head may rebel. If you're driving yourself, it's best to ask directions at the square in Pétionville to be sure of taking the proper route.

The castle is a tongue-in-cheek re-creation of a German fortress, constructed whimsically over the past 30 years by Rudolf Linge, the charming and articulate German-Jewish husband of Jane Barbancourt. The de Barbancourt family, incidentally, began its Haitian history after receiving a land grant here from the governor of Bordeaux in 1736. They've been distilling rum since the 1760s, recently adding exotic and highly successful versions of the spirit based on the knowledge Rudolf gained while concocting perfumes in the south of France before World War II. The coconut rum, in particular, is worth writing home about.

At the castle, you'll be shown to a terrace which overlooks a deep valley with steep hillsides dotted here and there with color when the jacarandas and poinsettias are in bloom, or you can be comfortable in the barrel-stooled sampling room. It's recommended that you sit outdoors if possible, where you relax in the peaceful quiet, broken rarely with a complaint from a goat somewhere down the mountain, while you taste the varied rums the Barbancourt distillery produced from sugarcane. They range from light, liqueur-like drinks to the dark five-star rum that is more like a brandy. Flavors include hibiscus, coconut, coffee, orange, and chocolate, among others. You can sample them all, from glasses, and they'll keep pouring as long as you want to keep tasting, even allowing repeats on any flavor you like and wish to be sure of. It's a heady experience, and you don't have to purchase anything at all, although you're sure to want to. Bottles of the drinks are available at low cost (about $5 a fifth) if you wish.

LEOGANE: Less somnolent than Jacmel, less frentic than Port-au-Prince, Leogane, on the south coast of the bay, a few miles west of the capital city, was once Haiti's capital, and you can still see traces of its hauteur in stately but too often dilapidated wooden houses that have withstood the devastating forces of nature and of man. Efforts at establishing a boat-building industry there, on a small scale, are evident. This town was once called Yagunana, having been an ancient Indian settlement known for its heroic Queen Anacaona. Spanish invaders captured the Indian Caonabo here.

A large soccer field in the center of the town is the scene of much action and can provide a matchless opportunity to see Haitians at play. It attracts crowds from the capital.

The road west from Port-au-Prince to Leogane was paved many years ago and maintained in fair condition to permit the constant passage of *camions* laden with goods and people to and from the capital, together with people on donkeys, people walking, people on bicycles, and people just standing to watch the passing parade. Just outside the town is the new road leading south to Jacmel.

There's a tiny black sand beach not presently recommended for swimming or sunning, but a place to get a close look at this unique sand found here and there in the Caribbean and reminding that once volcanoes were a part of the hazards of life in this area of the world.

7. North to Cap-Haitien

Until recently, the only recommendable way to travel between the capital city and Cap-Haitien was by plane, as the only road was a nightmare of broken pavement, washed out in many places, requiring detours through streambeds and around boulders. If you were lucky an had a valiant driver, you might make the trip in 12 hours. Today, thanks to the engineering and financial aid of France, a fine, two-lane, blacktop highway permits you to make the trip in about four hours. It's a worthwhile journey, giving a view of scenic mountains, verdant valleys, desert sections, little towns, and a glimpse of Africa.

The town of **Duvalierville,** between Port-au-Prince and St-Marc, is becoming more populated every year. Built to honor President-for-Life François Duvalier (Papa Doc), who had an ambitious plan to move the capital there, the town appeared in the movie *The Comedians,* based on Graham Greene's novel, as a ghost town, with dilapidated buildings and shredded banners lapping in the breeze. Not so today, as many middle-class Haitians are seeing it as a place to live outside the city, within easy commuting distance.

En route to Cap-Haitien, you go through only two towns of any size:

St-Marc, on the Gulf of Gonâve, is a flat, dun-colored town which was the second city of the French colony and still has some of the steep-roofed wooden buildings from that time.

Gonaïves, on the gulf farther north, has in its area irrigation ditches and rice paddies. The town itself is also flat and dun colored, with nothing of architectural interest.

You observe, as you drive along, that the people all through the Artibonite Valley seem to feel that the new highway is their personal mall. Literally hordes of them flock the road, especially on weekends, sauntering along or just standing or squatting. Drivers honk their horns, and with the utmost nonchalance the Haitians, their goats, dogs, and chickens, move slowly out of the way.

Through the valleys, it is startling to see many little villages of **cailles,** one-room thatched huts of wattle and daub with dirt floors, exact replicas of such villages in remote areas of Africa. You learn that when the slaves were brought to Hispaniola to work in the cane fields and on the estates of the French settlers, they were obliged to erect their own shelters, and the only construction they knew was the one they had learned in their African homeland.

When the French were ousted and the independent nation of Haiti instituted at the beginning of the 19th century, time stood still for the tiny country villages, and they look today just as they did then, some sitting close beside the modern highway. They have no electricity, no telephones, no waterlines.

The cailles vary slightly in different villages, some of those closer to the capital no longer using thatching for the roofs. Some villages may have cailles with a higher roof line, a different arrangement of the one door and small window, because the original Africans who were placed in the different areas came from diverse tribes and followed their own heritage, as knowledgeable anthropologists attest. Some have shutters and doors painted in bright colors—blue, pink, yellow, or green—and overall they look like little houses drawn by a child in the early grades of school—frequently lopsided.

As you look into the open doors, you may see a table, which is usually the only piece of furniture, but the whole family sleeps in the hut, on thick straw mats spread on the dirt floor and rolled up and stacked along a wall in the daytime. The little windows, usually only one to a house, have no glass, but each has wooden slat shutters. At night when the family goes to bed, all shutters are closed and barred, as is the door, to keep out the stray spirits which most Haitians believe to be constantly roaming.

Cooking and eating are done outside, where the mother or grandmother squats beside a tiny charcoal fire, stirring the family's dinner in an iron pot.

Whatever you may be told, the belief in voodoo is still strong, particularly among the country people, and each village or group of villages still has its houngan, who is the leader of the community and skilled at curing ills, besides playing the lead role in the religious ceremonies which are still held in outlying areas as serious events, not as tourist attractions.

When you leave the valley and go into the mountains, now and then you will see a little hut standing alone, an orange tree laden with fruit, or a small herd of goats nibbling the vegetation by the roadside. Not many people are usually to be seen in this high country, possibly for reasons of superstition. My driver said that if the car broke down in the mountains late in the day, we must stay in the car, roll up the windows, and wait until the sun rose the next day to find help, because zombies who lurk in the forests would find us otherwise.

Miles and miles of sugarcane fields are still in use south of Cap-Haitien, the source of wealth for their owners even today, although not to the extent that they were in the days of slavery. The habitations of the Haitians who are born, live, work, and die in the humid mist of the cane fields are variations of the cailles found elsewhere in the country.

Among interesting signs you will note on the drive as you near Cap-Haitien are ones directing you to **Limonade** and **Marmalade,** and you learn that King Christophe, in setting up a Haitian nobility, created a Duke of Limonade and a Duke of Marmalade.

A *word of caution:* Do not expect to find restroom facilities along this Cap-Haitien/Port-au-Prince highway, or along any Haitien road. In the towns you can get gasoline, but there are no service stations in Haiti such as North Americans are accustomed to. You may, in a pinch, have to stop alongside the road and do as the Haitians do. In the towns, you might be directed to a decrepit outhouse, shared by men and women, but frankly I'd raher seek a secluded spot along a mountain road. Of course, the hotels have adequate facilities, and there's even an outhouse behind the government buildings in Milot, with separate men's and women's cubicles.

CAP-HAITIEN: Selden Rodman, poet, anthologist, and art critic who has encouraged artists who have beome internationally renowned, calls Cap-Haitien "the most subtly beautiful city in the West Indies." It was a favorite and stronghold of the French before their expulsion following the insurrection led by L'Ouverture and Dessalines in the last years of the 18th century and the beginning of the 19th. In 1802, King Henri Christophe, self-proclaimed ruler of northern Haiti, burned the city, so that of some 2000 houses, only about 60 survived.

Today, Cap-Haitien, a city of more than 30,000 people, is slowly awakening from a long sleep. Miles of fine beaches stretch out "to either side of the town. Not too far away, to the west, lies Île de la Tortue, or Tortuga Island, about ten miles off the northern coast of Haiti, off which Columbus's flagship, the *Santa Maria,* sank. Efforts are mounted with increasing frequency to find and recover the remains of this historic vessel.

"Le Cap," as Haitians call it, is today a mixture of structures which look as if they have been there forever, built from or on the ruins of the buildings Christophe destroyed, and painted in shades of blue, pink, and earth tones. Many are built of bricks retrieved from the ruins, bricks that were brought to the island as ballast for the French ships which came to take away loads of sugar produced in the cane fields, which still survive.

Among the giants of Haitian art the name Obin looms high. Cap-Haitien is the place of origin of the Obins, and the works of Philomé, Seneque, and Antoine Obin and their talented descendants and protégés may be found in studios in the city.

Sans Souci

In spite of his anger and vengeance wreaked on Cap-Haitien, King Henri Christophe obviously liked the general area on or near the north coast, because it was at Milot, a tiny village nearby, that he built his Sans Souci palace, nestling in splendor at the base of the 3000-foot mountain on which he had constructed the towering fortress known as the Citadel, called one of the Seven Wonders of the Modern World.

To reach Milot, you go about ten miles inland from Cap-Haitien, if the bridge is passable. If the bridge is out—and sometimes is, for rather long periods —you must take a longer route which starts off via a paved road but soons turns onto a bumpy, rutted, unpaved road, through sugarcane fields, along which you have to ford streams and endure the horrible stench of the sour effluent from the cane mills, which clogs the shallow ditches along the road.

A reminder of the past is afforded by the sight here and there of huge decorated stone gateposts and massive brick chimneys which are all that is left of the palatial homes and great estates of the early French overlords.

Sans Souci, completed in 1813, is now in ruins. What remains is part of the massive facade, some of the mosaic marble floors, staircases, and Christophe's domed chapel, which you can visit with the permission of the nuns who have an adjacent school. The dome is a restoration, but a good one. You can roam through the remainder of the ruins at will, and I advise doing so *before* making the long trek on horseback up to the Citadel. You'll have more strength beforehand to drink in the full splendor of the ruins.

Built of stuccoed brick, four stories high, the palace complex covered 20 acres of ground in the valley. In what was surely Christophe's effort to outdo Versailles, the palace boasted conduits carrying a cold mountain stream under the floors and numerous bathrooms.

It was here that Christophe, as legend has it, shot himself through the head with a silver bullet. He'd suffered a stroke months earlier and had become increasingly incapacitated.

The Citadel

It is no longer necessary to either hike or ride a horse or mule from Milot to the awe-inspiring mountain fastness Henri Christophe had constructed high in the tropical wilderness, although such ascents are still possible if you prefer. You can, however, now go by Jeep or other tough vehicle up the narrow, pot-holed, curving road leading to a parking lot on the mountain. (On muddy days, only a Jeep should dare try it.) From the parking area, you can proceed by horseback (costing about $3) or on foot (free) to the Citadel, this last leg taking about 20 minutes for the round trip.

If you're in Cap-Haitien, you can arrange for a Jeep with driver to transport you from the town all the way to the parking lot for $25 for two persons. Guests at Hotel Mont-Joli, described below, are offered an informative guided tour from the hotel and back to Milot, San Souci, via Jeep to the parking lot, and on to the fortress by horse or mule, at a cost of $25 per person.

Henri Christophe had the mountain fastness built, as ghastly expense in blood, sweat, and lives, rising nearly 200 feet from the peak, to be an impregnable fortress from which any attack forces by land or sea could be seen. The walls are 20 to 30 feet thick, of brick, mortar, and stone, and the **Citadelle La Ferrière,** as it was named, could house 15,000 troops. You can tour through for a small fee to the caretaker, but walk carefully, as there are no guard rails around the top to protect you from the 200-foot plunge. Also, some of the stone steps down below are moss-encrusted and may be damp and slippery.

The fort held a 40-room section for Christophe and his family and staff, plus ammunition storerooms, a hospital area, dungeons, and treasure chambers. Giant cannons of English, French, and Spanish origin which you will see lying about were dragged up the steep mountain trail by manpower alone, a monumental undertaking. There's a whole, immense storeroom full of cannonballs left as they were when Christophe died. He is believed to have been interred in a quicklime pit somewhere within the fort, the actual spot unknown.

FOOD AND LODGING: At **Hotel Mont-Joli,** P.O. Box 12 (tel. 2-0300), about five minutes from the center of town, Walter Bussenius will make you welcome. The ambience at this first-class hotel is provided by the best features of Haiti—

colorful fabrics, art and craftwork, pleasing music, and the soft voices of the Haitian staff, blending to let you know this is a special place. You can enjoy drinks at the bar or on the deck overlooking the pool, as the mysterious Haitian night falls.

Standing tall on a hill with vine-covered terraces, Mont-Joli was originally a private home that grew into the present popular inn, opening onto view of sea and mountain. It became a hotel in 1956. Air conditioning has been added to the bedrooms. In the main part of the inn are pleasantly furnished rooms, each with private bath. Some of these have private terraces and balconies as well, opening onto those spectacular views mentioned. From some of the balconies you can see the Citadel in the distance. If you're "hiding out," ask for one of the fully equipped villas some distance away.

All year, singles on the MAP pay from $60 to $65 daily; doubles, $85 to $90 daily. Ask for one of the older rooms (which I prefer), as you'll likely find century-old French colonial beds and lots of mahogany antiques.

Good-tasting créole, French, and American food is served in the ground-floor dining room by polite waiters. The hotel kitchen will pack a lunch for you to take along if you're going to the Citadel, and Mr. Bussenius will organize a Jeep ride to the beautiful beach at Labadie, about a half hour's ride from the hotel, where you can snorkel and spearfish or just lounge around. A short stroll from the hotel will take you to almost anyplace in town. For information you can call toll free in the U.S. 800/223-6510.

Hotel Beck, Bel Air, P.O. Box 48 (tel. 2-1400), is owned and operated by German-born Kurt Beck, who speaks English and is dedicated to offering spotlessly clean accommodations. His small hotel stands on grounds richly planted with orange trees, banana, hibiscus, and bougainvillea, a flower-filled estate which even has its own "private mountain."

Constructed from stone, the rooms are furnished in part with solid mahogany pieces, handcrafted, in some cases, from trees which once grew on the grounds. Air conditioning is provided, but you might not need it. On the MAP, the cost of a single ranges from $35 to $52 daily, from $50 to $72 in a double, these tariffs in effect all year.

If you're just visiting Cap-Haitien, you might want to go to the Mahogany Cocktail Lounge, reputed to serve the best rum punches in the city (I've never made a survey). Music is often played at night, and you can dance to the merengue. Native voodoo dances are staged every Thursday, and when cruise-ship passengers show up at the place, folkloric shows are presented. The cuisine is French, American, créole, and to honor the fatherland, German, all backed up by a good wine list.

The hotel makes arrangements for you to go to its own private beach at Cormier, and tennis, snorkeling, fishing, and sailing can also be arranged, as well as trips to the Citadel with a packed lunch provided.

Roi Christophe Hotel, rue 24B (tel. 2-0414), built in 1724, was the home of the French governor, and later used by General Leclerc and Pauline Bonaparte. When Henri Christophe placed prisoners there, the appointments were so sumptuous the natives called it the "Golden Jail." Patios, arcades, rambling old gardens, and courtyards recapture the charm of yesterday, although the hotel has been considerably modernized for today's visitors.

Accommodations come in a variety of styles and sizes, the most elaborate being the Pauline Bonaparte Suite, furnished with antiques. Rooms rated superior are air-conditioned and have small terraces. On the MAP, singles rates (year round) range from $42 to $60 daily; doubles, $62 to $82 daily.

The Cordon Bleu cuisine, with many Haitian specialties, is tempting. The dining room is vaulted and thick walled, suggesting Iberia in mood. Around the swimming pool is a bar. There is also a small casino. The hotel has a private beach at Rival, about one mile from the Roi Christophe.

Cormier Plage, P.O. Box 70 (tel. 2-1000), is a remote spot for special people seeking a secluded oasis on several acres of beachfront property. One newspaper reviewer called it "one of the least known hotels in Haiti."

The owner-manager, Kathy Dicquemare, offers ten well-furnished bungalows directly on the beach. In all, she rents out 35 units. The hotel is about a 40-minute drive along a dirt road lying to the west of Cap-Haitien. The location is about six miles from the town, some ten miles from the airport.

The food served in two restaurants consists mainly of French and créole recipes (I hope you'll have a chance to try their freshly caught lobster). Many guests spend their time at one of the hotel's two bars, or on the beach. Save your fancy resort wear for another occasion: it's strictly casual and informal around here.

A local band provides the entertainment, and there's an occasional voodoo show or a *combat de coqs* (cockfight). If you want more strenuous activity, a program of water sports can be arranged. MAP rates throughout the year range from $60 to $70 daily in a single and $80 to $900 in a double. Some triple units, also on the MAP, cost from $100 to $110 daily. Anoter 15% is for service and taxes.

Brise de Mer, Carénage (tel. 2-0821), advertises itself as the "bargain of the Caribbean," and it is! With a simple island ambience, it is a long, low, one-story building with a covered portico which has suggested a Mexican house to some of its clients. Running the length of the building, the portico has handmade chairs set out for meals, and as you dine, you look across the wall to a swimming beach. There's a narrow strip of garden with tall palm trees and brightly colored chairs set out for relaxation. Here you can have a cooling rum punch or an after-dinner Haitian coffee. Bedrooms are simplicity itself, and the food is French créole. Expect frog legs and good French wines. Roger Pinkcombe, the owner-manager, charges only $40 per person daily with two meals, but I don't know how long he can hold that price.

8. Jacmel in the South

For many years this once-thriving coffee export "capital" was difficult to visit from other parts of Haiti, lying as it does 50 miles from Port-au-Prince on the south shore of the republic. It was accessible only by boat, by airplane, or for the truly adventurous, by a so-called road which followed the rocky bed of a shallow stream, requiring frequent crossings at fords and sometimes making use of the streambed itself as a route called the **Route de l'Amitié.**

Since 1977, however, a good, two-lane blacktop highway has been in use, leading from Port-au-Prince to Jacmel via Leogane. The well-graded road, built with financial and engineering assistance from the government of France, provides a drive which will take you through beautiful high country to Jacmel in less than two hours, probably even less if you hire a Haitian driver.

Warning: There are no service stations or comfort stops along the road, so make your preparations accordingly.

JACMEL: Here is a quiet little sun-drenched town with a strong French flavor, shown in its public buildings and three-storied balconied homes, now in various stages of disrepair. A walk through its narrow streets will take you past coffee warehouses, most now unused but still redolent of the lush shipments of other days. Women who sit under porticos use the centuries-old hand method of sorting and sizing huge piles of coffee beans for export. Down at the docks you can see bags of coffee for shipment overseas.

An Iron Market, facing the cathedral, is a smaller version of the vast market in Port-au-Prince, with the same sights, sounds, smells, and sales items.

There is a good beach about five miles east of Jacmel. A voodoo-blessed little beach is called **Cy-Va-Dieu,** meaning God goes here.

Selden Rodman, poet, anthologist, and art critic, has a gallery, **Renaissance II,** rue du Commerce, which is open to visitors, with a good exhibition of Haitian art selectively displayed, so you are not overwhelmed. Also, you are not pressured to purchase. Rodman has a patio behind the gallery and his living quarters are above. The people of Jacmel treat him and his gallery as showpieces.

Ask at your hotel about making the horseback ride to the legendary **Blue Pool** ("Bassin Bleu" in French) in the nearby hills. *Warning:* This is a rough journey, involving taking a trail along a steep chasm, walking up and down hills, and fording streams. Figure on spending most of the day. Water nymphs, according to the natives of Jacmel, live here in three mountain grottoes. The goddess is said to sit on a rock on Palm Lake, combing her hair but disappearing at the sound of mortal footsteps. According to legend, if you find her golden comb, you'll become as rich as a king.

FOOD AND LODGING: La Jacmelienne, P.O. Box 916 (tel. 2-4899). This hotel on the beach is partly the result of the love affair between Erick Danies and his wife, Marlene, who met in New York while she was an art director for RCA and he was marketing pharmaceuticals. Deciding to return to an enchanted corner of Mr. Danies's homeland, Haiti, in 1972, they commissioned the innovative design of this hotel from a Canadian architect and set up business in what had been a grove of coconut palm on the water. Although this is technically a beach resort, it benefits from an ideal location close to the center of the gingerbread town, within sight of a parade of colorfully dressed women carrying food on their heads, field workers carrying machetes, and fishermen mending their nets, all using the street as a passage between their tiny nearby village and the center of Jacmel.

You'll enter the hotel through a covered breezeway flanked with soaring palms, the leaves of which shade the upper-level dining room. The sound of the surf is heard in the attractive bedrooms, each of which contains a covered balcony screened with wooden louvers, wicker furniture, and a view over the palm grove, the pool, and the black sand beach.

The attractive and helpful staff is dressed in colonial-style garb of gracefully draped cotton, complete with headdress, all designed by Marlene and worn with a shy kind of style by the girls. The cuisine is derived from Haitian recipes of long ago, with a scattering of French-inspired dishes. Elegant lunches, served on the palm terrace, cost around $12, while dinners go for around $18 apiece. Year-round MAP packages cost about $72 in a single, $110 in a double, and $145 in a triple. The Danieses offer a special package of $250 a week per person, MAP, for guests who want to really explore Jacmel.

Pension Craft, P.O. Box 916 (tel. 8-3331), stands on the north side of the town square, a pleasant place to stay only a short walk from the local Iron Market. The Jacmel-born proprietor is one of the kindest and most colorful persons in town. She is Adeline Danies (sister of Erick Danies, owner of La Jacmelienne), and by all accounts, she's the premier chef of Jacmel. Even if you're just passing through town, you can feel safe about leaving the menu up to her. Often (if she has it) she'll prepare fresh lobster, as well as Haitian bouillon, a vegetable soup with spinach, beans, and potatoes. Other specialties include pisquet (the caviar of Jacmel), crab with eggplant, Haitian chicken from the nearby mountains (reputed to be stronger and more flavorful than its lowland cousins), lambi (conch) with lima beans and rice, pumpkin soup, guinea hen with cabbage, Haitian turkey, leeks gratinée, and what is reputed to be the best goat meat in Jacmel. Meals are served in the high-ceilinged, simply decorated dining room or on the adjoining veranda.

The original house on this spot was rebuilt in 1860 after a disastrous fire wiped out much of the town. The new building was constructed mainly with materials from France, following techniques in use in Europe at the time. Adeline, in her time as operator of the Craft, has hosted dignitaries ranging from the late President Duvalier to Mike Wallace, to culinary historians eager to record her folkloric recipes as part of the popular history of Haiti.

The building's grandly proportioned stairwell is lined with portraits representing all branches of Adeline's family: she is by descent part Italian, part English, part Jewish, and part Haitian. At the top of the stairs, visitors can find wood-walled bedrooms that have been subdivided from the original chambers of the spaciously elegant house. The units today are functional, simple, and modern—solid, no-frills accommodations. The dozen rooms rent all year for $42 in a double, breakfast included. Dinner costs an additional $9. Ten of the 12 units have private bath.

Le Manoir Alexandra, P.O. Box 916, 36 rue d'Orléans (tel. 8-2711), is a handsome, tiered mansion one block down from the town square, looking out on the Bay of Jacmel, with steps leading from floor to floor outside and down to the street below, through well-kept gardens. Meals are served on the bougainvillea-framed, top-floor porch which provides a view of the bay and the mountains in the distance. When it was built some 70 years ago, it was the private family home of one of the most important merchants in the region. French antiques are used in many parts of the hotel, and some of the main rooms have ornate ceilings.

Enjoyment of the créole and French cuisine is heightened by the sound of a donkey braying in the distance, laundry women chattering in the island patois in the courtyard three stories below, and the rustle of fronds at eye level topping tall palm trees growing in the lower garden.

Most of the comfortable, clean rooms, only six in all (none with private bath), have good views. The owner of the hotel is Mme Alexandre Vital. She charges $30 per person daily, with breakfast and dinner included, plus tax and service. If you visit just for a meal, the cost is $12.

NIGHTLIFE: If you're adventurous, you can ask at your hotel to attend a voodoo ceremony. You're likely to be taken up a dusty hill road at night, lined with primitive little huts. You arrive at a tin-roofed "temple of voodoo." To the beat of conga drums, the high priestess (called *hougoun* locally) chants and rings a little bell. The devout undulate. Perhaps it's all staged just for tourists. Perhaps no.

9. Petit Goâve—Cocoyer Beach

Cocoyer Beach, off Petit Goâve, is one of the best beaches in Haiti, and the natives use it themselves, the women going in topless and looking like poses from *National Geographic*. Here Oliver Coquelin, who used to own the Habitation Leclerc (which he has now sold), has created an idyllic world devoted to the sybaritic life in the Caribbean.

A Pullman-bus will take you from Port-au-Prince, and rum punch is provided along the way. You'll be delivered to a private launch in Petit Goâve, which will then take you to Cocoyer Beach, where hammocks and straw couches abound. In addition to a 150-foot swimming pool, you'll find a croquet field, barbecue, equipment for an array of water sports, and marina facilities if you sail over. In time, Monsieur Coquelin plans to turn this into one of the most spectacular resort colonies in the Caribbean, certainly in Haiti.

A day's outing to Cocoyer Beach from Port-au-Prince includes round-trip bus and sea transport, rum drinks, and a barbecue lunch at Cocoyer Beach, all for a cost of $60. From Petit Goâve, including round-trip boat transport, the rum drinks, and the lunch at Cocoyer Beach, the cost is $50 per person. For information and reservations, telephone 2-9557 in Port-au-Prince. Or else ask at the front desk at your hotel.

One of the country's most extraordinary hotels is in Petit Goâve, about 30 miles along the coast from Port-au-Prince. It is the **Relais de L'Empéur** (tel. 2-9557). Some have suggested that the retreat is "decadent," but the owner, Monsieur Coquelin, defines decadent as "a beautiful way of life, where everything is lazy, and all you have to do is raise your hand and you get service." A bon vivant, M Coquelin founded New York's Hippopotamus, Port-au-Prince's now-closed Habitation Leclerc, and Haiti's most elegant beach club, the Plantation Cocoyer.

A member of the prestigious Relais de Campagne, the hotel is housed in the former residence of Haitian emperor Faustin I, who ruled Haiti from 1849 to 1856. (He was eventually exiled to Jamaica, but Haitian authorities in power allowed him to return here to die. His burial place is within five minutes of the village.) Faustin constructed his home in a grandly arched format of red brick which had come into the country from France as ships' ballast, placing it in the corner of what is now one of the most colorful villages in Haiti.

Day or night, visitors can peer through the louvers of their shutters or over the edges of their spacious balconies to watch women carrying bundles on their heads, donkeys, men with machetes, and the entire richly varied street life of rural Haiti. Before the building was renovated by M Coquelin, years of deterioration and it use as a warehouse had transformed the once-proud structure into a dim shadow of its former self.

Designer Lawrence Carleton Peabody II, member of a prominent Boston family, designed each of the ten bedrooms as well as the glamorous public rooms. Visitors enjoy such touches as a caged leopard in the outside courtyard, pairs of silver-filigreed elephant tusks, richly carved antiques, unusual paintings, an accommodating staff, and even a Tibetan wind chime serving as a doorbell.

The bedrooms have been called the most beautiful in Haiti, each individually decorated. The focal points are the oversize beds, bathtubs which are usually place between mirrors with an open view of the chamber, and the balcony beyond. The hotel's affable manager, Englishman Michael Febraro, confides that the tubs were arranged in such a prominent position "because we have no TV at the Relais." From each suite, a view over the tin-roofed village unfolds, reminiscent of a page out of *National Geographic*. Don't be timid about taking off your clothes, if that appeals to you. However, if that is not your choice, the management keeps more than 200 videotapes on the premises, one of which could contribute to the grandly exalted pastime of doing nothing while enveloped in an aura of indulgent attention.

Dinners are served in common, guests mingling at long tables under the high-ceilinged reception area. For nonresidents of the hotel, fixed-price dinners cost around $30 each, while set lunches go for around $18 and ample breakfasts about $9 each.

Single rooms here cost $230 in winter; doubles are priced at $300. *In summer, singles rent for $180 and doubles for $240.*

Included in the hotel tariffs are day outings at the nearby island of Cocoyer Beach, described above, going first by automobile and then by boat.

Chapter VI

THE DOMINICAN REPUBLIC

FIVE CENTURIES OF CULTURE and tradition converge in the mountainous country of the Dominican Republic, which has been called "the best kept secret in the Caribbean." The 54-mile-wide Mona Passage separates the Dominican Republic from Puerto Rico. In the Dominican interior, the fertile Valley of the Cibao (this is rich sugarcane country) ends its upward sweep at the Pico Duarte, formerly Pico Trujillo, the highest mountain peak in the West Indies, soaring to a height of 10,417 feet.

Nestled amid Cuba, Jamaica, and Puerto Rico, the island of Hispaniola (Little Spain) consists of both Haiti (which takes up the westernmost third of the island), and the Dominican Republic, which has a lush land mass equal to that of Vermont and New Hampshire combined.

Columbus sighted the coral-edged Caribbean coastline on his first voyage to the New World—"There is no more beautiful island in the world." The first permanent European settlement in the New World was founded on November 7, 1493, the ruins still remaining near Montecristi in the northeast. Primitive Indian tribes had called the island Quisqueya, "mother earth," before the arrival of the Spaniards to butcher them.

Much of what Columbus first sighted still remains in a natural, unspoiled condition, but that may change. The country is building and expanding rapidly, launching itself in the Caribbean resort race as fast as time and money will allow. The Dominican Republic is becoming a fast-growing tourist destination.

Gulf + Western created a fabulous resort on the southeastern coast of La Romana; and the northern shore, centered around Puerto Plata, is still a vast sweep of shimmering surf and sand, and is itself currently the scene of heavy resort development.

In the heart of the Caribbean archipelago, the country has an 870-mile coastline, about a third of which is given to magnificent beach. The average temperature is 77° Fahrenheit. August is the warmest month and January the coolest period, although even then it is still warm enough to swim at the beaches and enjoy the tropical sun.

That being so, you may ask why the Dominican Republic has been relatively undiscovered by visitors. The answer is largely political. The country has been steeped in misery and bloodshed almost from the beginning, climaxed by the infamous reign of Rafael Trujillo and the civil wars that followed.

The seeds of trouble were sown early. Hispaniola is divided today largely because of 1697 treaty with Spain granted the western part of the island to France. In 1795, another treaty between France and Spain granted the eastern part to France too.

But the French weren't in control for long. Their possession gave rise to the War for Reconquest in which the French colonials were defeated, the country returning to Spanish domination. José Nuñez de Caceres in 1821 proclaimed the "Ephemeral Independence," but after that Charles Boyer, the Haitian president, declared the Dominican Republic a part of Haiti, an occupation that lasted for nearly a quarter of a century.

It wasn't until February 27, 1844, that "La Trinitaria" was founded. This freedom movement, begun by Juan Duarte, made him the father of the Dominican Republic.

The country's problems weren't solved easily, as it once more became a pawn in the colonial possession game. The Spanish claimed the country until they were ousted.

In 1916 the United States established a military occupation which lasted until July 12, 1924. After their departure, Rafael Trujillo eventually overthrew the elected president in 1930, gaining power and dominating the country until his assassination in 1961. He wanted to be known as "El Benefactor," but more often his oppressed peopled called him "The Goat," because of his revolting excesses.

Now, with much of their often notorious past a subject of history books, the Dominicans are rapidly rebuilding and restoring their country. It does offer the visitor a chance to enjoy the sun and sea as well as an opportunity to learn something historically or even politically if the problems of a developing society should interest you.

GETTING THERE: American Airlines offers a once-a-day morning flight from New York's JFK airport to Santo Dominto, leaving enough time after your arrival for a leisurely afternoon on the beach. The lowest fares on the DC-10s are usually offered from Monday to Friday, during the periods from sometime in February till June and from early September till late November. Special promotion fares at the time of this writing for the periods listed above were as low as $319 if certain restrictions were observed. These special fares require an advance purchase of at least seven days and a wait of between 3 and 31 days before using the return half of the ticket.

Dominicana and Prinair airlines offer frequent flights from San Juan, Puerto Rico, to Santo Domingo.

From Miami, Eastern operates once-a-day service nonstop to Santo Domingo on L-1011 wide-body planes, departing in the early part of every afternoon. In-flight time is about two hours.

From New York to San Juan, Dominicana offers flights to Puerto Plata. American Airlines has expressed strong interest in establishing a route from New York to the north-coast city, but at the time this book was written, service had not yet been established.

PRACTICAL FACTS: The official language, of course, is Spanish, but English is making inroads. Even if they can't understand you (too often the case with waiters in hotels), they'll give you a friendly smile.

Since 1947 the Dominican peso has been on par with U.S. dollar, at least theoretically, and price quotations in this chapter appear in both American and Dominican **currency.** The latter is identified by the prefix RD $. As of this writing, you get about RD $2.80 to $1 U.S. dollar (RD $1 equals about 36¢ U.S.), but this rate will probably fluctuate many times during the lifetime of this guide. You should always check with your bank or the tourist office before planning your budget for the Dominican Republic. At the international airports and major hotels, there are bank booths where you can get your American currency converted into Dominican money at the rate of exchange prevailing in the free market. This rate is established periodically and therefore fluctuates. You will be given a receipt for the amount of foreign currency you have exchanged. If you don't spend all your Dominican currency, you can present the receipt with the remaining pesos (RD $s) at the Banco de Reservas booth at the airport and receive the equivalent in American dollars to take out of the country. Payments by credit card are charged to you at the rate of exchange of the free market. In the Dominican Republic, exchange banks (bancos de cambio) can convert foreign currency into Dominican money and vice versa. Commercial banks can exchange dollars for pesos but not the reverse.

Note: All currency quotations in this chapter are in U.S. dollars unless RD $ is specifically designated.

Upon your arrival at the airport, you must purchase a tourist card for $5 in U.S. currency. To enter, citizens of the U.S. and Canada need only proof of citizenship such as a passport or an original birth certificate, although U.S. citizens may have trouble returning home without a passport. A reproduced birth certificate is not acceptable. In addition, upon leaving the Dominican Republic, **a departure tax** RD $20 ($7.20) is assessed. This should be paid in pesos. If you pay in U.S. currency, the exchange rate for this tax will be calculated at 1:1.

It's Atlantic Standard Time throughout the country. When New York and Miami are on Eastern Standard Time, and it's 6 a.m. in either city, it is 7 a.m. in Santo Domingo. However, during Daylight Saving Time, when it's noon on the east coast mainland, it is the same time in Santo Domingo.

In most **restaurants and hotels,** a 10% service charge is added to check to include service. Most well-bred citizens of the country usually add from 5% to 10% more, especially if the service has been good. The government imposes a 5% tax on hotel rooms.

The Dominican Republic celebrates the usual **holidays,** such as Christmas and New Year's, but also has some of its own. They include January 21 (Our Lady of La Altagracia); January 26 (Duarte's Birthday); February 27 (National Independence Day); Movable feast (60 days after Good Friday), a Corpus Christi holiday; August 16 (Restoration Day); and September 24 (Our Lady of Las Mercedes).

In Santo Domingo, the U.S. Embassy is on César Nicolas Penson Street (tel. 682-2171).

The country has the same electricity as the U.S.—that is, 110 volts AC, 60 cycles—so adapters are not necessary.

Once the hassle of Customs (you get a very thorough check!) is over, some four million Dominicans extend a *bienvenido*.

GETTING AROUND: This is not always easy if your hotel is remotely perched. The most convenient means of transport is provided by:

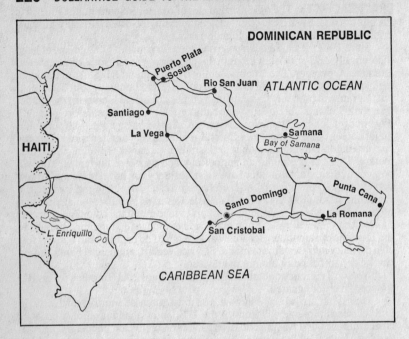

Taxis

Taxis aren't metered, and determining the cost in advance (which you should do) may be difficult if you and your driver have a language problem. Taxis can be hailed in the streets, and you'll definitely find them stationed outside the major hotels, most definitely outside the airport as you emerge from Customs. The minimum charge is $5. To go from the airport, Las Americas, into the heart of Santo Domingo will cost from $22.

Car Rentals

The best way to see the Dominican Republic is by car, particularly since intra-island transport by bus tends to erratic. Rail transport is virtually nonexistent. Several car-rental companies maintain agencies here, among them **Budget, Hertz,** and a local company called **Nelly Rent-a-Car.** All of them offer attractive rates and relatively well-maintained cars.

Two of Budget Rent-a-Car's best Caribbean agencies are in Santo Dominto and in Puerto Plata. Cars are mainly Daihatsus, Isuzus, and Hondas. If you're between the ages of 25 and 70, the cheapest rates are available by reserving a car at least 36 business hours before your arrival and keeping it for at least five days. The least expensive car begins at around $98 per week, with unlimited mileage and no tax. If you plan to arrive at either airport late at night, your reservation can be guaranteed by giving the number of your American Express card to a phone clerk at Budget's phone reservations (tel. toll free 800/527-0700) when you call for information and current prices.

Whether you travel inexpensively or in first-class luxury, Budget has a wide selection of cars in many price categories. These range from a peppy Daihatsu 550 with manual transmission to a miniature bus capable of carrying up to 15 passengers in air-conditioned comfort. In Santo Dominto, Budget is at the corner of John F. Kennedy and Lope de Vega (tel. 562-7211). In Puerto Plata, the office is on the Avenue 30 de Marzo at the corner of Belen (tel. 586-3141). The agencies maintain branches at the airports of both Santo Domingo and Puerto Plata.

If you're planning to travel to the hinterlands of the Dominican Republic, many of which merit the visit, you might be interested in a domestic car-rental company known as Nelly Rent-a-Car. It maintains more branches than any of its Stateside-based competitors, with branches in La Romana, Santiago, downtown Santo Domingo, at the airports of both Santo Domingo and Puerto Plata, and in the lobbies of several hotels in the capital. Nelly has mechanics on duty 24 hours a day. A wide range of cars, mostly Japanese, is offered, including popular luxury models. Options are available for daily rates wtih mileage or for weekly rates with unlimited mileage included.

The cheapest weekly rate for a Daihatsu STD is RD $215 ($77.40) a week. Like its American competitors, Nelly insists that drivers be at least 25 years of age. For a reservation, prospective clients can call collect at 809/532-7346.

Finally, Hertz maintains a single office at Santo Domingo, with a branch at the airport. It has a fleet of mostly Japanese cars also, although its cheapest model, a Lada, is made in Eastern Europe. When I compared Hertz, Nelly, and Budget as to cheapest weekly offers, Hertz's price was almost twice as high as either of the other two: $231 for a weekly rental of their least expensive car, with a seven-day advance booking required. If you're still interested, call Hertz's international booking desk, toll free 800/651-3001, for information.

Driving requirements include a valid Canadian or American driver's license. Unlike many places in the Caribbean, you drive on the right side of the road.

Buses

This is a cheap means of transportation for covering the city of Santo Domingo, but they are likely to be crowded. The cost is about 25¢ per ride. For schedules and information, get in touch with **Autobuses Metro,** 154 San Martín (tel. 566-3919), or **Expresos Dominicanos,** 11 Ave. Independencia (tel. 682-6610).

Sightseeing Tours

Taxis can also be rented for sightseeing tours if you prefer this costlier method of travel and if you don't mind negotiating a price with your driver before the beginning of the tour and then tipping him for extra services. Such prices can vary wildly, depending on your negotiating skills and how many monuments you wish to include, although the usual price is around $30, more if lunch is included. Some visitors prefer to escape the congestion of Santo Domingo and visit the beaches at Boca Chica by taxi. Some hotels in the capital, including the Embajador and the Concorde, include excursions to these beaches as part of their packages. If such trips are not covered in your hotel rates, except to pay around $35 round trip for the excursion, which requires a 30-minute drive each way. If there are more than two in your party, you might consider a taxi trip to La Romana, costing $70 to $80 and up. You have to be pretty affluent to pay for a taxi tour to Puerto Plata, around $120 each way, although you may be able to negotiate a lower tariff. The cheapest way is to go there by bus, costing around $5 each way.

The bus is, in fact, the cheapest way to tour sections of the Dominican Republic. At your hotel desk, someone can put you in touch with one of at least four bus operators, all of whom basically offer the same kind of full- or half-day journey. Some of them are interesting and sometimes quite creative. Tours of the colonial city are usually offered both morning and afternoon, costing around $18 for a half-day excursion.

Tour operators include: **Fantasy Tours,** Hotel Embajador (tel. 533-2131); **Prieto Tours,** 125 Francia Ave. (tel. 685-0101); **Metro Tours,** Winston Churchill Avenue (tel. 567-3138); and **Tour Inter,** 4 Leopoldo Navarro St. (tel. 685-4020).

SANTO DOMINGO

Bartholomew Columbus, brother of the discoverer, founded the city of New Isabella on August 4, 1496. It was later renamed Santo Domingo. That makes it the oldest city in the New World, a haven for history buffs, built on the banks of the Ozama River.

On the southeastern Caribbean coast, Santo Domingo—known as Ciudad Trujillo from 1936 to 1961—is, of course, the capital of the Dominican Republic. It has had a long, sometimes glorious, more often sad, history. At the peak of its power, Diego de Valasquez sailed from here to settle Cuba; Ponce de Leon went forth to discover and settle Puerto Rico and Florida; and Cortes was launched in the direction of Mexico.

The city today still reflects its long history—French, Haitian, and especially Spanish.

I'll first review its modern (for the most part) hotels and restaurants before picking up the sightseeing trail.

1. Hotels in Santo Domingo

Hotel Santo Domingo, Avenida Independencia (tel. 532-1511), Gulf + Western, has a tasteful extravagance, the designs of William Cox, and the styling of the famed Dominican haute couturier, Oscar de la Renta. Their flair has made this ochre stucco structure, 15 minutes from the downtown area, the most prestigious—and best—hotel in Santo Domingo, often attracting presidents of other Latin American countries. Opening into the sea, the deluxe hotel stands on 14 acres of landscaped ground of tropical planting, some of which form a pleasing backdrop for an Olympic-size swimming pool area.

Air-conditioned rooms spread out in two structures, three stories tall, these framing latticework loggias, one dedicated to orange trees. Most of the rooms open onto views of the water, but some face the garden, which isn't bad either. A fine collection of antiques, marble, wicker and bamboo pieces, and color—lots of color—set a high level of style that borrows at times from both the Moroccans and the Aztecs. Mr. de la Renta had local artists produce bold, primitive paintings for the bedrooms. A superior room—that is, extra-large with two double beds—rents for $95 in winter, going up to $106 in a deluxe unit with a balcony overlooking the Caribbean. Rates are for either double or single occupany. *In summer, these rates are reduced to $55 and $60 daily.* Add 15% for tax and service.

Just off the lobby, guests gather for drinks at La Cabuya, enjoying dinner at El Alcazar (see the dining recommendations). At a fountain is the informal restaurant El Cafetal, and you can also enjoy a poolside lunch at Las Brisas. The piano bar, Las Palmas, draws a lively crowd at night. Of the hotel's three professional tennis courts, two are lit for night games.

Hotel Santo Domingo North Hispaniola, Avenida Independencia (tel. 533-7111), has done an amazing Cinderella act. Gulf + Western practically rebuilt and completely transformed it. The location is across from its sister establishment, the deluxe Hotel Santo Domingo, already recommended. The designs of

William Cox and the color and fabrics of Oscar de la Renta have transformed the hotel into a resort.

On ten beautifully landscaped acres, it is a six-story structure, with an attractive swimming pool and a thatched coffeehouse (a bohio), where you can order breakfast, lunches, or drinks. The top-floor rooms, which are preferable, offer seaside views. The rooms reflect Dominican styling, and it is the fabric as well as the colors that give them excitement. I feel the designer wisely allowed the 1950s-style baths to remain as they are, a comment on an era. A standard room with balcony costs $65 daily in winter, and there are more than a dozen garden rooms going for $75 daily, either single or double occupancy, plus 15% for service and taxes. *In summer, these tariffs are considerably reduced, a standard unit going for only $38 daily, a garden room for $43, either single or double occupancy.*

The hotel's restaurant, Vivero, serves international specialties, as you sit on locally made ladderback chairs against a backdrop of gigantic blow-ups of local flowers, the handiwork of the well-known Dominican artist Ada Balcacer. The evening hot spot is the vibrant disco Neon 2002, attracting a great deal of local trade. Guests at the Hispaniola are entitled to use the facilities at the Hotel Santo Domingo, including its professional tennis courts, for which there is a charge.

Santo Domingo Sheraton, 365 Avenida George Washington (tel. 685-5151), is a high-rise right on the Malecón, with a splashy, dramatic entrance, along a boutique-lined drive that passes a waterfall, arriving at a vast lobby that is really a solarium. Vibrant colors and handsomely styled bamboo and rattan furnishings greet you, setting the taste and tone of the hotel. The bedrooms have personal Sheraton flair, traditional with Caribbean overtones (such as bamboo headboards), a small refrigerator for drinks, and room to lounge a bit. Beds are large, and music is piped in. There are 260 rooms, all doubles, plus 18 suites. *In summer the single rate ranges from $75 to $80 daily, and doubles go for $90 to $95. Suites are more expensive.* In winter, singles rent for $95 to $100 and doubles for $100 to $110. A third person in a room pays $20 extra. Suites rent for $130 to $230 in high season. Units are equipped with color TV showing free English movies. A Casino is also within the building. At the plant-filled Petit Café, overlooking the lobby, you can enjoy a sundowner before heading for Yarey's Lounge, a piano bar with good entertainment. Dining is at Antoine's (see the recommendations to follow), an elegant continental place. Breakfast or lunch is taken at La Terraza coffeehouse, which opens onto a poolside terrace. Try the tropical fruit salad served in a fresh pineapple. Other additions to the hotel are La Canasta, a restaurant featuring Dominican food, and the Omni Disco.

The hotel is a good bet for the commercial traveler, as it offers direct-dial phones, 24-hour room service, babysitters, laundry and dry-cleaning services, secretarial and translation services, and mail and telegram service, as well as an Avis car rental on the premises.

Dominican Concorde, Avenida Anacaona, Mirador del Sur (tel. 532-2531), is a complete resort with a casino outside the city, about half an hour's drive from the airport. The Paseo de los Indios is a five-mile park right outside the hotel's grounds. The only ingredient missing at the Dominicana is a beach. Instead it places emphasis on its geometrically designed swimming pool with its lavish surroundings, including a bar jutting out into the pool with underwater seats. The main building is a high-rise, with many built-in playground facilities. The pool is placed adjacent to eight tennis courts, which are lit at night. The bedrooms, 316 in all, utilize island colors and furnishings, and each has a double bed, refrigerator, radio, an intimate sitting area, plus private balconies where you can see clearly a view of faraway mountains or the nearby sea. In winter, singles or doubles range in price from $65 to $81. *Off-season, singles or doubles range from $50 to $66 daily.* Service and taxes are added to all bills. Even more expensive suites are available.

The lobby is in colorful warm hues, and the most advanced design is El Mercado coffeeshop, which uses wooden packing cases and baskets of island-grown produce such as bananas. You can order everything from such Stateside specialties as a hamburger to such local delicacies as pumpkin bisque. A luncheon buffet is featured. The main dining room, La Casa, was decorated to evoke a colonial Dominican mansion. Both seafood and international dishes are offered here, including lobster thermidor.

The rooftop lounge, L'Azotea, offers a magnificent view at night. You'll want to have at least a drink here. Other facilities include eight lit tennis courts, basketball, volleyball, a health club, and a sauna.

Hostal Nicolas de Ovando, 53 Calle las Damas (tel. 687-3101), stands in the Atarazana, created from two 15th-century mansions, a brilliant restoration that makes it one of the most charming inns in the Caribbean. Once it was the home of the governor of Hispaniola from 1502 to 1509 (the hostal is named after him), an example of a fortified house, with its own mirador or observation tower overlooking the Ozama River. The spearhead of the restoration program in the historic city, the hostal will serve you a good dinner in its restaurant (see the Extramadura, under "Where to Dine"), even if you can't stay here.

The public rooms are gracious, furnished in part with heraldic tapestries and bronze mirrors. The furniture, produced in Spain, is typical of the colonial era, and you might see some interesting Isabeline Gothic ornamentations. Bedrooms are furnished with good reproductions of antique spoolbeds. Baths contain hand-painted tiles from Talavera. Rates, in effect all year, range from $60 to $70 daily in a double or twin, from $50 in a single.

Inside, the original patios with arched colonnades have been returned to their former glory. There's always a vista of the water-splashing central fountain. In the Caceres Bar you can enjoy an apéritif before dinner, and in the heat of the day, you can refresh yourself in a swimming pool set in a tropical garden.

El Embajador Hotel Casino, Avenida Sarasota (tel. 533-2131), was created by Trujillo as a concrete-and-glass deluxe hotel with a luxury penthouse for his own use. It was built at the western outskirts of the city on the grounds of a horse-racing track, but today modern high-rise buildings have made inroads on the land where, in the Trujillo era, playboy Porfirio Rubirosa and El Jefe's son, Ramfis Trujillo, use to play polo. Perhaps no hotel in Santo Domingo has undergone such a metamorphosis in spirit as this place, although the 1950s aura still lingers a bit in style and decor. The Oriental owners, however, have given it a major refurbishing. The seven-story modern building has 309 air-conditioned bedrooms, French provincial in style, with both king- and queen-size beds, walk-in closets, color TV via satellite, and private terraces. Singles range in price during winter from RD $90 ($32.40) daily; doubles, from RD $110 ($39.60). For breakfast and dinner, guests pay an additional charge of $25 per person daily. *In summer, a single ranges from RD $75 ($27) to RD $80 ($28.80) daily; doubles, from RD $85 ($30.60) to RD $90 ($32.40). For breakfast and dinner, summer guests pay an additional charge of RD $29 ($10.44) per person daily.*

Among the best restaurants in Santo Domingo are the Jade Garden, featuring Chinese cuisine, and Le Diplomat, the deluxe restaurant with an international cuisine, which is known for its flambé dishes. You can drink and dance in

La Fontana lounge. On the grounds are tennis courts and an undulating swimming pool with a waterside terrace for refreshments. Its casino is previewed in the After Dark section.

Hotel Lina, Avenidas Maximo Gomez and 27 de Febrero (tel. 689-5185), is the modern, six-story outgrowth of the restaurant that was begun by Lina Aguado, a Spanish woman who came to Santo Domingo to cook for Trujillo. The restaurant has grown into one of the best known in the Caribbean (see the dining recommendations to follow). The hotel, one of the most famous in the Dominican Republic, has attracted everybody from Julio Iglesias to David Rockefeller to Latin American presidents to "The Incredible Hulk." Under the direction of Angel Montero, the hotel is better than ever. After a much-needed renovation, its facilities have been considerbly upgraded, including a gym for both men and women, along with a sauna and whirlpool. There is also a piano bar, a Kiosko Bar, and a gambling casino. There are also two swimming pools and tennis courts.

The hotel offers 225 well-furnished rooms, each with private bath and air conditioning. *On the EP, singles in summer cost from $95 to $100 daily, while doubles go for $105 to $110.* Even more expensive suites are available. Another 15% is added for service and tax. In winter, singles are $65, doubles run $70, and triples cost $85; suites go for $100 to $120 daily.

Hotel Continental, 16 Avenida Maximo Gomez (tel. 689-1151), is one of the best buys in Santo Domingo, a 100-room hotel facing the Palace of the Fine Arts, with pleasantly styled bedrooms, each with private bath and air conditioning. Fabrics in bold, primitive colors have been coordinated in the bedrooms, and sliding glass doors open onto private balconies. Year-round rates in a single range from $39 to $44, and doubles cost from $43 to $48 daily. For breakfast and dinner, add another $12, plus another 15% for service and taxes.

Off the street-floor lounge is an intimate free-form swimming pool, giving the Continental a resort touch. The main lounge is traditionally designed with ornate tile walls and wood paneling. The coffeeshop has been given a contemporary tropical look, with wood trim and terracotta pots of greenery. The bar has an angular wood-paneled ceiling, comfortable stools, and a "sitdown" drinking area. You can dine in the hotel's French restaurant, Le Jardin, later dancing nightly in the disco.

Comodoro, 193 Bolívar (tel. 687-7141), is a well-designed hotel in the northwest sector of Santo Domingo. Its facade rises four stories high, with rows of half-enclosed bay windows. On the rooftop is an open-air swimming pool with sundeck furniture in pastel colors. The hotel is good if you're watching the budget, as it offers simple, air-conditioned rooms, each with two double beds, color TV, a refrigerator, and background music. They are well-equipped and adequate for short stays. Year round, doubles rent for $73 daily, although singles cost only $65. The hotel draws a heavy patronage from business people. Guests dine in Le Gourmet Restaurant and enjoy the ambience of the lively boîte Salon Rojo Lounge. The airport is about a 45-minute cab ride from the hotel.

Hotel Caribe, corner of Avenidas Maximo Gomez and Sanchez Ramírez (tel. 688-8141), is one of the newest hostelries in town, a 36-room edifice in a heavily commercial area. The white- and coral-colored facade rises in an uninterrupted rectangle pierced with wide expanses of glass. Each of the units is a double, and some suites with full kitchens are available. Visitors will find a small swimming pool in an area of the hotel's roof, a piano bar, and attractively simple rooms with tile floors and neutral colors. You may find yourself among part of a tour group from Switzerland or Italy if you choose this hotel. *In low season,* *single rooms cost RD $70 ($25.20); doubles go for RD $80 ($28.80), and suites for RD $115 ($41.40).* In winter, you pay RD $84 ($30.24) for a single, RD $96 ($34.56) for a double, and RD $138 ($49.68) for a suite.

Hotel Naco, 22 Avenida Tiradentes (tel. 562-3100), is one of the best bargains of Santo Domingo. Good for families, it lies in the center of a residential area and is very popular with the Dominicans. It's not what you think of as a resort hotel, but it has a vaguely tropical feeling, with an open-air courtyard and swimming pool. The hotel offers 108 simply furnished rooms, each a double. Many of the units have kitchenettes. Year round, a single rents for $60; a double, $68; and a triple, $75 daily—plus 15% for service and tax. There is a coffeeshop on the premises, along with a cafeteria and restaurant. The food is international, ranging from seabass ceviche to garlic shrimp. Meals begin at RD $15 ($5.40).

Hotel El Napolitano, Avenida George Washington (tel. 689-5531), is a safe haven—and a good bargain—along the Malecón, which is usually lively until the wee hours. Popular with Dominicans, as is the Naco, El Napolitano rents out 72 comfortably furnished units, many of which are family rooms. There is a swimming pool on the second floor. The units have central air conditioning, and most rooms are equipped with two double beds. Year round, the charge is RD $65 ($23.40) for one person, going up to RD $73 ($26.28) for two. All accommodations open onto the sea. The café is open 24 hours a day, and the hotel also has a good restaurant, specializing in seafood, especially lobsters (kept in a tank). There is also a disco and a piano bar, with both live and recorded music. If you like crowds, lots of action, and informality, El Napolitano may be for you.

2. Where to Dine

In Santo Domingo, guests are not forced to dine every night in their hotels. The city has a host of restaurants serving good food. Dining rooms offering European cuisine, especially Italian, abound. Most of the restaurants stretch along the seaside-bordering Avenida George Washington, popularly known as Malecón.

The national dish is sancocho, a thick stew made with meats (maybe seven different ones), vegetables, and herbs, especially marjoram. Another national favorite is chicharrones de pollo, pieces of fried chicken and fried green bananas flavored with pungent spices.

Everything tastes better with a good local beer known as El Presidente. Wines, under strict and limited control by Customs, are imported, and the prices tend to run high. Dominican coffee is compared favorably with that of Colombia and Brazil.

Lina, in the Hotel Aguado Lina, Avenida Maximo Gomez (tel. 689-5185). Spanish-born Lina Aguado originally came to Santo Domingo when it was Ciudad Trujillo. Her culinary fame was so great in Madrid that she'd been hired as the personal *chef de rang* of the dictator Trujillo. She served El Jefe well until she left to open her own fonda. It was a small place, but the restaurant grew in international renown, and she became the number one restauratrice of the Dominican Republic.

Today, her nephew Armando Alvarez runs this modern hotel and restaurant, and it has nothing to do with the old place, except that Dona Lina taught the cooks her secret recipes. Four master chefs now rule in the kitchen. Mr. Alvarez is considered a gastronomic expert and a connoisseur of the finest wines. He offers one of the best Spanish, French, and Dominican cuisines on the island, and he's not at all disappointed if you tell him Lina is "one of the world's greatest eating places."

The place is known for its paella Valencian style and its paella with seafood.

Seabass is prepared in two different ways, both good—one flambéed with brandy, another in Lina's familiar Basque style.

I'm also fond of the tempting mixed seafood au Pernod cooked in a casserole. Tender steak is also prepared in three different ways, roquefort, pepper, and mustard. Appetizers are large in number and unusual, more than just your regular shrimp cocktail. For example, I recently ordered a pâté of wild boar's head. Naturally, the chefs will prepare a cold Andalusian gazpacho. One good main dish you might like is stewed lima beans, Asturian style.

The menu is vast, and you may give up and order something before you finish reading it. For dessert, you can ask for flaming apples with Cointreau. Other classic desserts are also rewarding. The prices are among the highest in the capital, from $25 for dinner, but the food is deserving. Reservations are suggested.

El Alcazar, in the Hotel Santo Domingo, Avenida Independencia (tel. 532-1511), was created by Dominican designer Oscar de la Renta in a Moroccan motif, with aged mother-of-pearl, small mirrors, and lots of fabric. All of this forms a setting to show off the culinary skills of the restaurant's chef. Perhaps here you'll enjoy your most elegant evening in Santo Domingo and you should save it for your final night. The preparation of dishes from the extensive international menu is always acceptable, and sometimes excellent. Good materials are used, and well-made sauces add further zest to dining. The presentation of the food, as well as the service from a well-trained staff, provides yet another reason to dine here.

Appetizers range from French snails bourguignonne to a local oyster cocktail on the half shell. In season, a creamy avocado vichyssoise, a rarity among soups, is a feature. Among main dishes, I'd recommend filet of red snapper amandine, sauteed frog legs Provençale, and seabass filet with crabmeat au gratin. Flambé dishes are a specialty. Rewarding desserts include banana flambé Santo Domingo. A dinner will cost around RD $70 ($25.20). Always call ahead for a reservation.

Antoine's, 361 Avenida George Washington, in the Santo Domingo Sheraton (tel. 685-5151), is the place where the well-dressed Dominican family goes to celebrate a special occasion. Of course, the well-run restaurant in this deluxe hotel also draws an international crowd among the guests staying at the Sheraton. Elegantly decorated, the restaurant also offers entertainment from the piano bar.

The cookery is international, and the service is among the finest in the capital. Unusual appetizers include squid in garlic dressing. I am very fond of the black-bean soup and also of the baked garlic soup with egg. The waiters often suggest the lobster thermidor, but I've found the red snapper Basque style more interesting, and it costs less. If you don't want fish, perhaps the tournedos Rossini will intrigue you.

One night I asked the chef to suggest something, and he told me I'd like his Madras hot pot of stewed beef, pork, and crab—and I did. While I was assured that his stewed seafood imperial is even better, that will have to wait until next time. For dessert, I happily settle for Spanish coffee, but the next table on my most recent visit preferred baked Alaska. Tabs tend to be wide-ranging here, but count on at least RD $30 ($10.80).

Vesuvio I, 521 Avenida George Washington (tel. 682-2766), is the most famous trattoria in the Dominican Republic, possibly Santo Domingo's most heavily patronized restaurant. Both visitors and local business people crowd in here for tasty, reasonably priced Italian fare, about every dish you can think of from that country's vast culinary repertoire. On the way to your table you can inspect the display counter of antipasti. In the hot months, guests seem to stay inside in air-conditioned comfort, but in winter they may prefer to dine under the canopy outside. White-jacketed waiters are efficient, maybe too much so, and before you've read the menu your meal has arrived. If you have the time between courses, you can contemplate the colorful paintings placed on the walls.

What to order? That is always a problem here, as the Neopolitan owners, the Bonarelli family, have worked since 1954 to perfect and enlarge their menu. Their homemade soups are excellent. I prefer either the seafood soup or the clam soup (in season only), but you may go for a Roman-style stracciatella. The chefs claim to be the pioneer of pizza in the country, and you can order at least a dozen different varieties.

From their north coast, the restaurant receives fresh fish such as red snapper, seabass, and oysters, and prepares them in imaginative and interesting ways. Lobsters from Azua de Compostela and Ocoa Bay are priced according to the season (one specialty is stuffed squid with marinara sauce). Meats come from the Hacienda El Rancho, at La Romana, in the eastern part of the country. A favorite is veal chops with peppers. An average meal begains at RD $35 ($12.60). The restaurant is closed Wednesday. If you want more Italian food, then go to **Vesuvio II,** 17 Tiradentes (tel. 565-9797).

Il Buco, 152-A Arzobispo Meriño (tel. 685-0884), is currently one of the most popular dining choices in the capital, drawing haut Santo Domingo to its precincts, where they are served an array of countrywide Italian and international specialties. Giuseppe Storniolo is the guiding light behind this successful enterprise in a restored 16th-century house accented with brick, stucco, and flowered tablecloths. All in-the-know diners request his antipasti, an array of both hot and cold Italian-style hors d'oeuvres. Follow with a pasta if you have the appetite, as it's homemade and likely to be served in a savory sauce. Fresh seafood, including bass and lobster, are served as well, depending on what looked good that day at the market. The waiters are polite and efficient, and often there is entertainment, all of which makes for a romantic dining choice. On Friday and Saturday nights the restaurant is likely to be crowded, so it's prudent to call for a reservation. Count on spending around $20 or more for one of your finest meals in the capital.

Juan Carlos, 7 Gustavo Mejía Ricart (tel. 562-6444), is a top-quality restaurant, handsomely decorated in pinks and mauves. Local paintings add to the attractiveness of the place. But it is the food that attracts the repeat clientele, mostly Dominicans. Several years ago the restaurant with a bodega was opened by Carlos Gil from Valencia, Spain. His specialties include tripe in the Madrid style, rabbit in a wine sauce, a seafood paella (prepared for at least two persons), roast lamb, and a seafood casserole. You can also order quail stew and seabass in orange sauce. Count on spending from RD $50 ($18) and up. The restaurant is open from noon to midnight seven days a week.

La Fromagerie, Plaza Criolla (tel. 567-9430), has a regional tavern-style decor, and it's one of the most attractive restaurants in Santo Domingo. It's air-conditioned inside, but you also have a choice of outside tables as well. The staff is accommodating, and the list of dishes is international, including Dominican specialties. At lunch, you may prefer to sample one of the crêpes, stuffed with a variety of fillings. Classic dishes include stuffed pot roast, duckling in an orange sauce, and bouillabaisse. More unusual fare is likely to feature a shellfish fondue, frog legs in a champagne sauce, and crabmeat in a red sauce. Meals cost from RD $40 ($14.40). Reservations are rarely needed.

Fonda La Atarazana, La Atarazana Street (tel. 689-2900). For native food in a colonial atmosphere, with night music for dancing as well, this patio restaurant often has forkloric festivals. Just across from the Alcázar, the restored structure can easily be visited as you're shopping and sightseeing in the old city. This friendly place retains plenty of character, without being deliberately self-conscious abut it. A cheap, good dish is "chicharrones de pollo," which is tasty fried bits of Dominican chicken. Otherwise, you might try curried goat in a sherry sauce. Sometimes the chef cooks guinea fowl in wine. I also like the Spanish-style seabass. If you don't mind waiting half an hour, you can order the sopa de ajo (garlic soup). The pork dishes attract many fans, who come here especially for the fricassé pork chops. An average repast will cost from $15 to $20.

Extremadura, in the Hostal Nicolas de Ovando, 53 Calle las Damas (tel. 687-0450). In the most enchanting old-world hotel in Santo Domingo, you get good dishes, well prepared and served in a typically Iberian ambience of terracotta floors, soaring timbered ceilings, leather-bottomed wooden chairs, gilded chandeliers, and an imposing grandeur. Each table contains a square-columned silver candlestick crafted from the metal the Spaniards fought for throughout the New World. The restaurant presents a long menu of favorite foods that borrow from many of Spain's provincial kitchens, from Castile to Valencia, from the province of Asturias to Andalusia. As an appetizer, you might like the snails Ovando bourguignonne style or a cup of either garlic soup or onion soup. Main dishes include a pottery casserole of seafood flambéed in rum, roast chicken or rabbit in garlic sauce, two types of paella, and stewed lobster. For dessert, you might choose caramel custard or flambéed bananas for two persons. Most meals range from $18. Waiters wear uniforms of bandarilleros from the province of Extremadura in Spain, from which the restaurant takes its name. Hours are noon to 3 p.m. and 7 to 11 p.m.

San Michel, 24 Avenida de Lope de Vega (tel. 562-4141), on a traffic-clogged street in a section of town called Naco, is a popular restaurant which may have its finest hour daily at lunchtime, when local business people come here with their friends, lovers, and clients. The wood-trimmed facade opens into an interior of light-grained wood, stone trim, and a curved black-accented bar which is open daily from noon to midnight. Menu items include many different kinds of beefsteak, seabass, red snapper, shrimp, lobster prepared in several ways, caesar salad, spinach lasagne, soufflés of shrimp or spinach, cream of pumpkin soup, gazpacho, and a series of flavorful chicken breast dishes, each stuffed in a different way. A dessert spectacular is soufflé Grand Marnier. Full meals here cost around RD $35 ($12.60) per person.

Restaurant/Bar Jai-Alai, 411 Avenida Independencia, corner of José Joaquin Pérez (tel. 685-2409). The original owner of this cosmopolitan restaurant left his home in Bilbao, Spain, when he was 18. After running a successful eatery in Lima, Peru, he came to Santo Domingo, where he set up this restaurant named after the favorite sport of his Basque ancestors. The establishment is housed in what used to be a wealthy private home. It's decorated like an informal gathering place in a Spanish plantation house, with lime-green tile floors, dark wood accents, and a rather dark dining area set behind thick walls. Today the restaurant is directed by the founder's son, Luís Llaque Gordillo, and his wife, Goyi, who welcomes guests with a smile and a fluency in several languages.

Shellfish is famous here, with such offerings as lobster creole, shrimp Jai-Alai, seafood casserole, and oysters in red sauce. Other dishes include octopus creole, garlic soup, Spanish-style pork chops, rabbit in garlic sauce, and seabass, both Basque and Breton style. As a before-dinner drink you might enjoy a glass of the Peruvian pick-me-up called *pisco.* Full meals cost from RD $40 ($14.40). The restaurant, which you'll find just back of the Sheraton Hotel, is open for lunch and dinner daily.

Restaurante Café-Concierto El Bodegón, 152 Arzobispo Meriño (tel. 682-

6864), occupies several elegant rooms in the heart of the oldest part of the city, immediately opposite the cathedral. The building is a house whose oldest parts date from the 15th century, all of it decorated with heavy ceiling timbers, massive wrought-iron chandeliers, old furniture, and scores of pictures by well-known Dominican artists.

Many of the artists are friends of the owner, Frank Salcedo, whose cuisine has won gastronomic awards and whose devotees include luminaries. The bar has received an international award for the house special, a rum caña.

Full meals, costing from around RD $35 ($12.60), can include international dishes such as zarzuela de mariscos (fish and shellfish in a casserole), tripe with ham and Spanish sausage, paella valenciana, seabass with shrimp and clams, rabbit in a special sauce, gazpacho, garlic soup, or a special cassoulet made with lamb, pork stew, sausage, and beans. For dessert you might like to try the pineapple custard. Meals are served daily except Sunday. If you happen to be in the neighborhood on Monday after 11 p.m., the establishment hosts live jazz concerts.

De Ciro, 38 Avenida Independencia (tel. 689-6046). As you approach this well-known rendezvous point, you may imagine you're arriving at an embassy rather than at a restaurant. This feeling is engendered by the fact that the ochre-colored villa was originally intended to house the Dominican/American cultural center before it became a restaurant in 1971. Guests usually enjoy a drink in the warmly paneled Piccolo Bar before entering the light-blue dining room.

Full meals usually cost from RD $35 ($12.60) and may include such specialties as spaghetti with red or white clam sauce, a full array of pasta dishes, chateaubriand, chicken cacciatore, grilled lobster, deviled shrimp, Sicilian-style seabass, minestrone, or stracciatella—in all, a wide selection of Italian foods. The restaurant is open daily except Tuesday for lunch and dinner.

Restaurant Chez François, 53 Padre Billini (tel. 688-2619). A large woven tapestry from Ecuador, decorated with orange dragons, serves as a visual focal point of this high-ceilinged French restaurant in the old city, about a block from the cathedral. The air-conditioned establishment serves French specialties amid bouquets of colorful flowers in clay vases, terracotta tiles, a collection of cane-backed chairs, bentwood chairs, and posters showing scenes of the French countryside. The Swiss owner is François.

Specialties include fondue bourguignonne, pork curry, grilled crayfish with three sauces, frog legs, onion soup, and a variety of other dishes. The restaurant is especially noted for the array of tempting savory sauces that the chef pours over his meat dishes. Expect to pay about RD $30 ($10.80) for a full meal here. The restaurant is open every day, and reservations are advised, since the number of tables is limited.

El Rincon Argentino, 501 Avenida George Washington (tel. 685-4411), serves Argentinian specialties amid a decor of roughly finished ceilings and walls fashioned from planking. Cowhides attached to the walls along with South American memorabilia make you think you're somewhere out on the pampas. Tango music is usually played around 11:30 p.m., and some of the crowd is likely to get up from the long wooden tables to dance. A featured dish here is lomitos, farina patties stuffed with different kinds of meat. If a buffet isn't featured the night of your visit, the meal might consist of grilled shrimp, shrimp creole, seabass filet, seabass with garlic, flambéed meats, steak Diane, a seafood platter, or filete al pimienta. Appetizers include ceviche and fried cheese balls. All dishes are served with potatoes, salad, yucca, or plantain. Full meals usually begin at RD $30 ($10.80). The restaurant is open seven days a week after 2 p.m.

An authentic German-Bavarian inn in Santo Domingo is **Gerd's Hoff-bräuhaus,** 417 Padre Billini (tel. 685-9802), a gemütlich restaurant serving real south German food. For a change from Spanish-influenced cuisine, you can enjoy sauerkraut, sauerbraten, roast pork with dumplings (schweinebraten mit knödel), or schnitzel, among other specialties of the house. A full meal will cost around RD $20 ($7.20). Gerd's is closed Thursday but open from 11 a.m. to 1 a.m. the rest of the week.

La Bahia, 1 Avenida George Washington (tel. 682-4022), is an unprepossessing type of place right on the Malecón. You'd never know that it serves some of the best, and freshest, seafood in the Dominican Republic. One predawn morning as I passed by, early-rising fishermen were waiting outside to sell the chef their latest catch. Rarely in the Caribbean will you find a restaurant with such a diversity of seafood offerings. For your appetizer, you might prefer ceviche, seabass marinated in lime juice, or lobster cocktail. Soups come from the sea and are likely to contain big chunks of lobster as well as shrimp. See if any of these specialties tempt you—kingfish in coconut sauce, seabass Ukrainian style (a specialty—how did they get the recipe?), baked red snapper, and seafood in the pot. A lot of unusual offerings show up on the menu. Conch is a special favorite with the chef, who knows how to prepare it in many ways. After a big seafood dinner here, costing from RD $30 ($10.80), desserts are superfluous. No reservations are needed.

Jade Garden, Hotel Embajador, Avenida Sarasota (tel. 533-2131), is clearly in the front rank in Chinese cookery in Santo Domingo. The management even sent its cooks to Hong Kong to learn some of the secret methods of Peking and northern Chinese cookery, and they returned to please customers with an array of specialties, including such delectables as minced pigeon, soya bean chicken, sweet corn soup (superb), lemon duck (even better!), sweet-and-sour pork, deep-fried fish, and fortune chicken, finished off with a toffee banana. The pièce de résistance is the Peking duck, which the chef roasts in an open-fire stove. Before peeling it with a special knife, it is presented to the diners who ordered it. Most of Jade Garden's ducks come from Tientsin, China, where they are well fed and restricted from movement to give their meat a special texture. Depending on what dinner you select, your tab might be as little as RD $20 ($7.20), going up to RD $30 ($10.80). Luncheons are great buys, one set meal costing from RD $10 ($3.60), another from RD $15 ($5.40). Hours are noon to 3 p.m. and 7:30 to 11:30 p.m.

Ananda, 7 Casimiro de Moya, corner of Pasteur (tel. 682-4465), is a vegetarian restaurant where you can enjoy good food in an informal, cozy room with Oriental or classical music supplying the background effect. The menu here, under the direction of Cristina Rosario de Pérez, includes a dish of the day as well as other foods all combining natural products. You can feast on a salad made of cucumber, tomato, celery, and spinach, black beans and rice with vegetables, while rice cooked in Chinese or Hindu style with fruits or vegetables, or even a "grilled steak"—actually made of glutin and served with a tasty sauce. Try the ripe plantain pudding for dessert with a local flavor, or perhaps you'd like the peanut or whole-bread pudding. All the desserts at Ananda are made with brown sugar or honey. A meal will cost from RD $20 ($7.30) at this health-oriented restaurant.

La Canasta, in the Santo Domingo Sheraton, 365 Avenida George Washington (tel. 685-5151), is the best late-night dining spot in the capital. Between the Omni Casino and the Omni Disco (both recommended separately in the nightlife section), the restaurant is not only economical, but it serves until 6 a.m. If you're an early diner, you can also drop in. The best news is that the restaurant serves the most popular Dominican dishes, culled from favorite recipes throughout the country. A complete meal costs from RD $15 ($5.40) and up. Among the favorite local offerings are sancocho, a typical stew with a variety of meats and yucca, and mondongo (tripe cooked with tomatoes and peppers). Unusual offerings include goatmeat braised in a rum sauce and beefsteak creole style. One section of the menu is labeled the "Dominican inflation fighter" and includes such offerings as crunchy chicken wings. You can also order soups such as fish or black bean and a selection from the sandwich basket.

3. Exploring the Capital

Spruced, as never before, Santo Domingo, a treasure trove, is part of a major government-sponsored restoration. The old town is still partially enclosed by remnants of its original city wall. Its narrow streets, old stone buildings, and forts are like nothing else in the Caribbean. The only thing missing is the clank of the armor of the conquistadores.

Old and modern Santo Domingo meet at the **Parque Independencia,** a big city square whose most prominent feature is its Altar de la Patria, a shrine dedicated to the three fathers of the country, Duarte, Sanchez, and Mella, all of whom are buried here. These men led the country's fight for freedom from Haiti in 1844. As in provincial Spanish cities, the square is a popular gathering point for families on Sunday afternoon. Old men sit in the sun and play Dominoes. El Conde Gate stands at the entrance to the plaza. It was named in 1955 for Count (El Conde) de Penalva, the governor who resisted the forces of Admiral Penn, the leader of a British invasion. It was also the site of the March for Independence in 1844, and holds a special place in the hearts of Dominicans.

Heading east along El Conde Street—a microcosm of Dominican life— you reach Columbus Square, with a large bronze statue honoring the discoverer. The statue was made in 1897 by a French sculptor, Gilbert. On the south side of the plaza, the **Cathedral of Santa Maria la Menor** is the oldest cathedral in the Americas, built in 1514. Characterized by a gold coral limestone facade, it is a stunning example of the Spanish Renaissance style. In the 450-year-old nave, four baroque columns, carved to resemble royal palms, support a marble sarcophagus holding what is believed to be the remains of Columbus. (It must be pointed out that several other locations make this same claim.) The cathedral was visited by Pope John Paul II in 1979, who was shown its elaborate altars and shrines and delicate carvings. A masterpiece, the carved high altar is faced with silver from the country's mines. A guide will probably attach himself to you, and he may be worth it. Get him to show you the *Madonna* by Murillo, the silver carillon by Cellini, and a crown, studded with emeralds, once worn by Queen Isabella of Spain.

The most outstanding structure in the old city is the Alcázar, the palace built for the son of Columbus, Diego, and his wife, the niece of Ferdinand, king of Spain. Diego became the colony's governor in 1509, and Santo Domingo rose as the hub of Spanish commerce and culture in America. Constructed of native coral limestone, it stands on the bluffs of the Ozama River. For more than 60 years it was the center of the Spanish court, entertaining such distinguished visitors as Cortes, Ponce de Leon, and Balboa. After its heyday, it fell on bad days, or rather two disastrous centuries, as invaders pillaged it. By 1835 it lay in virtual ruins; and it wasn't until 1957, in Trujillo's day, that the Dominican government finally restored it to its former splendor. Its nearly two dozen rooms and open-air loggias are decorated with paintings and period tapestries, as well as 16th-century antiques. It is open from 9 a.m. to noon and 2:30 to 5:30 p.m. daily, except Tuesday, charging 75¢ admission for adults, 25¢ for children. The same ticket entitles you to visit the **Museu Virreinal** or Museum of the Viceroys, adjacent to the Alcázar. It houses period furnishings and tapestries, as well as paintings dating from the colonial period.

The **Casa del Cordon,** or "Cord House," stands near the Alcázar at the corner of Calles Emiliano Tejera and Isabel la Católica. It was named for the cord of the Franciscan order which is carved above the door. Francisco de Garay, who came to Hispaniola with Columbus, built the casa in 1503–1504, making it the oldest stone house in the western hemisphere. Among important events that took place within the walls of the Casa del Cordon was the time it lodged the first Royal Audience of the New World which performed as the Supreme Court of Justice in the island and the rest of the West Indies. On another occasion, in January 1586, as a memorable gesture, the noble ladies of Santo Domingo gathered here to donate their jewelry as ransom demanded by Sir Francis Drake in return for his promise to leave the city. The restoration of this historical manor was financed by the Banco Popular Dominicano, where its executive offices are found.

Also in the shadow of the Alcázar, **La Atarazana** is a fully restored section which centered around one of the New World's first arsenals, serving the conquistadores. It extends for a city block, catacombed with merchandise-loaded shops, art galleries (both Haitian and Dominican paintings), and boutiques, as well as some good native and international restaurants, some of which have been recommmended previously.

Just behind river moorings, the oldest street in the New World is called Calle las Damas, or "Street of the Ladies." Some visitors assume this was a bordello district. Actually it wasn't. Rather, the elegant ladies of the viceregal court used to promenade there in the evening. It is lined with colonial buildings, including the government-owned and already-recommended Hostal Nicolas de Ovando.

Across the street, the **National Pantheon**—a fine example of Spanish American colonial architecture—was originally a Jesuit monastery in 1714, although it was later used as a warehouse for storing tobacco. Once it was a theater as well, and its massive size is characterized by austere lines. Trujillo had restored it in 1955, projecting it as his burial place, but instead one chapel preserves the ashes of the martyrs of June 14, 1959, who tried vainly to overthrow the dictator. Admisstion free, it can be visited Monday through Saturday.

From here you can walk a few steps north to visit the chapel of **Our Lady of Remedies,** where the first inhabitants of the city used to attend Mass before the cathedral was erected.

The **Museo de las Casas Reales,** or Museum of the Royal Houses, also stands on the Calle las Damas (tel. 682-4202). Originally it was the Palace of Justice and the governor's residence. Through artifacts, tapestries, maps, including a re-created courtroom, it traces Santo Domingo's history from 1492 to 1821. Gilded, elegant furniture, pieces of armor, and other colonial artifacts, all inspected by King Juan Carlos of Spain in 1976, make it the most interesting of all museums of Old Santo Domingo. It contains replicas of the three ships commanded by Columbus, and one exhibit is said to hold part of the ashes of the famed explorer. You can see, in addition to pre-Columbian art, parts of two galleons sunk in 1724 on their way from Spain to Mexico, along with remnants of the Spanish ship *Concepción*. There's even a bottle of wine dating from 1724. Hours are daily, except Monday from 9 a.m. to 5 p.m., and admission is 50¢.

On Padre Billini, formerly University Street, at the corner of Arzobispo Meriño, is the **Casa de Tostado** (Tostado House) whose beautiful Gothic double window (geminated window) is the only one existing today in the New World. The house was first owned by the scribe Francisco Tostado, and inherited by his son of the same name, a professor, writer, and poet who was the victim in 1586 of a shot fired during Drake's bombardment of Santo Domingo. The Casa de Tostado, which at one time was the archbishop's palace, now houses the **Museum of the Dominican Family,** showing how life was in the 19th century for a well-to-do household. It can be visited daily except Monday from 9 a.m. to 5:30 p.m. Admission is 50¢ for adults, 25¢ for children.

Museo del Hombre Dominicano, Plaza de la Cultura, Calle Pedro Henríquez Ureña (tel. 687-3622), houses the most important collection in the world of artifacts made by the Taino Indians, who greeted Columbus in 1492. Thousands of magnificently sculptured ceramic, stone, bone, and shell works are on display. Daily, except Monday, hours are 10 a.m. to 5 p.m., and admission is 50¢.

If time remains, try also to see the **Puerta de la Misericordia.** Part of the original city wall, this "Gate of Mercy" was once a refuge for colonists fleeing hurricanes and earthquakes.

The **Monastery of San Francisco** is but a mere ruin, lit at night. That any part of it still is standing must be counted as a miracle. It was destroyed by earthquakes, pillaged by Drake, bombarded by French artillery.

In total contrast to the colonial city, modern Santo Domingo dates from the Trujillo era. A city of broad, palm-shaded avenues, its seaside drive is called **Avenida George Washington,** more popularly known as the **Malecón.** This boulevard is filled with restaurants, as well as hotels and nightclubs.

In downtown Santo Domingo, it is now possible to visit the **National Palace,** the three-story, domed structure ordered built by President Trujillo in 1939 and used as the seat of government since its inauguration in 1947. The edifice, considered an architectural triumph in the Dominican Republic, was designed by Italian architect Guido D'Alessandro. It stands in landscaped gardens, where concerts are sometimes held. Because the first floor is mainly occupied by staff offices, visits start on the second floor, where you'll see the Gallery of Presidents. Paintings of the Dominican coat-of-arms from the first design to the one now in use are also displayed. In this room too are the velvet-upholstered, carved mahogany chair used by Trujillo and a mammoth conference table. Of particular interest is the Hall of Caryatides on the third floor, surrounded by 44 marble columns topped by carvings of female figures, separated by mirrors. A presidential suite on this floor is used to house visiting dignitaries. Visitors are sure to be impressed by the extensive use of marble throughout the palace, most of it the country's own product. For a guided tour of the palace, call 689-1131, ext. 211. Admission is free.

The former site of the Trujillo mansion, the **Plaza de la Cultura** has been turned into a large, attractive park, containing the National Library and the National Theater, which sponsors folkloric dances, opera, outdoor jazz concerts, traveling art exhibits, classical ballet, and music concerts. Also in the center, the Gallery of Modern Art has an exhibition of national and international paintings (the emphasis on native-born artists), as well as antiques.

I'd also suggest a visit to the **Paseo de los Indios,** that sprawling five-mile park with a restaurant, fountain displays, and a lake.

About a 20-minute drive from the heart of the city is **Los Tres Ojos** or "three eyes," which stare at you across the Ozama River from Old Santo Domingo. There is a trio of lagoons set in scenic caverns, with lots of stalactites and stalagmites. One lagoon is 40 feet deep, another 20 feet, and yet a third—known as "Ladies Bath"—only 5 feet deep. A Dominican Tarzan will sometimes dive off the walls of the cavern into the deepest lagoon. The area is equipped with walkways. The location is off the Autopista de las Americas on the way to the airport and the beach at Boca Chica.

In the northern sector of Santo Domingo, the **Botanical Gardens** at Arroyo Hondo are the biggest with the most varied plant life in all of Latin America. In 1.8 milion square meters, all the flowers and lush vegetation of the Dominican Republic can be seen anytime from 9 a.m. to noon and 2 to 6 p.m., and admission is 50¢ for adults, 25¢ for children. Seek out, in particular, the Japanese

Park, the Great Ravine, and the largest floral clock in the world. You can tour the grounds by horse carriage or else take a boat. The gardens are closed Monday.

4. Sports, Shopping, Nightlife

Typical of Latin cities, Santo Domingo has a pulsating life both day and night. I'll preview some of the action in the sections ahead, beginning with—

THE SPORTING LIFE: The Dominican Republic may have some great beaches, but they aren't in Santo Domingo. The principal beach resort in the area of the capital is at **Boca Chica,** five miles east of the airport, about a 45-minute taxi ride. The great beaches are at **Puerto Plata,** but that's a rough, three-hour drive from the capital, and at **La Romana,** a two-hour drive to the east. Most of the major Santo Domingo hotels have swimming pools.

Snorkeling and Scuba

Divers rate the Dominican Republic high for its so-called virgin coral reefs, where you can explore ancient shipwrecks and undersea gardens with an endless variety of marine life.

Mundo Submarino, 99 Gustavo Mejia Ricart (tel. 566-0340), is the best in Santo Domingo. It offers a snorkel tour from 9 a.m. to 1:30 p.m. from the beach or a secluded cove. A minimum of three divers is required, paying $30 per head. Advanced scuba tours are featured at the same time—daily diving by boat, in both a shallow and a deep reef with steep walls. The possibilities for photography are excellent. All equipment is included at a cost of $30 for one dive, $45 for two dives.

Golf

Serious golfers head for **La Romana** or the course that Robert Trent Jones designed at **Playa Dorada,** in the vicinity of Puerto Plata. Golf is also available in the capital at the **Santo Domingo Country Club,** an 18-hole course which grants privileges to guests of most of the major hotels. The rule here is members first, which means it's impossible for weekend games.

Tennis

The major hotels have very good courts, especially at the **Hotel Santo Domingo** (three courts, two lit for night play), **Santo Domingo Sheraton, Embajador, Lina,** and the **Dominican Concorde** (eight championship courts). The cost is usually $10 per hour at night. Some of these courts are lit for night games.

Polo

Made so famous during Trujillo's day, polo is still a popular sport. Polo fields are in Santo Domingo at Sierra Prieta, with games played on weekends.

Baseball

As in America, the most popular spectator sport is baseball, and many of the country's native-born sons have gone on to the major leagues. From October through February, games are played at stadiums in Santo Domingo. Check the local newspaper for schedules and locations of the nearest game.

Horse Racing

Santo Domingo's race track, **Perla Antillana,** schedules races on Tuesday, Wednesday, Thursday, and Saturday. You can make it a day here, having lunch at the track's restaurant.

Cock Fighting

Dominicans like this brutal "sport," but it offends many foreign visitors. However, if you want to see a cockfight, go to the **Santo Domingo Cockfighting Coliseum,** Avenida Luperton (tel. 565-3844), across from the Alas del Caribe Airport. This is a modern installation, and you'll see the spectators reach fever excitement. Stakes are high, and the cocks are well trained. The action is followed on closed-circuit TV, as guests sit in air conditioning on comfortable seats.

Deep-Sea Fishing

Prize-winning marlins, sailfish, dolphins, tuna, barracuda, and snappers are regularly caught in Dominican waters. **Mundo Submarino,** 99 Gustavo Mejia Ricart (tel. 566-0340), will rent you a boat with crew, gear, bait, and drinks. The company's fully rigged vessels range from 24 to 46 feet. The cost is $50 per person.

For other descriptions of sporting activities, refer to the sections under La Romana and Puerta Plata.

SHOPPING: The best buys are in handcrafted native items, especially amber jewelry, the national gem, a petrified fossil resin millions of years old. The pine from which the resin came disappeared from the earth long ago. The origins of amber were a mystery until the beginning of the 19th century when scientists determined the source of the gem.

Look for pieces of amber with trapped objects such as insects and spiders inside the enveloping material. Colors range from a bright yellow to black, but most of the gems are golden in tone. Amber deposits in the Dominican Republic were only discovered in the past three decades. Fine-quality amber jewelry is sold throughout the country.

A semiprecious stone of light blue (sometimes a dark-blue color), larimar is the Dominican turquoise. The Dominican Republic is the only country in the world where this variety of turquoise is found. It often makes striking jewelry, and is sometimes mounted with wild boar's teeth, but you may prefer to make a less obvious statement with silver.

Ever since the Dominicans presented John F. Kennedy with what became his favorite rocker, visitors have wanted to take home a rocking chair, a piece of furniture popular throughout the country. To simplify transport, these rockers are often sold unassembled (you put them together when you get home).

Other good buys include Dominican rum, hand-knit articles, macramé, ceramics, and crafts in native mahogany. Always haggle over the price, particularly in the open-air markets. No stallkeeper expects you to pay the first price asked. The best shopping streets are El Conde, the oldest and most traditional shop-flanked avenue, and Avenida Mella.

In the colonial section, **La Atarazana** is filled with galleries and gift and jewelry stores, charging inflated prices. Duty-free shops are found at the airport, in the capital at the **Centro de los Heroes,** and at both the Hotel Santo Domingo and the Hotel Embajador. Shopping hours are generally from 9 a.m. to 12:30 p.m. and from 2 to 5 p.m., Monday through Saturday.

Head first for the **Mercado Modelo,** the National Market, on the Avenida Mella, filled with stall after stall of craft products. Of course, this is a workaday market, catering to the needs of the capital's citizens, so it also overflows with spices, fruits, and vegetables. The merchants will be most eager to sell, and you can easily get lost in the crunch. Remember to bargain for any item that strikes your fancy. You'll see a lot of tortoise-shell work here, but exercise caution, since many species, especially the hawksbill, are on the endangered-species list and could be impounded by U.S. Customs if discovered in your luggage. The already-mentioned rockers are for sale here, as are mahogany ware, sandals, baskets, hats, clay braziers for grilling fish, whatever.

If you're worried that that piece of amber you like may be plastic (and you don't want to strike a match to it in front of the stallkeeper), then you can be assured of the real thing at **Ambar Marie,** 19 Rosa Duarte (tel. 682-7539). At this small shop, you can even design your own setting for your choice gem. Look especially for the tear-drop earrings. The shop is in the house of its owner, Marie Louise Taule, who had a Dominican mother and a French father. In a residential area, the shop is open at regular business hours Monday to Friday (closed weekends).

Novo Atarazana, 21 La Atarazana (tel. 689-0582). Although its name would imply that it's new, this is actually one of the best established shops in town. Inside you can purchase pieces of amber, black coral, tortoise shell, leather goods, woodcarvings, and even rocking chairs. It's open every day, closing at noon on Sunday.

Ambar Tres, 3 La Atarazana (tel. 688-0474), lies in the colonial section of the old city. This shop sells jewelry made from coconut shells, cow-horn earrings, mahogany carvings, watercolors, oil paintings, and tortoise shell. The shop is open seven days a week, but it closes at noon on Sunday.

Galería de Arte Nader, 9 La Atarazana (tel. 688-0969), in the center of the most historical section of town, is a well-known gallery that sells so many Dominican and Haitian paintings that they're sometimes stacked in rows against the walls. There's an ancient courtyard in back if you want a glimpse of how things looked in the Spanish colonies hundreds of years ago. The gallery is open daily except Sunday from 9:30 a.m. to 1 p.m. and 3:30 to 7 p.m.

The **Plaza Criolla** is a modern shopping complex, with a distinguished design theme. A complex of shops is set in gardens with tropical shrubbery and flowers, facing the Olympic Center on 27 de Febrero. The architecture makes generous use of natural woods, and a covered wooden walkway links the stalls together.

NIGHTLIFE: From a hectic night of merengue to gambling casinos to disco dancing, Santo Domingo has some of the most varied nightlife in the Caribbean.

Nightclubs

Meson de la Cueva, Avenida Mirador del Sur (tel. 533-2818), is a charming restaurant and nightclub built in a natural cave 50 feet under the ground, providing live music for dancing. Shows with merengue music are offered. To reach it, you descend a perilous open-backed iron stairway. At first I thought this was a mere gimmicky club until I sampled the food, finding it among the best in the capital.

Waiters bring in one good-tasting platter after another, placing them on your table perched under stalagmites and stalactites if you've been sent to the grottoes. For an appetizer you're faced with the usual selection—shrimp cocktail, onion soup, or gazpacho. Instead of those, however, you may go for the bisque of seafood or red snapper chowder. Among the main-course selections, you'll find "gourmet" beefsteak, fresh seabass in red sauce, tournedos, and coq au vin. You can finish off with a sorbet. Meals begin at RD $30 ($10.80) per person, plus the cost of your drinks. If you go just for the music and dancing, and many do, you'll be charged an entrance fee of $3 per person. After midnight, the waiters present a show of their own. The place is open every day.

José, 555 Avenida George Washington (tel. 688-8242), is one of the leading nightclubs in town, costing from RD $25 ($9) and up, depending on the attraction. A different show (usually Vegas style) is presented every night. Monday to Thursday, show time is 11:30 p.m. On Friday and Saturday there are two shows, an "early" one at 11:30 p.m. and a late revue at 4 a.m. There is also music for disco dancing when the show isn't on.

Sexto Sentido (Sixth Sense), 7 Padre Billini (tel. 688-7550), presents a complete nightclub show, with dancing girls, comedians, and singers. The Fantasia Erotica portion of the show combines costumes, dancing, and lights in lively display. The club, with red curtains and carpets, charges from RD $25 ($9), depending on the show, and music is provided for dancing when the stage is dark. Even if you don't understand Spanish and can't appreciate the comic passages, the sensual performance of the dancers need no interpreter. The club is open from 10 p.m. to 4 a.m.

Pubs and Bars

Three of the leading rendezvous points of Santo Domingo are close to one another, in the oldest section of the city. **The Village Pub,** Calle Hostos (tel. 689-5408), is my favorite nightlife spot in town, and if you appreciate lively places, you may like it too. At this sprawling complex, you can talk quietly in the tropical garden below one of the soaring trees or enjoy watching the oversize video screen where films of the world's greatest rock stars compete for attention with the crowds jostling at the stand-up bar. Just off the entrance vestibule you'll discover what looks like someone's elegant private living room, complete with unusual busts and old musical instruments. The place is open daily from 5 p.m. Most drinks cost around $2.

When you're ready for a change, you can drop into **Raffles,** next door on Calle Hostos. You'll be greeted by a John Lennon collage near the entrance. You may have to hunt around for a table somewhere in the series of high-ceilinged Spanish-style rooms with heavy beams, masses of plants, soothing candlelight, dimly lit Indian art, and textured baskets hanging beneath staircases leading to nowhere. Any lone woman who ventures in here will probably be approached whether she's looking for it or not. The bar opens at 7 p.m. daily except Sunday. You'll pay $2 for most drinks.

Drake's Pub, 25 La Atarazana (tel. 685-3036), is one of the most popular and atmospheric bars in the colonial zone. An American and English enterprise, it is run by John Gillin and Gary Hampton. Usually packed in the evening, it has an enclosed wine cellar and a wooden bar made from wild almond. Most people come here just to drink, although you can order barbecue beef, ham and cheese, or a pastrami sandwich in the $2.50 range. One of the more loyal patrons even brings his alcoholic dog.

Piano Bars

Most of the "chic stops" are in the big hotels. **Las Palmas,** at the Hotel Santo Domingo, Avenida Independencia (tel. 532-1511), was decorated by the country's best known designer, Oscar de la Renta. Under a high-vaulted ceiling, mirrored walls are painted with palm fronds. This is the best piano bar in town. A terrace, open to the sea, adjoins the bar. Music starts at 6 p.m., the "happy hour," when hors d'oeuvres are free. Romantic music is often played, and you can hear, on occasion, jazz, samba, and the bossa nova. Dancing music is played on certain nights. There is never a cover charge, and beer costs from RD $3 ($1.08).

The **Fontana Bar** of El Embajador hotel, Avenida Sarasota (tel. 533-2131), is a place to enjoy good music whether it's by the piano player and vocalist early in the evening or the orchestra later, with a variety of tunes for listening or dancing. The rhythms range from Dominican folk songs to samba to the highly popular merengue. The bar, which faces the front door of the hotel's lobby, is inviting, with rattan chairs and wooden tables, plus cozy candlelit corners in the evening. The Fontana also looks out on a patio leading to a swimming pool. Drinks cost from RD $8 ($2.88).

Disco Action

Disco-hopping in the Dominican Republic is an after-dinner ritual, although many couples postpone their almost-obligatory visits until after the end of a movie or whatever. At that time, even the most dedicated career woman may don sequins and other alluring garments for an evening out at such places as—

Bella Blu, The Malecón (tel. 689-2911). At this popular disco, a visitor will get a chance to watch some of the most turned-on dancers in the country strutting their stuff. Because of its location, Dominican wits claim that the party inside is only an extension of the carnival going on along the Malecón outside. The establishment has light-blue canopies attached to a vivid pink exterior which has art deco accents and curved-glass walls. Service is prompt, which pleases the energetic clientele whose average age is between 20 and 40. Everyone in the capital knows the Bella Blu, which opens around 9 p.m. and stays busy as late as 4 a.m. The cover charge is around RD $10 ($3.60), and drinks cost RD $7 ($2.52).

Columbus Disco, in front of the National Therater, is the favorite of many Dominicans, and the sophisticated interior decor certainly contributes to its popularity. The entrance area is painted purple and black and funnels guests into a labyrinthine interior filled with intimate nooks and crannies—areas of discreet intimacy. Of course, if someone wants to dance, which a lot of people do here, there's a vivid red dance floor surrounded with chairs. Entrance here costs around RD $10 ($3.60) and a beer at the mirrored bar goes for RD $7 ($2.52). The establishment is closed on Monday. The Columbus is near the Hotel Lina.

Alexander's, 23 Avenida Pasteur (no phone), caters to a young crowd which appreciates the electronic decor and the punk rock music. If you're looking for a Latin version of the Mudd Club in New York, this may be the place for you. If you're in town only on a Tuesday, you'll probably find Alexander's closed.

The **Neon Discotheque,** Hotel Santo Domingo North/Hispaniola, Avenida Independencia (tel. 533-7111), is one of the town's best established discos. It offers Latin jazz with different guest stars each week, although disco dancing under flashing lights is one of the main reasons for its popularity. The clientele tends to be somewhat formal compared to that of other nightclubs of Santo Domingo. You might see Oscar de la Renta and some of his friends among the well-dressed patrons, most of whom seem to be over 30. The decor is done in purple, blue, and red, contributing a colorful note to the sensuous merengue music and dancing. The Neon charges cover charge of around RD $6 ($2.16) on weekends, RD $4 ($1.44) the rest of the week. The place is closed on Monday.

The **Omni Disco** at the Sheraton Santo Domingo, 365 Avenida George Washington (tel. 685-5151), is popular with tourists and some of the sons and daughters of the country's most prestigious families, who come here to drink and dance. The action goes on late at night, and the setting is plush. The cover charge ranges from RD $5 ($1.80) to RD $10 ($3.60), depending on the day of the week.

L'Azotea, Dominican Concorde Hotel, Avenida Anacaona, Mirador del Sur (tel. 532-2531), has the most dramatic premises of any disco in town. On the top floor of this first-class hotel, it is one of the most attractive after-dark rendezvous points in Santo Domingo, with stunning views. Occasionally, live entertainment is featured, and there is always recorded music. The entrance ranges from RD $15 ($5.40) to RD $20 ($7.20), depending on what act is booked.

Jazz

Café-Concierto El Bodegon, 152 Arzobispo Meriño (tel. 682-6864), oppostie the cathedral in the most historical section of town, is the place to go late Monday night if you're a jazz aficionado. That's when concerts are given in this 15th-century house, beginning at 11 p.m. However, this popular bar, attached to one of the capital's leading restaurants (see my dining recommendation), is always a good place to stop in for a drink, served for around RD $3 ($1.08) amid a collection of Dominican pictures. The house special is the rum caña, made with rum, orange juice, and sugarcane. On Monday, when the changing series of jazz bands plays under the stone arches behind the bar area, the cover charge is RD $4 ($1.44).

Casinos

Santo Domingo has several major gambling casinos. The largest is **El Embadajor Casino,** Avenida Sarasota (tel. 533-2131), where you'll hear the whirr and clicks from the gaming tables. The popular games of blackjack, craps, and roulette are offered from 3 p.m. to 4 a.m. In between gaming sessions, you can spend an intimate moment at La Fontana, their casual bar where hors d'oeuvres are served.

Hotel Naco Casino, 22 Avenida Tiradentes (tel. 562-6191), also offers roulette, craps, and blackjack. The doors open at 4 p.m., shutting again at 4 a.m.

One of the most stylish casinos is at the Sheraton Santo Domingo, 365 Avenida George Washington (tel. 685-5151). Called the **Omni Casino,** it has a bilingual staff offering blackjack, craps, baccarat, and keno, among other popular games. It's open daily from 3 p.m. to 4 a.m., and players get free cigarettes and drinks.

Yet another casino, a bit far from the heart of the city for my taste, is the **Dominican Concorde Casino,** Avenida Anacaona, Mirador del Sur (tel. 532-2531), which is about half an hour's drive from the airport, bordering the Paseo de los Indios. If you're a high roller, you'll find that it has the highest limits in the city. The most popular games are wheel of fortune and keno, along with blackjack, baccarat, and roulette.

5. East to La Romana

On the southest coast of the Dominican Republic, about a two-hour drive east of Santo Domingo, lies this rich sugarcane and cattle-raising country that was turned into a tropical paradise resort of refinement and luxury living by Gulf + Western. A typical Dominican town, La Romana itself contains one of the largest sugar mills in the world.

THE ULTIMATE RESORT: Casa de Campo (tel. 682-2111) offers the greatest resort in the entire Caribbean area—and the competition is stiff. It brings a whole new dimension to a holiday. Gulf + Western took a vast hunk of coastal land, more than 7000 acres in all, allowing enough breathing space for everyone, and carved out this stunningly chic resort. The hotel attracts many celebrities as well as titans of industry. Some have built private homes on the grounds, including Oscar de la Renta. The ubiquitous Miami architect, William Cox, helped create it, and de la Renta provided the style and flair in some of the interiors, even designing the long, white flowing gowns, with pink bows and turbans, the waitresses wear when they serve you a piña colada.

Most of the buildings are one or two stories high, and they never go beyond three. Built of native stone, they are finished in stucco, with red corrugated roofs and local mahogany. Tiles, Dominican paintings, and louvered doors, as well as those flamboyant de la Renta patterned fabrics, characterize most of the interiors. The main buildings form a network, constructed of native-grown unpainted wood, each connected by walkways and sheltered by roofs, a combination of naturalism and the late Frank Lloyd Wright. Gardens blossom with flowering shrubbery and scenic vistas confront you in every direction.

Red-roofed casitas are situated in two-story structures around the main building, and these are the least expensive accommodations. *In summer, charges are only $70 to $85, based on either single or double occupancy. Suites rent from $120.* In the high season these same accommodations rent for $200, either single or double occupancy, and from $300 in a suite.

Villas cluster along the golf course, using the broad Bermuda fairways as common lawns; and there are more villas built along the sea. The tennis village cluster of villas at **La Terraza** is perched high on the hills, looking out across the cane, fairway, and meadows to the Caribbean. Villas, furnished with a kind of rustic Dominican elegance, come with bath and shower, a large living room, kitchen, refrigerator, and balcony.

Mr. Cox designed each villa so that it offers either a private terrace or veranda overlooking some land or sea vista. *In summer, a one-bedroom villa rents for $120.* In winter, these golf and tennis villas go up in price—from $275 for one bedroom.

At the core of everything is a wonderland swimming pool—three, in fact—each on a different level, with thatch huts on stilts to provide beverages and light meals. Perched over the pool is La Caña, the two-level bar and lounge, with a thatched roof but no walls. Dinner is on a rustic roofed terrace. The food is among the best in the Dominican Republic, and the chefs always make it interesting. Perhaps they'll throw a roast suckling pig barbecue right on the beach, or tempt you with some locally caught frog legs. Most of the beef used is grown right on the plains of La Romana.

SPORTS: La Romana, on 7000 acres of lush tropical turf, you'll find two Pete Dye golf courses, a stable of horses with twice-weekly polo, a private marina with deep-sea and river trips, snorkeling on live reefs, skeet and trap ranges, plus 17 tennis courts.

Golf

The **Casa de Campo** courses are known to dedicated golfers everywhere—in fact, *Golf* magazine called it "the finest golf resort in the world." The course, Teeth of the Dog, has also been called "a thing of almighty beauty," and it is. The site of the "Eisenhower Cup" World Amateur Tournament in 1974, it is a ruggedly natural terrain, with seven holes skirting the ocean. Opened in 1977, the Links is the inland course, built on sandy soil away from the beach. Greens fees are $20; cart fees (two persons), is also $20. Québec-born Gilles Gagnon, the head golf professional, will answer your questions (call him at 692-6956, ext. 3115). Hours are 7 a.m. to 6 p.m.

Beaches

Bayahibe is a large, palm-fringed sandy crescent reached by a 20-minute launch trip or else by road, a 30-minute drive from La Romana. In addition, **La Minitas** is tiny, but nice, an immaculate little beach and lagoon. Free transportation is by horse-drawn buckboard, leaving from Casa de Campo every hour.

Tennis

A total of 13 clay and four hard-surface courts at Casa de Campo, the best on the island, are lit for night play. Tennis pro Juan Rios and his assistant, Emilio Vasquez, are available for lessons and frequently arrange some of the biggest tennis tournaments in the Caribbean. The courts are available seven days a week from 8 a.m. to 10 p.m., and an hour of daylight net time costs RD $20 ($7.20), while 60 minutes of nighttime play is RD $24 ($8.64). You can rent a racquet for RD $5 ($1.80) an hour. The services of a ball boy cost between RD $5 ($1.80) and RD $6 ($2.16) an hour.

Water Sports

The **Casa de Campo Yachting and Beach Club** (tel. 682-2111) is one of the most complete water-sports facilities anywhere in the Dominican Republic. Reservations and information on any seaside activity can be arranged through the resort's concierge. A sampling of what's available includes the following:

Half-day snorkeling trips costing around RD $33 ($11.88) per person last either from 8:30 to 11:30 a.m. or from 2 to 5 p.m. A minimum of six persons is required for this. Full-day outings are organized to nearby reefs if enough people are interested, lasting from 8:30 a.m. to 2 p.m., costing around RD $50 ($18) per person.

You can charter a boat for a cruise to snorkel or fish. The resort maintains two Bertram boats, with a minimum of eight persons required per outing. Only four can fish at a time. A half-day cruise costs RD $750 ($205.20); a full day, RD $660 ($237.60).

Deep-sea fishing with all equipment provided is available for RD $440 ($158.40) for a full day, RD $308 ($110.88) for a half day. For outings like these, the hotel's room-service facility will pack a box lunch.

There are no on-site arrangements for scuba-diving, but the hotel will put interested clients in touch with a nearby place which leads such trips.

Patrons interested in river fishing on the Chavón can arrange trips there through the hotel as well. Some of the biggest snook ever recorded have been caught here. Half-day trips, lasting from 8 a.m. to noon or noon to 4 p.m., cost RD $44 ($15.84) per person. This is a more private form of activity, as only two persons are permitted in any single boat.

If you only want a look at the famous river which gave Altos de Chavón its name, Casa de Campo arranges river tours from 4 to 6 p.m. daily, costing RD $27.50 ($9.90) per person. Each boat holds a maximum of four.

If all you're looking for is a secluded beach with everything from palm trees to sailboats for rent, you'll appreciate the club's Minitas Beach, where the following rental items are available: snorkeling gear, sunfloats, canoe, Sunfish sailboats, windsurfers, and Hobiecats. The resort offers free transportation to the beach by horse-drawn buckboard every hour. There's a snackbar on the beach.

Polo and Horseback Riding

Jabar Singh, the nephew of the maharajah of Jodhpur, was brought to the Dominican Republic by Trujillo. He's given pointers on polo to such personages as Porfírio Rubirosa and Ramfis Trujillo (in fact, he was in Paris with them, recovering from a match, when word was flashed that the dictator had been assassinated). Now Mr. Singh has found more peaceful employment at Casa de Campo. Here the riding horses are the best in the Caribbean. Mr. Singh never assigns you a horse until he's talked to you and knows your experience. Riding horses with a gaucho rent for about RD $20 ($7.20) per hour. On occasion you can watch a mini-rodeo at La Roma, featuring Dominican cowboys. The riding stable at **Rancho Cajuiles** has quarterhorses bred and trained for the terrain of La Romana.

ALTOS DE CHAVÓN: Again under the daring guiding eye—and purse—of Gulf + Western, an international arts center, known as Altos de Chavón, was created at a point six miles from La Romana and three miles east of Casa de Campo. At the edge of its acreage, on the high banks of the Chavón River, an entire hamlet has been built to house artisans, both local and international, who come here on a rotating basis, teaching sculpture, pottery, silkscreen printing, weaving, dance, and music, among other artistic pursuits.

Here they can work in their craft shops and display their finished wares for sale. The construction was under the energetic guidance of an Italian builder, who was seemingly inspired by a hill town in the Tuscan countryside. He did a stunning job of creating an old-world village. To many, the village already looks as if it has stood there for centuries. It almost suggests a Hollywood movie set, except that everything here is real.

In the center is the red-tiled Church of St. Stanislaus. Surrounding it are "old" houses, along with restaurants on the main plaza, an inn, and other buildings, all over looking the valley with its river. Arcaded shops sell merchandise, and stairways lead to studio apartments for the artisans and their private loggias.

Frank Sinatra inaugurated the 5000-seat auditorium, an ampitheater modeled after the Greek antiquity at Epidaurus. Local and international artists appear here frequently. "Sunset performances" are usually on Friday and Sunday evening.

In addition, the museum, **Museo Arqueologico Regional,** open from 9 a.m. to 9 p.m., is devoted to the legacy of the vanished Taino Indian, displaying artifacts found along the banks of the river.

A narrow walk leads down over a small arched bridge, wending its way to the river below. Before you arrive at the village, there's a large parking area. A bus runs between the Casa de Campo and Altos de Chavón every hour.

A few artists from other cultures are invited to be "in residence" so they can teach the Dominicans how to perfect their art forms.

Where to Stay

La Posada, Altos de Chavón (tel. 682-9656, ext. 2312), is a charming, ten-room, regional-style inn, evoking something that might have been known to El Greco in Toledo, but with far more refined touches, including modern plumbing facilities. The air-conditioned inn has rustic stucco and massive ceiling beams. The location is near a parapet overlooking the gorge. It might be hard to get in here, as many artisans like to book these accommodations, so reservations are absolutely essential. *Summer tariffs are only $60 daily for a room, either single or double occupancy.* This rate rises in winter to $105 daily, either single or double occupancy. For your dining, you can a choice of all the little restaurants in Altos de Chavón (see below).

Where to Dine

La Piazzetta, Altos de Chavón (tel. 682-1239), snuggles happily within the 16th-century-style "village" set high above the Chavón River. Well-prepared and attractively served Italian dinners are served here. The decor is regional, with colorful tiles, high ceilings, and timbers. You might begin with an antipasto misto, following with filet of seabass pizzaiola or rib steak in the Florentine style. Chicken saltimbocca, with sage and prosciutto, is also popular. Your fellow diners are likely to be guests from the deluxe Casa de Campo nearby, enjoying a respite from living in Eden. You'll spend from $18 for dinner, but this tab could rise much higher if you order a costly wine. Dinner is served daily except Monday from 7 to 11 p.m.

La Fonda, Altos de Chavón (tel. 682-2350), styles its cookery as "creole," but what you get is a lovely array of some Dominican dishes not readily available in most of the major resort hotels. By that, I don't mean just rice-and-bean dishes either. Beef and fresh seafood appear regularly on the menu, and vegetables are interesting, including when available, fried yucca (casava). Count yourself lucky if you're here on a night the chef prepares "sancocho," a thick goat stew, the national dish of the Dominican Republic. You can also order lobster Dominican style and conch creole. The decor is regional, including examples of Dominican pottery. There are ceiling fans and stucco walls. and dining is partially al fresco. Dinner, depending on what you order of course, will likely begin at $12, going up to around $22 with wine. La Fonda serves daily except Monday from 11 a.m. to 11 p.m.

Caso del Río, Altos de Chavón (tel. 682-1596), stands high on a cliff, with panoramic vistas of the winding Chavón River. In such a setting, the chef presents an international repertoire of dishes, including fresh fish and seafood dishes. A Valencian-style paella is one of his specialties. Also try his river shrimp with fresh vegetables and herbs. Service is on ceramics made locally in the country, and like all the places at Altos de Chavón, the decor is in a regional style, with locally made furnishings. If you order the most expensive seafood entrees, as do the luxury-minded guests of the Casa de Campo, you might end up spending from $25 for dinner. Go here for one of your most romantic evenings in the Dominican Republic. It is open for dinner, Thursday to Sunday, from 7 to 11 p.m.

Café de Sol (tel. 682-2346). If you want a refreshing snack after your exploration of the mosaic-dotted plaza near the church, you'll probably enjoy this stone-floored indoor/outdoor café. To reach it, you climb a graciously proportioned flight of exterior stone steps to the rooftop of a building whose ground floor houses a jewelry shop. This is the only true outdoor café in the village, and it's so popular that you may encounter most of the executive staff and many of the artists and students who make Altos de Chavón a full-time residence. The outdoor area is ringed with flowers, shaded with an arbor, and accented with unusual masonry that merits a close examination. Open from 7 a.m. to 11 p.m., the café serves simple and appetizing meals with warm-weather specialties including two kinds of salad, croissant sandwiches, three kinds of pizza, Texas-style chili, and burgers. An unadorned burger or a bowl of chili costs around RD $7 ($2.52). The place is closed Monday.

After Dark

Genesis Disco (tel. 682-2340) features just about every kind of music at least once each evening. Clients are wide-ranging in tastes, from the most avant-garde artists to relatively conservative visitors from the resort's corporate headquarters in New York. In any event, if you've always wanted to dance your way through the gamut from rock, blues, salsa, merengue, to a good dose of romantic "music for lovers," this is the place for you. The illuminated and translucent dance floor is studded with multicolored pieces of coral. Open at 8 each night, the disco levies a cover charge of around RD $6 ($2.16). A domestic beer costs around RD $3 ($1.08).

PUNTA CAÑA: At the far eastern tip of the island of Hispaniola, the newest Club Mcd in the Caribbean opened in 1981. The village lies along a reef-protected white beach, said to have some of the best diving areas in the island. It was here that the beleaguered crews of the *Pinta, Niña,* and *Santa Maria* put ashore.

The crew of Columbus wouldn't recognize the place. Some 600 rooms fill three-story clusters of bungalows strung along the beach. Units contain twin beds and open either on the sea or onto a coconut grove. Each is air-conditioned with red tile floors and a private shower/bathroom. Rates vary throughout the year, and there's a $30 membership fee that must be faced if you havn't joined before.

You fly to San Juan, then connect with the club's free flight to Punta Caña's $1.4-million airport, El Aeropuerto del Este, lying just 20 minutes from Club Med village. Land rates for one-week stays from December 8 to April 6 are likely to range from $650 to $820 per person, based on double occupancy. The range in prices depends on the dates chosen. Warning: Tariffs go up during the Christmas and New Year's weeks. During Christmas and New Year's, when air space is the tightest, Club Med (at least in the past) has had its own charter flights to Punta Caña from New York, a round-trip fare costing around $480 (subject to change). *Land rates in summer are around $600 per week for everything.*

Sports include sailing, windsurfing, snorkeling, waterskiing, swimming, archery, and tennis on ten courts (four of which are lit for night games). You get the usual Club Med activities: picnics, boat rides, nightly dancing, shows, and optional excursions. There's even a computer workshop with 14 Atari computers.

Activities spin around a combined dining room/bar/dance floor and theater complex facing the sea in the center of the village. In front of this beehive of activity is a big swimming pool; a small restaurant and disco, nearby, are built beside the sea.

For reservations and information in New York, call 212/750-1670; otherwise, dial toll free 800/528-3100 nationwide.

6. North to Puerto Plata

Originally it was Columbus's intention to found America's first city at Puerto Plata, naming it La Isabela. But a tempest detained him, and it wasn't until 1502 that Nicolas de Ovando founded Puerto Plata, or "port of silver," lying 130 miles northwest of Santo Domingo. The port in time became the last stop for ships going back to Europe, their holds laden with treasures taken from the New World.

From Santo Domingo, the 3½-hour drive directly north passes through the lush Cibao Valley, home of the tobacco industry and Bermudez rum. You arrive first at Santiago, the second-largest city in the country, 90 miles north of Santo Domingo. The longest airport landing strip in the Dominican Republic is now in operation on this hitherto-undeveloped north coast of Hispaniola, which is the locale of the country's most ambitious development since Gulf + Western transformed a sugarcane plantation in another part of the island into the superluxurious (and more expensive) Casa de Campo.

Puerto Plata shows signs of offering a broad-based appeal to a market which may shun more expensive resorts, with some hotels boasting a nearly full occupancy rate almost all year. It is already casting a shadow on business at longer established resorts throughout the Caribbean, especially in Puerto Rico.

The backers of this sun-drenched spot have poured vast amounts of money into a flat area between a pond and the curved and verdant shoreline.

Four major hotels have been constructed, as well as a scattering of secluded condominiums and villas and a Robert Trent Jones–designed golf course, plus a riding stable with a complement of horses for each of the major properties.

Fort San Felipe, considered to be the oldest fort in the New World, is a popular attraction. Philip II of Spain ordered its construction in 1564, a task that took 33 years to complete. Built with eight-foot-thick walls, the fort was virtually impenetrable, and the moat surrounding it was treacherous. The Spaniards sharpened swords and embedded them in coral below the surface of the water to discourage use of the moat for entrance or exit purposes. The doors of the fort are only four feet high, another deterrent to swift passage. During the rule of Trujillo, Fort San Felipe was used as a prison. Standing at the end of the Malecón, the fort was restored in the early 1970s. On cruise-ship days, usually Tuesday and Thursday, it's likely to be overcrowded. The entrance fee is RD $1 (36¢).

Isabel de Torres, a tower with a fort built when Trujillo was in power, affords a magnificent view of the Amber Coast from a point near the top, 2565 feet above sea level. You reach the observation point by cable car *(teleférico),* a seven-minute ascent. Once there, you are also treated to seven square acres of botanical gardens. The round trip costs RD $2 (72¢). The aerial ride is operated daily except Monday and Wednesday from 8 a.m. to 6 p.m. Be warned: There is often a long wait in line for the cable car.

You can see a fascinating collection of rare amber specimens at the **Museum of Dominican Amber,** 61 Duarte St. (tel. 586-2848), owned and operated by Didi and Also Costa. The museum, open Monday to Saturday from 9 a.m. to 5 p.m., is near Puerto Plata's Central Park. Guided tours in English are offered. Admission is $1.

GETTING AROUND: If you prefer to be free to come and go as you wish, you may choose to rent a **car.** For information on this, see the discussion of car rentals in the Santo Domingo introduction. You might even find that a **motor scooter** will be suitable for transportation in Puerto Plata or Sosua.

If you take a **taxi,** make an agreement with the driver on the fare before your trip starts, as the vehicles are not metered. You'll find taxis in Central Park. At night it's wise to estalish your cab ride on a round-trip basis. If you go in the daytime by taxi to any of the other beach resorts or villages, check on reserving a vehicle for your return trip.

For a much cheaper ride, you can take a **publico,** a multipassenger taxi that travels on the main road. If you take one from Central Park, be sure it's really a publico and not a regular taxi. You can also flag down these vehicles on the highway, but you have to wave at all cars as the publicos are not designated on the outside. If it is one, and if there's room for another passenger, it will stop for you. A ride to anywhere in Puerto Plata will cost about 20¢, and you can go one-way to Sosua for about $1 per person.

Guaguas are public buses which you can take to the gate of Playa Dorada about every 20 minutes as well as to other destinations in the area. You can catch a guagua on the main street corners in Puerto Plata, a ride costing less than 10¢. Buses run from 7 a.m. to 7 p.m. daily.

WHERE TO STAY: Playa Dorado Hotel, P.O. Box 272 (tel. 586-3988), a dramatically designed Holiday Inn, set new standards for the Puerto Plata community when it opened in time for Christmas season of 1983. It is in fact not only the poshest hotel along the north coast of the Dominican Republic but one of the few hotels in all the Caribbean which can boast nearly full occupancy during most of the year.

The resort is designed in a style that might be called "Aztec Modern," arranged in massive blocks of coral-colored stucco, some with angled walls, soaring stairwells, and verdant greenery lacing itself throughout well-decorated spaces where the outdoors frequently blends pleasingly with the interior. Behind the reception desk is one of the biggest swimming pools in Puerto Plata, around which the hotel management hosts barbecues, buffet suppers, and weekly entertainment which includes singers and dancers known throughout the Spanish-speaking world.

The reception area is an air-conditioned oasis of Victorian-style lattice-work set whimsically beneath the soaring ceiling.

The 253 bedrooms are arranged along rambling corridors which, at the end of a long day on the well-maintained beach, may seem almost endless. Once you reach your room, however, you'll enjoy beautifully upholstered surroundings with up-to-date colors. More than two-thirds of the hotel's units are set into red-roofed wings which face the golden sands of the 1½-mile beach.

In addition to La Palma restaurant and the many bars and entertainment facilities, guests have access to a full range of boating, water sports, and golf activities (See "Sports," below). Three tennis courts are lit for night games. There's a cocktail lounge, Las Olas, where live entertainment is presented every night, as well as one of the hottest discos in town on the premises. Among the amenities are a babysitting service, laundry and valet service, and video movies. Resident manager Manuel Domenech is excellent as master of ceremonies at his weekly entertainment extravaganzas.

Not including taxes and service, winter rates for a single or double range from $100 to $160 per room. *In summer, the price goes from $60 to $100 per room, either single or double.* MAP is available for an additional $18 per person per day. The sports package is included in all tarriffs. There are also specially designed rooms for handicapped patrons within the hotel.

Montemar, Avenida Circunvalación del Norte, P.O. Box 382 (tel. 586-2800), is a glistening hotel complex that plays a double role: it's one of the pioneer resorts in the area, and it houses the local hotel school. Its buff-colored stucco facade is pierced with rows of brick-lined windows angled to catch the sunlight. Near Long Beach, the Montemar's rear entrance faces a copy of Michelangelo's *David,* set near the popular beach filled with residents of the town.

The pine-trimmed lobby is one of the most distinctive in the area. Enormous bamboo chandeliers illuminate the sea-green and pink upholstery, where images of birds flit across the comfortable couches and the naturalistic mural behind the reception desk. Your needs will be cared for by a battalion of eager students. A lounge nearby engages a merengue band which plays every night beside the illuminated palms.

The hotel opened a new wing as part of a major expansion in 1984, now offering a total of 96 attractively decorated units, most with views of palms and the sea and all with fresh colors and plush fabrics. *During low season, single rooms cost from RD $50 ($18) to RD $60 ($21.60), while double rooms rent for RD $60 ($21.60) to RD $75 ($27), and triples range from RD $75 ($27) to RD $85 ($30.60).* Rates in winter range from RD $110 ($39.60) in a single and from RD $150 ($54) in a double. MAP can be arranged for an additional RD $25 ($9) per person per day. The on-the-premises restaurant, La Isabella (see my dining recommendation) is one of the best decorated and most sophisticated restaurants in town. There are three tennis courts in the hotel complex.

The **Villa Doradas,** Villas Doradas Beach Resort, Playa Dorada (tel. 586-3000), is a pleasant collection of town houses arranged in landscaped clusters, usually around a courtyard. There's no beachfront here. Rather, part of your experience will be almost a community feeling, with neighbors all around in the groups of small villages set up around a series of green areas. The complex is within walking distance of sand beaches and golf facilities.

A focal point of the resort is the restaurant, Las Garzas, where a musical trio entertains guests every evening beneath the soaring pine ceiling. The management also features barbecues around the kidney-shaped pool area, where a net is sometimes set up for volleyball games. Of course, it would be tempting never to leave the shade of the cone-shaped thatched-roof pool bar, which is one of the most attractive and popular parts of the whole resort.

Many guests choose to cook in their villas for at least part of their daily meals, since kitchenettes are a part of each accommodation. Each unit is pleasantly furnished and attractively unpretentious, with louvered doors and windows to make your temporary home either open or closed to the outside world. There's a TV in each villa. *In summer, single rooms cost $80, doubles cost $95, one-bedroom are suites $155, and two-bedroom suites run $190.* In winter, the prices go up to $110 for a single, $125 for double, $205 for a one-bedroom suite, and $245 for a two-bedroom unit. The in-house restaurant offers simple meals for $25 and up.

Jack Tar Village, Playa Dorada (tel. 586-3800). Recently purchased by an investment group from Texas, this all-inclusive resort may represent the shape of things to come. Set at the edge of the sea and clustered around an L-shaped pool, the facility offers drinks, all meals, most water sports, and entertainment within its compound, so that you need never leave the grounds.

In the central, cement-covered core of the resort, you'll find dozens of vacationing adults and swarms of children noisily playing shuffleboard, cards, Ping-Pong, or volleyball, or just whiling away the time. If you prefer to simply linger beside one of the indoor/outdoor bars, where everything is free (even cigarettes), you'll have plenty of company. If you're more energetic, many water and land sports are offered, most of them included in the overall price of your accommodation in one of the white-walled villas.

The 240 units rent for $150 per person double occupancy in high season, for $180 single occupancy. *In low season, the charge is $110 per person for double occupancy, $150 for single occupancy. Children under 12 staying in their parents' room pay $25 each in low season,* $36 in high season. Four nights a week, dinners are sit-down affairs in the high-ceilinged dining room, with waiter service and frequent musical entertainment. The rest of the time, and often at lunch, meals are buffet style.

For reservations, call toll free 800/527-9299.

When **Dorado Naco,** P.O. Box 162 (tel. 596-2019), was built in 1982, there was only one other hotel in the entire Playa Dorado area. It's designed almost like a suburban apartment complex in the American sunbelt, yet at night when the merengue bands begin, the flavor is wholly Latin.

A flight of exterior wooden stairs passes under a portico and into a monochromatic lobby whose soaring ceiling is trussed with laminated pine beams. After registering, you'll be ushered past the poolside bar and restaurant complex, down a series of flowered walkways into one of the 150 units. A wide range of sports and entertainment available to guests.

A beach bar and grill lie a short walk from every room. The hotel has live music every night and live shows Thursday through Sunday. Wednesday, the manager hosts a cocktail party, and Thursday night, there's a beach party, complete with a bonfire, when you can dance on a raised floor. Throughout the week, guests find a full range of planned activities emanating from the charming social director. A nightly buffet is served under a portico near the pool, and à la carte meals are available in a covered dining room. A snackbar also does a brisk business.

Each unit contains comfortable furniture, a fully equipped kitchen, and a creative arrangement of interior space. Many guests choose to spend some of their evenings *en famille,* cooking at home, although a popular weekly meal plan includes seven breakfasts and four dinners for around $60 in high season. Many of the units are clustered along parapets or around well-planted atriums, and some of the larger ones include duplex floor plans and about as much spacious luxury as a vacationer could hope for. *In summer, the price is $85 in a one-bedroom apartment. A two-bedroom unit costs $120, while a penthouse, suitable for up to six persons, rents for $145.* In winter, a one-bedroom accommodation costs $120; a two-bedroom unit, $180; and a penthouse, $240. These prices do not include meals, taxes, or service.

Hotel Castilla, 34 John F. Kennedy (tel. 586-2559), is almost a second home to many of the resident "gringos" on the island. It's so laden with nostalgic spirit and handcrafted details that it might have been used as a backdrop for scenes in *Casablanca*. In keeping with this, just below the ceiling fans of the high-ceilinged dining room owner Jeff Ashil has placed posters of Bogart. His likeness goes well with the white-painted dadoes and nautical memorabilia attached to the walls of this 150-year-old frame building in the center of town.

By no stretch of the imagination is this a resort hotel. Its philosophy—"This ain't the Ritz"—is displayed near the bar, where European and North American painters, poets, yachtsmen, and various types of companions will be found enjoying drinks at any time of day.

The in-house restaurant is about as rustically "retro" as anything you'll find in the Caribbean and could serve as a model for newer eating places trying to create a similar feeling. The menu includes such Stateside specialties as sandwiches, hamburgers, chicken or conch salad, and filet of pork, as well as a shish kebab, piña coladas, Spanish wine, and beer. Meals begin at around $12.

The establishment contains 17 bedrooms, some with private baths. A few have four-poster mahogany beds, and all have ceiling fans. Modestly appointed but usually fairly clean, they rent for $22 to $36 year round, depending on the accommodation and the plumbing.

Costambar Beach Resort, P.O. Box 186 (tel. 586-3828), has more land connected to it—almost three square miles—than any other hotel property in the country. The section closest to the beach contains 50 low-lying villas, each pleasantly furnished in summertime colors and functional furniture. Many of the units belong to absentee investors, but the only rental arrangements which the average visitor will make are with the charming Dominican/Yugoslav partnership of Cecilia Ochao and her husband, Jovan.

Each of the 50 villas comes with a kitchenette, daily maid service, and access to the nearby Costambar Country Club. Visitors will find both a supermarket and an 18-hole golf course within easy reach, and there's a freshwater pond nearby. Babysitters are readily available. The various units contain from one to three bedrooms, complete with housekeeping accessories which include linens and kitchen utensils.

Daily winter rates range from $66 for a one-bedroom apartment, $110 for a two-bedroom villa, and $135 for a three-bedroom apartment. *Summer prices are about $10 less per category per day.* Government tax and a service charge are not included in the prices. To help assure the tranquility of the guests, there are no phones in any of the units, but calls can be placed and received at the reception area.

WHERE TO EAT: Porto Fino, Hermanas Mirabel Boulevard (tel. 586-2858), is a good Italian restaurant just across from the entrance of the Hotel Montemar. You can dine in the bright, lively dining room, which is trimmed in pink and white, or in the garden at a secluded table on a covered terrace surrounded by shrubbery. Italo Arandelli's Italian dishes have made this place popular in the Puerto Plata area. Parmesan breast of chicken, eggplant parmesan, spaghetti, ravioli, and pizzas are served in generous helpings. Expect to pay from $16 for a complete meal, although you'll get off much cheaper if you only order pizza. The restaurant is open daily from 11 a.m. to midnight.

Tainos Bar and Los Pinos Restaurant, Hermanas Mirabel Boulevard (tel. 586-3222). The rough-hewn walls of this darkly intimate retreat are covered with the religious drawings of the Tainos Indians, the original inhabitants of the island. A South Seas bar provides a convenient perch for daiquiri drinkers, although many customers prefer the comfortable banquettes ringing the tables which lookout over a verdant forest.

Alyce Remvidas, the owner, a Leo from New York, set this bar up in 1979, at which time she implanted her footprints in concrete near the front entrance.

After a couple of drinks in the bar, many patrons pass through an indoor/outdoor passage to the adjoining restaurant. There, in a decor of lacy cast-iron armchairs, big windows, colorful parakeets in cages, and hanging plants, diners enjoy the simple but well-prepared specialties of Alyce's kitchen. These include gazpacho, ham crêpes with sweet mustard sauce, four kinds of filet mignon, baked chicken with orange Cointreau sauce, seabass casserole, seabass filet with shrimp sauce, and grilled pork chops. These can be followed by one of six kinds of coffee, each made with a different after-dinner drink. Full meals here usually begin at around RD $35 ($12.60). If you want a less expensive meals, soups and sandwiches are available in the Tainos Bar. The establishment is open for lunch and dinner every day.

Restaurant La Carreta, Separación at the corner of Antera Mota (tel. 586-3418), is a converted Victorian home whose wrap-around veranda now contains tables, plants, and strolling minstrels. The walls are decked with a number of Dominican paintings, all of which are for sale.

After choosing a seat at one of the scattered tables in the spacious interior, you can select from the specialties which include lobster, fresh shrimp, seabass fritters with béchamel sauce, avocado salads, soups of the day, paella valenciana, crêpes with shellfish, and a variety of other creole and international dishes. Segundo Severino, the award-winning chef, charges around RD $35 ($12.60) for a full meal, although if you order lobster, you'll pay more. The restaurant, near Central Park, is open from 9 a.m. to 1 a.m. seven days a week.

Restaurant La Isabella, Hotel Montemar (tel. 586-2800). Because many of the staff of this restaurant are students at the adjoining hotel school, the service is probably better than at places where the help has become jaded. The decor is one of the most elegant in Puerto Plata. You enter a spacious, split-level room with subtle lighting, where the combined effect is like a page from an avant-garde fashion magazine. The carpets, walls, and upholstery are patterned in muted shades of dusty rose, turquoise, and white, with insertions of chrome at just the right places. One of the focal points is a quilted wall hanging whose patterns emphasize the art nouveau design of curved chairs and table settings.

Only dinner is served here, a polite staff of uniformed waiters looking after you. Specialties are filet of seabass à l'orange, beef tenderloin flambé, paella valenciana for two persons, Spanish-style garlic soup, a lobster/chicken casserole, pork chops, and a well-prepared chateaubriand. A fixed-price menu is offered for RD $22 ($7.92). Reservations are suggested.

Lowenbrau Restaurant, 72 Beller (no phone), affords a choice from a varied menu on which are listed Hungarian dishes along with German and Dominican specialties. You'll hear the voice of owner Franz Lowenberg booming from the kitchen as he directs his three young sons who serve the tables. You can choose from such tasty dishes as Hungarian goulash, Stroganoff, German bratwurst and sauerkraut, veal Swiss style, or leg of lamb Greek style, and local specialties include poached goat and various seafood items. An à la carte meal will cost from RD $20 ($7.20). You can dine at this rather no-frills restaurant in the 19th-century Gothic house from 6 to 11 p.m. daily except Monday.

WHERE TO SHOP: The Factory Gift Shop, 23 Duarte St. (tel. 586-3834), is the best place in town to purchase fairly priced samples of the two stones for which the Dominican Republic is noted. Amber from the island's north shore and larimar turquoise from the south shore are sold in a wide and attractive variety, or you can buy black coral, bull's horn, or Dominican pictures. Ramon Ortiz and his pleasant family will show you their workshop, where they polish different grades of their raw material into cunningly shaped figures, representing everything from frogs to rabbits. Some of the rare (and expensive) pieces contain well-preserved insects, and one even has in it a (petrified) lizard. Anything you buy can be mounted in silver or gold. Jewelry here ranges in price from $1 to $1000, depending on the quality. The store is open daily from 8 a.m. to 6 p.m.

SPORTS: Because of the location of Puerto Plata and Playa Dorada on the Atlantic Ocean, this is not the best spot in the Caribbean for water sports. At times, the sea tends to be rough.

Tennis, on the other hand, is a popular pastime at such hotels as Jack Tar Village and Playa Dorada.

Robert Trent Jones Jr. designed the par-72 18-hole **Playa Dorada championship golf course** which surrounds the resorts and runs along the coast. Greens fees are $25. An obligatory caddy (for each player) costs $6. You can rent a golf cart for $12, and golfing equipment is available at reasonable prices. Even nongolfers can stop at the clubhouse for a drink or a snack to enjoy the views.

You'll find superb **beaches** to the east and west of Puerto Plata. Among the better known are Playa Dorada, Sosua, Long Beach, Cofresi, Jack Tar, and Cabarete.

Fishing equipment and boats are available for rent. Get in touch with **Santiago Campo** (tel. 586-2632). You can also rent boats at Sosua and Jack Tar.

AFTER DARK: Vivaldi's, corner of Hermanas Mirabel Boulevard and the Malecón (tel. 586-3752), is a heavily patronized disco. Many non-Dominicans wouldn't think of coming back to Puerto Plata without rendezvousing with their acquaintances here. There's a restaurant on the upper floor, but most of the people who stream in head immediately for the ground-floor disco, where a combination of everything from salsa to reggae to New York City's recent dance releases is played practically all night. The entire interior is ringed with what you might call wrap-around neon. If you want a breath of cool air, there a little-used terrace in front. There's a cover charge of RD $10 ($3.60) on weekends. A drink costs around RD $3 ($1.08), although you can buy a full bottle of rum for you and your party to use throughout the evening for around RD $15 ($5.40).

The disco at the **Playa Dorada Hotel** is among the most animated nightspots in Puerto Plata. Head for the central core of the hotel on the ground level, and pass through the orchid-colored lobby to reach it. The entrance fee is RD $6 ($2.16), which you should pay in Dominican money if you have it, to avoid an unfavorable exchange rate. Once inside, you're faced with a dance floor (which is usually packed by the end of the evening) and lots of banquette seating, tiny tables, and flashing lights.

7. Sosua

Just ten miles east of Puerto Plata, Sosua is a small town on the ocean, with some unspoiled beaches nearby. It played a bizarre episode in history. For reasons known only to himself, the late Dominican dictator Trujillo invited 100,000 Jews to settle in his country, where they would escape Nazi terror on a banana plantation. Apparently, one of the reasons behind the offer was allegedly to "whiten the blood of the islanders."

Actually, only 600 or so Jews were allowed to immigrate, and of those, only about a dozen or so remain. However, there are some 36 Jewish families living in Sosua.

For the most part they are engaged in the dairy and smoked-meat industry which the refugees began during the war. Nowadays, with the dwindling Jewish population, many German expatriates are found in the town.

There is a local one-room synagogue, rescued from the termites, but rarely used except on holidays. Many of the Jews intermarried with Dominicans, and the town has taken on an increasingly Spanish flavor. Women of the town are often seen wearing both the Star of David and the Virgin de Alta Gracia.

WHERE TO STAY: Hotel Sosua, El Batey (tel 571-2683), is an aquamarine-color hotel in the suburban community about two minutes by car from the center of town. Its simple and attractive layout includes a reception area designed to conceal a flagstone-rimmed pool from the quiet residential street outside. The bedrooms are strung along a wing extending beside the pool. Amid an unpretentious decor of sea-green accessories, the rooms contain air conditioning, ceiling fans, and an occasional pine balcony. *In summer, the 24 accommodations rent for RD $55 ($19.80) in a double, RD $70 ($25.20) in a suite.* In winter, they cost RD $70 ($25.20) in a double, RD $88 ($31.68) in a suite. The hotel restaurant, on a a tree-shaded terrace, serves sandwiches and snacks.

El Mirador (formerly Sosuamar) (tel. 571-2202) is high on a hill above Sosua, a collection of Spanish-style villas commanding a sweeping view of the faraway sea. From its hilltop location, the resort maintains hourly bus service to and from the area's beaches. Each of the bungalows is landscaped around cultivated shrubbery, sinuous walkways, and rolling hills covered with lush grass.

The 40 units are privately owned by absentee investors, who leave the rental arrangements to a manager. Visitors enjoy the on-the-premises restaurant, the two pools, the tennis courts, the 35 riding horses, and the luxurious clubhouse/bar whose view sweeps over the seascape below.

The bungalows contain pleasantly appealing furnishings, walled terraces, and differing floor plans. When guests tire of being indoors, they can take advantage of organized activities such as Spanish lessons, aerobic pool exercises, crab races, casino tours to Santiago, and use of boats (usually free) at the resort's beach.

In summer, each unit rents for approximately RD $110 ($39.60) single or double, service and taxes not included. In winter, tariffs go up to RD $150 ($54) per unit, either single or double. Breakfast and dinner meal plans cost an additional RD $30 ($10.80) per person. The Tuesday-night barbecues here have become a traditional outing even for the residents of Sosua. Beginning at 6 p.m., a full meal costs around RD $15 ($5.40) per person, which allows you to enjoy a full evening of entertainment with native dancers, fire eaters, and music.

WHERE TO DINE: El Coral, El Batey (tel. 571-2645), is the best and arguably the most pleasant restaurant in town. It's in a Spanish-style building roofed with red tiles and set at the bottom of the cultivated garden near the end of Sosua Beach. The place looks smaller than it actually is as you aproach it from the front, but as soon as you pass through the heavy doors, you are in a spacious area with terracotta tiles, wooden accents, and stark white walls opening onto a panoramic view of the ocean. If you look out over the rear garden from one of the flowered terraces or through one of the big windows, you see an elliptical pool midway down the hill leading to the ocean. There's a bar in a room adjoining the dining room, covered with slickly modern brass accents and vertical metallic lines, each reflecting the spinning motion of the wicker ceiling fans. The specialties include lobster cocktail, grilled seabass, conch creole style, pork chops with pineapple, lobster thermidor, octopus creole style, shrimps with garlic, filet mignon, and flan. Full meals begin at around RD $20 ($7.20).

La Roca, El Batey (tel. 571-2216), is a banana warehouse when it was built almost 85 years ago, and it later became a general store. That was before two German expatriates and Rene Kirchheimer, the son of one of Sosua's original settlers, decided to transform it into the leading nightlife choice of Sosua.

The architect wisely chose to retain many of the massive structural beams and the darkly stained planks of the interior, achieving an exotic touch in the decor. This has been called a combination of the Black Forest and a Latin American pirate's lair. Even the sign displayed in front, "Cocina alemana," has a touch of the mixture.

Many guests opt for dinner on the breeze-cooled terrace which stretches to the side of the disco and interior bar. Full meals cost from around RD $20 ($7.20) and might include chef Kaj Albrech's special curry dishes (chicken is a favorite), chef's salads, fish soup, goulash soup, wienerschnitzel, chateaubriand for two persons, a mixed fish fry, arroz con pollo (chicken and yellow rice), lobster and shrimp, tournedos mexicaine, and beef Stroganoff. Many of the more expensive specialties are served flambéed, which adds a dramatic touch accompanied by the music pulsing from the dance floor inside the main section of the club.

Dining patrons are free to use a separate entrance after their meal to enter the disco. Nondinners guests pay an entrance fee of RD $7 ($2.52), after which drinks cost around RD $5 ($1.80). Both the disco and the restaurant are open seven days a week, although dancing doesn't usually begin until quite late.

Roma III, Emilio Prud'homme (no phone), is the best for the budget. Open to the breezes, this popular little place is more than just a pizzeria. The proprietor, George Sas, offers such unusual dishes as spaghetti octopus. You can also order the more conventional spaghetti carbonara. In addition, he features seabass in orange sauce and various concoctions of lobster, fresh fish, and shrimp dishes. There is also a meat specialty, steak chito. Open from noon to midnight, the little street-corner place charges very reasonable prices. If you want a pizza from the wood-fired oven, count on spending from RD $10 ($3.60); otherwise you'll pay from RD $20 ($7.20) for most main meals.

8. Río San Juan

The best reason for going to this sleepy town is to explore the Laguna Gri-gri (see below), requiring a 1½-hour drive from Puerto Plata. If you decide to spend the night or even a few relaxing days, the **Hotel Río San Juan** (tel. 589-2379) is a simple and attractive hostelry which usually caters to a Dominican clientele. The various sections of the structure are connected by catwalks and breezeways, most of which are raised above a series of cultivated gardens. The building is outfitted in a modern interpretation of a plantation style and contains a piano bar. Here, amid a color scheme with red accents and exposed wood, the management hosts Friday- and Saturday-night combo entertainment. Each of the 38 rooms has a private bath, painted cinderblock walls, mahogany trim, wall-to-wall carpeting, and air conditioning.

In winter, tariffs are RD $150 ($54) in a single, rising to RD $150 ($36) per person based on double occupancy. *In summer, expect reductions of around 20%.*

LAGUNA GRI-GRI: Lots of people dream about embarking (safely, of course) on a tour of a prehistoric swamp, but few realize that in the Dominican Republic, the opportunity exists for one of the most exotically beautiful trips anywhere in the Caribbean. Near the spot where the waters of the Arroyo Grande feed into the ocean, a wilderness of mangrove swampland has thrived in isolation for centuries.

Today, almost completely unspoiled, it's a refuge for hundreds of tropical and migrant birds, with surprisingly few insects in residence. At a well-marked departure point in Río San Juan, you can negotiate for the services of a motor-boat and its crew for between one and ten persons. The well-maintained, wide-bottomed boats embark on tours of an area which is reminiscent of the most secluded sections of the Florida Everglades.

You might suggest that the end point of your tour be **La Cueva de las Galondrinas,** which lies beyond the mouth of the river several miles along the rocky coastline. The cost will be around RD $40 ($14.40) per boatload. Along the way, note the soaring gri-gri trees, whose roots descend like tentacles into the water, plus the bizarre rock formations along the coast. Their forms include everything from natural arches to configurations resembling skulls. The end point of the tour, the cave of the galondrinas, was formed by a rockslide in 1846. Today the grotto takes its name from the bird, the galondrina, resembling the swallow, which migrates to South America in winter. If the water isn't too rough, a boat can be navigated right into the azure waters of the eerily echoing grotto, which some visitors say is just as blue as, and much less crowded than, anything along the Neapolitan coast of Italy.

Chapter VII

BRITISH LEEWARD ISLANDS

**1. Antigua and Barbuda
2. Montserrat
3. St. Kitts
4. Nevis
5. Anguilla**

ONCE A BRITISH COLONY, the Leeward Islands, except for Montserrat, have moved into more independent seas.

An aviator once said that these islands look like "a fleet of cockleshells set afloat in the sea." Between French-controlled Guadeloupe and the U.S. Virgins, at a bend of an archipelago, the British Leewards consist of Antigua (in association with isolated Barbuda), Montserrat, the twin state of St. Kitts and Nevis, and little Anguilla. Of them all, Antigua with its many beaches and resort hotels is the best equipped for mass tourism.

Once only Antigua and St. Kitts were visited by tourists, except for some curious, adventurous voyagers. However, the opening of more hotels and the providing of modern tourist facilities are now drawing thousands to Montserrat, Nevis, and to more remote Anguilla.

U.S. and Canadian citizens do not have to have a visa, but they will be asked for some means of identification such as a birth certificate or voter registration card. An outbound ticket for transportation is also required. Antigua makes a good base for going almost anywhere in the West Indies.

All the islands in this chapter use the Eastern Caribbean dollar (EC$), also called the "Bee Wee." However, no one faints if you give them a U.S. dollar. Nearly all hotels bill you in U.S. dollars. Only certain tiny restaurants present their prices in EC dollars. Make sure you know which dollars are referred to when you inquire about the price of something. The "Bee Wee" is worth about 38¢ in U.S. currency. Unless otherwise specified, rates quoted in this chapter are given in U.S. dollars.

1. Antigua and Barbuda

Antigua boasts a different beach for every day of the year—365 of them! Most of these beaches are protected by coral reefs, and the color of the sand is often sugar-white.

Antigua, Barbuda, and Redonda form the State of Antigua, an associated state within the British Commonwealth. (Redonda is an uninhabited rocky islet of less than one square mile, located 20 miles southwest of Antigua; and sparsely populated Barbuda is previewed at the end of this section.)

BRITISH LEEWARD ISLANDS

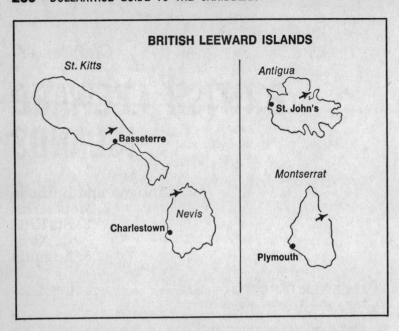

From a poverty-stricken sugar island, Antigua has risen to the position of a 20th-century vacation haven. Yankee millionaires seeking British serenity under a tropical sun turned Antigua into a citadel of elegance around the exclusive Mill Reef Club. The island has now developed a broader base of tourism—attracting not just the rich, but the middle-, even lower-income voyager.

Rolling, rustic Antigua (pronounced An-*tee*-ga) has as its highest point Babby Peak, 1360 feet above sea level. Stone towers, once sugar mills, dot the landscape; but in inland scenery Antigua isn't as dramatic as some of the British Leewards such as St. Kitts. But, oh, those beaches!

Discovered by Columbus on his second voyage in 1493, Antigua has a population of about 75,000 and an area of 108 square miles. The average all-year temperature ranges from 75° to 85° Fahrenheit.

Independence has come, but Antigua is still British in many of its traditions. English planters settled Antigua in 1623. In 1666 the French occupied the island, but Antigua was ceded to England the following year by the Treaty of Breda.

The summer carnival takes place on the first Monday and Tuesday in August and the preceding week. Included in this festival of fun and spectacle are a beauty competition, as well as calypso and steel-band competitions. Carnival envelops the streets in exotic costumes that recall the people's African heritage. The spring highlight is Antigua's annual sailing week in April.

The capital is **St. John's,** a neatly laid out large town, six miles from the airport and less than a mile from the deep-water Harbour Terminal. The port is the focal point of commerce and industry, as well as the seat of government and tourist shopping. Trade winds keep the streets fairly cool, as they were built wide just for that purpose. Protected in the throat of a narrow bay, the port city consists of cobblestone sidewalks, weather-beaten wooden houses (painted or not), corrugated iron roofs, and louvered West Indian verandas.

PRACTICAL FACTS: Arriving passengers are allowed 200 cigarettes and one quart of liquor, plus six ounces of perfume. Upon departing, a **departure tax** of EC $10 ($3.80) is imposed.

In addition, the government imposes a 5% **government tax,** which is added to all hotel bills. There is also a 10% service charge added to most hotels.

Most of the island's electricity is 220 volts AC, 60 cycles. However, the Hodges Bay area and some hotels are supplied with 110 volts, 60 cycles.

Holberton Hospital (tel. 2-0251) on Queen Elizabeth Highway is the principal **medical facility** on Antigua. Water is desalinated and therefore safe to drink.

Antigua falls within the **Atlantic Time Zone,** placing it one hour ahead of the east coast of the U.S. However, both Antigua and the U.S. East Coast keep the same time when the U.S. goes on Daylight Saving Time.

For emergencies, the **U.S. Embassy** is at Redcliffe Street, St. John's (tel. 2-3511).

Bank hours are usually Monday to Wednesday from 8 a.m. to 2 p.m. (on Thursday to 1 p.m.) and on Friday from 8 a.m. to 1 p.m. and 3 to 5 p.m.

Shops are most often open from 8:30 to noon and 1 to 4 p.m. But this rule varies greatly from store to store. Antiguan shopkeepers are an independent lot. Many of them close on Thursday at noon.

GETTING THERE: Many airlines consider Antigua an important link in their Caribbean networks. **Eastern Airlines** makes daily direct flights from Miami, through which dozens of American cities can be connected efficiently. Flights on Eastern's fleet of 757s make only one intermediate stop in Dutch St. Maarten before continuing on to Antigua. If you prefer to arrive in Antigua via San Juan, Puerto Rico, or St. Thomas/St. Croix, Eastern also offers service to those areas.

Eastern's rate structure is understandably cheapest when a Caribbean vacationer books his or her hotel reservations at the same time as booking airline tickets. Eastern's tour desk will describe its various options, but for those wishing to arrange their own accommodations, the least expensive ticket on Eastern is an excursion fare. The only restriction on this type of ticket is that a period of from 3 to 21 days must elapse before a customer uses the return half of his or her ticket. There's no advance purchase required. Round-trip passage from New York costs $495 in high season, $467 in low season. Round-trip passage from Miami is available in any season for only $350. The exact fare at the time of your trip is available from a reservations clerk at Eastern (look for the number in your telephone directory) or from your travel agent.

Other airlines offering service to Antigua include **American,** which has a nonstop flight from New York every day, with easy connections from Boston and slightly less convenient connections from Los Angeles and San Francisco. Luggage, of course, is routed through to a passenger's final destination. Passengers on this flight benefit from its nonstop convenience, but they find that on weekends, in high season, the round-trip excursion fare with the same restrictions cost about $45 more than the fare charged by Eastern. Passengers benefit from the convenience of American's nonstop service, but rock-bottom budgeteers may want to know about the savings.

Pan Am, after touching down in Dutch St. Maarten, continues with direct service to Antigua from New York every day. Pan Am also operates a daily direct flight from Miami. Fares are similar to those charged by American and Eastern, but a word of caution: in high season, Pan Am's cheapest APEX ticket, costing $492, requires a 7-day advance purchase and a delay of between 6 and 21 days before using the return half of the ticket. Substantial penalties are imposed if a passenger needs to change the return date. For only about $20 more, a customer doesn't have to book in advance and can leave the return half of the ticket as an "open return" for a date to be determined later.

BWIA flies nonstop from New York to Antigua three times a week. It also flies nonstop from Miami twice a week and five times per week from San Juan.

Canadians usually prefer to fly their domestic carrier, **Air Canada,** on nonstop flights that leave Toronto every Saturday and Sunday in winter, returning the same day. In summer, Air Canada maintains only a Saturday flight, but in any season, easy connections are made from Montréal through Toronto.

HOTELS: Antigua's hotels are among the best and most plentiful in the eastern Caribbean, and generally they are small—a 100-room hotel is rare on the island. Check summer closings, which often depend on the caprice of the owners who will decide to shut down if business isn't good. Incidentally, air conditioning, except in first-class hotels, isn't as plentiful as some visitors think it should be. Chances are, your hotel will be on a beach. You can also rent an apartment or cottage if you want to cook for yourself.

The Leaders in Luxury

Curtain Bluff, Old Road, P.O. Box 288 (tel. 3-1115), lies in southwest Antigua, the most tropical-looking section of the resort-studded island. A world set apart on a finger of land, it was built on Curtain Bluff Peninsula, with two beaches, about 14 miles from the airport. The setting is like a subtropical forest, with sky-high coconut trees off each of its leeward and windward beaches. I'd rate Curtain Bluff as the outstanding hotel on the island, where competition is stiff. The chairman, Howard Hulford, once a pilot for Texaco, and the managing director, Edward Sherrin, demand and get the best staff on the island, maintaining a private-club atmosphere that appeals to everybody from Herman Wouk to *The Sensuous Woman.*

Architecturally, the resort's buildings are original, suggesting the South Seas. Guests meet for drinks in the round bar, inspired by the early stone sugar mills. Ship models are set against the stone walls, and the round ceiling is beamed. Low modern sofas make it easy to while away the hours.

The peaked-roof bedrooms, only 50 in all, have open, covered verandas where you can take your breakfast. The white bamboo furnishings set the right taste tone. With its own secluded balcony and private bath, each unit faces the sea and is cooled by the breezes. The tariffs are expensive, but you get a lot of extras for your money, including Sunfish sailboats, waterskiing from a fiberglass speedboat, skindiving (masks, snorkels, and flippers furnished), Aqualungs (complete equipment for certified divers), boating (guided trips to Cades Reef), tennis (four championship Plexipave courts), and golf (a putting green). In winter, doubles on the full-board plan peak at $340 daily; a single, $290. *In summer, these tariffs are reduced: from $250 in a double, from $185 in a single, both on the full-board plan.* The hotel is closed from May 1 to mid-October.

After dining (men should wear a jacket and tie after 7 p.m.), there is entertainment. It might be a steel band or else calypso music for dancing. Beach cocktail parties are staged weekly. A European chef, Ruedi Portmann, prepares a very good continental cuisine, his menu backed up by a well-chosen and extensive wine cellar. Be sure to try his deep-fried ice cream!

The **St. James Club,** P.O. Box 63, St. John's (tel. 3-1430). This luxurious resort on Marmora Bay offers an example of how $12 million, careful planning, and construction expertise can whip an abandoned hotel into a glamorous and sought-after resort in an astonishingly short time. The 100-acre setting, which today blossoms with hundreds of tropical plants, is on a sun-drenched spit of land jutting into the Caribbean.

The pedigrees of both the resort, a branch of a sophisticated private club in London, and its owner, Peter de Savary (who financed one of Britain's recent contenders for the America's Cup), are as good as sterling silver. Just to launch the Antigua resort's first season, Mr. de Savary flew in an army of celebrities, which included everyone from Liza Minnelli to Joan Collins.

In a deep harbor dug out of what had been a shallow cove, the builders constructed a full-service marina with permanent berths for 30 vessels and moorings for 80 more.

The tons of sand pumped out to deepen the harbor were used, topped with white sand from neighboring Barbuda, to form a pair of beautiful beaches on the curved and palm-lined opposite side of the peninsula. In addition to beach activities there are five floodlit tennis courts flanked with observation gazebos. A stable houses about a dozen Texas quarterhorses guests can use to ride along woodland and hillside trails carved out of the surrounding landscape. A fleet of sportfishing boats is used for deep-sea expeditions and for snorkeling trips, and a complete Nautilus-equipped gymnasium has its own whirlpool.

Each accommodation looks like a page out of a decorator's magazine. Shades of imaginative pastels intertwine with vivid Dominican paintings, wicker and bentwood furniture, commodious canopy beds, sweeping views of the seascapes, and soundproof doors covered with hand-painted murals. Many rooms are reached by passing by a Japanese-style garden near the swimming pool. With MAP, *double occupancy rates range from $180 in low season* to a maximum of $450 in high season for studio accommodations. *Lodgings in suites go from $270 per couple with MAP off-season* to as much as $1200 per couple with MAP in winter. For single guests, the hotel deducts $25 per day from the rate charged for a double. No tipping is expected, since a 10% service charge is added to all bills.

The Jacaranda Supper Club and Disco is a see-and-be-seen kind of place, with zebra-striped chairs, lacquered tables, and the elements for one of the most sophisticated audio-visual systems in the Caribbean. There's also a high-ceilinged in-house casino whose walls are covered in a riveting combination of Italian-made art deco columns and glittering vertical stripes.

The Reef Deck restaurant serves poolside meals within the shelter of an ocean-view windbreak. The main dining room is especially dramatic. It contains a soaring white ceiling, a dinnertime pianist perched on a platform eyrie high above the floor, and a "rebuilt" tree which a crew of designers reassembled from a nearby forest and festooned with iridescent crystals. There's a harborside bar and open-air restaurant which serves as the perfect getaway. Every day at sundown, a steel band plays, seated on a floating pier set up in the harbor.

For reservations throughout the United States, call 800/235-3505 toll free; in New York state, 212/689-3048, and in Canada, 800/268-9051 toll free.

Half Moon Bay, P.O. Box 144, at Half Moon Bay (tel. 3-2101), is run like the country club of Antigua. Seventeen miles from St. John's, it has as its neighbor the exclusive Mill Reef Club, and ranks with Curtain Bluff as one of the leading resorts on the island, run with extreme professionalism and expertise. First, the mile-long, crescent-shaped beach of white powdery sand in front of Half Moon is splendid, the surf powerful. Families are generally separated from "couples only," a wise decision for those seeking tranquility. The serene white of the complex greets the travel-weary who are soon enjoying a rum punch under the palms. About the most excitement that ever occurred around here was in the winter of 1969 when former Beatle, Paul McCartney, and

Mrs. McCartney stayed here, distributing "Bee Wee" dollars—autographed, of course. Elton John sponsors a tennis tournament in January, and has made Half Moon his annual "get fit vacation" where he plays tennis four hours per day. There are other professional tennis tournaments in April and November.

A medium-sized hotel, set on 150 acres, managed by Keith Woodhouse, Half Moon offers 100 oceanfront deluxe rooms, each with a private balcony or patio overlooking the beach and sea. As you sip your orange juice at breakfast, you'll see little birds darting among the bright-red hibiscus and the purple bougainvillea. On the MAP, doubles in winter rent for anywhere from $230 to $265 daily, singles on the same terms for $180 to $220 daily. You can also reserve an oceanfront suite at $325 for two persons, complete with a veranda and a sitting room with convertible sofas. *In summer, rates go down: the single MAP is $100 to $120, going up to $150 to $190 in a double, and peaking at $225 for two persons occupying a suite.*

Not only does this hotel have a nine-hole tropical golf course, but it also offers some of the finest tennis on the island on five all-weather Plexipave courts. Water sports include Sunfish sailboats, snorkeling equipment, surfboards, and a glass-bottomed rowboat. Those who tire of the reef-protected beach will find a freshwater swimming pool. Nightly entertainment is offered, featuring dancing to a steel band. The food is good, and emphasis is placed on what comes from local waters, everything from grouper to lobster and turtle. Weekly steak barbecues are prepared. A European chef supervises the international cuisine.

Long Island Resort, P.O. Box 243 (tel. 3-2176), is an exclusive little island resort, 300 acres in all, lying off the eastern coast of Antigua and reached after a 12-minute motor launch ride. The site was selected for its powdery white sandy beaches, along a coastline protected by coral reefs. In gin-clear waters, guests can snorkel, go scuba-diving, or swim when they're not playing tennis, going fishing or sailing, or perhaps waterskiing.

The grounds have been handsomely landscaped in part with loblolly and white cedar trees. The resort at its peak can accommodate about 56 guests, and with such a low house count the place often takes on a house-party atmosphere.

Pampered guests are housed in one of a dozen cottage rooms, each with a large master bedroom and its own patio overlooking the water, or else in one of 16 guest units fronting the ocean on Jumby Bay Beach. These latter units have a living and sitting area as well as a "wet bar." Some of them even have a private "no curtains" shower courtyard which can provide entertainment to your roommate if you've kept your figure in shape.

In the shoulder and off-season, the full-board rate ranges from $225 to $275 daily in a single, from $275 to $325 in a double. In winter, the single AP rate peaks at $400 daily, the double going for $450, plus tax.

The hotel is built on the site of what had been the private home of a plantation owner engaged in growing sugarcane. In the 200-year-old vastly restored estate house, there is now a lounge, along with a library and games room. Dinner is served here, often attracting the yachting crowd who put into the 750-foot dock. The food is excellent, and picnic lunches can be arranged.

For reservations, get in touch with Resorts Management, Inc., The Carriage House, 201½ East 29th St., New York, NY 10016 (tel. 212/696-4566). Elsewhere, call toll free 800/225-4255.

First-Class Hotels

Halcyon Cove Beach Resort and Casino, P.O. Box 251, Dickenson Bay (tel. 2-0256), is a total resort with plenty of glamour and a casino. There, in the midst of waterfront gardens, are clusters of two-story buildings overlooking either the sea or well-tended grounds spread out around the swimming pool area. A total of 150 deluxe, stylish bedrooms are equipped for discerning guests. The decorating has authority, usually fine furnishings and coordinated fabrics. You have your own furnished private veranda; however, if you're on the ground floor you may get a lot of inspection from fellow guests, providing you are interesting enough. In winter, rooms (either single or double occupancy) rent for anywhere from $200 to $235 daily, *dropping to $105 to $130 from mid-April to mid-December.*

The Arawak Terrace, the hotel's main dining room, is open for breakfast and dinner. You can also lunch or dine on the elongated Warri Pier, standing on stilts 200 feet from the shore. It's reached by a boardwalk over the sea. You dine and drink under a thatched and shingled open-air café. There seems nearly half a mile of beach, and at one end is one of the major centers of Antigua's watersports program. Often there are buffet dinners. Other activities include playing tennis on the hotel's own courts and horseback riding.

The hotel is perched on an elevation, and it's but a three-minute walk down to the beach. Deck chairs and umbrellas are placed around a bar built right at the freshwater swimming pool, and a large airy dining room has a view of the sea. The hotel also has an ice-cream parlor-coffeeshop as well as a cocktail lounge that occasionally has entertainment. Tennis players will find three courts lit for night play. In season, the management brings in a steel band to provide poolside entertainment on Sunday. The location is 1½ miles from the airport and seven miles from St. John's, about a 15-minute taxi ride.

Blue Waters, P.O. Box 257, Soldier Bay (tel. 2-0292), curves around a private sandy beach, where you can lie in a hammock as a waiter serves you a stawberry-red rum punch. The location is four miles (about a 15-minute ride) from St. John's, to which the management provides a shuttle service at $3 per person. At his shore-hugging place, Osmund Kelsick, the chairman, has created a thoroughly refined little Caribbean inn where all rooms except the garden suites are beachfront and air-conditioned, surrounded by luxurious flowers and shrubs with coconut palms and shade trees in the extensive grounds. In winter, singles and doubles pay from $124 to $162 daily, EP. The MAP supplement is $32 per person daily. The resort is likely to be closed from mid-May to mid-July. *Otherwise, the single rate off-season ranges from $74 to $94 daily, going up to $80 to $106 in a double, plus another $30 per person for the MAP supplement.*

The Sunday brunch is deservedly praised. A lavish buffet table, decorated with coconuts and bougainvillea, is spread before you; and on Tuesday and Friday, outdoor barbecues with continental and West Indian dishes, among the best in Antigua, attract a lively crowd. In season, you can dance to combos, steel bands, or disco music, and every Wednesday night the management throws a house party featuring crab racing.

Water sports, tennis, sailing, archery, and fishing are all complimentary, or you may prefer just to relax in the clear freshwater pool or enjoy a sundowner from the gazebo. Deep-sea fishing and coastal trips to nearby islands are available.

The Anchorage, P.O. Box 147, Dickenson Bay (tel. 2-0267), is a special retreat and compound right on the beach. Guests face a choice of staying in a large, well-furnished room or a tropical thatched-roofed rondavel, with a private patio overlooking the sea. The cheapest way to stay here is to take one of the air-conditioned cottage rooms, costing $160 daily in season, either single or double occupancy. *These cottages drop to only $95 daily in summer, either single or double.* The most luxurious way to live here is in one of the air-conditioned deluxe beach rooms and rondavels. They rent for $200 daily in winter, *dropping* *to only $125 in summer,* either single or double occupancy. For breakfast and dinner, add another $38 per person daily.

Many thoughtful extras go into making the Anchorage one of the best run hotels on the island. For example, the maid comes around twice a day. The beachfront setting is in a coconut grove, and there's a wide assortment of water sports, plus three championship tennis courts. The chef can also accommodate special diets. Native bands and special guest performers are brought in to entertain, and down the beach you can enjoy casino action at the Halcyon Cove Hotel.

Antigua Beach Hotel, P.O. Box 60 (tel. 3-0048). The main building of this panoramic establishment was erected in 1939 as the first major resort hotel in Antigua. During World War II it was used as a British army barracks. Today, because of its well-maintained beauty, you'd never know that the high-ceilinged and breeze-swept public rooms were once home to Tommy Atkins. Although the hotel is set on a garden-ringed bluff and surrounded with fields, it's only a few minutes' walk to a long stretch of white sandy beach.

Many of the accommodations are quite large, suitable for entire families. In winter, singles range from $100 to $130, while doubles cost from $110 to $145, plus service. *Summer rates go from $72 to $110 in a single, with doubles costing $85 to $120, plus service.* A third person can lodge in any double for an extra $12 per day. MAP can be arranged for $30 per person per day.

There's a warmly furnished cocktail lounge, decorated with unusual photographs of street life in turn-of-the century Antigua, where live entertainment is presented weekly. The hotel has a freshwater pool with its own well-stocked bar, a floodlit tennis court, a games room, and a friendly staff whose management includes the Algeria-born Al Nait. The restaurant, whose entrance is marked with a rickshaw, was recently refurbished in a Moroccan-style decor of peacock chairs, hammered brass, and stained-glass lanterns, with sweeping views of the sea.

Jolly Beach, P.O. Box 744 (tel. 2-0061), is a sprawling hotel, near 1½ miles of sandy beach and about 12 minutes from St. John's. It caters to a mass-market clientele that often includes several tour groups at the same time. You're likely to hear recorded music, which is piped through the public areas much of the day. This is one of the largest hotels in the Eastern Caribbean basin, containing 76 units and two suites in the "Original Jolly Beach," plus a massive 368 accommodations and 16 junior suites in the "New Jolly Beach." Most units are air-conditioned (some with ceiling fans) and have private patio or balcony, radio, phone, hair dryer, and private bath.

The newer section is cheaper than the older. In winter, MAP singles begin at a low of $90 (ceiling fans only), rising to $145 daily, with MAP doubles costing from $150 to $190. *In summer, MAP rates range from $90 to $130 in a single, from $130 to $170 in a double.* Suites are more expensive, of course.

The free-form swimming pool is connected at its narrowest part by a wooden footbridge, while, with repetitive arches, parts of the living quarters—at least from the gardens—look vaguely Moorish in the New Jolly. By the animated splashing, gossiping, and partying of vacationing guests, however, you can tell that the milieu is pure North American.

In the older section, guests spend much time around the beach bar, the Coconut Wharf, later dining in the Flamboyant Bar and restaurant, which has music for dancing. In the newer section, La Taverne sells drinks and light fare in the daytime, and in the evening the Palm Bar and Restaurant is the magnet, with its continental fare, Stateside specialties, and occasional West Indian dishes. Buffets and barbecues are regular features. Night-owls dance until the early hours at Jaybee's Disco.

The resort offers a range of outside water sports such as scuba-diving and deep-sea fishing, which can be arranged at extra cost. Free activites include the use of two floodlit tennis courts, Sunfish, sailboats, windsurf boards, paddleboats, rowboats, and waterskiing and snorkeling equipment.

Flamingo Antigua Hotel and Casino, Michael's Mount, St. John's (tel. 2-1266), once known as Castle Harbour, is set on a somewhat bleak hill just outside the commercial center of the capital. It isn't near any beach, although it has a pool on its premises that affords a glimpse of the sea. Business people visiting from other parts of the Caribbean seem to like this hotel, but there's a casino here which also makes it a gambler's favorite. In fact, many never leave the confines of the hotel once they check in.

Its well-furnished suites are air-conditioned and include phones. Winter rates range from $92 to $115 for a single, $115 to $125 for a double. A third person can stay in any double for an additional $15 a day. MAP can be arranged for an extra $40 per day. *Visitors can expect reductions of around 20% in summer.* Bookings can be made through Flamingo Tours, 1304 E. Broward Blvd., Fort Lauderdale, FL 33301 (tel. 305/763-5877).

Antigua Village, P.O. Box 649, Dickenson Bay (tel. 2-2930), set on a peninsula stretching into the turquoise waters around it, is more of a self-contained community than a holiday resort. The road leading to it winds through hilly country until it eventually passes through large groves of palm trees scattered on both sides of a seaside area that is generously ringed with white sandy beaches. A freshwater pool, a restaurant, a bar, and a mini-market are on the premises, with a casino and neighboring restaurants within walking distance. Most water sports can be arranged through the resort's reception desk. You can use the tennis court, and there's an 18-hole golf course nearby.

The Village has studio apartments and villas, all of which have kitchenettes, patios or balconies, twin beds in the bedrooms, and sofa beds in the living rooms. One-bedroom apartments in winter cost $145 to $240 daily, depending on the number of occupants, the accommodation's design, and its location beside the sea or the pool. Two-bedroom villas in winter cost $320 to $400. *In summer, one-bedroom villas cost $60 to $145, while two-bedroom units cost $145 to $300.* These prices do not include service or a charge of $5 per day additional for air conditioning.

Small, Special Inns

The **Admiral's Inn,** P.O. Box 713, English Harbour (tel. 3-1027), as a building, was planned in 1785, the year Nelson sailed into the harbor as captain of the H.M.S. *Boreas.* Completed in 1788, the building's ground floor was used to store lead, turpentine, and pitch, with offices for dockyard engineers upstairs. Today it has been converted into one of the most atmospheric inns in Antigua. In the heart of Nelson's Dockyard, and loaded with West Indian charm, the hostelry is constructed of weathered brick brought from England as ships' ballast. The facade is eye-captivating, with white shutters, dormers, and a terrace opening onto a centuries-old garden. The look is that of a small manor house, and it's hangout for the yachting set. The ground floor, with its brick walls, giant ship beams, and island-made furniture, has a tavern atmosphere, with decorative copper, boat lanterns, and old oil paintings, everything lit at night by wrought-iron chandeliers.

Antilles ambience collectors will find that whatever room they're assigned will be full of character. There are three types of accommodations. Highest tariffs are charged for some ground-floor rooms in a tiny brick building—on the site of a provisional warehouse for Nelson's troops—across the pillared courtyard from the main structure. Each of these rooms has a little patio and a garden entry. Ceiling fans keep these spacious and airy rooms cool. A medium-priced rate applies to the rooms on the second floor of the main building, some of which open onto a view over the lawn. Others have air conditioning. The least expensive rate is for small chambers on the third floor, which get hot in summer but are quiet, with dormer-window views over the yacht-filled harbor. All rooms have ceiling fans and private baths and showers. Only 14 twin-bedded rooms are rented out, so reservations are imperative. One bedchamber has a four-poster bed, but it didn't belong to Nelson, or even Lady Hamilton.

Miss Ethelyn Philip, who has been with the inn for some 20 years, will welcome you and see to your needs. *In summer, singles on the EP stay here at rates that range from $38 to $46 daily; doubles, $44 to $52.* In winter, EP rates go up—$54 to $58 for a single, $64 to $72 for a double. The inn is closed in September.

Rates entitle you to use the inn's snorkeling equipment and Sunfish craft. Free transportation is also provided to two nearby beaches. On Saturday night a steel band plays. For the inn's restaurant, refer to the section on where to dine.

Galley Bay Surf Club, P.O. Box 305, Five Islands (tel. 2-0302). When she created this place west of St. John's, Edee Holbert had a fantasy of Gauguin and Polynesia—grass roofs and lily ponds. She's a gracious, lively hostess who knows how to run an exciting resort with just enough whimsy to make it an amusing vacation on the beach. American magazine editors have already showered it with compliments. *Mademoiselle* found it "an undiscovered gem with a half mile beach, unusual and amusing," and *The Tattler* rated it "the most imaginative of the island's hotels, run on rather house party lines." That beach referred to was the same beach where Greta Garbo was caught unaware by a nosy magazine photographer. Never happy having her picture taken in past decades, the great actress was even more distressed this time, as she was without her bathing suit.

A variety of accommodations is offered. For tranquility seekers, the Gauguin Village, with 12 units, is 150 feet off the beach, built around a salt pond under a leafy coconut grove. Each of these units consists of two villas—one with a spacious bedroom, the other with a good-sized bath and dressing room. Furnishings are in rattan, the wall hangings from Haiti. Directly on the beach, advertised as "four seconds from bed to sea," are a dozen beach rooms with a South Seas decor of white walls, including a sunken tub in the bathroom and private lanai and hand-woven palm leaf shutters, which Ms. Holbert says are "just for fun"! In addition, a quartet of executive beach rooms are also on the beach. These are big double rooms, decorated with style and imagination, including a private lounge, private bar, dining porch, and kitchen. The price depends not only on the season, but the accommodation you select. *In summer, a beach room rents for $105 (single or double), an executive beach room is $120, and a Gauguin villa, $140.* In winter, these prices rise to $175 in a double, $200 in a beach room for two, and $275 in a Gauguin villa. All these are EP tariffs. For MAP, add another $35 per person daily. A ten-day minimum stay is required at Christmas and in February.

Horses suitable even for beginning riders are available—"on the house." Also included free are hard-surface tennis courts, snorkeling (a sunken schooner is nearby), and a dinghy for fishing. In season, dancing is nightly to West Indian bands, particularly at the barbecues. The food is especially good, and *Gourmet* magazine has published some of the recipes. Outstanding are the Caribbean fish chowder, flambé desserts, roast duckling with banana stuffing, paper-thin crêpes, callaloo soup, coq au vin, and lobster thermidor.

The Inn, P.O. Box 187, English Harbour (tel. 3-1014), is one of my favorite nooks, and I enjoy sharing it with others. Owned by Peter and Ann Deeth, it stands in a corner of Freeman's Bay. Guests have a choice of pleasingly furnished hillside studios and suites, or else beachfront units, the latter naturally costing more money.

In winter, hillside singles on the MAP rent for $180 daily, rising to $200 to $250 on the beach. A MAP double on the hillside goes for $230, increasing to anywhere from $225 to $285 daily on the beach. In summer, hillside units are shut down. *However, regular off-season rates for the beachfront rooms with kitchenette, either single or double occupancy, range from $85 to $95 and up daily.*

The Inn has one of the finest sites in Antigua, with views over Nelson's Dockyard and English Harbour from its terrace. Have a before-dinner drink in the old-style English Bar, with its stone walls and low-overhead beams. Lunch is served both at the beach house and in the main dining room, and the Inn is known for the quality of its cookery. The hotel also has its own waterski boat, Sailfish, and a yacht for sailing; other activities on the agenda include tennis, horseback riding, swimming, and snorkeling. Tennis and golf are nearby.

Long Bay Hotel, P.O. Box 442 (tel. 3-2005), is dramatically situated on a spit of land between the open sea and a sheltered lagoon, on the eastern shore, beyond the hamlet of Willikie's. Many repeat visitors consider it more of an inn than a large-scale hotel. It features 20 breeze-filled rooms as well as five furnished cottages for more reclusive guests.

From early November till mid-December rates are $160 in a double, $100 in a single, and $60 for each additional person in a double room. From mid-December till mid-April doubles cost $230 and singles run $170; an extra person is charged $75. *Summer rates, mid-April to mid-July, range from $190 in a double to $110 in a single, with an extra person paying $75.* These prices include breakfast and dinner. The management prefers that no tipping be done, since 10% is automatically added to each bill as a gratuity. The hotel is closed between mid-July and early November each year.

The resort is centered around a hip-roof clubhouse whose stone-walled dining room and artifact-dotted bar provide a relaxing environment. There's a championship tennis court, plus complete scuba facilities and a full array of rental sailboats on the premises. Golf is nearby.

Babysitters are available when needed, and there is a special dinner sitting just for children. The hotel has a library and games room, a separate building for the dining room, and a beach house restaurant and bar.

To make reservations before coming to the island, call 800/223-9868, toll free.

Lord Nelson Club, P.O. Box 155 (tel. 2-3094), is a self-contained resort about a mile from the airport, some five miles from St. John's. The club occupies 19 acres, opening onto its own private sandy beach. The pink-walled hotel may look a bit ramshackle in places, but it has a lot of character and personality, which has made it a secret address to many a discriminating client over the years. Expatriates, both English and American, flock here. The inn has American owners, the Fuller family. One of its members, Nick, was a former U.S. consul. Somehow the purchase of the property involved a swap that included a battleship.

Rooms vary widely, and I prefer the pleasantly decorated twin-bedded rooms, each with a private tiled bath and a terrace with a view of the water. The trade winds keep it cool at night. In season, two persons can stay here on the MAP for $120 daily, a single person paying $90 daily. *From mid-April to mid-December, reductions are granted: $95 for two on the MAP, $75 for one person, plus tax and service.* The old-fashioned dining room offers a cuisine that includes some of the island specialties, as well as the partial hull of a beached dinghy set up in its center as a serving station. The stone-walled bar, shaped like a cabana, contains hanging fishnets and a portrait which looks like Lord Nelson above the serving area. Set directly on the sand, the bar is ready to serve you a tropical drink at your request. The lounge and bar have a few decorative antiques to add zest. The beach is fringed with tropical trees and shrubbery.

The **Catamaran Hotel and Marina**, P.O. Box 958, Falmouth (tel. 3-1036), is a small West Indian inn, a kind of Pago-Pago hideaway, right on the historic shores of Falmouth Harbour, 20 minutes from the airport. It's adjacent to Nelson's Dockyard. Hugh Bailey, an Antiguan sailor, founded this place, naming it after his catamaran. Soon boating types started filling up the cottages by the gently lapping sea, and more pink stucco buildings were added.

The atmosphere is very casual, and many repeat guests come here, enjoying the carefree tropical living. Soft pines and palms cast shadows over most of the buildings. Many guests prefer an intimate cottage set apart from the rest. In addition to two housekeeping cottages, suitable for triple occupancy, Mr. Bailey has converted four of his twin-bedded rooms into housekeeping efficiencies. In winter, the owner charges $52 daily in a single, $60 in a double, $100 in a triple. *Off-season, tariffs are reduced to $45 in a single, $54 in a double, and $75 in a triple.* Meals are extra. Guests who often share tables family style enjoy the low wooden dining room, with its antique tables and chairs. Facilities include free Sunfish sailing, rowboating in the bay, and fishing off the dock. Someone will probably teach you the popular Antiguan "Warri Game." The 30-foot, hotel-owned catamaran, *Sagitoo II,* is available for full- or half-day charters. You'll see it at the 27-berth marina added to the property in 1983. There is also the *Octo Pussy,* a 31-foot Bertram sportfisherman cabin cruiser which is available for deep-sea fishing and pleasure cruising on full- or half-day charters.

Best for the Budget

Barrymore, just off Fort Road, P.O. Box 244, Runaway Bay, St. John's (tel. 2-1055), has its own special niche in resort-crowded Antigua. First, it's a good bargain. Second, it's Antiguan, run by the LaBarries, and offers an inexpensive holiday in a completely unpretentious setting. A small bungalow colony with a freshwater swimming pool, it stands on three acres of private grounds, about a mile from the nearest beach and the capital. Free transportation is provided to the beach, incidentally. The place does a good family business, and children are free to romp on the lawn planted with poinsettia bushes. Rooms and efficiencies are in blue and white modern bungalows scattered about the grounds, bordered by flowering shrubbery.

Bedrooms have modern appointments motel style, private baths, and patios. Some, not all, contain air conditioning. In winter, singles on the EP range from $52 to $60 daily; doubles, $70 to $78. *Off-season, singles are charged from $40 to $48; doubles, $52 to $60 daily.* The LaBarries enjoy a good reputation on the island for serving West Indian dishes, especially Antiguan lobster, at their popular restaurant, Dubarry's (see "Where to Eat," below). You can dine inside or out on the porch, enjoying the breezes if there are any. The LaBarrie family is descended from Madame du Barry, and their French heritage is evident in the charm and grace with which they run their romantic, cozy restaurant.

Spanish Main, P.O. Box 655, East Street, St. John's (tel. 2-0660), is a restored town house facing St. John's Park, the center of sporting events and the annual carnival. Architecturally it reflects a romantic past, with twin gables and an upper and lower balcony. Its restaurant alone has won honorable mention from *Gourmet* magazine (see the dining recommendations). There are 15 second-floor bedrooms, furnished in the main with rattan, all consistently appealing. At this small, intimate inn, you pay $30 in a single, $45 in a double, including service and taxes. No meals are included for that, just a room and a bath. The owners, Bob and Janice Branker, are gentle, sweet, low-key people who have lived in New York and have won many friends, whom they welcome back again and again to their charming little place, one of the most delightful inns on the island. They preside over their garden-level bar and restaurant, always taking time out for some friendly gossip over a tall rum drink.

Pigottsville Hotel, P.O. Box 521, Clare Hall (tel. 2-0592). Your West Indian hosts, Hugh and Naomi Pigott, will take you in as if you're a member of their family, and Mrs. Pigott will show you her prize flowers. Their four-story, modern hotel sparkles with cleanliness. It is not lavishly appointed in any way, but the friendliness of the Pigotts and their good local food make this a fine buy. On the MAP, singles pay $25 daily, the cost rising to $40 for two persons in a double. A few family rooms are also rented out. All bedrooms on the ground floor have shared baths, although those on the upper floors have their own private facilities.

Hugh Pigott is a founder of the Small Hotels & Guest House Association in Antigua, and is trying to see that the lower cost properties get their fair shake. For example, in peak season, when some of the luxury hotels have more than 90% occupancy (or no rooms at all), the budget lodgings have reported plenty of empty rooms. Mr. Pigott feels that if some of the smaller hotels were better known, they'd fill up too in these days of the dwindling dollar—and I feel the man has a point.

Additional services arranged at extra cost include daily bus service to a nearby beach, horseback riding, buggy rides to the city and beach, transportation to the casino and nightclubs, and tours of historical sites. Pigottsville can accommodate groups of students 12 years old and over and other organizations.

Self-Sufficient Accommodations

The **Copper and Lumber Store,** P.O. Box 184, Nelson's Dockyard, English Harbour (tel. 3-1058), is an 18th-century building originally the purveyor of wood and sheet copper for the construction and/or repair of sailing ships of the British fleet plying the waters of the Caribbean. Today the louvered and shuttered windows of its dignified Georgian facade look out on increasing numbers of guests who recognize that in many ways this is the most understatedly elegant hotel in Antigua.

The store and its adjacent harbor structures were built of brick brought from England in the holds of ships as ballast, to be replaced on return voyages with sugar, rum, and other rich products of the West Indies. These bricks imbue the building with 18th-century English charm and sometimes serve to carefully conceal its necessary modern amenities.

You enter the hostelry into what looks like a private salon in an English manor house, and you can pass through into an arcaded inner courtyard where a sailmaker stitching huge expanses of canvas and a mammoth iron pot once used for boiling sugarcane recall an earlier era of the building's history.

The courtyard represents the kind of weathered charm that Gillian Gutteridge and her husband, a former British navy commander, worked for years to restore and preserve. Mrs. Gutteridge personally researched the wallpaper patterns and the exquisite moldings as the interior was restored by a battalion of expert carpenters. Rotted floors were replaced with insect-resistant purpleheart, and the massive post and beam ceilings were substituted with nearly exact copies of the hand-hewn and pegged originals.

Each of the 14 brick-lined accommodations has its own design and is named after one of the ships which fought at the battle of Trafalgar. Each is a well-proportioned study in high-quality 18th-century decorating. They're filled with fine Chippendale and Queen Anne reproductions, antiques, gleaming brass chandeliers, hardwood paneling, and hand-stenciled floors, all with a curator's eye for detail. Even the showers look like cabinetry in a sailing vessel, being lined with thick paneled slabs of mahogany, accented with polished brass fittings, then carefully shielded with many coats of waterproofing. The hotel has four one-level rooms and ten duplexes, each with a self-contained kitchen. Most have wide-angle views over the harbor where boats come and go much as they did 200 years ago.

The establishment's hostess, Patricia Hodges, or her assistant, Liisu Carlson, are usually around to welcome guests into the 18th-century games room or the elegantly symmetrical salon.

Since you don't come here looking for a beach or a pool, the "store" is more for those who want to revel in about as much atmosphere as you'll find anywhere in the Caribbean. Of course, Mrs. Hodges can describe a wide variety of water-sports facilities in the area if you're looking for an outing.

Maid service is included in the price of the rooms, which in winter cost $150 in a studio sleeping up to three persons and $215 in a one-bedroom suite which sleeps up to four. *In summer, the rates go down to $74 in a studio, $110 in a one-bedroom suite.* These tariffs are for double occupancy. Extra persons cost an additional $20 to $30 per day, depending on the season and the accommodation.

Mrs. Hodges can arrange lodgings in comfortable and charming contemporary accommodations as well. While not awash in the Georgian authenticity of the period rooms, they represent a reasonable investment at $85 for a studio and $125 for a one-bedroom suite (double occupancy) in winter. *Summer rates, double occupancy, are $50 in a studio and $70 in a one-bedroom suite.*

Barrymore Beach Apartments, P.O. Box 244, Runaway Bay, St. John's (tel. 2-4101). Recently designed and built by a Scottish architect, these are probably the most pleasantly finished and furnished apartments in the area. They're managed by one of the charming co-owners of the nearby Barrymore Hotel, Linda Gordon, who decorated the on-the-premises restaurant, the Satay Hut (see "Where to Eat," below), with Indonesian art she collected in the Far East.

There are 20 one- and two-bedroom apartments within this sun-drenched resort, where Linda, her husband, Brian, and the friendly staff do everything they can to create a "kick off your shoes" kind of ambience. The apartments are clustered within a handful of contemporary buildings whose cruciform design makes them look vaguely like Eastern Orthodox churches pierced with large windows.

The apartments contain kitchenettes, which Linda stocks with breakfast items before the arrival of guests, and sea-view terraces, original paintings, and collections of rattan and bentwood furnishings. In winter, a room for two with bath costs $80 to $90 daily, one-bedroom apartments are $110 to $130, and two-bedroom units, suitable for four, run $170 to $190. *In summer, a double with bath costs from $50 to $60 daily, a one-bedroom apartment runs $75 to $85, and a two-bedroom accommodation for four goes for $100 to $110,* plus service.

Galleon Beach Club and Hotel, P.O. Box 1003, English Harbour (tel. 3-1024), is built on a flat sandy area dotted with palms, only a few feet above the level of the nearby harbor. Accommodations are in a handful of low-slung cottages with big verandas and large plate-glass windows. The decor includes louvered shutters, tile floors, vertical slats of varnished pine paneling, and bentwood or rattan chairs and tables in natural colors.

In winter, one-bedroom studios cost $130 daily; one-bedroom cottages, $160; and two-bedroom cottages, $190. Two-bedroom deluxe villas go for $240. *In summer, one-bedroom studios are $80, one-bedroom cottages run $100, two-*

bedroom cottages cost $120, and two-bedroom deluxe villas, $140. These rates *do* include service.

Guests tend to socialize on the veranda of the on-site Colombo's Restaurant (see "Where to Eat," below).

WHERE TO EAT: Traditionally, hotels were the answer if you wanted to dine out in Antigua. That is no longer true. In addition to the hotel facilities, many independently operated restaurants have opened in and around St. Johns's, serving West Indian food not readily available in the hotel dining rooms. Many dishes, especially the curries, show an East Indian influence. Lobster is a specialty. In the 1980s, "gourmet" restaurants, charging inflated prices in some cases, started sprouting up on the island. Several of these are previewed in the section called "Elsewhere on the Island."

In and Around St. John's

Spanish Main Inn, P.O. Box 655, East Street (tel. 2-0660), looks like a Tennessee Williams setting, a relaxed atmosphere combined with an old-world elegance. Bordering the park, it serves some of the best food in town, with a heavy emphasis on local specialties, including those from the neighboring island of Barbuda. For example, as an appetizer you can order stuffed crab back, perhaps shark puffs, or a clams casino Bee Wee.

Their fish is always delivered fresh daily, so certain selections may not be available. However, if available I'd recommend Barbuda lobster. Try also the conch Barbuda style or the chef's special shark. Janice and Bob Branker once lived in New York—Janice working in an office, Bob digging for Con Edison. But they headed south after that with only $500 in savings and high hopes. They purchased this shingled house on Newgate Street, painting it white with red shutters. Gradually, because of their food and hospitality, the world came to their door.

In honor of their New York years, they still feature kosher knockwurst with sauerkraut. In season, they offer two rare delicacies—Barbuda guinea fowl and Barbuda venison.

You might begin your meal with one of their good-tasting soups, such as goat water, red bean, clam or fish chowder. Their vegetables, a wide selection, are also tasty, composed, as they are, mainly of fresh home-grown produce.

For dessert, I suggest Antigua Black Diamond pineapple. At lunch, hot dishes such as salisbury steak are served, or you may prefer a cheeseburger. Their club sandwiches are New York style. Expect to spend from $12 for lunch, $20 for dinner.

Brother B's, Long Street and Soul Alley (tel. 2-0616), is preferred for West Indian food, attracting a faithful crowd as well as a scattering of visitors. You can dine out on the patio, enjoying lobster caught fresh daily, plus fresh vegetables from Antiguan farms. The restaurant opens early (8 a.m.), remaining so until 11 p.m. Antiguan specials, prepared from recipes known for a century or two by oldtime island cooks, are served daily. For example, on Monday you might enjoy dumplings and mackerel, or pepperpot and fungi the following day, perhaps ducana (like a dumpling, made with sweet potatoes) and saltfish, or else curried conch. At night, hot plates include grilled lobster, baked chicken legs, and breaded pork chops, Antiguan style. Bottles of Susie's hot sauce (and Susie means that!) are placed on every table. Expect to spend from $15 and up. Sometimes a little jazz band plays on weekends.

Darcy's, Kensington Court, on St. Mary's Street, (tel. 2-1323), is an outdoor restaurant right in the heart of the shopping district. If a cruise ship isn't in dock, I'd recommend it for lunch. At that time a good steel band entertains.

Everything from a cheeseburger to West Indian dishes is featured. Each day a house specialty is selected from the local Antiguan cuisine and placed on the menu. The price of these specialties varies, of course, depending on the ingredients, but the cost is low. Another favorite luncheon selection is a lobster sandwich, or you can order hot plates of fish or chicken. If you're in town early, you'll find that Darcy's will prepare you a good breakfast. Should you want to hear the steel band, try to go early and select a preferred table under either a palm or a mango drop, admiring the bougainvillea. The jumbo-size pineapple and banana daiquiris are soothing, if you drop in for refreshment in the midafternoon. Your final bill will most likely come to $15. Closed Sunday.

18 Carat, Church Street, St. John's (tel. 2-4219). The sign above the broken pavement outside is hard to see, but this is nonetheless one of the best lunchtime stopovers in town. Its location is in the center, under a lattice-trimmed parapet which the owners have built at the edge of an attractive sheltered garden. The blackboard menu appeals to a wide array of well-dressed local residents.

The kitchen produces flavorful versions of chicken and corn chowder, club sandwiches, liver and bacon, cheeseburgers and hamburgers, seafood platters, and chicken-stuffed baked potatoes. Full meals cost EC$40 ($15.20) and are served only at lunchtime. In the evening, the garden becomes a conversation area for one of the most popular discos in town (see my nightlife recommendations, below).

Cockleshell Inn, Lower Fort Road (tel. 2-0471), may be hard to find, but it's one of the most economical and best dining spots on the island. Its chef-owner, Winston Derrick, who once lived in Canada, uses the produce of Antigua—cucumbers, potatoes, eggplant, papaya, pineapple. His rolls are homemade: "You've got to cook for people so they come back." A complete dinner costs around $15, although up this to $25 if you want lobster. Red snapper is often featured. The inn is open daily from 6 p.m. until midnight.

Golden Peanut, High Street (tel. 2-1415), is a carousel-like place in the heart of town, the domain of Rolston Anthony who was "born and bred on this island." His restaurant is unpretentious, and you might not imagine at first that its specialty is lobster thermidor, which the chef prepares better than anyone else on the island. The lobster salad is also tempting, particulary at lunch. Mr. Anthony gets the finest of fresh lobster from his brother, a local fisherman, and that seems to be part of his secret. Every day he offers two local specials, perhaps mutton stew, pepperpot, or curried goat, each a typical West Indian dish. If you're dropping in for lunch during a shopping expedition, you can also ask for sandwiches. The Peanut opens early—at 8 a.m.—for breakfast. In addition, grill specialties such as lamb chops are also a feature. Your final tab will come to anywhere from $15 to $20. The Peanut snaps shut at 11 p.m.

Country Pond Restaurant, Upper Nevis Street, St. John's (tel. 2-4508). When Liz Mellor entered the scene, this pink colonial town house needed virtually all of the interior floors and walls replaced. Built in 1796, it housed various merchant families until, in greatly reduced circumstances, it served as the run-down office of a local doctor. Today the refurbished structure welcomes residents and visitors alike into its interior with its high, white ceiling. It's only a few steps away from a freshwater pond on the edge of the commercial center of town.

If you're on a shopping expedition in St. John's, this might be the ideal place for you to have a light lunch. There's a terrace for al fresco dining, although the interior is kept cool by the slowly turning ceiling fans. Open daily except Sunday, the restaurant serves from 11 to 3 p.m. and 6 to 11 p.m. Full meals, ranging upward from EC$80 ($30.40), include red snapper, steak au poivre, veal piccata, chicken Kiev, shrimp and conch salad, and a full array of hamburgers and pizza.

The Yard, Upper Long Street (tel. 2-1856), gives you the feeling of dining in a living, growing garden. The tranquility demands that you relax. There is no decor added. The food is first rate. For lunch, the stuffed crab back is a specialty. There is a sumptuous Sunday brunch with a traditional local breakfast including fungi and shark. Dinner is from a well-chosen menu, costing from $18. A first-timer to the Yard should dine on the most delectable garlic shrimp in the region.

Elsewhere on the Island

Le Bistro, P.O. Box 390, Hodge's Bay (tel. 2-3881). The charming owners of this pleasant auberge are Yves Robert and his attractive wife, Chantale. Having emigrated from Nantes, after a sojourn in St. Martin they decided to open a French inn in Antigua, where everything, from the beamed ceiling to the well-polished paneling, is reminiscent of a country restaurant in central France.

By candlelight, you'll be offered menu choices such as crayfish bisque, pâté maison, escargots en croûte with tomatoes and basil, vol-au-vent with seafood, a white mushroom mousse, christophenes with lobster and curry, medallions of lobster printanière, filet of snapper au gratin Bistro style (with lobster, shrimp, scallops, and cream sauce), and duckling with apples and Calvados. Only dinner is served here. Full meals range upward from EC$80 ($30.40), lobster and some other entrees sending the price up. Le Bistro is closed Tuesday.

Pelican Club, P.O. Box 390, Hodge's Bay (tel. 2-2300), is set behind a low white wall between a road and the sea. The restaurant is filled with modern, country-style touches which include stone columns, brass ceiling fans, sloping wooden ceilings fashioned from varnished pine, and candlelit pink napery. When they're not gazing at the French-inspired menu, diners can look out at the seaside terrace and the view beyond. Established by French-born François Robert (whose brother, Yves, runs the neighboring restaurant, Le Bistro, reviewed above), this rambling place occasionally accepts groups of diners who fill every available table. It's best to reserve in advance, which gives you a chance to evaluate the dining situation on the evening of your choice.

Full meals cost from EC$100 ($38) and might include such specialties as Pelican Club salad made with shrimp and Tahitian-style scallops, conch stew in garlic and tomato sauce, freshly grilled Antiguan lobster, spaghetti carbonara, roast duck in honey and raspberry sauce, and veal Cordon Bleu. Serving only dinner, the restaurant is open every night of the week except Monday.

L'Auberge de Paris, Tradewinds, above Dickenson Bay (tel. 2-1223). Among all the restaurants of Antigua, this one offers the most sophisticated decor. It's reminiscent of a trendy bistro in the south of France, although both the accents and the attitude of the staff are pure Parisian. Masses of flowers set off the glossy collection of cocktail tables, low-slung sofas, and soft lights of the bar area, where a pianist (sometimes imported from Paris) creates music until late in the evening. Most guests enjoy a cocktail in the bar before heading for the slope-ceilinged dining room, where the view is that of an ornamental swimming pool gracefully set between several wings of outlying buildings.

Menu specialties usually include artichoke hearts with crayfish, turtle soup, salad with hot chavignol cheese, confit of duckling, aiguillettes of duckling with pepper, saddle of lamb with herbs for two, and filet of sole with tarragon. Full meals with wine cost from EC$60 ($22.80) per person.

It's on a hillside on the extreme northern end of the island, not far from the Halcyon Cove Hotel.

Dubarry's, Barrymore Hotel, P.O. Box 244, Runaway Bay, St. John's (tel. 2-1055), is one of the best restaurants in town. In a modern, low-slung building adjacent to the Barrymore Hotel, it's divided into two distinctly different dining rooms and a pleasant paneled bar dotted with Indonesian art. On a chilly evening, you'll be seated inside in an elegant modern room capped with a well-finished ceiling of Douglas fir and pitch pine. In warm weather and during informal lunches, diners are seated behind an iron railing on an al fresco terrace overlooking the blue rectangle of an outdoor pool.

Strictly local vegetables are used as accompaniments to the specialties served by candlelight. They include seafood-stuffed tomatoes, lobster bouchées, quiche maison, seafood bisque, spicy pumpkin or red bean soup, fresh salads, and main dishes such as potatoes stuffed with kingfish, fish and lobster mornay, deviled egg and shrimp casserole, curried coconut chicken served in coconut shells, spicy Malaysian lamb, and four different recipes for lobster, including a creole-style "Fra Diavolo." For dessert, you may want to try the chocolate-fudge-sundae pie which the chef considers his signature. Other dessert choices include a collection of homemade ice creams and coconut meringue pudding.

Pub lunches are served, but the real emphasis is on the dinner menu, which is offered every day except Sunday from 7:30 to 10 p.m. Full meals range from EC$85 ($32.30), if you don't order expensive lobster. Reservations are suggested.

Colombo's Restaurant, Galleon Beach Club, P.O. Box 1003, English Harbour (tel. 3-1024), is a Polynesian-style open-air terrace sheltered from the sun and rain by a ceiling crafted from woven palm fronds suspended on top of vertical posts. It's only a few steps across the flat sands to the water.

Lunches in this sprawling place cost EC$40 ($15.20) and might include spaghetti marinara, lobster salad, and sandwiches. Dinners are more elaborate, around EC$100 ($38), and include daily specials from a classic Italian inventory of veal scaloppine, red snapper, tagliatelle Colombo, veal pizzaiola, and lobster mornay. These can be accompanied by a wide assortment of French or Italian wines. Lunch and dinner are served daily except for the annual vacation between early September and early October.

Admiral's Inn, P.O. Box 713 (tel. 3-1027), has already been previewed in the hotel selections, a historic building in Nelson's Dockyard. If you're touring the southern coast, as most visitors do, it also makes an intriguing and pleasant stopover for lunch. In a 17th-century setting, lobster, seafood, and steaks are served, a lunch costing between $9 and $12, the price rising to about $20 for a full dinner, plus service and tax. To get you started, the chef is likely to tempt you with anything from pumpkin soup to shrimp cocktail. For your main course, you're usually given four or five choices daily—perhaps lobster thermidor, roast duckling, broiled kingfish, or lamb chops with mint sauce. If coconut custard pudding is on the menu, I'd recommend it highly. Before dinner, have a drink in the bar. There you can read the names of sailors carved in wood more than a century ago. The service is friendly and agreeable, and the setting is heavy on atmosphere. In season, you should make a reservation for dinner.

Shirley Heights Lookout, Shirley Heights (tel. 3-1274). In the 1790s this was the lookout station for advance warning of unfriendly ships heading toward English Harbour. To strengthen Britain's position in this strategic spot, Nelson ordered the construction of a powder magazine which, by the time Russell Hodge leased the heights from the government, had fallen into almost total ruin. Today the panoramic spot is one of the most romantic in Antigua.

Mr. Hodge, who is also a commercial pilot, is the dedicated restaurateur who directs the ground-floor pub and the elegant, breezy upstairs dining room which he leases on a long-term basis. This is my favorite lookout point in the Caribbean. If visitors want to bring a picnic onto the stone battlements below the restaurant, they're welcome to sit in the shade of the palm-thatch-covered parasols.

A far more desirable experience to me is to dine under the angled rafters of the upstairs restaurant, where large, old-fashioned windows surround the room on all sides. Specialties include pumpkin soup, grilled lobster in lime butter, garlic-flavored shrimp, and good desserts, such as banana flambé and carrot cake. Full meals range from EC$80 ($30.40), although less expensive hamburgers and sandwiches are available from the pub downstairs. A Sunday-afternoon tradition with many of the area's residents are the steel band concerts beginning at 3 p.m., accompanying the "end of the week" barbecues. The establishment is open from 10 a.m. to 10 p.m. daily. It never has a water shortage—part of Mr. Hodge's renovation included revamping the 200-year-old cistern.

The **Catamaran Hotel,** Falmouth Harbour (tel. 3-1036), was also previewed earlier in the hotel section. Even if you don't stay there, I suggest ringing up its owner and find out what's cooking. Just 20 minutes from the airport and 20 minutes from St. John's, the hotel is near Nelson's Dockyard at English Harbour. The menu is written on a board, and it changes daily. Only locally grown vegetables are cooked, always in the West Indian style. Soups are savory, including such unusual selections as okra or pumpkin. "We're not a hamburger-type restaurant," the owner proudly admits. The staff does a number of perfectly seasoned curry dishes, including conch, mutton, and chicken. Always there is fish just freshly caught, and sometimes lobster. For a complete dinner, figure on spending $20. Your bill may climb higher than $25 if you order lobster. A large patio with individual tables for outdoor dining has been added to the restaurant and bar, and the Catamaran can now accommodate up to 80 diners.

The **Satay Hut,** P.O. Box 244, Runaway Bay, St. John's (tel. 2-4101), is a simple and friendly restaurant which could serve as the focal point for a day at the beach. It sits directly on the sands of Runaway Bay, with breezes and the tropical drinks served by a smiling waitress keeping you cool. The interior is filled with Indonesian art which owner Linda Gordon picked up during her years in Jakarta.

No one will mind if you just come here for a drink. Piña coladas and rum punch cost $1 each during happy hour, held during a part of every afternoon. If you want a nourishing and good-tasting lunch or dinner, complete meals begin at around EC$50 ($19). Weekend specials are Indian curry, Antiguan lobster, and several different red snapper dishes. In keeping with the decor, the restaurant specializes in Indonesian satay, made with skewered pork, chicken, and beef, served with nasi goreng (fried rice), peanut sauce, and pickled vegetables. Less exotic and less expensive fare includes several kinds of hamburgers, cheeseburgers, club sandwiches, and chili dogs. The setting is informal, a fact appreciated by guests at the adjacent Barrymore Hotel.

Bach-Lien, Hodge's Bay (tel. 2-3293). One of the most delightfully isolated spots in Antigua is the veranda of a former plantation house on a tree-lined country road. The domain is the property of the beautiful and charming Claire Marchand, whose mixed Swiss-Vietnamese heritage has contributed to her becoming fluent in several languages and dialects, any of which she may be called on to use in communication with guests. Be sure to have a drink seated on one of the elaborately carved Chinese bar chairs. The antiques that line the room include an intricately embroidered Thai wedding dress draped over a mannequin whose elaborate headdress could grace the shelves of a museum. Some of the furniture took years of bureaucratic haggling to export from Vietnam, but the unusual carving and inlay work make it worth the effort.

Many of the food specialties include herbs, soya sprouts, lime leaves, and fresh mint which Mme Marchand grows in her garden. Menu choices include stuffed crab claws, Vietnamese duck, beef with lime leaves, bamboo chicken, Vietnamese salads, ginger chicken, and Saigon-style soup. Everything is delicately flavored, served on the candlelit veranda with views of the old, old trees on the lawn outside, making for a delightful evening. Lunches are served only on special reservation, although dinners are offered from 7 to 10:30 every evening except Wednesday. Full meals cost from EC$80 ($30.40).

EXPLORING ANTIGUA: In the southern part of St. John's, the **market** is colorful and interesting, especially on Saturday morning. Hucksters busy selling their fruits and vegetables bargain and gossip. The semi-open-air market lies at the lower end of Market Street. Scenery is provided by both dress and food.

Also in town, **St. John's Cathedral,** the Anglican cathedral, has had a disastrous history. Originally built in 1683, it was replaced by a stone building in 1745. That, however, was destroyed by an earthquake in 1843. The present pitch-pine interior, dating from 1847, shores up the stone walls against earthquakes. The interior was being restored when, in 1973, the twin towers and structure were badly damaged by an earthquake. The towers and the southern section have been restored, but restoring the northern part is estimated to cost thousands of dollars, for which contributions are gratefully received. At the entrance, iron gates were erected by the vestry in 1789. The figures of St. John the Baptist and St. John the Divine, at the south gate, were said to have been taken from one of the Napoleonic ships and brought to Antigua by a British man-of-war. The cathedral is between Long and Newgate Streets at Church Lane.

After leaving St. John's, the average visitor heads for one of the biggest attractions in the eastern Caribbean, **Nelson's Dockyard.**

One of the safest landlocked harbors in the world, the restored dockyard was used by Admirals Nelson, Rodney, and Hood. It was the home of the British fleet at the time of the Napoleonic wars. From 1784 Nelson was the commander of the British navy in the Leeward Islands, having his headquarters at English Harbour.

English ships used the harbor as early as 1671, finding it a refuge from hurricanes. The era of privateers, pirates, and great sea battles in the 18th century revolved around the dockyard.

Restored by the Friends of English Harbour, the dockyard is sometimes known as a Caribbean Williamsburg. Its colonial-style naval buildings stand now as they did when Nelson was there (1784–1787). However, Nelson never lived at the Admiral's House, as it was built in 1855. It does contain what may have been his bed, a four-poster of gilded ivory-colored wood. The house has been turned into a museum of nautical memorabilia. (For accommodations at English Harbour, refer to my earlier recommendations.)

A footpath leads to **Fort Barclay,** the fort at the entrance to English Harbour. The path starts just outside the gate of the dockyard, and it's about half a mile away. The fort is interesting, a fine specimen of oldtime military engineering.

If you're at English Harbour at sunset, head for **Shirley Heights,** named after General Shirley, governor of the Leeward Islands in 1781. He fortified the hills guarding the harbor. Standing are Palladian arches, once part of the barracks. The Block House, one of the main buildings, was put up as a stronghold in case of siege. The nearby Victorian cemetery contains an obelisk to the officers and men of the 54th Regiment.

On a low hill overlooking Nelson's Dockyard, **Clarence House** was built by English stonemasons to accommodate Prince William Henry, later known as the Duke of Clarence (even later he became King William IV). The future king stayed here when he was in command of the *Pegasus* in 1787. At present, it is the country home of the governor of Antigua, and is open to visitors when His Excellency is not in residence. A caretaker will show you through (it's customary to tip him, of course), and you'll see many pieces of furniture on loan from the National Trust. In days of yore, Princess Margaret and Lord Snowdon stayed here on their honeymoon.

On the way back, take **Fig Tree Drive,** a 20-some-mile circular drive across the main mountain range. It passes through lush tropical hills and fishing villages along the southern coast. You can pick up the road just outside Liberta, north of Falmouth. Winding through a rain forest, it passes thatched villages, and every village has a church with lots of goats and children running about. However, don't expect fig trees. Fig is an Antiguan name for bananas.

About half a mile before reaching St. John's, you come to **Fort James,** which was begun in 1704 as a main lookout post for the port. It was named after James II in whose reign efforts were made to build the fort on the point known as St. John's.

Other places on the island worth seeking out include the following:

Parkham Church: The origin of this church is unknown. However, a church stood on this spot in 1755. The church, overlooking Parkham Town, was destroyed by fire, and the present structure was erected in 1840 in the so-called Italian style. Richly adorned with stucco work, it was damaged by an earthquake in 1843. Much of the ceiling was destroyed and very little of the stucco work remains, but the octagonal structure is still worth a visit.

Potsworks Dam: This is the largest man-made lake in Antigua, surrounded by an area of natural beauty. The dam has a capacity of 1000 million gallons of water, protection for Antigua in case of a drought.

Indian Town: One of Antigua's national parks, Indian Town is at a northeastern point on the island. Over the centuries Atlantic breakers have lashed against the rocks, carving a natural bridge known as Devil's Bridge. It is surrounded by numerous blowholes spouting surf.

Megaliths: At Greencastle Hill, a long climb will reveal these megaliths, said to have been set up by human hands for the worship of a sun god and a moon goddess. Some experts, however, believe that the arrangement is an unusual geological formation, a volcanic rockfall.

Antigua Rum Distillery: This production plant at Rat Island turns out two fine rums, Cavalier and Old Mill. Check at the tourist office about arranging a visit. Established in 1932, the plant is next to Deep Water Harbour. Its annual production rate is in excess of 250,000 imperial-proof gallons.

GETTING AROUND: Taxis meet every airplane, and drivers wait outside the major hotels hoping to pick up passengers. In fact, if you're going to be in Antigua for a few days, you may find that a particular driver has "adopted" you. A typical fare from, say, the airport to Halcyon Cove is $8.50 for a one-way trip. From the airport to Curtain Bluff, however, will cost from $20, as it's a long run. The government of Antigua fixes the rates, but the taxis have no meters. While it's costly, the best way to see Antigua is by private taxi. Drivers are also guides. Most taxi tours, taking in all the major sights, including lunch at Admiral's Inn, last 3½ hours and cost $50 to $60.

Buses are not recommended for the average visitor, although they do exist. Service seems erratic and undependable. The official hours of operation between St. John's and the villages are between 5:30 a.m. and 6 p.m., but don't count on it. However, if you're adventurous, you'll find buses the cheapest means of transport, costing EC$1.50 (57¢) for most fares. In St. John's, buses leave from the West Bus Station for Falmouth and English Harbour, the major goal of most travelers.

Car Rentals: A self-drive car may be more practical for some visitors. Note that as a holdover of British tradition, Antiguans *drive on the left*. Many car-rental agencies operate in Antigua.

However, there is one important requirement. You must obtain a driver's license, costing $10. To obtain one, you must produce a valid U.S. or Canadian license. It is no longer necessary to go to the police station to obtain this license. Most car-rental firms are authorized to issue it to you in exchange for a fee.

Car-rental firms in Antigua are local operations, although two or three are affiliated with major car-rental firms in the United States. The exception is **Hertz,** which has folded its Antigua operation. **Avis** is represented by a local firm with a different name (see below), and you also have a choice of some very local and often small operations (one of which I recommend). However, several others rent cars that aren't in the best of condition, and with the pot-holed roads of Antigua you need the best-maintained vehicle you can get.

Operating under its own banner, **Budget Rent-a-Car** maintains a local office in Antigua at the corner of American and Factory Road (tel. 2-2544). When you arrive at the Coolidge Airport, a Budget representative will see that you are delivered to Budget's island headquarters.

There, the cheapest car available is usually a manual-transmission Toyota Corolla without air conditioning. In high season it rents for $180 a week, with each additional day costing $30. However, you must notify Budget at least two business days in advance to get this rate. You also must be at least 25 years old, but not older than 65.

If your heart is set on a Datsun Sunny, with air conditioning and automatic transmission (either two- or four-door, seating four passengers comfortably), the charge is $204 weekly, with each additional day costing $34.

Budget charges $7 per day for a collision damage waiver, which in the event of an accident will void your financial responsibility for repairs. Without that waiver, the renter is responsible for the first $250 worth of damage to the vehicle.

These rates may change during the lifetime of this edition. Before making your travel plans, you can call Budget toll free at 800/527-0700.

Another rental agency is **Antigua Car Rentals,** P.O. Box 244, which holds the local Avis license. It's run by Martin A. LaBarrie, whose Barrymore Hotel (tel. 2-1815) was previously recommended. One-day rentals cost from $35; weekly rentals, from $210. The person renting the car must be between the ages of 25 and 65.

Carib Car Rentals, P.O. Box 1258, Hodge's Bay (tel. 2-2062), will pick you up and deliver you anywhere on Antigua. It rents vehicles that are clean, modern, and reliable. For one day expect to pay from $35, with a free choice of automatic or stick shift. If you keep the car from seven days, the charge is lowered to only $29 per day. Hours are 8 a.m. to 5 p.m. seven days a week.

SHOPPING: Most of the shops are clustered on St. Mary's Street or High Street in St. John's.

There are many duty-free items for sale, including English woolens and linens, and you can also purchase several specialized items made in Antigua. These include original pottery, local straw work, Antigua rum, and silk-screened, hand-printed local designs on fabrics, as well as mammy bags, floppy foldable hats, and shell curios.

Sea island cotton products are good buys, and some of the best are found at the **West Indian Sea Island Cotton Shop,** St. Mary's Street, St. John's. The shop is an outlet for the Romney Manor workshop on St. Kitts. The Caribelle label consists of batik and tie-dye, offering beach wraps, swimwear, and head ties.

The **Studio,** Cross Street, opposite Government House (tel. 2-1034). Heike Petersen came to Antigua in 1964, restoring this lovely old town house. When it was finished, the designer was ready to show off a collection of island fashions. The clothes are island-inspired originals, and Heike designs all of them herself, using fabrics from all over the world. The originals are hand-finished and styled in Antigua, however. Beach fashions are displayed, along with striking day wear, even evening gowns and coordinated accessories. The style is that of casual elegance. Heike is also available for consultation and custom designing.

The **Industrial School for the Blind** stands next to the public market. Here the government helps the handicapped in training programs. On sale are the results of some of their work—pieces of straw work, including floormats, baskets, chairs, mats, hats, and other small household items. You'll also see the craftspeople at work.

Coco Shop, the "brown house on St. Mary's Street" (tel. 2-1128), is one of the best equipped marts in town. It's a West Indian beach and shore fashion center, utilizing sea island cottons, even prints from Liberty of London. You can purchase these fabrics either made up or by the yard. Men's shirts have a tropical flair, and some of the carefree clothes are hand-embroidered. Men, women, and children will find a selection of shirts, dresses, blouses, and bikinis. Placed on the counters are handcrafted ceramics, all made in Antigua. The most popular are the famous steel bandsmen. Ask for Antiguan Frangipani Perfume.

Shouls Chief Store, St. Mary's Street, a large corner store opposite Barclay's Bank, is an emporium selling hard-to-find imported fabrics by the yard or skirt length, including colorful prints from Bali and France. Men's shirts are also fashioned out of some of the fabrics.

Shipwreck, St. Mary's Street at Kensington Court, seems to have everything. Its walls, ceilings, and counters are loaded with merchandise, either from Antigua or some neighboring island. "Nothing from Japan or Hoboken," a sign proclaims. Many of the items might be labeled "trinkets," but you might find something you're looking for—wooden bowls, coconuts, flour sacks (with original but faded ads for the brand, made into shirts for men), figurines of wood and ceramic, stuffed rag dolls, Indian sandals, straw mats, or block prints of tropical flowers and island birds. At one side of the Shipwreck is an open doorway leading to an open-air patio where you can purchase tropical beverages and listen to a steel band at noon.

Bay Boutique, St. Mary's Street (tel. 2-2183), is for women who are offered a choice line of ready-made clothes for sale. Hostess gowns are well styled, and there are both long and short skirts, and blouses. All of the items were sewn on the island from imported fabrics. Lots of English flowery fabrics were in evidence on my most recent rounds.

Sugar Mill Boutique, St. Mary's Street (tel. 2-4523), set amid a collection of other clothing stores and shops, sells garments whose fabrics have been silkscreened by local artist Ruth Clarage. The designs tend to include depictions of birds, fish, flowers, and shells indigenous to the region. The store sells a wide array of vibrantly colorful swimwear, evening wear, and casual clothes for men and women. Everything sold here is advertised as hand-washable.

Quin Farara's Liquor Store, Long Street and Corn Alley (tel. 2-0463). Antigua has some of the lowest liquor prices in the Caribbean, and this shop has one of the largest collections of wines and liquors on the island. Often you'll save up to 50% on what you'd pay in the States. The staff will show you how to take home a "gallon," pay the duty, and still save. Don Diego (originally Cuban) cigars are also on sale.

The **Halcyon Cove Hotel** boutique at Dickenson Bay always has 100 or so casual dresses on hangers. There is a vast selection of attractive floral prints. For the most part the dresses are full length and strapless, some with spaghetti straps.

Kel-Print, Coolidge Airport and also St. Mary's Street in St. John's (tel. 2-2189), offers silkscreened, hand-print fabrics and T-shirts. Some children's wear is also sold.

If you want an island-made bead necklace, don't bother to go to any shop. Just lie on the beach—anywhere—and some "bead lady" will find you.

NIGHTLIFE: Most nightlife revolves around the hotels, unless you want to roam Antigua at night looking for that "hot native club." If you're going out for the night, make arrangements to have a taxi pick you up—otherwise, you could be stranded in the wilds somewhere. Antigua has some of the best steel bands in the Caribbean.

18 Carat, Church Street, St. John's (tel. 2-4219). Although it serves well-prepared lunches, this place's real identity comes from its function as St. John's leading nightclub. Guests go through a pleasant garden, past a lattice-trimmed arbor, and then enter the cozy building at the garden's far end. The club's ambience is heightened by its small dimensions. There's occasionally a live singer in the disco, but most of the time the crowd seems to prefer to dance the night away to the sounds of the recorded music. This place opened in 1984 under the watchful eye of Lebanon-born Souheil Hechme and his beautiful Antiguan wife, Gaye. The disco opens at 9:30 p.m. Wednesday through Sunday, charging an entrance fee of EC$6 ($2.28). Red Stripe beer costs EC$3.50 ($1.33).

After dinner, you might also want to patronize the **Halcyon Cove Casino** (tel. 2-0256). It offers all the games of chance, giving you an opportunity to try your luck at roulette, blackjack, American craps, and super-jackpot slots.

Flamingo Antigua Hotel and Casino, on Michael's Mount (tel. 2-1266), is a gambling complex that's part of the hotel of the same name, about half a mile from the center. It offers blackjack and craps tables, plus a large assortment of slot machines and roulette.

THE SPORTING LIFE: Beaches, beaches and more beaches—Antigua has, as mentioned, some 365 of them. Some are superior. There's a lovely beach at Pigeon Point, in Falmouth Harbour, about a four-minute drive from the Admiral's Inn. The beach at **Dickenson Bay,** near the Halcyon Cove Hotel, is also superior, and for a break, you can enjoy meals and drinks on the hotel's Warri Pier, built on stilts in the water (this beach is also a center for water sports). Chances are, however, you'll swim at your own hotel.

Golf

In golf, Antigua doesn't have the facilities of some of the other islands such as Puerto Rico. But what it has is good. The 18-hole **Cedar Valley Golf Club** is three miles out of St. John's, near the airport. It has been improved and expanded in recent years. Greens fees are about $16 per person. A golf cart can be rented for $20 for 18 holes, and caddy fees are $3.50 per nine holes.

The other course of note is the one at **Half Moon Bay** (tel. 2-2726), on the southeast corner of Antigua. It's a nine-holer. In season, guests of the hotel are guaranteed a space—and you may not be.

Horseback Riding

It may no longer be prudent to ride a horse along the beach (there have been problems in the past), but this sport is still popular, costing $12 per hour.

Riding is possible at the **Galley Bay Surf Club** (tel. 2-0302), 15 minutes from St. John's by taxi.

Tennis

Tennis buffs will find courts at most of the major hotels. Some are lit for night games. I don't recommend playing tennis at noon in Antigua unless you're a "mad dog or an Englishman." It's just too hot! If your hotel doesn't have a court, you'll find them available at the **Halcyon Cove, Anchorage, Half Moon Bay, Cedar Valley Golf Club,** and **Curtain Bluff.** If you're not a guest, you'll have to book a court, paying about $4 per hour, a price which can vary from hotel to hotel. Some hotels require a $25 deposit for the rental of balls and racquets, but the full amount is refunded if the equipment is returned.

Fishing

Deep-sea fishing can usually be arranged at your hotel desk. If you want to negotiate on your own, check out **Long Bay Hotel,** P.O. Box 442 (tel. 3-2005), which offers a half-day inshore fishing at $20 per person if there are two or more in your party. For deep-sea fishing, including guide, bait, and tackle, the cost is $125 per half-day trip.

Windsurfing

The **Blue Waters Beach Hotel,** Soldier Bay (tel. 2-0290), claims nearly everybody can learn this sport. It's one of the leading facilities on the island for windsurfing, giving an introductory lesson for $35 for 1½ hours. If you already know how to windsurf, the cost is $12 per hour.

Another establishment that specializes in helping newcomers to become windsurfers is **Windsurfing Antigua** (tel. 2-0068, ext. 300), at the south end of the Jolly Beach Hotel, although it is an independent operation not connected with the hotel. Thea Ramsey and André de St. Phalle are the enthusiastic operators of this business which dispenses information on where, how, and what windsurfing in Antigua is all about. They've certified dozens of visitors since they began their operation and will rent several brands of sailboards for $6 to $8 an hour.

For safety reasons, only certified windsurfers are allowed to rent boards and to pursue the sport with the proper facilities anywhere in the world. Thea and André offer courses which, depending on the season, cost between $45 and $65 for two lessons, stressing what Thea calls "sailing geometry," self-rescue, and water safety. If purchased in conjunction with the lessons, three hours of subsequent windsurfing time costs only $10. A series of advanced lessons, stressing jibing, upwind sailing, uses of a harness and footstraps, and body dips, cost $20 each. A free half-hour introductory lesson is held every day at noon.

Water Sports

Snorkeling and scuba-diving are best arranged through **Dive Antigua,** at the Halcyon Cove Beach Resort and Casino on Dickenson Bay (tel. 2-0256), and at the Jolly Beach Hotel on Morris Bay (tel. 2-0061). The cost of scuba-diving is $30, with one tank provided. Snorkelers are welcomed at a cost of $12 per person. A resort scuba course costs $50 and up per person, including all equipment and one dive.

Long Bay Hotel (tel. 3-2005), on the northeastern coast of the island at Long Bay, is another good location for water sports—swimming, sailing, water-skiing, deep-sea fishing, windsurfing, and scuba-diving. The hotel has complete scuba facilities. Diving rates (per dive) are $40 for a boat trip and guide for one.

Individual instruction is $30 per person if there are two or more. Both beginning snorkelers and experienced divers are welcomed. You're taken on snorkel trips by boat to Green Island at a cost of $10 per person (if there are two or more) and to Great Bird Island for $15 per person (again if there are two or more). The shallow side of the double reef across Long Bay is ideal for the neophyte, and the whole area on the northeastern tip has many reefs of varying depths.

The **Blue Waters Beach Hotel,** Soldier Bay (tel. 2-0290), has one of the best water-sports programs on the island. Waterskiing is available at about $10 per ski per person. They also have parasailing at $25 per ten-minute ride. In addition, they offer snorkeling gear free to their guests.

Sailing

Since Admiral Nelson's day, sailing has been popular in Antigua. I prefer the **Servabo Fun Cruise** taken in a character-type vessel, the last constructed of a British sailing fishing trawler popular from 1750 to 1927. Based off the shores of Dickenson Bay, the 64-ton *Servabo* celebrated her 50th anniversary some time back. She even appeared before the cameras, in the Omar Sharif film *The Mysterious Island.* The vessel's barbecue cruise costs $40 per person. Out at sea you're given barbecued steak and lobster, and you're gone from 10 a.m. to 4 p.m. The cruise departs from Antigua Village. The day is filled with calypso music, snorkeling, and rum punches. Telephone 2-1581 for reservations.

All major hotel desks can book you on a day cruise on the 108-foot "pirate ship," the **Jolly Roger.** For $36, you are taken sightseeing on a fun-filled day, with drinks and a barbecue steak lunch. The *Jolly Roger* is the largest sailing ship in Antiguan waters. Lunch is combined with a snorkel trip. Dancing is on the poop deck, and members of the crew teach passengers how to dance calypso. Everything's a little corny, but most passengers love it. If you want to make reservations on your own, telephone 2-2064 or write to P.O. Box 301. There are daily sailings from Dickenson Bay.

Other sailing expeditions can be arranged on the 46-foot Bermuda Cutter **Pride of Orca,** which is capably skippered by Antiguan Capt. Nash Edwards. Built of teak and mahogany in Southhampton, England, she was originally designed as a racing craft. Today you can sail aboard her on cocktail or luncheon cruises.

The cocktail cruise, when featured, leaves at 2 p.m., providing opportunities for snorkeling and as many rum punches as you can contain, before the 5 p.m. return. The cost is $25 per person. Sometimes a luncheon cruise departs at 10 a.m., returning at 5 p.m. Lunch is served at an anchorage on the lee coast of Antigua. Guests swim, snorkel, and imbibe all the rum punch they want. The cost is $40 per person.

For information and reservations, call 2-1569 or inquire at your hotel desk.

BARBUDA: Known by the Spanish as Dulcina, sparsely populated Barbuda, part of an associated state with Antigua, was discovered by Columbus in 1493. The island lies 28 miles to the north of Antigua, and is about 15 miles long by 5 miles wide with a population of some 1200 hardy souls, most of whom live around the unattractive village of Codrington.

Don't come here seeking lush, tropical scenery, as flat Barbuda consists of coral rock. Yet it is the flatness that gives the island some fine beaches that stretch for miles on both the leeward and the windward coasts.

Hunters, fishermen, and just plain beachcombers are attracted to the island, as it has some fallow deer, guinea fowl, pigeon, and wild pig. Barbuda also has a few deer. Those interested in fishing negotiate with the owners of small boats which hire them out. Bonefish and tarpon are frequently caught.

The main town is named after Christopher Codrington, who was once the governor of the Leeward Islands. He is believed to have deliberately wrecked ships on the reefs circling Barbuda. What is known is that he used the island, which he'd received in 1691 from the Crown, for the purposes of breeding slaves. He was given the island in return for "one fat pig per year, if asked."

Barbuda has a temperature that seldom falls below an average of 75° Fahrenheit.

The island is reached after a ten-minute flight from Antigua's Coolidge Airport. It has two airfields, one at Codrington, the other a private facility, "Kelly Field," at Coco Point. Both are served by Leeward Islands Air Transport (LIAT) on both a scheduled and charter service.

Wadadli Travel and Tours Ltd., P.O. Box 589, in the Murdoch Building, Market Street in St. John's (tel. 2-2227), runs tours to the island, attracting those interested in rookery, snorkeling, turtle watching, or in exploring chartered wrecks, whatever.

Paradise Tours, High Street, St. John's (tel. 2-4786), also conducts a round-trip tour to Barbuda for the day, including a picnic lunch.

Prices are subject to variation, but count on spending some $100 for the day tour, including air flight.

Those trippers over just for the day usually head for **Wa'Omoni Beach Park,** where they can visit a frigate bird sanctuary, snorkel for lobster, and eat barbecue.

Curiosities of the island include a **"Dividing Wall,"** which once separated the Codringtons from the black people, and the **Martello Tower,** which predates the known history of the island. Tours also cover interesting underground caves on the island. Stamp collectors might want to call at the **Philatelic Bureau** in Codrington.

Where to Stay

Coco Point Lodge (tel. 2-3206) is like a private club, occupying a 164-acre peninsula with more than 2½ miles of white sandy beach at the southern tip of Barbuda. Guests are housed either in the main building or in one of the newer cottages such as Spanish Point, Martello Tower, or Sea Crescent, a total of 32 accommodations with beachfront patios. Coco Point caters to everybody from a small-town banker to titans of industry, actresses who want to escape from it all, even Princess Margaret.

On the full-board plan, single peak-season rates range from $400 to $550 daily, with doubles costing from $425 to $620 on the same plan. An additional person in a room is another $140. At least the booze is included in the rate.

The food is flown in from Miami, except some fresh produce which may be shipped in from Dominica and St. Kitts. The venison is left for the natives to live on. Their seafood and homemade bisques are superb.

A lot of wicker is used, making the lodge evoke a summer home in the Hamptons. The designer did the exclusive Mill Reef Club on Antigua. The inn is definitely understated, and that's how its clients like it. The social hub is the clubhouse. The lodge receives only from December 1 to May 1. Usually there are rarely more than 50 guests at one time, perhaps 60 at the very most, and it's estimated that some three-quarters of them are repeat customers. Dress is casual, and ties and jackets are certainly not required.

About 40% of the guests come here to enjoy the good fishing. A 43-foot motor sailer is placed at the disposal of guests. Guests who land on the lodge's own 3000-foot strip are picked up quickly, and 15 minutes later are found sitting on the beach with a rum punch. Included in the rate is air transportation from Coolidge Airport in Antigua.

Other facilities include waterskiing and two very fine all-weather tennis courts.

The owner is Bill Kelly, who once lived next door to the Kennedys in Hyannis Port. His son, Patrick, is now in charge. His most helpful on-the-spot managers are Martin and Caroline Price.

Frankly, Mr. Kelly prefers to keep the crowds out. After all, this is an exclusive resort. Therefore if you're planning to drop in for a drink or a meal, forget it, unless you're a paying guest. Many a visiting yachtsman has been turned away disappointed. At the rates charged, Coco Point guests demand—and get—their privacy.

For reservations in the U.S., telephone 212/696-4750 in New York.

Le Village Soleil, P.O. Box 1104, St. John's, Antigua (tel. 462-3147 in Antigua). If you've ever wanted to practice your French in as remote an environment as possible, you might enjoy this isolated guest house whose charming owners come from Québec. André Cloutier and his attractive wife, Danie, maintain this tiny resort on Barbuda as if it were an extension of their private home.

Most of the accommodations contain large bedrooms, verandas, private baths, thatched roofs, and imaginatively rustic ceilings. Between mid-December and the end of April, single units cost $120 to $125 and doubles run $200 to $220. All meals are included in the tariffs, wine also. A 10% service charge is added to all bills.

The public rooms revolve around a steep-roofed, cedar-sided bar and restaurant open to a sweeping view of the wide, curved beach of white clear sand. Meals are usually eaten at long tables with the other guests, where nightfall parties feast on the French and Caribbean cuisine. Since there are no telephones, television, or newspapers, most guests succumb to the temptation of simply relaxing.

There's room for only 16 guests at this congenial establishment, many of whom come yearly from Québec, like the owners. The hotel is not open in summer, at which time inquiries should be sent to P.O. Box 72, Roberval, Québec G8H 2N4, Canada (tel. 418/275-3861).

2. Montserrat

Vacationers often visit the volcanic island of Montserrat just for the day, and later are sorry they hadn't booked more time. Called tritely "The Emerald Isle of the Caribbean," Montserrat is some 27 miles southwest of Antigua, lying between Guadeloupe and Nevis. The pear-shaped island is mountainous with lush green forests, much tropical vegetation, and some licorice beaches of volcanic sand that are powdery but black as midnight.

Montserrat was discovered by the ubiquitous Columbus in 1493 and named after the famous sawtoothed mountain near Barcelona. However, it wasn't until 1632 that Irish settlers colonized the island, when Oliver Cromwell, it is believed, shipped out a band of reluctant colonists who'd been captured after a rebellion. Sending the unwilling band to the ruggedly beautiful island was Cromwell's way of getting rid of them.

Today, Montserrat's more than 15,000 hardworking, friendly people, most of whom were descended from African slaves, often speak with an Irish brogue as a heritage left by those early settlers.

Customs officials stamp your passport with the official Montserrat three-leaf clover.

The island was captured by the French in 1644, restored to England in 1668, and retaken by the French in 1782, who ceded it to Britain in 1783. Popular as a retiree resort, the island has political stability, its officials having elected to remain a British Crown Colony, as they don't have the financial independence to go it alone.

The capital, Plymouth, is reputed to be one of the cleanest in the Caribbean. It's best viewed on Saturday market day, when gossip is traded along with fruit. A shamrock adorns the center gable of Government House, which may be visited.

The mean temperature of Montserrat ranges from a high of 86.5° to a low of 73.5° Fahrenheit.

George Martin, best known as the producer of the Beatles, has launched a contemporary electronic studio in a Belham Valley estate, and he uses Olveston House, the residence of an early lime-juice magnate, as a private residence for the Aire recording company (tel. 491-5656).

Therefore don't be surprised if, when exploring Montserrat, you encounter such artists as Paul McCartney or Elton John, both of whom come here for weeks at a time to record music and to "wind down." Also attracted to the island are such performers as The Police, Jimmy Buffet, and Stevie Wonder. Yes, Ringo Starr as well. So along with being a tourist attraction, Aire Studios is also a source of local employment.

PRACTICAL FACTS: Montserrat is on Atlantic Standard Time. When it's 6 a.m. in Plymouth, it's 5 a.m. in New York or Miami. However, island clocks match those of the mainland when the East Coast goes on Daylight Saving Time.

You'll need an electrical adapter for all U.S.-made appliances, as the island has 220–230 volts, 60 cycles, AC.

Most hotels add a 10% surcharge to your final tab to cover tips. If they don't, it's customary to tip from 10% to 15%.

As you leave Montserrat, the government will impose a $5 departure tax. They also charge a government hotel tax of 7%.

GETTING THERE: Antigua is the "gateway" to Montserrat. The government of Montserrat purchased two planes from LIAT, calling their new airline the **Montserrat Air Service** (MAS for short). MAS still uses LIAT's ticketing facilities. In other words, a passenger might fly MAS and still think he or she was doing business with LIAT. There are several morning and afternoon flights every day of the week. The round-trip passage between Antigua and Montserrat is EC$134 ($50.92).

HOTELS: Montserrat has a very limited range of accommodations and these are wide-ranging in style, from plantation-style guest houses to modest inns to condominium colonies. The trade winds, more than air conditioning, will keep you cool. Extreme informality is the keynote.

Vue Pointe Hotel, Old Towne, P.O. Box 65 (tel. 5211), is a family-run cottage colony of octagonal, shingle-roofed villas, on a slope overlooking Isles Bay and the golf course. At the bottom is the Isles Bay Beach. Offered are 28 individual rondavels, plus 12 bedrooms, constructed in the main with natural lumber with open-beamed ceilings, and furnished with sleekly modern pieces. Each has a private bath, a sitting room area, and twin beds. The location is just 11 miles from the Montserrat airport.

Your host is Cedric R. Osborne, a bright, charming West Indian aristocrat who welcomes guests with his customary style and grace, and does what he can to keep you from becoming bored, even though Montserrat is supposed to be "sleepy." His father built Vue Point, and he's assisted by Carole, his wife. If it's your second visit, he welcomes you as "part of the family."

In winter, two persons pay $175 daily in a cottage, while a single person is charged only $135, all on the MAP. A double room, also on the MAP, rents for $135 daily, a single for $110. *In summer, tariffs are lowered, with two persons on the MAP paying from $60 daily; a single, from $50.*

A natural breeze sweeps through accommodations in lieu of air conditioning. Besides the freshwater swimming pool, there are two tennis courts, lit for evening games.

The cuisine is the best on the island, and as proof of that, everybody seems to show up for the West Indian barbecue on Wednesday night. Food is served family style, which means that no one faints if you ask for second helpings. However, the first helpings are usually generous enough to suffice.

There are two attractive bars, one at the rambling main house, the other, called the Nest, at water's edge.

Mr. Osborne has selected what is the finest staff on the island, with Augustus Cruickshank as manager. They are unobtrusive, but so well trained they seem to anticipate your needs. When they can, they offer music and dancing to a steel-band beat. They'll even show movies.

The location is just two minutes from the challenging seaside Montserrat Golf Club. The staff will arrange for fishing, sailing, and snorkeling. Dress is informal, except on Monday and Saturday nights in season, when custom dictates that the men spruce up a bit.

Coconut Hill Hotel, P.O. Box 337 (tel. 2144), in the residential suburbs half a mile outside Plymouth, once belonged to an English surgeon and plantation owner who settled in Montserrat at the time of the American Civil War. This antique Montserratian mansion has roots deep in the soil of the island. The son of the original owner converted the property into a hotel way back in 1908, adding half a dozen rooms on the top floor. Other renovations have been carried out to improve the facilities.

This is a very casual West Indian guest house, surrounded by park-like grounds. It's also classic in style—the facade has remained the same over the years, with a long upper and lower balcony across the front. Across the rear of the building, a dining room, serving island-style meals, offers an unmarred view. The furnishings are unusually fine, with a generous collection of Caribbean antiques. All but one of the bedrooms have private baths, and are furnished with a mixture of the old and new. Each room also has a phone, but don't expect air conditioning. However, you may sleep blissfully in a four-poster bed.

In winter, guests on the MAP are charged $75 daily in a single, $85 in a double. *Off-season reductions drop the prices to $65 daily in a single, $85 in a double, both MAP tariffs.*

Montserrat Springs Hotel, P.O. Box 259, Richmond (tel. 2481), is a 16-room inn and health spa nestled on a hillside, with a superb view of Plymouth, a mile and a half away. The manager runs a quiet, subdued, small hotel, welcoming you into a split-level house with its trade-wind-swept, open-air terrace built around a swimming pool that juts out on the hill. Guest rooms extend down a breezy corridor. You often must keep the jalousied windows open for air, and this definitely interferes with privacy. Your other wall opens onto a picture window with a small patio. Baths are big and tiled, however. A few rooms have air conditioning. The hotel has a Jacuzzi and a hot-water mineral bath.

In the modest open-air lounge, you can enjoy a before-dinner drink before walking up to the mezzanine for a big, hearty West Indian dinner. In winter, singles on the EP pay $90 to $96 daily (the higher price is for an air-conditioned accommodation). Doubles are $102 to $108. *Off-season, singles are $54 to $60, while doubles cost $66 to $72.* A third adult in a room pays $24, but there is no charge for children up to 12 sharing a room with adults. The beach is a taxi ride away. On some nights there is live music and entertainment, perhaps crab racing.

Wade Inn, Parliament Street, right in the heart of Plymouth (tel. 2881), is simple and handy for anyone on a budget wanting to stay in the center. The furnishings may be a bit mail-order catalogue, with plastic where you might hope for rattan, but I like it nevertheless, and so did a group of young American schoolteachers vacationing there on my most recent visit. It offers ten small but immaculately kept nests, each with a private bath. *In summer, singles on the MAP rent for $45 daily; doubles, $65.* In winter, rates go up to $50 daily in a single, to $75 in a double, both MAP tariffs.

SELF-SUFFICIENT VACATIONS: Shamrock Villas, P.O. Box 180, Plymouth (tel. 2434), is a recently built condominium hillside colony, suggesting an Iberian village of white, balcony-studded houses. Owners have arranged for their villas to be rented in their absence. The interiors are decorated in the taste of their owners. You might, for example, find a style that is imaginative, with high walls of rugged stone, lofty ceilings with open beams, and furnishings that combine bamboo with locally made mahogany and cedar pieces. From all villas there are views of the sea, the black sandy beaches, and Plymouth.

Up for rent are one- and two-bedroom apartments as well as penthouses. In season (December to April), the rates for one-bedroom one-bath apartments are $60 per night, $375 weekly, and $1400 monthly. Furnished two-bedroom two-bath units are $70 per night, $475 weekly, and $1700 monthly. For the penthouses, the charge is $80 per night, $500 per week, and $1800 per month. *Off-season, the rates drop to $45 per night, $275 weekly, and $1000 monthly for a one-bedroom apartment; $60 nightly, $375 weekly, and $1300 monthly for a two-bedroom unit; and $65 per night, $400 weekly, and $1400 monthly for a penthouse.* Linen and cutlery are included, even for short-term rentals. Maid service is available at an extra cost. Services are close by. Bread comes fresh from the baker, and at the local market you can sample the produce grown on the island, especially the abundant tomatoes, carrots, and pineapples. A beach and tennis court are adjacent.

Lime Court Apartments, P.O. Box 250, Plymouth (tel. 2513), is an apartment colony right in the center of town, one minute from the harbor and beach. The property is walled in, making the gardens private. Fully furnished one- and two-bedroom apartments are available with well-equipped kitchens and electric cooking. Each unit has a hot-water shower for the bedroom, and all utilities and maid service are included in the tariffs. The most luxuriously equipped unit (no. 1) is a two-bedroom apartment with private baths—very well furnished, with a large kitchen, complete with ice maker, washing machine and dryer, and a living room (37 by 21 feet) with a TV and stereo, plus a veranda in front and back. This honey goes for $350 weekly year round. Four one-bedroom units with private patios cost $135 weekly. Some other two-bedroom units go for $200. In winter, all bookings should be made at least two months in advance.

The **Belham Valley Hotel,** P.O. Box 420 (tel. 5553), is a series of cottages rented out by Chris and Barbara Crowe, two British expatriates. The cottages stand on a hillside overlooking the Belham Valley and its river. The entrance to the Montserrat Golf Course is directly below the property. The beach is about a seven-minute walk, and you can also stroll over for an evening at the already-previewed Vue Pointe Hotel.

The Crowes call the Frangipani studio cottage their "showpiece," as it's surrounded by tropical shrubs and coconut palms. It consists of a large bed-sitting room, fully equipped kitchen, private bath, and balcony. *In low-season, it rents for $195 weekly,* increasing to $275 weekly in season.

The Jasmine studio apartment, adjacent to their restaurant, the leading one on the island, consists of a large bed-sitting room, a small dinette area, a private bath, and a completely stocked kitchen. There is also a private patio for viewing the sea or the mountains in the distance. *It rents for only $135 weekly, in low season.* In winter, prices rise to $200 weekly.

A new apartment, the Mignonette, contains two bedrooms, a bath, and a living area with a fully equipped kitchen. Its large patio faces the golf course and the sea. *You can stay here for $250 weekly off-season,* $380 weekly in season.

WHERE TO EAT: Some of the best fruit and vegetables in the Caribbean are grown in the rich, volcanic soil of Montserrat. The island is known for its toma-toes, carrots, and mangoes; and "goat water" (a mutton stew) is the best known local dish. Another island specialty is "mountain chicken," as locally caught frog legs are called.

The **Belham Valley Restaurant,** near the Vue Pointe Hotel (tel. 5553), is the premier restaurant of Montserrat. Britishers Chris and Barbara Crowe are most hospitable hosts, and they cater well to their diners. Naturally, they have to alter their menu a lot, as their biggest headache (the problem of the island itself) is the availability of supplies.

But they're very inventive in the kitchen, and you'll probably not only get a good meal but have a good time, especially if Valerie is still around at the piano.

The setting is tropical romantic, and the location is in a former private home, standing on a hillside overlooking the Belham River and its valley. It's also convenient for guests at the Montserrat Golf Course.

Among their island dishes, you might enjoy chilled breadfruit vichyssoise, or a creole crab and callaloo soup. However, they do the classic ones as well, including French onion with cheese and croutons.

They generally have a steak on the grill, served with garlic butter or else their own mushroom and red wine sauce. Among the unusual items that might appear is fresh baby shark steak. Fondue bourguignonne is regularly featured, and occasionally that ubiquitous Montserrat "mountain chicken" or frog legs, a staple of the island.

Their desserts are luscious, including fresh coconut pie or a Belham super sundae. Calypso coffee is served, but true to heritage, an Irish coffee as well. The ice creams are a special feature, as they are homemade and come in such unusual flavors as soursop and guava. Meals average around EC$75 ($28.50).

The restaurant is open only in the evening and preferably by reservation. In winter it's open every night except Monday. During the summer, it's open four nights a week: Thursday, Friday, Saturday, and Sunday. It is usually closed for three weeks in September.

Wade Inn, Parliament Street, right in the heart of Plymouth (tel. 2881), has long been a favorite in-town dining spot. The owner serves island-style meals on a sheltered side terrace, with hanging pots of ferns. When you arrive, tell him what kind of food you like and chances are you'll get it, with a few suggestions of his own. He has a set meal, perhaps chicken legs, cabbage, macaroni, and cole slaw for EC$10 ($3.80), and many people who work in town drop in to enjoy it. Most popular are his barbecued pork chops, spare ribs, and chicken on Sunday night. I'd also recommend his red snapper and, when available, mountain chick-en (frog legs).

EXPLORING MONTSERRAT: The island is small, only 11 miles long and 7 miles across at its widest point. Its gently rolling hills and mountains reach their zenith at **Chances Peak,** rising to 3000 feet. From its vantage point, a panoramic vista of the island unfolds. To climb the mountain, serious hikers need a guide, which your hotel can arrange. Near the airport, the mountain can be hazardous, and it's best to have an experienced hand along.

Galway's Soufrière, in the south-central region of the island, is a crater which bubbles and steams with sulfur smoke. A journey of exploration here is recommended for nature lovers. The government has a shortcut path, allowing you to drive up to within a 15-minute walk of the vents. The crater is a natural wonder, and it's reached by a mountain road lined with tree ferns. Look also for the exotic incense tree. Yellow sulfur spills over the side in stark contrast to the verdant green of the forest. Again, you should have your hotel arrange a mountain guide who will boil an egg in the hot sulfur.

Another natural wonder, the **Great Alps Waterfall,** is reached by first taking a 15-minute taxi ride south from Plymouth. After the driver lets you off, the waterfall lies a leisurely hour's walk through a lush interior. You come upon a horseshoe-shaped formation with crystal water plunging some 70 feet into a mountain pool. The noonday sun turns the mist into rainbow colors, reflecting the shadows of the rich surrounding foliage, a mystical effect of great beauty and worth the trek.

On the outskirts of Plymouth, **St. Anthony's Church**—the main Anglican church on the island—was built between 1632 and 1666, then rebuilt in 1730. Freed slaves, upon their emancipation, donated two beautiful silver chalices, on display. Next to the church is a gnarled tamarind tree two centuries old.

About a 15-minute drive from town, the ruined **Fort St. George** dates from the 18th century, and from it a magnificent panorama unfolds. The fort is 1184 feet above sea level. Another ruin is **Fort Barrington,** also built in the 18th century.

The **Montserrat Museum** (tel. 5443) is housed in an old sugar mill at Richmond Hill. Here is displayed a collection of Montserratian artifacts, including pictures of island life at the turn of the century. Some of the artifacts relate to the island's pre-Columbian history. The featured exhibit is a small replica of a wind-driven sugar mill. Admission is free, but donations maintain the museum. Hours are 2:30 to 5 p.m. on Wednesday and Sunday. Curator Edward Laroussini will answer your questions.

GETTING AROUND: There are 130 miles of surfaced roads, and taxis and buses are the most popular means of transport. **Taxi** drivers meet every plane, and fares to most hotels around the island range from $10 to $13. Sightseeing taxi tours cost about $8 per hour or about $30 per day. Motor **buses** run between Plymouth and most areas at fees ranging from $1 to $2.

If you don't mind driving on the left, you can rent a car in Montserrat, although you must go to the police station where you'll be given a temporary driver's license upon presentation of a valid U.S. or Canadian license and payment of a $3 fee. Rental cars, ranging in price from $26 to $35 per day, unlimited mileage, are generally booked at your hotel, or you can get in touch with **Pauline's Car Rental** (tel. 2345) or **Jefferson Car Rental** (tel. 2126). Incidentally, car rentals aren't allowed to operate out of the airport, so one must board a taxi for the cross-island trip to Plymouth. It's important to bear in mind that there are only two gasoline stations (they call it petrol here) in Montserrat. One is the Texaco station, north of Old Towne, and the other is opposite the public market.

THE SPORTING LIFE: There are many isolated areas for swimming and sunning;

and hopefully you'll like black sand. Most hotels have pools and lounging areas, however. One good beach is reached by boat. If there are four or more in your party, you can book the yacht *Queen of Scots* at the Vue Pointe Hotel (tel. 5210). It charges $35 per person from 9:30 a.m. to 4 p.m. for a sailing, sunning, and snorkeling trip to Rendezvous Bay. You're given lunch, along with rum punches and an open bar.

Snorkelers and scuba-divers should bring their own equipment, however, as none may be available for rent when you arrive in Montserrat. Experienced guides are always available, however.

People interested in fishing should ask at their hotel about the availability of small boats for rent. Sunfish sailing and deep-sea fishing are available, and a fully equipped cruiser can cost about $300 per day.

Tennis buffs will find asphalt courts at the Vue Pointe Hotel. There are also two courts at Montserrat Springs, which are lit for night games.

The **Montserrat Golf Course,** while it is only nine holes, is considered one of the finest in the eastern Caribbean. Even though it has only 11 greens, a full round of 18 holes can be played, by doubling up. The second hole, the best known, is about 600 yards across two branches of the Belham River. It covers an area of some 100 acres, and greens fees are EC$30 ($11.40) per day. The club-house was once part of an old cotton gin on the plantation. Neophyte caddies are paid EC$1.50 (57¢); juniors get EC$2 (76¢); and professionals get EC$2.50 (95¢).

SHOPPING: There is no duty-free shopping, but some interesting locally made handicrafts are for sale. Straw goods and small ceramic souvenirs predominate, along with sea island cotton fabrics.

The **Montserrat Sea Island Cotton Company** sales outlet, at the corner of George and Strand Streets (tel. 2557), offers exclusive hand-woven sea island cotton products and such souvenir items as leather goods and pottery. The outlet is open from 8 a.m., closing at 4 p.m. on Monday, Tuesday, Thursday, and Friday, and at noon on Wednesday and Saturday.

Outside of town, the government-owned and -operated **Montserrat Leather Craft** (tel. 2378) is in an actual leathercraft shop at the Groves. There, artistic handcrafted leather goods are offered for sale. All items—belts, wallets, handbags, sandals, purses—are made from locally tanned genuine leather. See in particular the batik belts. The factory is closed on Saturday and Sunday.

The **Spinning Plant** (tel. 2825) and **Hand-Weaving Studio** (tel. 2915), both owned and operated by the government, are at sites on the Industrial Estate. Sea island cotton yarn and roving (a step in turning fiber into soft yarn), manufactured by the plant, are hand-woven into a variety of end products. Clara Davidson, who came from Nova Scotia, founded the Hand-Weaving Studio, teaching the young women of Montserrat the craft. The products are unique, and the spun cotton is locally grown. Various designs of placemats, tablecloths, skirt-length material, clutch bags, stoles, scarves, baby blankets, and belts are offered for sale.

The **John Bull Shop,** over the bridge in Wapping just outside Plymouth, has many local crafts and gift items. Robert and Marilyn Townsend, formerly of Connecticut, have operated the shop since 1980. You can buy merchandise here for moderate to expensive prices. They have beautiful dress and decorating fabrics, tapestries of Montserrat, distinctive rugs, and wall decor that is locally made.

Dutcher's Studio (tel. 5253) is a glass and ceramic studio in Olveston just outside Plymouth. Items are made of hand-cut and hand-painted glass, with many signed and collectors' pieces. Featured are wind chimes made of bottles, hand-painted dishes, mobiles, and ceramic works of art, all made on Montserrat. Studio hours are 8:30 a.m. to 2:30 p.m. Monday to Friday. If you wish to go there on Saturday, Sunday, or holidays, you must call for an appointment. The studio is near the Vue Pointe Hotel and Salem.

AFTER DARK: Montserrat may be sleepy during the day, but it gets even quieter at night. The most activity is at the **Vue Pointe Hotel,** Old Towne (tel. 5210), where a steel band plays every Wednesday night, and there is nightly entertainment by local musicians in season. At the Wednesday-night bash, a barbecue dinner is cooked, costing $25 per person.

If you've never seen a West Indian disco, attracting just the local crowd, then you can drop in at either 747, Harney Street, or **La Cave,** Strand Street. Both are in Plymouth, and both are extremely modest little places, playing records for dancers. Some of the local dancers are very talented. The discos charge an entrance fee of $3 and up.

3. St. Kitts

The volcanic central island of the British Leewards is not really a resort mecca in the way Antigua is. Its major crop is sugar, and has been since the mid-17th century.

At some point in your visit, you'll want to eat sugar directly from the cane. Any St. Kitts farmer will sell you a huge stalk, and there are sugarcane plantations all over the island. Just ask your taxi driver to take you to one. You strip off the hard exterior of the stalk and bite into it, chewing on the tasty reeds and swallowing the juice. It's best with a side glass of rum.

The Caribs, the early settlers, called St. Kitts "Liamuiga," or "fertile isle." Its mountain ranges reach up to nearly 4000 feet, and in its interior are virgin rain forests, alive with the sound of hummingbirds and the chatter of green-backed monkeys (the early French colonists brought them here).

Sugarcane climbs right up the slopes, and there are palm-lined beaches around the island as well. As you travel around St. Kitts, you'll notice ruins of old mills and plantation houses. You'll also see an island rich in trees and vegetation—frangipani, bougainvillea, hibiscus, and flamboyant trees (the treasured poinciana was first cultivated in the Caribbean by Count de Poincy).

St. Kitts is 33 miles long and 6½ miles wide, riding the crest of that arc of islands known as the northerly Leeward group of the Lesser Antilles. It is separated from its sister state of Nevis by a two-mile-wide strait. Its administrative capital is Basseterre.

In 1967 St. Kitts was given internal self-government and, along with Nevis, became a state in association with Britain (Anguilla broke away).

On his second voyage in 1493, Columbus spotted St. Kitts, naming it Saint Christopher, but the English later changed that to St. Kitts. In 1623 the Europeans colonized St. Kitts when Sir Thomas Warner landed with his wife and son, and a party of 14 farmers. This settlement made St. Kitts the oldest British colony in the West Indies. When the island later sent out parties of settlers to neighboring islands, St. Kitts became known as "the mother colony of the West Indies."

Shortly after their arrival, the English were soon joined by the French. In 1627 they divided the island between them and, united, they withstood attacks from the Caribs and the Spanish. But in time the British and French fought among themselves, and the island changed hands several times until it was finally given to the British by the Treaty of Versailles.

The annual average temperature is 78° Fahrenheit. St. Kitts is in the path of the northeast trade winds, making for a steady cooling breeze throughout the year.

The capital, **Basseterre,** an 18th-century-print port with its waterfront intact, lies on the Caribbean shore near the southern end of the island, about a mile from Golden Rock Airport, where you will land. With its white-painted colonial houses with toothpick balconies and wide, palm-lined streets, it looks like a Hollywood version of a West Indian port.

The bustling harbor is filled with schooners from Antigua, St. Martin, and Nevis which carry the rich produce of St. Kitts to neighboring islands. You'll also spot freighters from the U.S. and Canada. The men of St. Kitts are known as good sailors, and it's interesting to see them in action, skillfully handling their boats.

This British colonial town is built around a so-called Circus, the town's round square. A tall green Victorian clock tower stands in the center of the Circus. In the old days, wealthy plantation owners and their families used to promenade here.

At some point, try to visit the marketplace. There, country women bring baskets brimming with mangoes, guavas, soursop, mammy apples, and wild strawberries and cherries just picked in the fields. You can see the vegetables you may eat later in the day—yams, breadfruit, hearts of palm, pumpkins, christophines. Tropical flowers abound.

Another major square is called Pall Mall, once a thriving slave market. It is surrounded by private homes of Georgian architecture.

GETTING THERE: LIAT operates a daily scheduled service from Antigua to St. Kitts, but flights are often late in departing. Although LIAT also flies to St. Kitts from St. Thomas, St. Croix, and St. Maarten, **Prinair** offers more frequent service from the latter three islands as well as from its home base in San Juan.

BWIA flies nonstop once a week, on Sunday, from New York to St. Kitts, returning the same day to JFK.

Most passengers, however, if they want to fly direct from New York or Miami, use the services of **Pan American.** Pan Am operates thrice-weekly flights from New York to St. Kitts, leaving New York at 12:30 p.m. and touching down briefly at St. Thomas before winging on to St. Kitts. Returning flights leave St. Kitts three times a week at 8 a.m., requiring passengers to make an efficient connection in St. Thomas. Although passengers change aircraft during the brief stopover there, their luggage is routed directly through to New York.

Pan Am also offers service from Miami to St. Kitts. Southbound passengers change planes in St. Thomas during the three-times-a-week service, although their luggage is routed directly to their final destinations. Passengers returning to Miami from St. Kitts remain on the same aircraft as it touches down briefly in St. Thomas during the regular runs.

PRACTICAL FACTS: Entry requirements, money, and language were previewed in the introductory section to this chapter.

St. Kitts is on **Atlantic Standard Time,** and its clocks never change all year. That means that in winter when it's 6 a.m. in Basseterre, it's 5 a.m. in Miami or New York. When the U.S. goes on Daylight Saving Time, Basseterre and the East Coast mainland keep the same time.

The water supply of the island is good and safe for drinking. However, since its electricity is 230 volts, 60 cycles, AC, you'll need an adapter for U.S.-made appliances.

Customs allows you in duty free with personal belongings.

Again, reflecting British tradition, **driving is on the left!** However, you'll need a local driver's license, which can be obtained at the Traffic Department in Basseterre for about $4.

If you want to exchange your dollars into Eastern Caribbean currency, you'll find **banks** open Monday to Friday from 8 a.m. till noon (also on Friday from 3 to 5 p.m.). **Store hours,** on the other hand, are 8 a.m. to noon and 1 to 4 p.m. except Sunday (this is likely to vary greatly, depending on the individual shopkeeper).

Most hotels add a service charge of 10% to cover tipping. If not, tip from 10% to 15%.

The government also imposes a 5% tax on rooms and meals, plus another $5 airport departure tax.

HOTELS: This is no resort-studded island like Antigua. Rather, the island has hotels of character, small and special, ranging from plantation-style living to retreats so remote they're accessible only by a bumpy boat ride.

Ocean Terrace Inn, P.O. Box 65 (tel. 465-2380), is affectionately known as the O.T.I. If you want to be near Basseterre, it's the best hotel around the port (it also has an excellent cuisine and the island's leading disco, and is the chief center for water sports, all detailed in the section to follow). The O.T.I. commands a view of the harbor and the capital, with oceanfront verandas. With its many terraces and different levels, it is so compact that a stay here is like a house party on a great liner.

All the handsomely decorated, air-conditioned bedrooms overlook the "great open-air living room"—that is, a well-planted terrace with a flagstone-edged swimming pool (which has a row of underwater stools where you'll be served well-made drinks while still immersed). Another adjoining bar is placed under tropical trees and flowering shrubbery. The furnishings are color coordinated, with a light, tropical feeling. In winter, singles on the MAP range from $95 to $150 daily, with doubles costing from $230 to $150. *Off-season MAP rates range from $80 to $115 in a single, from $125 to $160 in a double.* Some more expensive suites are available, and guests can stay here on the EP if they wish, for somewhat lower prices. A third person in a room on the MAP costs $60 year round. Colin Pereira, who is from St. Kitts, is your host, and he runs a tight ship.

Fairview Inn, P.O. Box 212 (tel. 465-2472), was originally the 18th-century great house of a wealthy French plantation owner. Set on the rise of a hill, and surrounded by tropical flowers and blooming flamboyant trees, it is only five miles from the jetport and three miles west of the city, about a ten-minute run by taxi. It has its own swimming pool and sundeck, and there is a secluded beach just a 12-minute walk from the inn. Prince Charles danced the carnival queen around the pool. The manor house has plenty of character, with its lacy front verandas, louvered windows, and long, covered loggia. Some of the bedrooms are in the main building, and others are in cottages in the rear garden where the plantation outbuildings of yesteryear used to stand.

Each of the 30 twin-bedded rooms has a private bath as well as its own patio. You can ask for air conditioning (available in some of the rooms), but trade winds usually suffice. I prefer the bedrooms that have been converted from stone stables. Natural-stone walls have been incorporated into the scheme. The rooms are clean and comfortable.

What makes Fairview Inn such a success, drawing repeat visitors, is its ownership. A Trinidadian, Freddy Lam, and his wife, Betty (she's from St. Kitts), extend old-fashioned hospitality. Betty's island background is reflected in her cuisine. For example, she grows her own papaya, making green papaya pie to delight her diners. The Lams also grow their own vegetables and pineapples, and often use breadfruit as well as making a superb callaloo soup. In winter, for about four nights a week a calypso band will come in to entertain. In season, singles rent for $70 to $80 daily on the EP; doubles, from $80 to $90. *Off-season, a single pays only $50 to $60; two persons, $60 to $70.* Breakfast and dinner carry an additional daily supplement of $28 per person. In my opinion, the Fairview Inn is one of the best tourist buys in the Caribbean.

The **Royal St. Kitts Hotel and Casino,** P.O. Box 406, Frigate Bay (tel. 465-8651), popular with charter tour groups, is like an elaborate country club. It's completely self-contained and has four tennis courts (lit at night) and an 18-hole championship golf course. Completely rebuilt in 1983, the Royal has charm. In sports facilities it is unparalleled in both St. Kitts and Nevis, and it's also the scene of whatever action there is on the island, housing a casino on the premises.

The hotel does a thriving business in package bookings, as this 138-room luxury structure is the first big-time resort ever erected on St. Kitts. Modern rooms are in attractively designed villas. The special rooms are a dozen duplex suites with large living rooms, fully equipped kitchens, and private balconies on the second floor. A spiral staircase goes up to oversize bedrooms with double beds and sitting areas. In winter, either singles or doubles, EP, rent for $160, and suites cost $190. *In summer, rates are $67, single or double, and $125 in a suite, all EP.*

The Royal dining room offers a wide range of continental cuisine, with local seafood dishes featured. The Garden Restaurant is open 24 hours a day in season. A patio entertainment area is the scene of weekly programs, including the manager's cocktail party and fashion show, a West Indian evening with a Kittitian buffet and local entertainers, a show featuring the hotel staff, and a weekly beach barbecue.

The location is unique, on Frigate Bay between the Atlantic Ocean and the Caribbean Sea. In just ten minutes you can enjoy the waves of the Atlantic, then swim in more tranquil Caribbean waters.

Golden Lemon, Dieppe Bay (tel. 465-7260), was created by Arthur Leaman, onetime decorating editor of *House & Garden* magazine. With his taste and background, he has formed a tiny oasis that is a citadel of charm in the British Leewards. Mr. Leaman found this ramshackle 18th-century plantation house, set back from the road, near a coconut grove and a black volcanic sand beach opening onto the Atlantic toward the northern end of St. Kitts. Slaves were once shipped to this French section of the island, which was named after a more famous bay in the home country. Originally a 17th-century French manor stood here, and a Georgian upper story was added in the 18th century.

The two-story house, with its covered galleries, was for a time a former sugar storehouse. Like a page ripped from *House & Garden,* the high-ceilinged bedrooms are spacious and the rare antiques "are from everywhere." Some were purchased at auctions when estates were sold. Most of the bedrooms (there are 17) have graceful canopy beds. Everywhere you look, the Golden Lemon is swathed in color. Even the baths weren't neglected, and are often furnished with one-of-a-kind wicker. Overhead, slow-whirling ceiling fans keep the air moving. Before retiring, you can state your breakfast preference—served on your own open gallery or in your bedroom.

The rooms always contain fresh flowers, and the management has hired a well-trained staff, who work in chic costumes. In days gone by you were likely to spot everybody from Loretta Young to Graham Greene to Michael York walking around the premises. And at the small pool in the entry courtyard no one faints if you wish to remove your bikini and reveal your charms (or do they?). "Sophisticated" and "discriminating" are the words most often used around here.

A minimum stay of seven days in season is required (Mr. Leaman feels it takes guests that long just to wind down). Off-season, the minimum is three days. Surprisingly, he limits guests to a maximum stay of two weeks, fearing (and I'm guessing) that they might get restless, even in paradise.

In winter, the MAP rates (and that means afternoon tea as well) cost $160 daily in a single. A twin or double rents for $260 to $300. *Off-season, on the MAP, singles pay $140 daily; two persons, $175 to $200.*

Rawlins Plantation, Mount Pleasant, P.O. Box 340 (tel. 465-6221), is a small, family-owned hotel, set on a former plantation among the remains of a muscovado sugar factory. The original great house burned in 1790, but was replaced by the present Walwyn family in 1970, who have turned it into an English country-home-type place. (Incidentally, the first Walwyn arrived in Nevis in 1677, moving his family to St. Kitts and founding the Rawlins Plantation in 1790.) Near Dieppe Bay on the northeast coast, the former plantation is 350 feet above sea level, enjoying cooling breezes from both ocean and mountains. Behind the grounds the land rises to a rain forest and Mount Misery.

Rawlins is unique on St. Kitts, evoking certain plantation hotels on neighboring Nevis. A 17th-century windmill has become converted into a charming suite, complete with private bath and sitting room; and the boiling houses, formerly a caldron of molasses, have been turned into a cool courtyard where guests dine, enjoying the flowers and tropical birds. Accommodations are rented in the main house, as well as pleasantly decorated cottages which have been equipped with modern facilities.

The plantation is run by Mr. and Mrs. Philip Walwyn, who graciously let you swim in their pool (fed from their own mountain spring), or eat at their table, offering peace and tranquility for the discriminating few who find their way to their door. Vegetables usually come from their own gardens and they raise their own beef. *On the MAP, singles are welcomed off-season for $130 daily; doubles, $190.* In winter, prices rise to $210 in a single, $275 in a double, all on the MAP. In season, a minimum stay of four days is required. You can also go for a sail on Philip's 45-foot catamaran on Sunday.

Frigate Bay Beach Hotel, P.O. Box 398, Basseterre (tel. 465-8935), is set on a verdant hillside above a point where English settlers used to watch the passing frigates. Accommodations are in gleaming-white condominiums administered as hotel units for their absentee owners. The villas housing these "second homes" have alternating red and yellow tile roofs. The central core of the resort contains a pair of round swimming pools and a cabana-style bar where you can enjoy a drink while partially immersed if you choose. Green hills rise up behind the hotel, while on either side are beaches lined with rugged cliffs. An 18-hole golf course and tennis courts are within easy walking distance.

Units are nicely furnished to the taste of the owner and painted in an array of pastel colors. They have cool tile floors, ceiling fans, sliding glass doors leading onto verandas, private baths, and air conditioning. Winter rates are $120 daily for a double, $200 for a one-bedroom suite suitable for two persons, and $300 for a two-bedroom suite for up to four persons. *In summer, doubles go for $60 per day, a one-bedroom suite for $90, and a two-bedroom suite for $150.* Service is added to all bills. MAP is available for an additional $35 per day per person.

Banana Bay Beach Hotel, c/o Palmco Ltd., The Circus, Basseterre (tel. 465-2860). This secluded gem is accessible only by boat. Guests are met at the airport and taken to the pier where the *Careebo* waits to take them on the scenic cruise to Banana Bay. The creativity put into the physical side of this ten-room hideaway is evident immediately from use of fantastic colors and attention to details capturing the perfect setting for a Caribbean vacation.

The spiritual side is no less a factor, for the accent is on nothingness, allowing one to walk quietly along sandy beaches and absorb the beauty of surrounding landscape. Activity focuses on the beach, although reading and good conversation have high priorities. The food is excellent with a good balance of local and continental dishes. There is no pretense here of elegance or fanciness. It is simply good food well served without fanfare.

Year-round rates on the AP are $235 double, $185 single, including the cost of transportation on arrival and departure.

The **Cockleshell**, P.O. Box 430 (no phone). Laddie Hamilton, your host, entertains guests as if they'd been invited to a private house party. This is a self-contained little resort on the southeastern tip of St. Kitts, two miles across the channel from Nevis, accessible only by boat, a splashy 45-minute run from Basseterre, where you will be met if you've notified the staff of your arrival. Here the escapist will find informality and friendliness, as well as a somewhat fashionable atmosphere, with all-white interiors and an occasional exposed beam. At a bamboo bar you mix your own drinks, and if you're so inclined, you'll find some puzzles and games waiting to be played. The living-dining room is furnished with Oriental rugs, antique paintings, and enough books to satisfy the most voracious reader. The food is good native cuisine.

Each of the bedrooms has twin beds, a private bath, and its own veranda overlooking the sea. Year-round rates are $175 in a double, on the MAP. Swimming, snorkeling, sailing, tennis, fishing, and waterskiing are available, and the beach and sea are at your doorstep.

Back in Basseterre, I offer two simple St. Kitts guest houses for those who must sacrifice amenities to keep costs bone-trimmed.

Blackeney Hotel, P.O. Box 168, Church Street (tel. 465-2222), is a utilitarian budget hotel, often favored by traveling West Indian athletic teams. Its exterior is a natural stone with white clapboard and faded pink shutters. The hotel sprawls across the second floor of an old structure built more than a century ago. From its roofdeck you can watch the sun set over Mount Misery. At a bar there you can order a rum swizzle. The rooms are lofty, with walls painted in various hues of pastels. The lounge is furnished with basic modern settees and armchairs. Guests pay $20 a day in a single, the cost going up to $25 in a double, EP. The same tariffs are in effect all year.

Park View Guest House, P.O. Box 164, Victoria Road (tel. 465-2100), is a modest old corner building with a peaked roof, verandas, and a view of either Warner Park where major sports events occur, or opposite the Church of England and its surrounding garden. You'll see an excellent specimen of a banyan tree which has spread its branches to nearly 100 feet. The owner has renovated the place, installing air conditioning in all the rooms. Year-round rates are $20 daily in a single, $35 in a double.

At these prices, you can't expect the rooms to be very modern or even especially attractive. However, you can expect them to be well kept and immaculate. You can make arrangements to have your meals if you want them.

WHERE TO DINE: Most guests eat at their hotels; however, St. Kitts has a scattering of good restaurants where you are likely to have turtle stews, spiny lobster, crab back, pepperpot, breadfruit, and curried conch.

I'd recommend that you dine with a local family at least once. That way, you'll get to meet Kittitians in their homes as well as enjoy a good local cuisine. Your hotel will make such arrangements. Two of the family-run establishments, one operated by a fifth-generation island family, are **Harbour Lights** and **The Patio** (no phones).

The **Georgian House**, South Square Street (tel. 465-4049), fronts Independence Square. As the name suggests, this is a restored Georgian manor, decorated with Queen Anne reproductions, and said to be the oldest habitable building in St. Kitts. Long, long before its present reincarnation as the leading restaurant on the island, it was the exclusive Planters' Club.

New Yorker Georgiana Bowers, the owner and chef, offers a well-prepared and sophisticated menu that changes nightly. You may be there on the night peanut soup is served, but you also might settle happily for chilled cucumber soup. Main courses are likely to include roast leg of lamb, chicken breasts in garlic, and lobster thermidor. Desserts are luscious here. Maybe it'll be Tia Maria mousse. If not, then coconut cream pie or most definitely guava ice cream. The menu is à la carte. With a drink or two, count on spending around $25 per person. Hours are 11 a.m. to 2 p.m. and 6:30 to 9 p.m., except Sunday.

Dinner is served in the beautifully restored dining room, and lunch is presented in a large walled garden. Lunch, of course, is much simpler. You're given a choice of two soups and four main courses, along with a couple of desserts. Lobster salad is a favorite at $12, and so is the chicken salad at a more reasonably priced $8.50. Perhaps a club sandwich at $4.50 would tempt you. Each of these luncheon orders is accompanied by potato salad, lettuce, and tomato.

The restaurant shuts down in summer when business in St. Kitts is at a minimum.

In Basseterre, some of the finest cuisine is found at the **Ocean Terrace Inn** (tel. 465-2754). It also offers the best view, especially at night when you can sit and watch the lights in the harbor. Native food is featured every night, and standard dishes from the international repertoire are invariably included as well. My most recent dinner, costing EC$45 ($17.10), began with curried chicken broth, followed by sliced hard-boiled eggs in a mushroom sauce served on the half shell. Then came an order of tasty fish cakes, accompanied by breaded carrot slices, creamed spinach, a stuffed potato, Johnny cake, a corn-meal dumpling, and a green banana in a lime butter sauce, topped off by a tropical fruit pie and coffee! Dining is on an open-air veranda. On some nights the main dish might be a large breadfruit stuffed with chicken. On Sunday there's a chicken luncheon barbecue around the pool, costing EC$15 ($5.70).

Jong's, Conaree Beach (tel. 465-2062), is an Oriental restaurant combined with Cisco's Hide-Away Bar. It serves the best Oriental food in St. Kitts, the dishes well prepared, the service friendly and efficient. A complete meal costs about $20. The bar opens at 11 a.m., remaining so until midnight. Lunch is from noon to 2:30 p.m., and dinner from 6:30 to 10 p.m. On Wednesday, dinner hours are 6 p.m. to midnight. It's important that you call and make a reservation.

For the best native food in St. Kitts, I prefer **Avondale House,** George Street (tel. 465-2487), an old West Indian town house with tables placed out on the porch. As you dine, you'll hear an occasional rooster crow. There's a little garden out front, and one room is a bar. In the center of town, right off Pall Mall Square, this is a very simple place, attracting the locals of St. Kitts. The specialty is goat water (a mutton stew). Corn and fish is also good, as is chicken and rice. Sauteed chicken legs are another favorite dish. Expect to pay from $10 to $15 for a complete meal.

If you're touring St. Kitts, the best luncheon stopover is at the **Golden Lemon,** Dieppe Bay (tel. 465-7260), the 18th-century house converted into a hotel by Arthur Leaman, former decorating editor of *House & Garden* magazine (see the description above). Always call in advance for a reservation. Before dining, you may want to enjoy a Bloody Mary, rum punch, or piña colada at poolside. Lunch is in a lush tropical setting of ferns, bougainvillea, and flitting hummingbirds and finches. The food is very good, and the service is polite. A complete luncheon costs around $15, and special drinks are priced at $3.50. Dinner costs from $12 to $25 à la carte, and is served in an elegant, candlelit dining room. The cuisine features creole, continental, and American dishes, and the menu changes daily. Dress is casual chic. Lunch is served from noon to 2:30 p.m., dinner from 7 to 9:30 p.m.

The **Ballahoo Bar and Restaurant,** on the Circus just beside the Spencer Cameron Art Gallery, offers a wide array of seafood and other local dishes. It boasts a long, open-air veranda, allowing diners a cool table where they can enjoy gazing over the town center while they enjoy their meals. Expect to pay from $7 to $12 for a complete lunch or dinner.

EXPLORING ST. KITTS: The chief sight is **Brimstone Hill,** which was once known as the "Gibraltar of the West Indies." In size, this 18th-century fortress rivaled the pyramids of Egypt. A car can be driven up the winding road, almost to the top. When your driver lets you out, you have to climb stairs to the main fortifications. In 1782 the fort was besieged and captured by the French, but Britain regained it the following year.

Although the hurricanes of 1834 and 1852 brought great damage, the citadel has been partially reconstructed, its guns remounted. Today you can see the ruins of the officers' quarters, barracks, the ordnance store, a cemetery, and the redoubts.

Thousands of slaves worked for more than a century to complete this fortress. From its precincts there is a magnificent view with a radius of 70 miles. You can see Saba and St. Eustatius to the northwest, St. Barts and St. Maarten to the north, and Montserrat and Nevis to the southeast. The fortress dominates the southwest of St. Kitts.

Rugged visitors also make the eight-hour excursion to **Mount Misery** (at least you'll get a lot of exercise). A Land Rover will take you part of the way, and you should hire a guide. After that, it's a long, steady climb to the lip of the crater at 2600 feet (the peak is 3792 feet). Hikers can descend into the crater, clinging to vines and roots.

At the hamlet of **Half-Way Tree,** a large tamarind marked the boundary in the old days between the British-held sector and the French half.

It was near the hamlet of **Old Road Town** that Sir Thomas Warner landed with the first band of settlers, establishing the first permanent colony, to the northwest at Sandy Point. Sir Thomas's grave is in the cemetery of St. Thomas Church.

A sign in the middle of Old Road Town points the way to **Carib Rock Drawings,** all the evidence that remains of the former inhabitants. The markings are on black boulders, the pictographs dating back to prehistoric days.

Two commercial tours interest visitors. Get your driver to take you to the **Sugar Factory,** which is best seen from February through July, when the cane is ground. You don't need a reservation, and you'll see the process from when the raw cane enters the factory until it emerges as bulk sugar.

Guests are also allowed to visit the **Carib Beer Plant,** an English lager beer-processing house. Carib Beer is considered the best in the West Indies, if sales are any indication. At the end of the tour through the plant, visitors are given cold Carib in the lounge. The plant doesn't always operate, so check before heading there to see if it's open.

GETTING AROUND: A good road encircles the island. I'll preview the major means of transport.

Car Rentals

Hertz and Budget are not represented on St. Kitts, but **Avis** has an office at Delisle Walwyn and Company in Liverpool Row (tel. 2631 locally or, better yet, call toll free 800/331-1212 at least three days in advance to have a car reserved).

Your best deal with Avis in St. Kitts is a four-door Suzuki at $170 weekly, unlimited mileage. If you want a bigger car, try the five-passenger Mazda at $196 per week, also with unlimited mileage.

My advice is to purchase a collision damage waiver at an extra $5 per day. Drivers, who must be at least 25 years old, have to take a taxi from the airport to the Avis subsidiary.

Taxis

Since most taxi drivers are also guides, this is the best means of getting around. You don't even have to find a driver at the airport (one will find you). Drivers also wait outside the major hotels, so getting around is fairly easy. Before heading out on an expedition, however, you must agree on the price—taxis aren't metered. Also, ask if the rates quoted to you are in U.S. dollars or the "Bee Wee" dollar. Taxi rates may have risen considerably by the time you read this, so check the fares. At the time of writing, you could go from the airport to, say, the Fairview Inn for $6, or all the way to Sandy Point for $10.

Sightseeing Tours

You can negotiate with a taxi driver to take you on a tour of the island for about $45. Most drivers are well versed in the lore of the island, and all of them of course speak English. Lunch can be arranged either at the Rawlins Plantation Inn or the Golden Lemon.

Inter-Island Ferries

Most visitors to St. Kitts or Nevis like to spend a least one day on the sister island, and the government passenger ferry M.V. *Caribe Queen* provides such an opportunity. The schedule permits departures from either island between the hours of 7:30 and 8:30 a.m. daily except Thursday and Sunday, returning at 4 and 6 p.m. (check the time at your hotel or the tourist office). The cost is EC$7 ($2.66) one way. Passengers are allowed one hand package free, with a minimal fee for additional pieces.

Local Air Service

LIAT (Leeward Islands Air Transport) provides daily morning and afternoon flights to and from Nevis at a cost of $15 per person. Make reservations at the LIAT office in Basseterre instead of at the airport.

SHOPPING: The good buys here are in local handicrafts, including leather items made from goatskin, baskets, ceramic figurines, and coconut shells (the natives know how to make almost anything from these items). Some good values are also to be found in clothing and fabrics, especially sea island cottons.

Caribelle Batik, at Romney Manor (tel. 465-6253), qualifies as a sightseeing attraction as well as a shopping expedition. Its workroom and sales showrooms are in the most romantic setting of any shopping recommendation in this guide—the entire Romney Manor, a plantation established in the 17th century. You'll need a car, as it's reached via a short, steep road off the coast. It's right off Old Road, in the shade of a flamboyant tree. On the way to the manor, ask your driver to show you the Carib petroglyphs carved on stones (right near Old Road Town).

In the showroom a chart explains the batik process. You can watch as island workers apply different layers of molten wax and color, both required in the printing process. Also there are facilities for tie-dye fabrics. Items include wall hangings made of West Indian sea island cotton. Take your time and you'll usually find someone willing to explain the process to you. The shop offers beautiful caftans, T-shirts (preshrunk), and batik pictures. U.S. citizens may make duty-free purchases here. If you want to create your own ensemble, you can do so by purchasing lengths of fabric. Visiting hours are Monday to Friday, 8 a.m. to 4 p.m.

Losada's Boutique, Wigley Avenue, Portlands (tel. 465-2564), near the Ocean Terrace Inn and the Fort Thomas Hotel, is a cozy "antiques and everything" shop in premises with access to a flower and shrub garden. It's owned by Mrs. Ghislaine Cramer, who keeps her eye on anything on the island that could be classified as an antique. She's at every estate sale and knows value. Her boutique has a collection of old gold watches, silver service, antique and contemporary jewelry in gold and silver, decanters, and teapots. She always has some antiques on consignment, and also offers local craftware such as bamboo fans and fabric hats. She encourages young, talented craftspeople on St. Kitts to sell their creations at her store.

You'll find the **Spencer Cameron Art Gallery** (tel. 465-4047) by the Circus, with its entrance on Bay Road. Here, two British women, Kate Spencer and Rosey Cameron-Smith, produce watercolors and limited-edition prints of Kittitian and Nevisian scenes. The two arrived here about six years ago and were captivated by the island's charms. They made an effort to reproduce in art some of the essence of true West Indian life, particularly the humor that sneaks into all its aspects. A somewhat unusual aspect of their work is that when the paintings are for reproduction, the women work on the same picture, even both working on the same one at the same time when deadlines are involved. Kate is especially good at buildings and the general background, while Rosey's forte includes flora, fauna, and incidentals. Original paintings, however, are generally attacked individually. There's a wide selection of artwork available, ranging from small prints for $5, large prints around $15, and hand-colored prints for $35, to original paintings ranging from $40 to $300. The women also produce a variety of greeting cards, postcards, calendars, and hand-printed, silkscreened T-shirts.

For the most luxurious shopping suggestion of all, I suggest **A Slice of the Lemon,** all white and mirrored inside. In 1979 Martin Kreiner opened a duty-free shop at the already-previewed Golden Lemon. However, the main store is in the Palms at the Circus in Basseterre. There is an arcade of shops with duty-free perfumes and jewelry, Palm Crafts with all-Caribbean handicrafts, hand-blocked print fabrics by Jean-Ives Froment from St. Bart's, silkscreen fabrics and accessories from the Saba Artisans Studio, and the renowned Batik Caribe fabrics and clothes from St. Vinand.

Palm Crafts has three outlets on St. Kitts: on Princes Street, Basseterre; at the Sun 'n Sand Hotel, Frigate Bay; and at the Golden Lemon Hotel, Dieppe Bay. Kathleen Fallon has combined her Kittitian Kitchen with Palm Crafts, going into partnership with Arthur Leaman to operate the three shops. Among the merchandise sold here are jams, jellies, chutneys; skin oils, creams, and lotions made from coconut oil and other essential ingredients; straw items; postcards of the island; island-made gifts; straw rugs; teas; some island clothing and T-shirts; pottery; coconut wind chimes and bird feeders; books on the Caribbean; carved wooden bowls; animals and fruit of the tropics; and wall hangings.

THE SPORTING LIFE: Sporting activities aren't as developed on St. Kitts as they are on more tourist-oriented islands, but the outlook is improving. Beaches are the primary concern of most visitors, who find the swimming best at Conaree Beach (two miles from Basseterre), Frigate Bay, and Friar's Bay. The narrow peninsula in the southeast that contains the island's salt ponds also boasts its best beaches.

Snorkeling and Scuba

Most of the major hotels have equipment, but these sports are not as avidly pursued in St. Kitts as they are elsewhere in the Caribbean. Colin Pereira of the **Ocean Terrace Inn,** P.O. Box 65 (tel. 465-2754 or 465-2380), arranges trips on a fully equipped 33-foot cabin cruiser. Scuba-diving courses are available from experienced dive masters. The rate is $30 per person per dive for a scuba-diving trip, with equipment available for rent. A night dive costs $36 per person.

Another good center is **Caribbean Water Sports.** To make contact, get in touch with Paul Harman, c/o Royal St. Kitts Hotel, P.O. Box 406, Frigate Bay (tel. 465-8651).

The trips are off secluded beaches on the peninsula and along the coast between Frigate Bay and Salt Pond.

Waterskiing

Fisherman's Wharf at Pelican Cove, Ocean Terrace Inn, offers waterskiing in sheltered waters off the peninsula at a rate of $15 per person for 15 minutes.

Boating

Charters are available to Cockleshell Bay and Banana Bay Hotels at the southern tip of St. Kitts. Reservations must be made one day in advance (your hotel can arrange it). Charter groups are limited to six persons. The Ocean Terrace Inn can also arrange for you to join a special charter to Cockleshell or Major Bay on Saturday and Sunday. However, a minimum of 15 passengers must agree to go along.

Beachcomber Sailboats Rental, Frigate Bay, P.O. Box 168, offers snorkeling, windsurfing, Sunfish sailing, and waterskiing in the Caribbean at reasonable hourly rates. Instruction is available.

Spearfishing

This is legal in St. Kitts. **St. Kitts Water Sports,** at Frigate Bay, will make arrangements for sports people to go spearfishing on the reefs off the peninsula at the southern end of St. Kitts. The cost is $20 per person. A minimum of two is required.

Deep-Sea Fishing

Again, you must turn to Colin Pereira at the Ocean Terrace Inn (tel. 465-2754). If six persons want to go out, he can arrange a half-day fishing jaunt at a cost of $40 per hour, tackle and bait included.

Golfing

At **Frigate Bay** there is an 18-hole championship golf course, and there's a nine-hole course at **Golden Rock.** Robert Trent Jones designed the course at the Royal St. Kitts at Frigate Bay. Greens fees are $15 per round. Caddies get $5 per round per bag.

Tennis

The **Royal St. Kitts** at Frigate Bay has four courts, which are lit at night.

NIGHTLIFE: There isn't much. The **Royal St. Kitts Hotel and Casino,** Frigate Bay (tel. 465-8651), has crap tables, roulette wheels, blackjack tables, and slot machines. Sometimes a steel band plays at the hotel on Saturday night. Also, Mr. Z's Disco is open nightly from 10 p.m.

In Basseterre, the **Bitter End** is a disco at the Ocean Terrace Inn (tel. 465-2380). There, on most Wednesday and Friday nights, you'll see some action after 9 p.m.

If you decide to venture into one of the local bars around the island, you just might be served a concoction known as "Halfway Three." It's made of bootleg and white lightning, along with moonshine, and is to be drunk at your own risk!

4. Nevis

Two miles south of St. Kitts, Nevis *(Nee-vis)* was discovered by Columbus in 1493. He called it Las Nieves, Spanish for "snows," because its cloud-capped mountains reminded him of the snow-capped range in the Pyrenees. The island, almost circular, appears like a perfect cone when viewed from St. Kitts, its sister state. The cone rises gradually to a height of 3596 feet. A saddle joins the mountain to two smaller peaks, Saddle Hill (1432 feet) in the south, and Hurricane Hill (1192 feet) in the north. Coral reefs rim the shoreline, and there is mile after mile of palm-shaded white sandy beaches.

Columbus may have discovered the island, but it was settled by the British in 1628. The volcanic island is famous as the birthplace of Alexander Hamilton, drafter of the U.S. Constitution. It was also at Nevis that Admiral Nelson harbored his fleet in Napoleonic days, marrying a rich, young window, Frances Nisbet. His best man was the Duke of Clarence, later King William IV of England.

In the 18th century, Nevis, "The Queen of the Caribees," was the leading spa of the West Indies, made so by its hot mineral springs.

Once Nevis was peppered with prosperous sugarcane estates, which are gone now (many converted into some of the most intriguing character hotels in the Caribbean). Sea island cotton is the chief crop today.

As you drive around the nostalgic island, going through tiny hamlets such as Gingerland (named for the spice it used to export), you'll reach the heavily wooded slopes of Nevis Peak. From that vantage point there are magnificent views of the neighboring islands. Nevis is an island of exceptional beauty and has remained unspoiled. Its people, in the main, are black descendants of slaves. Nevis is usually approached by ferry boat or air from **St. Kitts.**

On the Caribbean side, **Charlestown,** the capital of Nevis, was very fashionable in the 18th century, as sugar planters were carried around in carriages and sedan chairs. Houses are of locally quarried volcanic stone, often supporting a clapboard second story, encircled by West Indian fretted verandas. A town of wide, quiet streets, this port only gets busy when its major link to the world, the ferry from St. Kitts, docks at the harbor. Then it becomes a cascade of activity. You can also fly over on Four Island Air, a division of LIAT, which has regularly scheduled service. Carib Aviation is available for charters, and will fly from two to five passengers. The trip by air takes only five minutes.

Its major attraction is the **Birthplace of Alexander Hamilton,** now in ruins, lying on the bayfront. Only the foundation of the old house and a staircase remain. Mr. Hamilton was born illegitimate in 1757, the son of a Scotsman, James Hamilton, and a Creole, Rachael Fawcett. As a boy, he left Nevis to work in the

Virgin Islands before heading to the United States and into history books. Above the town, Hamilton Estate was once the property of Alexander Hamilton's father.

PRACTICAL FACTS: Language, currency, and entry requirements have already been discussed in this chapter's introductory section. Most visitors will clear Customs in St. Kitts, so arrival in Nevis should not be complicated.

As in St. Kitts, an **electrical** transformer will be needed for most U.S. and Canadian appliances. The current is 230 volts, 60 cycles.

The **water** supply is good and safe to drink.

To **drive** in Nevis, you must obtain a permit from the Traffic Department, costing about $4 and valid for three months. Remember, all the vehicles must be driven on the *left-hand side of the road.*

The **post office** is open from 8 a.m. to 3 p.m. daily, except Thursday when it closes at 11:30 a.m.

Banking hours are 8 a.m. to noon daily except Saturday and Sunday. However, most banks reopen from 3:30 to 5:30 p.m. on Friday.

Normal **business hours** are 8 a.m. to noon and 1 to 4 p.m., except on Thursday.

The **Tourist Bureau** is on Chapel Street in Charlestown.

As in St. Kitts, Nevis is on **Atlantic Standard Time,** which means it's usually one hour ahead of the U.S. East Coast, except when the mainland goes on Daylight Saving Time. Then clocks are the same.

A 10% **service charge** is added to your hotel bill. In restaurants, it is customary to tip from 10% to 15% of the tab.

The government imposes a 5% **tax** on hotel bills.

HOTELS: Several of the inns of Nevis have been adapted from long-decayed sugar plantations. The style and amenities may transport you back to a bygone era. In addition, there are a scattering of air-conditioned motel-type accommodations for those who prefer that.

Croney's Old Manor Estate. P.O. Box 70, Gingerland (tel. 465-5445), dates back in Nevis history to 1690, and has operated continuously as a sugar plantation and cattle ranch. For part of its life, it was a stud farm for slave breeding, according to local legend. Now owned by Vicki Knorr, the estate has been turned into a miniature resort. If you like the old style of life and dislike the plastic hotel style, you may fit in just fine here, finding the pace slow and easy. The courtyard is ablaze with geraniums, antherium, and red hibiscus. Yet as you contemplate nature, you live quite luxuriously.

Built at an 800-foot elevation on the breeze-swept trade-wind side of the island, the present cut-stone structures of Croney's were erected between 1810 and 1832 around the great house and a sugar mill. At the death of the former owner, Bertie Croney, in 1967, the great house was the longest continually lived-in such place in the West Indies.

A major restoration program has saved the buildings, which now have a modern Neiman-Marcus interior decor. The Executive House, a former carriage hall, livery stable, and attendants' quarters, was turned into a bar, kitchen, and dining room, as well as a trio of bedrooms. The estate workers' clapboard huts have been replaced by the Admiral's Building, containing two one-bedroom suites, plus one two-bedroom suite. From another era, the smokehouse and jail were replaced with the Overseers Building, with a one- and a two-bedroom suite. Most of the bedrooms have king-size beds, a net canopy, an overhead fan, and rattan furnishings.

EP rates in winter are $90 daily in a single, $120 in a double. *The summer*

EP rates are $59 in a single, $70 in a double. For breakfast and dinner, the charge is only $28 per person per day year round. With the best cook on the island, the charming, witty Bernice Morton ("as in Morton salt"), that is a very good price indeed. Try her barbecued lobster. The beef placed on the table is raised right on the estate, and they grow their own vegetables. Try also the tangy pumpkin soup, the moist red snapper, the super-fresh vegetables, topped off by banana grits.

As in olden days, ladies still sip tea on the veranda and gentlemen ride fine horses and talk politics. However, guests in bygone eras didn't have a large freshwater swimming pool or today's conveniences. If you want a drink, you just help yourself. It's an open-bar policy around here. The misnamed Tea Garden is actually the site of sundowners, string and pan band dances, movies, or whatever.

Nisbet Plantation Inn, Newcastle (tel. 465-5325), is a gracious estate house on a copra farm where gentility and a respect for fine living prevail. This is the former home of Frances Nisbet, who married Lord Nelson at the age of 22. (Enamored of Miss Nisbet at the time, he later fell in love with Lady Hamilton, and Frances Nisbet died a bitter old woman in England, one of history's pathetic figures.) The present main building on the 30-acre plantation was rebuilt on the foundations of the original 18th-century great house. The ruins of a circular sugar mill stand at the entrance, covered with cassia, frangipani, hibiscus, and poinciana.

Sitting on a veranda, after helping yourself to a sideboard breakfast, you look down a wide, grassy lawn, lined with sentinel palm trees, which leads to a half-mile-long sandy beach, the best in Nevis. Two neighboring bays combine to make a total of three miles for beachcombing and shelling. An offshore reef protects the swimming area, providing good snorkeling. At the hotel, snorkeling and spearfishing equipment are available. Set in the palm grove are octagonal yellow and white frame guest cottages, with covered verandas, all with private baths, overhead fans, and louvered windows. Two of the guest rooms have ornate four-poster beds. The living room of the main house is furnished with English antiques.

The managers are easygoing, innately hospitable, seeing to your needs, showing you their shelves of books, or guiding you to horseback riding, tennis (a hard court with racquets and balls provided), fishing, and sailing on the island. At the end of the day they share a tranquil evening meal (with wine included), perhaps a creole concoction such as curried chicken or lamb kebab. Dinner is always a social occasion, guests gathering first on the veranda for sundowners, then being seated at tables holding four or six. The bar is self-service, based on the honor system. Sunday is barbecue time on the beach. If visitors drop in, they are charged $20.

On the MAP, winter rates are $135 to $160 daily in a single, $220 to $260 in a double. *In summer, EP guests are accepted at a rate ranging from $45 to $65 daily in a single, from $65 to $95 in a double. For breakfast and dinner, add another $35 per person daily.*

Zetland Plantation, Gingerland, P.O. Box 448 (tel. 465-5454), originally a sugar plantation, was converted into an exceptional hotel, occupying a 750-acre site with good views of both the Atlantic and the Caribbean Sea. The former plantation lies 1000 to 2000 feet up on the slopes of Mount Nevis, from which you can view Antigua and Montserrat. Its name is derived from Scotland's Shetland Islands.

Today, Zetland is more like a country-club lodge. More than a dozen plantation suites (square one-story houses) are rented, containing fully equipped, compact kitchens. Hotel-type maid service is included in the tariffs. Scattered about the grounds, all rental units are within easy walking distance of the main complex. Because of its mountain perch, trade-wind breezes keep the plantation cooled.

In summer, a single room rents for $80 daily on the MAP, going up to $110 daily in a double, also on the MAP. In winter, singles are charged $95 on the MAP, and two persons pay $150 daily. Rates include wake-up coffee and transportation to the hotel beach hut. When making reservations, inquire about package rates and family plans. The Sugar Mill has been transformed into a family unit, housing up to six persons.

As only 40 guests can be accommodated at a time, everybody quickly gets to know everybody else. The manager is Michael Reeves, who has had experience in restaurant and tourist enterprises in England and Africa. He'll outline the sports program to you, including hikes through an unspoiled tropical forest, tennis, horseback riding, or swimming at the plantation pool. Or you can drive to Zetland's beach for ocean swimming. A place for the discriminating traveler, Zetland also serves good food (see my dining recommendations). Most of it is grown on the plantation. People staying here on EP rates are charged extra for gas for cooking in their units.

Cliff Dwellers, Tamarind Bay (tel. 465-5262), offers 14 guest cottages and a dining room which hang virtually suspended in a cluster between the hills and the water. Facing St. Kitts, the hotel may be difficult to reach, but once you've arrived at the altitudinal perch, you're rewarded with a panoramic view in all directions. The hotel managers, Richard and Maureen Lupinacci, are warm, capable, and knowing people who have had much experience in the Caribbean. They're most obliging, provide transportation by van down the steep hill to the 100-foot-long swimming pool and tennis court. (By the time you arrive, a tram to perform this function may have been restored.)

Completely redecorated and vastly improved, the hotel's guest rooms have been called sumptuous. Each cottage is spacious—20 feet by 24 feet, according to the hotel's own measurements—and each has a private balcony with a view of mountain and sea. King-size or twin beds have been placed in each cottage, which, incidentally, come with private baths.

On its own 17 acres, the hotel has some 2000 feet of oceanfront. MAP tariffs are $150 in a single in season, $190 in a double. *In the off-season, tariffs are lowered to $85 in a single, from $160 in a double, plus service, both MAP rates.*

Cliff Dwellers, likely to be closed in September and October, is considered by many as the best hotel on Nevis, and some have suggested that it is among the half dozen fine small hotels in the area. The food is ranked the finest on Nevis. Lobster and fish come from local waters, and the cook does many continental dishes well too. Breakfast can be taken on your own private balcony, and you'll live very well indeed here.

Golden Rock Estate, P.O. Box 493, Gingerland (tel. 465-5346), a sugar estate built on 1815, high in the hills of Nevis, has been converted into one of the most charming and atmospheric inns in the Caribbean. You walk through a 25-acre garden in a tropical setting of about 150 acres, lush and lovely. The original windmill, a stone tower, has been turned into a duplex honeymoon retreat (or else accommodataions for a family of four), with an elaborate four-poster bed. The inn has 12 double rooms in all, spread about the garden, shaded by hibiscus and allamanda, yet within a minute's walk of the freshwater swimming pool and shady terrace where tropical rum punches are served.

Each villa has been decorated with flair, and the king-size beds are four-posters made of bamboo. The fabrics used are island made, with tropical flower designs. Everything seems handsome and personal. In addition, the rooms have large porches for relaxing, reading, or just looking out at the sea. In winter, a single rents for $110 daily and a double goes for $140, plus another $35 per person extra for breakfast and dinner. *In summer, a single costs only $50 daily, a double renting for $80.* The hotel is not recommended for children under 12.

The managers, Pam and Frank Barry, came to Nevis on a project involving tanning of sheepskin and goatskin. They fell in love with the island, and their enthusiasm is contagious.

Wine is included at dinner, which is likely to be a West Indian meal (ever had stuffed pumpkin?) served at the 175-year-old "long house." Before dinner, you will surely have had a tall drink in the hotel's bar.

Pam will show you to the tennis court or start you on a hike through a rain forest, where you might spot a wild monkey. The hotel's bus takes guests to one of Golden Rock's beaches every day at no extra cost. The estate owns one beach on the leeward side, part of the famous Pinney's Beach, and another on the windward side where you can surf. The shuttle runs once a day (round trip) to both beaches, with a shopping stop in Charlestown if you want it. In addition, a 20-foot fiberglass day-sailer and a 16-foot Boston whaler are offered for waterskiing, light offshore fishing, and snorkel and scuba-diving. Scuba is available to accredited divers only. A private car, either a Mini-Moke or a Volkswagen, is available for one or two couples, including insurance and mileage. After dark, the Barries might produce a string band for your amusement.

Montpelier Plantation Inn, P.O. Box 474, Montpelier (tel. 465-5462), 700 feet up the slopes of Mount Nevis, is owned by the Milnes Gaskell family from Yorkshire. Sixteen rooms with private terraces and baths are in modern cottages and are kept cool and fresh by the almost constant light breeze. Other portions were set on the foundations of the ruins of the great Montpelier estate. Much use has been made of local stonework and traditional architectural styles. The magnificent and extensive gardens have, at their center, the 18th-century sugar mill, a mammoth swimming pool and pool bar, and at the periphery a hard tennis court. The year 1980 saw renovations and complete redecoration. The atmosphere is of informal West Indian grandeur.

The hotel concentrates on the quality of its food, providing organically grown produce from its own three-acre fruit and vegetable garden. Winter rates on the MAP are $120 daily in a single and $150 to $165 daily in a double. *Off-season, MAP rates are $80 daily in a single and $105 in a double.*

The inn has its own speedboat, a 17-foot Boston whaler with 85-h.p. outboard engine for waterskiing and snorkeling. Horseback riding, sailing, and deep-sea fishing can be arranged. In season, several nights a week there are dances at nearby establishments. Montpelier occasionally has a grand affair, featuring the Honey Bees Scratch Band and the Nevis Folklore Dancers.

Pinney's Beach Hotel, P.O. Box 61, Charlestown (tel. 465-5207), is the only hotel on one of the most spectacular beaches in Nevis. A miniature resort, it is a bungalow colony, 48 double rooms, including six family-type units, clustered around a waterside patio where you can have cooling drinks, lunch, or take a dip. The decor is traditional, with a certain amount of clutter, but guests seem to like such informality. Rooms are modestly equipped, yet supplied with the basic necessities. Some are air-conditioned. Each unit comes with a private bath and a patio, and a view of the palm-fringed coastline is thrown in as well. The cheaper bungalows are set back a bit, overlooking an inner flower garden, while the others have their own direct entrance onto the beach. In winter, double rooms rent for $105 daily on the MAP, and singles go for $70. In one of the cottages, two to four persons can be housed at MAP rates that range from $105 to $140 daily. *In summer, the manager reduces the tariffs to $55 daily in a single, $85 in a double, all MAP. Summer cottages, for two to four persons, rent from $90 to $110 daily, all MAP rates.*

Horseback riding, sailing, and deep-sea fishing can be arranged by the hotel, and there's a tennis club about 50 yards from Pinney's.

Many business people from the town come here for lunch, as the hotel is only a seven-minute walk into Charlestown (about a 15-minute drive from the airport).

Rest Haven Inn, P.O. Box 209, Old Hospital Road in Charlestown (tel. 465-5208), is a collection of bungalows standing on 2½ acres of grounds. I prefer the newer units which the soft-spoken owner, Almon Nisbett (with two Ts, no relation to Frances), has built at water's edge. Each with a private patio opening onto the Caribbean, these are his deluxe units—spacious, air-conditioned, containing twin-size and single beds. For these, of course, he charges his highest tariffs. The older rooms containing twin beds are set back a bit, located within the pool and dining area compound, facing each other with private patios. Some of these have simple efficiency units for light cooking.

Summer rates, depending on the accommodation, range from $40 to $75 daily in a single, from $60 to $95 in a double, MAP. In winter, MAP tariffs are $65 to $85 daily in a single, from $95 to $115 in a double. A studio apartment with kitchenette accommodates two couples at a rate of $135 per day EP.

The hospitality is what counts here, not the grand surroundings, and you are close to Charlestown, a five-minute walk away. The location is also near Pinney's Beach, where you'll surely want to spend your days. Mr. Nisbett has a reputation for serving good-tasting island dishes, and if you want to go hiking, one of his staff will pack a picnic lunch for you. There is also a snackbar, where light lunches, including lobster, are served daily to those who don't want to leave the grounds. Tennis is available on the hotel's own courts.

WHERE TO EAT: Most people dine at their hotel. To break what could be monotony, many guests often take their lunch at one of the plantation hotels on the island, for which they should call in advance for a reservation—except at **Zetland Plantation,** Gingerland (tel. 465-5454), which accepts luncheon guests without prior notice. Some people consider the food here the best on the island, costing $12 for a midday meal. However, for one of its well-prepared $20 dinners, you'll need a reservation (for a fuller description, see my hotel recommendation).

Outside of the hotels, the **Rookery Nook,** a lava-stone corner pub, in Charlestown, past Barclay's Bank, is the most popular gathering spot on the island, but even it doesn't have enough business to remain open most evenings. You can drink or order light meals inside, or else go out to the patio near the waterfront, which is sheltered by a large flamboyant tree. Count on spending from $8 for a meal.

If you find yourself Charlestown at midday, you might do better gathering the makings for your own picnic lunch. One way to do this is to go to the **marketplace,** buying fresh fruit, such as mangoes, from the stallkeepers. Then head for the **Nevis Bakery,** where you can order coconut tarts, and fresh-baked bread. The friendly people at **Main Street Grocery Store** will provide the rest of the makings for your lunch, including canned pâté.

When you can get it, the native food is good. If you request sea urchin, the chef won't be surprised. Good local dishes include not only that, but turtle specialties as well (stew, steak, or pie). Suckling pig and pixilated pork are both roasted with many spices, and eggplant is used in a number of tasty ways, as is the avocado.

EXPLORING NEVIS: When you arrive at the airport, it's best to negotiate with a taxi driver to take you around Nevis. The distance is only 20 miles. You may find yourself taking much longer if you stop to see specific sights. The people are friendly and will often engage you in conversation.

At Bath Village, about half a mile from Charlestown, you'll find the **Bath House Hotel,** which was a grand place 200 years ago. In serious disrepair today, there is still talk of restoring it. Norman Fowler most recently started the present rebuilding, a project that came to an abrupt halt at his death. An antique store that never seems to open has been installed on the third floor. Pick your path carefully through the ruined building. John Huggins built the hotel in 1778 to accommodate some 50 guests, mostly wealthy planters in the West Indies who were afflicted with rheumatism and gout. The hotel had five hot baths built in which temperatures ranged up to 108° Fahrenheit. It shut down in 1870. Patched and proud, she stands today as a reminder of Nevis's heyday, although goats now tread the tired verandas instead of fancy, if ailing, gentlemen who courted their ladies here centuries ago.

Nearby, **St. John's Church** stands in the midst of a sprawling graveyard in Fig Tree Village. It is said to have been the parish church of Lady Nelson, wife of Horatio Lord Nelson. A church of gray stone, dating from the 18th century, it contains the record of Nelson's marriage in the church register.

At Morning Star, **Nelson's Museum** is privately owned and maintained. It contains a large collection of Nelson memorabilia gathered by Robert D. Abrahams, a Philadelphia lawyer. The museum can be visited free. Displayed among other items is a faded letter written by Nelson with his left hand, after he lost his right one. See also a grandfather clock that was deliberately (and permanently) stopped the moment Queen Elizabeth entered the museum on February 22, 1966, the most recent big event that has happened on Nevis. The museum is open daily but hours fluctuate.

Ashby Fort is not overgrown, but it was once used by Lord Nelson to guard his ships in Nevis while they took on fresh water and supplies. Nearby is **Nelson's Spring,** near Cotton Ground Village. In the 18th century, Nelson is said to have watered his ships here before they left to fight in the American Revolution. The fort, in bad ruin, overlooks the site of **Jamestown,** an early settlement that was devastated by a 1680 tidal wave.

The **Eden Brown Estate** lies about a mile and a half from New River and it's said to be haunted. Once it was the home of a wealthy planter, whose daughter was to be married, but her husband-to-be was killed in a duel at the prenuptial feast. The mansion was then closed forever and left to the ravages of nature. A gray solid stone still stands, and only the most adventurous go here on a moonlit night.

Outside the center of Charlestown, the **Jewish Cemetery** was restored in part by an American, Robert D. Abrahams, the Philadelphia lawyer already mentioned. At the lower end of Government Road, this necropolis was the resting place of many of the early shopkeepers of Nevis. At one time Sephardic Jews coming from Brazil made up a quarter of the population. It is believed that Jews introduced sugar production into the Leewards. Most of the tombstones date from between 1690 and 1710.

GETTING AROUND: Your ten-seater plane arrives at the airport, 14 minutes north of Charlestown; then you should stop at the police station in Charlestown if you plan to do any driving. Holders of a valid Canadian or American license can obtain a permit for about $4.

If you're prepared to face the rocky, pot-holed roads of Nevis, you can arrange for a rental car from **Budget** before going there (call toll free at 800/527-0700). Avis and Hertz maintain no offices in Nevis. The Budget office is on Main

Street in Charlestown (tel. within Nevis, 5390; from outside of Nevis, 809/465-5390). This particular subsidiary of Budget requires a customer to take a taxi from the airport or from his or her hotel to the car-rental headquarters to pick up a vehicle.

The cheapest car is a Dodge Colt with automatic transmission. The cost is $150 per week with unlimited mileage. Drivers must be at least 25 years old. It's advisable to take out a collision damage waiver.

You can also rent a **taxi** with a driver (who also doubles as a guide). You'll find them waiting at the airport at the arrival of every plane. A good 3½-hour tour that takes in most of the sightseeing attractions should cost no more than EC$90 ($34.20), but terms on these unmetered cabs should be firmly negotiated before you strike out. The average taxi holds up to four persons, so when the cost is sliced per passenger, it's a reasonable investment. No sightseeing bus companies operate tours on Nevis.

SHOPPING: Everybody, including Prince Charles, heads for **Eva Wilkin's Studio** on the grounds of the old sugar mill plantation her father owned. She is the most famous artist of Nevis, and invites visitors to come by her studio and home during the day, except from noon to 3 p.m. "when I need rest." A spry, elderly lady who doesn't "understand modern ways," she displays both black-and-white and color prints. Color prints sell from $35, although black-and-white ones are much less. Her studio is at Clay Ghaut Estate near Montpelier in Gingerland. She paints island people (using real models), local flowers and scenes. On the grounds near her house is a miniature reproduction of the original sugar factory. Ask your driver if she's in residence before starting out. Everybody knows when Miss Wilkins is on the island.

For one of the most bizarre shopping expeditions in this book, head for the home of **Mrs. Jones,** the last house on the right going east out of Newcastle, a tumbledown old village near the airport. Mrs. Jones doesn't put out a sign "because I don't need one." She candidly admits, "I'm known all over the world, but I've been no place from Nevis." An elderly peanut farmer, she turns out unglazed pottery: "I make every creature but man, and only God can put life into him." Her specialty is terracotta birds, and she also makes oversize clay pots.

The **Sand-Box Tree,** Chapel Street. Kitty Burke is the inspiration behind this unusual shop specializing in everything from island antiques to homemade fashions. Kitty will assist your selection from a line of ready-to-wear or custom-made bikinis, hats, and daytime, evening, and boating wear. There are even selections of toys for your favorite godchild, stationery for letters home, and jewelry for that special night out. Many of the fabrics, often stitched into garments for men and women, are silkscreened. You'll find this shop near the corner of Main Street.

The **Nevis Handicraft Cooperative Society,** Lower Happy Hill Alley, is a stone building about 200 feet from the wharf. Near the colorful marketplace (visit on Tuesday, Thursday, and Saturday mornings), the handicraft shop contains locally made gift items, including unusual objects of goatskin.

Heading up Government Road, you reach the **School for the Blind,** where the Nevisians make handicrafts for sale. Visiting hours are 9 a.m. to noon and 1 to 4 p.m. Monday through Wednesday (9 a.m. to noon on Saturday). Go only if you want to buy something, as it seems cruel to disturb these unfortunate people who have very little money and few prospects.

The best for last—**Caribee Clothes,** on Main Street (tel. 465-5217), features hand-embroidered styles. It's run by R. V. W. and Cathy Todd, who will sometimes grant customers permission to visit the factory. Nevis themes often form the motif in the patterns. Resort-type shirts and skirts are sold, and they're quite beautiful—and expensive. The little industry provides work for many craftspeople on the island, and Caribee Clothes are sold in many fine West Indian boutiques and in America.

THE SPORTING LIFE: The best beach on Nevis—in fact, one of the best beaches in the Caribbean—is the reef-protected **Pinney's Beach,** with its clear water and gradual slope. Just north of Charlestown, you'll have three miles of sand (often virtually to yourself), culminating in a sleepy lagoon that evokes a scene south of Pago-Pago.

In sports equipment, it's best to bring your own. However, hotels are stocked with limited gear (but equipment may often be in use by other guests).

Snorkeling and Scuba

Again, head for Pinney's Beach. You might also try the waters of Fort Ashby, where the settlement of Jamestown is said to have slid into the sea, and legend has it that the church bells can still be heard and the undersea town can still be seen when conditions are just right. So far, no diver, to my knowledge, has ever found the conditions "just right."

Your best bet is the **Oualie Beach Pub** (tel. 465-5329), at Mosquito Bay, which has snorkeling trips at a cost of $20 per person (minimum of two required).

Deep-Sea Fishing

The fishing is excellent, not only for snapper and grouper, but for bonita and kingfish as well. The best hotel for making boating arrangements is the **Golden Rock** (tel. 465-5346). It has its own 20-foot fiberglass day-sailer, and a 16-foot Boston whaler for waterskiing, light offshore fishing, and snorkel and scuba-diving. Most trips cost $75 per half day for the boat, and at least three fisherpeople are required.

Fishing trips can also be arranged by the **Oualie Beach Pub** (tel. 465-5329), at a cost of $20 per hour. The location is at Mosquito Bay.

Boating

The best arrangements are made at the **Golden Rock** (see above).

Oualie Beach Pub (tel. 465-5329), at Mosquito Bay, will rent you Sunfish, windsurfers and a Hobie Cat at costs ranging from $10 to $15 per hour. A daily sail and a picnic will cost $35 per person (a minimum of two required).

Waterskiing

Check with **Oualie Beach Pub** (tel. 465-5329), at Mosquito Bay, where the cost is $10 for every 15 minutes.

Tennis

Most of the major hotels have courts. The two courts at **Croney's Old Manor** (tel. 465-5445) are lit at night.

Golf

Addicts of this sport are invited to go to St. Kitts, a 45-minute boat ride or a 10-minute air hop, for a game.

Mountain Climbing

This is strenuous, recommended only to the stout of heart. Ask first at your hotel for a picnic lunch, and also the desk, to arrange a guide for you (he'll probably request about $20). Hikers climb Mount Nevis, 3500 feet up to the volcanic (extinct) crater and enjoy a hike to the rain forest to watch for wild monkeys.

Horseback Riding

Rare in the Caribbean, horseback riding is available at the **Nisbet Plantation** (tel. 465-5325), previewed earlier. Naturally, you ride English saddle. The cost is $15 per person for one hour, $10 for each hour to follow. With a guide, you are taken along mountain trails, and along the way you visit the site of long-forgotten plantations.

5. Anguilla

The most northerly of the Leeward Islands in the eastern Caribbean, Anguilla, known as "Eel Island" because of its shape, is only 16 miles long and a maximum of 3 miles wide. Anguilla lies five miles north of St. Martin. Flat as a pancake, long, slender Anguilla has very little rainfall. The soil is unproductive, with mainly low foliage and scrub vegetation.

Vegetation may be sparse, but the beaches of white coral sand around Anguilla are outstanding. Incidentally, these strips of sand are nearly deserted, as Anguilla attracts few tourists compared to an island such as Antigua.

Once Anguilla was part of a federation with St. Kitts and Nevis, but it declared its independence in 1967. Breaking away from that associated state, it is now a British dependency, and English, of course, is the official language. Most of the men on the island work as lobster fishermen or at the government-owned Salt Pond.

Upon leaving Anguilla, you must pay a departure tax of $3.

Columbus may have spotted the island, calling it Anguilla, Spanish for "eel." The island was first colonized by the British, in 1650. The colony was subjected to sporadic raids from Irish and French freebooters. In 1745 a French expedition of two frigates and some 700 soldiers launched an attack, but were repulsed by the governor and his militia. The French invaders landed again in 1796, an attack bravely resisted by heroic Anguillans who fed their cannons with lead balls from their sprat nets. The invasion failed and Anguilla went back to sleep under Britain's protection. It is said that the sea island cotton seed which spread to Georgia and the Carolinas in 1889 came originally from Anguilla.

One of the most popular beaches is Road Bay, framed by the crescent-shaped village of Sandy Ground and a large salt pond. There you can negotiate with one of the local fishermen to take you to **Sandy Island,** studded with palms, just 20 minutes from port. You can also go farther out to Prickly Pear Cay, stretching like a sweeping arc all the way to a sand spit populated by sea birds and rusty brown pelicans. The bay boasts some of Anguilla's best coral gardens, inhabited by small fish with iridescent markings.

Other good beaches include Shoal Bay, which apart from its silver sands boasts some of Anguilla's best coral gardens, the habitat of hundreds of tiny fish with iridescent, brilliantly colored markings. Crocus Bay is a long, golden beach, where a fisherman might take you out in search of snapper or grouper, or ferry you to such wee islands as Little Scrub.

At Island Harbour's horseshoe bay, fishermen bring in the lobster catch. On the beach they caulk colorful boats and mend their nets. You'll want to take plenty of pictures (if you've brought your own film—camera supplies are short here). Schooners are built on the shore at this hamlet, which lies at the east end of the island.

Boat trips can also be arranged to **Sombrero Island,** 38 miles northwest of Anguilla. This mysterious island, with its lone lighthouse, is 400 yards wide at its broadest point, three-quarters of a mile in length. Phosphate miners abandoned it in 1890; and limestone rocks, now eroded, rise in cliffs around the island. The treeless, waterless terrain evokes a moonscape. Once an 1869 lighthouse which stood here served the ships of the world. An old schooner, *Warspite,* leaves Anguilla twice a month (ask at the tourist office), taking mail and supplies to the hearty souls who inhabit the rock. The boat leaves at night, arriving at Sombrero Island at dawn, the rough trip taking four hours. This trip is recommended only to the stout of heart, more for travelers than tourists, as absolutely no comfort is provided.

The hottest months in Anguilla are from July to October, the coolest from December to February. The mean monthly temperature is about 80° Fahrenheit.

In all, Anguilla is for the adventuresome explorer. Its limited nightlife will bore many visitors, although it is that very unspoiled nature that attracts those who decide to visit it.

GETTING THERE: The nearest jet airports to Anguilla are the Juliana Airport on the Dutch-held St. Maarten and the Coolidge Airport in Antigua. **Winair** runs a scheduled service from its headquarters in St. Maarten, and several domestic air services link Anguilla with Antigua, St. Thomas, St. Kitts, and other neighboring islands.

For example, **LIAT** flies from either St. Kitts or Antigua twice a week. One way to get to Anguilla from North America is to take **Eastern Airlines** to San Juan, with an extension flight to St. Maarten on **Prinair.** Anguilla is reached in just 5 minutes' flying time from St. Maarten and 45 minutes' flying time from St. Thomas. **CrownAir** flies visitors to Anguilla from San Juan via St. Thomas four days a week. If you're flying to St. Maarten and don't want to wait around for a connecting flight, **Carib Air Service,** based in Anguilla, will go over and pick you up. You'll be met at immigration in St. Maarten and escorted right through with your luggage onto a waiting plane for the six-minute flight to Anguilla. A minimum of two passengers is required. Captain Leslie will pick you up, and the cost is $40 round trip per person. However, if you should need service after sunset, the charge goes up to $280 for the plane, plus an extra $75 per hour after 11 p.m. This is because of the high cost of landing and taking off in St. Maarten.

If you'd prefer to arrive in Anguilla by sea, a **ferry** called *Two Cheers* leaves the Marigot pier in French St. Martin every day except Monday at 9:30 a.m., 2:30 p.m., and 4:30 p.m. The trip takes only 20 minutes and costs $10 round trip. Reservations are not necessary.

GETTING AROUND: A **taxi** tour is the best way to see the island. In about two hours, one of the local drivers (all of them are guides) will show you everything. A driver costs about $35 for the day. If you're visiting just for the day (as most sightseers do), you can be let off at your favorite beach after a look around, then picked up and returned to the airport in time to catch your flight back to wherever.

Or if you'd prefer, you can rent an automatic- or standard-shift car from **Connor's Car Rental,** P.O. Box 65, South Hill (tel. 2433). Daily rates are $30 to $35 (the more expensive tariff is for air conditioning). Mileage is unlimited, but gas is extra. For reservations, write to Maurice Connor at the address given. *Remember to drive on the left!* Don't be surprised to find a vintage Japanese car waiting, as Connor's 50 cars are Toyotas, Hondas, and Datsuns. I found only one full-service petrol station on my latest rounds.

PRACTICAL FACTS: The Eastern Caribbean dollar is the official **currency** of Anguilla, although U.S. dollars are widely circulated. There are four banks in Anguilla, and the official exchange rate is EC$2.65 to $1 (U.S.).

In time, Anguilla is four hours behind Greenwich Mean Time and one hour ahead of Eastern Standard Time.

The main **post office** is in the Valley. Collectors consider Anguilla's stamps valuable, and the post office there also operates a philatelic bureau. Hours are 8 a.m. to noon and 1 to 3:30 p.m. Monday through Friday, and 8 a.m. to noon on Saturday. Hotel owners on Anguilla have told me that mail directed to them often ends up (for reasons known only to postal authorities) in either Bombay, India, or Sydney, Australia.

Cable and Wireless Ltd. operates the island's phone system as well as its Telex, cable, and phone links to the world.

Electricity, except in the Valley area, is provided by privately owned generators. Current is 110 volts.

In medical services, there is a **Cottage Hospital** on Anguilla, plus several district clinics.

A daily broadcast service is provided by **Radio Anguilla,** which operates on a frequency of 1505 kHz (200 meters) with a power of 1000 watts.

Special **holidays** include Constitution Day on February 10, Anguilla Day on May 30, and Separation Day on December 19.

ACCOMMODATIONS: Sleepy Anguilla is awakening to tourism, but the island has got a long way to go. In fact, it definitely doesn't want to become another St. Maarten. Development is being controlled, and it is emerging slowly. Some of the resorts recommended below are still under construction. Villas and cottages are being added, but no one seems in a hurry. Most of the operations are small, friendly, and informal, and there's a "touch of class" as well.

Malliouhana, Maids Bay (tel. 2741). Malliouhana was the Carib Indian word for Anguilla. But that's all that is primitive about this super-deluxe hostelry. A surprise in "sleepy" Anguilla, there are few places in the Caribbean Basin where you will be coddled in such splendor and comfort—for a price, of course. Whether they created it in a "fit of madness" or whatever, this major oasis of luxury in Anguilla was the dream of an Englishman, Robin Ricketts, and his wife, Sue. The resort is operated in conjunction with Cul de Sac (see below).

Today's hotel began with two luxury villas, named Orchid and Tamarind. They are still there, but the hotel has now grown, and it's got plenty of space for expansion, as it is set on 25 acres of property surrounded by two miles of white sandy beaches.

In the main house are 34 rooms and seven suites. In addition, there are three-bedroom villas opening onto the beach or onto well-planted and maintained gardens overlooking the water. To create this pocket of posh, the famed designer, Lawrence Carleton Peabody II, member of a prominent Boston family and celebrated designer, was called in. He used textured Haitian fabrics, Brazilian walnut, touches of bamboo and wicker, and lots of marble and mirrors to create an aura of refinement.

The marble and mirror were used most effectively in the bathrooms. The luxury suites, for example, have not only a large bedroom and mirrored bathroom, but a living room, dressing room, dining room, and cook's pantry, opening onto al fresco terraces.

Now the bad news: you must pay the piper. High-season tariffs are in effect from mid-December until the end of April. A luxury double, the least expensive way of staying here, rents for $250 to $325 daily, a one-bedroom suite for $400 to $500 daily, and those three-bedroom villas mentioned earlier for anywhere from $1000 to $1200 daily. Meals are extra. *From May 1 until the hotel shuts down at the end of August, the luxury double is reduced to $175 daily, the one-bedroom suite goes for $400 daily, and a three-bedroom villa costs $700 daily.*

The rooms are only part of the attraction of this resort. It has the finest food on the island (see below). Bar service is provided on both beaches and around the pools. One bar is by three cascading freshwater pools. On some evenings, quiet music is played for dancing, but for more vigorous entertainment, guests are taken on a shuttle bus over to the sister resort, Cul de Sac.

There is also a water-sports center (see below) and three tennis courts.

That's not all. The chic Italian boutique, La Romana, from St. Maarten has a branch at the hotel, selling fine clothing for both women and men, along with their jewelry collection. The beauty salon, Schumi of London, is available for pedicures, manicures, and hair dressing.

Incidentally, *The New York Times* predicted that Malliouhana may one day "be one of the world's most exclusive hotels."

Cinnamon Reef Beach Club, Little Harbour (tel. 2727), is one of the most sophisticated resorts in the British Leewards. No detail was overlooked in its design, from the uniforms of the friendly staff to the exquisite table settings that complement the culinary achievements of an experienced chef. Built slowly over many years, this resort officially opened in the autumn of 1984. Ringed with plants, its architectural style is a combination of ultramodern lines with a vaguely Moorish motif. Accommodations are contained within white stucco villas, the porticos of which are piereced with enormous portholes and large archways leading onto private terraces.

Inside the units, guests climb several steps to reach the well-appointed bedrooms and dressing rooms, which look down on a spacious living room filled with comfortable furniture. Ample quantities of water—both hot and cold—are available, since the Hauser family included a giant cistern as part of the property. Since there are only 14 accommodations, guests have the feeling of being in a wealthy private home, a feeling enhanced by the ministrations of the manager, New York–born Scott Hauser, the son of the owner.

With MAP, winter rates are $300 per day per couple. No children under 12 are allowed between January 15 and March 15, when winter rates are in effect. *Spring and autumn prices are $250 daily per couple, MAP. From May 15 to November 15, MAP costs $175 per day per couple.* Lodgings for single guests are reduced from $40 to $50 per accommodation, with MAP.

The dining room and bar areas are the focal points of this glamorous retreat, which has already attracted celebrities. The views over the veranda are of the reef-sheltered harbor where boats ride at anchor. The music greeting guests ranges from early Mozart or Vivaldi at breakfast to discreet dinner music. Some form of live entertainment and occasional dancing is offered at night.

On the premises is a freshwater rectangular pool big enough to swim laps in, two championship tennis courts, free sailboats, paddleboats, snorkeling equipment, windsurfers, and fishing equipment for the use of guests. Scuba-diving can also be arranged. The beach, sheltered by a reef, has tons and tons of fine coral sand which marine geologists pumped in over many seasons.

For reservations and information, call 800/223-1108 toll free nationwide (in New York state, phone 212/249-6840).

Cul de Sac, Blowing Point (tel. 2461), advertises itself as a place for those who seek "sun, sea, and tranquility." You get all that and a lot more around here. This expensive resort retreat is run by Robin and Sue Ricketts, who also own the super-deluxe Malliouhana just previewed. They offer six handsomely appointed and beautifully decorated studio apartments perched on the Caribbean at Blowing Point overlooking the mountains of St. Maarten. Each apartment has a bedroom/sitting room, bathroom, and kitchen/dining room with a large terrace opening onto the sea.

In the winter, a studio cottage rents for $140 daily, EP; *the tariff drops to $100 daily for two persons in summer.*

A swimming pool opens onto those mountains of St. Maarten already referred to. There is, as well, a private beach with a jetty which is known for its snorkeling possibilities.

The food at Cul de Sac (your meals are extra) are among the best on the island (see below). It is also the entertainment center of Anguilla (more about that later too). An added advantage is that guests of Cul de Sac are entitled to enjoy the full benefits as the pampered residents of Malliouhana. A shuttle bus takes guests, both day and night, between the two properties.

Guests at Cul de Sac can spend a lazy morning in the swimming pool placed in a garden setting, later enjoying a champagne and lobster picnic at one of the offshore cays. Maid service takes care of all cleaning and household laundry.

Merrywing, Cove Bay (tel. 2752), consists of some newly completed units, part of a much larger vacation resort on 49 acres of choice property fronting a beachfront of 850 feet. The first condo units to sprout up contain two-bedroom apartments with two baths and four one-bedroom units with bath. Fully equipped kitchens contain service for up to six persons and a large dining and living room area leading to one's own private terrace. Ceiling fans circulate trade winds in lieu of air conditioning. Perhaps by the time of your visit more units will be in operation.

In summer, a one-bedroom condo rents for $60 daily, $380 weekly for two persons. This goes up to $110 daily and $660 weekly for a two-bedroom apartment for four persons. A three-bedroom villa for six persons rents for $155 daily, $1080 weekly. In the winter season, the same one-bedroom condo costs $110 daily, $720 weekly; a two-bedroom apartment, $210 daily or $1440 weekly; and a three-bedroom villa, $335 daily, $2100 weekly.

Reservations for Anguilla's first condominium community can be made through Villa Vacations, P.O. Box 188, Cold Spring Harbor, NY 11724 (tel. 212/517-3088 in New York City, or 516/692-5525 in Long Island).

The **Mariners,** Sandy Ground (tel. 2671). Guests who appreciate a maximum of independence seem to prefer the type of vacation accommodation whose size can be almost tailor-made to fit their needs, as well as providing kitchen facilities if desired. This beachside resort is composed of nine gingerbread cottages, each of which contains a central living/dining room/kitchenette, with bedrooms on either side. Each bedroom has its own entrance, private bath, and veranda. The cottages can be rented as two-bedroom houses suitable for up to four persons, or as three separate self-sufficient accommodations. There's a bar, a dining room, and a sandy beach a few steps from any of the units for guests who have opted for a kitchenless bedroom or who prefer not to cook.

In winter, with no meals included, single persons can rent a kitchenless bedroom for $100 to $115, while couples pay $130 to $145. A studio with kitchenette rents for $110 to $120 for a single occupant, $145 to $155 for two persons. A one-bedroom suite for either one or two persons costs $215 to $230, while a two-bedroom cottage rents for $330 to $360. *In summer, single occupants of a kitchenless bedroom pay $85 to $95, while two pay $95. Studio apartments with kitchenettes rent for $95 single, $110 double. One-bedroom apartments go for $180, two-bedroom cottages for $260.* MAP can be arranged for an extra $40 per person in any season.

Anguilla Holiday Spa (see below for phone contact), is a 40-villa spa hotel on the north coast which is owned by the World Health Research Center. Each attractively furnished villa can accommodate up to four persons. Units include overhead fans, color TV, refrigerator, comfortable beds, and air conditioning. Villas also have sitting rooms which convert to a bedroom, with an extensive lounge or living room space, as well as a separate bedroom, bath, shower, and patio. Each villa also faces the ocean and the white sands of a bay. Year-round rates are $225 daily in a single, $250 in a double, and $275 in a triple, plus another $28 per person for breakfast and dinner.

The main pavilion houses a sauna, massage centers, table tennis, darts, as well as boutiques and a beauty salon. Saunas and massages must be arranged by appointment. A swimming pool (40 by 60 feet) is installed with a bar. The main pavilion houses three large restaurants, including the Palm Cove, serving American food, steaks, chops, and lobster; the Horizon Room, serving continental food, and finally, the Pelican Pub, offering fish and chips, lobster, and seafood. Entertainment, usually local music groups, perform at the Gazebo near the pool and barbecue pit.

For reservations, call Mary Gerold at 800/543-3722 toll free or 305/781-9544, or else write to 660 South Federal Hwy., Pompano Beach, FL 33062.

Rendezvous Bay Hotel, Rendezvous Bay (tel. 2549), opens onto sweeping, remote Rendezvous Bay, the most beautiful on the island, the place where the French landed in 1796. Set in the midst of soft pine trees, it evokes an inland hotel in Central America. Two long one-story guests houses with a covered portico provide each room with its own exterior lounge area. The rooms are very simple, furnished mostly in bamboo and rattan. While they are not air-conditioned, they do contain private baths (you are advised to be sparing with the water). The owner, Jeremiah Gumbs, was born in Anguilla and returned after spending many years in the U.S. In-season rates on the MAP are $90 daily in a single, $115 in a double. *In summer, these same MAP rates are lowered to $75 in a single, $90 in a double.* There is hot and cold water and 24-hour electric service. Mr. Gumbs holds forth on the longest and widest covered veranda in the Caribbean, often without his shirt (dress around here is very casual). Mr. Gumbs is known for his lobster lunches or dinners (he seemingly gets lobster when it's not available elsewhere). A lobster dinner, with salad, saffron rice, and dessert, costs about $20 per person, plus service and tax.

The **Seahorse,** P.O. Box 17 (tel. 2751), between Shaddick Point and Rendezvous Bay, features four one-bedroom apartments. Each unit is spacious, fully equipped, and well furnished, with bath and private gallery where you can view the sun set. The apartments are on the water on a small but ideal beach. At water's edge is a barbecue area for outdoor cooking or enjoying a drink. *The weekly rate in summer is $550 for two persons,* going up to $640 in winter. Included in that is maid service, as well as the use of the Seahorse's windsurfer and Sunfish. Dive tanks, air, and a dive boat are also available, and a few rental cars are offered at $120 per week. Reservations must be made with a deposit of $100 for each week's booking.

Loblolly Apartments, Sandy Hill (tel. 2250), was created by Capt. and Mrs. J. L. Wigley as a retirement retreat (he had been a London barrister). The apartments stand in the midst of tropical greenery, with an old smugglers' path leading down to a private beach. The apartments, along with a private residence, stand on a six-acre piece of property on a hill 100 feet above Sandy Hill Bay. The Wigleys offer two apartments, each with a double bedroom, kitchen, and bath. One has a dining room, the other a dinette. The apartments are ideal for two persons or else can be rented together to accommodate a family. Mahogany chests, fine chairs, and crystal chandeliers are in evidence. You can hire a cook, if needed, who will do your shopping, serving, and dish washing three times a day. In season, an apartment rents for $72 daily, $480 weekly, or $1900 monthly, *those prices dropping in summer to $60 daily, $420 weekly, or $1680 monthly.*

Shoal Bay Villas, P.O. Box 81, is directly on one of the finest beaches of the Caribbean—2½ miles of pure white sand. The Happy Jack beach bar and restaurant, open from 10 a.m. to 10 p.m., are popular island attractions. Water sports are also available. The villas are set in landscaped gardens. In winter, efficiencies for two persons rent for $135 per day, and a penthouse for two goes for $195 daily; a duplex for four costs $275 per day. An extra person in any accommodation pays $30 per day. *In summer, the prices are $75 in an efficiency, $110 in a penthouse, $150 for a duplex, and $20 per day for an extra person.* For reservations, contact the Jane Condon Corp., 211 East 43rd St., New York, NY 10017 (tel. 212/936-4373), or Jillian Carty, P.O. Box 256, Anguilla (tel. 809/497-2596). The villas are only ten minutes from the airport.

The **Inter-Island Hotel,** Lower South Hill (tel. 2259), is a two-story, residential-style villa with upper and lower covered verandas, overlooking the sea and neighboring St. Martin. Mr. Lewis, who runs it, rents out ten bedrooms, each with private bath and toilet. His living room is homey, with yellow and white tiles and organdy curtains. Everything is kept sparkling clean, although you'll definitely need a car to stay here. On the MAP, singles cost $55 daily; doubles, $85. The same tariffs are in effect all year, and tax and service are extra.

Lloyd's Guesthouse, The Valley, P.O. Box 52 (tel. 2351), is a simple Anguillan guest house run by a local politician, David Lloyd. He represented Anguilla when his country was part of the federation with St. Kitts and Nevis, and claims that any day he might go back into politics. In the meantime, he welcomes guests to his home where they gather in the living room in the evening after enjoying a big meal. A table holds a collection of family photographs. Fourteen simply furnished rooms are rented at year-round rates—$35 daily in a single, $62 in a double, MAP. Down by the water he rents out two cottages, very simple (there's that word again). Lloyd can also arrange boats for waterskiing and fishing.

Coral Bay Resort, The Valley (tel. 2345), is an 11-unit cottage community at a secluded beachfront point, with a good view of St. Martin. Accommodations are bedrooms or two- or three-bedroom villas, each self-contained and most opening onto a terrace with an ocean view. The furniture looks as if it were shipped in from Port-au-Prince. Maintenance is good, and the prices moderate. In winter, the single rate is $125 daily, or $750 on a special weekly rate. The cost in a double is $75 per person daily, or $900 per couple on a special weekly rate. MAP is available at another $25 per person daily. *In summer, expect reductions of 30%.* You can eat conch chips and grilled crayfish, each well prepared and attractively served in the regional-style restaurant.

Easy Corner Cottages, South Hill, P.O. Box 65 (tel. 2433), are owned by Maurice E. Connor, the same man who rents out most of the cars on the island. The nine one-, two-, and three-bedroom units are in landscaped settings with spectacular sunset views from the private porches, and you can also watch sailboats and beach frolickers. All units have full kitchens, combination living-dining rooms, porches, large and airy rooms, ceiling fans, bright and light rattan furniture, and TV. Children over the age of 2 are welcome, and daily maid service is available at an extra charge. *In summer, one-bedroom accommodations cost $55 daily and $360 weekly, two-bedroom units go for $75 daily and $510 weekly, and three-bedroom cottages for $90 per day and $630 per week.* In winter, one-bedroom facilities cost $85 and $540; two-bedroom units, $115 and $750; and three-bedroom accommodations, $145 and $960. Taxes and service are additional.

Skiffles Villas, P.O. Box 82, Isaac's Cliff (tel. 2619), is the personal creation of John and Susan Graff, who usually spend their summers at home in Indiana and their winters with their children on Anguilla. They offer six comfortably furnished villas of two bedrooms each, along with privacy and panoramic views, plus a freshwater pool. Weekly rates in high season are $750 for four guests (or $130 daily, *and 20% less in the off-season.* Address inquiries to John and Susan Graff, 1710 Lincolnway East, Goshen IN 46526 (tel. 809/497-2619), or write the villa directly in winter.

Rainbow Reef Villas, Seafeathers Bay, P.O. Box 130 (tel. 2817), is said to offer the finest snorkeling on the island from its beach off a three-acre site. Four two-bedroom self-catering villas are rented at $90 for two persons daily in season, or $560 weekly. Each additional person is charged $10. *In summer, the daily rate drops to $55, the weekly rental to $320 for two persons.*

Florencia Guest House, The Valley (tel. 2319), is a modest Anguillan guest house, rising two stories, painted green with a white trim. The house is over a grocery store, and each of the five bedrooms rented by Mr. and Mrs. Wilfred Daniel are tidy and shining clean. Don't expect air conditioning. Mrs. Daniel is a very good cook, so you may want to stay here on the MAP at $30 daily in a single, rising to $43 daily in a double. These rates are in effect all year. The welcome and hospitality extended are warm, although admittedly the facilities are very limited.

WHERE TO EAT: Order spiny lobster if you can get it. It's very good here and invariably fresh (many of the neighboring islands get their lobster from the fishermen of Anguilla). Home-grown vegetables, such as christophines and yams, accompany most dinners, with the inevitable rice.

Malliouhana Restaurant, Maids Bay (tel. 2741). Who would ever expect the celebrated Jo Rostang to turn up in such a remote outpost as Anguilla? Monsieur Rostang runs that deluxe citadel of haute cuisine, La Bonne Auberge, at Antibes on the French Riviera. The restaurant's nouvelle cuisine served there is ranked among the best along the Riviera. Mr. Rostang also operates the restaurant at Malliouhana, and his younger son runs it.

Admittedly, not the same ingredients from France are available to the Rostangs. Nevertheless their cuisine is still very French, but they also provide a Caribbean flair, making use of local ingredients not likely to be found in France. What they do with Anguillan fish, particularly red snapper, is amazing. They also have a French pastry chef who is among the finest in the Caribbean.

You get good food, ideal service, and glamorous surroundings. Meals can easily cost $50 and up, particularly with wine. The wine cellar has at least 30,000 carefully selected bottles from which you can make your choice. Reservations are imperative. Plan to make an evening of it.

Cul de Sac, Blowing Point (tel. 2461), is an elegant choice for gourmet dining. This small inn has a fine restaurant in a tropical setting overlooking the sea. Backed up by an excellent wine list, it specializes in French and Caribbean dishes. Jo Rostang of the famous three-star Michelin-rated La Bonne Auberge in Antibes, France, sends his young chefs to supervise the kitchen. You dine by candlelight in the open-air courtyard, surrounded by tropical ferns and exotic trees and flowers. Order spiny Anguillan lobster here, among other dishes, and expect to pay from $35 per person.

The Mariners, Sandy Ground (tel. 2671), has already been recommended as a hotel. Attracting a yachting crowd, it is also one of the finest places to dine on the island. The restaurant and bar serve both a Caribbean and continental cuisine, including spiny Anguillan lobster, along with freshly caught conch, grouper, and whelks from local waters. Try for a terrace table overlooking the calm Caribbean. On Thursday night there is usually a barbecue, and on Saturday night a West Indian buffet. My recent beautifully cooked crayfish was succulent. By flickering candlelight, you'll be presented a bill for around $25 to $30. The place usually rocks on a Saturday night with the Speckled Bird Band.

Harbour View, South Hill (tel. 2253), not only has the most attractive view on the island, but offers imaginatively prepared food. What makes it special is its owner, Lucy Halley, who lived in the French part of St. Martin, learning many secrets of the cuisine there. With a ring on every finger, she has the figure of a high-fashion model. She features both French and West Indian cookery, and her place is open seven days a week for lunch and dinner (she closes it when "the last person is served"). The visiting French are fond of the place, placed like a converted home on a cliff, overlooking the salt ponds, with a view of three islands. Lucy has just renovated and added to her place so that her 40-seat dining room now offers everyone a spectacular view of Sandy Ground and Road Bay. When you call or just arrive, ask Lucy what she has in the larder, or tell her what kind of food you like. If the catch is right, she'll make a lobster stew. She always has pork or lamb chops. Meals cost from $15 up. Live entertainment is often presented.

Barrel Stay Beach Bar & Restaurant, Sandy Ground (tel. 2831), is open all day, and meals are served from 11 a.m. to 3 p.m. and 6:30 to 10 p.m., costing $18 and up. A favorite is the fish soup served in the French fashion. The chef is noted for his fresh Anguilla seafood, including lobster, crayfish, red snapper, yellowtail, and conch. You can also order prime steaks, smoked ham, and chicken brochette. All dishes are served with a variety of fresh local West Indian vegetables. Desserts include homemade chocolate mousse and French ice cream. A selection of French wines is offered at reasonable prices.

The **Fish Trap Beach Bar & Restaurant,** Island Harbour (tel. 4488), lives up to its name. This is perhaps the best spot on the island if you like good seafood, very fresh, everything simply prepared, and that is likely to include snapper and grouper. When they're cooked in spices, the taste is similar to that you'd encounter in the Bayou country of Louisiana. The fishing boats also bring in that tasty spiny lobster which is so well prepared here (the most expensive item on the menu, however). You can also order stuffed crab and many other "fruits of the sea." Meals cost from $25. You're cooled by the trade winds as you dine. The place is not elegant in any way, but it's highly popular locally.

THE SPORTING LIFE: The major activity is swimming and lying on one of Anguilla's magnificent beaches (see the introduction). When you tire of that, the following are recommended:

Water Sports

Most of the coastline of Anguilla is fringed by coral reefs, and the island's waters are rich in marine life. Off the shore are sunken coral gardens and brilliantly colored fish. Fish include the torpedo-headed wrasse, the striped squirrelfish, and the sleek garfish. Conditions for scuba-diving and snorkeling on the island are ideal.

Tamariain Watersports (P.O. Box 247) has opened at Cul de Sac (tel. 2798), offering both diving instruction and a PADI certification course. For $250, you'll get five ocean dives including all the equipment and materials. For a three-hour pool course, plus one ocean dive and all the equipment, the price is $55. One tank rented in the morning or afternoon for a scuba-diving boat trip costs $25. An all-day snorkel trip with a picnic lunch included goes for $25 to $35 per person, but a minimum of six persons is needed to go out.

Malliouhana, Maids Bay (tel. 2741), also has a water-sports center. Instruction, if required, can be provided. The featured activities include scuba-diving, waterskiing, sailing, and perhaps parasailing.

Fishing

Fishing excursions can be made with the local fishermen. Your hotel can make the arrangements for you and the cost is about $40 a day. You should bring your own tackle. Absolutely agree on the cost, however, before setting out, as some misunderstandings have been reported.

A more organized form of this activity is available at **Tamariain Watersports,** P.O. Box 247, at the Cul de Sac (tel. 2798). Here, deep-sea fishing trips can be arranged, costing from $160 for a maximum of six persons for a half-day's adventure or $300 for a full day.

Malliouhana, Maids Bay (tel. 2741), can also make arrangements for guests to go deep-sea fishing. They also go on day trips to neighboring islands. The deluxe hotel has its own 34-foot cruiser and a 30-foot motor launch, plus a sailing yacht at its disposal.

Tennis

Malliouhana, Maids Bay (tel. 2741), has three championship Laykold tennis courts with a tennis pro and shop. Guests have the latest in video training techniques and a ball machine.

There are also two courts at **Cinnamon Reef,** Little Harbour (tel. 2727).

SHOPPING: Efforts have been made in recent years to develop handicrafts among the islanders. Island shops aren't very commercial as of yet.

The best known is the **Local Gift Shop** in the Quarter, a tiny little place where every item is homemade. Gifts made of shells are displayed along with wooden dolls. The hand-crocheted mats are quite beautiful, and tablecloths and bedspreads are woven into spidery lace designs, requiring awesome patience; but many of these are grabbed up by shops on neighboring islands and sold there at high prices. Baskets and mats are made from stripped corn husks and sisal rope. Model schooners and small pond boats are also for sale. Anguillan handicrafts are simple, an emerging industry deserving support.

Judy Henderson's **Sunshine Shop** (co-owned by the already-mentioned Maurice E. Connor) is in South Hill opposite Connor's Car Rental agency and is affiliated with Hilton Connor's Airport Hilton (not a hotel but a gift shop) where equally attractive locally made items are sold. Judy stocks fine cotton fun wear, including sarongs from Polynesia. She also has an assortment of beachwear, and such trinkets as hand-carved turtles, pelicans, and crayfish, each handcrafted by an Anguillan. You'll also find ivory and silver bracelets, perfume, and necklaces, perhaps a lithograph of an island scene. Large color photographs of the island's famous "Butterfly Wing" boats are on display, along with watercolors. The shops are full of many worthwhile carry-home items and contain a few hidden surprises.

Of course, stamp collectors will head for the already-mentioned **Valley Post Office** if they want to acquire unusual stamps from Anguilla.

NIGHTLIFE: There isn't much. The best of what there is centers around the hotels in season only. The major hotel for entertainment is **Cul de Sac,** Blowing Point (tel. 2461), where, in season, there is something going on at least six nights a week. A performance of the Mayoumba Folkloric Theatre is presented every Thursday night.

Chapter VIII

DUTCH WINDWARDS IN THE LEEWARDS

1. St. Maarten
2. St. Eustatius
3. Saba

THE DUTCH WINDWARDS have the same orientation to the northeast trades as do the British Leewards, documented in the previous chapter. However, the islands of St. Maarten, St. Eustatius (called "Statia"), and Saba—no more than dots in the Antilles—are called "The Dutch Windwards."

This is confusing to the visitor, but it makes sense in the Netherlands. The Dutch-held islands of Aruba, Bonaire, and Curaçao, lying off the coast of South America, go by the name of "The Dutch Leewards."

The Windwards, which are actually in the Leewards, were once inhabited by the fierce Carib Indians who believed that one acquired and assimilated the strength of his slain enemy by eating his flesh!

Columbus, on his second voyage to America, is said to have sighted the group of small islands on the name day of San Martino (St. Martin of Tours), hence, the present name of Sint (St.) Maarten.

Cooled by trade winds, the Windwards are comfortable to visit at any time of the year. The three Windward Islands, along with Aruba, Bonaire, and Curaçao, form the Netherlands Antilles.

In currency, the legal tender is the NAf (guilder), and the official rate at which the banks accept U.S. dollars is 1.77 NAf equals $1. Regardless, U.S. dollars are easily, willingly, and often eagerly accepted in the Dutch Windwards, especially St. Maarten. *Note:* Prices in this chapter are given in U.S. currency unless otherwise designated.

Even though the language is officially Dutch, everybody speaks English.

1. St. Maarten

It's small, only 37 square miles, about half the area of the District of Columbia. A split-personality island, St. Maarten is half Dutch, half French (who call their part St. Martin).

The divided island is considered the smallest territory in the world shared by two sovereign states (for a preview of St. Martin, refer to Chapter X on the French West Indies). The only way you know you're crossing an international border is when you see the sign—*"Bienvenue, Partie Française,"* a mon-

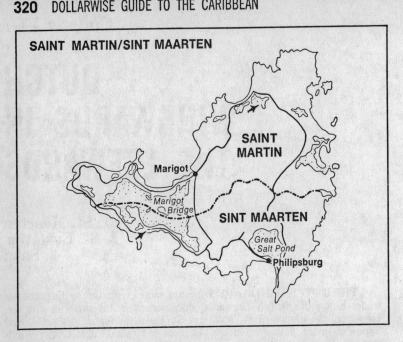

SAINT MARTIN/SINT MAARTEN

SAINT MARTIN

Marigot

Marigot Bridge

SINT MAARTEN

Great Salt Pond

Philipsburg

ument which commemorates the peaceful coexistence between the two nations.

The island was divided in 1648, and visitors still ascend Mount Concordia, near the border, where agreement was reached. Even so, St. Maarten was to change hands 16 times before becoming permanently Dutch.

Legend has it that a gin-drinking Dutchman and a wine-guzzling Frenchman walked around the island to see how much territory each could earmark for his side in one day. The Frenchman outwalked the Dutchman, but the canny Dutchman got the more valuable piece of property.

Northernmost of the Netherlands Antilles, St. Maarten lies some 150 miles southeast of Puerto Rico. A lush island, rimmed with bays and beaches, it has a year-round temperature of 80° Fahrenheit.

In addition to some 36 beaches—long, languorous coral strands—duty-free shopping and gambling casinos draw visitors to St. Maarten where there has been a rush of hotel building in the past few years.

The Dutch capital, **Philipsburg,** curves like a toy village along Great Bay. The town lies on a narrow sand isthmus separating Great Bay and Great Salt Pond. The capital was founded in 1763 by Commander John Philips, a Scot in Dutch employ. To protect Great Bay, Fort Amsterdam was built in 1737.

The town still retains some of its unique shingled architecture. The main thoroughfare is the traffic-clogged Front Street, stretching for about a mile. It's lined with stores selling international merchandise, such as French designer fashions and Swedish crystal. If you don't find what you want, you can take one of the little lanes, known as *steegijes,* that connect Front Street with Back Street, running parallel to it. Back Street is another shoppers' mart.

GETTING THERE: Necessitated by the heavy volume that makes the St.

Maarten airport the second busiest after Puerto Rico in the Caribbean, government authorities have expanded the island's landing facilities.

Many persons route themselves onto the convenient connections offered by **Eastern Airlines** through Miami. Since flights leave there daily at 5:25 p.m., dozens of daytime flights from elsewhere in the U.S. can make easy connections with a St. Maarten–bound flight. Most such connections require a minimum amount of time at the Miami airport. Luggage can be routed from the passenger's original takeoff point to his or her final destination.

Transport to St. Maarten is always cheapest when a person makes a simultaneous booking at a hotel through Eastern's tour desk (ask the Eastern telephone representative to connect you).

Among the high-season fares available, one of the most popular is the excursion ticket. This requires an advance purchase of 7 days and a wait of between 3 and 21 days before using the return section of the ticket. Round-trip fares from Miami cost $388 if the departure is on a weekday, $415 if it's on a weekend.

An even less expensive option of $350 round trip Miami/St. Maarten is available, as well as a special discounted first-class passage on the same routing for $504 round trip. Passengers who qualify for these fares must purchase their tickets at least 7 days in advance and delay their return from 6 to 20 days after their original takeoff.

Because these fares are likely to change, check with a flight representative or travel agent before you fly.

Eastern is not alone in servicing St. Maarten from the American northeast. **Pan Am** operates a daily flight nonstop from New York's JFK, routing passengers from Philadelphia, Boston, and Chicago through JFK, usually with fairly short waits for connections.

Likewise, **American Airlines** operates flights to St. Maarten from Dallas/Fort Worth as well as from New York.

Prinair operates flights from San Juan, which is an option some travelers decide to take, routing themselves through Puerto Rico if it works out to be cheaper. (It doesn't always, and a delay of luggage in Puerto Rico can foul up even your best organized plans).

PRACTICAL FACTS: To enter the Dutch-held side of St. Maarten, U.S. citizens should have **proof of citizenship** in the form of a passport (preferably valid but not more than five years expired), or else an original birth certificate with a raised seal or a photocopy with a notary seal, or, finally, a voter's registration card. Naturalized citizens may show their naturalization certificate, and resident aliens must provide the alien registration "green" card or a temporary card which allows them to leave and reenter the U.S. All visitors must have a confirmed room reservation before their arrival on the island. A return or ongoing ticket must also be shown. When leaving, a $5 departure tax is charged.

In general, hotels add a 10% to 15% **service charge,** plus a 5% government **tax.** Unless service has not been added (unlikely), it is customary to tip around 15% in restaurants.

St. Maarten is on **Atlantic Standard Time.** In winter, when the U.S. is on Eastern Standard Time, it will be 6 a.m. in Philipsburg when it's only 5 a.m. in New York. During Daylight Saving Time, the island keeps the same time as the U.S. East Coast.

Traffic moves *on the right,* and international road signs are observed.

The Dutch side of the island operates on 110 volts AC (60 cycles) of electricity, and chances are, you won't need an adapter (unless you're staying on the French side).

Hotels serve desalinated **water,** and the water is safe to drink.

Emergency telephone numbers include the police at 2299 and an ambulance at 2299 also.

If you need **medical assistance,** ask at your hotel. There is one hospital (tel. 2300) on the Dutch side and another on the French side.

Shopping hours in general are 8 a.m. to noon and 2 to 6 p.m. weekdays. If a cruise ship is in port, many shops open even if it's Sunday.

Most **banks** are open from 8:30 a.m. to 1 p.m. Monday to Friday, except on Friday they reopen between 4 and 5 p.m.

From Dutch St. Maarten, if you want **to call French St. Martin,** dial 06 plus the French number.

If you want information on any of the Dutch islands before you go, you can ask at the **St. Maarten, Saba, and St. Eustatius Tourist Office,** 1500 Broadway. New York, NY 10036 (tel. 212/840-6655).

HOTELS: Hotels in St. Maarten run the gamut—from big-time resort hotels, some with tennis courts and gambling casinos, to motel-like efficiency units where guests prepare their own meals, to simple West Indian guest houses. As a warning, I'll note that in general the Dutch hostelries charge higher tariffs than the French auberges on the other side of the island. (For my selection of inns and hotels on Saint Martin, refer to the chapter on the French West Indies.)

Inns of Character

Oyster Pond Yacht Club, P.O. Box 239 (tel. 2206), is splendidly chic, a Caribbean Shangri-La, eight miles from Philipsburg, reached by a twisting, scenic road. On the windward side of the island, a circular harbor on the eastern shore near the French border, the fortress-like structure stands guard over a 35-acre protected marina. Catering to a select clientele, it is not unlike a small Spanish parador in southern Spain, unflawed in architecture and decoration. With its own harbor for yachts, it also has a private half-moon sandy beach reached by passing along beautiful landscaped grounds.

The hotel is furnished in part with nautical antiques, like a great country house. It offers only 20 rooms, and these are accommodations of character. Some are duplexes with beds placed in balustraded galleries, and the decoration is often in the West Indian buccaneer style. Bedrooms open onto arches with a wooden balustraded balcony overlooking the pond or sea. In winter, two persons can stay here in units ranging from standard to deluxe at prices going from $230 to $270 daily, plus another $45 per person for MAP charged year round. The most elegant accommodations are the tower suites, costing $300 daily. *In the off-season, two persons are charged from $140 to $160 daily, with tower suites dropping to $190.*

Its central courtyard is open to the skies, and the living room, also al fresco, has an elegant touch, with wicker, fine paintings, an understatement of good taste. Off the courtyard, and opening onto the sea, is a bar/lounge, as warm and comfortable as one's private home. The dining room is exceptional, the chef turning out a well-prepared continental cuisine intermixed with some creole dishes. The service is superb, and the tables are set with the finest of china and linen. After dinner, guests sip coffee on the outer terrace under palm trees, watching the sea and listening to the waves crash against the cliff.

Mary's Fancy, P.O. Box 420, Dutch Cul-de-Sac (tel. 2665), is the most exotic, treasure-filled retreat on the island. Here, on five acres of lush tropical gardens is a guest house and top restaurant, occupying what was once a sugar plantation great house. One of the early rich settlers, Mary Van Ramondt, was given her choice of any spot on the island to build her plantation home 250 years ago, and she chose this valley property between two mountains, only a 15-minute drive to Philipsburg or the nearest beach. When asked why she settled here, she replied, "I just fancied it!" Later it became the governor's mansion, where every famed visitor on the island made an appearance, with many staying as guests.

Seven individualized and pastel-painted cottages have been built in the garden, making superb one-of-a-kind suites. There is also a quartet of rooms in the main house. The abundant foliage provides complete privacy. The cottages (too humble a name, I feel) are really glamorous studios, with cathedral beamed ceilings, turn-of-the-century fans, each having its own color theme and style of decorating, hand-quilted bedspreads, and macramé lamps. One may have a Tudor four-poster bed with a lounge area of wicker, a bath and kitchen. Another may have a Chinese theme, with a red-and-white scroll dominating the bed, which is red bamboo. Another has a Victorian high headboard. There is one with a Bali theme, with a wall hanging to carry out the concept. Still another has a stone wall, a pair of Edwardian brass beds, and a large living room area. The cottages sleep two to four comfortably. They stand amid huge oaks, sandbox trees, a 200-year-old silk cotton tree, grounds lushly planted with frangipani, oleander, monkey-no-climb, pope's cap cactus, rubber trees, kapok, and cashew, as well as solid mahogany, with gently curving walks bordered by flowers leading through a meadow to a free-form swimming pool.

A wooden bridge over an ancient slave wall cuts through a green meadow to the free-form swimming pool and sun patio. The main house, with its special rooms for before-dinner drinks, has one exceptionally furnished dining room after another. The service is gold, the linen the finest, and only fine china is used for your gourmet meal. On the veranda there must be 60 tall natural rattan peacock chairs for in- and outdoor dining, with candles flickering sofly.

In winter, the rate in a single or double ranges from $100 to $120 daily, going up to $140 to $160 daily in a junior suite. A room with a kitchen costs from $160 to $180 daily, and a two-bedroom suite is rented for $240 nightly. *In summer, rates are slashed by about 50%*.

The **Caravanserai**, P.O. Box 113, Maho Bay (tel. 4214), is an elegant oasis on its private coral promontory close to the airport, six miles west of Philipsburg. An occasional jet lands or takes off, but otherwise it's quiet around here. Its design concept, both original and tasteful, makes it special, and its many amenities cause it to rank as one of the finest resorts on the island. It was the creation of an exiled New Yorker, Dave Crane, who turned it into one of the most urbane inns in the West Indies. Both Juliana and Beatrix, from the Dutch royal family, have stayed here. The architecture utilizes natural woods and stone, with moorish arches, wooden frame octagonal structures, all decorated with tropical furnishings such as peacock bamboo and rattan chairs. Many potted palms and primitive paintings add a further decorative touch.

There are two tennis courts, every kind of water sport, a private beach, and two swimming pools (one saltwater). The larger pool opens onto a long, arched loggia, where you can have an American-style breakfast or an evening meal with wine. The cuisine is international, and most memorable are the Wednesday Caribbean buffet with a complimentary glass of wine, the Friday seafood feast (again a complimentary glass of wine), and the Sunday brunch with complimentary champagne from 11 a.m. to 2:30 p.m. The octagonal peak-roofed Ocean View bar is on the tip of the promontory.

Accommodations come in a wide range—one-bedroom apartments and studios facing the Caribbean, 15 superior rooms also facing the sea, and 7 standards opening onto the courtyard, plus a quartet of villas, ideal for lovers.

In winter, rooms range in price from $225 daily, based on either single or double occupancy. Apartments rent for anywhere from $300 to $350 daily. *In summer, rates, either double or single occupancy, are $98 in a standard bedroom, $120 in a studio, and $140 in a one-bedroom suite.* You can stay here on the full-board plan at an additional cost of $35 per person daily.

Mary's Boon, P.O. Box 278, Simpson Bay (tel. 4235), really a small casual inn, is a string of 12 oversize apartments with kitchenettes designed as private villas, with personalized style, directly on a three-mile sandy beach, just south of the Juliana Airport and 15 minutes from Philipsburg. It's near the airport, but big planes are rare, and when they do land, they do so only in the daytime.

A gingerbread trim on the main building is garlanded with flowering bushes, and the grounds are lushly planted with sea grape, coconut palms, and alamander. Reached by a long private road, Mary's Boon is set back from the sea, all pinky-beige with brown wooden balconies and stairs. The interior is imaginative, with peaked beamed cathedral ceilings and eclectic furnishings (English mahogany, ornate bamboo chairs and tables), plus a collection of Haitian paintings, tropical-style sofas, and a grand piano, which dominates the reception lounge. There's a dining gallery fronting Simpson Bay in case you decide to take the half-board arrangement, with punctured tin cones covering the overhead lights at the table, which gives a candlelit dinner atmosphere. The cuisine is Dutch/French West Indian. In the bar you fix your own drinks on the honor system.

The rooms are done in rattan and wicker, louvered windows open to sea breezes, and there is an occasional tile and flagstone antique floor. Most of the rooms are in separate cottages, but there are two units in the main house. The efficiencies have ceiling fans. *On the EP, two persons are charged $80 daily in summer, with a third person paying another $20.* Rates go up in winter to $120 daily in a double, plus another $30 for a third party sharing. No children under 16 are allowed. Service and tax are added to the tariffs.

Pasanggrahan, P.O. Box 151, Front Street (tel. 3588), is the Indonesian word for guest house, and this one maintains a clientele which favors old-style West Indian living. It's a marvelous bargain in high-priced St. Maarten. A small, charming, informal guest house, it's right on the busy, narrow main street of Philipsburg. It's set back under tall trees, with a building-wide white wooden veranda. The interior still has many old features, such as peacock bamboo chairs, a pair of Indian spool tables, and a gilt-framed oil portrait of Queen Wilhelmina. In fact, so many guests asked to see the bedroom where the queen and her daughter, Juliana, stayed in World War II that the management turned it into the Sydney Greenstreet Bar.

Set among the wild jungle of overgrown knep trees, coconut palms, and flowering shrubbery, is the dining area, Seaside by Candlelight. You reach the private beach, only 50 feet away, through the jungle filled with hummingbirds, yellowbirds, and mockingbirds. There are 26 newly renovated bedrooms with king-size beds and beautiful Mexican bedspreads, each with a private bath, some in the main building, others in an adjoining annex. Manager Dr. Peter de Zela has set excellent rates, priced according to room outlook.

All accommodations have tropical-style ceiling fans, and air conditioning is available for $7.50 extra per day. *In summer, singles range in price from $38 to $45 daily, and doubles go for $50 to $65.* In winter, tariffs range from $69 to $79 daily in a single, from $79 to $98 in a double, plus tax and service. Off-season bargain packages are often featured.

The Big Resort Hotels

Mullet Bay Resort and Casino, P.O. Box 309, Mullet Bay Beach (tel. 2801), is the best all-around complete resort in St. Maarten. With 595 condominium units clustered around a golf course, it's certainly the liveliest. The place is so big a roving jitney has to transport you around the grounds. It occupies 172 acres of the westernmost tip of St. Maarten, just a five-minute ride from Juliana Airport. It'll keep you busy just eating at each of the seven in- and outdoor restaurants, having exotic drinks at nine bars, or finding a new place for sea bathing along the half mile of white sandy beach. You'll be busy trying out a new tennis court every day, as there are 16 all-weather courts, with a fully stocked pro shop. Top-ranked Tom Okker supervises the tennis. And there is the Joseph Lee–designed 18-hole golf course with a resident pro, a full clubhouse, and a golfer's outdoor patio cocktail lounge.

Of the two swimming pools, one is Olympic-size, with a zigzag, geometric design, plus extensive lounge areas nearby for refreshments and sunbathing. Dining is casual overlooking the Caribbean waters in the Shipwreck restaurant, and for more formal dining in the evening there's the Gourmet Room. On the lagoon is the Frigate with its nautical atmosphere. Yet another spot for casual dining is the Hillside Restaurant. My favorite is Lil Oceanreef, an outdoor restaurant right on the beach, with a perfect Caribbean ambience, serving creole dishes, mainly seafood, from 6 to 10:30 p.m. nightly. When you eat in the Fish Joynt or the Prime Rib Restaurant, it's obvious what you'll be served. When you've dined, you might go to the Hillside Disco or even to the fully operating Casino.

The accommodations are spread discreetly through the gardens, some having water views. The rooms are classified as standard, superior, and deluxe. The suites have one bedroom, with or without ocean views. Then there are deluxe two-bedroom suites, where the rate you pay includes the use of a rental car. The rates I quote are for room only, and you must add $30 daily per person for half board, plus service and tax. All units contain private terraces except the twin-bedded standard accommodations. In winter, a twin-bedded room rents for $175 daily, a one-bedroom suite for $230, and a two-bedroom suite for $360, plus tax and service. *In summer, prices are drastically reduced to $108 daily in a twin, $135 in a one-bedroom suite, and $200 in a two-bedroom suite, plus service and tax.* The tone of the decor for most rooms, whether sleeping rooms or dining, is half traditional, half Caribbean, including flamboyant and light floral fabrics, and bamboo-style furniture. On the premises are a beauty shop, laundry service, babysitters, a fully staffed medical clinic, and a grocery store.

Reservations are available by calling 800/4-M-U-L-L-E-T toll free. The Mullet Bay Resort & Casino Sales and Reservations Office is at 25 West 39th St., Suite 907, New York, NY 10018. For additional information, call 212/819-1640.

The **Belair Beach Hotel**, P.O. Box 140, Little Bay (tel. 3362). One of the most surprising things about this breezy oceanfront hotel is the size of the accommodations. Checking in is like renting your own apartment home in the tropics, especially if you stay in one of the seaside rooms whose arched patios sit only a few paces from the white sandy beach. Each of the 72 units contains two bedrooms, two full baths, a fully equipped kitchen, satellite-beamed color TV, a 21-foot patio or veranda with a sweeping view of the sea, two phones, and full air conditioning. There's even an indoor pool, although most guests prefer the wash of the glistening white beach.

This handsome hotel is perfect for relaxing in the most convenient circumstances, particularly since the comfortable circumstances provide for an elegant, well-upholstered retreat. For vacationers who want the activities of a resort, the Little Bay Beach Resort and Casino, just a short walk down the beach, offers a full array of facilities (see below).

Jan Welage is the general manager of the Belair. With his staff, he provides many extras, such as a nightly turn-down of the beds and fresh-daily beach towels. Tariffs in winter for beach-level accommodations range from $330 to $390 for one or two persons, $360 to $440 for three, and $400 to $480 for four. Units facing the beach but on the upper floors, with verandas instead of patios, cost $25 less per room per day.

During summer and shoulder season, oceanfront units at beach level cost $130 to $150 daily for a single, $150 to $170 for a double, $170 to $190 for a triple, and $190 to $200 for a quad. Rooms on the upper floors cost around $20 less. MAP is available at around $35 per person per day. One popular meal option is for seven full American breakfasts and four dinners for $170 per person. All meals are taken in the adjacent Little Bay Beach Resort and Casino. Rates quoted do not include service and tax.

Great Bay Beach Hotel & Casino, P.O. Box 310, Voorstraat (tel. 2446), is a complete modern resort at the southwestern corner of the Great Bay of downtown Philipsburg. In fact, all the shops and restaurants of the old town are walkable from the hotel. Its five floors of cellular rooms—225 air-conditioned, suitably furnished units—have walk-in closets and tiled baths, each with a balcony and view of either the sea or hills. On the grounds are abundant facilities. Near the main building is a terracotta sun terrace, surrounded by palm trees and lounge furniture. At one end set in among the shrubbery is a poolside refreshment area. The main dining room has water-view windows, and features local foods in addition to Stateside cooking plus continental specialties from Great Bay's chef.

Summer EP rates in a single or double range from $70 to $95 daily. In winter, guests are accepted on the EP, for $105 to $126 daily in a single, from $115 to $135 for two persons. Naturally, suites are more expensive. Service and tax are added to all bills. Below the swimming pool terrace is a wide sandy beach, and skiing boats can be had at your request. Across the road are tennis courts. There is also a water-sports center on the premises. Evenings are enlivened by a steel band, with calypso entertainment. Many gamblers flock here to one of the important casinos on the island, which has one-arm bandits in addition to roulette and baccarat.

Pelican Resort and Casino, P.O. Box 431, Simpson Bay (tel. 2503), is a seaside resort whose architectural styles are about as varied as its clientele. The village-style sections are well separated with buffers of bougainvillea and hibiscus. The largest cluster contains only 20 units and, like all the others, is tucked into a hillside, with a sweeping view of the sea. Paths connecting the various elements are sometimes flanked by small waterways channeled into disciplined beds.

Scattered among the 12 acres are a lily pond, an orchid garden, a Jacuzzi, tennis courts, a swimming pool, 1400 feet of oceanfront, and a marina. Guests can arrange water sports through the hotel or outside agencies.

All accommodations are privately owned and leased through the hotel management to vacationing guests. Each has one or two bedrooms, a kitchen, a 24-hour color TV with satellite reception, a phone, and a cassette tape player. There's a convenience deli on the premises to make shopping easy, and a casino and restaurant, the Suisse Chalet, add to vacationing pleasure.

Rates for the 100 accommodations vary widely with the season and the exposure. Guests are required to remain for a minimum of seven to ten nights during the most popular periods of the winter season. In winter, studios rent for $140 daily, one-bedroom units for $170 to $190, and two-bedroom quarters for $300 to $350. Additional persons in any unit are charged $35 each. From shortly after the New Year until around the end of January, the prices are considerably less: studios cost $100; one-bedroom units, $120 to $145; and two-bedroom accommodations, $240 to $290. *In summer, the rentals are: studios, $60 daily; one-bedroom facilities, $85 to $110; and two-bedroom units, $145 to $170. An additional person pays $18.*

For reservations and information, call 800/223-9815 toll free; in New York state, call 212/840-6636.

Smaller Resort Hotels

Dawn Beach Hotel, P.O. Box 389 (tel. 2929), stands on the Atlantic side of the island, near the Dutch-French border. It cuddles next to a tall mountain at Oyster Pond. The location is about eight miles from Philipsburg, reached by a scenic but twisting road. Each of the 155 individual villas along the beach and on the mountain offers a choice of air conditioning or ceiling fans. *Summer EP rates range from $75 to $105 daily in a double,* going up in winter to $145 to $180.

It's really villa condo living, and the owners of this resort complex have emphasized luxury and style. Beds are big enough to stretch out in and units are equipped with small kitchenettes. A large Bali-style restaurant, capped by a pagoda roof, is a potent lure, serving good meals. There is also a bar on the premises. The Oriental gardens use such Japanese-like touches as a bridge over the swimming pool. Sprawling sea grape trees provide cover from the sun, as do umbrellas around the freshwater pool with a cascading waterfall.

The hotel has made many improvements, including two composition tennis courts lit for night play. A water-sports desk will make arrangements for cruising, windsurfing, waterskiing, snorkeling, and sailing, including all-day charters to St. Bart, Saba, and Anguilla. A shuttle to and from Philipsburg operates three times a day.

Little Bay Resort and Casino, P.O. Box 61, Little Bay (tel. 2333), the first of the island's resort hotels, is a very complete resort, with its private 1000-foot beach, within a short distance of the shops and restaurants of Philipsburg. The hotel opened in 1955 with only 20 rooms, and Queen Juliana, and her husband, Prince Bernhard, were the first guests. Princess Margaret came here on her honeymoon. Other royalty has visited as well, including Queen Beatrix. Queen Juliana came back in 1983 for a farewell visit.

You'll find everything you might need on the premises, whether it's water sports, a beauty parlor, a Las Vegas–style casino, or a freshwater pool. There are three tennis courts, plus regular local entertainment. At a beach bar, you can order those long, cool, intoxicating drinks, and a deluxe snackbar is appealing for a light lunch. Continental dishes, Stateside favorites, and authentic Dutch and West Indian specialties are served in the historic Fort Amsterdam Room. The restaurant overlooks the Caribbean, and diners enjoy a candlelit atmosphere. The food is prepared by a chef, André, from Lyon. Guests gather at Le Café to enjoy the piano bar. A late breakfast/late-night coffeeshop, La Primavera, is open from 11 a.m. to 1 p.m.

You'll find the decor of the bedrooms warm and inviting, with private bath and terrace or balcony, as well as air conditioning and wall-to-wall carpeting. The best rooms are the beachfront accommodations. *In summer, singles range in price from $90 to $108 daily, with doubles going for $100 to $135,* plus another $35 per person charged year round for breakfast and dinner. Winter prices jump to $175 to $300 daily in a single, from $185 to $300 in a double, the higher tariff, both single and double, for beach-level accommodation.

Cupecoy Beach Resort, P.O. Box 14 (tel. 4297), stands on a rocky bluff high above a pristine beach dotted with caves. Mediterranean in style, it is one of the most outstanding accommodations on the island. Each of its one- to three-bedroom suites has been elegantly designed to capture a Caribbean motif. You live in luxury here with plenty of style. Guests are housed either hillside or beachside, and the hillside units are cheaper, of course. *Two persons in the off-season pay from $80 to $200 daily in a standard, superior, and deluxe twin.* In winter, these same units rent for anywhere from $120 to $275 daily for two persons. The one-, two-, and three-bedroom suites are much more expensive. There is no MAP; dining is à la carte. Through your own private window you can look down at Cupecoy Beach, one of the best on the island. There are three pools, and like a mermaid (or man) you can "swim up" for a tropical rum punch. There's also a restaurant serving international specialties, plus a lounge. For golf you can use the 18-hole course at nearby Mullet Bay. Casino action, tennis courts—they're all here.

Summit Resort Hotel, P.O. Box 456, Simpson Bay Lagoon (tel. 42270), north of the airport near the French border, is a delightful miniature resort, small enough to be personal, yet avoiding the confusion often fund in a larger establishment. Here are 61 rooms in one- and two-story cottages, built like a little chalet village, Tudoresque in style, with decorative beams. The units are interconnected by walks through lush foliage and tall tress. Each unit is an individually owned condo, and some are for sale. With an 180-degree view, it sits on the side of a hill, facing Simpson Bay Lagoon, with an all-weather tennis court and swimming pool complex with a tiny informal bar and intimate restaurant.

Each of the air-conditioned chalets has a combined living room/bedroom with two double beds, a full private bath, and either a balcony or terrace running the full length of the chalet. Each also has its private entrance. The receptionist can arrange for deep-sea fishing, sailing, snorkeling, and free use of the beach buggy. If gambling is your interest, the management can provide free transportation to two of the island's largest casinos less than five minutes away. In winter, standard rooms cost from $120 daily for two perons, the cost going up to $145 in a superior, plus 20% extra for tax and service. Both are EP tariffs. *Rates are dramatically slashed off-season, ranging in price from $70 to $80 daily for two persons, plus tax and service. Singles are usually $10 cheaper in either unit.* For breakfast and dinner, add another $32 per person daily. Children under 12 are allowed to share a room with their parents. You might also ask a travel agent about special package rates offered at the Summit.

St. Maarten Beach Club Hotel & Casino, P.O. Box 465, at Front Street in Philipsburg (tel. 3434), is a modern 86-suite complex that stands on both sides of this main shopping street in the heart of the Dutch capital. Obviously, the commodious beachfront suites are the select units (they're also the most expensive). From their private patios, they look down on yacht-filled Great Bay, where trawlers unload cargoes of sugarcane, plantains, and bananas. Since its opening it's been a favorite of honeymooners, who haved found a chilled bottle of champagne waiting for their traditional toast.

Winter rates in a one-bedroom suite range from $180 to $220 daily, with a two-bedroom suite costing from $275 to $325. *Summer tariffs are considerably reduced: from $100 to $120 daily in a one-bedroom suite, and from $130 to $150 daily in a two-bedroom suite.* All tariffs quoted are EP. The suites are equipped with a well-supplied kitchenette in case you want to cook for yourself. You're within walking distance of a supermarket.

If you'd like to eat in, you'll find Fandango's Restaurant on the premises, plus the Heartbreak Bar, one of the most charming and lively tropical bars in Philipsburg. The intimate casino opens at 1 in the afternoon, and you can play until 6 p.m. It later reopens at 8 p.m. and remains so until 3 a.m.

Holland House, P.O. Box 393, Front Street (tel. 2572), shares the beach and water-sports center with the St. Maarten Beach Club, to which you also retire when you want some casino action. It rents 42 cozy apartments decorated with furnishings from the Netherlands. Each unit contains a very tiny kitchenette, ideal for cooking an omelet but not a big dinner. You're right on the beach, where you can order drinks at the bar. An open-air dining terrace fronts Great Bay. Some people like it, and maybe you will too. You're certainly near everything, including all the major restaurants and shops of Philipsburg. EP rates in a double in winter range from $135 to $155 daily. *Tariffs drop in summer to $75 to $85 daily for a double room, EP.* Even if you're not staying here, you might want to call and reserve a table for dinner. this is one of the few hotels that serves authentic Dutch specialties.

Seaview Beach Hotel, P.O. Box 65, Front Street (tel. 2323), is a 46-room, modest but fine, waterfront hotel right in the shopping and restaurant section of Philipsburg, with half of its rooms overlooking Great Bay and its beach. In this three-story stucco building, each room has furnishings with a Caribbean theme, and each comes with a ceiling fan and private bath. If you stay here on a plan to include dinners, you can enjoy the Saturday-night barbecue (chicken, beef, and pork—whatever you want). You are given free use of beach chairs and umbrellas when a guest. Winter EP rates range from $86 to $90 in a single, from $95 to $105 in a double. *In summer, in either a single or double, rates are $60 daily for a standard unit, $70 f or a beachfront accommodation.* A casino, Rouge et Noir, operates at Seaview.

Efficiency Units and Guest Houses

The **Horny Toad Guest House,** P.O. Box 397, Butterfish Road, Elizabeth (tel. 4323), was once an island governor's residence. The present owners, Betty and Earle Vaughan, continue the tradition of hospitality found there in former days: hosts and guests are soon on a first-name basis. What you get here for your money makes it very desirable, as it opens directly onto the beach at Simpson Bay. The second floor of their white frame building has an encircling covered West Indies balacony, and all of their efficiency units have kitchen areas and private baths. Two have separate bedrooms housing three guests per unit. Daily maid service is included. The furnishings are "family style" with a plentiful use of colorful floral fabrics, rattan chairs, hanging lamps, and wood-paneled walls. Everything is casual and congenial.

In summer season, the efficiencies are $75 daily; in winter, $140. An extra person is charged $28 per day. Three of the units will accommodate a family of four. Sports actitivies are informal: nightly surfing, and for a modest fee a fully equipped fishing and diving boat. *Note:* The guest house is near the airfield, and does have noisy moments.

To make reservations before traveling to the island, get in touch with Betty and Dave Harvey, 7 Warren St., Winchester, MA 01890 (tel. 617/729-3171).

The **Town House,** P.O. Box 347, Front Street (tel. 2989), is a group of ten two-story apartments at the edge of the restaurant and shopping district of Philipsburg. At your doorstep is Great Bay Beach, dotted with palms—it's all shut off from the main street by a rugged stone wall and a wrought-iron gate. The town houses are handsome, rather formal with slanted shingled mansard roofs, and set-in second-floor windows. It's all quite private and elegant. Each apartment has two large bedrooms and two bathrooms; the second-floor ones have a shower. There's a completely equipped kitchen, plus raised dining area in the long and well-furnished living room. Wide glass doors open onto a private terrace with lounge chairs. Whether dining or having conversation in the living room or drinks on your terrace, you can enjoy a view of the bay. To make it a holiday, a cook can also be provided inexpensively. *Off-season, the town houses rent for $125 a day,* rising to $230 daily in winter. At the rates quoted, four persons are allowed in each villa.

The **Naked Boy,** P.O. Box 252, Philipsburg (tel. 2789; or 516/692-7878 in

New York for information), is a small, modern two-story apartment house standing in a garden of trees, with covered balconies overlooking Great Bay. Here there is no surf, and the bathing is gentle. Each unit as an adequately furnished living room with two sofa beds, studio style, plus a fully equipped kitchenette. A bedroom has either singles or a king-size bed, a dressing room area, and a shower in the bath. Units are air-conditioned, and maid service in included. Within walking distance are shops for groceries and restaurants. If your apartment faces the sea, the rate is slightly higher. In winter, two persons pay from $90 daily for a unit, the tariff going up to $105 if oceanfront. Each additional person is assessed $20 per day. *In the off-season, the daily tab is $55 to $65 for two persons, depending on the room's location.* Tax and 15% service are added to all bills. There's a modest surcharge for use of air conditioning.

RESTAURANTS: Half-Dutch, half-French St. Maarten/St. Martin has dozens of good international restaurants, and visitors on each side must decide each night if they want to "cross the border" to dine. Specialities range from créole through continental, with a decided French accent. Dutch cooking is harder to come by.

La Coupole and **Le Bec Fin,** 109 Front St. (tel. 2979). First, there is La Coupole, built on a patio in the back, opening onto the water. Here, at your own leisure, you can enjoy breakfast and, if you linger long enough over coffee, lunch. This enclave of French gastronomy dates back to the mid-19th century. In her old home, La Coupole turns out croissants fresh from the oven, as well as other French pastries and homemade ice cream.

But, deservedly, most of the attention focuses on Le Bec Fin, which is across the courtyard and up a flight of stairs. It is considered one of the best restaurants in St. Maarten, either on the French or Dutch side of the island. Monsieur Pascal Petit is a chef still in his 20s, but his nouvelle cuisine has already been much awarded, not only in his native France, but in St. Maarten where he won the 1984–1985 gourmet award.

Try his burgundy snails, his beef tenderloin in a pepper sauce, his veal scaloppine with morels, his fresh "salmon cucumbers," his lobster en croûte with a spinach mousse, finishing with a raspberry soufflé with apricot sauce that is among the best I've ever had, all for about $35 or so. Reservations are essential, as there are only about a dozen tables.

Bilboquet, Pointe Blanche (no phone). For specialties unique in the Caribbean, this private house provides cookery that is imaginative and prepared with flair. With devotion to service and cuisine, Bill Ahlstrom and Bob Donn, former language teachers from Minnesota and New York, have opened this place providing two prix-fixe dinners for about $35 nightly. The five-course meals are served from 7:30 to 8:30 p.m., except Monday. The trick is, you must visit the place first to make a reservation (24 hours in advance). Perhaps that proves you can find it at night. Follow the road to Pointe Blanche, turning left at the Pot Rum factory, then taking another left at Vinomar. It's the first uphill left turn from that point. Once there, you write your name on a waiting list.

Their cuisine is completely international, and they can travel from Thailand to Greece with little problem in translation (after all, they are language experts). For example, one meal might begin with a Cuban black-bean soup or callaloo soup with crabmeat, follow with scampi fritti, then a Greek moussaka with a green salad, topped off by a southern pecan pie. You'll like it so well you might come back the following evening, enjoying a lemon-zested shrimp soup or green papaya vichyssoise (a first for me), followed by seafood on the half shell, East or West Indian curries, stuffed eggplants, cucumber salad, and a rum and bourbon pudding. The view is of St. Barts.

L'Escargot, Front Street (tel. 2483), is my favorite French bistro, right in the heart of Philipsburg where the competition is keen. It's perched in a gaily decorated 100-year-old Antillean house, with a red tin roof, celebrating its namesake by serving snails in pâte à choux, with mushrooms, in omelets, or in the more traditional escargots à la Provençale. For good-tasting *bonne cuisine française,* and some of the nicest, friendliest people around, you'll do well here, and the prices, although not cheap, seem reasonable to most diners.

If you arrive before your reservation, you can relax in the bar to your left before being shown to your candlelit table. Not one bit of space is undecorated, and the decor may appear too gimmicky to some. But that shouldn't make you suspicious of the food. It is first rate—caviar blinis, duck in a pineapple and banana sauce, quail with raisin sauce, lobster thermidor, coq au vin. If you can handle it, the waiter will serve you a chocolate mousse to finish your repast, which should cost from $30, maybe a lot more. In season, reservations are absolutely necessary.

The Café Royal (tel. 3443), in the atrium of the Royal Palm Plaza, a few blocks from the Main Square in Philipsburg, is a local favorite. You can order lunch, dinner, and lavishly packed picnic baskets. You can eat for about $15 to $20. French pâtés and pastries, Dutch hams and cheeses, the local Caribbean spiny langouste, and fresh fruits such as papayas, magoes, pineapple, and avocados, along witlh American favorites, including hamburgers and cheesecake, make up the regular fare.

Rene Florijn, owner of the Café Royal, which is also locally known as the jazz headquarters of St. Maarten, invites you to the Saturday jazz matinees from 4:30 to 6:30 p.m. He'll also buy you a drink if you can get Francesca, that great-looking blonde on the bar stool who sits there from early in the morning until late at night, to smile or say hello to you. Many patrons have tried, but so far none has succeeded.

In the rear section of the Café Royal you'll discover a gourmet shop, "Eat Royal," with Ella ("Smiles") Sluis behind the counter. This small shop is brimful of local and international delicacies, and has had many a satisfied customer, including Princess Margaret. If given notice, you'll be prepared an elegant picnic basket for two, costing $28. In addition to gift items, most of them packable, you'll be tempted with smoked salmon, pâté, caviar, lobster, and fresh croissants.

Antoine's, Front Street (tel. 2964), offers *la belle cuisine* in an atmospheric building next to the Little Pier in the center of Philipsburg. Wear your casual-chic resort wear here at night, enjoying the view of Great Bay from the seafronting terrace. You can also dine inside where the glow of candles makes everything more romantic. Be sure to make a reservation in season. The entrance is through a breezeway alive with greenery. You can enjoy an apértif in the cocktail bar.

If the crowd is right (usually in winter), Antoine's takes on worldly sophistication, and the staff will prove that you don't have to cross the border for impressive wines, top-quality service, and a long list of Gallic specialities. Fresh local fish is always available, but well-sauced beef and chicken dishes are also served, at a cost of around $35 for dinner, perhaps $20 for lunch. Every restaurant owner seems to specialize in the increasingly hard-to-get lobster, and Antoine's is no exception. The spiny Caribbean langouste is regularly featured and prepared very well indeed.

Hours are daily from 11:30 a.m. to 4 p.m. and from 6:30 to 11 p.m.

La Grenouille, Dutchman's Walk (tel. 2269), stands next to the Pasang-grahan and is reached by going up a flight of steps. It's been around for some time, having survived when many of its Gallic competitors bit the dust. Your host is "Johnny" (that's how he's known—no last name), and he'll guide you through the menu selections. Again, fresh local fish and Caribbean spiny langouste appear when available, but the chef also does some delectable main dishes such as pepper steak flambé in cognac and Dover sole. In season live oysters are flown in straight from Brittany. Tables have a view of the bay, and both lunch and dinner are served, the hours being from noon to 2:30 p.m. and 7 to 11 p.m. daily. Expect to pay from $25 for a full meal. The place is informal, but you should dress a tiny bit for dinner.

Felix's, Simpson Bay (tel. 5237), is one of the island's best choices for an al fresco meal with a view of the sea. Because of its location a few paces from the white sands of a popular beach, many guests turn their outings here into full afternoon excursions. Chaise longues are available from the owners, Margaret and Richard (Felix) Ducrat, who describe their cuisine as "typically French." Felix's grandfather owns the well-known Felix's in Cannes.

This place is at its most romantic during candlelit dinners where seating choices range from intimately sheltered booths to outdoor tables set within sight and sound of the sea.

Many of the seafood specialties come from the lobster tank whose waters bubble at ground level near the lounge. Full dinners can total $50 per person and might include chateaubriand for two, rack of lamb, fish caught locally that day and sometimes served with an exquisite sorrel-flavored hollandaise, a wide selection of lobster dishes, and a Felix salad.

Lunches are less formal and less expensive, costing $20 per person. A midday meal features several kinds of salad (including lobster), scrumptious omelets, and lightly whimsical dishes, some made with snails. Open daily except Tuesday from November 1 to May 1, the restaurant serves lunch from noon to 2 p.m. and dinner from 7 to 10 p.m.

La Caravelle, Front Street (tel. 3011), is a little culinary Gallic pocket, run with charming flair by its patrons, Jacqueline and José, across from the Caribbean Hotel. Tables open onto a view of Great Bay Harbor. Unlike many of the French restaurants in town, this one is moderately priced, with meals costing from $25. As you enjoy a comfortable atmosphere and air cooled by trade winds, you can select from a well-chosen menu. You don't get daring recipes here: what you are served instead is a classic repertoire of dishes well prepared and cordially presented. These include French onion soup gratinée, vichyssoise, snails in garlic butter, frog legs, the chef's pâté, duckling with fresh orange sauce, a rack of lamb with herbs, and shrimps in the style of Provence. Their sauces for steak are especially good, including their Bordelaise red wine sauce or their moutarde with French mustard and white wine. A 15% service charge is extra. The wine list is limited, but select.

Asha's, Front Street (no phone). Elegantly handcrafted birds are suspended in mobiles from above the brass-trimmed bar, while riveting examples of northern Indian art hang by the dozen from the lattice-covered walls.

The family operating Asha's brought with them from Bombay an array of specialties that they categorize as nouvelle Indian cuisine. Dishes are relatively inexpensive, ranging from the "totally unspiced" to tandoori, awash with subtle flavors and herb-laden fragrances. A *tandoor* is a vat-shaped clay oven heated with charcoal. Cooked within it are skewered sections of chicken and other heavily marinated meats, which cook quickly, sealing in their juices.

Asha's offers an array of tandoori dishes, as well as curried seafoods such as shrimp Bengal and lobster Bombay style. Vegetarian dishes, Indian-style beef, and unspiced Western foods such as lamb chops, breast of chicken, and filet mignon are served sizzling on wooden platters.

Full meals range upward from around $10 to as much as $30. Lunch is served from noon to 3 p.m., while dinner lasts from 5 to 11 p.m. The establishment is closed on Monday.

Le Pavillon, Simpson Bay Village (tel. 4254), is one of the tiniest French restaurant in St. Maarten, providing just the right kind of intimacy for some of the best and most carefully prepared French food on the island. The owner-chef, Max Petit, runs everything, supervising the service and personally shopping for the fresh ingredients which he shapes into a gourmet meal, costing around $25 and up for dinner.

Food is served in an open-air pavilion in this oldtime fishing village. Monsieur Petit learned his culinary skills in his native Toulouse, although he also picked up gastronomic secrets when he worked in other provinces of his native country. He's also cooked in Paris and Guadeloupe. His French and creole repertoire includes lobster and crab omelets, cold platters, quiches, escargots, pepper steaks, crisp salad, and his specialty, a tasty duckling with pineapple sauce instead of the usual orange. For dessert, ask him for his bananas flambé. You can enjoy a before-dinner drink at the bar and terrace. Reservations are advised.

A place to go if you have an insatiable sweet tooth is **Etna Gardens** (tel. 3424), set in a palm-shaded courtyard at the end of a fern-draped passageway a few steps from the Main Square in Philipsburg. Here you can dip into such frosty concoctions as banana, amaretto, or marron glacé ice creams, and lemon, mango, soursop, and pineapple sherbets. Owners Paolo and Betty Smiraldo make the confections right on the premises, using natural ingredients such as fresh fruit. And while Paolo is turning out the frozen items on the menu, Betty is busy in the kitchen, baking cookies and macaroons that are as light as a tropical breeze. The six cozy tables and the minuscule counter are always crowded with on- and off-islanders continuing the time-honored tradition of "cooling out," as they call it locally. The minimum tab is around $3. For a recommendation of the original Etna Shop, at Port La Royale, Marigot, refer to the St. Martin section in Chapter X on the French West Indies.

Your ice-cream passions can be satisfied from 9 a.m. to midnight weekdays (on Sunday, from noon to 6 p.m.). **Ristorante Da Livio,** Front Street (tel. 2690), is the place to go for the classic Italian cuisine. The best of its kind in St. Maarten, it is run by Livio Bergamasco, who was the maître d' of the Great Bay Beach Resort before going into business for himself. A traditional dinner here might include linguine alle vongole (clams) or perhaps saltimbocco alla Romana, a popular Roman specialty that literally means "jump in your mouth." It's made with ham and veal. The pasta specialty, fettuccine alla Livio, is prepared right at your table. Another one of Mr. Bergamasco's dishes, for which he is known, is fresh snapper, which I most recently enjoyed.

For dessert, save room for the spumone salsa cioccolato, followed by café stravagante. He also has a good wine selection. Expect to spend from $25 for dinner, and in season a reservation would be wise. Lunch is also served, costing around $18.

You can dine al fresco, overlooking Great Bay.

Pinocchio, Italian Village, Front Street (tel. 2166), has other entrances, but the preferred way to go in is through an authentically restored tunnel-shaped cistern, leading into the Italian patio. In the heart of town, it can also be entered from the beach, luring diners to its terrace swept by trade winds and its al fresco patio bar, which is known for its frozen fruit daiquiris. The intricate latticework in the dining room frames the harbor, and you take a seat at a large community table. Most guests seem to prefer pasta and pizza, but you can also order many other Italian specialties, as well as fresh local fish and lobster. Try the conch parmesan. Dinner costs from $18. You can also visit for lunch, even breakfast (it opens at 9 a.m.). The luncheon offering includes the usual array of burgers, sandwiches, and salads, along with tropical fruit drinks. Naturally, you can order a café espresso, and children's specials are also offered. This place usually stays active until 2 a.m. with live entertainment.

Chesterfields, Great Bay Marina, Pointe Blanche Road (tel. 3484), has a special attraction other its good food—which, incidentally, is among the best served on the Dutch side. It offers pierside dining with a view of the harbor, on a trade-wind-swept veranda right close to Great Bay Marina. When the yachting set gathers here (everybody seems to know everybody else), the atmosphere becomes almost like that of your friendly "local."

The setting and the dress are both casual, and you dine on several international specialties, with fresh seafood and French-inspired cookery a highlight. Dinners average around $20. In season there's always some lively activity going on, such as champagne brunches on Sunday, "happy hours," or whatever. It's been an enduring favorite because it gives good service, and the staff makes you feel welcome.

Sam's Place (tel. 2989), at the end of Front Street, is where Bogie might land if he were alive and in St. Maarten today. Locals and tourists alike use Sam's "front porch" as a rendezvous point, practically at any time of the day. Boatmen come in here at breakfast ordering steak and eggs; vacationing southerners like the pancakes in syrup; and homesick New Yorkers ask for a toasted bagel with cream cheese.

At lunch the item to order is on of the locally well-known "Samburgers," followed by a slice of fruit pie, with ice cream on the side if you wish. Dinner on the "back porch" turns to heartier fare, such as charcoal-broiled steak. When available, try the fresh local fish or the Caribbean spiny langouste. Barbecue is also a feature. The place is inexpensive: you can get by for around $18 unless you order the expensive lobster or steak. The "side porch" serves hors d'-oeuvres at happy hour. It's open from 7:30 a.m. to 2 a.m.

West Indian Tavern, at the "head" of Front Street (tel. 2965), is like a primitive island painting, exploding with vibrant colors such as turkey red and lime green. A buccaneerish place, it was built from local cedar early in the 1800s on the site of a Jewish synagogue. An Irishman, Stephen Thompson, runs this place where, after 5 p.m., everybody in St. Maarten seems to gather for a sundowner. The place has plenty of atmosphere—bamboo and rattan chairs, big potted ferns, tropical plants, slow-turning overhead fans, and old-world nautical prints. If conversation slackens, a noisy parrot keeps it lively.

The chef specializes in fresh local lobster, which he does in six different ways, all a treat. Some of his other good-tasting dishes include fresh local grouper sauteed with bacon, hazelnuts, and served in a cream sauce, yellowtail with medallions of lobster in a mornay sauce, and fisherman's pie (lobster, crab, shrimp, and snapper in champagne). I'm also fond of the black Javanese pepper steak. The dessert specialty is real key lime pie. An average meal will cost about $18, unless you order lobster. Then count on dinner going for $30 or more. You dine in a garden patio, shaded by tamarind, frangipani, and lime tree. Dinner is from 6 p.m. to 1 a.m. Backgammon is played until 2 in the morning, and there is live entertainment on most nights.

Calypso, Simpson Bay (no phone), an unpretentious place, is the newest and largest West Indian restaurant on the island.

The large rectangular room contains about 100 simple chairs pulled up to plain tables where the only real decor comes from the specialties hauled in copious quantities from he kitchen. A fixed-price dinner costs $28 and provides a sampling of many items for which the owner, Melford Hazel, has become known.

Dishes include Calypso stuffed crab backs, fish soup, saltfish cakes, red snapper prepared many different ways, conch done in various ways (including in fritters), twice-baked christophene, and lobster creole style, broiled, or stuffed. A Calypso salad includes avocado and pineapple. Fried biscuits (johnnycakes) can accompany your meal.

Lunches are much less elaborate, costing around $12. They include an array of creole dishes, pizzas, sandwiches, and hamburgers. If you drop in for an afternoon drink, since the place is open daily from 11 a.m. till midnight, you may want to try the one guaranteed to make a calypso artist out of anyone—the Calypso Treat. It's concocted from Galliano, apricot brandy, coconut cream, and rum. The Calypso is closed Monday.

Rusty Pelican, end of Front Street (tel. 2941), is a seafood restaurant, right on the harbor of Great Bay, adjacent to Bobby's Marina. Naturally, it has a nautical decor. Many young American boys, who apparently are on an "endless summer," adopt this popular place as their local club. But it's more than a "beer, booze, and burger" joint, even though it has all three of those. Tables placed on tile floors open onto the sea breezes.

If you arrive in time for a sundowner, take it in the "sunken bar," which stays open until 1 a.m. At night, seafood is a specialty, including a lobster pot, kingfish, dolphin, grouper, and stuffed crab backs, a local delicacy, along with the charbroiled red snapper and conch done in imaginative ways. As a surprise, escargots à la romaine is one of the chef's specialties. They'll also cook steak and chicken. Dinner is likely to run around $25, with lunch costing from $15. Lunch is from 10:30 a.m. to 3:30 p.m., dinner from 6:30 to 10:30 p.m.

GETTING AROUND: Transportation is not difficult, with a variety of methods available.

Taxis

Taxis are unmetered, but St. Maarten law required drivers to have a list which details fares for major targets on the island. Typical fares, say, from Juliana Airport to the Sheraton Mullet Bay Resort and Casino are $4; from Philipsburg to Juliana Airport, $8. There are minimum fares for two passengers, and each additional passenger pays another $1. Passengers are entitled to one piece of luggage free, and each additional piece is assessed 50¢ extra. Fares are higher by 25% between 10 p.m. anad midnight, and 50% higher between midnight and 6 a.m. Even if you're renting a car, taxi regulations require you to take a cab to your hotel, where your car will be delivered.

Buses

This is a reasonable means of transport in St. Maarten if you don't mind inconveniences, and at times overcrowding. The fare is only 85¢, and buses run between 7 a.m. and midnight, serving most of the major locations in St. Maarten. The most popular run is from Philipsburg to Marigot on the French side. In Philipsburg, catch the bus in front of the Record Shop.

Car Rentals

Unlike some of the islands in the Caribbean, car rentals are a practical means of transport in St. Maarten, particularly if you're staying out near Oyster Pond Marina.

Budget Rent-a-Car maintains a booth at the airport, although because of local regulations the cars are kept at a different place. When you arrive by plane, a counter attendant will help you with the necessary forms and will arrange for a car to be delivered to your hotel. If your arrival is late at night, a phone call next day to Budget's local office, 95 Cole Bay, P.O. Box 374, Philipsburg (tel. 4308), will set things moving.

Clients should reserve a vehicle through Budget's reservation center at least three days in advance. In the United States, a toll-free number is 800/527-0700. The least expensive car is a peppy Toyota Starlet, suitable for up to four persons. The weekly rate in high season, with unlimited mileage, is $175 per week, or $25 per day. In this rental, as in all others, a 5% tax is added to the bill.

Drivers must be between 21 and 70 and must present a valid driver's license and a major credit card in lieu of a cash deposit. Clients who do not arrange for additional insurance at the time of rental will be fully responsible for the first $1000 worth of damage to their car in the event of an accident.

If your comfort is a priority, Budget will rent you a Toyota Corolla, wiith either manual or automatic transmission and air conditioning, for $280 per week, unlimited mileage included, with each additional day costing an extra $40.

Avis and **Hertz** are also represented in St. Maarten, although when I investigated their prices, I found that each charged $85 per week more for their least expensive car than Budget was charging during the same time period.

Of course, any dollarwise shopper should compare last-minute Avis and Hertz rates before embarking on a trip. You can call toll free: Hertz at 800/654-3131 and Avis at 800/331-1212.

Sightseeing Taxi Tours

If you don't want to drive, you can negotiate with a taxi driver who will also serve as your guide. One or two passengers are charged $30 for a 2½-hour tour, and an additional passenger pays around $5.

Motorcycles and Mopeds

Carter's, Bush Road, Cul-de-Sac and Simpson Bay (tel. 2621 and 4251), rents motorcycles and mopeds. Moped rentals begin at about $16.50 per day, and cheaper weekly tariffs are assessed. Call for their courtesy bus.

SHOPPING: St. Maarten is not only a free port, but there are no local taxes. Prices are sometimes lower than anywhere else in the Caribbean. However,the problem is that you must know what you're looking for, what is actually a bargain. Too many cruise-ship passengers have returned home to find the same Japanese camera selling for less in their local discount store! Many well-known shops in Curaçao offer branches here, in case you're not going on to the ABC islands.

Except for the boutiques at resort hotels, the main shopping center is in downtown Philipsburg. Most of the shops are on two leading strccts, Front Street (called Voorstraat in Dutch), which is closer to the bay, and Back Street (Achterstraat), which runs parallel.

I'll only mention a few shops to get you started, as nearly every building in Philipsburg seems to be a store ready to sell.

Shipwreck Shop, Front Street (tel. 2962), is a West Indian store selling hammocks, colorful beach towels, steak plates and salad bowls, baskets, hand-made jewelry, T-shirts, postcards, stamps, books, and much more. It is the home of Caribelle Batik and Lord & Hunter seasalt, cane sugar, and spices.

Java Wraps has opened a store in Royal Palm Plaza (tel. 3568). It is all white tile, with traditional Javanese straw matting on the walls decorated with exotic Balinese woodcarvings. Locals and tourists alike buy the hand-batiked resort wear line specializing in shorts, shirts, sundresses, and children's clothing. Java Wraps is known for its sarong pieces. You can have a demonstration of how to tie them in at least 15 different ways.

The New Amsterdam Store, Front Street (tel. 2787), offers novelty items, T-shirts, and costume jewelry, hand-embroidered blouses for women, and porcelain figurines from Italy and Spain. They also feature St. Maarten's largest linen department. Beachwear for women is also on display, including on my latest rounds Gottex and Oberson swimwear from Israel. They sell men's and women's elegant sportswear from leading French and Italian designers, as well as accessories and shoes. You will find everything from jogging suits to watches to 14- and 18-karat gold and silver jewelry.

Gulmohar's, Front Street (tel. 2956), could save you a shopping trip to the Orient. It's a real bazaar. On display are linen and drip-dry tablecloths, batik dresses and shirts, silk blouses, Japanese kimonos, and elegantly beaded handbags. Look for meerschaum pipes, musical jewel boxes, fine silk scarves, souvenirs, and, of course, liquor at duty-free prices.

Spritzer & Fuhrmann's, 42 Front St. (tel. 2523), is another good center for selective buyers, a branch of the famous firm founded in Curaçao more than half a century ago. The shop in St. Maarten sells "name" watches, as well as a collection of quality china and porcelain with lines from Royal Worcester, Royal Doulton, Wedgwood, Royal Copenhagen, and Lladró, plus Baccarat, Lalique, Waterford, and Swarovski crystal.

La Romana, Royal Palm Plaza (tel. 21818), is arguably the chicest international boutique in St. Maarten. On two floors, you'll find a display of designer wares, including Italian sportswear and beach outfits. Their shoe salon, for both men and women, is superb. Names designers such as Giorgio Armani are regularly featured here with merchandise that is often 25% lower than it is in the United States. You're welcomed by Jolanda and Augusto Marini.

Oro de Sol Jewelers, Front Street (tel. 2520), is a well-stocked store offering one of the most imaginative selections in St. Maarten. Included in the inventory is an array of gold watches, as well as high-fashion jewelry studded with precious stones. The establishment also has a branch on the rue de la République in Marigot, which carries perfumes and fragrances as well as jewelry. The Rosell family—Donna and Jacques—buy their inventory from around the world, often offering discounts of up to 50% over Stateside prices.

Yellow House (Casa Amarilla), De Ruyterplein (tel. 2332). Residents of the Dutch-speaking islands know this place as the branch of a century-old establishment in Curaçao. All kinds of perfumes and luxury items are sold here, including fine porcelain dishes and figurines, plus a full range of jewelry from the biggest names in gems. Everything is sold at duty-free prices, so it's easy to find bargains.

Thimbles & Things, Back Street (tel. 2898), north of the post office, is for noteworthy needlework with flair. Housed in a little pink home, it features West Indian batiks, as well as pillows that are appliquéed or hand-embroidered. If it's something made by hand, with fine needlework, you'll surely be drawn to the items here. Take special note of hand-painted island scenes in needlepoint made by Nusza. The shop also sells Dutch kits for do-it-yourself needlepoint.

Two handsome shops now offer their distinctive presentations under the same roof. To the right as you enter a handsomely restored old stone building is **Around the Bend,** where you'll find Gottex swimwear and supple eelskin products along with gifts and beachtops mostly island made. **Sergio Moreta** shares the left-hand side of the carefully restored property and features elegant European women's wear and accessories displayed in a charming manner, with Sergio on hand to help you with your selections. Look for the Sergio Moreta and Around the Bend signs opposite Marshalls Mall at the head of Front Street.

Danielle Boutique, 119 Front St. (tel. 2343), is a sophisticated shop carrying one of the most imaginative selections possible for French-designed fashion sportswear, whimsical accessories, Italian handbags, and reasonably priced jewelry. The boutique is next door to the previously recommended restaurant, Le Bec Fin.

As you're leaving, you might drop in at **Antillean Liquors,** at Juliana Airport (tel. 4267). This duty-free shop which attracts the last-minute shopper is open seven days a week, 365 days a year, from 8 a.m. until the last plane has left. It has a complete assortment of all the leading brands of liquor and liqueurs, as well as cigarettes and Cuban cigars.

THE SPORTING LIFE: Regardless of what hotel you select in St. Maarten, you're never far from the water. On the Dutch side, you'll find a magnificent collection of white sandy beaches, perhaps your own hidden cove. If you're a beach-sampler, you can often use the changing facilities at some of the bigger resorts for a fee of about $3. (Nudists should head for the French side of the island, although the Dutch side is getting more liberal about those who prefer to take their sand sans attire).

Windsurfing and jet-skiing are especially popular on St. Maarten. The unruffled waters of Simpson Bay Lagoon, the largest in the West Indies, are ideal for these sports, as well as for the more traditional waterskiing. For the truly daring, parasailing is also available.

Snorkeling and Scuba

Both the serious snorkeler and the scuba-diver are attacted to St. Maarten's crystal-clear bays and the countless coves which honeycomb the island. Underwater visibility reportedly runs from 75 to 125 feet. The biggest attraction for scuba-divers is the 1801 British man-o-war, H.M.S. *Proselyte,* which came to a watery grave on a reef a mile off the coast. Divers today can see her cannons and anchors. Most of the big resort hotels have facilities for scuba-diving, and someone on the staff will provide information about underwater tours, for photography as well as night diving.

One of the major water-sports centers is **Maho Watersports,** with headquarters in a pair of harborfront cottages near the Mullet Bay Resort (tel. 4387). Directed by ex-Californians, it issues NAUI certification to clients who successfully complete their $250 course. LeRoy (Lee) French is a highly experienced diver, one of the world's few surivors of an attack by a white shark. With his English wife, Barbara, he and his partner, Mike Meyers, offer a three-hour introductory scuba lesson costing $45. Clients who choose to continue their diving can elect a series of dives for $45 each. Snorkeling trips last half a day, leaving daily at 9:30 a.m. and returning at 1:30 p.m. Rum punches and soft drinks are included in the per-person price of $35.

READER'S DIVING SUGGESTION: "For diving in St. Maarten, I strongly recommend **Sint Maarten Divers,** P.O. Box 310 (tel. 2446), with their shop at the Great Bay Hotel in Philipsburg. The owner, Pierre DeCelles, is a young French-Canadian who opened his shop several years ago and provides an excellent service. The trips are boat dives and are exciting and colorful, more so even than St. Thomas. Reefs, wrecks (1801, H.M.S. *Proselyte*), and a fascinating maze of tunnels and coral valleys, as well as interesting night dives, make his trips the highlight of a visit to St. Maarten. Rates are cheaper than in St. Thomas: $35 for a single-tank boat dive" (Dr. Larry A. Robinson, Omaha, Neb.).

Windsurfing

Windsurfing is available at the following water-sports centers:

Little Bay Beach Hotel Watersports Center (tel. 2333). The sailboards are for rent for $12 per hour, for $20 per hour with instruction.

Maho Watersports, Mullet Bay Resort and Casino (tel. 2801). Equipment rental is $15 per hour. With instruction for one person the price if $25 per hour; for two persons, $35 per hour.

Red Ensign Watersports, Dawn Beach Hotel. Board rental with instruction is $15 per hour.

St. Maarten Beach Club (tel. 3434). Rental is $10 per hour.

Tennis

You can try the courts at any of the large hotels. **Mullet Bay Resort and Casino** (tel. 2801) takes tennis more seriously than anyplace else on the island, but if you're not a guest there you will have to book a court, paying about $5 per hour. A trio of Mullet Bay's courts are lit at night.

Great Bay Beach Hotel and Casino (tel. 2447) has one court. Night play costs $5 per hour. There is no pro or pro shop. Guests are allowed to use the court free.

Little Bay Beach Hotel (tel. 2333) and **Belair Beach Hotel** (tel. 3560) each have three asphalt courts, some of them available for night play, at a charge of $4. A pro to give instruction, a pro shop, and a tennis clinic are among the amentities. Guests of the hotels are allowed free court time.

Golf

Mullet Bay Resort and Casino (tel. 2801) also has a splendid 18-hole course designed by Joseph Lee, stretching along the shores of Mullet Pond and Simpson Bay Lagoon. Greens fees are $16, and carts cost $18. Rental clubs are $6. Pros and assistants are always on hand, and there's also a good pro shop. Naturally, house residents get the first chance on the starting times.

Boating

The **Cheshire Cat** is a 50-foot catamaran sailing every day from the small pier right in the heart of Philipsburg. Jim Hapgood leaves at 9 a.m. for a two-hour sail to the French-held island of St. Barts. Passengers are allowed four hours on the island to go shopping, shelling, or snorkeling, and to have lunch. The sail back to St. Maarten takes two hours. For a price of $45 per guest, you're given an open bar, snacks, and champagne. For reservation, call 2572 day, 2088 evening.

On the power yacht **Maison Maru,** passengers sail along the shoreline while the captian, Larry Berkowitz, points out landmarks and regales his listeners with amusing tales of island life. During the day-long excursion, lunch with wine is served. An hour's layover in Marigot allows time for shopping and sightseeing, perhaps swimming and snorkeling in a secluded cove. The 57-foot *Maison Maru* departs from the Little Pier in Philipsburg at 9:30 a.m., costing $45 per person.

Picnic Sails

One of the most popular fair-weather pastimes for vacationers to St. Maarten is to sign on or a day of picknicking, sailing, snorkeling, and sightseeing aboard one of several boats providing this service. The sleek sailboats usually pack large wicker hampers full of vituals and stretch tarpaulins over sections of the deck to protect sun-shy visitors.

The **Orotava** operates daily out of Bobby's Marina, Philipsburg harbor, leaving at 9 a.m. for one of the dozens of outlying islands which can be reached only by water. Ton and Rosa, the skippers, maintain an open bar, serve copious lunches, and act as guides throughout the day. The cost of the day-long outing is $55 per person.

A 60-foot schooner, the **Gandalf,** which docks alongside the *Orotava* at the marina, sails daily to the island of Tintamarre (Flat Island), where for 30 years beginning in 1902 the locally dubbed "King of Tintamarre" and his 100 workers operated a cotton plantation. Swimming and snorkeling are good here, benefiting from the outlying reef which keeps the waters calm and full of sea life. Luncheon on the *Gandalf* includes a barbecue, with shish kebab, spare ribs, hearty salads, and fresh-baked bread. Snorkeling equipment is provided. The cost is $55 per person.

Another picnic sail is offered on the **Gabrielle,** which also sails from Bobby's Marina, leaving at 9 a.m. and returning at 5 p.m. The *Gabrielle* is a 46-foot ketch, with a spacious cockpit and large decks. Its $55-per-person price includes lunch, beer, French wine, and use of all equipment. You're taken to a secluded cove on a small island where you can sunbathe, swim, and snorkel. Boston-born Jerry Rosen is your skipper. Call 3170 after 6 p.m., 2366 during the day.

In most cases you can make reservations for any of these cruises at the activities desk of your hotel.

Deep-Sea Fishing

Fishermen come to St. Maarten to seek out such game fish as bonito, red snapper, marlin, and albacore. Those interested should walk over to **Bobby's Marina** (tel. 2167), where *Long George* or the *Gemini Two* are berthed. Prices average $120 for a half day and $200 for a full day, with a maximum of four persons. Rates usually include the use of tackle, plus lunch and refreshments.

Sailing to Other Island Countries

Vacationers to St. Maarten have the opportunity to visit other inhabited Caribbean islands on day trips. Experienced skippers make voyages to St. Barts in the French West Indies and to Saba, another of the islands comprising the Dutch Windwards in the Leewards, stopping long enough for passengers to familiarize themselves with the island ports, to shop, and to have lunch if they wish, returning to St. Maarten the same day. The trips are available several times each week.

The **Eagle,** one of the most beautiful catamarans home-ported in Philipsburg, sails for St. Barts daily except Friday and Sunday at 9:30 a.m., returning to St. Maarten at 5 p.m. The boat, with double hulls painted black with gold trim and propelled by a billowing spinnaker, takes passengers for a charge of $45 per person on the cruise which includes snacks, open bar, use of snorkeling gear, and spectacular views.

The *Eagle* makes an excursion to Saba once a week, Friday, leaving at 8 a.m. and returning at around 5:30 p.m. Snacks, open bar, a lunch at a restaurant on Saba, and a bus tour of the island are all included in the $80-per-person charge.

The **White Octopus,** a 70-foot motor-driven catamaran, offers spacious upper and lower decks for passengers going from St. Maarten to St. Barts, a trip lasting 1½ hours and costing $45. The boat leaves Philipsburg every Tuesday through Saturday at 9:15 a.m., returning at 5 p.m.

Other possibilities for the trip to St. Barts are **El Tigre** and **Bluebeard,** catamarans leaving Great Bay Marina in Philipsburg every Tuesday through Sunday at 9 a.m. and returning at 5 p.m. The cost is $45 per person.

Also making the St. Barts run is the 90-passenger **M.V. Henry D,** a large vessel providing air-conditioned comfort on the voyage and charging $35 per person. It sails Wednesday, Thursday, Friday, and Saturday at 9:30 a.m., returning at 5 p.m. The *Henry D* sails from the little pier in Philipsburg.

Coastal and Sunset Cruises

The **Ferotolos** is a 60-foot cruising yacht which, before coming to ply the waters off St. Maarten, ran between scattered points in the Mediterranean. A coastal cruise leaving from Great Bay Marina, Simpson Bay, circumnavigates the island, stopping at many coves and inlets before breaking for a buffet luncheon. Departing at 9:30 a.m. Friday, Saturday, and Sunday, and returning at 5:30 p.m., the trip costs $65 per person. Sunset cruises, beginning at 4:30 p.m. and returning after dark, leave Tuesday, Wednesday, and Thursday. You're welcomed aboard at a cost of $25 per person. An open bar is maintained on all cruises. No children under 11 are accepted on the cruises. For reservations, call 2572 in the daytime, 2038 in the evening, or else inquire at your hotel activities desk.

Horseback Riding

Crazy Acres, Wathey Estate, Cole Bay (tel. 2503, ext. 201). Riding expeditions here, led by Ottawa-born Linda Russell, invariably end on an isolated beach where the horses, with or without their riders, enjoy the cool waters in an after-ride romp. Ms. Russell is an avid rider who, with another escort, often accompanies eight-person outings which begin at 9 a.m. every weekday, returning about noon. The per-person price if $40. Riders of all levels of experience are welcome, with the single provision that they wear bathing suits under their jeans for a grand finale on the beach. Private lessons can be arranged with a trainer and one of the stable's 16 mounts for around $25 an hour. It's recommended that reservations for any activity be made at least two days in advance. On weekends, families wishing to picnic together can arrange horseback outings *en famille* through the stable.

NIGHTLIFE: On the Dutch side of St. Maarten, there are no nightclubs to speak of. After-dark activities begin early here, as guest select their favorite nook for a sundowner, perhaps the veranda of the **West Indian Tavern,** the **Rusty Pelican** on the water, or the beautiful garden patio of **Pasanggrahan,** all of these establishments having been previously recommended.

A favorite spot for sunset watching is at the **Caravanserai,** a luxury hotel also previously recommended. An airy octagonal gazebo caps a rocky outcropping at Burgeaux Bay. From here, guest watch for the legendary "green flash," an atmospheric phenomenon written about by Hemingway that sometimes occurs in these latitudes just as the sun drops below the horizon. Each evening guests wait expectantly, and have been known to break into a round of applause at a particularly spectacular sunset.

Most of the combos and **gambling casinos** as well are in the big hotels such as the **Mullet Bay Resort and Casino,** the **Maho Reef Beach Resort, Little Bay, Great Bay,** the **Seaview Beach Hotel,** and the **St. Maarten Beach Club** (refer to the previous recommendations for descriptions and locations). Casino action is usually from 8 p.m. till 3 a.m., but the casino at the St. Maarten Beach Club opens at 1 in the afternoon. The island's newest casino opened at the **Pelican Resort** (tel. 2503) in 1984, built to a Swiss design incorporating a panoramic view of Simpson Bay. It features Las Vegas rules.

The big hotels, and some of the smaller ones too, sponsor **beachside barbecues** (particularly in season), bringing in steel bands and offering native music and folk dancing. Outsiders are welcomed at most of these events, but call ahead to see if it's a private catered affair.

Hemingway's, Front Street (tel. 2976), is the most unusual club on the island. At the top of a sweeping flight of steps, you'll see nostalgic Hollywood photos, a panoramic sweep of ocean, and an international collection of guests. The club combines chic with ribald comedy presented in its mini-theater at 11 p.m. by female impersonators portraying such stars at Bette Davis, Gloria Swanson, Josephine Baker, and Marlene Dietrich. Some of the performers come from as far away as Zurich. Occasionally one of them will really be a woman born. In addition to the wide assortment of drinks, full dinners are served, costing from $30 to $35, with lunches for $18, both featuring an international cuisine. Hemingway's is open from 11 a.m. to 3 a.m. Reservations for the 11 p.m. show as well as for dinner are a good idea.

Many hotels have discos as well. The best is the **Hillside Disco,** at the Mullet Bay Resort and Casino (tel. 2801). Drinks cost from $3.50.

2. St. Eustatius

Called "Statia," this Dutch-held island is just an eight-square-mile pinpoint in the Netherlands Antilles, still basking in its 18th-century heritage as the "Golden Rock." One of the true backwaters of the West Indies, it is just awakening to tourism. The location is 150 miles east of Puerto Rico, 90 miles east of St. Croix, 38 miles due south of St. Maarten, and 17 miles southeast of Saba.

Two extinct volcanoes, the Quill, and "Little Mountain," are linked by a sloping agricultural plain, growing yams and sweet potatoes, forming the topography of Stratia. The valley is known as De Cultuurvlakte.

Overlooking the Caribbean on the western edge of the plain, Oranjestad (Orange City) is the capital and the only village, consisting of both an Upper and Lower Town, connected by stone-paved, dogleg Fort Road.

Statia was sighted by Columbus in 1493, on his second voyage, and the island was claimed for Holland by Jan Snouck in 1640. The island's history was turbulent before it settled down to peaceful slumber under Dutch protection. From 1650 to 1816, Statia changed flags 22 times!

Once the trading hub of the Caribbean, Statia was a thriving market, both for goods and for slaves. Benjamin Franklin directed his mail to Europe through Statia.

Before the American Revolution, the population of Statia did not exceed 1200, most of whom were slaves engaged in raising sugarcane. When war came and Britain blockaded the North American coast, Europe's trade was diverted to the West Indies. Dutch neutrality lured many traders, which led to the construction of a mile and a half of warehouses in Lower Town. The Americans obtained gunpowder and ammunition shipped through Statia.

Statia's historical links are strong with the United States. Its Fort Oranje was the first fortress to salute the Stars and Stripes, flying from the 14-gun brigantine *Andrew Doria.* The date was November 16, 1776. Satia paid for such early recognition of a revolutionary government. In reprisal in 1781, Great Britain's Admiral Rodney seized and sacked Statia, luring unsuspecting vessels into anchorage by continuing to fly the Dutch flag. It is estimated that when Rodney sailed away, he carried from $15 to $20 million of booty from Statia.

Contrary to legend, Statia was not destroyed by Rodney. After his forces left, the island bounced back to reach the pinnacle of its prosperity in 1790, with a population put at 8125 persons. Its gradual decay came about when it was no longer needed as a transit port for the American colonies. Also it was bled by exorbitant demands of interim French and English governments unprotected warehouses eventually tumbled into the sea, and only their barest shells and raw foundations remain, skeletal stone walls that one historian dubbed "the Pompeii of the Caribbean."

GETTING THERE: St. Eustatius can be reached from St. Maarten's Juliana Airport via **Windward Islands Airways** (called Winair). The flight, leaving both in the morning and the afternoon, takes only 30 minutes. Connections can be made on Statia for either Saba or St. Kitts.

It's also possible to take an **excursion boat,** M.V. *Henry D,* leaving from the little Pier in Philipsburg, St. Maarten.

PRACTICAL FACTS: Dutch is the official **language,** although English is commonly spoken. The official unit of **currency** is the Netherlands Antilles guilder (NAf), but nearly all places will quote you prices in U.S. dollars.

Arrival is at Franklin Delano Roosevelt Airport, where there is no Customs (the island is a free port). U.S. and Canadian citizens need **proof of citizenship,** such as a passort, voter registration card, or a birth certificate, along with an ongoing ticket.

There is no **departure tax** if you are returning to the Dutch-held islands of St. Maarten or Saba. If going elsewhere, you'll be charged $5.

Once on the island, visitors find a climate with an average daytime temperature of 78° to 82° F. The annual rainfall is only 45 inches.

The **time** is the same as Eastern Daylight Saving Time. **Electricity** is 110 volts AC, 60 cycles, the same as the U.S.

The **water** is considered safe to drink.

At the **Princess Beatrix Hospital,** 25 Prinsesweg (tel. 2211), in Oranjestad, a licensed physician is on duty.

Most **shops,** what few there are, are open from 8 a.m. to noon and 1:30 to 5:30 p.m. weekdays (on Saturday, hours are 10 a.m. to noon and 2:30 to 5:30 p.m.). Of course, this could vary widely.

Tipping is at the visitor's discretion, and most hotels, guest houses, and restaurants include a 10% service charge.

Ask at your hotel if you need to send a cable. St. Eustatius maintains a 24-hour-a-day **telephone service** to the world, and sometimes it takes about that much time to get a call through!

The **Banco Popular Antiliano** is open from 8:30 a.m. to 1 p.m. Monday to Friday and also from 4 to 5 p.m. on Friday.

The **Tourist Bureau** is at 3 Fort Oranjestraat (tel. 2225).

At last, it's a place in the world where crime is almost nonexistent. If there is any trouble at all, it is likely to be caused by your fellow tourists, not by the locals.

HOTELS: Don't expect deluxe hotels or high-rises. Statia is strictly for escapists. Sometimes guests are placed in private homes. There are, as well, some small guest houses on the island.

The Old Gin House, P.O. Box 172 Bay Road, Lower Town (tel. 2319), is a two-in-one hotel, with half a dozen rooms facing the beach in Oranjestad, the other 14 built across the street and opening onto a pool. What used to be known as the "Mooshay Bay Publick House"—the hotel set back from the beach—is of more recent vintage than the Old Gin House. However, it was built on the ruins of 18th-century warehouses once used to store molasses.

It is run by John May and Marty Scofield, two expatriate Americans. Before coming to the island, Mr. Scofield was an art director for J. Walter Thompson in New York, and Mr. May taught art classes in Greenwich, Connecticut. In their inn, they have mixed antiques with practical and well-chosen pieces. They have shown a healthy respect for the past but were not trapped by it, remembering that this was an inn to be used and enjoyed by modern-day travelers.

From a decaying cistern a small pool was shaped, and an old cannon was discovered while digging the swimming hole. It's been retired to a peaceful nook. The rooms at the Publick House are set in a brick building with a double row of balconies. An overseer's gallery has been turned into a library and backgammon room. Cooled by overhead fans and sea breezes, each accommodation has sophisticated touches, including paintings and wrought-iron wall hangings from Haiti. The floral lightness evokes a touch of Matisse. Terracotta plaques were imported from New Orleans for the brick walls, and flowering plants cascade from terraces and large ceramic urns.

Across the street, the Old Gin House originally began as a hotdog stand in 1972, and like Topsy it just grew and grew, becoming a six-room inn of character, small but special. On the ruins of an old cotton gin, the house was designed by Mr. May, who with the help of his partner has made it a comfortable haven. He used red brick brought to Statia as ballast from Holland.

The decision to build grew out of a response from clients who came here to eat and stayed around looking for a place to stay. Antiques "gathered from all over" are scattered about the place—a wooden candelabrum came from Louisiana, a rare 18th-century Bristol clock "from wherever." A two-story unit faces the sea, the rooms cooled by breezes. The ceilings are high, and balconies open onto the waterfront from which you can see Statia's fishermen leaving early in the morning.

In winter, the oceanfront deluxe double accommodations rent for $120. *Single or double occupancy in summer is $100 daily.* For breakfast and dinner (with complimentary wine), there is an additional charge of $35 per person daily, plus tax and service.

La Maison Sur la Plage, P.O. Box 157 (tel. 2256), is a delight. Once known to many readers as the Golden Rock Resort, it has been taken over by Michelle Bonnachaux, a French woman noted for her remarkable French cuisine, which has many nouvelle touches. The location is on the opposite side of the island at Zeelandia, on a two-mile stretch of beach nestling at the end of curving Concordia Bay.

This fairly remote 20-room waterfront complex offers comfortable cabanas around a pool. Guest quarters, for the most part, are in ranch-style rooms containing Mexican arches. The units are pleasantly furnished and attractively maintained. In winter, the rate, including breakfast, ranges from $65 to $85 a day, single or double. Some triples cost from $90 to $115 daily. *Summer rates, either single or double occupancy, cost $55 daily, with breakfast included.*

The **Golden Era,** Lower Town (tel. 2345), is a 20-room hotel recently built on Statia. Its angular, functional modernity provides a striking contrast to the other-days style of the Old Gin House which lies near by. Each of the pleasant accommodations is clean, comfortable, and filled with sea breezes that come through the windows. All rooms face the water and have wall-to-wall carpeting, air conditioning, and telephones. Winter rates are $95 daily for a single, $100 for a double, plus service. *In summer, prices are reduced by about 25%.* The hotel has a bar and restaurant on the premises.

Ocean View Guest House, Upper Town (tel. 2271), stands at the edge of town, a modest two-story building, offering eight bedrooms, all with a view of the water. Youngish guests swear by its cleanliness, and pass it along to their Statia-abound friends as a true bargain. Units are small but well kept, with tiny showers and toilets. At certain times of the year it gets very hot here. The charge if $34 daily for two persons with a breakfast "cooked as you wish." If you want lunch or dinner, the additional charge is only $10, and for this you might be served two pieces of chicken, vegetables, potatoes, a salad, and dessert. A band sometimes plays downstairs, and the bar is open nightly, except Sunday.

Gloria Hotel, Rosemary Lane (tel. 2378), is a large, square utilitarian structure, each of its modestly furnished bedrooms opening off an enormous hallway. Each unit has a set of twin beds, as well as a tiled bath and shower. The accommodations resemble monks' cells, but all is tidy and neat. Cooling is by electric fans. The owner charges $48 daily in a single, $58 in a double, these tariffs including a continental breakfast and a well-prepared three-course dinner which features fresh fish and locally grown produce when available.

WHERE TO DINE: The **Old Gin House and Mooshay Publick House,** Lower Town (tel. 2319). In a nostalgic atmosphere, guests at lunch can enjoy the shady treillage terrace of this little charmer, overlooking the beach. Perhaps you'll begin with a soursop or strawberry daiquiri. If featured, I'd suggest the peanut soup (so good its recipe was published in *Gourmet* magazine). The secret is dry-roasted peanuts and a dollop or so of *ketjap bentang*. You might also order conch chowder.

Recipes are the creation of American expatriate Marty Scofield. He's an inspired cook, depending on his own inventiveness: "I certainly didn't learn from my mother, who always served boiled peas and carrots." Some of is luncheon specialties include lobster Antillean, skewered chicken with peanut sauce, and red snapper mousse. I'm also fond of the chicken and coconut salad or the beef crêpes, although you can also order a hamburger if you're so inclined. Fresh pineapple is the preferred dessert. Expect to spend from $15 to $20, depending on your selection. For dinner all you have to do is walk across the street.

Try to arrive before the dinner setting, so you can enjoy a drink in the pub, a structure of wooden beams and old ship-ballast bricks. The chefs are likely to feature a delicate quiche Niçoise with a light, flaky crust, or perhaps fish chowder—"I can't make it unless the catch is good." Specialties (among a wide-ranging repertoire) includes the bisque de homard with rouille, made with lobster legs, perfectly balanced with Mediterranean spicing. Perhaps he'll offer snapper mousse with broccoli.

Service is on pewter tranchers and Spode china, and the staff is friendly and smiling. Complimentary wine is included, and the total cost is $30, well-spent money. In homage to the 18th century, Delft and pewter are used generously. Dining is by candlelight in either of two rooms, connected by brick arches with an eclectic collection of ship models, old clocks, and primitive paintings. The owners went to Haiti to order the hardwood chairs wth rush seats. But everything is just a showcase of Mr. Scofield's creative cookery.

Talk of the Town, Golden Rock (tel. 2236), offers the largest menu on the island, but don't expect all the dishes listed to be available. However, the cook, Melvina Nias, if given sufficient notice can prepare an international array of dishes that ranges from Dutch favorites to creole cookery, with side trips to the Orient. Anyone who's eaten in the airport restaurant in Aruba may find the menu vaguely familiar. Ms. Nias used to cook there at the 7 Nations restaurant, and when she returned to her native Statia, she brought back with her the secrets she'd learned.

She's taken me on a tour of her well-stocked freezers in back. Bulging with food, her larder has an unbelievable array of foodsuffs, but as most of it's frozen, you've got to call her in time to allow her to thaw it out.

To get you started, she might offer shark-fin soup or perhaps her own native fish soup. I prefer her Dutch green pea soup, really good. Among her main dishes, I'd recommend any of her curry concoctions, her soy sauce duck, which is served with an orange-flavored Curaçao sauce, her Caribbean red snapper with a Spanish sauce, or her beef Stroganoff. You might also enjoy her spaghetti Bolognese, her nasi-goreng special, her Chinese rice (a meal in itself), or her pepper steak with oyster sauce. Another special, which she secretly labels "Happy Family," is her self-styled Chinese concoction. Meals begin at $18 per head. Although she doesn't like to say she's the best native cook on the island, some refer to her as such; she modestly admits, "I try." Drop in for lunch or dinner "anytime."

L'Étoile, 6 Van Rheeweg (tel. 2299), is a second-floor native restaurant with a few simple tables. Eric and Caren Henriquez have had this place for some time, and they are well known in Statia for their local cuisine, but you don't run into too many tourists here. In fact, it's one of the few places on the island that quotes menu prices in Netherland Antillean guilders. Favored and recommended main dishes include the ubiquitous "goat water" (a stew), fried liver and onions, stuffed crab backs, stewed whelks, as well as tasty spare ribs. Caren is also known for her pastechis, deep-fried turnovers stuffed with meat. Expect to pay from $18 for a complete and very filling meal.

If you want a really cheap place to stay in Statia, they'll put you up in their ten-room guest house in Oranjestad, where a *single room in off-season rents for only $20 daily, going up to $33 in a double.* In winter, singles rent for $22 daily; doubles, $36.

GETTING AROUND: Taxis are your bet bet. They meet all incoming flights and will drive from there to your hotel. On the way to the hotel, I assure you that your driver will offer himself as a guide during your stay on the island. Taxi rates are inexpensive, probably no more than a $3 ride to your hotel from the airport. If you book a 3½-hour tour later in the day (and in that time you should be able to cover all the sights on Statia), the cost is about $30 per vehicle.

Car rentals are also available, although I don't think you'll need one.

Maduro Car Rental (tel. 2225) has Toyota Starlites available for rent. The daily rate, subject to change, is about $30 with unlimited mileage. Gas is extra.

SEEING THE SIGHTS: The capital, Oranjestad, stands on a cliff looking out upon a beach and the island's calm anchorage, where in the 18th century you might see 200 vessels offshore. Fort Oranje was built in 1636 and restored in honor of the U.S. Bicentennial celebration of 1976. Today it is perched like one of the island's seabirds atop the cliffs. Its terraced rampart is lined with old cannons. You'll see a bronze plaque honoring the fact that "Here the sovereignty of the United States of America was first formally acknowledged to a national vessel by a foreign official." The plaque was presented by Franklin D. Roosevelt. The fort is now used for government offices.

One of the island's most attractive buildings stands across from the square. Once this house belonged to Johannes de Graaff, Statia's most famous governor. It was de Graaff who ordered the salute to the Stars and Stripes. The plundering Rodney also stayed here in 1781.

A few steps away, a cluster of 18th-century buildings is called Three Widows' Corner, surrounding a quiet courtyard.

Nearby are the ruins of the first Dutch Reformed church. To reach it, turn west from Three Widows' Corner onto Kerkweg. On tilting headstones are recorded the names of the characters in the island's past. The St. Eustatius Historical Foundation recently completed restoration of the church. Visitors may climb to the top level of the tower and see the bay as lookouts did many years before.

In the center, Honen Dalim, a Jewish synagogue, the second in the western hemisphere, can be explored, although it is in ruins. Once Statia had a large

Jewish colony of traders. This house of prayer was begun about 1740 and was damaged by a hurricane in 1772. It fel into disuse at the dawn of the 19th century. The synagogue stands beside Synagogpad, a narrow lane whose entrance faces Madam Theatre on the square.

The walls of a ritual mikvah rise beside the **Jewish burial ground** on the edge of town. The oldest stone in the cemetery is that of Abraham Hisquiau de la Motta, who died in 1742. The inscription is in both Portuguese and Hebrew. The most recent marker is that of Moses Waag, who died February 25, 1825. Most poignant is the memorial of David Haim Hezeciah de Lion, who died in 1760 at the age of "2 years, 8 months, 26 days." Carved into the baroque surface is an angel releasing a tiny songbird from its cage.

In addition, a short ride from Oranjestad takes you to the road's end at White Wall. There on you left is **Sugarloaf,** a mini replica of Rio's famed cone. On the right is a panoramic view of **St. Kitts.**

At the base of the pink-gray cliff beneath Fort Oranje, **Lower Town** was the mercantile center of Statia in the 18th century. Bulging with sugar, rum, and tobacco, Lower Town was once filled with row upon row of brick warehouses. Part of the rich cargo of some of these warehouses was human, slaves held in bondage awaiting shipment to other islands in the Caribbean. You can wander at leisure through the ruins, stopping later at the Old Gin House for a drink.

The **Quill** is an extinct volcano, called "the most perfect" in the Caribbean, sheltering a lush tropical rain forest, a botanical wonderland, in its deep wide crater. The Quill rises to 1960 feet on the southern edge of the island. Hikers climb it.

Birdwatchers come here for a glimpse of the blue pigeon, a rare bird known to frequent the breadfruit and cottonwood trees in the mountains.

SHOPPING: Merchandise is very limited, but you may want to pick up a local item or two as a reminder of a pleasant stay.

The **Golden Rock Artisan Foundation,** Upper Town, is a wood-working concern set up for training as well as production. Orders for custom-made furniture, carved signs, doors, windows, gates, and other items of wood are welcomed at its workshop on Rosemary Lane or the office on Van Tonningenweg any weekday from 8 a.m. to noon and 1 to 5 p.m.

The **Mazinga Gift Shop,** Upper Town (tel. 2245), is a general store where you can buy trinkets and gifts. Some Dutch clocks, Colombian woodcarvings, woven hangings, and jewelry are on sale. At the entrance is a caged monkey. Statia is known throughout the Caribbean for its famous "Blue Beads." Inquire if they have any here for sale.

THE SPORTING LIFE: There are few organized sports activities. Life here is casual.

Water Sports

On the Atlantic side of the island, at Concordia Bay, surfing possibilities are best. However, there is no lifeguard protection.

Snorkeling through the Caribbean Sea and exploring the remnants of an 18th-century man-of-war and the walls of warehouses, taverns, and shops that sank below the surface of Oranje Bay more than 200 years ago are available for a $5-per-day price for fins and snorkel rental. Snorkeling and fishing trips with a local guide in native long boats holding up to six persons is $35 per hour. A motor yacht with skipper, including fuel and deep-sea fishing gear is available for rental at $340 per day. The yacht holds up to ten persons. Inquire at the **Old Gin House Sports Activity Center,** P.O. Box 172 (tel. 2319).

Tennis

Tennis, available for the first time on Statia, can be played at Madam Estate at the **Community Center.** The court has a concrete surface and is lit for night play. Changing facilities are also available. It should cost about $2 or less to use the court. The center and the tennis facilities were dedicated on Statia-American Day, November 16. Bring your own equipment.

Crab Catching

I'm perfectly serious. If you're interested in this sport, you an join Statians in a crab hunt. The Quill's crater is the breeding ground for these large crustaceans. At night they emerge from their holes to forage, and that's when they're caught. Men, either with flashlights or else relying on moonlight, climb the Quill, catch a crab, and take the local delicacy back to the favorite cooks on the island who prepare stuffed crab back.

Hiking

Perhaps this is the most popular sporting activity. Those with the stamina can climb the slopes of the Quill. Hikers make their way through a lush rain forest which grew when volcanic activity died down. The trip takes about half a day, and you can ask the tourist office to arrange for a guide for you. He'll expect at least $12.

Bicycling

The **Old Gin House Sports Activity Center** (tel. 2319) rents bicycles for $10 per day, $6 per half day, or $1.75 per hour.

Swimming

On the southwestern shore of Statia are the best volcanic beaches for swimming. Any taxi driver can take you to what he thinks is the best spot.

3. Saba

An extinct volcano, exotic, cone-shaped Saba is five square miles of rock carpeted in lush foliage such as orchids (which grow in profusion), giant elephant ear, and Eucharist lilies. At its zenith, it reaches a height of 2900 feet at Mount Scenery, which the locals call simply "The Mountain." The Dutch settled it in the middle of the 17th century, and out of such an unusual piece of jagged geography they created an experiment in living that has continued to grow.

Saba is in the Netherlands' Windward Islands at the top of the Lesser Antilles arc. The location is 150 miles east of Puerto Rico and 90 miles east of St. Croix. Most visitors fly over from the Dutch-held section of St. Maarten (Saba is 28 miles to the south).

Columbus is credited with sighting Saba in 1493. Before it became permanently Dutch, it was passed back and forth among its European masters a total of 12 times. At one time it was English, then French, then Spanish, and so forth.

Sabans have been known in days of yore to take advantage of their special topography—that is, they pelted invaders from above with rocks and boulders. Because of the influence of English missionaries and Scottish seamen from the remote Shetland Islands who settled on the island, Saba has always been English speaking. The official language, however, is Dutch.

Because of those early settlers from Europe, 60% of the population is white. Don't be surprised to run into natives with red hair and freckled fair skin. Since the men often have to leave to work in the oil refineries of Aruba and Curaçao, Saban women outnumber the men two to one.

On Saba, tidy white houses cling to the mountainside, and small family cemeteries adjoin each dwelling. Lace-curtained gingerbread-trimmed cottages give a Disneyland aura.

The first Jeep arrived on Saba in 1947. Before that, Sabans went about on foot, climbing from village to village. Hundreds of steps had been chiseled out of rock by the early Dutch settlers in 1640.

Engineers told them it was impossible, but Sabans built a single cross-island road by hand. It's filled with hairpin turns, zigzagging from Fort Bay, where a deep-water pier accommodates large tenders from cruise ships, to a height of 1600 feet. Along the way it has fortress-like supporting walls.

Past storybook villages, the road goes over the crest to **The Bottom.** Derived from the Dutch word *botte,* which means bowl-shaped, this village is nestled on a plateau and surrounded by rocky volcanic domes. It occupies about the only bit of ground, 800 feet above the sea. It's also the official capital of Saba, a Dutch village of charm, with chimneys, gabled roofs, and gardens.

From the Bottom you can take a taxi up the hill to the mountain village of **Windwardside,** perched on the crest of two ravines at about 1500 above sea level. This village of red-roofed houses, the second most important in Saba, is the site of the two biggest inns and most of the shops. From Windwardside, you can climb steep steps cut in the rock to yet another village, **Hell's Gate,** teetering on the edge of a mountain. Only the most athletic go from here to the lip of the volcanic crater.

In Windwardside, the **Harry L. Johnson Memorial Museum** is housed in an old sea captain's home, with antique furnishings, everything evoking an 1890s aura. Filled with family memorabilia, the house can be visited throughout the day, and admission is $1. The surprise visit of Jacqueline Kennedy Onassis is still vividly recalled.

GETTING THERE: You can leave New York's JFK airport in the morning and be at Captain's Quarters in Saba for dinner that night. To do that, you can take a direct flight on any of several major carriers from JFK to St. Maarten. From Juliana Airport there, you can fly to Saba on **Winair.**

Many guests at hotels on St. Maarten fly over to Saba on the morning flight, spend the day sightseeing, then return to St. Maarten on the afternoon fight. Air connections can also be made in Saba to St. Kitts and Statia.

If you're returning to St. Maarten or else flying over to Statia, you don't have to pay a departure tax. However, if you're going elsewhere, such as to St. Kitts, a $5 departure tax wil be imposed on you.

Arriving by air from St. Maarten, the traveler steps from Windward Island Airways' 20-passenger STOL (short take off and landing) plane onto the tarmac runway of the Juancho Yrausquin Airport. The airstrip stretches 1312 feet along the aptly named Flat Point, one of the few level area on the island. From there, the road rises in 20 serpentine curves to the village of Hell's Gate which, despite its name, nestles in the shadow of the island's largest church.

PRACTICAL FACTS: The Netherlands Antilles guilder (NAF 1.77 to the $1 U.S.) is the official unit of currency, but U.S. dollars are accepted by almost everybody here.

Arrival is at **Juancho Yrausquin Airport** at Flat Point where there is no

Customs, as this is a free port. Once off the plane, you encounter a temperature of 78° to 82°F (the annual rainfall is 42 inches). The government does require that all U.S. and Canadian citizens show proof of citizenship, such as a passport or voter registation card. An ongoing ticket must also be produced.

The time is Eastern Daylight Time, and the electricity is 110 volts AC, 60 cycles, so most U.S.-made appliances do not need converters.

Licensed physicians practice at the Princess Irene Hospital, St. John's (tel. 2232).

Cables and international **telephone calls** can be placed at the Cable and Wireless office in Windwardside.

Most restaurants and hotels add a 10% or 15% service charge to cover tipping. The government imposes a 5% tax on hotel rooms.

Whatever your problems, you can take them to Will Johnson, who is the chairman of the Saba Tourist Board. He operates out of a small office, the **Tourist Bureau** (tel. 2231), next door to the post office in Windwardside.

HOTELS: The island has a few inns of character, extremely limited in accommodations, yet special and charming for that reason. If you check into an address here, you could safely say you're "hiding out."

Captain's Quarters, Windwardside (tel. 2201), is a restored 19th-century sea captain's house converted into a guest house where many visitors spend secluded holidays. Just off the village center of Windwardside, it's a complex of several wood-frame guest cottages surrounding the main house with its traditional verandas and covered porches. You make your way here by going down a narrow, steep lane, brushing a hibiscus branch out of your face. Thrust out toward the water, almost as if ready to tumble down to the sea, is a freshwater swimming pool surrounded on two sides by a terrace where you can sunbathe or order refreshments from an open-air bar. This is the only swimming pool on the island.

The main house was built by a Saban sea captain and serves as office, library, sitting room, and kitchen on the first floor, with two private accommodations above (one is a honeymoon suite). The house is furnished with antiques gathered from many ports of the world. About half of the ten bedrooms contain four-poster beds, and each is complete with a private bath and balcony overelooking the sea and Mount Scenery. Well designed and cozy, studio rooms stand in the garden. Everything seems a quaint reminder of New England. The hotel, open all year (except in June), *charges $65 in a single in summer, $80 in a double, and a third or fourth person sharing a room is assessed another $20.* In winter, the single tariff is $75, going up to $95 in a double. These are tariffs for rooms only. For breakfast and dinner, add another $25 per person daily. Modern comfort and infinite charm combine to form a tasteful, distinctive Saban atmosphere.

The manager, **Steve Hassell** (everybody in Saba seems to be named Hassell), handles the inn with style, and he's rightly proud of his chef, well known in the islands as "Sugar." Meals are served in the garden pavilions surrounded by breadfruit and mango trees.

Scout's Place, Windwardside (tel. 2205), right in the center of the village, is hidden from the street. It's set on the ledge of a hill, giving every table a view of the sea. This old guest house was transformed by Ohio-born Scout Thirkield into an inn of atmosphere. It is sheltered in an old house, with a large covered but open-walled dining room. It's an informal-type place, witlh a highly individualistic decor that might include everything from Surinam hand-carvings to peacock chairs in red and black wicker to silver samovars. Don't be surprised either if you see a plastic chair or two.

Rooms open on to an interior courtyard filled with flowers, and each unit has a view of the sea. Furnishings are fairly coordinated, unpretentious, and very informal. Most of the rooms have private baths; others must share. Rates are the same all year—$60 daily for two persons with private bath, $45 per single. These tariffs include breakfast and dinner, plus service. Manager Diana Madero makes guests feel right at home.

Cranston's Antique Inn, The Bottom (tel. 3203), is a frame inn standing near the village roadway, with a front terrace where everyone congregates for rum drinks and gossip. It's an old-fashioned house, more than 100 years old at least, and every bedroom has antique four-poster beds. Mr. Cranston, the owner, will gladly rent you the same room where Queen Juliana once spent a holiday. It's on the second floor, on your left, facing the rear garden. Aside from the impressive wooden beds, the furnishings are mostly hit or miss. Rates, in effect all year, are $32 daily in a single, rising to $42 in a double, including breakfast. Local dishes are offered, such as roast pork from island pigs, red snapper, and broiled grouper. Mr. Cranston has a good island cook, who makes use of locally grown spices. Meals are served on a covered terrace in the garden. The house is within walking distance of **Ladder Bay.**

Carib Guest House, The Bottom (tel. 3259), is a bungalow with a red roof and a wide front porch, a combination private home and guest house owned by a jolly, rotund taxi driver, John Woods. His living room is divided from the dining area, and all is plain, very clean, and comfortable. Mr. Woods asks $55 daily for a double room, including three meals a day. Singles pay only $35 daily on the same plan. These tariffs are in effect all year. Mr. Woods has a cook who offers spicy local dishes. Set back from the road, the house is very quiet. It's a friendly little oasis, in a secluded woodsy area of the Bottom. Naturally, Mr. Woods can arrange for you to go on a tour of the island.

WHERE TO EAT: Scout's Place, Windwardside (tel. 2205), is a favorite dining spot for those visitors over for the day, but you should have your driver stop by early and make a reservation for lunch for you. Food at Scout's is simple and good, rewarding and filling, and the price is low too, about $12 for lunch. Dinner is more elaborate, and because of the limited staff reservations are definitely necessary. For your evening meal, expect to pay about $18. Tables are placed on an open-side terrace, the ideal spot for a Heineken at sundown. Local vegetables, homemade bread, and fruit are served.

Captain's Quarters, Windwardside (tel. 2201), is an alternative choice for dinner, and again you must reserve a table. Dining is al fresco; however, if it rains, don't worry—they have a roof. Large, hearty appetites are catered to here, at a cost averaging around $18 for dinner.

Perhaps you'll be there on the night they have fresh grouper. It's one of the best selections in the Caribbean. Soups are homemade and often quite good. Because of the limited suplies on Saba, vegetables are often frozen. Likewise, the wine list is very limited. Lunch will cost much less, about $10, and you can also stop in here for a very filling breakfast at around $6. The dining room is open every day of the year except during the June closing.

For native cookery, really fine West Indian specialties, head for the **Blue Wave Restaurant and Bar** in the Bottom. It's run by J. C. Cranston, manager of the already-previewed Cranston's Antique Inn. Blue Wave serves breakfast at $6, lunch at $10, and dinner at $18 daily. A meal plan for guests at Cranston's Inn is also available. Devotees of creole cookery will ask for some of the freshly caught seafood, such as red snapper and grouper. Local vegetables, when available, are also served. The setting is informal and casual, but air-conditioned. For reservations, call 3202.

GETTING AROUND: Transport is mostly on foot, but taxis and five rental cars are available. In the unlikely event you should dare want to drive a car on Saba, your hotel can make arrangements for you at a cost of about $30 a day. Again, I don't recommend this.

Taxis

Taxis meet every flight, and you can use one to take you to your hotel or book one for a tour of the island at a cost of about $25 per day for six passengers.

Alvin "Bobby" Every seems to be every visitor's favorite driver in his "Red Devil Taxi," painted in you guess what color. He knows the "ups and downs" of Saba, and he'll fill you witlh lots of tales about the island, and I trust they're true.

Hitchhiking

Now frowned upon in much of the world, hitchhiking has long been an acceptable means of transport in Saba, where everybody seemingly knows everybody else. On my latest rounds, my taxi rushed a sick child to the plane and picked up an old man to take him up the hill because he'd fallen and hurt himself —all on my sightseeing tour! I welcomed this friendly and cooperative spirit. At least by hitchhiking, you'll get to know everybody else.

Walking

The oldest and most traditional means of getting around on Saba is still much in evidence. But I suggest that only the sturdy in heart and limb walk from the Bottom up to Windwardside. Many do, but you'd better have some shoes that grip the ground, particularly after a recent rain.

SHOPPING: After lunch you can go for a stroll in Windwardside, stopping in at the boutiques, which often look like the living room of someone's private home. Most stores are open from 9 a.m. to noon and 2 to around 5:30 p.m.

Stitched by Saban wives when their fishermen husbands were off to sea, the traditional drawn threadwork of the island is famous. You don't even have to go to a shop to find it either. Chances are, your driver will stop along the road as women, mostly descendants of Europeans, crowd around you. You'll find out later that the shy woman selling the drawn threadwork is the sister of your taxi driver.

Sometimes this work, introduced by a local woman named Gertrude Johnson in the 1870s, is called Spanish work, because it was believed to have been perfected by nuns in Caracas. Selected threads are drawn and tied in a piece of linen to produce an ornamental pattern. It can be expensive if a quality linen has been used, not to mention the amount of painstaking human detail that went into its creation.

The **Island Craft Shop,** Windwardside, has a good selection of drawn threadwork if you didn't buy some along the road.

The **Saba Artisan Foundation,** The Bottom (tel. 3260), has in recent years made a name for itself in the world of fashion with hand-screened resort fashions. The clothes are casual and colorful. Among the items sold are men's bush jacket shirts, numerous styles of dresses and skirts, napkins, and placemats, as well as yard goods. Island motifs are used in many designs, and you might like a fern or casava-leaf print. Also popular are the famous Saba drawn lace patterns. The fashions are designed, printed, sewn, and marketed by Sabans. Mail-order as well as wholesale distributorship inquiries are invited.

As a final shopping note, try to come home with some "Saba Spice," an aromatic blend of 150-proof cask rum, with such spices as fennel seed, cinnamon, cloves, and nutmeg, straight from someone's home brew. It's not for eveyrone (too sweet), but will make an exotic bottle to show off in your liquor cabinet.

THE SPORTING LIFE: Don't come here for beaches. Saba has only one sand beach, and it's about 20 feet long. Sports here are mostly do-it-yourself. John F. Kennedy, Jr., likes to visit Saba to enjoy the underwater scenery and dark, volcanic sands and coral formations.

Saba, according to some divers, is said to offer "some of the most spectacular diving in the Caribbean." **Saba Deep** (tel. 3347) operates out of Captain's Quarters (see my hotel recommendation) and is run by Edward Arnold (he's called "Tat") and his partner, Lou Bourque. Their diving operation is small, and they're concerned with individual attention. In spite of the size of the island, they have at their disposal a minimum of two dozen dive sites, ranging from shallow-water caves to spectacular dropoffs. A single one-tank dive goes for $35, everything included, a two-tank dive for $60. There's also a three-hour resort course in diving, with a single dive, priced at $60.

For the less energetic, Lou and Tat offer a half-hour sunset cruise, complete witlh drinks and hors d'oeuvres, for $20 per person. However, a minimum of four persons must sign up for this before they will go out. Package rates for divers, including accommodations, meals, and underwater activities, are available upon request.

Tennis buffs will find a public court in the Bottom. It's a cement court and doesn't charge players.

Mountain walking is actually the major sport, and the top of **Mount Scenery** is a goal of eager bands of hikers. Allow more than a day and take your time, climbing the 1064 concrete steps up to the cloud-reefed mountain. One of the inns will pack you a picnic lunch. The higher you limb, the cooler it grows, about a drop of 1° Fahrenheit every 328 feet. On a hot day this can be an incentive.

Others not so athletic may settle for a hike up Booby Hills, 66 terraced steps leading to a peak of 1500 feet. Beautiful views unfold in every direction.

NIGHTLIFE: Believe it or not, there is some. The **Lido Club,** Windwardside, is open only on Saturday night, when practically the entire island turns out.

Chapter IX

JAMAICA

1. Kingston
2. Port Antonio
3. Ocho Rios
4. Montego Bay
5. Negril
6. Mandeville

JAMAICA, 90 MILES south of Cuba, is the third largest of the Caribbean islands, with some 4400 square miles of predominantly green land, a mountain ridge peaking to 7400 feet above sea level, and on the north coast, many beautiful white sand beaches with clear blue sea.

First populated in A.D. 700 by Arawak Indians, gentle people from South America who named the island "Xaymaca," Jamaica was first discovered by Christopher Columbus, who called it "the fairest isle eyes have seen" in 1494— Jamaicans will tell you that he was their first tourist and was a repeat visitor. Spain settled the island in 1509. In due course, Africans were imported by the Spanish as slaves to supplement the Indian labor force, which was gradually depleted by European disease and overwork. By 1655, when the English captured the island, there were no Arawaks left.

Until 1962 Jamaica was a Crown Colony of Great Britain but has now achieved full independence within the Commonwealth. The island's motto is, appropriately, "Out of Many, One People." The islanders are mostly of African or Afro-European descent, with a minority of British, Chinese, Indians, Portuguese, Germans, and people from other West Indian islands, all intermarried to create one people. the government is similar to that of Great Britain, the queen being represented by a governor-general appointed on the advice of the prime minister of Jamaica, who is elected. English is the official language, but with delightful adaptations, and you'll probably hear "Jamaica talk" when you take your *bankra* (basket) and *dunny* (money) to the market or have a meal of fish tea, rundown, and skyjuice.

Tourism has become the biggest industry in Jamaica, surpassing the traditional leaders, bauxite and aluminum.

The average Jamaican is friendly, and responds to a smile and a cheerful hello with a kindness that will almost overwhelm you. Of course, there are rogues in every country and common sense has to prevail when you travel, but most visitors find only friendliness and helpfulness in Jamaica.

In general, if you like people, you will like the Jamaicans. Don't call them natives, however. They feel it's insulting, and they are proud of just being called Jamaicans.

MONEY: Be careful! There are Jamaican dollars and there are U.S. dollars. Unless it is clearly stated, either in shops or when agreeing to a rate with a taxi driver or in a restaurant, always insist on knowing which dollar they are quoting. Actually, tourists are required to pay their bills in Jamaican dollars, written J$. However, shopkeepers and hotel owners still, in many cases, quote tourists prices in U.S. dollars. Jamaica adopted the policy of excluding U.S. currency from circulation so that the impact of two recent devaluations could be reflected in the economy of the island. For purposes of clarification, in this book prices quoted in Jamaican dollars will be given as J$, with the U.S. conversion in parentheses after that quotation. Otherwise, the dollar figures given are in U.S. currency. As of this writing, there is confusion regarding the value of the Jamaican dollar. Any comment made by me will likely be out of date by the time you actually reach Jamaica. At the time of research for this edition, a visitor could get about J$4.60 to $1 U.S. (J$1 equals about 22¢). But that rate has fluctuated greatly, and is certainly likely to continue upward or downward during the lifetime of this edition. However, to give you a rough idea of what certain services will cost, I will convert at the prevailing rate at the time of research. But remember to check with your bank or a Jamaican tourist office to find what the prevailing rate of exchange will be during your visit.

You should use your immigration card when making bank transactions and also when converting Jamaican dollars back into U.S. dollars.

Jamaican currency comes in different sizes: J$1, J$2, J$5, J$10, and J$20. Coins are 1¢, 10¢, 20¢, 25¢, and 50¢. There is no limit to the amount of foreign currency you can bring in, but it is illegal to import or export Jamaican currency. Duty-free shops, banks and hotels change money. But wherever you change money, get a currency receipt—you must present it when changing your surplus Jamaican dollars at the end of your stay. Both international airports have banks.

PRACTICAL FACTS: To ease your orientation to an often bewildering island, I have some important information you should know in advance of your arrival:

Airport Tax: On departure, you will be charged J$20 ($4.40). All air flights must be reconfirmed no later than 72 hours before departure.

Banks: Open from 9 a.m. to 2 p.m. Monday through Thursday, 9 a.m. to noon and 2:30 to 5 p.m. on Friday. In rural towns there is a slight difference in closing times, but you are safe between 9 a.m. and noon.

Camping: The **Jamaican Alternative Tourism, Camping, and Hiking Association (JATCHA)**, P. O. Box 216, Kingston (tel. 927-5409), will supply information about hiking in the beautiful mountainous regions of Jamaica, either by foot or bicycle. For information, you should write them. They furnish data about rawboned accommodations along the way, as well as a map showing campsites. It is suggested that you bring your own bicycle. All-inclusive adventure tours range in price from $35 to $80 per day.

Climate: Expect temperatures around 80° to 90° Fahrenheit on the coast. Winter is a little cooler. In the mountains, it can get as low as 40°. There is generally a breeze, which in winter is noticeably cool. The rainy periods are October to early November, and May to early June. Normally rain comes in short, sharp showers; then the sun shines.

Driving: As in other British-influenced countries, *you drive on the left.* Speed limits in town are 30 miles per hour; elsewhere, 50 mph. Gas costs J$9 ($1.98) per imperial gallon, payable only in Jamaican dollars—no credit cards are accepted. (The cost of gasoline may be higher by the time you visit.) Your own driver's license is acceptable.

Drugs: Hard drugs and *ganja* (marijuana) are illegal and imprisonment is the penalty for violation. Prescriptions are accepted only if issued by a Jamaican doctor. Hotels have doctors on call. If you need any particular medicine or treatment, bring evidence, such as a letter from your own doctor.

Electric Current: Most places have the standard voltage of 110, as in the U.S. However, some establishments operate on 220 volts, 50 cycles. If your hotel is on a different current from your U.S.-made appliance, ask for a converter.

Marriages: You can get a license after 48 hours' residence on the island, and then marry as soon as it can be arranged. You will need your birth certificates, and where applicable, divorce documents. Apply to the Ministry of Justic, Kingston, and then many Jamaican hotels will arrange the rest.

Nude Bathing: There are a number of hotels, clubs, and beaches, especially in Negril, which are signposted "Swimsuits Optional." Elsewhere, the law will not even allow topless sunbathing.

Passports: U.S. and Canadian residents do not need passports but must hold a return or ongoing ticket and proof of citizenship. Other visitors need passports, for a maximum stay of six months.

Room Tax: In summer the government imposes a room tax, ranging from $4 to $8 per room. This goes up in winter to $8 to $12. The higher price is, naturally, for the more deluxe and first-class hotels. Hotels sometimes also impose an energy tax.

Store Hours: These vary widely, but as a general rule most business establishments open at 8:30 a.m., closing at 5 p.m. (or in some places, earlier at 4:30 p.m.). Some shops are open on Saturday until noon.

Taking Pictures: Some Jamaicans don't like having their pictures taken, for various reasons. Ask permission first.

Telephone: All overseas calls outside your hotel incur a government tax of 50% over what the hotel will charge!

Time: In winter, Jamaica is on Eastern Standard Time. However, when the U.S. is on Daylight Saving Time, when it's 6 a.m. in Miami it's 5 a.m. in Kingston.

Tipping: A general 10% or 15% is expected in hotels and restaurants on occasions where you would normally tip. Some places add a service charge to the bill.

Water: It's safe to drink water from the tap at your hotel, as it is piped, filtered, and chlorinated.

MEET THE PEOPLE: Throughout the island, the Jamaican Tourist Offices in the various towns can arrange for visitors to be hosted by Jamaican families. More than 650 families are registered in the scheme with the Tourist Board, which keeps a list of their interests and hobbies. All you have to do is give the board a rough idea of your own interests, and they will arrange for you to spend the day with a similar family.

Once with them, you just go along with whatever they plan to do, sharing their life, eating at their table, joining them at a dinner party. You may end up at a beach barbecue, afternoon tea with the neighbors, or selling fruit at the roadside, working quietly in the garden, or just sitting and expounding theories, arguing, and talking far into the night.

If you have a particular interest—birds, butterflies, music, ham radio, stamp collecting, or spelunking (there are many caves to explore)—the Tourist Board will find you a fellow enthusiast. Many lasting friendships have been developed because of this unique opportunity to meet the people exactly as they are.

It is important to know that this service is entirely free. You need not even take your hostess a gift, but she will certainly appreciate a bunch of flowers after your visit. In Jamaica, apply at any of the tourist boards: 79-81 Knutsford Blvd., New Kingston (tel. 929-8070); Cornwall Beach, Montego Bay (tel. 952-4425); Visitor's Service Bureau in Negril (tel. 957-4243); Ocean Village Shopping Centre in Ocho Rios (tel. 974-2570); or at the City Centre Plaza in Port Antonio (tel. 993-3051).

FOOD AND DRINK: Because this is an island, there is great emphasis on seafood. Rock lobster is a regular dish on every menu, appearing grilled, thermidor, cold, hot. Codfish and akee is the national dish, a concoction of salt fish and a brightly colored vegetable that tastes something like scrambled eggs. Escaveche (marinated fish) is usually fried and then simmered in vinegar with onions and peppers. Curried mutton and goat are popular, as is pepperpot stew, all highly seasoned and guaranteed to reduce your body temperature.

Jerk pork is peculiar to country areas, where it is barbecued slowly over wood fires until crisp and brown. Apart from rice and peas (which are really red beans), usually served as a sort of risotto with added onions, spices, and salt pork, vegetables are exotic: breadfruit, imported by Captain Bligh in 1723 when he arrived aboard H.M.S. *Bounty;* callaloo, rather like spinach, used in pepperpot soup (not to be confused with the stew of the same name); cho-cho, served boiled and buttered or stuffed; and green bananas and plantains, fried or boiled and served with almost everything. Then there is pumpkin, which goes into a soup or is served on the side, boiled and mashed with butter.

Coconut water is a refreshing drink, especially when you stop by the roadside to have a local vendor chop the top from a fresh nut straight from the tree. Sweet potatoes appear with main courses, but there is also a sweet potato pudding made with sugar and coconut milk, flavored with cinnamon, nutmeg, and vanilla. You'll meet the intriguing *stamp and go,* salt fish cakes to eat as an appetizer; *fall back,* salty stew with bananas and dumplings; and *rundown,* mackerel cooked in coconut milk, often eaten for breakfast. For the really adventurous, *mannish water,* a soup made from goat offal and tripe, is said to increase virility. Patties—the best in the island are at Montego Bay—are another staple snack. Pastry filled with highly seasoned meat and breadcrumbs, to be eaten at any time of the day or night, is sold with boiled corn, roast yams, and roast salt fish at roadside stands, gas stations, and snack counters.

Rum punches are everywhere, and the local beer is Red Stripe. The island produces many liqueurs, the most famous being Tia Maria, made from coffee beans. Rumona is another good one to take home with you. Bellywash, the local name for lemonade, will supply the extra liquid you may need to counteract the heat of the tropics. Blue Mountain coffee is the best, but tea, cocoa, and milk are usually available to round off a meal.

REGGAE FESTIVAL: The annual Reggae festival, usually held the second week in August, also in Montego Bay, features Jamaican artists. Arrangements to atttend can be made by May of every year. Many local hotels are fully booked for the festival, so advance reservations are necessary. The Jamaican Tourist Boards can give information (see above) about tour packages and group rates for the festival.

GETTING THERE: The most popular routings to Jamaica are from New York or Miami. **Eastern** flies every day from Miami to both Kingston and Montego Bay (Eastern, of course, has many connections throughout the U.S. via Miami). **Air Jamaica,** the national carrier, flies to Jamaica from Atlanta, Los Angeles, Toronto, New York, Philadelphia, and Baltimore. **Air Canada** flies three times a week in high season to Kingston from Toronto, with connecting service from Montréal.

The single most popular routing is the **American Airlines** connection from New York, which departs daily to both Montego Bay and Kingston. The aircraft is usually a DC-10, which makes a brief stopover in Montego Bay before continuing to Kingston. Later in the day, the same aircraft reverses its path, returning to New York's JFK via Montego Bay.

A wide array of fares is available. The cheapest ones are contingent on the availability for the particular day of travel of whatever block of seats American has set aside for its promotional fares. At press time, round-trip high-season fares from New York to Kingston were as low as $275 for weekday travel (Monday through Thursday), or $295 at other times (Friday through Sunday). A limited number of these rock-bottom fares are available to the public only if reservations are made at least 14 days in advance and if the return half of the round-trip ticket is used within 3 to 21 days of the original departure date.

If travelers can live with the uncertainty of not knowing until the last minute if they will be on a certain flight, American also offers a limited quantity of similarly priced first-come, first-served seats to passengers who simply show up at the flight gate on the day of departure. This latter system, however, could be discontinued at any time.

If American's quota of inexpensive seats to Jamaica is filled by the time of your hoped-for departure date, it might be necessary to book a regular excursion ticket for which no advance reservations are necessary. From New York to Kingston in high season, the round-trip excursion fare is $463 (subject to change) for midweek travel and $508 for weekend travel. The prices of regularly scheduled excursion tickets in low season is substantially less expensive.

So many ticket options are available that only a call to an American Airlines ticketing agent (or else your travel agent) will clarify the exact price at the time of your intended departure.

It's important to remember that American, like most of the other major carriers, maintains a tour desk which can often arrange hotel accommodations for your trip as well as your flight. Because the major carriers book in such volume, you might save money this way than if you book hotels on your own at what is called "the rack rate."

GETTING AROUND: Many people like to see more of Jamaica than just their resort hotel. If so, I have the following suggestions for getting around the countryside:

By Air

The bulk of travelers to Jamaica, particularly tourists, enter Jamaica via Montego Bay. The island service is by **Trans-Jamaican Airlines Ltd.**, P.O. Box 218, Montego Bay (tel. 952-3418). The international **Air Jamaica** handles sales and provides information overseas. Trans-Jamaican flies between the major towns of the island. Sample prices are $45 from Montego Bay to Negril, $52 from Montego Bay to Ocho Rios, and $66 from Montego Bay to Port Antonio. Fares are reduced slightly in low season. Incidentally, there are two Kingston airports, which are connected by taxi. One is for domestic flights, the other for international. Car-rental facilities are only available at the international airport.

By Car

Jamaica is big enough and public transportation is unreliable enough that a car is not really a luxury but is almost a necessity if you plan to do any sightseeing beyond the confines of your hotel. Over the years, I have tried and recommended all the major car-rental firms. On my most recent trip, I used the **Budget Rent-a-Car** subsidiary at the Montego Bay airport. Budget maintains three locations in Jamaica—one at the Kingston International airport, one at Montego Bay airport, and one in downtown Ocho Rios.

Renting a car in Jamaica is easy, but there are several things you should be aware of before starting out. Drivers must be between the ages of 25 and 70 and must present their driver's license and a credit card when filling out the forms. Travelers without a credit card must pay a deposit of $500 in cash at the time of rental.

Budget's insurance policies declare that any driver is responsible for the first $500 of damage to the car, regardless of whether he or she has signed a collision damage waiver. (The potential liability is even greater with several other car-rental companies.) If a driver decides to purchase such a waiver, costing $6 per day, his or her eventual liability in the event of an accident will be limited to the first $500 damage. If the driver forgoes the waiver, the responsibility is limited to the first $2500 worth of damage.

Budget offers a wide variety of vehicles, mainly Japanese. Any rental is cheaper by the week, although daily rentals are also possible. The following prices apply to vehicles reserved at least two full business days in advance through Budget's toll-free reservation system. A Nissan Sunny, with manual transmission and a seating capacity of four, costs $216 per week, with each additional day costing an extra $36. Daily rentals of less than a week cost $41 per day. Unlimited mileage is included in all rates, and there is no government tax added. Automatic-transmission cars are also available: a Sunny costs $227 per week with this equipment, and extra days cost an additional $38. Daily rentals of less than a week cost $43 per day. An air-conditioned car with manual transmission costs $268 per week, with each extra day costing $45. Per-day rentals of less than a week are $51.

A clerk at Budget's toll-free reservations center will be glad to explain the rates to you in greater detail. The extended-hour toll-free number is 800/527-1700. Budget's rates for both rentals and insurance in Jamaica are substantially cheaper than those at Avis or Hertz. To compare prices before you start your trip, you can call **Hertz** toll free at 800/654-3131 or **Avis** toll free at 800/331-1212.

By Train

A leisurely sort of travel, but a marvelous way to see the country, is by rail. At each station, peddlers leap onto the train to sell their wares, jumping off at the last possible second as the train leaves the station. Expect to pay about J$10

($2.20) per mile for second-class rail travel, nearly J$20 ($4.40) per mile for first-class travel. The journey from Kingston to Montego Bay takes about 4½ hours, and there are two departures a day. Check at local stations to see when trains are expected to run.

By Bus

Both Kingston and Montego Bay have in-town buses, but you will find them slow, crowded, hot, and noisy, loaded with market produce and livestock as well as people. They make so many stops en route that the progress is slow, and they don't cover the entire island. The cost in town is about J$1 (22¢) per ten miles.

By Taxi

Kingston has taxis with meters, but not many of them work so agree on a price before you get in. In Kingston and the rest of the island, taxis are operated by JUTA, Jamaican Union of Travellers Association, and have the union's emblem on the side of the vehicle. All prices are controlled, and any local JUTA office will supply a list of rate. JUTA drivers do all the touring and guiding on the island. I've found them a pleasant, friendly, and, in the main, knowledgeable group of people, and good drivers. Most of the cabs are of U.S. origin, but they are old.

Bike, Moped, and Honda Rentals

These can be rented in Montego Bay, and you'll need a valid driver's license for anything mechanized. **Montego Bike Rentals,** 21 Gloucester Ave. (tel. 952-4984), rents Hondas for $35 per day, requiring a $100 deposit. Ten-speed bicycles cost only $15 per day. Ten-speed bicycles cost only $15 per day. Deposits are refundable if vehicles are returned in good shape. Mopeds can be rented at the **Holiday Inn (Rose Hall)** (tel. 953-2485) and at the **Americana Ocho Rios** (tel. 974-2150, ext. 1272).

THE SPORTING LIFE: If sports are important to your vacation, you may want to review the offerings of Jamaica before deciding on a particular resort. Sports are so spread out, and Jamaica so large, that it isn't feasible to go on a long day's excursion just to play golf, for example. The cost of most activities is generally the same throughout the island, except for golf, which is more expensive in Kingston.

Golf

In all the West Indies, Jamaica has the best courses. Montego Bay alone has four championship courses, including the newest one, **Rose Hall Intercontinental** (tel. 953-2650). Others include the challenging **Tryall** (tel. 952-5110), in Hanover, 12 miles from town, the Robert Trent Jones–designed **Half Moon** (tel. 953-2560), and the **Ironside Golf Club** (tel. 953-2800).

On the north coast, **Jamaica, Jamaica** (tel. 973-3435) has another 18-hole course.

In Kingston, check out **Constant Spring Golf Club** (tel. 924-1610), an 18-hole course in the foothills of the Blue Mountains, and **Caymanas Country Club** (no phone), in the midst of sugarcane fields.

In Mandeville, there's the 9-hole **Manchester Golf Club** (tel. 962-2403). Greens fees vary little. In season, expect to spend from $9 (U.S.) to $16 for

18 holes and from $8 to $15 in summer. Caddy charges are about $5 for 9 holes and anywhere from $6 to $10 for 18 holes. Rental motorized carts are usually available, costing from $15 to $20 a round, maybe more in Montego Bay at the more exclusive courses.

Water Sports

Water options for the sports lover proliferate throughout Jamaica, with many activities offered as part of all-inclusive packages by the island's major hotels. However, there are other well-maintained facilities for water sports not connected to the hotel offerings.

Jamaica has some of the finest diving waters in the world. The average diving depth ranges from 35 to 95 feet. Visibility is usually from 60 to 120 feet. Most of the diving is done on coral reefs, which are protected by underwater parks where fish, shells, coral, and sponges are plentiful. Experienced divers can also see wrecks, hedges, caves, dropoffs, and tunnels.

Tojo Water Sports, at the Trelawny Beach Hotel in Falmouth (tel. 954-2450), offers scuba-diving programs to the offshore coral reefs that are considered some of the most spectacular of the Caribbean. Johnny Wright and Steve McClure direct seven PADI-certified dive guides, four dive boats, and all the necessary equipment for either inexperienced or already-certified divers.

Guests of the Trelawny benefit from free introductory lessons and the availability of a free daily dive. Persons not registered at the hotel can sign up for supervised dives which cost $35 per tank, although the price goes down to $30 if you bring your own equipment. A two-dive package costs $45, while a package for experienced divers only of five two-tank dives is offered for $215. This is conducted partly offshore of the hotel and partly near the reefs at Ocho Rios. Night dives are also offered, and transportation is provided to all dive sites.

Trelawny beach also offers free snorkeling, Sunfish sailing, windsurfing, glass-bottomed boat rides, and tennis.

Horseback Riding

The best riding is in Ocho Rios, where **Prospect Plantation** (tel. 974-2058) provides horses and guides. Montego Bay has a number of stables in the area: the **Good Hope** (tel. 954-3289), inland from Falmouth at Trelawny, is the best.

Tennis

Most hotels have their own courts, many floodlit for night games. If your hotel does not have a court, expect to pay about $6 to $8 per hour at the local country club.

Deep-Sea Fishing

Port Antonio is perhaps the best center, with fine deep-sea fishing areas. Most major hotels have facilities. Charter rates for boat and tackle are around $210 for half a day, $420 for seven hours, for a party of four to six persons.

Water Sports

Waterskiing: It costs about $12 for a 20-minute ski run, and many hotels have training facilities. Apply locally.

A Sunfish: Many hotels and some public beaches have Sunfish sailboats for rent at about $10 per hour. Hotels with their own fleets will charge less.

Snorkeling: Equipment for snorkeling is available in many places, for $8 to $12 per day.

Windsurfing: Some hotels have boards for windsurfing available. Expect to pay about $35 for a day, including a basic lesson on the sport.

Many hotels offer some of the above facilities free to their guests. See separate entries for more detailed facilities and prices.

1. Kingston

Kingston, the largest English-speaking city in the Caribbean, is the capital of Jamaica, with a population of some 700,000 people living on the plains between Blue Mountain and the sea.

The buildings are a mixture of very modern, graceful old, and plain ramshackle. It's a busy city, as you might expect, with a natural harbor which is the seventh largest in the world. The University of the West Indies has its campus on the edge of the city. The cultural center of Jamaica is here, along with industry, finance, and government. Now covering some 40 square miles, the city was founded by the survivors of the 1692 Port Royal earthquake, and in 1872 it became the capital, superseding Spanish Town.

WHERE TO STAY: Kingston has accommodations in all price ranges, but I'll begin with—

The Leading Hotels

Security-conscious Kingston now provides all leading hotels with guards, not unlike the deluxe apartments in New York.

Wyndham Hotel New Kingston, 85 Knutsford Blvd., P.O. Box 112 (tel. 926-8232). One of the most dynamic of the new hotel chains has completely renovated what used to be a strictly commercial hotel in a suburb of Kingston, reopening officially early in 1985. It rises in an imposing mass of pink-colored stucco pierced with oversize sheets of tinted glass. Each unit has a white metal balcony, emphasizing to viewers the distinctive rose tint (the designers call it "Wyndham Red Rock") that is the trademark of the Wyndham chain. The $8-million property renovation added scores of improvements.

The first thing guests are likely to notice in the reception ar₃a, aside from the white marble floors, is the oak paneling and the most beautiful jungle mural in the country, set above the computerized desk where a staff of well-trained, uniformed clerks make check-in easy. On the premises is a gathering place called the Rendezvous Bar where live entertainment is presented in a setting of live plants and soft lights, and a disco called the Jonkanoo Lounge (see "Kingston After Dark," below).

The designers of the hotel included lots of extras. The air-conditioning capacity has been more than doubled in anticipation of a new generation of guests whose tastes have been honed by exposure to posh hotels elsewhere. The engineers have added an on-site generator, activated during the occasional city power failure. The hotel contains around 400 rooms, three restaurants, four bars, an Olympic-size swimming pool, floodlit tennis courts, a fully equipped health club, and all the amenities to make what was a commercial hotel into an inner-city resort.

Each of the bedrooms and suites contains cable TV. Units capable of accommodating from one to two persons are priced from $145 and $170 daily, while suites usually begin at $350 per night. An additional person can stay in any double room for an extra $25 per night, while children under 18 stay free in their parents' room. MAP can be arranged for an additional $50 per person per day. Use of the tennis courts is free daily until 4 p.m. after which they rent for $12 per hour.

For reservations in the U.S., call toll free 800/822-4200. In Canada, phone 800/631-4200.

Hotel Oceana, P.O. Box 986, corner of King Street and Ocean Boulevard (tel. 922-0920), is a modern 12-story structure overlooking Kingston Harbor and close to the cruise-ship piers, some 30 minutes from Norman Manley Airport and within easy walking distance of the Victoria Crafts Market and downtown Kingston. Its rooms go for $82 to $92 single daily, $92 to $102 double, all year, plus tax and service. An extra person in a room costs $19. For bed, breakfast, and an evening meal, you'll pay an extra $35 per person.

The hotel has many amenities: air conditioning, laundry and room service, cable and Telex facilities, hairdressing and barbershops, a drugstore, and a newsstand. The Oceana is a safe choice. It is used mainly by business people who need efficient service and good value for their money. The staff is impeccable; the food, mentioned later in "Where to Dine," is of good international standard. This hotel is not in a resort area, but it provides a number of recreational facilities. It has a swimming pool and health club, and arrangements are made for water activities and land sports. It is in a development area, but the hotel is unaffected, as it is surrounded by already-developed land. The Spanish Town Square, the hotel's cocktail lounge, is open until 1 a.m., and the Oceana Disco operates on Friday, Saturday, and Sunday nights, opening at 8 p.m.

Jamaica Pegasus, 81 Knutsford Blvd. (tel. 926-3690), is a 17-story modern hotel in New Kingston with accommodations for 700 guests. Each bedroom is air-conditioned and has its own private balcony and bath/shower. Rooms are pleasantly furnished, and studio and luxury suites are available on request. Rates year round range from $135 to $145 in a single, and $155 to $170 in a twin-bedded room. For breakfast and dinner, add $50 per person daily to the room tariff. (For dining, see the recommendations following.) At the rooftop restaurant, nightly entertainment is offered. The hotel has a swimming pool and a golf driving range, plus tennis and squash nearby.

The Courtleigh, 31 Trafalgar Rd. (tel. 926-8174), one of my favorite hotels in Kingston, is housed in a symmetrical, white-painted, two-story building that sprawls amid a flowering garden set back from the busy street. Jamaican owned, the establishment contains a covered reception area with no exterior walls, a plantation-inspired series of verandas and gardens, and extended balconied wings containing the pleasant, simple accommodations. The central core of all this is the flower-bordered pool area, sheltered from the suburbs outside by the hotel as well as by shrubs and trees which a team of gardeners works hard to maintain. Being here strongly evokes plantation living in the middle of Kingston.

The polite and charming staff, dressed in red waistcoats, black bow ties and black trousers, will usher you down open-air hallways to your comfortable room, opening in most cases onto a view of the flowering patio, the pool area, and the bar and restaurant. On the premises is a popular disco, Mingles (see "Kingston After Dark," below), and the recommended Plantation Restaurant (see "Where to Dine"). Year-round prices for the pleasant rooms, each of which has a modern veranda or balcony of its own, a private bath, air conditioning, and a phone, range from J$275 ($60.50) to J$300 ($66) for a single, from J$310 ($68.20) to J$325 ($71.50) for a double, depending on the accommodation.

Small Budget Hotels

Terra Nova Hotel, 17 Waterloo Rd. (tel. 926-2211), is a gem among small, independently run hotels. Built in 1924 as a wedding present for a young bride, the house has had a varied career. It was once the family seat of the Myers rum dynasty, and the birthplace and home of Christopher Blackwell, promoter of many Jamaican singers and musical groups, among which were Bob Marley and the Wailers and Millie Small. In 1959 the house was converted into a hotel, and, set in 2½ acres of well-kept gardens with a backdrop of greenery and mountains, is now considered one of the best small Jamaican hotels. There is a swimming pool behind the hotel.

You arrive at the colonial-style house by following a sweeping driveway, to be greeted in the cool reception area and led to your well-equipped, simply furnished, air-conditioned bedroom. Most of the 34 bedrooms are in a new wing. All have balconies or patios looking out onto the gardens. Tariffs are $75 daily in a single, $80 in a double, all year, plus service and tax.

Your à la carte breakfast is served on the balcony or in the dining room. Above the portico is a balcony roof bar. The Spanish-style dining room, a fairly recent addititon to the old building, with a stone floor, wide windows, and spotless linens, offers some of the best international food on the island (see "Where to Dine").

The **Indies Hotel,** 5 Holborn Rd. (tel. 926-2952), is set in one of the small side streets of New Kingston opening onto a flower garden. The pleasant, half-timbered building with double gables has a small reception area decorated with potted plants, a lounge, and a TV lounge. The bedrooms, restaurant, and bar are grouped around a cool patio, all spotless. Ike Shaw, a Canadian, and his wife, Jean, a Jamaican, have operated the hotel for some 17 years. They have built up a reputation among the locals for friendly atmosphere and good-quality, budget meals. Their fish and chips is renowned, although Jean claims that their specialty is pizza. They also serve steak with all the trimmings, and when they get fancy, prepare lobster thermidor.

The 16 rooms go for $18 to $34 daily in a single, $32 to $42 in a double. All have shower and toilet and are air-conditioned. Breakfast is J$5 ($1.10) to J$12 ($2.64) per person.

Four Seasons Hotel, 18 Ruthven Rd. (tel. 926-8805), is a nice old house with a colonial-style veranda along the front, looking onto mango trees and a pleasant wooded garden through which you drive. There is good car parking, and you enter through the columns of the veranda to the tiled reception area of this friendly hotel. The rooms are simple and air-conditioned, with telephones and private baths or showers. They rent for $34 to $42 daily for a single, $38 to $50 for a double. Breakfast is extra. There is an arrangement for swimming at one of the large hotels. The hotel has two bars (one inside, one out), and a TV lounge through which you reach the restaurant. A buffet lunch, consisting of a interesting selection of hot dishes, vegetable salads, and desserts, is available to both residents and nonresidents from Monday to Friday. Dinner is served to both hotel guests and outsiders also.

The **Tropical Inn Hotel,** 19 Cliveden Ave. (tel. 927-9917), is a white-walled apartment/hotel complex offering refuge to peace-loving guests in a section of the city called "uptown Kingston." The complex is clustered around a shallow swimming pool and an outdoor bar. On the premises is a popular disco called Scruplez (see "Kingston After Dark," below). Partially air-conditioned accommodations without kitchenettes rent for $55 daily in a single, $65 in a double. With a kitchenette and full air conditioning, a one-bedroom unit costs $85 and a two-bedroom accommodation goes for $120. All the rooms have color TV.

A Guest House

Wyncliff Guest House, 222 Mountain View Ave. (tel. 927-5553), near the National Stadium, charges $15 per person per night for bed and breakfast. The owner has nine rooms, each with bath or shower, in this small, neat, one-story house, surrounded by a well-kept garden. The bedrooms are at the back, none with air conditioning. Breakfast is served in your room. The house is on a busy road, with driveway parking only. No evening meals are served, and the nearest eating places are some five to ten minutes away.

On the Outskirts

Outside the town, in the St. Andrews Hills toward the Blue Mountain, is the **Hotel Casa Monte,** Old Stony Hill Road (tel. 942-2471), which has panoramic views over Kingston, the sea, and the mountains. The hotel offers 20 rooms, all with air conditioning and bathrooms. *In summer, standard rooms rent for $40 per night, going up to $52 in a superior, either single or double occupancy.* In winter, standard units cost from $44 a night, with superior accommodations going for $55, either single or double occupancy. The difference in the prices of the rooms is in the furnishings (stone floors or full carpeting) and in the view (sea or mountain).

There is a swimming pool, an attractive bar with live music on occasion, and drink service at the pool. In this nonresort area, the dining room provides good food. The chef's special is stuffed lobster, or grilled filet of snapper. The restaurant is open from noon to 2 p.m. for lunch and from 7 to 10 p.m. for dinner.

Farther up Blue Mountain, for back-to-nature buffs and backpackers, is **Whitfield Hall,** about six miles from Mavis Bank. Usually people drive to Mahogany Vale, leave their cars in the field of a friendly farmer, and walk or use a Land Rover for J$50 ($11) there or back. The last four miles are rough and steep. Whitfield Hall was originally an old coffee plantation house, and is the last inhabited house before the peak, some 4000 feet above sea level. It's a hostel, providing accommodations for some 30 persons, in twin-bedded rooms or those containing three or more beds. Blankets and linen are provided, but no personal items such as towels, soap, or food. There is a deep-freeze and a refrigerator as well as good cooking facilities. All water comes from the local freshwater spring, and all lighting is by gas lanterns (called Tilleys) or by kerosene lamps. Wood fires warm the hostel and its guests, for it gets cold in the mountains at night.

The charge for one night is $6 per person all year. You bring your own food and share the communal kitchen. You can stay here for one night, one week, or if you really want to get away from it all, for longer. Most visitors tend to aim for seeing the sunrise from the summit of Blue Mountain, which means getting up at around 2 to 3 a.m. to walk the additional 3402 feet to the summit along bridle paths through the forest. The route is clearly marked, and all you really need is a good flashlight and warm clothing to go with your hiking boots. It's a three-hour walk each way. It is possible to hire a mule or horse to make the jaunt, accompanied by a guide, for approximately J$50 ($11) round trip for the 13-mile journey.

It is quite possible to spend a week or more in the mountains, just walking to see the vast variety of flowers and trees, the largest number of different varieties of ferns in the world, to listen to the crickets, and to watch the birds. There are many trails, and the hostel has information on various routes to take. However, for those who are apprehensive (people have been lost in these mountains), it is possible to arrange for a guide, negotiable locally.

For reservations at the hostel, write to John Allgrove, 8 Armon Jones Crescent, Kingston 6 (tel. 922-4759), office; 927-0986, home). He has a brochure available, but send an International Reply Paid coupon if you write for one.

Staying at Port Royal

Morgan's Harbour Hotel, Beach Club and Marina (tel. 924-8464) has a holiday beach-club atmosphere. To get to Port Royal, you either take the ferry from Victoria Pier off Ocean Boulevard, Kingston, costing J$1 (22¢), or a taxi past the airport and along the quay. Boats are moored along the jetty, and the hotel grounds run down to the water. If you take the ferryboat, it will deposit you in Port Royal, about a two-minute taxi ride from the hotel. Also, the hotel operates twice-weekly ferryboats from the Victoria Pier directly to the hotel.

The marina was substantially upgraded a few years ago. It and its docking facilities are among the most modern and up-to-date in the Caribbean. Morgan's Harbour, in essence, is a complete complex of facilities for the visitor, member, boater, sports-minded devotee, restaurant or bar user, and outdoor types in general. It easily mixes an international clientele with local Jamaican members.

The accommodations are on ground level around a large seafront patio, which during the day is the hub of all activities, and the room count is expected to be expanded greatly during the lifetime of this edition. The rooms are well furnished with Jamaican-made carved mahogany furniture, large photomurals with pirate and flower themes, and floor coverings. *Room rates in summer are $48 in a single, $80 in a double.* Winter rates are $55 in a single and $90 in a double. A 10% service charge is added to each bill at checkout time. MAP can be arranged for an additional $22 per person. Each room is fully air-conditioned and contains a ceiling fan.

At the seafood restaurant, you either eat in an air-conditioned area or in the open air. The restaurant serves seafood and fresh fish, among other dishes. It is similar to such places in Fort Lauderdale or Marina del Rey.

At the bar, next to the jetty, the bartender makes a big boast: that he serves the "world's greatest fruit daiquiris." Here you can sit and watch the boats or look across to Kingston in the distance. The saltwater swimming area is roped off from the boat anchorage and is safe for all ages and abilities to swim in the clear, blue water. A constant cool breeze off the sea tempers the heat of the sun. This is an ideal place for children, as everything is centered around the main patio, and there is little chance of their wandering away.

During the evening, various entertainment is offered: local groups of dancers or singers, talks and slide shows on the history of the island, disco dancing. There is a friendly, relaxed atmosphere where everybody seems to know everybody else.

An overseas club membership costs about $30 and allows hotel guests to sign for use of any facilities at published costs and pay for them as part of the hotel bill at the end of a stay. Your card can be used by members of your family and by guests if they want to make use of the swimming facilities with you. You can also rent Sunfish for J$35 ($7.70) per hour, waterski for J$48 ($10.56) per half hour, or arrange scuba expeditions with an outside agency nearby. All club facilities, and they are extensive, are open to tourists. This includes bathhouses, swimming, waterskiing, sailing, boat tours to offshores cays, deep-sea fishing, diving, and jogging trails along the club's half-mile of waterfront property. A large membership clubhouse includes lounges, game rooms, bar facilities, and deluxe accommodations.

WHERE TO DINE: Kingston has a good range of places to eat, whether you're seeking stately meals in plantation houses, hotel buffets, or fast-food shops.

Blue Mountain Inn (tel. 927-3606) is about a 20-minute drive from downtown Kingston, an 18th-century coffee plantation house set on the slopes of Blue Mountain, surrounded by trees and flowers on the bank of the Mammee River. At night, fireflies add their lights to the stars while you relax on the verandas overlooking the river below and the floodlit forest beyond. The house is furnished with fine antiques, set off by the plain white walls. On cold nights, log fires blaze, and the dining room gleams with silver and sparkling glass under the discreet table lights. The inn is one of Jamaica's most famous restaurants, not only for food but for atmosphere and service. Men are required to wear jackets (ties are optional), but the effort is worth it and the cool night air justifies it. Women are advised to take a wrap.

For appetizers, you choose from akee quiche or the chef's pumpkin soup. Main dishes include roast rib of beef with Yorkshire pudding and horseradish, ocean sole filet, lobster thermidor, or beef Wellington. All are served with a selection of fresh vegetables.

Top off your meal with tropical fruit salad and cream, Tia Maria parfait, baked Alaska, crêpes suzette, or a more ambitious banana or pineapple flambé. The wine list includes European varieties together with local beverages. A complete meal costs about $30. Reservations are essential, as it is popular all year.

In Devon House, 26 Hope Rd., is the National Picture Gallery. Beside the lovely old house is the restaurant, the **Port Royal Grogg Shoppe** (tel. 926-3589), with its weathered swinging sign, open for lunch, dinner, morning coffee, and snacks. You can eat in one of the old outbuildings or on patios under the trees, in sight of the royal palms and the fountain in front of the main building. The terraces are called either "mango" or "mahogany."

Your meal will have a traditional Jamaican character, and the bar serves 11 different rum punches and 10 fruit punches, such as a tamarind fizz or a papaya (paw-paw) punch. Snacks include coffee and sandwiches. Lunch, from noon to 3 p.m., includes appetizers, among them a "tidbit" of jerk pork or a bowl of soup (perhaps Jamaican red pea—really bean—or pumpkin soup). The cost of the meal, ranging from J$40 ($8.80) to J$75 ($16.50), will depend on your selection, either a sandwich and soup or a complete hot meal. Main dishes include offerings such as Jamaican akee and salt fish, barbecued chicken, or steamed snapper. Also tasty is their unusual homemade ice creams made of local fruits such as soursop. Blue Mountain tea or coffee is also served, and a 10% service charge is added to all bills. The waiters, who are dressed like pirates, serve daily except Sunday from 9 a.m. to midnight.

Terra Nova Hotel Restaurant, 17 Waterloo Rd. (tel. 926-9334), in one of the choice small hotels of Kingston, welcomes an enthusiastic crowd of local business people and other dignitaries at mealtimes into a formal dining room. It's owned by Jamaican brothers, Peter and Pat Rousseau, who recently refurbished the restaurant's Hepplewhite chairs, terracotta walls, high ceilings, and lattice-bordered windows. The palatial dining room was at one time the family headquarters of a large private home. The grounds once included stables, but acres of land and buildings have gradually been sold off to accommodate the encroaching sprawl of Kingston. Today the grandeur of the portico, the elaborate moldings of the hotel reception area, and the restaurant are souvenirs of the affluent one-time owners.

The dining room serves a combination of international and Jamaican specialties, with emphasis on fish and shellfish dishes. These include snapper, sweet-and-sour conch, kingfish, curried lobster, prime rib of beef, filet au poivre, sirloin Café de Paris, and many other items. Complete lunches cost from around J$65 ($14.30), while dinners average $J100 ($22) per person, wine not included. Every day a fixed-price business lunch is served for J$35 ($7.70). On Friday at lunchtime, one of the most popular dining choices is the seafood buffet, served from 12:30 to 2:30 p.m., costing J$50 ($11).

Rumours, 3 Dumfries Rd. (tel. 929-7904). From the outside this looks more like a well-designed modern house than the most popular and most informally sophisticated restaurant in Kingston, but that, by most accounts, is just what it is. The building, which now has well-varnished wood trim, lots of exposed brick and stucco, and a sometimes-obscured sign in front, at one time housed one of the sleaziest go-go bars in town, but today the new ownership has brought about a dramatic change. The charming and hardworking Colin Machado (who is pure Jamaican, although his grandparents were Cuban) is the vibrant force behind Rumours. The mango-shaded back terrace attracts Italian yachtsmen, European aristocrats, Old Yankee millionaires, and just plain folks who happen to be in town. There is also always a healthy dollop of the trendiest and most attractive Jamaicans on the island. In fact people come here in such numbers that it is sometimes necessary to post a security guard at the front gate.

Many visitors appreciate the place for the "informally formal" dining room set in one of the beautifully decorated side rooms, where the decor is reminiscent of an updated Louis XIV salon. Specialties are pepperpot soup, conch chowder, and an array of seafood which may include grouper, dolphin, red snapper, stuffed lobster Rumour style (an old family recipe), shrimp tempura, and shrimp florentine. Full sit-down dinners cost around J$70 ($15.40), while a full lunch goes for J$40 ($8.80). Reservations are necessary. Barbecues are held on Wednesday, Thursday, Friday, and Saturday outdoors, costing from J$18 ($3.96) to J$25 ($5.50), depending on what you order.

No one will stop you from showing up just for a drink at the rectangular bar or for the backyard concerts and buffets, where sometimes as many as 25 musicians at a time will play, usually on a Thursday night. Every evening after 10:30 people show up, depending on the night, for the live music or the pulse of the disco, which goes on until early in the morning. Red Stripe beer costs about J$5 ($1.10), while a scotch and soda goes for about J$12 ($2.64).

Rumours, which opened in mid-1984, is about a 15-minute drive from downtown Kingston and may be difficult to find without detailed directions or the help of a taxi.

The **Plantation Terrace,** the Courtleigh Hotel, 31 Trafalgar Rd. (tel. 926-8174), is a pleasant place to dine and escape from the traffic of Kingston. Meals are served under a covered parapet lined with tropical plants near an outdoor cabana-style poolside bar. Seated on green-painted iron armchairs you'll enjoy à la carte breakfasts, Sunday-night barbecues, Wednesday Jamaican evenings, and popular lunches and dinners. The other guests may include a scattering of business people as well as the employees of the American and Australian consulates nearby.

The uniformed staff will serve such specialties as pepperpot soup, lobster thermidor, shrimp sauté, filet of fish including red snapper and grouper, chicken suprême, chicken gumbo, pork piccata, surf and turf, chicken Cordon Bleu, baked crab backs, and many other dishes which vary according to the culinary culture being emphasized on a particular evening. There's even an occasional Chinese specialty, as well as Jamaican dishes of akee and codfish, hog's tail, and stewed beef served on Wednesday. Complete dinners begin at J$35 ($7.70), while lunches are slightly less expensive. Full Jamaican breakfasts are served even to nonresidents for J$12 ($2.64). The restaurant, which sometimes has live music in the evening, is open seven days a week.

The **Orchid,** 3 Waterloo Ave. (tel. 926-8202), is in a former aristocratic house whose grounds are covered with an array of orchids. The 150 varieties would fascinate any botanist. They, plus many other tropical plants, entwine themselves with the breezy lattices that shelter this garden restaurant from the city around it. About 150 years ago a wealthy planter built the great house as his family quarters, but that was long before Ohio-born Michelle Swann opened her popular restaurant.

The more perceptive guests discover that the orchid hand-painted on the daily menu matches the color of the blossoms placed on the candlelit tables. Full lunches, priced at upward of J$48 ($6.16), may include such items as "orchid burgers," sandwiches, soups, an orchid pizza with akee, or a fruit plate "exotica." Dinner is more expensive, priced from J$90 ($19.80), and could include daily specials such as butterfly shrimp, chicken tetrazzini, fettuccine, filet mignon, bread pudding, and carrot cake.

The ideal way to spend an evening here is to dine first in the pavilion in the front garden, then adjourn to the piano bar inside. There, surrounded by cut orchids on each table, unusual paintings by Edna Manley (the mother of the former prime minister of Jamaica), and a florid pastel color scheme, you'll enjoy tall drinks and music from the massive, carved Empire-style piano. Live music is presented in the bar on Wednesday through Sunday from 7 to 11 p.m. On Thursday night guests are encouraged to sing along. One night one of the patrons was Brooke Shields, who scarcely made a ripple next to the members of the foreign embassies and the fashion designers who accompanied her.

The **Jamaica Pegasus Hotel,** 81 Knutsford Blvd. (tel. 926-3690), offers gourmet dining in its rooftop Talk of the Town restaurant from an à la carte menu which features an excellent four-course meal at about J$100 ($22). Discreet, attentive service is provided. Main dishes include red snapper in lime butter or grilled lobster in garlic butter, preceded by smoked salmon or pepperpot soup. Le Pavillon features nouvelle cuisine and is open Monday to Friday from noon to 3 p.m. For something light, enjoy snacks, high tea, cakes, or pastries in the Café Orangerie at the Pavillon, open Monday to Friday from 11 a.m. to 8 p.m. In short, there's something to suit everyone's taste.

The **Surrey Tavern,** beside and part of the Jamaica Pegasus (tel. 926-3690), with its own entrance, is a pub-style place with wooden tables and chairs, low lighting, and a long, wood-paneled bar in the English tradition. Lunchtime, noon to 3 p.m., a cold pub buffet is served, featuring a daily hot special. Meals cost from J$5.45 ($11.99). Enjoy a long glass of cold draft beer while tapping to the jazz beat of Sonny Bradshaw and his friends, while Tuesday and Thursday evening beginning at 8:30 p.m. The pub is closed on Sunday.

Fort Charles Restaurant, in the Oceana Hotel (tel. 922-0920), is open seven days a week from 7 a.m. until 11 p.m. You can use it as a coffeeshop-style place for a quick snack or else as a more formal restaurant. Lunches cost from J$50 ($11). You can order a cold roast beef open-face sandwich. There is also barbecued chicken, and the more exotic lobster thermidor, seafood Newburg, or rock lobster. From 7 p.m., the dinner menu includes a variety of appetizers, soups, steaks, and other meat dishes in addition to the daytime menu. Tenderloin tips with mushrooms is a specialty, as are a filet mignon with madeira sauce and lobster and shrimp diablo. Their steaks are called the juiciest in town. Depending on your selection of a main course, dinner prices will begin at J$80 ($17.60) and range upward.

The **Indies Pub and Grill,** 8 Holborn Rd. (tel. 926-2952), was designed around a garden terrace which on hot nights is the best place to sit. Of course, you can always go into the inner rooms, which are haphazardly but pleasantly decorated with caribou horns, tortoise shells, half-timbered walls, an aquarium sometimes stocked with baby sharks, and even a Canadian moosehead. The establishment offers a full sandwich menu at lunchtime. In the evening you can enjoy grilled lobster, fish and chips, barbecued quail, chicken Kiev, or roast beef. You can eat here for about J$45 ($9.90) every day of the week from 11 a.m. to 1 a.m.

WHAT TO SEE: Even if you're staying at one of the resorts, such as Montego Bay or Ocho Rios, you may want to come into Kingston for sightseeing, and for visits to nearby Port Royal and Spanish Town.

Devon House, 26 Hope Rd., was built in 1881 by George Stiebel, a Jamaican who, after mining in South America, became one of the first black millionaires in the Caribbean. A striking building of classical style, the house has been restored to its original beauty by the Jamaican National Trust. The grounds contain craft shops, boutiques, and a museum of African art and history. The main house also displays furniture of various periods and styles. The former coach house is now the Port Royal Grogg Shoppe (described earlier).

Admission to Devon House is free, but you are expected to buy a catalog of the exhibits. The house is open daily from 10 a.m. to 5 p.m., except Sunday.

Almost next door to Devon House are the sentried gates of **Jamaica House,** residence of the prime minister, a fine, white-columned building set well back from the road.

Continuing along Hope Road, at the crossroads of Lady Musgrave Road and King's House Road, turn left and you will see a gate on the left with its own personal traffic light. This leads to **King's House,** the official residence of the governor-general of Jamaica, the queen's representative on the island. The gracious residence, set in 200 acres of well-tended parkland, is open to view from 10 a.m. to 5 p.m., Monday to Friday. The secretarial offices are housed next door in an old wooden building set on brick arches. In front of the house is a gigantic banyan tree in whose roots, legend says, *duppies* (as ghosts are called in Jamaica) take refuge when they are not living in the cotton trees.

On Old Hope Road, behind the Colleges of Arts, Science, and Technoloy, are the **Hope Botanical Gardens** occupying 200 acres on the grounds of the Hope Sugar Estate. It was one of the three largest estates in this area. The others are King's House and the University of the West Indies. The aqueduct constructed in 1759 still brings water to the gardens and augments the city's supply. The pride of the gardens is the fine orchid house containing specimens of some 200 native Jamaican species. There are a cactus garden and more than 600 different types of trees, including an impressive palm avenue, flowering trees, fruit trees, and creepers. For those interested in the plants, a guide is available to escort you and answer your questions. The guide's services are free, as is admission to the gardens, but it is the practice to tip.

A quick tour will take about an hour. You may find that you prefer to wander along the tree-lined paths among the flowers and listen to the incessant chirping of the birds hidden in the leaves. A new fountain has been constructed just to the front of the Palm Avenue, and several new picnic structures have been set up.

Coconut Park (tel. 927-7552), also in Hope Gardens, is next door. It's a "funland" and canteen owned by the Ministry of Agriculture and leased to two charities, the Polio Foundation and the Jamaica Association for Mentally Handicapped Children. You can usually buy fresh coconut and enjoy the refreshing milk. A small zoo at the end contains monkeys and snakes, to mention a few of the inmates. There are nine rides, costing from 35¢, and the gates are open from noon to 5 p.m. The canteen is open from 10 a.m. to 5 p.m. daily.

Between Old Hope Road and Mona Road, a short distance from the Botanic Gardens, is the **University of the West Indies,** built in 1948 on the Mona Sugar Estate, the third of the large estates in this area. Ruins of old mills, storehouses, and aqueducts are jostled by the modern buildings on what must be the most beautifully situated campus in the world. The chapel, an old sugar factory building, was transported stone by stone from Trelawny and rebuilt on the campus close to the old sugar factory, the remains of which are well preserved and give a good idea of how sugar was made in slave days.

The **National Stadium,** Briggs Park, of which Jamaica is justly proud, has a magnificent aluminum statue of Arthur Wint, national athlete, at the entrance. The stadium is used for such activities as soccer, field sports, and cycling, and in

1966 was the site of the Commonwealth Games. Beside the stadium is the **National Arena,** used for indoor sports, exhibitions, and concerts, and there is an Olympic-size pool for water sports. Admission prices vary according to activities.

In downtown Kingston, if you go north on King Street, you come to Upper King Street and **National Heroes Park,** formerly known as George VI Memorial Park. This was the old Kingston race course. An assortment of large office blocks, including the offices of the prime minister and various ministries, overlooks the park and the statues of Simón Bolívar, and of George Gordon and Paul Bogle, martyrs of the Morant Bay revolt. Sir Donald Sangster, Norman Manley, and Alexander Bustamente, national heroes of Jamaica, are buried here.

Just north of Heroes Park, on Marescaux Road, is **Mico College** (tel. 929-5260), for "lady" training. Lacy Mico, a rich London widow, left her fortune to a favorite nephew on the condition that he marry one of her six nieces. He did not, and the inheritance was invested, the interest being used to ransom victims of the Barbary pirates. With the end of piracy in the early 19th century, it was decided that the capital would be devoted to founding schools for newly emancipated slaves, and, among others, Mico College was established.

Running between National Heroes Park and the harbor is the **Institute of Jamaica,** 12 East St., which is open from 9 a.m. to 5 p.m. The institute, founded in 1879, has as its main functions the fostering and encouragement of development of culture, science, and history in the national interest. Among the divisions of institute responsibility are museums, the National Art Gallery, a cultural center for training in the fine arts, a research center, the national library (see below), and a large natural history museum with examples of most types of the island's indigenous animals and plants.

The **National Library of Jamaica** (formerly the West India Reference Library), Institute of Jamaica, 12–16 East St. (tel. 922-0620), a storehouse of the history, culture, and traditions of Jamaica and the Caribbean, is the finest working library for West Indian studies in the world. It has the most comprehensive, up-to-date, and balanced collection of materials, including books, photographs, maps, and prints, to be found anywhere in the Caribbean. Of special interest to visitors are the regular exhibitions which attractively and professionally highlight different aspects of Jamaica and West Indian life.

Tuff Gong, 56 Hope St. (tel. 927-7103), is said to be the most visited sight in Kingston, although unless you're a Bob Marley fan, it may not mean much to you. The beige clapboard house with its garden and high surrounding wall was Marley's home and recording studio until his death. Since then, its function has changed several times. It contains rehearsal space for local musicians trying to develop the musical ideas Marley made famous to reggae lovers around the world. By the time you visit, some other use may be initiated.

If you want a glimpse of the house, you pass through a heavily guarded iron gate where you describe your purpose in coming. Entrance is (technically) free. It's open Monday through Friday from 8 a.m. to 5 p.m.

SHOPPING: Downtown Kingston, the old part of the town, is centered around Victoria Park, a walled, nondecript park of little interest, overpowered by the bustling main shopping area of **King Street** and by the heavy, fast-moving traffic on all four sides. King Street runs north from the harbor.

Here you will find covered walkways, with peddlers at small stands selling anything from cooked shrimp and melon slices to cool drinks, cigarettes, chocolates, fruit, matches, and anything else they can find a buyer for. The sidewalks are shaded from the sun by light roofs from which hang a variety of intriguingly worded advertisements and swinging signs: Hanna's Hub, Ready-Made Dresses; Golly Trotters, and Garment People; Buzzers Impossible, Closing-Down Sale (which has been going on for years); Cosmotologist Hair-Stylist; Men's Shop 79½.

Cool arcades lead off from the main street, but everywhere there is a teeming mass of people going about their business. There are some beggars and the inevitable salesmen who sidle up and offer "hot stuff, man," frequently highly polished brass lightly dipped in gold and offered at high prices as real gold. The hucksters do accept a polite but firm "no," but don't let them keep you talking or you'll end up buying. They are very persuasive!

On this street are the General Post Office, the Law Courts, and the bus terminal.

Sangster's Old Jamaica Spirits, 17 Holborn Rd. (tel. 926-8888), has a full array of unusual rum-based liqueurs available in this well-scrubbed factory outlet on a back street of Kingston. The entrance isn't well marked, but once you enter the showroom, you know from the hundreds of bottles on display that you're in a rum lovers' mecca. The prices vary, based on the quality and size of the container, not on the contents. You can pay from J$18 ($3.96) to J$60 ($13.20) for such tempting flavors as coconut rum (my personal favorite), coffee-orange liqueur, pimiento dram, Blue Mountain coffee liqueur, and Old Jamaica 100 proof. The store is open Monday to Friday from 8:30 a.m. to 4:30 p.m. There's a large trolley filled with samples of the various rums which you can sample from small paper cups before you buy.

Kingston Crafts Market, at the west end of Harbour Street, is a large, covered area of small stalls individually owned, reached through such thoroughfares as Straw Avenue, Drummer's Lane, and Cheapside. All kinds of island crafts products are on sale: wooden plates and bowls, trays, ashtrays, and pepperpots made from mahoe, the national wood of the island. Straw hats, mats, baskets are also on display. Batik shirts and cotton shirts with gaudy designs are sold. Banners for wall decoration are inscribed with the Jamaican coat-of-arms, and wood masks often have elaborately carved faces. Apart from being a good place to buy worthwhile souvenirs, the market is where you can learn the art of bargaining and ask for a *brawta,* a free bonus. Only pay around one-half to two-thirds of the asking price, since to the stallholder the bargaining is half the fun and is expected. Don't forget to take your *dunny* (money) with you.

SIGHTS IN THE ENVIRONS: Not far from Kingston are two centers for sightseeing worth a visit—Port Royal and Spanish Town.

PORT ROYAL

From West Beach Dock, Kingston, a J$1 (22¢) ferry ride of 20 to 30 minutes will take you to Port Royal, or you can drive west instead of east along the Palisadoes from Kingston's international airport, and about 13 miles between sea-pounded white beaches and saltwater mangrove swamps.

Port Royal, once the island's capital, conjures up pictures of swashbuckling pirates led by Henry Morgan, swilling grog in harbor taverns. This was once one of the largest trading centers of the New World, with a reputation of being the wickedest city on earth (Blackbeard stopped here regularly on his Caribbean trips). But the whole thing came to an end at 11:43 a.m. on June 7, 1692, when a third of the town disappeared under water as the result of a devastating earthquake. Nowadays, Port Royal, with its memories of the past, has been designated by the government for redevelopment as a tourist destination.

As you drive along the Palisadoes, you arrive first at **St. Peter's Church.** It's usually closed, but you may persuade the caretaker, who lives opposite, to open it if you want to see the silver plate, said to be spoils captured by Henry Morgan from the cathedral in Panama. In the ill-kept graveyard is the tomb of one Lewis Galdy, a Frenchman swallowed up and subsequently regurgitated by the 1692 earthquake.

You next arrive at the gates of the **Police Training Depot,** where the constable on duty will record your name and purpose. When passage is permitted, you follow the road across the edge of the parade ground to the entrance to **Fort Charles,** the only remaining one of Port Royal's six forts. It has withstood attack, earthquake, fire, and hurricane. Built in 1656 and later strengthened by Morgan for his own purposes, the fort was expanded and further armed in the 1700s, until its firepower boasted more than 100 cannons, covering both the land and the sea approaches. After subsequent earthquakes and tremors, the fort ceased to be at the water's edge and is now well inland. For a few short weeks in 1779, Horatio Nelson was commander of the fort and trod the wooden walkway inside the western parapet as he kept watch for the French invasion fleet.

Giddy House, once the Royal Artillery storehouse, is another example of what earth movements can do. Walking across the tilted floor is an eerie and disturbing experience.

On the land side of the fort is the **Old Naval Hospital,** which now houses the **Archaeological Museum and Research Centre.** This building was completed in 1818 and is the oldest cast-iron prefabricated building in the western hemisphere. It contains many artifacts unearthed from digs and underwater searches around Port Royal, including a watch which had stopped at the moment of the 1692 earthquake, now in pieces, but totally authentic; a Chinese porcelain madonna, of which only three exist in the world, recovered from the sea; Spanish armor; slave shackles; and much weaponry, together with models and descriptive tableaux of the Port Royal of the past.

Admission to the upstairs museum is gained by ringing the 19th-century bell for the guide. You can see such things as Prince Henry's Polygon Battery, the Old Coaling Wharf, the Jail House, and the Victoria and Albert Battery complex, not to mention the Chocolata Hole.

Spanish Town

From 1662 to 1872 Spanish Town was the capital of the island. Originally founded by the Spaniards as Villa de la Vega, it was sacked by Cromwell's men in 1655 and all traces of papism were obliterated. The English cathedral, surprisingly retaining a Spanish name, **St. Jago de la Vega,** was built in 1666 and rebuilt after being destroyed by a hurricane in 1712. As you drive into the town from Kingston, the new cathedral, built in 1714, catches your eye, with its brick tower and two-tiered wooden steeple, which was not added until 1831. As the cathedral was built on the foundation and remains of the old Spanish church, it is half-English, half-Spanish, showing two definite styles, one Romanesque, the other Gothic.

Of cruciform design and built mostly of brick, the cathedral is historically one of the most interesting buildings on the island. The black and white marble stones of the aisles are interspersed with ancient tombstones, and the walls are heavy with marble memorials which are almost a chronicle of Jamaica's history, dating back as far as 1662. Episcopalian services are held regularly on Sunday at 7 and 10:30 a.m. and at 6:30 p.m., sometimes conducted by the bishop of Jamaica, whose see this is.

Beyond the cathedral, turn right and two blocks along you will reach Constitution Street and the **Town Square.** This delightful little square is surrounded by towering royal palms. On each side of the square is one perfectly designed building, creating what has been described as the finest Georgian square in the western hemisphere.

On the west side is **King's House,** gutted by fire in 1925 and not as yet restored because no plans, drawings, or designs of the original have been found. This was the residence of the governor-general, and many celebrated guests, among them Lord Nelson, Admiral Rodney, Captain Bligh of H.M.S. *Bounty* fame, and King William IV, have stayed here.

Behind the house is the **Jamaica People's Museum of Craft and Technology,** open daily from 10 a.m. to 5 p.m. The garden contains examples of old farm machinery, an old water mill wheel, a hand-turned sugar mill, a coffee pulper, an old hearse, and a fire engine. An outbuilding contains a museum of crafts and technology, together with a number of smaller agricultural implements. In the small archeological museum are old prints, models (including one of King's House based on a written description), and maps of the town's grid layout from the 1700s. For information, phone 922-0620.

On the north side of the square is the Rodney Memorial, perhaps the most dramatic of the buldings on the square, commissioned by a grateful assembly to commemorate the victory in 1782 of Baron George Rodney, English admiral, over the French fleet, which saved the island from invasion.

Opposite the Rodney Memorial is the **Court House,** the most recent of the four buildings. The court occupies the gound floor, and when in session, overflows onto the pavement and road, an animated throng of court attendants, defendants, witnesses, and spectators, all apparently accompanied by relatives and friends.

The final side of the square, the east, contains the most attractive building, the **House of Assembly,** with a shady brick colonnade running the length of the ground floor and above it a wooden pillared balcony. This was the stormy center of the bitter debates for Jamaica's governing body. Now the ground floor is the parish library, and council officers occupy the upper floor, along with the Mayor's Parlour.

The streets around the old Town Square contain many fine Georgian town houses intermixed with tin-roofed shacks of dubious durability. Nearby is the market, so busy in the morning you will find it difficult, almost dangerous, to drive through. It provides, however, a colorful and bustling scene of Jamaican life.

Driving to Spanish Town from Kingston on the A1 (Washington Boulevard), at Central Village you come to the **Arawak Museum,** on the right. The entrance appears to lead to a quarry, but don't be put off. Drive down to the museum, a hexagonal building on the site of one of the largest Arawak settlements in the island. It is open Monday to Friday from 10 a.m. to 5 p.m. The small, well-planned museum contains drawings, pictures, and diagrams of Arawak life, plus old flints and other artifacts which help you to understand the early history or prehistoric period of Jamaica. Smoking of tobacco seems to have been a habit even in 1518, when Arawaks were recorded as lighting hollow tubes at one end and sucking the other. The visitor can also see signs of an original Arawak settlement at White Marl, around the museum building.

KINGSTON AFTER DARK: There are safer places to be. Use caution when going out.

Nightspots

The **Red Hills Strip** in downtown Kingston has a number of nightclubs, all of which I make it a point to avoid.

The **Jonkanno Lounge,** Wyndham Hotel New Kingston, 85 Knutsford Blvd. (tel. 926-8282), is within the walls of one of Kingston's recently upgraded hotels. This glamorous disco thrives on the friendly rivalry between the batteries of synchronized lights and the rhythms from recently released music. Entrance is free during the daily happy hour, lasting from 5 to 7 p.m. After that, there's a cover charge of J$12 ($2.64) for singles and J$18 ($3.96) for couples on weeknights, when recorded disco is *de rigueur.* On Friday and Saturday when the music is live, singles are charged J$18 ($3.96) and couples pay J$24 ($5.28).

Mingles Disco, Courtleigh Hotel, 31 Trafalgar Rd. (tel. 926-8174), is set into the innards of the hotel at the far end of the reception area. This popular disco is furnished with a simple dark-grained decor of movable tables, parquet floors, and large expanses of both bar space and dancing areas. Residents of Kingston sometimes pour in here for the live concerts that are held every weekend. On other evenings, disco is featured. There's no cover charge. Red Stripe beer costs around J$4 (88¢). On weekdays the disco and bar are open from 5 p.m. to 2 a.m. and on Saturday from 8 p.m. to 2 a.m. It's closed Sunday.

Rumours, 3 Dumfries Rd. (tel. 929-7904), one of my favorite restaurants in Kingston, also attracts an enthusiastic, attractive, and alert crowd of supertrendies every evening for live music or disco. The type of entertainment varies from steel band to reggae concerts to recorded music. What's certain is that if anyone in the music or yachting business is in town for an evening, he or she may turn up for a late-night drink at this unusual house on a quiet street about 15 minutes from downtown Kingston. You can phone Colin Machado, the savvy and friendly owner, for news on what's going on for any particular night. Musical evenings, especially Thursday, have been known to draw huge numbers of jazz lovers from around the capital. Red Stripe beer costs J$5 ($1.10) and scotch is around J$12 ($2.64). For more information, see "Where to Dine," above.

Scruplez Disco, 19 Cliveden Ave. (tel. 927-9917), attracts a middle-class Jamaican clientele to its second-story interior. To get there, you pass through the garden-style Tropical Inn Hotel. Disco lovers can select a place at the long curving bar or on one of the beige naugahyde banquettes which are clustered tightly together around the room. A J$12 ($2.64) cover charge applies only to people who enter after 9 p.m. except on Saturday when the charge is levied all night long. A Red Stripe beer costs around J$5 ($1.10). This disco opened in 1984.

Live Theater

Kingston is called the cultural heart of the West Indies. There are several theaters, presenting live performances: **Ward Theatre** on North Parade (tel. 922-0318), **Little Theatre** on Tom Redcam Drive near the National Stadium (tel. 926-6129), the **Barn** on Norwood Avenue off Oxford Road (tel. 926-6469), and the **Creative Arts Centre** at the University of the West Indies (tel. 927-7546 or 927-0746). All stage local or imported plays and musicals, light opera, and revues. You may be fortunate enough to catch a performance by the Jamaica National Dance Theatre or the Jamaica Folk Singers, whose vivid and spontaneous performances show the true Jamaican folk culture.

Most entertainment of this sort is listed in the daily press, along with one-time attractions and sporting activities.

2. Port Antonio

Port Antonio is a seaport on the northeast coast of Jamaica, 63 miles from Kingston, where Brooke Shields filmed *The Blue Lagoon.* It has been called the Jamaica of 100 years ago. In seasons, Port Antonio has long drawn the titled and the wealthy, those European royalty with titles of duchesses and barons, along with an assortment of film stars, such as Bette Davis and Ginger Rogers.

To reach it from the capital, you have a choice between taking the A4 road through Port Morant and up the east coast, or driving north on the A3 through Castleton and approaching along the north coast, where Jamaica's tourist industry started. In other days, visitors arrived by banana boat and stayed at the Titchfield Hotel (now a school) in a lush, tropical part of the island unspoiled by gimmicks. The small, bustling town of Port Antonio is like many on the island: both clean and untidy, with sidewalks around a market filled with vendors; tin-roofed shacks competing with old Georgian and modern brick and concrete buildings; lots of people busy shopping, talking, laughing, and some just loafing, others sitting and playing Dominoes, loudly banging the pieces down on the table, which is very much part of the game.

The market is a place to browse among local craftwork, spices, and fruits. Captain Bligh landed here in 1793 with the first breadfruit plants, and Port Antonio claims that the ones grown in this area are the best on the island. Visitors still arrive by water, but now it's in cruise ships which moor close to Navy Island, and the passengers come ashore just for the day.

Navy Island and the old Titchfield Hotel were owned for a short time by film star Errol Flynn. The story is that after suffering damage to his yacht, he put into Kingston for repairs, visited Port Antonio by motorbike, fell in love with the area, and in due course acquired Navy Island, some say in a gambling game. Later, he either lost or sold it and bought a nearby plantation, Comfort Castle, stilled owned by his widow, Patrice Wymore, who spends most of her time there and hopes to open a museum honoring Flynn (refer to "What to See," below). He was much loved and admired by the Jamaicans and was totally integrated into the community. They still talk of him in Port Antonio, especially the men, who refer to his womanizing and drinking skills in reverent tones.

WHERE TO STAY: Trident Villas and Hotel, P.O. Box 119 (tel. 993-2602), is about 2½ miles east along the coast toward Frenchman's Cove. This interesting hotel complex, rebuilt after hurricane damage, is a good all-year bet for those who want a quiet, relaxing Jamaican holiday, away from the more publicized tourist areas of the north and northwest coasts. The main building is furnished with many antique reproductions, indigenous flowers decorate the cool lobby, and there is a small boutique owned, incidentally, by Patrice Wymore Flynn.

After checking in, you will be conducted to your room by a cheerful uniformed porter, through gardens bright with flowers and filled with the screech of peacocks—which fly up and roost on the roofs, pick their way among the parked cars, and are so tame they come and demand food.

Your room will be in a studio cottage reached by a pathway through the tidy gardens. You have your own cottage key. A large bedroom with ample sitting area opens onto a private patio with nothing between you and the sea except grass and a low stone wall. All cottages have their own bathrooms with tub, shower, and toilet. There is plenty of storage space. Jugs of ice and water are constantly replenished, and fresh Jamaican flowers grace the dressing table. The high-peaked wooden roof is fitted with a ceiling fan which produces a highly satisfactory form of air conditioning. Most of the furnishings are made of local materials. Chaise longues provide sunbathing on the patio.

There is a small private sand beach and a large freshwater pool overlooking the sea, which will tempt even the nonswimmer. Lounges, tables, chairs, and bar service add to your pleasure. If you want a sandwich or a drink at lunchtime, you can adjourn to the main building where there are two patios, one covered. Breakfast is served either on the public patio or on your own private patio by your personal butler at no extra charge. He'll soon know your preferences, and you have the advantage of personal service.

At dinner, men are required to wear jackets and ties. That meal is served in one wing of the main block. Silver service, crystal, and Port Royal pewter sparkle on the tables. Dinner is a many-course set meal, and for those who are concerned with diets and phobias, it is advisable that requirements be made known early so that alternative food can be served. This is essentially a relaxing place. People who want to indulge in energetic activities are likely to look elsewhere.

Studios, obviously, are cheaper than the one-bedroom villas. *In summer, the single rate begins at $220, the double at $320, both MAP tariffs.* In winter, MAP singles range from $280 to $320 daily, while doubles go for $185 to $280 per person. Tennis, horseback riding, and such water sports as sailing and snorkeling are included in the tariffs.

Marbella Club at Dragon Bay (tel. 993-3281), almost like a private village, offers the ideal in vacation living. You can either relax by the pool or on the shores of the Caribbean, or you can indulge in more active pursuits. The hotel has a tennis pro, and there are facilities for sailing, waterskiing, snorkeling, and deep-sea fishing.

An estate of well-tended trees and lawns surrounds the private bay, and the chalets are spread among the trees and shrubs. There's a large aviary, with parrots, parakeets, and other exotic birds. All the chalets have views from private verandas, and all are air-conditioned and self-contained. Full room service is, of course, available.

The hotel is owned by Prince Alfonso Hohenlohe, who built the chic Marbella Club on the Costa del Sol in Spain. Descended from 12th-century Prussian royalty, he was the former brother-in-law of Prince Egon Von Furstenberg. It is Prince Hohenlohe's plan to restore some of the chic to Port Antonio that it used to know when it was patronized by movie stars, European royalty, and the very rich. He has engaged Manfred Ernst to manage the hotel for him. After a major refurbishing, the inn launched itself on its new career. Many of its present cottages are for sale.

The Italianate main building has a terrace for al fresco dining in the Dragon Square. At night you dine beneath the stars with candles flickering on the tables and enjoy the entertainment provided by both local and international performers. A singer, a steel band, a novelty act, or quiet background music may be presented from a raised terrace backed by a conservatory of tropical plants. Breakfast is served in your cottage or in the Beach Club Pavilion overlooking the bay. Lunch in the Beach Club is a light snack or a choice from the extensive menu. There's no requirement to dress for lunch—a swimsuit will do. But at dinner, casually formal attire is obligatory.

Nightlife centers around the Clifftop Disco, far enough away from all accommodations, but the pulsating beat of the music will lure you on as you walk through the trees. Don't be put off by feeling you must dance, because as well as the reverberating dance floor, there is a bar with comfortable chairs where you can hear the music without vibrating and can enjoy conversation. From the terrace, drink in the nighttime view across the bay. If you don't care to go to the disco, you may want to play tennis on the floodlit courts or just sit in one of the quiet little nooks and enjoy a nightcap under the stars. There is also a large bar off the Dragon Terrace, where, if it rains at night, evening meals are served.

Single rates in winter range from $225 to $450 daily, with doubles going for $280 and $475, MAP included. Special packages are also available. *In summer, rates are lowered to $110 to $150 daily in a single, from $155 to $280 in a double, EP.*

The hotel has its own boats for waterskiing and sailing. You can also take a small boat through the cut below the disco and into the Blue Lagoon. The use of the tennis courts is free to hotel guests, and there is a pro to sharpen up your game or to partner a match at a nominal fee.

If you flee this haven of good living to explore the island, a box lunch will be provided for you if you order it the night before. Also, exchange dining with the Trident Hotel can be arranged.

Bonnie View Hotel, P.O. Box 82 (tel. 993-2752), a hillside hugger, opens onto Port Antonio, Navy Island in the middle of the harbor, and the Caribbean. At the hotel's rear is a banana plantation and the cloud-shrouded peaks of the Blue Mountains. The bedrooms are simply but adequately furnished, with private bathrooms. There is no air conditioning, as the hotel has the advantage of the mountain breezes which lower the temperature by some ten degrees. All rooms have balconies, some toward the sea, others toward the mountains. The lounge patio and the veranda are pleasant places to sit and drink a rum punch or nibble a lunchtime snack.

Breakfast is served either in your room or in the dining room set back from the patio. At both lunch and dinner, a mixture of tasty Jamaican and international dishes is offered. At night during the season, a calypso band provides music for dancing after dinner. The pool has a bar and a large lounging area where you can relax under the sun with the mountains for company. Hotel guests can use the free staff bus down to Port Antonio and back at scheduled times. There are tennis courts, and most other sporting activities can be arranged for you. Bunches of bananas hang in the entrance and guests can help themselves to a quick snack at will.

All year round, a single is charged $35. Two persons in a double pay $55. Add $20 per person per day for breakfast and a set dinner.

De Montevin Lodge Private Hotel, 21 Fort George St. (tel. 993-2604), is a small guest house-style private hotel owned for many years by Mr. Mullings, a well-known figure in Port Antonio, who is a justice of the peace. In his 1881 Victorian house, a former sea captain's home done in bright colors of yellow, green, purple, and pink, he has built up a reputation for a friendly atmosphere and reasonable prices. The 13 rooms are rented all year for $35 in a twin-bedded unit with bath. These rates are EP.

There is a lounge with TV and a small bar and patio at the side of the house. Typical Jamaican dishes are served in the cool dining room. There is usually a breeze, and hence no need for air conditioning. Arrangements are easily made for any sports activities guests wish to pursue. The hotel is only three or four minutes' walk from the center of town.

Trident Villas at San San, P.O. Box 26 (tel. 993-3049), formerly known as Goblin Hill, is run by the already-previewed Trident Villas and Hotel but owned by the Jamaican government.

High above the sea, in manicured grounds, 28 villas are set in rows, with eveey room having a view of the San San Bay and the mountains. Guests have a choice of one- or two-bedroom villas, each with a living room and a dining room. There are floodlit tennis courts with free instruction, snorkeling equipment and instruction, a vine-draped pool, horseback riding, use of a beach, glass-bottomed boat rides, bicycling, and lawn sports. On a 700-acre estate adjacent to the Blue Lagoon, the hotel lies seven miles from Port Antonio. Continental cuisine as well as local Jamaican delicacies are served.

In summer, guests can stay here on the MAP at a charge of $110 in a single and $90 per person in a double. Winter rates on the EP are $175 in a single and $100 per person in a double, plus tax.

WHERE TO DINE: A surprising array of atmospheric choices awaits you.

Trident Hotel Restaurant (tel. 993-2602) has for a long time been frequented by those seeking gourmet cuisine. Part of the main hotel building, the restaurant has an air of elegance. The high-pitched wooden roof set on white stone walls holds several ceiling fans which gently stir the air. The antique tables for two, four, or more are set with old china, English silver, and Port Royal pewter. Warm place settings and candles complete the picture.

Dinner is served at 8 o'clock, and men are required to wear jackets and ties. A butler shows you to your table, where warm bread, cold butter, and ice water await. A waiter, resplendent in uniform and white starched shirt, and, to complete the picture, pristine white cotton gloves, will help you choose your wine. The waiter whispers the name of each course as he serves it: Jamaican salad; coconut soup; dolphin with mayonnaise and mustard sauce; French salad with wine vinaigrette; steak with broccoli and sauteed potatoes; peach Melba and Blue Mountain coffee with Wild Orange, a Jamaican liqueur. "More coffee, sir, and more—as much as you want." The cost of the meal is $35 per person. Tip at your discretion. Wine is extra. The six-course menu varies each day, but there is no à la carte service. The meal is expertly cooked and beautifully served. Reservations are required. After dinner, join the crowd around the bar, where a small combo plays tunes on request.

Marbella Club at Dragon Bay Restaurant (tel. 993-3281) is as different from the restaurant at the Trident Hotel as chalk from cheese—a relaxed, open-air dining spot beneath the stars on an Italianate terrace sheltered from the cool wind. On all sides, flowers, trees, and soft lights give a tropical ambience as people in casually formal dress enjoy good food. Dinner is served from 7:30 to 9:30 p.m. to the sound of music on the raised terrace at the end of the dining area.

Your meal starts with light hors d'oeuvres such as tomato elegante, followed by a fish chowder or some other soup. The fish course will be snapper or perhaps a lobster or shellfish dish. Main courses include chicken or beef dishes served with fresh vegetables. Desserts may be fresh fruit salad or a Melba, and then there is tea, coffee, or hot chocolate. You can order a hamburger, omelet, or a steak, even lobster salad, served with french fries. Expect to spend about $35 per head for dinner.

The **De Montevin Lodge Restaurant,** 21 Fort George St. (tel. 993-2604), is *the* place for a true Jamaican dinner. Start with pepperpot or pumpkin soup, then cod with akee. Follow these with curried lobster and chicken Jamaican style with local vegetables. Top the meal off with coconut or banana cream pie, washed down with coffee, a meal fit for a good trencherman or woman, for around $15 and up. An ice-cold Red Stripe beer goes well with such a meal. The menu changes according to the availability of fresh supplies, but the standard of cooking and the full Jamaican character of the meal are constant. The friendly staff will explain the intricacies of any particular dish that takes your fancy. Always call the day before to let them know you're coming. Mrs. Mullings is considered the best cook in Port Antonio. She was Errol Flynn's cook, incidentally.

WHAT TO DO: For the experience of a lifetime, most guests follow the lead of a legendary film star and go—

Rafting on the Rio Grande

Rafting started on the Rio Grande and on the Martha Brae River as a means of transporting bananas from the plantations to the waiting freighters. In 1871 a Yankee skipper, Lorenzo Dow Baker, decided that a seat on one of the rafts was better than walking, but it was not until Errol Flynn arrived that the rafts became popular as a tourist attraction. Flynn used to hire the craft for his friends and encouraged the drivers to race down the Rio Grande, spurred on by bets on the winner. Now that the bananas are transported by road, the raft skippers make one or maybe two trips a day down the waterway.

The rafts are some 33 feet long and only about 3 feet wide, propelled by stout bamboo poles. There is a raised double seat about two-thirds of the way back for the two passengers. The skipper stands in the front, trousers rolled up to his knees, the water washing his feet, and guides the lively craft down the river, about eight miles between steep hills covered with coconut palms, banana plantations, and flowers, through limestone rock cliffs pitted with caves, through the Tunnel of Love, a narrow cleft in the rocks, then on to wider, gentler water. The whole trip takes about two or three hours, but there may be stops for chats with bankside residents whom the rafters know well. You can disembark and get a drink at a small shop on the way.

The day starts at Rafter's Rest, a few miles west of Port Antonio at Burlington on St. Margaret's Bay. Buy your raft ticket, $32 for two, and leave your valuables in the specially provided lockers. A driver will take you to the starting point and pick you up again in your rental car. He is fully insured to do so. If you feel like it, take a picnic lunch. Bring enough for your skipper too, and he will find a peaceful spot for your meal and perhaps a swim, regaling you with lively stories of the river, laughing, and talking—a good companion for an exciting trip.

A Trip to the Blue Lagoon

A cool, tranquil, 185-foot-deep body of crystal-clear, dark-blue water surrounded by trees, the Blue Lagoon is one of the most photographed sights in Jamaica. Islanders call it simply the "blue hole." Driving, you follow the signs off the main road past the Frenchman's Cove Hotel down to the beach. Walk through the gate into the palm-leaf-roofed bar and restaurant overlooking the lagoon. From 10 a.m. to 10 p.m. daily, you can lie by the water, drop into the sea to cool off, or soak in the waters of the mineral spring which is said to cure rheumatic pains.

For the more energetic, waterskiing is available. A trip in a glass-bottomed boat to see the coral and tropical fish for 20 minutes is $8 per person. A mask, flippers, and snorkel cost $8 a day to rent, and if you want to scuba-dive out along the reef, $32 is the cost of a 45-minute dive, rental of all equipment, a boat out to the reef, and the services of an experienced guide. Renting a 14-foot inflatable dinghy with outboard motor costs $32 per hour, including fuel.

Going Swimming

There is public swimming at **Boston Bay Beach,** past the Blue Lagoon, where you can sample the famous jerk pork, priced by weight and served from the barbecue.

WHAT TO SEE: Continuing our energetic activities, I have the following suggestions:

Somerset Falls is ten miles west of Port Antonio, just past Hope Bay on the A4. The waters of the Daniels River pour down a deep gorge through the rain forest, with waterfalls and foaming cascades. There are picnic spots, and you can swim in the deep rock pools. You can buy sandwiches, light meals, beer, soft drinks, and even liquor at the snackbar. Admission to the falls is J$2 (44¢) for adults, J$1 ($22¢) for children.

The **Caves of Nonsuch** and the **Gardens of Athenry** are east from Port Antonio past the Blue Lagoon. Turn right, and follow the signs about six miles up into the hills through small villages to the caves. It is an easy drive and an easy walk to see the stalagmites, fossilized marine remains, evidence of Arawak civilization, and signs of volcanic activity, adding up to 1½ million years of life on earth.

From the Gardens of Athenry there are panoramic views over the island and the sea. The gardens are filled with coconut palms, flowers, and trees.

Admission to the caves and gardens is $4 per person. The facilities are open seven days a week, and complete guided tours are given from 9 a.m. to 5 p.m. Rates include a guide for both the caves and gardens. Refreshments are available at the Athenry Pavilion, and one beverage is included in the tour.

The **Folly Great House** lies on the outskirts of Port Antonio. The remains of the two-story mansion can be visited free. It was built, it is said, in 1905 by Arthur Mitchell, an American millionaire, for his wife, Annie, daughter of Charles Tiffany, founder of the famous New York store. Sea water was used in the construction, and the house collapsed shortly after they moved in.

Because of the beautiful location, it is easy to see what a fine great house it must have been, but the years and vandals have not added to its attractiveness. Decay and graffiti mar the ruins.

Someone once said, "Anything is possible in Jamaica." Although I can't promise it, it is sometimes possible to arrange a trip of the **Errol Flynn Plantation** (check with the tourist office). Of course, the more in your party, the better your chances of getting to see the land so beloved by the film star and author of the autobiography *My Wicked, Wicked Ways*. The widow of the film star, Patrice Wymore Flynn (you may remember her from several films she made in the '50s), is now the owner of the working plantation which lies in the area of Priestman's River. Sometimes she personally shows visitors about the property where coconut and pimiento are grown. You can also visit a wicker factory—not a large operation—and see how coconut is processed into copra.

3. Ocho Rios

A north coast resort some two hours by road from Montego Bay, Ocho Rios was once a small banana and fishing port, but in recent years tourism has become the leading industry. The bay is dominated on one side by a bauxite loading terminal and on the other by a range of hotels with sandy beaches fringed by palm trees. Runaway Bay, once only a satellite of Ocho Rios but now a resort area in its own right, is presented at the end of this section.

Many readers of this guide have expressed strong objections to a holiday in Ocho Rios. Culled from several reports, here are the main problems. The rainy months are in May and October. The town is so commercial you won't find the real Jamaica there. Three cruise ships arrive every week (four every other week). The young men on the streets are very aggressive toward selling you any kind of drugs and worthless souvenirs. Therefore it's hard to just walk around the town to see the sights and eat in the local restaurants.

WHERE TO STAY: The area of Ocho Rios is a formidable rival of Montego Bay. Some inns of character remain, holding out against the newer developments that may sweep away what is left of the former colonial life of the resort.

The Luxury Leaders

Jamaica Inn, off Route 4 (tel. 974-2514), is a long, low, U-shaped building set close to the sea, surrounded by grass and palm trees with oleander and bougainvillea. The cool, comfortable lounge with books, and the games room with cards and jigsaw puzzles, will provide you with something to do in case of rain, but it's the outdoor attractions that bring people to the inn. Lovely patios open onto the lawns, and the bedrooms, which face the sea, are reached along garden paths. There is a small pool almost at the water's edge, where a wide, white sand beach invites you to swim or lounge. Arthur, the boatman, will arrange sailing trips. The sea close in is almost too clear to make snorkeling an adventure, but farther out it is rewarding. For the nonaquatic there is tennis, with golf close by at the Upton Country Club.

The inn is proud of its cuisine. The chef was trained in Europe and lends his expertise to the production of dishes both international and Jamaican. You can have breakfast served in your room, selecting from kippers, an omelet, or pancakes with maple syrup, or you can enjoy it in the dining room. Lunch is a pleasant à la carte affair, with a wide menu choice. Dinner, for a set charge of $24, may start with mango nectar, caviar on toast, or stuffed sweet peppers, followed by soup. For the main course, there may be lobster thermidor, broiled tenderloin with béarnaise sauce or fried chicken. You can finish with a dessert or cheese, and Blue Mountain coffee. The management requires men to wear a jacket and tie at night. (One New Jersey man didn't bring a tie and had to spend one whole day in search of one, finally finding the item in a small native dry-goods store.)

Winter rates, including three meals and tea, are $215 daily in a single (not ocean view), rising to $250 to $300 in a double. *Summer tariffs go from $135 daily in a single and from $175 to $185 in a double.* The expensive White Suite, incidentally, was a favorite of Winston Churchill.

Plantation Inn (tel. 974-2501) is a magnificent hotel evoking a southern antebellum mansion, reached by a sweeping driveway and entered through a colonnaded portico, set above the beach in pleasant gardens. All bedrooms open off balconies and have their own patios overlooking the sea. The rooms are attractively decorated with chintz and comfortable furnishings, and are air cooled by slowly revolving fans. There is an inside dining room, but most of the action takes place under the tropical sky. The beach is 50 steps down from the garden, and seats on the way provide resting spots. Water sports are available: skindiving, Sunfish sailing, and waterskiing. There is a glass-bottomed boat on one of the two private beaches, or you can just take it easy and get a tan while doing nothing at all.

English tea is served on the terrace every afternoon from 4 to 5:30 p.m. You can have breakfast on your patio. Lunch is served outdoors, with a choice of chilled native nectars of mango, pineapple, guava, or tomato to start, followed by a sandwich, or perhaps you'll enjoy a chicken and onion omelet.

In winter, men are required to wear jackets at dinner (and jackets *and* ties, on Friday and Saturday night). In summer the dress code is more relaxed. Men are required to wear jackets only for dinner on Friday and Saturday night. The menu comes at a set price of $28 for five courses and coffee, plus 10% service. On Sunday a Jamaica night buffet is offered, and you can feast and dance to calypso music.

On the MAP, two persons can stay here in winter at prices ranging from $250 to $315 daily, the latter for occupancy of a junior suite. *In summer, prices are reduced: the same MAP is offered for $185 to $220 daily for two persons.* For single occupancy in either season, deduct $40 a night. Apart from the regular hotel, there are two units that provide more private living. Plantana Cottage above the east beach sleeps two to six persons. The Family House with garden view sleeps up to five persons. These, naturally, are far more expensive than the regular rates.

Eden II, Mammee Bay, P.O. Box 51 (tel. 972-2300), knew life as the Jamaica Hilton before becoming an all-inclusive couples resort. It is set on the seafront between Ocho Rios and St. Ann's Bay, facing Mammee Bay in 22 acres of landscaped gardens, reached along an avenue of royal palms.

The resort is very sports oriented, with, among other facilities, a Nautilus Fitness Centre that features a hot tub and aerobic exercise classes. Tennis is played both day and night, and other activities include dance lessons, volleyball, and backgammon. You can go horseback riding about 2000 feet above sea level, jog along a marked trail, and partake of such water sports as skiing, windsurfing, scuba-diving, snorkeling, and sailboat racing.

Rooms are attractively furnished, each with a private balcony if overhead or a patio if on ground level. As in most couples-only resorts in Jamaica, a client gets the works: that is, three meals a day, along with "happy hour" hors d'oeuvres, Sunday champagne brunches, and all bar drinks (even cigarettes). A choice of four wines is available at lunch and dinner.

Transfers are arranged between the airport and the hotel. Most guests book in here on the seven-night plan, and during certain peak periods they must arrive on Friday, Saturday, or Sunday only. The rate for three nights in high season ranges from $370 to $450 per person, based obviously on double occupancy. The seven-night deal goes from $950 to around $1100. *After April 12, prices are lowered. A seven-night package ranges from $830 to $1050 per person; a three-night night package goes for $320 to $420.* The least expensive rooms are called lanai. The second most expensive category is labeled mountain-view, and the ocean-view rooms carry the highest price tags.

Sans Souci, P.O. Box 103 (tel. 974-2353). As you enter the driveway, past large pink posts and well-tended foliage, you may be fooled. You'll think Sans Souci has been here for more than a century. The central hillside hotel, pink with lacy trim balconies and encircling galleries, recaptures the romantic past. Yet the hotel is most up-to-date, as it recently spent three million Jamaican dollars on refurbishing all the rooms and adding a spa. The hotel is a collection of Mediterranean-style villas standing on garden terraces, presenting a quiet elegance. The villas are set in the midst of foliage on terraced hills, with an elevator tower taking you down to the lower waterfront swimming pool and docks. Around the main house is yet another pool.

Lovers seek out garden nooks placed strategically along winding pathways, which have resting perches with white furniture. A whimsical idea is to order the "fertile turtle" at Charlie's Bar. Here you can continue your suntanning while playing chess on the large and most unusual outdoor chessboard.

Whether you have a room, a penthouse, or a suite, all the bedroom appointments are tasteful, a subdued statement. Units come with fully equipped kitchens, and each bedroom has its own bath. Each suite has an ocean view and private balcony. In winter, EP singles range from $140 to $230 daily; doubles, from $160 to $330. The Royal Suite, a three-bedroom penthouse, costs $1200 a day for up to six guests. *In summer, a single goes for $110 to $170, doubles for $130 to $230, and the three-bedroom penthouse for $500 to $620 daily.* For a full American breakfast and five-course à la carte dinner, you'll pay an additional $40 per person per day. A 10% service charge is extra.

The hotel's restaurant, Casanova, is one of the finest dining spots along the north shore. The Sans Souci chefs won numerous high awards in the 1984 Jamaica Festival of Culinary Arts. Delroy entertains on the grand piano during the cocktail hour, and the Nostalgics play danceable music during and after dinner. There are two Laykold hard tennis courts, and Sans Souci guests have complimentary greens fees at the Upton Country Club 18-hole golf course.

Americana Ocho Rios, P.O. Box 100 (tel. 974-2151), is a 325-room citadel opening onto a long, sandy beach. Its next-door neighbor is the Ocho Rios Sheraton, and guests often wander back and forth between the two hotels, checking out the action. Once they were linked almost like Siamese twins when they were run under the same banner and known then as the Intercontinental Ocho Rios and the Mallards Beach-Hyatt. Many returning guests still remember them under their old names.

The Americana is a modern, high-rise building, with air-conditioned units, a large cool lobby, and a shopping arcade which is handy if you don't want to walk to nearby Ocho Rios and the Ocean Village Shopping Centre.

There is a coffeeshop as well as the Victoria Restaurant on the premises, but most meals are taken on the terrace amid tropical plants. After dark, a disco might (maybe not) hum with life, and native floor shows and calypso music on some occasions could add to your entertainment.

Two tennis courts, horseback riding, and golf are available at the Upton Country Club. Waterskiing, fishing, and scuba-diving can be arranged for a small cost.

Guests check in here in summer for $65 to $85 daily, EP, either single or double occupancy. In winter, the EP rate for either single or double occupancy is $100 to $125.

The **Ocho Rios Sheraton**, P.O. Box 245 (tel. 974-2201), which as mentioned was known as the Mallards Beach-Hyatt in a former lifetime, is a similar high-rise on the beach like its neighbor, the Americana. The upper lobby and reception area of the Sheraton is graced by a fountain and pool. The decor is tropical, and maximum use is made of bamboo, rattan, and batik. A shopping arcade, three bars, and three restaurants are part of the hotel. Waterskiing, snorkeling, sailing, jet skiing, windsurfing, deep-sea fishing, and tennis are avilable at the hotel, and golf can be played a couple of miles away.

In winter, singles (room only) cost from $125 to $145 daily, and doubles pay from $130 to $150. *In summer, singles range in price from $70 to $85 daily, while doubles cost from $75 to $90. It's also possible to stay here in summer on MAP rates, going from $106 to $121 daily in a single and from $147 to $162 in a double.*

Couples, P.O. Box 330, Tower Isle Post Office, St. Mary (tel. 974-4271). Don't come here alone—you won't get in! You're asked to bring a "little love here," and that means your lover. The management defines couples here as "any two people in love." Everything is in couplets, even the double chairs by the moon-drenched beach. Once you've paid the initial fee, you have free use of all facilities—there will be no more bills. It's a taboo subject. Even the cigarettes and whiskey are free. You get three meals a day too, including all the wine you want. And tips are not permitted.

Every bedroom has either a king-size bed or two doubles, and furnishings are pleasantly traditional. Breakfasts are bountiful. Every room has a patio fronting either the sea or the beach; if not that, then gardens or the mountains.

Packaged by Lotus Hedonism Holidays of New York (tel. 212/832-7830), the hotel accepts bookings for eight days, seven nights, Sunday to Sunday. Ten different rate structures are offered, depending on the time of year. The highest winter tab is an ocean-view room at $2200 per week for two, and the lowest winter tariff is a mountain-view room at $2000 per week per couple. *Summer prices are reduced, costing approximately $820 to $1000 per person per week.*

Dinners are four courses, and afterward there is dancing on the terrace every evening, with a different kind of entertainment. The piano bar opens at 7 p.m., and stays that way until the last guest retires (this is sometimes at 7 a.m.).

You can play tennis on one of the five world-class courts, three of which are lit, or else cycle, go horseback riding, sailing, or snorkeling. Or you may want to slip away to their private island where you can bask in the buff.

The only criticism I have of the resort is that it does away with the mating game, unless you cast a roving eye on someone else's other half.

Less Expensive Choices

Shaw Park Beach Hotel, P.O. Box 17, Cutlass Bay (tel. 974-2552), is an elegant Jamaica Georgian property with all rooms directly on the beach, facing the ocean. It has three bars, two inside and the Beach Bar on the Caribbean Terrace under the sky. The reception area looks like a colonial version of a Georgian living room, and the terrace one floor below is built right up to the crashing waves. All rooms are air-conditioned and comfortably furnished. Most have full bathrooms, but some in the east wing have showers. There is a swimming pool, and ocean water sports—sailing, fishing, windsurfing, waterskiing, snorkeling —are available from the beach at nominal charges. The hotel has its own tennis courts and reciprocity with Upton Golf Club. A resident band plays for dancing nightly. Floor shows are arranged most nights. The nightclub, **Silks,** vibrates to disco music and has an intimate Jockey Bar.

In summer, singles range in price from $99 to $115 daily; doubles, $120 to $130. Four persons can occupy a deluxe two-bedroom apartment suite for about $300. Winter rates rise to $155 to $165 daily in a single, from $166 to $175 in a double, with a two-bedroom apartment suite costing four persons about $400 daily. One reader, Gregory Speck of New York City, noted that Bergen Davis, the chef here, "prepares just about the best lobster I've ever encountered, and has a degree from the University of Miami in culinary arts."

Shaw Park Gardens (described under "Boonoonoonoos") are owned and operated by the hotel and provide a pleasant afternoon's sightseeing trip.

Hibiscus Lodge Hotel, P.O. Box 52 (tel. 974-2676), is an intimate, friendly little inn in the hills for those who enjoy the character of old architecture surrounded by abundant greenery. You get atmosphere at low prices—from J$175 ($38.50) daily in a single in winter, J$225 ($49.50) in a double, and J$280 ($61.60) in a triple. *Off-season, reductions are granted: J$140 ($30.80) in a single, J$185 ($40.70) in a double, and J$200 ($44) in a triple, all EP.* The lodge is an old building with a wide veranda and newer extensions built in the same style. Your brightly furnished bedroom opens onto upper and lower verandas.

Bedrooms are in natural wood with reed and bamboo. Some have air conditioning, and all the units contain ceiling fans. Every kind of island tree and flowering vine seems to grow in the three-acre compound. There's a tiny beach, and within walking distance is a larger wide sandy beach. At the inn, a dining room opens onto views of trees and becomes quite cozy when candles are lit at night. The food is good, including many Jamaican specialties. Alfred Doswald and Richard Powell run the lodge.

Inn on the Beach, P.O. Box 342, St. Ann (tel. 974-2782), just behind the sprawling Ocean Village Shopping Center, is an attractively decorated, Jamaican-run inn at the edge of a public beach in the center of town. Its accommodations are as comfortable as those in larger, more expensive resort hotels nearby. If you don't mind the absence of the varied on-the-premises entertainment facilities of the larger hotels, this may be the place for you.

Open-air hallways lead to the pleasantly sunny bedrooms, each of which has two double beds, large windows, a terrace, air conditioning, a tiled bath, and attractive furnishings, some upholstered in springtime colors. There's no elevator, no bar, and no restaurant in the hotel, but you'll find a number of watering spots within walking distance, and two restaurants, under different management, are connected architecturally with the rear side of the inn.

In winter, the 46 accommodations rent for $72 daily in a single, $80 in a double, $95 in a triple, and $105 in a quad. *In summer, rates go down to $48 in a single, $58 in a double, $65 in a triple, and $72 in a quad.*

Orchid Hill Great House and Guest House, 98 Main St., P.O. Box 366 (tel.

974-2926), is the central address for what is actually two different guest houses. Mrs. Jean Shell, a transplanted Virginian, and her daughter, Lynn, are the proprietors of both properties, which are about a mile apart. The bigger house, on Main Street, served at the turn of the century as the great house for a plantation, which since then has been subdivided into many different parcels of land.

The ten bedrooms each contain a private bath and air conditioning, although climate control costs an additional $6 per room per day. The Great House has a miniature menagerie on the premises. An additional four bedrooms are available in the guest house, at 12 Scarnes Ave. (tel. 974-5118). The guest house contains a large living/dining area for the use of the building's occupants.

Rates in both houses are $36 in a single or double and $50 for a triple. This place is definitely not for everybody, but if you're an independent-minded traveler looking for a simple accommodation not far from the beaches, it may serve you well. Don't expect the amenities of a grand hotel, and remember that making friends with the animals in the mini-zoo is considered part of the experience.

WHERE TO EAT: Ruins Restaurant (tel. 974-2442) is one of the most captivating eating places anywhere in Jamaica. You dine in a spot at the foot of a series of waterfalls which can be considered a tourist attraction in their own right. In 1831 a British entrepreneur constructed a sugar mill on the site, using the powerful stream to drive his water wheels. Today, all that remains is a jumble of ruins, hence the restaurant's name.

After you cross a covered bridge, perhaps stopping off for a drink at the bar in the outbuilding first, you find yourself in a fairyland where the only sounds come from the tree frogs, the falling water from about a dozen cascades, and the discreet clink of silver and china. Tables are set on a wooden deck leading all the way up to the pool at the foot of the falls, where moss and other vegetation line the stones at the base. As part of the evening's enjoyment you may want to climb a flight of stairs to the top of the falls, where bobbing lanterns and the illuminated waters below afford one of the most delightful experiences on the island.

Reservations are important, since in season this restaurant draws crowds. Menu items, since the place was taken over by Messrs. HoSang and Lee in 1982, include a wide range of Chinese food, such as sweet-and-sour pork or chicken, several kinds of chow mein or chop suey, chicken and pineapple, beef in oyster sauce, and a house specialty—lobster sauteed in a special sauce. International dishes include lamb or pork chops, chicken Kiev, surf and turf, two kinds of steak, and an array of fish. Full meals range from J$90 ($19.80) and are served daily except at lunchtime Sunday.

The **Almond Tree Restaurant** (tel. 974-2813), behind the Hibiscus Lodge Hotel, is run by Dick Powell, from Morden, Surrey, England. Originally a catering manager for one of England's finest hotels, Dick was invited by his partner, Freddie Dosewald, to run this restaurant. Freddie was trained in Switzerland, was executive chef at Couples, and also owns and runs the Pâtisserie and Bread Shop in Ocean Villiage.

The Almond Tree patio, with trees growing up through the roof, overlooks the blue waters of the Caribbean over floodlit trees at night. Wrought-iron tables and chairs make this a choice place for indoor-outdoor lunch or dinner. Lunch, served from noon to 3 p.m., offers several possibilities from a limited menu, which is likely to include red pea soup, red snapper with sweet-and-sour sauce, rice, and salad, and callay and fried plantain. The cost for lunch will probably be about $10.

Dinner is served from 7 p.m., with a wide choice of appetizers, including fish cakes, native style. Soups include pepperpot and pumpkin. Almond Tree specialties include a wide range of continental dishes. I prefer the seafood dishes from the Caribbean, including bouillabaisse (not only pieces of conch, but lobster) and broiled red snapper with a creole sauce. The chef also prepares a Caribbean seafood fondue. Lobster is the most expensive item on the menu. Expect to spend from $15 to $25 for dinner. The wine list offers a variety of vintages, including Spanish and Jamaican wines.

Have an apéritif in the Port of Call Bar beside the hotel before dinner.

Moxons of Boscobel, St. Mary (tel. 974-3234), is open seven nights a week. This enchanting place, six miles out of Ocho Rios on the A3 going east, is so popular that a reservation is imperative. It was opened about 12 years ago by Oliver and Benita Moxon, when they came to Jamaica from England in search of what they discribe as "a middle-age challenge." They arrived on the island, found their cliff-edge site, literally built their restaurant, and trained their staff from waiter to chef. The Moxons built a school in the village, and are totally integrated into the life of the island. Noted diners at their restaurant have included famous authors and prime ministers, and the Moxons claim that in high season they turn down business rather than hurry their guests.

Enter through the stout wooden doors and have a before-dinner drink in the white, tree-covered patio; then dine on the terrace with a fantastic view over the lagoon. The tables are candlelit and fresh flowers, arranged by a talented waiter, center each. The musical background complements the scenery.

For an appetizer, try liver pâté or oeuf Florentine. There is fresh fish and a variety of lobster dishes served with rice and salad. The steaks are good, but a particular delicacy that is often available is poussin français (the Moxons even taught a farmer how to fatten the chicks). French-fried, creamed, or steamed potatoes come with the meal. The chef's selections are shown daily on a menu board. Homemade desserts are excellent. Count on parting with at least $25 per person. The maître d'hôtel, Warren Perry, is happy to assist you.

Carib Inn Restaurant and Bar (tel. 974-2445) is a place where you can stop in just for a drink or do what many patrons do—visit for an entire day. On the premises you'll find one of the most charming restaurants in town and a bar where you can spend a drawn-out evening or a lazy afternoon soothed by the sound of flowing water in stone-walled canals. The complex is set in a 17-acre garden lush with coconut palms flowering shrubs. At one time the well-kept villas were rental facilities. Today, however, most of them are privately owned vacation homes, but the central bar and restaurant, the pool, and the wide, sandy beach are open to anyone who wishes to enjoy them.

To enter, you walk through shrubbery and, over a footbridge to the open-air restaurant with its cluster of teepee-shaped roofs. There's a bar at the far end where the swiftly flowing stream in the canal provides a soft sound and where the steep and verdant hillside complements the vividly patterned fabrics covering the wicker furniture.

In winter, dinner guests are treated to a glass of Jamaican rum punch mixed at the spacious hexagonal bar. If you decide to stay for dinner, you'll be served by a formally dressed staff in high season. You can feast on such specialties as akee on toast, fresh fish, crab backs, flambéed lobster tails, seafood casserole, "brown stew kingfish," or marinated shrimp. The many meat dishes include a "koral kebab" of beef and pork marinated in wine. Full dinners range upward from J$40 ($8.80), while a simpler lunch menu, which offers chicken or lobster salads, BLTs, and daily specials such as curried goat and boiled rice or stewed beef, usually begins at J$18 ($3.96). A 10% service charge is added to your tab.

Dick Turpin, Coconut Grove Shopping Centre (tel. 974-2717), is an English pub and retaurant in this shopping center. Decorated with the newspapers of London as its theme, it has an active, friendly pub, a favorite rendezvous point for both visitors and locals. Lunch, costing around J$50 ($11), is served daily from noon to 3:30 and includes some Chinese dishes, and dinner for around $25 is offered from 6:30 to 10:30 p.m. On Sunday, hours are 6 p.m. to midnight.

Appetizers are enticing, including stuffed crab back, Jamaican patties, and smoked marlin. A host of entrees are offered, featuring curried lobster, barbecued spare ribs, and steak and shrimp fondue. Roast prime ribs of beef is the specialty. Fresh homemade desserts are a regular feature, along with Dick Turpin's "grog mug." Dinner is by candlelight.

The host is Bill Letchford, from Wiltshire, England, who likes to see that his produce, meats, and seafood are fresh. Try also his homemade breads.

The **Little Pub Restaurant and Cocktail Bar** (tel. 974-2324) is in a tropical patio surrounded by souvenir shops bordered with gingerbread fretwork. This indoor-outdoor pub's inner rooms focus on a small stage area for native bands. No one will mind if you just enjoy a drink while you sit in one of the pub's barrel chairs, but if you want dinner, you can proceed to one of the linen-covered tables capped with cut flowers and candlelight.

Menu items include lobster thermidor, lobster creole, a shrimp-filled pineapple boat, barbecued chicken, grilled steaks, grilled kingfish, brown fish stew with peppery brown gravy (a Jamaican specialty), and banana flambé. Dinners cost J$120 ($26.40) and up.

To add to the ambience of this already-colorful spot, live music is offered during dinner, as well as a live show at 10 p.m. during high season. During the show, limbo and cabaret acts are featured. Many guests find that the live music is better than that offered in similar places around town. The pub is immediately west of the Ocho Rios roundabout behind a crumbled fortification and lots of verdant shrubs. Keith Foote is the charming and humorous owner/manager.

The **Victoria Restaurant,** Americana Hotel (tel. 974-2151), offers a relaxed but formal ambience for good food with attentive service. The setting is Victorian, fitting the name, with soft lights and red plush furnishings. Air conditioning adds to guests' comfort. The à la carte menu is decorated with pictures of a fictitious visit of Queen Victoria to Jamaica in which she is seen enjoying such pleasures as balloon hopping, rafting, and being fired from a cannon!

Dishes include fresh fish and lobster with such delicacies as filet mignon wrapped in bacon, veal cutlets, and chicken Kiev. A good selection of desserts includes chocolate soufflé, bombé surprise, and crêpes suzette. A meal will cost around $30.

The staff, unlike that in many large international hotels, is friendly and helpful. One of the waiters, hearing that a young couple would be leaving the next morning, produced the woman's favorite dessert on the house—"Just to remind you of us until your next trip."

Chez Robert (tel. 974-5007) is the result of a happy marriage between the Swiss-born Paul Moser and his Jamaican wife, Pearline. Together they direct the modern second-floor restaurant whose window seats offer a view of the beach and the palms at its edge. Opening at 6 p.m. seven nights a week for dinner, the establishment serves specialties such as steaks, cassoulet d'escargots, oysters au gratin, pepperpot, vichyssoise, veal Chez Robert (served with rösti, the potato specialty from Switzerland), tournedos Rossini, chicken paprika, and beef Stroganoff. Full meals range upward from J$120 ($26.40).

The **Beach Bowl,** Ocean Villiage Shopping Center (tel. 974-5007), is a simple coffeeshop serving well-prepared snacks and meals to guests retreating from the sunshine of the nearby beach. It's directed by Mrs. Pearline Moser, who divides her time between this place and the more formal Chez Robert, upstairs.

Mrs. Moser opens for business daily at 7 a.m. for breakfast and closes at 10 p.m. after dinner. Menu items include steaks, curried lobster, milkshakes, Chinese dishes, and fried chicken (cooked either southern or Jamaican style). Full meals cost from J$45 ($9.90) up. If you just want a drink, the Mosers also operate a nearby cedar-roofed beach cabana dispensing beer and cold drinks during the day.

WHAT TO DO: A pleasant drive out of Ocho Rios along the A3 will take you inland through **Fern Gully.** This was originally a riverbed, but now the main road winds up some 700 feet between a profusion of wild ferns, a tall rain forest, hardwood trees, and lianas. For the botanist, there are hundreds of varieties of ferns, and for the less plant-minded, roadside stands offer fruit and vegetables, carved wood souvenirs, and basketwork. The road runs for about four miles, sometimes with a large pool of sunlight, sometimes fingers of light just penetrating the overhanging vegetation. Then at the top of the hill, you come to a right-hand turn, onto a narrow road leading to Golden Grove.

You pass Lydford with the remains of **Edinburgh Castle,** built in 1763, the lair of one of Jamaica's most infamous murderers, a Scot named Lewis Hutchinson who used to shoot passersby and toss their bodies into a deep pit built for the purpose. The authorities got wind of his activities, and although he tried to escape by canoe, he was captured by the navy under the command of Admiral Rodney and was hanged. Rather proud of his achievements (evidence of at least 43 murders was found), he left £100 and instructions for a memorial to be built. It never was, but the castle ruins remain.

Continue down the A1 to **St. Ann's Bay,** the site of the first Spanish settlement on the island, where you can see the **Statue of Christopher Columbus,** cast in his hometown of Genoa, erected near St. Ann's Hospital on the west side of town, close to the coast road. There are a number of Georgian buildings in the town. The **Court House** near the parish church, built in 1866, is most interesting.

Follow the A3 back toward Ocho Rios and you will pass **Dunn's River Falls.** There is plenty of parking space, and for a charge of J$2 (44¢) you can relax on the beach or else climb with a guide to the top of the 600-foot falls. Dressing rooms are available. You can splash in the waters at the bottom of the falls or drop into the cool pools higher up between the cascades of water. The beach restaurant provides snacks and refreshing drinks. If you're visiting the falls, wear old tennis shoes, whatever, anything to protect your feet from the sharp rocks and to prevent slipping.

The **Green Grotto Caves** are at Runaway Bay, 40 minutes west from Ocho Rios on the A1 past St. Ann's Bay. In 1658 the Spanish governor is said to have hidden here from the English before escaping through an underground passage on to Cuba. Tours of the caves take about 45 minutes. You descend some 120 meters underground, and your guide, flashlight in hand, will show such natural rock formations as the Madonna and Child, with a draping like jeweled lace, or the Spanish conquistador, so lifelike that one is almost convinced he was carved by human hand. At the bottom is the Green Grotto Lake, across which you will take a boat to the bar for a free cool drink. With luck, your guide will play the Arawak piano, which sounds a little like the chimes of Big Ben, before you return to the surface. The caves are open from 9 a.m. to 5 p.m. daily. Admission is J$10 ($2.20) for adults.

Prospect Plantation (tel. 974-2058), 4½ miles east of Ocho Rios, is a working property. A visit to this plantation combines the opportunity to take an educational, relaxing, and enjoyable tour. On your leisurely ride by covered jitney through the scenic beauty of Prospect, you'll readily see why this section of Jamaica is called "the garden parish of the island." You can view the many trees planted by such visitors as Sir Winston Churchill, Henry Kissinger, Charlie Chaplin, Pierre Trudeau, Sir Noël Coward, and many others. You will learn about and see growing pimento (allspice), bananas, cassava, sugarcane, coffee, cocoa, coconut, pineapple, and the famous leucaena "Tree of Life." You'll see Jamaica's first hydroelectric plant and Jamaica red poll cattle at the feedlot, and sample some of the exotic fruit and drinks. Your guide will be a cadet from **Prospect Training College,** founded more than 25 years ago by Col. Sir Harold Mitchell, Bt.

Horseback riding is available on three scenic trails at Prospect. The rides vary from 1 to 2¼ hours. Advance booking of one hour is necessary to reserve horses.

Tours, costing from $25, depart Monday through Saturday at 10:30 a.m. and at 2 and 3:30 p.m., and on Sunday at 11 a.m. and 1:30 and 3 p.m. Children under 12 go free.

Brimmer Hall Estate is farther east from Ochos Rios in the hills behind Port Maria, an ideal place to spend a day, where you can relax beside the pool and sample a wide variety of brews and concoctions, including an interestingly different one called "Wow!" The Plantation Tour Eating House offers typical Jamaican dishes for lunch, and there is a souvenir shop with a good selection of ceramics, art, straw goods, woodcarvings, rums, liqueurs, and cigars. All this is on a working plantation where you are driven around in a tractor-drawn jitney to see the tropical fruit trees and coffee plants, and learn from the knowledgeable guides about the various processes necessary to produce the fine fruits of the island. The plantation tours are at 11 a.m. and 1:30 and 3:30 p.m. daily. The cost is J$31 ($6.82).

Firefly, 20 miles east of Ocho Rios above Oracabessa, was the home of Sir Noël Coward and his longtime companion, Graham Payn, who, as executor of Coward's estate, donated it to the Jamaica National Trust. Now open daily from 10 a.m. to 4 p.m. for an admission of J$5 ($1.10), the house has been kept exactly as it was on the day Sir Noël died in 1973, even to the clothes, including Hawaiian print shirts, hanging in the closet in his austere bedroom with its heavy mahogany four-poster. The library contains his large collection of books, and the living room is warm and comfortable with big armchairs and two grand pianos where he composed several famous tunes. Here the English Queen Mother was entertained. When the lobster mousse he was serving her melted, Coward opened a can of pea soup. Guests—Coward's "bloody loved ones"—who spent a night or more were housed in Blue Harbour, a villa nearer to Port Maria, where Sir Noël lived before building Firefly. Celebrated guests included Evelyn Waugh, Winston Churchill, Errol Flynn and his wife, Patrice Wymore, Laurence Olivier and Vivien Leigh, and such theatrical and cinema greats as Claudette Colbert, Katharine Hepburn, and Mary Martin. Paintings by the noted playwright, actor, author, and composer adorn the walls. An open patio looks out over the pool and the sea, and across the lawn, on his simple, flat white marble grave is inscribed simply: "Sir Noel Coward, born December 16, 1899, died March 26, 1973."

Coward was a frequent guest of Ian Fleming at **Goldeneye,** on the north shore, made fashionable in the 1950s. It was here that the most famous secret agent in the world, 007, was born in 1952. Fleming built the house in 1946, and wrote each of the 13 original Bond thrillers in it. The island permeates many of the Bond thrillers. Through the large gates, with bronze pineapples on the top, came a host of international celebrities: Evelyn Waugh, Truman Capote, Graham Greene.

The house was closed and dilapidated for some time after the writer's death. However, its present owner, Christopher Blackwell, has restored the property. It is furnished with "just the basics," the way Fleming wanted it, and the beachfront house can be rented (at a rate to be negotiated). Otherwise, unless you're a guest of the tenant, you aren't allowed to visit as it is private property. However, all 007 fans in this part of the world like to go by, hoping for a look. Inquiries about the property should be directed to Mrs. Blanche Blackwell, P.O. Box 31, Port Maria, St. Mary, Jamaica.

Harmony Hall (tel. 974-4233), was built near the end of the 19th century as another one of the "great houses" of Jamaica, this one connected with a pimento estate. Today, after a restoration, it's a center for a gallery selling paintings and other works by Jamaican artists. Arts and crafts are also sold, and some very good ones at that, not the usual junky assortment you often find on the beach. A bar in mahogany paneling has a collection of Victorian memorabilia. The gallery is open from 10 a.m. to 6 p.m., and the pub and restaurant from 11 a.m. to midnight. If you're at Harmony Hall for lunch, you can enjoy a British-style restaurant, the King's Arms, serving such dishes as fish and chips, steak-and-kidney pie, and shepherd's pie, a light luncheon costing around $15 per person. To reach it, you can drive about four miles east of Ocho Rios on the main road to Oracabessa. Or else call and inquire about their free shuttle service.

St. Ann's Polo Club at Drax Hall, going toward Runaway Bay, is reached by a turnoff to the right on a blind corner on the main road. Day membership of J$2 (44¢) allows a Saturday afternoon's enjoyment watching a polo game. The first chukka is at 2:30 p.m., and the game goes on throughout the afternoon. It is great fun to watch the noble sport of princes.

Columbus Park Museum is a large, open area between the main coast road and the sea at Discovery Bay. Admission is free. You just pull off the road and then walk among the fantastic collection of exhibits, which range from a canoe made of a solid piece of cottonwood in the same way the Arawaks did it more than five centuries ago, to a stone cross, a monument originally placed on the Barrett estate at Retreat by Edward Barrett, whose sister Elizabeth became the wife of the poet Robert Browning.

You'll see a tally, used to count bananas carried on men's heads from plantation to ship, as well as a planter's strongbox with a weighted lead base to prevent its theft. Also among the exhibits are 18th-century cannons used in the French and Spanish hostilities and during the American Revolution, and a Spanish water cooler and calcifier, a fish pot made from bamboo, a corn husker, a manual grass chopper, and a waterwheel of the type used on the sugar estates in the mid-19th century for all motive power. You can follow the history of sugar since its introduction in 1495 by Columbus, who brought canes from Gomera in the Canary Islands, and see how Khus Khus, a Jamaican perfume, is made from the roots of a plant, and how black dye is extracted from logwood. Pimento trees, from which allspice, used for curing meat, is produced, dominate the park. There is a large mural by Eugene S. Hyde, depicting the first landing of Columbus at Puerto Bueno (Discovery Bay) on May 4, 1494. The museum is well worth a visit to learn of the varied cultures which have influenced the development of Jamaica.

New Gallery Joe James, Rio Bueno (tel. 953-2392), is halfway between Ocho Rios and Montego Bay, 30 miles each way. Joe is one of those rare, gentle men in whose company you could happily spend a day or a year, listening to his talk about art, his life in England and Jamaica, his enthusiasm for painting and carving, and his hopes for the future development of art in Jamaica. He says he owes much of his success as an artist to the years he spent in flat, monochromatic Suffolk, England, but his pictures by contrast capture with ease the color and gaiety of the Jamaicans, their character, and their island. After a prior visit,

James returned to Jamaica in 1966 and opened a gallery at Runaway Bay, moving to this site in 1968 where he built the present gallery and restaurant with his own bare hands—including putting in the plumbing and making most of the furnishings. He now employs a staff of 25 in the woodcraft workshop, where he personally supervises production of the delicately carved sculptures and woodcarvings which, with his own striking paintings, fill the gallery.

Enter the gallery from the parking lot. It is brilliant with portraits, landscapes, color, and life. Indigenous woods are used to create carvings of heads, small birds, or bowls. A carved crocodile, a crab, a turtle, or a turtle-shaped ashtray are among the interesting souvenirs.

Early visitors can have breakfast for J$15 ($3.30). Lunch is served inside or on the patio with the water almost lapping your feet. For dinner, the cost of the main dish includes soup, salad, dessert, coffee, and a Tia Maria, plus a main course of grilled or broiled lobster, sirloin steak, or fresh turtle steak. The wine list includes a wide variety, or you can order Red Stripe beer. The menu is kept small so that the quality of each dish is high. Lunch costs from J$50 ($11); dinner, from J$80 ($17.60).

Warning: Don't try to bargain for the items on sale here. Joe will voluntarily offer a discount if you buy a number of objects of reasonable value. Otherwise, the prices are as marked.

Golf and Horseback Riding

Upton Country Club (tel. 974-2528) is above Ocho Rios. At the golf course, greens fees are J$60 ($13.20) a day. There are reductions for three or seven days' play, and after 4 p.m. Rental of a golf cart for 18 holes is J$64 ($14.08). A caddy charges J$28 ($6.16) for 18 holes. The course is open from 9 a.m. to dusk. Par for the course is 71. There is a bar and a card room, and light lunches are served.

Horseback riding through the allspice and coconut palms can be arranged, with the services of a guide who knows the best routes to take. The cost is about $12 for two hours with a guide.

Boonoonoonoos

Boonoonoonoos is Jamaican for "very nice" or "super," and also stands for a "happening" in Jamaica.

At **Shaw Park Gardens,** you can stroll through the magnificent gardens to Lookout Point, where a 17th-century cannon points you to a spectacular view over Ocho Rios and Turtle Bay. Other paths lead past rushing waterfalls and babbling streams, and a flight of 100 steps takes you up or down, through the trees and bushes that are a sanctuary for a rich variety of bird life. There is a saying about this path, that those who walk together here will never forget the experience. Don't forget your camera. Hours are 9 a.m. to 5 p.m., and admission is J$10 ($2.20). On most Tuesdays, a Boonoonoonoos Tea is served, along with a fashion show, followed by a band concert.

For **Dunn's River Cruise,** on Sunday and Friday at 10 a.m. and 2 p.m., bookings can be made at **JADCO** in the Ocean Village Shopping Centre (tel. 974-2092). Your hotel can make individual arrangements for you to go on this tour.

Dunn's River Feast takes place on Wednesday at 7 p.m. It's a top-notch barbecue banquet on the beach beside the tumbling waters of the falls, with roast suckling pig, chicken, rice and peas, fried bananas, and breadfruit, washed down with as much as you can drink from the Jamaican open bar. There is a lively steel band and calypso music for dancing on the sand. Many of the Ocho

Rios hotels allow a rebate for those on half-board or full-board arrangements, but the cost of the evening for others is only J$110 ($24.20). For reservations, call 274-2570.

All year on Monday and Tuesday at 7 p.m. you can enjoy a **Jamaican Night on the White River,** a few miles to the east of Ocho Rios. The boat trip takes you up the torchlit river for a picnic supper on the banks. There is an open bar for as much as you can drink. A native folklore show precedes dancing under the stars. Telephone 974-2619 for reservations. The cost is J$110 ($24.20) and the food is the same as for the Dunn's River Feast.

SHOPPING: There are three main shopping plazas—Ocean Village, Pineapple Place, and Coconut Grove—all open daily except Sunday from 9 a.m. to 5 p.m. Almost everything is offered to shoppers, including food, clothing, and souvenirs.

At **Ocean Village Shopping Centre,** a self-service laundromat offers ten-hour-a-day service. On Sunday it's only open until 2 p.m. Other facilities include Art Mart, Fantasia Boutique, Pretty Feet Shoeshop and the Honey Bee Pastry Shop. The Pharmacy (tel. 974-2041) sells most proprietary brands, perfumes, plasters for sore heels, and suntan lotions, among its many wares. The Swiss Stores offer silver and gold charms with a general Jamaican theme. In addition, there are a commercial bank, Family Foods supermarket, the Beach Bowl coffeeshop, a souvenir stand, a boutique for "ladies and gents," and shops selling in-bond perfumes, liquors, and crystal.

Pineapple Place Shopping Centre, just east of Ocho Rios, is a pleasant collection of cedar-shingle-roofed cottages set amid tropical flowers. Many shops are represented, including **Ruth Clarage** (tel. 974-2658), who specializes in beautifully colored hand-silkscreened prints. Many are embroidered by hand in her Montego Bay workshops, and if you wish, you can buy ready-made dresses, evening wear, and sports clothes. Tasteful matching ceramic jewelry can be bought also.

El Dorado (no phone) is a mass of jewelry and souvenirs including pendants of black coral, silver rings with black coral, and earrings. Paintings by local artists are also sold.

Ocho Rios Craft Park is a complex of some 150 stalls through which to browse. At the stalls, an eager seller will weave you a hat or a basket while you wait, or you can buy from the mixture of ready-made hats, hampers, handbags, placemats, and lampshades. Other stands stock hand-embroidered goods and will make up small items while you wait. Alongside all this activity, woodcarvers work on bowls, ashtrays, native heads, and statues chipped from lignum vitae, and make cups from local bamboo. Even if you don't want to buy, the park is worth a visit for it is lively and colorful.

The **Coconut Grove Shopping Plaza** is a collection of low-lying shops linked by walkways and shrubs. The merchandise consists mainly of local craft items. Many of your fellow shoppers may be cruise-ship passengers looking for something to buy.

You can see and purchase work by Jamaican artists at the **Frame Centre Gallery,** above the Little Pub on Main Street (tel. 974-2374). Work of established painters and up-and-coming talent can be seen here.

RUNAWAY BAY: Once this resort was a mere satellite of Ocho Rios. However, with the opening of some large resort hotels, plus a colony of smaller hostelries, Runaway Bay is now a destination in its own right. The place was named for escaped slaves who hid out in local caves.

Jack Tar Village, P. O. Box 112, Runaway Bay (tel. 973-3504), is a restored original plantation hall that has been turned into an all-inclusive package-deal resort similar to the chain's operation in Montego Bay. The brick foundation walls are probably those of an English fort dating from the 17th or 18th century. A subterranean passage, now bricked up, leads from the living room to the coral cliffs behind the house. The hall is named for Timothy Eaton, a Canadian who bought the house in the late 19th century.

The property is a successful coordination of the old blended with newer rooms added in wings that maintain the same architectural tradition. There are suites containing carved mahogany four-poster beds and other furnishings of the 18th-century period. Some of the bedrooms of the great house open onto an arched portico, and four units in the main house front the sea. On each side of the hall are bedroom wings with ocean views. These are furnished in a more restrained way, but with good judgment, utilizing tropical fabric designs and older mahogany pieces. Directly on the beach are the villas, with four bedrooms. Your veranda here will extend out over a rocky ledge, and the water is six feet below you. The mahogany trim used in parts of the hotel is beautiful.

In the winter season, the inclusive rate in a single is $175 daily, dropping to $150 per person, based on double occupancy. A third person sharing a double room is charged another $90 per night, and children under 12 sharing a room with their parents pay $35 a night. *In summer, tariffs are reduced to $150 a night in a single, from $135 per person based on double occupancy.* Suites cost extra, of course.

Massages are free, as are cigarettes. And drinks, including wine at lunch and dinner, are also included in the package deal. There is no scuba-diving, but other water sports are free. Each week a barbecue is offered, along with midnight snacks. Once a week there is a Jamaican buffet with a show; otherwise, the piano bar provides nightly entertainment.

The ambience of the great house and its surrounding garden is memorable. The entry lounge has smart styling, with old beams, an open fireplace, traditional wing chairs, and mahogany antiques. The dining room is dignified yet warm as you sit on carved high-backed chairs. After your meal, you can walk to an adjoining lounge and terrace for a nightcap, watching the flickering lights from the swimming pool. On the grounds is a tennis court.

Jamaica, Jamaica, P.O. Box 58, St. Ann (tel. 973-2436), is the catchy new name of this couples-type resort that offers inclusive one-week packages. Fronting the beach, it is the latest incarnation of the old Runaway Bay Hotel and Golf Club. The location is 18 miles west of Ocho Rios toward Montego Bay, which is a further 42 miles along the coast. The hotel is made up of long, low, two-story structures, set among palm trees around shady gardens leading to the pool and white sand beach. The emphasis is on comfort and relaxation. All units are air-conditioned and have private balconies overlooking the sea.

Freddie DePass, the general manager, offers high-season weekly rates of around $850 per person, based on double occupancy in a shared twin. Summer rates had not been announced at press time, but you can expect 20% or more reductions. This package rate includes three meals a day, with table wine at lunch and dinner. Drinks are paid for with tallies, an old currency of Jamaica (the currency was immortalized in the line "Come, Mr. Tallyman, tally me banana.") Guests check in at the lobby area, with two large waterfalls. As they register, they sip a complimentary rum punch.

Tariffs include use of sports equipment, including two tennis courts, a gym, a gigantic swimming pool, a Jacuzzi, sailing, and volleyball. Entertainment such as cruises and horse-and-buggy rides are also offered.

Caribbean Isle Hotel, P.O. Box 119, Runaway Bay (tel. 973-2364), is a small place with an informal atmosphere, a TV in the bar-lounge, and a dining room leading onto a sea-view patio where budget meals are served throughout the day by the swimming pool. The 14 rooms overlook the small beach and ocean, and are tastefully furnished, with private bath and shower and air conditioning. The hotel offers excellent value for your money, with a friendly atmosphere and good food.

A full breakfast costs J$15 ($3.30), and throughout the day a variety of sandwiches are offered. Dinner includes lobster and shrimp, fish, steak, pork chops, and chicken, all with a choice of french fries or creamed potato. A service charge is added. *In summer, room rates are $40 daily in a double, $35 in a single.* Daily winter rates are $60 in a double, $50 in a single.

4. Montego Bay

Montego Bay first attracted tourists in the 1940s when Doctor's Cave Beach was popular with the wealthy who bathed in the warm water fed by mineral springs. The town, now Jamaica's second-largest city, is on the northwest coast of the island. In spite of the large influx of visitors, it still retains its own identity with a thriving business and commercial center, and functions as the market town for most of western Jamaica. The history of Mo Bay, as the islanders call it, goes back to 1494 when it was discovered as an Arawak settlement.

As Montego Bay has its own international airport, those who vacation here have little need to visit Kingston, the island's capital, unless they are seeking the cultural pleasures of museums and galleries. Otherwise, you have everything in Mo Bay, the most cosmopolitan of Jamaica's resorts.

WHERE TO STAY: Montego Bay offers accommodations in all brackets, from the luxurious Round Hill to guest houses. I'll begin with—

The Luxury Leaders

Round Hill (tel. 952-5150) is one of the most distinguished hotels in the Caribbean, a gathering place of the elite. It stands on a 98-acre peninsula, once part of Lord Monson's sugar plantation, lying eight miles west of Montego Bay. Everybody from the Kennedys to Sir Noel Coward to Cole Porter has driven up the casuarina-lined, curving driveway. Perhaps as they got out of the car, they'd hear Irving Berlin trying out one of his new pieces. As a watering spa for the rich and famous, Round Hill helped make Mo Bay a well-known resort when it opened its doors in 1954.

Surrounded by gardens, Round Hill accommodates 200 well-heeled guests, who enjoy the private beach, the view of Jamaica's north shore, the vista of the mountains, and those ever-present hummingbirds. On handsome grounds, accommodations are in a couple of main units fronting the beach or in more than two dozen shingle-roofed villas scattered over the hillside, some of which have their own pools. Some of the villas are privately owned (rented when the landlords are away.) Many of these owners have stylish furnishings, including one-of-a-kind antiques and brass beds with pineapple-topped finials.

In winter, room rates range from $320 daily, double occupancy, MAP; and villa suites go for anywhere from $350 to $450 daily, double occupancy, also MAP. *Even though the hotel is closed in summer, villas are available on a weekly rental basis, ranging from $1500 for a two-bedroom selection all the way to $2500 weekly for the deluxe choice, a four-bedroom honey with a private pool.* Tariffs include maid, cook, and gardener. Michael J. Kemp is the friendly, helpful, and considerate managing director.

At the little sandy bay is an intimate straw hut and an open terrace where guests congregate for informal luncheons. At the core of the building you'll find the celebrted piano bar which used to be familiar to Rodgers and Hammerstein. Dining is on a candlelit terrace beneath a giant banyan tree, or else you'll be served in the roofed-over Georgian colonial room overlooking the sea. The cuisine is a mixture of Jamaican and continental dishes. At times the finest buffet meals in Jamaica are set out here. Guests still dress for dinner, and black tie is more or less the rule on Saturday night.

The place is sedate, and entertainment is varied—a bonfire beach picnic on Monday, a calypso barbecue on Wednesday, and dancing nightly. A program of water sports is offered, and guests can play tennis on the hotel's all-weather courts.

Tryall Golf and Beach Club, in Hanover Parish (tel. 952-5110), is a complex of elegant villas and a stately stone and glass great house built in 1834 and vastly restored. The location is on a 2200-acre sugarcane plantation, about 14 miles from the airport at Montego Bay and some 12 miles from the heart of the resort itself, a pleasant 20-minute drive. It has been called one of the grande dames of Jamaican resorts, and it is. For my money it's one of the most beautifully decorated resorts on the island, almost a cliché of Caribbean charm, with much use of chintz and vivid floral patterns, everything harmoniously color coordinated in sea blue and canary yellow.

A total of 44 recently refurbished units, all air-conditioned, are offered. The hotel offers large handsomely furnished guest rooms with picture windows and in some cases four-posters. The most expensive rentals are the luxuriously furnished villas, set in lush tropical foliage, and designed and placed on the grounds for privacy. Villas come with full-time staff, including a cook, maid, laundress, and gardener. It's the ultimate in luxury for the island, and very expensive.

The regular guest accommodations in winter range from $280 to $320 daily for two persons on the MAP. A two-bedroom villa rents from $2000 per week, EP. However, there is a shoulder season between the first of November and mid-December when great house acommodations are reduced. There is another shoulder season for one month from mid-April to mid-May. At those times, two persons can stay in the great house at prices ranging from $190 to $230 daily, MAP.

The great house closes in summer, but the villas, beach café, and all recreational facilities remain open. *In summer, a two-bedroom villa rents for $1200 weekly, a three-bedroom villa for $1900 weekly, both EP.*

Josef Berger, the general manager, runs a superb operation. Born in Austria, yet a resident of the Caribbean for many years, Mr. Berger draws on a wealth of experience in managing properties as diverse as the Dominican Republic's Casa de Campo and Puerto Rico's Palmas del Mar. He has instituted the daily ritual of afternoon tea in the Brisith tradition, served at four with little "finger" sandwiches.

Before-dinner drinks are served in a sitting room opening onto a glass-enclosed veranda lit by candles. International specialties along with Jamaican dishes are served in the multitiered dining room. On many nights in season, music and dancing are presented. The deliciously varied meals are prepared by a staff directed by Paul Redihan and beautifully served by a batallion of impeccably dressed waiters. Lunch is at the beach bar, where equipment is available for snorkeling, sailing, or windsurfing. Deep-sea fishing can also be arranged.

The pride of the estate is the fairways of the 18-hole golf course, a 6680-yard, par-71 course. Six Laykold tennis courts, two lit for night games, are also offered. Horseback rides along century-old trails can also be arranged.

The pool has a swim-up bar. If you want to go on a tour, ask Vincent, the concièrge. He seemingly knows everything about Jamaica.

For reservations and more information, get in touch with a travel agent or Tryall Golf and Beach Club, P.O. Box 3492, Alexandria, VA 22303; call 800/336-4571 nationwide; in Virginia, call 703/370-8377.

The **Half Moon Club** (tel. 953-2211) lies about eight miles from Montego Bay and some six miles from the international airport. Set in a 400-acre estate alongside one of the finest white sandy beaches in Jamaica, it's better than ever, having undergone a much-needed $3-million refurbishing. Its managing director, Heinz E. W. Simonitsch, was awarded the "Golden Conch" as the most outstanding hotelier in the West Indies.

Set in pleasant gardens, the resort complex consists of hotel rooms, cottages, apartments, and golf villas. Over the years it has attracted many a distinguished guest, including Vice-President George Bush.

From the west side of the property, which offers a mile of swimming beach, a guest can sail, windsurf, or snorkel, and from the east side it's possible to go scuba-diving or deep-sea fishing. One can swim in the club's two major freshwater pools or play tennis on one of the club's 13 courts (four of which are floodlit at night). There are also four lit squash courts (British tradition lives on), and of course the 18-hole Robert Trent Jones–designed golf course is another lure.

From mid-April to mid-December, daily rates start at $120 per person, based on double occupancy, rising to $180 per person for a deluxe suite with a private pool, both MAP. Villas directly on the beach on the EP range from $90 to $120 per person. In winter, these same accommodations rent for $160 per person, based on double occupancy, up to $260 per person, MAP. Villas, on the EP, cost from $120 to $190 per person.

The clubhouse grill has a personal touch, set as it is beside a working water wheel from a bygone sugar estate. For my comments on the cuisine served here, refer to the restaurant section. The club has a calypso group, a resident band, nightly shows, and one can also taxi into Montego Bay to sample the nightlife there. The Half Moon also has a shopping arcade with a pharmacy and boutiques. There is also a beauty salon, as well as a sauna and massage facilities.

First-Class Choices

The **Royal Caribbean Hotel**, P.O. Box 167 (tel. 953-2231), was in 1966, the choice of Queen Elizabeth II and Prince Philip when they visited the island. The building lies on its own private beach, and all its ground-floor rooms and public areas are paved with marble. There are three bars, the Gazebo, the Almond Beach Bar, and the Captain's Bar close to the boat dock. The maître d'hôtel, Wilford Samuels, and the chef, Albert Spence, have looked after the dining experiences of the regulars and newcomers for more than 20 years at the Patio Restaurant where you can dine under the stars. A new addition is La Parisienne Coffee Shop, open from 10:30 a.m. to 8 p.m.

The double room rates from mid-December to mid-April are $150 to $200, including an American breakfast. *In summer the cost is $100 to $150.*

Activities include day and night tennis, snorkeling, Sunfish sailing, and windsurfing, all free. If you require lessons, there is a charge of $5 per half hour. Also available are scuba-diving, $15 per half hour, and deep-sea fishing, $187.50 per half day and $300 per full day. A full entertainment program is offered year round, and for the young at heart the hotel has added a late-night disco. Under the management of Michael Knox-Johnston, the Royal Caribbean has undergone considerable refurbishment to enhance its "Old Jamaican" atmosphere.

Sandals Resort Beach Club, P.O. Box 100 (tel. 952-5510), is a couples-only resort, in the familiar Club Med theme, but more specifically a spin-off of the famous "Couples" in Ocho Rios. Accommodations are either in villas spread along 1700 feet of white sand beach or in the main house where all bedrooms face the sea and have private balconies.

All are air-conditioned and well furnished. You can have a drink at the large indoor bar or at the one by the pool. Most meals are served in the open air, or if you prefer, there's a delightful dining room. The Olympic-size pool supplements sea bathing, and the beach is dotted with thatched roofs under which loungers beckon. The resort has its own tennis courts, a croquet lawn, and a sauna. Water sports are provided at the beach.

Sandals is one of the most romantic hideaways in Mo Bay. Incidentally, you don't have to be married: all you need do is check in here as a male-female couple. Naturally, children are not welcome. For the inclusive weekly rates (the minimum stay, incidentally), nearly everything is taken care of except your air fare. That means all meals, sports activities, accommodations, entertainment, wine, drinks, even some costume parties. *Summer packages range from around $830 to $1200 weekly, these rates being for two, of course.* The same deal is available for friendly couples in winter but at around $2000 to $2400 weekly.

Trelawny Beach Hotel (tel. 954-2450) is a 350-room, self-contained resort in Falmouth, about half an hour's drive from Sangster International Airport in Montego Bay, under Warwick International Hotels. It recently underwent a $2-million renovation program. The end result is an open-air, tropical feeling. Locally made materials, in keeping with the policy of the "New Jamaica," were used when possible, including wicker furniture along with Jamaican floral fabrics. The focal point of Trelawny is the circular lobby. The 1400-foot beach area was more than tripled with the leasing of 1100 feet of adjacent frontage. Bohíos were built around the pool area, and many new trees and flowers have been planted in the gardens to give everything a lusher look.

In winter, the daily MAP rates per person are $125 in a single, $103 in a double, and $95 in a triple. Children 12 and under may share a room with an adult at $24, MAP. Accommodations are in air-conditioned rooms with private balconies and an ocean or mountain view. *Daily MAP rates in summer are $112 in a single, $88 per person in a double, and $80 per person in a triple.* There is a maximum of three persons to a room. Lunch is an extra $14 daily if desired. Taxes and service are extra. A honeymoon package is available.

Rates include complimentary tennis, water sports, live entertainment nightly, shuttle bus service to Mo Bay, and parties. Free lessons are given in scuba-diving, snorkeling, Sunfish sailing, windsurfing, and waterskiing, even reggae dancing. The resort has four lit Laykold tennis courts, plus a swimming pool.

Meals are served in the Jamaican Room, an indoor, air-conditioned dining room that has been decorated with wicker chairs, cedar tables, and carpeting. On the Palm Terrace you can order from an à la carte menu, as well as the adjacent Almond Tree coffeeshop and by poolside.

Holiday Inn Rose Hall, P. O. Box 480 (tel. 952-2485), is an oceanside hotel whose stone facade is separated from the busy street outside by a screen of palm trees. The hotel assures its guests' privacy by having a guard at the entrance to screen persons coming in. Inside you find numerous amenities, including a free-form pool whose narrowest section is spanned by an arched footbridge. A sandy beach, a variety of water sports (glass-bottomed boats, sailboats, and scuba- and skindiving), a disco, a Jamaica-style nightclub with limbo dancers and fire-eating entertainers, and tennis courts are also available for the patrons' enjoyment. Other facilities are a children's playground and a choice of five bars—one in an inner atrium—plus four restaurants.

In winter, singles range from $111 to $150 daily. Doubles go for $116 to

$160. *In summer, singles are priced from $84 to $103 while doubles cost $90 to $110.* In any season, an extra person can be lodged in any unit for an additional $10 per night. Taxes are added to the bill. MAP is available for $45 more per adult, $35 per child under 12.

Wyndham Rose Hall Beach Hotel and Country Club, P. O. Box 999 (tel. 953-2650), is at the bottom of a rolling parcel of land along the north-coast highway. The hotel is constructed of several ochre-colored rectangular cubes set amid flowering gardens with palms, shrubs, fountains, and winding access roads. Although it's popular as a convention site, the hotel also caters to a family-oriented market where children are considered an important part of the clientele.

Behind the reception area at the bottom of a flight of stairs there are three pools—one for wading, one for swimming, and a third for diving. It's never more than a short walk to one of the many bars scattered around the hotel property, and a sandy beach, rental sailboats, and a top-rated golf course meandering over a part of the hotel grounds are here for the enjoyment of the guests. You'll also find three reataurants, three tennis courts, and a busy staff of social organizers. Every night a live band performs in the Junkanoo nightclub and disco whose jungle theme is furnished in a tropical motif of big murals and comfortable banquettes. It opens every night at 8:30.

Owned by a worldwide and rapidly expanding hotel chain based in Dallas, Texas, the hotel charges between $145 and $200 daily in high season for a single or double room. A third person sharing a double room pays an additional $25 per day. MAP costs another $40 or $50 per person. For individual reservations, call toll free 800/822-4200 in the continental U.S.

Jack Tar Village, P. O. Box 144 (tel. 952-4340), is called simply "The Village" in Mo Bay. Like its sister hotels in Puerto Plata, Runaway Bay, and Grand Bahama, it offers one of those "all-inclusive" package deals, including, while you're here: all meals; unlimited wine with lunch and dinner; unlimited beer, wine, and liquor both day and night; daytime tennis; water sports such as windsurfing, snorkeling, and sailing; nightly entertainment; sauna and massages; free use of the tennis clinic; and even reggae dance lessons.

Its policy, as of this writing, is to require no minimum stay. That means a rate in winter of $175 daily in a single, $150 per person in a double. Children under 12 sharing a full double with their parents are charged only $35. *Rates go down in summer to $140 daily in a single, $125 per person in a double, plus another $35 for a child under 12 (sharing).*

Private balconies open directly onto Montego Bay, and guests practically live in their swimsuits (and skimpy ones at that). A few steps from your private room lead directly to the beach. Lunch is served at beachside or in the main dining room.

For reservations, call toll free 800/527-9299.

Less Expensive Choices

Wexford Court Hotel, Gloucester Avenue (tel. 952-2854), is on the main road about ten minutes to downtown Mo Bay and close to Doctor's Cave Beach. The small hotel has a pleasant pool and a patio where in season calypso is enjoyed. The rooms are air-conditioned, and some have nice living/dining areas, bathrooms, and kitchenettes, if you wish to cook for yourself. All rooms have patios shaded by gables and Swiss chalet-style roofs. *In summer, singles range in price from $50 to $60 daily, and doubles go for $60 to $70. Triple rooms are also available, costing from $70 to $80.* In winter, rates go up: from $65 to $80 daily in a single, from $75 to $90 in a double, and from $85 to $100 in a triple. For breakfast and dinner, add another $32 per person daily.

The Wexford Grill includes a good selection of Jamaican dishes, such as chicken deep fried with honey. Guests can enjoy drinks in the Wayside Pub.

The hotel is owned and operated by Godfrey Dyer, who has led an interesting life, being a former policeman, detective, and taxi business entrepreneur. When he found that his other ventures were getting to be too demanding, he settled for just running the hotel.

Royal Court Hotel, Sewell Avenue (tel. 952-4531), is a budget accommodation set on the hillside overlooking Montego Bay, with a swimming pool. The rooms are furnished with bright, tasteful colors. All have air conditioning, private bathrooms, and patios. The larger ones have fully equipped kitchenettes. *The charge in summer for a single is $50; for a double, $65.* In winter, a single costs $58 to $79; a double $39 to $50 per person, all EP, plus tax.

Meals are served in the Grotto Bar, and dinner is a set meal. On Sunday evening, a Jamaican buffet is served around the pool. Nightly, a resident band plays soft music on the patio under the stars, for dancing or listening.

Free transportation is provided to the town, the beach, and the golf course and tennis club, where special rates can be arranged for hotel guests. This hotel is spotlessly clean, attractive, has a charming atmosphere, and is good value.

Carlyle Beach Hotel, P. O. Box 412 (tel. 952-4140), is an excellent choice for a budget stay. Separated from the sea by the main road, the hotel is built around the large pool and patio, but you can walk over to the beach if you prefer to swim in the sea. All 52 rooms are air-conditioned and have large, cool balconies with a view of the Caribbean. The lobby is cheerful and spacious, and there is a quiet lounge with comfortable chairs. The Pub Bar and Restaurant is decorated in a British old-world style.

For lunch, you can select cold salads, sandwiches, or something from the grill for $8 and up. Dinner, from $20, might begin with a seafood cocktail and follow with lobster, steak, or fresh fish. Freshly cooked vegetables are served with all main courses. Desserts, cheeses, and excellent coffee will add the finishing touches to your meal.

The hotel has a pleasant atmosphere and offers good value. It's on Kent Avenue and is within walking distance of Montego Bay's best shopping area. *In summer, a single costs $54 daily; a double, $64; a triple, $74.* Winter rates are $75 daily for a single, $85 for a double, and $95 for a triple. Children under 12 are free when sharing a room with their parents.

Ocean View Guest House, Sunset Avenue, P. O. Box 210 (tel. 952-2662), is half a mile from the airport and the same distance from the public beach. Buses pass the door for the ride down into Mo Bay, and the owner runs his own bus to and from the airport. There is a small library and TV room. You can use a stock of Jamaican music tapes to provide background, or you might want to hurl a few darts. All the rooms are either air-conditioned or have fans. Each has hot and cold running water, and most open onto a veranda or the spacious front porch. It's quietest at the back.

In the off-season, room rates are $12 in a single, $9 or $9.75 per person in a double. In winter, the costs rise to $18 in a single, $14 or $15 per person in a double. The owner will arrange for you to play tennis or golf, and water sports can also be arranged.

Toby Inn, P. O. Box 467 (tel. 952-4370), is another budget accommodation. It's not on the sea, but the famous Doctor's Cave Beach is a short walk away. There is a pool, and the Cozy Tree Bay will cater for your immediate needs if you don't want to go into town. In season, live entertainment is presented most nights of the week, but things are quiet off-season. All rooms are air-conditioned and have bathrooms. In winter, singles on the EP range from $70 daily; doubles $80 and up, all EP. Room tax is extra. *In the off-season, prices* *drop to $55 daily in a single, $60 in a double.* You'll be served a good breakfast and a pleasant dinner, including Jamaican dishes, in the air-conditioned dining room or on the patio. There is also a Chinese-Polynesian restaurant, the Pagoda Kai.

Beach View Hotel, P.O. Box 86 (tel. 952-4420), is right across from the Doctor's Cave Beach, or you can go to Cornwall Beach to swim. This is a good budget place with a pool on the roof and a patio area with a stone floor where, in the Bistro Restaurant and Bar, you can while away many pleasant hours listening to live music or talking. *In summer, singles range in price from $40 daily; doubles, $45 to $60. An extra person pays $16.* In winter, a single goes from $55; a double, $60 to $80. An extra person pays $18. For breakfast and dinner, add $35 per person.

Doctor's Cave Beach Hotel, P.O. Box 94 (tel. 952-4355), across the highway from the famous beach, is backed by lush vegetation and has a small garden patio among the trees, with a dance floor. There's a pool and a game room for wet days. Meals are taken on the terrace surrounded by trees, which are floodlit at night. In the Cascade bar, with stone walls and wooden roof, you can listen to music.

EP singles in the off-season rent from $55 daily; doubles, from $75, EP. In winter, tariffs in a single increase to $60 daily; in a double, from $80. For breakfast and dinner, add $25 per person per day extra to the charges quoted.

Along one of the passages are pictures of all the national figures from Admirals Rodney and Nelson to the present prime minister.

Richmond Hill, Union Street, P.O. Box 362 (tel. 952-3859), is visited primarily by diners (see the recommendations to follow), but it's also an inn, a remodeled historic manor house built in the 1700s. The property was owned by the Dewars, a Scottish clan from which the famous whisky takes its name. Units are scattered in a series of outbuildings surrounding the pool. The bedrooms aren't spacious, but are in keeping with the character of the old house. A few of the accommodations have kitchens and air conditioning, and all open onto verandas. In winter, singles pay $70 daily; doubles, $90—plus a supplement of $42 for breakfast and dinner. *In summer, rates are lowered: singles cost from $55, doubles $70.*

FOOD IN MO BAY: The resort has some of the finest—and most expensive—dining on the island. But if you're watching your wallet, you'll find that food is often sold right on the street. For example, on Kent Avenue you might try jerk pork, a delicacy peculiar to Jamaica. Seasoned spare ribs are also grilled over charcoal fires and sold with extra-hot sauce. Naturally, you order a Red Stripe beer to go with it.

Cooked shrimp are also sold on the streets of Mo Bay. They don't look it, but they're very hotly spiced, so be warned. If you have an efficiency unit with a kitchenette, you might also want to buy fresh lobster or the "catch of the day" from Mo Bay fishermen. It's easily and readily available.

Now, my more formal dining selections below.

Brigadoon Restaurant, 2 Sewell Ave., off Queen's Drive (tel. 952-1723), offers free limousine service from and to your Mo Bay hotel. The restaurant is open from 5 p.m. to midnight. The pleasant entrance leads to the bar, where you can sit on a comfortable stool and try a Veta's Special before dinner. There is an inside dining room in case of bad weather, but most of the time you eat on the wide, half-covered patio between the tropical forest and the sea, with candles on the tables and wicker-shaded lights flickering among the trees. A friendly staff knows what good service is and makes sure you enjoy your meal.

From the menu of interesting dishes, why not try a Brigadoon conch maska of shellfish with a rum and garlic sauce? You might like the smoked dolphin with lemon sauce or escargots bourguignonnes before embarking on the main meal, which includes soup, hot bread and butter, salad, and fresh vegetables in the price of the main course. Among the main dishes, fresh fish, especially red snapper and kingfish, are the big drawing cards. You can also order U.S. T-bone steaks and prime sirloin. One specialty is labeled simply "Jamaican National Dish," and the chef asks you to trust him! Among the desserts, try the Jamaican banana flambé, followed by coffee from the Blue Mountain. My last dining tab here came to $30.

Dress at the Brigadoon is informal, and you can dance after dinner or just listen to calypso music or the latest reggae. There is no cover and no minimum.

The **Diplomat,** 9 Queen's Dr. (tel. 952-3353), offers a delightful, informal yet elegant evening. Hidden behind a long white wall, gates lead to a sweeping driveway through clipped lawns, old trees, and colorful flower beds to a gracious house, not as old as its columned style would suggest. The marble-floored entrance with an Italianate water garden leads into the hall where there is a small bar, and down two steps into the tastefully simple drawing room and lounge. Comfortable sofas and armchairs are gathered around coffee tables. A grand piano in the corner is played softly by a Jamaican, Crawford, who seems to know every tune ever written. The bar waiter takes your drink order, and you will probably be greeted by the manager, Georg Kahl, who has spent more than 30 years in the restaurant business. He was born in Poland of German parents, and has traveled widely.

The restaurant does not require ties and jackets for men, but shorts and T-shirts are frowned on. Georg will call the maître d' to take your order from the well-balanced menu. Guests dine on the terrace overlooking a floodlit ornamental pool with fountains playing and trees silhouetted with lights leading down toward the sea. The calm efficiency of the waiters completes a pleasant evening. Liqueurs are served at your table or in the drawing room. Expect to spend $25 per person.

Georg is in partnership with Ralph Chapman, a retired English businessman who built the house as his private home. The other body on the management team is a big, sloppy, friendly mastiff, Caesar, and his son, Sonny, who always greet guests and see them into their home. This is a good place from which to watch Mo Bay's famous sunsets.

The **Half-Moon Club,** P.O. Box 80 (tel. 953-2211). Franz V. Eichenauer, the general manager of the resort hotel containing this restaurant, is a tireless, German-born chef who participated over the years in winning 189 gold medals for cuisine. He is also a clever inventor of new dishes. Today he applies his talents to the constant upgrading of the food facilities at the Half-Moon Club and is recognized as one of the main driving forces behind what island hoteliers call the "New Caribbean Cuisine."

Specialties include such savory dishes as lobster and callaloo soup, deboned curried goat, cubed lamb marinated in papaya juice with coconut butter and yogurt, roast of veal stuffed with lobster, shrimp and chicken creole, breast of chicken stuffed with lobster, and many other concoctions, each of which combines local and imported ingredients in dramatically new twists.

In fact, the kind of dishes that helped win the Culinary Olympics for the Caribbean team in 1984 (a team headed by Mr. Eichenauer) are served on the tree-shaded outdoor terrace—such viands as shrimp calypso (stuffed with banana, sauteed in coconut butter, and served with a curry sauce), chicken paradise (stuffed with pineapple and cashew nuts and served with an apricot rum sauce), and tropical strudel capped with a Jamaican rum sauce.

Meals on the outdoor terrace are served under the spreading branches of an 80-year-old sea grape tree whose limbs are festooned with colorful lanterns. A lattice-trimmed gazebo adds decoration, while a covered veranda offers shelter in case of rain. Dinner is a six-course, fixed-price affair costing about $18 per person. Those wishing to order à la carte in the slightly more formal surroundings of the clubhouse will pay around $27 for a full meal.

Marguerite's by the Sea, Gloucester Avenue (tel. 952-4777), is a well-known Mo Bay eatery, which, as its name implies, overlooks the sea. You can dine on a terrace overlooking the water, enjoying the fresh food which is usually well prepared and served by a friendly staff, along with a tasteful atmosphere. The menu changes, depending on the availability of fresh produce. You can, however, generally count on getting lobster or a grilled New York sirloin. Invariably there is a "catch of the day," and you can ask the chef to steam it in coconut milk if you prefer. International dishes include the likes of chicken chasseur or a seafood crêpe, the latter an especially good luncheon choice. For a complete dinner, the tab is likely to be $30. It's best to call for a reservation. You may not need it, but why take a chance?

The **Wexford Grill,** in the Wexford Court Hotel (tel. 952-2854), is one of the finest dining choices for an authentic Jamaican cuisine. It's also one of the bargain dinners of the island, costing around J$75 ($16.50) for a complete meal. The cuisine on any given night might be curried goat, which tastes much better than it sounds, or fresh kingfish. The cook does wonders with chicken, and someone on the staff once boasted to me, "All Jamaicans know how to cook—and cook good. They learn it early." Don't go here for decor, but for "jerk pork" or akee and saltfish, the national dish. If that goat didn't turn up, perhaps it will be mutton instead. The fruits are ripe and fresh, properly considered delicacies. "Paw-paw" turns out to be papaya, and you'll also find juicy mangoes and pineapple. The restaurant, open 24 hours a day, stands at the southern tip of the Mo Bay hotel district.

Richmond Hill Inn, Union Street (tel. 952-3859), is an old plantation house above the bustle of the bay area. The restaurant overlooks, and is part of, a large patio with a swimming pool and romanesque statues on low plinths beside it. A stone balustrade runs around the patio, which has views over the town and the bay. Music is muted and classical in the early evening, but calypso is introduced later on.

You might begin your repast with a shrimp and lobster cocktail, which for many years I have found their best appetizer. Dolphin (the fish, that is) is regularly featured among the "catch of the day." I generally skip over surf and turf to order their well-prepared wienerschnitzel. If you're traditional, try the sirloin or lamb chops, and don't plan to escape for less than $35 for dinner.

The **Calabash Restaurant,** Queen's Drive (tel. 952-3891), perched 500 feet above sea level, has a great view from the Garden Terrace and Roman Balcony, where you dine among the flowers to the sound of classical music. Authentic national dishes of Jamaica, such as curried goat as a main course or akee and saltfish as an appetizer, are served daily. The menu is a blend of Jamaican and continental cuisine highlighted by seafoods of the Caribbean. Good wines accompany a well-planned menu. You can also find a juicy filet mignon, lamb chops, or veal mixed in the fare. To the average tab of $25 per person, there is a 15% service charge. Free transportation from your hotel is provided. The restaurant is open daily for dinner from 6 to 9:30 p.m. The Calabash is quiet, comfortable, and well run.

The **Pelican,** Gloucester Avenue (tel. 952-3171), is informal and popular both with polite and well-mannered Jamaicans themselves as well as visitors. In air-conditioned comfort, it starts early serving breakfast. Later at lunch you might prefer a burger or a Jamaican fruit salad. Milkshakes, beer, milk, and lemonade are also sold. At night you might be ready for a lobster, the most expensive item on the bill of fare. A meal here should come to about $20 per person. The atmosphere is relaxing, enhanced by natural cedar, cut stone, and tropical foliage. The Pelican is convenient to many Mo Bay hotels.

The **Town House,** 16 Church St. (tel. 952-2660), is a lovely old, dark-brick house built in 1765. The restaurant has recommendations from, among others, *Gourmet* magazine. You find the bar and restaurant around at the back of the house in what used to be the cellars, now air-conditioned with tables set around the walls. Old ship lanterns give a warm light, and pictures of bygone days and of soldiers of the past adorn the walls. Straight-back chairs with cane seats surround tables on which lamps flicker. Flagstones lead from the bar to the restaurant, and you sip your apéritif while choosing your meal. Orders are individually prepared by the chef, James H. Snead.

The place is a tranquil, cool luncheon choice, if you want to dine lightly, enjoying sandwiches and salads—or more elaborate fare if you're hungry—far removed from the noonday glare of Mo Bay. If you return for dinner, it becomes more atmospheric, and you're faced with a wide and good selection of main courses. Everybody seemingly talks favorably of red snapper en papillotte, that is, baked in a paper bag. You might also try stuffed lobster. I'm fond of the chef's large rack of barbecued spare ribs with the owner's special Tennessee sauce. Another specialty is "surf and turf kebabs." You'll easily spend from $25 for dinner.

House of Lords Supper Club and Seafood Palace, in W. G. Hilcram's entertainment complex, Holiday Village, Rose Hall (tel. 953-2113), is set back from the traffic of the north-coast highway across from the Holiday Inn. This Jamaican-owned restaurant is on the upper floor of a concrete and glass building whose lower level contains a popular disco and a snackbar. To go to the dining room, you climb a winding, red-carpeted stairway to reach the slightly faded red-and-white supper club. Here you'll be treated to such specialties as lobster or shrimp cocktail, conch or fish chowder, Jamaican pepperpot soup, three kinds of lobster, a selection of fish, chicken creole or Cordon Bleu, or sirloin steak. The waiters are formally dressed and usually quite courteous. Full dinners begin at around J$110 ($24.20). The restaurant is open only for dinner seven days a week, but if you're in the neighborhood at lunchtime, the snackbar on the ground floor is open 24 hours every day. Many dinner guests end their evening with a stop at the ground-floor Disco Inferno (see "After Dark," below).

Dolphin Grill, Holiday Village (tel. 953-2676), is a well-planned complex of eating facilities clustered around a kidney-shaped pool where many guests choose to spend at least part of the afternoon. Near the Holiday Inn, the Jamaican-owned establishment features the pool surrounded with tables, and the Quarterdeck bar's raised and covered platform just a few steps away. If you wish, you can have your meal in the main dining room, a high-ceilinged Jamaica-style facility with exposed wood and lots of windows overlooking the pool. The beach is only a few steps away.

You may choose seafood cocktail, canapé Diane with bacon and banana, lobster bisque, three kinds of lobster, many varieties of fish including snapper, and several meat dishes such as sirloin steak. The average dinner costs around J$115 ($25.30); the average lunch, J$30 ($6.60). In addition, the establishment boasts a piano bar where live music begins at 9:30 every evening and breakfast facilities where meals are served every morning beginning at 6. A rum punch at the cabana bar costs around J$8 ($1.76) any time of day.

If all you want is a light meal, sandwich, or salad, a snackbar near the main road away from the pool will be happy to serve it to you.

Kentucky Fried Chicken, 23 Orange St. (tel. 952-4555), by City Centre Shopping, amid art stores, duty-free shops, and women's clothing stores, offers a family bucket with 15 pieces of chicken, plus rolls, for J$46 ($10.12). There are 11 other stores, in Ocho Rios, Kingston, May Pen, Spanish Town, and Mandeville.

Butterflakes Pastries Ltd., 19 Harbour St. (tel. 952-2314), is the best such shop for selling the famous Jamaican "patties." They cost J$1(22¢), and a line forms early in the morning to get the patties piping hot from the oven. The shop, run by Orientals, also sells a wide variety of other pastries as well.

Dining in Falmouth

Glistening Waters Inn and Marina, Falmouth (tel. 954-2229). Residents of Montego Bay sometimes make the 22-mile drive out here just to sample an ambience of the almost-forgotten Jamaica of another era. The restaurant is housed in what was originally a private clubhouse of the aristocrats of nearby Trelawny. About six years ago Pat and Patricia Hastings transformed the wood-frame building into a neighborhood restaurant, where one of the few decisions that patrons need to make is whether to sit behind the screens of the wood-walled plantation-style interior or on the outside veranda overlooking the quiet lagoon. The furniture here may remind you of a stage set for *Night of the Iguana*. Wicker chairs alternate with simple wooden tables for the kind of place where you wouldn't be surprised to see a retired minister quietly reading the newspaper next to a faded debutante.

If you want a tour of the property, English-born Patricia will show you the rapidly growing menagerie in the backyard. You'll probably see a baby crocodile caged in a beached fishing boat, a tidal pool of oxbill turtles (each of which Patricia, a former nurse, stitched together after their various mishaps in the wild), and a host of tame birds, including geese and ducks, plus a friendly assortment of canines. On the premises there's a cabana bar with a thatched roof and a nearby boat mooring.

Menu items may include many local fish dishes such as snapper or kingfish, often marinated in a vinegar sauce (with onions, carrots, pimento, peppers, and allspice), served with bammy (a form of cassava bread). Other specialties are three different lobster dishes, three different preparations of shrimp, three different conch viands, fried rice, and pork served as chops or in a stew. Full meals begin at J$42 ($9.24).

Many guests look forward to coming here because the waters of the lagoon are memorable. They contain a rare form of phosphorescent microbes which, when the waters are agitated, glow in the dark, the glistening usually starting between 7 and 7:30 p.m. Every Wednesday and Saturday the Hastingses offer boat cruises which include transportation from the Trelawny Beach Hotel, although they are open to anyone. A two-hour tour around the lagoon, costing around $18 per person, with an open bar included, is a pleasant way to spend an early evening. If you'd like to combine the cruise with a full dinner afterward, the combined fee is $30 per person, including a glass of wine. Depending on the arrangements for that particular night, short tours of about 30 minutes, costing $15, are sometimes possible if guests phone ahead. This includes a set-menu dinner, although transportation to Glistening Waters is the guest's responsibility.

WHAT TO DO: Rafting on the Martha Brae is an exciting adventure. To reach the starting point, drive east to Falmouth and turn approximately three miles inland to Martha's Brae Rafters Village. The rafts are similar to those on the Rio

Grande, and charge about J$82 ($18.04) per raft, with only two persons allowed on a raft, plus a small child if accompanied by an adult. The raft trips, lasting about an hour, operate seven days a week until 4:30 p.m. You sit on a raised dais on bamboo logs. The rafters supplement their incomes by selling carved gourds. Along the way you can stop and order cool drinks or beer along the banks of the river. There is a bar, a restaurant, and a souvenir shop in the village. Later you get a souvenir rafting certificate.

Cornwall Beach, opposite the Casa Monte Hotel, is Jamaica's finest underwater marine park and fun complex, a long stretch of white sand beach with dressing cabanas. Water sports, scuba-diving, and snorkeling are available. Admission to the beach is J$2 (44¢) per adult, J$1 (22¢) for children, for the entire day. A bar and cafeteria offer refreshment.

Doctor's Cave Beach, across from the Montego Bay Club, helped launch Mo Bay as a resort in the 1940s. Admission to the beach is J$2 (44¢) for adults, J$1 (22¢) for children. You can participate in water sports here. Dressing rooms, chairs, umbrellas, and rafts are available.

For a plantation tour and even a hot-air balloon ride to get a bird's-eye view of the countryside, go on a **Hilton High Day Tour** (tel. 952-3343), with an office on Beach View Plaza. Round-trip transportation on a scenic drive through historic plantation areas is included. Your day starts at the plantation, with the balloon ride if you choose, the next thing being a continental breakfast at the old plantation house on a patio overlooking the fields and hills. You can roam around the 100 acres of the plantation and visit the German village of Seaford Town or St. Leonards village nearby. A Jamaican lunch of roast suckling pig with rum punch is served at 1 p.m. Horseback riding is available for $6 extra per half hour. The charge for the day is $55 per person with the balloon ride included, $45 per person just for the plantation tour, breakfast, lunch, and transportation.

Jamaican Swamp Safari at Falmouth has tours daily every hour on the hour from 10 a.m. to 4 p.m. The tours lead through the crocodile pens and breeding centers. A 1000-pound crocodile can move at 120 miles an hour, and the reptiles' love calls are original, to say the least. Prices of the tour are J$10 ($2.20) for adults.

For reservations and tickets to any of the major attractions of the island, call Jadco, Gloucester Avenue (tel. 952-4425), in Montego Bay.

Rocklands Feeding Station, Anchovy (tel. 952-2009), otherwise called Rocklands Bird Sanctuary, was established by Lisa Salmon, known as the Bird Lady of Anchovy, attracting nature lovers and birdwatchers. It's a unique experience to have a Jamaican doctor bird perch on your finger to drink syrup, and to feed small doves and finches millet from your hand, plus watching dozens of other birds flying in for their evening meal. The feeding station is open every afternoon throughout the year from 3:15 until half an hour before sundown (varying with the time of year). Admission is J$10 ($2.20) for two adults and their children. Do not take children age 5 and under, as they tend to worry the birds. Smoking and playing transistor radio are forbidden. Rocklands is about a mile outside Anchovy on the road from Montego Bay.

Montego Bay's most famous trip is the Governor's Coach Tour, a railway tour in a coach, which is a second-class European version and not air-conditioned. The trip takes you some 40 miles into the heartland, through banana and coconut groves and coffee plantations, stopping frequently at little villages. At one such stop, Catadupa, you can order men's Jamaican shirts and women's dresses made to measure in the style and material you select. You collect your garments on the return journey.

The tour visits the Appleton Estate Rum Distillery, where you can drink a complimentary rum punch. You also pass Anchovy and Cambridge; and at Ipswich, a visit is made to the famous caves to see the fascinating rock formations. The tour takes all day, from 9:30 a.m. until 4:30 p.m. The cost is $35 per person, which includes a picnic lunch with rum punch.

Touring the Great Houses

Occupied by plantation owners, the great houses of Jamaica were always built on high ground so that they overlooked the plantation itself and could see the next house in the distance. It was the custom for the owners to offer hospitality to travelers crossing the island by road. They were spotted by the lookout, who noted the rising dust. Bed and food were then made ready for the traveler's arrival.

The most famous great house in Jamaica is the legendary **Rose Hall** (tel. 953-2341), a nine-mile jaunt east from Montego Bay along the coast road. The subject of at least a dozen Gothic novels, Rose Hall was immortalized in the H. G. deLisser book *White Witch of Rosehall*. The house was built about two centuries ago by a John Palmer. However, it was Annie Palmer, wife of the builder's grandnephew, who became the focal point of fiction and fact.

Called "Infamous Annie," she was said to have dabbled in witchcraft. She took slaves as lovers, killing them off when they bored her. Those servants called her "the Obeah woman" (Jamaican for voodoo). Annie was said to have murdered several of her coterie of husbands while they slept, and eventually suffered the same fate herself in a kind of poetic justice.

Long in ruins, the house has now been restored and can be visited by the public at a cost of $5. Hours are daily from 9 a.m. to 5 p.m.

Greenwood (no phone) is even more interesting to some house tourers than Rose Hall. On its hillside perch, it lies 14 miles to the east of Montego Bay and seven miles west of Falmouth. Hours are 9 a.m. to 6 p.m. daily, and admission is J$20 ($4.40) for adults. Erected in the early 19th century, the Georgian-style building was once the residence of Richard Barrett between 1780 and 1800. He was of the same family as Elizabeth Barrett Browning. On display are the original library of the Barrett family, with rare books dating from 1697, along with oil paintings of the Barrett family, china made by Wedgwood for the family, and a rare exhibition of musical instruments in working order, plus a fine collection of antique furniture. The house today is privately owned by Bob and Ann Betton, who have decided to open it to the public.

MONTEGO BAY SHOPPING: The main shopping areas are the **City Centre** (where most of the in-bond shops are, aside from at the large hotels), **Overton Plaza, Holiday Village Shopping Centre,** and **Westgate Shopping Centre.**

Blue Mountain Gems Workshop (tel. 953-2338), at the Holiday Village Shopping Centre, offers a tour of the workshops to see the process from raw stone to the finished product you can buy later.

Throughout the island, Appleton's overproof, special, and punch rums are excellent value. Tia Maria and Rumona (the one coffee-, the other rum-flavored) are the best liqueurs. Khus Khus is the local perfume.

Caribatik Island Fabrics, at Rock Wharf on the Luminous Lagoon (tel. 954-2314), is two miles east of Falmouth on the north-coast road. You'll recognize the place easily, as it has a huge sign painted across the building's side. This is the private living and work domain of Muriel and Keith Chandler, who escaped the snows of Chicago years ago to introduce a batik studio and clothing factory to Jamaica as a pioneer industry in 1970. Today the batiks of Muriel Chandler are viewed as stylish and sensual garments by chic boutiques from Padre Island, Texas, to fashion enclaves in the American Northeast.

Muriel's original dresses are printed on cotton or Chinese silk, and range in price from $85 to around $750 for a top-of-the-line couture creation.

There is also a full range of scarves and wall hangings, some patterned after themes such as a parade of the endangered animal species of the world, as well as abstract patterns reminiscent of a painting by Jackson Pollack. Original batik paintings, each one of a kind, range from $300 to as much as $2500. The shop, which contains a factory in back where either Muriel or Keith will describe the intricate process of batiking, is open daily except Sunday and Monday from 10 a.m. to 3 p.m.

For visitors who want an out-of-the-way retreat along the Jamaican coast, Muriel and Keith Chandler have recently added a handful of guest bungalows behind their batik studio. Three units, appropriately named Rivendell after the elfin house in the Tolkien trilogy, include access to a raised swimming pool and views of the hibiscus-lined garden, where a concrete cobra, a prop from an old Ginger Rogers movie, guards the entrance. Before being renovated by the Chandlers, the thick walls of the apartments housed a rum warehouse. Inside, the bathrooms are discreetly open-air, with trailing vines and lots of exposed hardwood. Each apartment contains a fully stocked refrigerator and bar, the contents of which guests pay for when they check out. The units cost $120 a day, breakfast included, and are suitable for two persons.

At the **crafts market** near Harbour Street in downtown Montego Bay you can find a wide selection of handmade souvenirs of Jamaica, including straw hats and bags, wooden platters, straw baskets, musical instruments, beads, carved objects, and toys. That "jippa jappa" hat is important if you're going to be out in the island sun.

AFTER DARK: There are a lot more activities to pursue in Montego Bay in the evenings than going to the discos, but the resort certainly has those too.

Currently, the hottest disco action in Mo Bay is at the **Disco Inferno,** W. G. Hilcram's entertainment complex, Holiday Village, Rose Hall (tel. 953-2113). On the ground floor of the same building that contains both the House of Lords restaurant and a 24-hour snackbar, this spacious gathering place is furnished in a vaguely Spanish style of somber wood and flashing lights. Disco alternates here with live reggae bands, sometimes two per night, each playing to the enthusiastic response of the Jamaican crowds which pour in. Concerts usually begin at 9 p.m., after which, at around 10:30 p.m., disco music takes over. Women are invited free to this nightclub/disco on Monday and Thursday. Otherwise the entrance fee is J$7 (1.54). There's a long bar which serves rum punch for J$9 ($1.98) and beer for J$6 ($1.32). The Inferno is across from the Holiday Inn on the north-coast highway.

Witch's Hideaway at the Holiday Inn (tel. 953-2485) is for those on a macabre after-dark circuit. You can in fact disco-hop throughout most of the evening, if that is your somewhat dated desire. Drinks here also begin at $3. Sometimes instead of recorded music you get live entertainment here. One night I saw a fire-eater; on another occasion it might be a limbo dancer or calypso singer. One always hopes (so far in vain) to hear another Jamaican, the equal of Harry Belafonte, "tally me banana." The Holiday Inn has more recently opened the **Thriller Disco** in the nightclub. It is free to hotel guests, and it's open seven days a week at 8 p.m. Movies are sometimes shown.

The **Hell Fire Club** at the Rose Hall Beach & Country Club (tel. 953-2650) apparently bears no relationship to its namesake in England. It's not that daring! Some ten miles or 18 minutes from the airport at Mo Bay, the disco club is decorated in a flaming scarlet. Live combos are brought in here to perform, and some of the shows have been quite good. Drinks begin at $3.

But for more "life-seeing" adventures, I have the following recommendations:

Cornwall Beach Party, on Wednesday and Friday night at 7, features a barbecue, open bar, and for entertainment, fire eating, limbo, singing, and dancing far into the night. It costs $25 per person. I've seen this beach party turn into an X-rated event, depending on the crowd. It's no place to take the kiddies.

Every Sunday, Tuesday, and Thursday, there is an **Evening on the Great River,** during which you ride in a fishing canoe up the river ten miles west of Montego Bay. A torchlit path leads to a re-created Arawak Indian village, where you eat, drink as much as you like at the open bar, and watch a floor show. The Country Store offers jackass rope (tobacco by the yard), nutmeg, cinnamon, brown sugar, and all sorts of country items for sale. The cost, with transportation, is $28 per person.

For both the Cornwall Beach Party and An Evening on the Great River, make reservations through **Jadco,** on Gloucester Avenue in Montego Bay (tel. 952-4425).

5. Negril

Jamaica's newest resort, on the western tip of the island, is famed for its seven-mile beach, the pride of the area. A place of legend, Negril recalls Buccaneer Calico Jack (his name derived from his fondness for calico undershorts) and his carousings with his infamous women pirates, Mary Read and Ann Bonney.

Emerging Negril is 50 miles and about a two-hour drive from Montego Bay's airport along a good road, past ruins of sugar estates and great houses. From Kingston, it's about a four-hour drive, a distance of 150 miles.

This once-sleepy village has turned into a tourist mecca, visitors drawn to its beaches along three well-protected bays—Long Bay, Bloody Bay, and Orange Bay. Negril became famous in the late 1960s when it attracted laid-back American and Canadian youth, who liked the idea of a place with no phones, no electricity. They rented modest digs in little houses where the local people extended their hospitality.

At some point you'll want to explore Booby Cay, a tiny islet off the Negril Coast. Once it was featured in the Walt Disney film *20,000 Leagues Under the Sea,* but now it's rampant with nudists from Hedonism II.

Chances are, however, you'll stake out your own favorite spot along Negril's own seven-mile beach. You don't need to get up for anything, as somebody will be along to serve you. Perhaps it'll be the "banana lady," with a basket of fruit perched on her head. Maybe the "ice cream man" will set up a stand right under a coconut palm. Surely the "beer lady" will find you as she strolls along the beach, a carton of Jamaican beer on her head, a bucket of ice in her hand.

WHERE TO STAY: Hedonism II, P.O. Box 25 (tel. 957-4200), is called the "home of hedonism." In the familiar Club Med theme, it includes "the works" in a one-package deal, except at Hedonism they even give you all the booze you want to drink. Some abuse the privilege, but most guests seemingly drink in moderation.

The resort is closed to the general public. There is no tender of any sort, and tipping is not permitted. In two-story clusters, 280 rooms are stacked, dotted around a gently sloping 22-acre site. You enter under a cedar-roofed portico to find a miniature "city," totally equipped with everything and a staff usually willing to serve your needs. There is a large covered area filled with rest tables, bars, and at the end, a swimming pool. Most of the guests, who must be above

16 years of age, are Americans, with a significant number of Canadians, some Europeans, and a few South Americans.

A minimum stay of one week is required. Rates given below are per person weekly, based on double occupancy. This is not a "couples-only" resort. Singles are accepted, but the rooms are doubles. Therefore you are likely to be assigned a same-sex roommate if you should arrive alone. Arrivals are on Friday, Saturday, Sunday, or Monday. Weekly tariffs in winter range from a low of $910 to a high of $1010 and up. *In summer, you get a major reduction, paying from $740 to $810 per person weekly, all inclusive.* In the open-sided dining room, Jamaican and international buffets are served.

There are six tournament-class tennis courts, along with two badminton courts and a basketball court. There's also a small gymnasium. You can go horseback riding, sailing, snorkeling, waterskiing, scuba-diving, or windsurfing. Nightly entertainment is presented, along with a live band, show disco, and piano bar.

On one section of the beach "clothing is optional," as the management states. Some women prefer to go merely topless. On some nights guests dress up in sheets which they like to think of as Roman togas. Provocative beauty contests are staged as well, including one with wet T-shirts.

The resort also has a secluded beach on nearby Booby Key (originally cay) where guests are taken twice a week for a picnic.

Sundowner Hotel, P.O. Box 5 (tel. 957-4225), is the traditional beachside favorite—in fact, some say it "invented" Negril as a resort. It was once the secret hideaway of the *Saturday Evening Post* cover artist, Norman Rockwell. The crowd is (usually) convivial, decidedly informal, and often young. At a point north of Negril, Rita Hojan opened this place to an uncertain future. Over the years it's grown steadily, increasing in popularity with a beach-oriented crowd who like the sleepy lifestyle here. Ms. Hojan's staff is most loyal, and many members have been with her almost from the beginning. A family atmosphere prevails.

The Sundowner is a two-story, motel-like structure, and rooms are simple, but comfortable enough. Bedrooms are nicely coordinated, with one-color themes plus fine fruitwood furnishings, and each unit has a private terrace where you can enjoy breakfast overlooking the sea. For the higher priced units you get more room and a tiny refrigerator. In winter, two persons can stay here on the MAP at rates ranging from $175 daily, a single person paying from $150. *In summer, two persons are charged from $130; one person $90—all MAP tariffs.*

The cook's creativity reaches its peak at the Wednesday and Saturday buffets when a live calypso band comes in to entertain guests. Meals are served under a spreading breadfruit tree right at the water's edge. Before dining, you can perch at a bar table made from seashell-filled barrels. The main house is the core of the original inn, which has been turned into public rooms. The beach is enough for most people, and you can also partake of water sports at the Negril Beach Village nearby. The Sundowner is a great getaway place.

Rockhouse (for reservations, write to P.O. Box 78, Park Ridge, IL 60068; tel. 312/296-1894) looks, as you approach it, like a remote African village ready to be photographed for *National Geographic*. It lies on the lighthouse road, just south of Negril. Frankly, this place isn't for everyone. It caters to surf lovers who like its lack of phones and limited electricity. Other than the stars, kerosene lamps—the ones used in "My Old Kentucky Home"—provide the main illumination at night.

These thatched rondavels, rustic style, with their peaked roofs, cling to the trees and cliffs above coves and pools. On the water doesn't mean on the beach. You go swimming "off the rocks." Walls are built of woven split bamboo, but glass doors, big ones, let in the view. Your particular hut might be perched on a rock formation just ten feet above the water. A lot of divers like to lodge here, exploring the crystal-blue coves.

The cottages may look primitive from the outside, but actually they have the desired amenities tucked away. There are studios and villas for two guests, with a sleepling loft for additional beds. The beach house has two bedrooms, a living and a dining room, plus a bath and a kitchen with a two-burner gas plate. There's a private shower with palm trees and sky for a ceiling.

This is primarily an adult retreat, but children over 12 are welcomed. In winter, two persons pay from $90 daily in a studio, $120 in a villa. *In the off-season, two persons are charged from $70 to $90 daily.*

For the beach house, meals are prepared in your room, or else you can go over to Rick's on the beach. If you'd like to have supper at the complex, ask the management, giving them a 24-hour notice. On my most recent visit, a Jamaican cook taught me how to prepare curried god-a-mi, a shiny black fish from the nearby Cabaritta River.

Charela Inn, P.O. Box 33 (tel. 957-4277), is a seafront inn reminiscent of a Spanish country-style hacienda. It's not the place for social types on the see-and-be-seen circuit, but for those wanting genuine hospitality where they're treated like one of the family. The warmth of the place stems from your hosts, Daniel and Sylvia Grizzle, who personally run and supervise everything. Homey meals and an informal atmosphere attract a loyal following to this site, on the A1, north of Negril.

The main house and its addition have a row of arches with air-conditioned bedrooms, all with a tropical architecture and decorative details. In winter, singles can stay here on half-board terms ranging from $120 daily; doubles (also half board) cost from $80 to $95 per person. *In summer, MAP singles range from $85 to $100 daily, doubles costing from $60 to $65 per person.*

The graciously appointed dining room with its high-backed colonial chairs carries out the Spanish theme, and overlooks a garden as well. At sunset most guests gather at the fountain terrace to sample the various rum drinks. At this time your hosts like to introduce fellow guests. Ask about snorkeling, waterskiing, fishing, boating, tennis, golf, horseback riding, and sightseeing.

Negril Beach Club Hotel, P.O. Box 7 (tel. 957-4220), is a resort designed around a series of white stucco cubes adorned with exterior stairways and terraces. The entire complex is clustered like a horseshoe around a rectangular garden whose end abuts a sandy beach. There's ample parking on the premises and easy access to a full range of sporting facilities including snorkeling, a pool, volleyball, table tennis, and windsurfing. Other activities can be organized nearby, and beach barbecues and buffet breakfasts are ample and frequent.

This place has been compared to Aggie Grey's old place in Samoa, especially since there's a kind of communal feeling among the residents of the angular accommodations, which range from simply furnished units to one-bedroom suites with kitchens. *In summer, singles range from $48 to $80; doubles, from $60 to $90; and triples, from $72 to $100.* In winter, singles go from $72 to $110, doubles cost $85 to $120, and triples run $95 to $120. MAP can be arranged for $20 per person per day.

WHERE TO DINE: Most people eat at their hotel. However, there are some other possibilities.

Whether you have a meal or not, everybody in Negril at sundown seems to head for **Rick's Café** (no phone), the name inspired by the old watering hole of Bogie's *Casablanca.* Here the sunset is said to be the most glorious at the resort, and after a few fresh fruit daiquiris (pineapple, bananna, or papaya) you'll give whoever's claiming that no argument. I recently drank the night away with a group of divers staying at Rockhouse, a stroll down the road. At this cliffside proximity to nature, "casual" is the word in dress. The location where you order your eggs Benedict, Jamaican style, or fresh lobster is right on the westernmost promontory. Ham omelets are good here, and there are lots of Stateside specialties. The fish is always fresh, and you might have red snapper or grouper. Try the chef's Jamaican fish chowder. Expect to pay from $10 to $22 for dinner. You can also buy plastic bar tokens at the door, which you can use instead of money à la Club Med.

Rick's also has a fully equipped dive shop, snorkel rentals, scuba tours of the coral cliffs, and lessons with a fully qualified instructor.

Mariners Inn and Restaurant, West End (no phone). The main reason most guests come here is for the boat-shaped bar and the adjoining restaurant whose access is through a tropical garden which eventually slopes down to the beach. As you drink or dine, the breezes will waft in under the most pleasant and relaxed experiences in Negril. You can lunch here for around J$25 ($5.50), although if you want a conch steak or a portion of red snapper, it may cost you twice as much. Lobster, chicken, and tuna salads are also available, as are cheese omelets, club sandwiches, homemade pâté, and—if you really want to dine properly—lobster thermidor. Manley Wallace is the Jamaican owner who, with his attractive staff, works seven days a week from 8:30 a.m. till very late at night.

A handful of three- and four-unit bungalows is connected to this restaurant, renting for around $100 each, including breakfast, for two persons. Each contains a private bath, ceiling fan, louvered doors, a garden setting, and simple furniture.

Negril Sands (no phone) is a large-scale cabana where the owner may greet you in a Dorothy Lamour sarong as you disembark from your car near the sandy frontyard between the roadside trees and the water. This is the kind of place where you can arrive sometime in the morning and spend a carefree day on the immaculate beach of this establishment, the first of its kind ever to be built on the sands of Negril. The owner is the cultivated and humorous Elinor Gubler, a Jamaican who married a Swiss expatriate named Hans years ago. You're likely to see a score of well-proportioned Germans and Swedes basking in the tropical sun along with friendly Jamaicans (often artists and diplomats) and a goodly number of North American refugees from urban centers.

The headquarters and base from which all of the beach action (or non-action, as you prefer) emanates is an octagonal thatched-roof cabana where the convivial bar is open all day and where luncheon buffets are served daily from 12:30 to 3 p.m. A full buffet, which sometimes includes half a grilled lobster, costs $9 per person. Othewise, a meatless salad bar goes for $3 per person. À la carte items are hamburgers, barbecued chicken and pork chops, and fish of the day with herbs and garlic sauce. You'll always be welcome to stay through dinner, since the bar is open daily until midnight. Live music is featured from 8 p.m. on Saturday and from noon to 4 p.m. on Sunday.

If you're in Negril on a Wednesday night, head over to the **Sundowner** (tel. 957-4225; see the hotel recommendations). There you can sample fine cookery at a West Indian buffet, featuring Jamaican specialties. The evening will cost you about J$90 ($19.80), and it's well worth it. At beachside, you dine under a thatched roof, watching the sun set. In fact, you spend a lot of time in Negril watching sunsets. To top your meal, you can order Jamaican coffee.

Café au Lait, Lighthouse Road, West End (tel. 957-4277). Both the furniture and the building here were made as a learning project by the students at a nearby technical school. You'll quickly learn, however, that there's nothing experimental about the well-prepared French and Jamaican cuisine served here, where the walls are open to the breezes coming through from the surrounding forest. Daniel and Sylvie Grizzle are the Jamaican/French couple who prepare the cuisine served by a charming staff participating in the well-organized teamwork of this place.

Menu items include quiches, escargots, lobster prepared several ways (including in salads and bisques), and an unusual crêpe made with cheese and callaloo. There are four kinds of pizza (one with lobster) and several kinds of salad, one made with fish. The menu also features roast lamb, pork, and chicken, as well as a wine list stressing French products. Dessert may be lime tart with ice cream, concluding a full meal which costs from J$100 ($22). This restaurant is open only for dinner, beginning at 5 every evening.

Kaiser's Café, West End (no phone). The place is so laid back that you might end up spending an entire afternoon under its thatched-roof bar and restaurant. Platters of ham and eggs, sandwiches, and salads are offered in simple surroundings near a rocky beach. You can order simple food from a service window at one end of the terrace or dine inside under the high rafters of a room where live Jamaican music is sometimes featured. In the event there's entertainment, you pay a cover charge of J$25 ($5.50). The café is open every day for breakfast, lunch, and dinner. Swing time usually stretches from 8:30 p.m. until after midnight. You may be tempted to walk across the causeway connecting the mainland to a small island after you finish your breakfast or lunch. Here you'll probably find people sunning themselves and willing to chat.

The most economical way to dine in Negril is to walk along the lighthouse road, where you'll see a string of about ten or so good little restaurants. Ignore their "plain Jane" entrances and think instead of the good food served.

I've found that **Chicken Lavish,** Westend, whose name I love, is the best of the lot. Don't ever call here—in fact, there's no phone. Just show up on the doorstep and see what's cooking. Curried goat is a specialty, as is fresh fried fish. Fresh Caribbean lobster is prepared to perfection here, as is the red snapper caught in local waters.

But the main reason I've recommended the joint is because of the namesake. Ask the chef to make his special Jamaican chicken. He'll tell you, and you may agree, that it's the best on the island. Along with a salad and dessert, expect to spend around $15 for a complete meal. The location is south of the town

What to wear here? Dress as you would to clean up your backyard on a hot August day.

6. Mandeville

The "English Town" Mandeville is certainly situated on a plateau more than 2000 feet above the sea in the tropical highlands. The commercial part of the town is small, surrounded by a sprawling residential area popular with the large North American expatriate population mostly involved with the bauxite-mining industry. Much cooler than the coastal resorts, it's an ideal center from which to explore the entire land.

Shopping in the town is a pleasure, whether in the old center or in one or the modern shopping complexes such as Grove Court. The market in the center of town teems with life, particularly on weekends when the country folk bus into town for their weekly visit. The town has several interesting old buildings. The square-towered church built in 1820 has fine stained glass, and the little churchyard tells an interesting story of past inhabitants of Mandeville. The Court House was built in 1816, a fine old Georgian stone-and-wood building with a pillared portico reached by a steep, sweeping double staircase.

Among the interesting attractions, **Marshall's Pen** (tel. 962-2260) is one of the great houses, an old coffee plantation home some 200 years old and filled with antique furniture, fine grandfather clocks, beautiful carpets, and valuable rugs. The house is a history lesson in itself, as it was once owned by the Earl of Balcaris, the island's governor. In 1939 Arthur Sutton, who traces his family back to the old Dutch colony of New Amsterdam, acquired the property. Now, with his son, Robert, he farms the 300 acres, breeding mainly Jamaican red poll cattle. The Suttons have a large collection of seashells, some fine Arawak relics, and a large general stamp collection.

Arthur Sutton, with charm and wit, will entertain you with the history of his home and the island and with anecdotes of the origin of local words. This is very much a private home, and should be treated as such. Reservations to view it are usually made by applying to the Hotel Astra, P.O. Box 60 in Mandeville (tel. 962-3265 for further information). Admission is J$15 ($3.30).

WHERE TO STAY: Hotel Astra, 62 Ward Ave. (tel. 962-3265), is my top choice for a stay in this area. It's a family-run hotel, the home of the McIntyres, who do all they can to ensure that visitors and local people alike are satisfied. Diana McIntyre-Pike, known to her family and friends as Thunderbird (she is always coming to the rescue of guests), happily picks up people in her own car, taking them around to see the sights and organizing introductions to people of the island.

The hotel has 20 double rooms and two suites, mainly in two buildings reached along open walkways. The Zodiac Room, entered from the lounge area, offers excellent meals served by friendly staff members. Lunch or dinner is a choice of chilled juice, beef and vegetable soup, or pumpkin soup; followed by shrimp rice, meatballs Italiano, or braised steak. All main dishes are served with a selection of rice, buttered cho-cho, scalloped potatoes, and other vegetables. A large salad bowl is also included at dinner. The kitchen is under the personal control of Diana, who is always collecting awards in Jamaican culinary competitions, and someone is on hand to explain to you the niceties of any particular Jamaican dish. A complete meal costs around $25.

The Revival Room is the name of the bar, where everything including the bar stools is made from rum-soaked barrels. Try the family's own homemade liqueur and "reviver," a pick-me-up concocted from Guinness, rum, egg, condensed milk, and nutmeg—guaranteed not to fail. There is a dart board for a game, if the locals haven't beaten you to it. English pub hours are kept, from 11 a.m. to 3 p.m. and from 4 to 11 p.m. Bar snacks, including pizzas, are served if you don't want a full meal.

Friday night is barbecue night, when guests and townfolk gather around the pool to dine. Spare ribs, chicken, and steak are delectable, costing from J$25 ($5.50) to J$65 ($14.30), depending on your selection of meat. In addition to the pool, there is a sauna, or you can spend the afternoon at the Manchester Country Club, where tennis and golf are available. Horses can be provided for cross-country treks.

The tariff all year is $35 to $80 single or double. No meals are included in the rates.

Mandeville Hotel, Hotel Street (tel. 962-2138), is a modern place but lacks the intimate atmosphere of the Astra. It has a large indoor bar and a spacious lounge where daily papers and weekly magazines are laid out on a large round table. Activity at the hotel centers mainly around the pool and the coffeeship, where substantial meals are served at moderate prices and at rates good all year.

Room rates range from $30 to $60 single and $35 to $70 double, no meals included, plus the usual taxes. There are attractive gardens with many fine old trees and lovely roses, and golf and tennis at the Manchester Country Club.

Horseback riding can also be arranged.

WHERE TO EAT: Bill Laurie's Steak House, Bloomfield Gardens (tel. 962-3116), 100 feet above Mandeville, is a long, two-story wooden house with a veranda stretching the length of the upper floor. Outside you are likely to find 14½ cars, none less than 30 years old, including an old London taxi which used to take customers home after a heavy meal. The front end of an old Wolseley makes up the total count.

Going upstairs to the bar and restaurant, you meet even more examples of Bill's squirrel-like habits—more than 500 vehicle license plates decorate the walls, pictures of cars fill all available extra space, along with visiting cards by the thousand, beer mats, and model cars vying for space among pewter tankards left there permanently by regulars who are set in their ways. "Play it if you like," says Bill of the old piano. You can even try the old Western Electric telephone to see whether the operator will respond to a turn of the crank.

In the lounge beside the restaurant is a wireless with knobs and fabric-covered loudspeaker. The kitchen still has a wood-burning stove in excellent condition, carefully blacked but no longer used. Bill, not middle-aged, came from Scotland 30 years ago and loves his island highland home in the sun, where he can indulge his love of old cars and collecting things.

The food consists of appetizers such as fruit punch or mango nectar, soups, and steaks varying in size and cut. Ground beef steak, mixed grill, and lamb chops are among the main-dish offerings. All meals are cooked to order and come with french fries, salad, and vegetables. You'll spend about $20.

The **Mandeville Hotel,** Hotel Street (tel. 962-2460), is close to the city center and popular with local business people who use the coffeeshop by the pool for a quick, appetizing luncheon stop. A wide selection of sandwiches is available. You can order milkshakes, tea, or coffee.

In the hotel restaurant, open for lunch (you must reserve for dinner but not necessarily for lunch), the à la carte menu offers such foods as Jamaican pepperpot soup, lobster thermidor, fresh snapper, and kingfish. Potatoes and vegetables in season are included in the main-dish prices. A complete meal can cost from $18. If you happen to be there at breakfast, a full Jamaican meal costs from $6.

WHAT TO SEE AND DO: Mandeville is the sort of place where you can become well acquainted with the people and feel like part of the community. One of the most interesting persons in the area is **Dr. James W. Lee,** a Canadian from British Columbia, who has lived in Jamaica for more than 30 years and works as a geologist at the Alpart plant. He has devoted much of his spare time to making a collection of old prints, dating back as far as 1561, all connected in some way with the island's history. Being a geologist, he can talk for hours about the formation and development of Jamaica and is happy to do so. You should also ask to see his amusing photo collection of offbeat and incredible advertising signs collected from around Jamaica.

To meet him, you should write well in advance of your visit to Dr. James W. Lee, P.O. Box 206, Mandeville, Jamaica.

For the speleologist, at Oxford, about nine miles northwest of Mandeville, is one of the largest and driest caves on the island. Signs direct you to it after you leave Mile Gully, a village dominated by St. George's Church, some 175 years old.

Birdwatching

Marshall's Pen estate boasts 23 endemic species of bird, as well as many winter and summer migrants, mainly warblers from North America which seek shelter among the shrubs and unusual plants in the wildlife reserve. Small parties of six can be taken on early-morning guided tours at prices to be negotiated.

Day tours are also arranged to the Cockpit Country, where if you're lucky you can see a golden swallow.

For further information, get in touch with **Robert L. Sutton,** P.O. Box 58, Mandeville (tel. 962-2260).

Taking the Waters

Milk River Mineral Bath, Milk River, P. O. Clarendon (tel. 986-2521), lies nine miles south of the Kingston–Mandeville highway. It boasts the world's most radioactive mineral waters, recommended for the treatment of arthritis, rheumatism, lumbago, neuralgia, sciatica, and liver disorders. These mineral-laden waters are available to guests of the hotel as well as casual visitors to the enclosed baths or the mineral swimming pool. The restaurant offers fine Jamaican cuisine, health drinks, and special diets in an old-world atmosphere of relaxation. The nearby Milk River affords boating and fishing. Accommodations are available at MAP rates, ranging from J$85 ($18.70) to J$100 ($22) in a single, J$150 ($33) to J$160 ($35.20) in a double, per night.

Tennis, Golf, Horseback Riding

The **Manchester Club,** 1 Caledonia Rd., P.O. Box 17 (tel. 962-2403), is the oldest membership club on the island. Close to Mandeville town center, it offers fine facilities for tennis and golf. The four hard tennis courts are used each August for the All Jamaica Hardcourt Championships, but you can use them at other times. Overseas membership is invited at a cost of $50 per year, dating from November 1 to October 31.

The clubhouse has a bar and snackbar, and there is a full-size pool table for indoor entertainment.

The international show-jumping champion, **Mrs. Goodwin,** lives at Godfrey Lands, close to Mandeville, where horseback riding and instruction can be arranged for visitors. Further inquiries should be made to Westway Enterprises Ltd., 62 Ward Ave., P.O. Box 60, Mandeville (tel. 962-3265).

Chapter X

FRENCH WEST INDIES

1. Martinique
2. Guadeloupe
3. St. Martin
4. St. Barthélemy

FRENCH CHARM and tropical beauty combine in the great curve of the Lesser Antilles. A long way from Europe, France's western border is composed mainly of Guadeloupe and Martinique, with a scattering of tiny offshore dependencies, such as the six little clustered Îles des Saintes.

Almond-shaped Martinique is the northernmost of the Windwards, while butterfly-shaped Guadeloupe is near the southern stretch of the Leewards. These are not colonies, as many visitors wrongly assume, but the westernmost *départements* of France, meaning that these cinnamon-colored *citoyens* are full-fledged citizens of la belle France.

Other satellites of the French West Indies include St. Martin (which shares an island with the Dutch-held St. Maarten; see Chapter VIII), St. Barthélemy, Marie-Galante, and Désirade, a former leper colony.

Unlike Barbados and Jamaica, the French West Indies are Johnny-come-latelies to tourism. Although cruise-ship passengers had arrived long before, mass tourism began in these islands only in the 1970s. Before that, Jacques Cousteau or David Rockefeller could retreat here, enjoying a hideaway, but that soon may no longer be possible, as Martinique and Guadeloupe move up as vacation targets. Micro-bikinis now bobble on the beach sites. Incidentally, top-less bathing is commonplace on French beaches, and areas are set aside for nudists. Créole customs make these islands unique in the Caribbean. The inhabitants also serve some of the best food. Don't be afraid if I've sent you to a dilapidated wooden shack. You may find the *New York Times* food editor there too, sampling a sumptuous gourmet meal.

1. Martinique

France's anchor in the Caribbean world, Martinique is the land of the Empress Josephine. In her youth, Madame de Maintenon, mistress of Louis XIV, also lived here in the small fishing village of Precheur.

Martinique still has remarkable women, considered the most beautiful in the West Indies. A mingling of African and French blood has produced a classic, limpid-eyed Créole beauty, famous for her *madras et foulard* costume, a dress reserved now more for special occasions. Presumably, the flair of the knots of the madras reveals whether the girl is engaged, married, or available (or any combination of the above).

Columbus discovered Martinique, and the French settled the island when the king's gentleman, Belain d'Esnambuc took possession in the name of Louis XIII. The year was 1635. In spite of some intrusions by British forces, the French have remained in Martinique ever since. Immigration from France produced sugarcane plantations and rum distilleries.

Early in the beginning of their colonization, the French imported black slaves from Africa to work the plantations. In spite of segregation, the blacks and whites mixed freely. The sensuous young women of Martinique seemed to take delight in capturing the hearts of their white masters from their less experienced brides. The mixed blood that resulted produced the saffron-colored Créole look.

At the time of the French Revolution, slavery began to decline on Martinique. But it wasn't until the mid-19th century that its abolition was obtained by Victor Schoelcher, a Paris-born deputy from Alsace. Since 1946, Martinique has been a part of France.

Martinique is part of the Lesser Antilles and lies in the semitropical zone, its western shore facing the Caribbean, its eastern shore the livelier Atlantic. It is some 4340 miles from France, 2000 miles from New York, 2300 miles from Montréal, and 1450 miles from Miami.

The surface of the island is only 420 square miles—50 miles at its longest dimension, 21 miles at its widest point.

The ground is mountainous, especially in the rain-forested northern part where Mount Pelée, a volcano, rises to a height of 4656 feet. In the center of the island the mountains are smaller, Carbet Peak reaching a 3960-foot summit. The high hills rising among the peaks or mountains are called "Morne." The southern part of Martinique has only big hills, reaching peaks of 1500 feet at Vauclin, 1400 feet at Diamant. The irregular coastline of the island provides five bays, dozens of coves, and miles of sandy beaches.

The climate is relatively mild, and the heat is rarely uncomfortable, the average temperature in the 75° to 85° Fahrenheit range. At higher elevations, it is considerably cooler. The island is cooled by a wind the French called *alizé*, and rain is frequent but doesn't last very long. From September to November might be called the rainy season. April to September are the hottest months.

The early Carib Indians, who gave Columbus such a hostile reception, called Martinique "the island of flowers," and indeed it has remained so. The vegetation is lush, including hibiscus, poinsettias, bougainvillea, everything enhanced by such trees as the flamboyant, the royal palm, coconut, giant bamboo, mango, orange, and the locust tree. Almost any fruit that can grow in the ground sprouts out of Martinique's soil—pineapples, avocados, bananas, papayas, and custard apples.

Birdwatchers are often pleased at the number of hummingbirds, while spotting the mountain whistler and blackbird as well. The mongoose is common, and multicolored butterflies add to the panorama of nature. After sunset, there's a permanent concert of grasshoppers, frogs, and crickets.

GETTING THERE: Many travelers fly **Eastern Airlines,** especially if their home airport has a nonstop flight to Eastern's Caribbean hub, Miami. The company's service has traditionally reached passengers along the East Coast, although persons coming from the Midwest (through the airline's new hub, Kansas City) and the West Coast also benefit from easy connections to and from Miami.

Eastern's afternoon flight to Martinique leaves Miami five days a week at

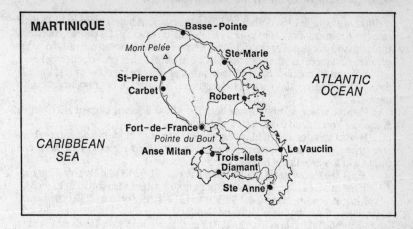

5:05 p.m., giving passengers in transit plenty of time for daytime connections from other cities. Varying with the day of the week, Eastern's flight is either nonstop or direct. When the plane does stop, it makes a brief touchdown in Guadeloupe before continuing on to Martinique. An Eastern representative greets planes arriving in Miami to direct passengers to their next connection.

The cheapest way to fly to Martinique is to book a "land package" (prearranged and prepaid hotel accommodations at one of several selected hotels) through Eastern's tour desk.

Otherwise, if passengers can reserve and pay for a round-trip ticket at least 7 full days before takeoff and wait for between 6 and 21 days before using the return half, they might be interested in an APEX ticket. The current APEX round-trip fare in high season between Miami and Fort-de-France is $467. A slightly more expensive fare is a 21-day excursion fare, which requires no advance reservations and allows delays of between 3 and 21 days before the return ticket is used. Prices for weekday travel round trip from Miami to Fort-de-France are $472, and for weekend travel, $527.

Residents of New York City whose schedules are flexible may be more interested in the weekend flights on **American Airlines,** which makes round-trip journeys from JFK to Martinique every Saturday and Sunday.

Likewise, **Pan American** flies four times a week direct from New York, touching down briefly in St. Thomas before continuing on the same aircraft to Martinique. Passengers returning from Martinique must change airplanes in an efficient connection at St. Thomas before returning to New York.

Air France flies to Martinique from Miami and San Juan, and **Air Canada** from Montréal to Toronto. Both **Air Martinique** and **LIAT** make connections to surrounding islands.

PRACTICAL FACTS: French is the official **language,** spoken by everyone. The local Créoles patois uses words borrowed from France, England, Spain, and Africa. In the wake of increased tourism, English is now understood and occasionally spoken in the major hotels and restaurants. But don't count on driving around the countryside and asking for directions in English. The Martiniquais aren't that bilingual yet.

The **French franc** is legal tender here. You should exchange your money at banks as they give much better rates than the hotels. Currency quotations in this chapter are both in U.S. dollars and French francs, as hotels often publish their rates in American dollars to visitors from North America. Of course, exchange rates are subject to dollar fluctuations. Exchange rates quoted are only for your general guidance, and may not actually be in effect at the time of your visit.

U.S. and Canadian citizens need **proof of identity** for stays of less than 21 days. After that, a valid passport is required. A return or ongoing ticket is also necessary.

Potable **water** is found throughout the island. **Electric current** is 220 volts, 50 cycles. You'll need a converter or adapter.

Health services and medical equipment are both modern and comprehensive (there are some 18 hospitals and clinics). In an emergency, your hotel can put you in touch with the nearest one.

The **U.S. Consulate** is at 14 rue Blénac (tel. 71-93-01), in Fort-de-France.

Time in Martinique is one hour later than Eastern Standard Time.

Most stores are open from 9 a.m. to 12:30 p.m. and 3 to 5:30 p.m. weekdays; closed Saturday afternoon and Sunday.

A helpful address on the island: **Office Départemental du Tourisme** (Tourist Office), Boulevard Alfassa (Bord de Mer), 97206 Fort-de-France (tel. 71-79-60).

GETTING AROUND: Travel by **taxi** is the most popular method, and rates are expensive. Most of the cabs aren't metered, and you'll have to agree on the price of the ride before getting in. Most visitors arriving at Lamentin Airport head for one of the resorts along the peninsula of Pointe du Bout. To do so costs about $16 during the day, about $22 for two in the evening. Night fares are in effect from 10 p.m. to 6 a.m. The trip from Pointe du Bout to Fort-de-France for a day's sightseeing or shopping is about $20. However, the night drive over to Fort-de-France from Pointe du Bout is about $28. It's much better to take the ferry that runs back and forth.

The famous Leyritz Plantation in the north will provide a transfer from the airport for 228F ($22.80). If you're staying at Manoir de Beauregard in the south, expect a taxi fare of 210F ($21) during the day.

If you want to rent a taxi for the day, it's better to have a party of at least three or four persons to keep costs low. Depending on the size of the car, expect to pay from 255F ($25.50) for a four-hour trip. Only a few of the drivers will be able to speak English, however.

Buses

There is no railway system in Martinique, but buses are operated from Fort-de-France, linking every single village on the island. Depending on the distance, fares run from 50¢ to $3. However, for those taking this local means of transport, I must point out that mama, her kids, or even a chicken may ride on your lap.

"**Taxis collectifs**" are preferred. These are usually limos or vans holding from about eight to ten passengers, charging fares in the 5F (50¢) to 20F ($2) range, depending on where you're going. They are faster than the buses and much less crowded. In Fort-de-France, the departure point for these CTs is at Pointe Simon on the harborfront.

Car Rentals

Many companies, both domestic and international, rent cars on Martinique. The leaders maintain airport offices which are open weekdays from 8 a.m. to noon and 2:30 to 5:30 p.m. On Saturday, car-rental offices are open from 8 a.m. to noon. In large hotels you can obtain a car at a reception desk, or through a small office the rental company might have on the premises, if the place is big enough. For 20 days, your own driver's license, if valid, is good for Martinique. If you rent a car, you must be at least 21 to 25 years old, depending on the company. Driving is on the right.

If you drive in Martinique, expect to maintain a very slow average speed, because of the island's zigzagging, narrow roads, most of which are in good condition. Expect the local driver to do anything. Incidentally, traffic laws are fiercely enforced by French gendarmes.

The prices of the major car-rental companies in Martinique are roughtly the same. I recently used the services of **Budget Rent-a-Car.** A Peugeot 104 with manual transmission and either two or four doors rents for $175 per week, unlimited mileage, or $25 per day. In addition, clients are advised to take the $4.85 collision damage waiver.

In high season, demand for cars can exceed the supply if you don't reserve well in advance while still on the mainland. The toll-free number for Budget is 800/527-0700. Budget maintains an office at the Martinique airport (tel. 79-22-88) and at the hotel complex at Pointe du Bout (tel. 76-30-45). The latter office is convenient if you prefer to check into a room before arranging to pick up your car.

Dollarwise shoppers should also compare the rates at **Avis** (tel. toll free 800/331-1212), and at **Hertz** (tel. toll free 800/654-3131).

In addition to these U.S.-based companies, there are several local companies, some of which maintain reservations facilities at the reception desks of the major hotels.

Scooter Rentals

Vespa Martinique, 3 rue Jules-Monnerot, Fort-de-France (tel. 71-60-03), has a fleet of motorcycles, motorbikes, mopeds, and scooters. For a Vespa, prices range from 90F ($9) a day to 450F ($45) a week. Reservations should be made one day in advance.

THE SPORTING LIFE: The Martiniquais don't work at their sports as hard as North Americans do. Yet they have an active sports program.

Scuba-diving, snorkeling, fishing, and waterskiing can be enjoyed all along the coastline. Golf clubs are at your disposal in all the first-class hotels, where prices are obtainable (tariffs vary considerably, depending on the duration and season).

Tennis

This game is widely practiced on the island, and each large hotel has courts. Residents play free during the day, and night games usually require a 14F ($1.40) surcharge for lighting for 30 minutes. Nonguests are faced with a playing-time charge that could range from $8 to $10 per half hour.

Your best bet is to play at one of the three new courts that have opened on the grounds of **Golf de l'Impératrice Josephine** (tel. 76-32-81; see below), at Trois-Îlets, a five-minute drive from one of the major hotels at Pointe du Bout. The setting here is one of the most beautiful in Martinique.

Scuba-Diving and Snorkeling

Scuba-divers come here to explore the St-Pierre shipwrecks sunk in the 1902 volcano eruption and the Diamond Rock caves and walls. Small scuba centers operate at many of the hotels.

Snorkeling equipment is usually available free to hotel guests, who quickly learn that coral, fish, and ferns abound in the waters around the Pointe du Bout hotels.

The Latitude, at Carbet, about a half-hour drive north of Fort-de-France, is tucked neatly into a U-shaped lagoon. Its **Carib Scuba Club** (tel. 73-69-89) is headed by Mark Balssa as well as by Michel Metery, the hotel's director, and has an impressive stock of equipment, including double and single tanks, adaptors, wet suits, and Spirotechnique regulators. A single dive costs 150F ($15), five cost 650F ($65), and a week of 13 dives costs 1200F ($120). Dives of all types can be made from nearby coves and beaches or from sites as far away as an hour by boat. One sample of the latter is the offshore landmark, Îlet la Perle, whose backdrop is the lush, mountainous northern part of Martinque.

From Latitude, waterborne excursions can be made to St-Pierre where shipwrecks from the already mentioned 1902 volcanic eruption of Mt. Pelée can be seen and explored. The most prominent, filmed for TV by Jacques Cousteau, is the metal-hulled *Roraimi*, which rests on a slant in 150 to 200 feet of water. It takes several dives to cover the entire hulk.

Other special trips, such as the all-day **Pique-Nique Nautique,** can be arranged by Latitude. Two or three times a week a boat—minimum ten passengers—departs at 9 a.m. for an hour-long voyage to an offshore fishermen's island. Guests swim and dive among angelfish, batfish, butterfish, grouper, needlefish, rock beauties, soldierfish, trumpetfish, and a long black-and-white fish locally called "Monsieur l'Abbé." After a meal of freshly caught and cooked fish, the boat returns to the hotel at around 5:30 p.m. The cost of this excursion is 250F ($25) for Latitude guests, 290F ($29) for outsiders.

To the south, **Bathy's Club** in the Hotel Méridien (tel. 66-00-00), is the scuba center for Pointe du Bout, serving neighboring hotels Bakoua and Frantel. Jean-Marc and Bertrand Sailly operate the club and, with an assistant, escort daily dive trips on the 37-foot *Egg Harbor* that leaves from the Méridien pier. Individual dives through Bathy's Club are priced at about $20. A package of six dives costs $100, and a package of 12, $166. Prices include equipment rental, transportation, guide, and drinks on board. Dives are conducted twice daily, from 9 a.m. to noon and 3 to 6 p.m., and full-day charters can be arranged. The dive shop on Méridien's beach stocks everything from weight belts and tanks to partial wetsuits and underwater cameras.

Buccaneer's Creek / Club Med (tel. 76-72-72) has long made scuba a part of its weekly packages. The dive school goes to the reefs around Ste-Anne at the southern tip of Martinique, where the club is situated.

Two other Martinique hotels also have scuba centers. The Hotel Casino La Batelière (tel. 71-90-41) houses the **Club Caraibe Subaquatique,** headed by Louis Burle and Antoinette Hartmann, both fully licensed and certified divemasters. Individual dives are about $17, six run dives $73, and ten cost $100. The boat leaves directly from the hotel.

Facing historic Diamond Rock off the southwestern coast is **Diamant-Novotel** (tel. 73-66-15), which boasts scuba facilities and a prime diving location. The crystal-clear underwater world here is challenging to the diver but presents such rewards as coral formations, multicolored fish, sponges, and a cannon or two. Inquire at the hotel about excursions, rates, and the type of scuba instruction.

Windsurfing

This is the most popular sport in the French West Indies. Equipment and lessons are available at all hotel water-sports operators, especially the **Hotel Méridien** (tel. 66-00-00), where the cost is 50F ($5) for a one-hour rental.

Waterskiing

This is available at every beach near the large hotels, the cost about 60F ($6) for 10- to 15-minute rides.

The Beaches

The beaches south of Fort-de-France are white while the northern strands are composed mostly of gray sand. Outstanding in the south is the **Plage des Salines,** near Ste-Anne, with palm trees and miles of white sand, and **Diamant,** with the landmark Diamond Rock offshore. Swimming on the Atlantic coast is for experts only, except at **Cap Chevalier** and **Presqu'île de la Caravelle Nature Preserve.** Public beaches do not as a rule have changing cabins or showers. Some hotels charge nonguests for the use of changing and beach facilities, and request a deposit for rental of towels.

Hiking

Inexpensive and guided excursions in which tourists can participate are organized by the personnel of the Parc Régional de la Martinique year round. Special excursions can be organized on request of small groups by getting in touch with the **Parc Naturel Régional de la Martinique,** Caserne Bouillé, Fort-de-France (tel. 73-19-30). A folder is available at the Martinique Tourist Office.

The Presqu'île de la Caravelle Nature Preserve, a well-protected peninsula jutting into the Atlantic Ocean, has safe beaches and well-marked trails to the ruins of historic Château Debuc and through tropical wetlands.

Serious hiking excursions to climb Mt. Pelée and explore the Gorges de la Falaise or the thick coastal rain forest between Grand'Rivière and Precheur are organized with local guides at certain times of the year by the park staff.

Camping

Camping is permitted almost everywhere, including in the mountains and forests and on many beaches. It is advisable to check with the local mayor's office or property owner before setting up camp. Campsites are usually basic, although comfortable camps with cold showers and toilets are on the southeast coast at Macabou; at Ste-Luce, Le Marin, and Ste-Anne on the south coast; and Anse-à-l'Âne near Trois-Îlets. For tent rentals, get in touch with **Chanteur Vacances,** 65 rue Perrinon, Fort-de-France (tel. 71-66-19).

Camping cars, fully equipped for five persons, can be rented from **D.L.C. Villa Vacances,** Anse-à-l'Âne (tel. 76-34-52).

Horseback Riding

Ranch Jack de Golocha (tel. 76-43-97) will arrange this for you from its starting point, about ten minutes from Pointe du Bout. You can ride through the neighboring hills, across sugarcane fields, and by sea coves. A half-day ride costs from 250F ($25).

Golf

The famous golf course designer, Robert Trent Jones, visited Martinique and left behind the 18-hole **Golf de l'Impératrice Josephine** at Trois-Îlets (tel. 76-32-81), a five-minute, one-mile drive from the leading resort area of Pointe du Bout and about 18 miles from Fort-de-France. The course unfolds its greens from the birthplace of Empress Josephine for whom it is named, across rolling hills with scenic vistas down to the sea. Greens fees for the day are 125F ($12.50) per person, 230F ($23) per couple. Electric carts rent for 150F ($15) for 18 holes, hand carts for 25F ($2.50), and a bag of clubs for 50F ($5). Under Philippe Rosier, full-time president of the club, new amenities added include a pro shop, a new bar, and a restaurant. Roland Lameynardie is the hospitable director, and the pro is Frederik Dissat.

Sailing

This is a big pastime in Martinique. It's also a big cost unless there are enough in your party.

Dufour Antilles, Marina Pointe du Bout (tel. 76-35-35), at Trois-Îlets, can arrange yacht charters with crew or bareboat.

But only a select few can afford such costs. If you want to see the waters around Martinique, it's better to go on one of the sailboat excursions in the bay of Fort-de-France and the southeast coast of the island.

A 79-foot ketch, **Captain Cap,** sails regularly from the Méridien Hotel at Pointe du Bout. Reservations can be made by calling 66-02-52. A full-day excursion with lunch is offered, and no more than 60 passengers go out at a time. Also, sunset cruises are offered as well. The day excursion is on Wednesday and Friday, with a 9 a.m. departure, returning at 5 p.m. The cost is 200F ($20) per person. The sunset cruise, with music and rum punch, is on Friday at 5 p.m., returning at 7:30 p.m., at a cost of 90F ($9) per person.

Glass-Bottomed Boat

L'Aquarius at the Méridien Hotel (tel. 66-00-00), at Pointe du Bout, departs every day at 3 p.m., returning at 5:30 p.m., at a cost of 90F ($9) per person. You might also want to go on their "Pirate Night," leaving at 6:30 p.m., returning at 10:30 p.m. At a cost of 220F ($22) per person, you're given a look at the murky depths at night with a spotlight beam and provided with a fish dinner, music, and drinks.

Sea Fishing

You can make arrangements at the **Hotel Méridien,** Pointe du Bout (tel. 66-00-00). Equipment and a motorboat leader are provided, with departures every day at 6 a.m. and again at 9:30 a.m., at a cost of 130F ($13) per person.

The Mongoose vs. the Snake

Some people say you've not really seen Martinique until you've attended a match between a mongoose and a snake. Said to have been imported by East Indian workers, this is a to-the-death struggle. If you attend such an event, you're to remain deadly still. Even lighting a cigarette is supposed to break the concentration of the combatants. Incidentally, the mongoose almost always wins. Some taxi drivers or small inkeepers on the island will tell you where to go to watch this "sport." Frankly, I think you can skip it.

CARNIVAL: If you like masquerades and dancing in the streets, you should attend carnival, or "Vaval" as it is known here. The event of the year, carnival begins right after the New Year, as each village prepares costumes and floats. Weekend after weekend, frenzied celebrations take place, reaching fever pitch just before Lent.

Fort-de-France is the focal point, and the spirit of the carnival envelops the island, as narrow streets are jammed with floats. On Ash Wednesday the streets of Fort-de-France are filled with *diablesses,* or she-devils (including members of both sexes). They are costumed in black and white, crowding the streets to form King Carnival's funeral procession. As devils cavort about and the rum flows, a funeral pyre is built at La Savane. When it is set on fire, the dancing of those "she-devils" becomes frantic (many are thoroughly drunk at this point).

Long past dusk, the cortège takes the coffin to its burial, ending carnival until another year.

FORT-DE-FRANCE: A lovely melange of New Orleans and Menton (French Riviera), Fort-de-France is the main town of Martinique, lying at the end of a large bay, surrounded by evergeen hills. Iron-grillwork balconies overflowing with flowers are commonpalce here.

The people of Martinique are even more fascinating than the town. Today the café-au-lait Créole beauties are likely to be seen in jeans instead of their traditional turbans and Empress Josephine-style gowns, but they still have the same walk. Heads held high, shoulders up, they have a jaunty spring. They're a proud, sprightly people, and I miss their massive earrings that used to jounce and sway as they sauntered along.

Narrow streets climb up the steep hills on which houses have been built to catch the overflow of the capital's more than 100,000 inhabitants.

At the center of the town lies a broad garden planted with many palms and mangoes, **La Savane,** a handsome savannah with shops and cafés lining its sides. In the middle of this grande place stands a statue of Josephine, "Napoleon's little Créole," made of white marble, the work of Vital Debray. With the grace of a Greek goddess, she poses in a Regency gown, her half-exposed breasts cooled by trade winds. She looks toward Trois Ilets where she was born.

On my latest rounds to pay my respects to the empress, the square was full of young men in drag celebrating carnival. With red paint on their petulant lips, they headed on high heels for the cathedral. A native told me that as part of a religious ceremony they represented those "she-devils" referred to earlier.

You too can join the procession to the **St. Louis Roman Catholic Cathedral,** built in 1875. It's an extraordinary iron building, which someone once likened to "a sort of Catholic railway station."

There's another statue of the island's second main historical figure, Victor Schoelcher (you'll see his name a lot in Martinique). As mentioned, he worked to free the slaves more than a century ago. This statue stands in front of the Palais de Justice.

The **Library Schoelcher** also honors this popular hero. It was first displayed at the Paris Exposition of 1889. However, the Romanesque portal, in red and blue, the Egyptian lotus-petal columns, even the turquoise tiles, were imported piece by piece from Paris, reassembled finally in this West Indian setting of royal palms and tamarinds.

Guarding the port is **Fort St-Louis,** built in the Vauban style on a rocky promontory. In addition, **Fort Tartenson** and **Fort Desaix** stand on hills overlooking the port.

The **Musée Départemental de la Martinique** (tel. 71-57-05) is the one bastion on Martinique that preserves its pre-Columbian past, the relics left from the early settlers, the peaceful Arawaks and the cannibalistic Caribs. Exhibits depict in artifacts and garments the life of these Indians. The location is along the rue de la Liberté, at the same location as the government-sponsored Caribbean Art Center, facing the Savane. The museum is open Monday to Friday from 8 a.m. to noon and 3 to 6 p.m. (from 8 a.m. to noon on Saturday), charging a 5F (50¢) admission.

Finally, **Sacré-Coeur de Balata Cathedral,** also overlooking Fort-de-France, is a copy of the one looking down upon Montmartre in Paris—and this one is just as incongruous, maybe more so.

Hotels in and around Fort-de-France

Hotel Casino La Batelière, Schoelcher (tel. 71-90-41), stands on the west coast in a chic new reincarnation. It attracts social types on the see-and-be-seen circuit. The 18-acre estate lies in La Batelière, a residential suburb about a mile from Fort-de-France. This waterside French-modern hotel is a 215-room, air-conditioned white stucco structure, set back in a garden from its wide private beach. The hotel itself lacks super-glamour but serves successfully as a center of many water sports, social activities, dining choices, and nightlife activities with its casino and disco action at the Club 21.

Furnishings are conservative, brightened considerably by the use of fabrics against a backdrop of immaculate white walls. Each unit contains a tiled bath, but best of all are the room-wide glass doors opening onto your own water-view terrace. In winter, you can stay here (with a continental breakfast included) in a single for 600F ($60) to 1200F ($120) daily, for 720F ($72) to 1400F ($140) in a double; a third person pays 220F ($22). *Off-season, singles are accepted for anywhere from 400F ($40) to 620F ($62) daily; doubles, 540F ($53) to 740F ($74).* For dinner, add 180F ($18) per person to the prices quoted.

You may enjoy a span of dredged sand or else the super-size, round-shaped swimming pool. You can order a drink under the canopied bar as you sit comfortably on blue cushions. Sports such as scuba-diving, snorkeling, windsurfing, sailing, and waterskiing are available at rates which depend on the season and duration. Tennis is free, however, except at night when there's a surcharge. On the premises are a beauty salon and barbershop, a sauna, plus a deluxe boutique called Samantha.

In the Laffitte dining room, a French, international, and créole cuisine is served, and there's a pizzeria near the swimming pool.

Hôtel l'Impératrice, Place de la Savane, rue de la Liberté (tel. 71-06-82), favored by business persons, faces a landscaped mall. Named for Josephine, it's a 1950s "layer-cake" stucco hotel, with encircling balconies overlooking the traffic at the west side of the Savane. The lounge has large, white wickerwork chairs. Adjoining is a bar with white furniture set on its tiled floor. If you don't like to perch there, you may prefer the bar on the next level, with its harmonious green and white decor.

The bedrooms are modern and functional, each air-conditioned with private bath. The front rooms tend to be noisy; yet, to compensate, windows overlook the fascinating life along the Savane. Since this is not a resort hotel, rates stay more or less the same year round. Singles pay from 220F ($22) to 280F ($28), with doubles costing from 300F ($30) to 325F ($32.50). Some triple rooms are rented for 400F ($40) daily.

If you're in Fort-de-France on a shopping excursion, you might want to consider dining at Le Joséphine, the hotel's restaurant (see my dining recommendations).

Le Lafayette, 5 rue de la Liberté, in Fort-de-France (tel. 73-80-50), is a modern hotel right on La Savane. You enter through the rue Victor-Hugo, reaching the reception hall after climbing a few steps of red stone. The dark-brown wood doors are offset handsomely by the soft beige walls. Inside the bedrooms, Japanese wall tapestries form the decorative motif, and most rooms contain twin beds in a dark-brown wood. The windows have small panes, and the brown curtains are color coordinated with the bedspreads. Bathrooms are in pure white, and the overall impression is of a neat, clean, but simple, hostelry.

In the off-season, rooms range from 225F ($22.50) to 260F ($26) in a single, the difference in price depending on the location of the unit. Doubles go from 270F ($27) to 305F ($30.50), and some triple rooms are rented for 435F ($43.50). In winter, EP singles rent for 285F ($28.50), doubles for 320F ($32), and triples for 470F ($47). A continental breakfast is an additional 25F ($2.50) per person.

The restaurant is decorated in the bistro style. Tables of hors d'oeuvres are placed in each corner of the room. All main dishes include a selection of these delectable appetizers. For a main course, I'd recommend a brochette of scallops or grilled steak. Broiled lobster, when available, is featured, or you may be attracted to the full rib of beef in a butter sauce. Meat is grilled on the charcoal. Desserts are tempting. An average repast will cost from 120F ($12).

Bristol, rue Martin-Luther-King (tel. 71-31-80), is a converted colonial home, standing on a hill on Bellevue Road, providing only ten simple rooms, each air-conditioned, with its tidy bath. Rooms are nicely furnished nothing elaborate, and all is comfortable and immaculate. This could be a good base for an inexpensive Martinique holiday.

The three-story house has veranda extensions on all sides, providing spots where sea breezes keep your conversation cool. Mr. Solis is a good host, filled with helpful suggestions about touring in Martinique. While he's got everything well organized, he runs the place in an informal way, offering a good créole cuisine in his dining room.

It's best to book in here on the half-board plan, which year round is 300F ($30) in a single, 400F ($40) in a double, and 500F ($50) in a triple. You'll need a car if you stay here and want to reach the beaches. The house overlooks the bay, about a five-minute walk from the center.

Victoria, Rond Point de Didier (tel. 60-56-78), about two minutes from the center of Fort-de-France, is a colonial house built some 100 years ago and surrounded by 30 personalized bungalows, each air-conditioned. From its encircling veranda, trimmed in gingerbread, you can look out on views of the bay. Not on the beach itself, the Victoria has a garden swimming pool. The main living room is in a traditional style, with wooden walls, an arched room divider, and louvered windows.

Year round, you pay from 225F ($22.50) to 230F ($23) daily in a single, from 260F ($26) to 280F ($28) in a double. A first-class French restaurant is right on the premises.

Le Balisier, 21 rue Victor-Hugo (tel. 71-46-54), has built its reputation mainly on its food (see my dining recommendations), but its rooms are also recommendable. A little hotel right in the heart of Fort-de-France, it houses guests in 19 rooms on its upper floors where you get better air and views. The furnishings are contemporary and functional, and units are air-conditioned and equipped with shower baths. The location's really not bad if you want to stay right in the center.

Year round, singles with showers range in price from 175F ($17.50) to 195F ($19.50) daily; doubles with the same plumbing run from 220F ($22).

Le Gommier, 3 rue Jacques-Cazotte (tel. 71-88-55), stands in a thriving sector, centrally located only a short block from the ferry pier that takes you to various beaches for swimming. However, the little hotel is tucked away on a side street, with a white-stucco and red-brick facade. Rather rawboned, the hotel is puritan bleak, with 16 air-conditioned bedrooms, scrubbed and polished clean. There is hot and cold water, as well as showers. The furniture is spartan but neat and immaculate, with matching, flowering cretonne used on the spreads and at the windows on draperies. Rates year round range from 125F ($12.50) to 165F ($16.50) in a single, from 155F ($15.50) to 180F ($18) in a double, and from 220F ($22) to 260F ($26) in a triple.

Dining in and around Fort-de-France

Many travel-wise visitors wing in to Martinique just to sample its créole cookery. The food served here, at least in my opinion, is the best in the Caribbean. The island's chefs and Créole mamas have been called "seasoned sorcerers." They took not only their native talent for good cooking, but have borrowed freely from Spain and Africa. They've even thrown in a bit of Hindu and a touch of Asian cuisine.

In honor of its African roots, créole cooking is based on seafood, often bought by the chef "fresh from the Caribbean Sea." Out in the country, every cook has his or her own herb garden, as the Martinique cuisine is highly seasoned with herbs and spices. Except in the major hotels, most restaurants are family run, offering real homemade cooking. Best of all, you usually get to dine al fresco.

Stuffed, stewed, skewered, or broiled langoustes, turtles, clams, conchs, oysters, and octopuses are presented to you with French taste and subtlety but with Martiniquais skill and invention. Every good chef knows how to make *colombo*, a spicy rich stew of pork (or beef), served with rice, herbs, sauces, and a variety of seeds. Another Créole favorite is *calalou* (callaloo in English), a soup flavored with savory herbs.

Incidentally, watch those Sunday closings.

Tiffany, La Croix Bellevue, route de Bellevue (tel. 71-33-82), is an elegant little restaurant that's my personal favorite. It may be the best table on the island, and there are those who suggest that it's one of the best restaurants in all the Caribbean. Four miles north of town, it faces the Institut Vivioz. Its owner, Claude Pradines, who also owns an antique shop in Paris, has created an enticing atmosphere in which to serve his exquisite French specialties. It's an old pink-and-white gingerbread house. Louvered windows let in the sea breezes, which are then whirled about by the ceiling fans.

He's taken over an old colonial mansion once owned by Victor Severe, a famous Martiniquais. Monsieur Pradines has brought his knowledge of antiques and their use into play here. For example, an old chest he found in the mansion is now used as a server in the dining room. In the hallway is a large shell once used in a church to hold holy water. The walls are bright with watercolors and flamboyant Haitian primitives which are in contrast to the dark-wood furniture.

In the garden are lime trees, banana, and papaya loaded with fruit, and darting trips are made there to gather produce for some of the dishes served. When Monsieur Pradines is in a good mood, he'll entertain guests with magic and card tricks.

I suggest you let Monsieur Pradines propose a dinner for you. It might be baby pullet in a tarragon or a créole sauce, perhaps duck magret with raspberry vinegar. His red snapper is delicately flavored with basil, and he might also suggest a fish filet with green peppercorns. The choice depends on what fresh produce was imported from France. I recently dined on his filet mignon with a buttery roquefort sauce. That was preceded by his asparagus in puff pastry with a herb cream sauce. The finish came with his velvety chocolate cake and a Martinique coffee. To improve his culinary skills, he journeys to France every year to learn "what's cooking." Dining here as well as speaking to him is a pleasure, especially if you're sipping his first-class wine. The typical price of an à la carte menu is 275F ($27.50). However, on the newly installed terrace, there is a set meal for 175F ($17.50), including wine and service.

La Grand'Voile, Pointe Simon (tel. 70-29-29), serves some of the finest food in Martinique. "The Big Sail" is at the stylish Yacht Club, and from its second-floor windows a panoramic view of the bay unfolds. Before dinner it's customary to have a drink in the amusing, intimate bar which has a sailing theme, with a pair of dark wood chests, low white tables, and low white seats. Overhead hang multicolored life buoys. The first-class restaurant is large, the style of decor often described as "early American."

The cuisine is excellent—French, créole, and provincial specialties, with fine seafood selections. Lyonnaise specialties lead the menu, and these include such dishes as tripe cooked with white wine, tomatoes, onions, and flavored with mustard. My favorite vegetable dish is artichokes in morels with a cream sauce. Among the West Indian specialties, stuffed crab is preferred. Sea urchin is considered a delicacy here (its taste, when cooked, is not unlike crayfish). A sea urchin blaff, or fish stew, is the chef's specialty. Another local specialty is blood sausage (boudin) créole.

Among more classical dishes, you can select beef filet Bearn, flap mushrooms à la Provençale, and scallops Grand'Voile. After all that rich food, a slice of fresh pineapple is an easy finish. My last meal here came to about $32, and you can pay far more, of course. In winter, be sure you nail down a reservation. Lyons-born Raymond and Christiane Benoit set the style for this fashionable restaurant. Closed Sunday.

La Belle Époque, 2 km. 500, route de Didier (tel. 71-89-26). Some of the best known chefs in Martinique have collaborated in the establishment of this restaurant. In a turn-of-the-century house, it was recently opened by Marcel Provost, who began his culinary apprenticeship when he was 15. His list of teachers sounds like a Who's Who of French cuisine—Bocuse, Alex Imbert, the Troisgros brothers, and some others. Since Provost spends part of his time managing a family restaurant in Caracas, he has imparted some of his skill to Yves Coyac, a Martinique-born chef whose own list of credits is long and impressive.

Cuisine here is imaginatively French, accompanied by impeccable service. Among the specialties are veal kidneys in mustard sauce, pork piccata with curry, sarde (a local fish) with cider, julienne of chicken livers with morels, seafood in puff pastry with mint, oeufs en cocotte with caviar, quenelle of sarde with cream sauce, shrimp with passionfruit juice, and an unusual concoction of beef with capers. Reservations are suggested. Full meals cost from $30.

D'Esnambuc, rue de la Liberté (tel. 71-46-51), is small, select, and elegant, the domain of Josette Kleinpeter since 1981. Stylish in decor and clientele, it overlooks the harbor near La Savane. You climb to the third floor, enjoying not only good food but a view of the bay and a refreshing atmosphere. The staircase foreshadows the abundance of green plants and vines in the dining room. The cool rectangular room is spotlessly white, the basketware chairs also white, with green cushions.

Both lunch and dinner are served. A noonday table d'hôte costs 80F ($8), and a set dinner goes for 115F ($11.50). However, if you order à la carte, your tab could easily run to 200F ($20) or more. Among the chef's specialties are a coquille of conch, a fresh green salad with lardoons, shrimp créole, and a plate of sauteed frog legs. There are also many meat dishes, mostly French in style.

El Raco, 23 rue Lazare-Carnot (tel. 72-29-16), is somewhat hard to find on a side street. It has a Spanish atmosphere with white crude walls and black ornate grated doors and windows. The Spanish owners serve a cuisine typical of many of their native regions—Catalonia, Valencia, and Andalusia. The visiting French are fond of going here to sample the paella Valenciana, washed down with plenty of sangría, of course. However, you can also order grilled shrimp provençal and stuffed mussels. Panchito (which we call ham and melon) is a good beginnng. The favorite dish around Seville is kidneys in sherry sauce, and it's served here too. If you prefer it, there's a tourist menu for 120F ($12), or else expect to spend from 200F ($20) if you order à la carte. The restaurant is closed all day Sunday and for lunch on both Saturday and Monday.

L'Escalier, 19 rue de la République (tel. 71-25-22), is a downtown balconied restaurant which you reach by climbing to the second floor. It has a long, devoted following because of its zesty créole specialties. The front balcony is inviting, with vines and bright flowers. The ambience is intimate, reflecting the local island atmosphere, with walls of light lacquered natural wood, the furniture in darker tones.

À la carte dishes include a superb crayfish tart. Here you can order that popular blaff (fish stew) made with sea urchin. Depending on the catch of the day, there's always a fish on the grill. If available, grilled lobster is served, its price based on weight, naturally. The filet mignon is very good, as is the stuffed crab. Expect to spend from 200F ($20) here, plus the cost of your wine. The restaurant is open only for lunch, every day except Sunday.

La Biguine, 11 route de la Folie (tel. 71-40-07), has been rated by some food critics as one of the finest restaurants in Martinique. It's the personal statement of a master chef, Gérard Padra, who for a long time was associated with the Bakoua. Wanting to leave the hotel trade and branch out on his own, he found this clapboard colonial-style house in teeming Fort-de-France. In it he installed a restaurant, bar, and tea salon (dining is on the second floor).

It is. Few who try his 200F ($20) gastronomic menu are disappointed. It is a showcase for the many fine dishes for which he is known, including a créole mutton soup, shrimp fricassée, broiled lobster, veal cooked with vermouth, a blaff of fish, coq au vin, and duck with pineapple sauce. For a perfect ending to one of his repasts, try one of his sorbets (sherbet) made with local fruits. He serves lunch and dinner daily except Sunday. Because he has very few tables but a big reputation as a chef, reservations are essential.

Le Coq Hardi, 0.6 km. rue Martin-Luther-King (tel. 71-59-64). If the chef/proprietor isn't too busy, he might take time out to tell you about his days of serving in the French Foreign Legion in Algeria and Indochina. Le Coq Hardi is a no-nonsense type of place which, gastronomically speaking, is known for its meats grilled over a wood fire. This is a place for hearty eaters who don't mind spending about $22 for a worthy dinner. In some ways, Le Coq Hardi is the type of bistro that the famous food critic Waverley Root was always discovering in some working-class arrondissement of Paris. It is open every day except Wednesday.

Balisier, 21 rue Victor-Hugo (tel. 71-46-54), right in the heart of Fort-de-France, has already been recommended as a hotel. But it's also a good place to dine. You are likely to get such Martinique dishes as a gratin de lambi (conch), perhaps accras de morue (cod fritters) or a salade Niçoise with entrecôte. If you're there the day the chef makes his turtle ragoût, I suggest you order it. An average meal here will cost from 175F ($17.50).

On the ground floor you can eat in the self-service section at low prices, ordering a blaff of sea urchins, a colombo of curried chicken or pork, or a plate of cured country ham.

Le Joséphine, rue de la Liberté (tel. 71-06-82), on the premises of the previously recommended Hôtel Impératrice, may remind you of an old créole inn. Right in the center of town, it looks out upon the Place de la Savane. On the set menu for 80F ($8), you may be served a pâté en pot, followed by spare ribs with curry and rice, plus dessert. On the à la carte, costing around 130F ($13), you can order such dishes as conch soup with basil, codfish fritters, stuffed crabs, grilled fish with hot sauce, a fricassée of crayfish, or grilled lamb cutlets temptingly flavored with herbs.

Typic Bellevue, 83 Blvd. de la Marne (tel. 71-68-87), a few minutes from the center of town, is a rustic rural house, with eye-catching blue walls and light-brown shutters. Operated by Bruno Raphael-Amanrich, it's frequented by local residents because of its well-prepared créole dishes, which are served at reasonable prices. As you dine on the terrace, you'll get the feeling of stopping over at a roadside inn. Among the specialties are seafood such as lobster and local shrimp, curried chicken or pork colombo, fricassée of goat, fish soup, turtle steak, steamed baby shark, escargots, and frog legs. A meal of créole specialties will lead to a final tab in the neighborhood of 120F ($12) to 175F ($17.50). It shuts down on Saturday afternoon and Sunday.

Shopping in Fort-de-France

Your best buys in Martinique are French luxury imports, such as perfumes, fashions, Vuitton luggage, Lalique crystal, or Limoges dinnerware. Sometimes (but don't count on it) prices are as much as 30% to 40% below Stateside levels.

A cautious reader who is nobody's fool sounds a warning to all readers. He points out that if you pay in dollars, store owners supposedly will give you a 20% discount, which is the "Value Added Tax" imposed on countries of Europe that are members of the Common Market. He proposes a hypothetical example. That is, a shopper will make a purchase for 1000F. Less 20%, that becomes 800F. However, when you pay in dollars the rates vary considerably from store to store, and almost invariably they are far lower than that proposed at one of the local banks. He writes: "The net result is that you received a 20% discount, but then they take away from 9% to 15% on the dollar exchange, giving you a net savings of only 5% to 11%—not 20%." He further notes, "Actually, you're probably better off shopping in the smaller stores where prices are 8% to 12% less on comparable items and paying in francs that you have exchanged at a local bank."

The main shopping street is rue Victor-Hugo. The other two leading shopping streets are the rues Schoelcher and St-Louis.

Facing the tourist office and alongside Quai Desnambuc is an open market where you can purchase local handicrafts and souvenirs. Many of these are tacky, however.

Far more interesting is the display of vegetables and fruit, quite a show, at the open-air stalls along rue Isambert. Don't miss it for its local ambience, and you can't help but smell the fish market alongside the Levassor River.

Try to postpone your shopping trip if a cruise ship is in town.

Roger Albert, 7 rue Victor-Hugo (tel. 71-71-71), offers most of the Paris articles of fashion, with all the big names in design, as well as crystal from Daum and Lalique, French perfumes, and chinaware from Limoges. The location is just off the Savane. The merchandise is definitely of high quality, and it's the finest selection on Martinique. Long established, this is the best known store in Martinique.

Across the street from Roger Albert, **Beaufrand,** rue Victor-Hugo (tel. 70-24-01), is a gift shop providing many similar items but on a smaller scale, along with leather goods, copper, ceramics, and French-made cottons imprinted with typical island design.

Au Printemps, 10 rue Schoelcher, near the cathedral (tel. 71-30-92), is one of the finest department stores in the Caribbean. French fashions are sold, along with china, crystal, and Baccarat, and such famous names in perfume as Lanvin, Chanel, Jean Patou, and Guerlain.

Likewise, I suggest a visit to **Prisunic,** rue Lamartine, another branch of a famous French department store. Here you'll find everything from St. Tropez bikinis to enough gourmet kitchenware to please Julia Child. Of course, if you're booked in a "housekeeping holiday," you can always pick up gastronomic goodies such as sauerkraut cooked in champagne.

On that same note, gourmet chefs will find all sorts of spices in the open-air markets of the capital, or such goodies as tinned pâté or canned quail in the local *supermarchés*.

The best place to go for handicrafts and souvenirs is the **Caribbean Art Center,** rue E-Deproge (tel. 70-25-01), facing the Savane, next to the tourist office and Air France. Everything here is handmade, and you can visit the shop from 9 a.m. to 12:30 p.m. and 3 to 6:30 p.m. All the craftwork of the island is represented here, particularly basketwork and clay crafts. You'll find madras, napkins, and table settings; bags in coconut husks, moon fishes, and boubous (large multicolored gowns), the latter at much lower prices than in the hotel shops. Look also for the Martiniquais doll in her *madras et foulard.*

For the ubiquitous local fabric, madras, there are shops on every street with bolts and bolts of it, all colorful and inexpensive, from about $4 to $7 per yard. Haute couture and chic resortwear are sold in many boutiques dotting downtown Fort-de-France.

Some boutiques, such as **Olympe,** 20–24 rue Lamartine (tel. 71-38-48), are long established *pret-à-porter* (ready-to-wear) shops carrying jeans, slacks, and fashionable sports wear from Paris and Côte d'Azur designers.

Young Martinique designers also present their own collections, usually showing on Thursday in their respective shops. The most prominent haute couture name is **Yves Gérard.** For ready-to-wear clothing, look for such names as **Daniel Rodap, Monique Louisor,** and **Gilbert Basson,** whose label is "Gigi." In fashion-conscious Martinique, a new crop of boutiques seems to blossom each season, although some, such as **Gisele,** 14 rue Victor-Hugo (tel. 71-38-67), have been around a while.

The above places are mostly for women, but some shops also carry fashions for men. Among these is **Prune,** 109 rue Lamartine (tel. 73-41-87).

Cadet-Daniel, 72 rue Antoine-Siger (tel. 71-41-48), which opened in 1840, sells Christofle silver, Limoges china, and crystal from Daum, Baccarat, Lalique, and Sèvres. Like some nearby stores, it also sells island-made 18-karat gold baubles, including the beaded *collier chou,* or "darling's necklace," long a required ornament for a créole costume.

Before leaving Martinique, you may want to purchase some rum, considered by aficionados to be one of the world's finest distilled drinks. Hemingway in *A Moveable Feast* lauded it as the perfect antidote to a rainy day. I suggest you try Vieux Acajou, a dark, mellow Old Mahogany, or else a blood-red brown liqueur-like rum bottled by Bally. The best place for browsing is **La Case à Rhum,** Galerie Marchande, 5 avenue de la Liberté (tel. 73-73-20).

Shopping Elsewhere on the Island

If you're staying at one of the hotels on the peninsula of Pointe du Bout, you'll find that the Marina complex there has a number of interesting boutiques. Several sell handicrafts and curios from Martinique. They are of very good quality, and are quite expensive, regrettably, particularly if you purchase some of their batiks of natural silk and their enameled jewel boxes.

North of the capital in the village of Bezaudin near Ste-Marie, Madame Nogard's little *boutique gourmande,* **Ella,** specializes in exotic home-grown spices, homemade preserves of island fruits, and original syrups.

There are the sturdy, attractive straw food baskets in the shops of nearby Morne-des-Esses, the *vannerie* (basket-making) capital of Martinique.

Another homemade delicacy that makes a distinctive gift is rillette Landaise au foie gras, prepared and put up in glass jars by Mme Laurent de Meillac at her 1500-duck farm, **Habitation Durocher,** near Lamentin. At Christmas, her specialty is a terrine of foie gras made with armagnac and presented in a lovely crock made by the **Poterie de Trois-Îlets** (tel. 76-03-44), an excellent place on Martinique to buy ceramics.

A Side Trip to Trois-Îlets

Marie-Josephe Rose Tasher de la Pagerié was born here in 1763. As Josephine, she was to become the wife of Napoléon I and empress of France from 1804 to 1809. She'd been married before to Alexandre de Beauharnais, who'd actually wanted to wed either of her two more attractive sisters, taking her as a consolation prize. Six years older than Napoleon, she pretended she'd lost her birth certificate so he wouldn't find out her true age. Although some historians call her ruthless and selfish (certainly unfaithful), she is still revered in Martinique as an uncommonly gracious lady.

After 20 miles of driving from Fort-de-France, you reach Trois-Îlets, a charming little village. One mile outside of the hamlet, you turn left to **La Pagerié,** where a small museum of mementos relating to Josephine has been installed in the former estate kitchen. Along with her childhood bed in the kitchen, you'll see a smouldering letter from Napoleon. The collection was compiled by Dr. Robert Rose-Rosette, who lives next door. Here Josephine gossiped with her slaves and played the guitar.

Still remaining are the partially restored ruins of the Pagerié sugar mill and the church (in the village itself) where she was christened in 1763. The plantation was destroyed in the 1766 hurricane. The museum is open daily, except Monday, from 9 a.m. to 5:30 p.m., charging 8F (80¢) for admission.

A vast botanical garden, **Parc des Floralies,** is adjacent to the Golf de l'Impératrice Joséphine, as is the museum devoted to Josephine described above.

POINTE DU BOUT: Pointe du Bout is a narrow, irregularly shaped peninsula across the bay from Fort-de-France. Over the past few years it's become the major resort area of Martinique. This is because of four major hotels—the Frantel, de la Marina, Bakoua, and the Méridien.

In addition to the hotels. you'll find a Robert Trent Jones–designed golf course, a dozen tennis courts, several restaurants, a marina, a gambling casino, discos, swimming pools, facilities for horseback riding, waterskiing, scubadiving, snorkeling, and volleyball courts.

To drive there from Fort-de-France, leave by Route 1, which takes you for a few minutes along the autoroute. You cross the plain of Lamentin, the industrial area of Fort-de-France and the site of the international airport. Very frequently the air is filled with the fragrance of caramel because of the large sugarcane factories in the area.

After 20 miles of driving, you reach Trois-Îlets, Josephine's hometown, previewed above. Three miles farther on your right, take the D38 to Pointe du Bout.

For those who want to reach Pointe du Bout by sea, there's a ferry service running all day long (until midnight) from Fort-de-France for a 9F (90¢) fare.

The Resort Hotels

Bakoua Beach Hotel, Pointe du Bout (tel. 76-33-95), has buildings that are not overpowering, allowing the natural beauty of the landscape to survive. The 90-room hotel consists of two hillside buildings in the center of the garden of frangipani and coconut palms, plus another building, a bungalow type, right on the beach. The hotel often draws a list of celebrities, including Jean-Paul Belmondo, Paul McCartney, and Mike Douglas. Of course, they book the imperial suite, with its green marble sunken bathtub and yellow four-poster bed.

The style of the rooms is more or less colonial, not really typical of the West Indies. All the units, however, are comfortable, with a refined polish. In the high season, a double, including a full American breakfast, rents for $145 to $185, with singles going for $120 to $145. *In summer, tariffs are lowered to 680F ($68) to 800F ($80) in a double, from 500F ($50) to 600F ($60) in a single.*

The bar welcomes you to its circular site, dominating an oval-shaped swimming pool right over the beach. The bar, La Rotonde, has a ceiling which is partly in bamboo, partly in striped linen.

If you want a snack, you can eat right on the beach, but for an elegant repast I'd suggest Le Chateaubriand with its award-winning French chef.

Sports are free here, including tennis, volleyball, snorkeling, and sailing. The hotel closes in September. In high season it provides dancing every night (only four times a week in the off-season). The Ballets Martiniquais usually show up every Friday night.

Hotel Méridien, Trois-Îlets (tel. 66-00-00), is actually a miniature village, a dramatically designed Air France property offering first-class accommodations in 300 rooms. It has excellent facilities, including a dramatically designed reception area open to the palm-fringed swimming pool and the waters of the bay. Among the restaurants and bars of this hostelry, the Anthurium offers gourmet dining accompanied by a dance band and served by Créole waitresses dressed in native costume. The Von Von disco features electronic rhythms for the international crowd, while the casino provides glitter and excitement.

The hotel is slightly angled to follow the line of the shore. Because of that, all units benefit from a view of either the Caribbean or the bay, at the far end of which you'll be able to see the lights of Fort-de-France. Around the huge block of rooms are a waterside garden, a 100-foot marina, and a cabana-style bar near the swimming pool.

The bedrooms provide much comfort, with luxurious baths, private balconies, king-size beds, and attractively modern furnishings. Room service is available 24 hours a day. In winter, singles range from $100 to $145, doubles run from $120 to $170, and triples cost from $170 to $220. *In summer, singles cost $80 to $95; doubles, $95 to $115; and triples, $130 to $140.* Children under 12 stay free in their parents' room.

Fixed-price meals are available for around $9 at the buffet breadfast, $21 at lunch, and $23 at dinner. On certain nights of the week the hotel hosts vibrantly colorful Ballets Martiniquais near the pool. A créole buffet supper followed by the folkloric show costs 150F ($15) for residents of the hotel, 200F ($20) for non-residents.

Further out on the point is an old fort where you can walk at night, breathing air filled with tropical fragrance..

For reservations, call toll free 800/223-9918 in the U.S., 800/361-8234 in Canada. In Montréal, call 514/285-1450, and in New York state, 800/442-5917.

Frantel Martinique, Pointe du Bout (tel. 73-63-03). One of the advantages of staying here is that you don't realize you're entering a hotel. Rather, you think you've come for a walk in a tropical garden. It's easy to forget that behind the scenes are 200 bedrooms. The buildings are encircled by large lawns planted with coconut or palm trees and many flowering bushes. The rooms are in two-story bungalows, each having a balcony. The view from your abode will be of gardens, a marina, or the bay of Fort-de-France. In the center of everything is a circular swimming pool, also with a view of the bay. The curving beach provides safe swimming as well.

Also taking advantage of that bay view, La Paillote, a bar, is nicely decorated and lit by original cord lamps. It's a dramatic setting in which to meet friends or make new ones.

The bedrooms are handsomely coordinated, with white walls and beamed ceilings. The draperies and bedcovers match, in deep yellows, light browns, and mustards. The furnishings are in a contemporary style, with wickerwork. On the EP in winter, singles range in price from $80 to $92 daily, with doubles going for $93 to $110. *Tariffs drop in summer: from 350F ($35) to 475F ($47.50) daily in a single and from 450F ($45) to 750F ($75) in a double.*

In the Café Créole, you can order a quick snack lunch, without interference with your suntanning schedule. It connects the beach to the pool and acts as an open passage. On the buffet, you'll have a choice of salads and desserts and can select the plat du jour. The café is also open for dinner. It serves some of the best food on Pointe du Bout, tasty and attractively presented.

La Boucau is the principal restaurant, created with an island atmosphere of white ceilings and wooden beams. The view over the bay is dramatic at night. In the background is a stage where a local combo plays during dinner. While the atmosphere is quite exotic, the restaurant may also be noisy at times. Fish is the specialty, and créole cookery is done with flair here. Main dishes include red snapper, stuffed crabs, conch ragoût, or a blaff (stew) of sea urchin. The cuisine is first class, the portions rather generous.

Rates include free use of the sports equipment, except for waterskiing. However, you're admitted free to the hotel's disco, **Vesou.**

PLM ETAP Pagerié, Pointe du Bout (tel. 66-05-30), gives you a chance to have the independence of your own personal apartment. In neat, efficient, streamlined designs, the club offers 98 air-conditioned rooms, some with fully equipped kitchenettes and balconies opening onto a view of the bay. The location is across the road from the action swirling around the Bakoua.

Units are not only comfortable but attractive, with tile floors and white walls, in contrast to the bright pastel draperies and bedspreads. Furnishings are in a clean-cut contemporary style. In winter, EP rates are $58 daily in a single, $77 in a double, with full hotel services. *In summer, prices are 225F ($22.50) daily in a single, 285F ($28.50) in a double, a remarkable bargain that I hope is still in effect at the time of your visit if you go at that time of year.*

If you don't want to cook, you can order a meal at one of several restaurants at your doorstep. There is also a large swimming pool.

Small Inns (Budget to Moderate)

Hôtel Calalou (tel. 76-31-67), Anse-à-l'Âne, Trois-Îlets, rests languidly in a small lushly planted park facing the water and a view of Fort-de-France. Managed by Patrick de Reynal, it is built on a white sand beach and can be reached by launch from Fort-de-France in less than 30 minutes.

Aside from the beach, most of the social life of this bungalow hotel centers around a large sun terrace. This dining room is open to the sea breezes under a high-ceilinged, tepee-shaped roof, making the meals even more pleasant. White wrought-iron garden furniture adds a fresh note. The cooks are island born, preparing spicy créole dishes among others. Even if you're not a guest here, you might want to visit for a meal. You can order a table d'hôte at 80F ($8), or else à la carte, enjoying fresh grilled fish, pork Caribbean style, escalope de veau with shrimp, and, a delightful dish, chicken stuffed with conch.

Bedrooms have a minimum of style, but they are roomy enough. All are equipped with air conditioning and a private bath with plenty of hot water. In winter, singles are accepted for 460F ($46) daily on the half-board plan; doubles pay 680F ($68) for the same arrangement. *In the off-season, the single half-board* *price is 380F ($38) daily, 600F ($60) for two persons,* plus service. You can fish, waterski, snorkel, windsurf, or skindive here. The hotel takes a vacation in October.

Madinina Sidonie, Marina Pointe du Bout (tel. 66-00-54), is an appealing 15-room hotel, directly on the marina. The clean-cut rooms are modern, with built-in headboards and your own bath. Units are air-conditioned, with stream-lined furniture and bright colors used in the draperies and spreads. In season, prices are 180F ($18) daily in a single, 270F ($27) in a double. Breakfast is an extra 40F ($4) per person. *In the off-season, the double rate is 210F ($21) daily; the single tariff, 150F ($15).* The rooms, however, are not the main reason to stay here. Its owner, Mme Sidonie Pamphile, is a famous woman cook, serving some of the island's best créole dishes (see my dining recommendations).

Auberge de l'Anse Mitan, Anse Mitan, Trois-Îlets (tel. 66-01-12). Many of the residents of Fort-de-France, 20 minutes away by hourly launch, come here for their weekend retreat at the end of a beach frequented by Martiniquais. Once this place was the core of a little fishing village before hordes of tourists started arriving. In a three-story-bungalow, stucco box-type structure, with two one-bedroom cottages strung along the beach, the simple little inn rents singles on the MAP for 300F ($30) nightly, and doubles cost 400F ($40) on the same plan, plus service and tax. Rates are the same all year.

From the veranda you can look out on the beach and the yachts tied up at the marina across the way. The little lounge has a grouping of blond Danish chairs, gathered around a central table with flowers. The dining room has wide windows providing views of the water, and there's a tiny wood-paneled bar for nightcaps.

Le Matador, Anse Mitan (tel. 66-05-36), is a simple inn where you might spend most of your vacation in your bikini. That bikini is likely to be even snugger after a stay here at this inn. It was launched by François, the former Bakoua chef, and Raymonde Crico. They rent out 11 pleasant rooms, which are comfortable in spite of their simplicity. In season, a single, with breakfast included, ranges from 260F ($26) daily, a double going from 400F ($40). *Off-season, tariffs are lowered by about 20%.* The food served here is among the best on the island (see my dining recommendations).

Le Caraibe Auberge, Anse Mitan (tel. 66-03-19), is run by a friendly manager, Louis Yank Ting. The auberge is not antique; rather, it is a contemporary structure at beachside, with blond furniture. The bar on a terrace opens onto a good view of the bay of Fort-de-France.

French-speaking visitors will fit in better here. The rooms have functional, clean-cut pieces, and are equipped with showers, private toilets, and air conditioning. For a single in high season, you pay from 300F ($30), the price increasing to 340F ($34) in a double, these tariffs including a continental breakfast. *In summer, the single rate is 220F ($22), going up to 260F ($26) in a double, a real bargain.*

The food is good, with many créole specialties featured. Expect to pay from 150F ($15) for a three-course meal.

Rivage Hotel, Anse Mitan, Trois-Îlets (tel. 66-00-53), opened in 1984. If you want a small French Antillean hotel with friendly innkeepers and bargain prices, this is it. Jean-Claude and Maryelle Riveti are most hospitable. They bring a freshness of spirit to welcoming their guests, both French- and English-speaking, and housing them in one of their eight pleasantly furnished and air-conditioned units, opening onto the seaside. The location is between the previously recommended Caraibe Auberge and the Matador. Four of the units also contain kitchenettes, and they will tell you where to pick up supplies if you're cutting down on your food costs. With a continental breakfast included, a single can stay here in winter at a cost of 250F ($25) daily, a double going for 310F ($31). *In summer, tariffs are lowered to 195F ($19.50) in a single and 290F ($29) in a double.* They also have a snackbar, and, on occasion, many guests have gotten together for their own barbecue dinner.

Dining Outside "The Big Four"

Chez Sidonie, in the Hotel Madinina, Marina Pointe du Bout (tel. 66-00-54), is the best restaurant on the peninsula for true créole cookery (see my previous recommendation of the hotel). Its charming owner, who is reputed to be the queen of the créole cuisine, Mme Sidonie Pamphile, is also known as the island's most attractive patronne.

There are two dining rooms, and most guests favor the one at the edge of the marina. If you want your dinner really fresh, you can make your selections from a large aquarium. The second floor is more secluded, with a view of the harbor.

Mme Pamphile knows a lot of créole secrets, and she uses her knowledge expertly in her dishes. Her fish soup is one of the finest, and she also does another well-known Martinique specialty, pâté en pot. Some of her favorite dishes include crab en fricassé, créole pudding, crayfish in the style of Mme Pamphile, and squid, also prepared créole style. You might also try her grilled fish in a créole sauce or her colombo of curried mutton. She also serves such exotica as beef testicles on a spit. For desserts, I'd suggest bananas Juanita.

Of course, the kitchen also knows how to turn out a traditional French cuisine as well—veal scallops, chateaubriand au poivre vert, and crêpes suzette. You'll easily spend 200F ($20) per person here.

La Vila Créole, Anse Mitan (tel. 76-35-53), was revealed to me by a reader from Rochester, N.Y., Lili Wildenheim. She wrote: "I won't tell you about the place. Go and discover it for yourself. It's exceptional." After having one of my finest meals in Martinique there, I totally concur. Run by an enterprising and most cordial young Martiniquais, Guy, the restaurant offers outdoor dining on the garden veranda of a charming little Antillean home. Guy entertains with his guitar, while his sister, Edith, prepares a savory créole cuisine. Specialties are grilled meat and langouste, and each is done to perfection. I applaud their use of such local vegetables as the christophine. Fish with bananas? Don't knock it until you've tried it. As in all good créole cookery, a lot of fresh herbs are used. Expect to spend from $25 or more for a complete dinner, and plan to make an evening of it.

Le Cantonnais, Pointe du Bout la Marina (tel. 66-02-33), is decorated in the classic Chinese fashion of red and gold. Your host, a Martiniquais, Tien-You Guy, offers not only excellent change-of-pace fare, but his tariffs are also kept low. For example, I'd suggest broiled shark fin (I'm perfectly serious). His sliced duckling with black bean sauce and green pepper is excellent too. You might also prefer the fried crab claw, the lemon chicken, barbecued pork Chinese style, and fish with fresh mushrooms. Soups include braised bird's nest with minced chicken. A simple set meal is offered for 65F ($6.50); otherwise, count on spending from 150F ($15). Either meal is a fine bargain.

Le Matador, Anse Mitan (tel. 66-05-36), has long enjoyed a position as one of the best créole restaurants in Martinique, and I want only to add to that well-deserved reputation. François and Raymond Crico, your friendly, sophisticated hosts, will present you a selection of such savory dishes as crabes farcis (this is a land crab which has been deviled and flavored with a hot seasoning and tossed in breadcrumbs, then baked in its own shell). Some of the most exotic sea denizens in the Caribbean come out of the kitchen, including octopi, conch, and sea urchins; however, I always gravitate to their classic red snapper, which they simmer in a well-flavored court bouillon.

For a main course, the most obvious choice is a colombo of mutton, which is a Créole version of curry. The Martiniquais who dine here often say the Americans make a wrong decision in sticking to the hotel dining rooms, instead of venturing out on the island to sample the locally run inns, which offer the best food. Le Matador lies across the bay from Fort-de-France near the hotels of Pointe du Bout which include the Bakoua Beach and the Frantel Martinique. The Cricos like to take Tuesday off, but are there every other night, serving you a fine repast for around $20 to $25.

Incidentally, the matador in the title has caused some to believe this might be a Spanish restaurant. Actually, the name is Créole for "arrogant woman in full dress."

L'Ecrevisse, Plage de l'Anse Mitan (tel. 66-05-15), offers romantic candlelit dining at the seaside. The restaurant is the personal statement of Hector Trefle, the former manager of another restaurant in Martinique. He oversees practically everything about this intimate restaurant on a patio overlooking the bay at l'Anse Mitan. Mr. Trefle is always attentive to the needs of his guests, and has been known to pick them up at their hotel and redeposit them at the end of a meal. His food is a savory blend of créole and classic French. Specialties include the restaurant's namesake, crayfish, along with lobster and grilled meat. He usually presents a local fish in a créole sauce of island-grown vegetables and spices. Occasionally, he'll have turtle steak. Count on spending from $20 per person.

THE SOUTH LOOP: We now leave Pointe du Bout, heading south for more sun and beaches. Centers here include Le Diamant, Sainte-Anne, and Le François.

From Trois-Îlets, you can follow a small curved road which brings you to Anse-à-l'Âne, Grande Anse, and Anse d'Arlet. At any of these places are small beaches, quite safe and usually not crowded.

At Anse d'Arlet, for example, the scenery is beautiful. Fishing boats draw up on the beach, the men drying their nets in the sun.

From Anse d'Arlet, two winding roads may be chosen to take you to Diamant. One follows the coastline, the other forcing its way through the hills. Both of them offer pleasant scenery.

Anse-à-l'Âne

Reflet de la Mer, Trois-Îlets (tel. 76-32-14). A ferryboat from Fort-de-France lands every hour at a spot a few steps away from a simple cement building at the edge of the beach housing this restaurant and small hotel. Mme Pauline Achille and her daughter, Paulette Vendenberghe, serve créole specialties on checked tablecloths. Menu items include blaff of fish and conch, blaff of sea urchin, conch fricassée, colombo of chicken and mutton, stuffed crabs, and fish soup. Full meals are served at lunch and dinner daily except Monday. If you want to make a day of it, you can bring your beach clothes for an after-lunch swim. The women also rent six very simple rooms which, with half board included, cost 200F ($20) in a single, 350F ($35) for a double. The rooms contain sinks, showers, and toilets as part of the bedroom, not set off in a separate bathroom.

Grande Anse

Le Tamarin Plage, Anse d'Arlet (tel. 76-48-26), is a place little changed since the time when Paul Gauguin visited this part of Martinique. Sugarcane leaves cover the ceiling, and a rough-textured veranda overlooks the beach.

Don't be put off by its rustic appearance. You come here for the food, not for deluxe accouterments. Locals sit at the bar most of the day, while Mr. Perronette, the owner, mixes drinks. Set meals cost 55F ($5.50), with service included. À la carte meals are from 135F ($13.50). Menu items include several kinds of accras, fish soup, stuffed crab, chicken fricassée, sea crab fricassée, and grilled lobster. This restaurant opens every day at 6 a.m., remaining in business until after the last diner has gone home.

Anse d'Arlet

La Case à Cha-Cha (tel. 76-42-28) is an intensely local kind of restaurant which developed when Ginette Adé, her husband, André, and their five children expanded their bakery to include an adjacent eating place. Today the bakery is still in business, yet the main focus of the family's energy is the restaurant's kitchen. Frankly, the building is a makeshift affair filled with the simplest of accessories. Your fellow diners are likely to be Martiniquais rather than tourists. You'll reach the dining room by going through a corridor-style bar. Menu choices usually include pig with pineapple, coconut and pumpkin flan, soup z'habitant, seafood tart, boudin, fish blaff, grilled fish, goat colombo, grilled lobster, and conch fricassée. Full meals cost from 130F ($13). You'll find this place near the center of town.

Le Diamant

Here is a village with quite a good beach open to the winds from the south. **Diamond Rock** juts from the sea rising to a height of 573 feet. In a daring maneuver in 1804, the British carried ammunition and 110 sailors to the top. There, in spite of French coastal artillery bombardment, they held out for 18 months, commanding the passage between the rock and Martinique. You can visit it, but the access by small boat is considered risky.

Diamond Beach is excellent, with surf and bathing possibilities. It's lined with the familiar groves of swaying palms.

In the area, **Hôtel Diamant les Bains** (tel. 76-40-14) is a small, beachfront, family-style hotel, with a cluster of recently added cottages. Close to the water, everything rests under palm trees. The cultivated gardens surrounding the bungalows have lounge chairs, where you can sit and enjoy the view of Diamond Rock. Hubert Andrieu is a thoughtful, concerned host. When his father founded the hotel in 1954, it was one of the first to open on the island.

The main building, with its upper-deck bedrooms, houses the restaurant where you can dine on the terrace with a view of the sea. The cuisine is mostly créole, with some French dishes. The chef pays liberal attention to locally caught fish. A special menu is offered at 150F ($15). You can sample classic créole specialties, such as stuffed sand or sea crabs, spicy black pudding, shrimp fritters, créole steak, a boiled fish blaff, conch in tomato sauce, fricassée of squid, finishing with a coconut flan. However, if you're touring the island, you should note that the restaurant is closed on Wednesday.

The air-conditioned beachside bungalows have red tile floors, light beamed ceilings, and built-in fruitwood headboards, set on a raised level. Baths have tiles and French showers. In high season, a single can stay here, with breakfast and dinner included, for 275F ($27.50) daily; two persons pay 420F ($42). *In the off-season, half-board rates are 250F ($25) in a single, 335F ($33.50) in a double.*

Novotel Le Diamant (tel. 76-42-42) stands about two miles outside the village on a half island. Architecturally, it's an esthetic success. The reception, opening onto a large pool is decorated in honey brown and sunflower yellow.

You cross the pool on a Chinese-style wooden bridge to connect with the buildings where the rooms are located. The bedroom units face either the pool or else the coast with its expansive view of the famous Diamond Rock. The furniture in the bedrooms is typically functional and neutral in styling. *The prices off-season are 320F ($32) in a single, 400F ($40) in a double, and 500F ($50) in a triple, all EP.* In winter, the EP rates are 500F ($50) for a single, 650F ($65) in a double, and 800F ($80) for a triple. Breakfast is another 44F ($4.40); lunch and dinner, from 150F ($15) up. Half board must be taken from December 20 to January 6, costing 150F ($15) per person per day extra.

Outside of the hotel, the neighboring beaches aren't too crowded, and the view of the Caribbean is splendid in most directions. If you don't want to leave the hotel, you can of course relax around the pool, sipping your rum punch at the bar. Lawns and gardens, as well as tennis courts, surround the hotel. Water sports and many divertissements are also offered by management.

The trip from the airport to the hotel in a taxi will take half an hour, and the cost will be about 150F ($15).

As you follow the road south to Trois Rivières you'll come to **Sainte-Luce,** perhaps one of the island's most charming villages. Beautiful beaches surround the town, and it's the site of the Forest Montravail. Continuing, you'll reach Rivière Pilote, quite a large town, and Le Marin, at the bottom of a bay of the same name. From Le Marin, a five-mile drive brings you to—

Sainte-Anne

At the extreme southern tip of Martinique, this is a sleepy little village, with white sand beaches. It opens onto views of the Sainte Lucia Canal, and nearby is the site of the Petrified Savannah Forest. The French call it **Savane des Pétrifications.** It's a field of petrified volcanic boulders in the shape of logs. The eerie, desert-like site, no man's land, is studded with cacti. The region is so barren you'll not want to linger long.

Before reaching Sainte-Anne, on your right as you head south is the route des Boucaniers which brings you to the **Club Méditerranée,** at Buccaneer's Creek (tel. 76-72-72). Nestled on a peaceful cove, designed like a Créole village, the club is set on the 48-acre site of a former pirate's hideaway. It stands in a forest of coconut palms.

In the typical Cub Med style, it features around-the-clock activities. Sports such as sailing, waterskiing, and snorkeling are provided for the overall package cost. In a domed two-level building in the heart of the resort, you'll find the dining places, the amusement center, a theater, dance floor, and bar. On one part of the white sandy beach you can go in the buff.

A walk along rue du Port (the main street of Club Med) leads to a conically roofed cirvular Café du Port, the main restaurant, which overlooks the sailboat fleet anchored in the marina.

Accommodations are in comfortable, air-conditioned bungalows which are booked for double occupancy, each with twin beds and private shower baths. *In summer and fall, one-week land rates with everything included costs from $500 per person.* Winter and spring land rates range from around $1000 to $1100 per person weekly (it's most expensive at Christmas, of course).

Activities include day-long picnics, dance classes, boat rides, a language lab, and disco dancing at the opposite end of the village.

Nonguests on a tour of Martinique are welcome to stop in here for a meal, enjoying a large buffet for 200F ($20), with créole specialties where you help yourself to all you want. Every Tuesday night the club throws an Antilles folklore evening, also costing 200F ($20) per person, including food and entertainment. Other facilities include the Café du Port, a small café for afternoon drinks and leisure talk, and the Maison Créole, a restaurant annex opening every night with a different theme, such as Russian, Créole, or Italian.

Hotel Caritan, also known as Caritan Beach Village (tel. 76-74-12), is a comfortably modern collection of yellow and beige Mediterranean-style villas set side by side on a gently graded hillside. In the center are a swimming pool, a pleasant restaurant, and a bar. Separated from the resort's central core by a green-tree buffer is a wide sandy beach.

Each accommodation has its own kitchenette and a terrace set up for family dining. Singles cost 300F ($30) daily, while doubles go for 350F ($35). Extra beds can be set up in any double room for an additional 65F ($6.50) per night.

Some of the public areas are accented with vividly colored murals, including the breezy and very pleasant dining room, where fixed-price meals cost from 85F ($8.50). Occasionally a limbo artist and an orchestra will entertain guests in the evening. A full range of water sports can be organized on request. This establishment is about five minutes along the coast from the center of town. In many ways, it is a self-contained community.

If you want to stay in Sainte-Anne, I recommend **La Dunette** (tel. 76-73-90), a motel-like structure on the water. It's near the Club Med and the white sandy beaches of the Salines as well. It has only 17 rooms, all of which are air-conditioned. Most of them have large flower-filled balconies which open onto views of the Caribbean. The seaside inn is protected by a garden filled with flowers and tropical plants. Mme Marie-Louise Kambona is the owner.

In winter, a single ranges in price from 175F ($17.50) to 250F ($25), with doubles going for 220F ($22) to a peak of 400F ($40). *In summer, singles cost from 180F ($18) to 210F ($21) and doubles run from 210F ($21) to 325F ($32.50).* The furnishings are in casual modern, and some of the units are quite small.

In the evenings, guests gather for drinks in the bar, La Galiote. From the terrace over the sea, you can catch your own lobster and enjoy it cooked for you later in the hotel's restaurant, which serves many French and créole specialties. Sports and excursions can be arranged for you, even a jaunt to watch a mongoose fight a snake.

Restaurant Poï et Virginie (tel. 76-72-22). Yvan Thiedu used to play drums with Dizzy Gillespie, but today he's better known as the owner and occasional performer at what is one of my favorite restaurants on the island. The establishment's name is a Caribbean pun on the name of a 19th-century French romance that every French person has at least heard about.

Built on a narrow strip of land between the road and the sea, the Créole-inspired decor includes bright-red chairs, bamboo walls, a canopied ceiling printed with figures of sailboats and pineapples, and vividly contrasting patterned tablecloths and wall hangings. Shutters open onto a view of the boats which might have caught the ingredients for the evening's French and créole seafood specialties. Among these are palourdes (local small clams), a Caribbean-style salade Niçoise, a rémoulade of christophine, grilled conch, turtle steak, sea urchin blaff, and Caribbean bouillabaisse. Full meals, costing from 170F ($17), are served from 12:30 to 3 p.m. for lunch and from 7:30 to 9 p.m. for dinner daily except Monday.

Aux Filets Bleus (tel. 76-73-42), set on a flat area close to the beach, is a family-run restaurant flanked by a pair of blue canopies and separated from the road by a hedge. Once you've entered, the seaside exposure of the al fresco dining room and its terrace make you feel like you're in an isolated tropical retreat, where the only sound is the splash of waves and the tinkling of ice in glasses.

What you think is a glass-covered reflecting pool set into the floor is actually a lobster tank. From it come many specialties, which include several preparations of lobster. Also featured are stuffed crab, turtle soup, fried sea urchins, and many kinds of grilled fish. Fixed-price menus begin at 75F ($7.50), while à la carte meals cost from 180F ($18). The Anglio family, the owners, serve lunch from 10 a.m. to 4 p.m. and dinner from 7 to 10 p.m. The place is closed Sunday and Monday nights.

At the end of the main street of Sainte-Anne, turn on your left and head for the **Manoir de Beauregard** (tel. 76-73-40), an 18th-century manor house where Madame Marcelle Saint-Cyr, the owner, has brought a tasteful, personalized touch. The present relais was built somewhere between 1700 and 1720, and the name probably comes from one of its early owners, a settler named d'Orient, whose daughter married a knight called "de la Touche de Beauregard."

While its location is near some of the most beautiful beaches on the island, most guests seem to prefer to splash around the swimming pool in the briefest of bikinis. The manoir is a white building under a tile roof, its arches evoking Spain. The interior has been skillfully adapted to make it a comfortable place for paying guests, yet the old architectural features have been religiously respected.

Your bedroom will probably have a four-poster bed made from island trees. Fabrics for windows, beds, and chairs are often in flowering chintz. Each room is air-conditioned, containing a private bath (each one individually decorated). In high season, two persons pay $74 for bed and breakfast; singles go for $56. *Off-season, these same rates are reduced to 280F ($28) in a single and 320F ($32) in a double.*

The hallway has bronze candelabra and a clock on a 19th-century console. The lounge hall is not grand—rather, it's furnished in a Créole style, with pieces handmade by local artisans from island-grown timber. The floors are black-and-white checkerboard-style tiles, and the ceiling is beamed.

Ornate wrought-iron reredos rescued from a cathedral at Fort-de-France serve as room dividers. The stair rail was once the communion rail.

The main dining room is an enclosure of a long terrace with simple handmade chairs. Another room is used mainly for informal breakfasts, although most guests prefer the terrace.

Madame Saint-Cyr draws many distinguished guests, including Prince Napoléon, a charming French aristocrat, who is descended from Napoléon III.

Even is you don't stay here, know that many guests make a reservation for meals to sample the créole cookery. Meals cost from 75F ($7.50) to 125F ($12.50).

After passing Le Marin, you reach **Vauclin,** a fishing port and market town that is pre-Columbian. If you have time, stop in at the Chapel of the Holy Virgin, dating from the 18th century. Visitors like to make an excursion to **Mount Vauclin,** the highest point in southern Martinique. There they are rewarded with one of the most panoramic views in the West Indies.

After that, continuing on Route N6, you reach—

Le François

This town is known for its sailing competitions when owners of yawls compete. It also enjoys a reputation for cookery, which is best a **Club Nautique,** Pointe Bateau (tel. 54-31-00). Every morning you can see the owner, Georges Amalis, out checking over the early-morning catch. His keen eye selects only the best. To get to his club, you cross the main street, heading for the sea. Stay along the shoreline until you reach Nautique. Only lunch is served.

Before you order, you can sample various rum punches at a bar on the terrace. You might begin with a *décollage*, which translates into "takeoff" as in jet, but here means a potent rum drink aged with herbs until it turns green. The less heady *planteur* is concocted of local rums and fruit juices. Then you descend a few steps to the simple but scrubbed-clean dining room. Don't be discouraged by the almost desolate look of the place, or the bleak furnishings and surroundings. The food is very fresh, the kitchen clean. You can even dip your feet in water if you've just emerged from the sands.

A set menu is offered for 175F ($17.50), which includes such delectable items as sea urchin fritters, sweet clams, shellfish, lobster, or broiled fish, perhaps turtle steak along with flambé bananas and aromatic coffee. He also makes a good-tasting fish soup. You can ask for fish in court-bouillon. Lobster is prepared any style, especially charcoal broiled. A taste sensation is the butter-yellow urchin roe.

Lunch might be preceded by a boat trip to the nearby coral reefs where Josephine used to bathe. Boat excursions leave every day at 10 a.m.

After dining in Le François, you can easily return to Fort-de-France by passing through Le Lamentin, or you can go the Pointe du Bout route through Ducos and Rivière Salée.

THE NORTH LOOP: As we swing north from Fort-de-France, our main targets are Le Carbet, St-Pierre, Montagne Pelée, and Leyritz. However, I'll sandwich in many fascinating stopovers along the way.

From Fort-de-France there are three ways to head north to the Montagne Pelée. The first way is to follow Route N4 up to St-Joseph. There you take the left fork for three miles after St-Joseph, turning onto the D15 toward Marigot.

At Morne des Esses, you might want to stop for lunch at **Le Colibri** (The Hummingbird; tel. 75-32-12), which is the private Créole home of Madame Clotilde Palladino and her daughters. She has been called a sorceress in the kitchen. Here you'll get some of the finest West Indian cookery on the island. The place is somewhat hidden, however. If you take the little lane on your right after the post office, you'll find it.

Tables are set up in a small dining room on a terrace with black-and-white tile floor. The furnishings are island-made wood pieces. If the terrace fills up with weekenders from Fort-de-France, you'll be seated on another smaller veranda where you can survey the cooking. You'll seem close enough to the church steeple to touch it, or else to reach out and grab a coconut tree.

The place is decidedly informal, and it exudes the warmth of madame. The typically créole cookery is first class. For example, you might begin with a callaloo soup with crab or a sea urchin tart. Try also calalou aux crabes or the avocado salade aux crabes. Among the dishes I recommend are a buisson d'ecrevisses (crayfish), stuffed pigeon, chicken with coconut, and roast suckling pig. For dessert, try a coconut flan. The tab comes to about $18 for a complete meal. The French wines are inexpensively priced.

Alternative Routes

Another way to Montagne Pelée is to take the N3 through the vegetation-rich Mornes until you reach Le Morne Rouge. This road is known as "Route de la Trace," and is now the center of the Parc Naturel de la Martinique.

A different way to reach Montagne Pelée is to follow Route N2 along the coast. Close to Fort-de-France, the first town you reach is **Schoelcher.**

Right in town, near to the sea, is a good restaurant called **Le Foulard** (tel. 71-05-72). The restaurant is in a private mansion facing the Mer des Antilles. Because of its large number of habitués, reservations are necessary. The view of the small harbor is great, and the place is very much typically Créole, its atmosphere and surroundings successfully evoking the island spirit. There's a fixed menu for 100F ($10) which offers you a choice of créole specialties, three courses in all. Le Foulard shuts down on Saturday at lunch, on Sunday evening, and all day on Monday and Tuesday.

Farther along Route N2 you reach Case Pilote, and then Bellefontaine. This portion, along the most frequented tourist route in Martinique—that is, Fort-de-France to St-Pierre—will remind many a traveler of the French Riviera. Bellefontaine is a small fishing village, with boats stretched along the beach. As an architectural curiosity, note the many houses also built in the shape of boats.

Leaving Bellefontaine, a five-mile drive north will deliver you to—

Le Carbet

Columbus landed here in 1502 and the first French settlers arrived in 1635. In 1887 Gauguin lived here for four months before going on to Tahiti. You can stop for a swim at an Olympic-size pool set into the hills, or else look upon flocks of native women scrubbing clothes in a stream.

The **Musée Paul Gauguin** (tel. 77-22-66) is at Anse Turin, near Carbet. This small building commemorates the French artist's stay in Martinique in 1887, with books, prints, letters, and other memorabilia. There are also changing exhibits of works by local artists, regrettably none as great as the master himself. The museum is open daily from 10 a.m. to 5 p.m., charging an admission of 6F (60¢).

Like Gauguin, you may be tempted to spend some time here. If so, I'd suggest a stay at **Latitude Martinique** (tel. 73-69-99). The place is like an exotic back-to-nature adventure with amenities. Built on the site of an old plantation, the resort is a collection of prefabricated rondavels with peaked roofs shipped from Lyon, directly on the beach. Everything seems to center around the disco, Le Rocher, which will keep you up late if you retire early. The music lasts till 11:30 p.m. Even though right on the beach, many of these units are air-conditioned because of the lack of cross ventilation.

Some of the rondavels are actually modular, and in some instances several are interconnected. The furnishings are often in bamboo, and bright patterned fabrics on the bedspreads give warmth. However, the units are quite small, as most people live outdoors here, not in their rooms.

Each bungalow has a small open porch facing the beach. In winter, the MAP rate in a double is 420F ($42) per person, rising to 480F ($48) in a single. *In the off-season, the MAP rate is 380F ($38) per person in a double, 440F ($44) in a single.*

The dining room is open on three sides, looking out onto the sea. Every Tuesday a typical créole dinner is offered, and every Thursday there's a barbecue. On the beach you can play a game of pétanque or go waterskiing and Sunfish sailing.

L'Imprévu, Grande Anse (tel. 78-08-01). It would be difficult to find a less formal restaurant than this, although it's a preferred stopover for many residents who return to it every time they're in the area. Vertical sections of bamboo support the palm-frond roof, below which groups of friends play an unusual form of tarot. Unlike many card players, they're usually happy to decipher the symbols for visitors.

You can order a drink at the stand-up bar or choose a table under the sunshield overlooking the beach. The house specialty is a libation called golden apple *(prune de cythère)* juice. Menu items include accras made with codfish, titiris (a small river fish), crayfish, stuffed crab, fish soup, callaloo with crab, blaff, grilled conch, and pigeon with sauce Imprévu. Several dishes require a 24-hour advance notice. Full meals range from around 135F ($13.50). Since its annual closing varies each year, it's a good idea to call ahead before making a special trip. The restaurant is closed Monday.

St-Pierre

At the beginning of this century, St-Pierre was known as the "Little Paris of the West Indies." Home to 30,000 inhabitants, it was the cultural and economic capital of Martinique. On May 7, 1902, the citizens read in their daily newspaper that "Montagne Pelée does not present any more risk to the population than Vesuvius does to the Neapolitans."

However, on May 8, at 8 a.m., the southwest side of Montagne Pelée exploded, raining down fire and lava. At 8:02 a.m., all 30,000 inhabitants were dead—that is, all except one. A black convict in his underground cell was spared, saved by the thickness of the wall. When islanders reached the site, the convict was paroled, leaving Martinique to tour in Barnum and Bailey's circus.

St-Pierre never recovered its past splendor. Now it could be called the Pompeii of the West Indies. Ruins of the church, the theater, and some other buildings can be seen along the coast.

The **Musée Volcanologique** was created by an American volcanologist Franck Alvard Perret, who turned the museum over to the city in 1933. Here in pictures and relics dug from the debris you can trace the story of what happened to St-Pierre. Dug from the lava is a clock that stopped at the exact moment the volcano erupted. The museum is open from 9 a.m. to noon and 3 to 5 p.m., charging an entrance fee of 5F (50¢).

La Factorerie, Centre de Formation Rurale (tel. 77-12-53). Many patrons of this restaurant, which was built by a young people's co-op, make it a point to stop in the stone church a few paces away either before or after a meal. Both buildings are set near the top of a steep hill high above the town, with a view that sweeps out over a well-kept lawn, a verdant forest, and the sea. In an al fresco setting under a sloping beamed ceiling, you'll be able to choose créole specialties such as grilled fish with spicy sauce, fish soup, brochette of conch, grilled lobster, accras of shrimp, and the local recipes for blaff and chicken colombo. Set meals are offered for 65F ($6.50) and 115F ($11.50). The restaurant is open for lunch and dinner every day.

From St-Pierre, you can climb to—

Montagne Pelée

A spectacular and winding road takes you through a tropical rain forest. The curves are of the hairpin variety, and the road is twisty and not always kept in good shape. However, you're rewarded with tropical flowers, baby ferns, plumed bamboo, and valleys so deep green you'll think you're wearing cheap sunglasses.

You reach the village of Morne Rouge, right at the foot of Montagne Pelée, a popular vacation spot for Martiniquais. From there on, a narrow and unreliable road brings you to a level of 2500 feet above sea level, 1600 feet under the round summit of the volcano that destroyed St-Pierre. Montagne Pelée itself rises 4656 feet above sea level.

If you're a trained mountain climber, you can scale the peak, reaching Grand Rivière—that is, if you don't mind four or five hours of hiking. Realize that this is a mountain, that rain is frequent, and that temperatures drop very low. Tropical growth often hides deep crevices in the earth, and there are other dangers. That's why if you're really serious about this climb, you should hire an experienced guide. As for the volcano, its death-dealing rain in 1902 apparently satisfied it, at least for the time being!

On the small road you can halt for lunch at **Montauberge** (tel. 77-34-11), a panoramic restaurant facing Montagne Pelée. It was built in a one-story format of big windows to capture the power as well as the tranquility of the view of the volcano. You dine on a veranda. The furnishings are traditional, with white napery.

The view alone could suffice, but the chef doesn't rely on that. The food is quite good. Depending on your taste and your palate, you can order boudin à la créole, the popular blood sausage. Other suggested orders include a crab cocktail, frog legs à la Provençale, shrimp fritters, broiled fish, and flambéed quail with mushrooms. A complete meal averages 150F ($15). The restaurant is closed on Monday at lunch.

If you wish to stay over, a few rooms are available, costing from 170F ($17) daily in a single, 210F ($21) in a double, including breakfast. Full board is 275F ($27.50) per person daily.

Upon your descent from Montagne Pelée, you can drive down to Ajoupa Bouillon and Basse-Pointe. A mile before reaching the latter town, you turn on your left and follow a road that goes deeply into sugarcane country to—

Leyritz

Here you can explore the best restored plantation in Martinique, perhaps stopping by for lunch.

Hôtel Plantation de Leyritz, Basse-Pointe (tel. 75-53-92), the pride of Martinique, was built around 1700 by a plantation owner, Bordeaux-born Michel de Leyritz. It was the site of the "swimming pool summit meeting" in 1974 between Presidents Gerald Ford and Valéry Giscard d'Estaing. It's still a working banana plantation which (since 1970) has been restored by Charles and Yveline de Lucy de Fossarieu to its original and authentic character. You can live here in style and elegance, surrounded by an atmosphere of long ago.

There are 16 acres of tropical gardens through which guests ride on horseback, and at the core is an 18th-century stone great house. From the grounds, the view sweeps across the Atlantic taking in fearsome Montagne Pelée.

The owners have kept the best of the old, such as the rugged stone walls, 20 inches thick, the beamed ceilings, and the tile and flagstone floors. They have created a cozy setting of mahogany tables, overstuffed sofas, and gilt mirrors.

A few of the outbuildings, former slave quarters with bamboo roofs and stone walls, now house guests, and new ones have been added. I prefer the units —ten in all—in the manor, because they are probably the most attractive, certainly the most authentic. You can also stay in the carriage house across the lawn. Don't expect luxury—that's not the style here.

The proprietors have installed a fully equipped two-story spa center. The spa's ground floor includes three massage rooms, two Jacuzzis, salons for facial and body care, and a lounge for yoga and gymnastics. On the upper level is an open-air terrace with a Jacuzzi and solarium. In residence are a medical doctor, esthetician, yoga instructor, masseur, and a hairdresser. Twenty-one new spa rooms have also been built. They are air-conditioned and furnished in antiques. A covered path links them with the spa center.

The dining room is in a rum distillery, incorporating the fresh spring water running down from the hillside. Eating here is dramatic at night, and the cuisine is of a high level, authentically créole. Afternoon tea or apéritifs are served in the salon, with flickering lights from a 19th-century bronze and globed chandelier. You sit on Martinique-style rockers. On the surrounding walls are gilt-framed family portraits, plus scenic views of the island and Paris. Tour bus crowds predominate at lunch.

The swimming pool is at the edge of the compound, with grassy lawns and parasol tables where you can order *un punch vieux,* the traditional French plantation owner's libation. Bring your tennis racquet, as there is always someone ready to join you in a set. A horse can be brought for a ride through the woods.

Most guests visit just for lunch, heading south for the night. If that's the case with you, expect to pay from 120F ($12) to have a meal here. On my most recent rounds, I enjoyed a first-class créole lunch, which was really like a dinner. The main course was grilled chicken covered in coconut milk sauce, along with *oussous,* a freshwater crayfish which came in a herb sauce. Vegetables consisted of sauteed breadfruit and sauteed bananas.

In winter, guests can stay here on the continental plan, paying from $55 to $105 in a single and from $73 to $125 in a double. *In the off-season, with breakfast included, singles run 200F ($20) to 260F ($26) daily, and doubles cost from 230F ($23) to 310F ($31).*

Basse-Pointe

At the northernmost point on the island, Basse-Pointe is a land of pineapple and banana plantation fields, covering the Atlantic-side slopes of Mount Pelée volcano.

Chez Mally Edjam (tel. 75-51-18) is a local legend. Many visitors prefer to drive all the way from Pointe du Bout to dine with her instead of at the Leyritz Plantation. Of course, never arrive without calling for a reservation—it's like visiting a private home, which is what it is. You sit out on one of a handful of tables on her side porch. Grandmotherly Mally obviously likes hibiscus, and hummingbirds as well, but most of the time she's busy in the kitchen, turning out her créole delicacies. She knows how to do all the dishes for which the island is known: stuffed land crab with a hot seasoning, small pieces of conch in a tart shell, langouste, sea urchins (which are made suprisingly tasty), and a classic colombo de porc, the créole version of pork curry. She is known also for her lobster vinaigrette, her papaya soufflé, and her highly original confitures, which are tiny portions of fresh island fruits, such as pineapple and guava, that have been preserved in a vanilla syrup. Expect to spend from $20 for lunch.

After Basse-Pointe, the town you reach on your northward trek is Grand Rivière. From there, you must turn back. Before doing so, you may want to stop at **Chez Vava,** a good restaurant right at the entrance to the town. With its bright-orange tiling, it's easy to spot. You'll also find plenty of space to park your car.

The style is like a simple country inn. For 100F ($10) you can order a tomato salad, broiled fish with rice, and a dessert. À la carte menu items are also offered, including créole soup, a blaff of sea urchins, and lobster. An old rum punch, a specialty of the house, is also offered. If you order the most elaborate items on the menu, your tab could climb to 175F ($17.50).

Lorrain

Even though Lorrain is called the "kingdom of bananas," you might pass through this charming hamlet on the northeastern coast in short time. That is, unless you knew about the restaurant recommended below.

Relais des Îles, rue Chaumereau-Lamotte (tel. 75-43-85), is one of the least known restaurants on the island. Its lack of fame is underserved, since its créole food is among the best in Martinique. It's as if it's just awaiting discovery by the major food magazines. It's housed in an old Martiniquais house with shutters, clapboard siding, gingerbread fretwork, and a large veranda looking down on a curve in the road near the center of town.

Antoine and Gabrielle Duventru are the hospitable owners of this refreshingly simple place, where specialties vary with the availability of ingredients and where much of the art depends on the inspiration Mme Duventru might feel at the moment. Since she was born within a few miles of this spot, she's been able to pick up many gems of culinary lore.

Your meal might include pâté en pot (which, despite its name, is a kind of lamb soup), soup with crabs, Caribbean lobster, créole shrimp, six kinds of soufflé including varieties with conch and crayfish, a particularly tasty fish soup, eggplant or codfish fritters, stuffed eggplant, and a unique and original recipe of stuffed cucumbers and onions. Other possibilities are four kinds of tarts (made with sea urchins, onions, crayfish, or conch), stuffed crab, colombo of chicken, a flan of christophine au gratin, and a soupe z'habitants made with such vegetables as cabbage, leeks, onions, celery, and locally grown leaves. Set meals cost from 55F ($5.50), while à la carte menus cost from 135F ($13.50). The restaurant is open every day from 6 a.m. till after dinner. Reservations are a good idea.

Trinité

If you head back south along the coastal route, you'll pass through the small village of Trinité on the Atlantic side of Martinique. It would hardly merit a stopover were it not for the following hotel.

Saint-Aubin Hôtel at Trinité (tel. 75-34-77) is one of the loveliest inns in the Caribbean basin. A former restaurant owner, Normandy-born Guy Forêt has sunk his fortune into restoring this three-story Victorian-style house and turning it into a three-star hostelry.

In pink beige with fancy gingerbread, it was once a plantation house, sitting on a hillside above sugarcane fields and Trinité's bay. A long excursion from Pointe du Bout or Fort-de-France, it would make the perfect luncheon stopover or the ideal retreat for a vacation in Martinique. The location is 14½ miles from the airport, 19 miles from Fort-de-France, and 2 miles from the seaside village of Trinité itself. There are 800 yards of private beach as a further enticement, plus a swimming pool on the grounds.

All rooms are air-conditioned, with wall-to-wall carpeting and modern (not antique) furniture. There are some family rooms as well. After dinner you can sit on the veranda on the first and second floors, enjoying life as lived long ago. Rooms have a view of either the garden or the sea. In winter, two persons can stay here on the MAP at a rate of 550F ($55) daily, while singles pay from 340F ($34). *In summer, guests on the room-only (with breakfast included) plan need pay only 240F ($24) in a single, 325F ($32.50) in a double.* If you're stopping in only to dine (always call to reserve), expect a tab in the neighborhood of 120F ($12) per person.

AFTER DARK: Everybody who goes to Martinique wants to see the show performed by **Les Ballets Martiniquais,** a bouncy group of about two dozen dancers, along with musicians, singers, and choreographers. Many members of the troupe look no more than 17 years old. Launched in the early '60s, this group performs the traditional dances of Martinique and has been acclaimed in both Europe and the States.

The other folk ballet troupe is called **Les Grands Ballets de la Martinique.** With a swoosh of gaily striped skirts, a gentle swaying of hips, and clever acting, youthful dancers capture all the exuberance of the island's soul.

The groups have toured abroad with great success, but they perform best on home ground. Dressed in traditional costumes—madras headdresses, gold earrings, lace blouses, silk scarves, billowing skirts, and crisply starched petticoats—the island girls are led by their young men through such dances as the spirited mazurka, which was brought from the ballrooms of Europe, and the exotic beguine. The newer Grands Ballets, with 25 young performers under the direction of Jean-Pierre Bonjour, is considered one of the best ensembles in the Caribbean.

Cole Porter, incidentally, did not invent the beguine. It's a Martinique dance—some would call it a way of life. Instead of having me try to explain it, it's best to see it. Or dance it if you think you can.

Both groups present tableaux that tell of jealous brides and faithless husbands, demanding overseers and toiling cane cutters. There's a dreamy "Créole Waltz" and an erotic "Calenda," danced to the beat of an African drum. The "Parasol Dance" and "Carnival" add sparkle to the performance, and the show may end with the last mentioned dance or with "Adieu Foulard, Adieu Madras," a tale of a Créole girl's hopeless love for a French naval officer who must leave her.

Les Grands Ballets perform Monday at the Hotel Diamant-Novotel, Wednesday at the Frantel, and Friday at the Bakoua Beach. In addition, the troupe gives mini-performances aboard visiting cruise ships. The Ballets Martiniquais can be seen Thursday at the Méridien and Saturday at the Hotel Casino La Batelière. To enjoy a buffet dinner and a ballet show at one of the hotels costs from 160F ($16) to 200F ($20).

There's also a lot of nightlife revolving around the four major hotels at Pointe du Bout—**Bakoua Beach, Frantel Martinique, Méridien Martinique,** and **PLM ETAP Pagerié.** As mentioned, on certain nights you can watch Les Ballets Martiniquais. In addition, musicians, some of them quite young, play nightly in the larger hotels.

Hotel guests are allowed in free at three of the nightclubs, **Vesou** in the Frantel, **Vonvon** in the Méridien, and **Hutte** in Bakoua. However, figure on spending 50F ($5) per drink. If you're not a resident of one of the hotels, you'll be charged an entrance fee of around 60F ($6). It's hard to say which club is the best, as a mainly young crowd wanders from one to the other on a warm night. My preference, however, is for **Vesou.**

Club 21 at the Hôtel PLM La Batelière, Schoelcher (tel. 71-90-41), about a mile from Fort-de-France, swings into action every night at 10, except Monday. Rumor has it that the best-looking people on Martinique are likely to be found here on any given night. The special attraction of the place is a covered terrace hanging over the sea. The entrance fee is 60F ($6) per person. For that price, you'll have the rest of the night to fish for one of the lovely sirens (or handsome guys) who haunt the place.

The **Casino Trois-Îlets,** on the premises of the Méridien Martinique, Pointe du Bout (tel. 66-00-30) is open every night from 9 a.m. to 3 a.m. Here you can try to win the cost of your vacation by playing roulette, blackjack, or chemin-de-fer. Some form of identification with picture is required at the entrance. You present it along with 55F ($5.50).

You might also try your luck at the **Casino Hôtel PLM La Batelière** (tel. 71-90-41), Schoelcher, outside Fort-de-France. Not as glamorous as Las Vegas, it attracts a leisure crowd who play roulette, French chemin-de-fer, craps, or blackjack. An identity card such as a passport is required. The entrance fee is 50F ($5), and hours are from 9 p.m. to 3 a.m.

I'd advise you to spend your nights in the big hotel clubs. There are other native clubs frequented by the Martiniquais. However, some "incidents" have been reported when tourists strayed in. If you insist on going to one of these clubs "to see the real beguine," I suggest you go there with some local friends who know the island.

2. Guadeloupe

"The time is near, I believe, when thousands of American tourists will come to spend the winter among the beautiful countryside and friendly people of Guadeloupe." Or so Theodore Roosevelt accurately predicted on February 21, 1916. Guadeloupe isn't the same place it was when the Rough Rider himself rode through, but the natural beauty he witnessed, and certainly the people, are still there to be enjoyed.

Guadeloupe is part of the Lesser Antilles, lying about 200 miles north of Martinique, closer to the United States than its sister island. In addition to tourism, sugar production and rum beef up the local economy. The total surface of Guadeloupe and its satellite islands is close to 700 square miles. There is a lot of similarity in climate, animals, and vegetation between Martinique and Guadeloupe. So no one is surprised coming from one island to the other.

Guadeloupe is, in fact, formed by two different islands, separated by a narrow sea-water channel, known as Rivière Salée. **Grande Terre,** the eastern island, is typical of charm of the Antilles, with its rolling hills and sugar plantations.

On the other hand, **Basse Terre,** to the west, is a rugged mountainous island, dominated by the 4800-foot volcano La Soufrière, which is still alive. Its mountains are covered with tropical forests, impenetrable in many places. Bananas grown on plantations are the main crop. The island is ringed by beautiful beaches which have attracted much tourism, especially in the '70s and '80s

Among the celebrities from the island, Saint-John Perse (alias Alexis Saint-Leger) was born in St. Leger des Feuilles, a small islet in Pointe-à-Pitre bay, in 1887. The French diplomat was better known as a poet, the Nobel Prize winner in 1960. During all his life he wrote a constant song to the beauty of his island.

Guadeloupe was first called Karukera by the Arawaks, meaning "the island of the beautiful waters." On November 3, 1493, Columbus landed, naming the island Santa Maria de Guadelupe de Estramaduros, which in time became Guadeloupe. The island's modern history is very much related to that of Martinique. Guadeloupe was settled by Sir Lienard de l'Olive and Sir Duplessis d'Ossonville, who were detached from Martinique by its commander, Belain d'Esnambuc. These men arrived with a group of some 500 settlers on June 28, 1635.

The British seized the island in 1759. They gave it back, but took it once more in 1794. A mulatto, Victor Hugues, attacked them with his revolutionary army of blacks and whites, but he faded after Napoleon came to power, allowing the British to move in again in 1810. The island returned to French hands in 1815.

For 100 years Guadeloupe was a dependency of Martinique. In 1946 Guadeloupe became a full-fledged French *département* (the French equivalent of an American state), and its people are citizens of France with all the privileges that that implies.

GETTING THERE: As an overseas *département* of France, Guadeloupe is connected by Air France to Paris, Bordeaux, Lyon, Mulhouse, and large sections of South America. Most U.S. passengers, however, will be interested in **Eastern Airlines'** twice-weekly flights from Miami, for which APEX tickets in high season cost $467 round trip. This type of ticket requires an advance purchase of at least 7 days, and passengers must delay the ticketed return flight for between 6 and 21 days after takeoff date.

Clients unable to qualify for these requirements should ask about Eastern's excursion tickets, which require no advance purchase and a delay of only 3 to 21 days before returning home. This type of ticket for high-season travel costs $472 for midweek flights, $527 on weekends.

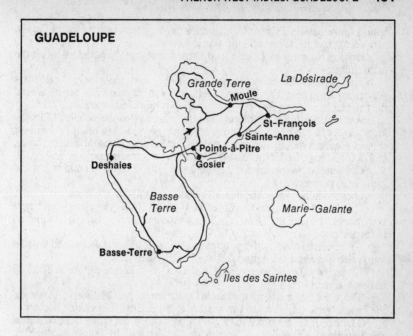

GUADELOUPE

Grande Terre
Moule
La Désirade
St-François
Sainte-Anne
Pointe-à-Pitre
Deshaies
Gosier
Basse Terre
Marie-Galante
Basse-Terre
Îles des Saintes

Eastern's flights to Guadeloupe from dozens of North American cities connect efficiently through Miami. For more information, get in touch with Eastern or a travel agent and inquire at the same time about discounts available on air transport when "land packages" (prepaid accommodations at selected hotels) are arranged through the airline's tour desk.

Other airlines servicing Guadeloupe include **American,** which flies direct from New York's JFK every Saturday and Sunday, making a brief stop in Martinique before continuing on to Guadeloupe.

Pan Am offers more service from New York than any other airline, flying from JFK nonstop every Saturday and Sunday and flying direct (with a brief touchdown at St. Thomas) every Monday, Wednesday, and Friday. Pan Am also makes flights from Miami to Guadeloupe three times a week, with a change of planes in St. Thomas.

Air Canada flies once a week from Toronto and Montréal, while **LIAT, Air Guadeloupe,** and **Air St. Barth** service the neighboring islands.

PRACTICAL FACTS: The official **language** is French, and Créole is the unofficial second language. As in Martinique, English is spoken only in the major tourist centers, rarely in the countryside. The official **currency** is the French franc, and some shops will take U.S. dollars. For stays of less than 21 days, **proof of identity** is needed, plus a return or ongoing plane ticket. For a longer stay, a valid passport is required.

Guadeloupe **time** is one hour later than Eastern Standard Time (when it's 6 a.m. in New York, it's 7 a.m. in Guadeloupe). When Eastern Daylight Saving Time is in effect, Guadeloupe and New York keep the same clocks.

The local **electricity** is 220 volts AC, 50 cycles, which means you'll need an adapter. Some of the big resorts lend these to guests, but don't count on it. One hotel I know had only six in stock, and a long, long waiting list (and of the six, two were broken!). Clients should take their own.

Driving is on the right side, and there are several gas stations along the main routes.

The **pharmacies** carry French medicines, and most over-the-counter American drugs have French equivalents. Prescribed medicines can be filled if the traveler has a prescription. Guadeloupe has modern hospitals.

As an important note, it must be remembered that the people of Guadeloupe do not like to be photographed unless they are camera-ready in their best clothes. Tourists should always ask permission before photographing anybody, and don't be surprised if the answer is a flat and resounding no.

Customs allows items for personal use, "in limited quantities," to be brought in tax free.

On scheduled flights, the **departure tax** is included in the fares.

Hotels and restaurants usually add a 10% to 15% **service charge,** and most taxi drivers who own their own cars do not expect a **tip.** Surprisingly, neither do hotel porters.

American tobacco and cigarettes are available at hotel shops, and Guadeloupe also has some **café-tabacs,** selling foreign cigarettes.

If you have a police emergency, call 82-00-05 in Pointe-à-Pitre or 81-11-55 in Basse Terre.

There are five modern **hospitals** in Guadeloupe, plus 23 clinics. Hotels and the Guadeloupe tourist office can assist in locating English-speaking doctors.

The major tourist office in Guadeloupe is called the **Office Départemental du Tourisme,** B.P. 1099, 5 Square de la Banque, in Pointe-à-Pitre (tel. 82-09-30).

GETTING AROUND: You'll find taxis when you arrive at the airport but no limousines or buses waiting to serve you. Chances are, you'll be heading for one of the resorts in Gosier. If so, count on spending about 55F ($5.50) to be taken there. After 9 p.m., until 7 a.m., cabbies are legally entitled to charge you 40% more.

Buses

As in Martinique, there is no rail service. But buses link almost every hamlet to Pointe-à-Pitre. However, you may need to know some high school French to use the system. From Pointe-à-Pitre you can catch one of these jitney vans, either at the Gare Routière de Bergevin if you're going to Basse Terre, or the Gare Routière de Mortenol if Grande Terre is your destination. The cost, for example, from Pointe-à-Pitre to Basse Terre is only $2.95.

Car Rentals

This is easy to arrange, since as many as ten local and international companies have offices in Guadeloupe. Car-rental kiosks at the airport are open to meet each international arrival. Rental rates at the various agencies vary only slightly, but if you want to be sure of getting a car when you arrive, it's usually best to reserve one in advance through the nationwide toll-free number maintained by at least three of these agencies.

Budget Rent-a-Car requires only 48 hours' advance notice for the reservation of a peppy Toyota Starlet with manual transmission. During high season the weekly rate for this car is $144, with unlimited mileage. Customers needing a car for less than a week pay $24 per day, unlimited mileage. French government tax is added to all rentals. Customers requiring air conditioning must go to Budget's top-of-the-line car, which is a Toyota Tercel with automatic transmission. This rents for $198 per week in high season, unlimited mileage included, or $33 per day. Drivers at Budget must be between 21 and 75, and must present a valid driver's license at the time of rental.

Avis has rates that are roughly comparable when a car is rented for a full week, although rentals of less than a week require a fee for every kilometer driven. This might or might not be more expensive than Budget's rates, depending on the distances you plan to drive.

Hertz is also represented in Guadeloupe, with a total of four locations throughout the island, although its rates tend to be higher than at either Avis or Budget.

I strongly advise car renters to accept the additional insurance that the counter attendant will offer at the time of rental. Budget charges around $4.30 per day for what it calls a collision damage waiver. If you accept it, you waive any financial responsibility for any damage inflicted on your car in an accident. If you do not accept it, you will be fully responsible for the repairs. The amount of liability differs from company to company, so it's always a good idea to check out the conditions in advance.

For more information, call Budget in the U.S. toll free at 800/527-0700. Hertz can be reached toll free at 800/654-3131 and Avis at 800/331-1212.

Taxi Tours

If you're traveling with people or imaginative in putting a party together, it's best to sightsee by taxi. Usually the concierge at your hotel will help you make this arrangement. Depending on the size of car you order, you can expect to pay from $60 a day for this service. Split four ways, the tab is much easier to handle, of course.

POINTE-À-PITRE: The port and chief city of Guadeloupe, Pointe-à-Pitre lies in Grande Terre. Unfortunately, it doesn't have the old-world charm of Fort-de-France in Martinique. What beauty it does possess is often hidden behind closed doors.

Having been burned and rebuilt so many times, the port has now emerged as a town lacking in character, with modern apartments and condominiums forming a high-rise backdrop over jerry-built shacks and industrial suburbs. The rather narrow streets are jammed during the day with a colorful crowd creating a permanent traffic tie-up. However, at sunset the town becomes quiet again and almost deserted.

The real point of interest in Pointe-à-Pitre is shopping. It's best to visit the town in the morning—you can easily cover it in a half day—taking in the waterfront and outdoor market (the latter is livelier in the early hours).

Open-air stalls surround the **covered market** at the corner of rue Frébault and rue Thiers. Here you can discover the many fruits, spices, and vegetables which are enjoyable just to view if not to taste. A deep fragrance of a Créole market permeates the place. In madras turbans local Créole women make deals over their strings of fire-red pimientos. The bright, colorful fabrics they wear compete with the rich tones of oranges, papayas, bananas, mangoes, and pineapples. The sounds of an African-accented French fill the air.

The town center is the Place de la Victoire, a park shaded by palm trees and poincianas. Here you'll see some old sandbox trees said to have been planted by Victor Hugues, the mulatto who organized a revolutionary army of both whites and blacks to establish a dictatorship. In this square he kept a guillotine busy, and the death-dealing instrument still stood there (but not in use) until modern times.

Sloops that travel through the islands, as well as fishing schooners, tie up at the old port, La Darse. Farther out, Caribbean cruise ships drop anchor to allow their passengers to go on shopping expeditions. We might as well follow their lead.

Shopping

Frankly, if you're going on to Fort-de-France in Martinique, I suggest you skip a shopping tour of Pointe-à-Pitre, as you'll find far more merchandise there, and perhaps friendlier service. However, if you're not, I'd recommend the following shops, some of which line the rue Frébault.

Of course, your best buys will be anything French—perfumes from Channel, silk scarfs from Hermès, cosmetics from Dior, crystal from Lalique and Baccarat. I've found (but not often) some of these items discounted as much as 30% lower than Stateside or Canadian prices.

Shops, which accept U.S. dollars, give these discounts only to purchases made by travelers check. Purchases are duty free if brought directly from store to airplane. In addition to the places below, there are also duty-free shops at Raizet Airport, selling liquor, rums, perfumes, crystal, and cigarettes.

Most shops open at 9 a.m., closing at 1 p.m., then reopening between 3 and 6 p.m. They are closed on Saturday afternoon, Sunday, and holidays. When the cruise ships are in port, many eager shopkeepers naturally change these hours, stretching them out, even on weekends, much to the regret of the clerks.

One of the best places to buy French perfumes, at prices often lower than those charged in Paris, is **Phoenicia.** It has three locations: 8 rue Frébault (tel. 83-50-36); 121 rue Frébault (tel. 82-22-22); and 93 rue de Nozières (tel. 82-71-93).

Rosébleu, 5 rue Frébault (tel. 82-93-44), has one of the biggest stocks in Pointe-à-Pitre of jewelry, crystal, perfumes, gifts, and fashion accessories. If you pay with travelers checks, you'll get discounts of 10% to 20%.

Seven Sins, 6 rue Frébault (tel. 82-10-35) sells any kind of alcoholic beverage, and it specializes in rum, including one so fiery white it is sipped like a liqueur.

Vendôme, 8-10 rue Frébault (tel. 83-42-84), has imported fashions for both men and women, most of them quite stylish, as well as a large selection of gifts and perfumes, including the big names. Usually you can find someone who speaks English to sell you a Cardin watch.

You can order anthurium, Bird of Paradise, and other island flowers, packaged for home shipment, at **Floral Antilles,** 80 rue Schoelcher (tel. 82-18-63).

TIM TIM, 15 rue Henri-IV (no phone), is a shop that should be better known. It is officially an antique store, but I go there mainly seeking old engravings and maps which can be attractively framed for the walls of your study when you return home.

Actually, if you're adventurous you may want to seek out some native goods found in little shops along the back streets of Pointe-à-Pitre. Considered collector's items are the straw hats or salacos made in Les Saintes islands. They look distinctly related to Chinese coolie hats and are usually well designed, often made of split bamboo. Native doudou dolls are also popular gift items.

Where to Stay

For convenience to terminals, if you'd like to seek lodgings in Pointe-à-Pitre, I have the following suggestions:

Bougainvillée, 9 rue Frébault (tel. 82-07-56), right on the corner of this major shopping drag and rue Delgres, draws people in town on business who book rooms spread over several floors, 32 fully air-conditioned units of comfort, with modern, functionally styled furnishings. Either single or double occupancy costs from 320F ($32) to 430F ($43) in winter. *In the off-season, singles or doubles range from 250F ($25) to 285F ($28.50), all EP tariffs.*

At its ground-floor restaurant you can order a set menu for 100F ($10) in a fairly pleasant setting. À la carte specialties include crayfish with its créole fragrance and hint of a fiery aftertaste and bouillabaisse.

Saint-John Perse once wrote about the fine old time sailors had when they arrived in Pointe-à-Pitre when it was used as a stopover anchorage on the famous Route du Rhum. But since that day is long gone, you may not want to linger; you can take a different route instead, this one to the "South Riviera," from Pointe-à-Pitre to Pointe de Châteaux.

Where to Dine

La Canne à Sucre, 17 rue Henri-IV (tel. 82-10-19), is one "sugarcane" that has created a local sensation, and in spite of its youth has already become the most select rendezvous for a superbly prepared Guadeloupean cuisine in Pointe-à-Pitre. Gérard Virginius, along with his wife, Marie, have restored this colonial house, with a kitchen from which emerge all the tempting dishes of the créole cuisine. You dine in a parlor setting with a choice of two rooms.

For an appetizer, try one of their fritters made with malange, which tastes like sweet potatoes to me, and another with a vegetable known as giraumon, a squashy-like pumpkin. Their stuffed land crabs (called crabes farcis here) are among the best sampled on the island. Conch is queen around here, and it's likely to be served in a variety of ways, put in everything from a tart to soup. I consider it best here when it's cooked with eggplant.

For a main course, try the grilled lemon chicken with onion rings, or sea urchins made even more delectable with a gently squeeze of lime. Fresh fish is served in papillotte, and occasionally they have turtle steak. Desserts are lavish and sinful: a soursop sherbet or a coupe Canne à Sucre (a rondelle with old rum, coconut sherbet, whipped cream, banana, caramel, and a touch of cinnamon). It's traditional to begin your meal with a small rum punch. The restaurant is closed on Saturday for lunch and all day Sunday, but open otherwise for those who make a reservation. Expect to spend from $35 per person for dinner.

LE BAS DU FORT: The first tourist complex, lying just two miles from Pointe-à-Pitre, is called Le Bas du Fort, in the vicinity of Gosier. Two large hotels previewed below are found there.

Where to Stay

Frantel Guadeloupe, Le Bas du Fort, Gosier (tel.83-64-44), is a secluded bungalow colony of two- and three-story structures, set away from the main road, occupying grounds from a secondary route to the shoreline. In a setting of banana trees and lawns, it offers first-class comfort in 200 air-conditioned rooms, either in bungalows or in the two wings, which open onto a view of the park-like grounds or the water. The furnishings are in "sober modern," and the floors are tiled, the baths having a separate toilet. In high season, a single room rents for 475F ($47.50) daily, *dropping to 350F ($35) in low season.* Two persons in a double pay 620F ($62) in high season, *475F ($47.50) in the off-season.* All units have either twin or double beds.

The beach is small, but you'll have the use of a large swimming pool. The Frantel is a complete resort with lots of sports activities. Next to the pool is a circular bar, Le Wahoo.

The hotel's deluxe restaurant, Le Grand Baie, opens onto a terrace where you can order both local créole specialties or the traditional French cuisine. The set menu of four courses goes from 120F ($12). Sicali is an open grill lying halfway between the beach and the pool, providing simple but savory meals, with grilled meat or fish, as well as a serve-yourself salad bar and a dessert buffet. The hut-shaped restaurant enjoys much favor from guests.

Fleur d'Épée Novotel, Le Bas du Fort, Gosier (tel. 83-49-49), is a sister resort to its neighbor, the Frantel. Both share the same beach facilities, and guests mingle freely. The Novotel is a string of connected modular units, 191 in all, with diamond-shaped roofs. At its center is a larger white-roofed restaurant where you can order authentic French dinners, with West Indian overtones. Expect to pay $21 for a complete meal.

There are plenty of grounds for relaxation, as well as a generous-size pool where guests sometimes remove *le minimum.* Groupings of parasols, with low white lounges, make it a popular spot.

The accommodations offer much comfort, although they are in a simple modern with a few island touches such as bamboo chairs. There are private, angular balconies with unblocked views. The cost is $72 daily in a single in high season. In a double, you pay $60 in high season. *In summer, a single rents for $50 daily, and a double goes for $60.*

Included in the tariffs quoted are free use of pedalboats, sailboats, and snorkeling equipment, along with Sunfish, Ping-Pong, tennis, and volleyball. Those chaises longues at the swimming pool and beach are given out free to the hotel's guests. All rooms come with an ocean view, and there is usually entertainment offered at dinner, including perhaps a local band or a folkoric group. Children up to 12 years are housed free if they share a rorom with their parents.

PLM Sun Village (also called PLM Village Soleil), Bas du Fort (tel. 83-05-76). Because of its position on a hill above the yacht basin, many of this hotel's rooms can scan just about anything entering or leaving the harbor. Many of the residents of the attractive apartments are boating people who appreciate the resort's position near many of the area's marina and yacht-rental facilities. Pointe-à-Pitre is within a ten-minute drive of the 100 units, which include 36 duplexes each sleeping up to four persons. Each apartment contains a kitchenette, a balcony, and comes with maid service. In winter, singles cost between $42 and $56, while doubles go for $48 to $66. *The summer rates are 280F ($28) for singles, 340F ($34) for doubles.*

On the premises are a large pool, a food market, a cocktail bar, and a restaurant, Le Boucanier, with both French and créole specialties.

Where to Dine

La Plantation, Bas du Fort, in the Port de Plaisance shopping center (tel. 82-39-63). Never judge a restaurant by its location. This shopping center, at a marina complex, could easily be on Long Island. The food at this stylish pink-and-green confection is not ordinary in any sense, and is in fact one of the finest dining establishments on the island, serving dinner only, for which it is most important that you reserve a table.

In an intimate and modern setting (also air-conditioned), a French and nouvelle cuisine is presented nightly except Sunday. Monsieur François Delage of Bordeaux is the chef de cuisine, and he's one of Guadeloupe's hottest kitchen properties, who knows all about raspberry vinegar. His array of delicate new dishes brings a creative touch to the cookery of Guadeloupe. For a beginning, try either the pumpkin soup, or if featured, a superb hors d'oeuvre of gésier d'oie, a goose giblet salad with a warm vinaigrette, served with walnuts and crisp croûtons. You'll also find staples from the classic repertoire of cooks in France, including a côte de boeuf rôtie with sauce moëlle. You might also be served duck breast with pears, perhaps red snapper in a cream sauce flavored with small baby clams and saffron. Many of his other dishes are outstanding, and he does wonders with crayfish, called ouassous, which he serves with a creamy dressing tinged with carapace and wine. It's easy to spend from $35 for dinner, including wine.

L'Albatros, Bas du Fort (tel. 82-52-64), is the challenger. It has a far more romantic location, as it opens onto the water near the already-recommended Hôtel Frantel. In season, diners wanting to escape the confines of either the Frantel or the Fleur d'Épée are likely to fill up all 24 tables, so reservations are important. The most in-the-know diners ask for a table on a big veranda with a glass floor over an aquarium.

The decor is subdued in autumnal tones with just the right tones of rose to make it interesting. The owner, Rosell Aurières, over the years has collected a cookbook of recipes, and she passes them on to her chef, regardless of who is cooking on any given night.

One of the most acclaimed dishes is lobster, small clams, and conch that have been gratinéed in a béchamel. Another local savory treat is crab claws in a spicy créole sauce, even baby shark in a perfect sauce made with green peppercorns instead of the fashionable pink ones. Try also a salade meli-melo, which is made with lumpfish roe, ham, fruit, and potatoes. A colombo of goat or chicken is regularly featured. Meals cost around $30. The restaurant serves until 11 p.m. except Sunday, and on Friday a band plays for dancing.

GOSIER: Some of the biggest and most important hotels of Guadeloupe are found at this holiday center, with its nearly five miles of beach, stretching east from Pointe-à-Pitre.

For an excursion, you can climb to **Fort Fleur d'Épée,** dating from the 18th century. Its dungeons and battlements are testaments remaining of the ferocious fighting between the French and British armies in 1794 seeking to control the island. The well-preserved ruins command the crown of a hill. From there you'll have good views over the bay of Pointe-à-Pitre, and on a clear day you can see the neighboring offshore islands of Marie-Galante and Îles des Saintes.

Where to Stay

Ecotel Guadeloupe, Gosier (tel. 84-15-66), is a restful retreat surrounded by lush gardens. Within an eight-minute drive of the capital and ten minutes from the airport, the hotel is maintained by students from the local hotel school. One part of the building is constructed in the shape of an H, with flower-bordered walkways connecting the segments. It was designed by Gilbert Corbin, who also conceived the Raizet Airport. It's modern in styling, yet its restaurant, bar, and bedrooms are West Indian in feeling.

Each of the accommodations, 44 in all, opens onto a view of the enticing pool, the gardens, or the adjoining forest. The units contain many built-in pieces, as well as white molded furniture. The air conditioning is occasionally not strong enough for some guests, but it is silent. Breakfast is served on an al fresco extension of the comfortably furnished reception area. To stay here costs 320F ($32) daily in a single in high season, 500F ($50) in a double, breakfast included. *These prices drop to 240F ($24) daily in a single off-season, 310F ($31) in a double.* With dinner included, add 120F ($12) per person per day to the tariffs quoted.

At the restaurant, Le Galion, serving dinner only, you get not only student waiters but also student cooks, the latter under the tutelage of a trained chef from France. Among the specialties is a filet de machoiran, a fleshy fish shipped in from Guyana. Also try their local red snapper done in a variety of ways. They also do a gâteau de langouste (spiny lobster) with whiskey. Snails come with Pernod and walnuts. In winter, the director, Monsieur Castell, presents two gastronomic evenings each with the best chefs of France. Similar evenings are held with the best créole cooks on Guadeloupe. Expect to pay around $25 for a meal.

If you choose, you can dine on much lighter fare alongside the swimming pool at Pap-Pap. Here a meal will average 95F ($9.50).

Another quarter of a mile farther on, you come to the tourist complex of—

Callinago Beach Hotel and Village, Gosier (tel. 84-12-93), named after a Carib Indian hero. Built along the Gosier beachfront, the hotel lies between the Auberge de la Vieille Tour and the Salako. The hotel is run like a small resort inn along the Mediterranean, and the host, Jacques Savariau, has a friendly, helpful staff.

In buildings of white stucco, some 41 rooms, with private baths, air conditioning, and private balconies, are rented. In high season, the cost is 420F ($42) daily in a single, rising to 575F ($57.50) in a double, EP. *In the off-season, the single tariff is 250F ($25) daily, and the double, 340F ($34).*

In the residential village complex, next to the hotel, the management offers 96 studios and 22 duplex apartments. The studios, for example, are spacious, with a combination living room and bedroom furnished in Nordic modern, with complete kitchens and baths. A sliding glass wall opens onto a private balcony overlooking Gosier Bay. The duplexes, of course, are larger. You ascend a spiral staircase to your upstairs bedroom, with a private bath and another small terrace. On the premises is a little, well-stocked market if you'd like to do light housekeeping.

In winter, rates are $58 for a studio single, $65 for a studio double, $120 for a duplex suitable for three to four persons, and $135 for a duplex suitable for five guests, all EP tariffs. *Expect 20% reductions in summer.* The prices are for rooms only. If you want to dine out, you can eat in the hotel's restaurant, offering both French and créole foods, a good meal costing from 120F ($12) and up.

The hotel opens onto a white sand beach, and on the grounds is a freshwater pool. Such sports as waterskiing, sailing, snorkeling, pedal boating, windsurfing, and rides on a 36-foot sailing boat are available as well, but you'll pay extra for these. There are two tennis courts as well.

Hôtel Salako, Pointe de la Verdure (tel. 84-14-90), is a six-floor building in a modern block with an extension opening onto a vast swimming pool and built on the beachfront. Popular with tour groups, it offers a view of the lagoon and a white sandy beach. Five minutes from Gosier, it has 120 air-conditioned bedrooms, each with bath, phone, radio, and balcony. Rates in winter are 420F ($42) in a single, 560F ($56) in a double. *In summer, tariffs are lowered to 280F ($28) in a single, 340F ($34) in a double.*

Lunch can be taken at the al fresco restaurant and bar, with its vista of water and mountains, and dinner is served in a candlelit main room where créole specialties and classic French dishes are featured. Their buffet is considered one of the best on the island. Full dinners at the restaurant, Saintois, cost from 140F ($14) and up. Live entertainment is often featured here.

La Créole Beach Hotel, Pointe de la Verdure, Gosier (tel. 84-15-00), formerly the Holiday Inn, has the nicest hotel design of any of the Gosier establishments. Half New Orleans, half colonial, the hotel stands alongside two beaches in a setting of lawns and trees, as well as hibiscus and bougainvillea.

The bedrooms, 156 regular ones plus six duplexes, are traditional in tone, with dark wood pieces, carpeted floors, phones, TVs, and individually controlled air conditioning. The comfortable beds are in a beige color. Your balcony will be large enough to be your breakfast spot or a perch for your sundowner.

High-season rates, including a full American breakfast, are $82 daily in a single, $125 in a double, and $141 in a triple, plus another $23-per-person supplement for MAP. *In summer, the cost of a double is 480F ($48) daily, with a single going for 380F ($38).*

The gourmet restaurant is called Ste-Anne, and it is attractively decorated with plants. Many local specials are served here, along with a more familiar international cuisine. During the day guests enjoy drinks at the poolside bar, St. Tropez, or a lunch at the beach snackbar named Beethoven. The newest restaurant, Les Alizés, stands on an airy terrace near the pool and is full of handsome greenery. Its kitchen is run by an expert French chef, Jean-Paul Gulotta, featuring a Lyonnaise cuisine. For a nightcap, guests head for the American bar, Le Voile d'Or. Many water sports as well as tennis are provided. In addition, hotel guests are admitted free to the nightclub, Ti Racoon, which offers occasional shows and nightly dancing.

Hôtel PLM Arawak, Pointe de la Verdure, Gosier (tel. 84-12-74), was one of the first hotels to be built in the area, a forecast of what was to come. It's a high-rise, ten-floor white building, with its exterior in cellular patterns, tiers of balcony inserts with brown iron railings.

All 150 rooms are fully air-conditioned, and the overall furnishings and ambience was once described as "modern Créole." Bedrooms have a French Caribbean look, with strong colors used against white and with white plastic furnishings. A few of the larger rooms are more conservative. In winter, a single ranges in price from $58 to $88 daily, with doubles going for $79 to $112. Suites are more expensive, of course. *In summer, singles cost from 295F ($29.50) to 400F ($40) daily, and two persons pay from 365F ($36.50) to 525F ($52.50).*

The hotel is built in the middle of a tropical garden, and you can enjoy the swimming pool. The reception is wide and open to the bar, which mixes some excellent drinks. The restaurant has a fair reputation for turning out créole specialties or French cookery. Expect to pay from $20 to have lunch here. Finally, all water sports as well as tennis are featured.

A casino, Gosier-les-Bains, is open nightly at 9. Men aren't required to wear a jacket and tie, but are cautioned to "dress elegantly."

Auberge de la Vieille Tour, Gosier (tel. 84-12-04), is a harmonious combination of the old and the practical new, where you get vintage charm and an authentic Créole quality. Directed by the Frantel interests, the complex encircles an 1835 sugar mill whose thick-walled tower (which looks like a lighthouse) is now the reception area. To that original structure, 82 rooms of first-class standard, with balconies overlooking the gardens and a small private beach, have been added. As you enter the driveway, you pass old mechanical parts of the former mill—dented wheels, the furnace, whatever. The modern bedroom extensions flow out into the tropical garden. For those who want even more privacy than that provided by the regular units, there are three intimate bungalows.

If you want to stay here, figure on spending 480F ($48) daily in a single and up to 600F ($60) in a double in high season. *These rates drop to 400F ($40) daily in a single and 450F ($45) in a double in low season.* For 180F ($18) in addition to the room tariff, you can have breakfast and dinner, taking your meals on an exchange system with the Callinago and Frantel.

The waterfront garden is the social center, with its large swimming pool. If you'd like to eat at the hotel, refer to the recommendations in "Dining at Gosier." At the Ajoupa Club beach grill you can dance for free if you're a hotel guest, enjoying the sounds of a local steel band almost every night in season. Sometimes limbo dancers are brought in, and buffets and barbecues are planned. Most sports are available at the hotel, and on the premises is a shop providing local handicrafts at reasonable tariffs. You can take a short boat ride to the nude beach on the island of Gosier facing the auberge. Or if you're not daring, the hotel has a freshwater pool. Tennis is played on three composition courts, which are floodlit for night play.

Serge's Guest House, Perinette Gosier (tel. 84-10-25), right in the middle of town, gives you a chance to live in a Créole family house with an encircling garden awash with tropical flowers and vegetation. Each of the 25 modestly furnished rooms contains air conditioning and a private bath, while several of the units have verandas. A swimming pool is set amid the greenery. Meals are consumed in a sunny room whose glass louvers open onto a view of the lush garden. There, an octagonal gazebo serves as a daytime bar and a nighttime rendezvous for occasional live entertainment. Serge Helene, the owner, includes a continental breakfast as part of his rates. Year round, these range from 150F ($15) to 215F ($21.50) in a single, from 200F ($20) to 240F ($24) in a double. The white concrete structure lies just over half a mile from the nearest beach.

Dining at Gosier

In addition to the hotels, many small restaurants are found in Gosier and the vicinity. At some of these places you'll get créole cookery with a relaxed atmosphere, and often relaxed service too. Many of these places you may discover on your own. I'll suggest the following. First, I'll document the best in-hotel dining, then the independent places.

Auberge de la Vieille Tour, Gosier (tel. 84-12-04), is one of the finest restaurants on the island. The main dining room is decorated in the French country style, with beamed ceilings, paneled walls, and chandeliers. The service from a staff hired by the famous Frantel chain in France, is among the best on the island. Waitresses, many of them trained at hotel schools, serve you, clad in their Guadeloupe madras Créole garb.

The menu will probably change many times during the lifetime of this edition, but you'll get, in whatever form, French nouvelle cuisine here. The fish soup with fennel will get you going, then you are likely to be faced with such temptations as veal sweetbreads delicately braised with honey or roast lamb with a saffron sabayon. The locally caught red snapper is likely to be accompanied by cucumber balls and mango butter (yes, mango butter). My most recent guinea fowl was perfectly cooked and served with fresh cabbage leaves, a garlic cream sauce, and giraumon, the local pumpkin. The price is high, about $35 per head, but it's worth it.

Balata, route de Morne Labrousse (tel. 82-85-29). From the gastronomic capital of France (Lyon) to a panoramic site in Grande-Terre, Pierre Cecillon has come a long way. But so far he, along with his wife, Marie, are having much success with their charming little restaurant which combines the classic Lyonnaise cuisine with créole cookery, and does so exceedingly well.

Those who reserve early enough get a table on the terrace. Waitresses in *madras et foulard* dress bring out an array of tempting fare which might include a fish mousse with lobster sauce, perhaps chicken liver in aspic as an appetizer. On the créole side, raw conch is often marinated in lime juice and olive oil, and blood pudding is invariably featured. The fish of the day might be served simply with parsley and butter, or with chive-flecked butter and tangy capers.

A table d'hôte meal is offered for 120F ($12), and you'll spend far more, from 200F ($20), ordering à la carte. A choice of desserts from the trolley is offered. The restaurant serves lunch and dinner except on Sunday night (it is also shut all day on Monday).

Chez Violetta, at the far eastern end of Gosier Village, en route to Ste-Anne (tel. 84-10-34), is run by the high priestess of créole cookery, who still presides in her kitchen. Her name is Violetta Chaville, and in her domain you'll know you're getting the finest of native cuisine. On the à la carte menu, try her stuffed crabs, her blaff of seafood, her fresh fish of the day (perhaps red snapper), and her turtle ragoût. For an appetizer, you might ask for cod fritters or beignets called "accra." The classic blood sausage, boudin, is also served here. In addition to the turtle ragoût, she does a fine conch ragoût, superb in texture and flavor. It's best when served with hot chilis grown on Guadeloupe. On occasion, she'll even prepare a brochette of shark, if available. Fresh pineapple makes an ideal dessert, or you can try her banana cake. The restaurant serves seven days a week, both lunch and dinner. For a really fine meal on the à la carte, expect to pay from 175F ($17.50). Waitresses here dress in *madras et foulard*.

Le Jardin des Gourmets, Montauban–Le Gosier (tel. 84-00-55), was created by a Créole beauty named Elisabeth, who returned to Guadeloupe after a career as an actress and model for Paco-Rabanne in Paris. This establishment is increasingly talked about for its nouvelle créole cuisine. It sits behind a wall and a flowering garden, in an upper-crust Antillean home.

Most diners prefer the wide porch whose wicker furniture has supported the well-dressed contours of such French celebrities as Giscard d'Estaing and bevies of Parisians who seem to relish being photographed here. A pair of porcelain leopards flanks the entrance to the inner room, where personalized touches include a fringed throw on the piano, an ornately woven hammock, and dozens of palms and plants.

Specialties served at the beautifully set tables combine classic recipes with a select mixture of local ingredients. They include a cassoulet of conch and octopus with small mushrooms and lardoons, a petite marmite fisherman's style with root vegetables, a blaff of créole-style fish, cassoulette of lobster, a side of veal with scallions (in a sauce forestière and coconut milk), curried baby shark with green tomatoes, terrine of seafood in saffron-colored aspic, and ouassous (local crayfish) in the Provençale style. Full meals range upward from 230F ($23). The restaurant is open daily from noon to 1 a.m. Most patrons seem to prefer dining late, when piano music accompanies their meal. Reservations are advised.

Chez Rosette, route de Gosier (tel. 84-11-32), is centered near many of the previously recommended hotels whose guests, even though on the half-board plan, come here for dinner. They know they'll get créole cookery that is zesty and beautifully flavored with spices and herbs. Chez Rosette is one of the largest créole places in Guadeloupe. It grew from a "front porch" restaurant made famous by Madame Rosette, whose successors carry on today, serving 120 patrons.

The restaurant is known mostly for fish dishes, which are often stewed or curried, as reflected by the colombo de poisson. The pièce de résistance is roast suckling pig, perfectly prepared, although I'm just as fond of the lobster flambé and the crabes farcis. In season, a tourist menu is offered at 100F ($10), which might include an appetizer of shellfish, a garnished grilled meat dish, salad or cheese, followed by dessert. For 120F ($12) you can sample the hors d'oeuvres buffet, taking as much as you want of vegetables and salads, to be followed by fish or grilled meat, plus dessert. Otherwise, if you order à la carte, sampling the authentic créole cookery, you'll pay from 150F ($15) to 200F ($20). Service is by a bevy of Guadeloupiennes dressed in the traditional *madras et foulard*.

Chez Back-Lien, Boulevard Amédé-Clara, Gosier Village (tel. 84-10-91), is the best Oriental restaurant in Guadeloupe. It's on the upper floor of a concrete building whose walls are covered with Cambodian art. The elegantly beautiful Kim Thomas is the Vietnamese owner who came to Guadeloupe via Paris to set up this establishment in 1979. When I was here, the chef (who happened to be her teenage son) produced delicately flavored Vietnamese specialties which showed his innate flair for culinary pursuits. You can enjoy five kinds of duckling, duck soup, pork with caramel sauce, beef with black mushrooms, and brochettes of chicken in hot sauce. The restaurant is open only for dinner, 7 to 11 p.m., and serves copious meals costing from $25. It's closed on Wednesday.

La Chaubette, route de la Riviera (tel. 84-14-29). Begin with a rum punch, made with white rum and served with a lime wedge and sugar. But don't order too much—it's lethal, and you won't be able to get through the rest of dinner. This is a "front porch" créole restaurant with lots of local color. About a 12-minute run from Pointe-à-Pitre, it's big and immaculately kept, almost like the Guadeloupe version of a roadside inn, with its red checked tablecloths and curtains made of bamboo.

Mme Gitane Chavalin is in charge, and she's known in the area for her créole recipes, using, whenever possible, the fish and produce of her island. She gets the name of her restaurant from a small clam that lives in the Caribbean basin, and she makes a broth with these clams to honor the namesake. When it's available, her langouste is peerless, as is her hog's head cheese with a minced onion vinaigrette. Of course she knows how to pound and season conch to perfection, and often she'll prepare turtle steak when she can get it. Her ragoût of chatrou (a tiny octopus) is served in a tomato sauce, and I heartily endorse it for those seeking real local cookery.

She's closed Sunday, but otherwise will top off a fine meal for you by serving either coconut ice cream or a banana flaming with rum. For her trouble, expect a bill around $25 per person for a complete meal. Service is until 11 p.m.

ST-FÉLIX: At a distance of some two miles from Gosier, on the road to Ste-Anne, I suggest a stopover in the hamlet of St-Félix. Right in the middle of the fields, past running chickens and jumping kids, you'll come across **Chez Lydie** (tel. 84-13-63). The dining room looks like a ballroom in a country village—no great compliment—but the food is very good, and everything is clean. You are served on madras tablecloths. The best items to order here are fresh fish, goat ragoût, or turtle ragoût (the latter, if you catch the cook on a good night, is absolutely a delight and beautifully flavored). Prices are quite low for the area. You'll not only have a good-tasting luncheon or dinner, but a memorable experience, all for the cost of $15 to $20.

Auberge Landaise, Trois-Chemins, Pliane-St-Félix (tel. 84-06-53). The natives in and around Bordeaux have always been known for their appreciation of good food and wine. This restaurant takes its name from Les Landes, the name of the region from which the owners, Michel and Yvette Chantegreil, emerged. They offer not only Landaise cookery, but Basque specialties as well, along with a fine selection of bordeaux wines.

To begin your repast, you might ask for their jambon de Bayonne, the famed cured ham of Bayonne, or a Basque-style fish soup. Try also the crab soup with vermicelli. Bordeaux snails come en croûte, and there is a wide variety of duck dishes, such as confit or lacquered duck. In winter, game is often featured. She is also noted for her *pâtisseries et glaces maison.* Count on spending from $25 and up. Although Monsieur and Madame Chantegreil can take up to 50 diners, it is always important to call on weekends because of the popularity of this place. They are closed on Monday.

PETIT HAVRE: Just off the main highway, between Gosier and Ste-Anne, you'll come upon **Le Bistrot** (tel. 88-91-82), where Danny and Annie Rossard, who came here from the south of France, run what was always considered one of the island's finest dining rooms. They have continued the same high standards set by the former owners, and if anything, are even better at the reception and the cuisine.

The panoramic view of this hilltop restaurant has always been a potent attraction. During the day you get a sweep of the sea, and at night, of twinkling island lights. The accent is casual here, but in an elegantly chic way. The dining room is open to the trade winds, but concealed under a thatched roof.

To open your repast, try the féroce d'avocat, which is puréed avocado with onion, cod, and cassava in the fruit's shell. You might also try the fish soup with aioli, that wonderfully garlic flavor found on the French Riviera. On occasion you can have baby shark or a zesty red snapper, everything depending on the catch of the day. That might included pisquettes, which are tiny fish lightly fried, evoking some Mediterranean meal. For dessert they do a tarte tatin to perfection (the apples are, naturally, imported). Count on spending from $30. They are closed on Sunday and Monday, and they take an annual vacation in August and September.

STE-ANNE: About nine miles from Gosier, little Ste-Anne is a sugar town and a small resort, offering many fine beaches and lodging facilities. In many ways it's the most charming of the villages of Guadeloupe, with its town hall in pastel colors, its church, and its principal square, Place de la Victoire, where a statue of Schoelcher commemorates the abolition of slavery in 1848.

Where to Stay

Its best known resort is **Club Méditerranée Caravelle** (tel. 84-12-00), a 45-acre tourist complex hidden alongside a cape covered with palm trees. Its beach is one of the finest in the French West Indies. Beads are legal tender here, and rooms are shared. If you're a single man, you'll be assigned a room with a member of the same sex. But that arrangement isn't necessarily how you'll end up after the game of musical beds played around here.

The core of this open-air duplex structure contains the dance floor, cabaret, disco, dining room, and bar. Radiating from this heart are the rooms, twin-bedded, air-conditioned units with private shower baths. Most of the accommodations open onto a private terrace. More units are housed in yet another complex a short walk from the main building.

You can stay here for a week, with most everything included. *In summer and fall, land arrangements are about $650 per person weekly,* rising to anywhere from $820 to $1100 weekly in winter and spring. The highest tariffs are in effect during the Christmas holidays. These tariffs are only approximate and subject to change. Nonguests can drop in for lunch, eating all they want from the buffet for 200F ($20) per person. Local créole specialties are featured. Sometimes folklore evenings are presented, and there is dancing to live bands.

Sports don't cost extra—six tennis courts (lit for night games), scuba-diving (deep dives at Pigeon Island), sailing, snorkeling, swimming in either the pool or ocean, pétanque, yoga, windsurfing, archery. Scuba-divers and snorkelers find at government-protected Pigeon Bay an underwater reserve. With the assistance of the Alliance Française, specially trained teachers offer classes in French for all levels throughout the day, followed by helpful language-lab practice sessions. And to keep members computer literate, the village offers an Atari Computer Workshop, with a year-round complement of 25 sophisticated computers. Buffets are served at the club's intimate hillside restaurant overlooking the bay. There's even a nude bathing area included.

Hôtel La Toubana (tel. 88-25-57) is a hostelry centered around a low-lying stone building on a cliff overlooking the bay. Many guests come here just for the view, which on a clear day encompasses Marie-Galante, Dominica, La Désirade, and the Îles des Saintes, but you'll quickly learn that there's far more to this charming place than just a panorama. After parking, you walk into a circular forecourt whose side is flanked with a reflecting pool which doubles as a lobster tank. Registration takes place at an al fresco countertop away from the main building.

You'll be shown to one of the 64 attractive rooms, each of which occupies half of one of the 32 red-roofed bungalows that lie scattered among the tropical shrubs along the adjacent hillsides. *Toubana* is the Arawak word for "small house," and your toubana-away-from-home will cost 480F ($48) to 660F ($66) per person per day for double occupancy, half board included. Single occupants of double accommodations pay between 570F ($57) and 800F ($80) per day, with half board. A third bed for a child under 12 can be set up in any accommodation, although the hotel doesn't allow more than two adults per room. Guests who stay for an entire week receive a discount of 300F ($30) to 400F ($40) off the total half-board price. *Expect 20% reductions off-season.*

The capable manager of this resort is Patrick Vial-Collet, who studied innkeeping in Switzerland and trained in London. His ideas contributed to the designer's inspiration of lining the dining room walls with illuminated aquariums from which schools of fish and crayfish stare back at curious visitors. The dining room, painted in shades of aqua and white, decked out at dinnertime with immaculate napery, offers both indoor and al fresco dining stretching right up to the edge of the pool. Chef Jean-François Dalremont offers a small but varied menu of seafood and meat. One particularly tasty specialty is fish soup in the style of Toulon.

The beach is only a five-minute walk from any lodging, while tennis courts are on the premises. Deep-sea fishing and other water sports can be arranged.

Le Rotabas (tel. 88-25060) is near the Caravelle Club Med, on a gravel road running into the highway between Ste-Anne and Pointe-à-Pitre. The reception area is in a high-ceilinged A-frame structure recently erected by Guadeloupian entrepreneurs Julien and Amalie Bastaraud.

Accommodations are in 28 bungalows scattered over the landscape where trees and shrubs compete for space with the network of tile walks connecting the buildings. One of the social centers is under the parapet-style roof of the al fresco lounge, where comfortable sofas and chairs receive refreshing breezes. Breakfast and lunch are served in a waterside villa, while dinner is a more formal affair in a modern open-air building with paneled walls, a high ceiling, and a bar furnished with wicker.

Most guests take a short walk to the beach of the nearby Club Med, where they can bathe *au naturel* if they wish. The Rotabas waterfront, however, does contain a popular windsurfing concession run by two émigrés from the French Jura region. Evelyn and Alain Perret rent boards for around 45F ($4.50) per hour at this spot where the winds are said to be almost constant.

The establishment's bungalows are simple, clean, and economical. Each has its own tile bath, air conditioning, and patio. In winter, doubles range from 460F ($46) to 500F ($50), depending on the view. MAP can be arranged for 120F ($12) per person per day. *In summer, single or double rooms cost 260F ($26) each, and MAP is an additional 100F ($10) per person.*

Incongruously named, the ten-room **Hôtel Le Grand Large** (tel. 88-20-06), at the edge of town, is close to the municipal beach. It's nestled in the midst of tropical greenery, including coconut palms, on a two-acre site. Life here is informal and casual, everything beach oriented. The hostess is charming Mme Georges Damico, and English for her is definitely not even a second language.

Accommodations are white bungalows with twin beds and private baths, all air-conditioned. That may not really be necessary as they're exposed to the trade winds. Guests can stay here year round, either single or double occupancy, for 380F ($38) daily, plus tax and service. The restaurant has been closed, but salads, sandwiches, and light platters are still available. Tea, if desired, is served on a big veranda with an angled bamboo ceiling.

Le Relais du Moulin, Chateaubrun, near Ste-Anne (tel. 88-23-96), is a tranquil oasis run by Patricia Marie, where you can go horseback riding around the grounds. A cluster of bungalows was built around an old sugar mill, from which the hotel takes its name. These private bungalows, suitable for up to four guests (ideal for families), contain a terrace with a hammock strung up, two beds, air conditioning, a refrigerator, and a bathroom with shower. It's best to book in here on the MAP, costing 650F ($65) for two persons, the tab rising to 820F ($82) for three guests, including service. One person is charged 440F ($44). The hotel restaurant, Le Tap Tap d'Haiti, features first-rate créole cookery. It has beige and brown napery, stylish crystal, natural-wood chairs and tables, and a beamed ceiling.

If you want to go horseback riding, the charge is 70F ($7) per hour. Nearby is a wild, long beach, about a 20-minute walk from the moulin. However, the hotel has a swimming pool as well. Other activities include archery, windsurfing, and tennis. Mostly this is a little place to retreat to if you like sun. Better take along some companions.

Where to Dine

L'Amour en Fleurs, Ste-Anne (tel. 88-23-72). If anyone can lure guests away from the groaning buffet tables at Club Med, it's Mme Trésor Amanthe, who is considered a sorceress of créole cookery. It is certainly not lavish surrounding that attracts patrons to her West Indian bistro by the roadside, across from a local cemetery. It's customary to have one of her special rum punches in a tiny bar, before heading to one of a dozen tables. Paper streamers and macramé light shades will have to do in lieu of decor.

On her menu of around two dozen items (key words are written in English), you make your selection from the classic créole repertoire of blood pudding, a blaff of seafood, spiny lobster, and some of the best court-bouillon on the island. Generally, guests finish off with her homemade coconut ice cream. Meals cost from around $15.

ST-FRANÇOIS: Continuing east from Ste-Anne, you'll notice many old round towers named for Father Labat, the Dominican founder of the sugarcane industry. These towers were once used as mills to grind the cane. St-François, 25 miles south of Pointe-à-Pitre, used to be a sleepy fishing village, known for its native créole restaurants. Then Air France discovered it and opened a Méridien hotel with a casino. That was followed by the promotional activities of J. F. Rozan, a native, who has invested heavily to make St-François a jet-set resort. Now the once-sleepy village possesses first-class accommodations, as well as an airport available to private jets, a golf course, and a marina.

Seven miles from St-François is **Pointe des Châteaux,** the easternmost tip of Grande Terre, at the point where the Atlantic meets the Caribbean. Here, where crashing waves sound around you, you'll see a cliff sculpted by the sea into castle-like formations, the erosion typical of France's Brittany coast. The view from here is splendid. At the top is an old cross put there back in the 19th century.

Motorists in this part of the island might like to stop in for a meal at **La Mouette** (tel. 84-40-57), which has only a dozen tables or so but very good créole cookery. You can eat here in your bathing suit if that is your desire. The place is decidedly informal. Jacques Nainan is your host. The food consists of not only the local dishes, the goat or chicken colombos, the accras, and the blaffs of sea urchin, but an occasional interesting variation, such as stuffed poisson coffré, a local fish. Expect to spend around $15, and don't show up on Sunday.

If you wish, you can walk to the Pointe des Colibris, the extreme end of Guadeloupe. From there you'll have a view of the northeastern sector of Guadeloupe, and to the east a look at La Désirade, an island which seems to be a huge vessel anchored far away. Among the coved beaches found around here, Pointe Tarare is the au naturel one.

In hotels, **Méridien Guadeloupe** (tel. 84-41-00) is one of the first Méridien hotels built for Air France, standing alongside one of the best beaches in Guadeloupe on 150 acres of land. The climate, quite dry here, is refreshed by trade winds. A four-star hotel, it offers 272 rooms either overlooking the sea or the Robert Trent Jones–designed golf course.

The rooms are fully equipped with many amenities to add to your comfort, and furnishings are in a modern style combined with Créole overtones. The hotel was refurbished in 1984. *In low season, a single pays $76 to $81 daily; a double, $90 to $100.* However, in high season, prices go up to $96 to $132 daily in a single, $110 to $150 in a double. The hotel is booked more or less year round by groups. Included in the tariffs are use of the swimming pool, tennis courts, and windsurfers.

St-Charles, which offers only an à la carte menu, is in the style of a deluxe restaurant, charging from 250F ($25) for a good meal, either from the French cuisine or the créole repertoire. Or perhaps you'll prefer Balaou, a terraced restaurant in a more relaxed and exotic mood, where your dinner will cost from $80F ($8) to 125F ($12.50). In addition, the hotel has a grill and barbecue snackbar, Le Casa Zomar, right on the beach, where the prices are quite high, especially if you order lobster. Alongside the swimming pool, the Lele is a tropical bar serving punches and other drinks. At night you can dance at Le Bête à Feu, the hotel's disco.

For people who care for more independence, I suggest a bungalow at Guadeloupe's poshest property, **Hamak** (tel. 84-41-80), founded by J. F. Rozan, the French entrepreneur, who built it right alongside the marina, a quarter of a mile from the Méridien. Its port, its little nearby beach, and its proximity to golf and a tiny airport make it popular with weekend jet-setters from Paris, or perhaps "the divine friends" of nightclub impresario Régine. "Les amis" like to be elegant, but informally so. It was the site of the 1979 international summit that brought President Carter, among others, here.

Spread on a 250-acre estate, accommodations are in villas (each with two individual tropical suites with twin beds opening onto a walled garden patio where you can sunbathe au naturel); studios (with intimate living/bedrooms combined, a kitchenette, and a large terrace facing a garden and the marina), and in duplexes (same as the studio designs, except with an indoor staircase leading to an additional bedroom on the second landing).

Each bungalow houses one to four guests. In peak season, a single ranges in price from $225 to $275 daily, and a double goes for $265 to $300, with a continental breakfast. *In the off-season, charges are $135 daily in a single, $165 in a double.* These prices include the suite, water sports, greens fees, tennis, taxes, and service. A nearby supermarket provides the supplies you'll need if you're housekeeping. Otherwise, you may take your meals in a popular tavern setting where you can enjoy seafood hors d'oeuvres, fish platters, and bouillabaisse for two. They say this place is the "poor rich man's restaurant."

Les Marines de St-François (tel. 84-45-15) is one of the newest clusters of residences in Guadeloupe, set in ten acres of well-planted seashore with views looking over a marina. The 132 fully furnished condominium units differ in floor plan and size, ranging from the central three-story headquarters to a handful of two-story town houses scattered throughout the property.

Each accommodation has air conditioning, a fully equipped kitchenette, and a tasteful collection of furniture crafted from light-colored woods and imaginative fabrics. The charge in apartments or bungalows suitable for two to four persons range from $295 to $420 in winter. *Expect reductions of 20% or more in summer.* Guests can arrange for maid service if they wish.

A large swimming pool, a wading pool for children, and two tennis courts are on the premises, while an 18-hole Robert Trent Jones–designed golf course is a short distance away. Water sports, especially sailing, are available at the marina or at the nearby Méridien Hôtel.

Trois Mats Hôtel (Three Masts; tel. 84-42-90) is only about a mile from the center of town, although many of its occupants never leave the area surrounding its marina. The hotel is a trio of modern buildings that sit directly on the water a short walk from the Hôtel Méridien.

Each of the 36 accommodations has its own kitchen, although cooking facilities are on either a balcony or a patio, depending on the unit's design. In midwinter, studio apartments cost around $70 for a single $90 for a double. Duplexes rent for $115 for three persons and $145 for four. *Expect reductions of around 20% in summer.* Beaches, tennis courts, golf, discos, and restaurants are all easily accessible.

Where to Dine

Guests at the big hotels might also want to head for the village of St-François, about a 20-minute walk from the Méridien, about 15 miles from Hamak. At night, you can dine at **Madame Jerco,** right in the middle of town. When you see the tin-roofed shack, oilcloths on the table, maybe a clucking chicken running across the floor, you may think you've come to the wrong address (on rue Egalité; tel. 84-40-19). But don't be snobbish. If you dine here under madame's tin roof, you'll be following in the gastronomic footsteps of many a famous personage.

Mme Jerco seemingly couldn't care less about such chic. She likes her decor strictly from the five-and-dime. But mostly she concentrates on her cuisine, which offers many créole specialties—"not sophisticated, but eternal," as one pleased diner recently put it.

The place is nearly always packed. The last time I was there, more than three dozen diners, mostly French-speaking ones, had crowded in. Accras are excellent, lambi (conch) in sauce even more enjoyable; and better yet is the court-bouillon of fish, the colombo of curried goat, the cod fritters, blood sausage, breadfruit, and lobster. Mango sherbet is a special treat. Go only for lunch and expect to pay from $20. It is closed on Tuesday.

La Pecherie, rue de la République (tel. 84-48-94), is another good choice in the area. It's a restored 200-year-old stone warehouse with a veranda overlooking the water. While the tropical breezes cool you, you can ask the owner and chef, Camille Rotin, what freshly caught seafood he has that day. His seafood is so fresh it seems just plucked from the Caribbean. The food is not only food, but many dishes seemingly are prepared with original recipes, based on oldtime Créole secrets passed along from one generation to the next. The decor is rustic with wooden tables. Camille is a fisherman himself, and he knows not only the fish of his island and how to catch them, but also how to cook them. His turtle stew is excellent, as is his fish soup. Try also his parrot fish and red snapper. If he decides to make it, try his caviar d'aubergine (puréed eggplant with cod, garlic, and hot spices). Prices are reasonable, about $20 per head for a meal. No lunch is served on Monday.

To go back to Pointe-à-Pitre from Pointe des Châteaux, you can use an alternative route, the N5 from St-François. After a nine-mile drive, you reach the village of—

LE MOULE: Founded at the end of the 17th century, Le Moule was known long before Pointe-à-Pitre. It used to be a major shipping port for sugar. Now a tiny coastal fishing village, it never regained its importance after it was devastated in the hurricane of 1928, like so many other villages of Grand Terre. Because of its more than ten-mile crescent-shaped beach, it is developing as a holiday center. Modern hotels, built along the beaches, have opened to accommodate visitors.

Nearby the sea unearthed skulls, grim reminders of the fierce battles fought among the Caribs and the French and English. It's called "The Beach of Skulls and Bones."

The new **Edgar Clerc Archeological Museum** shows a collection of both Carib and Arawak Indian artifacts gathered from various islands of the Lesser Antilles. The museum can be visited daily except Tuesday from 10:30 a.m. to 6:30 p.m.

Where to Dine

Restaurants here are simple but good, and also surprisingly inexpensive.

Chez Lucile, 3 rue Saint-Jean (tel. 84-51-63), is known locally for its *spécialités Antillaises*. It's open for lunch and dinner every day of the week, with meals costing from 65F ($6.50). It's a very basic, tin-roofed structure, with oilcloth-draped tables. The staff is friendly and polite, and the food is good. You might begin with a court-bouillon de poissons, following with spiny lobster, blood pudding, crisp codfish fritters known as accras, and whatever the "catch of the day" turned up.

An alternative choice is **L'Arbe à Pain,** 17 rue Ste-Anne (tel. 84-54-29), which is known for concocting 50 different kinds of rum punches. After downing one or two, you'll be ready for one of the specialties, such as chicken flavored with coconut or grilled spiny lobster. They also offer good fresh fish. Count on spending $15 at night, maybe less.

To return to Pointe-à-Pitre, I suggest you use the D3 toward Abymes. The road winds around as you plunge deeply into Grand Terre. As a curiosity, about halfway along the way, a road will bring you to **Jabrun du Nord** and **Jabrun du Sud.** These two villages are inhabited by white peasants with blond hair. They are said to be survivors of aristocrats slaughtered during the Revolution. Those members of their families who escaped found safety by hiding out in Les Grands Fonds. The most important family here is named Matignon, giving its name to the colony known as "les Blancs Matignon." These aristocratic peasants are said to be related to Prince Rainier of Monaco.

Pointe-à-Pitre lies only ten miles from Les Grand Fonds.

THE ROAD NORTH: From Pointe-à-Pitre, head northeast toward Abymes, passing next through Morne à l'Eau, reaching **Petit Canal** after 13 miles. This is Guadeloupe's sugarcane country, and a sweet smell fills the air. It is worth stopping over in the charming but sleepy town of Petit Canal to sample the following restaurant.

Restaurant Le Barbaroc, rue Schoelcher, Petit Canal (tel. 84-72-71). One of the most dedicated cooks in Guadeloupe is Mme Félicité Doloir. In the 1983 edition of the *Annual Book of Cooks* by H. J. Heinz, she was featured as "one of the ten outstanding cooks in the world." She has researched local recipes since her youth and has made trips to such faraway cities as New York to teach her lore to audiences of enthusiastic students.

Her restaurant, not far from her birthplace, lies on the main street of town in an unpretentious concrete building whose terrace is reached by climbing a flight of stairs. The daily specials are written on a chalkboard hanging over the street. One of Madame Doloir's goals, which she describes fervently, is the promotion of locally produced ingredients in their most flavorful combinations.

Her unique recipes are served in an upstairs room whose decor includes country-French furniture, flowers, wooden balustrades, and large, prominently displayed slogans advocating the dignity of mankind with special stress on the rights of women. Go here as much for an experience as for a good meal.

The restaurant is open every day for lunch and dinner, serving such dishes as codfish accras (whose pastry shell is made from carrots, eggplant, pumpkins, wheat flour, and breadfruit), burgots (sea snails) gratinée, purée of breadfruit, crab pâté, poulet du pays cuit fumé (smoked chicken), and sweet potato noodles. Even homemade beer is served here, as well as a house drink, maby, made from ingredients which include tree bark and which tastes a little like absinthe. Meals cost from $20 up.

Continuing northwest along the coast from Petit Canal, you come to **Port Louis** which is well known for its beautiful beach, La Plage du Souffleur, which I find best in the spring. Then the brilliant white sand is effectively shown off against a contrast of the flaming red poinciana. During the week, the beach is an especially quiet spot. The little port town is asleep under a heavy sun, and it has some good restaurants.

Le Poisson d'Or, rue Sadi Carnot, Port Louis (tel. 84-90-22), is a little Antillean house, entered by going down a narrow corridor, emerging into a rustic room. You can climb the steps to the second floor, an open terrace overlooking the sea and the fishing boats gently swaying in the water. It's run by Mme Eleanore Boulate.

In spite of its simple setting, the food is excellent. Try, for example, the stuffed crabs, the court-bouillon, topped off by coconut ice cream, which is homemade and tastes it. With a bottle of good wine, your bill will come to about $15. The place is a fine choice for an experience with créole cookery.

Also in Port Louis, you may want to patronize **Chez Odette,** rue Gambette (tel. 84-90-16). On a weekend, residents of Guadeloupe are likely to drive all the way from Basse Terre to sample the créole viands offered by Rose Mozar, the *cuisinière patronne,* the daughter of founding mother, Odette. The accras (fritters) here are not made with just saltcod, but also from giraumon, the local pumpkin. They're a savory treat. Her colombos, made with either curried local goat or chicken, are among the best in this part of Guadeloupe. She also stuffs and seasons crabs to perfection. Among the local vegetables served is a delectable christophine (a chayote) gratinée. The dining room is exposed to the trade winds, if there are any, and the place is aggressively simple—and that's how the local diners like it. Meals cost around $15.

About five miles from Port Louis lies **Anse Bertrand,** the northernmost village of Guadeloupe. What is now a fishing village was the last refuge of the Carib tribes, and a reserve was once created here. Everything now, however, is lazy and sleepy.

Folie Plage (also known as Chez Prudence; tel. 84-91-17) lies directly north of Anse Bertrand at Anse Laborde. Its owner, Prudence Marcelin, is another *cuisiniè*re patronne, who enjoys much local acclaim for her créole cookery. She too draws people from all over the island, especially on Sunday when this place is its most crowded. Island children frolic in the pool, and in between courses, diners can shop for handicrafts, clothes, and souvenirs sold locally. On weekends there is disco action. But at this popular rendezvous the food is still the attraction. Her court-bouillon is excellent, as is either her goat or chicken (curried) colombo. The way she handles palourdes (clams) also attests to her imagination. She also knows how to make a zesty sauce to serve with fish. Her crabes farcis are done to perfection as well. The place is relaxed and casual, and the bill rarely comes to more than $15.

From Anse Bertrand, you can drive along a graveled road heading for **Pointe de la Grande Vigie,** the northernmost tip of the island, which you reach after four miles of what I hope will be eautious driving. Park your car and walk carefully along a narrow lane which will bring you to the northernmost rock of Guadeloupe. The view of the sweeping Atlantic from the top of rocky cliffs is remarkable—you stand at a distance of about 280 feet above the sea. If the day is clear, you can see the island of Antigua, about 35 miles away.

Afterward, a four-mile drive south on quite a good road will bring you to the **Porte d'Enfer** or "gateway to hell." Once there, you'll find that the sea comes violently against two narrow cliffs.

After this kind of awesome experience in the remote part of the island, you can head back, going either to Morne à l'Eau or Le Moule before connecting to the road taking you in to Pointe-à-Pitre.

A BASSE TERRE ROUND-UP: Leaving Pointe-à-Pitre by Route N1, you can explore the lesser windward coast. After a mile and a half, you cross the Rivière Salée at Pont de la Gabarre. This narrow strait separates the two islands that form Guadeloupe. For the next four miles, the road runs straight through sugarcane fields.

At the sign, on a main crossing, turn right on the N2 toward **Baie Mahault.** Leaving that town on the right, head for **Lamentin.** This village was settled by corsairs at the beginning of the 18th century. Scattered about are some old colonial mansions.

If you should be in the area for lunch, try **Ravine Chaude** (tel. 85-60-53). The hot springs around here attracted so many visitors that this little bistro was opened to satisfy a demand. It's a relaxed, casual place, attracting mainly French-speaking diners who enjoy the local crayfish prepared in a variety of ways. If you're up for it, one of the specialties is a blood pudding omelet (it's called boudin on the menu). Should that not interest you, perhaps the spiny lobster or the lamb brochette will. Meals cost from $15.

Ste-Rose

From Lamentin, you can drive for 6½ miles to **Ste-Rose,** where you'll find several good beaches. On your left, a small road leads to Sofaia, from which you'll have a splendid view over the coast and forest preserve. The natives claim that a sulfur spring here has curative powers.

Chez Clara (tel. 28-72-79) is the culinary statement of Clara Lesueur and her talented and charming mother, Justine. Clara, her hair tightly braided with flashing gold thread, has the manner and appearance of a chic Parisienne, a role she filled when she lived in the French capital and appeared as a model in fashion layouts in *France-Soir*. She said good-bye to that life, however, when she returned to Guadeloupe, her home, and set up her breeze-cooled restaurant. Try for a table on the open patio, where young palm trees complement the color scheme.

Clara and Justine artfully meld the French style of fine dining with authentic, spicy créole cookery. Specialties listed on the blackboard menu may include crayfish, curried skate, lobster, clams, boudin (blood pudding), ouassous (local crayfish), brochette of swordfish, palourdes (small clams), even crabes farcis (red-orange crabs with a spicy filling). The *sauce chien* served with many of the dishes is a blend of hot peppers, garlic, lime juice, and "secret things" that go well with the house drink, made with six local fruits and ample quantities of rum. To further cool your palate, your dessert might consist of a choice of sherbets such as guava, soursop, or passionfruit. Full meals cost around $18 per person and are served daily except Sunday night and all day Wednesday.

At Deshaies

A few miles farther along, you reach Pointe Allegre, the northernmost point of Basse Terre. At Clugny Beach, you'll be at the site where the first settler landed in Guadeloupe.

This is also the site of **Club Méditerranée Fort-Royal,** Deshaies (tel. 85-81-10), the most intimate of their chain in the Caribbean. It's set against a backdrop of mountains, its grounds winding down to two wide beaches. Covered with tropical foliage, conical double cottages are placed alongside the beach, while the hotel stands on a high promontory. Of all the Club Meds in the Caribbean, this one is best for families with children. A special French joie de vivre seems to permeate the place. Its backers shelled out millions, and complete informality reigns. That pertains to dress too. Almost everybody, both male and female, seems a little bit on display here. Only problem is, don't display it too quickly. On my latest rounds, everybody booked in a group seemed to be suffering from sunburn. Instead of the classic golden tan, the color was definitely lobster red.

Couples and singles are housed in the bungalows, and more conservative-minded families get the hotel rooms. All units and bungalows, incidentally, are air-conditioned, each containing private shower baths and twin beds. Land rates are at their lowest in September and October, reaching their painful peak around the Christmas holidays. *In summer and fall, the charge is $600 weekly.* In spring and winter, tariffs can range from a low of $780 weekly, land arrangements only to a peak of $1100.

The hotel is on two beaches, but I've found the northern half too dangerous. However, if you're timid, there's an Olympic-size freshwater pool. The Mini Club keeps children, ages 4 to 12, busy all day under the guidance of trained counselors.

There's a special dining room for dinner, plus a bar and nightclub. The disco adjoins, a thatch-roofed terrace overlooking the bay. Lunch can be taken al fresco at the poolside bar. Sports are here galore, including four tennis courts (two lit at night), scuba-diving (deep dives and classes at Pigeon Island), snorkeling, archery, yoga, and water polo, even pétanque. Sometimes the management has folklore evenings, and always the eat-all-you-want buffet lunches with créole specialties. Nonguests come here for those, paying 200F ($20) for the privilege.

A couple of miles farther will bring you to **Grand Anse,** one of the best beaches in Guadeloupe. It's very large and still secluded, sheltered by many tropical trees.

Next to the beach is a good restaurant, **Le Karacoli** (tel. 28-41-17). To get here, you turn off the main highway onto a secondary road leading to the tree-shaded beach. The restaurant, with a facade that looks like a Caribbean adaptation of a Norman house, stands behind a wall and a large parking lot. There's a pleasant high-ceilinged dining room, but my preferred spot is on the jungle-like terrace. There, dozens of tropical trees almost erupt out of holes in the concrete, allowing shafts of sunlight to dapple the napery of the tables.

This is the domain of Mme Lucienne Salcède. Her accras (saltcod fritters) are considered some of the best on the island. She's also known for her fish, crab, or squid tarts, turtle ragoût, spiny lobster, small clams (palourdes), and her superb version of curried chicken colombo. The place is open for midday meals daily except Friday. Fixed-price lunches cost 70F ($7) to 85F ($8.50); à la carte meals go from 135F ($13.50). No dinner is served. In winter, an adjacent disco attracts local residents at night.

For years yachters have tried to keep Mme Racine's **Les Mouillages** (tel. 85-81-12), overlooking the Deshaies marina, a secret address. They succeeded for a long while, but now the word is out. Mme Racine's place can fill up quickly on certain good days. That's because she's known for her inexpensive prices and grilled lobster served with a piquant créole sauce that has been a house specialty around here for nearly 20 years. She also does those beautifully flavored red-orange crabs which pop stuffed from the oven. Her least expensive meals cost from around $12.

At Deshaies, snorkeling and fishing are popular pastimes. The narrow road winds up and down and has a corniche look to it, with the blue sea underneath, the view of green mountains studded with colorful hamlets.

Nine miles from Deshaies, **Pointe Noire** comes into view. Its name comes from black volcanic rocks. Look for the odd polychrome cenotaph in town.

Route de la Traversée

Four miles from Pointe Noire, you reach Mahaut. On your left begins the Route de la Traversée, the Transcoastal Highway. This is the best way to explore the scenic wonders of **Parc Naturel** when traveling between the capital, Basse-Terre, and Pointe-à-Pitre. I recommend going this way, as you pass through a tropical forest.

To preserve the Parc Naturel, Guadeloupe has set aside 74,100 acres or about one-fifth of its entire terrain. Reached by modern roads, this is a huge tract of mountains, tropical forests, and magnificent scenery.

The park is home to a variety of tame animals, including Titi (a raccoon adopted as its official mascot), and such birds as the wood pigeon, turtledove, and thrush. Small exhibition huts, devoted to the volcano, the forest, or to coffee, sugarcane, and rum, are scattered throughout the park.

The Parc Naturel has no gates, no opening or closing hours, and no admission fee.

From Mahaut you climb slowly in a setting of giant ferns and luxuriant vegetation. Four miles after the fork, you reach **Les Deux Mamelles** (The Two Breasts), where you can park your car and go for a hike. Some of the trails are for experts only; others, such as the Pigeon Trail, will bring you to a summit of about 2600 feet where the view is impressive. Expect to spend at least three hours going each way. Halfway along the trail you can stop at Forest House. From that point, many lanes, all signposted, branch off on trails that will last anywhere from 20 minutes to two hours. Try to find the **Chute de l'Écrevisse,** the "Crayfish Waterfall," a little pond of very cold water which you'll discover after a quarter of a mile. Male hikers are likely to encounter some local beauties swimming here. If so, you can join them for a cooling dip.

After the hike, the main road descends toward Versailles, a hamlet about five miles from Pointe-à-Pitre.

Back in Mahaut, you can stop at **Chez Vaneauck** (tel. 86-21-71) before going along the Route de la Traversée. The place is a simple bistro with a modern terrace overlooking a Mediterranean-style calanque. Here the crayfish is known as ouassous, and it's made into a soup, or else you can order it as a main course. Specialties include colombo of goat or chicken, ragoût of stewed goat in a savory sauce, lambi (conch), and octopus. Also good is stewed fish in a sauce or grilled or broiled fish. A typical meal will cost from 120F ($12).

From Mahaut, you reach the village of **Bouillante,** which is exciting for only one reason: you might encounter Brigitte Bardot here, as she's a part-time resident.

Try not to miss seeing the small island called Îlet à **Goyave** or Îlet du **Pigeon.** Jacques Cousteau often explores its silent depths.

Facing the islet is the best choice for a luncheon on the whole island:

La Touna, Malendure (tel. 86-70-10), is built on a narrow strip of sand between the road and the sea, its foundation almost touching the water. This gives patrons of this charming restaurant a marine panorama which complements the seafood specialties that the youthful Marc Haag and Michel Rebre concoct so skillfully in the kitchen.

Most of the dining tables are in a side veranda whose ceiling is covered with palm fronds. Despite its allure, many of the guests delay a meal until after a drink in the sunken bar whose encircling banquettes give the impression of the cabin of a ship. One of the most appealing rituals in Guadeloupe has become a habit here: you are brought a tray on which are seven or eight carafes, each filled with a rum-soaked tropical fruit such as guava, maracoja, pineapple, and passionfruit. You select the ingredients you prefer and mix your own drink. This you can savor as you observe your fellow diners or look out at the glittering waves. Of course if you prefer the house specialty, you'll have a combination of fruit with or without rum, one of the most refreshing drinks on the island.

Menu items make use of the freshest local ingredients. You may be tempted by the three-fresh terrine, a mousse made from locally smoked fish, poached crayfish with avocado sauce, accras or codfish, or crabmeat with sage sauce in puff pastry. Other delicacies include a fish brochette with six sauces, crayfish ragoût, sliced marlin, colombo of goat, faux filet au poivre vert, and chatoux façon Monique, named for the employee who invented it. Full meals usually cost from 145F ($14.50) and are served daily at lunch and every evening except Sunday and Monday.

After a meal at La Touna, you can explore around the village of Bouillante, the country known for its thermal springs. In some places if you scratch the ground for only a few inches you'll feel the heat.

Another choice for lunch is **Chez Loulouse** (tel. 86-70-34), at Malendure, also opposite Pigeon Island. Right on Malendure Beach, this bistro, another one of the many "chez" restaurants dotting the island, is spacious and furnished rustically with wooden tables. It offers a simple table d'hôte for only $12. You get typically créole cookery here, including saltcod fritters, blood pudding, grilled red snapper, and court-bouillon. This place is known to divers and snorkelers returning famished from Pigeon Island. You are likely to hear drinking songs in five languages at least. There are changing facilities if you want to beach it or else go snorkeling.

Vieux Habitants

The winding coast road brings you to Vieux Habitants (Old Settlers), one of the oldest villages on the island, founded back in 1636. The name comes from the people who settled it. After serving in the employment of the West Indies Company, they retired here. But they preferred to call themselves inhabitants, so as not to be confused with slaves.

For those who'd like to find lodgings in the vicinity, I suggest **Hôtel de Rocroy,** Plage de Recroy (tel. 81-12-25), which lies just outside Vieux Habitants, at a point about four miles from Basse-Terre.

A typical French beachside place, the hotel is at the water's edge, offering 11 rooms furnished with Nordic modern and lots of plastic. In winter, the single MAP rate is $55 daily, rising to $68 in a double. *In summer, two persons can stay here for anywhere from 380F ($38) to 420F ($42) daily, MAP.* The food, served on an al fresco terrace, is quite nice, and the bungalows scattered along the grounds are air-conditioned.

Basse-Terre

Another ten miles of winding roads bring you to Basse-Terre, the seat of the government of Guadeloupe, lying between the water and La Soufrière, the volcano. Founded in 1634, it is the oldest town on the island, and still has a lot of charm, its market squares shaded by tamarind and palm trees.

The town suffered heavy destruction at the hands of British troops in 1691 and again in 1702. It was also the center of fierce fighting during the Revolution. The story of Colonel Delgres blowing himself up in 1802, along with his troops, is like a Guadeloupe Fort Alamo.

In spite of its history, there isn't much to see except for a 17th-century cathedral and Fort St-Charles, which has guarded the city (not always well) since it was established.

Unlike most capitals, Basse-Terre doesn't have many interesting hotels or restaurants.

La Soufrière

The big attraction of Basse Terre is the famous, sulfur-puffing Soufrière volcano, which is still alive, but dormant—for the moment at least. Rising to a height of some 4800 feet, it is flanked by banana plantations and lush foliage.

After leaving the capital at Basse-Terre, you can drive to **St-Claude,** a wealthy suburb, four miles up the mountainside to a distance of 1900 feet. It has an elegant reputation for its perfect climate and luxurious tropical gardens.

In one of the nicest mansions there, you'll find the **Relais de la Grande Soufrière,** St-Claude (tel. 81-41-27). It was said to have been built as a recreation center for Emperor Maximillian's French troops who'd fought in Mexico. The place was rebuilt in 1965 at a cost of three-quarters of a million dollars. Today it is run as a government hotel school, the École Hôtelière.

Of course, that makes the guests the guinea pigs, but have no fear about that. I've received better service, concern, and care here than in many of the so-called deluxe hotels of Guadeloupe.

The building is a large colonial-style mansion with shutters, standing right in the middle of a tropical garden, which itself lies in the midst of verdant banana plantations. It has the charm of a Créole country house of many years ago.

Rooms are air-conditioned, well designed, and outfitted with many comforts. Most of the units are on the second floor, double-height chambers. Some of the units, incidentally, are duplexes, with the bedrooms perched on the second level.

If you stop here only for a meal, you can order from a set menu, and you'll get four courses of classical French cooking. Although temporarily shut down at the time of my last visit, the relais should be open and fully functioning by the time of your trip. Check with one of the French tourist offices for new rates in effect.

The place is an excellent base for exploring the volcano or even for those who want to live close to the excitement. The management claims La Grande Soufrière is "harmless."

Instead of going to St-Claude, you can head for **Matouba,** in a country of clear mountain spring water. The only sound you're likely to hear at this idyllically quiet place is of birds and the running water of thousands of springs. The village was settled long ago by Hindus.

You'll find good food at **Chez Paul de Matouba** (tel. 81-41-77), on the banks of the small Rivière Rouge (Red River). The dining room on the second floor is enclosed by windows, allowing you to drink in the surrounding dark-green foliage of the mountains. The cookery is créole, and crayfish dishes are the specialty. However, because of the influence of the early settlers, Hindu meals are also available. By all means, drink the mineral or spring water of Matouba. Expect to pay around 110F ($11) for what one diner called "an honest meal." Specialties include stuffed crab, rabbit in a marengo sauce, colombo (curried) chicken, as well as an array of both French, Créole, and Hindu specialties. It is open only for lunch, but not on Monday. Regrettably, if you're an independent traveler, you're likely to find the place overcrowded in the winter season with the tour-bus crowd.

Back in St-Claude, you can now begin the climb up the narrow, winding road the Guadeloupeans say leads to hell—that is, **La Soufrière.** Now reopened, the road ends at a car park at La Savane à Mulets, at an altitude of 3300 feet. That is the ultimate point to be reached by car. Hikers are able to climb right to the mouth of the volcano. However, in 1975, ashes, mud, billowing smoke, and earthquake-like tremors proved that the old beast was still alive.

In the resettlement process, 75,000 inhabitants were relocated to Grande Terre. However, no deaths were reported. But the inhabitants in Basse Terre still keep a watchful eye on the smoking giant.

Before leaving the parking lot, you can feel the heat of the volcano merely by touching ground. Steam emerges from fumaroles and sulfurous fumes from the volcano's "burps." Of course, fumes come from its pit and mud cauldrons as well.

A throw of a stone or a leak of mud or a groan will prove the danger to you. Many scientists are there to sound the call for withdrawal if it should become necessary.

The Windward Coast

From Basse Terre to Pointe-à-Pitre, the road follows the east coast, called the Windward Coast. The country here is richer and greener than any I've seen so far on the island.

To reach **Trois Rivières** you have a choice of two routes. One goes along the coastline, coming eventually to Vieux Fort, from where you can see Les Saintes archipelago. The other heads across the hills, Monts Caraibes.

Near the pier in Trois Rivières you'll see some pre-Columbian petroglyphs carved by the original inhabitants, the Arawaks. They are called merely "Roches Gravées," or carved rocks. In this archeological park, the rock engravings are of animal and human figures, dating most likely from A.D. 300 or 400. You'll also see specimens of plants, including the calabash, cassava, cocoa, pimento, and banana, that the Arawaks cultivated long before the Europeans set foot on Guadeloupe. From Trois Rivières, you can take boats to Les Saintes.

After leaving Trois Rivières, you continue on Route 1. Passing through the village of Banaier, you turn on your left at Anse Saint-Sauveur to reach the famous **Chutes du Carbet,** a trio of waterfalls. The road of two of them is a narrow, winding one, along many steep hills, passing through banana plantations as you move deeper into a tropical forest.

After three miles, a lane, suitable only for hikers, brings you to Zombie Pool. Half a mile farther along, a fork to the left takes you to Grand Etang, or large pool. At a point six miles from the main road, a parking area is available and you'll have to walk the rest of the way on an uneasy trail toward the second fall, Le Carbet. Expect to spend around 20 to 30 minutes, depending on how slippery the lane is. Then you'll be at the foot of this second fall where the water drops from 230 feet. The waters here aren't too cold, averaging 70° Fahrenheit, which is pretty warm for a mountain spring.

The first fall is the most impressive, but it takes two hours of rough hiking to get there. The third fall is reached from Capesterre on the main road by climbing to Routhiers. This fall is less impressive in height, only 70 feet. When the Carbet water runs out of Soufrière, it is almost boiling.

After Capesterre, you can go along for 4½ miles to see the statue of the first tourist who landed in Guadeloupe. It stands in the town square of Ste-Marie. The tourist was Christopher Columbus, who anchored a quarter of a mile from Ste-Marie on November 4, 1493. In the journal of his second voyage, he wrote, "We arrived, seeing ahead of us a large mountain which seemed to want to rise up to the sky, in the middle of which was a peak higher than all the rest of the mountains from which flowed a living stream."

However, when Caribs started shooting arrows at him, he left quickly, heading for new adventures.

After Ste-Marie, you pass through Goyave, then Petit Bourg, seeing on your left the Route de la Traversée before reaching Pointe-à-Pitre. You will have just completed the most fascinating scenic tour Guadeloupe has to offer.

THE SPORTING LIFE: Most visitors come to Guadeloupe for swimming and sunning. There are many well-sheltered beaches where you can enjoy not only this, but fishing, skindiving, and waterskiing. Chances are, your hotel will be built right on a beach, or else will lie no more than 20 minutes from a good one. There is a plenitude of natural beaches dotting the island from the surf-brushed dark strands of western Basse Terre to the long stretches of white sand encircling Grande Terre. Public beaches are generally free, but some charge for parking. Unlike hotel beaches, they have few facilities. Hotels welcome nonguests, but charge for changing facilities, beach chairs, and towels.

Sunday is family day at the beach. You'll see how the local folk enjoy their day off. Topless sunbathing is common at hotels, less so on village beaches.

Guadeloupe is known for its nudist beaches. All of them are reached by bus (or course, on the bus you should wear something). Places on Grande Terre where you can go sans bikini include the beach of Gosier Islet; the beach of Caravelle, Club Med, Ste-Anne; and the beach between Pointe Tarare and Pointe de la Gourde, called Pointe des Châteaux. In Basse Terre, nudists can use the Plage de Clugny, between Ste-Rose and Deshaies, and the beach of Club Med at Fort-Royal in Deshaies. The beach at Vieux Habitants is also nudist, as is the beach of Islet Fortune facing Goyave.

Golf

The **Golf de St-François**, adjacent to the Hamak (tel. 84-41-80), is the St-François, about 25 miles east of Raizet Airport. The golf course runs alongside an 800-acre lagoon where windsurfing, waterskiing, and sailing prevail. The course, designed by Robert Trent Jones, is a 6755-yard, par-71 course, which presents many challenges to the golfer, with water traps on 6 of the 18 holes, massive bunkers, prevailing trade winds, and a particularly fiendish 400-yard par-4 ninth hole. The par-5 third is the toughest hole on the course. Its 450 yards must be negotiated into the constant easterly winds. The tennis pro is Michel Saige.

Greens fees for 18 holes is 180F ($18) per day. There is a clubhouse, along with a pro shop, lockers, and a bar. The course is equipped with 24 electric carts, renting for 150F ($15) all day for two persons.

Scuba and Snorkeling

Hot on the trail of Jacques Cousteau, who spends much time in local waters, scuba-divers are drawn to Guadeloupe. The best waters are those off the southern and western coasts of Grande Terre. Divers go to either Club Med to use the facilities of the club and scuba school on Pigeon Island, composed of volcanic stone and scrub trees, where Cousteau is a frequent visitor. Pigeon Island has everything divers want: colorful reefs, shipwrecks, wall diving, caves, slopes, and drop-offs.

Other dive sites are Mouton Vert, Mouchoir Carré, and Cay Ismini. They are close by the major hotels, in the bay of Petit Cul-de-Sac Marin, south of Rivière Salée, the river separating the two halves of Guadeloupe. North of the Salée is another bay, Grand Cul-de-Sac Marin, where the small islets of Fajou and Caret also boast fine diving.

The scuba schools at Guadeloupe's hotels all offer dive operations. Every day around noon there is a free trial in the hotel pool. Sea dives in the area around the major hotels of Gosier cost about 175F ($17.50), individually. Excursions of Pigeon Island usually include a glass-bottomed boat ride in addition to the dives, and prices per dive are about 275F ($27.50).

A leading booster of the sport is divemaster Stephane Bailly, whose **Karukera Scuba Club** (tel. 84-12-93) is based at the Hôtel PLM Callinago in Gosier, a resort area 15 miles east of Pointe-à-Pitre. Bailly's school, whose clients come mostly from hotels in Gosier, has five French-licensed instructors who conduct two dives daily from a glass-bottomed boat at Pigeon. The school is equipped with compressors, tanks, and gear, as well as a 32-foot Chris-Craft Cavalier and its own Peugeot minibus.

A second dive center on Guadeloupe is **Club International** (tel. 83-64-44), at the Hôtel Frantel in Bas du Fort, just minutes from Gosier. Englishman John Lehew instructs and supervises French-licensed teachers. Two dives per day for five days cost $30 per person daily. An extra $5 is charged for night dives. Included in the price are transportation to and from the dive spot on board the *Providencia*, a 47-foot powerboat, instruction by a certified diver, free daily lessons in the Frantel pool, and use of U.S. standard equipment, including a compressor and cascade system, tanks, regulators, masks, fins, safety vests, backpacks, snorkels, and underwater cameras with flash.

Le Créole Beach Hotel (tel. 84-15-00), also in Gosier, has its own school called **Holiday Sports.** The underwater trips, supervised by certified diver Alain Verdonck, explore the remains of two sunken ships, Pointe-à-Pitre Bay, nearby coral reefs, and Pigeon Island. Individual dives range from 150F ($15) to 275F ($27.50), depending on the dive site. A special five-dive package is offered, including insurance and equipment. A day-long excursion to Guadeloupe's offshore islands of Les Saintes, with transportation by boat from the hotel to the dive site, costs 500F ($50).

Sailing

Sailboats of varying sizes, crewed or bareboat, are plentiful. Information can be secured at any hotel desk. Excursions on the catamaran *Silverheels* (tel. 85-16-71) are popular, as are day and moonlight sails on the *Papyrus* (tel. 82-87-26 or 82-91-73). Sunfish sailing can be done at almost every beachfront hotel.

Yachting

Yachting is a challenging sport in Guadeloupe. Facilities are available at Pointe-à-Pitre's **Carénage** and at **Deshaies,** a village on northeastern Basse Terre, as well as at three fairly recently opened marinas. They are **Bas du Fort Port de Plaisance** (tel. 82-54-85), ten minutes from Raizet Airport, five minutes from Pointe-à-Pitre and the same distance from Gosier; **Marina de St-François** in the St-François resort area; and **Marina de Rivière-Sens,** at Gourbeyre, a five-minute drive from the capital of Basse Terre.

Deep-Sea Fishing

The season for barracuda and kingfish is January to May. For tuna, dolphin, and bonito, it's December to March. Hotel desks recommend such fishing boats as the *Thalassa,* based at the **Port de Plaisance Marina** (tel. 82-74-94). Inquire also at the **Fishing Club Antilles** in Bouillante (tel. 86-73-77) and **Guadeloupe Chartaire** in Pointe-à-Pitre (tel. 82-34-47).

Waterskiing

Most seaside hotels can arrange this at a cost of $13 for 30 minutes' boating time.

Windsurfing

This is the hottest sport in Guadeloupe today, and it's available with lessons at all the major beach hotels.

Tennis

All the large resort hotels have tennis courts, many of which they light at night for games. The noonday sun is often too hot for most players. If you're a guest, tennis is free at most of these hotels. But you will be charged for night play. If your hotel doesn't have a court, you can play at the **Club of St-François** (tel. 84-40-01). Also you might consider an outing to **Le Relais du Moulin,** Châteaubrun, near Ste-Anne (tel. 88-23-96). There you can play tennis at 35F ($3.50) per hour.

Horseback Riding

The **Relais due Moulin Hôtel,** at Châteaubrun near Ste-Anne (tel. 88-23-96), has six English thoroughbred horses which it rents on accompanied tours through sugarcane fields and the local countryside at a rate of 70F ($7) per hour or 300F ($30) for a full day's excursion with picnic.

Cycling

A popular pastime on Guadeloupe, cycling is a preferred means of transport for many. **Chez Erick,** 9 rue de la République at Pointe-à-Pitre (tel. 82-21-86), rents motorbikes only for about $8 per day. The minimum age is 18 years.

Hiking

The **Parc Naturel** is the best hiking grounds in the Caribbean, in my opinion (please refer to the touring notes on Route de la Traversée). Marked trails cut through the deep foliage of rain forests until you come upon a waterfall or perhaps a cool mountain pool. The big excursion country, of course, if around the volcano, La Soufrière. However, because of the dangers involved, I recommend that you go out only with a guide. Hiking brochures are available from the tourist office, and guided excursions are arranged by by the **Organization des Guides de Montagne,** Maison Forestière, Parc Naturel, Basse Terre (contact M. Berry; tel. 81-45-79). Guided hiking tours, such as a four-hour scale of La Soufrière, cost about 300F ($30).

Camping

Campsites are basic, except at **Les Sables d'Or** (tel. 81-39-10), Grande Anse Beach near Deshaies, which has good facilities and rents tents. Fully equipped Toyota camping cars sleeping two to four can be rented from **Caraibes Loisirs,** Villa Caille, Petit Bourg (tel. 85-42-38).

AFTER DARK: Guadeloupeans claim that the beguine was invented here, not on Martinique. Regardless, the people dance the beguine as if they truly did own it. Of course, calypso, the merengue, whatever, moves rhythmically along, as the people of the island are known for their dancing.

Ask at your hotel where the folkloric **Ballets Guadeloupeans** will be appearing. This troupe makes frequent appearances at the big hotels, although they don't enjoy the fame of the Ballets Martiniquais, the troupe already described on the sister island.

L'Enfer Vert, Galerie Nozières (tel. 91-53-82), in Pointe-à-Pitre, has been called the new "hot spot." In French, it's name translates as "Green Inferno." Both the local people on the island and many vacationing French and others show up here for a créole version of nouvelle cuisine. In the heart of town, reached by going to the second floor, this is a bar and lounge combined with a restaurant where meals cost from $20. It reaches its peak on Friday and Saturday nights when a live jazz band is brought in. South American combos often perform, and sometimes on slow nights, between bites of hot camembert crêpes, guests get up and tinkle the ivories. Diners can also play billiards or chess here. It is closed all day Sunday and for lunch on Saturday.

Le Foufou is a disco on the grounds of the Hôtel Frantel Guadeloupe, Le Bas du Fort, Gosier (tel. 82-64-44), two miles from Pointe-à-Pitre. It is open only from Tuesday to Saturday, and the action begins at 11 p.m. You're charged an entrance fee of 50F ($5) which entitles you to your first drink. After that, drinks cost from 35F ($3.50).

Guests from surrounding hotels often head for the **Hôtel Salako,** Pointe de la Verdure (tel. 84-14-90). The after-dark attraction is the Club Caraibe, a disco nightclub. If the crowd is right, the place can be fun. For your first drink you pay 50F ($5), which includes the price of your entrance fee.

The **Casino de la Marina** (tel. 84-41-41) stands near the Méridien Hôtel in St-François. It is open from 9 p.m. to 3 a.m. to persons over 21, providing they have proof of identity in the form of a driver's license with a photo (or else a valid passport). The entrance fee is 60F ($6), and once inside, you can play American roulette, chemin-de-fer, and blackjack. Dress is casual. The nightclub in the open garden offers dancing under the stars to a live band or disco.

Another casino is **Gosier-les-Bains,** on the grounds of the Hôtel PLM Arawak (tel. 84-18-33) in Gosier. Entrance fee is 60F ($6). Coat and tie are not required, but dress tends to be casually elegant. An identity card with photo is required for admission. It opens at 9 p.m., and the most popular games are blackjack, roulette, and chemin-de-fer. There is not only a restaurant, but a disco.

ÎLES DES SAINTES:
A cluster of eight islands off the southern coast of Guadeloupe, the Îles des Saintes are certainly off the beaten track. The two main islands and six rocks are Terre-de-Haut, Terre-de-Bas, Îlet-à-Cabrit, La Coche, Les Augustins, Grand Îlet, Le Redonde, and Le Pâté. Of all those Saints, only Terre-de-Haut ("land of high") and to a lesser extent Terre-de-Bas, ("land below") attract visitors, mostly Guadeloupeans wanting an escape.

If you're planning a visit, Terre-de-Haut is the most interesting Saint to call upon. It's the only one with facilities for overnight guests.

Some claim Les Saintes has one of the nicest bays in the world, a lilliput Rio de Janeiro with a sugarloaf. The isles, just six miles from the main island, were discovered by Columbus (who else?) on November 4, 1493, who named them "Los Santos."

The history of Les Saintes is very much the history of Guadeloupe itself. In years past the islands have been heavily fortified, as they were considered

Guadeloupe's Gibraltar. The climate is very dry, and until the desalinization plant opened, water was often rationed.

The population of Terre-de-Haut is mainly white, all fishermen or sailors and their families who descended from Breton corsairs. The fishermen are very skilled sailors, maneuvering large boats called "saintois." They wear coolie-like headgear called a salaco, which is shallow and white with sun shades covered in cloth built on radiating ribs of thick bamboo. Frankly, they look like small parasols. Of course, all visitors want to photograph these sailors, and they seem to resent that. If you can't resist taking a picture, please make a polite request (in French, no less; otherwise they won't know what you're talking about). Women like to buy these hats (if they can find them) for use as beach wear. They are often likened to inverted saucers.

Terre-de-Haut is a place for discovery and lovers of nature, many of whom stake out their exhibitionistic space on the nude beach at Anse Crawen.

Part of the fun of Les Saintes is in getting there. From Pointe-à-Pitre you can drive to Trois Rivières in about an hour. From there, a boat to Les Saintes leaves twice a day, at 8:30 a.m. and 4 p.m., Monday to Saturday. On Sunday, sailing time is 8:30 a.m. Les Saintes can also be reached from the capital, Basse Terre, a schooner leaving every day at 6 a.m., if anyone wants to get up for that. The ride is over choppy seas, and the round-trip fare is 52F ($5.20). Flights from Pointe-à-Pitre on Air Guadeloupe take just 15 minutes, and depart daily.

At Terre-de-Haut, you'll find the main settlement at **Bourg**, a single street which follows the curve of the fishing harbor. A charming hamlet, it has little houses with red or blue doorways, balconies, and Victorian gingerbread gewgaws. Donkeys are the beasts of burden, and everywhere you look are fish nets drying in the brilliant sunshine. You can also explore the ruins of Fort Napoleon, which is left over from those 17th-century wars, including the famous naval encounter known in European history books as "The Battle of the Saints." You can see the barracks and prison cells, as well as the drawbridge and art musuem. Occasionally you'll spot an iguana scurrying up the ramparts. Directly across the bay, atop Îlet-à-Cabrit, sits the fort named in honor of the Empress Josephine.

You might also get a Breton sailor to take you on his boat to the other main island, Terre-de-Bas, which has no accommodations, incidentally. Or you can stay in Terre-de-Haut and go on a hike to Le Grand Souffleur with its beautiful cliffs, and to Le Chameau, the highest point on the island, rising to a peak of 1000 feet.

Scuba-diving centers are not limited to mainland Guadeloupe. The underwater world off Les Saintes has attracted deep-sea divers as renowned as Jacques Cousteau, but even the less experienced may explore its challenging depths and milticolored reefs. Denis Collins's **Centre Nautique** is on the pier in Terre-de-Huat. This fully equipped scuba operation offers both beginner's lessons in the calm waters of the Pain du Sucre and excursions for experienced divers near the Îlet-à-Cabrit. Intriguing underwater grottoes found near Fort Napoléon on Terre-de-Haut are also explored. Dives cost from 150F ($15) to 18F ($18) per person.

There are no roads and no more than a dozen or so cars. A few bistros will be found—I can recommend **Le Mouillage** (tel. 81-05-76), which lies on the main street and has a simple decor with dark wooden tables and benches, and the chef, naturally, specializes in seafood.

You might also try **Le Coq d'Or** (tel. 81-36-15), on the dock square, with an outdoor terrace one flight up and an excellent view of the harbor.

Just down the street from the town hall you'll find **Le Caraibe** (no phone).

Here you can sample some of the fish caught in local waters: red snapper, king-fish, conch, rock lobster, and the silvery dorade.

At some of these places you'll have your chance to eat a roasted iguana, the giant lizard found on many of these islands. It's quite tasty, and I guarantee that! But if the idea revolts you, you'll also find lots of conch (lambi), Caribbean lobster, and fresh fish. I've never paid more than 85F ($8.50) for a good meal in any of these places. For your dessert, you can sample the savory island specialty, *tourment d'amour* (agony of love), a coconut pastry available in the restaurants but best sampled from the barefoot children who sell the delicacy near the boat dock.

Hôtel La Saintoise, Terre-de-Haut (tel. 92-52-50), is a modern, two-story building across from the principal plaza, with its almond trees and widespread poinciana. As in a small French village, the inn places tables and chairs on the sidewalk, where you can sit out and observe what action there is.

Paris-born Jacques Cauet, the owner, will welcome you, showing you through his uncluttered lobby to one of his modest bedrooms, of which he has only ten, each outfitted with a tile bath. They are on the second floor, and the furnishings are admittedly modest. Everything is kept immaculately clean. In winter or summer, the single MAP rate is 335F ($33.50), going up to 440F ($44) in a double.

If you're over just for the day, you'll find the hotel perched at water's edge, near where the boat from Trois Rivières on Basse Terre comes in. You can make arrangements to have lunch here, costing from 110F ($11) per person, plus 10% service. The restaurant at La Saintoise is called Le Foyal, and it serves a créole cuisine on an open-air terrace at the water's edge.

Bois Joli, Terre-de-Haut (tel. 99-50-38), lies in the western part of the islands, overlooking a fine beach. In confectionery white, the stucco block sits on a palm-studded rise of a slope, the home of Monsieur and Madame Philippe Blandin.

Accommodations are spread between the main house and in some cottages on the hillside. Bold patterned fabrics are used on the beds, and the rooms are furnished in basic modern. About half the units are air-conditioned, with various combinations of shower bath arrangements. The inn offers 21 rooms in all. Bathless singles (but with a sink and bidet) rent for 235F ($23.50) daily, going up to 260F ($26) for the best units, those with private showers and air conditioning. Doubles, depending on the room assigned, cost from 245F ($24.50) daily to a high of 270F ($27). Dinner is another 110F ($11) per person, but tax, service, and a continental breakfast are included in the rates quoted.

Her food is good créole-style cooking. Mr. Blandin can arrange for water-skiing, sailing, boat trips to some of the islets or rocks that form Les Saintes, and snorkeling. The place is for those who like their Caribbean holidays remote.

Jeanne d'Arc, Fond du Curé (tel. 99-50-41), lies on a beach in a village, less than a mile from the airport. Frenchman Guy Janin and his wife, Mary, run this ten-room, two-story concrete building at the edge of the water. Units are modest in style, but they compensate with private showers (likely to be cold) and views of the water. English is spoken, and pedal boats and windsurfing on the beach can be arranged. Two persons can stay here at a half-board bargain rate of about $40 per person daily, a remarkable bargain for the Caribbean. Fresh fish and other seafood and créole dishes are served on the simple seaside terrace restaurant. Monsieur Janin is an excellent cook, and he sells the fish he smokes to other hotels in Guadeloupe.

Kanaoa, Terre-de-Haut (tel. 99-51-36), is a modern structure, utterly plain, that was erected on a little beach at Pointe Coquelet. Théo Giorgi owns this

14-room inn, including five units with views of the sea and Anse Mire Cove. All accommodations contain private showers, and a limited amount of English is spoken. The location is 1¼ miles from the airport, or about five minutes on foot from town. If the furnishings are spartan, so is the tariff: two persons can take one of the doubles at a cost of about $35 nightly. A good créole meal for 75F ($7.50) is served in the open-air restaurant at the water's edge.

MARIE-GALANTE: The island, an offshore dependency of Guadeloupe, is an almost perfect circle of about 60 square miles. Possessing such rustic charm, it lies 20 miles to the south of Guadeloupe's Grand Terre.

Columbus noticed it before he did Guadeloupe, discovering it on November 3, 1493. He named it for his own vessel, but didn't land there. In fact, for the next 150 years no European set foot on its shoreline.

The first French governor of the island was Constant d'Aubigne, father of the Marquise de Maintenon. Several captains from the West Indies Company attempted settlement, but none of them succeeded. In 1674 Marie-Galante was given to the Crown, and from that point on its history was closely linked to that of Guadeloupe.

However, since 1816 the island settled down to a quiet slumber. You could hear the sugarcane growing on the plantations, and that was about it. Many windmills have been built to crush the cane, and lots of tropical fruits are grown here.

Now, some 30,000 inhabitants live here, making their living from sugar and rum, the latter said to be the best in the Caribbean. The island's climate is rather dry, and there are many good beaches. One of these stretches of sand covers at least five miles—brilliantly white, a real paradise.

Air Guadeloupe will bring you to the island in just 20 minutes from Pointe-à-Pitre.

Les Basse airport on Marie-Galante lies about two miles from Grand-Bourg, the main town with an 1845 baroque church. The 18th-century Grand Anse rum distillery can be visited, as can the historic fishing hamlet of Vieux Fort. The island is almost exclusively French speaking.

You can also go over by boat, as there is daily service on the *Général Dugommier,* connecting Grand-Bourg to Pointe-à-Pitre. The round-trip fare is 120F ($12).

A limited number of taxis are available at the airport, and prices are to be negotiated. If you'd like to rent a car, get in touch with **Maga,** 16 rue Beaurenom in Grand-Bourg (tel. 97-81-97).

The best way to see the island, especially if you don't speak French, is to call **Philippe Bavardy,** rue du Presbytère (tel. 85-90-38). For a price of 185F ($18.50) per person, based on a minimum of six passengers, he'll take you on an extensive tour of the island, with visits to the rum distillery referred to, and a stopover at the 18th-century Château Murat, Vieux Fort, and Saint-Louis. Lunch and swimming are included.

There are many white sandy beaches on the coastline, but swimming can be dangerous in some places. The best beach is at Petite Anse, 6½ miles from Grand-Bourg.

Food and Lodging

There are only a few little accommodations on the island, which, even if they aren't very up-to-date in amenities, are clean and hearty. At least the greetings are friendly. They may also be bewildering if you speak no French.

I prefer the **Auberge de Soledad** (tel. 87-22-24), which lies about two miles from the airport on the outskirts of Grand-Bourg. In a setting of sugarcane fields, it rents out eight simply furnished, air-conditioned rooms, each with private shower. Rooms are also equipped with refrigerators and TV sets (the latter of little use to most English guests). The hotel also rents bicycles and small motorcycles to guests. On the grounds are tennis courts and a woman's hairdressing salon. Mme Emma Avril prefers her guests to stay at least a week, but if you're rushed, she'll probably charge by the day. Either single or double occupancy will cost from 200F ($20) to 250F ($25) daily. Meals are extra in her créole restaurant.

There are some native places serving typical créole meals in Grand-Bourg, among which **Au P'tit Pêcheur** (The Little Fisherman) stands out. It's a popular local place built right on the water in Plage de la Feuillère (tel. 87-22-24). For around 85F ($8.50) you can enjoy a meal of Caribbean langouste or conch in a spicy sauce. The restaurant, lying on the road to Savane, is also known as "Chez Verin," the name of the owner.

For about the same price, you can also dine at **Touloulou,** a beachfront restaurant at Petite Anse (tel. 87-22-63).

LA DÉSIRADE: The ubiquitous Columbus spotted this terre désirée or "sought-after land" after his Atlantic crossing in 1493. Named La Désirade, the island, which is less than seven miles long and more than 1½ miles wide, lies just five miles off the eastern tip of Guadeloupe. This former leper colony is often visited on a day's excursion (Club Med types like it a lot).

The island has fewer than 2000 inhabitants, including the descendants of Europeans exiled here by royal command. Tourism has hardly touched the place, if you can forget about those "day trippers," and there are almost no facilities for overnighting, with an exception or two.

The main hamlet is Grande Anse, which has a lovely small church with a presbytery and flower garden, and the homes of the local inhabitants. Le Souffleur is a village where boats are constructed; and at Baie Mahault are the ruins of an old leper colony from the early 18th century.

From Pointe-à-Pitre, Air Guadeloupe flies to Désirade three times daily on a 20-minute flight. The airstrip on Désirade accommodates up to 19-seat aircraft. Under no circumstance should you ever go by sea (unless you have your own yacht). The crossing is rough, and mainly cargo ships go here.

On Désirade, three minibuses run between the airport and the towns. To get around, you might negotiate with a local driver. Bicycles are also available.

The best beaches are Souffleur, a peaceful and tranquil oasis near the boatbuilding hamlet, and Baie Mahault, a small beach that is a Caribbean cliché with white sand and palm trees.

For food and lodging, go to **La Guitoune,** near the sea in Grande Anse (tel. 82-94-08), where Mme Jeanville will welcome you to her native-style hotel. She rents out only five modestly furnished rooms with private cold-water showers (toilets in the hallway) for around $25 per night. Her local restaurant is good, serving créole meals for about 75F ($7.50), with the emphasis on fresh fish. It is 7½ miles from the airport and is exceptionally basic, but it's all that's available here.

3. St. Martin

Partitioned between the Netherlands and France, the divided island of St. Martin (Sint or St. Maarten in Dutch) has a split personality. The 37-square-mile island is shaped like a lazy triangle. The northern part of the island, a land area of about 21 square miles, belong to France, the southern part of the Netherlands.

The island has two jurisdictions, but there is complete freedom of move-

SAINT MARTIN/SINT MAARTEN

SAINT
MARTIN

Marigot

Marigot
Bridge

SINT MAARTEN

Great
Salt Pond

Philipsburg

ment between the two sectors. If you arrive on the Dutch side and clear Customs there, you need not worry anymore with red-tape formalities when crossing over to the French side—either for shopping, perhaps a hotel, and certainly for eating, as it has the best food (with some notable exceptions).

French St. Martin is governed from Guadeloupe and has direct representation in the government in Paris. Lying between Guadeloupe and Puerto Rico, the tiny island has been half French, half Dutch since 1648.

The principal town on the French side is **Marigot,** the seat of the subperfect and municipal council. Visitors come here not only for shopping, as the island is a free port, but also to enjoy the excellent cookery in the créole bistros.

Marigot is not quite the same size as its counterpart, Philipsburg, in the Dutch sector. It has none of the frenzied pace of Philipsburg, which is often overrun with cruise-ship passengers. In fact, Marigot looks like a tiny French village transplanted to the West Indies. The policeman on the beat is a gendarme.

If you climb the hill over this tiny port, you'll be rewarded with a view from the old fort there.

About 20 minutes by car beyond Marigot takes you to **Grand Case,** a small fishing village, an outpost of French civilization that has some very good local créole restaurants and a few places to stay.

St. Martin hardly has the attractions of St. Thomas, Puerto Rico, Jamaica, or whatever. You may ask, "Why come here?" There are no dazzling sights, no spectacular nightlife. Even the sports program on St. Martin isn't as organized as it is on most Caribbean islands, although the Dutch side has golf and other diversions.

Most people come to St. Martin just to relax. They can do that on the island's many fine beaches, where you can sometimes sunbathe in the buff. In spite of its many drawbacks, the island has become such a popular tourist destination in the past few years that it's practically impossible to get a room in winter without reserving in advance.

Not just the beaches, but the hospitality of St. Martin is important too. This is a friendly island whose local population welcomes visitors. Some 70% of the residents work in the tourist business. In spite of its lack of great scenic beauty, the island has been called "civilized."

Its major "archeological site" is actually of recent vintage. It's the ruins of La Belle Créole at Pointe du Bluff. This was the report that never was. A multi-million-dollar dream, it was conceived by Claude Philippe, the erstwhile maître d' at the Waldorf in New York. But sieges of bankruptcy and legal tangles left a group of half-finished Mediterranean-style units unoccupied. It's a grandiose ghost town slowly being eaten away by the natural elements of the Caribbean.

GETTING THERE: Chances are, you will set down on the Dutch side (St. Maarten) at the Queen Juliana Airport. For a more detailed description of transportation to the island, refer to the "Getting There" section of St. Maarten in Chapter VIII.

To sum up, however, **American Airlines** serves St. Maarten from New York and Dallas/Fort Worth. **Pan American** flies in from New York, and **Eastern** earns its wings from Miami.

Air Guadeloupe also flies in daily to and from Guadeloupe, and **LIAT, Prinair, Windward Islands Airways** (Winair), and **Air Martinique** have regularly scheduled inter-island service. All these airlines use the Juliana International Airport on the Dutch side, where there is a $5 airport departure tax.

For its daily ten-minute flights to St. Barts (coming up), Air Guadeloupe uses the Espérance Airport, a small domestic airport near Grand Case on the French side.

PRACTICAL FACTS: English is widely spoken in St. Martin, even though it is a French possession. A patois is spoken only by a small segment of the local populace.

The **currency,** officially at least, is the French franc, yet U.S. dollars seem acceptable as legal tender wherever you go. Canadians should convert their dollars, however.

French St. Martin is linked to the Guadeloupe **telephone system,** which can place calls to and from the U.S. To call Dutch St. Maarten from the French side, dial 93 plus the four digits of the St. Maarten number. To call from the Dutch side to the French side, dial 06, then the six-digit French number.

Most arrivals are at the Dutch-controlled **Juliana International Airport;** however, French St. Martin has **Espérance Airport** at Grand Case (tel. 87-51-21), where Air Guadeloupe flies in. The departure tax at Espérance Airport is now included in the published fare.

U.S. and Canadian citizens should have either a passport, voter registration card, or a birth certificate, plus an ongoing or a return ticket.

The island is on **Atlantic Standard Time,** which means that the only time the U.S. and St. Martin are in step is during the Daylight Saving Time of summer.

Banks generally are open from 8:30 a.m. to 1 p.m. Monday to Thursday. On Friday they're open during the day but also from 4 to 5 p.m.

The **electric current** is 220 volts, 50 cycles, which of course will necessitate a converter or adapter if you plan to use your appliances such as a hair dryer.

The **water** is safe to drink, and most hotels serve desalinated water. That same hotel is likely to add a 10% to 15% service charge to your bill to cover tipping. Likewise, most restaurants include the service charge on your bill.

There is a **hospital** in Marigot (tel. 87-50-07), and hotels will help visitors in contacting English-speaking doctors.

The **tourist board,** called Syndicat d'Initiative, is at Mairie de Saint-Martin at Marigot (tel. 87-50-04).

GETTING AROUND: For visitors, the most common means of transport is the taxi. A **Taxi Service & Information Center** operates at the port of Marigot (tel. 87-56-54), headed by Raymond Helligar. Always agree on the rate before getting into an unmetered cab. Here are some sample fares, subject to change: for one or or two persons in a taxi from the center of Marigot to Expérance Airport or the Grand Case Beach Club, $7; to La Samanna Hotel, $8, and to Orient Bay or Le Galion Beach, $12. These fares are in effect from 7 a.m. to 9 p.m. After that, they go up by 25% until midnight, rising by 50% after midnight.

You can also book 2½-hour sightseeing trips of the island, either through the organization listed above or at any hotel desk. The cost is $25 for one or two passengers, plus $7.50 for each additional guest.

It's much cheaper to go by one of the island's **buses,** running from 6 a.m. until midnight. For example, one departs from Grand Case to Marigot every 20 minutes. There's a departure every hour from Marigot to the Dutch side. The one-way fare from Marigot to Philipsburg on the Dutch side is only 85¢, increasing to $1.50 from Grand Case.

Several **car-rental companies** operate on the island, but vehicles can't be picked up at the Dutch Juliana Airport and have to be delivered free to your hotel. Chances are, you'll make your car-rental arrangements at Juliana Airport before going over to your hotel by taxi on the French side. If so, you may want to refer to the transportation section for St. Maarten in Chapter VIII. **Budget, Avis, Hertz**—all the big names—are represented in the Dutch side. Compact cars cost about $35 a day.

If you want to make local arrangements in French St. Martin, you'll find such firms serving you as **Romeo Fleming Rent-a-Car,** Galisbay, Marigot (tel. 87-50-81), and **Saint Martin Auto,** in both Grand Case (tel. 87-50-86) and Marigot (tel. 87-54-72).

Most hotels will reserve a car for guests in advance, and this is highly recommended in winter, when there is often a shortage of rental cars. Most companies insist that drivers be at least 23 to 25 years old. All foreign driver's licenses are honored. One tank of gas should last a week.

WHERE TO STAY: Most of the hotels are on the Dutch side. The French side seems to specialize in efficiency apartments with kitchenettes, and the hotels that do exist are more continental in flavor than some of the beachside hostelries bordering the sands outside of Philipsburg in St. Maarten.

At a few of the St. Martin inns, guests are likely to be French speaking—so be duly warned if you fear a language problem.

The Luxury Leaders

La Samanna, Baie Longue (tel. 87-51-22), admits it's "not for everyone." However, if you're Mick Jagger, or just a person devoted to good, wholehearted, unabashed sybaritism—and have lots of money—you should fit in beautifully here. Set on a landscaped 55-acre piece of choice property, the confectionery **La Samanna** opens onto a mile and a half of white sandy beach, filled with some of the best stuffed bikinis you're likely to see this side of St. Tropez. In fact, the resort, like so many places in St. Martin, is more evocative of the Côte d'Azur or Morocco than the Caribbean.

The place is what the French call *intime, tranquille, et informal.* Yes, *informal,* like *le weekend,* is creeping in to bastardize the French language. Around the blue-green waters of the Moorish-style pool you are likely to see some chic guests.

The place itself is a curious melange of styles. At one minute you'll think you're in Fez, yet another look convinces you you're in a setting typical of Arizona (even Beverly Hills), and still another glance makes you think you've stopped off at a hotel somewhere in the Aegean Sea. Arches and balconies in pure "Greek fishing village white" are set off effectively by the use of stunning royal-blue doors and umbrellas. Splashes of bold fabrics are used on the puffy cushions on the Haitian furniture which is mostly in wicker and rattan. The colors are like a flamboyant flower garden.

The choice of rooms is complicated. In the main building you'll find more than a dozen twin-bedded rooms. These have balconies and are screened from the terrace by a thatched ramada roof. Otherwise, you can ask for one of the two dozen one-bedroom apartments, one of the 16 two-bedroom units, or one of the six villas with three bedrooms each—each with fully equipped kitchens, living rooms, dining areas, and large patios. People often speak in awe of the rates charged here, so I'd better get them off my chest fast. On the EP in winter, La Samanna charges from $380 to $480 daily, either single or double occupancy, and from $760 to $1050 daily in one of the two- or three-bedroom villas. *Two persons can stay here in summer in a twin-bedroom unit, paying from $280 to $360 daily, or from $500 daily in a two-bedroom villa.* The hotel is closed in October.

Before dinner, enjoying an apéritif in the bar, where an Indian wedding robe serves as the colorful ceiling. Dining is al fresco with a French and créole cuisine prepared by some of the best chefs on the island. You eat out on a candlelit terrace overlooking Baie Longue. A recent lunch for two set me back $75. After dinner, the bar becomes a disco.

Down below at the beach, snorkeling, waterskiing, sailing, and island exploring can be arranged. Scuba-diving and other sports are always available, as is tennis.

Happy Bay Hotel, Baie Heureuse (tel. 87-55-20), is one of the newest resorts on the island, a 60-unit complex set on a luxuriantly verdant 35-acre tract of land along the beach. Owner and general manager Guy Comperin did everything he could to seclude each villa as thoroughly as possible from its neighbors. Each of the handsome accommodations is constructed on the side of the hill, offering views down to the waters off the white sand beach. Efforts have been made to establish this as one of the most exclusive properties on St. Martin.

Each cottage contains an all-marble private bath, color TV, phone, and a terrace facing the tropical garden. In winter, the cost is $355 daily in a single, $460 in a double, with a full American breakfast included. *Summer rates are about 20% lower.* A concierge is at the service of guests for the arrangement of a range of water sports, with free use of snorkeling equipment included in the rates, as well as for the rentals of yachts, aircraft, cars, or limousines. Secretarial or translation services are also available on request. On the premises you'll find a florist, a hairdresser and masseuse, a private beach with deck chairs and chaise longues, two tennis courts, a freshwater pool, and two restaurants.

First Class

Le Grand St-Martin Hôtel and Beach Resort, P.O. Box 99, Marigot (tel. 87-56-50). In 1983 the developers of this property transformed an already-existing hotel into one of the most comfortable resorts in the French West Indies.

You'll find it at the end of several back streets at the edge of town. Sunk into lush green acreage is the largest swimming pool on the island, surrounded with a wrap-around terracotta terrace a few steps from a wide sandy beach.

Guests register at an open-air kiosk in the garden-style courtyard before going to their rooms. The 83 condominium accommodations, ranging from studios to three-bedroom apartments, are in a trio of elongated, hip-roofed buildings with balconies accented by fretwork, almost at the water's edge. Each accommodation has a kitchenette, a veranda or balcony, stylish tropical furniture, cable color TV, and a private bath.

In winter, studio apartments, suitable for one or two persons, cost $120 to $180 per night. One-bedroom suites for one to four persons go to $230 per night; two-bedroom suites for two to six persons, $275; and three-bedroom units for three to eight persons, $420 to $540. *In summer, studios cost $66 to $90; one-bedroom suites, $125; two-bedroom units, $160; and three-bedroom accommodations, $225 to $340.*

For reservations, call 212/935-9279 in New York City.

Marina Royale, Port La Royale, Marigot (tel. 87-57-28). Guests here have freedom that a central location can provide. The apartment-style building is only a few steps from one of the richest assortments of boutiques, restaurants, and cafés on the island. Each of the standard studios has a vista over the hills, while all the other accommodations enjoy views of the sea. The establishment's super-modern design includes 72 units, each with a private patio or veranda, big windows, a fully equipped kitchenette, air conditioning, and lots of well-organized space.

In winter, singles rent for $90 to $115; doubles, $115 to $132; and two-bedroom duplexes, $170. *In summer, singles range from $40 to $65; doubles, $50 to $80; and two-bedroom units, $120.*

There's a freshwater pool on the property, as well as a water-sports instructor who can organize participation in most activities. One of these is a $35 day-long excursion to Prickly Pear Island near Anguilla, with a picnic lunch and the use of snorkeling equipment included in the price.

For reservations and information, call toll free 800/221-4542 (residents of New York state should call 212/354-3722 collect).

Grand Case Beach Club (tel. 87-51-87) is a beachfront condominium hotel, run by the Acciani family from New York City and lying within walking distance of Grand Case. The two-story buildings are elongated and honeycombed, and most units open onto ocean-view terraces. You have a choice of several studios, mezzanine studios, one-bedroom apartments, and two-bedroom town houses. Each apartment contains a fully equipped kitchen and a private bathroom. Units are airy, with tile floors, air conditioning, rattan furnishings, and daily maid service. Accommodations, from studios to two-bedroom duplexes, *range off-season from $85 to $200 for one or two persons daily, all inclusive.* In winter, the rates go from $200 to $425 for two persons, similarly inclusive. Gratuities are optional.

There are two beaches, water-sports facilities including a 52-foot yacht, and the first artificial grass tennis court in the Caribbean. The Waves Restaurant (see "Where to Dine," below), an architectural gem, extends out on a bluff overlooking Grand Case. The ambience at the hotel is informal. This is the type of place where you make friends with other guests and plan to see them the "same time next year."

The Moderate Range

Le Galion (tel. 87-51-77) attracts devotees of water sports and beachcombers in general to its laidback premises. Reached by a bad road, this informal resort could use some sprucing up, but it has its loyal following, often booked by mainland French visitors. Just over the border from the Dutch side, this hotel opens onto a two-mile stretch of white sandy beach where most guests spend their days.

One of the most secluded resorts in St. Martin, Le Galion is set on grounds planted with casuarinas and hibiscus (but not always well kept). The rooms, for the most part, are spacious, with a total of 48 suites and doubles. Each suite comes complete with a sitting room, as well as a bedroom and bath. French families often double up here in intriguing ways. Fully equipped one- and two-bedroom cottages are also rented. Furnishings, for the most part, are hit and miss. You get few fancy trimmings.

In winter, singles range in price from $110 to $160 daily, with doubles going for $130 to $175. *In summer, singles drop to $60 to $85 and doubles pay from $70 to $95.* A one-bedroom cottage in winter rents for $240 for two persons; a two-bedroom cottage for four costs $350. *In summer, a one-bedroom cottage is only $130 daily; a two-bedroom cottage, $220.* Add 10% for service.

Food is both French and créole, and meals are served at an oceanside dining room which is candlelit. Only an à la carte menu is offered. Many water sports, such as snorkeling, sailing, and waterskiing, can be arranged, as can tennis.

Petite Plage, Grand Case (tel. 87-50-65), is an attractive motel-style accommodation at the far end of the Grand Case Beach, with food markets and restaurants in easy walking distance. Eight one- and two-bedroom units have baths with showers, air conditioning, kitchenettes, and dining areas. Six "superior" apartments have recently been added to the complex. Each of these has a bedroom, bath, living room, kitchen, dining area, and balcony. In winter, rentals, either single or double, cost around $160 per day. Part of the complex closes down in summer. Owner John Laurence is likely to be on hand to greet you when you arrive.

For reservations and information, call 305/666-4083.

Best for the Budget

Beauséjour, in Marigot (tel. 87-52-18), is like a Créole auberge, a small place, only a block from the harbor. The owners offer ten simple rooms, each air-conditioned and each containing a private shower and refrigerator.

In summer, singles are accepted for 225F ($22.50) daily, doubles for 285F ($28.50), including a breakfast of good coffee and croissants. Winter rates are 245F ($24.50) daily in a single, 305F ($30.50) in a double; a third person pays another 100F ($10). Breakfast is served on an outdoor terrace.

Chez Martine, Grand Case (tel. 87-51-59), offers relaxed informality in a small white villa on a white sand beach. Rooms downstairs with twin beds rent for $50 in the high season and upstairs with a double bed and terrace for $70 a day, both with a continental breakfast included. *Off-season, the rates are lowered to $35 downstairs and $40 upstairs, including a continental breakfast.* This modern two-story building contains only eight rooms at the water's edge. All units are air-conditioned with a private shower, tile floor, and hammock. There's an extra charge for air conditioning. The place is young and friendly. The hotel also offers an excellent open-air French restaurant overlooking the beach, serving lunch and dinner daily (see below).

For Nudists

Club Orient, Baie Orientale (tel. 87-53-85), is the only nude resort in the Caribbean. A peaceful back-to-nature place, it lies on the northeast side of the island, north of Le Galion. Its beautifully secluded beach is one of the best on the island. About 61 pinewood chalets imported from Finland are scattered along the peninsula. If you'll forgive the expression, it's bonebare simple around here. About two dozen chalets each have one bedroom with ceiling fan, private bath, kitchen, and a living room that sleeps two. The shower's outside, as no one has to worry about privacy around here. The rest of the units are studios, with a living area, kitchenette, private shower, and porch. At the daytime beach bar and in the restaurant, dress is optional. *In summer, a chalet or studio rents for $72 to $84 daily in a single, and a double costs from $84 to $134.* Rates go up in winter: from $110 to $130 daily in a single, from $126 to $208 in a double.

WHERE TO DINE: The classic French haute cuisine, with a big touch of the West Indies, is waiting to greet your taste buds. St. Martin has some of the finest food in the Caribbean.

Baie Longue

Even though you may not be staying at **La Samanna,** you might want to make a reservation to enjoy a meal on the resort's dining terrace. Sitting a few feet above the white sands of the glistening beach, it contains dining alcoves where the only sound may be the discreet tinkling of crystal and china and the lapping of the waves. Your fellow diners come here for the well-prepared specialties of the Lyon-born chef. Critics of this cuisine, created by Jean-Pierre Jury and his assistant, Bernard Malanesset, have declared it among the best in the Caribbean. The high prices reflect its image.

Your meal could include à la carte specialties such as roast pigeon with puréed green cabbage, red snapper with mint and lemon preserves, fresh foie gras of duckling, lobster with sweetbreads, curry, and squash, and desserts such as pear soufflé. Full dinners, served from 7 to 9:30 p.m., cost from $75 per person. Lunches, where a theatrically prepared steak tartare is a favorite, are less expensive. Reservations are almost essential at any time. Call 87-51-22.

In and Around Marigot

Le Santal, over the Marigot Bridge (tel. 87-53-48), serves fine French fare from its location between PLM's St-Tropez Hôtel and the deluxe, exclusive La Samanna. In fact, many of the guests at either place, wanting a retreat from hotel life, come to call on Evelyne and Jean Dupont. They know they'll not only get a warm welcome, but will be served well-prepared specialties while enjoying a view of such distant points as tiny Anguilla, the eel-shaped island. The Duponts keep their place buzzing seven nights a week, serving dinner only, from 6:30 p.m. The restaurant is in a surprisingly large room whose blue tablecloths reflect the same color as the sea that can be seen from where you dine. One entire wall is removed for the view.

Depending on their shopping that day, they are likely to tempt you with medallions of lobster with avocado and hearts of palm, a fresh mushroom salad with caramelized onion fritters that is perfection itself, broiled red snapper with fennel (flambéed with Pernod and served with "white butter"), or ocean scallops and mussels glazed with dry vermouth and served with a julienne of leeks and celery. You might try their veal tenderloin with wild mushrooms. They are also known for their lacquered pineapple duck, which is served with a sauce of five fragrances. In addition to the superbly prepared food, they also have an extensive wine list. For dessert, try the apple flambé or one of those delicately light, fluffy pastries Jean is fond of turning out to perfection. Prices are among the most lethal on the island. It takes no talent to spend $50 (or perhaps a lot more) on a single meal here. Service is another 15%.

Le Poisson d'Or (tel. 87-50-33), one of the island's newest restaurants, has already attracted a sophisticated international clientele. The owners of La Vie en Rose brought many of the successful ideas of that establishment to the seaside terrace of what had been an old stone warehouse. A small alley off the rue d'Anguille leads to this place. When a chef smokes his own lobster and serves it with butter laced with champagne, you know the cost will be steep. Specialties include a mousse of wild mushrooms and tarragon sauce, scallops in a cabbage and bacon sauce, and many more delicacies. For dessert, I recommend the chef's chocolate cake, although if you prefer something lighter, the mousse made with passionfruit merits attention. Full meals cost from $50 per person.

Le Nadaillac, Galerie Périgourdine, rue d'Anguille (tel. 87-53-77). On the waterfront side of this gallery, a little terrace restaurant is like a transplanted pocket of France in the Caribbean. The chef-owner, Fernand Malard, a native of the Périgord region of France (which is famous for its truffles and foie gras), operates a splendid but expensive restaurant, with meals costing from $35. His skilled touch is seen in such dishes as giblet salad (it appears as salade de gésiers aux lardons) and in his preserved goose, or confit d'oie. Portions of goose are cooked in goose fat and preserved in stoneware pots. He gets many of his products from France, but also has imaginative touches with what emerged from local waters, such as red snapper. The service is polite and often quite stylish. Dinner is served nightly except Sunday, and reservations are always recommended.

La Calanque, Boulevard de France, along the Baie de Marigot (tel. 87-50-82), has a devoted clientele, some of whom acclaim it as the finest French restaurant on the island. Dispensing the haute cuisine with West Indian overtones, this bistro primarily features the cookery of Provence, with nouvelle cuisine variations. Calanque is "Mediterranean French" for "the bay." The decor is Marseille style, and specialties include snails in the style of Bourgogne and a tasty onion soup, followed by frog legs Provençale. My recent meal, and a splendid one it was, included crêpes stuffed with tender lobster, plus duck in an imaginative banana sauce. For dessert, ask for "the crazy pineapple." However, expect to pay for what you get, as my tab for two, along with wine and service, came to $60, and could easily have been more.

L'Aventure (tel. 87-53-58) is in a high-ceilinged building which was once a movie theater on the harbor. The owners have covered the ceiling with palm fronds to give the interior a tropical note to complement the mainland France touches. There's an airy bar area, accented with blue and white tiles and cooled with ceiling fans. The real soul of the restaurant, however, is on the narrow second-floor veranda overlooking the market and the yachts in the harbor. About 70% of the establishment's tables are there.

The Swiss-born chef, Thierry Pultau, formerly of Girardet in Lausanne, prepares the kind of foods that draw French visitors in ever-increasing quantities. The house salad is made of avocado, shrimp, artichoke hearts, and marinated salmon. A fish terrine is filled with pieces of salmon and yellowtail. Shellfish lovers might order the lobster rolls in cabbage leaves, served with a fricassée of sweet red peppers. Other specialites include cream of crayfish soup, filet of sole on a bed of snowpeas baked in puff pastry with truffles, scallop mousse with whole scallops and dill, a pasta lobster turnover in a creamy zucchini sauce, scallops in lime sauce served on a bed of frayed endive, and poached filet of yellowtail with a broccoli mousse.

To top it off, your dessert could include a fruit or tea-flavored sherbet, iced pear soufflé with passionfruit sauce, or warm chocolate puff pastry with cold cacão sauce. Full meals, for which reservations are important, range from $35. The restaurant is open for lunch and dinner seven days a week.

Mini Club, rue de la Liberté, Marigot (tel. 87-50-69). After parking, you'll pass behind the building, climb a gently sloped flight of wooden stairs, and find yourself in an environment once described as a treehouse built among coconut palms. Suspended on a wooden deck above the sands of the beach, this establishment is filled with such accessories as Haitian-style murals, grass carpeting, and immaculate napery.

You might begin your meal with a glass of kir royale, made with a healthy dose of champagne. The French and créole specialties include lobster soufflé (made for four persons), an array of fish and vegetable terrines, several kinds of poached or broiled fish, including red snapper with créole sauce, sweetbreads in puff pastry, and many kinds of salad, including one with fresh hearts of palm. Dessert might consist of bananas flambéed with cognac.

Dinner is served nightly, while lunch is offered every day except Sunday. The owners of the Mini are Claude and Pierre Plessis, who hold lavish buffets every Wednesday and Saturday night, with unlimited wine included, for $35 per person. À la carte lunches cost around $12, while dinners go for $22 on the fixed-price offering. Otherwise, an à la carte dinner costs from $30.

La Vie en Rose, on the harbor in Marigot (tel. 87-54-42), is a balconied second-floor restaurant whose cozy dining room, with ceiling fans and candle-light, evokes for many observers the nostalgia of the 1920s. If you don't like the parlor, you can gravitate to one of the tables on a little veranda overlooking the harbor, providing you requested one when you made a reservation. A French gourmet rendezvous, the restaurant is not unreasonably expensive, dinner costing from $30 per person. Red snapper is bedded in a spinach mousse. The soupe de poisson is served with a rouille sauce and garlicky croûtons. In the nouvelle cuisine tradition, the duck breast is served rare on a bed of spinach and mush-rooms. Try also lobster casserole and sauteed scallops with an orange sauce. The desserts are some of the best made on the island. La Vie en Rose serves both lunch and dinner seven days a week, but is closed on Sunday in the off-season.

Le Boucanier (tel. 87-69-83) is a terraced restaurant reached through an alleyway just opposite the post office. The charming hostess is Yvonne Reming-ton, whose garden-style establishment serves French and Caribbean dishes that make the most of the wealth of native seafoods from the nearby waters. No one will mind if you enjoy a before- or after-dinner drink in the restaurant's sea-view sitting room, although a bar ringed with plants and yellow accessories offers stools if you prefer a perch with a view of the other customers. This is one of the best established restaurants in town, with a list of special dishes that have been savored by most of the island's residents and many visitors since it opened more than a decade ago. Menu items include tasty preparations of fish and lobster, filet of duck, sweetbreads sauteed in Calvados, and a savory rack of baby lamb. Open daily from noon to 3 p.m. and 6 to 11 p.m., Le Boucanier serves full meals costing from $25.

Native food? Try **Cas' Anny** (tel. 87-53-38), which used to be known as Chez Lolotte. It's on the rue de la Liberté in Marigot. The chef has made exper-tise in turning out a French Antillean cuisine. If you break bread here, you sit in a garden planted with lush foliage. Mme Anne-Marie Boissard came from Mar-tinique to open this restaurant, which serves both lunch and dinner, costing around $25 and up. Here you can order such local dishes as boudin créole, a créole blood sausage. When available, turtle steak is featured. You might also try her conch in the style of Provence (it appears on the menu as lambi), and crabe farci or stuffed crab backs. Even if that weren't reason enough to recom-mend the place, it is also possible to ask for more traditional dishes from the French repertoire, such as soupe de poisson. Desserts are also good.

La Maison sur le Port (tel. 87-56-38). Images of St. Tropez may come to mind as visitors approach this restaurant whose bar lies within one of the oldest houses in Marigot. Many guests drop in just for a drink, especially at sundown, when the yachts bobbing in the harbor and the building's aubergine-colored trim catch the fiery rays of the sun. Lunch and dinner guests are treated to one of the most refreshing indoor/outdoor experiences on the island. Candlelit tables have been placed between crisscross balustrades of the covered terrace where polite service is provided by Christian Verdeau and his attractive staff.

The French chef, Bruno Godefroy, prepares appetizers which, at dinner, include snails in garlic and shallot-flavored butter, a fricassée of lobster and seafood, and French onion soup. Among the main dishes are suprême of salmon with sorrel and watercress, red snapper with mustard sauce, duck filet Montmorency with brandy sauce, veal scallops with morels, hot chicken pâté stuffed with shrimp and served with a pink peppercorn sauce, and many others.

Full dinners cost from $30 and are served between 7 and 11 p.m. Lunches are simpler, with salads, several kinds of fish, and various elegant main courses. These are served from 11 a.m. to 2:30 p.m. and cost around $20. Salads and drinks are available throughout the day, and breakfast is an option many yachting people take advantage of.

Davids, rue de la Liberté in Marigot (tel. 87-51-58), is run by two Englishmen, both of whom used to be at sea, hence the attraction for visiting yachting people to its casual expatriate ambience. A red, white, and blue spinnaker hangs from the rafters. Appetizers include everything from conch fritters to potato skins, and good soups are served too, especially fish chowder and baked onion. Fresh dorado is prepared three different ways, and local lobster is done by the chef any way you want it. The specialty of the house is beef Wellington, served with a red wine sauce. Chicken banzai, marinated in Indonesian soy sauce, is a recent addition, as is the jumbo shrimp kebab with spicy garlic butter. The steaks are prime quality and can be served with Dijonnaise or black pepper sauce. Your final bill will probably run from $25 per person. Light lunch is served from 11:30 a.m. to 4 p.m. and dinner from 6 to 10:15 p.m. The bar is open until midnight seven days a week.

In and Around Grand Case

This beach town, a scant mile-long brush stroke, has probably the greatest concentration of fine dining spots in the Caribbean. On the town's one and only street, there are more than 18 restaurants, serving the cuisines of half a dozen cultures.

La Nacelle, Grand Case (tel. 87-53-63), has an elegant atmosphere with a whimsical pink trim and a selective menu, which was created by Charles Chevillot of New York's celebrated La Petite Ferme. He has handsomely restored a *gendarmerie* built at the turn of the century, across from the pier. Lying about a ten-minute ride from Marigot, La Nacelle is expensive but worth it. At dinner here, your leek bisque, followed by lobster Caribbean style, is served under an almond tree in a beautiful, flower-filled garden. Outside the courtyard, shaded by palm fronds, is a bright mural of a balloonist (a *nacelle* is the basket of a hot-air balloon). You can also dine inside, enjoying the immaculate service and fine napery and tableware. Dinner is likely to cost around $35. A winter-only restaurant, La Nacelle wisely employs masters of the French cuisine. For dessert, try, if featured, a sherbet made with guava. It's necessary to make a reservation.

L'Auberge-Gourmande, Grand Case (no phone), has generated a lot of local excitement, and deservedly so. You have to go to a bit of trouble to dine here, but it's worth it. Since there is no phone, you must drop by and make a reservation for dinner that night. The chef-owner, Burgundy-born Daniel Passerie, has opened this small, romantic dining room that is like a little country inn, perhaps somewhere in the heartland of France. Both classic French dishes, plus some with a touch of Burgundy, are served in this old Antillean home. Begin with a duck pâté with walnuts. The salads are well made here, using crisp fresh greens, often mixed with bits of ham, cheese, and walnuts. For a main course, the langouste is the most preferred and expensive selection, and the red snapper is equally as good. Filet of beef is served with morels, which are probably flown in from France. You might also try poultry breast with red wine sauce, sweetbreads with mushrooms, frog legs with mustard sauce, or scallops and shrimp with a fresh herb sauce. For dessert, try apple crêpe drenched in Calvados. For a complete meal, expect to spend from $30. The restaurant serves dinner six nights a week, closing Wednesday. Trade winds cool the place in lieu of air conditioning. You can also dine at **Taste-vin**, a sea terrace dining room across the road from Auberge-Gourmande and slightly higher in price. Both restaurants are closed in August and September.

Chez Martine, Grand Case (tel. 87-51-59), was recommended as a good little budget hotel. Diners sit at a well-set table on a gingerbread terrace overlooking the sea. This is a very French Antillean place, and the staff has been well selected, giving friendly, capable service.

You get a number of dazzling choices in cuisine. To begin your meal, you're faced with such appetizers as uncooked salmon (marinated in a sauce of fresh herbs), a savory fish soup, garlicky frog legs in a fluffy puff pastry case, snails in garlic butter, or foie gras in a jellied turnip concoction. The most tempting part of the menu is that listed under les poissons. My favorite is a pot-au-feu de la mer, which they translate here as "homemade sea stew." You can also order lobster in a number of ways, as well as scallops on a bed of endive. Duck filet is given a nouvelle cuisine touch with raspberry vinegar, and the lamb chops are flavored with saffron. Meals cost around $30. For dessert, try a French pastry.

Hévéa (tel. 87-56-85). Because of its tiny size, this Vietnamese restaurant gives its patrons the impression of dining in a private home. The trappings are unashamedly upper class and include dinner service of English china, antique colonial accessories, and a live pianist to create a kind of sophistication that less experienced restaurants sometimes find hard to achieve. The proprietor, Hoa Maï (Spring Flower), formerly operated another Vietnamese restaurant which still bears her name (see below), and her sense of fashion style and culinary skill have created a loyal island clientele. Assisted by her French-born husband, Jean-Pierre Petra, she prepares specialties which include veal flambéed in vodka and tournedos with sauce financière. These and many other dishes might be preceded by an artfully arranged assortment of crudités named for their daughter, Candice. Reservations are suggested. Full meals cost from $35.

L'Escapade (no phone). Many dinners from the capital combine a weekend excursion to the beach with a meal at this restored house on the main street of town. Although the village of Grand Case surrounds you here, you'd never know it because of the masses of plants which the owners cultivate in the garden. Scattered tastefully in the pair of nautically decorated dining rooms are candlelit tables covered with coral-colored napery. Guests are encouraged to enjoy after-dinner drinks on the moonlit terrace overlooking the water. The menu here includes a limited number of specialties whose inspiration comes from conservative applications of nouvelle cuisine. Your dinner might include almond soup, a mousse of avocado and smoked salmon, Cornish game hen with vinegar sauce, carré d'agneau, terrine of fish and vegetables, crayfish with tomatoes, basil, and truffles, and scallops with cream and white wine sauce. Full meals cost $35 per person and up.

Rainbow (tel. 87-56-85) is a popular restaurant created through the professional cooperation of Dutch-born Fleur Raad and American-born David Hendrich. Together, they've taken French St. Martin by storm, serving some of the most original and excellent dishes on the island. Since there are only a few tables, reservations, which can be made through Hévéa, a neighboring restaurant also recommended, are important for the evening seatings which begin at 7 and at 9:30 p.m. Views from the elegantly casual beachside dining room encompass Grand Case Bay.

The chef has imagination, cooking a varied menu that changes night after night. Specialties such as mousse of duckling, salmon, or chicken are often served, as are such delicacies as grilled snapper with fennel, medallions of veal in a special sauce, steak au poivre, roast duckling with brandied cherries, several kinds of fresh pasta, and scallop chowder. The restaurant is closed from June to October. The rest of the year, full meals cost from $35 each.

Hoa-Maï, Grand Case (tel. 87-59-69), is a family-run Vietnamese eating house in a pleasantly furnished cottage, on the lagoon side of the main street of Grand Case. Near the Grand Case Beach Club, Hoa-Maï is a surprising choice for the Caribbean, which is not known for its Vietnamese restaurants. The fare is superb, and spicy. Try, for example, crisp shrimp fritters in a sauce that's not too sweet, not too sour; or beef cooked with vegetables that have been seasoned with herbs (perhaps cardamom). I personally prefer the hot chili sauce a lot, but those without an asbestos palate may order sesame seed or soy sauce. The chicken with peanuts is another favorite. Only dinner is served, and it's likely to cost from $25 per person.

The **Waves Restaurant,** Grand Case Beach Club (tel. 87-53-90), is perched on a tiny promontory between two beaches. The Accianis, a charming family from Brooklyn, manage the restaurant and the already-recommended hotel that adjoins it. There's a casual, relaxed atmosphere at lunch, and dinners are illuminated by candlelight. Many of the specialties are prepared on the outdoor grill. Accompanied by crisp fresh salads, they could include locally caught fish such as red snapper, spiny lobster, and, naturally, steaks like they do them Stateside. The conch salad here tastes like ceviche and might be accompanied by a selection from the French wine list. Dan Acciani created this place, including a sea terrace bar, before appointing his son, Michael, as its manager. Full meals cost around $25.

Inland to Colombier

Minutes from Marigot, in the tiny hamlet of Colombier, is one of the best créole restaurants on St. Martin, **La Rhumerie** (no phone). Owners Yannick Le Moine from Brittany and his West Indian wife, Francillette, serve with finesse dishes that have influenced many residents on the island to declare this their favorite restaurant. For years, I recommended their Chez Lolotte when they were in business in Marigot. There, as here, Yannick's experience in the dining rooms of the Lasserre and Ledoyen in Paris has enabled his island restaurants to become well known.

In this new, country setting, the Le Moines have taken a private home and turned it into a charming créole restaurant which also serves traditional French dishes. These include salade Niçoise, escargots, and onion soup gratinée. Despite their skill at mainland dishes, they are best known for créole cuisine, offering such dishes as curried goat, a salad of coffre (a local fish), conch in fresh herbs, and poulet boucanne créole (home-smoked chicken served with baked green papayas and steamed, buttered cabbage hearts).

You have to drive out here to make a reservation, although you can make it as simple as possible by stopping in on your way between Marigot and Grand

Case. There are two servings every day at dinner, one at 7 and another at 9 p.m. Full meals cost from $30 per person.

THE SPORTING LIFE: The island as a whole has 32 perfect white sandy beaches. The hotels, for the most part, have grabbed up the choicest sands, and usually for a fee of $3 nonguests can use their beach and changing facilities. Topless sunbathing is practiced commonly at the beaches on the French side. Club Orient Hôtel (see below) has the only nudist beach on the island, but nude or mono-kini (as opposed to bikini) is relatively common, even though total nudity is not officially endorsed. Îlet Pinel, a tiny island off St. Martin, is perfect for beach recluses. Le Galion Beach Hôtel (tel. 87-51-77) will take visitors over to Pinel on request. The trip can also be made by negotiating with a passing fisherman to provide transport back and forth.

Scuba-Diving

Scuba is excellent around St. Martin. The types of diving are reef, wreck, night, cave, and drift, and the depth of dives is from 40 to 50 feet. Off the northeast coast on the French side, dive sites include Îlet Pinel for shallow diving, Green Key, a barrier reef; Flat Island for sheltered coves and geologic faults; and Tintamarre, known for its shipwreck. To the north, Anse Marcel and neighboring Anguilla are good choices. Wilson McQueen, a certified divemaster, works out of **Grand Case Beach Club** (tel. 87-51-87) and **Le Galion Beach Hôtel** (tel. 87-51-77). He has all types of equipment and charges $25 per lesson, $30 for a one-tank dive. Most hotels will arrange for scuba excursions on request.

Snorkeling

The calm waters ringing the shallow reefs and tiny coves found throughout the island make it a snorkeler's heaven. Equipment is readily available at almost any hotel.

Le Grand St-Martin, P.O. Box 99, in Marigot (tel. 87-56-50), has a 40-foot sloop, *Clochar Celeste,* anchored right at the hotel beach. For $50, you can have an all-day excursion of snorkeling, swimming, and picnicking on a nearby island. For $30, an all-morning snorkeling trip is conducted to Rocher Créole, and for another $20 you can cap the day's activities with a three-hour sunset sail with drinks and snacks.

Tennis

If tennis is your game, Le Galion and Happy Bay have two courts, and PLM St-Tropez has one. La Samanna has three courts (but these are reserved for guests only). Grand Case Beach Club has installed the first artificial grass tennis surface in the Caribbean (lit for night play) called Omnicourt. If you're not a guest of one of these hotels, fees can range from $8 to $10 an hour.

Waterskiing

This activity can be organized at Grand Case Beach Club (in season only), at La Samanna, at Galion, and at PLM St-Tropez. The cost can range from $15 an hour.

Windsurfing

Almost every beachfront hotel has facilities for this sport, and many offer instructions for beginners.

Golf

An 18-hole golf course is at Mullet Bay on the Dutch side. See Chapter VIII.

Deep-Sea Fishing

A number of good fishing boats are available for either charter by the half day, the day, or the week. Charters usually include tackle, bait, food, and drink. The average cost is $300 for a half day, $550 for a full day. Check the activities desk at any hotel for information. The season for dolphin, kingfish, and barracuda is December to April; for tuna, year round.

Sailing

Boats of all kinds are available for charter, most with crews rather than bareboat. Information is available at most hotels and at **Team Number One,** Marina Port Royale, Marigot. Sailing excursions often include snorkeling, open bar, and picnics.

SHOPPING: Many day-trippers come over to Marigot from the Dutch side just to look at the collection of boutiques from here. Marigot's streets, lined with neat little boutiques and shopping arcades, invite you to walk and browse.

It is a completely duty-free port, and because of that you'll find some of the best shopping in the Caribbean. There is a wide selection of French goods, including crystal, perfumes, jewelry, and fashions at 25% to 50% less than in the U.S. and Canada. There are also fine liqueurs, cognacs, and cigars. If you're seeking anything from jewelry to perfume to St. Tropez bikinis, you'll find most of the boutiques, often in mellow old buildings, along the rue de la République and rue de la Liberté in Marigot.

Most of the boutiques on the French side are open from 9 a.m. to noon or 12:30 p.m. and from 2 to 6 p.m. from Monday to Saturday. When cruise ships are in on Sunday and holidays, some of the larger shops open again.

Prices are often quoted in U.S. dollars, and salespeople, for the most part, frequently speak English. Credit cards and travelers checks are generally accepted.

Look especially for French luxury items, such as Lalique crystal, Vuitton bags, and Chanel perfume.

At Marigot

At harborside in Marigot, there is a frisky morning market with vendors selling spices, fruit, shells, and local handicrafts.

At **Port La Royale,** the bustling new center of everything, mornings are even more alive: schooners unloading produce from the neighboring islands; boats boarding guests from the Hôtel Marina Royale for picnics on deserted beaches; a brigantine setting out on a sightseeing sail. And throughout the handsome complex, the owners of a dozen different little dining spots are setting the stage for the daily ritual of a leisurely lunch. This is the *French* Caribbean, so meals are very important.

The largest shopping arcade in St. Martin, Port La Royale has many boutiques, some of which come and go with great rapidity. When I last strolled through, **Anaël,** La Haliote Marina (No. 18), enjoyed a reputation for French fashion. **Elle Boutique** offers designer footwear for women, as well as leather bags. Try **Lipstick** for cosmetics and beauty preparations by such name designers as Dior and Yves St. Laurent (you can also get facial cleaning and massages here).

Should the heat of the day get to you, stop in at **Etna Ice Cream Per Dolce**

Vita on Kennedy Avenue in Port La Royale. Here, Betty Smiraldo operates a gelateria-pasticciere, with many homemade ice creams created from fresh fruit, with specialties costing from $1.25 to $3. You get such delights as a tartufo as good as the one served on the Piazza Navona in Rome, as well as spumoni, cassata, espresso, along with French croissants and mouthwatering pastries. A fresh fruit drink, Frullato, is prepared in front of you so you can see what goes into it. The "sweet life" holds forth here from 9 a.m. to midnight.

If you opt for a housekeeping holiday in St. Martin, know that the best food is at the **Gourmet Shop** in Marigot (tel. 87-52-23). This is a French *supermarché* where you can order pâté, elegant mustards (especially from Dijon), fine French cheese and wine, and all sorts of fresh and canned goodies.

At another shopping complex, the **Galerie Périgourdine,** facing the post office, you'll find another cluster of boutiques. Here you might pick up some interesting kitchen and tablewear, as well as designer wear for both men and women, including items from the collection of Ted Lapidus. If you're interested in dining here, the Malards own the waterfront terrace restaurant, Le Nadaillac, part of the complex, which has been previously recommended.

Maneks, rue de la République (tel. 87-54-91), is worth a stopover, as it has a little bit of everything: hand-carved figurines, tobacco products, liquors, gifts, souvenirs, cameras, radio casettes, Kodak film, and swimming wear and T-shirts.

Little Switzerland (tel. 87-50-03), also in Marigot, has a better known branch in Philipsburg on the Dutch side. But the shop here is a fine one too. In fact it is one of the best places in the country if you're seeking European imports at prices lower than Stateside. You get not only name china and crystal, but Swiss precision watches. There is also a large selection of jewelry. The jewelry collection in both the Dutch and French stores is perhaps the biggest in the West Indies. There are many gift items as well, and you can pick up your favorite fragrance.

Spritzer & Fuhrmann, the famous Dutch store, has a branch in Marigot on the rue de la République, just off the bay. It offers a wide range of merchandise (but not as much stock as its Philipsburg branch). Included in its collection are crystal, china, clocks, and a superb array of 14- and 18-karat jewelry.

Oro de Sol, whose branch in St. Maarten was already reviewed, also operates out of Marigot (tel. 87-57-02). Here you'll find a wide selection of watches, Italian and French linens, Cuban cigars, crystal, china, silver, fine jewelry, and home accessories.

Grand Case

Pierre Lapin (tel. 87-52-10) is a *tiny* store selling original designs of clothes made from hand-printed fabrics, paintings, books, and gifts. It's well known and *intime,* owned by an American mystery writer.

l'Atelier (no phone) is run by Mr. and Mrs. Etchegoyen (Charles and Régine), who sell a wide array of handicrafts from their shop within an old Créole house. The inventory includes lathe-turned wooden objects, woodcarvings, enamelware, leather goods, macramé, woven goods, silkscreen prints, and pottery. For anyone interested in one of mankind's oldest crafts, the Etchegoyens open their pottery studio every Wednesday afternoon and all day on Saturday for visitors who'd like to throw their own pot on the wheel. If you plan to do this, wear something from which the splatter will wash off.

Local artist **Roland Richardson,** who lives in Orléans, welcomes visitors into his house for viewing and purchasing of his original watercolors and prints of island vistas. It's open Monday through Friday from 9:30 a.m. to 1 p.m.

NIGHTLIFE: Some French St. Martin hotels have dinner-dancing, cocktail lounge music, and even disco dancing, but the most popular after-dark pastime is leisurely dining. The **Jardin Bresilien** on the rue de la République in Marigot presents live music, often from South America, in season, and a disco, **Night Fever,** is in Colombier, outside Marigot. There is casino gambling on the Dutch side. Refer to Chapter VIII.

4. St. Barthélemy

Friends call it "St. Barts" (also St. Barths). That's short for St. Barthélemy —named by its discoverer Columbus in 1493 and pronounced "San Bar-te-le-*mee.*" The uppermost corner of the French West Indies, it is the only Caribbean island with a touch of Sweden in its personality.

French adventurers first occupied it, selling out to the Knights of Malta in 1651. When the Caribs pushed the knights out in 1656, France regained control, eventually ceding her rights to Sweden, which ruled from 1784 to 1877.

Louis XVI had traded the island and its people to Sweden in exchange for trading rights in Hothenburg.

Once, in the 19th century, Britain also held control. However, in 1878 a plebiscite returned permanent control to France, and today St. Barts is a dependency of Guadeloupe.

For a long time the island was a paradise for a few millionaires such as David Rockefeller who has a magnificent parabolic-roofed hideaway on the northwest shore, or Edmond de Rothschild who occupies some fabulous acres at the "other end" of the island. The Biddles of Philadelphia are in the middle. Nowadays, however, St. Barts is developing a broader base of tourism, as it opens more hotels.

For the most part, St. Bartians are descendants of Breton and Norman fishermen. The mostly white population is small, about 3000, living in some eight square miles, 15 miles southeast of St. Martin and 140 miles north of Guadeloupe.

Often you'll see St. Bartians dressed in the provincial costumes of Normandy, and when you hear them speak Norman French, you'll think you're back in the old country—until you feel the temperature. Some of the old ladies (who often go barefoot) still wear their big white sunbonnets called *quichenottes.* They are camera-shy, however, and won't stand still to be photographed. They spend their days weaving straw hats, baskets, and placemats to sell to visitors. Many of the girls are long limbed and very attractive, showing Swedish ancestry with their blonde hair and blue eyes.

The island's capital town is **Gustavia,** named after a Swedish king. In fact, Gustavia is St. Barts' only town and seaport. It's a landlocked, hurricane-proof harbor, looking like a little dollhouse-scale port.

GETTING THERE: From the U.S., the principal gateways are St. Maarten (see Chapter VIII), St. Thomas (see Chapter III), and Guadeloupe (included in this chapter). At either of these islands, connections to St. Barts can be made on inter-island carriers.

It is just a ten-minute flight from Juliana Airport on Dutch-held St. Maarten by **Windward Island Airways** or from Espérance Airport on French St. Martin by **Air Guadeloupe.** It is a one-hour flight from Guadeloupe on Air Guadeloupe. There is also charter service to and from Guadeloupe and nearby islands on **Air St. Barthélemy** (tel. 27-61-01).

Many jokes have been made about the makeshift landing strip at St. Barts. It's short to begin with, accommodating small craft. The biggest plane it can land is a 19-seat STOL (short takeoff and landing craft). As a chilling sight, a cemetery adjoins the strip! Natives pray to the white cross that stands between two hills flanking the field. Your plane has to make a curving swoop through a hilltop pass. Others suggest that a good belt of scotch should be downed before takeoff. No matter, everybody seems to arrive in one piece.

If you're flying in, you'll need an **identification card** which is required for a stay not exceeding ten days. After that, a valid passport is needed, or a visa for a period longer than three months.

The **official monetary unit** is the French franc, but most stores and restaurants accept payment in U.S. dollars. Most hotels also quote their rates in American currency. For the most part, I will stick to that same policy.

PRACTICAL FACTS: There are two **banks** on the island, both in Gustavia. The Banque Française Commerciale, rue du Général-de-Gaulle (tel. 27-62-62), is open from 8 a.m. to noon and 2 to 3:30 p.m. The Banque Nationale de Paris, rue du Bord de Mer (tel. 27-63-70), is open from 8:15 a.m. to noon and from 2 to 4 p.m.

The **climate** of St. Barts is ideal: it's dry with an average temperature of 72° to 86° Fahrenheit.

In **government,** St. Barts is a dependency of Guadeloupe, which in turn is an overseas *département* of France. As such, the citizens of St. Barts are allowed to participate in French elections. It has its own mayor (elected every seven years), a town constable, and a security force of six policemen and fewer than a dozen gendarmes.

French is the official **language,** and the type spoken by St. Bartians is a quaint Norman dialect. Some of the populace speak English, however, and there is seldom a language problem at hotels, restaurants, and shops.

St. Barts' **Customs** allows you to bring in items for personal use, such as tobacco, cameras, and film.

In **electric current,** voltage is 200 AC, 50 cycles; therefore, American-made appliances require French plugs, converters, and transformers.

In **medical facilities,** Gustavia has one clinic, five doctors, and three dentists. Your hotel reception desk will put you in touch with one if the need should arise.

There is no arrival or departure tax for visitors.

For information while on the island, go to the **Office du Tourisme,** Mairie de St-Barth, rue August-Nyman, in Gustavia (tel. 27-60-08).

There is one-hour **time** difference between St. Barts and the East Coast of the U.S. when Standard Time is in effect in the U.S. and Canada. Thus, when it's 7 p.m. in St. Barts, it is only 6 p.m. in New York or Toronto. The island tells time the French way: 1 p.m., for example, is 13 hours; midnight is 24 hours.

To make a direct **telephone call** from the U.S., dial 011-596 plus the St. Barts number for station-to-station calls; dial 01-596 plus the St. Barts number for person-to-person calls.

GETTING AROUND: The principal means are taxis, car rentals, sightseeing tours, even bikes, all of which are outlined below.

Taxis

They meet all flights. Once you've gone through the minor check at Customs, you can take one of these cabs to your St. Jean Bay hotel or go into Gustavia. Taxis are not very expensive, mostly because no one destination is all that far from any other. There are more than two dozen taxi operators on St.

Barts. Sample fares: from the airport to Castelets, $3.90; to Gustavia, $1.65; to Flamands, $2.20; to St-Jean, $1.65; to Grand Cul-de-Sac, $3.90; and to L'Orient, $2.20. If you need a taxi at night, call Mr. Janin (tel. 27-61-86).

Car Rentals

Some of the companies are very strict about the driver they'll rent to. For example, you may have to be more than 25 years old, with two years' driving experience behind the wheel. If you qualify, you'll find a fleet of small Volkswagen Beetles and little open Gurgels, as well as Mini-Mokes, available. The terrain is hilly, so these vehicles are more practical. You must know how to operate a stick-shift car.

Rentals are fairly standardized. Cars average $35 to $40 for the first day and are sometimes on a sliding scale downward thereafter. Rates include unlimited mileage, collision-damage insurance, and free delivery. Gas is extra. Tanks carry enough to get you to a gas station, of which there are three; but only one, the Shell station at the airport, is open on Sunday, and then only from 8 to 11 a.m. All valid foreign driver's licenses are honored. In season, it is necessary to make reservations at least one month in advance.

The main car-rental agencies (no big international companies operate here) include **St. Barth Car Rental,** whose location is at the Gustavia Airport (tel. 87-60-07). It's run by Mr. Hippolyte Lédée, who offers minimum rentals of two days. Others are **Constant Gumbs,** Colombier (tel. 27-61-93); **Henry's Car Rental,** at the airport (tel. 27-60-21), managed by Henry Greaus; and **Carlos Car Rental,** operated by Charles Geaux, in Gustavia and at the airport (tel. 27-61-90).

Sightseeing Tours

Group tours are scaled to the island's size: eight passengers per minibus, with a charge of $5 per person. In a private taxi, two persons can tour for 150F ($15). Operators include **René Bernier** (tel. 27-61-24), **Claude Lédée** (tel. 27-60-54), and Hugo Cagan's **St. Barth Tours** (tel. 27-61-28).

Motorbikes

These are plentiful, with Yamahas renting for about $15 per day. A driver's license is required. Try Ernest Lédée or Denis Duffau, both in Gustavia (no phone), if you're interested in this means of transport.

Boat Service to St. Martin

There is a variety of service between St. Barts and St. Martin, but schedules vary with the season, so it's best to check on the spot. For **catamarans,** call 27-66-30 or contact the skippers of the *White Octopus, Maho,* or *El Tigre* who arrive in St. Barts around noon after a one-hour crossing from St. Martin. They depart late the same afternoon.

The motorboat *Princess* goes from La Marine Restaurant's dock in St. Barts to Philipsburg in Dutch-held St. Maarten in 30 to 45 minutes on Monday, Wednesday, and Friday at 8:30 a.m., returning at 4:30 p.m. Some 12 to 15 passengers are carried. The round-trip ticket costs 230F ($23). **Patrick Siou,** the captain, or Dany, his mate, can be reached in advance by calling 27-61-33 during the day.

WHERE TO STAY: With the exception of Les Castelets and PLM Jean Bart, most places here are homey, comfortable, and casual. Everything is small, as tiny St. Barts is hardly in the mainstream of tourism. Some furnished hillside and beach cottages are rented out by the week or month. In March it's often hard to get in here unless you've made reservations far in advance. Rates throughout the island, with some exceptions, are moderate, attracting a good family trade, usually French speaking.

Les Castelets, Morne Lurin (tel. 27-61-73), is a luxurious private retreat perched on a hillside commanding spectacular views of Gustavia harbor and the offshore islands. It's exclusive and exceptional, lying a steep 1.7 miles from the airport, about three-quarters of a mile from Gustavia. It's owned by financier Justin Colin, a board member of the American Ballet Theater. Because of the owner's theater connections and friendships, you're likely to encounter such illustrious fellow guests as Mikhail Barishnikov. The former president of France, Valéry Giscard d'Estaing, has also stayed here. Mrs. Geneviève Jouany is the capable manager, a most cordial and gracious hostess.

Do not expect a beach and the seaside at your doorstep. However, you'll find a small swimming pool with a view on the grounds.

A fashionable hideaway, this retreat of quiet comfort and relaxed luxury houses its guests in a number of different accommodations, including two small bedrooms in the main building. Villas have two bedrooms, a gracious two-story living room with a marble floor, complete kitchens, carpeted bathrooms (with bidets), and a private terrace for that view. Each villa has a tapedeck.

The price of this style comes high. The hotel is likely to be closed from September to November 1. In high season, it charges from $130 to $140 daily, either single or double occupancy, in one of the club accommodations. Villas begin at $150 daily for two persons, going up to $450. However, three or four persons can stay in one of the private two-bedroom villas at a cost of $600. *During the off-season, club accommodations, either single or double, cost from $100 daily; villas, double occupancy, rent for anywhere from $130 to $330 daily.* All tariffs include a continental breakfast.

Even if you're not staying here, you might try to nail down a reservation for dinner, as the place serves the finest food on St. Barts (see the dining recommendations to follow).

For reservations or information, call or write to Jane Martin, Castelets, c/o Bear, Stearns & Co, 55 Water St., 49th Floor, New York, NY 10041 (tel. 212/571-0336).

Manapany, Anse des Cayes (tel. 27-66-55), is a recently opened resort that its developers claim is the most luxurious cottage cluster on the island. Created around 20 bungalows perched on a hillside above the white sands of the Anse des Cayes developed by French entrepreneur Guy Roy, the Manapany has an oblong swimming pool, a Jacuzzi, a wide range of water sports, and floodlit tennis courts.

The accommodations range from comfortable bedrooms with refrigerators and many extras to one- and two-bedroom suites with full kitchens and bars. Regardless of size, each lodging contains a private terrace, color TV, full maid service, radio, and phone. The furnishings are brightly colored contemporary pieces with a strong West Indian flavor. In winter, rooms suitable for one or two persons cost $200. One-bedroom suites go for $300 and up, while full cottages, suitable for two to four persons, cost $440 to $500. *Summer rates for one or two are $120 to $170 daily, while one-bedroom suites begin at $175, and full cottages cost $220 to $420.*

The resort has full room service to all accommodations, a piano bar, and two restaurants. The young cuisinier studied classic cookery from some of France's best known chefs. À la carte lunches are $15 per person, while à la carte dinners in the restaurant cost $30 and up.

For reservations, call 800/847-4249 toll free. In New York state, call 212/757-0225.

PLM Hôtel Jean Bart, St. Jean Bay (tel. 27-63-27), next to the beach in Gustavia, is a bungalow resort. Red-tiled "casitas" are terraced up the hillside from St. Jean Bay. Run by France's PLM chain, which has hotels in Guadeloupe, St. Martin, and Martinique, it offers 50 comfortably appointed, air-conditioned rooms. A total of 35 have kitchenettes where you can prepare simple meals. There's a small market near the hotel. Each unit has a balcony covered with tropical foliage where you can sit out and enjoy the view.

The location is a mile and a half from the airport, 2½ miles from Gustavia. The service is about the finest on St. Barts, as the manager has employed a courteous, helpful staff.

In high season, singles cost from $95 to $115 daily. Doubles rent for $115 to $140 daily. A continental breakfast is included in the tariffs quoted, but no other meals are offered. The hotel is closed during the entire summer and early autumn.

Most of the beds are twins, but some are king-size. Guests usually like the tile showers with bidets, and rattan furnishings are used effectively with coordinated fabrics.

The hotel is one of the few on the island that offers much sports, including tennis and snorkeling facilities. Windsurfing, diving, and sailing can also be arranged, as can a leisurely boat cruise. On the grounds is a large freshwater swimming pool, as well as a disco.

Village St-Jean, St. Jean, P.O. Box 23 (tel. 27-61-39), is a group of redwood chalets, about a mile from the airport, 1½ miles from Gustavia. It's about a four-minute walk down the hill to a good beach. The atmosphere is totally relaxed and informal—you do more or less what you want in this quiet, breezy location.

Of the 25 rooms rented out, five are two-story chalets. Some have a private garden or terrace overlooking the bay. Functionally furnished accommodations are in twin-bedded units, with private showers, air conditioning, and kitchenettes. Incidentally, Craig Claiborne, food critic of the *New York Times,* often stays here, where he prepares many a meal, including Christmas feasts.

Families or groups who can get along seem to like it here, enjoying the hospitality of manager Gaby Charneau. The design is tasteful, the decor agreeable. Expect to pay from $62 daily in a single in winter, from $86 to $168 in a double. *In summer, singles, plus service charges, cost from $43 daily; doubles, from $50 to $86.*

If you don't have Claiborne's touch in the kitchen, you can dine at the hotel's restaurant, Le Patio, a duplex serving both breakfast and dinner daily except Wednesday. Selections include fine classic Italian cuisine and also French dishes.

St. Barths Beach Hôtel, Grand Cul-de-Sac (tel. 27-62-73), is a favorite with the sports crowd who enjoy snorkeling at the coral reef offshore. The manager, Guy Turbé, will arrange for Sunfish sailboats and pedal boats. Tennis fans can bounce around the asphalt court. The hotel is built on a quiet cove in spartan French modern.

It has a casual, family atmosphere, attracting self-sufficient types to its 36 air-conditioned rooms, with private showers and balconies with ocean views. The units are austerely furnished, but few people spend much time inside here. The two-story structure, housing the rooms, is stretched along a long, white sandy beach which forms a narrow peninsula between the bay and the lagoon. *To stay here costs 340F ($34), EP, in a double in summer, from 280F ($28) in a single.* In winter, the EP rate for two persons is $135 daily, going down to $106 in a single.

The location is three miles from the airport, four miles from Gustavia. On the grounds you'll find a panoramic bar and restaurant, serving what the kitchen calls "a family cuisine."

Grand Cul-de-Sac Beach (tel. 27-60-70) is Guy Turbé's "other place." Since it's also under the wing of the St. Barths Beach Hôtel, guests are allowed to use the tennis court there. At the Cul-de-Sac (the "grand" in its name is a misnomer), 8 of its 16 rooms are air-conditioned and are superior beachfront units with terrace and a fully equipped kitchen. Winter rates in a single range from $78 to $108 daily, and doubles go for $100 to $134. *Expect $20 reductions in summer.*

Baie des Flamands, Anse des Flamands (tel. 27-64-85), attracts French holiday-makers, many from Guadeloupe, who like this two-story block run by the efficient Mrs. Solange Greaux. With the green hills as a backdrop and the enticing islets seaward, the 24-room hotel perches right on the scenic Baie des Flamands.

The beach of white sand and gentle waves is favored by lots of families who anchor here in this two-story modern structure, in one of the functionally furnished, air-conditioned rooms with private showers and balconies opening onto sea views. *In summer, special package deals are offered.* Otherwise, expect to pay $84 in a single, $115 in a double. *Summer rates are $44 for a single, $60 for a double.* All tariffs are EP.

The location is two miles from the airport, 2¾ miles from Gustavia. The place is sports oriented, having not only a seawater pool, but opportunities for sailing, snorkeling, fishing, and boat excursions. At the 90-seat restaurant, glass doors open onto a veranda with a bar. There's also a pool bar. Drinking is definitely encouraged. The chef's specialty here is the largest lobsters I've seen in St. Barts.

L'Hibiscus, rue Thiers in Gustavia (tel. 27-64-82), is set in the midst of a landscape of hibiscus bushes, from which the place takes its name. The little estate has sweeping views of Gustavia harbor; and the tone, welcome, and pleasant atmosphere are set by the hospitable owner-managers, Henri and Laurence Thellin-Mourie. Incidentally, Laurence is the wife, having married Belgium-born Henri, who used to be a well-known soccer star. Their pretty little cluster of bungalows is set just below the old clock tower, a landmark and legacy of Sweden's 100-year-old rule over St. Barts.

The yachting set (Henri is also adept at sailing), among others, is attracted to the 11 one-bedroom bungalows plus a two-bedroom duplex with a living room that is among the best accommodations on the island. All units are attractively furnished, utilizing designer fabrics, and contain twin beds, private showers, kitchenettes, living rooms, TV, and terraces with views. *In summer, the bungalows cost $77 daily, single or double occupancy.* In season, the price is $96, again either double or single.

Occasionally there are musical cocktail hours in the bar, a favorite rendezvous point for those yachtsmen. The inn's restaurant, Du Vieux Clocher, is named for the old bell tower, and is festooned with hanging plants. The opensided dining room fronts a swimming pool (so does the bar), and features a lunch or dinner menu for around $25 that includes help-yourself hors d'oeuvres, along with poultry, fresh fish, steaks done just right, and the wine of the house.

El Sereno Beach Hôtel, at Grand Cul-de-Sac (tel. 27-64-80), is a chic choice. In fact, it's a little bit of faraway St. Tropez in the tropics. A lot of the Riviera crowd is attracted to it. Their initial lure was its former owner, René Sereno, whose Da Lolo is a much publicized and frequented restaurant in St. Tropez. Its present owner, Lyon-born Marc Llepez, and his wife, Christine, aim to make the hotel "the most beautiful" place in St. Barts.

The beachside location is four miles from Gustavia, only three miles from the airport. Should you shun the beach, you can swim in a freshwater pool in the shade of a sheltering palm, with a floating garden, or else go windsurfing, a very popular sport here.

Each of the 20 white stucco rooms comes with a small terrace and garden, which are built around a courtyard opening onto the water. Each bedroom has two beds, an individual safe, air conditioning, and a refrigerator. Including the classic French *petit déjeuner, a single rents for 420F ($42) to 490F ($49) daily in summer, from 530F ($53) to 650F ($65) in a double.* In high season, a single room rents from $150 daily and a double goes for $180.

The bar is an elegant rendezvous. For example, on my last visit I chatted with a textile designer (formerly from Tunis, now living in Paris), and a Scottish poet, while everybody looked (but no one spoke) to a Brazilian singer in a see-through blouse. The restaurant, also open to nonresidents, is one of the best on the island, serving a classic French cuisine, with a well-chosen wine list. The restaurant, on the sea, has a dining room built around an aquarium for lobsters.

Filao Beach, St. Jean (tel. 27-64-84), is a crescent-shaped, 30-unit, white stucco, bungalow-style hotel, where each room is named for a château in France. All rooms are air-conditioned, with two beds in each unit, plus a sitting area, phone, radio, wall-to-wall carpeting, full bath (nicely equipped, even a hair dryer is provided), and a little terrace where you can sit and read or whatever. Units open onto a freshwater swimming pool and the gardens or the sea.

This exceptional holiday choice is run by Albert Veille, the former manager of the Bakoua Hôtel in Martinique. Right on the beach, it stands across the road from the Village St-Jean and next to the Eden Rock. Try to get Bungalow 40, near the beach.

The hotel is likely to be closed in September and during part of October. *Otherwise, its summer tariffs range from 400F ($40) to 450F ($45) daily in a single, from 500F ($50) in a double.* In season, a minimum stay of seven nights is required. On the CP, singles rent at $155 daily, and doubles go for $180.

The light meals served here at lunch are superb, including French-style omelets, stuffed land crabs, select cold cuts, and fresh, crisp salads. They're served either at the café-bar or around the swimming pool.

Tropical Hotel, St. Jean, P.O. Box 147 (tel. 87-64-87), is a little picture-postcard-type inn, trimmed in gingerbread, offering an intimate and restful atmosphere under the hospitality umbrella of its manager, Alain Jeanney. It's perched on a hillside spot, about 50 yards above St. Jean Beach (a mile from the airport and a mile and a half from Gustavia). The hotel (almost a bungalow inn) rents out some 20 air-conditioned, twin-bedded units, each with private shower, tile floor, color-coordinated schemes, plus a phone and a refrigerator to cool your tropical drinks. Nine of the units come with a sea view and balcony, and 11 contain a porch opening onto the garden.

There's a hospitality center, where guests read, listen to music, or order drinks at the bar. The freshwater swimming pool is small, but water sports are available on the beach. Breakfast is served at the poolside terrace.

In season, a minimum stay of four days is required. For that privilege, guests pay from $115 daily in a single, from $145 in a double. *In summer, tariffs range from $50 daily in a single and from $60 in a double.*

Eden Rock, St. Jean (tel 27-60-01), has now become part of the lore of the island. Once it was the only place to stay in St. Barts. Before being turned into a hotel, it was the private home of the island's former mayor, Remy de Haenen. This longtime mayor, who has unofficially been called "Mr. St. Barts," lives on the top floor. This "bare rock" was originally purchased for $100, and its old woman owner laughed at Monsieur de Haenen for paying "so many francs for it."

Nowadays, guests are accommodated in the main house with its bright-red roof, or are put up in three hillside cottages. The buildings are perched on a boulder jutting into the sea and flanked by beaches. The location is in the center of St. Jean's Bay, on the north coast, about a mile from the airport and 1½ miles from Gustavia. Eden Rock is furnished with many antiques, including some family prints and massive four-posters. In the units, there is hot running water but cold showers. To stay here in winter costs $130 per night, either double or single occupancy, in Room 1 or 4, $100 in Room 2, 3, 5, or 6. *Off-season prices are $80 in room 1 or 4, $65 in the other four units.* Breakfast is included in all tariffs.

Hôtel Emeraude Plage, St. Jean (tel. 27-64-78), right below the Eden Rock, is a perennial favorite. The hotel was designed by Dominique Celerié, a St. Bartian architect. It is just a stone's throw from the water-sports facilities and excellent restaurants of St. Jean. The setting is in a tropical garden a mile from the airport, a mile and a half from Gustavia. Guests can climb up to the Eden Rock for a sundowner. Some occupants have complained of mosquitoes, but the regular spraying of a repellent keeps the numbers down considerably.

The hotel has 24 bungalows. All rooms are air-conditioned, with a fully equipped kitchenette, private baths, and terraces. The manager is an extremely pleasant young woman, Geneviève Nouy, who has a lot of experience in hotel management. She's always on hand to welcome visitors, many of whom prefer to return year after year.

In summer, either single or double occupancy costs 450F ($45) to 650F ($65) daily. In winter, rates are $85 to $145 daily for a standard bungalow for one or two persons, rising to $180 for two-bedroom bungalows housing up to four persons. A villa is available at $250. All rates are EP.

Autour du Rocher, L'Orient (tel. 27-60-73), has been given a new lease on life, and it's been completely refurbished by its proprietors, Florence and André Lenoble. Now this breezy retreat, a favorite with young couples, is better than ever. It sits on a hilltop perch above L'Orient Beach, about 1¼ miles from the airport and more than 1½ miles from Gustavia. It's also one of the best places on the island for dining (see the recommendations to follow).

There are only two double rooms—each twin-bedded in the main building—and one suite, a cottage with two large bedrooms. The hotel is built around and atop a large rock. Much antique furniture is used, including some four-poster beds. All units contain private showers and ceiling fans. The hotel is likely to be closed during most of the summer. However, for winter tabs, two persons pay from $175 daily on the CP.

La Presqu'île, Gustavia (tel. 27-64-60), is a typical French Antilles house with a veranda, right on the waterfront in Gustavia harbor. It is mellow, slow moving, and very casual, luring those who like its lack of pretension.

If your orientation is to the sea and you don't mind modestly furnished rooms, you can try for one of the dozen or so sleeperies offered here. Rooms have air conditioners and showers.

In summer, EP rates are 240F ($24) in a single, rising to 300F ($30) in a double. Winter rates are 300F ($30) in a single, 360F($36) in a double. Life here is so relaxed and informal that one French-speaking visitor told me it should be recommended only "for connoisseurs." The atmosphere downstairs is Somerset Maugham, and a few Sadie Thompsons might show up at the bar. The place offers good value for the money, and the food, usually fresh fish, is good too. It's cooked by Mme Jacqua, perhaps the best known local chef. She was noted for her créole cuisine *à la martiniquaise* when she ran her own little restaurant, Auberge du Fort Oscar.

Club Banane, L'Orient (tel. 27-60-80), about a mile from the airport, has only four accommodations in its bungalows. The buildings are set into a tropical garden cultivated around the swimming pool. An expedition to L'Orient Beach requires a five-minute walk, although may guests prefer to relax in the antique-filled clubhouse where they can watch a choice of French or American films in the video room near the bar. The films can also be shown in the one- or two-bedroom apartments on special request.

Two of the four units contain kitchenettes, while all have refrigerators. Gérard Joffes, the manager, charges winter rates of between $100 and $125 per day per accommodation suitable for one or two persons. *Summer rates are $80 to $105.*

L'Hostellerie des Trois Forces, Vitet (tel. 27-61-25). The owner, Hubert de la Motte, takes Oriental philosophy almost as seriously as he does the administration of this unusual hotel in the mountains about three miles from Gustavia. It offers a total of 12 rooms scattered among a series of small St. Barts–style wooden cottages, each named after a sign of the zodiac. A resident astrologer as well as a few visiting star students are usually on hand for forecasts and advice. Small pets often accompany the array of cosmic-minded guests. A network of paths crisscrosses the surrounding forest for nature walks or jogging, and yoga is taught every day around the swimming pool.

Furnishings in the cottages, each of which contains a private bath and a terrace, include handmade wooden pieces in keeping with the natural outdoorsy feeling of the place. With MAP included, single accommodations cost $75 in winter, between $85 and $180 for a double. The establishment is closed off-season.

WHERE TO EAT: For the most part, you're served an essentially French cuisine with local adaptations, reflecting the island's unusual mixed European heritage. I've found few truly local dishes. However, at a private home I was once served "Madame Jackass," a red fish dish with hot peppers. As a warning, I'd like to note that many of these restaurants shut down on a whim if there's no business. This is true particularly in the autumn.

Most guests will want to swim and have lunch at one of the clubs right on the beach. See the writeup below on Chez Francine, as an example. Most of these clubs are rustic lean-tos, built of wood, more Tahiti in style than St. Barts. From tiny cooking galleys, battle-trained chefs often turn out an amazingly good cuisine, and not just hamburgers either. You might get breast of duck or charcoal-grilled lobster. A favorite specialty of mine is the puffy fritters of salt cod.

In Gustavia

Le Brigantin, rue Jeanne-d'Arc (tel. 27-60-89). Habitués of St. Barts never visit the island without a meal at one of the most cosmopolitan restaurants in Gustavia. Frenchman Dantes Magras and his Swedish wife, Maria, restored the stone and brick walls of what had been the island's yacht club into a historically accurate copy of the original 19th-century design. Today, seating choices stretch from the warmly decorated interior into the garden-style rear courtyard which at night is one of the most intimately romantic spots I know of. It's also a lot of fun, according to the clients who line up near the plank-covered bar that at one time sheathed the hull of a sailing ship. There's likely to be live jazz presented in the evening. Specialties include a full range of delectable seafood. Reservations are often needed well in advance, especially in high season. Full meals, costing $35 per person, are served daily except Wednesday.

L'Ananas, rue Sadi-Carnot (tel. 27-63-77), is sought out by many visitors for its sweeping view of the yacht-clogged harbor and its fruit drinks. Many choose to remain for an evening meal, especially if the sophsticated decor appeals to them. The furnishings are rattan, covered with neutral-color cloth and illuminated with lights shaded by Oriental fans. No lunch is served, but dinner, for which reservations are necessary, is offered every night, costing around $35 per person. Specialties include lottefish with a purée of endive, leg of lamb, filet mignon with green peppercorns, and eggplant soufflé.

Au Port, rue Sadi-Carnot (tel. 27-62-36). There is only a very limited number of tables on the balcony overlooking the harbor, and these are grabbed up fast. The view, however, is not the major attraction; rather, it is the cuisine of Gérard Balageas. He caters to "the selective, discriminating palate." How such a small place manages to turn out almost three dozen dishes a night, along with at least a dozen desserts, I'm not sure. But somehow Monsieur Balageas manages, and does so admirably well. His foie gras is flown in fresh weekly from Paris, and that's but one of the many thoughtful and exciting extras about this place. For this luxurious cuisine, count on spending about $25 per person. Make a reservation and go only in the evening except Sunday. The restaurant operates from January to April.

La Crémaillère, rue du Général-de-Gaulle (tel. 27-63-89), stands next to the fashionable Jean-Yves Froment boutique. It is easily one of St. Barts' finest restaurants in all respects—service, menu (in the classic French tradition), carefully selected ingredients, and a fine wine list. Chef Michel Brunet, a traditionalist in the kitchen, operates a country-style dining room, with lacy white cloths. Service is also al fresco in the garden. He turns out such dishes as a velvety-smooth langouste bisque, along with such time-tested dishes as red snapper flambé, frog legs, onion soup, and Caribbean lobster thermidor. My favorite specialty is his gratin de poisson. Regardless of what you select as a main course, by all means order his pommes soufflées. The desserts are carefully prepared and imaginative. It is important to reserve at this expensive citadel, where a meal with wine will cost about $28 per person.

Rôtisserie Bertrand, rue Lafayette and rue du Roi Oscar II (tel. 27-63-13), right in the heart of Gustavia, has been called "the best take-out service in the western hemisphere." The much-overworked owners, a young French couple, are Pierre-Marie L'Hermite and his wife, Evelyne. If you don't want to cook, they'll prepare dinner for you. Order it in the morning, give them time to cook it, then pick it up later in the day.

They turn out everything from French pizzas to many types of tarts (such as onion), to langouste mayonnaise, to pâté de campagne, to canard à l'orange. If you're here during the Yule season, you can enjoy oysters flown in from Brittany and fresh foie gras. It's no ordinary "deli." It's favored by locals (read that "well-heeled" locals), and it's the best place in St. Barts to pick up items if you're planning a picnic or a boat excursion to a neighboring island. Their casseroles to go include beef bourguignonne.

Prices are high, with some pâtés costing from $7 to $12 per pound and casseroles priced from $10 and up. The rôtisserie shuts down Sunday afternoon and all day Monday, but is closed otherwise in the afternoon from 12:30 to 4 p.m. Across the street, the bakery is the place to shop for croissants, pastries, and a loaf of French bread to go with all that pâté.

La Langouste, rue du Roi Oscar II (tel. 27-66-40), used to be known as "Annie's." Annie, of the island family of Turbé, is still around, but she prefers to name her place in honor of the clawless Caribbean lobster instead of herself. In a century-old building, erected during the Swedish domain over the island, her zesty little restaurant is flanked by the Gendarmerie and the Galerie Molinard. You get down-to-earth créole cookery here, and that means stuffed land crabs, cod fritters (called accra de morue), the namesake langouste, always fresh fish, and a custard made with a local fish, coco. Expect to spend about 130F ($13) for a filling repast. Lunches are light, but dinner, served daily except Thursday, is a créole delight.

In the St. Jean Beach Area

Le Pelican Gourmand! (tel. 27-64-64) is a French/Japanese affair, which may sound like "the odd couple." But the result is perfection, making it one of the finest dining choices in St. Barts. Mr. and Mrs. Robert Quistrebert, who used to operate a successful restaurant in Brittany, hired a Japanese chef, Shigao (Tony) Torigai, and after tasting *his* nouvelle cuisine, satisfied diners have pronounced him the culinary rage of the island.

Try his delicate salad of sweetbreads, or a fricassée of lobster in raspberry vinegar. In honor of his distant homeland, there is a breast of duck à la Japonaise instead of the familiar à l'orange, and few diners complain when the omelettes soufflées are presented majestically before them. Dessert could be an enticingly familiar platter of sorbets with fresh fruit or you can take "pot luck" and order the tart of the day.

No one ever said it was cheap: count on some $30 or more per person for dinner, and always make a reservation. The restaurant is air-conditioned, and is open daily in winter from 6:30 to 10 p.m. In summer, it's closed every Monday, and from the end of September until the end of October.

Incidentally, you can also enjoy a light lunch here, offered every day of the year from noon to 4 p.m. (with no seasonal closing). Food is served on a terrace overlooking the bay. You can order a hamburger, an omelet, or a salad, perhaps a selection of grilled fish, or merely a sandwich. Prices begin at $4.50, unless you go for the grilled lobster, and then you might be staring a $25 bill (or more) in the face.

Chez Francine stands right on St. Jean Beach (tel. 27-60-49). Your host, Alain Van den Haute, maintains a delightfully informal atmosphere. The ladies at an adjoining table are likely to be dining topless. Checking out the action in winter, Sylvester Stallone, Alain Delon, or Lino Ventura might give them an eye. That is, until Lee Radziwill arrives to capture the most attention. People from all over the island come here, mingling with the tourists over a casual lunch, served from 11:30 a.m. to 4 p.m.

For such a simple-looking place, the cuisine is surprisingly sophisticated. Crudités are likely to be followed by black pudding, créole style, or a tasty shish kebab, along with a glass of French wine. Caribbean lobster is dished up on a wooden platter. Piled to one side is a mound of freshly made pommes-frites along with fresh vegetables. Desserts are also rich tasting, especially the tartes maisons. Expect to spend from 125F ($12.50) to 175F ($17.50) per person for a meal. It serves lunch every day but Monday.

Morne Lurin

Les Castelets, Morne Lurin (tel. 27-61-73), was already previewed as the chicest place to stay in St. Barts. Likewise, this eagle's-nest retreat is the most elegant dining choice. The elite meet in luxury, as celebrities from both sides of the Atlantic enjoy their apéritif on the terrace, said to have the best view on the island.

The dining room turns out a classic French and nouvelle cuisine, and the food is backed up by a fine wine cellar, considered one of the finest in the Caribbean. The chef, Michel Viali, was born in Marseilles, but he has long gone beyond the cookery of Provence. An artist of considerable skill, his cookery is not only beautifully prepared (he makes his own pasta and smokes his own fish), it is also well served. In a setting of French provincial antiques, the well-chosen napery and glassware add to the dignity of the occasion.

Guest Jessica Lange, the actress, preferred a salad named for Aphrodite (cubed lobster with mayonnaise and peach bits), while the late Tennessee Williams found a local fish, known as cola (baked en papillote), his favorite. It's served with a shrimp and lobster sauce. I personally gravitate to a warm salad of walnut-flecked goose giblets. Other specialties include clams in a garlic-flavored tartar sauce and fish mousse on a bed of spinach served with a perfectly made hollandaise. Whatever you select, it will usually be superb, especially the tarte maison, often presented with homemade ice cream. Castelets is closed all day Tuesday and for lunch only on Wednesday. It is imperative to telephone for a reservation, and for the privilege of dining here, expect to pay from $35 per person.

If you're in the area during day or night, head up to **Café Santa Fé** (tel. 27-61-04), which lies high up beyond Castelets. Here you'll get the best American-style hamburgers on the island, juicy ones at that. You can take in the view for free. Most checks are under $10 unless you have a lot to drink.

L'Orient Bay

Autour de Rocher (tel. 27-60-73) was previously suggested as a small hotel. However, it's also one of the best known and most frequented restaurants on the island, seemingly holding its own against the onslaught of new restaurants popping up at about the rate of one a month (don't hold me to that!).

Florence and André, if you've been there before (or Mr. and Mrs. Lenoble if you're a first-timer), operate this first-rate establishment somewhat like a private club. It's worth it almost for the view. But the Lenoble couple don't rely just on that.

If you go at lunch, there's a sushi bar (something not too often encountered in the West Indies). Most diners prefer to go there deep in the night, ordering such well-prepared and tasty classic French dishes as bouillabaisse. It may not taste exactly as it does on the Mediterranean, but the version here is special and different, well worth trying. Try to reserve, and anticipate a check ranging from $30 per person. It's closed Monday in low season.

Grande Saline

Each season has a special spot that seems to attract sophisticated diners more than other places. Currently chic, the favored place in the sun is **Le Tamarin** (no phone), which picks up the beach traffic—many in stunningly revealing bikinis—from the nearby Plage de Saline.

If you'd like either lunch or dinner on the beach, paying from $17.50 to $25 for the privilege, join the hungry diners at Le Tamarin. I've never seen more than two dozen guests here at the same time, each eagerly reading the blackboard menu for the chef's suggestions.

If you have to wait, diners can order an apéritif in one of the lazy hammocks stretched under a tamarind tree (hence the name of the restaurant). Fresh fish is invariably featured, but meat dishes and poultry also are cooked well. Service can be hectic, but if you're in a rush you shouldn't be here. It's for a lazy afternoon on the beach or a relaxed dinner under the stars.

Grand Cul-de-Sac

Club Lafayette (tel. 27-62-51), near the Sereno Beach Hôtel, lies at a cove on the eastern end of the island. Lunching here is like taking a meal at your own private beach club. After a dip in the ocean or a pool, you can order a planteur in the shade of a sea grape, and later proceed to lunch itself: a roquefort-and-walnut salad, a créole version of boudin noir (black sausage), charcoaled langouste, grilled fresh fish, and breast of duck. In other words, this is no hamburger fast-food beach joint. Afterward, have a refreshing citrus-flavored sherbet. Prices begin at $25 for a good and satisfying meal. It is open daily.

Chez Tatie, at Public, on the road to Corossol (tel. 27-61-61), is known throughout the island. It's outside Gustavia. Mme Tatie, to judge from her size, likes her own cookery. I can well understand why: she's considered the best local chef on the island. Many residents call her when they want a "special supper" catered. If you have a housekeeping cottage on St. Bart and don't want to cook one night, she'll help you out, providing you with such fare as stuffed spiced land crabs and a blood sausage known in the Caribbean as boudin.

For the most fun of all, go to her own little place with its six tables covered with oilcloth. There you can order her specialty, colombo. Every créole chef has her or his own closely guarded recipe for colombo, but essentially it's a spicy rich stew of beef or pork, flavored with herbs, sauces, and seeds, and served with rice.

From the kitchen of Mme Tatie comes an array of good things. Her ground conch, used in crêpes, is tempting in taste and texture, as are her cod fritters. You might also order her langouste, a clawless Caribbean version of lobster. She uses the fresh vegetables of the islands, including the christophine, likely to be stuffed with crabmeat. Expect to spend $20 or more, per head, and try, if possible, to call a day ahead for a reservation if you plan to eat on the premises.

THE SPORTING LIFE: Unlike the other French islands in the West Indies, total nudism is illegal on St. Barts. However, women can bathe topless in most places. Bikinied casualness seems to be the rule. The most popular beach is St. Jean, which has some waterfront cafés where you can get drinks and light meals. Grand Cul-de-Sac, with its St. Barths Beach Hôtel, and Anse des Flamands are other attractive beaches. (Golfers please note: There are no golf courses on the island.)

Snorkeling and Scuba

The clear waters around St. Barts are good for snorkeling. The large hotels, such as PLM Jean-Bart, have fins, flippers, and masks to rent.

St. Barths Water Sports and Scuba Diving (tel. 27-66-16) is licensed, fully accredited dive school at the corner of rue Oscar-II and rue de la Guadeloupe in Gustavia. It has available two compressors and two dive boats. For rent or purchase, there are bottles, regulators, and weights, but no fins or masks.

Windsurfing

This is becoming one of the most practiced sports in St. Barts. **Jack Windsurfing,** near Le Pelican at St. Jean (tel. 27-63-19), can arrange it. It costs about $10 an hour to rent a board.

Tennis

Mainly for its hotel guests, **Taiwana Club** (tel. 27-61-96) is a sports club on the Baie des Flamands. You can also enjoy lunch here and swim in the pool. There's another court at the **St. Barths Beach Hôtel,** Grand Cul-de-Sac (tel. 27-62-73).

The only court lit at night is at Hôtel Manapany (tel. 27-66-55).

Fishing

People who like to fish are fond of the waters of St. Barts. In March through July, they catch dolphin; in September, wahoo. Atlantic bonito, barracuda, and marlin also turn up with great frequency. I suggest you ask at your hotel to help arrange a trip out with one of the local fishermen, who prefer the handline, incidentally. It's best to bring your own speargun or rod and reel.

In addition, good charter boats are available each season. Names are posted on the pier not far from the Paul et Virginie Boutique in Gustavia, or you can inquire in front of the Banque Nationale de Paris on rue Bord-de-Mer.

Sailing

Jaunts also can be arranged at many of the hotels, parties booked for trips to neighboring islands. Sometimes these are combined with fishing trips. Some of the hotels, such as Baie des Flamands, have Sunfish craft which they offer free to guests. Yachting isn't organized, however. Yet, in winter, anything's negotiable when stray yachts sail into Gustavia harbor.

You can charter, for example, **Offshore Sailing's** 38-foot *Gin Fizz,* which accommodates six passengers. A full-day sail, costing $50 per person, leaves Gustavia at 9:30 a.m. for Île Fourchue, a tiny, uninhabited island northwest of St. Barts. You can enjoy swimming, snorkeling, and sunbathing, then cocktails and a cold gourmet lunch. The yacht then sails to Colombier and arrives back in Gustavia at 5:30 p.m. For information, call Sibarth (tel. 27-62-38).

Another charter to Île Fourchue and other nearby places can be had on the *Zavijava* operated by **Patrick Siou** and his mate, Dany. The *Zavijava* leaves at 9:30 a.m. and returns at 5:30 p.m., for a charge of 500F ($50) per person with lunch and open bar. You can make reservations by calling 27-61-33 from 9:30 a.m. to 12:30 p.m. or 3:30 to 5:30 p.m. Captain Patrick and Dany also run the thrice-weekly *Princess* crossings to St. Martin.

Waterskiing

Waterskiing is authorized between 9 a.m. and 1 p.m. and again from 4:40 p.m. to sundown. Because of the shape of the coastline, skiers must remain 80 yards from shore on the windward side of the island and 110 yards off on the leeward side. St. Barts has no licensed instructors or equipment for rent.

SHOPPING: You don't pay any duty in St. Barts. Everything is out-of-bond. The island, then, is a good place to buy liquor and French perfumes, among the lowest priced in the West Indies. Perfume, for example, is cheaper in St. Barts than it is in France itself. Champagne is cheaper than in Épernay, France. St. Barts is the only completely free-trading port in the world, with the exception of French St. Martin and Dutch St. Maarten.

Only trouble is, selections are limited. However, you'll find good buys in sportswear, crystal, porcelain, watches, and other luxuries.

If you're in the market for some island crafts, try to find those convertible-brim, fine straw hats St. Bartians like to wear. *Vogue* once featured this highcrown headwear in its fashion pages. While I've seen some interesting blockprinted resort clothes in cotton, St. Barts, admittedly, isn't a leader in this field.

Jean-Yves Froment, in Gustavia (tel. 27-62-11), in the vicinity of the post office, has a studio selling hand-blocked St. Barts prints. You have a choice of buying by the yard and making your own resort wear, or else selecting from the ready-made items.

Boutique du Quai has one of the best collections of Parisian cosmetics, along with some luxury leather items.

Near the waterfront, **Alma** (tel. 27-61-36) has the standard repertoire of those imported luxury items that I spoke of earlier—cameras, watches, crystal, and perfume.

NIGHTLIFE: Most guests consider a French créole dinner under the open stars near the sea (or with a view of the twinkling stars) enough of a noctural adventure. After that, there isn't a lot of excitement.

In Gustavia, the most popular gathering place is the **Select Café,** apparently named after its more famous granddaddy in the Montparnasse section of Paris. It's utterly simple, and a game of Dominoes might be under way as you walk in. The locals like it a lot, and outsiders are welcomed but not necessarily embraced until they get to know you a bit. If you want to spread a rumor and have it travel fast across the island, start it here. In an adjoining garden the talk is of the sea.

Nearby is **La Brasserie,** patterned after a Riviera Bistro, and a good spot for an in-town nightcap.

Also in Gustavia, overlooking the harbor, is the **Hôtel Hibiscus,** popular with visiting yachting people.

Dancing to a disco beat is not unheard of, but it's limited. Check with your hotel desk to see what's currently popular. The real nighttime experience for most visitors is dining in the most leisurely of fashions.

Chapter XI

THE BRITISH WINDWARDS

1. Dominica
2. St. Lucia
3. St. Vincent
4. The Grenadines
5. Grenada

THESE WINDWARD ISLANDS lie in the direct path of the trade winds, which swoop down from the northeast. British affiliated (now mainly independent), they are Gallic in manner, West Indian in outlook.

French habits often persist because of early Gallic invaders, as the islands changed hands many times before coming into Britain's orbit. On such islands as St. Lucia, and especially Dominica, you'll hear a Créole patois. English, however, is commonly spoken.

The British Windwards are made up of four main islands—St. Lucia, St. Vincent, Grenada, and Dominica—along with a scattering of isles or spits of land known as the Grenadines. Truly far-out islands, the Grenadines are a chain stretching from St. Vincent to Grenada. Some people group Barbados and Trinidad and Tobago in the British Windwards, but I have preferred, for convenience's sake, to treat these independent island nations separately in the following chapters.

Topped by mountains, bursting with greenery, the British Windwards in this chapter are still far enough off the mainline tourist circuit to make a visit to them something of an adventure. At some of the more remote oases, you'll have the sand crabs, iguanas, and sea birds to enjoy all by yourself.

For the most part the islands are small, volcanic in origin. They have no glittering casinos and dazzling resort hotels, but you'll not have a dull time, at least visually.

The islands use the same currency, the Eastern Caribbean dollar, worth about 38¢ U.S. *Note:* Prices in this chapter are given in U.S. dollars unless otherwise indicated. Most of the inhabitants live on their crops. There's little or no industry, and tourism is not overly developed, especially in Dominica.

1. Dominica

It has been called "the most original island in the Caribbean." Covered by a dense tropical rain forest that blankets its mountain slopes, including cloud-wreathed Morne Diablotin at 4747 feet, it has vegetation unique in the West

Indies. Untamed, unspoiled Dominica (pronounced Dom-in-*ee*-ka) is known for its crystal-clear rivers and waterfalls, its hot springs and boiling lakes. According to myth, it has 365 "rivers," one for each day of the year.

Nature lovers and adventurers are attracted to the almond-shaped island, seeking such endangered species as the sisserou and the imperial parrot. Dominica, not to be confused with the Dominican Republic, is also the last reservation of the once-fierce, cannibalistic Carib Indians, who managed to hold out against Europe's two grand armies of the 18th century.

SOME BACKGROUND: Largest of the British Windwards, Dominica (or Sunday Island) was discovered by Columbus in November of 1493. For centuries, British and French troops fought each other for its domination. The deadly game eventually turned in Britain's favor, and it had to pay a ransom of $65,000 to France to get that country to leave. In 1805 Britain assumed control, yet it still had to deal with Carib uprisings, including an Indian war which broke out as late as 1930.

On March 1, 1967, Dominica got a new constitution and was declared a state in association with Britain. On November 3, 1978, it became independent, and now faces a troubled future, as it needs financing to forge ahead.

Dominica, with a population of some 80,000 souls, lies in the eastern Caribbean, between Guadeloupe to the north and Martinique to the south. English is the official language, but a French patois is widely spoken.

The mountainous island is 29 miles long and 15 miles wide, with a total land area of 290 square miles, many of which have never been seen by explorers other than, presumably, the Carib Indians.

Most Dominicans earn their living from agriculture. In the past the government has made a strong bid for tourism, but not the type who would expect miles of white sandy beaches which the island doesn't have. Rather, Dominica is known for its river swimming. Because of the many shipwrecks around the island, scuba-diving is popular, particularly off the west coast.

The climate is quite hot, ranging during the day from 75° to 90° Fahrenheit. Nights are cooler, and rainfall varies from a dryness along the coast to a tropical rain forest downpour in the mountainous interior.

Clothing is casual, including light summer wear most of the year; however, taking along a sweater for those trips into the mountains. Bikinis and swimwear should not be worn in the capital city, Roseau, or in the villages.

To sum up, go here for the beauties of nature more than *la dolce vita*.

GETTING THERE: There are two airports in Dominica, neither of which is large enough to handle a jetliner. Therefore there are no direct flights from North America (there wouldn't be a large demand even if there were). The **Melville Hall Airport** is on the northeast coast of the island, almost diagonally across the island from its capital, Roseau.

Even though improvements have been made in this winding, narrow, very steep mountain road, it still shows devastation suffered from the attack of Hurricane David in 1979. However, should you land at Melville Hall, you are faced with a two-hour, bumpy taxi ride and a $40 fare. Therefore, try to avoid booking a flight that might land you at this airport if you have a choice.

It's much better to land at the newer **Canefield Airport,** an airstrip about an 18-minute taxi ride to the north of Roseau. This airfield takes smaller planes than those that can land at Melville Hall.

For many North Americans, the easiest way to reach Dominica is to take a flight to Antigua (see "Getting There" in Chapter VII). From there, you can

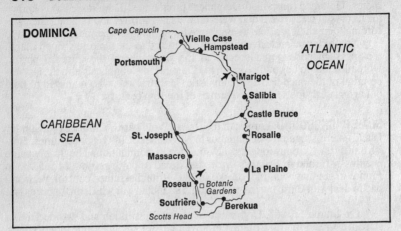

take a LIAT flight to Dominica—but even though it's scheduled, don't expect it to be on time.

It's also possible to fly from New York to Guadeloupe (see "Getting There" in Chapter X). Once in Guadeloupe, you can make a connection on Air Guadeloupe to Dominica. Air Martinique also flies in from Fort-de-France.

PRACTICAL FACTS: To enter, U.S. and Canadian residents need **proof of citizenship** such as a passport, voter registration card, or a birth certificate. In addition, an ongoing (or return) ticket must be produced.

Customs is lenient, allowing you personal and household effects, plus 200 cigarettes, 50 cigars, and 40 ounces of liquor or wine.

Dominica maintains **phone,** telegraph, teletype, and Telex services with the rest of the world, but don't count on getting calls through right away.

Its **currency,** as mentioned, is the Eastern Caribbean, or "Bee Wee," dollar.

For U.S.-made appliances, take along an adapter. The **electrical current** is 220 to 240 volts AC, 50 cycles. The **time** is also different, except in the summer when the U.S. goes on Daylight Saving time. Then Roseau and Miami (or New York) keep the same clocks. But in winter Dominica is one hour ahead of Miami and New York.

Most hotels and restaurants add a 10% service charge to bills. The real local island joints do not. In them, **tipping** is up to you. In addition, a 10% government **room tax** is added to every hotel accommodation bill, plus a 10% tax on the sale of alcohol in hotels. Anyone who remains in Dominica for 24 hours must pay an EC$8 ($3.04) **embarkation tax** (it may have risen by the time of your visit).

Regular **business hours** are from 8 a.m. to 4 p.m. daily except on Saturday (from 8 a.m. to 1 p.m.). Lunch break is from 1 to 2 p.m. **Banks** are open Monday to Friday from 8 a.m. to noon. They reopen on Friday from 3 to 5 p.m. to handle last-minute transactions for the weekend.

Water is drinkable from the taps or in the high mountains (pollution is hardly a problem here).

In **climate,** daytime temperatures average between 70° and 85° Fahrenheit. Nights, however, are much cooler, especially in the mountains. The rainy season is from June to October, when there can be warnings of hurricane activity. Remember to take a flashlight to Dominica.

GETTING AROUND: Roseau is the capital, and most of the places to stay are found there.

At either airport, you can rent a **taxi,** and prices are controlled by the government.

Even if you can find a **car** to rent, I most definitely recommend that you not try to drive by yourself on Dominica's roads. If a banana truck doesn't run you off the road, a timber-loaded vehicle will, or if not that, a pothole bigger than any you've ever seen will do you in. If you're a daredevil and prefer to ignore my warning, you can rent a Suzuki Jeep at most of the bigger hotels for about $35 per day, plus a $200 deposit. On top of that expense, you'll have to pay another $12 to the government to obtain a driver's license. I've found roads impassable in many parts of the island, except with a four-wheel drive. *Driving is officially on the left.*

There is no public transportation to speak of, except some private **minibus** service between Roseau and the rest of Dominica. These minibuses are filled mainly with schoolchildren, workers, and country people who need to come into the city to buy supplies. They are definitely not recommended to visitors, who should, as mentioned, stick to the taxis as a far more reliable means of transport.

Anchorage Tours, Castle Comfort (tel. 2638), run by Carl and Janice Armour, offer the best tours on the island, including hiking and photo safaris. The most popular tour is to the Carib Reservation and to Emerald Pool, a grotto in the heart of the rain forest. With lunch included, the six-hour safari costs $44.

The two-hour tour to Sulfur Springs, and a visit to the Botanical Gardens, goes for $12. I'd also recommend a combined tour of Trafalgar Triple Waterfalls, Sulfur Springs (via the Morne and Botanical Gardens), and Freshwater Lake, including a picnic lunch and rum punch, lasting six hours and going for $16.

Otherwise you can negotiate your own terms with the taxi drivers eagerly awaiting your business at the airport when the plane lands. Rates are about $15 per person for each hour of touring. As many as four passengers can go along at the same time.

HOTELS IN DOMINICA: There are several places to stay, but none of them is very large. Only small groups of people or individual travelers can be accommodated at one time. Air conditioning may be found in some hotels, but most establishments on Dominica are a far cry from luxury. As a compensation, the cost of living is low, and tariffs throughout the island entice the bargain seeker. At most of the hotels, you're quite isolated.

Anchorage Hotel, P.O. Box 34 (tel. 2638), lies at Castle Comfort, half a mile south of Roseau, an EC$5 ($1.90) ride into town. Carl and Janice Armour provide 36 air-conditioned rooms, each with two double beds, all with shower or bath, plus a balcony overlooking their private pool. Mr. and Mrs. Armour are the most helpful hosts I've encountered on the island. For a peaceful holiday hideaway, the Anchorage rents a single for $45 nightly, a double going for $55, both EP. For breakfast and dinner, a supplement of $20 per person is tacked on. Children under 12 are granted reductions of 50%. In the bedrooms, draperies and bedspreads are often in florid prints.

In spite of its location on shore, there is little or no beach available, so guests spend most of the day around the swimming pool. If you own a yacht, you can moor it alongside the hotel pier or use the dinghy to come over and enjoy a meal on the roof restaurant, with its view of the sea and Roseau harbor.

The hotel's French and Caribbean cuisine is the best on the island. The food is simple but good, with an emphasis on fresh fish and vegetables. A table d'hôte luncheon or dinner costs $15. But you can dine much lighter, perhaps ordering only fish, a salad, and rice for $5. Nonresidents aren't allowed to use the swimming pool, but they can drop in for meals. A West Indian band plays music twice a week for dancing.

Reigate Hall Hotel, Reigate (tel. 4031), lies about a mile from Roseau, to which it is connected by free shuttle service. Closed for a long time, it should be reopened and fully functioning at the time of your visit. Under new ownership (G. J. Harris), it has been extensively renovated and improved. Rates range from $60 to $100 daily for a double or twin room, these tariffs including a full English breakfast. All units are air-conditioned, containing private baths and balconies. The most expensive chambers are equipped with a private bar, TV, video, hi-fi, four-poster bed, and spa bath. Unique for Dominica, there is 24-hour room service. Facilities include a swimming pool, tennis court, sauna, games room, and gymnasium.

Guest Houses in Roseau

Cherry Lodge Guest House, Kennedy Avenue, P.O. Box 138 (tel. 2366), right in the heart of town, offers inexpensive accommodations. They rent out eight guest rooms, four of which are doubles with their own private toilet and bath with hot and cold running water. Four other units are singles, and guests in these share a common toilet with bath and hot and cold running water. All units are carpeted. Rates, in effect all year, are EC$60 ($22.80) per person, MAP, plus an extra 20% charge for service and government tax. There's a spacious dining room with a garden of green shrubs.

Kent Anthony Guest House (tel. 2730) also stands right in the heart of Roseau. Often filled with French visitors from Guadeloupe, it offers just minimum comfort, its 11 rooms containing no private baths or air conditioning. The charge is EC$28 ($10.64) per person just for the room (no meals). In addition, the guest house has built 11 new rooms with air conditioning and private bath. These rent for EC$50 ($19) daily in a single, rising to EC$75 ($28.50) in a double. Food and drink can be purchased at the restaurant and bar downstairs.

More Rooms in Castle Comfort

In Castle Comfort, just half a mile south of Roseau, where I have already previewed the Anchorage, other accommodations are available.

Castle Comfort Guest House, P.O. Box 63 (tel. 2188), stands right next to the Anchorage, but it's much smaller, offering only six rooms. However, these units contain private baths and air conditioning. The hotel, incidentally, lies right on the sea, but don't expect a beach. The year-round cost in the little guest house for half board is $42 to $44 in a single, $52 to $65 in a double. Scuba and snorkel gear are available for rent. Also standing next to the Anchorage, **Sisserou Hotel,** P.O. Box 134 (tel. 3111), is named after the island bird that is on the endangered-species list. It offers about the same class and comfort of accommodations as the Anchorage.

The friendly management lodges guests in one of 20 rooms, each with private bath, air conditioning, and a balcony overlooking the sea. The hotel stands right on the shoreline, but instead of swimming there, most guests dive into the hotel's pool. There's also a bar and restaurant on the premises. Year-round rates are $76 daily in a single, $96 in a double, both on the half-board plan. You can also stay here, taking just your room and breakfast, at a charge of $58 in a single, $76 in a double. An excursion tour group, Robinson Crusoe Safaris, works out of the Sisserou, charging the same tariffs as those proposed by the tours at the Anchorage.

A Beachfront Resort

The **Castaways Beach Hotel,** P.O. Box 5, Roseau (tel. 6244), is the island's first major resort along the coast north of Roseau, some 13 miles from the capital. Nestled between the tropical forest and a mile-long black sand beach, the hotel has 28 concrete-walled rooms shaded by tall coconut palms. Each accommodation has a private bath and is spacious, well ventilated, and filled with simple contemporary furniture. Linda Harris, the managing director, charges winter rates of $110 in a double and $85 in a single. *In summer, a double costs $70, and a single, $50.* A third person can stay in any double room for $25 to $35 per day. All tariffs include MAP.

Between the hotel units and the sea is an open-air bar built in a fashion similar to the *chikees* of the Seminole Indians in the Florida Everglades, thatched with palmetto fronds. Water sports can be arranged through the reception desk, as can guided excursions to the island's principal sights.

The hotel dining room serves some of the best food I've found on Dominica (see my recommendation below).

At Portsmouth

Portsmouth Beach Hotel, P.O. Box 34 (tel. 5142), is on a long sandy beach about a mile south of Portsmouth. The 100 rooms all have private baths. They rent on the EP for $48 in a single, $60 in a double. Children under 12 pay half price. For half board, the price per adult is $18, $9 per child under 12. The hotel has a freshwater swimming pool, a bar, a cocktail lounge, and a restaurant. Dinner dances are held on Saturday night, and a folkloric group presents entertainment once a week. Water sports available are canoeing up the Indian River, motorboat tours, sailing, scuba-diving, windsurfing, fishing, snorkeling, and waterskiing. The hotel has a laundry on the premises.

Canefield Airport is 25 miles south of the Portsmouth Beach by taxi along the coastal highway which passes through tiny fishing villages and scenic sea views. Melville Hall Airport is 20 miles away running along the northern part of Dominica through coconut and banana plantations. The hotel is much used by university students who study nearby.

Isolated Retreats

Springfield Plantation, P.O. Box 41 (tel. 1401), is a Victorian plantation house lying six miles inland from Roseau, about 1200 feet up. In the main house, furnished in part with antiques, you'll find seven attractive rooms. In addition to that, you can also rent one of the cottages or apartments that have been constructed on the grounds. In one of the bedrooms, the daily year-round rate ranges from $62 in a single, from $80 to $95 in a double, both half-board terms. However, if your vacation is extended, you can rent one of the apartments on the grounds for anywhere from $360 to $420 monthly, with maid service included.

Emerald Safari Hotel, P.O. Box 20 (tel. 4545), one mile from the Emerald Pool, is a small guest house in the mountain area, 1000 feet above sea level, close to the national park, Morne Trois Pitons, and the Carib Indian territory. Six wooden Carib Indian-style bungalows are for rent, costing a year-round rate of $17 in a single, $22 for a double. If you wish to stay here on the half-board rate, expect to pay $34 in a single, $40 in a double. The hotel sponsors regular safari tours along the Carib Indian territory and the interior of the island to Roseau, at reduced prices for its guests. Your host is Swiss-born Peter Kaufmann.

Papillote, P.O. Box 67 (tel. 2287), is a hotel and restaurant run by the Jean-Baptistes—Dominican-born Cuthbert, who handles the restaurant, and his wife, Florida-born Anne Grey, a marine scientist. Their place, four miles to the east of Roseau, stands right in the middle of Papillote Forest, at the foothills of Morne Macaque. In this remote setting they have created a unique rain-forest resort that is somewhat primitive. You can spend an Adam and Eve life here, surrounded by exotic fruits, flowers, and herb gardens.

They serve gourmet health foods in their own Shangri-La and can cater to some diets. On the MAP, singles can stay here for $55 daily, the cost rising to $98 in a double. As there are only six rooms available, you'd better reserve a long time in advance.

Hot mineral baths are available, and you'll be directed to a secluded waterfall where you can swim in the river. The Jean-Baptistes also run a boutique in which they sell Dominican products, including patchwork quilts, made by the local artisans.

Roxy's Mountain Lodge, P.O. Box 265, Laudat (tel. 4845), lies in the mountains at an elevation of 2200 feet. A guest house–type establishment, it rents out only six rooms, either for single or double occupancy, charging a year-round rate of $15 per person, including breakfast. On the MAP, a single costs $27 and a double room rents for $46 year round. A guide can be obtained for hikes to Boiling Lake, Trafalgar Falls, Freshwater Lake, and Titous Gorge.

Rivière La Croix Estate Hotel, P.O. Box 100 (tel. 1354), lies some ten miles inland from Roseau, about eight miles from the new Canefield Airport, on a plantation 1600 feet above sea level, offering a spectacular view of the mountains and the Caribbean Sea. Near Traverse Road, it features seven basic wooden cabins, each with hot/cold shower bath, private toilet, and veranda. Year-round rates are $42 in a single, $72 in a double, and $95 in a triple, including breakfast and dinner. Service and tax are extra. Children under 12 are given a 50% discount. Car rental as well as sightseeing tours and safaris can be arranged. Babysitting and laundry service are also available.

WHERE TO EAT: The local delicacy is the fine flesh of the crapaud (a frog) called "mountain chicken." Freshwater crayfish is another specialty, as is *tee-tee-ree,* fried cakes made from tiny fish. Stuffed crab back is usually a delight. The backs of red and black land crabs are stuffed with delicate crabmeat and creole seasonings. The fresh fruit juices of the island are divine nectar, and no true Dominican spends the day without at least one rum punch.

Some of the best island dining is at the already-recommended **Castaways Beach Hotel,** P.O. Box 5 (tel. 6244), 13 miles north of Roseau. In this resort setting, the managing director, Linda Harris, welcomes nonguests to her hotel dining room with its waterfront setting. Guests dress in casual resortwear and dine informally, enjoying the warm hospitality of the staff.

Here you get the cuisine for which Dominica is known, including the crapaud or mountain chicken. Prepared in a number of ways, it is almost always delicious. My frog legs were almost eight inches long. They have a delicacy most often compared to quail. You can also get lambi (conch), as well as island crab mixed with a savory creole stuffing. All dishes are garnished with the fruits and vegetables of Dominica's rich soil. Count on spending around $20 for dinner, less for lunch. Before dining, try a rum punch in the lounge or beach bar.

In Roseau, **La Robe Créole,** 3 Victoria St. (tel. 2896), is housed in an old colonial mansion with an open terrace on the second floor. This veranda, with its hanging plants and flower boxes, is a popular gathering spot, attracting both visitors and the town's business people. The choice of food is not wide, but it's rather inexpensive. You can order a hamburger or chicken in a basket. A specialty is the Erica salad bowl. Those soothing rum punches are good too. On some nights, depending on availability of produce, the cook gets fancy, offering "mountain chicken" and Caribbean langouste in the creole style. Expect to spend about $18 for a fine meal.

Also at the same address, **The Mouse Hole,** 3 Victoria St. (no phone), is good for food on the run. From its takeout service, you can enjoy freshly made sandwiches and salads; light meals cost $5. They make very good Trinidadian-inspired rôtis here. This is burrito-type food, a wheat pancake wrapping beef, chicken, or vegetables. In Dominica, these rôtis are most often flavored with curry.

Papillote (tel. 2287) was recommended separately as a hotel. But even if you're not staying there, negotiate with a taxi driver, call for a reservation, and ask to be taken there for a meal. The setting is a wilderness retreat and nature sanctuary. You're served exotic island specialties and gourmet health food. A meal will cost from $12 to $18 per person.

The restaurant is managed by Dominica-born Cuthbert Jean-Baptiste, and his wife, Anne Grey Jean-Baptiste, a Floridian, runs the little hotel. The salads and homemade breads are the finest on the island, and naturally you are served herbal tea on request. Vegetarian dishes are offered and fresh fish, including grilled dolphin with creole sauce. It is open during the day for lunch and snacks, but dinner must be by reservation, and you should have a way of getting back to your hotel.

Ti Kai (tel. 3261) is a local little eatery, very basic, on the edge of town, but it has a loyal local following. You get native dishes here, including the frogs that live in the mountains. Other specialties are freshwater crayfish and crab backs (the backs of the black and red land crabs stuffed with highly seasoned crabmeat). Its fruit juices and nectars are outstanding. Naturally, they serve Bello's pepper sauce, which is made on the island and seemingly used on half the main dishes. A meal will cost around $12, maybe even less.

Vena's Bar and Restaurant, Cork Street (tel. 3286), right in the heart of town, is about the best place to go for local cooking. Some say that Vena is the best cook on the island. She'll feed you on her little garden patio, and even has a few rooms to rent, should you need an accommodation for the night. Her prices are EC$18 ($6.84) to EC$35 ($13.30) for a full meal. Don't count on a big menu here—ask her what she's got in the kitchen. Maybe it will be crab backs, perhaps "tee-tee-ree," fried cakes made from tiny fish, or lambi (conch meat). She's said to make the best rum punches on the island as well, and they're a concoction of rich fruits blended with locally produced favorites such as D-Special and Bagatelle rums.

Guiyave, 15 Cork St. (tel. 2930), is a cheap place for a lunch if you're visiting Roseau for the day. It's often favored by the business community, who usually begin their meal with a refreshing rum punch made with such fresh local fruit as guava, papaya, and pineapple. At this walkup place, try to get a table on the porch if you're sticking around for dinner. Meals rarely cost more than $12.

TOURING THE ISLAND: Those making day trips to Dominica from other islands will want to see the **Carib Indian Reservation,** in the northeast. In 1903 Britain got the Caribs to agree to accept boundaries on 3700 acres of land set aside for them. Hence, this is the last remaining domain of this once-hostile tribe (now subdued) who gave their name to the archipelago—Caribbean.

Their look is Mongolian, and they are no longer "pure-blooded." Blacks and others have married into the tribe. However, no non-Carib males are accepted as part of the tribe. Men, however, are free to bring in women of other races.

Their reserve is accessible only by Land Rover. Today they survive by fishing, growing food, and weaving baskets and vertivert grass mats which they sell to the outside world. They still make dugout canoes too.

It's like going back in time when you explore **Morn Trois Pitons National Park,** a primordial rain forest, "me Tarzan, you Jane" country. Mists rise gently over lush, dark-green growth, drifting up to blue-green peaks that have earned for Dominica the title of "Switzerland of the Caribbean." Framed by banks of giant ferns, rivers rush and tumble. Trees sprout orchids, and everything seems blanketed with some type of parasitic growth. Green sunlight filters down through timeless trees, and the roar of a waterfall creates a blue mist.

Exploring this green heart of Dominica is for serious botanists and only the most skilled hikers, who should never penetrate unmarked trails without a very experienced guide.

Deep in the park is the **Emerald Pool Trail,** a nature trail of half a mile that forms a circuit loop on a footpath passing through the forest to a pool with a beautiful waterfall. Downpours are frequent in the rain forest, and at high elevations cold winds blow.

Five miles up from the **Roseau River Valley,** in the south-central sector of Dominica, **Trafalgar Falls** can be reached after your vehicle passes through the village of Trafalgar. There, however, you have to approach by foot, as the slopes are too steep for vehicles. After a 20-minute walk, you arrive at the base of the falls. A trio of falls converge into a rock-strewn pool. Boulders sprout vegetation, and tree ferns encircle this flowing water. On the way there you pause to pick ginger plants or vanilla orchids.

The **Sulfur Springs** are evidence of the island's volcanic past. Jeeps or Land Rovers get quite near. Not only Sulfur Springs but **Boiling Lake** are bubbling evidence of underground volcanic activity, which can be seen near Trafalgar Falls, north and east of Roseau. It's like a bubbling pool of gray mud. Sometimes you hear a belch of smelly sulfurous fumes—the odor is like a rotten egg. Only the very fit should attempt to go to Boiling Lake. Some Dominicans fear that volcanic activity will erupt again, but these poor people have enough trouble for the moment. Freshwater Lake lies at the foot of Mount Macaque.

On the northwest coast, **Portsmouth** is Dominica's second-largest settlement. Once there, you can row up the Indian River in native canoes to visit the ruins of old Fort Shirley and bathe at Sandy Beach on Douglas Bay.

THE SPORTING LIFE: There isn't much, but serious hikers find it a major challenge. Guides should be used for all unmarked trails. You can reach one by going to the office of the **Dominica National Park** on Victoria Street in Roseau (tel. 2732).

The best all-around sports center is at the previously recommended **Anchorage Hotel** (tel. 2638) at Castle Comfort, half a mile south of Roseau. There, Carl and Janice Armour do much to help sports-oriented guests on Dominica. Snorkeling and scuba-diving can also be arranged at the previously recommended Portsmouth Beach Hotel (tel. 5142) should you be interested in diving in the vicinity of the northwest coast. Scuba equipment and dives cost $35. If you want to go water-skiing, it will cost $20 per hour to rent a boat, and four passengers are allowed to go out for that price. Deep-sea fishing trips cost $300 daily for five persons.

Birdwatchers and collectors of tropical flora also visit the island, and photo safaris are possible, costing from $25 to $50, depending on where you want to go. Again, it's best to check with the Anchorage for what possibilities exist during your visit. Sometimes the people there have arranged for horseback riding on a farm in the hills.

As for **beaches,** there are good beaches in the northwest of the island around Portsmouth, the second town. There are also secluded beaches in the northeast, along with spectacular coastal scenery. But all of these are hard to reach, and you might settle instead for a freshwater swimming pool.

SHOPPING: There isn't a lot. In Roseau, **Tropicrafts Ltd.** on Turkey Lane (tel. 2747) offers the well-known grass rugs handmade and woven in several intricate patterns at Tropicrafts' factory. They also have for sale handmade bags, shopping bags, and placemats, all appliquéed by hand. The handmade dolls are popular with doll collectors. The Dominican vertivert-grass mats are known throughout the world.

Caribana Handcrafts, 31 Cork St. (tel. 2761), in Roseau offers similar merchandise. Some of the items were handcrafted by the Caribs.

It's a bit of a shopping adventure to check out the **Handcraft Center** at the Carib Reserve, which sells the vertivert-grass mats. The Caribs are noted for their basket weaving.

READER'S SHOPPING SUGGESTIONS: "We walked to **Trafalgar Village** where the U.S. has sponored a woodworking shop assisted by Peace Corps volunteers. There, you'll find mahogany carving, cane-seat chairs, bentwood rockers, and elegant beds and love seats. The furniture is really beautiful, especially the Lucas wood. It looks like cedar and is very hard and more expensive than mahogany. Shopping should also include a trip to the **Goodwill Workshop for the Blind,** at the northern sector of Roseau. This shop has reasonable bamboo basket work. . . . **Pots 'n Things,** on George Street in Roseau, is an unexpected treasure. The quality is as good as the potters of Nagoya and Kyoto, Japan, where I lived for four years. . . . Other good buys are the pineapple and grapefruit marmalade, curry (an original mix), vanilla extracts and Bello hot sauce, along with Rose's lime juice. These items are found at various stores in Rouseau" (Melodie Stokcs, Meridian, Miss.).

NIGHTLIFE: It's not very sophisticated, but there is some. A couple of the major hotels such as Castaways have entertainment on weekends, usually a combo playing for dancing until midnight. Sometimes there is live music at La Robe Créole (see my dining recommendations).

2. St. Lucia

Second largest of the Windward Islands, St. Lucia (pronounced *Loo*-sha) is a checkerboard of green-mantled mountains, gentle valleys, wide beaches, banana plantations, a bubbling volcano, giant tree ferns, wild orchids, and fishing villages. There's a smell of the South Pacific about it. With its mixed French and British heritage, it has year-round temperatures of 70° to 90° Fahrenheit.

The actual discovery of this football-shaped island is shrouded in conjecture, some maintaining that Columbus landed on December 13, 1502. However, this widely held opinion is considered a total myth. Records reveal that the explorer was far from St. Lucia on that date. It is often conceded that Spanish seamen discovered the island in some unknown year.

St. Lucia lies some 20 miles from Martinique. An English party coming from St. Kitts settled here in 1605, but the island was to change hands a total of 14 times, as the French and English fought intermittently for its control, their battles lasting for more than a century. Slaughter parties led by cannibalistic Caribs often deterred permanent settlements for years.

The island was a British colony from 1803 to 1967, when it became an associated state within the Commonwealth. St. Lucia arrived at its full sovereignty on February 22, 1979, and in spite of protests, became an independent country and a full-fledged sister in the British Commonwealth of nations.

A mountainous island of some 240 square miles, St. Lucia counts some 120,000 inhabitants. The capital, **Castries,** is built on the southern shore of a large, almost landlocked harbor—a "reliable shelter for ships"—surrounded by hills. The approach to the airport is almost a path between hills, and it's very impressive.

The capital was named for an 18th-century French secretary of state to the foreign colonies, Marshal de Castries. Fires have swept over the town many times, destroying its wooden buildings. The last catastrophe occurred in 1948. As a result, don't expect too many vintage structures.

GETTING THERE: Getting to St. Lucia has become much easier in recent years. From New York, **Pan American** is the best way to reach St. Lucia. Its flights leave twice a week, stopping briefly in Barbados before continuing on to Hewanorra Airport on the southeastern coast of St. Lucia.

BWIA also flies from New York once a week on a Saturday, touching down briefly at both St. Kitts and Barbados.

Other airlines eventually get to St. Lucia, but I strongly advise against the plane change onto LIAT at Barbados if you can possibly avoid it. Passenger bumping and cancelled flights seem to be a spectator sport there.

If there are no other options, both **American Airlines** (daily from New York) and **Air Canada** (once weekly from Montréal and three times weekly from Toronto) provide a link-up to Barbados, where LIAT supposedly takes over for the final leg to St. Lucia.

Passengers embarking at Miami can choose directly weekly flights on either BWIA or **Eastern Airlines,** each of which makes a stop along the way.

PRACTICAL FACTS: The official **currency** is the Eastern Caribbean dollar, popularly known as the "Bee Wee" dollar, or EC$. It's about 38¢ in U.S. currency. However, most of the quotations will be in American dollars, as they are accepted by nearly all hotels, restaurants, and shops.

English is the official **language,** but St. Lucians may not speak it as you do. Islanders also speak a French-Créole patois, similar to that heard in Martinique.

St. Lucia has two **airports.** Most international flights land at Hewanorra Airport in the south, 45 miles from Castries. If you fly in here and you're booked into a hotel in the north, you'll have to spend up to about an hour and a half going along the poorly maintained and potholed East Coast Highway. The average taxi cost is $35. Once this airport was known as "Beane Field," when Roosevelt and Churchill agreed to construct a big air base there.

However, inter-island flights land at Vigie Airport in the northeast, which is much more convenient as it brings you down just outside Castries. LIAT Airways with its small prop planes flies into Vigie.

Customs at either airport should be no major hassle. U.S. or Canadian citizens need **proof of citizenship,** such as a passport, voter registration card, or birth certificate, plus an ongoing or return ticket.

In winter, watch your clock. St. Lucia is on **Atlantic Standard Time,** placing it one hour ahead of New York or Miami. However, during Daylight Saving Time, it matches the clocks of the U.S. East Coast.

Electricity is a problem. Bring a converter, as St. Lucia has 220 to 230 volts, 50 cycles, AC.

Shopping hours are 8 a.m. to 4 p.m. in general, but watch those early closings on Wednesday.

Major **banks** in Castries include Chase Manhattan, and they close early, at noon, and even earlier on Saturday, at 11 a.m.

Cable & Wireless provides international telecommunications and also operates a dial **phone system** throughout the island. Cables may be handed in at hotel desks or at the offices of Cable & Wireless in the George Gordon Buildings on Bridge Street in Castries.

You'll find a **tourist information bureau** on the Queen Elizabeth II dock in Castries.

The **General Post Office** is on Bridge Street in Castries. It is open Monday to Friday from 8:30 a.m. to 4 p.m.

Most hotels add a 10% **service charge,** and restaurants do likewise.

The government imposes a 7% **occupancy tax** on hotel room rentals.

If you're flying to one of the islands in the Caribbean Commonwealth (English-speaking islands), you must pay a **departure tax** of EC$6 ($2.28). That is true also for the French West Indies and the U.S. Virgin Islands. However, if you're returning to the U.S. mainland or going elsewhere, the airport tax is EC$12 ($4.56). This tax must be paid in EC dollars.

GETTING AROUND: Taxis are ubiquitous on the island, and most drivers are friendly and eager to please. The drivers have to be quite experienced to cope with the narrow, hilly, switchback roads outside the capital. Special programs have trained them to serve as guides. Their cars are unmetered, but tariffs for all standard trips are fixed by the government.

In asking the fare for a ride, make sure you determine if the driver is quoting a rate in U.S. dollars or the "Bee Wee." Leisure drives cost about $20 per hour. For example, one of the most popular runs—from Castries to Sulfur Springs via Soufrière and back to the capital—goes for $75 and therefore is best when costs are shared with three or four passengers.

Car Rentals

First, remember to *drive on the left.* The price of a small car runs from $28 to $35 per day, depending on the type of vehicle, plus 35¢ per mile. You are usually given the first 30 miles free. National, Europcar, and Tilden are represented by **St. Lucia Car Rental Services,** P.O. Box 542, Castries, with locations at Hewanorra International Airport (tel. 454-6699), Vigie Airport (tel. 452-3050), Elliott Shell Servicentre at Gros Islet (tel. 452-8721), and Cariblue Hotel (tel. 452-8551).

You will need a St. Lucia's driver's license. This can most easily be obtained at either airport upon arrival. Present your valid home license to the immigration officer and pay a fee of approximately EC$15 ($5.70).

Local Buses

Wooden omnibuses, with names like "Lucian Love," and jitneys connect Castries with such main towns as Soufrière and Vieux Fort. They are generally overcrowded and often filled with produce on the way to market. Schedules are also unreliable. However, since taxis are expensive, it might be a reliable means of transport. At least it's cheap. Buses from Cap Estate, the northern part of the island, leave from Jeremy Street in Castries, near the market. Buses going to Vieux Fort, Soufrière, leave from Bridge Street in front of the department store.

Sightseeing Bus Tours

Most hotel front desks will make arrangements for excursions, taking in all the major sights of St. Lucia. For example, **St. Lucia Representative Services,** Manoel Street, Castries (tel. 452-2332), offers an island tour, taking visitors to the top of Morne Fortune. That's followed by a visit to a rum distillery and on through the banana plantations and the pretty little fishing villages. The most spectacular stop for a view is to look at the Pitons. The tour stops at a restaurant for lunch and then a swim before returning to Castries. The cost is about $30.

Sea Excursions

This type of tour can usually be arranged at your hotel's activities desk. One of the most popular tours, costing $38 per person, is aboard the *Brig Unicorn*, which takes you on a day's sail to Soufrière and the Pitons. The *Unicorn* starred as the slave ship in the TV series *Roots*, among other movie roles. Built in 1948 and captained by Bob Elliot, it is a 140-foot vessel with 16 square-rigged sails, carrying a crew of 13. You sail southward from Coal Pot, near Castries, at 9 a.m., heading for Soufrière's Sulfur Springs. On the return voyage, you're served a lunch aboard. Later, you swim at Anse Cochon and sail into Marigot Bay. You're back at dock at 4 p.m., where coaches await to return you to your hotel. To make reservations on your own, call 452-5643.

WHERE TO STAY: Most of the lead hotels on this island are in the same price range. You have to seek out the bargains (begin at the bottom of my list). Once you reach your hotel, chances are you'll feel pretty isolated, but that's what many guests want. Many St. Lucian hostelries have kitchenettes where you can prepare simple meals. Prices are quoted in U.S. dollars.

Couples, P.O. Box 190, Malabar Beach (tel. 452-4211), is, in my opinion, the best place to stay in St. Lucia. The logo—a silhouette of two lions coupling—is a provocative and sophisticated symbol of this unusual hotel, where all meals, drinks, cigarettes, entertainment, and most incidental expenses are included in the initial price. The center of the complex is under a gridword of peaked roofs floored with tasteful terracotta tiles. Set on the edge of a beach bordered with palm trees, the hotel has a sprawling garden centered around a 150-year-old saman tree. A saltwater swimming pool is graced with a lattice-sheltered bar area.

This is a resort for couples only, with no children allowed. (A couple, according to the sophisticated owner, Craig, and his beautiful wife, Penny, can be any two mutually interested persons.) Singles and triples are not accepted, which contributes to the relaxed ambience of lovers enjoying each other, making friends with other couples, and celebrating the beautiful physical plant as well as their relationships.

A member of the staff will meet your plane at the airport with a chest of cold beer and rum punches when you arrive. The bar opens early and closes late, acting as a precursor to the fine cuisine arranged by an expatriate Scotsman named Nigel. Most of the lunches are buffet style, and there's even a cold-cut buffet offered every evening after the end of the dinner hour. Evening action is fun, including a weekly pajama party the likes of which you may always have wanted to attend but never had the chance.

All of this goes for a reasonable *$1600 per couple per week in summer,* $2000 per couple per week from December till April.

The location is at the end of the Vigie runway, near Castries.

Canard La Toc Hotel and Villas, P.O. Box 399 (tel. 452-3081), some 2½ miles south of Castries, bills itself as tropical, tranquil, and luxurious, and here's one place that delivers what it promises. The site was purchased some 20 years ago when a Cunard executive spotted it and quickly decided that it would be ideal for a deluxe hotel. The resort hosts frequent luncheons and beach stopovers for the passengers of the Cunard vessels when they stop in St. Lucia. On 100 secluded acres at the edge of the island, the complex consists of both the Hotel La Toc, which has 160 handsomely furnished rooms, but also La Toc Villas with 60 one- and two-bedroom, beautifully appointed villas. The privately owned villas are rented as a whole or in sections. The hotel units are colorfully accented with a tropical-motif decor. Each accommodation includes a private bath, air conditioning, plus balconies or patios offering views of the ocean or the exotic gardens, planted with red ixora and pink-purple eranthemum.

This complex is about a ten-minute drive south from the capital, built on a half mile of curved beach. *In summer, twins range in price from $95 to $120 daily; singles cost $75.* In winter, two persons pay $160 to $180 daily; one person, $130 to $170. For breakfast and dinner, add another $30 per person.

La Toc Villas are like little dollhouses in pastel colors. *Town & Country* called them "one of the ten most luxurious villa complexes in the Caribbean." Set apart, each of the villas nestles against the mountainside facing the sea. They are connected by frequent jitney service to the main building. In winter, a superior two-bedroom villa costs $250 daily, rising to $300 in a deluxe two-bedroom villa with a private plunge pool. *In summer, these same villas cost from $190 to $230 daily.*

All guests have a choice of two swimming pools, one so big it has its own palm-studded island. Among the shops you'll find a beauty salon, souvenir shop, boutique, duty-free shop, and a drugstore. Dining is either at the Grill Restaurant, a carvery-type place, the Village Restaurant, which has some of the best food on the island, or the Créole Restaurant, which has highly seasoned food and operates only in the winter season.

On the grounds is a manicured 18-hole golf course with a resident pro. Tennis buffs enjoy any of La Toc's three Har-tru courts (lit for night games) or the two hard-surface courts with a resident tennis pro. The front-desk personnel can arrange for you to go fishing for dorado (dolphin), swordfish, cavalle, or barracuda. Watersports include Sunfish sailing, windsurfing, snorkeling, and waterskiing, all free to La Toc guests. La Toc's private 120-foot brig, the *Unicorn*, sails twice weekly. There is live entertainment nightly, plus two floor shows a week.

Steigenberger Cariblue, P.O. Box 437, Cap Estate (tel. 452-8551), is a citadel of first-class resort living, on a 1500-acre estate at the northernmost tip of the island. The famous German hotel chain has staked out this Anse du Cap entry in the Caribbean, within walking distance of the nine-hole golf course at Cap Estate. It is housed in a yellow colonial-style complex with white balconies and seemingly endless covered breezeways.

For a unique St. Lucian holiday, this place is number one for many Europeans and Americans seem to like it equally well. Informality and elegance go hand in hand here. Of course, you're an eight-mile run from Castries, but guests seem to prefer this isolation. Besides, if you want to go shopping, it's only a taxi ride across halfway passable roads. In addition, the hotel bus runs in three days a week for a shopping excursion.

Guests are housed in one of 102 individually air-conditioned rooms with their own private balconies overlooking those sunsets which, even though a cliché, still cause a thrill when everybody takes on a cantaloupe glow.

You might be reading the *New York Times* and the reader in the next room the *Frankfurter Allgemein,* but you'll share the same facilities—the Caribbean-style bamboo and rattan furnishings, the wall-to-wall carpeting, the polished oak. Most of the units are in the duo of four-story buildings, but I prefer the two-story beachfront wing. MAP singles in winter range in price from $126 to $182 daily, while doubles go for $175 to $235. *In summer, a single on the MAP rents for $89 to $119 daily, and a couple pays from $134 to $164 on the same plan.*

The grounds open onto a light-colored sandy beach. Garmisch-Partenkirchen–style walkways protect you from the sun's rays, but no one seems to need this shield, as they come here for the sun. Beside the beach stands an open-air dining pavilion with a bar, and you can also eat in an air-conditioned room with the French name Au Jardin du Cariblue (In the Garden of Cariblue).

The hotel is a complete resort, offering not only golf, but a swimming pool (as would be expected), and tennis, golf, water sports such as scuba-diving, even a riding stable which allows you to go horseback riding. Snorkeling can be arranged, as can Laser and Sailfish sailing, windsurfing, and waterskiing.

Dasheene, P.O. Box 255, Soufrière (tel. 454-7444), is one of the most inaccessible and peaceful resorts on St. Lucia, reached after a long, winding drive. The establishment, managed by Joe and Ellen Kinnebrew, who spend part of their year in Michigan running his design business, was built between 1970 and 1975 making use of local products such as hardwoods, especially greenheart, stone, and labor. This dramatically located hotel has a Tahitian-style collection of palm-thatched, umbrella-shaped shelters on a terrace overlooking the two Pitons, a moon-shaped bay, and a forest of palm trees.

Each accommodation is designed like a town house, joined to its neighbors in a complicated series of well-designed planes, each with several levels, open-air bedrooms angled so the rain can't come in, a scattering of antiques, and an aura of being very, very far from any urban center. *In summer, the daily rate ranges from a low of $65 in a studio apartment, going up to $100 in a deluxe suite with a private plunge pool.* The honeymoon suite and some other villas are even more expensive. In winter, a studio apartment rents for $600 weekly, a deluxe suite going for $925, plus service and tax. Rates given are for either single or double occupancy. The tariffs cited are for accommodation only. The required MAP will cost another $30 per person per day. In low season, a minimum stay of three days is required, seven days in high season.

À la carte lunches are available near the small swimming pool. Dasheen (without the final *e* in the hotel's name) is a local vegetable used frequently in the natural-style cuisine that makes use of as many local foodstuffs as possible. Ever had mango mousse? One winter visitor described the dining experience here as "like coming to a dinner party every evening."

Marigot Bay Resort, at Marigot Bay (tel. 453-4256), is a blanket name to cover a complex of inns, cottages, restaurants, bars, boutiques, and yachting berths lying about a 45-minute drive along the west coast. Much favored by the yachting set, the lagoon setting was described by the author James Michener as "the most beautiful bay in the Caribbean." On a low-lying spit of the palm-dotted island, the complex, part of which is reached only by ferry service, is the most idyllic spot on St. Lucia.

A cluster of colonial-style cottages is called Marigot des Roseaux, and they are spread along a hillside. Some are privately owned, others controlled by the hotel. Most are one- or two-bedroom buildings, attractively making use of both their indoor and outdoor areas. In winter, a one-bedroom cottage or a studio apartment rents for $140 a day, and a two-bedroom cottage costs $180. However, *in summer, a studio or one-bedroom cottage costs only $80 to $90 daily.*

The yachting set often stays at the Marigot Inn, which is decorated in the West Indian style. The double rooms here are comfortable and attractive, opening onto verandas where the occupants can look at their yachts. There's also a Hurricane Hole, a cottage hotel on the southeastern shore. It offers the only swimming pool in the complex, with a shark painted amusingly onto its cement bottom. Here most rooms have skylit baths.

Garvan Farley, the Australian-born manager, oversees the operation with efficiency and his own quiet style. In season, hotel rooms cost $100 daily in a single, going up to $120 in a double. *In summer, hotel rooms go for $80 in a double, $60 in a single.* Tax and service are extra.

The most popular restaurant is Doolittle's, built out over the water on stilts (it is recommended separately in the dining section).

Across the way, the Hurricane Hole's restaurant is the Rusty Anchor, where barbecues are offered on Friday, a traditional English roast beef on Sunday. On Friday and Saturday nights guests or visitors can attend a "jump-up."

Halcyon Beach Club, P.O. Box 388, Choc Bay (tel. 452-5331), a four-mile drive outside Castries, is almost the classic concept of a modern Caribbean hotel today. With 88 of the 98 rooms on the beach and the remaining 10 set in tropical gardens, this hotel offers the perfect vacation for the entire family. Water sports and sailing are free, as are tennis, volleyball, shuffleboard, and a host of indoor games. There is also a children's playground. You have a choice of two restaurants for dining, one of which, the Fisherman's Wharf, is built sea style over the ocean for cool evening enjoyment. Danish manager Peter Kouly, who trained at the leading hotel in Copenhagen and then owned a disco and restaurant on Jutland, offers one of the most copious breakfast buffets on the island. The evening menu is filled with an international cuisine, including Danish and French specialties. A barbecue, bar, and disco with the latest sound equipment extends on a platform out into the sea, creating a kind of man-made island. There is also a piano bar.

In winter, singles range in price from $90 to $110 daily, with twins costing from $110 to $140. *In summer, a single costs from $55 to $65 daily, and twins are priced from $70 to $80.* On the grounds you can see caged parrots and iguanas, for which St. Lucia is well known.

The **St. Lucian Hotel,** P.O. Box 512 (tel. 452-8351), 6½ miles from Castries, is a well-designed, 192-room hotel complex centered around the open-air restaurant and the oceanside pool. It has lots of flowering shrubs, swaying palms, and latticed breezeways connecting the outlying buildings which once formed two hotels. Accommodations face a sandy beach, where you can participate in such water sports as windsurfing, waterskiing, and sailing. Two tennis courts are lit at night. An in-house disco, Lucifer's, is a popular island nightspot.

Summer rates range from $70 to $80 daily in a single, from $90 to $100 in a double. In winter, the prices go up to $105 to $120 in a single, and $130 to $150 in a double. MAP supplement is $30 extra per person per day. The rooms are comfortable and the food good.

Taxi fare from the hotel to the main airport is set at $32.

Smugglers Village, Castries (tel. 452-0551), is a newish resort built on a flat, sandy area near the Steigenberger Cariblue hotel. Its bungalow accommodations are scattered over the surrounding landscape. The resort's core is a wooden building with decks from which you can look down on a free-form pool and the curved bay where smugglers used to bring in brandies, cognacs, and cigars from Martinique. A hexagonal wooden canopy covers the open-air bar which becomes a social center early in the day.

The Austrian-born manager, Helmut di Bernardo, operated a hotel in Kenya before coming here. He encourages tranquility and quiet, which is what the tile- and wood-accented bungalows offer in abundance. Each contains a kitchen, which residents can stock from the nearby minimarket. In winter, singles cost $85; doubles, $120. *In summer, the price of singles is $42, and doubles go for $65.* MAP can be arranged with the hotel for $20 extra per person per day.

A regular shuttle bus carries adventure-seeking guests to Rodney Bay and Reduit Beach.

Anse Chastanet, P.O. Box 216, Soufrière (tel. 454-7355), is a beachside hotel scattered along a hill site, above palm-fringed, lava-ash Anse Chastanet Beach, some two miles outside of Soufrière. General manager Peter N. Pietruszka provides 20 bungalows built in an octagonal shape. Some overlook the sea and the Pitons, those twin cones that soar abruptly from the sea. The core of the house is a small main building, with a bar and dining room, but there's also a beachside bar and restaurant as well. The latter comes in very handy, as it's 109 steps down to the sands. The climb back is Everest-like. When the sun grows too fierce there, you can always retreat under thatched bohíos. The place keeps you jogger-fit climbing up and down.

You can dine or drink on windswept terraces built along the hillside over the beach. Here the owner has provided tropical landscaping, with much use made of flowering bougainvillea, hibiscus, and allamander. The chalets have wrap-around terraces which frame views in every direction.

When a quartet of Canadians dropped anchor here many years ago and decided to build a hotel on the hillside-hugging site, many St. Lucians told them it couldn't be done. However, they succeeded, thanks to the poor laborers who had to lug up all that heavy material which had been dumped on the beach. Even if not elaborately decorated, some units have individuality. Cooling is by overhead fans or those sea breezes. In addition to the regular rooms, there are two villas with four bedrooms, two one-bedroom units, and two two-bedroom suites.

One room, described as "dark and jungle-like," sans view, has drawn the ire of at least two readers. It's to be avoided. In winter, a single rents for $116 daily; a double costs $128. *In summer, a single is $86 daily, with a double going for $104.* The MAP suplement is an extra $28 per person daily.

To reach the hotel requires some doing. It's about an hour and a half from the airport, a $35 taxi ride.

The **Islander,** P.O. Box 907, Rodney Bay (tel. 452-0255), is near Pat's Pub, the St. Lucian Hotel, and Reduit Beach. This well-recommended hotel has an entrance whose walls are festooned with hanging flowers. Botany-minded guests will appreciate the placques attached to plants throughout the property, giving the names of the various species that grow here in abundance. Many of the accommodations were completed in 1984, making them among the more up-to-date facilities on the island. All of this was open savanna before it became the ever-expanding hotel.

A brightly painted fishing boat serves as a buffet table near the pool, and there's a spacious covered bar area perfect for socializing with the owner, Greg Glacé. Mr. Glacé built this attractive property and serves as restaurateur and manager, using experience he gained during sojourns in Rochester, Los Angeles, New York, and Miami, before returning to St. Lucia.

Many of the accommodations are named after different Caribbean islands. Guests walk a few hundred feet to the beach and to shop in nearby markets, cooking, living, and entertaining in their compact yet tasteful self-contained units, each of which contains a kitchenette and private bath. In winter, daily rates are around $78 in a single, $99 in a double. *In summer, the tariffs are $36 in a single, $48 in a double.* Children under 12 stay free in their parents' room. Taxes and service are extra. A discount is given for stays of a full week.

Accommodations look over a grassy courtyard sheltered with vines and flowers, with a network of walkways leading to the convivial restaurant. There, the Friday-night barbecue is popular, costing EC$40 ($15.20) per person for grilled fish, steak, pork, and chicken. Other evenings, the Caribbean pepperpot dinners cost EC$30 ($11.40) per person, drawing an enthusiastic crowd of local residents as well as the hotel guests.

For reservations and information, call 212/840-6636 in New York City.

East Winds Inn, P.O. Box 193, Castries (tel. 452-8212), is a beach-comberish place on a private, white, powdery strand at La Brellotte Bay, a five-mile drive from Vigie Airport or Castries. The manager, Sylvia Marcellin, runs this beach haven in a relaxed, casual way, but has a sharp eye for anticipating the needs of her guests.

Tucked among sea grape, lime trees, oleander, wood rose, casuarinas, bright-red ixia, bougainvillea, and bird cages with parrots and parakeets are spacious and airy, hexagonal-shaped, wood cone-roofed cottages, all with kitchenettes, tile baths (with step-down tub and shower), even a thatched umbrella in the bohío style on your patio. Cooled by overhead fans, units are really thatched huts. The furnishings—wicker armchairs, rush rugs placed over cement floors—are not stylish in any way, but the units are clean and comfortable.

In winter, singles can stay here for $80 daily, from $90 in a double. *Summer rates go way down to $44 in a single, $52 in a double.* If you want to, say, prepare lunch for yourself, you need pay only another $22 per person for breakfast and dinner at the open seaside dining room and bar which serves a mixed West Indian and Stateside cuisine. You might get gazpacho one day, cold breadfruit soup the next, red snapper creole style, or local Caribbean lobster. The fish is very fresh and local men haul their pirogues right up on the sands, bringing dolphin perhaps, and someone from the kitchen picks out what the East Winds wants for dinner that night. The banana bread has been called "the best in the world."

Most people spend the day here in their bathing suits, and don't get much more formal in the evening. The Egerers have snorkeling equipment for your use, or else you can enjoy a book from their large lending library.

Harmony Apartel, P.O. Box 155, Castries (tel. 452-8756), near Rodney Bay Lagoon, is an attractive collection of two-story buildings outfitted with 21 big-windowed accommodations. More than half of these contain two bedrooms and one or two baths, while nine are studio efficiency apartments. Each has a kitchenette, a patio, and a token-operated air-conditioning system. The units are clustered around a pleasant swimming pool with a bar near by. The white sands of a wide beach are across the road. Visitors can cook in their rooms, shopping at a mini-mart not far away, or patronize the in-house restaurant. Winter rates are $55 for two persons in a studio, $80 in a one-bedroom unit, and $90 in a two-bedroom apartment suitable for four persons. Service and tax are extra. *Expect reductions of around 25% in summer, when promotional deals sometimes offer three weeks for the price of two.*

Caribbees Apartment Hotel, P.O. Box 547, La Pensée, Castries (tel. 452-2359). Accommodations in this well-landscaped apartment complex are set end to end under a series of angular roofs. Each comes with a fully equipped kitchenette, private bath, phone, and air conditioning. A garden-style open-air restaurant is near the swimming pool, while many water sports, a car-rental facility, and a mini-market are on the premises. The hotel offers transportation service to Vigie Beach, a five-minute drive. In winter, the simply furnished units rent for $42 in a single, $66 in a double, $78 in a triple, and $90 in a quad. *In summer, singles cost $30; doubles, $42; triples, $54; and quads, $66.* MAP can be arranged for an additional $25 per person per day.

The **Green Parrot Hotel,** Red Tape Lane, Morne Fortune (Good Luck Hill; tel. 452-3167). Connected to the Green Parrot restaurant, this hillside series of balconied accommodations winds sinuously up the side of one of the steepest slopes in Castries. Flanking both sides of the pathways are masses of flowering shrubs and vines, as well as a menagerie of monkeys in chicken-wire cages. (Be careful—they bite!) Near the top of the complex, the landscape architects designed a terraced swimming pool, where guests lounge in comfortable chairs with views of the harbor far below. A courtesy bus makes runs to the beach daily except Saturday. A sunken bar is set into the floor of the Pool Room restaurant, where no one minds if patrons show up in their bathing suits.

The 38 accommodations include a handful of apartments with kitchens. All of them are reached via brick-lined hallways whose sides are pierced with breezeway arches that open onto a view of the forest. In winter, singles cost $70, while doubles go for $105. *In summer, singles are $40, and doubles, $65.* A third person can stay in any double for an additional $30 to $35 per night. MAP supplements can be arranged for an extra $22 in the Pool Room restaurant and an extra $32 in the main restaurant. These prices do not include service and tax.

WHERE TO DINE: If possible, try to break free of your resort hotel and dine in one of St. Lucia's little character-loaded restaurants. The local food is excellent, including such West Indian specialties as pumpkin soup, fried flying fish, stuffed crab back, and stuffed breadfruit, as well as the inevitable callaloo soup.

In Castries
The **Green Parrot,** Red Tape Lane at Morne Fortune (Good Luck Hill; tel. 452-3167), about a mile and a half from the center, overlooks Castries harbor. Your ascent from downtown will take about 12 minutes. Once you get there, the effort will have been worth it as this is an elegant choice for dining. It's the home of its chef, Harry, who got his long years of training in prestigious restaurants and hotels in London, including Claridges.

Guests take their time and make an evening of it. Many enjoy a before-dinner drink in the Victorian-style salon near a talkative green cockatoo (caged) which Harry claims has been here almost as long as he has. The price of a meal in the English-style dining room includes entertainment: Harry can not only cook, he is also an entertainer of some note. Show nights are Wednesday and Saturday, beginning at around 10:30 p.m. They feature limbo dancers and fire-eaters, followed by music for dancing. Another special night is Monday—ladies' night. A woman who wears a flower in her hair, when accompanied by a man in a coat and tie, receives a free dinner. Everybody can listen to the music of the Shac-Shac band.

All of this may sound gimmicky, but the food doesn't suffer because of all the activity. There's an emphasis on St. Lucian specialties, using home-grown produce when it's available. The countertop of a stone platform in the dining room usually overflows with almost a week's supply, decoratively displayed like a Renaissance still-life. Try the christophine au gratin (a Caribbean squash with cheese) or the creole soup made with callaloo and pumpkin. There are also five kinds of curry with chutney as well as a selection of omelets and sandwiches at lunchtime. Some of the American guests seem to go for the steaks or the daily specials. Full meals cost around $25 and up.

To precede your meal you might enjoy a house special, the Grass Parrot (made from coconut cream, crème de menthe, bananas, white rum, and sugar). It costs around EC$11 ($4.18). If you choose it instead of a more conservative drink, you'll be in good company, since it's rumored to have been sampled by Michael Caine, Princess Margaret, and many of the prime ministers of the Caribbean islands.

Rain, Columbus Square (tel. 452-3022), has a touch of nostalgia, named as it is for that old Somerset Maugham story made into a film where Joan Crawford with her alarmingly enlarged lips did away forever with the rosebud mouth. Going behind its palm green and white facade and under its tin roof, you expect any of the actresses who played Sadie suddenly to come through the door—Gloria Swanson, June Havoc, Jeanne Eagles, Tallulah Bankhead, Rita Hayworth.

The inspired creation was the idea of Al Haman, a former advertising man. "Under one roof" he installed a bar, restaurant, and boutique, the latter selling batiks, sarongs, custom-designed bikinis, whatever. A popular rendezvous point, particularly with expatriates on the island, Rain keeps to the Maugham decor of ceiling fans, louvered doors, peacock chairs, and oil lamps. Try to head for the second-floor balcony—a gingerbread-frilled upper gallery—if you're dining. There you can not only order food, but can enjoy a view over the town square and its famous spreading saman tree. One day some lucky guests were treated to the sight of lovely Sophia Loren shopping in the ground-floor boutique while on the island for the filming of *Fire Power*. Rain catered for the crew, including such co-stars as James Coburn, O. J. Simpson, George Grizzard, and Anthony Franciosa.

Menus are chalked up on blackboards, and you read them when not looking at faded posters of *Mommie Dearest*. If you don't dine on the candlelit upper floor, you might prefer a nook in the garden courtyard, where an array of pizzas and pasta dishes are available in casually informal surroundings at bargain prices.

Good cooks turn out a repertoire of home-cooking in the evening that includes not only Stateside dishes, but West Indian specialties such as dolphin St-Jacques, pepperpot, stuffed crab, beef curries, and shrimp creole. The salads are crisp and fresh with tangy dressing. The homemade ice creams are mouthwatering, especially soursop which is featured in season. Aside from wine, expect to pay about $25 per person for dinner. Lunches cost from $12. Among drinks, I recommend such rum refreshers as Sadie's Sin and the Reverend's Downfall! Rain is closed Sunday and holidays.

Coal Pot, Gantner's Bay (tel. 452-5643), enjoys a waterside perch at historic Vigie Marina, and from that position attracts the yachting set or any stray boaters in the area. Set on its own wharf, the Coal Pot opens onto harbor views. Nautical touches abound, as in the fishnet-draped bar.

The Cordon Bleu and creole menu leans, naturally, to fresh seafood dishes, which are generally well prepared here, depending on what's available from the local catch. Lobster and flying fish are traditionally featured. Ask the owner about the wine list, reputed to be the best in St. Lucia. You might begin your meal by ordering the bartender's special, a Naked Virgin, made with a blend of OJ, rum, Galliano, and cream of coconut. One, I assure you, is enough. Expect to pay from $20 per person for dinner.

Le Boucan, Columbus Square (tel. 452-2415), is a local restaurant and bar, with a sidewalk café that is a casual rendezvous point for morning shoppers in Castries. If you come just for a drink, make it soursop, golden apple, or passionfruit juice or any of the delicious local fruit drink specials. If you stick around for a full lunch, snack, or dinner, that's possible too, and the price is right: about $12 more or less for a meal, depending on your selection. The food is simple and good, with emphasis on fresh local flavor as reflected by the curried shrimp, very fresh fish, creole lobster, and juicy steaks. Chicken Boucan is a specialty. It is open Monday to Saturday from 10 a.m. to 2 p.m. and 6 to 10 p.m. Thursday night is folk food night.

Calabash, Mongiraud Street (tel. 452-2864), is an unpretentious little eatery which serves inexpensive meals, a dinner costing from $12. Casually dressed people come here for the inviting, friendly atmosphere and polite service, and because they know they can get good creole cooking. The seafood is fresh, and juicy hamburgers are served along with such familiar fare as pork chops. Hours are from 9 a.m. to 11 p.m. The place has an old-English-pub atmosphere.

Pisces Restaurant, Choc Bay (tel. 452-5898), serves some of the best food on the island, in an unlikely location at the top of a forbiddingly steep flight of steps from the road just opposite the Halcyon Beach Club. Tables are set on a terraced balcony of a stucco building high above the graveled parking lot near the sea. Opened in 1980 by Eden Elius Xavier ("Eddie," to his friends), who was born under the sign of Pisces, assisted by Lawrence Hilton, also a Pisces, the establishment produces food that includes the best crab backs on the island, savory lobster in season, a shrimp creole worth writing home about, and my favorite island drink, a White Pigeon, made with vodka, white crème de menthe, milk, and bananas. Many of the accoutrements here are shaped like fish. All of the produce and practically everything except the shrimp (from Guyana) and the sirloin is locally produced. Full meals cost from EC$60 ($22.80) up, although snacks and sandwiches can come to EC$15 ($5.70) for a filling holdover. It is open every day, and you get two drinks for the price of one at happy hour from 5:30 to 6:30 p.m.

In Soufrière

The Still (tel. 454-7224) is the first thing you'll see as you drive up the hill from the harbor of Soufrière. It's a very old rum distillery set on a platform of thick timbers. The front garden blossoms with avocado pears, and a mahogany forest is a few steps away. All of this contributes to the country ambience of this stone-walled restaurant where Michael and Monica Du Boulay serve their freshly cooked specialties. The bar near the front veranda is furnished with glossy tables cut from cross sections of tropical tree trunks. A more formal and very spacious dining room is nearby. A three-course lunch costs around EC$25 ($9.50) and might include chicken, pepperpot, pork chops, or fish. A buffet, when available, costs EC$20 ($7.60) per person, while a chicken or fish salad plate is available for $11 each. Lunch and dinner are served every day. If you're coming with a big party, it's wise to phone ahead.

Captain Hooks Hideaway (tel. 454-7328) occupies what used to be a beautiful old French great house built some 150 years ago on the southwest coast. A restaurant and bar have been erected on the ruins. St. Lucian dishes and American specialties are served, and the food is well prepared, the ingredients carefully selected. You eat near a backyard fig tree, trimmed with conch shells.

I usually ignore the American dishes and concentrate instead on the mouthwatering Caribbean specialties, including a real Amerindian "pepperpot," my favorite, and fried plantain, along with langouste (local lobster). Fresh fish and vegetables change with the season, but breadfruit is most often available, as is lambi (conch). Expect to pay from EC$25 ($9.50) for dinner. Occasionally "brigands barbecues" are featured, and potent rum punches are served in the Skull & Crossbones Bar. An unusual selection of St. Lucian handicrafts is for sale.

The **Hummingbird** (tel. 454-7232) was named for the tiny, darting birds that fly around this restaurant and its adjoining boutique, which sells merchandise carefully handmade by owner Joan Alexander. An outdoor pool is free for use by persons who drop into the restaurant for a meal or just a drink. Patrons have included everyone from Mick Jagger to Christina Onassis.

The ceiling is covered with seafan coral. A few larger-than-life wooden statues of mermaids support the thatch roof in back, and near the entrance is a rock garden with a woodcarving made from the stump of a poinciana tree when its roots started interfering with the foundations of the building.

The wide-ranging menu features many tempting drinks (for example, a Hummingbird Hangover made of sambuca, golden rum, orange juice, and bitters) as well as such international food specialties as curry, English, Indian, or West Indian dishes including seafood crêpes, ceviche (raw marinated fish), beef Stroganoff, steak Diane, and chateaubriand. Full meals cost around EC$60 ($22.80).

The boutique, selling hand-painted batiks and silkscreen fabrics by Joan, is one of the best stores on the island for creations of women's clothes, wall hangings, and table services of a rare beauty.

Rodney Bay

Pat's Pub (tel. 452-8314) wouldn't exactly pass for a pub in the English Midlands, what with its native island music, the masses of bougainvillea, the open-air architecture, and the suntanned yacht enthusiasts. This sophisticated ambience draws upon the past experience of Elizabeth Dawson as the owner of a yacht charter service in Jamaica and a former English resident of West Africa.

At dinner, you might begin with a homemade pâté or crabe farcie, perhaps a homemade soup of the day. The main courses always include fresh fish of the day, lobster (when available), grilled prime sirloin steak, and beef Stroganoff, these dishes served with rice or potatoes and fresh vegetables. One of the chef's specialties is fondue bourgignonne, but most guests come here for the charbroiled steaks. Side orders of tasty garlic bread are invariably ordered. For dessert, you get a real English trifle with lots of sherry. Dinners cost around EC$75 ($28.50). A simple lunch is served every day for EC$40 ($15.20). Drinks cost EC$6.50 ($2.47).

Reservations are preferred for dinner, although no one minds if you drop into the bar area to mingle with the informal mariners waiting for the three-times-weekly evening music to begin. One of the singers, Boo Hinkson, is reputed to be the best in the Windward Islands, and Ms. Dawson sometimes joins in. The pub is open every day of the week except on Sunday at lunch.

The **Charthouse**, Rodney Bay (tel. 452-8115), is set in a large grange-like building with a skylit ceiling, thick teak tables, and blue and white upholstery. It's built several feet above the bobbing yachts of Rodney Bay, without walls, to allow an optimum view of the water. Its exterior is crafted from weathered planking into a series of pleasingly soft angles whose corners are masked with masses of hanging plants. Nautical charts of the region adorn the walls, reflecting the marine interests of Nick Ashworth, the Irish-born owner. Full meals, costing from EC$95 ($36.10), might include callaloo soup, St. Lucian crab backs, surf and turf, shrimp creole, local lobster (in season, a choice of local fish, and well-prepared steaks. The restaurant is open daily except Sunday.

An art gallery in a wood-sided building a few steps up the hill offers before-lunch diversions. Run by Paula, formerly of Memphis, Tennessee, the gallery sells paintings by local artists as well as by artists throughout the Caribbean. The gallery is open daily except Sunday from 9 a.m. to 1 p.m.

Marigot Bay

Dolittle's, Marigot Bay (tel. 452-4246), was named for the Rex Harrison movie which created a lot of local excitement but didn't generate that much interest from worldwide audiences. But it's a name that still means a lot around here. This popular restaurant, rated among the top three in St. Lucia, is right on the beach. You reach it by a miniature ferryboat which leaves every 20 minutes from the Marigot jetty. If it doesn't, sound your horn three times. That's the signal for the ferry to come over and pick you up.

Once at Dolittle's, you can also swim or snorkel before lunch or dinner. Before your meal, try their local bartender's specialty, called a "Love Bird." This is a mixture of fresh "paw-paw" (papaya to us), Sabra orange liqueur, cream, Cherry Heering, and a local rum.

A yachting crowd drops in here, and the place has a congenial atmosphere.

Perhaps you'll be there for one of their Caribbean evenings. On one night a big bowl of steaming callaloo soup was served in a big pot. Guests helped themselves.

Some of the St. Lucian specialties served include marinated red snapper, and you're given skewers of shrimp and beef which you cook yourselves over hot coals in the shish-kebab fashion. Locally grown vegetables such as christophine (a Caribbean squash) are also served, followed by homemade ice creams in unusual flavors. Expect to spend at least EC$60 ($22.80), maybe more, for a complete meal.

WHAT TO SEE: Towns, beaches, bays, bananas—even a volcano are here to visit.

Castries

The capital city has grown up around its harbor which occupies the crater of an extinct volcano. Charter captains and the yachting set drift in here, and large cruise ship wharfs welcome vessels from around the world. Because of those devastating fires mentioned earlier, the town today has a fresh, new look, its sterile glass-and-concrete (or steel) buildings replacing the French colonial or Victorian look typical of many West Indian capitals.

The **Saturday-morning market** in the old tin-roofed building on Jeremy Street in Castries is my favorite "people-watching" site on the island. Country women dress up in their traditional garb of cotton headdress and come into town for the occasion, which makes it all seem carnival-festive. The number of knotted points on top reveals their marital status (ask one of the locals to explain it to you). The luscious fresh fruits and vegetables of St. Lucia are sold, as again, weather-beaten men sit close by playing warrie, which is a fast pre-video game of pebbles on a carved board. You can also pick up St. Lucia handicrafts here, such as baskets and unglazed pottery.

Government House is a charming late Victorian building, and a Roman Catholic cathedral stands on Columbus Square, which has a few restored buildings.

Beyond Government House lies **Morne Fortune,** the name meaning "Hill of Good Luck." No one had much luck here, certainly not the battling French and British fighting for Fort Charlotte. The barracks and guard rooms changed nationalities many times. You can visit the 18th-century barracks complete with a military cemetery, a small museum, the Old Powder Magazine, and the "Four Apostles Battery" (the apostles being a quartet of grim muzzle-loading cannons). The view of the harbor of Castries is spectacular. You can see north to Pigeon Island or south to the Pitons.

Pigeon Point

This island is connected to the mainland of St. Lucia by a man-made causeway off Gros Islet Bay, on the west coast. Pirates such as 'Old Wooden Leg' used it as a retreat, as did Admiral Rodney's British fleet much later. It was from here that Rodney sailed to defeat De Grasse at the Battle of the Saints. Historic ruins of forts can still be seen. The island is called pigeon in honor of Rodney's hobby of breeding the birds here. There are also remnants of the Arawak Indians on the island. It's a perfect place for a picnic, after which you can go for a swim from its white sandy beaches.

Marigot Bay

Movie companies such as Rex Harrison's *Dr. Doolittle* or Sophia Loren's *Fire Power* like to use this bay, one of the most beautiful in the Caribbean, for background shots. It's narrow yet navigable for any size yacht. Here Admiral Ridney camouflaged his ships with palm leaves while lying in wait for French frigates. The shore, lined with palm trees, remains relatively unspoiled, but some building sites have been sold. Again, it's a delightful spot for a picnic if you didn't take your food basket to Pigeon Island.

Soufrière

This little fishing port, St. Lucia's second-largest settlement, is dominated by two pointed hills called **Petit Piton** and **Gros Piton.** These two hills, "The Pitons," have become the very symbol of St. Lucia. They are two volcanic cones rising to 2460 and 2619 feet. Once actively volcanic, they are now clothed in green vegetation. Their rise sheer from the sea makes them a spectacular landmark visible for miles around. Formed of lava and rock, they are the remains of St. Lucia's once-active volcanos. Waves crash around their bases.

In the vicinity of Soufrière lies the famous "drive-in" volcano. Called **Mt. Soufrière,** it's a rocky lunar landscape of bubbling mud and craters seething with fuming sulfur. You literally drive your car into an old (millions of years) crater, parking the vehicle and walking between the sulfur springs and pools of hissing steam. A local guide is usually waiting beside them shrouded with sulfurous fumes that are said to have medicinal properties. For a small fee, he'll point out the blackened waters which are among the few of their kind in the Caribbean.

Nearby are the **Diamond Mineral Baths,** surrounded by a tropical arboretum. Constructed on orders of Louis XVI in 1784, whose doctors told him that these waters were similar in mineral content to the waters at Aix-les-Bains, they were intended for recuperative effects for French soldiers fighting in the West Indies. Later destroyed, they were rebuilt after World War II. They have an average temperature of 106° and lie near one of the geological attractions of the island, a waterfall which changes colors (from yellow to black to green to gray) several times a day. For EC$5 ($1.90), you can bathe and benefit from the recuperative effects. This boiling caldron has not rained down any catastrophes to date, unlike its neighbors in St. Vincent and Martinique.

From Soufrière in the southwest, the road wends toward Fond St. Jacques where you'll have a good view of mountains and villages as you cut through St. Lucia's **Moule-à-Chique** tropical rain forest. You'll see the Barre de l'Isle divide.

Moule-à-Chique

At the southern tip of the island, Moule-à-Chique is where the Caribbean Sea merges with the Atlantic. This is the southernmost tip of St. Lucia, and the town of Vieux Fort can be seen, as can the neighboring island of St. Vincent, 26 miles away.

Banana Plantations

Bananas are the island's leading export. As you're being hauled around the island by a taxi driver, ask him to take you to one of these huge plantations which allow visitors to come on the grounds. I suggest a sightseeing look at one of the trio of big ones—the Cul-de-Sac, just north of Marigot Bay; La Caya, in Dennery on the East Coast; and the Roseau Estate, south of Marigot Bay.

THE SPORTING LIFE: Since most of the island hotels are built right on the beach, you won't have far to go for swimming. I prefer the beaches along the western coast. On the windward side, a rough surf makes swimming at least potentially dangerous. Pigeon Island, off the north shore, is a fine beach, as is Vigie, just north of the harbor of Castries. For a novelty, you might try the black volcanic sand at Soufrière. The beach there is called **La Toc.**

Snorkeling and Scuba

Arrangements for most water sports are made at your hotel. **La Toc, East Winds, Steigenberger Cariblue,** and **St. Lucian** are particularly well equipped for these sports.

Dive St. Lucia, P.O. Box 412, Vigie, Castries (tel. 452-4127), is a top-quality independent operator. Internationally certified instructors give an introductory scuba course for $55 and individual dives for certified divers go for $45. Equipment is supplied by the dive company. Accommodation and dive packages can also be arranged. In addition, snorkeling trips with all equipment can be provided for $18. Six-dive packages cost $185.

In Soufrière, the **Anse Chastenet Hotel,** P.O. Box 216 (tel. 454-7354), employs three professional PADI instructors who offer dive programs two or three times a day. Some of the most spectacular coral reefs in St. Lucia—many only 10 to 20 feet below the surface of the water—lie a short distance from the hotel's beach. Photographic equipment is available for rent (film can be processed on the premises), and instruction is offered in picture taking in price ranges depending on the time and equipment involved. An introductory three-hour course begins at $55. Single-tank dives, with all equipment included, cost $30; two-tank dives, $50; and a night dive, $35. An introductory lesson first-timers is $40. Experienced divers can rent the equipment they need on a per-item basis. One of the establishment's better bargains is its nonrefundable, nontransferable group rates for six or more persons diving together. With back tank, backpack, and weight belt included, each dive costs $22, while a package of 12 dives is $180 per person, when all six divers organize their dives together. Through participation in the establishment's "specialty" courses, divers can obtain PADI certification.

Horseback Riding

You can hire a horse at **Cap Estate Stables.** To make arrangements, call René Trim at 452-8626. The cost is EC$50 ($19) per 1½ hours. As an added feature, you can ask about a picnic trip to the Atlantic, with a barbecue lunch and drink included. Departures are at 10:15 a.m. on horseback, the return at 3:30 p.m. Nonriders can be included too, as they are transported to the site in a van. A rider pays EC$85 ($32.30) per person; a nonrider, EC$45 ($17.10).

Tennis

Most of the big hotels have their own courts. If yours doesn't, ask at the front desk for the nearest one. Some of the courts on St. Lucia are lit for night games for those who'd like to avoid the midday sun.

Golf

St. Lucia has two golf courses. A nine-hole one is at the **Cap Estate Golf Club** (tel. 452-8317) at the northern end of the island, and the larger one is at **Hotel La Toc** (tel. 452-3081), one of my featured recommendations toward the south. Non-residents are charged $7.50 per hour, but if you're a guest at La Toc it is included free. Clubs are leased out for $7.50 daily, and a St. Lucian caddy would like at least $2 per game on a nine-hole course.

Deep-Sea Fishing

The waters around St. Lucia are known for their gamefish, including the wahoo. Most of the major hotels can make arrangements for these. Among the independent operators, your best bet is **Dive St. Lucia,** P.O. Box 412, Vigie (tel.

452-4127). A maximum of four sportsmen will be taken out on a four-hour trip for around $175.

SHOPPING: Stores are generally open from 8 a.m. to 4 p.m., except Sunday. Most of the shopping is in Castries, where the principal streets are William Peter Boulevard and Bridge Street. Many stores will sell you goods at duty-free prices (providing you don't take the merchandise with you but have it delivered instead to the airport). There are some good buys—not remarkable—in bone china, jewelry, perfume, watches, liquor, and crystal. Souvenir items include bags and mats, local pottery, and straw hats, again nothing remarkable.

The **West Indian Sea Island Cotton Shop,** Bridge Street (tel. 452-3674), designs and creates original batik artwork entirely by hand. Wall hangings and clothing are among their merchandise which is exclusively available in the West Indies.

Bagshaws, just outside Castries, at La Toc (tel. 452-2139), are the leading hand-print silkscreeners. An American, Sydney Bagshaw, and family have devoted their considerable skills to turning out a line of fabric that are as colorful as the Caribbean. The birds and flowers of St. Lucia are incorporated into their designs. Linen placemats, men's shirts, women's skirts, wall handings, and dress kits are good buys. Each creation is an original Bagshaw design.

Rain Boutique, Columbus Square (tel. 452-3022; see my restaurant recommendation), is fashionable and petit. In the corner of this virtual landmark restaurant, the boutique promises that you can "sip and sup while you shop." Chicly styled cotton clothing is offered. Even Sophia Loren bought some of her clothes here, and O. J. Simpson dropped in too for some resortwear.

Y. de Lima's, William Peter Boulevard (tel. 452-2898), has a good range of jewelry in gold and silver, as well as an array of Swiss watches, cameras, and binoculars, all at duty-free prices.

Noah's Arkade, Post Office Lane, Bridge Street (tel. 452-2523), has an array of Caribbean handicrafts and gifts. Many of these are routine tourist items, yet you'll often find something interesting if you browse enough—local straw placemats and rugs, wall hangings, sandals, maracas, steel drums, shell necklaces, and warri boards. Many of the hotels have branches of this emporium. It's run by Mr. and Mrs. Arthur Skerrett.

St. Lucia Perfumes, Red Tape Lane, Morne Fortune (tel. 452-3890), next door to the Green Parrot restaurant, manufactures its own scents from local varieties of spices and flowers. Merchandise includes toilet waters and perfumes made from local essences such as vanilla, lime, sweet orange, musk, bergamot, anise, and frangipani. An adjacent room sells bathing suits and imaginative women's clothes from batiks and silkscreens. Open every weekday from 8:30 a.m. to 4:30 p.m., it closes at 1:30 p.m. on Saturday and all day Sunday.

Eudovic Art Studio, Goodlands, Morne Fortune (tel. 452-2747). Eudovic is a local artist and woodcarver whose sculptures have been exhibited in the O.A.S. headquarters in Washington, D.C., and have gained an increasing island fame. He usually carves his imaginative free-form sculptures from local tree roots, such as cobary, mahogany, and red cedar, and follows the natural pattern, sanding the grain until it's of almost satin smoothness. Prices range from EC$200 ($76). The studio is open seven days a week.

NIGHTLIFE: There isn't much except the entertainment offered by hotels. If your hotel is silent and you're in the mood for action, ask at your front desk what other hotel might be planning entertainment that evening. In the winter months, at least one hotel offers a steel band, calypso music, whatever, at least every night of the week. Otherwise, check to see what's happening at **Rain** (tel.

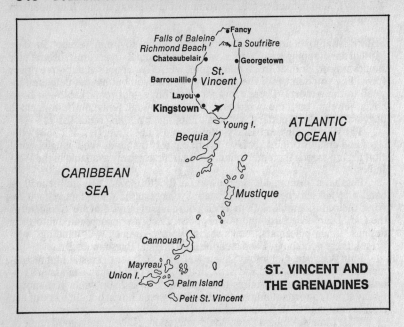

452-3022) and the **Green Parrot** (tel. 452-3167)—see the restaurant recommendations.

    Lucifer's, St. Lucian Hotel (tel. 452-8351), one of the best discos on the island, has a decor like a simulated version of the infernos of hell. Banquettes and love seats are cozily strewn amid roughly textured cave rocks, while stalactites hang from the ceiling, whose crevices glow with eerie red lights. This place can get crowded around 11 every evening, when guests from the Steigenberger Cariblue and Couples drop in for disco, calypso, or reggae. If you don't want beer at EC$5 ($1.90) or a gin and tonic at EC$6.50 ($2.47), you might try the house special, a St. Lucian Hurricane (grenadine, lime juice, sugar syrup, Cointreau, and rum) or a Pigeon Island Drum (lime juice, syrup, orange juice, brandy, white rum, bitters, and grenadine). There's a cover charge of EC$6 ($2.28) on Tuesday, Wednesday, and Thursday, and EC$12 ($4.56) on Friday and Saturday. Guests of the St. Lucian Hotel enter free. You get two drinks for the price of one during happy hour, from midnight to 1 a.m. daily. The disco opens every Tuesday through Saturday at 9 p.m.

3. St. Vincent

    An emerald island 18 miles long and 12 miles wide, St. Vincent was discovered by Columbus in 1498 on his third voyage. If the explorer had gone on a field expedition, and assuming he hadn't been devoured by the cannibalistic Caribs, he would have discovered an island of natural beauty.

    Amazing for such a small area, St. Vincent has fertile valleys, rich forests, lush jungles, rugged peaks, waterfalls, foam-whitened beaches, outstanding coral reefs (with what experts say is some of the world's clearest water), a volcano nestled in the sky and usually capped by its own private cloud, and 4000 feet up, Crater Lake.

    Fierce, aggressive, warlike, the Caribs held out longer on St. Vincent against the tide of European colonization than they did almost anywhere else. However, in a 1763 treaty the British won the right to possess the island. In 1779 French troups invaded. At the Treaty of Versailles in 1783 they gave it back to His Majesty's colonists.

A few years later Captain Bligh set off on the *Bounty* from England, going to Tahiti. There he loaded his vessel with breadfruit seedlings. Faced with mutiny, and after great difficulties (described in many historical novels), the captain in 1793 reached St. Vincent with his seedlings. The breadfruit trees took fantastically to St. Vincentian soil, earning for the island the title of "the Tahiti of the Caribbean."

In 1795, during the French Revolution, St. Vincent suffered yet another invasion. French revolutionaries, allied with the Caribs, burned British plantations and made a fierce war, only to be defeated by British forces the following year. The Caribs were rounded up and shipped off to British Honduras in Central America, where their descendants live to this day. The British decided St. Vincent was too small for both planters and Indians.

The island has remained under "Rule Britannia" from that day since, until it achieved statehood within the Commonwealth in 1969.

One of the major Windward Islands, it is only now awakening to tourism, which hasn't yet reached massive dimensions. Sailors and the yachting set have long known of St. Vincent and its satellite bays and beaches in the Grenadines. Trade winds keep the island cool all year, and the tropical temperature is in the 78° to 82° Fahrenheit range.

Much of its interior is inhabited and cultivated with coconut and banana groves. Arrowroot, often used as a thickening in baby foods, grows in abundance.

Unspoiled by the worst fallout which mass tourism sometimes brings, the people are very friendly and actually trest visitors like people, providing that courtesy is returned.

GETTING THERE: In the Eastern Caribbean, St. Vincent—the "gateway to the Grenadines" (see the next section)—lies 100 miles west of Barbados, where most visitors from North America fly first, making connections that will take them on to St. Vincent and the Grenadines. For transportation from North America to Barbados, refer to the "Getting There" section of the next chapter.

From Barbados, you can connect with a **LIAT** flight to St. Vincent. The flight from Barbados takes just 40 minutes, and at least two of them go out daily. LIAT also flies in from Trinidad, St. Lucia, and Martinique.

There is an airport, of course, at St. Vincent, but also a small one at Mustique, Union Island, and Canouan.

WINLINK, a charter service, also operates scheduled flights between St. Lucia and St. Vincent, going on to Union Island. In addition, **Inter-Island Air Services,** another charter company, also has scheduled runs between St. Lucia, St. Vincent, and on to Union Island where launch service can be used to take you on to Palm Island or Petit St. Vincent.

If you're not flying to the Grenadines, you can go by a boat, the M.V. *Grenadine Star,* which leaves St. Vincent twice daily for the Grenadines. Another vessel, *Friendship,* goes from St. Vincent to Bequia.

PRACTICAL FACTS: British customs are predominant, but with a distinct West Indian flair. Those invading French troops have also left their legacy, and Gallic cultural influences remain as delightful traces. English is the official language, of course, yet there's a French patois spoken on a number of the Grenadines, including St. Vincent.

Visitors arriving should have **proof of identity** and a return or ongoing ticket, providing they are either Canadian or U.S. citizens. The official **currency** of St. Vincent is the Eastern Caribbean dollar, or "Bee Wee," as it's called, worth about 38¢ in U.S. terms. *Note:* Most of the quotations in this chapter appear in U.S. dollars. Most restaurants, shops, and hotels will accept payment in American dollars or travelers checks.

Electric current is 220/240 volts, 50 cycles, AC, so you'll need an adapter. Some hotels have voltage converters, but it's best to bring your own.

Both St. Vincent and the Grenadines operate on **Atlantic Standard Time:** when it's 6 a.m. in St. Vincent, it's 5 a.m. in Miami. During Daylight Saving Time, St. Vincent keeps the same time as the U.S. East Coast.

Banks are open from 8 a.m. to noon Monday to Thursday and from 8 a.m. to noon and 3 to 5 p.m. on Friday (always check, as each bank may vary these hours slightly).

Most **shops** are open Monday to Friday from 8 a.m. to 4 p.m. Stores generally close from noon to 1 p.m. for lunch. Saturday hours are 8 a.m. to noon.

There is a general **hospital** in Kingstown and a smaller hospital in Georgetown on the Windward Coast. The Kingstown Hospital is fully equipped with an operating room, X-ray department, dental and eye clinics.

The government imposes an airport **departure tax** of EC$10 ($3.80) per person. A 5% government **occupancy tax** is charged for all hotel accommodations; and in addition to that, most hotels as well as restaurants add a 10% or 15% **service charge.**

Special events include the week-long Carnival in early July, one of the largest in the eastern Caribbean, with steel band and calypso competitions, along with the crowning of the king and queen of carnival.

GETTING AROUND: The government sets the rates for fares, but **taxis** are unmetered. The wise passenger, however, will always ask the fare and agree upon the charge before getting in. Figure on spending about $7 to go from the St. Vincent Arnos Vale Airport to your hotel, maybe more. Of course, you should tip about 12% of the fare.

If you don't want to drive yourself, you can also hire taxis to take you to the island's major attractions. Most drivers seem to be well-informed guides (it doesn't take long to learn everything you need to know about St. Vincent). Figure on spending about $15 per hour for a car holding two to four passengers.

Buses

Flamboyantly painted "al fresco" buses also travel the principal arteries of St. Vincent, linking the major towns and villages. The price is really low, depending on where you're going, and the experience will connect you with the people of the island. At least you'll get to see a preview of what's being taken to market, perhaps a burlap bag of arrowroot.

Car Rentals

Rentals can be arranged. However, driving on St. Vincent is a bit of an adventure because of the narrow, twisting roads and the *drive-on-the-left* requirement. To go motoring like a Vincentian, you'll soon learn to sound your horn a lot as you make the sharp curves and turns. If you present your valid U.S. or Canadian driver's license at the police department, and pay an EC$5 ($1.90) fee, you'll obtain a temporary permit to drive Go to the police station on Bay Street in Kingstown.

Among the many leasing agents, **Car Rentals Ltd.**, on Halifax Street in Kingstown (tel. 456-1862), rents Mazdas and Fiat 125s. **Choice Garage,** Grenville Street in Kingstown (tel. 456-1883), rents Toyotas. The cost is about $40 per day, but you usually get the first 50 miles free.

WHERE TO STAY: Accommodations range from tropical villas on their own private island to a guest house built back in the plantation era serving creole cookery. Don't expect massive high-rise resorts here, as everything is kept small, and many Vincentians hope it will always be this way. The West Indian lifestyle prevails here. The places are comfortable, not fancy, and you usually get a lot of personal attention from the staffs.

Young Island, P.O. Box 211, Young Island (tel. 458-4826), is a 25-acre resort that might have attracted Gauguin. Instead of that artist, it was supposed to be where a Carib Indian chieftain kept his harem. A paradise island promising barefoot happiness, it lies just 200 yards off the south shore of St. Vincent, to which it is linked by a ferry to the mainland from the pier right on Villa Beach, a five-minute ride.

Tropical villas—25 deluxe, two luxury, and three suites—are set in a tropical garden of hibiscus, crotons, ferns, and white ginger, as well as giant almond, breadfruit, nutmeg, and mango trees. The beach, however, is of a brilliant white sand. Hammocks are hung under thatched roofs if you want to rest. Carib canoes and Sailfish await your use at the beach's edge. Island specials are served at the Coconut Bar, a thatched bohío on stilts which actually serves many of its drinks in fresh coconuts. The free-form pool is set into landscaped grounds.

You're housed in Tahitian cottages with a bamboo decor and outdoor showers. Floors are of seashells and terrazzo, covered by rush rugs. *In low season, single guests on half-board arrangements pay $140 to $190 daily, the cost going up to $175 to $225 daily in a double.* In high season, half board is required. At that time a single person pays from $245 to $345 a day, the cost rising to $280 to $380 in a double. Ask about package rates for lovers, under the categories of "young lovers" and "lucky lovers." These are exceptional bargain deals offered during the off-season periods. The food is well prepared, with an emphasis on lots of fresh fish and lobster and plenty of island-grown vegetables. Dining is by candlelight, and dress is informal.

The hotel has one tennis court, which is lit for night games. All water sports, such as scuba-diving and waterskiing, are available. At the far end of the beach there's a saltwater lagoon-like pool where you can hear parrots and macaws chattering.

On some nights the hotel transports guests over to the rock on its other island, Fort Duvemette, for a cocktail party. There hors d'oeuvres are cooked over charcoal pits, and a local band plays under torchlight. Sometimes a steel band plays for dancing after dinner, and you're serenaded by strolling singers.

Waterloo House, Orange Hill (tel. 458-6330), is a historic private home, an hour's drive from the airport. It is the architectural highlight of what is still one of the largest working plantations in the western hemisphere, more than 2500 acres. Its sweeping verandas overlook views of the surrounding hills, the Atlantic, and the Caribbean. Over the years, additional rooms have been added to the great house to accommodate a maximum of six paying guests, who often incorporate a visit here with hiking expeditions to the nearby volcano of La Soufrière. Meals and picnics can be arranged with the owners.

Cyril Barnard and his wife, Hazel, are gracious hosts. When they're not visiting with their children, each of whom has a modern house constructed somewhere within the family compound, they're occupied with their love of yachting and horse breeding. Many of their yachting victories happened off the shores of Trinidad or Barbados (dozens of trophies attest to their skill).

The Barnards real love, however, is the English colonial family manor whose elegantly eclectic mix of antique silver, empire furniture, and toile-covered sofas make for some of the most memorable interiors in St. Vincent. A visit here includes a tour of the enormous kitchen, which is big enough for barbecues. Year-round rates, with three meals a day included, are $100 daily for a single, $210 for a double. After a walk through the coconut groves, you can go for a dip in the pool.

Sunset Shores Beach Hotel, P.O. Box 849, in Villa, about four miles from Kingstown (tel. 458-4411), is an attractively landscaped cluster of vacation accommodations set on terraces which descend to a sandy beach. An oblong swimming pool, flanked with a covered bar, is set just below the low-lying accommodations. These contain comfortable beds, sliding glass doors, hanging wicker lamps, private baths, and air conditioning. In winter, single rooms on the MAP cost $110 to $125, while doubles on the MAP range from $160 to $180. Triples rent for $210, MAP included. *In summer, on the MAP, singles cost $85 to $100; doubles, $120 to $140; and triples, $180.* Children between 2 and 12 who stay with their parents pay $45 per day for MAP in any season. Taxes and service charges are extra. Sailing and snorkeling can be arranged at no additional cost.

Villa Lodge Hotel, P.O. Box 222, Indian Bay Beach (tel. 458-4641). Only ten rooms are contained within this former West Indian private home set about 100 yards above the beach. The establishment is dotted with verandas, latticework accents, and big windows to allow the breezes to blow in from the well-cultivated gardens outside. There's a swimming pool on the premises and a restaurant decorated in the style of the Far East. *In summer, the pleasant rooms cost from $70 in a single, $110 in a double, $140 in a triple, and $170 in a quad.* In winter, singles go for $90; doubles, $130; triples, $170; and quads, $200. All tariffs include MAP but not service and tax.

The **Cobblestone Inn,** P.O. Box 867, Kingstown (tel. 456-1937), right on the waterfront, is sometimes called "the local Ritz." A converted 1814 sugar warehouse (it once stored arrowroot). St. Vincent craftsmen have returned it to its original Georgian look, with its cobblestone walkways and arches. A large, open-air stone stairway takes you from an inside courtyard passage to the reception on the upper floor.

There you'll find second-floor bedrooms that would not surprise you if you came upon them in the middle of Sussex. These air-conditioned units (11 doubles, 6 singles) are attractively furnished in an old style, each with its own private bath. Plantation-style furnishings were hewn by local craftsmen. Many guests heading for the Grenadines overnight here, paying EC$100 ($38) daily in one of the small singles or EC$145 ($55.10) in a double, these tariffs in effect all year and including breakfast. Rooms open onto a corridor, with a view either of the town or of the harborfront.

The hotel is convenient for those who want an anchor close to town. However, you'll have to drive about three miles if you want to bathe on the beach. It might be casually run here, yet the service is excellent.

Grand View Beach Hotel, P.O. Box 173, Villa Point (tel. 458-4811). The owner-manager, F. A. ("Tony") Sardine, named this place well. The "grand view" promised is of islets, bays, yachts, Young Island, headlands, lagoons, and sailing craft. Villa Point lies just five minutes from the airport and ten minutes from Kingstown. On well-manicured grounds, it is set on eight acres of tropical gardens, with bougainvillea and frangipani. Tennis and squash courts and a swimming pool are available.

A converted private home, the hotel is a large, white, two-story mansion which has a dozen rooms with private baths to rent. Some of these are air-conditioned. Units are simply furnished, with flowery spreads and wood floors. Everything is maintained spotlessly, however, *In the off-season, singles rent for*

$49 daily; doubles, $66. In winter, rates go up to $70 daily in a single, $88 in a double. For breakfast and dinner, add another $30 per person to the tariff quoted.

For that you get a table d'hôte menu which changes every day. Most of the meals are based on fresh fish and island-grown vegetables. The cuisine is served in bountiful portions. The cookery is sometimes like a West Indian nouvelle cuisine style. The house is not on the beach, but sits on a hill. You have to go down to the shore for a swim.

With a name like Sardine, you might suspect that the owners came from Portugal, but that was so far back no one much remembers when.

Heron Hotel, P.O. Box 26, Kingstown (tel. 457-1631), is one of the finest West Indian-style guest houses in the British Windwards. Mrs. Doreen McKenzie is the beacon that attracts people, as she is known for her warmth and hospitality. This is the type of place where you can sit out drinking a rum swizzle on the "Planter's Porch," while watching the action on the banana boat pier.

Her 15 rooms come in all shapes and sizes, and they're located on the second floor. All units are air-conditioned and have private baths and telephones. They are kept spotless.

Year-round rates go from $35 daily in a single, $58 to $65 daily in a double, with breakfast and dinner included. Taxes and service are added to the bills.

Coconut Beach Hotel, P.O. Box 355 (tel. 458-4231), is relaxed and informal. Its two owners, Rita and Gordon Mathews, are from Naples, Florida. After reading the Wouk book, *Don't Stop the Carnival,* they claim they decided to live the sequel. Their ten-room inn lies at water's edge, just two minutes from the airport and less than five miles from Kingstown.

In winter, they accept MAP singles at $60 daily, the cost going up to $90 in a double. *Summer tariffs range from $48 daily in a single to $78 in a double,* all MAP. EP and CP are cheaper.

The place is warm and friendly and affectionately called "the Coconut." The rooms, simply furnished, are scattered about the palm-tree-studded grounds. Bright flowery prints enliven the decor.

The West Indian food is another good reason to book here—local kingfish, callaloo or pumpkin soup, stuffed breadfruit, tannia, and native yams, as well as fresh fruits, including papaya, soursop, and passionfruit. They also serve a Coconut Beach hamburger under a sheltering palm. At the bar you can order gin and coconut water.

They can make arrangements for snorkeling, sailing, exploring, and fishing for the likes of oldwife, blem, and hind, three types of fish not all that well known.

Mariner's Inn, Villa Beach (tel. 458-4287), is an old colonial-type hotel, where the atmosphere is relaxing and informal, the staff friendly and polite. In a tropical garden setting, the hotel lies directly on the beach, only two miles from the airport, four from Kingstown. The house is of the converted West Indian variety, with four-poster beds in most of the rooms, along with other typical Vincentian touches. The bar is the congregating point for many of the yachting set who anchor in the harbor.

From this south-shore perch, you'll have a clear view of Young Island as well as of yachts. The inn is very casual, the way the guests prefer it. The owner rents 15 rooms, which, on the half-board plan, are $95 daily in a double, $72 in a single in winter. *In summer, two persons can stay here on half-board terms at $80 per day, a single paying $50 on the same arrangement.* Rooms contain private baths, as well as homemade built-in furniture—minimal accoutrements.

Drinks are good and strong in the boat-bar, and the food in the outdoor dining room is also well prepared and plentiful. Tables overlook the Caribbean.

A steel band is sometimes brought in to play at "jump-ups," and the special Friday night barbecue is island famous.

Tropic Breeze Apartment Hotel, P.O. Box 761 (tel. 458-4631), lies a five-minute drive from the airport. In the hills on the Queen's Drive, east of Kingstown, the apartment hotel is surrounded by attractively landscaped grounds offering a view of the Grenadines from every room. Tropic Breeze rents out a dozen large and airy units, each with a bedroom, bath, and a combined patio and living room. In addition, six units have kitchenettes.

The manager, Elizabeth Punnett, sees that everything is kept bright and spotless. The furnishings are comfortably modern, graced by potted plants. Trade winds provide cross ventilation, yet air conditioning is also offered. *In summer, a single rents for $48 daily, a double for $60, and a two-bedroom-two-bath apartment for $120.* In winter, the tariffs go up to $54 in a single, $72 in a double, and $168 in an apartment. All rates are EP.

You can also enjoy the tranquility of the garden with its large freshwater pool. If you don't want to cook for yourself, you can eat at the hotel's Patio Restaurant overlooking the pool. You have 12 choices at lunch or dinner as well as snacks and a breakfast menu. Meals are served from 7 a.m. to 11 p.m. The location's not on the beach, but on a mountainside free from noise. Complimentary transportation to the beach is provided once a day.

Rawacou, Stubbs (tel. 458-4459), stands right on two beaches on the breeze-swept windward coast. Units of the complex of ten cottages are scattered in the middle of 15 acres of grounds, at a point about nine miles from Kingstown. Two Canadians, Peter and Nan Mickles, conceived and planned this resort, offering each villa with a split-level living and bedroom area, a bath, a fully equipped kitchenette, and a private patio. All units open onto a superb ocean view.

You can cook for yourself, and, if not, the cuisine offered here has much variety and is well presented in a thatched dining room. *On the MAP rate off-season, a single costs $105.60; the daily charge in a double on the MAP is $128.40.* In season, the MAP charge is $108 daily in a single, $132 in a double. The apartment rate is $84 daily per cottage. Drinks are served in a glass-fronted lounge, or else you can observe the seascape below or on the open floodlit tropical gardens. The furnishings are fairly spartan, everything having an uncluttered look. Mr. and Mrs. Mickles also offer five riding horses.

Kingstown Park Guest House, P.O. Box 41 (tel. 456-1532), is one of the best bargains on the island. It's a century-old plantation house built in the colonial planter's style. It stands in a garden setting on a hill overlooking Kingstown. The owner, Miss Nesta Paynter, welcomes you to her home, and will point out the details of the pre-Victorian architecture, the stone-walled dining room, and the airy cathedral ceiling.

The house has a good view of the mountains and sea, and lies within walking distance of the main shops of the capital. Cooled by trade winds, both singles and doubles—simply furnished—are rented out at rates ranging from $18 to $22 per person daily for half board. This is remarkable value, considering the good creole food and large portions served here. Units are equipped with private showers. The personal service from the staff, and particularly from Miss Paynter, makes this a worthy choice.

WHERE TO DINE: Most guests eat at their hotels on the Modified American Plan. Unlike the situation on many Caribbean islands, many Vincentian hostelries serve an authentic West Indian cuisine. There are also a few independent eateries as well, but not many.

The **Cobblestone Inn**, Kingstown (tel. 456-1937), which was previously recommended as an in-town stopover, also serves some of the best local food in port. That is, if you can crowd out a yachtsman for a seat. You can enjoy lunch at its top-floor open-air grill—items such as rich-tasting, nutritious soup, a generous portion of fish and chips, or a T-bone steak, finished off by ice cream.

Or you may prefer the air-conditioned bar and restaurant on the ground level. This is an attractive room using the natural elements of stone and wood to form its decor. Here at dinner you can order more elaborate preparations, including the classic West Indian callaloo soup, perhaps langouste flambé. Expect to pay around $15 to $20 for dinner.

Before dinner, you may want to go up to the top floor to watch the sun go down. You won't be alone, and hopefully you'll know something about boating if you want to join in on the conversation.

Heron Hotel, Kingstown (tel. 457-1631), previously described as a hotel, is a simple, traditional West Indian inn that serves very good and bountiful Vincentian-style meals. Mrs. McKenzie has wisely chosen a small staff to see that you're fed and served properly. You're served family-style fare, utilizing fresh fish and island-grown vegetables. Of course, if she's fully booked with overnight guests, she might not be able to accommodate you, but it's worth calling her up and making the request if you like this type of food, and are very hungry (the portions are most generous). A table d'hôte menu served in the second-floor dining room will cost about $18.

Bounty, Back Street, Kingstown (tel. 456-1776), is a café-style snackbar in a light-green and white building, right opposite the main Barclays Bank branch. Local people who work in the shops nearby come here for a typical British-style breakfast. Later on they're back for a hamburger at lunch. You can enjoy a snack for $4.50, a meal for around $10. Everything is pleasantly casual, and it's a good luncheon choice if you're in the area at noon. Otherwise, I wouldn't suggest that you make a special trip here.

Harbour View (tel. 458-4922), across from Young Island, already previewed, consistently serves simple Gallic specialties such as snails in garlic butter and quenelles with tomato sauce as an appetizer. For your main course, you'd be wise to ask for fresh lobster (not always available) or their steamed "catch of the day," most often served in a sauce of fresh herbs. In ambience, it's also one of the nicest stopovers on the island. For dessert, the chef makes sherbets out of fresh fruit. Count on spending about $20 for dinner.

Juliette's, Middle Street, in Kingstown (tel. 457-1645), was so praised by readers that I decided to check it out for myself. A good break from the monotony of a hotel dining room, it is a simple place, but the food is reliable. Here you get unadorned Vincentian-type cookery served without pretense. That means plenty of local vegetables and whatever the fishermen brought in that day. But if you want steak, that's available too. Prices are about $15 for a big meal. Incidentally, this is not the kind of place where you flash a credit card at the end of your meal.

Another independent eatery that is a favorite locally, **Ikahya,** Middle Street, in Kingstown (tel. 456-1824), has very good fish dishes, along with local vegetables and luscious fruits. Service is polite and friendly, and no one seems in a particular rush. Count on parting with no more than $15 for a good meal. Dress is casual.

Pink Dolphin, Villa Beach (tel. 458-4238). The yachting crowd touring the Grenadines likes to stop off here. They get reliable food (that means fried chicken, hamburgers, steaks done just right—but nothing fancy). No one would have it any other way. Prices are reasonable too, with dinners costing from $15.

WHAT TO SEE: In the capital, Kingstown, you can still meet oldtime beachcombers if you stroll on Upper Bay Street. White haired and bearded, they can be seen loading their boats with produce grown on the mountain, before heading to some secluded beach in the Grenadines. This is a chief port and gateway to the Grenadines, and you can also view the small boats, dinghies, and yachts that have dropped anchor here. The place is a magnet for charter sailors.

Kingstown

Lushly tropical and solidly British, the capital isn't as architecturally fascinating as St. George's in Grenada. Some English-style houses do exist, many of them looking as if they belonged in Penzance, Cornwall, instead of the West Indies.

At the top of a winding road on the north side of Kingstown, **Fort Charlotte** was built on Johnson Point, enclosing one side of the bay. Constructed about the time of the American Revolution, it was named after Queen Charlotte, the German consort of George III. The ruins aren't much to inspect. Instead, the reason to go here is for the view. The fort sits atop a steep promontory some 640 feet above the sea. From its citadel, you'll have a commanding sweep of the leeward shores to the north, Kingstown to the south, and the Grenadines beyond. A trio of cannons used to fight off French troops are still in place. Admission is 50¢, and for that you'll see a series of oil murals depicting the history of black Caribs.

The second major sight is the **Botanic Garden,** on the north side of Kingstown, about a mile from the center. Founded in 1765 by Gov. George Melville, it is the oldest botanic garden in the West Indies. In this Windward Eden, you'll see 20 acres of such tropical exotics as teak, almond, cinnamon, nutmeg, cannonball trees, and mahogany. Some of the trees are more than two centuries old. One of the breadfruit trees, reputedly, was among those original seedlings brought to this island by Captain Bligh in 1793.

Back in the heart of town, you might pay a visit to **St. Mary's Catholic Church,** on Grenville Street, with its curious melange of architecture. Fancifully flawed, it was built in 1935 by a Belgian monk, Dom Carlos Verbeke. He incorporated Romanesque arches, Gothic spires, and almost Moorish embellishments. The result—a maze of balconies, turrets, battlements, and courtyards—creates a bizarre effect.

After Kingstown, the following targets might intrigue you.

The Leeward Highway

The leeward or west side of the island has the most dramatic scenery. North from Kingstown, you rise into lofty terrain before descending to the water again. There are views in all directions. On your right you'll pass the Aqueduct Golf Course (see "The Sporting Life") before reaching Layou. Here you can see the massive **Carib Rock,** with a human face carving dating back to A.D. 600. This is considered one of the finest petroglyphs in the Caribbean.

Continuing north you reach **Barrouallie,** where there is another Carib stone altar. Even if you're not a fisherman, you might want to spend some time in this whaling village where men still set out in brightly painted boats armed with harpoons, *Moby Dick*-style, to seek the elusive whale. However, "Save the Whale" devotees need not harpoon their way here in anger. Barrouallie may be one of the last few outposts in the world where such whale-hunting is carried on, but St. Vincentians point out that it does not endanger an already endangered species since so few are caught each year. If one is caught, it's an occasion for festivities and a lot of blubber.

The leeward highway continues to Chateaubelair, the end of the line. There you can swim at the attractive Richmond Beach before heading back to

Kingstown. In the distance, the volcano, La Soufrière, looms menacingly in the mountains.

The adventurous set out from here to see the **Falls of Baleine,** 7½ miles north of Richmond Beach on the northern tip of the island, accessible only by boat. Coming from a stream in the volcanic hills, Baleine is a dramatic freshwater fall. If you're interested in making the trip, check with the tourist office in Kingstown about a tour there.

The Windward Highway

This road runs along the eastern Atlantic coast from Kingstown. Waves pound the surf, and all along the rocky shores are splendid seascapes. If you want to go swimming along this often-dangerous coast, stick to the sandy spots, as they offer safer shores. Along this road you'll pass coconut and banana plantations and fields of arrowroot, a crop that St. Vincent seems to monopolize.

North of Georgetown lies the **Rabacca Dry River,** which was the flow of lava from the volcano at its eruption at the beginning of the 20th century. The journey from Kingstown to here is only 24 miles, but it will seem like much longer than that. For those who want to go the final 11 miles along a rugged road to **Fancy,** the northern tip of the island, a Land Rover, Jeep, or Moke will be needed.

La Soufrière

A safari to St. Vincent's hot volcano is possible. As you travel the island, you can't miss its cloud-capped splendor. On some occasions this volcano has captured the attention of the world.

The most recent eruption was in 1979, when the volcano threw ashes and spit lava and hot mud, covering the vegetation that grew on its slopes and sending thousands of Vincentians fleeing its fury. Without warning, belched-out rock and black curling smoke filled the blue Caribbean sky. Jets of steam spouted 20,000 feet into the air. About 17,000 persons were evacuated from a ten-mile ring around the volcano.

Fortunately, the eruption was in the sparsely settled northern part of the island. The volcano lies away from most of the tourism and commercial centers of St. Vincent, and even if it should erupt again in the future, volcanologists do not consider it a danger to visitors lodged at beachside hotels along the leeward coast.

The last major eruption of the volcano occurred in 1902, when 2000 persons were killed. Until its 1979 eruption, the volcano had been quiet since 1972. The activity that year produced a 324-foot-long island of lava rock called Crater Lake.

Even if you're an experienced hiker, don't attempt to explore this volcano without an experienced local guide, many of whom will charge around $25 for the trip. Also, wear suitable hiking clothes and know that you're in the best of health before making such an arduous journey.

A guide will direct you in your car through a rich countryside of coconut and banana trees, coming to a clearing at the foot of the mountain. After you get there, you go on foot through a rain forest, following the trail that will eventually lead to the crater rim of La Soufrière. Allow at least three hours, unless you're an Olympic athlete.

At the rim of the crater you'll be rewarded with one of the most panoramic views in the Caribbean. That is, if the wind doesn't blow too hard and make you topple over into the crater itself! Extreme caution is emphasized. Inside, you can see the steam rising from the crater.

The trail back down is much easier, I assure you.

Marriqua Valley

Sometimes known as the Mesopotamia Valley, this verdant land is considered one of the most lushly cultivated valleys in the eastern Caribbean. Surrounded by mountain ridges, the drive takes you through a dramatic landscape richly planted with nutmeg, cocoa, coconut, breadfruit, and bananas. The road begins at Vigie Highway, to the east of the Arnos Vale Airport runway. At the town of Montréal, you'll come upon natural mineral springs. Only rugged vehicles should make this trip.

Around Kingstown, you can also enjoy the **Queen's Drive,** a dramatically scenic loop into the high hills to the east of the capital. From there, the view is magnificent over Kingstown and its yacht-clogged harbor to the Grenadines in the distance.

THE SPORTING LIFE: In St. Vincent you skin-dive, fish, swim, or snorkel, and of course go sailing, mainly to the Grenadines.

All beaches on St. Vincent are public, and many of the best ones border hotel properties which you can patronize for drinks or luncheons. Most of the resorts are in the south, where the beaches have white or golden-yellow sand. However, many of the beaches in the north have sands that look like lava ash in color. The safest swimming is on the leeward beaches, as the windward beaches can be dangerous.

Tennis

Short-term visitors to St. Vincent can play at the **Kingstown Tennis Club,** Murray Road. Guests are charged a subscription of $10 per court per hour. You're asked to provide your own tennis balls and racquets and make arrangements through the chief steward in advance. Telephone 456-1288 for more information. Short-term visitors are allowed to play between 8:30 a.m. and noon.

Golf

The nine-hole course at the **Aqueduct Golf Club,** considered one of the most beautiful in the world, is in the Buccament Valley on the leeward coast. Greens fees are $6 per day, $30 per week. These fees also include use of the pool at the clubhouse, where you'll also find a restaurant and bar.

Snorkeling, Scuba, and Sailboat Charters

The best area for snorkeling and scuba-diving is the Indian Bay section on the southern end of the island. **Mariners Scuba Shop,** P.O. Box 639 (tel. 458-4228), is run by Sue Schaffer and Earl Halbich, directly across from Young Island. They offer full diving service; and you can rent equipment here, going on guided reef trips in the warm, fantastically clear waters. The shop also offers night dives, as well as beginner and advanced diving instruction, windsurfing, waterskiing, and yacht charters. The complete course costs $45 per person. If you're experienced and want to go out on dive trips, the rental of the boat, tank, kit, and weights will cost about $25 per person. A minimum of two divers is required.

Fishing

It's best to go to a native fisherman for advice if you're interested in this sport, which your hotel will usually arrange for you. The government of St. Vincent doesn't require visitors to take out a license. If you arrange things in time, it's sometimes possible to accompany the local fishermen on one of their trips, perhaps four or five miles from shore. A modest fee should suffice. The fishing fleet leaves from the leeward coast at Barrouallie. They've been known to return to shore with everything from a six-inch redfish to a 20-foot pilot whale.

Sailing and Yachting

St. Vincent and the Grenadines are one of the great sailing centers of the West Indies. Here you can obtain yachts that are fully provisioned if you want to go bare-boating, or else, if you're a well-heeled novice, you can hire a captain and a crew.

You can rent boats from **Caribbean Sailing Yachts** (CSY), at P.O. Box 491, Tenafly, NJ 07670 (tel. 201/568-0390), or in St. Vincent at its offices at the Blue Lagoon (tel. 458-4308). This company is now in the full-service charter business. The cost of your craft will depend on the season. You'll be asked to prove what kind of sailor you are.

WHERE TO SHOP: You don't come to St. Vincent to shop, but once there, you might pick up some items in sea island cotton fabrics and clothing which are specialties here. In addition, Vincentian artisans make pottery, jewelry, and baskets that have souvenir value at least.

Since the capital, Kingstown, consists of about 12 small blocks, you can walk and browse and see about everything in a morning's shopping jaunt. Try to be in town for the colorful, noisy **Saturday morning market.** You might not purchase anything. After all, you don't plan to bring fruit, fish, and poultry back on the plane with you, but you'll surely enjoy the riot of color.

In the **St. Vincent Handicraft Centre** (tel. 457-1288), up the road from the wharf in Kingstown, you'll see a large display of the handicrafts of the island. On the site of an old cotton gin, this shop offers you a chance to see craftspeople at work, perhaps on macramé or metal-work jewelry.

Batik Caribe, Bay Street, Kingstown (tel. 456-1666), sells the best selection of original hand-dyed batik prints in St. Vincent. If you're going to be on the island for about three days, the staff here will make you an outfit to order. The shop is open weekdays from 9 a.m. to 4 p.m. and on Saturday from 9 a.m. to noon. You'll be shown their large display of scarfs, dresses, and swimwear.

Norma's, on Egmont Street, is one of the leading boutiques of St. Vincent. On the second floor of a Kingstown building, the shop prices its dresses reasonably.

Stetchers Jewellery Ltd., Lot 19, Lane Bay Street in Kingstown (tel. 457-1142), offers a good selection of crystal, watches, china, porcelain, and jewelry.

The familiar **Y de Lima Ltd.** (tel. 457-1681) also has a branch in Kingstown, well stocked with cameras, stereo equipment, clocks, binoculars, and jewelry.

Noah's Arkade (tel. 457-1513) is a little shop on Bay Street in Kingstown, selling handicrafts from the West Indies, including woodcarvings. It also offers locally made clothing.

Finally, as you're leaving you'll be able to purchase duty-free liquors and cigarettes at **Gonsalves Liquors** (tel. 458-4753) at Arnos Vale Airport.

NIGHTLIFE: The focus is mainly on the hotels, and activities are likely to include nighttime barbecues and dancing to steel bands. In season, at least one hotel seems to have something planned every night during a week.

One of the liveliest spots is **Mariner's Inn,** at Villa Beach (tel. 458-4287). Island calypso and steel drum music are the featured attractions here, and local people show up to dance to good music. Nonresidents pay an entrance fee of $3, which includes their first drink.

Adjacent to the Aqueduct Golf Club is the **Emerald Isle Casino,** Penniston (tel. 457-1325). As you listen to music, you can also enjoy one of the best meals on the island, with dinners costing from $20. Here you can try your luck at blackjack, roulette, slot machines, punto banco, and keno.

Next to the Young Island landing pier, the best known spot for entertainment remains the **Aquatic Club** (tel. 458-4205), which "jumps up" with action, usually on Tuesday and Friday nights. Guests from all the hotels come here to enjoy the music and sing-alongs. Drinks range in price from $3 and up.

4. The Grenadines

South of St. Vincent, which administers them, this small chain of islands extends for more than 40 miles, offering the finest yachting area in the eastern Caribbean. They're strung like a necklace of precious stones, and have such wonderful names as Bequia, Mustique, Canouan, and Petit St. Vincent.

A few of the islands have accommodations which we'll explore, but many are so small and so completely undeveloped and unspoiled that they attract only beachcombers and stray boating people in the area.

Populated by the descendants of African slaves, the Grenadines collectively add up to a land mass of only 30 square miles.

The islands are called the Grenadines because they lead to Grenada. These bits of land, often dots on nautical charts, may lack natural resources, yet they're blessed with white sandy beaches, coral reefs, and their own kind of sleepy beauty. If you're not spending the night in the Grenadines, you may at least go over for the day to visit one of them, enjoying a picnic lunch (which your hotel will pack for you) on one of the long stretches of beach.

GETTING THERE: The ideal way to go, of course, is to rent your own yacht, and many visitors do just that. If you'd like to consider that, refer to "The Sporting Life" in the previous section on St. Vincent.

By Boat

The least expensive method of going is on a mail, cargo, and passenger boat. However, to do this, you should be a free-wheeling person with lots of time and patience.

It's a unique experience for adventuresome travelers and for those who've never been on this type of vessel. You should carry along a raincoat to protect you from those quick Caribbean showers or that occasional big wave. Price and times might fluctuate, so you should check at the tourist office in Kingstown, St. Vincent.

The government mail boat, *Friendship Rose,* a two-masted vessel, leaves Kingstown in St. Vincent headed for Bequia Monday through Friday at 1:30 p.m. It returns to Kingstown the following morning at 6:30.

Also on Monday and Thursday, the M.V. *Grenadine Star* leaves Kingstown for Bequia at 9 a.m. The same vessel returns to Kingstown on Tuesday and Friday at 4 p.m.

Transportation on each boat is $5 for a one-way passage.

There is no boat going in either direction on Saturday.

On Sunday, there's an excursion to Bequia from Kingstown on the M.V. *Seimstrand.* It leaves St. Vincent at 8:30 a.m., returning from Bequia at 7 p.m. the same day, also charging a $5 one-way fare.

Look for schedules posted in St. Vincentian newspapers. *Note:* Times given here are only for general guidance and are subject to change.

By Air

It's also possible to go to some of the islands by air. Refer to the "Getting There" section of St. Vincent.

BEQUIA: Only seven square miles of land, Bequia is the largest of St. Vincent's Grenadines. Descended from age-old seafarers, its population of some 5000 Bequians will probably give you a friendly greeting if you pass them along the road. A feeling of relaxation and informality prevails here.

Pronounced Beck-wee, the island lies nine miles south of St. Vincent and is reached by schooner.

Its main harbor village, **Port Elizabeth,** is known for its safe anchorage, Admiralty Bay. The yachting set "from anywhere" puts in here, often bringing a kind of dazzling excitement to the locals.

No rental cars are available in the port, but you can hire a taxi at the dock to take you around or to your hotel if you're spending the night. Before that, drop in at the circular-shaped Tourist Information Centre. You'll see it right on the beach. There you can ask for a driver who is familiar with the attractions of the island (nearly all of them are). You should negotiate the fare in advance, hopefully paying no more than $35 for a short day tour, the cost of which can be split among passengers.

One of the pleasant staff at the tourist office will show you the way to the shop of the **Sargent Brothers,** where you'll see craftspeople making meticulously accurate scale models of yachts or sailboats. They'll also make one to your specifications, perhaps of your own vessel, if you give them enough time.

If you want to see your boats in real life, just walk along the beach. There, craftsmen can be seen constructing vessels by hand, a method they learned from their fathers who learned it from their ancestors. Whalers set out from here in wooden boats with hand harpoons, just as they do from a port village on St. Vincent.

You can set out too. Ask at the tourist office for the way to get in touch with a British expatriate, Neil Sanders, who will take you out on his 40-foot yacht, the *Reve,* for a tour of almost-deserted beaches at a charge of about $150 a day. There are some shops scattered along the water where you can buy hand-screened cotton made by Bequians.

The best of these is the **Crab Hole** (tel. 458-3290), which sells hand-screened fabrics on it premises.

Noah's Arkade also has a branch on Bequia, near Barclays Bank, selling woodcarvings, resortwear, swimsuits, and handicrafts from the West Indies.

You might also check out **Lulley's Bequia,** a boutique and gift shop, which also sells fishing, boating, and dive gear.

Frankly, after you leave Port Elizabeth there aren't many sights, and you'll probably have your driver, booked for the day, drop you off for a long, leisurely lunch and some time on a beach. However, you'll pass a fort with a harbor view, driving on to Industry Estates which has a Beach House restaurant which serves a fair lunch. At Paget Farm, you can wander into a village of whalers, and maybe inspect a few jawbones left over from catches of yesterday.

At Moonhole, there's a vacation and retirement community built into the cliffs, really free-form sculpture. These are private homes of course, and you're not to enter without permission. For a final look at Bequia, head up an 800-foot hill which the local people call "The Mountain." From that perch, you'll have a 360° view of St. Vincent and the Grenadines to the south.

Back in Port Elizabeth, you'll find the **Whaleboner Inn** on the bay (tel. 458-3233), just 100 yards or so south of the bank. The entranceway is a huge whale's jawbones in the shape of an arch. Inside, the bar is carved from the jawbone of another giant whale and the bar stools are made from the vertebrae. If you haven't already had lunch, you'll enjoy a lobster, pizza or fish 'n chips, or a variety of other snacks. Don't miss one of their delicious dinners prepared by an excellent West Indian cook. The cost of a meal ranges from $10. In the boutique is a selection of holiday clothes all handmade, hand-printed, or batiked in their home factory. They have room for a few special guests for overnight or by the week.

Where to Stay

Hotel Frangipani (tel. 458-3255) is the family homestead of Son Mitchell, the premier of St. Vincent and the Grenadines. Canada-born Marie Kingston runs the small inn beside a sandy beach in a casual way. She's a friend of Son and Pat Mitchell. Mr. Mitchell's father, a sea captain, built the house, but he disappeared with his crew in the Bermuda Triangle (his schooner sailed on!).

Popular with yachting people, the inn offers fine West Indies–style accommodations. The newer rooms in the garden cottages are in a stone and hardwood construction, with beams, louvers, private baths, dressing rooms, and a larger sundeck draped with frangipani. The older units are simpler, perched on the second floor of what used to be the family home. Mosquito netting covers the beds. There is, however, a corridor bath, and each unit has a wash basin with running water.

In high season, the EP rate is $30 to $54 daily in a single, from $36 to $72 in a double. *In low season, the charge in a single goes from $18 to $36 daily, from $30 to $54 in a double.* Add $18 per person for MAP.

The hotel offers good food with plenty of fresh fruits and vegetables. Fishermen bring in their latest catch, which often includes lobster and conch. If you're arriving on a fleet of dinghies from the yachts moored offshore, you'll fit in just fine here, enjoying the nautical heritage of the place. Old charts and paintings of seascapes decorate the lounge, and after a few drinks you're given your place at the dinner table where a guest pays from $14.40 to $18 for a fine meal. The dining room, of course, borders the seafront.

Friendship Bay Hotel (for reservations, tel. toll free in the U.S. 800/223-6764, 458-3222 locally) is a beachfront resort offering 27 well-decorated rooms with private verandas nestled in 12 acres of tropical gardens and the shores of a mile-long white sandy beach. Guests have a sweeping view of the sea and neighboring islands. The owners are Eduardo and Joanne Guadagnino. Eduardo moved from his homeland, Argentina, a number of years ago, going to California, where he went into the restaurant and married native Californian Joanne.

Joanne has seen to redecorating the hotel, using brightly colored curtains, bedspreads, and handmade wall hangings telling a picture story of life in Bequia, as well as new grass rugs in the rooms, which are cooled by the trade winds. In winter, units rent for $90 per person on the MAP; *the summer rate is $55 per person on the same plan.* A single person occupying a room pays only $11 extra, regardless of the season.

The Guadagninos have added a beach bar in Caribbean style. They offer Saturday-night barbecues on the beach, with music provided by the hotel band, Exotica, a popular island combo. The food is good too, with many island specialties on the menu, along with Italian and Argentine cuisine.

You can enjoy water sports and tennis here, or take an excursion aboard the hotel's classic yacht, built in 1920 in Cardiff, Wales, and completely restored by Mr. Guadagnino. The yacht makes trips to and from Mustique and St. Vincent, lavishing guests with refreshments, for $55 per person round trip.

Sunny Caribbee, P.O. Box 16, Admiralty Bay (tel. 458-3425), was completely restored after its purchase by a British concern. Accommodations consist of 17 West Indian cabanas, each with its own private terrace, plus eight rooms in the old colonial-style wood-frame house. The property fronts a 700-foot white sandy beach, with a seafront bar and a beachside pool. The resort overlooks Admiralty Bay, and its ten acres of grounds are planted with flowering trees and shrubs.

In winter, a hotel room rents for $36 a day for two, a detached cabana for $60. *In summer, these tariffs drop to $24 in a double room, $48 daily in a cabana.* The hotel rooms don't have showers en suite, and the cabanas have twin beds, a small sitting area, a shower room, and a terrace (a few come with kitchenettes). Extra beds are available at $10 per person daily, and for breakfast and dinner add another $15 per person daily.

A wide-open veranda extends around three sides of the building, and people sit here with absolutely nothing to do but unwind or have another beer, or both. You can also swim, snorkel, sail, waterski, or fish. There's also a tennis court if anybody has that much energy.

Spring on Bequia (tel. 458-3414) offers 15 units in several cottages spread out on 28 acres of land, a working plantation which raises its own bananas, oranges, grapefruit, coconuts, plums, mangos, and breadfruit. Most of the cottages are clustered around the main house, where about six more people can overnight, and often do. Furnishings make for good comfort, and each unit has a terrace with a hammock already strung up. Cottages are built on a hillside to take advantage of the view.

Guests are accepted on the MAP, enjoying the West Indian cuisine, with its many exotic vegetables and fresh fish caught about five hours previously. The dining room is open to the view, and is often shared by hummingbirds.

Rates for half board in a double room are $175 per day, depending on the location and the size of the unit. Single occupancy, also MAP, costs from $120 per day. *After Easter, prices are lower, costing $145 per day, based on double occupancy, from $100 in a single,* all tariffs including breakfast and dinner. Each unit has a shower, but no hot water. Stored in a reservoir, the water is warmed by the Caribbean sun.

A concrete tennis court is available, and there is 500 feet of private sandy beach on a secluded bay. On Friday night there's a barbecue on this beach, with entertainment by a local group.

Julie's Guest House, in Port Elizabeth (tel. 458-3304), has nearly doubled in size in recent years, and now has 20 rooms. Its location is a five-minute walk from Port Elizabeth. If you stay here, you're right in the middle of island life, and you can sit out and swap fancy tales with some yachting people who often stop off here, wanting a break from being at sea all the time.

Rooms are modestly equipped, but kept very clean. Expect to pay $25 per person, including half board. At mealtimes, portions are large, and good West Indian–style food is served, including pumpkin fritters and curry dishes.

MUSTIQUE: This island, 15 miles south of St. Vincent, is so remote and small it almost deserves to be unknown, and it would be if it weren't for the escapades of Princess Margaret (called "Yvonne" here by her intimates). The princess has a cottage on this island of luxury villas which someone once called "Georgian West Indian." The island also received worldwide media attention during the visit of Prince Andrew and what is still locally called "his lady friend."

The island is privately owned by a consortium of businessmen. When splashed on front pages in London, describing Princess Margaret's retreat, it was then owned by beer baron Colin Tennant, a millionaire Scottish nobleman. An eccentric dandy, he was often photographed in silk scarfs and Panama hats. On the trail of Margaret, and her cousin the Earl of Lichfield, came a host of celebrities, including Truman Capote, Paul Newman, Mick Jagger, Raquel Welch, and Richard Avedon.

Attracting the elite, the island is only three miles long and one mile wide, and it has only one hotel (see below), the only place to stay unless you're a guest in one of the private villas. Chartered planes usually arrive on its small airstrip. Once there, you'll find no taxis. But chances are, someone at Cotton House will already have seen you land. After settling in, you'll find many good white sandy beaches against a backdrop of luxuriant foliage. My favorite is Macaroni Beach, where the water is like turquoise.

On the northern reef of Mustique you'll find the wreck of the French liner *Antilles*, which went aground on the Pillories in 1971. Today its massive hulk, now gutted, can be seen cracked and rusting a few yards offshore, an eerie sight.

If you wish to tour the small island, you can rent a Mini-Moke to see some of the most elegant homes in the Caribbean. If you'd like to follow in the trail of soft-porn star Koo Star and her handsome prince, you can rent *Les Jolies Eaux* (that is, if you can afford it). Designed by Oliver Messel, this is the Caribbean home of Princess Margaret. A four-bedroom-four-bath house, it has a large swimming pool, naturally. Accommodating eight well-heeled guests, it is available only when HRH is not in residence. If you rent it, the princess will require references.

The **Cotton House** (tel. 458-4621 is an exclusive hotel, once operating as a private club, a place casually elegant, as is its clientele. The main house is an 18th-century structure, built of coral and stone. The house was painstakingly restored, rebuilt, and redecorated by Oliver Messel. The architecture of the hotel, decor, and amenities suggest the graciousness of the plantation era (that is, providing you weren't a slave). The design of the hotel is characterized by arched louvered doors and cedar shutters. The antique loggia sets the style— everything from Lady Bateman's steamer trunks to a scallop-shell fountain on a quartz base. Guests sit here enjoying their sundowns. Perhaps earlier they had a swim at the pool surrounded by Messel's "Roman ruins" after a barbecue-style lunch by the pool.

Some of the rooms were also designed by Messel. Units are in two fully restored Georgian houses, a trio of cottages, or in a newer block of eight rooms, all of which open onto windswept balconies or patios.

Of course, you pay for all this—$330 daily in a double in winter from $252 in a single, including a full breakfast and dinner. *Off-season, the half-board tariffs are $174 daily in a double, $132 in a single.*

The hotel enjoys an outstanding reputation for its food and service. The cuisine has a West Indian flavor. Nonresidents are allowed to dine here, but they must make reservations. Lunch ranges from $18 to $25, and dinner costs about $22 a head, plus wines.

The hotel is managed by Robert Bernard Hoflund.

Nobody ever goes to this island of indigenous farmers and fisherfolk without spending a night drinking at **Basil's Beach Bar.** A "South Seas island"–type establishment, it is more authentic than any reproduction in an old Dorothy Lamour flick. The gathering place for yachting people, as well as owners of those luxurious villas, the bar, but mainly its owner, has received a lot of newspaper publicity. Its greeter, Basil, is a six-foot four-inch, heavily muscled "Mandingo," whom *Esquire* magazine called "the island's most famous product after its sandy beaches." Some people come here to drink and watch a beautiful view, but Basil's is also, by reputation, one of the finest seafood restaurants in the Caribbean. Both lunch and dinner are served daily, and American Express cards are accepted. Expect to spend from $30 for a meal here, and a good one at that. There is also a boutique on the premises. On Wednesday night you can "jump-up" at a barbecue.

CANOUAN: In the shape of a half circle, Canouan is surrounded by coral reefs and dramatic blue lagoons, a virgin paradise, almost totally unspoiled. The island is only 3½ miles by 1½ miles in size, and is visited mainly by those who want to enjoy its splendid long beaches. Canouan has a population of less than 1000 people, many of whom fish for a living.

The island does not have a public power plant (as of this writing), but its one hotel has its own generator.

You reach Canouan by first taking an international flight to Barbados. It is then 50 minutes by charter flight on Tropic Air to Canouan. Alternatively, you can fly to St. Vincent on LIAT. There you'll be able to fly direct to Canouan on Inter-Island Air Services. There are also flights from Grenada.

Charters are also available from a three-seater plane in St. Vincent which can fly to Canouan any day.

To get in touch with the three-seater, phone through to the Crystal Sands (see below). The cost of travel from St. Vincent to Canouan by the ferryboat M.V. *Grenadine Star* is usually EC$14 ($5.32).

The mother island, St. Vincent, lies 14 miles to the north and Grenada 20 miles to the south. Canouan rises from its sandy beaches to the 800-foot-high peak of Mount Royal in the north. There you'll find unspoiled forests of white cedar.

Crystal Sands Beach Hotel, Canouan Island (tel. 457-1077), right on the beach, offers its guests blissful isolation in a complex that includes five cabanas and a main facility. The first and only hotel erected on the island, Crystal Sands is the creation of Mr. and Mrs. Phileus de Roche, who recognized the tourist possibilities of the place while wanting to keep it unspoiled at the same time.

Each of their cabanas offers accommodations in twin beds, with private baths. Furnishings are simple West Indian–style pieces, with flamboyant fabrics. In winter, guests pay $48 daily in a single, $72 daily in a double, EP. *Summer EP tariffs are $60 daily in a double, $40 in a single.*

There's an al fresco dining area in the main building that offers both West Indian and Stateside specialties. The fish served seems so fresh because the management claims it comes "almost from the sea to your table." When the hotel was built, the owners found many pottery artifacts, probably made by Arawaks about the time of Christ.

Sailing trips and game fishing can be arranged by the de Roche family.

PALM ISLAND: Is this island a resort or is the resort the island? Casual elegance and privacy prevail on these 100 acres in the southern Grenadines. Surrounded by five white sand beaches, the island is sometimes called "Prune," so one can easily understand the more appealing name change.

A little islet in the sun, it offers complete peace and quiet with plenty of sea, sand, sun, and sailing. To reach the place, it's best to take a share-charter direct to Union Island (operated November through May), one mile west of Palm, where a launch will be waiting. The cost is around $125 per person each way, which is a bit more than commercial flights, but avoids delays and is more reliable.

If you're visiting in summer, you can book a charter plane on your own; or first overnight in Barbados, then fly the next morning to St. Vincent with LIAT. There you can connect with Inter-Island Air Services' scheduled flight to Union Island, where you take the launch over to Palm Island.

Most people don't come to Palm Island to shop, but once there, you might see what is available at **La Boutique,** which has a collection of jewelry, local handicrafts, gifts, swimwear, plus other casual resort attire for both men and women.

Palm Island Beach Club (tel. 458-4804) is one of those "mom and pop"–type resorts, the long-cherished wish fulfillment of the Caldwells—John and Mary—working together in the tropical paradise, along with the help of their West Indian friends. John himself is nicknamed "Coconut Johnny," because of his reforestation hobby of planting palms. At old Prune Island, he planted hundreds upon hundreds of trees until its name was changed to Palm Island.

An adventurer, this Texan once set out to sail by himself across the Pacific, coming to rest off the coast of Fiji. He made it to Australia, where he constructed his own ketch, loaded his family aboard, and took off again. Eventually he made it to the Grenadines where he operated a charter business. His exploits, including getting embroiled in a hurricane, were documented in the autobiographical book *Desperate Voyage,* an account of his 106-day, 8500-mile journey at sea. After that exploit, he operated a charter business in the Grenadines, often taking guests to Palm (née Prune) Island. As his clients would swim or lie on the beach, he'd plant coconut palms.

Just right for the Grenadine frame of mind, he eventually built this cottage colony with enough room for 50 guests spaced under palms on the white sandy beach. Accommodations are in the Beach Club duplex cabanas or in one of the villas, which are equipped for housekeeping. Bungalows are built of stone and wood, with louvered walls as well as sliding glass doors that open onto terraces. The furniture was built by the Caldwells. All rooms are superior.

In winter, a double with all meals rents for $264 daily, a single for $180, and a triple for $294. *In summer, a double, again with all meals, costs $210 per day; a single, $150; and a triple, $240.* Rates include afternoon tea served on the patio.

Dining is in a "South Seas island"–style pavilion where the food is good and plentiful. Nautically oriented guests like to have tall drinks at the circular beach bar.

The Caldwells also maintain a small charter fleet of yachts for day sails, with one of their amiable West Indian crewmen aboard to assist. These natives are experts on local history, customs, and tall tales.

UNION ISLAND: Midway between Grenada and St. Vincent, Union Island is the most southern of the Grenadines. It's known for its dramatic 900-foot peak, Mount Parnassus, which is seen by yachting people for miles away. If you're cruising in the area, Union is the port of entry for St. Vincent. Yachters are required to check with Customs upon entry.

Hopefully, you'll sail into Union on a night when the locals are having a "big drum" dance. Costumed islanders dance and chant to the beat of drums made of goatskin.

The island is reached either by chartered or scheduled aircraft, by cargo boat, or by private yacht.

On a shopping note, check out **Chic/Unique Boutique,** a gift and souvenir shop 50 yards from the airstrip. Even if you don't find something here, you'll have to love its name!

Accommodations are very limited and simple.

Try the **Anchorage Yacht Club** (tel. 458-8244), which is the best place to stay on the island. It's casual and comfortable, and some have called its luxurious. Only ten pleasantly furnished rooms are rented, and the prices are quite high. You have to book in here on half-board terms. The charge in winter is $175 for two persons, on the MAP. *In summer, expect reductions of 20%.*

It is by no means a plush place, yet it has its own kind of unpretentious style. Rooms are built right on the beach, and you look out at the crystal-clear water, waiting for the sun to dip below the horizon. The yacht club reflects the unspoiled, uncomplicated lifestyle that is typical of Union Island. The food is quite good on most nights, and you get plenty of it.

Clifton Beach Hotel (tel. 458-8235) also provides comfortable rooms right on the beach. The staff here is very friendly and helpful, and unlike many places in the West Indies, seem to appreciate your business. Its owner, Conrad Adams, rents out cottages on the beach, also. Some of the rooms have private baths, and the others have running water. Ten double rooms with private bath are rented. Two MAP guests can stay here in winter at a rate of EC$192 ($72.96), this tariff lowered to EC$102 ($38.76) in a single. *In summer, the MAP tariff is EC$162 ($61.56) in a double, from EC$90 ($34.20) in a single.* The furnishings are modest, but no one seems to care about such things. Each unit is equipped with a phone. There's nothing fancy here, just good value, which you will probably see best when dinner is served.

Sunny Grenadines (tel. 458-8327) provides simpler but still comfortable accommodations. This is a very relaxed, no-frills type of barefoot-and-boating establishment. You don't do much around here after a rugged day other than sample the West Indian atmosphere and have a good dinner. The best way to stay here is to ask for the MAP rate, which is $78 in a single in winter, $108 in a double. *Summer MAP tariffs are $102 in a double.*

PETIT ST. VINCENT: A private island four miles from Union, in the southern Grenadines, this speck of island is rimmed with white sandy beaches. On 113 acres, it's an out-of-this-world corner of the Caribbean that is only for self-sufficient types, who want to be away from just about everything.

To reach it, fly to Barbados, hopefully arriving there before 4 p.m. If so, you can be on "PSV," as it is affectionately called, the same day. Passengers fly a charter or scheduled service. A common departure time will be scheduled for guests arriving that afternoon in Barbados for the 45-minute flight direct to Union Island. At Union Island, the PSV boat will meet you and take you on a half-hour ride to PSV. Connections can also be made through Martinique.

However, in such an offbeat oasis there exists **Petit St. Vincent Resort** (tel. 458-4801), which has a kind of nautical chic. Open to the trade winds, this self-contained cottage colony was conceived by a Swedish architect, Arne Hasselquist, who used purpleheart wood and the local stone, blue birch, for the walls. The resort, incidentally, is the only place on the island, and if you don't like things here and want to check out, you'd better have a yacht waiting.

But, chances are, you'll be quite pleased with what you see. Cottages are built on a hillside or set close to the beach, in a 113-acre setting. Units open onto big outdoor patios, all of which have views. Winter AP rates range from $190 to $320 for one person, $255 to $400 for two. *In the off-season, AP tariffs drop to $160 to $268 daily in a single, $212 to $340 in a double.* Personal checks are accepted. The resort is closed in September and October. Wicker and rattan along with khus-khus rugs set the Caribbean tone of the place.

The resort was conceived by Haze Richardson, who had to do everything from plant trees to lay cables, and his partner, H.W. Nichols, a Cincinnati executive who acquired the island from a little old woman in Petit Martinque. Before that, the archbishop of Trinidad owned it.

The units have no phones. When you need something, write out your re-

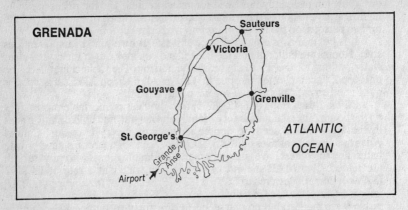

quest, place it in a slot in a bamboo flagpole, and run up the yellow flag! One of the waiters will arrive on a Mini-Moke to collect your order.

To make reservations, write to Petit St. Vincent, P.O. Box 12506, Cincinnati, OH 45212 (tel. 513/242-1333).

5. Grenada

The "Spice Island," Grenada is an independent three-island nation which includes Carriacou, the largest of the Grenadines, and Petit Martinque. The air in Grenada is full of the fragrance of spice and exotic fruits. The island has more spices per square mile than any other place in the world—cloves, cinnamon, mace, cocoa, tonka beans, ginger, and a third of the world's supply of nutmeg. "Drop a few seeds anywhere," the natives will tell you, "and you have an instant garden." The central area is like a jungle of palms, oleander, bougainvillea, purple and red hibiscus, crimson anthurium, bananas, breadfruit, birdsong, ferns, and palms.

Southernmost island of the Windward Antilles, Grenada (pronounced Gre-*nay*-dah) lies 60 miles southwest of St. Vincent and about 90 miles north of Trinidad. An oval-shaped island, it is 21 miles long and about 12 miles wide. Volcanic in origin, the island has an average yearly temperature of 83° Fahrenheit. Because of the constant trade winds, there is little humidity.

Like most of the Caribbean islands, it was discovered by Columbus, who sailed by it in 1498. Whether he landed or not is the subject of conjecture. Grenada was inhabited by the warmongering, cannibalistic Carib Indians. The first Europeans who visited Grenada were probably London seafaring merchants, who ended up, no doubt, in the Carib stewing pot.

The French in 1650 were the first to establish relations with the Caribs, buying their favors for two bottles of brandy and some baubles. But those peaceful relations didn't last too long when the Indians tired of their trinkets. The conflict ended in 1691 at **Morne du Sauteur** (Jumper Hill), as the last band of Caribs tossed their women and children into the sea, then in a suicide leap, plunged to their own deaths on the jagged rocks rather than submit to European domination.

After the inevitable British–French disputes and bloody wars for domination, Grenada has settled down to British rule since 1783. In 1967 it became an associated state within the Commonwealth. Before it achieved independence in early 1974, political squabbles virtually shut down the island, bringing havoc to the tourist season in late 1973 and early 1974. A general strike shut down the port, as electricity and water were turned off.

Grenada was dominated by a volatile black leader, Eric Gairy, who had been considered a practitioner of black magic and a UFO believer, performing voodoo-like rituals to keep himself in power. On three separate occasions he proposed before a stunned United Nations that it undertake a study of UFOs.

For 12 years he oppressively ruled over the island until he was overthrown in the spring of 1979. The revolution cost only three lives, and boatloads of tourists, including a Soviet cruise ship, hardly noticed they were in the middle of a revolution.

The man who ousted Gairy was Maurice Bishop, along with his radical New Jewel Movement. Bishop launched what is still a controversial 4½-year "revolution," cementing ties with the Soviet Union and Cuba. Dramatically, in 1983 Bishop was placed under house arrest. Later he was executed along with several key supporters. An even more radical Marxist-Leninist faction took over the government and installed a revolutionary military council.

President Reagan, however, looked upon these new leaders as "thugs." In October of that year, the U.S.—backed by other Caribbean countries—launched a successful invasion of Grenada, routing the military council and rounding up Cubans building the controversial Point Saline Airport.

Beefed up by financial aid from the U.S., Grenada has revived a sagging tourist industry. The anti-American slogans have long been down. Instead you are likely to see billboards proclaiming "Thank God for U.S." Grenada is a safe destination, and American tourists are genuinely welcomed there.

GETTING THERE: The controversial Point Saline International Airport—financed in part by the Soviet Union and Cuba (and finished by the United States)—opened in October 1984, on the anniversary of the U.S. rescue mission of the island. At the southwestern toe of Grenada, the airport not only makes it possible for jumbo jets to land, it makes most of the major hotels accessible in only 5 to 15 minutes by taxi.

Several major carriers may become interested in landing rights in Grenada during the lifetime of this edition, so a last-minute check with a travel agent is advised.

At the moment it's possible to fly BWIA on a direct flight from Miami to Grenada. Clients fly to Miami on several major carriers, then board a once-weekly flight to Grenada every Sunday at 2 p.m. The DC-9 makes touchdowns at Antigua and St. Lucia before continuing to Grenada's Point Saline Airport at 8:15 p.m.

This same BWIA flight returns every Sunday morning very early at 7, leaving for Miami via St. Lucia and Antigua. The plane lands in Miami at noon, in time for passengers to make daytime connections with other carriers for other cities.

Passengers from Toronto and New York can connect to Grenada via Trinidad on BWIA.

Passengers can also fly LIAT from Barbados, the traditional method of going to Grenada, but don't expect these flights to be on time

There is yet another airport on Grenada. It's tiny **Pearls Airport,** on the east coast, north of Grenville, the so-called second city of Grenada. Before the opening of the airport at Point Saline, all craft landed here. It is still in use by some small planes. However, in the unlikely event that your own plane sets down there, know that you must then take a long one-hour taxi drive across tortuous terrain with scenes evoking the colorful pages of *National Geographic*. That potholed road leads to the main hotels along Grand Anse beach.

PRACTICAL FACTS: English is commonly spoken on the island, because of the long years of British domination. **Proof of citizenship** is needed to enter the country. A passport is preferred, but a birth certificate or voter registration card will do. An ongoing or return ticket must be produced as well.

The official **currency** is the Eastern Caribbean dollar, or "Bee Wee." Always determine which dollars—EC or U.S.—you're talking about when someone on Grenada quotes you a price. In St. George's, the capital, you'll find such **banks** operating as the National Commercial Bank, Barclays, the Royal Bank of Canada, and the Bank of Nova Scotia.

The local **telephone system** maintains 24-hour daily service with the rest of the world. **Cable & Wireless Ltd.** offers a telegraphic service in St. George's from 7 a.m. to 7 p.m. daily (on Sunday and holidays from 7 a.m. to 10 a.m. and 4 to 8 p.m.).

The **General Post Office** in St. George's is open Monday through Thursday from 8 a.m. to 4 p.m., with a lunch break from 11:45 a.m. to 1 p.m. On Friday hours are 8 a.m. to 5 p.m. It is closed on weekends.

Radio Grenada, owned and operated by the government, broadcasts the news, and a lot of American pop and disco music.

Customs places no restrictions on the amount of money brought into the island.

Electricity, not always reliable, is supplied on the island by Grenada Electricity Services, and the current is 220/240 volts, 50 cycles, AC.

Grenada celebrates the usual **holidays.**

There is a **general hospital** in St. George's, with an X-ray department and operating theater. Private doctors and nurses are available on call.

Among newspapers, the *Grenadian Voice* is published weekly. You'll also find *Time* or *Newsweek*.

To most restaurant and hotel bills you are presented on the island, a 10% **service charge** will be added, plus another 7½% **government tax.**

Upon leaving Grenada, you must fill out an immigration card and pay a **departure tax** of EC$15 ($5.70).

For information, go to the **Grenada Tourist Department,** on the Carenage in St. George's (tel. 2001). It's open daily except Sunday from 9 to 11:45 a.m. and 1 to 4 p.m. At its location near the wharfside market (which, incidentally, is held every Tuesday), maps, guides, whatever are available. The young women who staff it seem to know everybody on the island, and they're adept at solving problems.

GETTING AROUND: You'll have to establish the price of a **taxi** before getting in. Most arriving visitors take a cab at the Point Saline Airport to one of the hotels near St. George's, at a cost ranging from $10 to $15.

You can also use most taxi drivers as a guide for a day's sightseeing, and the cost can be divided among three to four passengers. If so, count on about $60 per day. Again, this figure is to be negotiated.

Car Rentals

The rates are fairly modest if you want this often-difficult means of transport through the length and width of Grenada. First, you must remember to *drive on the left*. A U.S. or Canadian driver's license is valid in Grenada, so you don't have to obtain another permit from the police as you do on most Windward Islands.

A word of warning about local drivers: There's such a thing as a Grenadian driving machismo where the drivers take blind corners with abandon. An extraordinary number of accidents are reported in the lively local paper. It seems as if the drivers release much of their hostility on the road.

Royston's Rent-a-Car, at Blue Horizons (tel. 4316), rents Toyota automatics, Mazdas, and Mini-Mokes, among other vehicles. Rental fees, which include 50 free miles a day, are about $40 per day. Unlimited mileage is offered with a full week's rental, and American Express cards are accepted.

Buses

There are two types. The most colorful and traditional ones are painted in red, blue, gold, whatever, and are just as crazy as their names (one, for example, is called "Oo-la-la"). On plank seats, you're bounced until you're squealing just as much as the live pig with which you're likely to be sharing the ride! Most of these buses depart from Market Square in St. George's.

New minibuses have now been introduced as well, taking you on most rides for 50¢ to $1. They're not as colorful but are more comfortable.

Local Air Services

Many visitors like to fly over to Grenada's satellite island, Carriacou, for the day. **Inter-Island Air Services** makes the short takeoff and landing (STOL) flight in about ten minutes at a round-trip cost of EC$120 ($45.60) per person. To book a ticket, the Inter-Island telephone number is 7951.

Boat Excursions

The M.V. *Flamingo* bills its day riding the waves as an "escape to the sea." For about $30, you can enjoy casting off early from Grenada Yacht Services (see below). A guide will point out the many sights and the names of the islands you pass during your day on the water. Lunch is also available. For information about reservations, call 2508.

At the **Grenada Sailing School,** P.O. Box 220, St. George's (tel. 4458), you can charter the racer-cruiser *Damosel,* a 43-foot vessel, or the cutter ketch *Samantha II,* a 42-footer. The cost for a semi-bareboat charter aboard the *Damosel* costs $255 per day in winter, *$155 per day in summer.* The charge for a semi-bareboat charter aboard *Samantha II* is $317 per day in winter, *$200 per day in summer.* Provisions, either winter or summer, cost $16 per person per day. The maximum number of persons allowed on the semi-bareboat is six, and the maximum on the fully provisioned charter is four.

Carin Travel at Grand Anse (tel. 4363) offers day charters at $20 per person, along with fishing at $30 per person, and sunset cocktail cruises on Friday for $12.50 per person. A minimum of five persons is required.

Other charters can be arranged by getting in touch with **Grenada Yacht Services,** P.O. Box 183, St. George's (tel. 2508). They'll arrange a charter on a 40+-foot vessel between 9:30 a.m. and 4 p.m., with rum punch and juice supplied. However, you're to bring your own lunch. If several passengers, no more than six, share the ride, the per-person cost can be divided.

An excursion to Hog Island is a convenient destination for anyone who presents a letter from his yacht club and can afford the daily rental fee for a 40-foot Hughes II sailboat which is rented by **Spice Island Charters,** Prickly Bay, L Anse aux Épines (P.O. Box 449, St. George's; tel. 4342). They operate out of what has been called "the prettiest boatyard in the Caribbean." Bring a jug of the island's incomparable rum punch with you to really keep your party flowing. An even more exotic destination would be to the so-called Bird Island, an unmarked and unnamed rocky island off the south shore of Grenada. There, thousands of white egrets nest each evening at dusk, flying away in one white mass at daybreak. Yachts can be reserved in advance and sailed without supervision upon the presentation of documentation from a client's local yacht club. Face masks are provided with the boats free, and scuba equipment can be rented too, but only if you have a PADI certification. Both bareboat and crewed charters are available at Spice Island, along with skippered day charters. Windsurfers and Sunfish are also available to rent, hourly or daily.

WHERE TO STAY: Many of Grenada's hostelries evoke the Mediterranean more than the Caribbean in their architecture, perhaps in deference to the island's Spanish name. Innkeepers think small here. The Grenada Beach Hotel, scheduled to open by the time of your visit, is the biggest place at which you can overnight, and nearly everything else is tiny, usually containing no more than a dozen rooms.

Secret Harbour, P.O. Box 11, St. George's (tel. 4548), is an elegant site, five miles from the capital on the island's south coast. It's the creation of an English lady, expatriate Barbara Stevens. In her own country she'd been an accountant, but apparently that got to be too much for her one day. Along with her first husband, she sailed across the Atlantic in a ketch, eventually settling in Grenada, where she decided to build this hotel.

Seen from the water of Mount Hartman Bay, Secret Harbour reminds one of a Mediterranean complex on Spain's Costa del Sol—a tasteful one, that is, with white stucco arches, red tile roofs, and wrought-iron light fixtures. The design also has a Moorish touch in the tiles and terraces. Some of the decoration is opulent, including stained glass, hand-hewn beams, and two large mahogany four-poster beds in each room. From all over Grenada, including some island plantation homes, antiques were purchased, restored, and installed here. The bathrooms are also luxurious, with sunken tubs lined with color-rich Italian tiles, the lighting from unglazed medallion windows.

Each of Mrs. Stevens's 20 suites has a dressing room, living area, and patio overlooking the water. Steps lead down to the beach, as you pass along lime and papaya trees, palms, frangipani. Pathways take you to the tennis court, the freeform swimming pool, and the main building.

Winter EP rates are $138 daily in a double, $115 in a single. *In summer, guests are quoted an EP rate of $78 daily in a double, $66 in a single.*

In the dining room, decorated with style, a chef provides sumptuous meals. Arrangements can be made at the desk for car rentals, island tours, sports fishing, and golf.

Calabash, P.O. Box 382 (tel. 4234), fronts a protected bay and secluded sheltered L'Anse aux Épines beach, five miles south of St. George's. Eye-appealing in the best of the West Indian tradition, it is set in the midst of eight acres of tropical gardens, with many fragrant shrubs, including, naturally, the Calabash, for which the inn was named. Many repeat visitors come here to enjoy the hospitality of Charles de Gale and his friendly island staff.

In summer, singles on the MAP pay $80 daily, the cost rising to $120 for two persons sharing a double. The pool suite is my favorite, costing $150 per day for two on the half-board plan. In winter, prices rise to $160 in a single, MAP, $190 in a double, and a third person sharing a room pays yet another $95.

In the 22 suites with their own kitchens, maids prepare your breakfast, and they do a good job of it. Each unit has twin beds, an immaculately maintained private bath, a sitting room area, as well as a kitchenette and terrace. Louvered windows let in the fresh sea breezes.

Meals are West Indian in style and flavor, and occasional buffets are spread out for you. Ever had swordfish pie creole? A pool table and tennis court are also available to guests. The dining pavilion is made of local hardwood timber and natural gray stone.

Horse Shoe Bay, P.O. Box 174, St. George's (tel. 4410), is a little dream with vintage charm. Set on a hilltop, it is built in the elegant Mediterranean style, a total of 12 cozily furnished terracotta cottages—each with a canopied four-poster bed—all with private balconies and air conditioning. Breathing in the fragrant shrubs, you stroll leisurely down the hill to the beach and sea.

Constructed on a small promontory, the complex manages to capture the sea breezes at night, and you'll hear the rustling sound of wind blowing through acres of tropical gardens, filled with hibiscus and bougainvillea.

Guests are so well coddled here that they keep returning year after year, enjoying the appealingly furnished rooms. Many of the furnishings came from buying up antiques from old island family houses.

From the moment of your arrival, you know you've arrived at a warm, enchanting place in the tropics. The doorway to the Spanish stucco building is almost hidden by the foliage, including a towering banyan tree. You enter the Grenadian-Iberian dining pavilion and red-tiled lounge, with its cozy nooks and original oil paintings. The dining room frames views of the secluded beach and swimming pool, as well as of the gardens. On a star-studded night, you dine on good food, looking out onto a moonlit sea. If this place sounds like a cliché of Caribbean romance, it is.

Maids will come in to prepare breakfast in your own kitchen (one for every two rooms). In winter, guests must book in here on the half-board arrangement, no hardship really, considering the quality of the West Indian food. A double costs $165 daily, a single going for $125. *In the off-season, it's possible to stay here on room-only terms at $85 daily in a double, $75 in a single.*

Snorkeling and Sunfish sails are yours for the asking, or else you can just lie back and enjoy the bucolic serenity.

Spice Island Inn, P.O. Box 6, St. George's (tel. 4258), is a unique spot, set on an estate overlooking the Caribbean and built along 1200 feet of Grand Anse beach. The main house, reserved for dining and dancing, has a tropical aura and lots of nice touches, showing that taste and concern went into the design of the place. Twenty air-conditioned beach suites are offered, plus ten pool suites, all pleasantly contemporary, stretched along the white sands. About ten of them are set back a bit and have their own private plunge pools, surrounded by high walls where guests can skinny-dip. The waiter will arrive with your breakfast (a just-plucked red hibiscus resting on the tray), and you'll enjoy it (and, hopefully, who you're with) on a shaded patio, your very own.

In high season, the MAP rate costs from $165 to $190 a day in a single, from $185 to $220 for two persons sharing a double. *In low season, you can stay here on half-board terms at rates ranging from $112 to $130 daily in a single, from $130 to $150 in a double.* Furnishings in the rooms are not elaborate, with outdoor-type pieces such as wicker chairs.

The place is known for its Sunday buffet, and the cooks do not only a good Grenadian cuisine, but also deftly turn out an international cuisine, including soursop ice cream (nutmeg is also a specialty), breadfruit vichyssoise, green turtle soup, and Caribbean lobster. Sometimes a combo plays for dancing.

Cinnamon Hill and Beach Club, P.O. Box 292, St. George's (tel. 4301), was created by English expatriate Richard Gray, an actor, writer, producer, and architect. Cooperatively owned, Cinnamon Hill is a cluster of luxurious villas, like a Mediterranean-inspired village, surrounded by tropical gardens.

Some 20 hacienda-style suites are clustered on the hillside overlooking Grand Anse beach, each fully air-conditioned, with a living room, terrace, fully equipped kitchenette, one or two bedrooms, private bath, and balcony opening onto the sea.

The tiles, stonework, and woodwork come from Mr. Gray's own designing factory. A splash of red tile roofs, white stucco arches, hand-hewn beams—everything is in keeping with the Spanish-Mediterranean theme.

In the off-season, two persons can rent either a one- or two-bedroom villa for anywhere from $90 to $110 daily. A one-bedroom villa or suite can sleep four persons, and a two-bedroom villa can shelter six guests. Breakfast is cooked right in your own villa. In the high season, two guests are accepted for from $130 daily in a double with one bedroom, to $160 daily in a two-bedroom villa, each additional person paying $17.

Golf carts transport guests around the 12 acres of very steep hotel grounds. Sailing, snorkeling, waterskiing, skindiving, and fishing are arranged at the front desk. For its restaurant, see my dining recommendations.

Twelve Degrees North, P.O. Box 241, St. George's (tel. 4580), is operated by Joseph Gaylord, a former commercial real estate broker from New York, who greets visitors with a wide smile and an outstretched hand in front of a large flame tree on his front lawn. He owns this cluster of spotlessly clean efficiency apartments, not far from the new international airport at Point Saline.

Each unit (two with two bedrooms and six with one bedroom) comes with an individual uniformed attendant, who arrives at 8 each morning to perform the thousand small kindnesses that make Twelve Degres North a favorite lair for returning guests from America and Europe. Many of the staff members have been with Mr. Gaylord since he opened the place some 15 years ago, and are highly trustworthy. They'll cook breakfast, prepare lunch (perhaps pumpkin soup and the flying fish of Barbados), do the cleaning and laundry, go food shopping, and fix regional specialties for dinner (which you'll heat up for yourself later). Each unit is equipped with an efficiency kitchen with 12-cubic foot refrigerator, large enough to prevent the need for food shopping daily. The large beds can be separated or pushed together, depending on the mood of the guests.

The resort has its own tennis court, and a Sunfish and two sailing dinghies are provided for a small fee. A grass-roofed beach bar faces the water, and guests use an honor system.

The owner prefers to quote weekly rates for his apartments, because, as he says, "a few days isn't enough to get to know Grenada." In winter that rent begins at $670 weekly for two persons in a one-bedroom apartment. However, on a daily basis, a one-bedroom apartment for two persons is $96 a day, with each additional person paying another $42. *In summer, two persons in a one-bedroom unit pay $72 daily, and a two-bedroom apartment, suitable for four guests, rents for only $108 per day. The weekly rent on a one-bedroom apartment in summer is $504.*

Blue Horizons Cottage Hotel, Grand Anse (tel. 4316), was purchased by co-owners Royston and Arnold Hopkins from a bankrupt estate. Sons of the famous Grenadian hotelkeeprs Audrey and Curtis Hopkins, they transformed the neglected property into one of the finest on the island, with an occupancy rate second only to that of Spice Island. The cottages, 18 fully equipped one-bedroom suites, are spread throughout a lush and flowering garden of 3¼ acres. Each bungalow has an efficiency kitchen, comfortable furniture, and lots of the local hardwood, saman, which polishes to a beautiful rich-grained glow. Children are welcomed, and they can watch the 21 varieties of native birds said to inhabit the grounds.

High-season rates depend on the category of the cottage: standard, superior, or deluxe. On the EP, doubles in high season cost from $84 to $96 daily, singles go for $78 to $90 and an extra person pays $12. *In summer, rates are slashed to $66 to $78 daily in a double, EP, and $60 to $72 in a single.*

Guests who prefer to cook in their rooms can buy supplies from a Food Fair at Grand Anse, a ten-minute walk away. Most important, Grand Anse beach is only five minutes away by foot. On the grounds is one of the best restaurants on the island, La Belle Créole (see my dining recommendations). Lunch is served around a pool bar.

Apple Inn, Grand Anse beach (tel. 4557), is a simple West Indian guest house of only nine rooms, which is set way back from the beach. Its one of the most economical places to stay on the island, providing your tastes are not too demanding. The rooms are air-conditioned (well, almost) and they are doubles, each with a private shower and phone. Mrs. Germaine Woodroffe, your kindly Grenadian hostess, charges *$39 daily in a double and $33 if rented as a single in the off-season, EP.* Winter tariffs climb to $50 daily in a double and $40 in a single, both on the EP.

If you like native cookery, the food is some of the best along this beachfront. For an average price of $15, you're given a big and filling meal that might include pumpkin fritters, fresh seasonal greens, conch in ginger sauce, grilled fish of the day, and a special apple salad. At the bar, in addition to the usual libations, you can order sea moss and Spice Isle nectars.

WHERE TO DINE: You may eat in all the restaurants of the hotels previously described, but you should call first to make a reservation, as food supplies are often limited if the chef doesn't know to expect you. Table d'hôte luncheons or dinners run from $12 to $35 in most of these establishments. I've found hotel food better in Grenada than in the other British Windward Islands. Try, in particular, **Secret Harbour and Horse Shoe Bay,** already recommended. Many of the chefs are European or European trained, and native cooks are also on hand to prepare Grenadian specialties such as conch (called lambi here), lobster, callaloo soup (with greens and crab), conch-and-onion pie, turtle steaks, and soursop or avocado ice cream.

It is estimated that some 22 kinds of fish, including fresh tuna, dolphin, and barracuda, are caught off the island's shores. Most are good for eating. Naturally, the spices of the island, such as nutmeg, are used plentifully. The cookery is often served family style in an open-air setting, opening onto a vista of the sea.

Cinnamon Hill Restaurant, St. George's (tel. 4301), is the first condominium hotel to be built in Grenada, and it has already been recommended. At this scenic spot overlooking Grand Anse beach, a Swedish company operates a restaurant that specializes in the fresh seafood of Grenada, with many continental overtones. This same company also operates André's in Aspen, Colorado, and it's the first international firm to operate a restaurant in Grenada. A Swedish chef serves a superb cuisine nightly from 6 to midnight. The open-air, covered restaurant accepts nonresidents of the condo. Meals cost from $30 and up.

La Belle Créole, on the grounds at Blue Horizon's, Grand Anse beach (tel. 4316), is one of the best restaurants in Grenada. Arnold and Royston Hopkins, who run it, are sons of "Mama" Audrey Hopkins, long considered the best cook on the island if you're seeking West Indian specialties. Archways frame views of the mountains and the beach. Lunch is served from noon to 2 p.m. every day, featuring such summertime snacks as soups, chicken, fish, or lobster salads, plus a variety of sandwiches and omelets. Lunch can be taken poolside.

Dinner is table d'hôte, with a variety of choices featuring continental recipes with West Indian substitutions for foods not available on the island. A typical dinner might begin with dolphin (fish) mousse with callaloo, then conch chowder, followed by a main course such as creole veal roll stuffed with ham, chicken livers, onions, and seasonings, baked in a wine sauce, and served with local vegetables such as a dasheen soufflé and christophines, along with candied plantain. This, plus a dessert of mango delight, would cost around $25.

The walls and ceilings are covered with a type of island reed called roseau, which, strangely enough, must be cut only during a certain phase of the moon to provide a durable, long-lasting building surface. If cut at any other time of the month, experience has taught that the covering disintegrates into a powder within six months.

Dinner begins promptly at 7 p.m. until the last order is accepted at 8:30. Each of the items on the table d'hôte is priced separately, to allow a guest to order only an entree with coffee, for example.

Spice Island Inn, Grand Anse beach (tel. 4258). A favorite way to enjoy a meal in Grenada is on an uncrowded beachfront in the full outdoors, with only a well-designed parapet over your head to protect you from sudden tropical showers. At this inn, the view is of one of the best beaches in the Caribbean, miles of white sands, sprouting an occasional grove of sea grape or almond trees. The parapet looks like a Le Corbusier rooftop, built of imported pine and cedar, covering suntanned diners at immaculately table clothed place settings.

An à la carte lunch, which you can eat in a swimsuit if you elect, costs from $12. Dinner menus change frequently and can be cooked to your specifications. They are usually table d'hôte, costing about $25 each and offering enough selections to make everyone happy.

The Turtle Back, on the Carenage in St. George's (tel. 2206), at the entrance to the harbor, is built practically over the water. You can sip a rum punch or a Carib beer under a latticework of palm fronds on the somewhat rickety dock of this most informal restaurant, overlooking the offices of the prime minister. The place is a favorite rendezvous point for the owners of those sleek sailing craft that wander the islands of the Caribbean with their bikinied crew members.

Not all the items on the menu are always available, but you'll always get fresh fish, which is brought in daily to the kitchen here. The chef does it well, turning out a plate of, say, red snapper, a favorite. If you're here on a Friday, you can order an "oil down"—an island specialty of pork, turtle, pig snout, green bananas (known as "figs"), black pepper, curry, and sometimes an island goat, all simmering under callaloo leaves in coconut oil. Less exotic specialties include a conch steak which has been pounded tender and seasoned to perfection.

Pumpkin pie is offered in season, and you can usually get nutmeg ice cream. If you're dining light, sandwiches are offered. For dinner, count on spending from $15, plus the cost of your drinks.

The Turtle Back is open daily from 10 a.m. until midnight.

Rudolf's stands on the Carenage (tel. 2241), a deep, U-shaped inner harbor lined with commercial establishments in St. George's. Some people claim this is the best place for dining on the entire island. You might call it "tropical Swiss." The restaurant is open for both lunch and dinner. On the north corner of the Carenage, it's also a great spot for drinks in the late afternoon if you don't mind hearing the sexist remarks of the yachting machismo set.

If you stick around for dinner, you'll find that the food is well prepared, with more choices offered on the menu than in most places at Grenada. About 13 different steak dishes are offered, and if you're dining lighter, you're faced with a selection of some eight different omelets. Soups are both hot and cold, ranging from french onion to gazpacho. The owner is Austrian, Rudolf Hoschtaleik, and his menu reflects many Central European dishes. Try, for example, the specialty, cevapcici, minced beef with parsley potatoes and a salad.

Specials are posted daily. Dinners begin at $25, but will range much higher if you order either steak or lobster as a main course.

The Nutmeg, also at the Carenage (tel. 2539), is right on the harbor, over the Sea Change Shop where you can pick up paperbacks and souvenirs. It's another rendezvous point for the yachting set and a favorite with just about everybody, both expatriates living on the island and visitors. It is suitable for a snack or a full-fledged dinner. Its drinks are very good. Try one of the Grenadian rum punches made with Angostura bitters, grated nutmeg, rum, lime juice, and syrup.

An informal friendliness prevails, as you're served your filet of fish with potato croquettes and string beans. There's always fresh fish, and usually callaloo soup, maybe lobster too, on most days. Lambi (that ubiquitous conch) is also done very well here. It can be so disguised you don't know what you're tasting. Lobster thermidor is the most expensive food item on the menu. Meals cost from $20. There's a small wine list with some California, German, and Italian selections.

The sea view is good from the second-floor precincts, and you can drop in for just a glass of beer, staying as long as you wish. Sometimes, however, you'll be asked to share a table, but that's a great way to strike up a conversation. It is said that eventually, if you sit here long enough, everybody in Grenada will show up.

Hours are probably not observed exactly, but they are: breakfast from 9:30 to 11 a.m., lunch from 11 a.m. to 3 p.m., and dinner from 4 p.m. until "whenever."

The **St. James Hotel,** Grand Etang Road, in St. George's (tel. 2041), is a big, generously proportioned, old-fashioned, white-painted hotel on a hilltop overlooking the activity of St. George's. It caters to many local businessmen who consider it the best luncheon bargain in town. A fixed-price midday meal is offered every day except Sunday for EC$25 ($9.50), in an airy, light-filled dining room with immaculate tablecloths and good service. Dinner costs EC$35 ($13.30) and includes an extra fish course not offered at the table d'hôte luncheon.

Your meal might begin with an aromatic vegetable-and-chicken soup, then follow with a salad, along with conch casserole with tomatoes or a pungent beef stew with lots of hot peppers. An island dessert often featured is sopadilla delight. Lunch is from noon to 2 p.m. and dinner from 7 to 9 p.m.

The hotel has some of the bargain rooms of the island for those devotees of little West Indian inns that rarely attract the beach-seeking tourist. In season, a double room with private bath on the MAP rents for $57 per person daily, that rate *dropping to $54 in the off-season.*

Mama's (tel. 2299) is across from Butler House, on the road leading to Grenada Yacht Services. Every trip to the Caribbean should include a visit to an establishment like Mama's. Mama (alias Inslay Wardally), judging from her size, likes her own cookery, and serves copious meals out of her private home to brawny local mechanics playing friendly games of dominoes, quietly drunk fishermen stranded from nearby islands, Austrian yachtsmen escorting braless nymphets from California, and groups of initially bewildered foreign tourists.

Everyone goes to Mama's, to sit either on rickety chairs on the covered veranda or beside the bar in modest quarters that in the off-hours is Mama's living room.

Mama herself is as generous as her meals, which I am told come in two sizes: "the usual" and "the special." I telephoned ahead to order "the special," which, Mama eventually told me, was really the same as "the usual." It included such dishes as callaloo soup with coconut cream, shredded cold crab with lime juice, freshwater crayfish, fried conch, fried dolphin, breaded turtle served in its own shell, curried chicken with yellow chickpea sauce, mashed tannia root (deep fried in coconut oil), breadfruit salad flavored with three kinds of thyme, and a casserole of cooked bananas, yams, and dasheen, along with ripe baked plantain, and tortillas made of curry and yellow chickpeas, followed by sugar apple ice cream. I failed to try her rich, gamy opossum or her stewed armadillo. The specialty drink of the house is rum punch with cream, the ingredients of which are known only to Mama. Dinner here must be reserved in advance, and it costs EC$25 ($9.50) per person, drinks extra.

For change-of-pace dining, I suggest the **Bird's Nest,** also known as Yin Wo Restaurant, at the Grand Anse Shopping Centre (tel. 4264). This simple green-and-white restaurant is run by a Trinidadian-Grenadian couple, Derick and Lucy Steele, who give you a warm welcome. Their family business offers typical Chinese food, mainly Cantonese. The most expensive main courses, of course, are those with a lobster base. You'll see the familiar shrimp eggrolls along with eight different chow meins. Sweet-and-sour fish is a favorite, and daily specials are posted. A take-out service is available. Expect to spend from $18 for a meal, served Monday through Saturday from 11 a.m. to 3 p.m. and 6 to 11 p.m.

Elsewhere on the island, I'd suggest the **Red Crab,** at L'Anse aux Épines (tel. 4424), which is popular with many Americans. It's a favorite Grenadian luncheon spot, set out under the trees. However, I always like to approach it in the evening, as your vehicle hurtles through an inky night. It's like an English pub in the mock Tudor style, and is in fact run by an Englishman, Reg Blamphin. Before taking your order, one of the waiters will bring you a draft beer, and you can settle back to enjoy the classic fish and chips prepared here. The chef also does some of the best stuffed crab backs on the island. You can also order a savory seafood chowder, fried shrimp, or steamed turtle. Naturally, they offer callaloo soup. Dessert may perhaps be, say, blueberry pie à la mode. Your meal is likely to cost from EC$35 ($13.30). The pub is open daily from 11 a.m. to 2 p.m. and 6 to 11 p.m.

The name of **Mrs. Edgar Japal** (tel. 6346) is a closely guarded secret. This remarkable woman of East Indian descent lives in a village, Crochu, far off the beaten track (a taxi will take you there). Years ago she quietly established a reputation in Grenada as a superlative native cook, preparing tasty meals for parties who telephone far enough in advance.

Her specialty is curried goat, although her curried chicken is also talked about. A woman of great dignity, she will not cook for anyone or everybody, and sometimes is reluctant to quote prices over the phone. You'll probably end up paying about $22 per person, $38 per couple, for a gargantuan repast, including not only the curried goat and curried chicken, but pigeon peas, fried plantains, boiled green bananas (called "figs"), and sweet potatoes with island thyme.

The food is cooked in a 20-gallon iron pot, except for bread, pastries, cakes, roast chicken, and other items which are baked in a 45-gallon steel drum using coconut shells and sugarcane stalks for fuel. The whole experience encompasses far more than good food—it's likely to be one of your most memorable experiences of Grenada. Be sure to clarify in advance what drinks are to be provided, and make every effort to be on time.

WHAT TO SEE: The capital city of Grenada, St. George's, is considered one of the most attractive ports, the picture-postcard variety, in the West Indies. Its landlocked inner harbor is actually the deep crater of a long-dead volcano, or so one is told.

In the town you'll see some of the most charming Georgian colonial buildings to be found in the Caribbean, in spite of a devastating 1955 hurricane. The streets are mostly steep and narrow, and somehow this seems to enhance the attractiveness of the mellowed ballast bricks, wrought-iron balconies, the red tiles of the sloping roofs. Many of the pastel warehouses date back to the 18th century. Frangipani and flamboyant trees add to the palette of color.

The port, which some have compared to Portofino, if flanked by old forts and bold headlands. Among the town's attractions is an 18th-century pink-painted Anglican church, on Church Street, and a Market Square where colorfully attired farm women offer even more colorful produce for sale.

Fort George, built by the French, stands at the entrance to the bay, with subterranean passageways and old guardrooms and cells. It is now the headquarters of the Grenada police force.

Everybody strolls along the waterfront, called the **Carenage,** where bustling activity is connected with the loading and unloading of schooners and the coming and going of the people in their little dinghies from moored yachts. The Carenage is best viewed on Tuesday afternoon when crates and bags of fruit and vegetables are loaded and bound for Trinidad.

On this side of town, the **Grenada National Museum** is set in the foundations of an old French army barrack and prison built in 1704. Small but interesting, it houses finds from archeological digs, including the petroglyphs (the most recent found in the autumn of 1980), native fauna, the first telegraph installed on the island, a rum still, and memorabilia depicting Grenada's colorful history. The most comprehensive exhibit traces the Indian culture of Grenada. One of the exhibits shows two bathtubs—the wooden barrel used by the fort's prisoners and the carved marble tub used by Josephine Bonaparte during her adolescence on Martinique. The museum is also contemporary. In one section you get to see the blood-soaked clothes worn by Prime Minister Bishop on November 18, 1973, which is known in Grenada as "Bloody Sunday." You'll also see the stone responsible for bursting his head on that same date. Surprisingly, there's even an exhibition case devoted to the former prime minister (1974–1979), Sir Eric Gairy. You'll get to see his elaborate ceremonial garbs, among other tempting sights. Hours are 9 a.m. to 3 p.m. Monday to Friday.

The Outer Harbour is also called the **Esplanade.** It's connected to the Carenage by the Sendall Tunnel which is cut through the promontory known as St. George's Point, dividing the two bodies of water.

At the southern edge of town is the **Botanical Garden,** with a wide variety of tropical trees and flowers labeled so that you can identify them. Rare Caribbean animals and birds are kept in an adjoining zoo.

You can also take a drive up to Richmond Hill where **Fort Frederick** stands. The French built this fort in 1779, but before they could finish it, British troops had moved in. The English completed the structure in 1783. From its battlements, you'll have a superb view of the harbor and of the yacht marina.

An afternoon tour of St. George's and its environs should take you into the mountains northeast of the capital. There you'll find **Annandale Falls,** a tropical wonderland, where a cascade about 50 feet high falls into a basin. The overall beauty is almost Tahitian, and you can have a picnic surrounded by liana vines, elephant ears, and exotic tropical flora.

A few miles away is a lake called **Grand Etang,** at a height of 1800 feet. It's like the mirror of a dead volcano, lying in the midst of a forest preserve and bird sanctuary. Covering 13 acres, the water is a cobalt blue.

The next day you can head north out of St. George's along the western coast, taking in beaches, and spice plantations, and the fishing villages that are so typical of Grenada.

You pass through **Gouyave,** a spice town, the center of the nutmeg and mace industry. Both spices are produced from a single fruit. Before reaching the village you can stop at the Dougaldston Estate where you'll see most of the island's spices in their natural form. You'll witness the processing of nutmeg and mace.

At the **Grenada Cooperative Nutmeg Association,** huge quantities of the spice are aged, graded, and processed. Most of the work is done within the ochered walls of the factory, which sprouts such slogans as "Bring God's peace inside and leave the Devil's noise outside." Women sit on stools in the natural light from the open windows of the aging factory, laboriously sorting the raw nutmeg and its by-product, mace, into different baskets for grinding, peeling, and aging.

Proceeding along the coast, you reach **Sauteurs,** at the northern tip of Grenada. This is the third-largest town on the island. It was from this great cliff that the Caribs leaped to their deaths instead of facing enslavement by the French.

To the east of Sauteurs is the palm-lined **Levera Beach,** an idyll of sand where the Atlantic meets the Caribbean. This is a great spot for a picnic lunch, but swimming can sometimes be dangerous. On the distant horizon you'll see some of the Grenadines.

The **River Antoine Rum Distillery** is where you can get an insight into the conditions under which "demon rum" was made 300 years ago. At the site, a series of hand-operated sluice gates set a water-operated sugarcane pulverizer into motion. At first glance the process is shockingly unsanitary (remember, this was the way it was done hundreds of years ago), but the finished product is distilled to a crystal clearness. It's reputed to be one of the best rums produced in the Caribbean. Don't be alarmed by the bats living in the top of the distillery's roof—they only attack insects. It might be advisable to contribute to the "retirement fund" of the employees after touring the premises.

Heading down the east coast of Grenada, you reach **Grenville,** the island's second city. Hopefully, you'll pass through here on a Sunday morning when you'll enjoy the hubbub of the native fruit and vegetable market. There is also a fish market along the waterfront. A nutmeg factory here welcomes visitors.

From Grenville, you can cut inland into the heart of Grenada. Here you're in a world of luxuriant foliage, passing along nutmeg, banana, and cocoa plantations up to Grand Etang, previously mentioned. Your driver will then begin his descent from the mountains. Along the way you'll pass hanging carpets of mountain ferns. Going through the tiny hamlets of Snug Corner and Beaulieu, you eventually come back to the capital.

On yet another day, you can drive south from St. George's to the beaches and resorts spread along the already much-mentioned **Grand Anse,** which many people consider one of the most beautiful beaches in the West Indies. **Point Saline,** now the airport, is at the southwestern tip of Grenada. From the lighthouse, you'll have panoramic views in every direction. This tour of beaches and resorts is often called the "Royal Drive," named in honor of the route Queen Elizabeth II took on her visit to the island. Point Saline, as mentioned in the introduction, is the site of the new international airport of Grenada. Along with the beaches, it too is a sightseeing attraction.

Along the way you'll pass through the village of **Woburn,** which was featured in the film *Island in the Sun,* and go through the sugar belt of **Woodlands,** with its tiny sugarcane factory.

A Special Place

As you're touring north from the beach at Grand Anse and the capital at St. George's, one place is outstanding as a luncheon stopover. It's Betty Mascoll's **Morne Fendue,** in St. Patrick's (tel. 9330). This 1912 plantation house constructed the year she was born, is her ancestral home. It was built of carefully chiseled river rocks held together with a mixture of lime and molasses, as was the custom in that day. Only problem is, Betty Mascoll doesn't know whether she'll be receiving guests during the lifetime of this edition, so it is imperative to call.

Mrs. Mascoll has always lived in the house, except for a wartime stint in England. Her spacious living room is decorated with family portraits and heirlooms, including a patterned rug and heavily carved mahogany furniture. A collection of blue willow antique plates is displayed below the elaborate ceiling moldings.

Lunch, if available, costs from $15 for nonresidents. The noonday repast is likely to include such local delights as yam and sweet potato casserole, curried pork with lots of hot spices, and a hotpot of pork and oxtail.

If you fall in love with the place, you might also be able to stay here. She may (or may not) offer full board in one of her high-ceilinged rooms, renting for $45 to $65 daily in a double and only $30 in a single, which includes drinks and afternoon tea if desired.

Mrs. Mascoll is known for introducing her house guests to her friends and neighbors on the long verandas beneath the hanging vines of her house. Her garden is host to several varieties of hummingbirds.

THE SPORTING LIFE: The Spice Island can offer the kinds of diversions that urbanites yearn for, ranging from a few relaxing hours on a Sailfish cruising near the island's verdant coastline to a luxuriously catered week on a yacht. It could also include an afternoon in a small boat angling for the perfect dolphin, or a fiercely sunny day in search of that record-breaking big-game fish. Below the water's surface, other distractions appeal to sports lovers. Hundreds of varieties of fish and dozens of species of coral and sponges await your perusal, sometimes with underwater visibility stretching to 120 feet.

Beaches

Swimmers who simply enjoy the white sands of an almost perfect island might want to spend their days at one of the best beaches in the Caribbean. **Grand Anse,** three miles of sugar-white sands extending into deep waters far offshore. Grenada, by the way, has a strictly enforced policy of public ownership of all beaches (unlike Barbados, which has leased the prime beachfront property to private hotels, a cause célèbre for island dissidents). Most of Grenada's best hotels are within walking distance of Grand Anse. In the unlikely event that you get bored there, you can take off and discover dozens more beaches on your own.

Snorkeling and Scuba

Grenada offers the diver an underwater world, rich in submarine gardens, exotic fish, and coral formations. Off the coast is the wreck of the ocean liner *Bianca C,* which is nearly 600 feet long. If you get in touch with **Grenada Yacht Services** (tel. 2508 or 2883), they'll arrange two hours of snorkeling, but there must be a minimum of four. Scuba-diving is available at a cost of about $65 for a day's dive. Soft drinks and rum punch are included. Masks, fins, and snorkel rent for $5.

Novice divers might want to stick to the west coast of Grenada, while more experienced divers might search out the sights along the rougher Atlantic side. Divers should know that Grenada doesn't have a decompression chamber for the relief of bends. Should this happen to you, it would require an excruciatingly painful air trip to Trinidad.

If you'd rather strike out on your own, take a drive to Woburn and negotiate with a fisherman for a ride to Glovers Island, an old whaling station, and snorkel away.

Golf

The golf course of Woodlands is about six miles from St. George's. There you'll find a nine-hole course, charging greens fees of $8 a day. The course is open Monday to Saturday from 8 a.m. till sunset (on Sunday from 8 a.m. till noon). From the course you'll have a view of both the Caribbean Sea and the Atlantic. Telephone 4554 for information.

Water Sports

Water-sports fans gravitate to the beach near Spice Island Inn, where a collection of agencies rent boating equipment from 9 a.m. to 6 p.m. daily, including catamarans at $15 per hour, jet skis at $12 per hour, and windsurfers at $12 per hour. It's possible to take speedboat trips at $35 per hour. Many of the island's hotels have Sunfish craft for the use of their guests. The swimming, as mentioned, is particularly good off Grand Anse beach.

Deep-Sea Fishing

Fishermen come here from November to March in pursuit of both blue and white marlin, yellowfin tuna, wahoo, sailfish, and other catches. Most of the bigger hotels have a sports desk which will arrange fishing trips for you.

Tennis

Tennis, like cricket and football, is a popular everyday sport in Grenada. Guests at the Secret Harbour, Calabash Hotel, and Twelve Degrees North can avail themselves of those well-kept courts. Otherwise, the **Richmond Hill Tennis Club,** which has two hard courts, will arrange a temporary membership for EC$5 ($1.90). Or as a nonmember you can play for $3 per person hourly. In addition, the **Tanteen Tennis Club** will grant you a membership for $15. Nonmembers pay $3 per hour per person.

SHOPPING: The one item everybody who visits Grenada comes home with is a basket of spices, better than any you're likely to find in your local supermarket. These hand-woven panniers of palm leaf or straw are full of items grown on the island, including the inevitable nutmeg, as well as mace, cloves, cinnamon, bay leaf, vanilla, and ginger. The local stores also sell a lot of luxury-item imports, mainly from England, at prices that are almost (not quite) duty free.

Store hours, in general, are 8 to 11:45 a.m. and 1 to 3:45 p.m., Monday to Saturday.

For your introduction to shopping on the island, head to **Grencraft,** Melville Street in St. George's (tel. 2655), which is the government-run outlet for all handicrafts made on the island. You'll find selections of straw, sisal, and khus-khus mats, along with the baskets, rugs, and hats for which Grenada is known. A fine selection of island-grown spices is sold, along with such condiments as nutmeg jam and jelly, banana-guava nectar, mango nectar, hot sauce, and spice baskets. Many of the spices come in gift boxes. There are machinemade woodcarvings (of little interest), along with coral and coconut flex jewelry, plus calico dolls with spices inside. The shop enjoys a favorable waterside location which is reached by passing through Sendall Tunnel between the Carenage and the Esplanade.

One of the most interesting shops in St. George's is **Spice Island Perfumes Ltd.,** on the Carenage (tel. 2006). This small store and workshop is open from

8:30 a.m. to 4:30 p.m. Monday through Friday, and from 9 a.m. to noon on Saturday. It produces and sells perfumes, popourri, and teas made from the locally grown flowers and spices. The staff is pleased to show you the plants in their original states and explain the various processes. If you desire, they'll spray you with a number of desired scents, helping you choose among such temptations as island flower, spice, frangipani, jasmine, patchouli, and wild orchid. The store also serve as the outlet for Spice Island cosmetics products, a range of high-quality Grenadian shampoos, conditioners, lotions, and other toiletries. The shop stands near the harbor entrance, close to the Tourist Board, post office, public library, and Grencraft Handicraft Centre.

Veronica's Tropical Fashion, Grand Anse (tel. 4210), near the Grand Anse shopping Centre, is one of the more fashionable clothing outlets on the island. Nola Hamilton assists designer Veronica Adams in the manufacture and sale of her own designs. A floor-length evening dress in earth-colored floral patterns, called the "Cape Casual," is offered for $45. Likewise, a combination of sundress and formal skirt in a black and tropical pink cotton costs a reasonable $25.

Dinah's Originals, on the corner of Melville and Granby Streets, on the top floor, offers fashions selected by Dinah Ashton, who trained in the Traphagen School of Design in New York. Her resortwear is the best offer in Grenada. You can have items made to your specifications here and mailed back to your home. Both African and Liberty of London prints are fashionably shaped into bikinis, shifts, whatever.

Straw Mart, on Granby Street (tel. 2341), fronting Market Square, has beautiful hand-plaited and embroidered straw work. The spice dolls, woodcarvings, and sun hats you may find no less enticing.

The most interesting shop for souvenirs and artistic items is **Yellow Poui Art Gallery,** just past the Sendall Tunnel exit. It's open only from 9 a.m. to 1:30 p.m. on weekdays and on Saturday from 9 a.m. till noon. Oil paintings and watercolors are exhibited, as well as sculpture, prints, rare antique maps, engravings, and woodcuts, with prices beginning at $10 and going up. The galley serves as a showcase for Grenada's burgeoning talent. There's a second Yellow Poui out in the country which can be visited by appointment only (tel. 3001 or 2121).

Charles of Grenada, at Cross and Bruce Streets (tel. 2306), has a good selection of English import items in clothing—names such as Daks, Pringle sweaters, and Liberty fabrics. The shop lies on the esplanade side of Fort George.

NIGHTLIFE: This is not a compelling reason to come to Grenada. Most visitors seem to retire early. The major entertainment is at the **Spice Island Inn,** Grand Anse beach (tel. 4258). The manager offers crab-racing contests, with friendly betting against the house on Tuesday and Saturday nights. These races, where seven or eight sleepy hermit crabs are released in the center of a large painted circle, have been exported to Berlin, where they stole the show at a trade convention. On Monday and Wednesday nights, the inn features local jazz/pop/rock combos with dancing, and on Sunday and Thursday there are movies. On Friday guests can listen to a steel band play island rhythms.

The Sugar Mill, Grand Anse (tel. 4401), is rated the number one nightspot in Grenada. Open only on Wednesday and Saturday nights, this former rum distillery was built in 1750 and serves both as a disco and nightclub. It's usually much busier on Saturday than on Wednesday. Drinks cost EC$5 ($1.90). Sometimes it gets hot on Saturday night, when guests listen or dance to the sounds of reggae. *Warning:* You may be offered some of the potent local marijuana at this island gathering place (for a fee), but know that possession of marijuana is extremely illegal.

CARRIACOU: Largest of the Grenadines, Carriacou, "land of many reefs," is populated by about 8000 inhabitants, mainly of African descent, who are scattered over its 13 square miles of mountains, plains, and white sand beaches. There's also a Scottish colony, and you'll see names like MacFarland. In the small hamlet of Windward, on the east coast, villagers of mixed Scottish descent carry on the tradition of building wooden schooners. Large skeletons of boats in various stages of readiness line the beach where workmen labor with the most rudimentary of tools, building the West Indian trade schooner fleet. If you stop for a visit, a master boatsman will let you climb the ladder and peer inside the shell, and will explain which wood came from which island, and why he designed his boat in its particular way. Its two peaks shoot skyward to almost 1000 feet. Much of the population, according to reputation, is involved in smuggling. Otherwise, they are sailors, fishermen, shipwrights, and farmers.

The best time to visit Carriacou is in August in time for its **Regatta,** which was begun by J. Linton Rigg in 1965. It was started for work boats and schooners, for which the Grenadines are famous. Now work boats, three-masted schooners, and miniature "sailboats" propelled by hand join the festivities. Banana boats dock at the pier filed with people rather than bananas, and sailors from Bequia and Union camp on tiny Jack-a-Dan and Sandy Isle, only 20 minutes away by outboard motor from Hillsborough. The people of the Grenadines try their luck at the greased pole, foot races, and of course the sailing races. Music fills the air day and night, and impromptu parties are held. At the three-day celebration, Big Drum dancers perform in the Market Square, as the sound of conga drums fills the air.

Hillsborough is the chief port and administrative center, handling the commerce of the little island which is based mainly on growing limes and cotton. The capital bustles on Monday when the produce arrives, then settles down again until "mail day" on Saturday. The capital is nestled in a mile-long crescent of white sand.

The **Carriacou Museum** has a carefully selected display of Amerindian artifacts, European china and glass shards, and exhibits of African culture. In two small rooms, it preserves Carriacou's history, which parallels that of its sister island, Grenada.

Also in Carriacou is the **Sea Life Centre,** created by the North American Environmental Research Products organization and designed to educate both the islanders and visitors about sea life, especially the lambi (conch) and turtle. It features native paintings of fishermen at work, drawings of the life cycles of the sea's inhabitants, and microscopes and incubators set up for visitors to view the baby lambi and turtles that the center breeds.

The island attracts escapists, a sports-oriented crowd who spend their time fishing, snorkeling, waterskiing, and sailing. Of course, you can just go beachcombing.

Getting There

Visitors arrive on the twice-weekly produce and mail boats from Grenada, the trip taking five hours. A far faster method of transport is on a nine-seat plane, which takes just 25 minutes from the Point Saline International Airport in Grenada. A terminal building opened officially in 1984 at Carriacou's Lauriston Airport.

For those wanting a taste of Carriacou but having limited time, day tours are available from Grenada. An early-morning start gets you to Carriacou in time for breakfast at the Mermaid Beach Hotel, then on to swimming, snorkeling, and a picnic lunch at Sandy Isle and back to Grenada in time for dinner. The cost is $125 per person, including round-trip air transportation, all transfers, and two meals. Tours can be booked through any travel agent in Grenada.

Food and Lodging

The **Mermaid Inn,** Hillsborough (tel. Carriacou 23), is a small, two-story old building with wooden shutters. Rooms are furnished simply, but clean, and in some of the units you must share a bath. The inn stands at one end of Hillborough's main street, and its jasmine-and-hibiscus-filled courtyard leads to the dining veranda, just eight feet from the sea. Around the courtyard, doors lead to the accommodations, some of which have four-poster beds which have housed some of the Caribbean's most celebrated yachtsmen. The rum punch here is reported to be *the best* in the Caribbean.

In winter, two persons pay $65 daily in a room with bath; singles, $42. Without bath, the double rate is $55; the single rate, $32. All these tariffs include a continental breakfast and a good-tasting West Indian dinner. *In the off-season, doubles, depending on the plumbing, range from $55 daily; singles from $35, again including breakfast and dinner.*

Guests gather for an evening on the terrace, which at times seems to be the liveliest spot in town, particularly at the time of the annual summer regatta. Hopefully you'll be here when a boat is launched with a sprinkling of goat's blood and holy water. There may be dancing all night, the participants fueled up by the "ole debbil," Jack Iron rum.

The staff here is very helpful and will find boats for your use from their own little fleet. You can go snorkeling or else explore nearby islets, taking along a picnic. Nearby Sandy Island has some fascinating coral reef formations. The inn is closed in September.

Silver Beach Cottages, Beausejour Bay (tel. Carriacou 52), is a cottage colony lying about a five-minute walk north of the Hillsborough on a mile-long white sandy beach. Eight villas are offered, each quite spacious with both a bedroom and a living room along with private baths and fully equipped kitchenettes.

In winter, the double EP rate is $45 daily, dropping to $37 in a single. *In summer, the double EP rate is $35 daily, going down to $28 in a single.* Self-sufficient types are quoted special housekeeping rates of $175 weekly in winter, either single or double occupancy, *a tariff lowered to $120 weekly in the off-season.* The above charges include gas, electricity, linen, cutlery, and crockery.

The bar and dining pavilion is found between the cottages and the beach. At dinner you can sample some good local dishes prepared by native cooks and including lobster, conch, and fresh fish. Locally grown vegetables and fruits are served. Fishing, snorkeling, scuba-diving, and boating to nearby islands can be arranged, including World's End Reef in the Tobago Cays.

Camp Carriacou (tel. 4233 in Grenada or 63 in Carriacou for reservations) is sheltered in Belmont, on the island's southern tip. It offers eight rustic wooden cottages decorated in beiges and browns. Each has its own bath, bedroom, living room, and terrace overlooking the private beach. Two persons can stay here for $40 per night, including a continental breakfast.

The property is run by the government. Drinks are served in an open-air bar overlooking the beach, and the pace here is most relaxed, with an occasional disco party. In the Big Drum restaurant the cook will prepare you the local dishes of Carriacou, especially fresh seafood. Meals cost from $12. Motorboats, Sailfish, Kingfish, canoes, and snorkeling equipment are available, and island tours can be arranged, especially to four uninhabited islands with unspoiled sandy beaches.

BARBADOS

IN THE 19TH CENTURY, Barbados became famous as "the sanatorium of the West Indies," attracting mainly British guests suffering from the vapors who came here for the perfect climate and the relaxed, unhurried life.

In 1751 Maj. George Washington visited Barbados with his half brother Maj. Lawrence Washington, who had developed tuberculosis. Regrettably, the future American president contracted smallpox there which left him marked for life. Thus Barbados is said to have been the only place outside the United States that George Washington ever visited.

That danger long gone, Barbados still remains a salubrious island to visit, with its mixture of coral and lush green vegetation, along with seemingly endless miles of pink and white sandy beaches.

The most easterly of the long chain of Caribbean islands, it still retains its old-world charm, an imprint of grace and courtesy left over from 300 years of British tradition.

Barbados is renowned for the friendliness of its hospitable people and for having the oldest parliament in the western hemisphere, with a British heritage unbroken since the first landing by Englishmen in 1625 until its independence in 1966. Barbados is one Caribbean island *not* discovered by Columbus.

In a way, Barbados is like England in the tropics, with its bandbox cottages with neat little gardens, its centuries-old parish churches, and a scenic, hilly district in the north known as "Little Scotland" where a mist rises in the morning. Narrow roads ramble through green sugarcane fields trimmed in hedgerows. Sugar is king, and rum is its queen.

Once Barbados was the most heavily defended fortress island in the Caribbean, as 26 forts ran along its 21 miles of sheltered coast. Perhaps for that reason, the island was never invaded. Slavery was abolished in 1834, and independence within the Commonwealth was obtained in 1966.

Long before that, the first known inhabitants of Barbados were the Arawak Indians, who came over from South America. But they were gone by the time of the first British expedition in 1625. Two years later Capt. John Powell returned to colonize the island with 80 settlers who arrived at Jamestown (later renamed Holetown).

A thriving colony of Europeans and black slaves turned Barbados into a prosperous land, based on trading in tobacco and cotton, and by 1640, sugarcane. More and more slaves were imported to work these sugar plantations.

Many English families settled here in the 18th and 19th centuries, in spite of the usual plagues such as yellow fever or the intermittent wars. Because of the early importation of so many slaves, Barbados is the most densely populated of the West Indian islands, numbering some 258,000 souls.

A coral island, Barbados is flat compared to the wild, volcanic terrain of the Antilles, previewed in Chapter XI on the British Windwards. It is 21 miles long and 14 miles wide. Most of its hotels are on the western side, a sandy shoreline. The eastern side, fronting the Atlantic, is a breezy coastline with white-capped rollers. Experienced surfers like it, but it's not safe for amateur swimmers.

It's a land of hills and dales, limousines (carrying such residents as Claudette Colbert) and donkey carts. You'll find hills, but not mountains. The highest point is Mount Hillaby at 1115 feet. The island is shaped like a shoulder of mutton.

Barbados lies 200 miles from Trinidad and only 4½ jet hours from New York.

PRACTICAL FACTS: The Barbadians, or Bajans as they are called, speak English of course, but with their own island lilt. They live on an island where daytime temperatures are in the 75° to 85° Fahrenheit range throughout the year.

The Barbados dollar (BDS) is the official **currency,** available in $100, $20, $10, $5, and $1 notes, as well as $1, 25¢, and 10¢ silver coins, plus 5¢ and 1¢ copper coins. The Bajan dollar is worth slightly less than 50¢ in U.S. currency. Currency translations given in this chapter are only for the reader's convenience, and are subject to change. *Note:* Unless otherwise specified, currency quotations are in U.S. dollars. Most stores take travelers checks or U.S. dollars. However, it's best to convert your money at banks and pay your bills in Bajan dollars.

Citizens of the U.S. or Canada who embark in their own country and hold valid return tickets do not need a passport to enter the country for stays lasting not more than six months.

When you leave, you'll have to pay a $16 BDS ($8) **departure tax.** Not only that, but when you go to pay your hotel bill, you'll find you've been charged an 8% government **sales tax.** And while I'm on the subject, most hotels and restaurants add at least a 10% **service charge** to your bill.

The **electricity** is 110 volts, 50 cycles, AC, so at most establishments recommended you can use your U.S.-made appliances.

Most **banks** in Barbados are open from 8 a.m. to 3 p.m. Monday through Thursday and from 8 a.m. to 1 p.m. on Friday (later reopening from 3 to 5:30 p.m.). **Shopping hours,** in general, are 8 a.m. to 4 p.m. Monday to Friday and 8 a.m. to noon on Saturday.

You should have no trouble with telecommunications out of Barbados. Telegrams may be sent at your hotel front desk or at the **Barbados External Telecommunications, Ltd.,** offices on Lower Broad Street in Bridgetown, which is open from 9 a.m. to 5 p.m. weekdays and 8 a.m. to 1 p.m. on Saturday. Telex and data-access services are also available.

Most hotel desks can attend to your mailing; otherwise, the **Main Post Office** is in the Public Buildings of Bridgetown.

Barbados has a pure **water** supply. It's pumped from underground sources in the coral rock which covers six-sevenths of the island, and it's perfectly safe to drink.

In **medical facilities,** a 600-bed hospital, the Queen Elizabeth (tel. 436-6450), is in Bridgetown. There are as well several private clinics, including the 135-bed St. Joseph Hospital (tel. 422-2232), operated by a Roman Catholic order in St. Peter Parish.

Public **holidays** are January 1, Good Friday, Easter Monday, May Day (May 1), Whit Monday, Kadoment Day (a variable holiday), United Nations Day (first Monday in October), Independence Day (November 30), Christmas Day, and Boxing Day (December 26).

GETTING THERE: In the past, I've flown and recommended many airlines to and from Barbados, but on my most recent research trip, I chose the services of **Pan Am,** one of the most experienced airlines in the world. Pan Am offers non-stop daily service to Barbados' Grantley Adams Airport from New York's JFK and from Miami. Easy connections are available on Pan Am through New York from Boston, Washington, Philadelphia, Chicago, and Detroit, while travelers from Tampa, Orlando, New Orleans, and Houston can be routed through Miami. Luggage is always sent directly through to a passenger's final destination, to make inter-airport connections even easier.

All of Pan Am's flights into Barbados are on wide-bodied 747s, L-1011s, and A-300s. These frequently refurbished aircraft provide smooth, well-scheduled flights whose attentive in-flight service helps get a Bajan vacation off to a good start.

Pan Am's cheapest high-season ticket is an APEX (advance purchase excursion) fare. If a passenger pays for this ticket at least a week in advance and waits for a period of from 6 to 21 days before flying back to the original departure point, the fare during high season is $522 round trip from JFK and $459 from Miami. Fares are substantially less during low and shoulder season.

An important point to remember is that Pan Am's tour desk will lower round-trip APEX fares by as much as $100 per person if hotel accommodations are arranged through them. A wide range of hotels is available whose rates are usually cheaper when they're prearranged through a large-volume booking agent like Pan Am. Travelers can save substantial amounts of money on what major airlines call "land-based packages," and Pan Am's qualified staff will be happy to talk to you about this on their toll-free line (tel. 800/848-7777) seven days a week during extended hours.

For information and reservations for air fare without accompanying hotel reservations, call Pan Am through the number in your local telephone directory.

Transportation can also be arranged to Barbados through such airlines as **American,** which flies there daily from New York. **BWIA** also flies nonstop from New York. **Air Canada** operates nonstop service from Toronto every Friday and Saturday during high season, with easy connections on those same days from Montréal. Through service via Miami, **Eastern** services many cities throughout North America.

1. Hotels of Barbados

Per square inch, Barbados has the best hotels in the West Indies. Here you get elegant comfort, the atmosphere often that of an English house party. Most of the hotels are small and personally run, with a quiet, restrained dignity.

Most of my recommendations are sited on St. James Beach, the fashionable sector. However, you'll have to head south from Bridgetown to such places

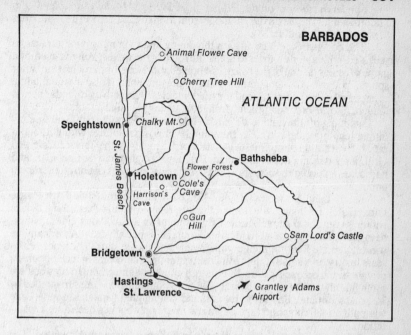

BARBADOS

Animal Flower Cave

Cherry Tree Hill

ATLANTIC OCEAN

Speightstown Chalky Mt.

St. James Beach

Bathsheba

Flower Forest

Holetown

Cole's Cave

Harrison's Cave

Gun Hill

Sam Lord's Castle

Bridgetown

Hastings
St. Lawrence

Grantley Adams Airport

as Hastings and Worthing for the best bargains, often in self-contained efficiencies or studio apartments where you can do your own cooking.

So as not to paint too rosy a picture, I'll give the bad news. Because of Barbados's long and continuing popularity, nowadays with back-to-back charter groups, the tariffs charged in these hotels often are, in my opinion, outrageous in high season. Many hotels will also insist that you take two meals at their establishments if you're there in the winter.

Know also that Barbados has some very good bargains as well, and I've surveyed the best of these too, on my most recent hotel hop around the island (see the end of this section).

Prices cited in this section, unless otherwise indicated, are in U.S. dollars.

The Top Resorts

Barbados Hilton, P.O. Box 510, on Needham's Point, St. Michael (tel. 426-0200), is a self-contained resort, built on a rugged peninsula around an old stone fort, surrounded on three sides by beaches, with more than 14 acres of landscaped gardens. On the heavily populated south edge of Bridgetown, it nevertheless has a remoteness that is appealing. The architecture of the building is among the most stunning of any Hilton worldwide. It's erected around a New Orleans–style central courtyard full of tropical gardens. Four floors of bedrooms with alcove terracing open toward the sea, and are reached via a glass elevator. A multitude of hanging baskets are suspended from the encircling inner balconies, and on the lower level is a circular staircase that takes you through palm trees and ferns.

The hotel opened in 1966, at the birth of the island's independence. Its outer silhouette is unpainted, a series of rooftop arches made of locally cut coral. The bedchambers are centrally air cooled and balconied, opening onto Carlisle Bay on the north side of the Atlantic on the south.

Singles in summer on the EP pay from $91 to $114 daily; doubles $99 to $122. In winter, tariffs on the EP range from $156 to $202 daily in a single, from $180 to $220 in a double.

The beach area, which adjoins the dining and swimming pool terraces, is secluded, with a stone barrier to break the force of the waves. You might enjoy a game of tennis on one of the courts, go horseback riding, or participate in water sports. You can go sailing, rent a boat, whatever. There's also a sauna, and a masseur who can be summoned for tired muscles. The activity calendar here is loaded, a social program ranging from goat racing to walking tours.

Opening off the inner core garden room is the Fort Charles Grill (see my dining recommendations). On the same level is a bar lounge with clusters of rattan chairs and sofas. Guests can also order meals in the Terrace Café and Grill, later dancing at the Flambeau Bar. Bajan nights here are popular, and barbecues and calypso shows are staged, along with movies and an international buffet.

Sandy Lane, St. James (tel. 432-1311), is a great house–style Trust House Forte Hotel. Ever since the days of the late Ronald Tree, it has been a deluxe winter haven for such well-heeled Englishmen as Sir Anthony Eden. Nowadays, however, it draws a broad base of tourism, especially from Americans. In winter, you are likely to mingle with royalty and movie stars. The place represents luxury on a small scale, with beautiful suites and rooms in a clubhouse, a private beach on one side, an 18-hole golf course on the other. In between are some fine all-weather tennis courts. The two swimming pools are surrounded by Italianate gardens, Roman fountains, and colonnaded verandas. Sandy Lane was built on 380 choice acres of Bajan real estate on what had been a sugar plantation.

The suites and apartments are set in gardens extravagantly planted. The buildings are in cut coral, with shingle roofs, baronial arches, high ceilings, and a porte cochère—in all, grand-estate-like with tall gates, a driveway, and ornamental steps. Rare butterflies and singing birds flit from water lilies to frangipani to bougainvillea to the flamboyant trees. The style is chicly casual.

Bedrooms are traditionally furnished, with white and gold chests and tables, along with Italian bronze wall lighting fixtures. The coloring is in pastel shades. Service is top-drawer, as there is a staff of some 400 persons ready to serve you. All of the 115 rooms and suites have private bath and air conditioning.

In the summer season, MAP guests are charged $280 daily for two persons in a double, $185 in a single. In winter, these same MAP tariffs rise to $385 to $435 for two persons, from $300 to $355 daily in a single. Even more expensive suites are available. Tax and service are extra.

You can order a cool salad at the pool at lunchtime, later enjoying a continental-inspired and candlelight dinner. Groaning buffet tables are frequent, as is regular native entertainment such as calypso. You can also dine in the Il Portico Italian restaurant.

Marriott's Sam Lord's Castle, St. Philip (tel. 423-7350). If you lodge here in the "Regency Rascal's" main house, it's like seeking an accommodation in a kind of Barbadian Mount Vernon. You can sleep in a four-poster canopied bed upstairs on the second floor of the crenellated manor house. However, there's a constant stream of visitors during the day exploring the ground-floor reception area. The great house was built in 1820 and craftsmen were sent over from England to reproduce the queen's castle at Windsor. These ceilings look down on the art of Reynolds, Raeburn, and Chippendale. According to legend, Samuel Hall Lord built the estate on money earned by piracy.

Set on 72 imaginatively landscaped acres with rare flowering trees, the estate has a wide, lengthy private sandy beach edged by tall coconut trees, as well as seven professional tennis courts which are lit at night. The location is about 14 miles out of Bridgetown, heading east beyond the airport. Depending on traffic, count on anywhere from a 30- to 45-minute drive.

You can swim in any of three pools which are built free form to look like small ponds or lakes. There are also a hydroptherapy pool and a children's pool. Other facilities include a games room, exercise room, shuffleboard, table tennis, library, beauty shop, and barbershop. Golf, sailing, horseback riding, snorkeling, waterskiing, fishing, luncheon and nighttime cruises, and other outside activities are available on the island and can be arranged by the activities director.

There are 259 guest rooms including 16 suites. All accommodations are air-conditioned with private bathrooms. There is a service charge and government tax added to all bills. In winter, rates range from $150 to $190 daily. Suites and cottages are more expensive. *Off-season, the tariff runs from $90 to $110 daily.* For breakfast and dinner, add another $40 per person daily to the room tariffs.

There is a whole list of dining and entertainment places, including the gourmet Cobbler's Reef Restaurant, open for dinner only. The Garden Restaurant, open for lunch and dinner, is more for family-style dining, featuring a full luncheon buffet. Breakfast and dinner are also served in the Wanderer Restaurant, and you can order a hamburger at Sam's Place, right on the beach. There are many bars as well.

A Bajan Fiesta night in the hotel's Bajan Village is offered once a week, as is a shipwreck barbecue and beach party with a steel drum band, a limbo show, and fire-eaters on South Beach. Slot machines are available for play every day, and goat races are held on the beach every Saturday. For more information, call Marriott toll free at 800/228-9290.

Colony Club, St. James Beach (tel. 422-2335). The entrance to this top-notch resort hotel is impressive, lined with Australian pines. This Bajan "residential club" lies about eight miles from Bridgetown on this well-known beach. An elegant feeling still prevails, even though the colony has grown from a small "house party"-type establishment to a complex of some 75 rooms which look out on shaded verandas and handsomely landscaped grounds. Twenty-eight of the colony's rooms are built directly on the beach, and all units have private patios and air conditioning. Accommodations are clustered in two- and three-story Mediterranean-style bungalows with red tile roofs.

The main building is the oldest, reflecting its serenity and Barbadian architecture. White walls and pitched beam ceilings are the perfect foil for the traditional wood furnishings. Sliding glass doors open onto sun terraces. Some units are so close to the pool you can almost dive in.

In summer, singles range from $60 to $85 daily, and doubles go for $75 to $100. In winter, singles are priced from $150 to $200, while doubles pay from $165 to $220. For MAP, add another $30 per person daily. Tax and services are extra.

Both a continental cuisine and West Indian specialties are served on a covered terrace, a gracious setting for dining. The beach barbecues are well known here, and deservedly so. Entertainment, such as calypso, limbo, and dancing to a combo, are occasionally provided.

Glitter Bay, St. James (tel. 422-4111), places its emphasis on luxury. Of the 46 available Moorish-style units, 7 are three-bedroom penthouses, 29 are two bedroom suites, which will convert into one-bedroom suites with kitchen, and the final 10 are one-bedroom suites. Each of the elegantly furnished accommodations has a private bath with double vanity, tub, and shower, as well as a fully carpeted and air-conditioned bedroom with a large private terrace. Suites feature fully equipped kitchens.

The resort lies on a ten-acre site. All its units are situated on a series of descending terraces, giving guests a view from either patio or balcony. The site was once owned by the Cunards, the aristocratic British family of shipping fame. From their elegant grand house and Venetian-style beach house, Glitter Bay was developed.

In winter, a single rents for $165 daily, a twin for $215. Twin occupancy of a one-bedroom suite costs $260. *In summer, a single rents for only $86, a twin going for $114, and a one-bedroom suite for two, from $153.* The MAP supplement is $55 per person daily.

The circular eatery here is Piperade, named after the Basque omelet so popular in Biarritz. It offers both classical and nouvelle cuisine, along with West Indian specialties. On Monday, a gala Bajan buffet is presented, and Friday is barbecue night. The Sunset Beach Bar is a popular rendezvous spot for a sundowner. Guests can dance under the stars and enjoy local entertainment such as steel band or calypso. Water cascades from a children's pool into the main pool spanned by a pine bridge. There is a full range of water sports provided on a complimentary basis, including waterskiing, windsurfing, snorkeling, and catamaran sailing. Many other activities, such as golf and horseback riding, can be arranged. Two tennis courts are lit at night.

Heywoods, St. Peter (tel. 422-4900), one of the island's newest resorts, is a government-built collection of colonial-style buildings set amid recently planted palm trees. The complex stands on a 31-acre, flat area near a mile-long sandy beach, a long haul north of Bridgetown. It cost $30 million to build, and when it was completed in 1983 it represented one of the most ambitious resort development projects ever undertaken in Barbados. Although owned by the Barbados Tourism Corporation, the resort is managed by an independent company.

On the premises are more than 300 rooms, clustered into seven architecturally different groupings, which contributes to a village-style ambience within each cluster. In winter, singles range from $100 to $138, while doubles cost from $130 to $175. A third person in any double pays an additional $30 per day. Use of a kitchenette is optional, costing in any season an extra $25 per day. *In summer, singles range from $78 to $90, while doubles go for $95 to $110.* MAP can be arranged for a $40 supplement per day per person, year round. Children under 12 sharing a room with their parents stay free.

The complex contains five floodlit tennis courts, a nine-hole golf course, squash courts, a collection of meeting rooms for the conventions sometimes held here, and an assortment of boutiques. It also has a coffeeshop, an outdoor restaurant, a formal dining room, a seafood restaurant, and two bars. The resort's disco, the Club Miliki, is open from Tuesday through Saturday from 9 p.m. to 3 a.m. (see my nightlife suggestions). There is also a wide selection of planned activities for guests and their children.

Holiday Inn Barbados–Carlisle Bay Beach Resort, St. Michael (tel. 426-0888), is definitely not from this chain's typical mold. It's a splendid, 138-room, high-rise resort on the beach at Carlisle Bay, slightly more than a mile from Bridgetown. You enter by going under widespread shade trees; the reception area is tropical and intimate, with white bamboo furnishings, and a cocktail lounge is done in natural bamboo.

Extending out into the water is the stilted Calypso Quay, an informal area for drinking, dining, and dancing. Ceiling fans circulate slowly and you drink sitting in natural bamboo chairs, overlooking an oval-shaped pool, all very "south of Pago-Pago" in style. There is also a seafood restaurant, Moorings.

You can dine on the pier, watching the yachts, before retiring to your air-conditioned bedroom which has many comforts and conveniences, including phones, plus balconies fronting the garden and the sea. A bamboo swing awaits your body on your own balcony. *In summer, one person pays $75 daily; two persons, $85.* In winter, a single rents for $95 daily, a double for $110. For breakfast and dinner, add a supplement of $30 per person daily to the rates quoted.

Added attractions include weekly barbecues, where there are tempting Bajan specialties, and nightly entertainment. The action-packed resort has a big program of water sports. Tennis can also be played nearby.

Cobblers Cove Hotel, Cobblers Cove (tel. 422-2291), on the northwest coast, grew out of a beachfront mansion built like a false fort with crenellations, which appealed to someone's fantasy. The home was erected over the site of a former British fort which used to protect His Majesty's vessels going into Speightstown, a mile away.

Today, after its remake, the hotel is a favorite honeymoon retreat, offering 38 first-class suites in a phalanx of ten Iberian-style villas, each with air conditioning. Overlooking a white sand beach, each unit has a spacious living room, private balcony or patio, and a kitchenette. A full American breakfast appears daily in your suite, and late in the afternoon another waiter returns to take your dinner order.

Beachfront units cost more than garden-view apartments. In winter, MAP twins range in price from $200 to $310 daily; singles on the same arrangement go for $150 to $250. *MAP couples in summer pay from $180 daily; a single, $95 to $120, also MAP.*

There are many acres of well-developed tropical gardens and lawns, including coconut palms and flowering shrubbery. A beach bar serves tropical drinks, which are more potent than you think at first. The suites have been wisely placed throughout the gardens in horseshoe patterns, each making use of natural woods. The open-air, shingle-roofed dining room overlooks the sea and is held up by huge posts. White tables and chairs give it an elegant touch. The loggia living room reflects the taste of its English owner, Alan Godsal, who uses well-selected antiques and country house chintz-covered sofas.

Crane Beach Hotel, Crane Beach, St. Philip (tel. 423-6220), is the most dramatic resort in Barbados. Its remote location on the southeast coast is on the edge of a rugged cliff, overlooking Cobblers Reef and its miles of unspoiled beach, yet it lies only two miles from Sam Lord's Castle and 12 wiggly miles from the capital, Bridgetown. Its core is an 18th-century mansion built of blocks of white coral. All has been carefully remodeled, and newer additions have given it more luxury and glamour.

One of Barbados's oldest hostelries, Crane has been known to generations upon generations of honeymooners from around the world. Once it was considered *the* resort on the island, lying on more than a dozen acres of sea-bordering land. Both the hotel and the Crane Beach Club overlook a coconut grove, with a 1000-foot ocean frontage on a white beach of coral sand. Sometimes young Bajans dive from this cliff as Mexican boys do in Acapulco.

Crane offers accommodations for 50 guests, giving them a choice of comfortably furnished double rooms, well-equipped apartments, or else individually decorated, large-size deluxe suites, furnished in part with antiques, including half-tester beds with canopy crowns, old paintings, chairs, and chests brought from England, Spain, and France. Each suite is different, with a special character.

In summer, singles range in price from $60 to $105; doubles, from $70 to $125 nightly. Single tariffs in winter rise to $80 to $140 daily, with doubles going for $90 to $170. Suites cost a little more.

All units have balconies, terraces, or sundecks, as well as private baths and phones. There are two swimming pools, the main one of Roman design, with a marble balustrade along the cliffside and rows of white marble fluted Greek columns standing in silhouette against the sea. A brick terrace for sunbathing has large white urns of flowers, and on the beach level is yet another pool. There are two refreshment bars, one dramatically cantilevered 60 feet above the beach.

Greensleeves, St. Peter (tel. 422-2275), is for well-heeled hedonists who like it posh and pretentious. In elegant trappings, Keith Laing and family operate this place off the main west-coast road, north of Holetown, about 20 minutes to the north of the capital. The main complex stands across the street from the beach area, but the property includes a private beach and enough sand for plenty of sunning.

Many of the apartments at Greensleeves are built in and around the swimming pool, and also overlooking an open-walled restaurant, with its row of Roman pillars (see my dining recommendations). In the individual units, lounges and patios are big enough to entertain friends, should you desire. Fully equipped kitchens serve as bars. Called "apartels" here, the units are furnished in a Caribbean motif with straw mats, occasional wicker sweetheart chairs, and color-coordinated draperies and spreads.

Two persons in a one-bedroom apartment pay $170 daily, the rate going up to $270 in a two-bedroom apartment sheltering four. *In the off-season, the rate is dramatically reduced: from $60 daily for two persons in the one-bedroom units, from $110 for four in the two-bedroom units.*

Greensleeves also boasts a restaurant on the ocean, specializing in Bajan seafood dishes with entertainment regularly in season.

Coral Reef Club, St. James Beach (tel. 422-2372). Private cottages surround a main building, which is the lobby and reading room, with some guest rooms on the second floor. The cottages, with names such as "Guava" and "Frangipani," are scattered over about a dozen handsomely landscaped acres with manchineels and casuarinas, fronting a long strip of pure white sandy beach, ideal for swimming.

Some furnishings have aesthetic appeal, others are in utilitarian modern. Whatever, there's maximum emphasis on beachside comfort. Rooms are air-conditioned and open onto private patios. Naturally, there's a bath with each unit, and some of the rooms have separate dressing rooms as well. Lacy straw carpets evoke the West Indian touch.

In summer, MAP singles range from a low of $86 daily to a high of $98; doubles, $138 to $176. In winter, the single full-board rate begins at $157, climbing to $206. A twin or double, also AP, starts at $230 daily, working up to $332.

When not on the sands, you can go for a dip in the pool before taking lunch in an open-air area, sharing your meal with the sugar birds. Dining and wining in the evening is most gracious, in an attractive room overlooking the ocean. A first-class continental chef is in the kitchen. There's a weekly folklore show and barbecue, and a Bajan buffet on Sunday evening.

Ginger Bay Beach Club, St. Philip (tel. 423-5810), contains a total of 16 units, each painted a vivid coral pink. They're built on top of low, rocky cliffs extending into the sand-bottomed waters of the Atlantic. From your comfortable perch at poolside, you'd never guess how dramatic the setting really is. A walk onto the nearby cliffs will reveal exotic grottoes carved by the action of the waves.

The focal point of the resort is the thatch-roofed restaurant called Ginger's, built inside the shelter of the pool area. Its decor includes a happy combination of tropical lattices set under a peaked roof whose open supports permit a free flow of air even when the ceiling fans are off. In formal contrast to the soft colors and tropical setting, the designer used scores of carved mahogany Chippendale-style armchairs, each crafted in Barbados, copied from 18th-century models.

Although the villas seem to huddle close to one another, the facades are staggered to permit a feeling of privacy on each accommodation's veranda. Each contains its own hammock, which visitors may soon discover is the perfect place for a midafternoon piña colada.

EP rates at this Atlantic resort in winter are $180 daily in a single, $230 in a double, and $275 in a triple. *In summer, prices go down to a more reasonable $80 in a single, $110 in a double, and $140 in a triple.* Children under 12 sharing a suite with their parents stay free.

Coconut Creek Club, St. James (tel. 420-4952), is an informal celebrity retreat on the fashionable coastline of Barbados. Rooms are snugly perched in a tropical garaden overlooking an intimate sandy cove. There is a polished yet rustic atmosphere.

Many of the bedrooms are built on the low cliff edge, overlooking the ocean. Others open onto the pool. The theme is Caribbean, with cut-out wooden balconies. Bedrooms are simple and uncluttered, with white walls, orange ceramic floors, and splashes of tropical colors on the beds. Each has a private bath, and a veranda or balcony where your breakfast is brought to you. There are some deluxe poolside apartments with small kitchenettes.

Rooms come in four different classifications, the cheapest being labeled "moderate." From that, you rise to apartment suites at poolside and superior and deluxe on the oceanfront. *In summer, two persons pay from $60 to $90 for a room; a single, from $45 to $65.* For breakfast and dinner, add another $30 per person year round. In winter, doubles cost from $130 to $170; singles $115 to $155.

General manager Trevor F. C. Ramsay has created an outpost of Britannic nostalgia in the English pub, the Cricketers. Bajan buffets and barbecues are served on a vine-covered open pergola, overlooking the gardens and the sea. In the inn's cozy restaurant, the food has been praised by *Gourmet* magazine. Architecturally, the room has upside-down stucco arches and rough beamed dividers. There's dancing to West Indian calypso and steel bands. Swimming is in the bay or else the freshwater pool, and complimentary water sports include waterskiing, windsurfing, and use of Hobie Cats.

Discovery Bay Inn, St. James (tel. 422-1301), is a first-class beachfront hotel on 4½ acres of tropical gardens. The main entrance is plantation style. The inn grew out of what had been a private beachside mansion built of coral stone. However, it's now firmly entrenched as a hotel on the casuarina-lined beach.

Guest rooms are contained in a stretched-out, two-story wing which was built along the garden. If you don't want to be inspected by passersby, select a second-story perch with raftered ceilings. A more recently built block containing three floors of rooms fronts the sandy beach, with its cluster of thatch shade huts. In the center of the complex is a swimming pool, and adjoining are two well-tended tennis courts.

In the entertainment area, a local combo often plays for dancing, and buffets are often spread under a covered portico.

In summer, singles range from $80 to $110 daily, and doubles cost from $90 to $120. Tariffs in winter rise to $160 to $210 daily, either single or double occupancy. For MAP, add another $30 per person daily, plus service and tax.

Sandpiper Inn, Holetown, St. James (tel. 422-2251), has more of a South Seas look than most of the hotels of Barbados. Affiliated with the also-recommended Coral Reef, it is a self-contained, intimate resort on the waterside, lying along the fashionable west coast. Avoiding sterile modern, it is Bajan in flavor, standing in a small grove of coconut palms and flowering trees. This cluster of rustic-chic villas and cottages surrounds a swimming pool, the focal point of communal life. Seductive bamboo chairs and overscale drinks make it a pleasant oasis. The sandy beach is only 25 feet away from the grounds, and you can jog along the water's edge.

The rooms—10 double ones and 11 ocean-view suites—open onto little terraces that stretch along the second story. Here you can order drinks or have breakfast. Villa rooms have a bamboo Caribbean motif and terracotta tile floors, with room-wide glass doors opening onto terraces or verandas. Bright bedcovers and matching lamps and pillows give the place a holiday resort look.

In winter, a MAP single ranges fom $192 to $204 daily; a double or twin, from $225 to $300. *On the same MAP, a single in summer costs from $90 daily; a double or twin, from $115 to $150.* Ask about special rates for three to four persons in one of the ocean-view suites.

Dining is under a wooden ceiling, and the cuisine is both continental and West Indian. Sometimes big buffets are spread out for you, with white-capped chefs in attendance.

Best Western Sandy Beach, Worthing, Christ Church (tel. 428-9033), is an 89-suite Bajan resort on the south shore of Barbados four miles from Bridgetown. It offers one- and two-bedroom suites, and features eight honeymoon suites with queen-size beds and completely private patios for sunning or whatever. You may be impressed with the tastefully decorated and spacious accommodations, the living and dining areas in the suites in harmonious blues and bronzes. All units also have fully equipped kitchenettes, bathrooms, and private balconies or patios, and all the furniture at this informal, friendly place is locally made.

The food and beach are good, the entertainment professional and low-key, and the water-sports program quite extensive, especially for so small a resort.

In summer, a one-bedroom suite costs from $85 for two persons, and four persons are sheltered in a two-bedroom suite for $125. In winter, one-bedroom suites rent at $155 for two persons, two-bedroom suites for two to four persons at $225. A MAP supplement of $45 allows guests unlimited choice from the breakfast and dinner à la carte menus in the Green House Restaurant and also offers a dine and cruise-around special which includes *Jolly Roger* evening cruises, *1627 and All That* folklore show, and *Barbados, Barbados,* a comedy play (see the nightlife section). Transportation, unlimited drinks, and dinners are all included in the specials.

The Green House Restaurant, specializing in seafood and steaks, is under a wood-shingled palapa and opens out to the beach and swimming pool. The open-air design and use of wood, hanging plants, browns in the tablecloths, and long skirts of the waitresses give the restaurant a natural look by day that becomes romantic by candlelight at night. Every Friday the resort sponsors a Bajan Cohoblopot buffet for $25, when outsiders are welcome. Caribbean specialties such as flying fish, cou-cou, curries, plantains, and pepperpot are served under the stars. Tuesday is barbecue night.

Another restaurant, the Ocean Terrace, opened in 1984, is a casual, open-air facility overlooking the beach, serving lighter, less expensive meals than the Green House. You have a choice of chicken, salads, flying-fish sandwiches, hamburgers, quiche, or omelets. The Ocean Terrace is open five nights a week from 6:30 to 10:30 p.m., but not during the Tuesday barbecue or the Friday Bajan buffet.

Complimentary water sports include three-hour snorkelings, windsurfing, paddle boats, Sailfish, scuba lessons, air mattresses, snorkels, fins, and masks, available to all resident guests.

Facilities for the handicapped are provided in four of the ground-floor suites.

Treasure Beach Hotel, St. James (tel. 432-1346), seems more like a highly stylized apartment complex than a hotel. Nevertheless, it is a full-service hotel, owned and managed by the Ward family. It lies only six miles from Bridgetown along the west coast. The one-bedroom suites are built in a set-back style, only two stories high, grouped around a free-form swimming pool in a tropical garden setting of well-tended local flora.

Most of the suites open directly onto the pool and garden or the sea. Standard twins do not have a pool or sea view. However, all suites have an overscale living and dining area, which seems even larger because it opens onto a private terrace. Adjoining the bath in these suites is a walk-in dressing room. Furnishings are tropical, light and airy, with an uncluttered look.

In summer, doubles range in price from $72 to $110 daily, with singles paying almost the same price. An extra person in a room in summer is $11. These rates do not include meals. In winter, a single or double costs from $125 to $175 daily, with an extra person paying another $45.

The hotel has an eye-catching in- and outdoor restaurant, with natural wood beams, rattan chairs, and three-tiered rattan lobster cages used as hanging lamps. Buffets and cocktail parties are regularly featured, and dancing to live music is possible all year.

Tamarind Cove, St. James Beach (tel. 432-1332). Lord Beaverbrook's daughter, the Hon. Janet Kidd, selected the site for this Mediterranean-style hotel of red-tiled roofs and wrought iron right on a beach alongside Buccaneer Bay. You get some style and luxury here, but informally so. Guests can enjoy the white sandy beach at their doorstep, or else lounge around the palm-shaded pool.

In a setting of tropical gardens, the modern hacienda-style units may lack personality but they're comfortable, with balconies overlooking the ocean. In all, there are 74 rooms, plus 12 suites. Standard and superior accommodations enjoy a pool view, and the deluxe and luxury units open onto the sea. *In summer, singles cost from $65 to $75 daily, and doubles go for $80 to $110.* In winter, charges in a single range from $135 to $195 daily, while doubles cost from $150 to $210, plus another $30 per person charged year round as a MAP supplement. Taxes and service charges are extra.

Guests gather in an attractive bar in the late afternoon for drinks. The food enjoys a good reputation.

Water sports such as skindiving, sailing, and waterskiing can easily be arranged, and golf, tennis, horseback riding, and polo are available nearby. Free transportation is provided for a shopping jaunt into Bridgetown, seven miles away.

Southwinds Hotel, St. Lawrence, Christ Church (tel. 429-7181). Repeat visitors to this two-part resort tend to have strong preferences for either its new or its old section, separated from one another by a busy road. The older section lies on the beachfront and consists of a comfortably unpretentious collection of buildings surrounded by palms and sea breezes. The real showplace of the resort, however, is the newer building. It lies just behind what may be the most beautiful bearded fig trees in Barbados (the tree that inspired Portuguese sailors in discovery days to give this island the name it bears).

This section looks like a tastefully interconnected series of urban town houses, with prominent wooden balconies and views of a large swimming pool. When you're not enjoying your room, you can appreciate a tropical drink in the cedar-shingled bar, where the roofline looks vaguely Chinese and the terrace is partially cantilevered above the pool.

In winter, hotel rooms cost between $90 and $120, and hold between one and three persons. Suites run between $145 and $240, the larger ones designed for up to four persons. *Summer rates in hotel rooms range from $55 in a single to $95 in a triple. Suites range from $95 in a one-bedroom garden unit to $200 for a two-bedroom poolside accommodation.* MAP can be arranged for an additional $32 per day year round. In the newer section, only suites are available.

Barbados Beach Village, St. James (tel. 425-1440), is indeed that—a white and multipasteled colony cluster created along a beautiful stretch of beach. Tucked in and around lawns and flowering shrubbery, rooms reflect a good standard of architecture and interior decorating which was tastefully conceived and executed, with natural wood ceilings, white beams, and tropical furnishings. Every room is air-conditioned and you'll have either a private balcony or terrace.

There are some hotel-style rooms, with large balconies and baths, comfortably furnished, in winter costing $110 daily in a single, $160 in a double on the half-board plan. *Off-season, tariffs are $40 daily in a single, $60 in a double, with no meals.* Otherwise, you can book apartments costing from $115 to $130 daily in season for two persons, *these tariffs reduced to $85 to $95 daily off-season, again with no meals.*

If you don't want to cook for yourself, you can order meals in a festive, oceanfront dining room. You can also dance later in the evening at the Village Night Club. It's open nightly till 4 a.m.

Southern Palms, St. Lawrence (tel. 428-7171), is a seafront club with a distinct personality, lying on the Pink Beach of Barbados, midway between the airport and Bridgetown. The core of the resort is an old pink-and-white manor house, built in the Dutch style with a garden-level colonnade of arches. Spread along the sands are multiarched two- and three-story buildings, on grounds planted with such foliage as oleander, bougainvillea, and hibiscus.

Italian fountains and statues add to the Mediterranean feeling, which was the inspiration of Lord Thompson, the Canadian-born British press boss. In its more modern block, an eclectic mixture of rooms includes some with kitchenettes, some facing the ocean, others opening onto the garden, and some with penthouse luxury.

On the EP, twin-bedded rooms in winter rent for $135 to $175 daily, and suites are more expensive, of course. *In summer, EP rates are from $85 to $97 daily in a double.* For MAP, add another $35 per person daily.

Linking the accommodations is a cluster of straw-roofed buildings, including the Khus-Khus Bar and Restaurant, serving both a West Indian and a continental cuisine. A native orchestra often entertains here, and you can dance the merengue to the music of a steel band. There's a terrace for sunning before you take a dip in the beachside freshwater swimming pool.

Paradise Beach Hotel, Black Rock, St. Michael (tel. 429-7151), one of the Cunard-Trafalgar Resorts, is the most sports-oriented resort in Barbados. It's generally conceded that the resort has the best water-sports program in the Caribbean—windsurfing, snorkeling, waterskiing, and Sunfish sailing are complimentary. A charge is made for scuba-diving. In addition, there are four championship Har-tru tennis courts under the direction of a pro.

Accommodations are wide ranging, from simple standard units to luxuriously appointed suites. All units are air-conditioned. *In summer, double rooms rent from $95 to $110 daily; singles, from $70 to $85.* In winter, double rooms rent from $145 to $175 daily; singles, from $120 to 150. All accommodation is EP. For breakfast and dinner, a supplement of $35 per person per day is charged. Bedrooms have contemporary styling and much comfort.

As lunch seems to be offered almost everywhere, I'd suggest a table beside the beach. Al fresco dining can be an elegant affair at the Dining Pavilion, and guests also go to the Carvery for a snack.

Two courteous and efficient social hostesses look after guests' needs and arrange for activities outside of the hotel, including golf, horseback riding, sightseeing tours, and shopping trips to Bridgetown.

The **Rockley Resort and Beach Club,** P.O. Box 35W, Worthing, Christ Church (tel. 427-5890). You'll pass five tennis courts on your drive up to the entrance of this resort, which gives an idea of how sports-oriented it is. If you stand on the terracotta tiles beside the pool, you can watch golfers tee off on the Rockley's nine-hole course or view squash games through a plate-glass window. If you prefer the beach to the pool, the hotel has a shuttle bus that makes a run there every 30 minutes.

There are two saunas on the premises, a poolside bar for after-sports relaxation, a breeze-filled restaurant, and a wide assortment of planned entertainment, including evening shows, belly-dancing, limbo contests, guest talent shows, a beach club, and a late-night disco.

The accommodations sprawl outward from the main reception area in long wings, some with views over the golf course. In winter, single units cost between $80 and $95 daily, while doubles range from $95 to $120. Two-bedroom suites, suitable for four persons, go for $155 to $210 in winter. *Singles in summer cost between $48 and $60 daily, while doubles go for $66 to $85, and an extra adult is $12 per day. Two-bedroom suites in summer cost between $110 and $120.* These rates do not include meals, but MAP can be arranged for a supplement of $30 per person per day in any season. MAP for children under 12 costs $15 per person.

Casuarina Beach Club, St. Lawrence Gap, Christ Church (tel. 428-3600). You'll approach this isolated resort through a forest of palm trees which sway gracefully above a well-maintained lawn. The main building has a series of arched windows leading onto verandas, although to get to your accommodation, you pass through the outlying reception building and beside the pair of swimming pools. These are separated from the wide sandy beach by a lawn area dotted with Caribbean pines and climbing roses. On the premises is an octagonal-roofed open-air bar and restaurant, as well as tennis and squash facilities. The front desk can arrange most seaside activities through outside agencies.

Each of the 64 accommodations is air-conditioned and has a ceiling fan, a kitchenette, and wicker furniture. In winter, two persons are charged $95 to $115 daily, *while during spring and autumn, the cost is $72 to $78, depending on their exposure. In summer, they represent good value at $60 to $66 for two guests.* Extra persons (more than two) staying in any unit pay $12 each per night, and children under 12 are accommodated free in their parents' room.

Settlers Beach, St. James (tel. 422-3052), is a seaside collection of well-appointed villas placed on four acres of beachfront property. Each air-conditioned apartment is self-contained, having two bedrooms with private bath, a spacious tile-floor lounge and dining room, plus a fully equipped kitchen.

In the shoulder and low season, an apartment for two begins at $85, going up to $125 daily. For breakfast and dinner, add a supplement of $30 per person daily. In high season, two persons stay here for $220 daily; three persons, $290. Tariffs go even higher at Christmas. The apartments have sunny colors, and the rates quoted include the services of a maid.

Adjoining the buildings is a swimming pool surrounded by palms and lawn. The square-roofed dining room and lounge bar serves good food and drink, and at dinner you can select a table in the moonlight. You can also dine around on the exchange plan, at the Coral Reef and the Sandpiper.

Ocean View, Hastings (tel. 427-7821), is an oldtimer that seems just as good as ever, maybe better. It's the oldest hotel in Barbados, founded in 1901. It still maintains some vintage niceties too. For example, your bed is turned down at night. Shoes left outside the door are waiting there polished the next morning. At dinner, vegetables are served from silver bowls.

Built between the busy road and the beach, the pink-and-white Ocean View has some of the graciousness of a colonial English house, with Queen Anne mahogany side tables, chintz-covered armchairs, an open staircase with an old balustrade, a drawing room richly furnished, and a seaside porch that's good for lounging.

The location is on the south coast in Christ Church, with Bridgetown about 5 minutes away; the international airport, 15 minutes. The staff of 57 has an average length of service of 17 years, and the two Bajan head cooks have been here for more than a quarter of a century.

The bedrooms are not decorated in the usual automatic style. Rather, every chamber is different—some large, some small and cozy—and an attractive use has been made of island antiques. In winter, singles range in price from $45 to $61 daily, a double costing from $64 to $73, all EP. *In summer, you pay from $40 to $52 daily in a single, from $62 to $70 in a double, EP.* For dining here, refer to "Barbados Cookery," below.

The Middle Bracket

Bagshot House, St. Lawrence, Christ Church (tel. 428-8125), was built about a quarter of a century ago by a charming Trinidadian, Mrs. Eileen Robinson. She has glamorized her house with flowering vines tumbling over the railing of the balconies. In front of the inn, the beach stretches out before you.

Some of the well-kept, simply furnished units have views of the water. All rentals, however, contain private baths. Twins cost $125 daily in winter; singles, $79—including breakfast and dinner. *In the off-season, these same twins go for $112 daily, singles for $74, both rates including half board as well.*

A front sunbathing deck is perched right at the edge of a lagoon. This is actually the living room, but there is a deckside lounge decorated with paintings by local artists. Bridgetown is about a 15-minute drive to the west.

The **Tides Inn,** Gibbes, St. Peter (tel. 422-2403), is a quiet retreat that appeals particularly to those who enjoy a small, friendly hotel with a relaxed, informal atmosphere. Lying on the St. Peter coast in the northern part of Barbados where the sea is calm, it has no swimming pool, but Gibbes Bay, with its clear, warm water, is only a short walk away. The area has been called by some visitors one of the three most beautiful beaches in the world.

The Tides is away from the rumble of main-road traffic and enjoys almost constant breezes. Guests are warmly welcomed with a complimentary rum punch, and there is no charge for use of beach and snorkeling equipment, personal laundry, daily newspaper, and room service. It offers a cozy bar near the main dining room which is outfitted in tropical decor of rattan furniture and colorful table linens, overlooking the garden. The varied menu includes West Indian and continental specialties.

The accommodations are in three separate buildings, each with veranda. All rooms are on the ground floor, with private bath and shower, and ceiling fans circulate the air. *In summer, two persons pay from $80 daily, MAP (or, for room only, $40).* MAP rates in winter for two persons are from $100. All units are completely screened. The Tides is a good bargain in the Caribbean.

Half Moon Beach Hotel, Dover Beach (tel. 428-7131), is a small waterside resort, popular with young people and families with children who want to keep costs low. The location is halfway between the airport and Bridgetown, the latter a 3½-mile run (it lies on a bus route). They rent 30 double, studio, and one-

and two-bedroom suites, the latter with a separate living room, bedroom, and fully equipped kitchen. Cooks and babysitters can be arranged by the management.

In summer, singles are a bargain at $20 daily, going up to $25 in a double. Two persons pay anywhere from $35 in a studio to $45 daily in a one-bedroom suite. The two-bedroom apartments for four cost $65 daily. In winter, single rooms cost $40 daily, going up anywhere from $45 to $60 daily in a double or studio. Two persons pay $85 daily in a one-bedroom apartment, and a two-bedroom apartment for four persons costs $100 daily. For breakfast and dinner, add a supplement of $15 per person daily to the room charges.

You can alternate between bathing in the sea in the cool freshwater pool, surrounded by coconut palms and a sunning terrace with thatched shade huts. Adjacent to the pool is the main bar, serving good tropical rum and fruit drinks. Dining is on an al fresco patio area. The dining room is actually on two levels, with a rustic wooden ceiling, hanging baskets, and round natural-pine tables, with bamboo chairs and rattan mats.

Welcome Inn, Maxwell Coast Road, Christ Church (tel. 428-9900), is an attractively priced, Mediterranean-style hotel whose seven stories curve and angle around a white sandy beach. Most of the social action happens in the vicinity of the hourglass-shaped pool on the edge of the beach and surrounded by foliage. The hotel looks vaguely like a large-scale pueblo dwelling, although many of its accents, particularly the textured stucco walls, are Mediterranean. You can hear the sound of the surf from some of the balconies, each of which is bordered by a log balustrade.

The accommodations contain refrigerators, stoves, air conditioning, and wall-to-wall carpeting. In winter, units suitable for either one or two persons range from $100 to $145, *while in summer, they cost between $55 and $90.* A third person in any room costs an additional $18, unless he or she is under 12, in which case the hotel charges $7. For reservations in the U.S., call 800/635-9900 toll free.

Sichris Apartment Hotel, 2 Worthing, Christ Church (tel. 427-5930), is shielded from the street by a row of shrubbery and a high wall. It contains a sheltered pool area, 24 one-bedroom apartments, and a friendly and attractive staff directed by David and Anne Walker. When they opened the hotel in 1978, the Walkers named it after their teenage children, Simon and Christopher, who occasionally help their parents in maintaining the place properly.

Each of the pleasant accommodations contain air conditioning, direct-dial phone, a kitchenette, and a veranda with louvered doors. Beach lovers will find the ocean a short walk away, and visitors who prefer to cook in their own units can shop at supermarkets close by. The in-house restaurant is a pleasantly informal place with an adjoining cabana bar and a series of scheduled barbecues and buffets with live music.

Summer rates in accommodations suitable for one or two persons range from $60 to $65, while winter prices go from $110 to $125, depending on whether your view is over the pool or over the road. The establishment charges an additional $15 for a third and fourth person in any apartment. Children under 12 stay free. MAP is available for a $48 supplement per person per day. For toll-free reservations in the United States, call 800/635-9900; in New York state, call 212/355-6605.

Good for the Budget

The **Island Inn,** Garrison, St. Michael (tel. 426-0057), is an old-style compound with bungalows placed in a maze of tropical trees and shrubbery, across the street from the Holiday Inn and down from the Hilton. On this site, a British army regiment in 1750 constructed an armory as part of the fort built to protect the harbor. The present unit, unfortunately, stands near a large Mobil refinery (but everyone assures me the wind doesn't blow in the direction of the Island Inn).

The inn has a loyal staff who run this place in a home-like way, housing you in one of their 27 air-conditioned garden cottages, each with a covered front veranda. Dollarwise travelers seem to like it here, especially the prices. In winter the single rate is $44 daily, rising to $62 in a double, with a third person paying another $28. *EP singles in summer cost $28 daily, rising to $40 in a double, plus tax and service.* Dark-wood floors, scatter rugs, louvered shutters, and straw mats set the style tone.

The location is on Needham's Point, about a ten-minute ride south of Bridgetown. At the edge of the patio garden is one of the finest restaurants on the island, Brown Sugar (see my dining recommendations). However, guests can also enjoy breakfast and perhaps a meal in Peter's Patio, the al fresco dining room for guests, with its vines clambering over an old English trellis. Perhaps they'll have a drink first in the informal lounge bar under a large tree. There's a mixture of antiques and simple modern in the public areas. Every Monday night the staff has an "Action at the Inn," with a full Caribbean buffet and native floor show.

Fairholme, Maxwell, Christ Church (tel. 428-9425), is a converted plantation house, once part of the Old Maxwell Plantation, lying five miles from the Grantley Adams Airport and six miles from Bridgetown. The main house with its original gardens is just off a major road, a five-minute walk to the beach, and across from its sister hotel the Sherringham Beach, with its waterfront café and bar which Fairholme guests are allowed to use.

The older part has 11 double rooms with private baths, a living room area, and a patio overlooking an orchard and swimming pool. Beside the pool is a grassy lawn for sunbathing and a bar for island beverages. More recently added are 20 Spanish-style studio apartments, all with balcony or patio, built within the walls of the old plantation, with high cathedral ceilings, dark beams, and traditional furnishings.

In summer, rooms rent for $30 daily in double occupancy, $22 in a single, with apartments going for $40 daily for two persons. In winter, rooms are $36 in a double, $24 in a single, with apartments costing $53 daily, double occupancy. Breakfast and dinner cost an additional $18 per person. The restaurant has a reputation for home-cooking—good, wholesome, nothing fancy, but the ingredients are fresh.

Seaview Hotel, Hastings Main Road (tel. 426-1450). Repeat guests like this mellow place and have told their friends, and they all keep coming back to some fine Bajan hospitality. Delightfully informal, the place is also a bargain, lying right on the seaside, with a tree-fringed beach.

You live here for the most part in your bathing suit. The inn lies on a main road, five minutes from Bridgetown, with lots of traffic, but fortunately most of its rooms face the sea. There's a large car park at the entrance, and the hotel has an encircling New Orleans–style wrought-iron railing. Air-conditioned bedrooms are pristine, with bright colors and private baths. In winter, a single rents for $62 daily, *the rate dropping to just $28 in summer.* A double costs $62 in winter, *only $33 in summer.*

On the premises is the Tamarind Tree Club, which is shaded by a large tree from which it derives its name. Here you can order breakfast, lunch, or snacks throughout the day. In addition, the Virginian Restaurant serves good island food nightly (see my dining recommendations).

Barbados Windsurfing Club Hotel, Benston Beach, Maxwell, Christ Church (tel. 428-9095), attracts many of its guests just because it's one of the most fun places in town. If you're an avid windsurfer, this could be the perfect place for you, also. Set between the road and the sea, the accommodations at this young-at-heart resort are within a brightly painted three-story rectangular building with angled balconies. The 15 units are spacious and simple, including basic kitchens and simple bathrooms. Phones are in the hallways (one per floor), and the reception area is sunny but spartan. In winter, singles cost $48, while doubles go for $60. *In summer, rates go down to $36 in a single and $48 in a double.*

Although the bedrooms are comfortable, no one comes here for the decor. It's the youthful ambience and the camaraderie that makes this place noteworthy. Experts say that the windsurfing just off the hotel's sea wall is as good as that in Hawaii, which appeals to nearly fanatical followers of the sport who come from all over the western hemisphere. On a sunny day when the wind is right, observers on the hotel's grassy terrace can see flotillas of sailboards riding the waves, heading either out into the Atlantic or back to shore. For rates and details, see "The Sporting Life," below.

An informal restaurant on the premises serves simple lunches (sandwiches and hamburgers) during the day for around $18 BDS ($9) for a meal, while more complete evening dinners, with such main dishes as steak, chicken, and dolphin, cost about $40 BDS ($20). Several musical evenings are usually planned per week, drawing an energetic crowd of fun-loving participants. For information about the week's entertainment, call the hotel.

The **Windsor,** Hastings, Christ Church (tel. 427-7831), is an art deco–inspired building set on a road across from the sea. Its large-scale interior contains a popular pub, a restaurant, a pool, and a series of comfortable rooms set in lattice-accented wings stretching to a garden in back. The pub contains a pool area where members of the on-the-premises gym may be playing and a bar area sheltered under a re-creation of a plantation-style veranda. In winter, singles range from $60 to $72, while doubles cost between $80 and $90. A third person in a double room is charged an additional $22 daily. *In summer, singles go from $42 to $48, and doubles cost $54 to $60. A third person in any double room in summer pays an extra $18.* All prices include a full English breakfast.

Atlantis Hotel, Bathsheba (tel. 433-9445), is housed in a slightly dilapidated, green-roofed villa built by a wealthy planter in 1882. In the unpretentious hostelry, set directly on the seacoast, simple bedrooms rent year round for $24 to $29 in a single, for $46 to $53 in a double. A third person in any double room is charged $19 to $22, although children staying with their parents pay $12 to $15. Surprisingly enough, these prices include all meals, which makes a stopover here one of the most economical along the Atlantic coast of Barbados.

Aside from inexpensive accommodations, this is the most popular luncheon spot on the east side of the island. Every day around noon, you're likely to see three or four tour buses and a fleet of private cars depositing crowds who flock into the sunny, breeze-filled interior.

There, with a sweeping view of the ocean, Enid I. Maxwell will be seated in a small booth, welcoming visitors into her restaurant. She bought the establishment in 1945, and ever since has served copious buffet lunches every Thursday and Sunday to just about everybody in Barbados. On those days, for around $31 BDS ($15.50) per person, patrons feast from an L-shaped table laden with buffet items that are replaced as quickly as they're emptied. On days when buffets are not scheduled, Mrs. Maxwell directs a handful of waitresses who take meal orders at your cloth-covered table. Main courses usually include fish and chicken, accompanied by pumpkin fritters and vegetables. Full meals cost from $25 BDS ($12.50). Dinners are also served from 7 p.m. every day of the week.

Your Own Apartment

Bresmay Apartment House, St. Lawrence Gap (tel. 428-6131), is an apartment cluster built right on the coast road, but with a 30- by 60-foot swimming pool and an open-air restaurant and bar, Strawberrys, facing its own beach. The units were constructed both for views and comforts, with today's less demanding traveler in mind. The place at times becomes intimate, almost club-like, particularly around the pool and seafront with its waterfront refreshment bar. You'll soon get to know your fellow guests.

Since every apartment has its own kitchen (there's a grocery nearby), you can cook your own meals or else dine at Semonne, a restaurant on the premises. Maid service is included in the rates. Extensive use is made of bamboo in the furnishings, setting a Caribbean motif in decor. All rates quoted are for two occupants. In winter, the cheapest way for two persons to stay here is in a poolside studio at $80 daily, although you'll pay $85 in a seaside studio. *In the off-season, rates dip to $40 to $45 for two, EP, plus tax and service.*

Sandhurst, St. Lawrence Gap (tel. 428-6595), 3½ miles west of Bridgetown, is a good housekeeping holiday complex, offering two types of accommodations—one-bedroom apartments (with a separate living and sleeping area) and studios (large rooms situated on the top floor). Nestled in tropical gardens, the complex opens onto half a mile of white sandy beach. All units are fully air-conditioned, and have private patios overlooking the beach and the palm-tree-shaded gardens. A private pool is thrust out almost onto the sea itself.

The apartments and studios are designed to give you a complete "at home" feeling, with all the necessities self-contained. The rates include a continental breakfast, and you'll find a fully equipped kitchen. You buy supplies at a nearby store, which will make you quite independent if you live here. There is daily maid service, however, and if you wish, a native cook can be employed reasonably. The furnishings are mostly in white wrought-iron patio style, with bamboo armchairs, everything lightened by tropical-color accents such as light orange and sunflower yellow.

In high season, two persons can stay here at rates ranging from $110 to $125 daily, *and these tariffs drop in summer to anywhere from $70 to $75.* Your hosts are Arthur and Jocelyne Graham.

Travelers' Palm, 265 Palm Ave., Sunset Crest, St. James (tel. 432-1841), is designed for those who want to be independent, a choice collection of 16 well-furnished apartments with fully equipped kitchens and air conditioning. Attracting a friendly young crowd, the apartments are filled with bright, resort-type colors and handcrafted furniture.

They open onto a well-kept lawn with a swimming pool. Serviced by maids, apartments can house one to three persons. The rate for one of these apartments costs from $60 daily in winter, *dropping to just $40 in summer.* Apartments also have a large living and dining room area, and a patio where you can have your breakfast or a candlelit dinner which you've prepared yourself.

Inn on the Beach, Holetown, St. James (tel. 432-0385), is an intimate, compact, miniature resort built as a suntrap directly on the beach. Its four floors of well-styled modern apartments give each occupant a protected private balcony which extends the size of the living rooms. Vaguely Aztec in design, it is white, in contrast to the sky blue of the swimming pool and the deep greens of the palms and fir trees.

The pool area becomes a communal living room. Before dinner, you'll surely have made friends at the loggia bar, with its tile floors, copper lanterns, and large colored rope and string hangings. Each of the 20 air-conditioned, self-contained studios holds a kitchenette where you can prepare your own meals, or you can dine at a poolside restaurant. Nearby is a shopping plaza where you can pick up supplies.

In summer, a single costs $60 daily, a double going for $65. The penthouse suite with a private balcony and a large sundeck rents for $100 daily for three persons. In winter, the single tariff rises to $95 daily, a double going for $105, and the penthouse suites costing $160.

Sherringham Beach Apartments, Christ Church (tel. 428-9339), is a gracious waterfront home, the core of which is a century-old estate of one of Barbados's plantation owners. With its sea-view verandas, it sits under a sloping red roof. To the vintage structure a block of 18 modern, self-contained, air-conditioned apartments has been added. Some have balcony perches for a look out at Oistin Bay.

The apartments are neat and simple, furnished in the typical Caribbean beachfront style, and all are air-conditioned. The more expensive units open onto the sea. *In summer, two persons can stay here for only $45 per day in a superior unit.* These tariffs range from $55 to $60 daily in winter, plus service and tax.

In the plantation house, you can take your meals in its restaurant if you don't want to cook yourself. Bajan specialties, among other dishes, are served. Guests can also use the facilities of its sister hotel nearby, the Fairholme, which has a swimming pool, bar and a more formal restaurant.

Maresol Beach Apartments, St. Lawrence, Christ Church (tel. 428-9300), is a cluster of one- and two-bedroom apartments in two-story buildings opening onto 1700 feet of beach. There are 17 units in all, which might be suitable if your requirements are minimal. In winter, a one-bedroom apartment suitable for two persons ranges in price from $450 to $500 weekly; a two-bedroom unit, accommodating four persons, costs from $600 to $900 weekly. *In summer, the one-bedroom apartment rents for $250 to $275 weekly, a two-bedroom unit (for four persons) ranging from $260 to $440.*

Apartments are appropriately furnished, and at the mini-mart on the premises you can obtain foodstuffs, liquor, and general supplies. In addition to that, vendors selling fresh fish and island-grown produce come right to your back door. Each apartment has a full kitchen, equipped with linens, cutlery, china, and other utensils. Mrs. Audrey Trotman can arrange for cooks, maids, or babysitters on request.

2. Barbados Cookery

The famous flying fish jumps up on every menu, and when prepared right it's a delicacy, moist and succulent, nutlike in flavor, approaching the subtlety of brook trout. Bajans boil it, steam it, bake it, stew it, fry it, stuff it, or whatever.

Try also the sea urchin, or oursin, which you may have already sampled in Martinique and Guadeloupe. Bajans often call these urchins "sea eggs." Crab-in-the-back is another specialty, as is langouste, the Barbadian lobster. Dolphin and salt fish cakes are other popular items on the menu.

Such vegetables typical of the Caribbean as yams, sweet potatoes, and eddoes are grown. And Barbadian fruits are luscious, including papaya, passionfruit, and mangos.

If you hear that any hotel or restaurant, such as Sandy Beach, is having a "Cohoblopot," call for a reservation. This is a Barbadian term which means to "cook up," and it inevitably will produce a host of Bajan specialties.

Bajan dishes are a blend of cookery styles: the British, and most definitely the East Indian and African. These recipes have been adapted to include the local meats, fruits, and vegetables. Pepperpot, stews, and curries are made with local chicken, pork, beef and fish. The secret of the flavorful dishes, as any Bajan cook will tell you, is in the "seasoning up." It is said that seasoning techniques have changed little since the 16th century.

At Christmas, when many U.S. visitors come to Barbados, roast ham or turkey is served with jug-jug, a rich casserole of Scottish derivation that includes salt beef, ground corn flour, green pigeon peas, and spices. Cou-cou, a side dish made from okra and cornmeal, accompanies fish, especially the "flying fish" of Barbados.

If possible, escape the dining requirements of your hotel and eat around, sampling the island's varied cuisine, which is interesting but not spicy exotic.

Note that most of the prices I'll cite are in U.S. dollars.

Bagatelle Restaurant, Highway 2A, three miles from Sunset Crest, St. Thomas (tel. 425-0666), is housed in the gubernatorial residence of Lord Willoughby of Parham, a plantation-style house dating back to 1645. The secluded, remote, sylvan retreat lies in the hills in the center of the island, retaining the aura of colonial days. It has been transformed into one of the island's finest and most elegant choices for dining, a sophisticated, popular rendezvous.

Cooled by overhead fans, you can dine in rambling cellars, with candles and lanterns illuminating the menu as well as the white coral walls and the old archways. Furnishings are mostly in a heavy black wood, adding a stately serenity and dignity to the place. Service is very gracious, among the best I found on Barbados.

You proceed first to a charming little bar where menu selections are made. Later you can select a cozy corner or dine outside, listening to the crickets.

For $35, you can select fom the set menu, ordering perhaps salmon mousse or a chicken liver pâté, going on to the callaloo soup or a fish chowder made mainly of flying fish, eddoes, and shrimp.

For a main course, you might enjoy superbly cooked rack of lamb or a "sort of beef Wellington." Desserts are such luscious concoctions as key lime pie, chocolate mousse, or crème brûlée. Hours are 7 p.m. to midnight, seven days a week.

Greensleeves, Greensleeves Hotel, St. Peter (tel. 422-2275), is the blue-ribbon choice for dining, exuding the discreet ambience of a patrician private home. The setting is at poolside, open to the stars, a romantic note for some of the continental and international dishes served here. The menu is perhaps the largest and most ambitious in Barbados.

Among the more interesting appetizers is rôti Greensleeves—selected meats, chopped and curried, wrapped in pastry, baked, and served with a demi-glacé. Try also the Greensleeves special fresh fish soup.

The fish dinners are excellent, especially the poisson volante Savannah. This is fresh flying fish cooked to an old créole recipe with tomatoes, onions, lime, herbs, and spices. You might prefer instead the mignons de boeuf (two thin filets, sauteed in butter with a sauce of cream and shallots). Desserts include the chef's special Austrian apfelstrudel. A meal begins at $35, but you could spend a lot more of course, and wine is extra.

In addition, there is a magnificent cellar of wines. The place has what the owners call civilized informality—that is, no jackets or ties are required at any time. The à la carte restaurant is open from 7 to 11:30 p.m.

Restaurant Flamboyant, Hastings Main Road, Christ Church (tel. 427-5588). If you dine here, you'll enter what used to be a private home, considerably simplified since it became a restaurant, with many of the interior walls removed. Still, the tapering columns of the veranda remain in place, and the view still encompasses a large flamboyant (poinciana) tree, which you may be lucky enough to see in full bloom, depending on the time of year of your visit to Barbados. Mr. and Mrs. Brian Cheeseman, the owners, direct a kitchen where, because everything is prepared to order, the food may take a while to be served. While you're waiting, you can enjoy drinks from the long wooden bar while studying the paintings of the whitewashed interior.

Menu items include pumpkin and potato soup, a seafood crêpe Flamboyant, wienerschnitzel, a half chicken stuffed Bajan style, shrimp in dill sauce, and apple pie à la mode. Full meals range upward from $60 BDS ($30) per person. Reservations are important, especially in high season.

Fort Charles Grill, Barbados Hilton, Needham's Point, St. Michael (tel. 426-0200), is an elegant setting for both a continental and a Bajan cuisine. Reservations are essential, however, as most of the tables, particularly in season, could be booked by the hotel's own guests.

For an opener, I suggest the Barbados pepperpot. It's a spicy gumbo with beef, chicken, pork, and duck, or you might prefer a breadfruit vichyssoise. I found the most interesting hors d'oeuvre is oysters Rockefeller. From the charcoal broiler, I suggest local lobster, sold by the pound at fluctuating prices. From the rôtisserie, you can order succulent sirloin steaks and lamb chops. Desserts tend to be spectacular—pineapple and banana flambé with old Bajan rum or crêpes suzettes. The Bajan coffee served here is flambéed with a ten-year-old cane brandy. You have a choice of ordering à la carte or from the table d'hôte menu (the latter usually includes about five main dishes, including roast prime rib of U.S. beef). From the set menu, expect to spend from $30 up, including an appetizer, soup, main course, the vegetable of the day, and a tempting dessert such as guava cheesecake, followed by American brewed coffee. On the à la carte menu, you are likely to spend from $40. Hours are from 6 to 11 p.m. You can dine and dance every Friday and Saturday night, and there is piano music on Sunday and Wednesday nights.

La Piperade, Glitter Bay, St. James (tel. 422-4111). Set at the back of the Glitter Bay Hotel, between a freshwater pool and a sandy beach, this restaurant is surrounded with lush and colorful vegetation. The building looks like a low-lying collection of whitewashed domes surrounded with Mediterranean-style terracotta roofs. Newcomers might compare its design to a village church in Greece, although that impression will quickly change at the hedonistic visual pleasure that this restaurant and the resort offer.

The restaurant is set in a series of contoured terraces leading on one side to the edge of the free-form pool. At lunchtime, the sun lovers from the hotel's beach may join you inside the Victorian-style interior, where ornate lattices and lathe-turned columns support the sparkling white ceilings. Meals are served on pink tablecloths by a battery of uniformed waiters. They may include such specialties as tournedos Piperade with brandy, lobster bisque with brandy, the chef's own chicken-liver pâté, whole Cornish game hen stuffed with wild rice and served with Périgueux sauce, a fresh fish of the day, and desserts such as key lime pie. In addition, the chef prepares daily special dishes which vary with the season. Full meals cost from $70 BDS ($35). Reservations are a good idea at this excellent restaurant.

Restaurant Château Créole, Porters, St. James (tel. 422-4116). In a spot near Glitter Bay, this stucco-and-tile house is set in a pleasant tropical garden dotted with statues of cherubs carrying lambs. After passing under a verdant arbor, you'll be invited to order a drink, served on one of the flowered banquettes filling various parts of the house. Meals are taken on the rear terrace, al fresco style, by candlelight. Barbara and Larry Tatem, formerly of Montréal, are the owners who welcome guests and direct the kitchens.

Menu specialties include creole dishes, which often make use of ample amounts of crabmeat, such as crab diablo and crabmeat au gratin. Perhaps you'd prefer shrimp rémoulade, creole red bean soup, New Orleans seafood gumbo, or chicken Pontalba. The establishment makes its own ice cream with local fruits several times a week. Full dinners, served every evening except Sunday, range from $45 BDS ($22.50) to $75 BDS ($37.50). The restaurant doesn't serve lunch. Dinner reservations are a good idea, especially in high season.

da Luciano, "Staten," Hastings, Highway 7, Christ Church (tel. 427-5518), is a lovely setting—in a Barbados National Trust–designated building of architectural interest—for a classical Italian cuisine. They offer some of the finest Italian dining in the southern Caribbean. The restaurant has gained in popularity with some of the island's outstanding residents who know they can get good service, top-quality ingredients, and skill and care reflected in what they order.

I recommend such specialties as cozze alla marinara (mussels in their shells sauteed in butter and parsley, with white wine and a lot of garlic). Try also the filetto battuto alla Luciano (flattened filet of beef flambéed in brandy, sauteed in butter, served with mustard, fresh cream, and mushrooms).

I'm also fond of spaghetti de cecco alla puttanesca (spaghetti sauteed with fresh tomato sauce, sliced olives, capers, anchovies, basil, and black pepper). The pièce de résistance is the quaglia nel nido alla wolfe (charcoal-broiled filet of beef topped with croutons of garlic bread, roast quail, and natural juice). For dessert, you can (in season) order fresh strawberries, finishing with an espresso. Your final bill will be from $30.

Brown Sugar, off Aquatic Gap next to the Island Inn in St. Michael (tel. 427-7684), is a beautiful al fresco dining room whose chefs prepare some of the tastiest Bajan specialties on the island. An efficient, friendly staff serves you.

The island house is hidden behind lush foliage. The ceiling is latticed, with slow-turning ceiling fans. Two walls open onto a lower garden dining room, with white plastic molded chairs set under parasols. The other walls are in stained pine, and there's an open veranda for dining in a setting of profuse hanging plants. You eat by candlelight.

For an unusual and imaginative opening, try Salomon Grundy, a spicy-hot Jamaican favorite—a pâté of smoked herring, allspice, wine vinegar, onion, chives, and hot bonnie peppers, served with Jamaican water crackers. You might also prefer Bol Jol, a Trinidadian special of salted codfish, seasoned and served with pickled cucumber and lime tips. Among the soups, I suggest hot gungo-pea soup (pigeon peas cooked in chicken broth and zested with fresh coconut milk, herbs, and a touch of white wine). The price of the main course includes one of these appetizers, plus soup, vegetables, dessert, and coffee.

Among the most recommendable main courses, tandoori chicken is that North Indian classic which is equally popular in the southern Caribbean. Or perhaps you'd like crabmeat Carlisle, a melange of flaked crabmeat, heavy cream, bread crumbs, local herbs and spices, heightened with a touch of brandy. A selection of locally grown fresh vegetables is offered nightly from the hot trolley, and you'll also be served a tossed green salad with a choice of dressing. For desserts, called confections here, I recommend the coconut cream mousse, which is smooth. You're faced with a $40 BDS ($20) or more dinner tab. The restaurant is also known for its superb luncheon buffet, costing from $30 BDS ($15) per person. Add another 18% for tax and service.

The **Witch Doctor,** St. Lawrence Gap, Christ Church (tel. 428-7856), hides behind a screen of thick foliage, across from another popular Barbadian eatery, the Pisces. There's a series of small dining rooms which open onto each other, with rustic wooden poles and shingled walls. Everything is decorated with African and island woodcarvings of witch doctors, in honor of its namesake.

The place purveys a fascinating African and Bajan cuisine with some unusual concoctions which, even if unfamiliar, are very tasty and well prepared, a big change from a lot of the bland hotel fare.

For an appetizer, try the split-pea and pumpkin soup. You'll also be offered kingfish shango (cold, soused in lime).

All main dishes are served with rice. Chef's specialties include shrimp creole, beef in wine, flying fish, lamb curry, kingfish, and chicken piri-piri (from Mozambique). Dinner, the only meal served here, should run about $20. Hours are 6 to 10:30 p.m. every night.

Pisces, St. Lawrence Gap, Christ Church (tel. 428-6558), is a private cottage, painted olive green with white trim, lodged right on the waterfront. The front garden is dominated by coconut trees, and the dining rooms extend along the water's edge. Cooled by sea breezes, you can enjoy fish and seafood in a setting that is rustic yet has a subdued Caribbean elegance.

With a name like Pisces, you expect and get well-prepared Neptunian dishes, including the famous flying fish of Barbados, served here stuffed with herbs. I'm very fond of the chef's turtle stew and his lobster chasseur. Try also the grilled shrimp kebab, which on my latest rounds was flavored to perfection. The pepper chicken and deviled crab are also good. For dessert, I'd endorse the Bajan trifle.

Expect to spend around $25 to $30 for a complete meal. Go for dinner only, served between 6:30 and 11 p.m., and be sure to make a reservation.

Restaurant Germania, St. Lawrence Main Road, Christ Church (tel. 428-4537). Sitting on the rear veranda of this charming restaurant is somehow reminiscent of looking out from a balcony in Venice. A well-maintained West Indian clapboard house (which used to house the Bajan telephone exchange), the building is painted lime with cream trim. It's owned by a German/Bajan couple, Clyde and Helga Cox. They met in London years ago, then moved to Helga's hometown of Essen, Germany, before coming to Barbados to follow the career they both like best—running a successful restaurant.

If you order a drink at the large curved bar in the front, Clyde won't stint on the whiskey. The libation he'll set on the pine boards will be a stiff one, guaranteed to please even the most hardfisted drinker. However, it's after a visitor moves to one of the nine tables on the back veranda that the Coxes' skill as restaurateurs shows itself. Specialties range from German traditional dishes to Bajan seafood and include fish soup, goulash soup, wienerschnitzel, filet of dolphin, sirloin steak, and a savory pepperpot, served with rice and a salad. The restaurant is open only for dinner from 6 to 11 p.m. daily except Monday. Full meals cost from $50 BDS ($25) up.

La Cage aux Folles, Paynes Bay, St. James (tel. 432-1203), on my latest rounds, seemed to be the most "trendy" restaurant on the island. It's the venture of Nick Hudson, who earned his fame when he worked at the popular Nick's Diner in London before coming to Barbados, where he was associated for a time with the Bagatelle Restaurant. In a "fit of madness," he decided to open this eatery, which takes its name from the noted French play and movie, later a successful Broadway musical, about two aging homosexuals on the Riviera. However, don't get the wrong idea. The place is aggressively straight, as a perusal of its wine list (with X-rated pictures) will reveal.

The menu, with dinners costing from $35, is a surprising combination of the French and Chinese cuisine. You may want to compose your meal from the repertoire of both those celebrated kitchens. I like the idea, having for years considered the Chinese and the French to be the finest cooks on earth. Perhaps you'll choose the sesame prawn pâté, crab au gratin, or creole fish soup. Other courses include a fresh fish of the day, Malaysian beef satay, sweet-and-sour shrimp, and crêpes with seafood.

Crane Beach Pavilion Restaurant, Crane Beach, St. Philip (tel. 423-6220). The setting is romantic, tables placed under a tented ceiling where food at night is served by candlelight. A continental touch prevails.

Appetizers are wide in scope, including deep-fried crane chubb (a rock fish) with tartar sauce. A platter with a selection of fresh, locally grown vegetables is offered with all main courses and is included in the price. I'd suggest seafood specialties, such as curried shrimps with a mango chutney, or perhaps grilled lobster. The chef also prepares good steaks. You might also prefer sauteed loin of pork, rack of lamb, or roast duckling. Dinners are likely to run from $85 BDS ($42.50). If you're touring the island and plan to visit just for lunch, you'll find such typical fare as sandwiches, omelets, burgers, and soups both hot and cold. Your tab is likely to be around $40 BDS ($20).

Try to attend one of the very popular Sunday buffets, beginning at 12:30 p.m. and costing $45 BDS ($22.50). Be sure to make a reservation. You're allowed to use the Roman swimming pool and can be entertained by a steel band.

The **Virginian Restaurant,** Seaview Hotel, Hastings, Main Road, Christ Church (tel. 427-7963), has good home cookery. The place is pleasant, the staff nice, and the prices reasonable. The restaurant opens for dinner at 6 p.m., and the chef prepares a number of good-tasting specialties, including roast prime rib of beef au jus, steamed Bajan flying fish, shrimp curry, and lasagne. Soups are good too, including the bouillabaisse. From the charcoal broiler you can ask for a 14-ounce T-bone. Desserts are luscious, including baked Alaska. A complete meal will cost around $25, plus the cost of your drink.

During the day, if you're in the area you can have lunch at the **Tamarind Tree Club,** which adjoins the Virginian. Every day a luncheon special is featured for $12.50 BDS ($6.25), including soup, a main course, vegetable, and dessert or coffee. An à la carte menu is available as well.

Khus-Khus Restaurant, Southern Palms Beach Club, St. Lawrence Gap, Christ Church (tel. 7171), is a breezy choice for fine barbecues and Bajan dishes. It also features such entertainment as a calypso band, a steel band, and pop music West Indian style. Casual party types who are hotel hopping often pop in here at night, and it also makes a good choice if you're beaching it in this area during the day. The cedar-shingle-roofed setting is attractive, and service is decidedly casual.

If you do succeed in getting some waiter's attention, you can order from a luncheon menu offering soup such as pumpkin, a local fish (different every day —usually snapper, kingfish, or dolphin), or chicken in a basket. Sandwiches are also offered. You need not spend more than $30 BDS ($15) for lunch.

At night a dinner will cost about $50 BDS ($25). Otherwise, you can select from a fairly well prepared à la carte menu which might offer grilled ribs or beef with pepper sauce, preceded by onion soup. A real West Indian appetizer is the melon cocktail (usually papaya) with rum. Another main course which I recently enjoyed was grilled Barbados red snapper in a choron sauce.

The Pebbles, off Aquatic Gap, St. Michael (tel. 426-4668), opens onto Carlisle Bay, and I prefer it sometimes when downtown Bridgetown seems too hot for survival. Here, in completely relaxed surroundings, you can dine watching the beach and boating activity. You don't need a reservation. The menu has nothing elaborate, just standard food prepared well and served until 10:30 p.m.

At this open-air pavilion, between the Holiday Inn and the Hilton, you can dine for around $15 unless you go crazy. Typical fare includes the most popular item, hamburgers, but for variety's sake you can also get a fish sandwich or a Spanish omelet. The cook usually does a good-tasting soup every day. If you're enjoying the beach, you can ask the waiter to give you a box of the nine-piece chicken "take-away."

The Ocean View, Hastings (tel. 427-7821), Barbados's oldest hostelry (previously recommended), also serves good food. The location is about a 5-minute drive from Bridgetown and some 15 minutes from the international airport. You will be shown to a table overlooking the sea on the south coast of the island. You can help yourself at the well-known Sunday planters' brunch, featuring, as was done in the olden days, a big spread with authentic Bajan specialties. Ernest Hemingway used to fill his plate high with flying fish and pepperpot, after having a big bowl of callaloo soup. The two Bajan head cooks have been at the hotel for some 30 years. Lunches are likely to cost from $20 BDS ($10), and dinners go for about $50 BDS ($25), plus tax and service. Most recently my party of four enjoyed such dishes as roast chicken with a savory stuffing and fish fondue. There is always a changing list of daily specialties. Perhaps you'll begin with a chilled shrimp soup, finishing off your repast with a moist coconut cake.

The **Captain's Carvery,** the Ship Inn, St. Lawrence Gap, Christ Church (tel. 428-9605). In a wing of my favorite pub in Barbados, this paneled restaurant is one of the most richly atmospheric of any place on the island. It's in a square, high-ceilinged room with an unused wooden balcony. The ambience is Old English, with lots of antique prints, thick paneling, and subdued lighting. Against one wall stands a uniformed carver who serves generous portions of meat and fowl to guests who line up for the heavily laden buffet table in the evening. Dinners go for a fixed price of $40 BDS ($20) and are served every day. You select from such specialties as pepperpot or a soup of the day, hot roasts with an array of sauces, a selection of cold cuts with homemade piccalilli, baked potatoes, a full range of green and vegetable salads, and several kinds of dessert.

Lunch is less expensive, costing around $17 BDS ($8.50) for access to the buffet table. There is no uniformed carver, and the buffet selection is simpler. Still, at the price, it represents one of the best bargains in Barbados. Lunch is served daily except Sunday.

Luigi's Restaurant, Dover Woods, St. Lawrence Gap (tel. 428-9218), is an open-air Italian trattoria with a Caribbean flavor. Since 1963 it has been operated in a well-maintained green-and-white house on a quiet road in the middle of a forest, making getting here somewhat of an expedition. Sue Chapman is the manager. From the rafters of this place are clustered hundreds of empty Chianti bottles which, when a breeze blows, tinkle gently against one another like wind chimes. The dining areas include a shrub-lined veranda and several inside rooms, one of which prominently displays a map of Italy.

Meals are prepared to order and may require as much as a 30-minute wait, but if at any time the conversation lags, you can always study the dozens of travel posters set edge to edge on many of the interior walls. This restaurant serves only dinner, opening its doors between 6 and 9:45 p.m. daily except Tuesday. Three fixed-price meals are offered, at $22 BDS ($11) per person. If ordering à la carte, count on spending from $45 BDS ($22.50). Both the fixed-price meals and the à la carte menus include such specialties as lasagne, spaghetti, shrimp cocktail, filet mignon, steak, chicken or shrimp cacciatora on rice, seafood casserole, grilled scampi with spaghetti, stuffed peppers and manicotti, and veal, chicken, and cheese cannelloni.

Waterfront Café, on the wharf of the Careenage, Bridgetown (tel. 427-0093), is an indoor/outdoor café, one of the best places to eat in town, set into a row of old warehouses on the harbor near the longest bridge in town. Its long bar holds jars filled with pickled lemons, which everyone should try at least once. The clientele may include anyone from a Swedish yachtsman to a Jamaican Rasta. When local musicians play here, the music usually begins at 7:30 p.m. No one will mind if you occupy one of the iron chairs while you have a drink or two. If you want a full meal, it will cost $15 for dinner and $8 for lunch. Menu choices include sesame chicken wings, pâté maison, flying fish salad, ceviche, gazpacho, and every Sunday a noontime, fish fry.

Peter the Fisherman, the Island Inn, Garrison, St. Michael (tel. 426-0057). Nestled between the reception area and a spacious barroom of this unpretentious hotel, you'll find a lattice-bordered restaurant whose tables are covered in immaculate napery. There's even a small reflecting pool at one end, near the tables crowded gregariously together. The menus here represent good value on an expensive island.

A fixed-price lunch might include baked flying fish, chicken salad, and vegetables, and usually costs $22 BDS ($11). Otherwise, à la carte lunches and dinners go for $36 BDS ($18), with simple but savory dishes—filet of red snapper Bajan style, steak platters, and roast chicken.

One of the establishment's most popular events is the Monday-night Bajan buffet and cabaret, which costs $48 BDS ($24) per person. Dinner is served seven nights a week from 6:30 to 9:30 p.m., although lunch is served only on weekdays. The restaurant is on the access road leading to the Barbados Hilton, across from the Holiday Inn.

Boomers, St. Lawrence Gap (tel. 428-8439), offers some of the best bargain meals on the island. An American/Bajan operation, it stands across from the Maresol Apartment Hotel. Set back from the road, it is a covered cabana with lots of exposed wood. Al fresco diners take one of the banquettes. The cook prepares a special catch of the day, and the fish is served with soup or salad, rice or baked potato, and a local vegetable. You can always count on seafood, steaks, and hamburgers. A two-egg breakfast with bacon costs only $8 BDS ($4), and a luncheon with a daily Bajan special goes for $12 BDS ($6). Dinner, depending on what you order, is likely to cost from $25 BDS ($12.50) to $35 BDS ($17.50). Children get a special welcome here.

3. Getting Around

TAXIS: Typical of this part of the world, taxis aren't metered, yet their rates are fixed by the government. Overcharging is infrequent, as most of the drivers have a reputation for courtesy and honesty. Taxis are plentiful, and most drivers will produce a list of standard rates, outlining fares between Grantley Adams International Airport and the major hotels. For example, it costs from $13 to $21 to be taken from the west coast to the airport.

BUSES: Unlike most of the British Windwards, Barbados has a reliable bus system. Haitian buses may be more colorful, but Bajan buses have springs and fan out from Bridgetown to almost every part of the island. On most of the major routes there are buses running every 15 minutes or so. Bus fares are 75¢ BDS (38¢) wherever you go.

CAR RENTALS: If you don't mind *driving on the left,* as you'll have to do in all the British Windward Islands, you may find a self-drive car ideal for a Bajan holiday. A temporary permit is needed if you don't have an International Driver's License. Go to the police desk upon your arrival at the airport. You're charged a registration fee of $30 BDS ($15), and you must have your own license. The speed limit is 20 miles per hour within the city limits, 30 mph elsewhere on the island.

All the big car-rental companies are represented including **Avis** (tel. 428-7202 at the airport) and **Hertz** (tel. 428-7878 at the airport). Count on spending from about $40 a day for a Mini-Moke to around $60 a day for a vehicle with automatic shift, both unlimited-mileage quotations. If you want to try your luck with a local firm, I can recommend **Dear's** (tel. 429-9277 or 427-7853, 24 hours a day). It offers self-drive cars, ranging from Mini Mokes to automatics, from economy to luxury.

SCOOTERS AND BICYCLES: Call **Rent-a-Bike,** on Rodney Beach (tel. 422-2112), if you're interested in renting a bicycle to tour Barbados. Bicycles usually cost about $6 per day or $35 per week. There's a delivery charge of $6 if you don't pick it up yourself.

To rent a motor scooter—they call it "hire" here—you must be 21 years of age and in possession of a valid motorcycle license. Mrs. Wells at **Jumbo Rentals** (tel. 426-5689) can make arrangements at a cost of $80 per week, plus a deposit of about $50.

SIGHTSEEING TAXI TOURS: Nearly all Bajan taxi drivers are familiar with the entire island, and usually like to show it off to visitors. If you can afford it, touring by taxi is far more relaxed than, and preferable to, taking one of the standardized bus tours. A four-hour tour of the island costs about $130 BDS ($65) for a party ranging from two to four persons.

SIGHTSEEING BUS TOURS: One of the leading minibus tour operators is **United Taxi Owners Association,** High Street, St. Michael (tel. 427-6868). Almost any type of land tour can be organized and negotiated with these people. A five-hour island tour is likely to cost from $60 to $80 for five passengers.

4. Touring the Island

Barbados is worth exploring, either in your own car or else with a taxidriver guide. Unlike so many islands of the Caribbean, the roads are fair and quite passable. Usually they are well marked with crossroad signs. If you get lost, the people in the countryside are generally friendly and speak English.

Often hot and traffic clogged, the capital, **Bridgetown,** merits no more than a morning's shopping jaunt. An architectural hodgepodge, it was founded by 64 settlers sent out by the Earl of Carlisle in 1628.

You might begin your tour at the **Carenage,** from the French word meaning to turn vessels over on their side for cleaning. This was a haven for the clipper ship, and even though today it doesn't have its yesteryear color, it is still worth exploring. Maybe you'll see a "mauby woman" making her rounds. In colorful dress, she wends her way among the harbor traffic with her bittersweet brew called mauby. With one raised hand, she turns the tap from which the frothy liquid pours into a glass held in the other hand. Perhaps she no longer calls out "Get your mauby, sweet sweet mauby," as was done in the donkey and horse-drawn cart period. To make the drink, dried bark is imported from neighboring islands. The bark is boiled until the water is dark brown and very bitter. This is called bitters and is the base of the drink to which sweetening, essences, and spices are added.

Perhaps you'll also see a Bajan harbor policeman in his Nelsonian sailor suit, with a wide-brimmed straw hat and a blue-collared middy.

At **Trafalgar Square** the long tradition of British colonization is perhaps immortalized forever. The monument here, honoring Lord Nelson, was executed by Sir Richard Westmacott and erected in 1813. The **Public Buildings** on the square are of the great, gray Victorian Gothic variety that you might expect to find in South Kensington, London. The east wing contains the meeting halls of the Senate and the House of Assembly, with some stained-glass windows representing the sovereigns of England from James I to Queen Victoria. Look for the Great Protector himself, Oliver Cromwell.

Behind the Financial Building, **St. Michael's Cathedral** is the symbol of the Church of England transplanted. This Anglican church was built in 1655, but was completely destroyed in a 1780 hurricane. Reconstructed in 1789, it was also damaged by a hurricane in 1831, but was not completely demolished as before. George Washington is said to have worshiped here on his ill-fated Barbados visit.

Some guides will tell you that the 18th-century "George Washington House" on Upper Bay Street is the spot where the future American president stayed during his Barbados journey. Historians doubt this claim.

At this point you can hail a taxi and visit **Garrison Savannah,** just south of the capital. Cricket matches and other games are played in this open-air space of some 50 acres. Horse races are also held at certain times of the year.

Installed here, the **Barbados Museum** (tel. 427-0201), housed in a former military prison, has a collection of furniture, glassware, birds, fish, and records of the island's history, plus a shop to sell souvenir books, prints, cards, jewelry, and handicrafts. The museum has a collection of Arawak artifacts which are at least 1500 years old. The museum can be visited from 9 a.m. to 6 p.m. Monday to Saturday. It charges adults $4 BDS ($2); children, $1 BDS (50¢).

Nearby, the russet-red **St. Ann's Fort,** on the fringe of the Savannah, garrisoned British soldiers in 1694. The fort wasn't completed until 1703. The Clock House survived the hurricane of 1831.

After Bridgetown, you pass through the middle-class resorts of Hastings, Rockley, Worthing, and St. Lawrence before arriving at **Oistin,** a former shipping port that today is a fishing village. Here the Charter of Barbados was signed at The Mermaid in 1652, as the island surrendered to Commonwealth forces. The inn, incidentally, was owned by a cousin of the John Turner who built the House of the Seven Gables in Salem, Massachusetts.

From here you can head on to **Sam Lord's Castle** (see the previous hotel recommendation). Although this is a hotel, it is also one of the major sightseeing attractions of Barbados. If you're not a guest, you'll have to pay $3 BDS ($1.50) to be admitted to the grounds. Built by slaves in 1820 and furnished with elegant Regency pieces, the house is like a Georgian plantation mansion. At the desk, you sign in and are then allowed to wander on your own, inspecting the paintings, silver, china, and antiques. Take note of the ornate ceilings, said to be the finest example of stucco work in the western hemisphere. At the entrance to the hotel are shops selling handicrafts and souvenirs.

In the neighboring section, you can visit **Ragged Point Lighthouse,** built in 1885 on a rugged cliff. Since then the beacon has gone out as a warning to ships approaching the dangerous reef, called "The Cobblers." The view from here is spectacular.

Continuing north along the jagged Atlantic coast, you reach **Codrington College,** which opened in 1745. A cabbage-palm-lined avenue leads to old coral block buildings, and on the grounds you can enjoy a picnic lunch. Today the gray stone buildings are the home of the teaching Order of the Resurrection.

Cutting inland at this point, head for the **Ashford Bird Park** (tel. 433-1268), which is home to many different birds from India, the Far East, South America, and Africa. In a tranquil setting, macaws and parrots can be seen. There are animals as well, including monkeys, and as a surprise, Shetland ponies brought over from Scotland. Charging an admission of $2 BDS ($1), the park is open to visitors every day from 10 a.m. to 5 p.m.

Before getting back on the coast road, ask in the neighborhood for directions to **St. John's Church,** perched on the edge of a cliff opening on the east coast, some 825 feet above sea level. The church dates from 1836 and in its graveyard rests a descendant of Emperor Constantine the Great, whose family was driven from the throne in Constantinople (Istanbul) by the Turks. He died in Barbados in 1678.

While in the area, you can go to **Villa Nova** (tel. 433-1524), built in 1834, a fine sugar plantation great house, furnished with period antiques in Barbadian mahogany and set in six acres of beautifully landscaped gardens, featuring wild orchids, flowering shrubs, and tropical fruit trees. It's open from 10 a.m. to 4 p.m. Monday to Friday, charging $5 BDS ($2.50) for admission.

The house was once owned by Sir Anthony Eden, Earl of Avon, the former prime minister of Great Britain. The earl and his countess had as their guests in 1966 Queen Elizabeth and Prince Philip, who planted two portlandias which still grow in the gardens. To reach the place, take Highway 3B toward St. John's Church, but turn left by the fire station at Four Cross Roads, toward Mt. Tabor Church. Go less than a mile before turning left again. Almost immediately turn right, and up the hill you'll see the entrance.

Before the day is over, if you move fast enough, you can also visit **Andromeda Gardens** (tel. 433-9454), on the outskirts of Bathsheba. On a cliff overlooking Bathsheba on the rugged east coast, limestone boulders make for a natural eight-acre rock-garden setting, where thousands of orchids are in bloom in the open air every day of the year along with hundreds of hibiscus and heliconia. Other plants are more seasonal, such as flamboyant and frangipani, jade vine and bougainvillea, lipstick tree, candlestick tree, mammee apple, and many more. My favorite is a rare jade vine from the Philippines with its blue-green flowers. Many varieties of ferns, bromeliads, and other species that are house plants in temperate climates grow here in splendid profusion. A new section is now being developed as a palm garden, with more than 100 species already here. A simple guide helps visitors to identify many of the plants.

The garden was started in 1954 by the present owner, Mrs. Iris Bannochie, on land that had belonged to her family for more than 200 years. On the grounds you'll occasionally see frogs, herons, guppies, and sometimes a mongoose or a monkey. Charging $4 BDS ($2) for admission, the gardens are open daily.

From the gardens, you can drive to the **Cotton Tower,** one of a chain of old landmark signal stations. English soldiers used these towers to warn when enemy ships were sighted along the coast. As the top of the tower is 1000 feet above sea level, you'll have a panoramic view of the eastern sector of Barbados. Admission is $1 BDS (50¢). It is open seven days a week from 9 a.m. to 5 p.m.

In the same area, **Hackleton's Cliff** also rises to a height of 1000 feet, giving you another view of the rugged Atlantic coast. The attraction and the view were described in the book *Cradle of the Deep* by Sir Frederick Treves.

Finally, you reach **Bathsheba,** the leading town along the east coast, where ocean rollers break, forming cascades of white foam. The same Sir Frederick compared this place to a "Cornwall in miniature." Today the old fishing village is a favorite resort among Bajans.

For the best dining choice in the area, refer to the previously recommended Atlantis Hotel.

The trail north from Bathsheba takes in the **East Coast Road** which runs for many miles with views of the Atlantic. Chalky Mount rises from the beach to 500 feet, forming a trio of peaks, and a little to the south, Barclays Park is a 15-acre natural wonder presented as a gift to the country by the banking people. There's a snackbar and picnic place here.

Stopping on the western side of Chalky Mount, you can visit Chalky Mount School, going out to see the **Potteries,** where potters turn out different products, some based on designs centuries old.

Back on the north trail, you can see and perhaps take a picture of **Morgan Lewis Mill,** the only windmill remaining in Barbados with its arms and wheel-houses intact. The impression may remind you of the countryside of Holland. You can go inside for $1 BDS (50¢). It is open seven days a week from 9 a.m. to 5 p.m.

The view from the top of **Cherry Tree Hill,** on Highway 1, is the finest in Barbados. You can look right down the eastern shore past Bathsheba to the lighthouse at Ragged Point, already described. The place is about 850 feet above sea level, and from its precincts you'll see out over "Little Scotland." The cherry trees from which the hill got its name no longer stand there, having given way to mahogany.

Most visitors to the area have come to go through **Farley Hill National Park,** which was used in the filming of *Island in the Sun.* The movie is now large-ly forgotten by the world, but it is still talked about a lot in Barbados. Paying $2 BDS ($1) per car to enter the park, you can explore the grounds and gracious ruins from 7 a.m. to 6 p.m. seven days a week. The filmmakers partially restored the shell of this once great house, but another fire destroyed the Hollywood re-make. The older section of the estate dates from 1818. Queen Elizabeth opened it as a national park in 1966.

From Farley Hill you can head due west to **Speightstown,** which was founded around 1635 and for a time was a whaling port. The "second city" of Barbados, the town has some colonial buildings constructed after the devastat-ing hurricane of 1831. The parish church, rebuilt in a half-Grecian style after the hurricane, is one of the places of interest. Its chancel rail is of carved mahogany.

South from Speightstown is what is known as the **Platinum Coast,** the pro-tected western shoreline which opens onto the gentler Caribbean. Along the shoreline of the parishes of St. James and St. Peter are found the island's plush-est hotels, which I've already previewed. Assorted British peers and an occa-sional movie actress live in mansions along the coast with its excellent white and pink sandy beaches.

Holetown is the center of the coast, taking its name from the town of Hole on the Thames River. Here the first English settlers landed in the winter of 1627. An obelisk marks the spot where the *Olive Blossom* landed the first Europeans. The monument, for some reason, lists the date erroneously as 1605.

Nearby **St. James Church** is Anglican, rebuilt in 1872 on the site of the early settlers' church of 1660. In the southern porch is an old bell, bearing the inscription "God Bless King William, 1696."

When you approach Highway 1, you can cut east of **Welchman's Hall Gully,** a lush tropical garden looked over by the National Trust of Barbados in the center of the island. Many of the tropical specimens are marked, and occa-sionally you'll spot a wild monkey. Here you'll see a ravine and limestone stalac-tites and stalagmites, as well as breadfruit trees which are claimed to be descended from the seedlings brought ashore by Captain Bligh of the *Bounty.* Admission is $3 BDS ($1.50). It is open seven days a week from 9 a.m. to 5 p.m.

I also suggest a visit to **St. Nicholas Abbey** (tel. 422-8725), the Jacobean plantation great house and sugarcane fields which have been around since 1640. It was never an abbey. An ambitious owner in about 1820 simply christened it as such. More than 200 acres are still cultivated each year. In the parish of St. Peter, the structure—at least the ground floor—is open to the public Monday through Friday from 10 a.m. to 3:30 p.m., charging an admission of $2.50 per person. The house is believed to be one of three Jacobean houses in the western hemisphere, and it's characterized by curved gables. Lt.-Col. Stephen Cave, the owner, is descended from the family who purchased the sugar plantation and great house in 1810. A movie made in 1934 with scenes of Barbados is shown at 11:30 a.m. and at 2:30 p.m. daily. Light refreshments are offered for sale.

Harrison's Cave at Welchman Hall in the parish of St. Thomas is the number one tourist attraction in Barbados, offering visitors a chance to view this beautiful natural underground world from aboard an electric tram and trailer. Before the tour, a color slide show of the cave is given in the presentation hall. During the tour, visitors see bubbling streams, tumbling cascades, and deep pools which are subtly lit, while all around stalactites hang overhead like icicles and stalagmites rise from the floor. Tours are daily from 9 a.m. to 4 p.m. except on Christmas, Good Friday, and Easter Sunday. You should book in advance by calling 432-8048. Admission is $10 BDS ($5).

The **Flower Forest** (tel. 433-8152) at Richmond Plantation, a mile from Harrison's Cave, is a recently established, 50-acre area dedicated to preserving and encouraging growth of the flowering shrubs, ferns, and trees native to the tropics, together with plantation crops on which the island's economy was once based. Richmond is an old sugar plantation with magnificent views of the Atlantic. The ruins are a relic of sugar cultivation. Local handicrafts and fresh fruit are available, as well as light refreshments. Hours are 9 a.m. to 5 p.m., and you can stay as long as you like. Admission is $6 BDS ($3).

The 300-year-old **Sunbury House** on Highway 5 has been turned by its owners, Mr. and Mrs. Keith Melville, into a museum showing how a family home looked in other days, with many Barbadian antiques in their collection. A feature also is a collection of old horse-drawn vehicles used in daily living in a bygone era. You may visit it from 10 a.m. to 4 p.m. from Monday to Friday. Admission is $6 BDS ($3) per person. The Melvilles are also horse lovers, and visitors are invited to see the ponies in the stable yard.

Finally, be sure to visit the recently opened **Barbados Wildlife Reserve** and **Primate Research Center** situated in a lush, natural mahogany forest across the road from Farley Hill National Park. Open 10 a.m. to 5 p.m. daily, with an admission $5 adults and $2.50 children.

5. Where to Shop

Barbados merchants can sometimes treat you to duty-free merchandise at prices 20% to 40% lower than in the United States and Canada. Duty-free shops have two prices listed on items of merchandise, the local retail price and the local retail price less the government-imposed tax.

Some of the best duty-free buys include cameras (such as Leica, Rollex, and Fiji), watches (names like Omega, Piaget, Seiko), beautiful crystal (such as Waterford and Lalique), gold (especially jewelry), bone china (such names as Wedgwood and Royal Doulton), cosmetics and perfumes, and liquor (including Barbados rum and liqueurs), along with tobacco products and cashmere sweaters, tweeds, and sportswear from Britain.

The outstanding item in Barbados handicrafts is black coral jewelry made into attractive earrings, pendants, and rings. Clay pottery is another Bajan craft. In the touring section I recommend a visit to Chalky Mount and the Potteries, where this special craft originated. In Barbados you'll find a selection of locally made vases, pots, pottery mugs, glazed plates, and ornaments.

From local grasses and dried flowers, beautiful wall hangings are made, and the island craftspeople also turn out straw mats, baskets, and bags with raffia embroidery.

Still in its infant stage, leatherwork is also found now in Barbados, particularly items such as handbags, belts, and sandals.

The best place to shop for duty-free items is **Cave Shepherd,** Broad Street in Bridgetown (tel. 426-3451), with branches at Sunset Crest, Speightstown, Hastings, and the Grantley Adams Airport. This is the largest department store in Barbados. One of the most modern such stores in the Caribbean, it was established back in 1906. After it was demolished in 1969, it went public in 1971. Up to then the Cave family had completely owned it, but was finally joined by the financial assistance of more than 2000 Bajans. The store is presently managed by the grandson of one of the founders.

The department store offers visitors the widest selection in Barbados of duty-free merchandise from all over the world, including select perfumes and cosmetics, liquor from more than 70 famous names, Swiss watches, gold and silver jewelry, Pringle woolens, Daks slacks, and Caribbean-made dashikis, plus an extensive range of Japanese cameras and photographic equipment. In addition, it has a handicraft department, with Barbados-made items in straw, black coral, or white coral.

While in Bridgetown, go down to the **Pelican Village** on Princess Alice Highway, leading down to the city's Deep Water Harbour. A collection of island-made crafts and souvenirs is sold here in a tiny colony of thatch-roofed shops, and you can wander from one to the other. Sometimes you can see craftspeople at work. Some of the shops to be found here are gimmicky and repetitive, although interesting items can be found.

Batik Caribe sells original hand-dyed batik in a number of outlets—at Gulf House on Broad Street in Bridgetown, at the Hilton Arcade, and at Marriott's Sam Lord's Castle. You are also welcome to visit their studio at the Colleton Estate in St. John where you can see craftspeople working at this ancient art. Original scarfs, wall hangings, Pareos dresses, jumpsuits, bikinis, and shirts are sold, among other items.

Sea Nymph Dress Shoppe, at the Skyway Shopping Plaza in Hastings (tel. 429-4242), specializes in swimwear (if you forgot your bathing suit), hostess gowns, blouses, shorts, slacks, and dresses made to order.

Antiquaria, St. Michael's Row, Bridgetown (tel. 426-0635), and the Barbados Hilton (tel. 436-3117), are shops I often visit for the collection of maps and prints of the West Indies. However, they also specialize in china, brass, glassware, old bottles and boxes, and some choice English antiques, including furniture.

At **Da Costas,** Broad Street in Bridgetown, and Sunset Crest, St. James (tel. 426-3451), you can find fine china, Waterford crystal, and Lladrò- and Capidemonte-style figurines at duty-free prices. The range of merchandise also includes French fragrances, cashmere, merino, and lamb's wool, as well as local mahogany sculpture.

Harrison's, whose main shop is at 1 Broad St., Bridgetown (tel. 426-0720), has a wide variety of duty-free merchandise, including china, crystal, jewelry, luggage, fashions, perfumes—what have you. They've been in business since the 19th century.

For a fine selection of Caribbean items, go to **West Indies Handicrafts,** on the first floor of Norman Centre, Broad Street in Bridgetown (tel. 426-4015). You'll find baskets, mahogany carvings, mats, bags, and other souvenirs.

The Loomhouse, Skyway Plaza, Hastings, Christ Church (tel. 426-0442), is one of the showcases for the hand-weaving work of Roslyn of Barbados, a talented Barbadian artist and designer. On the outskirts of Bridgetown, this craft boutique displays work by Roslyn Watson. The government of Barbados has selected some of her pieces to present to such dignitaries as the former Canadian prime minister, Pierre Trudeau. Works by other craftspeople are displayed, in mahogany, clay, and straw. There is also a collection of coral.

Articrafts, on the ground floor of Norman Centre, Bridgetown (tel. 427-5767), is another showcase of the weaving for Roslyn Watson. Other handicraft items are also sold.

6. The Sporting Life

The principal activity is swimming and sunning, which, as has been discussed, is far preferable on the western coast in the clear, buoyant waters, yet you may also want to visit the surf-pounded east. These Atlantic waters, however, might be better for viewing than swimming, because, as I've pointed out, they can be dangerous.

SNORKELING AND SCUBA: The Dive Shop, on Hilton Drive in St. Michael (tel. 426-9947), offers some of the best scuba-diving in Barbados (costing about $33 each). Each day two dive trips go out to the nearby reefs and wrecks. In addition, snorkeling trips and equipment rentals are possible. A one-hour trip to a shipwreck with equipment goes for $18.

Willie's Water Sports, at the Paradise Beach Hotel, Black Rock, St. Michael (tel. 425-1060). Here Willie Hassell will take you out on a dive boat designed especially for the scuba-diver. He takes interested parties diving through crystal-clear waters on some of the most beautiful coral reefs in the eastern Caribbean, including visits to two wrecks. He charges $36 per dive, with all gear and lessons included, only $30 if you have your own regulator. In addition he offers a five-dive package, which includes an introductory lesson if you need it, for $300 BDS ($150). Again, if you have your own regulator the cost of the package goes down—$240 BDS ($120). The five dives, of course, may be scattered over a five-day period if you like, or clustered together for more than one dive per day. The business operates out of an unpretentious wooden house next to the water and is open seven days a week.

Sandy Beach, Worthing, Christ Church (tel. 428-9033), takes guests, both resident and nonresident, on scuba-diving trips to reef and wrecks in both shallow and deep water. Instructions are $12 per hour, a one-tank dive is $30, and a package of five dives is $110. Guests can obtain a PADI Resort Certificate in scuba-diving by attending three pool classes, three classroom lectures, and one open-water dive. On completion of the entire course and test, this certificate will be awarded. The course can generally be completed within a seven-day vacation, and the cost if $110. Two-hour snorkeling cruises to a shallow wreck in Carlisle Bay, including snorkeling gear and rum punch on the return trip, cost $12 per person. At Carlisle Bay, snorkelers explore a wreck, a water barge that sank after World War II, which is about 60 feet long. Its top lies only about eight feet below the water's surface, and small tropical fish congregate near the wreck.

WINDSURFING: Experts say that the windsurfing off Bentson Beach is as good as any this side of Hawaii. Judging from the crowds of 20- to 35-year-olds who flock here, it's probably true. An establishment set up especially to handle the demand is the **Barbados Windsurfing Club,** Bentson Beach, Maxwell, Christ Church (tel. 428-9095). It rents boards and gives lessons to learners. A full week of unlimited sailboard usage costs around $200 BDS ($100), but less devoted aficionados might want to rent by the hour, which costs $18 BDS ($9) for the first hour, $25 BDS ($12.50) for the second.

HORSEBACK RIDING: Your best bet is **Sunbury Riding Stables,** Highway 5, St. Philip (tel. 423-6780), which has already been visited as a sightseeing attraction. The stables lie adjacent to one of Barbados's oldest surviving great houses, a 300-year-old plantation house. Horseback riders of all levels of experience can rent horses for pony treks through sugarcane fields and neighboring plantations for $20. The stables are open every Monday through Friday from 10 a.m. to 4 p.m. Riding sessions are followed by a tour of the antique horse-drawn vehicles inside the great house.

GOLF: Your best bet is the **Sandy Lane Hotel Golf Club,** St. James, on the west coast (tel. 432-1311), where greens fees cost from $22 in season for 18 holes, *$18 out of season.* Rental of clubs costs about $10, and a caddy costs $10 for 18 holes.

A nine-hole executive course is at the **Rockley Resort Hotel,** Golf Club Road, Worthing, Christ Church (tel. 427-5890), charging greens fees from $10. Clubs cost $4 for nine holes.

At the **Heywoods Resort,** St. Peter (tel. 422-4900), there is a popular nine-hole golf course. In season, greens fees are $14 for 18 holes, $9 for 9 holes. *Off-season, the charge is $13 for 18 holes, $9 for 9 holes.* Golf carts cost $4 for 18 holes.

TENNIS: Most of the major hotels have their own tennis courts, some of which are lit for night games. Generally, if you're not a guest, these hotels charge anywhere from $2 to $6 per hour of court time. Otherwise, you can play at the **Government Tennis Courts** at Garrison, St. Michael (tel. 427-5238). The grass court here costs $2 BDS ($1) per hour.

In addition, the **Paragon Tennis Club,** Dalkeith Ridge, Brittons Hill (tel. 427-2054), has courts for $10 BDS ($5) per hour.

DEEP-SEA FISHING: The fishing is first-rate in the waters around Barbados, where fishermen pursue dolphin, marlin, wahoo, barracuda, and sailfish, to name only the most popular catches. There's also an occasional cobia.

The Dive Shop, Hilton Drive, St. Michael (tel. 426-9947), can arrange half-day charters for one to six persons (all equipment and drinks included), costing $180 per boat. Under the same arrangement, the whole-day jaunt goes for $360. In other words, no discount.

Sandy Beach, Worthing, Christ Church (tel. 428-9033), offers deep-sea fishing on either *Jolly Jumper* or *Jolly Mariner,* two-luxury-class cabin cruisers. You can fish for wahoo, dolphin, marlin, sailfish, yellow-fin tuna, barracuda, and bonito. Rates are $35 per person for party fishing, or for private bookings, $180 per half day and $360 per full day. All charters have a maximum of six persons per trip, and the rates include ground transportation, soft drinks, rum, and beer. A sandwich lunch is provided on full-day charters.

BOAT TRIPS: If you want to see the fabulous world beneath the surface of the water, you can take a boat trip over the Underwater Park, and stop to snorkel or scuba-dive. Sailings are daily at 10:30 a.m. and 2:30 p.m. from **Les Wotton's Watersports** at the Coral Reef Hotel in St. James (tel. 422-3215 during the day or 432-0833 in the evening). The cost of a snorkel trip is $40 BDS ($20); the price of a scuba-dive, $65 BDS ($32.50)—all equipment included.

One of the most popular cruises is aboard the *Jolly Roger,* a full-size replica of a fighting ship. Aboard the vessel, you can enjoy drinks from an open bar, a full steak barbecue lunch, and nonstop music for dancing on the spacious sundeck. Later the boat stops at a sheltered cove where passengers can put on their bathing suits and go for a swim. At night passengers cruise and dance to the sounds of top local singing groups (in season only). The cost is $65 BDS ($32.50) for the day cruise, $75 BDS ($37.50) at night, both prices including meals. For information, telephone 436-6424, or visit the berth at Cavans Lane in Bridgetown.

In addition, most of the big hotels have Sailfish craft for rent, costing $15 per hour for one or two passengers.

7. After Dark in Barbados

Most of the big resort hotels feature entertainment nightly, often dancing to steel bands and occasional native floor shows. Sometimes beach barbecues are staged. Otherwise, here's the lineup.

The best place to head if you're in Barbados on a Thursday or Sunday is **1627 And All That** at the Barbados Museum in St. Michael's Parish (tel. 435-6900 for reservations). The show, 10 p.m., is a historical celebration of Barbadian culture. At the museum, once a British military prison, the evening features a traditional Bajan buffet dinner, with a liqueur, followed by a folk-dance extravaganza by the Barbados Dance Theatre Company. For the price of $60 BDS ($30) you are transported to and from the museum and are allowed to tour the exhibits. The drinks are complimentary as well. For your money, this is one of the best after-dark bargains in town, and you'll learn a lot as well as have fun.

The best dinner show on the island is **Barbados, Barbados,** a two-act musical comedy based on the life of one of the island's most colorful characters, Rachel Pringle. She was a sort of Bajan Polly Adler. This spectacular is staged every Tuesday in the Boiling House at Balls Estate, Christ Church (tel. 435-6900 for reservations). The price of $65 BDS ($32.50) includes transportation to and from your hotel, hors d'oeuvres, complimentary drinks all evening, government tax, the show, and dinner. Hours are 6:30 and 10 p.m.

The **Plantation Restaurant,** Highway 7, St. Lawrence (tel. 428-5048), stages two of the most popular dinner shows on the island. Every Tuesday the internationally known Merrymen perform their latest hits, and you can also see a Barbadian floor show featuring one of the island's top steel bands together with limbo dancing and fire-eating. The buffet dinner starts at 7 p.m. and show time is 8:30 p.m. On nights when shows are staged, the cost, including dinner, is $65 BDS ($32.50). Nondiners pay $20 BDS ($10). On Wednesday, the **Plantation Tropical Spectacular** is staged, a colorful cabaret dinner show with a cast of 30 dancers in scenes from the old marketplace, the mysteries of voodoo, and the splendor and excitement of carnival. A steel band provides dinner music. The dinner show, costing $60 BDS ($30), is from 6 to 9:30 p.m. On other evenings you can dine either on the veranda or inside this former great house. The Bajan fare served politely in romantic surroundings, costs from $36 BDS ($18). Reservations are necessary.

The **Flambeau Disco,** at the Barbados Hilton, on Needham's Point, St. Michael (tel. 426-0200), allows you to enjoy both nonstop disco and live music, on Friday and Saturday in a cozy nightclub setting from 9 p.m on. An experience in sound and vision, it charges from $2.50 for a drink. Cocktails are served from 5 to 9 p.m.

Club Milili, Heywoods, St. Peter (tel. 422-4900), plays disco music every evening except Sunday and Monday. There's a $12 BDS ($6) entrance charge, after which a beer costs $3 BDS ($1.50). The disco is in one of the many buildings (just follow the trail markers) at the government's Heywoods Resort, covered separately in the hotels section of this chapter.

Belair Jazz Club, Bay Street, Bridgetown (tel. 436-1664), is reputed to have been the leading jazz club in Barbados for the past 30 years, but it is so unpretentious in appearance from the street that you can miss it if you're not careful. It's inside a frame house near the center of town and affords some of the best listening on the island. Since it was remodeled in 1984 many Bajans claim the interior has lost its allure, but you'd never know it by the crowds of people who still come here. Sunday is steel-band night, but the rest of the week, beginning at 10 p.m. daily, the place welcomes both local and imported jazz talent. There's usually an entrance fee of $6 BDS ($3), after which a beer costs $3 BDS ($1.50). It's a difficult place to park anywhere near.

If you're in Barbados on a Thursday night, one of the most enjoyable evenings is to go to the **Barbados Hilton,** on Needham's Point, St. Michael (tel. 426-0200). There, a "night of the buccaneers" is staged at the old fort. Dinner is at 7 p.m., a floor show at 8:30 p.m. The Bajan cuisine features roast suckling pig, barbecued spare ribs, and grilled fish and lobster. The show that follows is lively. The cost is most reasonable as well: $55 BDS ($27.50) for adults, $32 BDS ($16) for children.

The **Holiday Inn–Carlisle Bay Beach Resort,** St. Michael (tel. 426-0890), offers a West Indian floor show every Friday night. A rum-punch party, beginning at 6:30 p.m., usually precedes the dinner, which is served from 7 to 10 p.m. This includes a steak and chicken barbecue, at the end of which a collection of calypso dancers, limbo artists, fire-eaters, acrobats, and musicians performs enthusiastically for the dinner audience. The total cost of the evening is around $50 BDS ($25) per person.

If you're in town on Wednesday night, the same hotel holds a West Indian buffet dinner, beginning at 7:30 p.m. The price of $40 BDS ($20) includes after-dinner music.

Party cruises aboard the ship **Bajan Queen** are held Thursday from 5 to 9 p.m., with a steel band, limbo dancer, and calypso singer providing entertainment. A limbo contest gives party-goers a chance to limber up and perhaps win a prize. A full Bajan buffet and open free bar are included in the price of $60 BDS ($30), as well as transport to and from your hotel. Other sunset cruises on the *Bajan Queen,* but not party time, are offered from 5 to 9 p.m. on Wednesday and Saturday.

A PUB CRAWL: The **Coach House,** Paynes Bay, St. James (tel. 432-1163). Fittingly, there's an antique coach sitting on the lawn of this ochre-colored house which the owners say is 200 years old. Looking at it from the outside, it's difficult to guess the building's age because of its recently added veranda. However, once you're inside under the ceiling beams, the atmosphere is very much that of an English pub. Business people and habitués of the nearby beaches enjoy this establishment's buffet lunches, where Bajan food is served daily except Saturday from noon to 3 p.m. The price is $17 BDS ($8.50) per person for an all-you-can-eat assortment of chicken, baked fish, salads, and local vegetables.

If you drop in between 6 and 11 p.m., you can accompany your drinks with bar meals such as flying fish and chips or chicken in a basket accompanied with a fresh salad for $12 BDS ($6) to $18 BDS ($9) per person.

There's also a more formal evening dining room on a lower floor, where fixed-price meals, excluding service and drinks, cost $45 BDS ($22.50). Menu specialties include pâté with brandy, homemade soup, beef braised in beer, fish creole, and chicken béchamel. Even if you don't want to eat, you can enjoy drinks here. Live music is presented almost every night, featuring everything from steel bands to country to calypso. The pub is on the main Bridgetown–Holetown road just south of Sandy Lane.

The **Ship Inn,** St. Lawrence Gap, Christ Church (tel. 428-9605), contains an attractive rough decor of dark ceiling beams, ship engravings, scattered banquettes accented with touches of gilt, and muted ship lanterns casting soft shadows. The large curved bar is peopled with handsome yacht owners and crews, local teenagers, and foreign trendsetters. Many guests come for the darts, others for the drinks, and still others for meeting friends and/or enjoying the live music on Wednesday and Friday night. On weekends and late on weeknights the place is sometimes packed with diplomats and other VIPs (including the Bajan prime minister), as well as visiting sailors from the various navies which come into port here.

The inn is both a pub and a restaurant, serving such food as steak-and-kidney pie, "bangers and mash," shepherd's pie, and flying fish and chips, brought to you by youthful bar helpers wearing shirts emblazoned with the word "crew." Full meals cost from $12. More substantial meals are served in the Captain's Carvery, reached through a passageway.

Chapter XIII

TRINIDAD AND TOBAGO

1. Hotels of Port-of-Spain
2. Food in Trinidad
3. Exploring Trinidad
4. Sports, Shops, Nightlife
5. A Side Trip to Tobago

DISCOVERED BY COLUMBUS on his third voyage in 1498, Trinidad has since then been peopled by immigrants from almost every corner of the world—Africa, the Middle East, Europe, India, China, and the Americas. It is against such a background that the island has become the fascinating mixture of cultures, races, and creeds that it is today.

Trinidad, which is about the size of Delaware, and its sister island, tiny Tobago, 20 miles to the northeast, together form a nation. The islands of the new country are the southernmost outposts of the West Indies. Trinidad lies only ten miles from the Paria Peninsula in Venezuela, to which in unrecorded times it was once connected.

Trinidad is completely different from the other islands of the Caribbean, and that forms part of its charm and appeal. Visitors in increasing numbers are drawn to this island of many rhythms, where the great swinging sounds of calypso, limbo, and steel-drum bands all began.

The people are part of the attraction, the most cosmopolitan island in the Caribbean. Its polyglot population includes Syrians, Chinese, Americans, Europeans, East Indians, Parsees, Madrasis, Venezuelans, and the last of the original Amerindians, the early Indian settlers of the island. You'll also find Hindustanis, Javanese, Lebanese, slave descendants, and Créole mixtures. The main religions are Christian, Hindu, and Muslim.

In all there are a million-plus inhabitants, who speak a strange argot, Trinibagianese, but English is spoken almost everywhere as well.

Port-of-Spain, in the northwest corner of the island, is the capital, with the largest concentration of the population, about 120,000. Every costume and fabric is worn on the streets of this city.

One of the richest and most industrialized nations in the Caribbean, and the third-largest exporter of oil in the western hemisphere, Trinidad, measuring 50 by 38 miles, is also blessed with a huge 114-acre Pitch Lake from which comes most of the world's asphalt. Further, it's also the home of Angostura Bitters, the recipe for which is a guarded secret.

The Spanish settled the island which the Indians had called Iere, or "land of the hummingbird." The Spaniards made their first permanent settlement in 1592 and held onto it longer than they did any of their other real estate in the Caribbean. The English captured Trinidad in 1797, and it remained British until the two-island nation declared its independence in 1962.

GETTING THERE: Residents of the New York area usually opt for transportation on the **American Airlines** 8 a.m. flight which leaves every day from JFK Airport. I've found that early departures from JFK avoid entanglement in rush-hour traffic jams around New York. You're airborne for about five hours, plus the time spent on a brief touchdown in Barbados.

The return from Trinidad leaves Port-of-Spain at 4:15 p.m. every day, allowing maximum beach time for passengers who want to delay coming home. Return flights touch down briefly to pick up more passengers in Barbados.

American's cheapest flights are available to passengers who simultaneously book a land package through one of their tour desks. This consists of prepaid hotel accommodations at six selected hotels throughout Trinidad, many of which are reviewed coming up.

Passengers who arrange land packages elsewhere, or who prefer not to be tied down to a prepaid choice, can opt for an APEX fare which requires a 7-day advance purchase and a delay of between 7 and 21 days before using the return portion of the ticket.

The round-trip high-season fares from New York cost $627 for weekday travel or $679 for weekend flights (Saturday and Sunday) in either direction. If you're going in summer, look for low-season discounts to be announced (or check with a travel agent).

You can make similar deals through **Pan American.** It operates daily flights from both New York's JFK and Miami, both of which stop briefly in Barbados before continuing to Trinidad. Both of these flights leave their departure points late enough in the day (10:30 a.m. from New York and 2:15 p.m. from Miami) that residents of other American cities can make daytime connections.

Eastern Airlines operates a daily flight from Miami, which leaves in the afternoon at 5:05 p.m., stopping in Barbados before continuing to Trinidad at 10:37 p.m. Be warned that although the service on Eastern is usually excellent, the late arrival in Port-of-Spain could involve you in the notoriously inefficient Trinidadian Customs system, and you might not get to your hotel until 3 a.m.!

Canadian passengers can connect with flights leaving from New York or Miami, or else take advantage of the **Air Canada** twice-weekly flights, leaving on Thursday and Sunday, flying from Toronto nonstop to Trinidad. Montréal-based passengers can connect with Air Canada's Sunday-morning flight to Barbados, then take a Pan Am flight from Barbados to Trinidad.

Finally, **BWIA** also flies from New York, Miami, and Toronto to Port-of-Spain.

PRACTICAL FACTS: Trinidad has a tropical climate all year, with constant trade winds maintaining mean temperatures of 84° Fahrenheit during the day, 74° at night. The rainy season runs from May to November, but that fact shouldn't deter a visit at that time. The rain usually lasts no more than two hours before the sun comes out again.

Trinidad and Tobago dollars are pegged to the U.S. dollar at an exchange rate of $1 U.S. to $2.40 TT. Ask what currency is being referred to when rates are quoted to you. I've used a combination of both in this chapter, depending on the establishment. U.S. and Canadian dollars are accepted in exchange for payment, particularly in places in Port-of-Spain, less so outside the capital. However, you'll do better by converting your Canadian or U.S. dollars into local currency.

Note: Unless otherwise specified, dollar quotations appearing in this chapter are in U.S. currency.

Visitors arriving in Trinidad and Tobago should have a valid passport and an ongoing or return ticket from their point of embarkation. You'll be asked to fill out an immigration card upon your arrival. The carbon copy of this should be saved, as it must be returned to immigration officials when you depart.

Going through **Customs** in Trinidad is one of the worst procedures in the West Indies. Officials almost deliberately move at a snail's pace, causing endless delays, and local arriving families seem to transport entire households of goods, of which officials insist on examining every parcel.

The **electric current** is 115 or 230 volts, 60 cycles, AC—so check before plugging in appliances. U.S.-made appliances will need a converter.

Banks stay open from 9 a.m. to 2 p.m. Monday to Thursday, and from 9 a.m. to 1 p.m. and 3 to 5 p.m. on Friday.

Trinidad and Tobago time is the same as the U.S. East Coast, except when the States go to Daylight Saving Time. Trinidad does not, so when it's 6 a.m. in Miami, it's still 5 a.m. in Trinidad.

As to the **climate,** Trinidad has a temperature range which varies between 70° and 90° Fahrenheit.

The big hotels and restaurants add at least a 10% to 15% **service charge** to your final tab; if not, you should tip from 12% to 15%. In addition, the government also imposes a 3% **occupancy tax** on room rates. It also imposes a **departure tax** of $20 TT ($8.40) on every passenger more than 5 years old.

Most **stores** are open from 8 a.m. to 4 p.m. Monday to Friday (some shops remain open until 5 p.m.). Liquor and food stores close at noon on Thursday, and nearly all shops, except liquor and food, close at noon on Saturday.

The **main post office** is on Wrightson Road, Port-of-Spain, and is open from 7 a.m. to 5 p.m. Monday to Friday. **Cables** may be handed in at the Tourist Bureau, Piarco Airport, at a hotel desk, or at the offices of Textel, 1 Edward St., Port-of-Spain.

The **Tourist Bureau,** 122–124 Frederick St., Port-of-Spain (tel. 623-1932), provides only the most routine of information.

CARNIVAL AND CALYPSO: Called "the world's most colorful festival," the Carnival of Trinidad is a spectacle of dazzling costumes and gaiety. Hundreds of bands of masqueraders parade through the cities on the Monday and Tuesday preceding Ash Wednesday. Traffic, except the human variety, comes to a standstill. The island seems to explode with music, fun-making, and dancing. It's been called a 48-hour orgy!

Hotel accommodations are booked months in advance, and all inns raise their prices at the time.

Some of the carnival costumes cost hundreds of dollars, and their owners spend all year making them, getting ready for next year's big event. For example, "bands" might depict the birds of Trinidad such as the scarlet ibis and the keskidee; or they might be a bevy of women in every shade from sapodilla to brown sugar, coming out in the streets dressed as pussy cats. Others are dragons, devils, and demons. Costumes are also satirical and comical.

The top calypsonian is proclaimed king. On one occasion, the King of Carnival appeared dressed as a "Devil Ray" with a gigantic "delta wing," his eyes glinting behind a black mask, his body bound in black leather studded with silver.

Trinidad, of course, is the land of calypso, which grew out of the folksong of the Afro-West Indian. The lyrics command the greatest attention, as they are rich in satire and innuendo. The calypsonian is considered a poet-musician, and lines have often been considered libelous and obscene, capable of toppling politicians from office as they have in the past.

In banter and bravado, the calypsonian reveals and gives voice to the sufferings, hopes, and aspirations of his people. At carnival time, the artist sings his compositions to spectators in places called by the traditional name of "tents."

GETTING AROUND: Taxis, which line up at the airport, are unmetered in Trinidad. When inquiring about the fare, ask if the rates quoted are in U.S. dollars or Trinidadian dollars. It makes quite a big difference. Cabs have an "H" as the first letter of their license plates. A taxi ride from the airport into Port-of-Spain generally costs about $85 TT ($35.70). Most drivers also serve as guides. Their rates, however, are based on route distances, so get an overall quotation and agree on the actual fare before setting off.

The Route Taxi

Trinidadians sometimes call these "pirate taxis." Launched in World War II, a route taxi is like a bus, stopping and taking on passengers or letting them off as they proceed through Port-of-Spain and its environs. Drivers take a maximum of five passengers. Fares vary depending on the route, of course. A typical ride in a pirate taxi costs only $2 TT (84¢).

Buses

All the cities of Trinidad are linked by regular bus service from Port-of-Spain. Fares are inexpensive, costing from 25¢ for runs within the capital. However, buses are likely to be very overcrowded. Always try to avoid them at rush hours.

Car Rentals

You have to drive on the left-hand side of the road, even though your rented car will probably have a right-hand mounted wheel. Trinidad has some 4500 miles of good roads, so touring is easy once you escape the fierce traffic jams of Port-of-Spain. That is, if you know where you're going. There are very few road signs, and good maps are practically nonexistent.

Unfortunately, it's next to impossible to rent a car for a short time in Port-of-Spain. Even persons who have reserved in advance often run into trouble getting one. The reason for this is that so many business people tie up all available cars that it becomes difficult for the tourist to rent one. Many local companies require a minimum of four days on all their vehicles. Many readers have expressed their disappointment at not getting to drive, say, to Pitch Lake. Of course, one can take a taxi, but for many they are far, far too expensive.

As a final rub, Trinidad requires prospective drivers to have an international driver's license.

Renting a car in Trinidad can cost far more than on other islands in the Caribbean. Rates are sometimes more than twice as much as, for example, in Curaçao, and the selection is often limited to one category.

Budget Rent-a-Car is probably the best bet in Trinidad, especially since Budget's phone reservations center can guarantee you a car with only a 36-hour advance notice. Budget maintains an office at Piarco Airport.

To rent a Datsun Sunny with air conditioning costs about $315 per week or

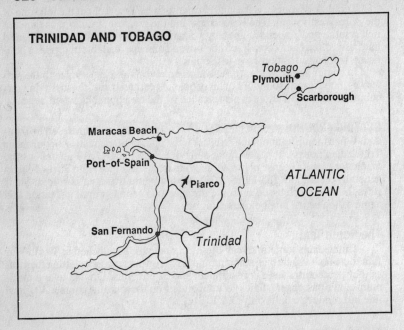

TRINIDAD AND TOBAGO

Tobago
Plymouth
Scarborough

Maracas Beach
Port-of-Spain
Piarco
ATLANTIC OCEAN
San Fernando
Trinidad

$45 per day on an unlimited-mileage arrangement with Budget. Drivers must be at least 25 years old. Additional insurance in the form of a collision damage waiver at $5 a day is advised.

The only other U.S.-based car-rental company in Trinidad is **Hertz.** Its rental cost is similar to that charged at Budget, although its collision damage waiver is more and air conditioning is not included in its standard rentals.

For toll-free information and reservations, call the international departments of Budget at 800/527-0700 or Hertz at 800/654-3001.

Organized Tours

After numerous complaints, I have stopped recommending local sightseeing tours. That's too bad too, because exploring Trinidad on your own is difficult because of the expensive taxis and the hard-to-get rental cars. But for many of our readers, the tour descriptions did not match the reality—and there are no refunds!

1. Hotels of Port-of-Spain

The number of hotels is extremely limited. Almost every hotel in Trinidad has a completely different personality, ranging from such posh hillside hostelries as the Hilton to a turn-of-the-century, ramshackle nature preserve center up in the mountains.

But don't check into any Port-of-Spain hotel expecting your room to open directly on a white sandy beach. The nearest beach is a long, costly taxi ride away.

Trinidad Hilton, P.O. Box 442, Port-of-Spain (tel. 624-3211). On a hilltop, Trinidad's most distinguished hotel is called upside-down because the lobby is at the top and the rooms are staggered down below. You press the down button if you want to go to the tenth floor. Because of its location just above Queen's Park Savannah, most of its rooms have a view of the sea and mountains.

You get a wide range of accommodations here, everything from a simple single to a suite with connecting doors. Rates, in effect all year, are $105 to $132 daily in a single, from $120 to $143 in a double. The MAP supplement is $42 per person. All rooms are air-conditioned and have balconies.

Most of the guests spend their time at the large tropical swimming pool, with its vast sunning areas and refreshment bar at the Gazebo where you can order the famous "rum and Coca-Cola."

The main dining room is La Boucan, stunningly dominated by a wide mural by Geoffrey Holder, the *The Wiz* man who is the unofficial "Prince of Trinidad." He charmingly and impishly painted serene Trinidadian women regally holding parasols with their backs to you! This dining room specializes in Trinidad cookery from the smoke oven. Live music is provided for entertainment and dancing. In fact, some of Trinidad's best native entertainment is booked by the Hilton management.

You can congregate at the Pool Terrace, a tropical dining room with a two-story-high metal sculpture and lighting chandelier. Wicker chairs are set out for breakfast and lunch, with ceiling-high glass walls. Music is played for dancing in the Carnival Bar until 2 a.m.

There's always plenty of activity around here, with pool barbecues featuring roast suckling pig, weekly fiestas, steel bands, limbo contests, whatever. The two all-weather tennis courts are lit for night games. Several shops, some offering handicrafts, are placed in the two-level arcade of the hotel.

For the business traveler, the Hilton is the best choice of the island. Of particular interest are the 24-hour Telex and cable facilities, a worldwide courière service for documents, and secretarial and translation services.

Holiday Inn, P.O. Box 1017, Wrightson Road, Port-of-Spain (tel. 625-3361), was wisely enough placed at the edge of the commercial area of the city, a skillful combination of a business person's hotel yet with resort "trimmings." It stands in gleaming white, a streamlined block topped by La Ronde, its circulating 14th-floor restaurant where diners have a view of the coastline of Venezuela, nine miles across the sea. A French menu is offered.

Adjoining the entrance lobby is a cloverleaf-shaped swimming pool, surrounded by Japanese sun parasols and a thatched poolside bar. You forget, at least for a while, the traffic of the city. The pool has some submerged bar stools for those who want to drink while they swim.

The Calypso Lounge on the 12th floor is considered the most sophisticated nightspot in Port-of-Spain, with music for dancing nightly. Carnival costumes form part of the decoration.

Most of the hotel bedrooms, 235 in all, have a freshness to them, with strongly colored fabrics on the beds and at the windows. The suites are more romantic, often with a decor inspired by the great house plantation style. Except for carnival, the year-round charge is $88 to $118 in a single, $86 to $129) in a double, but these are EP rates (no meals). The MAP supplement is another $35 per person. Rooms have private balconies, two double beds, phones, radios, and individually controlled air conditioning.

Chaconia Inn, 106 Saddle Rd., Maraval (tel. 629-2101), named for the country's scarlet national flower, is a miniature self-contained resort just north of Port-of-Spain in the cool mountain residential valley of Maraval. Its buildings are in simple style, and its furnishings in a contemporary motel idiom. Ken E. Duval, the managing director, runs one of Trinidad's finest small hotels, and does so with some flair. Personal hospitality is emphasized here by everybody from the management on down.

You'll be housed in one of the following category of rooms: 13 deluxe two-bedroom suites, 18 superior rooms with kitchenette and TV, or 10 standard rooms. All are equipped with private bath, air conditioning, phone, TV, and radio, and are tastefully decorated. There is also a swimming pool, as well as a dining room, lounge, and roof garden restaurant where barbecue dinners are served on Wednesday, Friday, and Saturday.

All year, tariffs are the same, except for Carnival. Singles range in price from $80 to $90; doubles and twins, from $95 to $105; and triples, from $110 to $120—all EP. For MAP, add $40 per person daily.

The lounge is open from 10 a.m. to 2 a.m. with music for dancing nightly and live entertainment on Wednesday from 9:30 p.m. to 2 a.m.

Normandie Hotel, P.O. Box 851, 10 Nook Ave. (tel. 624-1181), is a two-story hotel built around a swimming pool in the cool St. Ann's Valley, bordering the botanical gardens. Each of the bedrooms is neatly furnished, efficient, and air-conditioned. Doubles pay from $65 daily, with singles going from $60.

The focal point of the place is a freshwater swimming pool. Bedrooms on three sides open onto this pool. The other side is a covered dining terrace. The desk is also helpful in advising about tours and sightseeing, and arrangements can be made for tennis, fishing, and golfing.

Kapok Hotel and Restaurant, 16–18 Cotton Hill, St. Clair (tel. 622-6441), is a nine-floor modern little hotel at the corner of Queen's Park Savannah. From its lounge, you have not only a panoramic view of the park but of the Gulf of Paria. The lounge has been redecorated in pleasing, harmonious tones. Many guests who shun the Hilton seem to feel at home here, liking the slick neatness, the handsomely appointed bedrooms, and the rooftop restaurant serving Polynesian food. On the ground floor of the hotel is the Café Savanna, one of the finest restaurants in Trinidad. The location, in St. Clair, is in a pleasant and quiet residential area.

They rent 71 well-furnished rooms, each with private bath, phone service, and air conditioning. The rooms have been refurnished with wicker, adding a tropical warmth to the spacious accommodations. Year-round rates are $67 to $75 daily in a single, from $80 to $95 in a double, all EP. In the back is a small pool with a sunning area.

Moniques, 114 Saddle Rd., Maraval (tel. 629-2233), is a bungalow in the lush Maraval Valley, about eight minutes from the downtown sector of Port-of-Spain. It's the home of Mr. and Mrs. Charbonne. He has been the public relations head of the Angostura Bitters factory in Port-of-Spain.

They have an informal, freshly decorated, and most comfortable home where they have set aside seven rooms for paying guests. All units are air-conditioned, and each has its own bath. Singles range from $28 daily; doubles, $35. These tariffs are in effect all year.

Fellow guests like to gather on the tiny front lawn to exchange travel tips, and the owners allow guests to use their living room to watch TV. Arrangements are made for guests to go to a nearby swimming pool.

The **Errol J. Lau Hotel,** 66 Edward St., Port-of-Spain (tel. 62-54381), is a small personalized hotel in the heart of the shopping and restaurant district. Once it was an address known to every sailor in port (a four-star bordello!), but those days have long disappeared. Each of the modestly furnished bedrooms has a bath and toilet, and air conditioning has been installed. Rooms are spread across three elevatorless floors. Year round, singles with bath cost $28 daily; doubles, $40—a good bargain for Trinidad.

The owner, Errol Lau, hopes to make up with personalized service the usual shortcomings associated with big-city hotels. His staff is beautifully trained, and all are graduates of the Hotel and Catering School, which he has run. They'll post your laundry and get your dry cleaning done in 24 hours, see that your shoes are shined, whatever.

Bel Air International Airport Hotel (tel. 664-4771) is 400 yards from the Piarco International Airport and is built in a sprawling hacienda style. Its 58 rooms are all air-conditioned and have private showers. Standard rooms are in the main building, superior units around the swimming pool. Year-round rates are $52 to $57 in a single, $65 to $75 in a double. Triples cost $100, quads run $115, and suites go for $90. The dining room is open from 5 a.m. to 11:30 p.m. On Saturday night a barbecue is held with live entertainment and dancing.

Mount St. Benedict Guest House, Tunapuna (tel. 662-4084), is a friendly, well-run guest house occupying a substantial building nestled on the ledge of a hill halfway between the airport and Port-of-Spain. It's really like a spiritual retreat and was once used as such for Catholic Dutch fathers. Capping the hillsite are a church, monastery, and school, although the guest house is nonsectarian.

Nine miles east of Port-of-Spain, this hilltop hostelry charges from $40 to $45 per person daily for a room and three meals. The neat, clean, uncluttered rooms have twin beds with cold water. Guests use the corridor baths, which have hot water.

The food is above average, with an emphasis on local specialties. The dining room is spacious with two walls of windows providing a view of the valley. Long tables are covered in oilcloth, and meals are served family style. Against one wall is an ornate Victorian sideboard, and on yet another wall is a painting of the pink guest house as it once was.

The reception and living room has a few comfortable chairs, and there's also a wide front veranda from which you can look out onto vistas of hibiscus, bougainvillea, and poinsettia. Bus transport is possible, but of course it's better to have your own wheels.

Chagacabana Hotel, Chaguaramas, St. James on Beach (tel. 625-1021), is a modest beach resort frequented mostly by Trinidadians. From its grounds on a clear day you can see the coastline of Venezuela. About a half hour's drive from Port-of-Spain, the hotel sprawls on either side of the coast road, with 69 bungalows nestled in a garden against the hills, although the beach club is, of course, directly on the sea. The hotel was once used by the U.S. Navy for married petty officers' quarters.

There's a swimming pool at water's edge, as well as the Adam's Apple restaurant. The nightlife spot, the Heritage Disco, has rigid dress requirements, requiring an entrance fee of $15 TT ($6.30) per person or $25 TT ($10.50) per couple.

A regular room for two costs $105 TT ($44.10), going up to $185 TT ($77.70) daily in a two-bedroom unit with kitchenette. A one-bedroom unit with kitchenette costs $120 TT ($50.40), and you can house a family in a three-bedroom apartment with kitchenette at a cost of $220 TT ($92.40) daily, plus tax and service.

Asa Wright Nature Centre, P.O. Box 10, Spring Hill Estate, Arima (no phone), is one of the finest places in the Caribbean, where you can live in modest comfort surrounded by extraordinary wildlife, such as the rare lineated woodpecker which is but one of more than 150 species found in the Arima Valley. Others include toucans, oilbirds, bellbirds, and 12 species of hummingbirds. The 190-acre nature center is a trust established as a guest facility, study area, and refuge.

Spring Hill was once a cocoa, coffee, and citrus plantation, lodged in a lush rain forest. The white and green frame house where you'll stay is attractively painted and has great character. Charles William Meyer (1875–1948) built the house in 1907–1908 for his bride, and they reared 11 children here.

The winding road to the center takes you through the rain forest, lined with spice and fruit trees as well as ferns and great stands of bamboo growing from mountain stream banks. At the main house, high ceilinged and cool, you'll find guests on the large view veranda, sketching, photographing, or reading. The living room and library has large framed bird prints, carved chests, and a gilt-framed mirror that belonged to Jenny Lind. On another level is the very simple, family-style dining room.

Don't expect posh rooms, but a private bath and toilet is provided in each room. It's still rustic, just the way the guests prefer it. Meals are plentiful, Trinidadian in cuisine, with local fresh fruit and vegetables.

The daily rate charged is $70, including all meals, plus 10% service.

Tours for birdwatchers, ecologists, botanists, ornithologists, entomologists, and photographers are arranged from the center of various parts of Trinidad.

You can make toll-free reservations by calling 800/235-1216. Otherwise, write Caligo Ventures, 405 Greenwich Ave., Greenwich, CT 06830.

2. Food in Trinidad

The food in Trinidad is as varied and cosmopolitan as the islanders themselves. It was a British colony for years, yet the cookery of olde England never made much impression on Trinidadians. Red-hot curries remind one of the island's strong Indian influence, and some Chinese dishes are about as good here as any you'd find in Hong Kong. Creole and Spanish fare, as well as French, are also to be enjoyed.

A typical savory offering is a roti, a king-size crêpe, highly spiced, and rolled around a filling of chicken, shellfish, or meat. Of course, you may prefer to skip such local delicacies as opossum stew and fried armadillo! Naturally, your fresh rum punch will have a dash of Angostura bitters.

Le Cocrico, 117A Henry St. (tel. 623-8249), is perhaps the most elegant of Trinidad's restaurants outside the big hotels. The French food served here is considered among the best on the island, and Trinidadians rank it among their finest showplaces. The setting is part of the lure: a colonial-style evening in what was once a private and fashionable residence.

Simon Parkinson is your host, and he has a gracious, hospitable staff. Of course, many so-called classic dishes had to be changed considerably because of the lack of available produce or whatever in Trinidad. But that doesn't matter.

The chef used his imagination and what he has come up with is a fresh and imaginative cuisine that might begin with a pumpkin bisque and go on to some of the best, and best prepared, fish on the island, finishing off with a soufflé, perhaps flavored with citrus or rum. The cost is about $30 per person, and you should call for a reservation. The restaurant is open Tuesday to Friday. Lunch is served from 11:30 a.m. to 2 p.m., and the wine bar remains open until 6 p.m. Dinner is from 7:30 to 9 p.m. Tuesday to Friday. On Saturday, barbecued steak, chicken, and fish are featured from 7:30 to 9 p.m.

Café Savanna, Kapok Hotel, 16–18 Cotton Hill, St. Clair (tel. 622-6441), is currently the most fashionable dining spot in Trinidad. On the ground floor of a previously recommended hotel, it serves an excellent French-continental cuisine. You get refined service in a sophisticated and romantic setting. A complete dinner ranges from $20 to $30. Many of the specialties are prepared with imaginative flair, but they change seasonally so I can't recommend any particular dishes. There are always sizzling steaks, of course, and lobster when available. The café serves both lunch and dinner. Also in the same hotel is the equally popular Tiki Village (see below). The café is open Monday to Saturday. Lunch is Monday to Friday from noon to 2 p.m. and dinner from 7 to 10 p.m. On Saturday, only dinner is served.

Mangal's & Red Rooster Lounge, 13 Queen's Park East (tel. 624-1201), is the best place to go for Trinidadian and Indian specialties. It's set in a formal town house in a garden overlooking the Savannah. A converted, private home, it's decorated with red carpet and Trinidadian woodcarvings, opening onto a front terrace. You enter through a white gate with a bower of red bougainvillea and rows of white urns holding plants. The interior is bedecked with Indian masks and bronze plates, and service is by sari-clad hostesses.

You have a choice of curry—chicken, beef, mutton, goat, or shrimp. All these dishes here are real, honest-to-goodness, curry, with no attempt made to weaken or modify to please bland palates. With your dinner comes an oyster cocktail, mulligatawny soup, a roti, side dishes, plus dessert and either tea or coffee. Of course, you'll need lots of local beer to serve as a fire extinguisher. Temperatures always rise if you mix in a green mango relish.

The chef's specialty is captivating. It's a pepperpot of oxtail, cow heel, and pork, served with coconut rice and a fresh salad. It's actually a specialty of Guyana, made with casareep (which comes from the root of the cassava plant). A smooth opener is the turtle soup (when available). I'd also suggest you give the garnished Caribbean lobster a try, and the curried kingfish with roti and vegetables. You'll spend from $25 for a dinner. The restaurant is closed on Sunday. Otherwise, it's open for lunch Monday to Friday from 11 a.m. to 11 p.m. (on Saturday from 6 p.m. to midnight).

Shay Shay Tien, 81 Cipriani Blvd. (tel. 622-6294), stands near the Savannah, enjoying a local following who praise its Chinese viands, considered among the best in Trinidad. I suggest stopping in here for lunch if you're in Port-of-Spain shopping or sightseeing. No one will do a handstand just to get your business, but the food makes up for what may be lacking in hospitality. Shay Shay Tien is in a downtown corner building. Proceed by the cashier on the ground floor, heading for a table on the second landing.

To get you going (and I hope you're hungry), try a thick, well-stuffed eggroll, or perhaps a large bowl of bird's-nest soup. For a main course, I'm always fond of the sweet-and-sour chicken or the jumbo shrimp in black-bean sauce (with lots of garlic). The fried chicken in oyster sauce is one of the chef's better concoctions, and if you order it far enough in advance, he'll also prepare you sweet-and-sour fish. Lychee is the typical dessert, and the typical price is $20 for a big dinner.

Tiki Village, Kapok Hotel, 16–18 Cotton Hill, St. Clair (tel. 622-6441), perches on the top floor of this hotel, offering a panoramic view at night. Polynesian creations with a Chinese flair are presented nightly, except Monday, from 5:30 to 10:30 p.m. You can also have lunch here from 11:30 a.m. to 2:30 p.m. In the evening you should make a reservation. To get started, try the Polynesian delight, a combination of hor d'oeuvres. The egg roll is among the best I've ever ordered in the West Indies.

Among the main courses, I'd recommend the Hawaiian luau fish. This is a whole fish coated with water-chestnut flour and fried crisply before it's engulfed in a sweet-and-pungent sauce. The Tiki pork, which has been sauteed with plum sauce and garnished with shredded onion and sweet pepper, is superb. Chicken provincial is boneless cubes sauteed in a black-bean sauce. Desserts include an icebox cake, followed by Chinese tea, and then a bill of, say, $25. The village is open seven days a week, serving meals from 11:45 a.m. to 10:15 p.m.

Chaconia Inn, 106 Saddle Rd., Maraval (tel. 629-2101), recommended previously as a hotel, serves some of the best food of any hotel in Trinidad. Ken

E. Duval, the managing director, has a good wine list and lots of continental specialties as well as Trinidadian dishes. The staff is helpful, and the service quite good.

The dining choice is between the main dining room, noted for steaks, and the Roof Garden Restaurant. The main dining room is open daily from 6:30 a.m. for breakfast and 11:30 am. for lunch. Dinner is served à la carte on Monday, Tuesday, Thursday, and Sunday. Breakfast ranges from $5 to $9; lunch, from $20 to $35; and dinner, from $20 to $40. There is a large selection of appetizers, steaks, seafood, and poultry, as well as salads, desserts, and sandwiches. The Roof Garden Restaurant serves barbecue dinners on Wednesday, Friday, and Saturday. The cost for dinner here, including salad and dessert, is from $17 to $26. Reservations are recommended.

Veni Mangé, 13 Lucknow St. (no phone), lies on a tranquil street of private residences right off Western Main Road. If you can find this tiny home, you'll get a fine welcome from Allyson Hennessy and her sister, Rosemary Hezekiah, who usually serve about two dozen in-the-know Trinidadians every day at lunch, the only meal offered. It is open Monday to Friday, serving lunch from 11:30 a.m. to 2:30 p.m. The walls are decorated with the works of home-grown artists, and the tables are pleasant and inviting.

Start with their bartender's special, which is a coral-colored fruit punch, a rich, luscious mixture that combines the golden papaya with a banana whose skin is allowed to turn black so that its taste is most flavorsome.

On some days they do an authentic callaloo soup, which, according to Trinidadian legend, can make a man propose marriage, even if the idea hadn't occurred to him before. If not callaloo, then one of their other rich-tasting broths, such as pumpkin or red bean, will be served. Whatever, you'll get a kettle of hearty, provincial fare.

Save room for one of the main courses, such as curried crab or lobster au gratin, perhaps a vegetable lentil loaf. The helpings are large, and if you still have room, order their pineapple upside-down cake, which really isn't in honor of the "upside-down" Hilton. For all this, you'll pay from $22 or more for a fine meal and an example of local hospitality.

Copper Kettle Grill, 66–68 Edwards St. (tel. 625-4383), is a stylized "Pago-Pago" restaurant, where a trained staff will welcome you and feed you well. Considering the drab facade, the interior is much more inviting. The restaurant is named after a long copper kettle attached to one wall which was once used by slaves for cooking. An abstract mural adorns one wall. The small dining room has tables set with room dividers of white fencing, with basket lamps casting soft light on your table. The floors are in natural matting, and the bar is overscale, laden with local delicacies prepared by the ambitious kitchen. Before your meal, stop in at the bar on your right as you enter for an apéritif.

For an appetizer, you can order a shrimp cocktail or perhaps callaloo soup. The restaurant specializes in beef, ranging from an 8-ounce western steak to a 16-ounce U.S. choice T-bone. These main dishes are served with baked potato or french fries, as well as vegetables. You're allowed to help yourself at their salad bar. Dessert and coffee are included in the price of the main dishes, and a complete meal will cost from $22 per person. The pot simmers from 7 a.m. to 11 p.m.

The Outhouse, 82B Woodford St. (tel. 622-5737). Don't judge a restaurant by its name. This Edwardian-style little house offers some of the finest "creole vegetarian" dishes in Trinidad. Naturally, that includes callaloo soup, which is made here with chopped okra, onions, garlic, chives, and hot pepper. It's often accompanied by plantains. The restaurant also serves seafood, including some tasty crab dishes. The fresh fruits of the island, along with the homemade breads and ice creams, are excellent. Among the ice creams, you're likely to find featured on any day some exotic flavors unfamiliar to you. Try them! Lunch is offered during weekdays only (not on Saturday and Sunday) from 11:30 a.m. to 3 p.m. The cost of a complete meal is about from $18 per person.

3. Exploring Trinidad

AROUND THE CAPITAL: One of the busiest harbors in the Caribbean, Trinidad's capital, Port-of-Spain, can be explored on foot. Most tours begin at **Queen's Park Savannah,** on the northern edge of the city. Called "The Savannah," it consists of 199 acres, complete with a race course, cricket fields, and vendors hawking coconut water. What is now the park was once a sugar plantation until it was swept by a fire in 1808 which destroyed hundreds of homes.

Among the Savannah's outstanding buildings is the pink and blue Queen's Royal College, containing a clock tower with Westminister chimes. Today a school for boys, it stands on Maraval Road at the corner of St. Clair Avenue. On the same road, the family home of the Roodal clan is affectionately called "the gingerbread house" by Trinidadians. It was built in the baroque style of the French Second Empire.

In contrast, the family residence of the Stollmeyers was built in 1905 and is a copy of a German Rhenish castle. Nearby stands Whitehall, which was once a private mansion but today has been turned into the office of the prime minister of Trinidad and Tobago. In the Moorish style, it was erected in 1905 and served as the U.S. Army headquarters in World War II.

These houses, including Hayes Court, the residence of the Anglican bishop of Trinidad, and others form what is known as "the magnificent seven" big mansions standing in a row.

On the south side of the park stands the **National Museum and Art Gallery,** 117 Frederick St. (tel. 623-6419). It's open from 10 a.m. to 6 p.m. daily, except Monday, charging no admission. On the ground floor you'll see some Amerindian artifacts, traces of Trinidad's early Indian settlers.

At the southern end of Frederick Street, the main artery of Port-of-Spain's shopping district, stands **Woodford Square.** The gaudy **Red House** seen there is a large neo-Renaissance building built in 1906. It is the seat of the government of Trinidad and Tobago. Nearby stands **Holy Trinity Cathedral,** whose Gothic look may remind you of the churches of England. Inside, look for the marble monument to Sir Ralph Woodford made by the sculptor of Chantry.

Another of the town's important squares is called **Independence Square,** dating from Spanish days. Now mainly a car park, it stretches across the southern part of the capital from the **Cathedral of the Immaculate Conception** to Wrightson Road. The Roman Catholic church was built in 1815 in the neo-Gothic style and consecrated in 1832.

The cathedral has an outlet that leads to the **Central Market** on Beetham Highway, on the outskirts of Port-of-Spain. Here you can see all the spices and fruits for which Trinidad is known. It's one of the island's most colorful sights, made all the more so by the wide diversity of people who sell their wares here.

At the north of the Savannah, the **Botanic Gardens** covers 70 acres. Once part of a sugar plantation, the park is filled with flowering plants, shrubs, and rare and beautiful trees, including an orchid house. The cocaine bushes planted here always seem to intrigue visitors. Seek out also the raw beef tree. An incision made in its bark is said to resemble rare, bleeding roast beef. Licensed guides will take you through and explain the luxuriant foliage to you. In the garden is the President's House, the official residence of the president of Trinidad and Tobago. Victorian in style, it was built in 1875.

One part of the gardens is the **Emperor Valley Zoo,** which shows a good selection of the fauna of Trinidad as well as some of the usual exotic animals. The star attractions are a family of mandrills, a reptile house, and open bird parks. You can take shady jungle walks through tropical vegetation.

OUTSIDE PORT-OF-SPAIN: In the environs of Port-of-Spain, you may want to seek out the following sightseeing attractions:

Asa Wright Nature Center

On Spring Hill Estate (see the previous hotel recommendations), this preserve lies in a rain forest 1200 feet in the mountains of the Northern Range of Trinidad, seven miles north of the town of Arima. Once a private estate, the property came under the National Trust in 1967. Botanists, entomologists, and other naturalists come here to see squirrel cuckoos, toucans, and lesser species fly within sight of the front gallery. Tufted coquettes and a dozen other species of hummingbirds feed on vervain at the back gallery. It costs $1 to visit the estate and another $1 to explore Guacharo Cave, which is a breeding colony of the nocturnal oilbird of guacharo. A guide leaves three times daily between 9 a.m. and 3:30 p.m. Wear old, comfortable clothes.

Fort George

On a peak 1100 feet above Port-of-Spain, this fort was built by Gov. Sir Thomas Hislop in 1804 as a signal station in the days of the sailing ships. Once it could be reached only by hikers, but today it is accessible by an asphalt road. From its citadel you can see the mountains of Venezuela. The drive is only ten miles, but to play it safe, allow about two hours for the excursion.

Caroni Bird Sanctuary

At sundown, clouds of scarlet ibis, the national bird of Trinidad and Tobago, fly in from their feeding grounds to roost here. The 450-acre sanctuary couldn't be more idyllic, with blue, mauve, and white lilies, oysters growing on mangrove roots, and caimans resting on mudbanks. The sanctuary lies about a half hour's drive (actually seven miles) south of Port-of-Spain.

Blue Basin

This dell lies at the head of the Diego Martin Valley, a freshwater pool fed by a waterfall. The location is about 18 miles outside Port-of-Spain (the tour takes about 2½ hours). You can park your car less than a mile from the pool. From the car park you have to proceed by a footpath that is often steep in places. Once there you can take a dip in this pool. Regrettably, this once-enchanted place, widely touted in the tourist literature of Trinidad, is being allowed to serve in places as somewhat of a garbage dump. To reach the basin, the route begins on Western Main Road, goes through Four Roads and Diego Martin, and then passes through the government-owned River Estate. Don't get lost. Make sure you know where you're going if you succumb to the bait in the tourist pamphlets. It's hard to find, and what signs there are are inadequate.

Pitch Lake

One of the wonders of the world, its surface like elephant skin, the lake is 300 feet deep at its center. It's possible to walk on its rough hide, but I don't recommend that you proceed far. Legend has it that the lake devoured a tribe of

Chayma Indians, punishing them for eating hummingbirds in which the souls of their ancestors reposed. The bitumen mined here has been used for paving highways throughout the world. This lake was formed millions of years ago, and it is believed that at one time it was a huge mud volcano into which mud asphaltic oil seeped. Churned up and down by underground gases, the oil and mud eventually formed asphalt. Sir Walter Raleigh, according to legend, discovered the lake in 1595, using the asphalt to caulk his ships. However, don't believe those legends that no matter how much is dug out the lake is fully replenished in a day. Actually, the level of the lake drops at the rate of about six inches a year. Only problem is, to visit the lake is a tour of 120 miles, lasting ten hours.

The Saddle

This is a humped pass on a ridge dividing the Maraval Valley and the Santa Cruz Valley. Along this circular run you'll see the luxuriant growth of the island, as reflected by grapefruit, papaya, cassava, and cocoa. You leave Port-of-Spain by Saddle Road, going past the Trinidad Country Club. You pass through Maraval Village with its St. Andrew's Golf Course. Half a kilometer from Perseverance Estate there's a sharp turn. The road rises to cross the ridge at the spot from which "The Saddle" gets its name. After going over the hump, you descend through Santa Cruz Valley, rich with giant bamboo, into San Juan and back to the capital along Eastern Main Road or via Beetham Highway. You'll see splendid views in every direction. The tour recommended takes about two hours, covering 18 miles.

The North Coast Road

Nearly all cruise-ship passengers are hauled along Trinidad's "Skyline Highway" which opened in 1944. Starting at "The Saddle," previously recommended, it wends for seven miles across the Northern Range, and down to Maracas Bay. At one point, 100 feet above the Caribbean, you'll see on a clear day as far away as Venezuela in the west or Tobago in the east, a sweep of some 100 miles.

Most visitors take this route to **Maracas Beach,** one of the most splendid in Trinidad. Enclosed by mountains, it has the cliché charm of a Caribbean fantasy —white sands, swaying coconut palms, and crystal-clear water.

4. Sports, Shops, Nightlife

In Trinidad, you'll find much to see and do in the capital itself, beginning with your morning shopping tour of the Port-of-Spain bazaars, going on to water sports, ending with some calypso entertainment in the evening.

THE SPORTING LIFE: Whatever your sporting pleasure—hunting an alligator or playing a simple game of tennis—Trinidad has many possibilities for athletic activities. However, no one surely ever arrived in Port-of-Spain seeking these endeavors alone. In Trinidad, sports are integrated into daily life, and for golf and tennis holidays one should read some of the previous chapters where much more emphasis is placed on such pursuits.

Beaches

Trinidad isn't thought of as a beach, yet surprisingly it has more beach frontage than any other island in the West Indies. The only problem is that most of its beaches are undeveloped and found in distant, remote places, far removed from Port-of-Spain. The closest of the better beaches, Maracas, is a full 18 miles from Port-of-Spain. (For lovely, inviting beaches, see the section immediately following, on Tobago).

Tennis

The **Hilton** (tel. 624-3111) has the best courts, and you can also play at the **Trinidad Country Club** (tel. 622-3470) as well. On the grounds of the Prince's building, there are public courts in Port-of-Spain (ask at your hotel for directions to these).

Fishing

All year long good catches are possible either in the deep sea or in inland Trinidadian waters. In the waters of the Gulf of Paria and on the north shore, you can pursue salmon, snapper, and grouper, or troll for Spanish mackerel, kingfish, wahoo, dolphin, or bonita. **Hub Travel,** 68–78 Maraval Rd., Port-of-Spain (tel. 622-0936) can arrange fishing trips.

Hunting

Hunters bag everything from an armadillo to an alligator in Trinidad, and there's wild game in the forest too, including agouti, wild hog (called quenk), or deer. Ask at the Trinidad Tourist Bureau for particulars about hunting licenses.

Golf

The oldest golf club on the island, **Moka** (tel. 629-2314), is in Maraval, about two miles from Port-of-Spain. This 18-hole course has a clubhouse that offers every facility to all visitors, and the course has been internationally acclaimed since it was the setting for the 1976 Hoerman Cup Golf Tournament. Overcrowding can be a bother on weekends, as the course is popular with the Trinidadians.

WHERE TO SHOP: One of the large bazaars of the Caribbean, Port-of-Spain has luxury items from all over the globe, including Irish linens, English china, Scandinavian crystal, French perfumes, and of course, Swiss watches and Japanese cameras.

More interesting than these usual items are the Oriental bazaars where you can pick up items in ivory or brass, perhaps a carved chest. It takes only a day or two for a Hong Kong tailor to make you a suit or dress.

Reflecting the island's culture are calypso shirts (or dresses), sisal goods, woodwork, cascadura bracelets, silver jewelry in local motifs, and saris. For souvenir items, visitors often like to bring back figurines of limbo dancers, carnival masqueraders, calypso singers, or sari-draped Hindu lovelies.

For those luxury items mentioned, I suggest you pay a call at **Stecher's,** 27 Frederick St. (tel. 623-5912), which sells crystal, watches, jewelry, perfumes, Georg Jensen silver, handbags, Royal Copenhagen china, and other in-bond items which can be delivered to Piarco International Airport upon your departure. If you don't want to go downtown, there's a branch at the Hilton. Among the famous names represented here are Patek-Phillippe, Piaget, Girard Pérregaux, Royal Crown Derby, Bing & Grondahl, Belleek, Rosenthal, Lalique, Baccarat, and Swarovski. If you miss both shops, you can always pay a last-minute call at their tax-free airport branch, where they sell perfume, cigarettes, and cigars.

Y. de Lima, 23A Frederick St. (tel. 623-1364), is another good store for duty-free cameras, watches, and local jewelry. Its third-floor workroom will make what you want in goldwork, be it charms, brooches, pins, earrings, whatever. You may emerge with everything from steel-drum earrings to a hibiscus blossom brooch.

The **Trinidad and Tobago Blind Welfare Association,** 118 Duke St. (tel. 625-4659), makes everything from furniture to shopping baskets with rattan peel, rattan core, and sea grass. If you make a purchase here, you'll also be helping a sightless worker who is trying to help himself or herself.

The **Trinidad and Tobago Handicraft Cooperative** has its main shop at the Trinidad Hilton (tel. 624-3111). Here they offer items in fiber, straw, and wood, and they also sell small steel drums known locally as "ping pongs." Many other local products are sold, including everything from hammocks to salad bowls in purpleheart.

Lakhan's Bazaar, 32 West Main Rd. (tel. 622-4688), has an interesting selection of Indian merchandise, including beautifully designed saris, rugs, embroidered purses, as well as sandals. Go here also for ivory figurines, silk scarfs, and brass and copper ware.

AFTER DARK: At night in Port-of-Spain you'll hear the sounds of calypso and steel bands. Or hopefully you will.

Unfortunately, some of the best calypso is not in the capital, but at places such as **Sparrow's Hideaway,** my personal favorite. It costs only $12 TT ($5.04) to enter, but it's a nine-mile taxi ride from the center of Port-of-Spain. Go only on a Saturday night.

I recently asked three taxi drivers what it would cost to take me there and each one came up with a different figure, so I don't know what the going rate will be at the time of your visit. Of course, all collectors of calypso records know that "The Sparrow" is one of Trinidad's most famous singers. He is in fact known as the "calypso king of the world." If you're devotee enough to go, don't expect to see any fellow tourists. It's strictly a local crowd. Ask at your hotel reception desk for directions on how to get there. The club lies in Petit Valley at Diego Martin.

If you like your calypso in tamer surroundings than the famous but dangerous Independence Square, try the **Calypso Lounge** at the Holiday Inn, Wrightson Road (tel. 625-3361), in Port-of-Spain. A local combo plays for dancing and some of the best calypsonians are brought in to entertain guests, especially in the winter months. Special shows are staged on Friday and Saturday when the minimum charge is $5. The cover drops to just $3 on Wednesday and Thursday, when music is played for dancing.

At **Jay Bee's** in the Valpark Plaza (tel. 662-5837), the restaurant offers fine steaks and seafood, and is open weekdays for lunch and Monday to Saturday for dinner, costing from $25. The disco is open Wednesday to Saturday from 9 p.m. You should dress up a bit, as a dress code is strictly enforced. No reservations are necessary.

Finally, you may want to attend the **Hilton Poolside Fiesta** at the already-recommended Trinidad Hilton, Port-of-Spain (tel. 624-3211). For about $30 per person, every Monday night at 10 the Hilton presents a traditional native show with limbo dancers and a steel band. A barbecue at 7 p.m. precedes the entertainment.

5. A Side Trip to Tobago

Unlike bustling Trinidad, its sister island of Tobago is sleepy. Trinidadians go there, especially on weekends, to enjoy its wide sandy beaches. The legendary home of Robinson Crusoe, Tobago is only 27 miles long and 7½ miles wide.

The people are quiet and friendly, and their villages are so tiny they seem to blend with the landscape.

Fish-shaped Tobago was probably sighted by Columbus in 1498 when he discovered Trinidad, but the island was so tiny he paid no attention to it in his log. For the next 100 years it lay almost unexplored. In 1628 when Charles I of

England gave it to one of his nobles, the Earl of Pembroke, the maritime countries of Europe suddenly showed a belated interest. From then on, Tobago was fought over no less than 31 times by the Spanish, French, Dutch, and English, as well as marauding pirates and privateers.

After 1803 the island settled down to enjoy a sugar monopoly unbroken for decades. Great houses were built, and in London it used to be said of a wealthy man that he was "as rich as a Tobago planter." The island's economy collapsed in 1884 and Tobago entered an acute depression. The ruling monopoly, Gillespie Brothers, declared itself bankrupt and went out of business. The British government made Tobago a ward of Trinidad in 1889, and sugar was never revived.

Tobago lies 20 miles to the northeast of Trinidad, from which it is reached by frequent flights. It has long been known as a honeymooner's paradise. The physical beauty of Tobago is stunning, with its forests of breadfruit, mango, cocoa, and citrus, through which a chartreuse-colored iguana will suddenly dart. Jungle brooks dance over rocks.

The island's village-like capital is **Scarborough,** which is also the main port. Most of the shops are clustered in streets around the market. From Scarborough one can either go cross-country toward Plymouth or head toward the southwest part of Tobago.

For "Practical Facts," refer to Trinidad. Essentially the same customs apply.

Nearly all passengers arrive from Trinidad, where they have already cleared Customs.

GETTING THERE: First, you go to Trinidad (see "Getting There" in the preceding section). Between Trinidad and Tobago, **BWIA Air Bridge** links the two sister islands with flights every 30 minutes in the morning and evening, and every 60 minutes at midday. You're airborne only 20 minutes. Inter-island flights tend to be crowded on weekends when Trinidadians themselves head to Tobago and its beaches. On certain flights to Trinidad, the side trip to Tobago can be included for no extra charge (ask a travel agent before flying to Trinidad how this works).

If you want to go to Tobago by boat, the *Getling,* a coastal ferry with a bar and a trio of restaurants, makes the trip in about five hours, costing about $50 TT ($21) in cabin class round trip. Tourist class is only $30 TT ($12.60) round trip.

Tobago's small airport is at its southwestern tip, Crown Point.

GETTING AROUND: From the airport to your hotel, an unmetered taxi will charge about $12 to $20. You can also arrange (or have your hotel do it for you) a sightseeing tour by taxi. Rates have to be negotiated on an individual basis Count on spending from $45 on a day tour.

For car rentals, get in touch with **Tobago Travel,** Milford Road, Store Bay (tel. 639-8778), where the average cost of a small vehicle is about $40 to $45 per day, unlimited mileage. Gas, as of this writing, is $1.04 per gallon. An international driver's license, if valid, entitles you to drive on Tobago's often bad roads.

Public buses are sometimes modern and always very inexpensive. Buses travel from one end of the island to the other several times a day. Of course, expect an unscheduled stop at any passenger's doorstep, and never, but never, be in a hurry.

HOTELS OF TOBAGO: Quiet, tranquil oases, the hotels of Tobago are more for retreats, attracting those visitors who seek hideaways instead of action at high-rise resorts. Many of the hotels recommended below have been handsomely landscaped to blend into the natural terrain. Because of the shortage of restaurants on the island, it's best to take the MAP (breakfast and dinner) when booking a room.

Mount Irvine Bay Hotel, P.O. Box 222, Scarborough (tel. 639-8871), is Tobago's most expensive spa, built around an old sugar mill and bordering one of the finest golf courses in the Caribbean. On the north shore of the island, about a 20-minute drive from the airport, it brings to mind one of those luxurious country clubs, San Clemente style. The setting is on 150 acres of spread-out lawns, tropical gardens, areas for tennis, and an angular, free-form swimming pool with a swim-in bar and its surrounding terrace.

It's like a resort community. Built L-shaped around the pool, a two-story hacienda wing of guest rooms is all air-conditioned, each with a private bath and its own terrace or balcony. These units open toward the green lawns with their brilliantly colored blossoms on flowery shrubbery. The rest of the cottages are in small square houses covered with such planting as beliconia. Each of these cottages has two rooms which are rented separately, each with a private bath and patio and a view of the fairways or the water. Some Americans rent these cottages, but most often Germans and Italians. Golfers are of course attracted to the place, and a cosmopolitan crowd also comes here just to relax and enjoy the good life. Furnishings avoid a tropical theme, sticking more to the conservative and traditional.

In winter, single rates in the main building range from $175 to $190 daily, with doubles costing from $205 to $220, all half-board terms. Cottages cost $205 daily if occupied by one person, $235 if by two, both half-board rates. *In the off-season, it becomes cheaper, from $85 to $95 daily in a single, from $110 to $120 in a double, all MAP terms. Cottages cost a peak $105 daily in a single, from $130 in a double, again MAP.*

The most impressive place to dine is the Sugar Mill Restaurant, built around the 200-year-old circular stone mill, under a shingled, raftered conical roof. While enjoying the smell of jasmine, you dine at a candlelit table. The cuisine is of an acceptable international standard. You can order drinks in the Cocrico Lounge, named after the national bird of Tobago. There's dancing almost every evening either on the Sugar Mill Patio or in the Shamrock & Palms, a cellar disco under separate management, free to hotel guests. Calypso singers are brought in, barbecues are held, and limbo dancers and occasional shows entertain you, particularly in season.

Guests of the hotel also become temporary members of the golf club (see "The Sporting Life," below).

Arnos Vale, P.O. Box 208 (tel. 639-2881), was once a sugar plantation, but you wouldn't know that now. On the north coast about a mile from Plymouth, Arnos Vale is one of the oldest hotels on Tobago, an unusual retreat tucked away on 400 tropical acres opening directly on Arnos Vale Bay. A former English owner was a lover of nature, and he planted the place like a botanical garden, with frangipani and oleander predominating. In days of yore, you might have run into one of the Beatles sneaking through the lush foliage, or perhaps a married movie star with a wife not his own. A Mediterranean aura prevails, but the bananaquits and mot-mots keep it definitely in the Caribbean.

Its red-tile-roofed main house stands at the top of the hill. You can enjoy good drinks in the bar or on the al fresco patio, then go across to the dining room to be served one of the best meals on the island. Both an English fare and a Tobago cuisine are served, including such island dishes as callaloo soup, souse, and pelau. From this main house, you'll have a magnificent panorama of the sea.

Rooms come in many different styles and shapes, ranging from the Jacamar just off the beach to the Coral Cottage with an aerial view of the bay. Must of the furniture is custom made of local cedar. In winter, a single on the half-board arrangement rents for $125 daily, going up to $160 to $175 in a twin. *In summer, these rates are lowered to $90 daily in a single, from $110 to $130 in a twin.* All tariffs include breakfast, dinner, and afternoon tea.

On the richly planted grounds is a freshwater swimming pool. Peace and tranquility are stressed, but occasionally native steel bands are brought in to play, and there are beach barbecues. In addition, you'll find a tennis court.

Crown Reef Hotel, Store Bay (tel. 639-8571), is handsomely modern, standing on landscaped grounds with much tropical greenery and flowers. It also opens onto its own coral reef and an excellent, uncrowded beach. Don't come here seeking local island color. However, if you want some of the finest contemporary facilities Tobago has to offer, then you're at the right place, and can select from among 115 well-furnished suites and bedrooms, each with a private balcony or patio. A single rents for $180 daily, a double for $210 on the half-board plan, plus tax and service. *In the off-season, the half-board terms in a single are $110 daily, going up to $135 in a double.*

The dining room is approached from the lobby by a circular, open staircase, extending on rocks over water and encircling a large aviary. The terrazzo lounge has white deck chairs with pillows covered in flamboyant fabric. The menu has both Stateside and continental dishes, along with some Trinidadian specialties. Perched on a coral rock at water's edge is a thatched beach bar. Sometimes native dancers and steel bands are brought in.

A freshwater swimming pool is set in the midst of the lush gardens. Most water sports are offered, including scuba-diving and snorkeling, and you can play tennis on the hotel's courts. An 18-hole golf course is nearby.

Turtle Beach, P.O. Box 201 (tel. 639-2851), stands directly on one mile of sandy beach opening on Great Courtland Bay, on the leeward shore in the midst of a 600-acre coconut plantation. Housed in two-story units, all rooms are oceanfront and air-conditioned, with private baths containing both tub and shower, patio or balcony, and almost direct access to thc beach. The location is just eight miles from the airport, from which taxi transfers are available. The inn is also five miles from Scarborough.

The entrance loggia is the longest covered terrace on the island, where a slow pace sets the tempo of the relaxed, casual lifestyle of the hotel. While seated on sofas and in armchairs, you can enjoy tall fruit-and-rum drinks. Lunches are served around the garden pool or at the beach. Three times a week calypso music can be heard in the evenings. Perhaps a steel band will be brought in. If you don't want the beach, you can swim in a freshwater pool.

Bedroom accommodations are smartly tailored. Rooms on the second floor have sloped open-beamed ceilings, with white walls and shuttered doors which can be pushed back to enlarge the living areas. EP rates are $97 in a single, $99 in a double in winter, *dropping to $54 in a single and $56 in a double in summer.* Fishing trips can be arranged, as can snorkeling at Buccoo Reef. A dive and water-sports shop is on the hotel premises.

Sandy Point Beach Club, Crown Point (tel. 639-8533), is a winning miniature vacation village built somewhat in the style of a Riviera condominium. Each apartment has a kitchenette, allowing guests to be independent. It's just a three-minute run from the airport, but its shoreside position makes it seem remote. The little village of peaked and gabled roofs is landscaped all the way down to the sandy beach, where there's a rustic Steak Hut which serves meals throughout the day and evening.

The units, consisting of 20 suites and 22 studio apartments, are air-conditioned and fully equipped, each opening onto a patio, toward the sea, or onto a covered loggia. The rental units contain living and dining areas with pine trestle tables, plus a color TV. In some of the apartments is a rustic open stairway leading to a loft room with bunk beds, although there is a twin-bedded room on the lower level as well.

Double occupancy costs from $42 to $50 daily in the off-season, EP, and from $70 to $80 daily in winter. Service and tax are extra. The hotel has a sauna, and you can emerge from its intense heat to the shade of a banyan tree beside the swimming pool.

Crown Point, P.O. Box 223, Crown Point (tel. 639-8781), consists of 109 units on seven acres of landscaped tropical gardens within easy reach of the airport. It's condominium living, and you can choose from either a studio, cabana, or standard bedroom unit. You'll have a choice of preparing your own meals or else dining at the restaurant on the premises, featuring both island and continental foods. The main lobby opens onto a swimming pool.

The bedrooms have sheltered private balconies where you can have all your meals. On the premises is a modest mini-market. The units are simply furnished, with coordinated fabrics at the windows and on the beds. Each is air-conditioned, containing a private bath, a fully equipped kitchenette, and a phone, with daily maid service. In winter, singles or doubles on the EP cost $75. However, two persons can rent a cabana at $95 daily, a one-bedroom apartment at $100, plus service and tax. *In summer, the single EP rate ranges from $40, the double going from $47 to $58.*

Tropikist Beach Hotel, Crown Point (tel. 639-8513), is a self-contained resort that's not only comfortable but reasonably priced. A five-minute walk from the airport, the hotel is directly on the beach, two modern complexes opening onto a swimming pool. A little pathway leads down to the water. Bedrooms are in a modified tropical style, with bamboo and reed tables and muted floral prints on the beds and hanging from the windows. *In summer, a single rents for $60 daily, and a double goes for $80, including breakfast and dinner.* In winter, the single half-board tariff is $85 daily, increasing to $105 in a double. Island-style meals are served in a white dining room with bamboo armchairs. Other conveniences include a sauna and a nearby shopping area.

The **Della Mira Guest House,** Windward Road, Scarborough (tel. 639-2531), is a simple West Indian guest house where the warm hospitality of Neville Miranda and his wife Angela is extended. The place is modest and intimate—in reality a small inn where there's an open living room area with pleasantly provincial furnishings. In an adjoining dining room Angela serves authentic island dishes. Tobagoans are fond of coming here, as it has a real atmosphere which most of the other hotels lack.

The location is on a cool, airy site overlooking the sea, about half a mile from stores and churches and some 50 yards from the beach. You can also swim in a pool set in the lawn of the garden, around which a terrace has been built for sunning. The bedrooms overlook the garden and the pool, but some cheaper units look out onto the hills. The bedrooms, 14 in all, have a basic simplicity, nothing fancy, yet everything is clean and comfortable. All the rooms come with private bath, and about half of them are air-conditioned as well. *In the off-season, EP singles are accepted for $30 nightly, and doubles pay from $45.* On the half-board plan in season, single tariffs range from $65; doubles, $90.

On the premises is one of Tobago's leading nightclubs, La Tropicale, plus a beauty salon. Mrs. Miranda, incidentally, is the island's only licensed barber.

Man-o-War Bay Cottages, Charlotteville. If you're seeking a Caribbean hideaway—that is, a cluster of beach cottages—then the Man-o-War might be for you. Pat and Charles Turpin rent out five bungalows near a two-mile-long white sandy beach. Each unit comes complete with a bedroom, a spacious living and dining room, a private bath, and a porch opening onto the sea. Year round you can rent a two-bedroom cottage at $90 daily or a large four-bedroom bungalow (big enough to sleep ten) for only $150 a day. A maid and or cook can be hired for very little extra. For reservations, you have to write Mr. and Mrs. Turpin (you can't phone). Near the colony is a coral reef that is an ideal ground for snorkelers. The couple will also arrange a boat rental if you want to explore Lovers' Beach. Many birdwatchers looking for rare species often book one of these bungalows.

Blue Waters Inn, Batteaux Bay, Speyside (tel. 639-4341), is a little inn run by Barbara and Fred Zollna who escaped here from Trinidad. They are to be applauded for charging the same rates for foreign visitors as they do to local residents (unlike many, many places in the Caribbean which have two sets of tariffs). The remotely perched inn lies on the northeast coast of Tobago, about 24 miles from the airport and 20 miles from Scarborough. Figure either by private car or taxi that it's a 1½-hour drive along narrow, winding country roads.

They rent out 11 rooms and cabanas, each unit with private shower and toilet. On the EP, rates are $40 daily in a single, $52 in a double. Count on lunch costing another $15; dinner, $18. Meals are served in their casual restaurant, and there's also a bar dispensing tropical libations.

This is an extremely informal place, so leave your fancy resortwear at home. Fishing, tennis, shuffleboard, scuba, and skindiving can be arranged, as well as boat trips to Little Tobago. The property is a veritable bird sanctuary, a boon for nature lovers and birdwatchers.

Holiday Homes

There are 15 attractive, almost luxurious, privately owned holiday houses which can be rented throughout the year in Tobago. These rental units are among the most inexpensive ways of living well in the West Indies. Private owners have built and completely furnished these retreats for their own holidays. However, to cut back on expenses they rent these houses out to visitors, either weekly or monthly. When shared by a group of four to six persons, they become very cheap. Most houses accommodate at least six guests.

Houses vary greatly in shape, price, and size, but all of them have tiled baths, comfortable twin-bedded rooms, living rooms, fully equipped kitchens, patios, terraces, gardens, and private swimming pools. Half-day maid service is included, except on Sunday. Some of the houses have panoramic views of the coastline and the Buccoo Reef, and some are on a rise overlooking the 18-hole Mount Irvine Golf Course. All are close to fine beaches.

For further information, write to **Tobago Villas Agency**, P.O. Box 301, Scarborough (tel. 639-8737).

WHERE TO EAT: Most guests eat at their hotels, which seem to have a monopoly on the best chefs. The previously recommended **Mount Irvine Bay Hotel** (tel. 639-8871) and **Arnos Vale** (tel. 639-2881) are particularly noted for their cuisine, with dinners costing around $15. The Mount Irvine offers the Sugar Mill, al fresco dining around a cunning adaptation of a 200-year-old sugar mill. The cuisine is international, but with local seafood and creole specialties. At Arnos Vale, the creole buffet lunch on Sunday is the most attended event on the island, and you can also enjoy informal fare at the beachside restaurant.

Outside of the hotels, your best dining might be at the **Blue Haven Hotel,** Bacolet Street (tel. 629-2566). Up until some time in the '70s this was a famous hotel. You may already have seen it used as a backdrop in such films as *Robinson Crusoe Island* and *The Swiss Family Robinson*. A great house, set on about five acres, it has been taken over by Brian and Antonia Smith. Already they have established a restaurant here on the water. (Check to see what progress has been made in providing accommodations.)

Reflecting the French West Indian background of one of the owners, the menu has creole flair. Its cookery is among the best on the island. You get very fresh fish and vegetables. Sometimes entertainment is offered, and each week there is a buffet or two. Both lunch and dinner are served, with meals costing from $18. Call for a reservation.

I also suggest **Mon Cheri,** Grafton Road (no phone), where Theodore Irvine, the former chef at Arnos Vale, has distinguished himself in his own place. Lots of English guests who fell in love with his cuisine have followed him here to his new surroundings, a simple cement-block structure. The place is run on extremely casual lines. The last time I dropped in, a woman went to Mr. Irvine's home nearby, and he soon came down to open the restaurant and cook my party a meal. He usually has fish, such as red snapper, dolphin, or kingfish. On some occasions he'll cook goat, and perhaps will stuff some roti for you. My recent chicken lunch was so good I returned that night to enjoy an even better Caribbean lobster thermidor, the restaurant's specialty. Fresh fish of the day is another usually reliable choice, depending of course on what the "catch" was. A complete meal should run from $20. Before going there, always check on the status of this place. Since you can't phone, don't waste the trip if it should be shuttered.

The most colorful local restaurant in many ways is the **Old Donkey Cart House** (tel. 639-3551), on Bacolet Street in Scarborough. In this French-colonial-style house, it offers an array of local and continental dishes, a complete meal costing around $20. They have a selection of German wines, and among other distinctions, are noted for their homemade bread. The food is good, but it's the atmosphere of the place that draws many Trinidadians over for the weekend and makes this place hum. Sometimes, if the crowd warrants it, slide shows are shown outdoors. Always call in advance to make sure that it's open.

You might also consider a luncheon stopover at the **Bird of Paradise Inn** at Speyside (tel. 639-4376), which is on the northeast coast of Tobago, where trade winds blow on a private estate of 700 acres, which is a bird and wildlife sanctuary. The owners have encouraged the birds to live freely on the property in a natural condition. The drive from the airport takes 1½ hours on a winding scenic road. Always call in advance to make sure that something's cooking that day.

WHAT TO SEE: In Tobago's capital, **Scarborough,** you can enjoy a native market every morning except Sunday, listening to the sounds of a Créole patois.

The village-like place need claim your attention very little before you climb up the hill to **Fort King George,** about 430 feet above the town. Built by the English in 1779, it was later captured by the French. After that it jockeyed back and forth between various conquerors until nature decided to end it all in 1847, blowing off the roofs of its buildings. There's little left to see except the sunset over Tobago, which is spectacular.

From Scarborough you can drive northwest to **Plymouth,** Tobago's other town. In the graveyard of the little church is a tombstone dating from 1783 with a mysterious inscription: "She was a mother without knowing it, and a wife, without letting her husband know it, except by her kind indulgences to him."

Perched on a point at Plymouth is Fort James, which dates from 1768 when built by the British as a barracks. It is now mainly in ruins. You can stroll down to the tiny Botanic Gardens. But even more interesting, a little farther down, is **Graton Estate** where Mrs. Alefounder, an English woman, has established her veranda as a feeding place to which birds flock. She'll often let visitors come in the afternoon and watch the feeding.

From Speyside you can make arrangements with some local fisherman to go to **Little Tobago,** an offshore 450-acre island where a bird sanctuary attracts ornithologists. Threatened with extinction in New Guinea, many birds, perhaps 50 species in all, were brought over to this little island in the early part of this century.

Off Pigeon Point lies **Buccoo Reef** (see the "Sporting Life" section) where sea gardens of coral and hundreds of colorful fish can be seen in waist-deep water. This is the natural aquarium of Tobago. Nearly all the major hotels arrange boat trips here to these acres of submarine gardens which offer the best scuba-diving and snorkeling. You can get right in among the various types of tropical fish and other marine creatures. Even nonswimmers can wade knee-deep in the crystal-clear waters. Remember to protect your head and body from the tropical heat and to guard your feet against the sharp coral. A broad-brimmed hat plus an old shirt are necessary, as are canvas shoes.

After about half an hour at the reef, passengers reboard their boats and go over to Nylon Pool, with its cystal-clear waters. There in this white sand bottom, about a mile offshore, you can enjoy water only three to four feet deep. After a swim, the boatman returns you to Buccoo Village jetty in time for a goat and crab race.

At the **Museum of Tobago History,** on the grounds of the Mount Irvine Bay Hotel (tel. 639-8871), you'll find artifacts, implements, and pottery of the Caribs and Arawaks who used to inhabit Tobago. Tobago's archeological and historic past comes alive. The museum is open from 5:30 to 8:30 p.m. on Tuesday and Thursday, from 4:30 to 7:30 p.m. on Sunday. Admission is $2 for adults, 25¢ for children.

THE SPORTING LIFE: If beach-fringed Tobago wasn't in fact the alleged locale of Daniel Defoe's immortal story, the visitors who enjoy its superb beaches hardly seem to care. On Tobago sands you can still feel like Robinson Crusoe in a solitary cove, at least for most of the week before the Trinidadians fly over to sample the sands on a Saturday.

Bacolet Beach, about a 30-minute drive from Scarborough, can be reached by a taxi ride. At this beautiful beach, you can have a picnic lunch. The beach was featured in such movies as *The Swiss Family Robinson.*

Another good beach, **Back Bay,** is within an eight-minute walk of the Mount Irvine Bay Hotel. Along the way you'll pass a coconut plantation and an old cannon emplacement. Sometimes there can be dangerous currents here. But you can always enjoy exploring Rocky Point with its brilliantly colored parrot fish.

Other beautiful beaches include the one at **Englishman's Bay,** a small bay on the north side, about eight circuitous miles from the Mount Irvine Bay Hotel. Try also **Man O' War Bay,** one of the finest natural harbors in the West Indies, at the opposite end of the island. Once there, you'll find a long sandy beach, and you can also enjoy a picnic at a government-run rest house.

Finally, **Pigeon Point** on the island's northwest coast is the best known bathing area with a long coral beach. You'll find thatched shelters for changing into bathing attire, as well as tables and benches for picnics.

Golf

Tobago is the proud possessor of an 18-hole, 6800-yard golf course at Mount Irvine. Called the **Tobago Golf Club** (tel. 639-8871), it covers 150 acres of breeze-swept courses and was featured in the "Wonderful World of Golf" TV series. The course—and even beginners agree—is considered "friendly" to golfers. As a guest of the Mount Irvine Bay Hotel you are granted temporary membership and use of the clubhouse and facilities. Resident hotel guests are entitled to discounts of nearly 50% on normal greens fees. All serious golfers should stay at the Mount Irvine. Greens fees run about $18 daily.

Tennis

The Crown Reef (tel. 639-8571) and **Turtle Beach Hotels** (tel. 639-2851) have courts. The best courts, however, are at the **Mount Irvine Bay Hotel** (tel. 639-8871), where two good courts are available free to guests. There is a $3 surcharge for night games.

Water Sports

Snorkeling over the celebrated Buccoo Reef is one of the specialties of Tobago. Hotels arrange for their guests to visit this underwater wonderland.

Try **Turtle Beach** (tel. 639-2851), which has a dive shop and water-sports center on the hotel premises.

SHOPPING: Scarborough's stores have a limited range of merchandise, more to tempt the browser than the serious shopper. Both **Stecher's** and **Y. de Lima** (see the Trinidad descriptions) have a limited range of merchandise in Tobago.

NIGHTLIFE: **Mount Irvine Bay Hotel** (tel. 639-8871), as mentioned, has the most nightlife, luring the better-heeled visitor.

For the best island nightclub entertainment, head for **Club La Tropicale,** at the Della Mira Guest House, Windward Road, Scarborough (tel. 639-2531). In a tropical breeze-swept setting, it offers floor shows, steel bands, and calypso. Drinks begin at $3.

Chapter XIV

NETHERLANDS ANTILLES

1. Aruba
2. Bonaire
3. Curaçao

AS DUTCH AS a wooden shoe, the so-called ABC group of islands—Aruba, Bonaire, and Curaçao—lie just off the northern coast of Venezuela. the islands cover only 363 square miles, with a widely diversified population of some 225,000 people, many of whom speak Papiamento, a patois language, although Dutch is the official tongue.

Duty-free shopping and gambling are promoted by the government in all three islands. Curaçao has the most Dutch atmosphere, with a number of 18th-century buildings. Curaçao, along with Aruba, also has the most developed tourist centers, with Bonaire attracting the most dedicated scuba-divers. Someone once said that there are more flamingos than people in Bonaire. Aruba has the best beaches and the most hotel accommodations.

These spotless islands still retain old-world charm and are clean and prosperous.

The canny Dutch emerged from the European power struggle in the West Indies with these tiny specks of land, arid and for all appearances inconsequential. But they proceeded to turn these ugly duckling properties into some of the most valuable real estate in the Caribbean, an economy "fueled" by oil refineries.

Other Dutch-held islands in the Caribbean, including Saba, St. Eustatius (Statia), and St. Maarten, have already been previewed in Chapted VIII, "Dutch Windwards in the Leewards."

1. Aruba

At first you'll think you're on a movie set for a Hollywood western. The terrain is so similar. But instead of cowboys you'll meet a friendly people, many of whom speak Papiamento, a melange of Spanish, Portuguese, Dutch, and some Indian words.

Forget lush vegetation and palm-framed vistas in Aruba. That's impossible with only 17 inches of rainfall annually. Aruba is dry and sunny year round, its clean, exhilarating air desert-like. However, trade winds keep the island from becoming uncomfortably hot. At least you can be sure of the sun every day of your vacation in Aruba.

Cactus fences surround pastel-washed houses, Divi-Divi trees with their

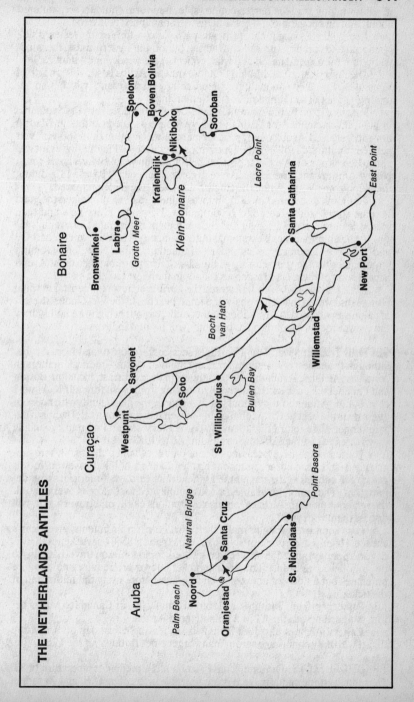

THE NETHERLANDS ANTILLES

Aruba

Palm Beach
Noord
Oranjestad
Santa Cruz
Natural Bridge
St. Nicholaas
Point Basora

Curaçao

Westpunt
Savonet
Soto
St. Willibrordus
Bullen Bay
Bocht van Hato
Willemstad
Santa Catharina
New Port
East Point

Bonaire

Bronswinkel
Labra
Grotto Meer
Klein Bonaire
Kralendijk
Spelonk
Boven Bolivia
Nikiboko
Soroban
Lacre Point

windblown look stud the barren countryside, free-form boulders are scattered about, and on occasion you'll come across an abandoned gold mine.

Aruba stands outside the hurricane path. Its coastline on the leeward side is smooth and serene, with sandy beaches; but on the eastern coast, the windward side, the look is rugged and wild, typical of the windswept Atlantic.

The most western of the Netherlands Antilles, Aruba lies 15 miles north of Venezuela. Some 40 nationalities live peacefully on the island, which is an autonomous part of the Kingdom of the Netherlands.

First inhabited by the Arawak Indians, Aruba was discovered by Spaniards in 1494. It was claimed for Spain in 1499 by Alonso de Ojeda, although Madrid never considered Aruba of any value. Near the culmination of the 80-year war between Spain and Holland, the Dutch took over in 1643. Pieter Stuyvesant was named governor of Aruba, a post he held for four years before going on to Nieuw Amsterdam. The English were in control between 1805 and 1816 during the Napoleonic Wars. When the English departed, the Dutch returned.

Gold was discovered in 1825 and was mined up until 1916 when the yield became so meager it ceased to be profitable. However, every now and then someone uncovers a big nugget and the excitement is generated all over again.

Aruba's rather bleak economic outlook changed in 1929 when Lago Oil and Transport Company, a subsidiary of Standard Oil of New Jersey, built a large refinery at the southeast tip of the island. Dating from those days, Aruba became one of the most prosperous islands in the West Indies.

Mainly in the 1970s Aruba entered the Caribbean resort sweepstakes when visitors discovered that it has one of the finest beaches in the West Indies stretching along its west coast. In addition to the sands, casinos in high-rise hotels draw the crowds today, as tourism has become Aruba's new industry.

GETTING THERE: Several major airlines service the route to and from Aruba, although the easiest connections for many areas of North America are through **American Airlines.** Aruba-bound passengers in the northeast, including Boston and Philadelphia, can catch a daily flight leaving from New York's JFK Airport at 9:30 a.m. After about 4½ hours of flying time, the plane lands with no stopovers near the beaches of Aruba, giving passengers time for a brief sunbath before dinner. The return flight leaves Aruba every day at 3:45 p.m., touching down briefly at Curaçao before continuing on to JFK.

The least expensive fare is included as part of a "land package," where prearranged and prepaid accommodations at selected hotels (reviewed in this guide) are booked at the same time as the airfare through American's tour department. The options available are too complicated for this brief overview, although an American Airlines' phone reservations clerk, or a travel agent, will discuss them with you.

For clients preferring to make their own hotel arrangements, American's cheapest high-season fare from New York to Aruba is $560 on weekends (Saturday and Sunday) and $515 on weekdays. (Look for low-season travel bargains to be announced as well.) The regular ticket, however, requires no advance purchase, but a delay of between 3 and 21 days before using the return half of the ticket.

Passengers from Toronto or Montréal usually fly **Air Canada** to Miami before connecting with the **ALM** 2 p.m. flight to Aruba.

Eastern Airlines also flies from Miami, leaving every day on a nonstop flight, with easy connections from many other cities throughout the U.S.

PRACTICAL FACTS: Dry and sunny, Aruba has a median temperature of 83° Fahrenheit (trade winds make it more bearable). To enter, U.S. and Canadian citizens may submit a **passport** or a birth certificate (or for U.S. citizens only, a voter registration card).

At your hotel, you'll find a 10% to 15% **service charge** on room, food, and beverages. **Tipping** (more politely known as a service charge) usually appears on the bill at 10% to 15% extra. Otherwise, it's up to you.

The **water** is pure (it comes from the world's second-largest desalinization plant). The **electrical current** is 110 volts AC, 60 cycles, the same as in the U.S. **Atlantic Standard Time** is observed year round.

The **currency** is the Netherlands Antillean florin or guilder which is divided into 100 cents. The current exchange rate is $1 U.S. to 1.77 NAf. U.S. dollars are accepted throughout the island, but you should carry along some small bills. It is difficult to get even a $10 bill changed outside of the casinos. *Note:* Unless otherwise stated, currency quotations in this chapter are in U.S. dollars.

Bank hours are Monday through Friday from 8 a.m. to noon and from 1:30 to 4 p.m. In taxes, you're hit with a 5% **room tax,** plus another $5.75 airport **departure tax.**

Telegrams and Telexes can be sent by the Government Telegraph and Radio Office at the Post Office Building in Oranjestad (or at your hotel). There is also an ITT office on Kerkstraat in Oranjestad. Local and international **telephone** calls can be made via hotel operators or from the Government Long Distance Telephone Office, also in the Post Office Building in Oranjestad.

In **medical services,** the Horacio Oduber Hospital (tel. 24300) opened in 1976. It's a modern building near Eagle Beach with excellent medical facilities. Hotels also have medical doctors on call, and there are good dental facilities as well (appointments can be made through your hotel).

For information, go to the **Aruba Tourist Bureau,** 2 A. Shuttestraat in Oranjestad (tel. 23777).

The official **language** is Dutch, but don't worry, as nearly everybody speaks English. They might also speak Papiamento. Spanish and Portuguese are also spoken.

GETTING AROUND: Taxis in Aruba are unmetered, but rates are fixed, so it's necessary to tell the driver your destination and ask the fare before getting in. A ride from the airport to most of the hotels, including those at Palm Beach, costs from $10 to $12 per car, and a maximum of four passengers are allowed to take the journey. Some of the local people don't tip, although it's good to give something extra, especially if the driver has helped you with a lot of luggage. Taxis can be found at the **Dispatch Office,** Boulevard Center in Oranjestad (tel. 22116 or 21604).

Buses

The cheapest way to go to your hotel is via one of the airport buses, costing about $4 per person. Aruba has a decent bus service as well. The bus stand for the return to most of the hotels is in Oranjestad, opposite the Tourist Bureau. The fare is only 70¢. Your hotel reception desk will know the approximate times the buses pass by where you're staying. There is regular service from 7:40 a.m. to 6:05 p.m.

Car Rentals

Unlike most Caribbean islands, Aruba makes it easy for the independent traveler to rent a car and explore on his or her own. The roads are fairly good, and a valid U.S. or Canadian driver's license is also accepted in Aruba. Most of the big hotels have desks which will rent cars for you. Always ask them a day in advance and you'll stand a better chance of getting the car you specify.

Three of the nation's major car-rental companies maintain offices in Aruba, usually with both airport branches as well as outlets at some of the major hotels. High-season rates offered by most of the companies are fairly consistent: a peppy two- and four-door car with manual transmission and unlimited mileage costs a minimum of around $140 a week. There's no tax imposed on car rentals in Aruba, and few hidden extras other than insurance.

Hertz, Avis, and **Budget Rent-a-Car** offer collision damage waivers to their clients. These policies, which cost about $6 a day at all three companies, reduce but do not always eliminate a driver's financial responsibility in the event of an accident. A close look at the fine print is needed.

Budget Rent-a-Car requires that each driver purchase the company's waiver, which then removes *all* financial responsibility from the driver for any collision damage. Although the policies at Hertz and Avis are not mandatory, they are less comprehensive than the one at Budget. Collision damage to cars rented through Hertz and Avis can cost a driver up to $10,000 if the damage is severe enough! Even if a renter opts for the purchase of the waiver, he or she is still responsible for the first $300 and $400 worth of damage at Avis and Hertz, respectively.

Air-conditioned cars at Hertz are substantially more expensive than air-conditioned vehicles at its competitors, costing about $100 more per week than the cheapest vehicle available at either Budget or Avis.

In a final comparison, underage or overage drivers might not be qualified for rentals at all three of the agencies. For insurance reasons, Budget requires that drivers in Aruba be between 23 and 65, Avis will rent only to qualified drivers between the ages of 23 and 60, and Hertz requires only that a qualified driver be older than 21.

For detailed information on rentals at the time of your trip, call the toll-free international departments of Budget (tel. 800/527-0700), Avis (tel. 800/331-2112), or Hertz (tel. 800/654-3001).

Sightseeing Taxi Tours

Taxis with English-speaking drivers are available as guides. Most of them seem well informed about their island and are anxious to share it with you. A one-hour tour (and you don't need much more than that) is offered at a cost of $22 per hour for a maximum of five passengers.

Sightseeing Bus Tours

De Palm Tours, 142 Lloyd Smith Blvd. in Oranjestad (tel. 24400 or 24401), seems to have a monopoly on the business, and their kiosk can be found at the major hotels. Their most popular jaunt is a 2½-hour excursion leaving at 9:30 a.m. and costing $15 per person. The tour takes in the island's major attractions, including a haul across the windswept countryside with its Divi-Divi trees, continuing on to the north coast to see Aruba's Natural Bridge.

WHERE TO STAY: Most of Aruba's hotels are of the resort variety, bustling, big, and self-contained. There's a tremendous dearth of family hotels or those of the budget variety. Guest houses are few and tend to be booked up early in winter by faithful returning visitors. In season, it's imperative to make reservations way, way in advance. Don't ever arrive expecting to find a room on the spot. You may end up spending the night under a cactus.

The Resort Hotels

Aruba Concorde Hotel-Casino, Palm Beach (tel. 24466), competes, rather successfully, for the title of "the biggest and best" along the Palm Beach strip. The 18-story property, owned by Concorde Hotels International of Venezuela, is a landmark on the horizon. It made its debut in 1978 on an expansive strip of the beach, with a full program of water sports. Management has selected a fine staff to run this excellent hotel.

The reception desk assigns one of the 500 ocean-view rooms, each with private balcony, closed-circuit color TV (movies shown from 11 a.m. to 3 a.m.), and radio with private channel music, as well as refrigerators and a vaguely continental decor. The designer was lavish in his colors, accented in vibrant walls, floors, and fabrics. Expensive suites are available, as you'd expect. Otherwise, single rooms range in price from $140 to $195 daily, with doubles going for $145 to $200, all winter tariffs. *In spring, summer, and fall, the single tariffs range from $85 to $115; the double, from $95 to $120 daily.* For breakfast and dinner, add another $42 per person per day.

The diamond-shaped swimming pool is Olympic size, and between the hotel and the sea is a tremendous playtime terrace with sunning areas and a multitude of lounge chairs. Professional tennis courts are lit for night games. Light lunches are served in the circular Kadushi Restaurant, with its balloon-like globe lighting and stylized tile cut-out murals on its pillars and walls.

Perhaps the best experience is to descend the central cantilevered interior staircase to the lower level. It's a flow of various rooms, Japaneses style, all open, with large planters and delicate screens setting off the various sections. Shimmering white floors and walls of glass give a sense of space. Somehow this warmness makes up for the coldness of the ultramodern reception area.

In the evening guests dine at La Serre, later playing baccarat or roulette in the casino, or else enjoying nightclub entertainment in the Arubesque.

Aruba Palm Beach Hotel & Casino, Palm Beach (tel. 23900), is a Delft blue-and-white palacio with Moorish arches. At this sleek, stylish, high-rise total resort, you are given all the trimmings. Built in 1968, it is placed firmly and luxuriously on a sizable portion of powdery Palm Beach. Lobby furnishings are contemporary, and the spaciousness is enchanced by an array of palm trees and other local vegetation. The Dutch Arcade houses a shopping center behind colorfully painted reproductions of Holland-type storefronts.

Staggered along its eight stories are 200 guest rooms, including pool-side lanais and oceanfront suites, all ultramodern and first class. Every unit has quality and character, with many amenities, including air conditioning. Bedrooms overlook the swimming pool or the gardens, and all are ocean view. In winter, singles range in price from $130 daily for standard units to $200 for an "ocean room," and doubles in the same category cost the same. For breakfast and dinner, add $42 per person daily to these tariffs. *In summer, May to December, big reductions are granted: a single costs from $75 to $95 daily, and a double, $80 to $100.*

This government-financed hotel spared little expense in developing a large sunning and sports area between the hotel and the sea. The Balashi Bar, informal and thatch-roofed, surrounds an overscale freshwater swimming pool, and there's a smaller pool for children. Strolling musicians make the poolside refreshment bar lively.

Surrounding gardens are well kept and planted with palms intermixed with more flamboyant varieties of shrubbery and trees. Scuba-diving, tennis, sailing, skindiving, even glass-bottomed boat rides, can easily be arranged at the sports desk.

For breakfast, choose from Arawak Coffeehouse, with a decorative theme of primitive hex signs and handsome Delft china, or the outdoor terrace buffet. Dine either in the elegant Rembrandt Room with walls of red velvet displaying many reproductions of the artist's finer works, where a dinner and floor show average $30, or at the outdoor Steak Pub, where the evening breeze carries the aromas of an open hearth cooking steaks, lobsters, and shrimp.

For nightly divertissement, the Club Galactica, with space-age design, offers a live band for dancing and a show, followed by a disco until the early-morning hours. Of course, the prime nighttime target is the modernized Grand Casino.

Americana Aruba, Palm Beach (tel. 24500), is a high-rise giant, boasting 206 double-bedded, air-conditioned, and colorfully decorated rooms. Opened in 1975, it staggers its rooms on ten floors, and all its units have balconies and room phones. The decorative style goes from a Caribbean motif to more traditional designs. *In the off-season, singles range from $75 to $95 daily, with doubles going for $120.* In winter, tariffs are raised to from $145 to a lethal $220, single or double occupancy.

The hotel rises from a splendid seaside setting. Contemporary paintings and shell wall hangings displayed in the corridors give the public areas a stylish effect. Much space has been devoted to sports and recreational facilities. A row of thatched shade huts was built along the water's edge, and there are two tennis courts. A buffet-style breakfast is served at Las Mananitas Café terrace, and you can order an al fresco luncheon here as well.

You can dine in the garden-style Villa Fiorita restaurant while seated in tall white wrought-iron banquettes. Happy hour guests gather in Le Club Lounge, with its purple and mauve carpeting. Between 6:30 and 7:30 p.m., this is a popular gathering point for tourists, as drinks are priced at only half price (for example, you can enjoy what is reputedly the best piña colada on the island). The Stellaris Supper Club has a theater-style setting (see my nightlife recommendations).

Holiday Inn, Palm Beach (tel. 23600), is the largest hotel on the island, with nearly 400 rooms. It's also the most action-packed hostelry along the sands of Palm Beach. Private balconies frame vistas of white sands, and each air-conditioned bedroom comes with a TV offering in-house video movies, a private tile bath, and a phone. Bedrooms, furnished in a sort of Holiday Inn traditional standard, have color coordination and are well furnished, with wall-to-wall carpeting, two double beds, and large closets. In winter, singles range from $110 to $160 daily, while doubles go for $110 to $175. *In the off-season, terms are lowered to anywhere from $70 to $100 daily in a single, from $76 to $106 in a double.* For breakfast and dinner, add another $35 per person daily.

The Olympic-size swimming pool with distilled fresh water seemingly has room for everybody, and it's surrounded by a sun terrace. There's a health club with a sauna, plus four tennis courts. The social hostess arranges a full program of water sports.

Strolling musicians serenade you as you dine in the Salon Internacional, with its continental menu (the specialty is lobster curry in a coconut shell). Adjacent to the salon is the supper club, the Palm Beach Room, which serves a continental cuisine and offers entertainment. A South American orchestra plays, often for the benefit of a Venezuelan clientele. In addition, within the hotel precincts is the King International Casino. Their Chinese restaurant, the Empress of China, features a fine cuisine.

Divi-Divi, Druif Bay Beach (tel. 23300), stands near the largest beach on the island. A rambling, low-rise structure, it has Iberian architectural accents, offering some rooms in the bungalow style, others in two-story buildings or lanais. In all, there are 152 rooms with private baths, all with tub and shower—92 units in the main buildings, 40 casitas, and 20 lanais, all of which have two double beds. Each accommodation has a private terrace or balcony and is fully air-conditioned. The Wiggins family of Ithaca, New York, have brought their own special touch to Divi-Divi, named after the famous wind-whipped tree, and to its companion accommodation, the nearby Tamarijn Beach Hotel. Casual and comfortable, the Divi-Divi is one of the island's friendliest oases.

Each member of the Wiggins family has added judgment, good taste, and a free spirit to this hotel on the outskirts of Oranjestad. The accommodations somehow seem connected with "the elements." Through a buying spree in Mexico, the Wiggins family gave the place a real Spanish flavor, with handmade mirrors, leather and dark-wood chairs, terracotta floors, and dark wooden shutters at the windows, along with hand-carved beds.

In winter, singles range in price from $150 to $170 daily and doubles run from $155 to $175. *However, in the off-season, rates are reduced to $90 to $120 in a single, $95 to $125 in a double.* For breakfast and dinner, add another $35 per person to the daily tariffs.

Meals are served on the casual Pelican Terrace or in the Red Parrot dining room. Sunday brunch is a popular occasion. On the grounds is a freshwater swimming pool, and the hotel has a tennis court. All year, dancing and entertainment are offered nightly. The Alhambra Casino stands across the road from Divi-Divi.

Tamarijn Beach Hotel, Druif Bay Beach (tel. 24150), is also owned by the Wiggins family, who run the Divi-Divi, previewed above. If you stay here, you can enjoy exchange privileges with the companion hotel, giving you greater choice in your selection of bars, meals, and entertainment. With 204 rooms, it is a cluster of white stucco buildings constructed in the Mediterranean style, with red tile roofs. The complex opens onto 1500 feet of private white sand beach.

In winter, the single tariff ranges from $120 to $145 daily, the double rate going from $125 to $150. *Rates are reduced in the off-season to anywhere from $65 to $95 daily in a single, from $70 to $100 in a double.* Breakfast and dinner cost an additional $35 per person daily.

Each unit has a private bath, two double beds, an oceanfront view, plus air conditioning. Sliding glass doors open onto a private porch or the garden. Placed around the seafront swimming pool is a thatched refreshment hut with sunshade parasols. You'll find barefoot elegance. The food is good too, with an American menu offered on the Cunucu Terrace. The more elegant Palm Court Restaurant specializes in fresh live lobster and Florida stone crabs. In addition to the freshwater swimming pool, there are also tennis courts on the grounds, dancing and entertainment nightly, and a shopping arcade.

Talk of the Town, Oranjestad (tel. 23380), was created by Mr. and Mrs. Ike Cohen, who'd lived in Jacksonville, Florida, before taking over this property in Aruba. Originally built as an eight-room structure in 1942, the Cohens in 1964 discovered it when it was the offices of a chemical plant. Learning, and occasionally making mistakes along the way, they transformed the moldy, termite-ridden building into a first-class resort hotel, the only one in the capital itself.

The hotel is best known for its restaurant, one of the most famous in the Caribbean. In fact, the name of the restaurant, Talk of the Town, eventually replaced the name of the hotel, Coral Strand. Between the hotel and its beachside sister, the Manchebo, there are five different places to eat, including the Moorish-style Surfside, serving Italian food, across from the Talk of the Town.

The hotel stands on the coastal road leading to the airport, and its two-floor bedroom units are built motel-like around a large swimming pool. The tiers of arches and rough plaster walls give it a Spanish look. There's also a heated hydrotherapy whirlpool bath. Traditional furnishings and strong colors are used, and all units have TV and refrigerators, and some have small kitchenettes.

In winter, singles range frrom $85 to $95 daily, and doubles go for $110 to

$125. For breakfast and dinner, add another $32 per person daily. *In summer, doubles drop to a low of $65 daily, with singles costing from $55 to $65.*

At poolside in a sheltered dining room, three meals are served every day, and a latticed gazebo is the setting for cocktail parties. Musicians entertain every evening.

Manchebo Beach Resort Hotel, Manchebo Beach (tel. 23444), with its spread-out beach-club facilities, is nearer to Oranjestad and its shops than the other beachfront properties in Aruba. Owned by the Cohens of Talk of the Town (guests have exchange privileges), the Manchebo consists of groups of two-story motel-like air-conditioned bedrooms, with balconies or patios overlooking the Caribbean. Its private-seeming 1600 feet of beach strip is ideal for suntanning and all water sports. Close to the surf line is a large freshwater swimming pool. On the grounds are facilities for volleyball, shuffleboard, and tennis.

The bedrooms—72 in all, each with private bath, TV, refrigerator, and phone—are light and airy in feeling, with white walls and bold patterned draperies and bedcovers. Many units have built-ins, and the baths are tiled and streamlined. In winter, singles pay from $125 for a room, and doubles cost the same. Add another $35 per person for breakfast and dinner. *In summer, the single tariff ranges from $65 to $75 and the double rate runs from $70 to $80.*

A relaxed, informal atmosphere prevails. On the grounds is the French Steak House (see my dining recommendations), plus a patio restaurant specializing in fish dishes. The hotel also has an "after hours" nightclub.

Bushiri Beach Hotel, 35 Lloyd G. Smith Blvd. (tel. 25471), is owned and operated by the Aruba Hospitality Trades Training Center, a well-staffed hotel set on an unblemished beach in the middle of an attractively landscaped garden. The students here make up in enthusiasm what they lack in experience—in fact the service is among the best on the island. They rent 50 spacious units which are carpeted and air-conditioned, usually containing two double beds per room. A double in high season, EP, ranges from $105 to $120 daily. Singles go for $100 to $110. *Off-season, rates are reduced to $70 to $85 in a double, $60 to $75 in a single.* The MAP supplement is $35 per person. Reservations in New York are handled by Reservation Systems, Inc., 6 East 46th St., New York, NY 10017 (tel. 212/661-4540). Nationwide, the toll-free number to call is 800/223-1588.

Apartments and Guest Houses

Many travelers prefer to visit Aruba on a much simpler basis than what we've been considering. There are some apartments and a handful of guest houses overlooking the sea or else within walking distance of a beach. Others are on a bus route, and still others require a car. My personal favorites follow.

The **Edge's,** 458 Lloyd G. Smith Blvd., Malmok-by-the-Sea (tel. 21072), owned by Virginians, is a guest-house complex of 11 units 50 yards across from the beach. It is less than a mile from the Holiday Inn Hotel and Casino going toward the lighthouse. A carpeted patio with chaise lounges separates two rows of motel-style units, and each apartment has a private entrance and patio with furniture for outdoor dining. These are really efficiency units with kitchenette, refrigerator, dishes, toaster, coffee pot, and all utensils for cooking. All apartments are air-conditioned with large tiled baths. Each unit has at least two beds and is pleasantly furnished and clean. There are two deluxe units with king-size beds, sitting rooms, full kitchens, and private patios with a view of the ocean. You'll receive a welcome from the owners or Filomena and Miranda, who smilingly take care of the needs of their guests. To the right of the entrance gate, you can watch sunsets from a whirlpool spa at no charge. The guest house lies only a 70¢ bus ride from Oranjestad. In winter, occupancy costs $62 to $89 per apartment daily. *In the off-season, tariffs are lowered to from $36 to $60 per apartment per day.* An extra $12 is charged for each person over two per apartment.

The **Vistalmar,** 28 Bucutiweg (tel. 28579), consists of eight complete waterfront apartments, each with an oversize front porch, offering a second living room. The apartments, with terrazzo floors, have a combination living room and kitchen area, plus space for dining, a large bedroom with spacious closets, and a private bath. The upper-floor apartments have white bamboo chairs set out on a porch, and all have Nordic interior furnishings, everything new and clean. There is also a laundry for guests.

Couches covered in tweedy fabric, hanging basket lamps, and white wicker chairs add a sophisticated touch. It's not unlike a chalet in the mountains of northern Spain with tiled roofs. A regular bus service goes by the hotel. The Vistalmar has put in a man-made private beach with a pier and sundeck next to a yacht club. Your friendly and most helpful hosts, Katy and Alby Yarzagaray, quote both daily and weekly rates. On a daily basis, the winter tariff is $70 in a double, *lowered to only $45 daily in a summer.*

Edward's Sea View, 19 Malmokweg, offers four air-conditioned bedrooms with kitchenettes in a residential area, a bus ride from Oranjestad. Furnishings are in a Scandinavian-Dutch style. An open porch-living room is shaded by blossoming trees. The apartments have private baths and two beds. Nearby is a famous cactus forest. *In summer, one-bedroom apartments rent for $35 daily; two-bedroom units, $45 daily.* In winter, tariffs rise to $50 per day for one-bedroom accommodations, $65 for two bedrooms.

ARUBA COOKERY: A few of Aruba's restaurants serve rijsttafel, the "Asian smörgåsbord," or nasi goreng, a "mini rijsttafel." In addition, a surprising number of Chinese restaurants operate in Oranjestad. Most of the major hotels have several dining options, ranging from fast food in coffeeshops to so-called gourmet restaurants. More and more Aruban specialties are beginning to appear on menus, although Stateside dishes such as hamburgers still predominate. French cuisine is the second major choice of most chefs. Sometimes, at least on off-season package deals, visitors on the MAP (breakfast and dinner) are allowed to dine around on an exchange plan with the other hotels.

La Dolce Vita, 164 Nassaustraat (tel. 25675). Once it was a private home, but since 1980 it has been the most acclaimed restaurant in Aruba, serving, as its name suggests, Italian specialties. It wasn't long before it was discovered by the food and wine critics of such prestigious Stateside magazines as *Gourmet.* Only dinner is served, costing from $35, and it's seven days a week from 6 p.m. to midnight. Because of the popularity of "The Sweet Life," it's best to call and reserve a table, especially in high season, when it can quickly fill up.

If you like pasta with salmon and cream (which became the rage in Italy in the 1980s), you'll find it served here. You might begin your repast, however, with a sampling of their antipasti, including fine Italian salami and cheese, along with artichokes and marinated squid. They also do a savory, perfectly flavored "kettle" of fruits de mer. Naturally you get some good veal, along with such familiar Italian standby dishes as baked clams and linguine. An espresso or perhaps some Italian ice cream will finish off your meal nicely.

Papagayo Restaurant, Lloyd G. Smith Boulevard Center (tel. 24140), is one of the most delightful restaurants in Aruba. It's decorated like a forest, with live birds, trees, and plants, along with a fish pond. In addition to that, it opens onto a view of the harbor. It has steadily grown in popularity ever since it opened in 1983. Managed by Divi Hotels, it offers such tempting fare as linguine with lobster and seafood and chicken Papagayo (one of the chef's many specialties—stuffed breast of chicken). In addition to that, you get excellent prime steaks along with the superb fare of the northern Italian kitchen. Prices are moderate, with a typical meal costing $20. Before dinner, you might want to have an apéritif in the lounge. It's open from 11 a.m. to 11 p.m. daily.

Bali Floating Restaurant, off Lloyd G. Smith Boulevard (tel. 22131), is moored in Oranjestad's harbor. The restaurant is housed in an Oriental house-boat decorated with bamboo and Indonesian art. Diners are treated to the popular Indonesian rijsttafel (rice table), a complete meal of rice surrounded by 21 different dishes, served at your table in individual portions. The rijsttafel is not spicy, but the sambal (hot, hot) is served on the side for the more adventurous to try. A mini-version is served for lunch, as well as sandwiches and snacks. Expect to pay from $20 for a full rijsttafel, which may be ordered per person, but try to go with a group if possible since it's a fun meal that everyone will enjoy. Besides the rijsttafel, the menu offers a fine selection of tenderloin steaks and fresh local fish dishes. Hours are noon to midnight daily.

Talk of the Town Restaurant, Airport Road (tel. 23380). As a boy when Ike Cohen was growing up in Rotterdam, he learned the meat business from his father. While still a boy he knew how to purchase meat for the family's wholesale butcher business. When he and his wife, Grete, founded the Talk of the Town Restaurant, Mr. Cohen applied that knowledge to his present business. Today his meat freezer is the best and most fully stocked on the island. A self-taught resort operator, Mr. Cohen now runs one of Aruba's best known restaurants, lying between the airport and Palm Beach (see the previous hotel recommendation).

From 6:30 p.m. candlelight dining is offered, backed up by a good wine list and live music. Mr. Cohen has always believed in feeding people well, and the portions here are gigantic. The setting could easily be Miami, and there's no view—but people don't come here for that. They want to dine well.

You can begin with escargots à la bourguignonne or perhaps vichyssoise. As mentioned, Mr. Cohen specializes in beef, and a favorite order is an ample cut of roast prime ribs of beef. The filet mignon Dutch style is also good. Other specialties include frog legs à la bourguignonne and veal Cordon Bleu. He also offers a selection of seafood dishes, including king crab legs and Dover sole meunière. Prices are high, but all items are imported, and you get a lot for your money. A complete meal could cost around $30 per person here. After 11 p.m., there's disco action.

The **Red Parrot,** Divi-Divi Beach Hotel, Druif Bay Beach (tel. 23300), is one of the better hotel restaurants. You dine on sturdy Spanish armchairs, and the view is through arched windows framed with vines and plants, opening onto the sea. The Iberian decor is reflected by the rough stone walls and wood paneling, as well as the archways. The menu leads off with a flourish, with an unusual appetizer—lightly salted frog legs with a combination of snails in a sauce with garlic and parsley. Or you may prefer a rich pea soup, Dutch style, with pig feet and geldersewurst.

Main-dish specialties include chicken Marengo, a roast young duckling in an orange sauce, and a local favorite, keshi yena, Dutch cheese filled with chicken and raisins and served with rice. In addition, the chefs prepare good seafood, including Alaska king crab leg, boiled and served with drawn butter, and a U.S. prime sirloin steak. A dessert selection is made from the trolley. Expect to spend from $28 to $35 per person here for a complete meal.

On Sunday night a buffet of local dishes is presented, everything enlivened by the Divi-Divi steel band. Reservations are needed on that night.

De Olde Molen, Palm Beach (tel. 22060), is housed in a landmark, standing just across the street from the Concorde. It can be reached on foot from a number of Palm Beach hotels. Originally, the windmill in which the restaurant is housed was built in 1804 in Friesland, Holland, but it was torn down and shipped to Aruba where it was reconstructed piece by piece. Since 1960 it has been a tourist-focused destination for dinner, served nightly except Sunday from 6 p.m. Jackets are suggested for men.

The chefs seem to change with some frequency here, but all of them know how to prepare an international cuisine with such classic offerings as pepper steak for two persons, veal Cordon Bleu, and shrimp Provençale. Try also, if offered, the red snapper amandine. Some guests begin with a shrimp cocktail, although I prefer the thick Dutch split-pea soup. For dessert, I suggest a pineapple mousse or Irish coffee. A complete meal can easily run around $20 to $35 per person. A 15% service charge is added to all bills.

Dragon-Phoenix, 31 Havenstraat (tel. 21928), in downtown Oranjestad, is run by a kindly gentleman who came from Canton province and brought his mild-flavored cuisine to Aruba with him. The setting is interesting, with some furniture made to order in Hong Kong and betasseled Chinatown light fixtures —in all, a soothing atmosphere for dining if you don't mind an occasional dragon.

In these cool, comfortable surroundings, you can make selections from a large menu. If you're confused by such a big choice, I'd suggest a special Chinese rice table. Perhaps there will be four or five persons in your party. Your party will receive the chef's special eggroll, sharkfin with chicken soup, chow kai kow with vegetables, shrimp in cashew nuts, lobster with oyster sauce, crabmeat with black-bean sauce, special fried rice, plus dessert.

At least 18 Cantonese dishes are offered, including lobster chop suey. In addition, the chef has at least 22 other specialties. A complete meal is likely to cost about $20 here.

Trocadéro, 152 Nassaustraat (tel. 21210), has a large, ambitious international menu, including Oriental dishes. As much as possible, the owners try to obtain foodstuffs from the Caribbean, including the waters along the coast of Venezuela.

Among their more tantalizing selections is baby shark steak meunière. They also serve turtle steak with a madeira sauce. Or try their squid marinara or their filet of barracuda meunière. For an appetizer, you might prefer half a dozen fresh clams. In addition, they have good steaks, including a U.S. prime sirloin. A complete meal will cost about $22.

The Spanishy-style restaurant is open for both lunch and dinner seven days a week from noon to 2:30 p.m. and from 6:30 to 10:30 p.m. Every night, a guitar player sings Caribbean songs.

Heidelberg, 136 Lloyd G. Smith Blvd. (tel. 33020). About the last place you'd expect to find a restaurant with a name like Heidelberg is the desert-like island of Aruba. But owner-chef Manfred Hein, along with his wife, Ilona, has brought such a dining room to Aruba, serving dinner nightly, except Wednesday, from 6 to 11 p.m. Established in 1982, it became immediately popular. Arubans even came here to celebrate Christmas by ordering the Heins' fat, juicy Christmas goose.

Here you get traditional German fare, including wienerschnitzel and goulash and noodles. In addition to goose, duck is well prepared. But before that, you may want to order the herring hausfrau style. Sauerbraten and good, rich-tasting soups are some of the other dishes served here. For dessert, select something from the trolley. Most diners, however, go for the strudel. Count on paying around $25 for a big, hearty, and altogether satisfying meal.

The **French Steak House,** Manchebo Beach Hotel, Manchebo Beach (tel. 23444), is a beachside bistro where the atmosphere is informal and the food is good. Guests from the other hotels often come here for the romantic candlelit dining, and no one need worry about putting on a jacket or tie. Service is friendly, and it's easy to make a night of it if you dine here in these relaxed surroundings. The place is owned by Ike and Grete Cohen, who also run the previously recommended Talk of the Town.

A table d'hôte dinner is offered nightly for about $20, plus service. Or else you can order à la carte, enjoying such chef's specialties as red snapper Provençale or the classic veal Stroganoff flamed with vodka and madeira. You can also help yourself at a New York–style salad bar. Of course, beef is the big feature here, including either the filet mignon or the New York sirloin, the latter a 14-ounce boneless strip charbroiled to your taste. You can also order either chateaubriand or pepper steak for two persons. If you order à la carte, chances are you'll end up paying from $30 per head.

Buccaneer, Casparito (tel. 26172), is a seafood restaurant with the only saltwater aquarium in the Caribbean. But you don't go here to watch the fish: you go to eat them. The atmosphere evokes (or means to) that of a ship's cabin. The location is near many of the major hotels, about two miles from Palm Beach (taxis are always waiting outside). The owners, Jozeh Munzenhofer and Peter Dorer, are also the chefs.

For an opener, the pirate's hotpot is a seaworthy choice (a native fish soup that somehow manages to taste different every night). Among the "fruits of the sea," the lobster thermidor is everybody's favorite. I always ask the waiter for the catch of the day, which he'll prepare with a creole sauce. Meats are frozen of course, but well prepared, including tournedos in a number of ways. Every main dish is served with the vegetable of the day, along with a stuffed potato and salad on the side. Coup Melba or homemade cheesecake are favored to finish off your meal, which most likely will cost from $25 per person or more. The service is excellent. Closed Sunday.

Outside of Oranjestad and the beach strip with its high-rise hotels, there aren't many eateries that can be safely recommended. An exception to that is **Brisas del Mar,** 222A Saveneta, near the police station (tel. 47718). It's like a place you might encounter in some outpost in Australia. Here in very simple surroundings, right at water's edge, Lucia Rasmijn opened this little hut with an air-conditioned bar in front at which the locals gather to drink the day away.

The place is often jammed on weekends with many of the same local people, who come here to drink and dance. On Friday, Saturday, and Sunday, Mrs. Lucia Rasmijn offers entertainment, with home-grown talent playing everything from the guitar to the harp.

In back the tables are open to the sea breezes, and nearby you can see a fisherman slicing the catch of the day, perhaps wahoo, selling it to local housewives. The cooks try to confine their menu to fish caught in the Caribbean. Perhaps you'll have the pan-broiled fish of the day, prepared Aruban style (with a creole sauce), or breaded conch cutlet. Try also the baby shark steak or the turtle steak with port wine. The breaded squid cutlet is yet another favorite.

For an appetizer, perhaps you'll select the "fisherman's fish soup." Desserts are simple, including fresh fruit or ice cream. Expect to spend from $20 per person. The restaurant is open for both lunch or dinner.

It's always best to call first for a reservation to avoid making the trip there, only to find the place full. Even with a reservation, you still may have to wait more than an hour or so to get a seat if the place is really jumping. To reach the restaurant's location at Savaneta, turn off to the right from the main road leading from Oranjestad to San Nicolas between Anthony Sales and the police station. You'll need a car to get there or else you'll have to take a cab. By bus it's more than an hour's trip.

EXPLORING ARUBA: The capital of Aruba, **Oranjestad** attracts mainly shoppers instead of sightseers. The bustling city has a very Caribbean flavor, and it's part Spanish, part Dutch in architecture. Cutting in from the airport, the main thoroughfare, Lloyd G. Smith Boulevard, goes along the waterfront and on to Palm Beach. But most visitors cross it heading for Nassaustraat or "Nassau Street." Here is where they find the best free-port shopping.

After a shopping trip, you might return to the harbor where fishing boats and schooners, many from Venezuela, are moored. Nearly all newcomers to Aruba like to take a picture of the **Schooner Harbor.** Not only does it have colorful boats docked along the quay, but boatmen display their wares in open stalls. The local patois predominates. A little farther along, at the fish market, fresh fish is sold directly from the boats. Also on the seaside of Oranjestad, **Wilhelmina Park** was named after Queen Wilhelmina of the Netherlands. A tropical garden has been planted along the water, and there's a sculpture of the Queen Mother.

Aside from shopping along Nassaustraat, the major attractions of Aruba are **Eagle Beach** and **Palm Beach,** considered among the finest in the Caribbean. Most of Aruba's hotels are stretched Las Vegas strip style along these pure-white sand stretches on the leeward coast.

If you can lift yourselves from the sands for one afternoon, you might like to drive into the **canucu,** which in Papiamento means the countryside. Here Arubans live in very modest but colorful pastel-washed houses. Of course, all visitors venturing into the center of Aruba want to see the strangely shaped Divi-Divi tree with its trade-wind-blown coiffure. Even though they live in a very dry climate where cactus thrives better than flowers, Arubans like to have bougainvillea, oleander, hibiscus, and other tropical plants around their homes. However, to grow them, they often use expensive desalinated water.

Rocks stud Aruba, and the most impressive ones are those found at **Ayo** and **Casibari,** to the northeast of Hooiberg. These stacks of diorite boulders are the size of buildings. The rocks, weighing several thousand tons, are a puzzle to geologists. On the rocks at Ayo are ancient Indian drawings. If the subject interests you, guides can also point out drawings on the walls and ceiling of the **Caves of Canashito,** south of Hooiberg. While there you may get to see the giant green parakeets.

Hooiberg is affectionately known as "The Haystack." It is Aruba's most outstanding landmark, and anybody with the stamina can take the steps all the way to the top of this 541-foot-high hill. One Aruban jogs up there every morning. From its precincts in the center of the island you can see Venezuela on a clear day.

On the jagged, windswept northern coast, the **Natural Bridge** has been carved out of the coral rock by the relentless surf. In a little café overlooking the coast you can order snacks. There you'll also find a souvenir shop with a large selection of trinkets, T-shirts, and wall hangings, all selling at reasonable prices.

You turn inland for the short trip to **Pirate's Castle** at Bushiribana, which stands on a cliff on the island's windward coast. This is actually a deserted gold mill from the island's now-defunct industry. Another gold mill is in the old ghost town on the west coast, **Balashi.**

You can continue to the village of Noord, known for its **St. Ann's Church** with a hand-carved Dutch altar dating from the 17th century.

At the opposite end of the island is **San Nicholas,** which is built around the **Lago Oil refinery.** This is a modern community which was designed and constructed for North Americans who work in the Exxon plant. The public relations department at the refinery grants permission to tour the plant.

THE SPORTING LIFE: Its western and southern shore, called the **"Turquoise Coast,"** is what attracts sun seekers to Aruba. Palm Beach and Eagle Beach (the latter closer to Oranjestad) are the best beaches. No hotel along the strip owns the beaches, all of which are open to the public. However, if you use any of the hotel's facilities you'll be charged, of course. You can also spread your towel on Manchebo or Druif Bay Beach—in fact, anywhere along seven miles of uninterrupted sugar-white sands. In total contrast to the leeward side, the north or windward shore is rugged and wild.

Snorkeling and Scuba

You can snorkel in rather shallow waters, and scuba-divers find stunning marine life with endless varieties of coral as well as tropical fish in infinite hues. At some point visibility is up to 90 feet. The goal of most divers is the German freighter *Antilia,* which was scuttled in the early years of World War II, lying off the northwest tip of Aruba, not too far from Palm Beach.

The best place to book water sports is from **De Palm Tours,** whose main office is at 142 Lloyd G. Smith Blvd. in Oranjestad (tel. 24400), although it also has offices at the major hotels as well. Here a certified teacher will give scuba-diving instruction at a cost of $50 per person. Subsequent dives can be arranged at $40 per person, as can scuba-diving trips for experienced divers. Snorkelers are often taken out on a boat ride to a site, with complete gear furnished, for $15 per person

Waterskiing

Most beach strip hotels offer this sport, charging about $10 for a quarter of an hour, or else giving lessons for around $25.

Golf

Visitors can play at the nine-hole **Aruba Golf Club,** 82 Golfweg (tel. 93485), near the oil refineries of San Nicolas at the eastern end of the island. Goats run across the course, and the oiled sand greens add zest to the game. Greens fees are $6 for as many holes as you can play in a day, and caddy fees run $3 for nine holes. You can rent clubs for $5 for the day. Fast-food items and sandwiches are available at the clubhouse and bar.

Tennis

Most of the island's beachfront hotels have tennis courts, and some have top pros on hand to give instruction. Many of the courts can also be lit for night games. (I don't advise playing in Aruba's noonday sun). Usually there's a $3 surcharge at night, although day games are free if you're a guest.

Deep-Sea Fishing

In the deep waters off the coast of Aruba you can test your skill and wits against the big ones such as the wahoo. Marlin, tuna, bonito, and sailfish are other popular catches. **De Palm Tours,** 142 Lloyd G. Smith Blvd. in Oranjestad (tel. 24400), takes out a maximum of six persons (four of whom can fish at the same time) on one of its charters, charging about $125 to $250 for a half day, depending on the size of the boat.

Boating

Usually your hotel will have boats and equipment. If not, you should go to **De Palm Tours,** 142 Lloyd G. Smith Blvd. in Oranjestad (tel. 24400). There you can rent sea Jeeps, those open-water buggies that have become a very popular sport in Aruba, costing about $15 per half hour.

Horseback Riding

Rancho El Paso, 44 Washington (tel. 23310), offers leisurely rides in the countryside, with horses for both beginners and advanced riders at the cost of $15 per hour.

SHOPPING: Aruba manages to compress six continents into the half-mile-long Nassaustraat in Oranjestad. Not technically a free port, the duty is so low (3.3%) that articles are very attractively priced. Aruba also has no sales tax. You'll find the usual array of Swiss watches, German and Japanese cameras, jewelry, liquor, English bone china and porcelain, Dutch, Swedish, and Danish silver and pewter, French perfume, British woolens, Indonesian specialties, and Madeira embroidery. Delft Blue pottery is an especially good buy. You'll find good buys on Holland cheese (Edam and Gouda), as well as Holand chocolate and English cigarettes in the airport departure area.

For handicrafts, you should wait for the Watapana Festival every Tuesday night (see "After Dark," below).

Store hours in general are Monday through Saturday from 8 a.m. to noon and from 2 to 6 p.m. Many stores are also closed on Tuesday afternoon and some seem to keep irregular hours in the off-season, especially in the fall and spring.

In the heart of Nassaustraat stands the legendary **Spritzer & Fuhrmann's,** with its main building and the much-photographed carillon chiming "Bon Bini" (welcome). Gold and diamond jewelry and fine watches are sold here, not only for the discriminating taste of the connoisseur but also for the budget buyer seeking good jewelry. In a new building, S&F has a collection of fine china, crystal, and flatware, in most of the better-known brands. If you can't make it into town, you'll find branches of the store at the Holiday Inn, the Concorde, and Divi-Divi.

The **Aruba Peasant Shop,** 70 Nassaustraat (tel. 22900), is the island's oldest gift shop and souvenir store. Handicrafts from more than 50 countries include the Delft Blue pottery as well as wooden shoes from Holland. Also sold are an extensive variety of exotic clothing and the largest Aruba T-shirt collection, along with exquisite figurines, miniatures, and other gifts at reasonable prices.

Photo El Globo Aruba (tel. 22900) is under one roof with the Aruba Peasant Shop at Nassaustraat. All your needs in photographic, hi-fi, and video equipment can be supplied in the world's best makes at good prices.

Aruba Book and Gift Store (Aröba Boekhandel), 94 Nassaustraat (tel. 21273), started as the island's first bookstore but has added an extensive collection of toys, gifts, and souvenirs.

Boulevard Book and Drugstore stands in the Boulevard Shopping Centre, with a full range of books, magazines, drugstore items, gifts, toys, and souvenirs. It is also open during lunch hour.

Kan Jewelers, 18 Nassaustraat (tel. 21192), has a good collection of contemporary 14- and 18-karat gold jewelry. These are jewelers from Holland, and they enjoy a good reputation in the Netherlands Antilles. They also carry a big variety of Swiss watches and Rosenthal china and crystal. Kan has eight locations in Aruba, including most of the large hotels, and one in Curaçao.

New Amsterdam Store, 18 Nassaustraat (tel. 21152), is best for linens, with its selection of napkins, placemats, and embroidered tablecloths with sources that range all the way from China. It has an extensive line of other merchandise as well, from Delft Blue pottery to beach wear and boutique items, along with an exquisite gold collection, gift items under $20, procelain figures by Lladro, watches, French and Italian women's wear, and leather bags and shoes.

Directly next door, the **Aruba Trading Company,** 14 Nassaustraat (tel. 22600), has all the popular tourist items—perfumes, souvenirs, plus liquor and cigarettes (the shop will deliver these in-bond items to your plane).

Casa del Mimbre, 76 Nassaustraat (tel. 27268), specializes in Colombian arts and crafts, including woolen ruanas, which are ponchos popularized by Avianca stewardesses. They also have souvenirs and gifts from Central America and other South American countries. Maya napkins from Guatemala, woven wall hangings from Mexico, cowhide golf bags from Colombia—the collection is wide ranging and intriguing.

AFTER DARK: The casinos of the big hotels along Palm Beach are the liveliest nighttime destinations. In plush gaming parlors, guests try their luck at roulette, craps, blackjack, and of course the one-armed bandits. The **Americana Aruba** (tel. 24500) opens daily at 1 p.m. for slots, 3 p.m. for blackjack and roulette, and at 9 p.m. for all games. Early birds go to the **Aruba Concorde** (tel. 24466) at 10 a.m. for slots, 1 p.m. for games. The **Holiday Inn** (tel. 23600) wins the prize for all-around action. Its casino doors are open 22 hours a day, closing only for two hours to clean. The **Aruba Palm Beach** (tel. 23900) opens its gambling tables from 9 p.m. on.

The latest casino is the **Alhambra,** Lloyd G. Smith Boulevard (tel. 23300), the first free-standing casino in Aruba (that is, one not connected with a hotel). Across from the Divi-Divi Beach Hotel, it is managed by Ron von Kaenel, and in many ways I like it more than all the others. It's owned and operated by Divi Hotels.

Nongamblers or those who grow tired of the slots and tables can patronize the hotel's cocktail lounges and supper clubs. You don't have to be a guest of the hotel to visit to see the shows, but you should make a reservation. Tables at the big shows, especially in season, are likely to be booked early in the day.

For my money, the best is the **Stellaris Gourmet Dinner Show** at the **Americana Aruba** (tel. 24500). In a theater-style setting, the club offers elegant dining and dancing plus an international floor show. For this you pay from about $22 per head. The club is open daily, except Monday, from 7 to 11 p.m. Show time is 9:15 p.m. nightly.

Also within the Americana Aruba complex is **Le Club Lounge,** which has disco action and tumba dancing from 9 p.m. to 3 a.m., and a midnight show as well. The place has its own drama in a setting of purple and mauve carpeting with red velvet chairs and subdued lighting. Everything seems restrained until the waiter comes soaring to your table, holding aloft a torch that is in fact a tall glass called "Island Fire," made with 100-proof rum. You'll be charged about $4 for this attention-getting concoction.

Usually you can go to one of the major hotel supper clubs and only order drinks. Expect to pay from $4 for most libations.

The **Holiday Inn** (tel. 23600) seems to have more action than most hotels. You might begin with a steak dinner in its Bon Bini Koffie Huis. On Wednesday there is often a poolside water ballet show. In the Palm Beach Room there is a dinner show nightly at 9:30 (closed Wednesday). The cocktail show usually begins right before midnight. Finally, to close down the evening, you can visit their disco, L'Esprit Club.

Every Tuesday evening from 7 to 10 there is a **Watapana Festival** in Oranjestad. At that time you can sample home-prepared native food, including bami, a beef-and-noodle dish. Elaborate drinks, such as rum punches, are prepared at booths set up by the major hotels, and there's local musical entertainment. The festival also makes for a shopping expedition. At this time you get your best buys in local handicrafts.

On the disco circuit, **Club Scaramouche** at the Boulevard Shopping Center in Oranjestad (tel. 24954), is clearly the leader. Technically, this is a private membership club, charging dues of $100 per year. Getting in without being a member is not a real problem, however. While residents of the island must be a member or the guest of a member to enter, island visitors may enjoy an evening for a charge of $5, or else obtain one of the VIP passes available in many of the leading hotels and some of the better restaurants. Jackets are required on weekends; jeans are not allowed, nor are tennis shoes or T-shirts. Hours are 9 p.m. to 5 a.m.

The elegantly decorated nightspot is like a sumptuous living room in grays and red burgundies. The floor has a sparkling star effect, created by tubes of lighting, and bubbles and fog rise to give a sometimes sensuous, often eerie effect. The acoustics are well conceived. You can sit at the bar and actually hear yourself talk.

The other leading disco is the **Contempo** at the Talk of the Town (tel. 21990). After 10:30 p.m. the tables are moved away in a part of this popular restaurant and there's dancing until 3 a.m. There's also a $6 entrance fee, including drinks, and tickets are on sale in the lobby. The management warns that prices are subject to change on special nights. Jackets are required, and no one under 18 is admitted.

A younger crowd is attracted to the disco directly across the street from Talk of the Town and under the same Cohen management. Called **Scorpio's**, it's at the Surfside Restaurant (tel. 23380). At this small Moorish-style place by the sea, you can dance to the sounds of live bands from 10 p.m. to 3 a.m. The atmosphere is casual, as is the dress. Many young Arubans are fond of going here. Couples pay $8 to enter (for that, one of the party of two gets a free drink).

The **Bamboo Bar,** on the Bali Pier (see my Bali Floating Restaurant recommendation under "Aruba Cookery"), is the home of Aruba's first piano bar. A "Happy Happy Hour" is featured from 6:30 to 7:30 p.m., while the sun sets over the harbor. Come in for drinks or open-air dining (same menu as the Bali Floating Restaurant) and enjoy the scene of boats and yachts bobbing at anchor. Romantic piano and guitar music sets the mood for a relaxing evening. The Bamboo Bar, open daily except Sunday, is one of Aruba's favorite meeting places.

2. Bonaire

Unlike some islands, Bonaire isn't just surrounded by coral reefs. It *is* the reef! And its shores are thick with rainbow-hued fish. Five miles wide and 24 miles long, Bonaire is poised in the Caribbean, close to the Spanish Main. The island attracts those seeking the out-of-the-way spot, the uncrowded shore.

Bonaire is best reached from its sister island of Curaçao, 30 miles to the west. Like Curaçao, it is equally desert-like, with a dry and brilliant atmosphere. Often it is visited by "day trippers," who rush through here in pursuit of the shy, elusive flamingo, the glamour bird of the Caribbean.

Boomerang-shaped Bonaire comprises about 112 square miles, making it the second largest of the ABC Dutch grouping. Its northern sector is hilly, tapering up to Brandaris Peak, all of 788 feet. However, the southern half, flat as a flapjack, is given over to bays, reefs, beaches, and a salt lake which attracts the flamingos.

The island has powdery white beaches and turquoise waters, where underwater photographers find a visibility of 100 feet or more. Unspoiled Bonaire is one of the world's best scuba and snorkeling grounds, a beachcomber's retreat, and a birdwatcher's heaven, with 145 different species—not only the graceful flamingo, but the big-billed pelican, as well as bright-green parrots, snipes, terns, parakeets, herons, hummingbirds, and others. Bring a pair of binoculars.

Contrary to a popular misconception often published in travel guides, Bonaire doesn't mean good air. Rather, it comes from the Indian, signifying low country.

Bonaireans zealously want to protect their environment. Even though they eagerly seek tourism, they aren't interested in creating "another Aruba" with its high-rise hotel blocks. Spearfishing isn't allowed in their waters, nor is the taking or destruction of any living animal or coral from the sea.

The island was discovered in 1499 by a party of explorers commanded by Amerigo Vespucci, who lent his name to the New World. Amerigo found some Indians living on the island in Stone Age conditions. After Spanish domination, Bonaire witnessed the arrival of the Dutch in 1634, perhaps seeking to protect Curaçao's flanks, an island they already occupied. Bonaire was assigned the duty of supplying livestock, corn, and salt.

Once the British occupied the island, eventually leasing it to a New York merchant for $2400 annually, including the services of 300 "salt-mine" slaves.

The Dutch came back in 1816, setting up plantations to grow dyewood, cochenille, and aloes. At the abolition of slavery in 1863, the economy collapsed. Bonaire settled into a long, dreary depression, relieved in part when its men in this century left their island to work in the refineries of Venezuela, Aruba, and Curaçao.

The revival of the salt works and the influx of tourism beginning in the 1960s have improved the island economically.

The big annual event is the **October Sailing Regatta,** a five-day festival of racing sponsored by the local tourist bureau. Now an international affair, the event attracts sailors and spectators from around the world, as a flotilla of sailboats and yachts anchor in Kralendijk Bay. If you're planning to visit during regatta days, make sure you have an iron-clad hotel reservation.

GETTING THERE: Bonaire gets one nonstop weekly flight, leaving from Miami every Saturday on **ALM Antillean Airlines,** which continues on to Curaçao.

Other visitors can fly to the island by going first to either Aruba or Curaçao (see the "Getting There" previews in each island section). From Curaçao, it's only a 15-minute flight to Bonaire on one of ALM's frequent flights (about seven daily). Depending on your connecting flight from the mainland, you can often be delayed for hours in the Curaçao airport.

PRACTICAL FACTS: Bonaire is known for its **climate,** with temperatures hovering at 82° Fahrenheit. The water temperature averages 80°.

Like Aruba and Curaçao, the Netherlands Antillean florin (NAf) or guilder (equal to 57¢ in U.S. dollars) is the coin of the realm. However, U.S. dollars are also accepted.

Upon leaving Bonaire, you'll be charged an airport **departure tax** of $5.75, so don't spend every penny.

Drinking **water** is safe (it comes from distilled and purified sea water).

To enter Bonaire, all you need is **proof of citizenship** and a return or continuing ticket.

English is widely spoken on the island, but you'll also hear Spanish, Dutch, and Papiamento.

The **electric current,** is 127 volts AC, 50 cycles. Divers with precise equipment should provide their own converters.

For tourist information in Bonaire, go to the **Tourist Office,** 1 Breedestraat in Kralendjik (tel. 8322 or 8649).

Banking hours are usually 8:30 a.m. to noon and 2 to 4 p.m., Monday to Friday.

Most **shops** are open from 8 a.m. to noon and 2 to 6 p.m., Monday to Saturday.

Bonaire operates on **Atlantic Standard Time** all year round

GETTING AROUND: As per usual, **taxis** are unmetered, but the government has established rates. Each driver should have a list of prices which he'll produce upon request. From the airport to your hotel costs from $5 to $10, depending on the time of day or night, and as many as four passengers can go along for the ride unless they have too much luggage. (*Note:* There are no public buses.)

Car Rentals

Too narrow for my tastes, roads in Bonaire are kept in fair condition. It's easy to drive in Bonaire, and car rentals are reasonable. I recommend **Budget/Boncar** (tel. 8300, ext. 225 in town, tel. 8315 at the airport). This firm rents VWs, Gurgels, Ford U-50s, Pony, Mazdas, and other vehicles starting at $25 per day with unlimited mileage. Your U.S. or Canadian driver's license, if valid, is acceptable for driving in Bonaire. Driving is on the right.

Sightseeing Taxi Tours

All taxi drivers are informed about Bonaire's sightseeing attractions, and will reveal them to you (as well as three other passengers) at a cost of about $18 for a half-day jaunt, which is plenty of time to take in the highlights, both north and south.

Sightseeing Bus Tours

Bonaire Sightseeing Tours (tel. 8300, ext. 225) hauls you on tours of the island, both north and south, taking in the flamingos, slave huts, conch shells, Goto Lake, the Indian inscriptions, and other sights. The northern tour, lasting two hours, costs $10 per person; the southern tour, also lasting two hours, costs the same. You can take a whole-island tour, lasting 3½ hours and costing $18 per person. A special four-hour tour of Washington National Park can be booked at a cost of $18 per person for a minimum of four.

Boat Excursions

The **Flamingo Beach Hotel** (tel. 8285) offers cruises on the *Gypsy Girl*. The boat goes out on sunset cruises, sangría afternoons, moonlight sails, or a full day's charter on request. Look for a copy of the daily sailing schedule in the hotel's lobby.

Every visitor to Bonaire wants to take a trip to uninhabited Klein Bonaire. The Beach Bonaire and Flamingo Beach Hotels offer trips daily. You'll be left in the morning for a day of snorkeling, beachcombing, and picnicking, then picked up later that afternoon.

HOTELS: Hotels are low-key and unhassled, and all of them face the sea. There are no high-rises here, only low-lying, personally run operations where everybody gets to know everybody else rather fast.

If you're planning to spend your vacation in Bonaire, perhaps with your family, you might consider an alternative to a hotel. Owners of more than 15 oceanfront rental cottages have banded together and are represented in the U.S. by **Bonaire Vacations,** a Long Island firm. Its toll-free number for calls outside New York state is 800/662-2742. In New York state the number is 516/627-5999.

Bonaire Beach Hotel, P.O.Box 34 (tel. 8448), is the most complete resort on Bonaire. Most of its facilities are in a low, central building, with a handsome, intimate dining room and a good-size casino. Long covered walkways lead to the blocks of modern bedroom units, furnished motel style. The buildings are surrounded by connecting gardens with palms and bougainvillea, giving a luxurious sense of space. Skill and taste have been demonstrated by the architect and designer.

Some buildings have rather deluxe rooms with impeccable decor. There are also units in the old wings with less style and no view of the water that nevertheless offer good value if you're on a tight budget. In winter, singles rent for $78 to $92 daily; doubles, $86 to $100. For breakfast and dinner, add another $30 per person to the tariffs quoted. *Low-season rates range from $62 to $74 daily in a single, from $72 to $84 in a double.* All units are comfortably air-conditioned, and contain private baths and phones.

The location, about half a mile north of town, is directly on its own beach of white sand, known as Playa Lechi or Milk Beach. You can also swim in a saltwater pool. A covered terrace bar/restaurant and parasols are on the beachfront, and it's here you can order a piña colada, lunch, or dinner. In the main building, facing the sea, is an in- and outdoor breakfast room.

The sports program is important here. Games are played on two asphalt tennis courts (there's a resident pro), and the hotel is also the site of one of the Netherlands Antilles' best known diving operations (see "The Sporting Life," below). The gaming tables in the casino are busy at night, but don't expect the big-time action of Aruba.

Cai-Cai, the official tourist guide, moonlights at night as a singer in the hotel's main restaurant (see my dining suggestions).

Flamingo Beach (tel. 8285) is one of the most personalized and charming hotels in the ABC islands. This complete beachfront resort, with its watersports facilities and stylized bedrooms, is the result of the Wiggins family of Ithaca, New York. They discovered a neglected, gone-to-seed hotel with a cluster of flimsy wooden bungalows that had been used as an internment camp for German prisoners of World War II. With foresight and taste, they turned it around to a top-notch resort, offering both individual cottages and modern seafront rooms with private balconies where you can stand out and watch rainbowhued tropical fish in the water below.

There are 110 good-size, air-conditioned rooms, facing either the sea or a large swimming pool in the garden courtyard. The bedrooms with sloping beamed ceilings have either Mexican styling, with imported carved beds and chairs, or island fashions, with bamboo tester headboards with half canopies. In high season, singles rent for $70 to $110 daily, the latter the price of a deluxe room. Doubles range from $75 to $115. *Off-season, tariffs go from $55 to $65 daily in a single, from $60 to $80 in a double.* For breakfast and dinner, add another $32 per person daily to the tariffs quoted.

A ten-minute walk from Kralendijk, the hotel serves meals in two different dining rooms, each delightfully capturing an island feeling. Breakfast, lunch, and dinner can be ordered at the Calabas Terrace, dinner in the Chibi Chibi al fresco dining facility built in tiers overhanging the clean waters of the Caribbean (see my dining suggestions). You can enjoy sunsets at the pool bar while sipping your favorite drink. Tuesday is Indonesian night with a rijsttafel in the Calabas, and on Saturday night there's a buffet on the outdoor terrace with local steelband entertainment.

A few palm-thatched sunshades are found along the swatch of beach. On the grounds is a professional dive shop (see "The Sporting Life," below).

Capt. Don's Habitat (tel. 8290) attracts divers and snorkelers. A unique Caribbean diving center, the compound consists of a cluster of modern little villas which can be enjoyed by nondivers as well. The hub, of course, is the building holding the diving gear, but there are adjoining terraced loggias, one for dining, another for an open bar lounge. Small terraces lead down to the water. Great attention is given to providing an informal setting in which to relax, drink, eat, whatever.

The Habitat is the creation of Capt. Don Stewart, a former Californian who sailed his schooner down here from San Francisco, going through the Panama Canal. Arriving on a reef in Bonaire, he's been here ever since. You'll spot him at once, with his one earring and his bare feet. Called "the godfather of diving on the island," the captain is a prime mover in the campaign to protect the reefs on Bonaire.

Cottages in winter range from $86 daily if occupied by one or two, going up to $100 to $110 daily for three to four guests. *In summer, one to two persons are charged only $62 daily for a cottage; three persons, $76; and four persons, $82.* Some economy rooms, known as "monk's cells," rent for only $28 in a single in winter, $50 in a double. *In summer, a single pays only $22; a double, $40.*

The little modern villas with sliding glass doors have simple, colorful furnishings—"the bare essentials," according to Captain Don. Breakfast or dinner, served on the terrace overlooking the reef, is the scene of lively swapping of underwater stories. Breakfast and an evening meal costs about $20, and at the bar you can order a good Amstel beer. Or if you prefer, you can cook your own meals in one of the kitchenettes in the bungalows. There's a mini-grocery store on the premises.

DINING OUT: The food is generally acceptable. Nearly everything has to be imported, of course. Your best bet is fresh-caught fish and an occasional rijsttafel, the traditional Indonesian rice table, or else try the local dishes.

The **Neptune Dining Room** in the Bonaire Beach Hotel (tel. 8448) is air-conditioned and attractively decorated in a nautical style. It has a well-selected international menu, with such hors d'oeuvres as a local version of breaded shrimp in garlic butter. Soups are well prepared, including callaloo with crab, the spicy West Indian soup, and the Antillean mock turtle soup.

Among the fish dishes I'd suggest the fresh Bonairean fish filet en papillotte. Among local specialties, keshi yena is familiar in Bonaire (that is, baked Edam cheese, stuffed with a good-tasting meat filling) or chicken laced with Curaçao liqueur. Desserts include a selection of French pastry from the wagon or Irish coffee. Count on spending from $15 for an average meal.

Entertainment is offered nightly, and after dinner you can try your luck at the casino.

The **Chibi-Chibi** at the Flamingo Beach Hotel (tel. 8285) offers open-air dining on multilevel terraces cantilevered over the surf. Before dinner, you may enjoy the sunset and your favorite cocktail at the Flamingo Nest.

The prix-fixe menu features local and continental cuisine. Specialties include seafood cocktail, gazpacho soup, native fish almondine, and filet mignon béarnaise, as well as a daily chef's special. Dinner is served from 6:30 to 10 p.m. for $20, plus 15% service per person. Reservations are suggested, and dress is casual.

The Chibi-Chibi is named for the yellow-breasted bird who'll visit your table, hoping to fly away with some sugar. Dinner without coat and tie is de rigueur.

Outside of the hotels, I prefer the **Beefeater,** 3 Calle Grandi (tel. 8081), in the heart of Kralendijk opposite the tourist office. Here a charming Englishman, Richard Dove, a former inspector for the Michelin guides, has created a handsome restaurant and decorated it with prints and pictures. It is housed in an old Bonairean town house. An apéritif is served in an intimate bar, and you're shown to your table where you'll enjoy excellent personal service in a dignified, somewhat elegant atmosphere.

Steaks and seafood are the main feature. The chef prepares an excellent steak au poivre. Before your main course, try his pâté, crêpe, or conch. Expect to pay from 30 NAf ($17.10) to 40 NAf ($22.80) for a three-course meal. The restaurant is open Monday through Saturday for dinner only from 6:30 to 11 p.m. In season, it's necessary to make a reservation.

Zeezicht, Curaçaostraat (tel. 8434), is the best place in the capital to go for a sundowner. You join the old salts or the people who live on boats to watch the sun go down, hoping to see the "green flash" that Hemingway wrote about. Pronounced "zay-zicht" and meaning sea view, this place has long been popular with fishermen who like the excellent local cookery and the Chinese dishes.

Rebuilt into a two-story operation, the restaurant offers an oyster soup that might be the best beginning. Perhaps you'll order a conch chop suey, a first for me. A small rijsttafel is also offered. Fried fish is invariably featured, the catch coming from the nearby fish market. Lobster à la Zeezicht is occasionally offered, and there's always the Zeezicht steak. Count on parting with about $20, unless you order the special dinner at $18. Zeezicht is open from 8:30 a.m. to 11 p.m.

China Garden, Calle Grandi (tel. 8480), is housed in a restored Bonairean mansion. Good-tasting Eastern dishes, with some Indonesian specialties, are served to West Indians. Portions are enormous, and prices are low, considering what you get. The chefs from Hong Kong also cook Chinese, American, and local dishes, and do so daily from 11:30 a.m. to 10 p.m. except Tuesday.

A variety of curries ranges from beef to lobster. Seafood dishes, prepared in a variety of styles, including lobster in black-bean sauce, are served. Special culinary features include a Java rijsttafel and the nasi goreng special. The place is air-conditioned, seating 60 guests, and it offers pleasant and courteous service. You can dine here for $18, but a lot of hungry scuba-divers spend a lot more, of course.

Mona Lisa Bar and Restaurant, Calle Grandi (tel. 8308), is known locally as Tom Spee's place. It stands across from his nightclub, "E Wowo," and is open from 9 a.m. to midnight, Wednesday through Monday. In spite of its name it has a definite Dutch touch. The best appetizers are cold, and they're from the sea. The chef does beef in exciting ways, ranging from pepper steak to a slab of beef covered in a béarnaise sauce. Dover sole is also a specialty. Many classic Central European dishes, including wienerschnitzel and Hungarian goulash, are served. Perhaps you'll settle instead for fresh local fish. Desserts are often elaborate, including a hot cherry jubilee. Expect to spend from $15 per person for a full meal, maybe more.

Den Laman Bar and Restaurant, Gouverneur Debrotweg (tel. 8955), next to the Hotel Bonaire, serves some of the best seafood on Bonaire. The restaurant has a huge 9000-gallon aquarium, covering two walls. Housed within are such creatures as sharks along with beautiful and fascinating tropical fish. The fish are not just for viewing, as you'll soon agree after ordering a cocktail as an appetizer (shrimp, lobster, or mixed seafood). Another excellent beginning is the fish soup, the chef's special. The fresh fish of the day depends on what was caught, of course. Perhaps you'll order conch flamingo, a local favorite, or lobster thermidor. When it's featured, I always go for the turtle steak or the red snapper creole. It's easy to spend $35 here, but also possible to dine for less.

Bistro des Amis, 1 Kerkweg (tel. 8003), is one of my favorites. It's intimate, it's friendly, and it serves good food. In the heart of Kralendijk, the bistro is owned by a woman known only as "Lucille." She will tell you her specials of the day, which are likely to include the best onion soup on the island, escargots served piping hot in garlic butter, and scallops swimming in a velvety cream sauce. The wine selection is limited, but among the best on the island. Incidentally, you dine in air-conditioned comfort. Hours are noon to 2 p.m. and 6:30 to 11 p.m. daily, except Monday, and there is often dancing so you can make a night of it. Count on a bill beginning at $18 for dinner. There's also a large bar if you'd like to drop in for a drink before dinner.

EXPLORING BONAIRE: The capital, **Kralendijk,** means "coral dike" and is pronounced "Krah-len-dike," although most denizens refer to it as "Playa," Spanish for beach. A dollhouse town of some 1600 persons, it is small, neat, and pretty, also Dutch clean, and its stucco buildings are painted in pastels of pink and orange, with an occasional lime green. The capital's jetty is lined with island sloops and fishing boats.

Kralendijk nestles in a bay on the west coast, opposite **Klein Bonaire** or Little Bonaire, an uninhabited (except for goats), low-lying islet a ten-minute swim from the capital.

The main street of town leads along the beachfront on the harbor. A Protestant church was built in 1834, and St. Bernard's Roman Catholic Church has some lovely stained-glass windows.

At Ford Oranje you'll see a lone cannon dating from the days of Napoleon. If possible, try to get up early to see the Fish Market on the waterfront, looking like a little pink Greek temple. Here you'll see a variety of strange and brilliantly colored fish.

The **Instituto Folklore Bonaire** on Helmundweg, in a fort near the waterfront, has some old utensils, Indian artifacts, and musical instruments. There are also a few costumes. It's open Monday, Wednesday, and Friday from 8 a.m. to noon and Saturday from 9 a.m. to 1 p.m.

Around town you'll probably see the official tourist guide and welcoming committee of one, Cai-Cai. In his sparkling white uniform and with his everpresent smile, he roams the streets, welcoming newcomers and offering advice and assistance. He's also a singer, having made records.

The Tour North

After leaving Kralendijk, and passing the Bonaire Beach Hotel and the desalinization plant, you'll come to Radio Nederland Wereld Omroep (Dutch World Radio). It's a 13-tower, 300,000-watter. Opposite the transmitting station is a lovers' promenade, built by nature. It's an ideal spot for a picnic.

The road north is one of the most beautiful stretches in the Antilles, with turquoise waters on your left, coral cliffs on your right. You can stop at several points along this road where you'll find paved paths for strolling or bicycling.

Continuing, you'll pass the storage tanks of the Bonaire Petroleum Corporation, the road heading to **Gotomeer,** the island's loveliest inland sector, with a saltwater lake. Several flamingos prefer this spot to the salt flats in the south.

Down the hill the road leads to a section called **"Dos Pos"** or two wells, which has palm trees and vegetation in contrast to the rest of the island, where only the drought-resistant kibraacha and Divi-Divi trees, tilted before the constant wind, can grow, along with forests of cacti.

Bonaire's oldest village is **Rincon.** Slaves who used to work in the salt flats in the south once lived here. There are a couple of bars, the Amstel and the Tropicana, where you can order beer before continuing on your journey. Above the bright roofs of the village is the crest of a hill called **Para Mira** or "stop and look."

A side path outside of Rincon leads to some Arawak Indian inscriptions supposedly 500 years old. The petroglyph designs are in pink-red dye. At nearby **Boca Onima,** you'll find grotesque grottos of coral.

Before going back to the capital, you might take a short bypass to **Seroe Larguy,** which has a good view of Kralendijk and the sea. Lovers frequent the spot at night.

At the northern tip of the island, **Washington/Slagbaai National Park** is an untamed wilderness with a road hacked through 50 kilometers (30 miles). It's open to the public daily, except Christmas Day, New Year's Day, Easter Sunday, and December 15, a national holiday, from 8 a.m. to 5 p.m., charging adults an admission of $2, although children under 15 are admitted free. This game preserve has at least 130 different species of birds. Hunting, fishing, and camping aren't permitted, however, without a special permit.

Visitors drive through a cactus forest with coral rock formations, and only the music of the birds breaks the silence. This 13,500-acre game preserve is the first of its kind in the Dutch Antilles. Birdwatchers come here early in the morning.

In touring the park, look for the Goto Lake and Salina Slagbaai where hundreds of flamingos may be searching for food. Playa Foenchi, in the preserve, is one of the best snorkeling areas in Bonaire.

Heading South

Leaving the capital again, you pass the Trans World Radio antennas, towering 500 feet in the air, transmitting with 810,000 watts. This is one of the hemisphere's most powerful medium-wave radio stations, the loudest voice in Christendom and the most powerful nongovernment broadcast station in the world. It beeps out interdenominational Gospel messages and hymns in 20 languages to countries as far away as the Iron Curtain and the Middle East.

Later, you come on the salt flats where the brilliantly colored pink flamingos live. Bonaire shelters the largest accessible nesting and breeding grounds in the world. The flamingos build high mud mounds to hold their eggs. In the background, mounds of salt look like snow mountains, glistening in the sun. The birds are best viewed in spring when they're usually nesting and tending their young.

The salt flats were once worked by slaves, and the government has rebuilt some primitive stone huts, bare shelters little more than waist high. The slaves slept in these huts, returning to their homes in Rincon in the north on weekends. The centuries-old salt pans have been reactivated by the International Salt Company. Near the salt pans you'll see some 30-foot obelisks in white, blue, and orange. They were built in 1838 to help mariners locate their proper anchorages.

Farther down the coast is the island's oldest lighthouse, Willemstoren, built in 1837. Still farther along, Sorobon Beach and Boca Cai come into view. They're at landlocked **Lac Bay** which is ideal for swimming and snorkeling. Conch shells are stacked up on the beach. The water here is so vivid and clear you can see coral 65 to 120 feet down in the reef-protected waters.

SHOPPING: Not technically duty free, prices on imported luxuries such as linens, jewelry, china, perfumes, and crystal represent substantial savings in Bonaire, as they do in Aruba and Curaçao. Walk along Calle Grandi in Kralendijk to sample the merchandise.

Of course, the famous **Spritzer & Fuhrmann's** has a branch on Calle Grandi, selling elegant Swiss watches, clocks, and jewelry, the largest collection on Bonaire. You can also buy English china and Scandinavian crystal here.

Littman Jewelers, 10 Calle Grandi (tel. 8160), has been around since the 1940s. It offers everything from a souvenir charm to an exquisite piece of jewelry from its location across from the tourist information office. In addition to Seiko, it also sells Pulsar, Oris, and Rolex, all at prices about 20% to 30% less than in the States. The director is Steven D. Littman.

Boolchand's, on Calle Grandi, has an interesting selection of beachwear, embroidered linens, Oriental curios, perfumes, colognes, souvenirs, and gift items.

Fundashon Arte Industria Bonairiano, on J. A. Abraham Boulevard, is the best shop for handicrafts, including woodcarvings, goatskin leather articles, tortoise-shell jewelry (could be seized by U.S. Customs), and best of all, black coral jewelry in silver settings.

Things Bonaire, on Calle Grandi, sells Jean Meiss hand-painted T-shirts as well as handmade sundresses. Also, you might want to look at some of their hand-painted pottery souvenirs.

Ki Bo Ke Pakus, at the Flamingo Beach Hotel, has some of the most imaginative merchandise on the island—Bonaire T-shirts, handbags, dashikis, locally made jewelry, batiks from Indonesia, Delft Blue items, and khangas, the African material which can be worn a dozen ways.

Both the Bonaire Beach and Flamingo Beach Hotels have interesting women's boutiques on the premises.

THE SPORTING LIFE: The true beauty on Bonaire is under the sea, where visibility is 100 feet 365 days of the year, and the water temperatures range from 78° to 82° Fahrenheit. Many dive sites can be reached directly from the beach, and sailing is another pastime. Birdwatching is among the best in the Caribbean, and for beachcombers there are acres and acres of driftwood, found along the shore from the salt flats to Lac.

Swimming

Bonaire has some of the whitest sand beaches in the West Indies. The major hotels have beaches, but you may want to wander down to the southeast coast for a swim at Sorobon and Boca Cai on Lac Bay. Here you can collect conch shells as souvenirs. In the north, you may want to swim at Playa Foenchi, on the coastline of the Washington/Slagbaai National Park.

Snorkeling

In an unusual development for snorkelers, an easily accessible trail along Bonaire's shoreline has been identified and marked off. Here a great many of the hundreds of fish and coral varieties to be found anywhere can be seen within a quarter-mile stretch of shallow water. This was a project of STINAPA, an organization sponsored jointly by the World Wildlife Fund and the government. The area attracts snorkelers from far and wide. While scuba enthusiasts come from all parts of the world to dive at Bonaire's 40-plus designated underwater scenic sites, snorkelers had not heretofore received special attention.

Equipment costing $5 to $6 per day can be rented at any of the dive centers outlined below.

Scuba

One of the richest reef communities in the entire West Indies, Bonaire has plunging walls which descend to a sand bottom at 130 or so feet, abounding with hard corals, numerous seawhips, black coral trees, basket sponges, gorgonia, and swarms of rainbow-hued tropical fish. One magazine said Bonaire had "the lushest, most colorful coral reefs to be found anywhere." Most of the diving is done on the leeward side where the ocean is lake flat. There are more than 40 dive sites on sharply sloping reefs.

Bonaire has a unique program for divers in that all three major hotels offer personalized, close-up encounters with the island's fish and other marine life. That way, the diver can experience underwater contacts in different dimensions under the expertise of Bonaire's dive guides.

The legendary Capt. Don Stewart runs **Dive Habitat** (tel. 8290), based at his hotel, already recommended. His is one of the best operated dive shops in the Netherlands Antilles. A conservationist, the captain likes ecology-minded divers. His diving company, standing on a reef 600 yards north of the Bonaire Beach Hotel, is designed to process 60 divers and provide equipment.

The captain takes guests to his own favorite spots each week. Otherwise, the divemaster is David Serlin, the only PADI-certified master instructor in the Netherlands Antilles. A total of six boat dives costs $150; a package of 12, $200. For a unique adventure, you can arrange to have Dee Scarr, an author, naturalist, and photo journalist, take you on one of her personalized dives.

Alice and Peter Hughes invite you to patronize their **Dive Bonaire** at the Flamingo Beach Hotel (tel. 8285), where they feature a package for $150 (six day boat dives, plus one night boat dive). A ten-dive package at $200 includes ten day boat dives, plus one boat night dive. The unlimited dive package at $225 offers you unlimited day boat dives, plus unlimited night boat dives. All these packages mentioned include tank, backpack, weights, weight belt, and use of a tank for unlimited day and night beach diving. Boat night dives are Monday through Friday, and beach night dives are nightly except Saturday. Scotland-born Peter Hughes also offers three-day reef snorkeling trips with all equipment for $33 per person.

The **Bonaire Scuba Center** lies on the 600-foot beach of the Bonaire Beach Hotel, where one of Bonaire's most spectacular reefs is located just 50 feet off-shore. The center's equipment includes three flat-top boats, two Mako compressors, and diving equipment for 80 divers. The center caters to both novice and experienced divers. It offers resort and certification courses, guided boat and night dives, mini photo courses, and still- and movie-camera rentals. Boats are available to experienced groups for exploration trips. For reservations, get in touch with Bonaire Tours, Inc., Box 775, Morgan, NJ 08879 (tel. 201/566-8866).

Golf

This is not a serious sport here. There's only a miniature course at the Bonaire Beach Hotel.

NETHERLANDS ANTILLES: BONAIRE **667**

Tennis

The Bonaire Beach Hotel (tel. 8448) has two good courts, which are free to residents, but cost $5 per hour for outsiders, day or night.

Waterskiing

Your hotel can arrange this for you at one of the dive operations at a cost of $10 for 15 minutes.

Boating

The major hotels rent Sunfish or windsurfers for about $10 per hour, although they are free to guests at the Bonaire Beach Hotel. Kralendijk Bay is ideal for sailing, and there's always a good breeze.

Deep-Sea Fishing

Both the **Bonaire Beach Hotel** and the **Flamingo Beach** can arrange for fishing charters. Fishermen are fond of the offshore fishing grounds surrounding Bonaire, and later, at sundowner time, they talk of the great kingfish, wahoo, swordfish, and barracuda they've caught. Both half-day and full-day charters are available, including food, tackle, and bait.

Birdwatching

Bonaire has 145 species of birds which lure one down untrafficked, paved roads into the hills, the lakes, and the "salinas." Of course, birdwatchers spend most of their time in pursuit of the flamingo, as Bonaire has one of the largest colonies in this hemisphere. Washington/Slagbaai National Park is best for birdwatching. A good post is Poos di Mangel, where many species of birds gather in the morning and late afternoon for a drink. The post is off on a road to the left on the way west to Boca Bartol. Hundreds of birds also come to drink at the foot of Brandaris at a place called Bronswinkel Well. You'll see blue pigeons, yellow breasts, and parakeets.

NIGHTLIFE: Outside of the hotels, check out the action at **"E Wowo"** ("The Eye" in Papiamento), which lies right in the heart of town near the tourist office, at the corner of Calle Grandi and Kerkweg. It's distinguished by two flashing op art eyes. The club caters to members, but if you ask at your hotel desk you'll usually be granted an admission pass. Hours are Wednesday through Sunday from 9 p.m. until the early hours. Once a disco, the club was redesigned by Tom Spee, who brought the Mona Lisa restaurant to the island. The club occupies the second floor of one of the oldest and most colorful Dutch Colonial buildings on the island. It is the only nightclub in Bonaire.

Upstairs over the already-recommended Zeezicht Bar and Restaurant, Curaçaostraat (tel. 8434), the same manager, Maddy Visser, also operates **Pirate House,** where you can eat and dance after 11 p.m. and occasionally see a show. Otherwise it's disco music. Drinks cost around $3.

The **casino** at the Bonaire Beach Hotel (tel. 8448) is a lively (for Bonaire) spot. The hotel is a good social center, with a Caribbean party held at its seaside beach hut twice weekly. On Tuesday there's a barbecue with a "jump-up" steel band, and on Friday a buffet and a folklore show.

As part of the Flamingo Beach Hotel (tel. 8285), a **casino** opened in 1984 in a former residence adjoining the property. It is being promoted as "The World's

First Barefoot Casino." Blackjack, roulette, poker, wheel of fortune, video games, and slot machines are available. Gambling on the island is under government regulations.

3. Curaçao

Just 35 miles off the coast of Venezuela, Curaçao, the "C" of the Dutch ABC islands of the Caribbean, is the most populated in the Netherlands Antilles. It attracts visitors because of its friendly people, who extend a big welcome, as well as its almost duty-free shopping, lively casinos, water sports, and international cuisine. Fleets of ocean-going tankers head out from its harbor to bring refined oil to all parts of the world.

A peaceful, self-governing part of the Netherlands, Curaçao has an average temperature of 81° Fahrenheit. Trade winds keep the island fairly cool, and it is flat and arid with an average rainfall of only 22 inches per year, hardly your idea of a lush, palm-studded tropical island.

Curaçao was discovered not by Colombus, but by one of his lieutenants, Alonso de Ojeda, as well as Amerigo Vespucci, in 1499. The Spaniards exterminated all but 75 members of a branch of the peaceful Arawak Indians. However, they in turn were ousted by the Dutch in 1634, who also had to fight off French and English invasions.

The Dutch made the island a tropical Holland in miniature. Pieter Stuyvesant, stomping on his peg, ruled Curaçao in 1644.

The island was turned into a Dutch Gibraltar, bristling with forts. Thick ramparts guarded the harbor's narrow entrance, the hilltop forts (many now converted into restaurants) protected the coastal approaches.

Because of all that early Dutch building, what one finds today is more European flavor than anywhere else in the Caribbean. Curaçao is the most important island architecturally in the entire West Indies.

In this century, it remained sleepy until 1915 when the Royal Dutch/Shell Campany built one of the world's largest oil refineries to process crude from Venezuela. Workers from some 50 countries poured into the island, turning Curaçao into a polyglot, cosmopolitan community.

Curaçao is only 37 miles long and 7 miles across at its widest point. After leaving the capital, Willemstad, you plunge into a strange, desert-like countryside that may remind you of the American Southwest. Three-pronged cactus studs the land, as do the spiny-leafed aloes and the weird Divi-Divi trees, with their coiffures bent by centuries of trade winds. The landscape is an amalgam of browns and russets.

Windmills that evoke Dorothy's in *The Wizard of Oz* are in and around Willemstad and in some parts of the countryside. These standard farm models pump water from wells to irrigate vegetation.

GETTING THERE: The air routes to Curaçao are strongly linked to those leading to and from Aruba, since several airlines combine flights from North America to both destinations.

American Airlines operates a daily flight to Curaçao which leaves from New York's JKF Airport at 9:30 a.m., in enough time to connect with incoming flights from many cities of the American Northeast and Middle West. It touches down briefly in Aruba before continuing to Curaçao.

The return flight from Curaçao to JFK is nonstop, landing at the New York airport after 4½ hours of flight time. Round-trip air fare is cheaper when a passenger arranges prepaid hotel accommodations through American's tour desk simultaneously with air transport. However, clients who want to arrange their own transport can opt for a 21-day excursion fare, where no advance booking is needed and where customers must wait for between 3 and 21 days before using the return half of their tickets. Round-trip fares for this kind of ticket cost $515 for midweek travel, $560 for weekend flights. However, look for low-season discounted fares if you plan to go in summer.

Eastern Airlines services Curaçao from Miami, combining many of its frequent flights with touchdowns in Aruba. Eastern's connections from many other cities of the U.S. link easily and efficiently with its flight leaving from Miami.

Likewise, **ALM** makes frequent trips to Curaçao from Miami.

PRACTICAL FACTS: To enter Curaçao, **proof of citizenship,** such as a voter registration card or a passport, is required, along with a return or continuing airline ticket out of the country. No visa or vaccination is required.

The drinking **water** comes from a modern desalinization plant and is perfectly safe to drink. The **electrical current** is 110–130 volts AC, 50 cycles, the same as in North America, although many hotels will have adapters if your appliances happen to be European.

While Canadian and U.S. dollars are accepted for purchases on the island, the official **currency** is the guilder (also called a florin), which is divided into 100 NA (Netherlands Antillean) cents. The exchange rate is tied to the dollar at a rate which never varies from $1 U.S. to 1.77 NAf. (Stated another way, 57¢ U.S. equals 1 NAf.)

Banks are open Monday to Friday from 8:30 a.m. till noon and 1:30 till 4:30 p.m. The only exceptions are the Banco Popular and the Bank of America, which remain open during lunch, from 9 a.m. till 3 p.m., Monday through Friday.

Curaçao is on **Atlantic Standard Time,** one hour ahead of Eastern Standard Time and the same as Eastern Daylight Saving Time.

Shops, hotels, and restaurants usually accept most major U.S. and Canadian credit cards.

Dutch, Spanish, and English are spoken in Curaçao, along with Papiamento, a language which combines the three major tongues with Indian and African dialects. The largest island in the Netherlands Antilles, Curaçao has 165,000 people representing more than 50 national groups.

A word of caution to swimmers: The sea water remains an almost constant 76° Fahrenheit year round, with good underwater visibility, but beware of stepping on spines of the sea urchins which sometimes abound in these waters. To give temporary first aid for an imbedded urchin's spine, try the local remedies of vinegar or lime juice, or as the natives advise, a burning match if you are tough. While the urchins are not fatal, they can cause several days of real discomfort.

There is a **departure tax** of $5.75.

For problems about passports or other matters, telephone the **U.S. Consulate** at 61-3066).

Medical facilities are well equipped, and the 820-bed St. Elisabeth Hospital, 193 Breedestraat (tel. 2-4900), near Otrabanda in Willemstad, is considered one of the most up-to-date facilities in the Caribbean.

For tourist information, go to the **Curaçao Tourist Board,** Plaza Pier (tel. 1-3397).

The **police emergency** number is 4-4444.

GETTING AROUND: Since **taxis** don't have meters, ask your driver to quote you the rate before getting in. Charges go up by 25% after 11 p.m. Drivers are supposed to carry an official tariff sheet which they'll produce upon request. Generally there is no need to tip, unless a driver helped you with your luggage. The cost from the airport to, say Las Palmas/Concorde is $10, and the charges can be split among four passengers. If a piece of luggage is so big the trunk lid won't close, you'll be assessed a surcharge of $1. In town, the best place to get a taxi is on the Otrabanda side of the floating bridge. To call a taxi, dial 8-4574.

Buses

Some of the hotels operate a free bus shuttle, taking you from the suburbs to the shopping district of Willemstad. A fleet of DAF yellow buses operate from Wilhelminapleim, near the shopping center, to most parts of Curaçao for a standard 2.50 NAf ($1.43) fare. Some limousines function as "C" buses. When you see one listing the destination you're heading for, you can hail it at any of the designated bus stops.

Sightseeing Taxi Tours

A tour by taxi costs about $15 per hour, and up to four passengers can go on the jaunt.

Sightseeing Bus Tours

Gray Line (tel. 1-3622) and **Taber Tours** (tel. 7-6713) operate sightseeing tours of the island. Most popular and recommendable is a city and country tour, leaving at 9:30 a.m. and again at 2:30 p.m., costing $12 per person, and lasting 2½ hours.

Car Rentals

Since all points of tourist interest are easily accessible by paved roads, you may want to rent a car. U.S. and Canadian citizens can use their own licenses, if valid, and traffic moves on the right. International road signs are observed. You drive on the right.

Several car-rental companies are represented in Curaçao, but **Budget Rent-a-Car**, the largest, offers one of the best high-season car-rental arrangements anywhere in the Caribbean. A four-passenger, two-door Daihatsu Charade without air conditioning is rented for an unlimited-mileage rate of $119 per week, $19 for each additional day. This rate requires an advance booking of two days (less than at many competing agencies) and a minimum rental of at least five days. Rentals of less than five days cost $26.85 per day, with unlimited mileage included. Visitors who prefer a car with air conditioning can reserve a manual-transmission four-door Toyota Corolla for a weekly rate of $288, with each additional day costing $41.15.

Purchase of insurance in the form of a collision damage waiver is required unless a renter prefers to make a $400 cash deposit. This costs between $8 and $11 per day, depending on the value of the car, and voids a driver's financial responsibility for collision damage in the event of an accident. Personal accident insurance is also available for an additional fee of around $1.75 per day.

Budget maintains five locations at major hotels throughout the island, as well as a branch at the airport. A phone call from 7 a.m. to 11 p.m. to Budget's island headquarters, 517 F. D. Rooseveltweg (tel. 8-3198), can help to arrange transportation to the nearest outlet.

Budget requires that drivers be between the ages of 23 and 65.

Visitors who don't meet these age requirements can try at **Avis**, since the minimum age there is 21, with no restrictions for drivers over 65. However, weekly rentals of cars at Avis are at least $85 more than the cheapest car at Budget. A Toyota Starlet at Avis costs $204 per week and requires an advance booking of at least seven days. Insurance benefits at Avis aren't as comprehensive as those at Budget, since drivers are responsible for about the first $100 worth of damage even if they opted to purchase a collision damage waiver. Such waivers cost around $9 per day.

Hertz is also represented in Curaçao, although its least expensive high-season rates ($228 for a week's rental for a Dodge Colt with unlimited mileage) are even more expensive than at Avis.

All three companies maintain toll-free numbers for callers. For rates and information while still in the States, call Budget at 800/527-0700, Avis at 800/331-2112, or Hertz at 800/654-3001.

WHERE TO STAY: Your hotel will be in Willemstad or in one of the suburbs, which lie only 10 to 15 minutes from the shopping center. The bigger hotels often have free shuttle buses running into town, and most of them have their own beaches and pools.

Remember that Curaçao is a bustling commercial center, and the downtown hotels often fill up fast with business travelers and Venezuelans on a shopping holiday. Therefore, reservations are always important.

Curaçao Concorde, P.O. Box 2133, Willemstad (tel. 2-5000), is a distinguished, "honeycomb-on-stilts" high-rise resort on the outskirts of Willemstad, with a free bus service to take you shopping in town. It's a self-contained complex, with a charming little beach and cove set among rocky bluffs where a dive shop offers the best water-sports program on the island, including skindiving, sailing, deep-sea fishing, and sea Jeeps. You have a choice of two Grasstex tennis courts lit for night games.

The structure is a block of rooms encased in a concrete facade, its arches not unlike Dutch lace. Most impressive to me is the wide, open lower lounge areas, giving everyone a trade-wind-swept view of Piscadera Bay. Furnished in wicker, the wall-less Pisca Terrace bar and restaurant opens onto an eight-pointed star-shaped pool and the ruins of a fort two centuries old. You can order breakfast on this terrace.

Glass-enclosed elevators built outside on the hotel offer a panoramic view as you're whisked to your room. The bedrooms have much space, immaculate baths with big towels, air conditioning that really works, and traditional furnishings, plus breeze-cooled private balconies, and an ice machine on each floor.

In winter, singles range in price from $135 to $230 daily, the difference based on the view. Doubles go from $140 to $180 daily. For breakfast and dinner, add another $35 per person daily. *In summer, the single tariff ranges from $85 to $105 daily; the twin, from $90 to $110.* Service and tax are added to all bills.

The Willemstad is an elegant, air-conditioned dining room offering meals from $25. Wednesday is barbecue night. To the left as you enter the hotel is a well-stocked shopping complex, including a branch of Spritzer & Fuhrmann.

Las Palmas Hotel and Vacation Village, P.O. Box 2179, Piscadera Bay, Willemstad (tel. 2-5200), across from the Curaçao Concorde, is ideal for those who seek a moderately priced Caribbean resort, one of the stated goals of this guide.

Not only do you get the most for your money here, you're able to enjoy a more intangible quality, imaginative good taste. The atmosphere is casual and convivial. The location is only two miles from Willemstad, on a breezy hillside location a few hundred yards from the sea and its own little beach with water sports. The cacti that used to stud the hillside have now given way to a botanical garden, a remarkable achievement considering how dry Curaçao is.

Accommodations are in a three-story, 100-room main building, or else in one of the little casitas with Samoan-style roofs sprinkled through the hillside gardens. Think of a casita as your own self-contained summer house, the kind you might have at a beach resort. The main building has attractive public rooms off the garden-style entry lounge. At its core is a courtyard, with a lily pond, bamboo, and flowering vines. Here you can start your day with a breakfast, later enjoying drinks and entertainment in the evening. Perhaps a family steel band will be brought in, or a fire-eating limbo dancer. Sometimes the guests themselves are asked to dance under the limbo pole, with prizes awarded to the winner—that is, the person who gets the most applause. Native-style buffet dinners are often hauled out of the kitchen.

Rooms in the main building have contemporary styling with bold colors, and each contains a private bath with air conditioning. A single rents for $85 daily in high season, the tariff going up to $103 in a twin-bedded room. For breakfast and dinner on the MAP, expect to pay from $22 per person in addition to the rates quoted. An island tax and a service charge of 10% are tacked on. *Rates for the off-season are about $69 daily in a single, going up to about $78 in a twin-bedded room.*

The casitas, 94 in all, can accommodate four persons and possibly six (although that would be crowded). Each villa has two well-furnished bedrooms, a living room for relaxation and entertaining, a kitchenette, and a porch where you can set up breakfast which you prepared yourself, after shopping at the grocery mini-market on the grounds. Even in the expensive winter months, these casitas cost $150 daily, *that rate dropping to about $119 in summer,* plus service and tax. The furnishings are in a rustic style, resting under beamed ceilings. The sliding doors enlarge the living room which can spill out onto the terrace.

A full equipped beach with a snackbar is less than 800 yards away from the entrance to the hotel. On the grounds is a tennis court lit for night games. Slot machines and croupiers are found inside the Las Palmas, although you can also go to the big casino at the Curaçao Concorde just across the way.

Other sporting facilites include two swimming pools—one Olympic size for adults, plus a tiny wading pool for children. In King Arthur's pub and restaurant, you can order Amstel beer, made with desalinated water, and good food, including some Antillean dishes. Every night there's dinner music, except on Saturday when a Caribbean night with a folklore show is presented.

Curaçao Plaza Hotel and Casino, Plaza Piar (tel. 1-2500), stands guard over the Punda side of St. Anna's Bay, as it's nestled in the ramparts of an 18th-century water fort on the eastern tip of the entrance to the harbor. It is in fact one of the harbor's two "lighthouses." Its designer saw fit to leave its ramparts intact, and now they serve as a promenade for guests. Of course, the hotel has to carry marine collision insurance, the only hostelry in the Caribbean with that distinction.

The original part of the hotel followed the style of the arcaded fort. However, now there is a tower of rooms stacked 15 stories high. In winter, singles range in price from $85 to $109 daily, with doubles going for $95 to $120. *From mid-April until mid-December, the charge is lowered to anywhere from $65 to $89 daily in a single, from $75 to $99 in a double.* For breakfast and dinner, add another $30 per person daily to the rates quoted. Each of the 245 bedrooms—your own crow's nest—is traditionally furnished with a private bath and phone.

The pool is placed inches away from the parapet of the fort. There's also a poolside bar and suntanning area, with a lobby-level bar. Crowning the tower is a rooftop dining room that offers the most spectacular sunset views over Willemstad. It's the Penthouse Cocktail Lounge and Gourmet Room, open from 7 to 11:30 p.m., and featuring not only dining but dancing. In the Waterfort Grill you can order New York–type sirloin steaks either at lunch or dinner. The Kini-Kini bar is an intimate oasis. The Waterfront offers buffet breakfasts and luncheons, and the Terrace Bar, with its view of the sea and the supertankers passing within a few feet, serves light lunches daily. The hotel also stages special events, including Caribbean nights and barbecue fiestas with dancing to local bands. It also has one of the most popular casinos on the island.

Holiday Beach Hotel & Casino, 31 Pater Eeuwensweg, P.O. Box 2178, Willemstad (tel. 2-5400), built about half a mile from the capital, opened in 1968, with 200 modern air-conditioned bedrooms. It has all the facilities of a complete resort hotel, erected along a sandy beach dotted with palm trees and a grassy land projection. The main part of the complex houses the Casino Royale and the principal dining spot, the Antillean Room. The recently refurbished lobby has a double-banked stairway, leading up to an even more luxuriously furnished second-floor lobby, which vaguely resembles an old European hotel.

The sleeping quarters are in two four-story wings, centering around a U-shaped garden with a large freshwater swimming pool. In size and amenities the bedrooms are well furnished, with two double beds in each unit, opening onto private balconies overlooking the water. Wall-to-wall carpeting, big tile baths, and lots of towels are just part of the comforts, along with phones and TV. In winter, singles cost from $90 to $100 and doubles go from $100 to $109. *In summer, singles cost $71 to $78; doubles, from $82 to $89. The summer rates include a full American breakfast.* Room rates are subject to service charge, tax, and a $3 daily energy surcharge per room.

In the main building are a drugstore and several unisex boutiques, plus the Cocolishi (shell) lounge with its daily happy hours. A nightclub in the upper lobby offers live entertainment. The water-sports center on the beach offers snorkeling, scuba, deep-sea fishing, waterskiing, windsurfing, and parasailing. Two asphalt tennis courts are on the premises.

Princess Beach Hotel, Martin Luther King Boulevard (tel. 61-4944), is a two-story, lanai-style waterfront resort, a short drive from the heart of the city, which is reached by frequent shuttle service. From a bird's-eye point of view, it's a huge chunk of sea-bordering property with its own docks for deep-sea fishing. All major water sports are featured, and a nine-hole golf course is nearby. On the grounds is a professional tennis court.

A large, elevated saltwater swimming pool is centered between the building blocks housing 140 units, all air-conditioned with private baths and either balconies or patios. The furnishings are in a modified tropical style, with low, white casual chairs and good, comfortable beds. Most of the rooms look out over the beach and contain verandas or loggias attractively shielded by tropical plants. *In the off-season, singles range in price from $50 to $63 daily; doubles, from $60 to $75.* In winter, rates go up to $65 to $71 daily in a single, from $80 to $87 in a double. For breakfast and dinner, add another $28 per person daily to the tariffs quoted.

The best spot is the terrace where you can sun and drink. The pool bar is one of the most popular hangouts in Curaçao at happy hour. There is also a casino which is the most modern on the island, filled with plants and arched windows. The main building, housing the casino, supper club, cabaret, and other places, is a reconstruction, following a fire that gutted the structure in the early 1980s.

Avila Beach Hotel, 130–134 Penstraat, P.O. Box 791 (tel. 1-4377), is a beautifully restored 200-year-old mansion standing on the shore road leading eastward out of the city from the shopping center. It is the only beachfront hotel in Willemstad, set on its own small but lovely private beach. The mansion was built by the English governor of Curaçao during the occupation of the island by the British at the time of the Napoleonic Wars. Subsequent governors, including Dutch ones, have used the place as a retreat.

Converted into a hotel in 1949, the mansion, now run by F. N. Moller, has added a modern bedroom wing opening toward the sea. It also has an open-air restaurant, Belle Terrace, with split-level dining and a bar area overlooking the beach (see my dining recommendations, below).

While the Dutch architecture and colonial style have been preserved on the exterior, the interior of the mansion has been totally rebuilt with a spacious lobby, conference room, offices, and guest rooms. The 45 guest rooms and two suites are all air-conditioned and furnished with Scandinavian modern pieces. In all, it's a comfortable, family-styled hotel. In winter, singles range from $59 to $82 daily; twins, from $65 to $88. *Off-season, singles cost $55 to $75; twins, $58 to $78.* MAP is an additional $28 per person.

The hotel stands next door to the Octagon Museum, where Bolívar the Liberator used to visit his sisters.

Trupial Inn, 5 Davelaarweg (tel. 7-8200), is named for a local bird, the trupial, one of which is caged near the pleasantly modern reception desk of this government-built hotel. The 74 accommodations are ringed abound a blacktop-covered courtyard. They are comfortable and well furnished, but there isn't much of a view from any of the windows. Each unit contains a private bath and a phone. Nine of the accommodations have kitchenettes, which can be stocked from a nearby supermarket. Year round, single rooms cost $45; doubles, $48; triples, $50; and quads, $60.

The inn has a sauna, tennis courts, and a swimming pool spanned by a Chinese-style bridge. Nighttime dancing is sometimes offered around the pool. Near the reception desk is a spacious breakfast and dining room, with big windows and a white tile floor.

Coral Cliff Resort and Beach Club, Santa Marta Bay, P.O. Box 3782 (tel. 4-1610), is *the* remote hotel of Curaçao. Set on a peninsula between the open sea and a harbor, its social center offers a wide covered terrace with a sweeping view of the ocean. The 35 accommodations are within a handful of red-roofed cement bungalows separated from the ocean only by a buffer of trees. Each unit has a covered arcade or veranda, a kitchenette, air conditioning, a phone, and a view of the water.

Single or double rooms, with breakfast included, cost $85 year round. Suites suitable for up to four persons go for $150. There's a nominal charge for children aged 4 to 12 who stay with their parents, and no charge for children under 4. Service and taxes are extra.

The resort's dining room adjoins a bar area whose surfaces are crafted from different kinds of polished hardwoods. Fixed-price lunches and dinners cost $15 and $20, respectively. Guests enjoy snorkeling, scuba-diving, sailing, and windsurfing on the 600-foot private beach, along with the relaxing feeling of being far removed from civilization. It takes about 30 minutes to drive from here to the capital.

Hotel Holland, 524 F. D. Rooseveltweg (tel. 8-1120), is a few minutes' drive from the airport and contains a bar that is a popular gathering place. For a few brief minutes of every day, you can see airplanes landing from your perch at the edge of the poolside terrace, where well-prepared meals are served during good weather (see my dining recommendation). This property is the domain of ex-navy frogman Hans Vrolijk and his wife, Henne. Hans still retains his interest in scuba, arranging dive packages for his guests. Assisted by his teenage daughter, Patricia, he also directs the service at his Dutch-style restaurant.

The 20 accommodations have baths, air conditioning, and balconies. Singles rent throughout the year for $36, doubles for $45, and triples for $55. Guests who remain for more than a week receive a free breakfast daily, as well as a slight discount on the room price.

San Marco, 7 Columbusstraat (tel. 1-2988), usually fills up with Venezuelans in Willemstad on a shopping jaunt from Caracas. It's a very basic hotel, painted a pale Mediterranean blue, its modestly furnished bedrooms, reached by an elevator, lying above an Italian restaurant (see my dining suggestions). Considerably modernized, it offers 60 air-conditioned bedrooms which have private baths of some sort. Singles range from $35 daily all year; doubles go from $40; and triples are rented from $55.

CURAÇAO COOKERY: The basic cuisine is Dutch, but there are many specialty items, particularly Latin American and Indonesian. The cuisine strikes many visitors as heavy for the tropics, and you may want to have a light lunch, ordering the more filling concoctions such as rijsttafel in the evening.

Erwtensoep, the well-known Dutch pea soup, is a popular dish, as is keshi yena, Edam cheese stuffed with meat, then baked. Funchi, a Caribbean tortilla, accompanies many local dishes. Sopito, fish soup often made with coconut water, is an especially good local dish, and conch is featured in curries and many other dishes.

Curaçao, the liqueur that made the island famous, is made from oranges.

The settings for dining are often dramatic, either in restored forts or haciendas, often al fresco.

De Taveerne, Landhuis Groot Develaar (tel. 7-0669), is a country manor house in a residential section. A red brick octagonal cupola rises over the roof of the building, and inside where the cows used to be sheltered Holland-born Jerry Wielinga has created a charming tavern atmosphere with an antique decor. He and his wife, Anna, scoured Curaçao's old homes, finding funishings for their charming restaurant, bar, and wine cellar. The setting is enhanced by burnished copper, white stucco walls, dark woods, and terracotta tiles.

The chef has created a number of specialties, including a steak à escargots. To begin your meal, perhaps he'll have smoked Dutch eel or lobster soup. He also has a winning way with snails bourguignonne.

Other recommendable dishes include shrimp thermidor and sole meunière. The chateaubriand Stroganoff for two persons is yet another specialty. A complete meal will set you back anywhere from $28 to $35. The restaurant is open for lunch from noon to 3 p.m. and for dinner from 7 to 11 p.m. daily except Sunday. You should definitely make a reservation.

Fort Nassau, near Point Juliana (tel. 1-3450), is a restored restuarant and bar built in the ruins of a formidably buttressed fort dating from 1792. From its Battery Terrace a 360-degree panorama unfolds of the sea, the harbor, and Willemstad, just a five-minute drive away. You'll even see the Shell refinery. A signal tower on the cliff sends out beacons to approaching ships.

The inn has retained an 18th-century decor. Before you approach the restaurant, you can enjoy an apéritif in a fashionably decorated bar. Many come up here just to have a drink and watch the sunset. On cruise-ship days, the place overflows.

The restaurant serves both lunch and dinner. Smoked salmon with horseradish leads off the list of appetizers, or you may prefer to begin with shrimp soup. From the grill, you can order a 16-ounce T-bone steak, or perhaps you may want to try one of the chef's specialties such as veal with fruit sauce. A limited selection of international desserts such as coffee mousse tops a most recommendable repast. You'll spend from $18 to $28. You can dress casually and enjoy your meal in air-conditioned comfort. Lunch is served from noon to 2 p.m. except on weekends. Dinner is nightly from 6:30 to 11 p.m. There's a cozy disco called Infinity in the lower depths, open from 9 p.m. to 2 a.m. daily.

La Bistroëlle, Astroidenweg/Schottegatweg in the Promenade Shopping Center (tel. 7-6929), is an elegant, family-run restaurant with an international cuisine and a good selection of wines, all served in a cozy, atmospheric place. The decor is one of high-backed red velvet chairs, brick accents, stucco, darkened beams, and rustic chandeliers, like a French country inn. The location is in a residential area east of the harbor, a short drive from the center of Willemstad.

The continental cuisine is largely French, beginning with such selections as snails in herb garlic butter. You might prefer instead mussels in a light whisky sauce. A rich fish soup is served and a steaming French onion soup. Some of the chef's specialties include octopus in a vinaigrette sauce, sole Picasso, lobster thermidor, and chicken saltimbocca. For dessert, you might prefer the crêpes suzette flavored with Curaçao, for two persons. A complete meal will run from 70 NAf ($39.90). The place is open daily from noon to 2 p.m. and 7 to 11 p.m.

Rijsttafel Restaurant Indonesia, 13 Mercuriusstraat in Cerrito (tel. 7-0917), is the best place to go on the island to sample the Indonesian rijsttafel, the traditional rice table with all the zesty side dishes. You're allowed to season your plate with peppers rated hot, very hot, and palate-melting. You must ask a taxi to take you to this villa in the suburbs. The site is near Salinja. Your host is Johan Dreijerink. The Holland Club bar is only for diners and their guests, who can visit daily from noon to 2 p.m. and from 6 to 9:30 p.m.

At lunchtime, the selection of dishes is more modest, but for dinner, Japanese cooks prepare the specialty of the house, a rijsttafel consisting of 16, 20, or 25 dishes. Warming trays are placed on your table and the service is buffet style. It's best to go to this place with a party so that all of you can share in the fun and feast. A dinner for two will cost between $25 and $40. Before going you should call to make a reservation.

Bistro Le Clochard, on the Otrabanda side of the pontoon bridge (tel. 2-5666), has been snugly fitted into the grim ramparts of Fort Rif at the gateway to the harbor. Its entrance is marked with a brown canopy, which leads into a series of rooms, each built under the stucco vaulting of the old Dutch fort. Only one table has a view of the water, since the only window is the rectangular opening that was formerly used to receive munitions from the adjacent stone quay. Overall, the colors are warm, reflecting copper utensils and exposed brick. A simulated grape arbor was installed above the bar of the pub area, Le Brick, where a piano sometimes provides live music.

The restaurant is open daily except Saturday at lunch and all day Sunday. The place is well run, and the owners seem to anticipate the needs of their patrons. Cuisine is basically French, including a few dishes from the Alps such as raclette and two kinds of fondue. Other specialties are roast hare flambéed in Calvados with a cream sauce, medallions of venison with a wild game sauce, guinea fowl with paprika, ham, garlic, and white wine, and wild boar chops in a mushroom cream sauce. A full dinner will cost from $30. Lunches are less expensive.

Wine Cellar, Ooststraat/Concordiastraat (tel. 1-2178), opposite the cathedral, is the domain of Nico Cornelisse, a *chevalier du tastevin,* who has one of the most extensive wine cartes on the island. He welcomes you to air-conditioned comfort in his Victoriana dining room, as you slowly make your wine selection for the evening. Food isn't ignored either. He has good meat dishes, well prepared, and a limited selection of seafood. Count on spending from $18 for a meal, plus the cost of your wine. There are only eight tables, so reservations are essential. Hours are noon to 2 p.m. and 6 p.m. till "whenever."

Le Recif (tel. 2-3824) is lodged under the arches of Fort Rif, near the shuttlebus stops for the Otrabanda hotels and the pontoon bridge. This place used to be a prison, but now it's one of the best places in town for Caribbean seafood. It's interior is festooned with fishnets and nautical implements hanging just below the vaulted ceilings. A terrace in front extends the darkly lit interior out into the sunshine. The owner of Le Recif is Don Llewellyn, a former police officer, who knows how to control any unruly member of his clientele.

After 11 p.m. the establishment becomes a disco, although visitors should be warned that there are occasional strip shows and soft-porn videos in a side room late at night. In the disco, beer costs 3.50 NAf ($2).

Full meals range from 60 NAf ($34.20) and might include shrimp creole, Curaçao fish stew, red snapper Cordon Bleu, conch soup, snails, curried crab, lobster thermidor, and turtle soup (when available). The ingredients for the seafood come either from neighboring waters, from Haiti, or from the Dominican Republic. Le Recif is open from noon to 2 p.m. and 7 p.m. to 3 a.m. seven days a week.

Belle Terrace, Avila Beach Hotel, 130–134 Penstraat (tel. 1-4377), is an open-air restaurant in a 200-year-old mansion on the beachfront of Willemstad. In a relaxed and informal atmosphere, it offers split-level dining. The Schooner Bar, where you can enjoy a rum punch, is shaped like a weather-beaten ship's prow looking out to sea, with a thatch roof projecting from its mast.

The restaurant, sheltered by an arbor of flamboyant branches, features Scandinavian and local cuisine with such special dishes as pickled herring, barracuda, and a Danish lunch platter. Local dishes, such as sopito (fish soup with coconut flavor) and keshi jena (Edam cheese stuffed with chicken, olives, raisins, and sweet peppers), are on the menu for both lunch and dinner. A special three-course meal is served every night except Saturday, in addition to a full à la carte menu.

On Saturday night the chef has a beef tenderloin barbecue and a help-yourself salad bar. Fish is always fresh at Belle Terrace, and the chef prepares the catch of the day to perfection: grilled, poached, meunière, or almondine. Desserts include Danish pastry and cakes, as well as a cocoa sherbet served in a coconut shell. Expect to spend $8 to $18 for lunch, $20 to $28 for dinner. The special three-course dinner costs $22.

Restaurant Larousse, 5 Penstraat (tel. 5-5418), built in 1742, is a typical little stone and plaster house with ornate edging on its roof. It was recently acquired by Holland-born Nico Cornelisse, who installed a collection of 19th-century artifacts under the original beamed ceiling and extended the dining area onto an alcove-style second floor. Amid Colombian-made copper and iron chandeliers, Victorian etched-globe lighting, and Oriental rugs, visitors are served on flowered china the foods they have chosen from well-prepared specialties.

These include cheese fondue for two persons, red snapper Curaçao style, a soup made from fresh cherry tomatoes, beef Stroganoff, and several kinds of steaks. A dessert specialty is Dutch egg liqueur and fresh whipped cream laced with vanilla or chocolate fondue according to an old Swiss recipe. Full meals range from 85 NAf ($48.45). The establishment is open only for dinner.

Fort Waakzaamheid Tavern, Seru di Domi, Otrabanda (tel. 2-3633), was the old fort that Captain Bligh of *Bounty* fame captured in 1804. He laid seige to Willemstad for almost a month. In the fort a stone-and-hardwood tavern and restaurant have been installed, opening onto a view of the Otrabanda and the harbor entrance. The atmosphere is that of a country tavern.

At lunch you can order from a simple menu that might include half a roast chicken or grilled pork chops. On the dinner menu, the fish soup will get you going, and you can follow with curried veal, wienerschnitzel, or garlic shrimp. Lobster is the most expensive item on the menu, and you may settle instead for Curaçao snapper. Each day a fresh fried fish is offered, with a salad. Meals run from $12 to $20. The fort is open daily except Tuesday from 7 to 11 p.m. The bar remains open until 1 a.m. (even later on weekends).

Restaurant San Marco, Columbusstraat (tel. 1-2988), just around the corner from the synagogue, offers a good Italian cuisine right in the heart of the shopping district. On the second floor of a previously recommended hotel, the restaurant serves food in a simply decorated, air-conditioned dining room. It's patronized mainly by those who like its large portions, tasty fare, and low prices.

Hors d'oeuvres San Marco might begin your repast, followed by minestrone Milanese style. Spaghetti is prepared in several ways here, including in the "Mafioso" style (that is, with olives and anchovies). Try also the lasagne Sorrentina.

I'm fond of the shrimps in garlic with parsley and a wine sauce, and of any number of scaloppine dishes. Caramel custard tops off the meal, which will probably cost from $12 to $20. The restaurant is open every day.

Rodeo Ranch Steakhouse, on Van Staverenweg in the suburban section of Cas Cora (tel. 7-0501), is a lot of fun. Stanley Gibbs and his Netherlands-born wife, Kathe, have created a touch of the Old West. There's a replica of a covered wagon set over the entrance, and an interior decor of rough-sawn planking, dark woods, and antique wagon wheels. So many guests of this popular place have attached their business cards to a bulletin board near the kitchen that it reads like a lesson in international geography. A "sheriff" (usually Stanley) greets visitors at the door in an outfit that includes a ten-gallon hat and a silver star.

No one will mind if you just stop off for a drink at the dimly lit bar, but if you want one of the most copious dinners in town, you'll be presented with a cowhide-covered menu by a cowgirl/waitress. To the sounds of country and western music, you'll enjoy the specialties of steak, soup from the kettle, a chuckwagon choice of potato specials, roast prime rib, and seafood. All steaks are U.S. prime beef, and are accompanied by as many visits as you want to make to the soup and salad bar. Don't dress up to go here. Casual is the keynote.

You'll spend $25 for a full meal, which you can enjoy in air-conditioned comfort. Hot hors d'oeuvres are served at the happy hour between 5 and 7 p.m. Lunch is offered daily from noon to 2 p.m., with the dinner bell ringing between 6 and 11 p.m. The bar remains open till "whenever."

Bellevue Restaurant, Baai Macolaweg, Parera (tel. 5-4291), is in an edifice built in 1942 by the Americans as headquarters for the naval base protecting the island's oil refineries. In 1948 it was purchased by the Den Dulk family, whose culinary skills quickly made it one of the leading restaurants on the island. A trio of imitation palm trees decks the sunny interior, which sometimes hosts some of the biggest landowners on the island. It's run by Martin and Curaçao-born Johanna, with their sons, Walter and Martin Jr. (winner of an island-wide contest to design the Curaçao national flag). They adhere strictly to local culinary lore in the preparation of their specialties.

Your meal could begin with a bandera. Loaded with cream, "secret ingredients," and Curaçao rum, it is the first blue drink many visitors have ever tried, and its smooth, not-too-sweet flavor is delicious. This could be followed with oyster soup, turtle soup, keshi yena, cactus soup, iguana soup, stewed goat meat, a tasty okra soup, sauerkraut stew, papaya stew, shark meat, turtle steak, stewed cucumbers, or Edam cheese stuffed with meat and spices. Patrons looking for a cross-sampling of the local dishes might try the funchi table, which includes five local viands on one savory platter. The restaurant is open seven days a week, from noon to 2:30 p.m. and 7 to 11 p.m. Full meals range upward in price from around 55 NAf ($31.35).

Pisces Seafood, 476 Caracasbaaiweg (tel. 7-2181). This West Indian restaurant may be difficult to find, set as it is on a flat industrial coastline near a marina and an oil refinery, about 20 minutes from the capital. There's been a restaurant here since the 1930s, when sailors and workers from the nearby Shell plant came for home-cooked meals. Today the simple frame building offers seating near the rough-hewn bar or in a breeze-swept inner room whose unglazed, open windows have hinged shutters to seal them off after closing.

Open from noon to midnight daily except Tuesday, the place serves combinations of seafood that depend on the catch of the local fishermen. Main courses, served with rice, vegetables, and plantains, might include sopi, "seacat" (squid), mula (similar to kingfish), shark meat, red snapper, or any of these served, if you wish, in copious quantities for two or more persons in the Pisces platter. Shrimp and conch are each prepared three different ways: with garlic, with curry, or creole style. Average meals cost 35 NAf ($19.95).

Golden Star, 2 Socratesstraat (tel. 5-4795), is the best place to go on the island for "criollo" or local food. Inland from the coast road, leading southeast from St. Anna Bay, the restaurant is very simple, evoking a roadside diner. But it has a large menu of native dishes that are very tasty.

Such Antillean dishes are featured as carco stoba or conch stew and bestia chiki (goat-meat stew). Try also bakijauw (salted cod) and concomber stoba (stewed meat and marble-size spiny cucumbers).

Other specialties include criollo shrimps (kiwa) and soppi carni. Everything is served with a side order of funchi, the cornmeal staple. Meals cost from 30 NAf ($17.10). The place is very friendly, and has a large local following with an occasional tourist dropping in. It's open daily from 11 a.m. till 11 p.m. The location is at the corner of Dr. Hugenholtzweg and Dr. Maalweg.

Kokkeltje, Hotel Holland, 524 F. D. Rooseveltweg (tel. 8-1120), is directed by Hans Vrolijk, an ex-frogman with the Dutch navy. This warmly decorated hideaway is especially popular around happy hour after most people finish daily work. You'll find the place on the scrub-bordered road leading to the airport, a few minutes away from the landing strips. If you want to follow your drinks with dinner, full meals cost from 55 NAf ($31.35) and include such specialties as nasi goreng, fresh fish in season, Dutch-style steak, wienerschnitzel, Caribbean-style chicken, and split-pea soup. All dishes are accompanied by fresh vegetables and Dutch-style potatoes. Patrons enjoy their meals around the pool outside or in a paneled and intimately lit room near the bar.

Playa Forti, in the Westpunt area (tel. 4-0273), is a good address to know if you're touring the island. The restaurant is built on the foundation of a fortress dating from Bonaparte's day. Not only do you get good local food here, but one of the most spectacular sea views on the island.

International dishes are presented, but it would be wiser to order some of the Antillean specialties, such as succulent goat stew which tastes a bit like veal. It's called cabrito. Try also keshi yena, a tasty mixture of beef and chicken, which has been pickled and cooked with tomatoes and onions, then wrapped in Edam cheese. Ayaca is a combination of chicken and beef, with olives, raisins, nuts, and spices wrapped in a soft corndough tortilla (it's packed and cooked in banana leaves). The fish soup makes a zesty opening. It's called sopi di plata. Or try the fried red snapper Curaçao style—that is, fried a golden brown, then covered in a sauce of tomatoes, onions, and green peppers. It's served with fried plantains and funchi, the local cornmeal preparation. Expect to pay from 35 NAf ($19.95) for a complete meal.

The waters of Westpunt are perfect for snorkeling and scuba-diving if you want to bring your own equipment. In the restaurant food is served from 10 a.m. to 6:30 p.m. except Monday. If you're touring, it's also possible to drop in for drinks in the afternoon.

EXPLORING CURAÇAO: Most cruise-ship passengers see only Willemstad—or, more accurately, the shops—but you may want to get out into the cunucu or countryside, exploring the towering cacti and rolling hills topped by landhuizen or plantation houses built more than three centuries ago. The 38-mile-long island is seen in a day or so.

Willemstad

In Willemstad the Dutch found a vast natural harbor, a perfect hideaway along the Spanish Main. Not only is Willemstad the capital of Curaçao, it is also the seat of government for the Netherlands Antilles.

The city grew up on both sides of the canal. Today it is divided into the **Punda** and the **Otrabanda,** the latter literally meaning "the other side." Both sections are connected by the **Queen Emma Pontoon Bridge,** a pedestrian walkway.

Originally, ferryboats linked the two sections of town, since by the mid-19th century Willemstad had spread to both sides of St. Anna Harbor. In 1887 the American consul, Leonard B. Smith, convinced the city fathers that a bridge was a good idea. One year later the swinging pontoon bridge across the harbor opened, and the tolls made Smith an extremely wealthy man. Powered by a diesel engine, it swings open many times every day to let ships from all over the globe pass in and out of the harbor.

The view from the bridge is of the old gabled houses in harmonized pastel shades such as lilac and ultramarine. The bright pastel colors, according to legend, are a holdover from the time when one of the island's early governors is said to have had eye trouble and flat white gave him headaches.

The colonial-style architecture, reflecting the Dutch influence, gives the town a "storybook" look, as is often said. Built three or four stories high, the houses are crowned by steep gables and roofed with orange Spanish tiles. Hemmed in by the sea, a tiny canal, and an inlet, the streets are narrow, and they're crosshatched by still narrower alleyways. Except for the pastel colors, Willemstad may remind you of old Amsterdam. It has one of the most intriguing townscapes in the Caribbean.

Replacing the pontoon bridge, **Queen Juliana Bridge** opened to vehicular traffic in 1973. Spanning the harbor, it rises 195 feet, the highest bridge in the Caribbean and one of the tallest in the world.

The **Waterfront** originally guarded the mouth of the canal on the eastern or Punda side. Now it's been incorporated into the Curaçao Plaza Hotel.

The task of standing guard has been taken over by **Fort Amsterdam,** site of the Governor's Palace and the 1769 Dutch Reformed Church. The church still has a British cannon ball embedded in it. The arches leading to the fort were tunneled under the official residence of the governor.

A corner of the fort stands at the intersection of Breedestraat and Handelskade, the starting point for a plunge into the island's major shopping district.

A few minutes' walk from the pontoon bridge, at the north end of Handelskade, is the **Floating Market,** where scores of schooners tie up alongside the canal, a few yards from the main shopping section. Docked boats arrive from Venezuela and Colombia, as well as other West Indian islands, to sell tropical fruits and vegetables, a little bit of everything in fact. The modern market under its vast cement cap has not replaced this unique shopping expedition which is fun to watch.

Between the I. H. (Sha) Capriles Kade and Fort Amsterdam stands the **Mikve Israel Emanuel Synagogue,** at the corner of Columbusstraat and Kerkstraat. Consecrated on the eve of the Passover in 1732, it antedates the first

U.S. synagogue in Newport, Rhode Island, by 31 years. It houses the oldest Jewish congregation in the New World, dating from 1651. One of the oldest synagogue buildings in the western hemisphere, it is a fine example of Dutch colonial architecture, covering about a square block in the heart of Willemstad.

It was built around a Spanish-style walled courtyard, with four large portals. Sand covers the sanctuary floor following a Portuguese Sephardic custom, representing the desert where Israelis camped when the Jews passed from slavery to freedom. Early settlers, led by Samuel Coheno, were Sephardic refugees from a Portuguese pogrom. Four brass chandeliers hang from the arched ceiling.

The theba (pulpit) is in the center, and the congregation surrounds it. Highlight of the east wall is the Holy Ark, rising 17 feet, and a raised banca, canopied in mahogany, is on the north wall. The synagogue has services every Friday at 6:30 p.m. and Saturday at 10 a.m.; as well as similar holiday service times. Visitors are welcome to all services, with appropriate dress required.

Adjacent to the synagogue courtyard is the **Curaçao Jewish Museum,** in a 200-year-old building which was once the rabbi's house (later it was a Chinese laundry). The courtyard revealed a 300-year-old mikvah, a bath used for prenuptial purification rituals. Displayed are utensils for kosher butchering, scrolls, styli, and various religious articles, which are still used by the congregation for holidays and life cycle events. During the week, the synagogue and museum are open from 9 to 11:45 a.m. and 2:30 to 5 p.m. There is a $1 entrance fee to the museum, and a gift shop is in the synagogue office.

A statue of Pedro Luís Brion dominates the square known as **Brionplein** right at the Otrabanda end of the pontoon bridge. Born in Curaçao in 1782, he became the island's favorite son and best known war hero. Under Simón Bolívar, he was an admiral of the fleet and fought for the independence of Venezuela and Colombia.

West of Willemstad

The **Curaçao Museum** on Van Leeuwenhoekstraat can be walked to from the pontoon bridge. Built in 1823 as a Seamen's Hospital, it has been carefully restored as a fine example of Dutch architecture. Furnished with paintings, objets d'art, and antiques, it re-creates a colonial atmosphere. A novelty is the polka-dot kitchen. The museum contains some relics of the Caiquetio Indians, the early settlers discovered by Vespucci, who claimed they were seven feet tall. You'll also see the cockpit of the Fokker F-XVIII trimotor which made the first commercial crossing of the southern Atlantic from the Netherlands to Curaçao in 1934. In the gardens are specimens of the island's trees and plants. Hours are 10 a.m. to noon and 2 to 5 p.m. daily except Sunday when they are open nonstop from 10 a.m. to 4 p.m. Admission is 2 NAf ($1.14).

Curaçao Seaquarium, Bapor Kibra (Sunken Ship; tel. 1-6666), has a worthwhile collection of local sea life protected behind thick sheets of glass—jewfish, live sponges, surgeon fish, moray eels, and brilliantly colored French angelfish among them. You reach this section by walking over a bridge that traverses a canal filled with sharks. The Seaquarium complex is in a collection of low-lying, beehive-shaped buildings erected on a point off which, in 1903, a large ship broke up on the rocks and sank. There is an informal al fresco restaurant here. The establishment is open daily from 10 a.m. to 6 p.m. Admission is 12 NAf ($6.84). It's a few minutes' walk along the rocky coast from the Princess Beach Hotel.

A new **underwater park,** opened in 1983, stretches to the eastern tip of the island and features 12½ miles of untouched coral reefs. Access is from the Princess Beach Hotel, less than a ten-minute drive from the city. For information on snorkeling, scuba-diving, and trips in a glass-bottomed boat to view the park, see "The Sporting Life," below.

Traveling northwest along the road, you reach the tip of the island. The **Landhuis Jan Kock,** on the road to Westpunt, is open to the public. Built in 1650, it is probably the oldest building on the island. The owner once stood on its adobe porch to watch slaves gather salt from huge flat fields flooded with sea water left to evaporate in the sun. The house, said to be haunted, was restored as a museum by the late Dr. Jan Diemont in 1960. Inside are many pieces from the 18th and early 19th centuries, including a hurdy-gurdy machine from this century. As it may not be open at the time of your visit, you should check in advance by phoning 8-8088.

Out toward the western tip of Curaçao, a high wire fence surrounds the entrance to the 4500-acre **Christoffel National Park,** about a 45-minute drive from the capital. A macadam road gives way to dirt, surrounded on all sides by abundant cactus and in the higher regions by rare orchids. Rising from flat, arid countryside, 1320-foot-high Mount Christoffel is the highest point in the Netherlands Antilles. Donkeys, wild goats, iguanas, the Curaçao deer, and many species of birds thrive in this preserve, and there are some Arawak Indian paintings on a coral cliff near the two caves (bring a flashlight). Piedra di Monton is nothing more than a rockheap accumulated by African slaves who worked on the former plantations. A folk legend passed down through the generations said that any worker would be able to climb to the top of the rockpile, jump off, and fly back home across the Atlantic. If, however, the slave had at any time in his life tasted a grain of salt, the magic would not work and he would crash to his death below. The park has 35 miles of one-way driving trails, with lots of flora and fauna along the way. The shortest trail is about 10 miles long, and because of the rough terrain, takes about 40 minutes to drive through. A walking trail is available also. It will take you to the top of Mount Christoffel in about 1½ hours. (Come early in the morning when it isn't so hot.) The park is open from 8 a.m. to 3 p.m. The last visitor is allowed in at 2 p.m. Admission is 2 NAf ($1.14) for adults, 1 NAf (57¢) for children. During the rainy season, October to January, the roads in the park are sometimes inaccessible. Make a phone call in advance to learn if the park is open to the public (tel. 4-0363). Also en route to Westpunt, you'll come across a dramatic seaside cavern known as **Boca Tabla,** one of many such grottos on this rugged, uninhabited north coast.

Playa Forti is a 45-minute ride from Punda in Willemstad. A stark region, it is characterized by soaring hills and towering cacti, along with 200-year-old Dutch land houses, the former mansions that housed the slaveowner plantation heads. For a dining suggestion, see the recommendation of the Playa Forti Restaurant.

North and East of Willemstad

Just northeast of the capital, **Fort Nassau** was completed in 1797 and christened by the Dutch as Fort Republic. It was built high on a hill, overlooking the harbor entrance to the south and St. Anna Bay to the north. It was fortified as a second line of defense in case Waterfort gave way. When the British invaded in 1807, they renamed it Fort George in honor of their own king. Later, when the Dutch regained control, they renamed it Orange Nassau in honor of the Dutch royal family. Today diners have replaced soldiers (see my restaurant recommendations).

Along the coast to the southeast of the town, the oddly shaped **Octagon House** on Penstraat was where the liberator, Bolívar, used to visit his two sisters during the wars for Venezuelan independence. Now a museum, it has been restored and furnished with antiques. It also contains some of the liberator's memorabilia. Hours are 8 a.m. to noon and 2 to 6 p.m., Monday through Saturday. No admission is charged.

From the house you can head north, going along the eastern side of the water, to the intersection of Rijkseenheid Boulevard, and Fokkerweg. There you'll see the **Autonomy Monument,** a vibrant 20th-century sculpture representing the Dutch islands as birds freed from their nest.

In the area, the **Amstel Brewery** allows visitors to tour its plant where Curaçao beer is brewed from desalinated seawater. Hours are Tuesday from 10 a.m. to noon (telephone 1-2944 for more information).

In addition, the **Curaçao Liqueur Distillery** offers free tours and tastes at Chobolobo, the 17th-century landhuis where the famous liqueur is made. Tours are Monday through Friday from 8 a.m. to noon and 1 to 5 p.m. (call 3-6322 for more information). The cordial, named after the region where it originated, is a distillate of dried peel of a particular strain of orange found only in Curaçao. (This strain grows only in Curaçao, where the soil and climate are unique.) Several herbs are added to give it an aromatic bouquet. It's made by a secret formula handed down through generations. One of the rewards of a visit here is a free snifter of the liqueur at the culmination of the tour.

On Schottegatweg West, lying northwest of Willemstad, past the Shell refineries, lies the **Beth Haim Cemetery,** oldest Caucasian burial site still in use in the western hemisphere. Meaning "House of Life," the cemetery was consecrated before 1659. On about three acres are some 2500 graves. The carving on some of the 17th- and 18th-century tombstones is exceptional.

Landhuis Brievengat, 4 Rheastraat (tel. 3-6229), gives visitors a chance to visit a Dutch version of an 18th-century West Indian plantation house. This stately building, set into a scrub-dotted landscape on the eastern side of the island, contains a few antiques, high ceilings, and a frontal gallery facing two entrance towers, said to have been used to imprison slaves and even for romantic trysts. The plantation was originally used for the cultivation of aloe and cattle, but an 1877 hurricane killed more than three-quarters of the livestock and the plantation operation ceased. The building was pulled down and the land purchased by Shell Oil. Around 1925 the remains of the structure were donated to the Society for the Preservation of Monuments, which rebuilt and restored it. Today it receives visitors for $1 daily from 9:30 a.m. to 12:30 p.m. and 3 to 6 p.m. There's an art gallery selling portrait busts on the rear terrace.

A SHOPPING EXPEDITION: The place is a shopper's paradise. Some 200 shops line the major shopping malls of such wooden-shoe-named streets as Heerenstraat and Breedestraat. Right in the heart of Willemstad, the **Punda** shopping area is a five-block district. Most stores are open Monday through Saturday from 8 a.m. to noon. When cruise ships are in port, stores are also open from noon to 2 p.m. and on Sunday and most holidays. To avoid the cruise-ship crowds, do your own shopping in the morning.

Look for good buys in French perfumes. Dutch Delft Blue souvenirs, finely woven Italian silks, Japanese and German cameras, jewelry, silver, Swiss watches, linens, leather goods, liquor, and island-made rum and liqueurs, especially Curaçao.

Incidentally, Curaçao is not technically a free port, but its prices are low because of its low import duty.

I always head first to the legendary **Spritzer & Fuhrmann** (tel. 1-2600), on a corner of vehicle-free Gomezplein, the leading jewelers of the Netherlands Antilles. This name stands for great values, service, and integrity, whether you buy a $50,000 diamond ring or a $50 gold chain. The finest Swiss watches are found here. In addition to the main store, there are other S&F specialty stores in the heart of Curaçao, carrying fine china and crystal. You will find names like Waterford, Baccarat, Lalique, Hummel, and Lladró among their stock.

Penha & Sons, 1 Herrenstraat (tel. 1-2266), occupies the oldest building in town, built in 1708. They're the distributor of such names as Chanel, Jean Patou, Yves Saint Laurent, and other perfumes, and cosmetics of Lancôme, Clinique, Orlane, and Estée Lauder, among others. The collection of merchandise at this prestigious store is quite varied—Hummel figurines, Delft Blue souvenirs, leather goods from Italy, even Guatemalan ponchos. Look also for cashmeres from Scotland.

Gandelman Jewelers, 35 Breedestraat (tel. 1-1854), is a family-run business, and they're the only manufacturing jewelers in the Netherlands Antilles They can supply North Americans with duty-free certificates on the jewelry which they make. Their specialty is jewelry with genuine gemstones such as diamonds, emeralds, rubies, sapphires, and others, which are also sold unmounted. In addition to their store in Willemstad, the family business also includes stores on St. Maarten and Aruba. The Gandelman family will welcome you, giving personal attention.

Kan, 44 Breedestraat, Punda (tel. 1-2111), has been in the jewelry business for more than half a century. Its Willemstad headquarters is in an 18th-century gabled building. Featured in a superb collection of 14- and 18-karat gold jewelry, as well as famous brand Swiss watches, such as Rolex. They also carry an exclusive line of Rosenthal china, crystal, and flatware.

The **Yellow House** (La Casa Amarilla), on Breedestraat (tel. 1-3222), is housed in a 19th-century yellow and white building. It's been operating since 1887, selling an intriguing collection of perfume from all over the world, and is the exclusive distributor of such names as Christian Dior. Some of their smaller departments have ready-to-wear items for men, women, and children.

Obra di Man, Plaza Piar (tel. 612-220), is filled with souvenirs and handicrafts, many items crafted by artisans on Curaçao. You'll find driftwood carvings, island fashions, black coral jewelry, and other items. Some of the merchandise is from the Netherlands. The shop is next to the Curaçao Plaza.

THE SPORTING LIFE: Its **beaches** are not as good as Aruba's seven-mile strip of sand, but Curaçao does have some 38 beaches, ranging from hotel sands to secluded coves. Thirty minutes from town, in the Willibrordus area on the south side of Curaçao, **Daaibooi** is a good beach. It's free but there are no changing facilities. Two good private beaches on the eastern side of the island are those of **Jan Thielbaai** and **Barbara Beach.** Jan Thielbaai has changing facilities and is good for snorkelers and scuba-divers. Locals are charged, but visitors are admitted free. Barbara Beach lies at the mouth of Spanish Water Bay on mining company property. It doesn't have facilities. Most hotels will pack you a picnic lunch.

Both these beaches give access to the new underwater park (see below under "Snorkeling and Scuba" and "Boating").

Snorkeling and Scuba

Most hotels offer water sports. The best equipped shop is **Piscadera Watersports** at the Curaçao Concorde (tel. 2-5000, ext. 177), which features snorkeling and scuba-diving trips to fascinating reefs and wrecks. Snorkeling trips leave at 11 a.m. and 3 p.m., costing $12 per hour. All these trips include a boat ride to and from the dive and snorkeling sites, complete and up-to-date equipment, as well as instructors and guides. Scuba lessons are offered for $25, and a reef dive goes for $30 ($35 at night). The shipwreck dive is popular at $30.

This is to a Venezuelan freighter that went down in 1979, right off the coast between Santa Ana Bay and Piscadera. It's about 100 feet below sea level.

Dive Curaçao & Watersports (tel. 1-4944), at the Princess Beach Hotel, offers scuba-diving at $25 for one dive, including tank, backpack, air, and weight, as well as equipment rental and trips to Barbara Beach for reef watching and snorkeling at a wreck. A 2½-hour trip with snorkeling gear and life vest costs $12 per person.

Scuba-divers and snorkelers can expect spectacular scenery in waters with visibility often exceeding 100 feet at the new **underwater park** off the Princess Beach Hotel. There are steep walls, two shallow wrecks, lush gardens of soft corals, and more than 30 species of hard corals. Although access from shore is possible at Jan Thielbaai and Barbara Beach, most people visit the park by boat. For easy and safe mooring, the park has 16 mooring buoys, placed at the best dive and snorkel sites. A snorkel trail with underwater interpretive markers has been laid out just east of the Princess Beach Hotel and is accessible from shore.

Golf

Curaçao Gold and Squash Club in Emmastad is open to the general public by arrangement only. Telephone Jan Cramar, the Holland-born golf pro, the day before you wish to play (tel. 6-2664). Greens fees are $12, and caddy charges run $4 for nine holes, $6 for 18. If the caddy has to carry two bags, the fee is $8 for 18 holes. Equipment can be rented at $4 for clubs, $2.50 for a pull cart. Hours are 8 a.m. to 4:30 p.m. on Monday, Wednesday, Thursday, and Friday, 8 a.m. to noon on Tuesday, Saturday, and Sunday. If oil company executives are using the course, you're out of luck. There's a bar and fast-food restaurant on the premises.

Boating

Again, **Piscadera Watersports** at the Curaçao Concorde (tel. 2-5000, ext. 177) are the people to see. They'll rent you a Sunfish at $20 per hour. You can also rent a waterscooter which can bear two persons, costing $20 per half hour. Pedalboats cost $10 per hour, and windsurfer boards, $20 per hour. You can also waterski for $20 per half hour.

The outfit offers a harbor tour, departing from the hotel and stopping at the Floating Market, going on for a look at Fort Nassau, ending up with a stop at the shipyards. The cost is $50 per hour for a minimum of four persons. In addition, a sightseeing tour—a beach hop by boat—cruises three different beaches, stopping at the fishing village of St. Michael's before going on to the Curaçao Oil Terminal, all for a cost of $50 per hour for a maximum of four persons.

Glass-bottomed boat rides can also be arranged at a cost of $6 per person. The tour takes in fish and coral life in Piscadera Bay, leaving the Concorde dock for a one-hour trip every day at 2 p.m.

Dive Curaçao & Watersports (tel. 1-4944), at the Princess Beach Hotel, offers glass-bottomed boat trips into the new underwater park at $6 per person for a one-hour trip.

Tennis

There are courts at the Curaçao Concorde, Las Palmas, Princess Beach, and Holiday Beach Hotels. Las Palmas's court is open 24 hours a day.

Deep-Sea Fishing

Our same reliable friends, **Piscadera Watersports** at the Curaçao Concorde (tel. 2-5000, ext. 177), have craft available for charter if you're interested in seeking sailfish, blue and white marlin, tuna, dolphin, and wahoo. Four persons pay $300 per half day. For a full day's fishing, four persons pay $500. Bottom fishing or light trolling costs four persons $100 per half day, $180 for a full day, and rental of fishing tackle is another $10 per day.

AFTER DARK: Most of the action spins around four casinos at the **Curaçao Concorde,** the **Holiday Beach,** the **Princess Beach,** and the **Curaçao Plaza.** These hotel gaming houses usually start their action at 2 p.m., and some of them remain open until 4 a.m. The Princess Beach serves complimentary drinks. The Concorde's room is the most dramatic. It's enclosed in natural stone walls and surrounded by a moat.

Nearly every sailor in port heads for **Campo Alegre,** sometimes known as "the compound." Others refer to it as "happy valley." This is the most famous, or notorious, bordello in the Caribbean. In the vicinity of the airport, the bordello is privately run, but under strict government controls.

The **Willemstad Room** at the Curaçao Concorde (tel. 2-5000) books some of the best acts on the island. There are two dinner seatings, one at 7 p.m. and again at 9 p.m., with meals costing from $25. For current shows, check the bulletin board in the hotel's lobby or else call. Remember to make a reservation in season, as the room can fill up quickly with the hotel's own guests. Live entertainment is offered nightly except Wednesday, with show time at 11 p.m. The minimum consumption is about $10 per person.

Royal Scotch Piano Bar, 6–10 Penstraat (tel. 1-6333), across the street from the Restaurant Larousse, is a 200-year-old ochre-colored building that used to be three row houses, each crumbling away. That was before ship's chef Herbert Haltmeyer, who worked most of his early life on the Holland-America shipping line, linked the interiors to form a nightlife spot. The decor includes a long, dark-grained bar, comfortable chairs and stools, row after row of wine and liquor bottles, and a white lacquered piano. There is live music from a talented pianist every day from 5 p.m. to 3 a.m. Heineken costs around 5 NAf ($2.85) and mixed drinks go for 6 NAf ($3.42). During happy hour, daily from 5 to 7 p.m., drinks are half price. The place is open every day except Sunday.

La Fontaine Discothèque Night Club, 78 Cas Coraweg (tel. 78596), about a ten-minute taxi ride from the center of Willemstad, is one of the most sophisticated after-dark spots on the island. It has a modern design and an array of psychedelic lighting. Andy Rhodes and Robby Dos Santos run this friendly disco/nightclub that occasionally has live shows. It's open from 10 p.m. to 4 p.m. Tuesday through Sunday, with drinks costing from $3.50.

The **Holiday Beach Hotel and Casino,** 31 Pater Euwensweg (tel. 2-5400), presents some of the splashiest musical comedies and revues in Curaçao. You get the show and dinner, along with wine, all for a package deal of $30. But you must make a reservation.

The **Temple Theater** is a restored landmark in the heart of Willemstad on the Wilhelminaplein by the Waterfort, built in 1867. A comfortable, air-conditioned, modern, multipurpose theater, it presents movies, plays, concerts, and stage shows.

NOW, SAVE MONEY ON ALL YOUR TRAVELS!
Join Arthur Frommer's $25-A-Day Travel Club

Saving money while traveling is never a simple matter, which is why, over 23 years ago, the **$25-A-Day Travel Club** was formed. Actually, the idea came from readers of the Arthur Frommer Publications who felt that such an organization could bring financial benefits, continuing travel information, and a sense of community to economy-minded travelers all over the world.

In keeping with the money-saving concept, the annual membership fee is low—$18 (U.S. residents) or $20 (Canadian, Mexican, and foreign residents)—and is immediately exceeded by the value of your benefits which include:

(1) The latest edition of any TWO of the books listed on the following page.

(2) An annual subscription to an 8-page quarterly newspaper *The Wonderful World of Budget Travel* which keeps you up-to-date on fastbreaking developments in low-cost travel in all parts of the world—bringing you the kind of information you'd have to pay over $25 a year to obtain elsewhere. This consumer-conscious publication also includes the following columns:

Hospitality Exchange—members all over the world who are willing to provide hospitality to other members as they pass through their home cities.

Share-a-Trip—requests from members for travel companions who can share costs and help avoid the burdensome single supplement.

Readers Ask ... Readers Reply—travel questions from members to which other members reply with authentic firsthand information.

(3) A copy of *Arthur Frommer's Guide to New York.*

(4) Your personal membership card which entitles you to purchase through the Club all Arthur Frommer Publications for a third to a half off their regular retail prices during the term of your membership.

So why not join this hardy band of international budgeteers NOW and participate in its exchange of information and hospitality? Simply send $18 (U.S. residents) or $20 U.S. (Canadian, Mexican, and other foreign residents) along with your name and address to: $25-A-Day Travel Club, Inc., 1230 Avenue of the Americas, New York, NY 10020. Remember to specify which *two* of the books in section (1) above you wish to receive in your initial package of members' benefits. Or tear out this page, check off any two books on the opposite side and send it to us with your membership fee.

FROMMER/PASMANTIER PUBLISHERS Date_____
1230 AVE. OF THE AMERICAS, NEW YORK, NY 10020

Friends, please send me the books checked below:

$-A-DAY GUIDES
(In-depth guides to low-cost tourist accommodations and facilities.)

☐ Europe on $25 a Day $11.95
☐ Australia on $25 a Day $10.95
☐ England on $35 a Day $10.95
☐ Greece on $25 a Day $10.95
☐ Hawaii on $35 a Day $10.95
☐ India on $15 & $25 a Day $9.95
☐ Ireland on $25 a Day $9.95
☐ Israel on $30 & $35 a Day $10.95
☐ Mexico on $20 a Day $9.95

☐ New Zealand on $25 a Day $10.95
☐ New York on $45 a Day............. $9.95
☐ Scandinavia on $35 a Day.......... $9.95
☐ Scotland and Wales on $35 a Day..... $10.95
☐ South America on $25 a Day $9.95
☐ Spain and Morocco (plus the Canary
  Is.) on $35 a Day $9.95
☐ Washington, D.C. on $40 a Day...... $10.95

DOLLARWISE GUIDES
(Guides to accommodations and facilities from budget to deluxe, with emphasis on the medium-priced.)

☐ Austria & Hungary $10.95
☐ Egypt........................... $11.95
☐ England & Scotland $10.95
☐ France.......................... $10.95
☐ Germany $11.95
☐ Italy............................ $10.95
☐ Japan & Hong Kong (avail. Apr. '86) . $11.95
☐ Portugal (incl. Madeira & the Azores) . $11.95
☐ Switzerland & Liechtenstein $11.95
☐ Bermuda & The Bahamas........... $10.95
☐ Canada $12.95

☐ Caribbean $12.95
☐ Cruises (incl. Alaska, Carib, Mex,
  Hawaii, Panama, Canada, & US)'..... $10.95
☐ California & Las Vegas $9.95
☐ Florida.......................... $10.95
☐ New England..................... $11.95
☐ Northwest $10.95
☐ Skiing USA—East $10.95
☐ Skiing USA—West $10.95
☐ Southeast & New Orleans.......... $11.95
☐ Southwest....................... $10.95

THE ARTHUR FROMMER GUIDES
(Pocket-size guides to tourist accommodations and facilities in all price ranges.)

☐ Amsterdam/Holland $4.95
☐ Athens........................... $4.95
☐ Atlantic City/Cape May $4.95
☐ Boston........................... $4.95
☐ Dublin/Ireland $4.95
☐ Hawaii $4.95
☐ Las Vegas $4.95
☐ Lisbon/Madrid/Costa del Sol........ $4.95
☐ London $4.95
☐ Los Angeles $4.95

☐ Mexico City/Acapulco $4.95
☐ Montreal/Quebec City $4.95
☐ New Orleans $4.95
☐ New York........................ $4.95
☐ Orlando/Disney World/EPCOT........ $4.95
☐ Paris $4.95
☐ Philadelphia...................... $4.95
☐ Rome $4.95
☐ San Francisco $4.95
☐ Washington, D.C................... $4.95

SPECIAL EDITIONS

☐ Bed & Breakfast—N. America $7.95
☐ Fast 'n' Easy Phrase Book
  (Fr/Ger/Ital/Sp in one vol.) $6.95
☐ Guide for the Disabled Traveler....... $10.95
☐ How to Beat the High Cost of Travel ... $4.95
☐ Marilyn Wood's Wonderful Weekends
  (NY, Conn, Mass, RI, Vt, NJ, Pa) $9.95

☐ Museums in New York $8.95
☐ Shopper's Guide to England, Scotland
  & Wales.......................... $10.95
☐ Swap and Go (Home Exchanging) $10.95
☐ Travel Diary and Record Book........ $5.95
☐ Urban Athlete (NYC sports guide) $9.95
☐ Where to Stay USA (Lodging from $3
  to $30 a night) $9.95

In U.S. include $1 post. & hdlg. for 1st book; 25¢ ea. add'l. book. Outside U.S. $2 and 50¢ respectively.

Enclosed is my check or money order for $_____

NAME_____

ADDRESS_____

CITY_____ STATE_____ ZIP_____